The Windows Serial Port Programming Handbook

OTHER AUERBACH PUBLICATIONS

The ABCs of IP Addressing
Gilbert Held
ISBN: 0-8493-1144-6

The ABCs of LDAP: How to Install, Run, and Administer LDAP Services
Reinhard Voglmaier
ISBN: 0-8493-1346-5

The ABCs of TCP/IP
Gilbert Held
ISBN: 0-8493-1463-1

Building a Wireless Office
Gilbert Held
ISBN: 0-8493-1271-X

The Complete Project Management Office Handbook
Gerald M. Hill
ISBN: 0-8493-2173-5

Enhancing LAN Performance, 4th Edition
Gilbert Held
ISBN: 0-8493-1942-0

Information Security Management Handbook, 5th Edition
Harold F. Tipton and Micki Krause, Editors
ISBN: 0-8493-1997-8

Information Security Policies and Procedures: A Practitioner's Reference 2nd Edition
Thomas R. Peltier
ISBN: 0-8493-1958-7

Information Security Policies, Procedures, and Standards: Guidelines for Effective Information Security Management
Thomas R. Peltier
ISBN: 0-8493-1137-3

Information Security Risk Analysis
Thomas R. Peltier
ISBN: 0-8493-0880-1

Information Technology for Manufacturing: Reducing Costs and Expanding Capabilities
Kevin Aki, John Clemons, and Mark Cubine
ISBN: 1-57444-359-3

Interpreting the CMMI: A Process Improvement Approach
Margaret Kulpa and Kurt Johnson
ISBN: 0-8493-1654-5

IS Management Handbook, 8th Edition
Carol V. Brown and Heikki Topi
ISBN: 0-8493-1595-6

ISO 9000:2000 for Software and Systems Providers
Robert Bamford and William Deibler, III
ISBN: 0-8493-2063-1

Managing a Network Vulnerability Assessment
Thomas R. Peltier and Justin Peltier
ISBN: 0-8493-1270-1

A Practical Approach to WBEM/CIM Management
Chris Hobbs
ISBN: 0-8493-2306-1

A Practical Guide to Security Engineering and Information Assurance
Debra Herrmann
ISBN: 0-8493-1163-2

Practical Network Design Techniques, 2nd Edition: A Complete Guide for WANs and LANs
Gilbert Held and S. Ravi Jagannathan
ISBN: 0-8493-2019-4

Real Process Improvement Using the CMMI
Michael West
ISBN: 0-8493-2109-3

Six Sigma Software Development
Christine B. Tayntor
ISBN: 0-8493-1193-4

Software Architecture Design Patterns in Java
Partha Kuchana
ISBN: 0-8493-2142-5

Software Configuration Management
Jessica Keyes
ISBN: 0-8493-1976-5

A Technical Guide to IPSec Virtual Private Networks
James S. Tiller
ISBN: 0-8493-0876-3

Telecommunications Cost Management
Brian DiMarsico, Thomas Phelps IV, and William A. Yarberry, Jr.
ISBN: 0-8493-1101-2

The Windows Serial Port Programming Handbook

Ying Bai

CRC Press is an imprint of the
Taylor & Francis Group, an **informa** business
AN AUERBACH BOOK

CRC Press
Taylor & Francis Group
6000 Broken Sound Parkway NW, Suite 300
Boca Raton, FL 33487-2742

First issued in paperback 2019

ISBN-13: 978-0-8493-2213-6 (hbk)
ISBN-13: 978-0-367-39358-8 (pbk)
Library of Congress Card Number 2004053125

Library of Congress Cataloging-in-Publication Data

Bai, Ying, 1956–
The windows serial port programming handbook / Ying Bai.
p. cm.
Includes bibliographical references and index.
ISBN 0-8493-2213-8
1. Computer interfaces. 2. Parallel programming (Computer science) 3. Ports (Electronic computer system) I. Title.

TK7887.5.B35 2004
005.2'75—dc22

2004053125

Visit the Taylor & Francis Web site at
http://www.taylorandfrancis.com

and the CRC Press Web site at
http://www.crcpress.com

Dedicated to my wife, Yan Wang,
and my daughter, Susan Bai

TRADEMARK ACKNOWLEDGMENTS

Visual C++ 6.0™ is a trademark and a product of Microsoft Corporation.
Visual Basic 6.0™ is a trademark and a product of Microsoft Corporation.
MSDN™ Library is a trademark and a product of Microsoft Corporation.
MAXIM™ is a registered trademark of Maxim Integrated Products, Inc.
Texas Instruments ™ is a registered trademark of Texas Instruments Incorporated.
MATLAB® is a trademark and product of The MathWorks, Inc.
MATLAB Compiler® is a trademark and product of The MathWorks, Inc.
MATLAB Instrument Control Toolbox® is a trademark and product of The MathWorks, Inc.
VisualWorks™ is a trademark of CinCom Systems, Inc.
VisualWorks DLL & C Connect™ is a trademark of CinCom Systems, Inc.
LabView™ is a trademark of National Instruments Corporation.
Java™ is a trademark of Sun Microsystems, Inc.

Table of Contents

Chapter 3

Chapter 4

Chapter 5

Chapter 6

About the Author

Dr. Ying Bai is an Assistant Professor in the Department of Computer Science and Engineering at Johnson C. Smith University. His special interests include computer architecture, software engineering, mixed-language programming, embedded controllers, automation and robot control, and robot calibration. His industry experience includes positions as a software engineer and senior software engineer at such corporations as Motorola MMS, Schlumberger ATE Technology, Immix TeleCom, and Lam Research. His work with these companies has involved applying various programming languages in the Windows environment to solutions for automation control, automation testing, and accuracy measurements.

Acknowledgments

The first thanks I give should go to my wife, Yan Wang. I could not have finished this book without her sincere encouragement and support, especially during the hard times.

Special thanks also to Mr. John Wyzalek, who has made my dream into a fact by making this book available to you readers. You would not have found this book on the market without John's deep perspective and hard work. The same thanks go to the editing team. Without these people's contributions, publishing the book would have been impossible.

I'd like to thank Mr. Jonathan Champ for taking the time to review my preface.

I also appreciate the help given by Dr. Attia Magdy and Dr. Bahalla Satish, both of whom provided me with very useful opinions as I was writing the book.

Finally, but not least, I wish to extend my thanks to all the people who supported me and helped me to finish this book.

1 The Fundamentals of Serial Port Communications

1.1 INTRODUCTION

With the rapid development of modern communications and computer technologies, communication between individuals, between individuals and groups, and between individuals and society has become more and more important. Almost all communication devices used today are closely related to computer technologies; these tools include digital telephones, cell phones, pagers, mobile phones, the Internet and Internet services, image phones, server/client communications, and fiber communication. All these modern communication technologies play a vital role in our society today.

The different communication technologies applied in all fields can be divided into two categories:

- Wire communications
- Wireless communications

Wire communication can be further divided into two subcategories:

- Electronic wire communications
- Fiber wire communications

Electronic wire communications can be categorized into analog and digital communication technologies. Most modern communication technologies use digital data transfer. Generally, the electronic wire communications used in computer technologies are digital technologies, and they come in two styles:

- Parallel communications
- Serial communications

Parallel communications can exchange or translate data between two devices in a parallel style, which means that multiple bits of data (such as 8-bit, 16-bit, or 32-bit data) can be transferred between two pieces of equipment simultaneously. Obviously, in parallel communication, the two devices must be connected with multiple wires; the relationship between the connected wires and the data to be translated is one to one, which means that one data bit travels over one wire.

Serial communications, on the other hand, can exchange or translate data between two devices only in a bit-by-bit fashion, like a sequence, by using a single wire. It should be noted that serial communication needs fewer wires, so the hardware connections are simpler. Figure 1.1 shows diagrams of both parallel and serial communications.

It can be seen in Figure 1.1 that a parallel interface port (a) needs to use more wires, which makes the interface more complicated. To compensate, those wires provide a high-speed data translation because the data is processed simultaneously by all the wires. The serial interface port (b) uses only a single wire to translate all the data bit by bit, which means that at any moment, only one bit of data can be translated from device I to device II. Figure 1.1 illustrates the translation of a binary data byte `(01100101)` through both parallel and serial interface ports. Relatively speaking, a slower translation speed is expected in the serial communication style.

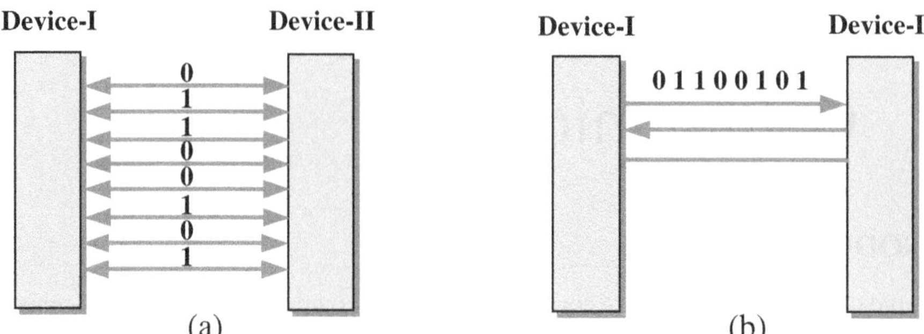

FIGURE 1.1 (a) Parallel and (b) serial data communications.

1.2 WHY SERIAL PORT COMMUNICATIONS ARE NECESSARY

Why are serial communications so important if the parallel interface port is available? To answer this question, an understanding of the following facts is required.

In the early days of computers, most data communications utilized parallel ports due to the slow running speed of the central processing unit (CPU). The typical CPU processing speed was between 10 and 200 MHz. The devices that used parallel port communications were hard disks, floppy disks, printers, scanners, and zip disk drives. The processing speed was the first priority for any slow computer. The disadvantages of using a parallel port interface included the complicated interface circuits, the high cost, and a limited data translation distance (less than 10 feet).

Since the twenty-first century, the running speed of CPUs has increased significantly. Today most normal computers can run at a speed of 1 or 2 GHz. Because running speed is no longer an obstacle, long-distance translation and low cost have become the main priorities in today's data communications. Serial port communications can now handle much longer-distance data translation (over 4,000 feet) at very low cost. Also, the hardware used for serial port communications is much simpler than that used for parallel port communications.

Most operating systems provide the appropriate communication drivers for serial ports; therefore, users aren't required to spend time developing (and learning to develop) serial port device drivers. Instead, they can spend time directly developing the user programs that talk to the serial ports to perform the data communications between computers, between servers and clients, and between the different devices that use serial ports.

For parallel port interfaces, it is a different story. Different parallel devices require that the associated device drivers be developed and installed, which is not an easy job even for experienced software developers. Some general-purpose parallel port interfaces are available, such as IEEE-488. If a user adopts such a general-purpose parallel port interface tool, he or she still needs to learn how to modify the equipment's subroutine to match the requirements of the interface.

Based on these facts, more and more peripheral devices (such as printers, zip drives, and scanners) are being expected to communicate with computers via serial port interfaces. Today universal serial bus (USB) drivers are the tools used most often for connecting computers to printers, scanners, floppy drives, and even hard disks (for example, the Iomega__HDD 250GB USB2.0/FireWire External Desktop Hard Drive). You can even find different sizes of USB flash memory on the market to increase the memory size of your computer.

It can be expected that the serial port interface will play an increasingly important role in today's computer technologies and communications. For this reason, it is important that developers understand the principles of serial communications so that they can develop sophisticated programs to support a variety of serial interfaces. Helping you achieve these dual goals is the objective of this book.

1.3 WHAT IS SERIAL PORT COMMUNICATION?

In the early 1960s, a standards committee, today known as the Electronic Industries Association (EIA), developed a common interface standard for data communications equipment. At that time, data communication was thought to mean a digital data exchange between a centrally located mainframe computer and a remote computer terminal, or possibly between two terminals without a computer involved. These devices were connected by telephone voice lines and consequently required a modem at each end for signal translation. Although simple in concept, the many opportunities for data errors that occurred when transmitting data through an analog channel required a relatively complex design. It was thought that a standard was needed first to ensure reliable communication, and second to enable the interconnection of equipment produced by different manufacturers, thereby fostering the benefits of mass production and competition. From these ideas, *Recommended Standard Number 232, Revision C* (RS232C) was born. It specified signal voltages, signal timing, signal function, protocols for information exchange, and mechanical connectors.

Over the more than 40 years since this standard was developed, the EIA published three modifications, the most recent being the EIA232E standard introduced in 1991. Beyond changing the standard's name from RS232 to EIA232, some signal lines were renamed and various new ones were defined, including a shield conductor.

Serial communications can be divided into different groups based on their operation principles. The following sections describe the different serial port communication groups.

1.3.1 RS-232

As previously mentioned, RS-232 is a protocol developed and defined by EIA in the 1960s that was used in early serial data communications. Because of its simplicity and popularity, RS-232 has been widely applied in all data communication fields, including industrial, commercial, educational, and even consumer electronics. RS-232 belongs to the *full-duplex* communication protocol, which means that both senders and receivers can exchange information simultaneously. The *half-duplex* communication protocol allows users (senders and receivers) to send or receive information between one another only at different periods of time; they cannot send and receive simultaneously. This means that the receiver has to wait until the sender finishes sending information; then the receiver can pick up and respond to the sender's information. At any moment, only one user, either sender or receiver, can control the transmission of data.

The simplest RS-232 protocol utilizes three wires: One wire is used to send information, one is used to receive information, and a third wire works as the ground or reference between the two devices. The information transmitted on RS-232 wires is represented as a sequence of binary bits, and the values of those binary bits are associated with two voltage levels: +12 volts (Space, or logical 1) and −12 volts (Mark, or logical 0). The data transmission speed is controlled by the *baud rate,* (the number of binary bits that can be transmitted per second), which can be indicated and set up by the user before the data transmission. In the early days, data transmission speed was relatively slow because of the slow CPU speeds, and typical baud rates were 1,200, 4,800, and 9,600. Baud rates applied in today's serial data communication have increased significantly and are typically 19,200, 38,400, and even higher. In short, the RS-232 port is designed to communicate with local devices and will support one driver and one receiver.

The typical transmission distance of the RS-232 protocol is less than 50 feet. To increase this distance and reduce noise and disturbance, RS-422 was developed.

1.3.2 RS-422

RS-232 serial port communication is part of a single-ended protocol, meaning that the value of each binary bit has an absolute voltage level relative to the ground. This single-ended protocol has shortcomings when it comes to data transmission. One of the most important disadvantages is its inability to overcome or reduce noise and disturbances during the information transmission. Even when ±12 volts is utilized as its signal level, the RS-232 still may encounter big, sharp pulses or other disturbances during data transmission or receipt, increasing the possibility that mistakes will occur in the signal transmission and that information will be made invalid.

To solve this problem, another serial communication protocol, RS-422, has emerged. RS-422 uses a differential signal transmission mode, which means that at any time, a binary bit value has a relative voltage flowing from the positive signal terminal to the negative signal terminal. Unlike the transmission wires used with RS-232, the wires for both the sending and receiving lines are doubled, and these double wires are twisted together to work as a single line (either a sending or a receiving line) to further reduce environmental disturbances.

When communicating at high baud rates or over long distances in real-world environments, single-ended methods are often inadequate. A differential data transmission (or a balanced differential signal) offers superior performance in most applications. Differential signals can help nullify the effects of ground shifts and induced noise signals that can appear as common mode voltages during the communication of data.

RS-422 is designed for greater distances and higher baud rates compared with RS-232. In its simplest form, a pair of converters from RS-232 to RS-422 (and back again) can be used to form an "RS-232 extension cord." Baud rates of up to 100 kbps and distances up to 4,000 feet can be accommodated with RS-422. RS-422 is also specified for multidrop (nodes) applications, where only one driver is connected to, and transmits on, a bus of up to 10 receivers.

Although a multidrop-type application has many desirable advantages, RS-422 devices cannot be used to build truly multipoint communication systems. A true multipoint communication system consists of multiple drivers and receivers connected on a single "bus," where any node can transmit or receive data.

Quasi-multidrop systems (four-wire systems) are often constructed from RS-422 devices. These systems are often used in a *half-duplex* mode, where a single master in a system sends a command to one of several slave devices on a network. Typically, one device (node) is addressed by the host computer, and a response is received from that device. This kind of system (four-wire, half-duplex) is often constructed to prevent data collision (or bus contention) problems on a multidrop network.

1.3.3 RS-485

RS-485 is similar to RS-422 in the differential signal transmission protocol, but the former has the capability to build a truly multipoint communication system. This means that multiple terminals or computers, which are considered nodes, can be connected to a common bus, and each node can work as either a sender or receiver of information from this bus. Each terminal or computer connected to the bus has a tristate control functionality and a unique address (or ID), and the communication between the sender and receiver is performed based on this ID.

RS-485 will support 32 drivers and 32 receivers in bidirectional, half-duplex, multidrop communications over single or dual twisted-pair wires. An RS-485 network can be connected in a two- or four-wire mode. The maximum cable length can be as much as 4,000 feet because of the differential voltage transmission system used. The typical use of RS-485 is for a single PC connected to several addressable devices that share the same cable. You can think of RS-485 as a party-line communications system. (The addressing is handled by the remote computer unit.) RS-232 may be converted to RS-485 with a simple interface converter; it can have optical isolation and surge suppression.

Electronic data communications between elements will generally fall into two broad categories: single-ended and differential communications. RS-422 and RS-485 belong to the differential mode data transmission category, but RS-232 is from the single-ended transmission mode. The specification of RS-232 allows for data transmission from one transmitter to one receiver at relatively slow data rates (up to 20 kbps) and short distances (up to 50 feet at the maximum data rate).

To solve the data collision problem often present in multidrop networks, hardware units (converters, repeaters, microprocessor controls) can be constructed to maintain a receive mode until they are ready to transmit data. Single-master systems (many other communications schemes are available) offer a straightforward and simple means of avoiding data collisions in a typical two-wire, half-duplex, multidrop system. The master initiates a communications request to a slave node by addressing that unit. The hardware detects the start bit of the transmission and automatically enables (on the fly) the RS-485 transmitter. Once a character is sent, the hardware reverts back to a receive mode in about one to two microseconds.

Any number of characters can be sent, and the transmitter will automatically be restarted with each new character (or in many cases a bit-oriented timing scheme is used in conjunction with network biasing for a fully automatic operation, including any baud rate and/or any communication specification). Once a slave unit is addressed, it can respond immediately because of the fast transmitter turn-off time of the automatic device. It is not necessary to introduce long delays in a network to avoid data collisions, because delays are not required and networks can be constructed to utilize the data communications bandwidth with up to 100 percent throughput.

1.3.4 Universal Serial Bus (USB)

USB provides an expandable, hot-plugging Plug and Play serial interface that ensures a standard, low-cost connection for peripheral devices such as keyboards, mice, joysticks, printers, scanners, storage devices, modems, and video conferencing cameras. Migration to USB is recommended for all peripheral devices that use legacy ports such as the PS/2, serial, and parallel ports.

USB was originally developed in 1995 by many of the same industry-leading companies currently working on USB 2.0. The major goal of USB is to define an external expansion bus that makes adding peripherals to a PC in a serial communication mode as easy as hooking up a telephone to a wall jack. The program's driving goals are ease of use and low cost. An external expansion architecture enables these goals and has the following highlights:

- PC host controller hardware and software
- Robust connectors and cable assemblies
- Peripheral friendly master-slave protocols
- Expandability through multiport hubs

The role of the system software is to provide a uniform view of the input/output (I/O) system for all applications software. It hides hardware implementation details so that application software is more portable. For the USB I/O subsystem in particular, the system software manages the dynamic attachment and detachment of peripherals. This phase, called *enumeration,* involves communicating with the peripheral to discover the identity of a device driver that it should load, if it is not already loaded. A unique address is assigned to each peripheral during enumeration to be used for run-time data transfers. During run time, the host PC initiates transactions to specific peripherals, and each peripheral accepts its transactions and responds accordingly. Additionally, the host PC software incorporates the peripheral into the system power-management scheme and can manage overall system power without user interaction.

All USB peripherals are slaves that obey a defined protocol. They must react to request transactions sent from the host PC. The peripheral responds to control transactions that, for example, request detailed information about the device and its configuration. The peripheral sends and receives data from the host using a standard USB data format. This standardized data movement to and from the PC host with interpretation by the peripheral gives USB enormous flexibility with little PC-host software changes. USB 1.1 peripherals can operate at 12 or 1.5 Mbps, but the USB 2.0 specification has a design data rate of 480 Mbps.

Although USB is a serial communication device, you cannot use serial device drivers to directly talk to any USB device because it works in a dynamic mode, and it can be hot-plugged to or hot-unplugged from a host computer. A special device driver is needed to successfully interface to any USB device. Microsoft provides some useful tools, such as Windows NT Device-Driver Development Kits (NT DDK) and Windows 2000 and 98 Device-Driver Development Kits (2000 and 98 DDKs), to help users to develop suitable drivers to interface with USB devices. Windows 2000 and 98 DDKs are free for downloading from the Microsoft Web site at www.microsoft.com/ddk. These DDKs also provide sample code and documentation to help you get started. Also, the developer's Webboard at this site contains postings of questions and solutions for writing drivers.

Today USB is enjoying tremendous success in the marketplace, with most peripheral vendors around the globe developing products to this specification. Virtually all new PCs come with one or more USB ports. In fact, USB has become a key enabler of the Easy PC Initiative, an industry initiative led by Intel and Microsoft to make PCs easier to use. This effort sprung from the recognition that users need simpler, easier-to-use PCs that don't sacrifice connectivity or expandability. USB is one of the key technologies used to provide this.

Early versions of USB include USB 1.0 and 1.1. Today USB version 2.0 provides system manufacturers with the ability to connect to high-performance peripherals in the least expensive way. The additional performance capabilities of USB 2.0 can be added with little impact to the overall system cost. Indeed, high-bandwidth interfaces such as small computer system interface (SCSI) adapters may no longer be required in some systems, leading to a net savings of system cost. Simpler construction will result because only USB connectors will be needed on many future PCs. Today's ubiquitous USB connectors will become USB 2.0, superceding USB 1.1, and today's USB devices will operate with full compatibility in a USB 2.0 system.

The added capabilities of USB 2.0 will expand the market segment for USB peripherals while enabling retail products to transition with the installed base. Support of USB 2.0 is recommended for hubs and higher-bandwidth peripherals.

Designing a USB 2.0 peripheral is an engineering effort similar to designing a USB 1.1 peripheral. Some low-speed peripherals, such as human interface devices (HIDs), may never be redesigned to support the USB 2.0 high-speed capability to maintain the absolute lowest cost.

1.3.5 Controller Area Network (CAN)

The controller area network (CAN) is a serial bus system specially suited to interconnect smart devices in order to build smart systems or subsystems. CAN was first developed from a Bosch internal project, which was to develop an in-vehicle network in 1983. In 1987, the first CAN controller chips from Intel and Philips Semiconductors emerged on the market. An international users and manufacturers group, CAN in Automation (CiA), was established in 1992.

Today you can find CAN in many different implementations, including a wide area of industrial and manufacturing fields. The automotive industry uses CAN as the in-vehicle network for engine management, body electronics such as door and roof control, air conditioning, lighting, and entertainment controls. Factory automation uses CAN to build smart factories, and the protocol known as DeviceNet is mainly used in this area. Such companies as Rockwell Automation (formerly Allen-Bradley) have made DeviceNet the most successful network in factory automation in the United States and in the Far East.

CAN is used as an embedded network for machine control within industries such as textiles, printing, injection molding, and packaging. Mainly, the protocol CANopen is used for such applications. Embedded controls can also be found in building automation, maritime functions, the medical field, and railway applications.

The CAN protocol is an international standard defined in ISO 11898. Beyond the CAN protocol itself, the conformance test for the CAN protocol is defined in the ISO 16845, which guarantees the interchangeability of the CAN chips. Figure 1.2 shows an operational diagram of a CAN system.

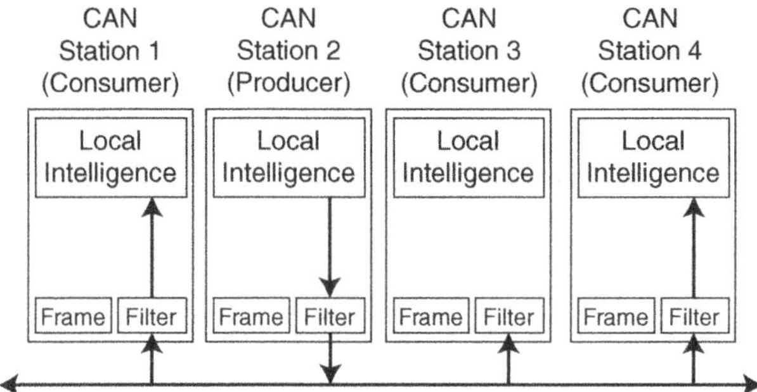

FIGURE 1.2 The operational diagram of a CAN system. (This section is reprinted by the permission of the CIA Web site http:www.can-cia.de/can/protocol/)

CAN is based on the broadcast communication mechanism. This broadcast communication is achieved by means of a message-oriented transmission protocol. Thus, it only defines messages, not stations or station addresses. These messages are identified by use of a message identifier. The message identifier has to be unique within the whole network, and the protocol defines not only the content, but also the priority of the message. The priority definition becomes important when several stations compete for bus access.

A high degree of system and configuration flexibility is achieved as a result of the content-oriented addressing scheme. It is easy to add stations to an existing CAN network without making any hardware or software modifications to the existing stations, as long as the new stations are purely receivers. This flexibility allows modular electronics to come into play, and it also permits multiple receptions and the synchronization of distributed processes. Data needed by several stations can be transmitted via the network in such a way that it is unnecessary for each station to have to know who the producer of the data is. Therefore, the servicing and upgrading of a network are relatively easy because the data transmission is not based on the availability of specific types of stations.

In real-time processing, the urgency to exchange messages over the network can differ greatly: A rapidly changing dimension (such as the engine load) has to be transmitted more frequently, and therefore with fewer delays, than do other dimensions (such as engine temperature).

The priority at which a message is transmitted, compared to another message, is specified by the identifier of each message. The priorities are laid down during system design in the form of corresponding binary values and cannot be changed dynamically. The identifier with the lowest binary number has the highest priority.

Bus access conflicts are resolved by bitwise arbitration of the identifiers involved by each station observing the bus level, bit for bit. This happens in accordance with the "wired and" mechanism, by which the dominant state overwrites the recessive state. The competition for bus allocation is lost by all stations (nodes) that have recessive transmission and dominant observation. All those "losers" automatically become receivers of the message with the highest priority and do not reattempt transmission until the bus is available again.

Transmission requests are handled by the messages' order of importance to the system as a whole. This system proves especially advantageous in overload situations. Because bus access is prioritized on the basis of the messages, it is possible to guarantee low individual latency times in real-time systems.

The CAN protocol supports two message frame formats; the only essential difference between the two is the length of the identifier. The CAN standard frame, also known as CAN 2.0 A, supports a length of 11 bits for the identifier, and the CAN extended frame (also known as CAN 2.0 B) supports a length of 29 bits for the identifier.

1.3.5.1 CAN Standard Frame

A message in the CAN standard-frame format begins with the start bit called the start of frame (SOF). This is followed by the Arbitration field, which consists of the identifier and the remote transmission request (RTR) bit used to distinguish between the data frame and the data request frame, also called the *remote frame.* The subsequent Control field contains the identifier extension (IDE) bit used to distinguish between the CAN standard frame and the CAN extended frame. The field also includes the data length code (DLC) used to indicate the number of following data bytes in the Data field. If the message is used as a remote frame, the DLC contains the number of requested data bytes.

The Data field that follows is able to hold up to 8 bytes of data. The integrity of the frame is guaranteed by the following cyclic redundancy check (CRC) sum. The Acknowledge (ACK) field compromises the ACK slot and the ACK delimiter. The bit in the ACK slot is sent as a recessive bit and is overwritten as a dominant bit by those receivers, which have at this time received the data correctly. Correct messages are acknowledged by the receivers regardless of the result of the acceptance test. The end of the message is indicated by the end of frame (EOF). The intermission frame space (IFS) is the minimum number of bits separating consecutive messages. If there is no subsequent bus access by any station, the bus remains idle.

1.3.5.2 CAN Extended Frame

A message in the CAN extended-frame format is likely the same as a message in CAN standard-frame format. The difference is the length of the identifier used. The identifier is made up of the existing 11-bit identifier (the base identifier) and an 18-bit extension (the identifier extension). The distinction between the CAN standard-frame format and the CAN extended-frame format is made by means of the IDE bit, which is transmitted as dominant if the frame is in CAN standard-frame format and is transmitted as recessive if the frame is in CAN extended-frame format. As the two formats have to coexist on one bus, the message with a higher priority on the bus is identified, in case of a bus access collision, with different formats and the same identifier or base identifier. A message in CAN standard-frame format always takes priority over a message in extended-frame format.

CAN controllers that support the messages in CAN extended-frame format are also able to send and receive messages in CAN standard-frame format. When CAN controllers covering only the CAN standard-frame format are used in one network, then only messages in CAN standard frame can be transmitted over the entire network. Messages in CAN extended-frame format will be misunderstood. However, some CAN controllers are available (such as version 2.0 B passive, for example) that support only CAN standard-frame format but that recognize messages in CAN extended-frame format and then ignore them.

1.3.5.3 Detecting and Signaling Errors

Unlike other bus systems, the CAN protocol does not use ACK messages, but instead signals any errors immediately as they occur. For error detection, the CAN protocol implements three mechanisms at the message level:

- **CRC:** The CRC safeguards information in the frame by adding redundant check bits at the transmission end. At the receiving end, these bits are recomputed and tested against the received bits. If they do not agree, a CRC error has occurred.

- **Frame check:** This mechanism verifies the structure of the transmitted frame by checking the bit fields against the fixed format and the frame size. Errors detected by frame checks are designated as format errors.
- **ACK errors:** As previously mentioned, received frames are acknowledged by all receivers through a positive ACK. If no ACK is received by the transmitter of the message, an ACK error is indicated.

The CAN protocol also implements two mechanisms for error detection at the bit level:

- **Monitoring:** The capability of the transmitter to detect errors is based on the monitoring of the bus signals. Each station that transmits also observes the bus level and thus detects differences between each bit sent and the corresponding bit received. This permits the reliable detection of global errors, as well as errors local to the transmitter.
- **Bit stuffing:** The coding of the individual bits is tested at bit level. The bit representation used by CAN is nonreturn to zero (NRZ) coding, which guarantees maximum efficiency in bit coding. The synchronization edges are generated by means of bit stuffing. This means that after five consecutive equal bits, the transmitter inserts into the bit stream a stuff bit with the complementary value, which is removed by the receivers.

If one or more errors are discovered by at least one station using the previous mechanisms, the current transmission is aborted by means of an error flag. This prevents other stations from accepting the message and thus ensures the consistency of data throughout the network. After the transmission of an erroneous message that has been aborted, the sender automatically reattempts transmission (automatic retransmission). There may again be competition for bus allocation.

However effective and efficient the method described may be, in the event of a defective station, all messages (including the correct ones) might be aborted. If no measures for self-monitoring are taken, the bus system will be blocked by this defective station. The CAN protocol therefore provides a mechanism for distinguishing sporadic errors from permanent errors and for local failures at the station. This is done by a statistical assessment of station error situations, with the aim of recognizing a station's own defects and possibly entering an operation mode that would not negatively affect the rest of the CAN network. This process may go as far as the station switching itself off to preventing messages erroneously from being recognized as incorrect.

1.3.6 Firewire

Firewire originally was developed by Apple Computer, Inc., as a high-speed serial bus. It was a kind of advanced digital broadcast (ADB) on lots of steroids. While it was being developed, many thought that it was actually too fast, and that some lower-speed interconnect devices, such as USB, would be cheaper to implement. After that, Firewire languished. Suddenly, in 1995, a tiny connector showed up on the first digital video (DV) camcorders shipped by Sony Corporation. DV was the killer application for Firewire. In late 1995, Firewire was accepted as a standard by the Institute of Electrical and Electronics Engineers (IEEE), henceforth called IEEE-1394.

The emergence of DV and multimedia applications have brought with them the need to move large amounts of data quickly between peripherals and PCs. As audio–video products migrate to digital technology, consumers and professionals alike stand to benefit from a simple high-speed connection that will make this transmission more efficient. Enter 1394, the digital cable. The IEEE-1394 serial bus is the industry-standard implementation of Apple Computer's 1394 digital I/O system. It is a versatile, high-speed, low-cost method for interconnecting a variety of personal computer peripherals and consumer electronics devices. Developed by the industry's leading technology companies, the specification was accepted as an industry standard by the IEEE Standards

Board on December 12, 1995, with succeeding revisions since then. The 1394 standard offers several advantages over other technologies. These benefits include the following:

- Guaranteed delivery of multiple data streams through isochronous data transport
- The capability to connect up to 63 devices without the need for additional hardware, such as hubs
- A flexible, six-wire cable
- Complete plug and play operation, including the hot-swapping of live devices
- Acceptance by over 40 leading manufacturers in the computer and electronics consumer industries

Figure 1.3 shows the physical structure of a typical Firewire port connector. The Firewire has two individually shielded pairs for data and two extra wires for power.

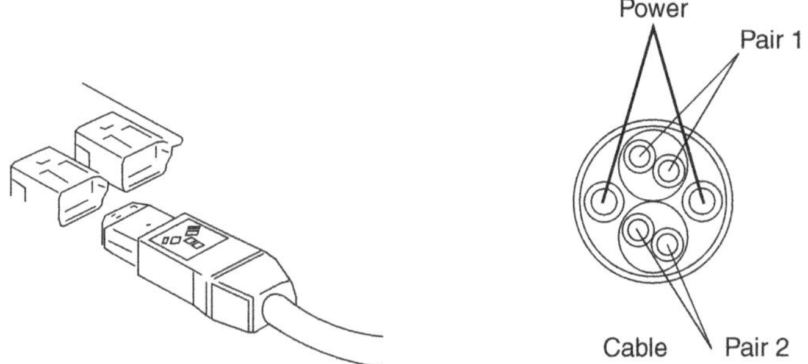

FIGURE 1.3 The physical structure of a typical Firewire port connector.

As shown in the figure, the standard Firewire cable actually consists of six wires. Data is sent via two separately shielded twisted-pair transmission lines. The two twisted pairs are crossed in each cable assembly to create a transmit–receive connection. Two more wires carry power (8 to 40V, 1.5A maximum) to remote devices. Currently, these power lines are rarely used. The wires terminate in Gameboy-style plugs, also shown in Figure 1.3.

Sony uses four-conductor cable for making connections to DV camcorders and DVCRs. Similar to the setup mentioned previously but without the power wires, these cables terminate in smaller, four-prong connectors. To connect a Sony DV camcorder or DVCR with a standard IEEE-1394 Firewire device or interface card, you need an adapter cable, with four prongs on one side and six on the other. It simply connects the data lines while omitting the power connection.

According to the standard, the IEEE-1394 "wire" is good for 400 Mbps over 4.5 meters. The standard cable uses 28 American wire gauge (AWG) signal pairs with 40 twists/meter. The power pair in the standard cable is 22 AWG.

Longer cable runs can be achieved by using thicker cable or by lowering the bit rate. DV users, keep in mind that the signaling rate of the Sony DV camcorders is only 100 Mbps. Can it use longer cables? The answer is Yes. Although such a connection lies outside of the product specifications, several people have reported successful 100 Mbps transmissions over more than 20 meters using standard cable. Reports have also been made of thicker cables being used to span lengths of 30 meters or more at 100 Mbps.

If you are the adventurous type, you can try using unshielded twisted-pair (UTP) cable. Don't notify the Federal Communications Commission (FCC) before doing this, and if your neighbors complain about strange stuff on their TV sets, stop the experiment. We have even heard reports about someone who was running 100 Mbps 1394 over 50 meters of Cat-5 UTP. According to lore, he ran isochronous video for several days without a single frame dropped due to errors.

1.4 SERIAL PORT COMMUNICATION PROTOCOLS

As previously mentioned, independent channels are established for two-way (full-duplex) communications. RS-232 signals are represented by voltage levels with respect to a common system (power/logic) ground. How can a single wire be used to transmit a sequence of data bit by bit between two devices effectively and without errors? This is a key concern: making sure our data communication is successful and reliable. To answer this question, let us now examine some terminologies applied in the serial data communications arena. Because of the similarity of the serial data definitions in RS-232, RS-422, and RS-485, we offer only an overview of the RS-232 serial data communication protocol, including both hardware and software protocols.

1.4.1 ASCII Code

Most serial data communications use ASCII code as the basic data unit for communicating among devices. ASCII code was defined by the American National Standards Institute (ANSI), and its full name is American Standard Code for Information Interchange. Basically, all information can be expressed in ASCII by a sequence or combination of 26 English characters, as well as some special characters, and each character can be expressed and transmitted by an associated 7-bit binary code. This representation method is the ASCII method. In serial communication programming, the ASCII code can be expressed in different formats, such as decimal or hexadecimal, and different subroutines can be utilized to translate between the different formats. Appendix A shows a typical ASCII code table that contains the popular characters used in normal data communications.

One point to remember is that in most computer data communications, each data unit is composed of 1 byte, or 8 bits, of binary code. For example, in Figure 1.1, a binary sequence, `01100101`, which is equivalent to a decimal of 101 or a hexadecimal of 65h in the standard ASCII table, is an 8-bit binary code. Only 7 bits are occupied when this code is represented as an ASCII code: `1100101`. The most significant bit (MSB) is not used. It can be concluded that the maximum binary code that can be expressed in ASCII code is `1111111`, which is equivalent to a decimal of 127.

However, in the real world of serial data communications, instead of using 7 bits, a data unit or an ASCII character is actually represented by a byte, or 8 bits, of binary code traveling between two devices. The MSB bit in an 8-bit binary code is often used as a parity bit for error checking, thus making ASCII, in practice, an 8-bit code.

The ASCII table in Appendix A shows the binary sequence represented in Figure 1.1, `01100101`, is equivalent to the ASCII character 'A'. By using the ASCII code, the data can be successfully expressed and transmitted through a single wire, bit by bit, byte by byte, character by character, from one device to another.

A potential problem exists in using ASCII code during data communications. The incompatibility of different spoken languages can be a challenge; for example, some countries use non-English languages. Special care must be taken to handle such incompatibilities.

Another issue is that most computers employ some human-readable characters as their data communication medium. One exception is IBM, which has developed its own character set, the Extended Binary Coded Decimal Interchange Code (EBCDIC); however, this character set is not compatible with ASCII code.

A solution to these potential problems has been the development of a new character set that extends the ASCII code to meet the requirements of different languages used for data communications in different countries. IBM, Apple, and a number of UNIX vendors have developed a Unicode standard to improve compatibility; it includes 16-bit encoding that encompasses all existing national character code standards. The International Organization for Standardization (ISO) adopted this Unicode standard as a superset of ISO 10646 in June 1992, but the 16-bit encoding set will not be adopted worldwide for quite some time.

1.4.2 DTE and DCE

For RS-232 serial port communication, if the full EIA232 standard is implemented as defined, the equipment at the far end of the connection is called the *data terminal equipment* (DTE). A DTE device is usually a computer or terminal. The interface connector can be either a DB-9 or DB-25 male connector, and it uses 6 of 9 or 22 of the 25 available pins for signals or grounding. Equipment at the near end of the connection (the telephone line or other device interface) is called the *data communications equipment* (DCE); it has a male DB-9 or DB-25 connector and uses the same 6 or 22 available pins for signals and grounding. The cable used for linking DTE and DCE devices is a parallel straight-through cable with no crossovers or self-connects in the connector hoods. Here the term *crossover* means that a null modem cable is used to connect two devices (in most cases, two computers). A more detailed discussion of null modem cabling will be given in Section 1.5.2.

If all devices followed this standard exactly, all cables would be identical, and there would be no chance of an incorrectly wired cable being used. Figure 1.4 shows the orientation and connector types for DTE and DCE devices.

Throughout this book, DTE will always refer to a computer, and DCE will refer to equipment or a device interfaced to a computer.

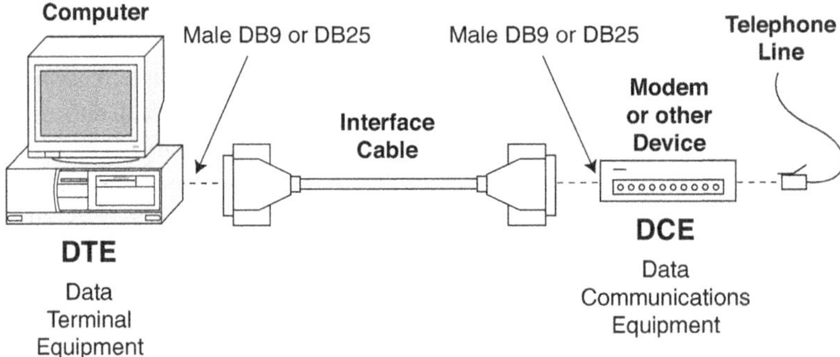

FIGURE 1.4 The connection between the DTE and the DCE. (This section is reprinted by the permission of the author, Christopher E. Strangio, CAMI Research Inc.)

1.4.3 Serial Data Format in TTL

Recall from Figure 1.1 that serial data communication uses three wires to transmit a sequence of binary bits, one by one, between two devices. This exact transmission has a certain requirement for data format and protocol. The actual data transmission between a DTE and a DCE utilizes two wires, or two RS-232 communication lines, a received data (RD) line and a transmitted data (TD) line, respectively. The TD line handles data to be transmitted from the DTE (PC computer) to the DCE, and the RD line works in reverse mode, processing data to be sent from the DCE to the DTE. The third line in Figure 1.1 is the common reference (or ground) line between the DTE and the DCE.

In the real world, serial data transmissions between the DTE and DCE can be divided into two categories: synchronous and asynchronous transmissions. A synchronous transmission takes place between the DTE and the DCE when both devices have the same transmission rate or speed. On the other hand, when the DTE has a different transmission rate than the DCE, an asynchronous transmission occurs. Wiring distances should be limited to 100 or 200 feet for asynchronous data and about 50 feet for synchronous data (and that may be pushing it in some cases). Synchronous data has a transmitting and receiving clock that limits the maximum distance that data can travel on a synchronous data line.

Almost all actual serial data communications are asynchronous, even when both devices use the same transmission rate (baud rate), because noise and disturbance from external factors and environmental conditions create a situation where the data must travel asynchronously between the DCE and the DTE. To coordinate this asynchronous transmission and make sure the communication between the two devices is correct (in other words, to synchronize the transmitted characters between the two devices), each serial data unit must have a certain format. A control unit called the *universal asynchronous receiver transmitter* (UART), which will be discussed in the following section, is always utilized to synchronize the data flow between the DTE and the DCE. Figure 1.5 shows a typical serial data unit format inside the DTE.

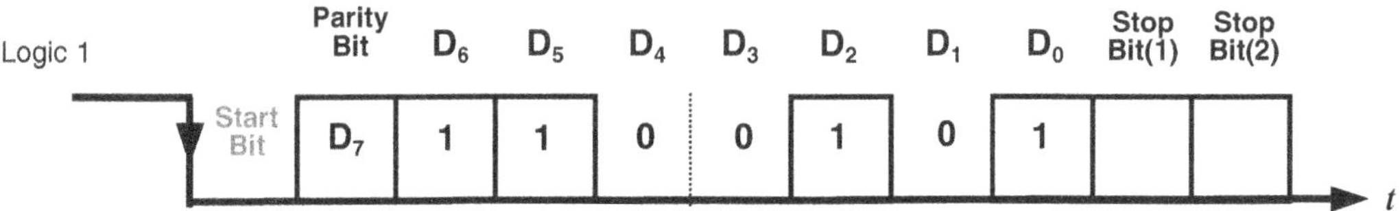

FIGURE 1.5 A typical serial data format—TTL/CMOS.

The serial data format is divided into the two categories, internal and external, which are equivalent to the data formats inside and outside the DTE or PC. The UART is an interface used to translate between the internal and external data formats of devices. Inside the DTE, the data is represented by the transistor-transistor-level (TTL) voltage, which is identical to the data format shown in Figure 1.5. Outside the DTE, the format in which the data is transmitted on the RS-232 transmission lines is different; this will be discussed in detail later in this section.

As shown in Figure 1.5, a total of 11 binary bits can be associated with an ASCII character to be transmitted. The first bit (or the start bit) is always logical 0 and always begins with a high-to-low transition. This high-to-low transition simply works as a synchronizing signal to indicate a new character will begin to be transmitted on the transmission lines. The idle state of the transmission lines (that is, when no character or data is being transmitted on the lines) is always logical 1. The next bit, bit 7, is utilized as a parity bit for error checking, and the value of this bit is determined by the number of binary 1's in the data unit. For example, if an `odd` parity is used for this data transmission, a value of `1` should be placed into this parity bit if the number of binary 1's in the data unit is an odd number. Otherwise, the value should be `0`. For our case, the data unit is an ASCII code 'A,' which is associated with a binary code of `1100101`, and it has four (`even`) binary 1's, so the parity bit value should be `0` if an odd parity is utilized.

When this character is transmitted from the DTE to the DCE, the receiver in the DCE side will check this parity bit value and count the number of the binary 1's from the received data unit to make sure this transmission is error-free. If the counted number of binary 1's of the received character matches with the received parity bit value, the transmission is successful. Otherwise, a transmission error occurs for this character transmission. For example, in Figure 1.5, the number of binary 1's is four, which is an even number, and a `0` should be placed in the *parity* bit position if an `odd` parity is utilized. The counting result of the binary 1's of the receiver should also be an even number, and the parity bit value should also be `0` if this transmission is successful.

Following the 7-bit ASCII code, the final two bits are stop bits. The values of these two stop bits are always logical `1`. When no data are being transmitted, a continuous `1` exists on the serial data line, indicating an idle state.

The duration of each bit sent across the lines determines the speed of the data transmission (the baud rate). Recall that the baud rate is commonly measured in bits per second (bps).

You can program the data format in your code to have different data transmission formats. For example, you can change the baud rate, the parity type (`odd` or `even`), the number of stop bits (1 or 2), and the number of binary bits (7 or 8) to be transmitted for each data unit.

Based on the serial data format discussed previously, the following parameters can be selected by a user to define his or her data transmission format:

- Baud rate
- Parity
- Stop bits
- Data bits

A more detailed discussion of some of these parameters will be provided later in this chapter.

1.4.4 Serial Data Format in Transmission Lines

When the data is transmitted on serial communication lines, a different data format is utilized to overcome some disturbances and noise. Figure 1.6 shows a typical data format for the transmission lines.

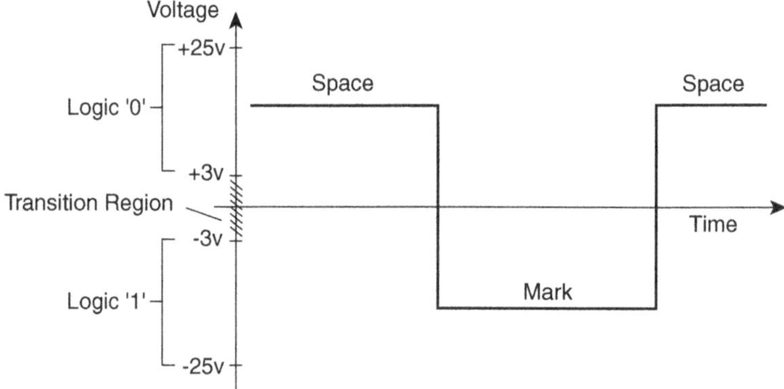

FIGURE 1.6 The real RS-232 signal.

Unlike the serial data format for TTL shown in Figure 1.5, the data format shown in Figure 1.6 is a real one that works for RS-232, RS-422, and RS-485 data communications. In long-distance data transmissions, for example, RS-485 can transmit data over more than 4,000 feet. Some factors, such as the signal attenuation, environmental disturbances, and noise should be considered to make sure that the data transmission is successful and reliable. For this purpose, the data format shown in Figure 1.6 should be adopted.

As previously mentioned, two transmission lines, RD and TD, are used to transmit data between the DTE and the DCE, respectively. TD and RD handle the data transmission asynchronously at a fixed baud rate, using start and stop bits for synchronization between the two devices. The data format shown in Figure 1.5 cannot be directly used for real data transmission. A UART should be used to translate that data format to the real data format shown in Figure 1.6, which can finally be transmitted over real communication lines.

In Figure 1.6, it should be noted that for real communication lines a low voltage of less than −3 volts is considered to be a logical `1` (called a Mark state) and a high voltage greater than 3 volts is read as a logical `0` (called a Space state). All the real RS-232 control lines use the opposite convention.

Figure 1.6 also shows that any voltage from −3 to −25 volts with respect to signal ground is considered a logical `1` (the Mark state), whereas a voltage from +3 to +25 volts is considered a logical `0` (the Space state). The range of voltages between −3 and +3 volts is considered a transition region for which signal states are not assigned.

Most contemporary applications will show an open-circuit signal voltage of −8 to −14 volts for logical 1 (Mark), and +8 to +14 volts for logical 0 (Space). Voltage magnitudes will be slightly less when the generator and receiver (the DTE and DCE devices) are connected with a cable. In some simple serial communication applications, two integrated circuits, MC1488 and MC1489, are used to finish these voltage-level translations. The MC1488 is called a *normal* voltage-level translator, which translates TTL voltages to transmission line voltages. The MC1489 is called an *inverse* voltage translator, and it translates voltages from the transmission-line level back to the TTL level.

The idle state (Mark) has the signal level negative with respect to common, and the active state (Space) has the signal level positive with respect to common. RS-232 has numerous handshaking lines (primarily used with modems) and also specifies a communications protocol. In general, if you are not connected to a modem, the handshaking lines can present a lot of problems if they are not disabled in the software or accounted for in the hardware (looped back or pulled up). Request to Send (RTS) does have some utility in certain applications. RS-423 is another single-ended specification with enhanced operation over RS-232; however, it has not been widely used in the industry.

RS-232 signals are represented by voltage levels with respect to system common (power ground). This type of signal works well in point-to-point communications at low data transmission rates. RS-232 ports on the PC are assigned to a single device. COM1 might be the mouse port, with COM2 used for a modem. This is an example of *point-to-point communications* (in which one port communicates with one device). RS-232 signals require a common ground between the PC and the associated device.

Before we can finish this section, we want to offer a little more detail regarding the two parameters mentioned previously: baud rate and parity.

1.4.5 Baud Rate

Baud rate is defined as the transmission speed of a sequence of binary bits in a transmission line, or in other words, the bps. Typical baud rates used in serial data communications are 9,600, 19,200, and 38,400. For example, a transmission speed of 300 characters per second is equivalent to a baud rate of 2,400 (300 bytes × 8 bits per second). Some specifically designed I/O serial/parallel interfacing cards have much higher baud rates, and the user can select different baud rates based on the clock frequency generated from the clock generator in the interfacing card.

1.4.6 Parity

A user can select from five parity values: `None`, `Even`, `Odd`, `Mark`, and `Space`:

`None` means that the data is transmitted without any parity bits. This is a popular setting when 8 bits of data are transmitted. For this kind of data transmission, no parity bits are available for transmission error checking.

`Even` means that the transmitting serial device will assign a logical `1` to the parity bit if an even number of binary 1's exist in the character's data bits. Otherwise, the parity bit is assigned a logical `0`.

`Odd` means that there will always be an odd number of logical 1s in the character's data bits. This setting will indicate an error if an even number of logical 1s is received.

`Mark` means that the DTE will send a logical `1s` parity bit before the character's data bits.

`Space` indicates that the transmitting serial device will send a logical `0` parity bit prior to the character's data bits.

Figure 1.7 shows a real serial data format in the transmission lines with an ASCII code 'A.' The parity is `even`, which is different from the parity bit in Figure 1.5, and two stop bits are present.

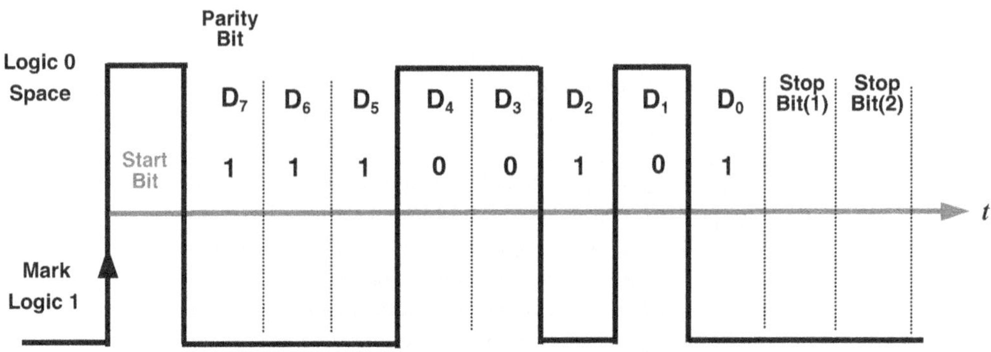

FIGURE 1.7 The RS-232 signal in transmission lines.

Now we have a basic understanding of serial data communications, as well as some useful terminologies. Before moving ahead to the UART, however, it's important to have some knowledge of how the serial port communicates with other devices and how the data is transmitted between the DTE and the DCE.

Data communication can be divided into the following four modes, based on its functionality: simplex, half-duplex, full-duplex, and multiplex:

- **Simplex:** In this mode, serial communication takes place in only one direction, either from the DTE to the DCE or vice versa.
- **Half-duplex:** In this mode, serial communication can take place in both directions, but the communication can take place in only one direction at a time. This means that either the sender or receiver can send or receive information at different times, but they cannot send and receive data simultaneously.
- **Full-duplex:** This mode allows serial communications to take place in both directions at the same time, which means that the sender and receiver can handle and exchange information simultaneously.
- **Multiplex:** This mode allows multiple serial communications channels to occur over the same serial communication line. Multiplex operations are performed by either allocating separate frequencies or by time slicing to the individual serial communication channels.

Most serial data communications belong to the full-duplex category.

Each data communication method mentioned here is based on a sequence of handshaking signals, and each signal is transmitted by a different signal line or RS-232 wire. All these handshaking signals are controlled by the UART, which works like a central headquarter. Let us now take a look at the signal distribution and the signal pin assignment on a physical RS-232 connector.

1.4.7 Serial Signal Handshaking and the Physical Connector

Figure 1.8 shows the RS-232 physical connector and pin assignments; (a) is for the DB-9 and (b) is for the DB-25 connector.

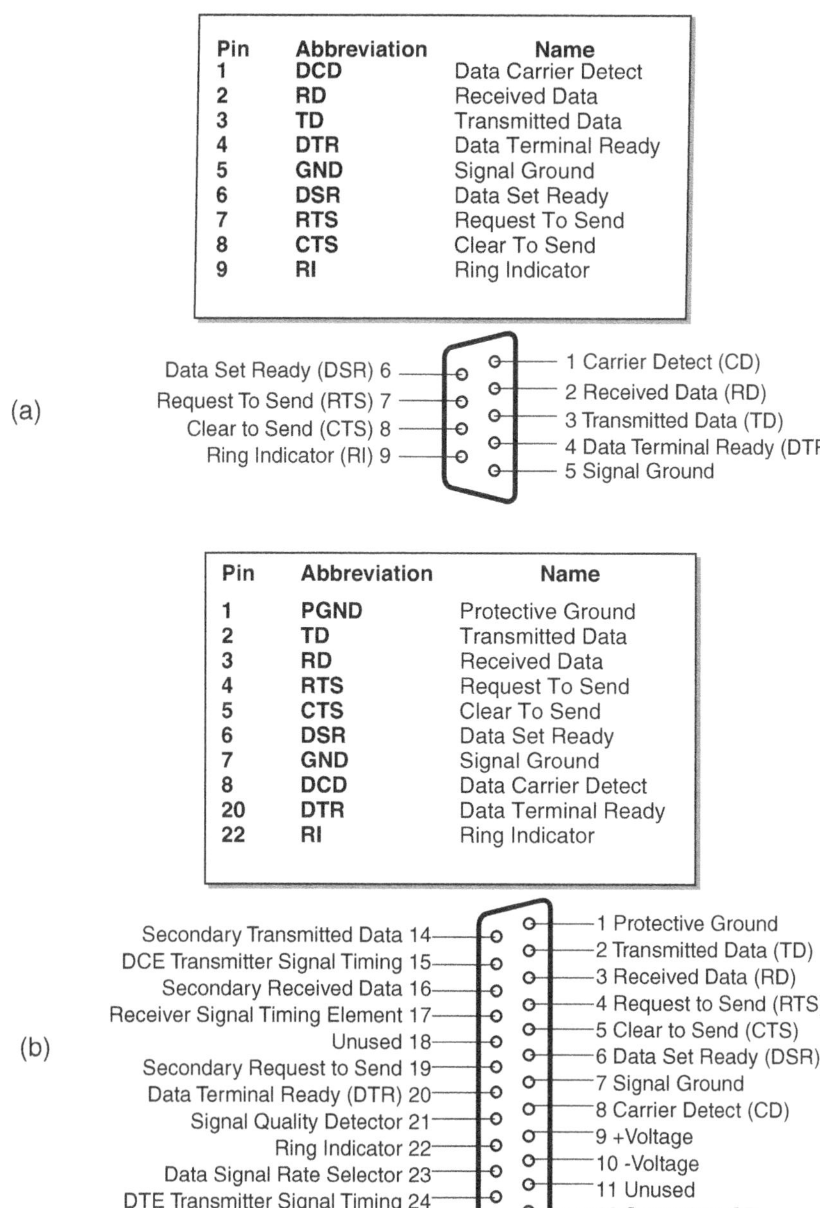

FIGURE 1.8 The RS-232 connectors: (a) DB-9 connector; (b) DB-25 connector.

Figure 1.10 shows a full EIA-232 signal definition for the DTE device (usually a PC). Figure 1.11 displays a full EIA-232 signal assignment for the DCE device. The most commonly used signals are shown in bold type.

Pin	DTE Side		DCE Side	Pin
1	Data Carrier Detect (DCD)	←	Data Carrier Detect (DCD)	1
2	Received Data (**RD**)	←	Transmitted Data (**TD**)	2
3	Transmitted Data (**TD**)	→	Received Data (**RD**)	3
4	Data Terminal Ready (**DTR**)	→	Data Terminal Ready (**DTR**)	4
5	Ground	—	Ground	5
6	Data Set Ready (**DSR**)	←	Data Set Ready (**DSR**)	6
7	Request To Send (**RTS**)	→	Clear To Send (**CTS**)	7
8	Clear To Send (**CTS**)	←	Request To Send (**RTS**)	8
9	Ring Indicator (RI)	←	Ring Indicator (RI)	9

FIGURE 1.9 The handshaking signal connection in DB-9.

1.4.7.1 DB-9 Connector

Many of the six signal lines in the EIA-232 DB-9 standard pertain to connections where the DCE device is a modem, and these lines are used only when the software protocol employs them. For any DCE device that is not a modem, or in situations where two DTE devices are directly linked, far fewer signal lines are necessary.

Figure 1.9 shows the handshaking signal connection of a DB-9 connector between the DTE and the DCE. A detailed explanation of those signal lines follows.

- **Pin 1—Data Carrier Detect (DCD):** The DCD line is set to logical `0` (high) whenever a data link is in progress. Generally, this line should be asserted by a DCE only when it has established a connection with another DCE, usually over a telephone line. This lets the DTE device know that communications can begin. The modem does not have a valid connection if this line is low.
  DCD is used by applications that have to wait for incoming calls. If a modem is programmed to auto-answer an incoming call, an application can simply scan the incoming lines for the assertion of DCD. If DCD goes high on a modem, it means that a call has been successfully answered.
- **Pin 2—Received Data (RD):** The RD line is utilized by the DCE to send data to the DTE. The EIA standard requires that an RD line be held at Mark level (between −3 and −25 volts), which is equivalent to a logical 1, when no carrier is present.
- **Pin 3—Transmitted Data (TD):** The TD line is used by the DTE to send data to the DCE. Similar to the RD line, this line should be kept at Mark level (between −3 and −25 volts), which is equivalent to a logical `1`, when no data is present on the line.
- **Pin 4—Data Terminal Ready (DTR):** The DTR line will be set to logical `0` (high) by the DTE when it is ready to begin a new communication with the DCE.
  All communication will be initiated by the DTE when it is ready, and the starting signal will set the DTR line to logical `0` (less than 3 volts). This value will be forwarded to the DCE, and the latter will then know that the DTE is ready to begin a communication. If the DCE is ready for this communication, it will respond to the DTE with a set DSR to indicate its readiness. The DTR and DSR can be used as a pair of handshaking signals to coordinate between the DTE and the DCE to initiate communication.

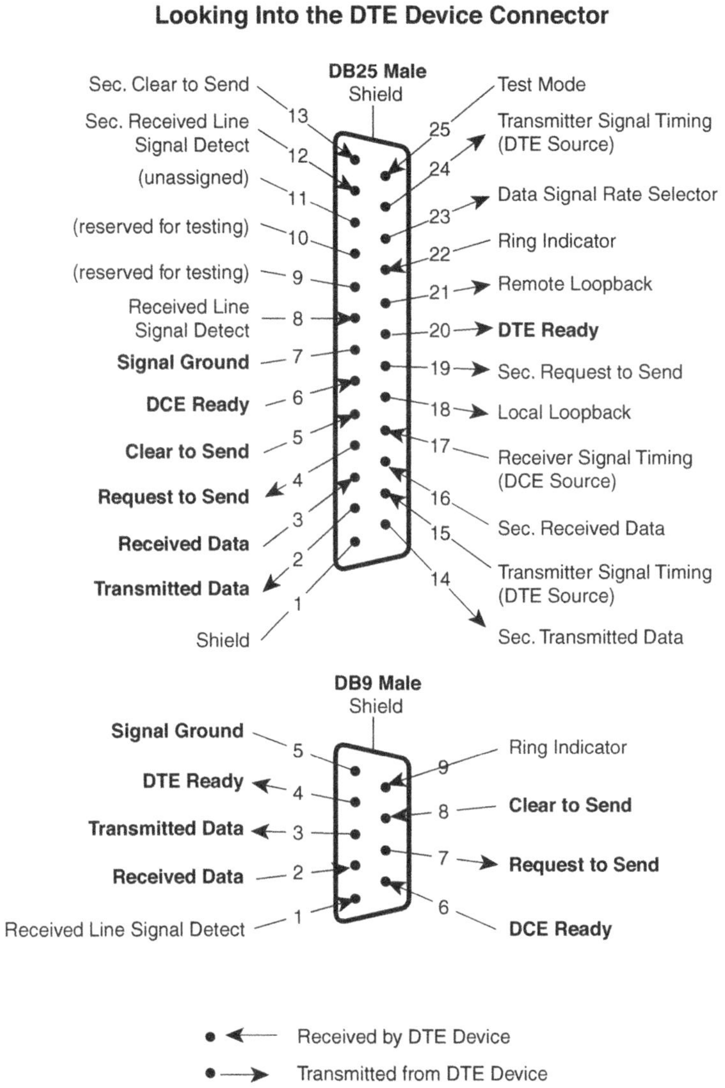

FIGURE 1.10 Pin assignments in DTE Side. (This figure is reprinted by the permission of the author, Christopher E. Strangio, CAMI Research Inc.)

- **Pin 5—Signal Ground (GND):** This is the common reference with respect to the signals for both the DTE and the DCE devices. In real data transmission, the GND on the DTE side and the GND on the DCE side need to be connected.
- **Pin 6—Data Set Ready (DSR):** The DSR line is set to logical 0 (high) by the DCE when it is ready to communicate with the DTE. Usually, the DSR line and the DTR line work together as a pair of handshaking signals. The DSR is used by the DCE to provide feedback to the DTE, inform it (by means of a logical 0 signal) that the DCE is ready to communicate with the DTE. Both the DTR and DSR should be kept at logical 0 (high) during a communication process until the communication is finished.

Looking Into the DCE Device Connector

DB25 Female

Shield — 13
Received Data — 12
Transmitted Data — 11
Clear to Send — 10
Request to Send — 9
DCE Ready — 8
Signal Ground — 7
Received Line Signal Detect — 6
(reserved for testing) — 5
(reserved for testing) — 4
(unassigned) — 3
Sec. Received Line Signal Detect — 2
Sec. Clear to Send — 1
Shield

14 — Sec. Transmitted Data
15 — Transmitter Signal Timing (DTE Source)
16 — Sec. Received Data
17 — Receiver Signal Timing (DCE Source)
18 — Local Loopback
19 — Sec. Request to Send
20 — **DTE Ready**
21 — Remote Loopback
22 — Ring Indicator
23 — Data Signal Rate Selector
24 — Transmitter Signal Timing (DTE Source)
25 — Test Mode

DB9 Female

Shield

Received Line Signal Detect — 5
Transmitted Data — 4
Received Data — 3
DTE Ready — 2
Signal Ground — 1

9 — **DCE Ready**
8 — **Clear to Send**
7 — **Request to Send**
6 — Ring Indicator

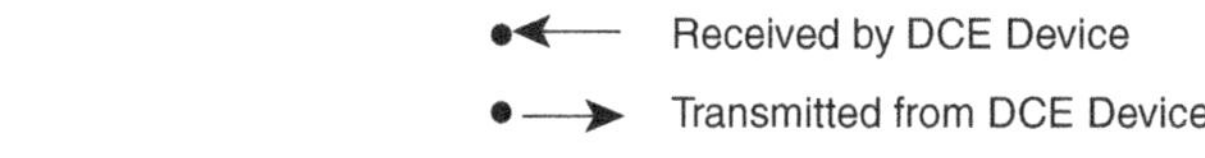

FIGURE 1.11 Pin assignments in DCE side. (This figure is reprinted by the permission of the author, Christopher E. Strangio, CAMI Research Inc.)

- **Pin 7—Request To Send (RTS):** The RTS line is set to logical `0` (high) by the DTE when it wants to transmit data to the DCE. In early applications of RS-232 equipment, such as half-duplex modems, both RTS and Clear to Send (CTS) lines were mainly used as handshaking signals between the DTE and the DCE. Today half-duplex modems are rarely used, and for the most part RTS and CTS are used almost exclusively to implement hardware handshaking.

  When the buffer in the DTE is empty and it is ready to receive more data, the DTE will set RTS to inform the DCE that the DTE is ready to get the next character from the DCE. This line will be kept at logical `1` (low) if the buffer of the DTE is full; this setting will inhibit the DCE from sending the next data.

- **Pin 8—Clear to Send (CTS):** The CTS line is set to logical `0` (high) by the DCE when it is ready to receive data from the DTE.
  This signal works as a feedback to (or a handshake with) the DTE to indicate whether the DCE is ready to receive the data.
- **Pin 9—Ring Indicator (RI):** The RI line will be set to logical `0` (high) by the DCE when a ring is detected.
  RI is used to indicate that the incoming phone line is ringing and it should rise and fall in lockstep with the ring cycle. This allows the software not only to detect incoming calls, but also to count rings.

1.4.7.2 DB-25 Connector

Recall from Figure 1.8 (b) that most signals in the DB-25 are not used for most general data communication, and only the most used signals are enclosed by parentheses and abbreviated. Those often used signals are also bolded in Figures 1-10 and 1-11.

Many of the 22 signal lines in the EIA-232 standard pertain to connections where the DCE device is a modem, and are used only when the software protocol employs them. For any DCE device that is not a modem, or in situations when two DTE devices are directly linked, fewer signal lines are required.

You may have noticed in the pin-out drawings a secondary channel that includes a duplicate set of flow-control signals. This secondary channel provides for management of the remote modem, enabling baud rates to be changed on the fly, retransmission to be requested if a parity error is detected, and other control functions to be managed. This secondary channel, when used, is typically set to operate at a much lower baud rate than that of the primary channel; this lower setting ensures reliability in the control path. In addition, it may operate as a simplex, half-duplex, or full-duplex channel, depending on the capabilities of the modem.

Transmitter and receiver timing signals (pins 15, 17, and 24) are used only for synchronous transmission protocol. For the standard asynchronous 8-bit protocol, external timing signals are unnecessary.

Signal names that imply direction, such as `Transmit Data` and `Receive Data`, are named from the point of view of the DTE device. If the EIA-232 standard were strictly followed, these signals would have the same name for the same pin number on the DCE side as well. Unfortunately, this has not been done in practice by most engineers, probably because no one can keep straight which side is DTE and which is DCE. As a result, direction-sensitive signal names are changed on the DCE end to reflect their drive direction at the DCE. Figure 1.12 gives the conventional usage of signal names.

1.4.7.2.1 Secondary Communications Channel Signal Lines

Most signals used in DB-25 are equivalent to those used in a DB-9 connector. The DB-25 signals that are different from DB-9 are listed here:

- **Pin 14—Secondary Transmitted Data (STD)**
- **Pin 16—Secondary Received Data (SRD)**
- **Pin 19—Secondary Request to Send (SRTS)**
- **Pin 13—Secondary Clear to Send (SCTS)**

These signals are equivalent to the corresponding signals in the primary communications channel. For the purpose of increased readability, however, the baud rate is typically much slower in the secondary channel.

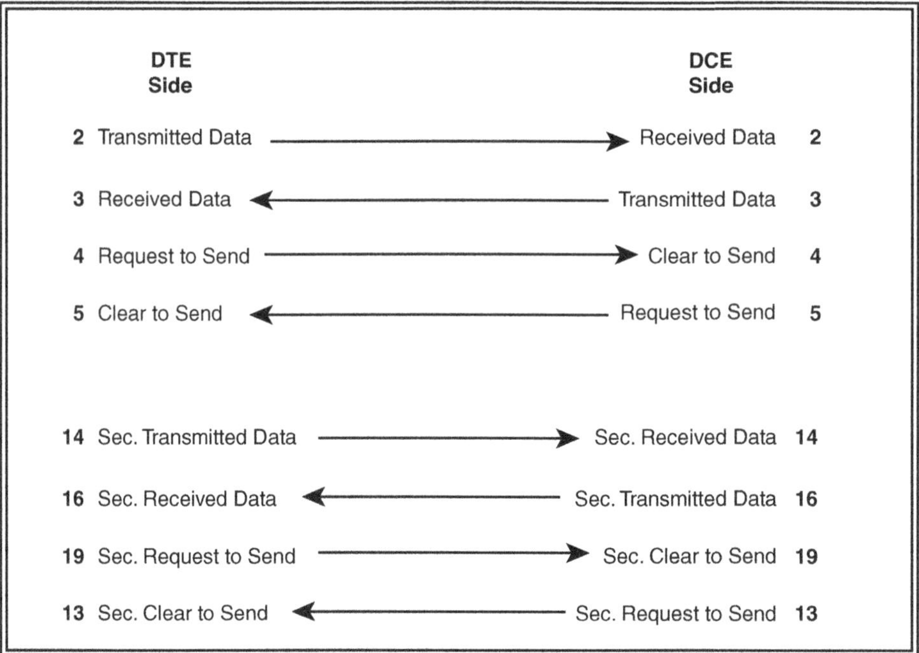

FIGURE 1.12 The connection between the DTE and the DCE in DB-25.

1.4.7.2.2 Modem Status and Control Signals

- **Pin 8—Received Line Signal Detector, also called Carrier Detect (CD):** This signal is relevant when the DCE device is a modem. It is asserted (logical `0`, positive voltage) by the modem when the telephone line is busy-when a connection has been established and an answer tone is being received from the remote modem. The signal is deasserted when no answer tone is being received or when the answer tone is of inadequate quality to meet the local modem's requirements (perhaps due to a noisy channel).
- **Pin 12—Secondary Received Line Signal Detector (SCD):** This signal is equivalent to the received line signal detector (pin 8), but refers to the secondary channel.
- **Pin 22—Ring Indicator (RI):** This signal is relevant when the DCE device is a modem and is asserted (logical `0`, positive voltage) when a ringing signal is being received from the telephone line. The assertion time of this signal approximately equals the duration of the ring signal, and it is deasserted between rings or when no ringing is present.
- **Pin 23—Data Signal Rate Selector:** This signal may originate either in the DTE or DCE device (but not both) and is used to select one of two prearranged baud rates. The asserted condition (logical `0`, positive voltage) selects the higher baud rate.

1.4.7.2.3 Transmitter and Receiver Timing Signals

- **Pin 15—Transmitter Signal Element Timing, also called Transmitter Clock (TC):** This signal is relevant only when the DCE device is a modem and is operating with a synchronous protocol. The modem generates this clock signal to control the rate at which data is sent on the transmitted data line (pin 2) from the DTE device to the DCE device. The transition from logical `1` to logical `0` (negative voltage to positive voltage) on this line causes a corresponding transition to the next data element on the transmitted data line. The modem generates this signal continuously, except when it is performing internal diagnostic functions.

- **Pin 17—Receiver Signal Element Timing, also called Receiver Clock (RC):** This signal is similar to TC (described previously), except that it provides timing information for the DTE receiver.
- **Pin 24—Transmitter Signal Element Timing, also called External Transmitter Clock (ETC):** Timing signals are provided by the DTE device for use by a modem. This signal is used only when TC and RC (pins 15 and 17) are not in use. The transition of logical `1` to logical `0` (negative voltage to positive voltage) indicates the time center of the data element. Timing signals will be provided whenever the DTE is turned on, regardless of other signal conditions.

1.4.7.2.4 Channel Test Signal Lines

- **Pin 18—Local Loopback (LL):** This signal is generated by the DTE device and is used to place the modem into a test state. When Local Loopback is asserted (logical `0`, positive voltage), the modem redirects its modulated output signal, which is normally fed into the telephone line, back into its receptive circuitry. This enables data generated by the DTE to be echoed back through the local modem to check the condition of the modem circuitry. The modem asserts its Test Mode signal on pin 25 to acknowledge that it has been placed in local loopback condition.
- **Pin 21—Remote Loopback (RL):** This signal is generated by the DTE device and is used to place the remote modem into a test state. When **Remote Loopback** is asserted (logical `0`, positive voltage), the remote modem redirects its received data back to its transmitted data input, thereby remodulating the received data and returning it to its source. When the DTE initiates such a test, transmitted data is passed through the local modem, the telephone line, the remote modem, and back, to exercise the channel and confirm its integrity. The remote modem signals the local modem to assert **Test Mode** on pin 25 when the remote loopback test is underway.
- **Pin 25—Test Mode (TM):** This signal is relevant only when the DCE device is a modem. When asserted (logical `0`, positive voltage), it indicates that the modem is in a **Local Loopback** or **Remote Loopback** condition. Other internal self-test conditions may also cause **Test Mode** to be asserted; these conditions depend on the modem and the network to which it is attached.

1.4.7.2.5 Signal Ground and Shield

- **Pin 7, pin 1**, and the **shell** are included in this category. Cables provide separate paths for each, but internal wiring often connects pin 1 and the cable shell/shield to signal ground on pin 7.
- **Pin 7—Ground:** All signals are referenced to a common ground, as defined by the voltage on pin 7. This conductor may or may not be connected to the protective ground inside the DCE device. The existence of a defined ground potential within the cable makes the EIA-232 standard different from a balanced differential voltage standard, such as EIA-530, which provides far greater noise immunity.

The EIA-232 standard includes a common ground reference on pin 7 and is frequently joined to pin 1 and a circular shield that surrounds all 25 cable conductors. Data, timing, and control signal voltages are measured with respect to this common ground. EIA-232 cannot be used in applications where the equipment on opposite ends of the connection must be electrically isolated.

1.4.8 Serial Signal Timing

The EIA-232 standard is applicable to data rates of up to 20,000 bits per second (the usual upper limit is 19,200 baud). Fixed baud rates are not set by the EIA-232 standard. However, the commonly used rates are 300, 1,200, 2,400, 9,600, and 19,200 baud. Other accepted values, which are not often used, include 110 (mechanical teletype machines), 600, and 4,800 baud.

Changes in signal state from logical `1` to logical `0` (or vice versa) must abide by several requirements:

1. Signals that enter the transition region during a change of state must move through the transition region to the opposite signal state without reversing direction or reentering.
2. For control signals, the transit time through the transition region should be less than 1ms.
3. For data and timing signals, the transit time through the transition region should be:
   a. less than 1ms for bit periods greater than 25ms
   b. 4 percent of the bit period for bit periods between 25ms and 125μs
   c. less than 5μs for bit periods less than 125μs
4. The slope of the rising and falling edges of a transition should not exceed 30v/μs. Rates higher than this may induce cross talk in adjacent conductors of a cable.

The rise and fall times of data and timing signals should (ideally) be equal, but in any case should vary by no more than a factor of three. Figure 1.13 shows a normal and some abnormal serial signals.

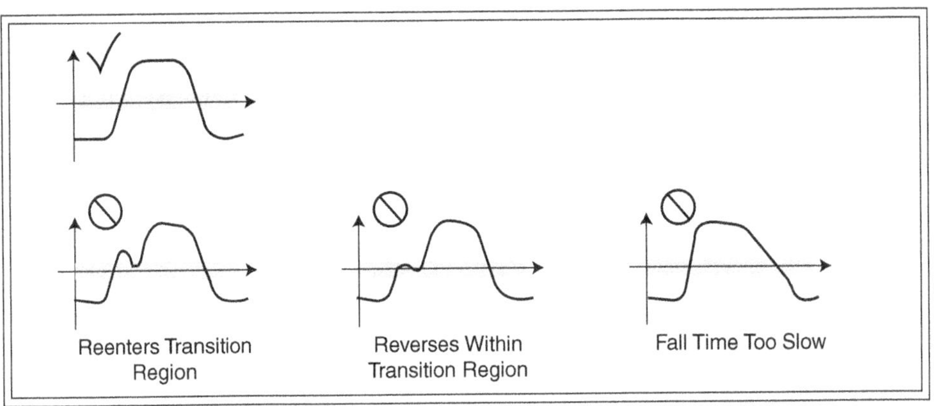

FIGURE 1.13 The normal and abnormal serial signals.

An acceptable pulse (top) moves through the transition region quickly and without hesitation or reversal. Defective pulses (bottom) can cause data errors. Note that neither the ASCII alphabet nor the asynchronous serial protocol that defines the start bit, number of data bits, parity bit, and stop bit is part of the EIA-232 specification.

1.5 SERIAL PORT CABLING

For the serial communications, different connections exist between the DTE and the DCE, the DTE and the DTE, the DCE and the DCE devices.

1.5.1 PC-TO-MODEM CABLING

The simplest type of connection between the DTE and the DCE is a PC-to-modem connection. In this type of connection, the male connector in the DTE device is directly connected to the female connector in the DCE device, pin by pin. Figure 1.14 shows a PC-to-modem connection. The cabling has DB-9 (a) and DB-25 (b) connectors.

DTE		DCE	
DCD	1	1	DCD
RD	2	2	RD
TD	3	3	TD
DTR	4	4	DTR
GND	5	5	GND
DSR	6	6	DSR
RTS	7	7	RTS
CTS	8	8	CTS
RI	9	9	RI

(a) DB-9 Connector.

DTE		DCE	
TD	2	2	TD
RD	3	3	RD
RTS	4	4	RTS
CTS	5	5	CTS
DSR	6	6	DSR
GND	7	7	GND
DCD	8	8	DCD
DTR	20	20	DTR
RI	22	22	RI

(b) DB-25 Connector.

FIGURE 1.14 The PC-to-modem connection.

Sometimes, a connection or a cabling between a DB-9 and a DB-25 connector is needed. In this case, the pins are shifted between DB-9 and DB-25 connectors to make sure that a correct connection is available for data communication.

Figure 1.15 shows a sample connection between DB-9 male (DTE) and a DB-25 (DCE) connectors.

DTE (9 Pin)		DCE (25 Pin)	
TD	3	2	TD
RD	2	3	RD
RTS	7	4	RTS
CTS	8	5	CTS
DSR	6	6	DSR
GND	5	7	GND
DCD	1	8	DCD
DTR	4	20	DTR
RI	9	22	RI

FIGURE 1.15 The PC-to-modem connection between DB-9 and DB-25.

1.5.2 Null Modem Cabling

Most serial data communications occur between DTE and the DCE devices (such as between a PC and a modem) or between a host computer and a peripheral device. In some implementations, communication between two computers or two devices is needed. In such a case, the communication occurs between two DTE or two DCE devices. The cable connection for this kind of data communication is called *null modem cabling*.

The term *null modem* refers to the fact that the cable takes the place of the pair of modems that should be connecting the two DTE devices. In other words, without going through modems, two DTE devices are directly connected together to perform the serial data transmissions between them. With null modem cabling, handshaking signals may not be necessary.

Several null modem configurations exist. The simplest one involves a three-wire null modem connection, as shown in Figure 1.16 (a) DB-9 and (b) DB-25.

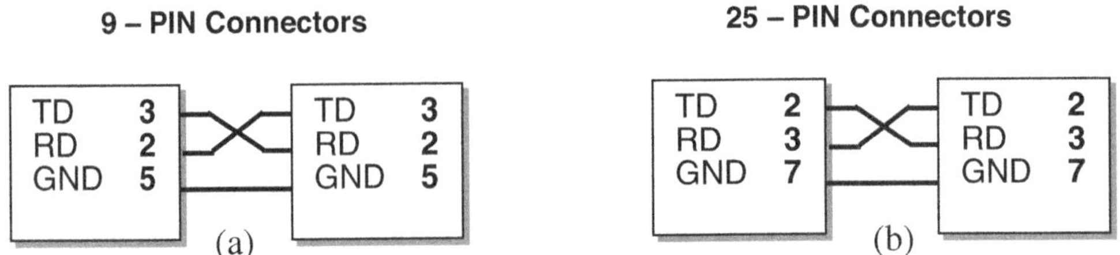

FIGURE 1.16 The simplest null modem connection.

Figure 1.16 shows that the most important connection on the null modem is the crossing of the transmitted data (TD) and received data (RD). This connection ensures that both the sender and the receiver have a correct data path.

Figure 1.17 shows a null modem configuration with full handshaking. Both the data and handshaking outputs connect to their corresponding inputs on the opposite device.

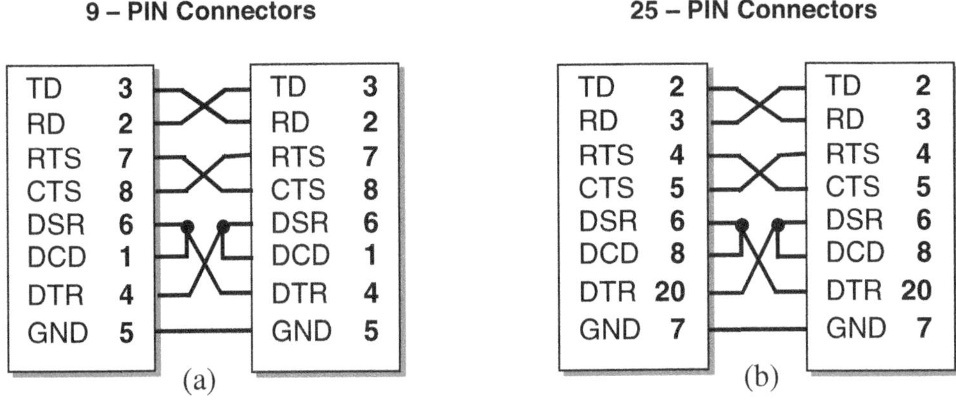

FIGURE 1.17 The null modem connection.

At this point, all the fundamentals and terms used in RS-232 serial data communications have been covered. You should have a basic understanding of RS-232 signals, physical connectors, cabling, and basic data transmission handshaking signals. The following section discusses the UART, which is a core unit in controlling and processing serial data communications in the real world.

1.6 THE UNIVERSAL ASYNCHRONOUS RECEIVER TRANSMITTER (UART)

As previously mentioned, the serial signal has different formats. Inside DTE devices and PC computers, all signals are transmitted on TTL level (0 to 5 volts), but on serial communication lines, the signal level is significantly different (−14 to +14 volts). Also, all signals inside a DTE or PC are transmitted in parallel mode, including signals between the CPU and memory, between the CPU and UART, and between the CPU and other I/O ports. At the same time, the signals transmitted between the DTE and the DCE are in the serial mode. To successfully connect a serial mode signal with a parallel data bus inside the DTE or PC, a control unit is needed. The control unit performs the following actions to work as an interface:

- **Receiving**
  Translating the received data from the serial format to the parallel format and feeding it to the CPU for further processing
  Translating the received signal from the transmission level to the TTL level, and feeding it to the CPU
- **Sending**
  Translating the outgoing data from the parallel format to the serial format, and sending it to the transmission line
  Translating the outgoing data from the TTL level to the transmission level

The control unit that performs these functions is the universal asynchronous receiver transmitter (UART).

In addition to converting between serial and parallel processing, the UART does some other things as a byproduct of its primary task. Extra bits, such as the start and stop bits, parity bits, are added to each byte before it can be transmitted. Almost all microcomputers use the UART to implement the RS-232 serial interface. The IBM PC and IBM compatibles use a UART that is based on National Semiconductor's INS8250 family of UARTs. Although some PC computers today still use the 8250 UART, most computers use the 16450 and 16550 UARTs. Basically, the 16450 UART is a higher-speed version of the 8250, and the 16550 is a special version of the 16450 that has what are called First Input First Output *(FIFO) buffers.* As today's high-speed modems and multitasking environments become more and more commonplace, the 16550 UART is gradually becoming the UART of choice in the PC world.

A UART is composed of a transmitter, a receiver, and a control unit. It contains a serial-to-parallel data converter, a parallel-to-serial converter, and voltage-level translators. A simple UART and its role in the data transmission are shown in Figure 1.18 (a) and (b), respectively.

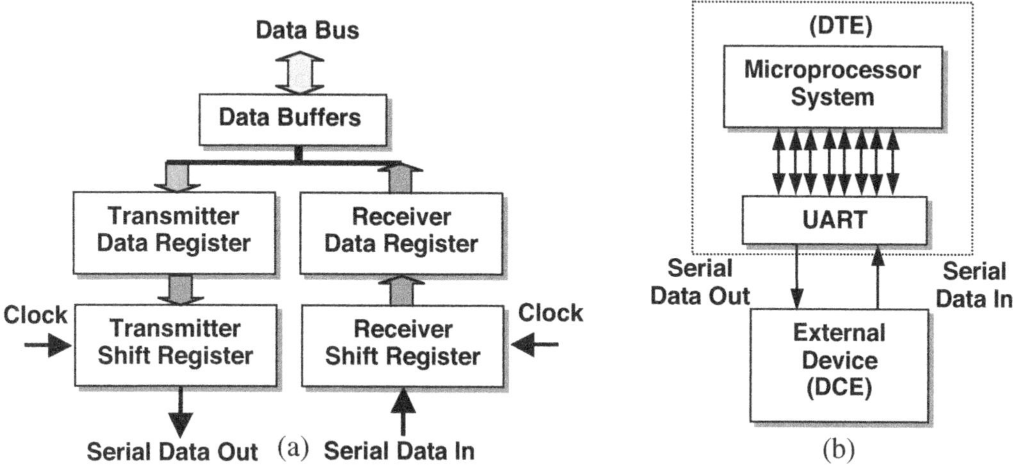

FIGURE 1.18 The UART structure and role.

Basically, the serial-to-parallel data converter is composed of shift registers and some clock control units. A simplified serial-to-parallel data converter is shown in Figure 1.19.

The serial data input is a sequence of serialized binary bits. With a high-to-low transition at the start bit, it sets the control flip-flop and makes the Q output a logical `1` (refer to Figure 1.19).

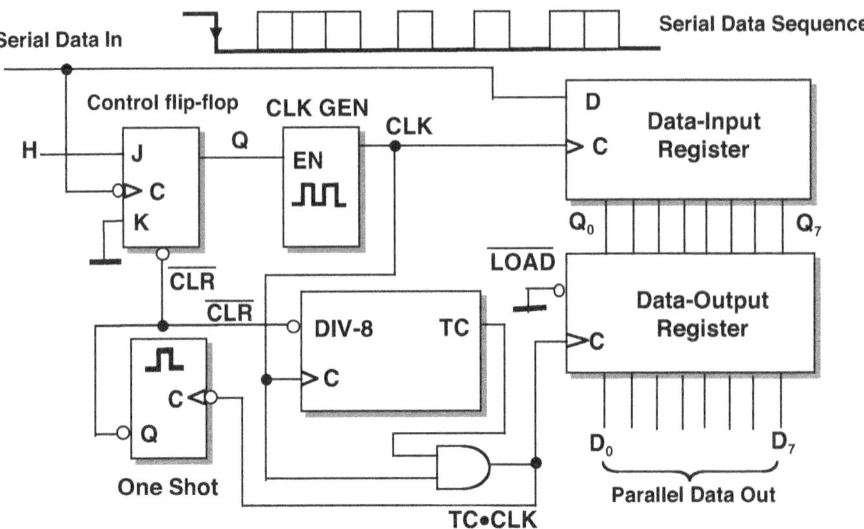

FIGURE 1.19 A serial-to-parallel unit in the UART.

The clock generator is enabled to generate a sequence of pulses to drive the data-input register, which is the shift register. After some delay, the logical `1` signal causes the input serial data to be moved, bit by bit, from left to right. The clock sequence also drives the divide-by-8 counter (DIV-8). The clock has a frequency accuracy equal to that of incoming serial data, and the first clock pulse after the start bit occurs simultaneously with the first data bit.

Under the control of this clock sequence, the 8-bit serial data, D_7 through D_0, are serially shifted into the data-input register. After the eighth clock pulse, a high-to-low transition of the terminal count (TC) output of the counter, ANDed with the clock (`TC. CLK`), loads the eight bits stored in the data-input register into the data-output register. This same transition triggers the one shot register, which generates a short-duration pulse to clear the counter and reset the control flip-flop, and thus disable the clock generator. The system is then ready for the next sequence of serial data inputs, and it waits for the next high-to-low transition at the beginning of the start bit.

To achieve a parallel-to-serial data converter, you would reverse this process.

1.6.1 Two Types of UARTs*

Two basic types of UARTs exist: dumb UARTS and FIFO UARTS. Dumb UARTs include the 8250, 16450, early 16550, and early 16650. They are obsolete, but if you understand how they work, it's easy to understand how the modern FIFO UARTS work (including the later versions 16550, 16550A, and higher numbers).

Some confusion regarding UART 16550 exists. Early models had a bug and worked properly only as 16450s (without FIFO). Later models with the bug fixed were named 16550A, but many manufacturers did not accept the name change and continued calling it the 16550. Most 16550 UARTs in use today are 16550As. Linux will report it as being a 16550A even though your hardware manual (or a label note) says it's a 16550. A similar situation exists for the 16650 (except that it's worse because the manufacturer allegedly didn't admit anything was wrong). Linux will report a

* This section is reprinted with permission of the author, David S. Lawyer, from the Web site www.ibiblio.org/mdw/HOWTO/Serial-HOWTO.html.

late 16650 as being a 16650V2. If Linux lists a UART as a 16650, the UART is one of the early versions; this is bad news and is used as if it had only a one-byte buffer.

Let's examine what happens when a UART has sent or received a byte. Then we can look at and begin to understand the differences between dumb and FIFO (or first in, first out queuing). The UART itself cannot do anything with the data passing through it; it simply receives and sends it. For the obsolete dumb UARTS, the CPU gets an interrupt signal from the serial device every time a byte has been sent or received. The CPU then moves the received byte out of the UART's buffer and into memory somewhere, or it gives the UART another byte to send. The obsolete 8250 and 16450 UARTs have only a one-byte buffer. This means that every time one byte is sent or received, the CPU is interrupted. At low transfer rates, this is no problem at all, but at high transfer rates, the CPU gets so busy dealing with the UART that it is does not have time to adequately process other tasks. In some cases, the CPU does not get around to servicing the interrupt in time, and the byte is overwritten because other bytes are coming in so quickly. This delay is called an *overrun* or *overflow*.

FIFO UARTs help solve this problem. Each 16550A (or 16550) FIFO chip comes with a 16-byte FIFO buffer. This means that it can receive up to 14 bytes, or send 16 bytes, before it has to interrupt the CPU. Not only can the CPU wait for more bytes, but it can also then transfer 14 to 16 bytes at a time. This is a significant advantage over the obsolete UARTs, which have only one-byte buffers. With a FIFO UART, the CPU receives fewer interrupts and is free to do other things, so data is rarely lost. Notice that the interrupt threshold (or trigger level) of FIFO buffers may be set at less than 14. Other possible choices include settings of 1, 4, and 8. As of late 2000, there was no way the Linux user could set these directly. Although many PCs only have a 16550 chip with a 16-byte buffer, better UARTS have even larger buffers.

The interrupt is issued slightly before the buffer gets full (at a trigger level of 14 bytes for a 16-byte buffer). This allows room for a couple more bytes to be received before the interrupt service routine is able to actually fetch all these bytes. The trigger level may be set to various permitted values by kernel software. A trigger level setting of `1` will be almost like an obsolete UART (except that it still has room for 15 more bytes after it issues the interrupt).

Now consider the case where you are on the Internet. Someone has just sent you a short Web page of text. All of this came in through the serial port. If you have a 16-byte buffer on the serial port that holds back characters until it has 14 of them, some of the last characters on the screen might be missing because the FIFO buffer has waited to get the 14th character. However, the 14th character has not arrived because you have been sent the entire page (over the phone line), and no more characters exist to be sent to you. It could be that these last characters are part of the HTML formatting and are not characters for display on the screen, but you don't want to lose format!

There is a timeout to prevent this problem, which works as follows for the receiving UART buffer: If characters arrive one after another, then an interrupt is issued only when, for instance, the 14th character reaches the buffer. If a character arrives and the next character does not arrive soon thereafter, an interrupt is issued anyway. Your computer will fetch all of the characters in the FIFO buffer, even if only a few (or only one) are present. There is also timeout for the transmitting buffer as well.

You may wonder why the FIFO buffers are not larger. After all, memory is cheap, and it does not cost much to use more buffers in the kilobyte range. The reason is *flow control*. Flow control stops the flow of data (bytes) on a serial line when necessary. If a stop signal is sent to the serial port, then the stop request is handled by the software (even if flow control is supposedly handled by the hardware). Remember, the serial port hardware really knows nothing about flow control.

If the serial port buffer contains 64 bytes that are ready to be sent when it receives a flow control signal to stop transmission, it will send the 64 bytes anyway in violation of the stop request. There is no stopping it, because it knows nothing about flow control. If the buffer is large, then many more bytes will be sent, in violation of the flow control's request to stop.

1.6.2 UART Model Numbers

Following is a list of some UARTs. (TL means trigger level.)

- **8250, 16450, early 16550:** Obsolete, with a one-byte buffer
- **16550, 16550A, 16C552:** 16-byte buffers, TL = 1,4,8,14; 115.2kbps standard; many UARTs support 230.4 or 460.8kbps
- **16650:** 32-byte buffers; 460.8kbps
- **16750:** 64-byte buffer for sending; 56-byte for receiving; 921.6kbps
- **16850, 16C850:** 128-byte buffers; 460.8kbps or 1.5Mbps
- **16950**
- **Hayes ESP:** 1-kB buffers

V.90 56k modems may be faster with a 16650 UART (especially if you are downloading large uncompressed files). The main advantage of the 16650 is its larger buffer size, as the extra speed is not needed unless the modem compression ratio is high. Some 56k internal modems may come with a 16650.

Non-UART and intelligent multiport boards use DSP chips to do additional buffering and control, thus relieving the CPU even more. For example, the Cyclades Cyclom and Stallion EasyIO boards use a Cirrus Logic CD1400 RISC UART, and many boards use 80186 CPUs or even special RISC CPUs, to handle the serial I/O.

Many 486 PCs (older machines) and all Pentiums (or similar PCs) should have 16550A UARTs (usually called simply 16550's) with FIFO. Some of the better motherboards (built in 2000 and beyond) even have 16650s.

1.6.3 The UART Transmitter

When a UART is used to transmit and receive serial data, it is unnecessary for both transmission and reception to have the same baud rate. In some full-duplex modem implementations, the control and handshaking signal is transmitted in the second reverse channel at a much lower baud rate than the baud rate in the main channel. In many UARTs, different clock inputs are provided for the transmitter and the receiver, and the system designer decides whether to use separate clocks or to use the same clock to perform data transmission.

The transmitter is composed of a transmitter buffer, a shift register, a master clock and baud generator, and control logic that loads the byte into the shift register in order to shift the byte to the transmission line bit by bit. The data to be transmitted is in bytes (8-bit) coming from the system data bus of the PC computer or the DTE device.

The tasks of a UART transmitter are as follows:

- Receiving and temporarily storing the parallel data coming from the system data bus inside the DTE or PC computer. This parallel data is to be transmitted serially to the transmission line
- Translating parallel data into serial format by adding additional necessary information, such as the start bit, parity bit, and stop bits
- Sending the formatted data to the shifted register, under control of the system clock and suitable baud clock. There the data is converted and transmitted in serial sequence, bit by bit, into the transmission line.

A system block diagram of a typical UART transmitter is shown in Figure 1.20.

The transmitted data comes from the system data bus, which in parallel eight-bit format. The data is first sent to the buffer, or transmitter holding register, to be translated to serial format. This

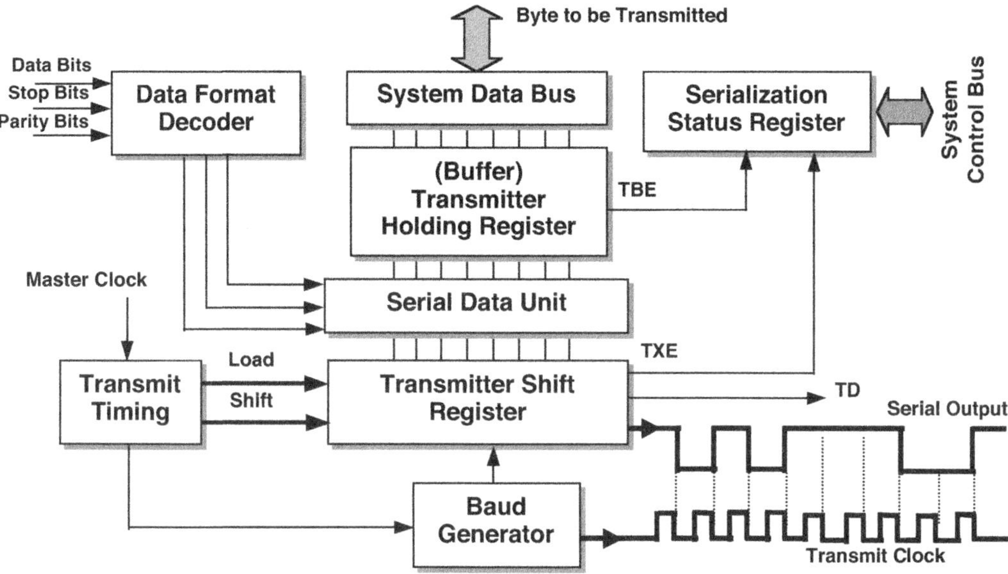

FIGURE 1.20 The UART transmitter unit.

buffer is very useful in speeding up the data conversion and transmission, and it allows the data formation and data shifting to be performed simultaneously. When the data is loaded from the system data bus into the UART buffer, where the parallel byte is translated to serial format, the preceding byte that is being shifted in the shift register can still be processed and moved to the transmission line as output. As mentioned in the previous section, dumb UARTs (the 8250, 16450 and early 16550) have only one-byte buffer. But the FIFO UARTs (16550 and 16550A) have a 16-byte buffer. Some advanced UARTs (16650 and 16750) have buffers of 64 bytes or more. Obviously, FIFO UARTs are better able to handle multiple byte transmission and multitasking processing than dumb UARTs.

The data format decoder is used to decode transmission parameters, such as the number of data bits, stop bits, and parity bits, and then to format the byte that is stored in the buffer based on the decoded result, using the serial data unit to obtain the serial format of the data. The start bit is automatically added to the beginning of the serial-formatted data. Then the serial-formatted data is loaded into the transmitter shift register, where the data (still in parallel form) is shifted to the output transmission line, bit by bit, under the control of the baud clock produced by the baud generator that is controlled by the transmission timing unit. The UART transmission status is then fed back to the serialization status register as status signals, which are collected by the CPU to monitor the UART's working process.

During the formatting process, unused bits in the serial data unit are left-filled with `0`s. The transmitter outputs a value of `1` when all the bits in the shift register have been shifted out. This value of `1` is used to indicate that the transmitter buffer will be empty after the next shift, or clock cycle. If the buffer is already empty, the next clock cycle will set the Transmitter Empty flag (TXE) to report to the serialization status register and stop further shifting. The TD line continues to assert the level of the final stop bit, and the line idles at the *Mark* level until the next byte is loaded into the transmitter holding register to begin a new transmission process.

Two statuses are important in programming the transmitter; one is the status of the transmitter holding register, and the other is the status of the transmitter shift register. The Transmitter Buffer Empty (TBE) signal is set if the data is loaded from the buffer into the shift register. When the serial data unit receives this signal, it passes the flag to the CPU, allowing the next byte to be loaded into the buffer. The TXE signal is set when the shift register is empty; this signal allows the shift register to accept a new serial-format byte from the buffer.

1.6.4 The UART Receiver

Similar to the UART transmitter, the UART receiver is composed of the receiver buffer, shift register, master clock, baud generator, and control logic unit. The job of the receiver is to translate the received, serially formatted data back to parallel format, or byte, and send the byte to the system data bus.

A system block diagram of a typical UART receiver is shown in Figure 1.21.

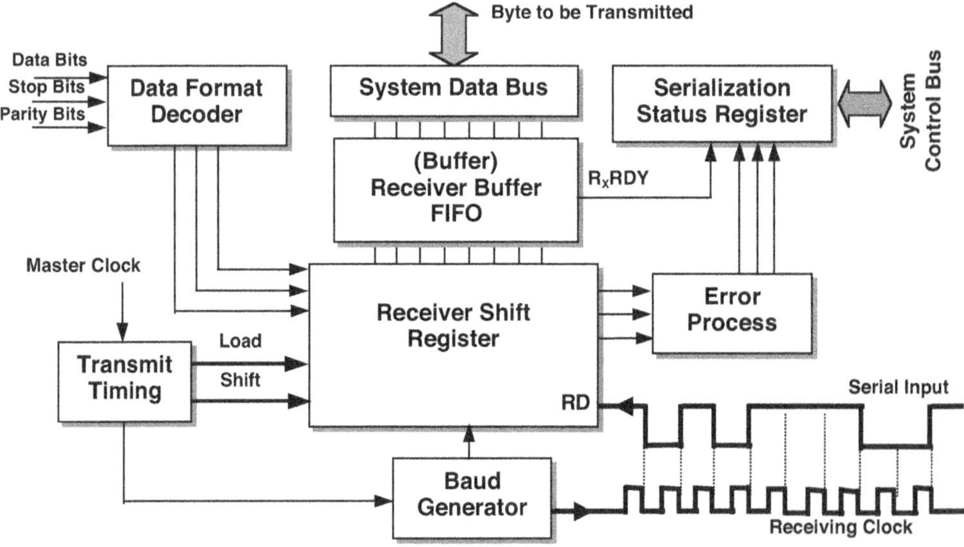

FIGURE 1.21 The UART receiver unit.

The receiver unit accesses the received data by reading the receiver buffer in the UART. The serial-formatted data is shifted into the receiver shift register from the RD line under the control of the baud clock that is produced by the baud generator. In idle status (when no data is transmitted in the transmission line), a `Mark` level is present in the RD line. The receiver keeps scanning the RD line until a start bit is present, which is a high-to-low transition (refer to Figure 1.5). As long as the start bit is detected, all successive bits on the transmission line will be shifted into the receiver shift register according to the format, which is defined in the data format decoder and is written by the user in the UART's user-programmable data format registers. Then the serial-formatted data stored in the receiver shift register is processed and extracted, and finally parallel-format data (a byte) is obtained. This parallel-format data is then loaded into the FIFO buffer and moved to the system data bus.

When the parallel-format data (byte) is moved into the receiver's FIFO, the R_XRDY signal is set to report to the serialization status register that converted data is available to be picked up by the CPU. This signal is reset when the CPU takes the converted data away and the FIFO becomes empty.

The error process unit is used to report any error during data transmission and reception. The UART itself does not handle mistakes occurring during the data transmission and receiving process; it only issues the errors or error sources. The errors are processed and handled by the software.

Errors that may occur during transmission and reception include the following:

- Transmitter overwrite errors
- Receiver overrun errors
- Receiver parity errors
- Receiver stop bits errors
- Receiver framing errors

All of these errors are reported to the serialization status register, and each one is mapped to a binary bit in this register. Figure 1.22 shows an example of the error bits assignment in the serialization status register (SSR), which is also called the *line status register* (LSR).

7	6	5	4	3	2	1	0
Transmitter Overwrite	Receiver Overrun	Break	Parity Error	Framing Error	TXE	TBE	R_XRDY

FIGURE 1.22 The 8250 serialization status register (SSR).

1.6.5 Addressing the UART

Each UART register has an address, and all UART registers can be accessed by their addresses. These registers are read from and written to an IBM PC or compatible computer through the use of I/O ports. All UART registers can be accessed based on the first register, whose address is called the *base address* and is equivalent to an associated port address. Figure 1.23 shows the relationship between the base address and the port address for COM1 to COM4.

Serial Port	Associated Base Register
COM1	3F8H
COM2	2F8H
COM3	3E8H
COM4	2E8H

FIGURE 1.23 The addresses of the UART's port.

In the following section, two typical UARTs, the UART 8250 and UART 16550, will be discussed.

1.6.6 The 8250 UART

Although 8250 is a relatively old UART, it is still widely used in data communications. Most advanced UARTs are developed based on the 8250, so it is valuable to dig a little deeper in this subject.

The 8250 has most of the functions needed in a typical UART. In particular, it supports the nine RS-232 lines utilized in most common RS-232 connections. In the IBM PC, it is addressed via eight consecutive register locations on the I/O bus. In the ISA bus, each UART has its own interrupt line. Two interrupt lines, COM1 and COM2, are used for the serial ports in an IBM PC. Additional port interruptions, such as COM3 and COM4, can share the interrupt lines of COM1 and COM2.

The 8250 has a built-in baud clock generator, which creates baud rates by dividing an input clock down by an integer. In the IBM PC, the master clock chosen for the baud rate generator produces a maximum baud rate of 115.2 kbps. That rate can be lowered further by dividing a factor of 115,200 by a 16-bit integer ranging from 1 to 65535.

Each 8250 UART has one or more registers. As with other programmable microprocessors, you can access and program the 8250 UART via these registers. The registers in the 8250 can be divided into three categories:

- Command and control registers
- Status register
- Data registers

The command and control registers are used to control and coordinate the operations of the 8250; all control commands come from the CPU. The status register is used to feed back the current working status, which is monitored by the CPU and other processors. The data registers are used to temporarily store the sent and received data.

In the 8250 UART, each register is assigned a unique base address., Generally, the base address is associated with the first register in the 8250 UART.

The 8250 UART can install and handle up to four serial ports, named COM1 through COM4. Each port's name is mapped to a base address of the associated register. Refer to Figure 1.23 for this mapping relationship.

1.6.6.1 8250 Architecture

Figure 1.24 shows the internal architecture of an 8250 UART.

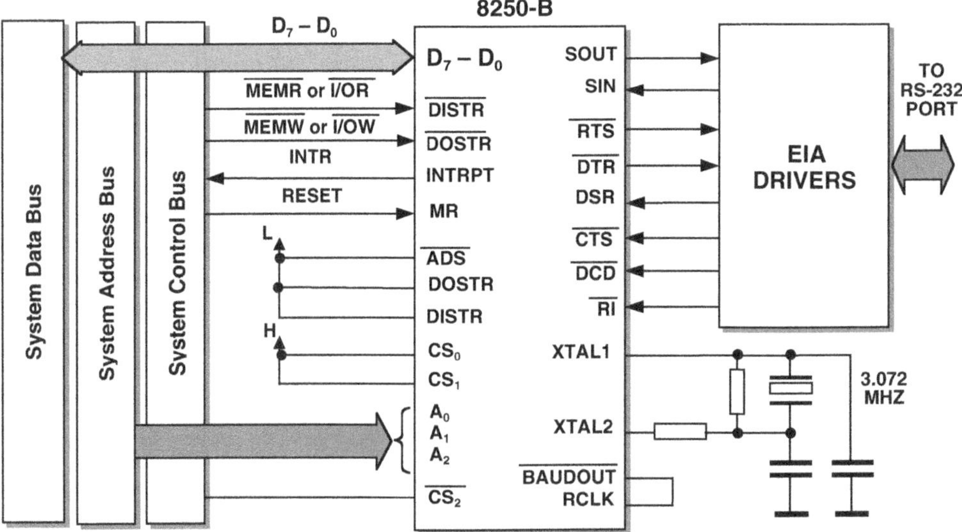

FIGURE 1.24 The 8250 architecture.

As shown in Figure 1.24, 8250 has three interfaces: the system I/O bus, the clock, and the RS-232 interface. The 8250 UART communicates with the system data bus with eight-bit data, which belongs to the low eight-bit data on the system data bus. The reading and writing operations are identified by two control signals, `DISTR` and `DOSTR`, respectively. An `INTR` signal is used for the interrupt operation.

Ten registers can be found in the 8250, and all of them can be accessed by their addresses. The CPU can access each register by selecting different combinations on the three low-system address lines in the system address bus, A_0, A_1, and A_2

The basic operations of the 8250 include transmitting and receiving bytes between the system and RS-232 port. Performing a data transmission involves the following steps:

- The CPU sends a byte to be transmitted to the system data bus, D_0 through D_7.
- The CPU selects the associated register by choosing the desired combination of the three low-system address lines, A_0, A_1, and A_2.
- The CPU activates the associated control signal from the system control bus, using a signal such as `DOSTR`, to move the byte from the system data bus into the 8250's transmitter register (buffer).
- If the shift register is empty, The 8250 moves the received byte from the transmitter register to the shift register under the control of the local clock cycle.
- The control is transferred to the 8250, which performs the data shifting and output of the serial-format data to the transmission line via EIA Drivers.

Data reception involves the following steps:

- The data register is selected by the CPU based on its address, a combination of A_0, A_1, and A_2.
- The CPU reads the data, activating the `DISTR` control signal from the system control bus.
- After the `DISTR` control signal is activated, the byte stored in the receiver register (buffer) is moved to the system data bus, D_0 through D_7.
- The CPU picks up the byte from the system data bus and stores it, either in the system memory or a register inside the CPU.

1.6.6.2 8250 Internal Registers

As mentioned previously, the 8250 has a total of ten registers, and each one can be accessed by its address. The address of each register should be a combination of three address lines on the system address bus: A_0, A_1, and A_2. A maximum of eight combinations of the three addresses exist, which means that only eight registers can be addressed. In other words, the 8250 contains eight "real" registers. So, how can we address ten registers with only three address lines?

First, both the transmitter and the receiver register have the same address. Second, by setting a different binary value (`0` or `1`) on the seventh bit of the data format register, a total of four different registers can be accessed. The seventh bit of the data format register is called the *divisor latch access bit,* or DLAB. When the DLAB is set to `1`, register `0` (the transmission and reception register) and register 1 (the interruption enabling register) become the low-order and high-order bytes of the baud rate divisor latch factor. Table 1-1 shows the relationship between the real registers and the addresses used in the 8250.

The address lines, A_2, A_1, and A_0 are the lowest three address lines. The different combinations of these address lines determined which register is accessed. The actual address of each register is also determined by the higher address or the base address of the first register. The formula used to calculate the destination address of a register is shown in Equation 1-1.

$$\text{Destination Register Address} = \text{Base Address} + \text{Combination of } A_2, A_1, \text{and } A_0 \quad \text{(Eq. 1-1)}$$

For instance, the base address of the port COM2 is 02F8H. The combination of A_2, A_1, and A_0 for the interrupt enable register (IER) of port COM2 is 001. As an example, the destination address

TABLE 1.1
Registers' Address Assignments

DLAB	A_2	A_1	A_0	IN/OUT	8250 Register
0	0	0	0	IN/OUT	Transmitted/Receiver Register (THR/RHR)
0	0	0	1	OUT	Interrupt Enable Register (IER)
1	0	0	0	OUT	Least significant bit (LSB) Baud Rate Divisor Latch
1	0	0	1	OUT	Most significant bit (MSB) Baud Rate Divisor Latch
X	0	1	0	IN	Interrupt Identification Register (IIR)
X	0	1	1	OUT	Data Format (Line Control) Register (LCR)
X	1	0	0	OUT	Modem Control Register (MCR)
X	1	0	1	IN	Serialization Status (Line Status) Register (LSR)
X	1	1	0	IN	Modem Status Register (MSR)
X	1	1	1	IN/OUT	Scratch Pad Register (SPR)

X—Any value

of the IER should be 02F8H + 001H = 02F9H. So the combination of A_2, A_1, and A_0 can be considered an offset.

On the other hand, if COM1 is used as a port, the base address or the first register's address is 03F8H, which is mapped to three registers: the transmitter holding register (THR), receiver holding register (RHR), and baud rate divisor (LSB). This means that anything above three registers shares one common address, 03F8H.

TIP: The seventh bit on the line control register must be set to `1` when the user wants to access the baud rate divisor (LSB) register by using the address 03F8H, and the seventh bit on the line control register must be set to `0` when the user wants to access the THR or RHR using the same address of 03F8H.

To make this mapping relationship clear, two real serial ports, COM1 and COM2, will be used as an example. Table 1-2 shows this mapping relationship.

TABLE 1.2
An Example of the 8250 Registers

Register	IN/OUT	COM1	COM2	Illustrations
Transmitter hold register	OUT	03F8H	02F8H	Bit 7 of line control register = `0`
Receiver hold register	IN	03F8H	02F8H	Bit 7 of line control register = `0`
Baud rate divisor (LSB)	OUT	03F8H	02F8H	Bit 7 of line control register = `1`
Baud rate divisor (MSB)	OUT	03F9H	02F9H	Bit 7 of line control register = `1`
Interrupt enable register	OUT	03F9H	02F9H	Bit 7 of line control register = `0`
Interrupt identification register	IN	03FAH	02FAH	
Line control register	OUT	03FBH	02FBH	
Modem control register	OUT	03FCH	02FCH	
Line status register	IN	03FDH	02FDH	
Modem status register	IN	03FEH	02FEH	

In the 8250, the transmitter register (or buffer) and receiver register are called the *transmitter holding register* (THR) (shown in Figure 1.20) and the *receiver holding register* (RHR), respectively.

In Table 1-2, the first column lists all 10 registers used in the 8250. The third and the fourth columns list seven real addresses associated with those 10 registers. The difference between the

THR, RHR, and baud rate divisor (LSB), which all use the same address, is determined by checking the value on the seventh bit of the line control register (LCR).

Another duplicated address is 03F9H (COM1) and 02F9H (COM2). Both the interrupt enable register (IER) and baud rate divisor (MSB) use this address. To distinguish them, you need to set or check the value of the seventh bit on the LCR.

Now we have a global picture of the registers used in the 8250 UART. Next we will explore the functionality and configuration of each register.

1.6.6.3 8250 Register Functionality

All 8250 registers do their job using the bit-function, which means that the different value on each binary bit of a register represents a different function.

1.6.6.3.1 The Transmitter Holding Register (THR)

As mentioned earlier, the THR works as a buffer to temporarily hold the byte to be transmitted from the 8250 to the transmission line. The THR is the first register in the 8250, so its address is the base address of a port. This register shares a common address with the RHR and the baud rate divisor LSB register.

All binary bits of this register are used to represent a transmitted byte. Figure 1.25 shows the bit functionality of the THR.

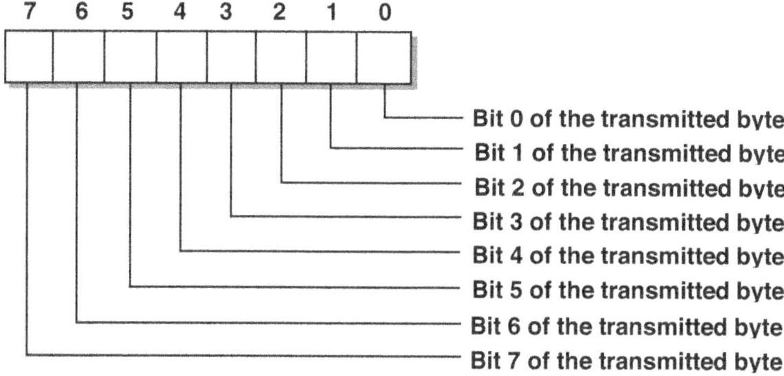

FIGURE 1.25 The 8250 transmitter holding register (THR).

1.6.6.3.2 The Receiver Holding Register (RHR)

The RHR is used to hold a received byte that is converted by the receiving shift register. The RHR shares the same address as the THR. The byte stored in the RHR can be accessed by reading the RHR's address. In COM1, this address is 03F8H.

Depending on the communication setup parameters defined by the user, the byte size received varies from five bits to eight bits. This is because prior to data communication, the user can select different data sizes to be transmitted. Figure 1.26 shows the bit function of the RHR.

1.6.6.3.3 The Interrupt Enable Register (IER)

This register is used to control the availability of the interrupt occurrences in the 8250. Each bit in this register is used to enable or disable one associated interrupt source. A bit value of logical `1` indicates that the associated interrupt is enabled; otherwise the associated interrupt is disabled or masked.

The availability of the interrupt can be determined by the user, and the IER can be either written or read by sending or reading a value from its address. In COM1, this address is 03F9H. Figure 1.27 shows each bit's function on the IER.

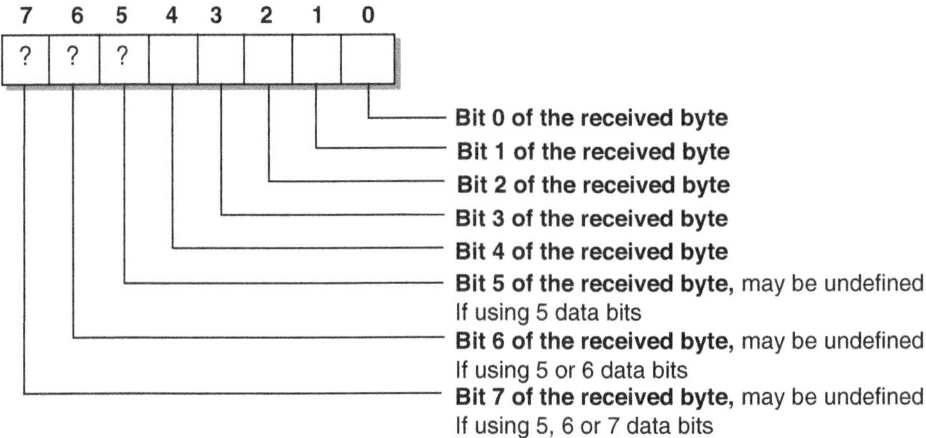

FIGURE 1.26 The 8250 receiver holding register (RHR).

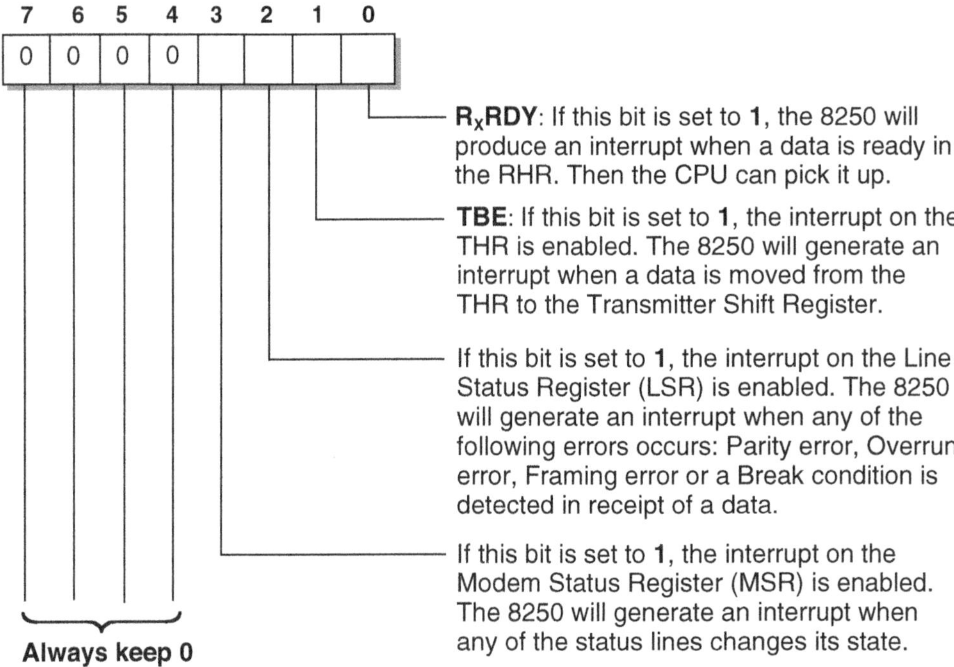

FIGURE 1.27 The 8250 interrupt enable register (IER).

1.6.6.3.4 The Interrupt Identification Register (IIR)

The purpose of the interrupt identification register (IIR) is to identify what kind of interruption has occurred if the CPU receives an interrupt request from the 8250. This is a read-only register, and it can be accessed by its address, which equals the serial port's base address plus 2. In COM1, the address of this register is 03F8H + 002 = 03FAH. The interrupt types and their bit assignments are shown in Figure 1.28.

Notice the value of bit 0 at the IIR in Figure 1.28. When this bit's value is equal to 0, which means that an interrupt has occurred, the CPU needs to temporarily stop running the current program and transfer control to the interrupt handling subroutine if the interrupt's priority level is higher

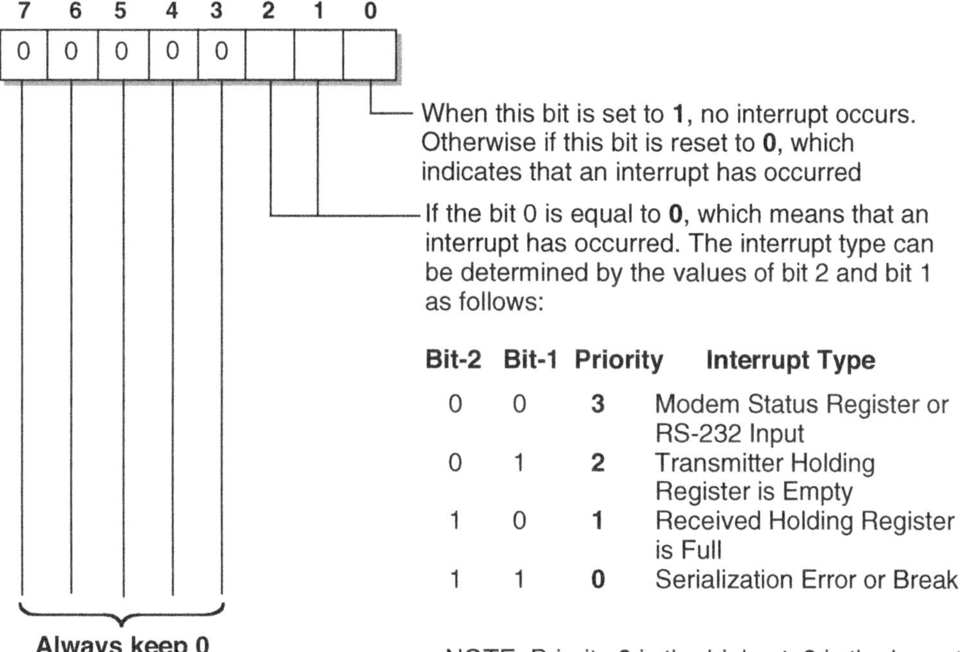

FIGURE 1.28 The 8250 interrupt identification register (IIR).

than that of the current program. This `0` value on bit 0 causes all four interrupt types to have an interval of 2. For example, the MSR interrupt (which includes bit 2, bit 1, and bit 0) has a value of `000`, the THR empty interrupt (which includes bit 2, bit 1, and bit 0) has a value of `010`, and the RHR full interrupt has a value of `100`. These numbers can be used as an index or a pointer stored in an interrupt vector table to point to the associated interrupt handling subroutine, which will handle the interrupt service procedure.

Notice that if you enable the interrupt sources in the 8250 by setting up the IER, but you do not want to use the interrupt mechanism in your program; you should use the polling method to interface to the 8250. The IIR can still set the correct bit value based on the associated interrupt source, and you can use the polling method in your program to periodically check those bits' values to determine which interrupt has occurred. This strategy is very useful and very efficient in some applications.

1.6.6.3.5 The Line Control Register (LCR)—Also Called the Data Format Register

The LCR is used to set up the format of the data to be transmitted to or received from the transmission lines. The data format includes the following parameters: the number of data bits, the number of stop bits, and the parity type. The possible format parameters and their bits distribution in the LCR are shown in Figure 1.29.

1.6.6.3.6 The Modem Control Register (MCR)

The MCR is also called the *RS-232 output control register*, and it controls the following outputs:

- Two RS-232 outputs, DTR and RTS
- Two non-RS-232 outputs, Output1 and Output2
- A loopback test bit
- The interrupt mask bit (Output2)

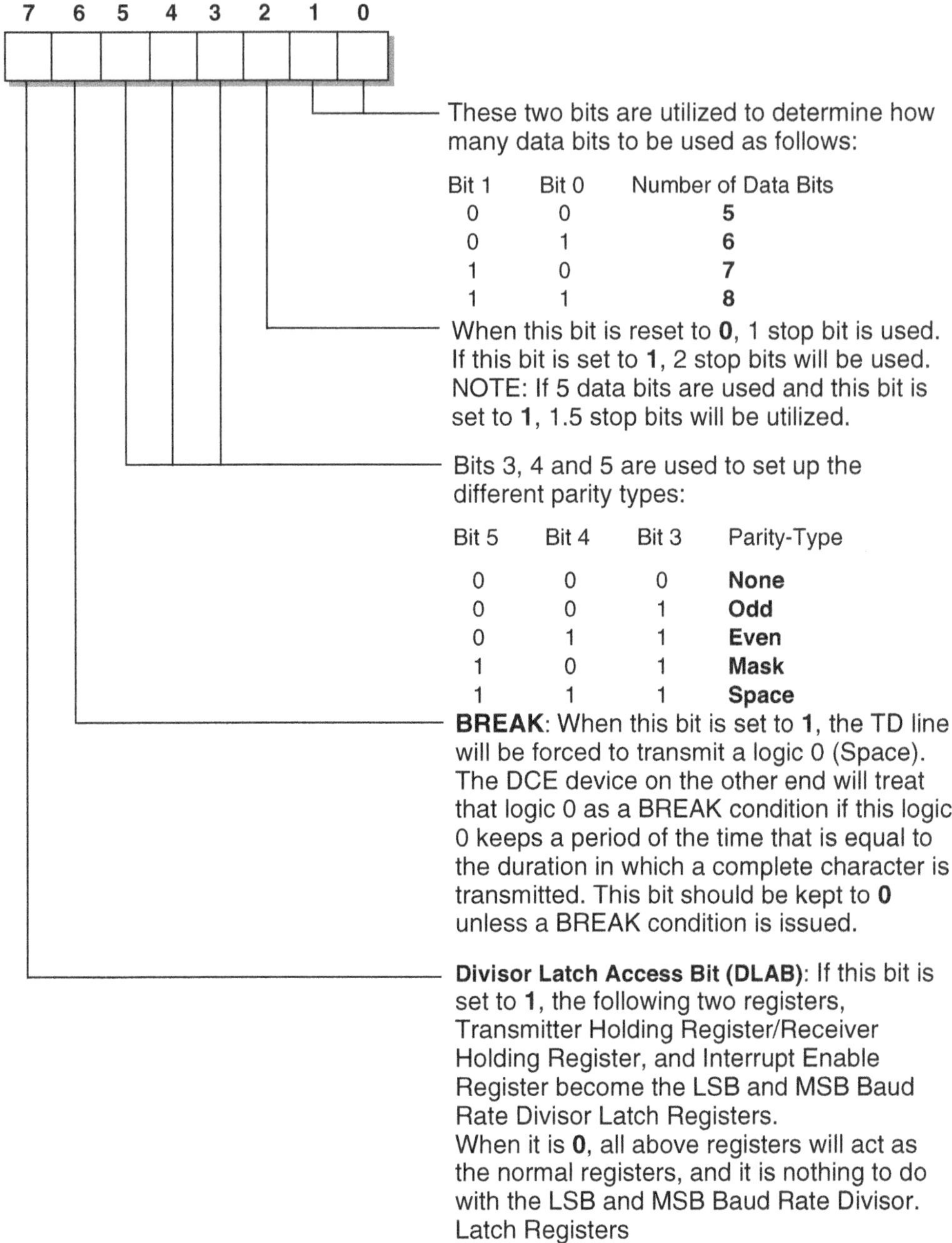

7 6 5 4 3 2 1 0
These two bits are utilized to determine how many data bits to be used as follows:
Bit 1 Bit 0 Number of Data Bits
0 0 5
0 1 6
1 0 7
1 1 8
When this bit is reset to 0, 1 stop bit is used. If this bit is set to 1, 2 stop bits will be used. NOTE: If 5 data bits are used and this bit is set to 1, 1.5 stop bits will be utilized.
Bits 3, 4 and 5 are used to set up the different parity types:
Bit 5 Bit 4 Bit 3 Parity-Type
0 0 0 None
0 0 1 Odd
0 1 1 Even
1 0 1 Mask
1 1 1 Space
BREAK: When this bit is set to 1, the TD line will be forced to transmit a logic 0 (Space). The DCE device on the other end will treat that logic 0 as a BREAK condition if this logic 0 keeps a period of the time that is equal to the duration in which a complete character is transmitted. This bit should be kept to 0 unless a BREAK condition is issued.
Divisor Latch Access Bit (DLAB): If this bit is set to 1, the following two registers, Transmitter Holding Register/Receiver Holding Register, and Interrupt Enable Register become the LSB and MSB Baud Rate Divisor Latch Registers.
When it is 0, all above registers will act as the normal registers, and it is nothing to do with the LSB and MSB Baud Rate Divisor. Latch Registers

FIGURE 1.29 The 8250 line control register (LCR).

TIP: The output control signals DTR and RTS are logically inverted, which simply means that if you set DTR to logical `1`, the DTR output will be a logical `0`. These signals are finally assumed to be reinverted to the same logic as you set on the associated bit in the MCR.

Output1 and Output2 are two non-RS-232 output control signals. Output2 has a special purpose in the interrupt control in the UART. This bit must be set to `1` to allow the interrupts you have enabled in the IER to take effect. Figure 1.30 shows the bit's functionality and assignment in the MCR.

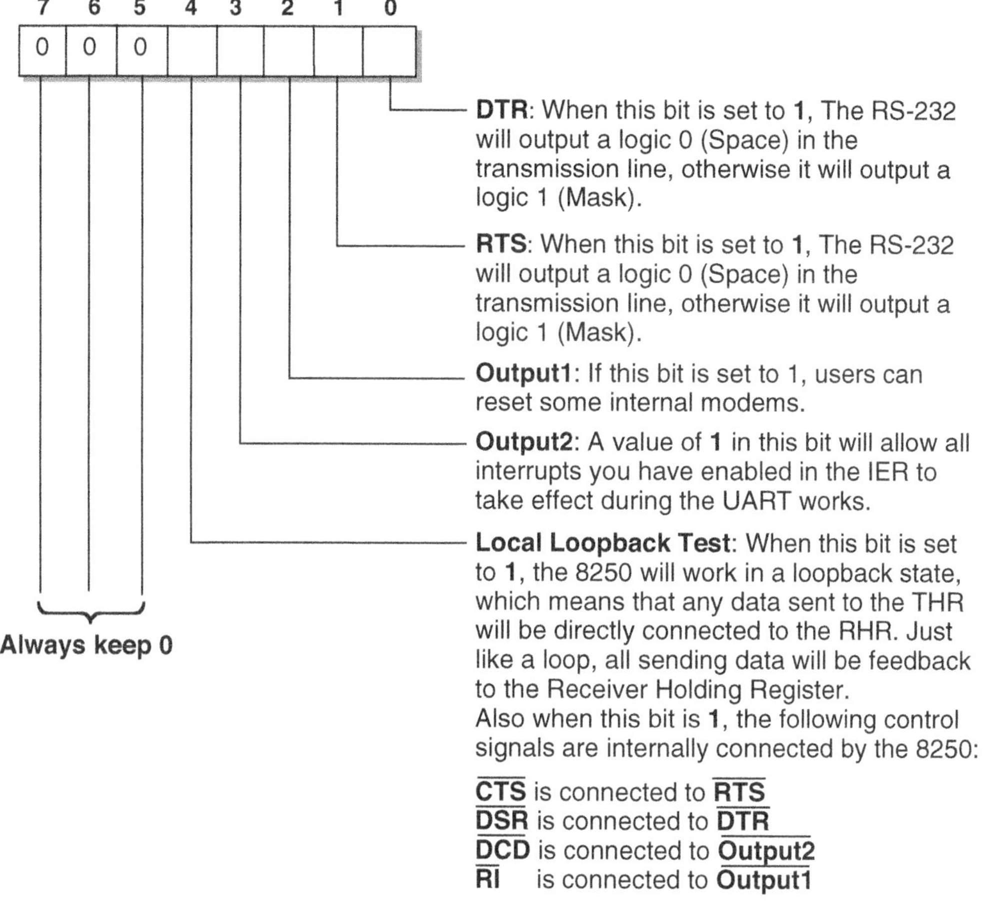

FIGURE 1.30 The 8250 modem control register (MCR).

1.6.6.3.7 The Line Status Register (LSR)-Serialization Status Register

The purpose of the LSR is to monitor and report the operation status of the UART. The following information needs to be monitored and reported by the 8250:

- Data is available in the UART's receiver holding register.
- The UART's transmitter holding register is empty.
- An error or a `BREAK` condition occurs.

The bit's functionality and assignment in the LSR is shown in Figure 1.31.

1.6.6.3.8 The Modem Status Register (MSR)

The MSR is also called RS-232 *input status register* (ISR) because it is used to reflect the current working status of the UART, such as the states of the CTS and DSR lines, the state of the ring indicator line, and the state of the data carrier detection line.

`Bit 0` ~ `bit 3` indicates a change of the associated line's state. A value of 1 means that its state has been changed since the last read operation of the MSR. When the MSR is read again, bit 0 ~ bit 3 will be cleared.

`Bit 4` ~ `bit 7` indicates the absolute state of the associated line.

Figure 1.32 shows the bits functions and assignments in the MSR.

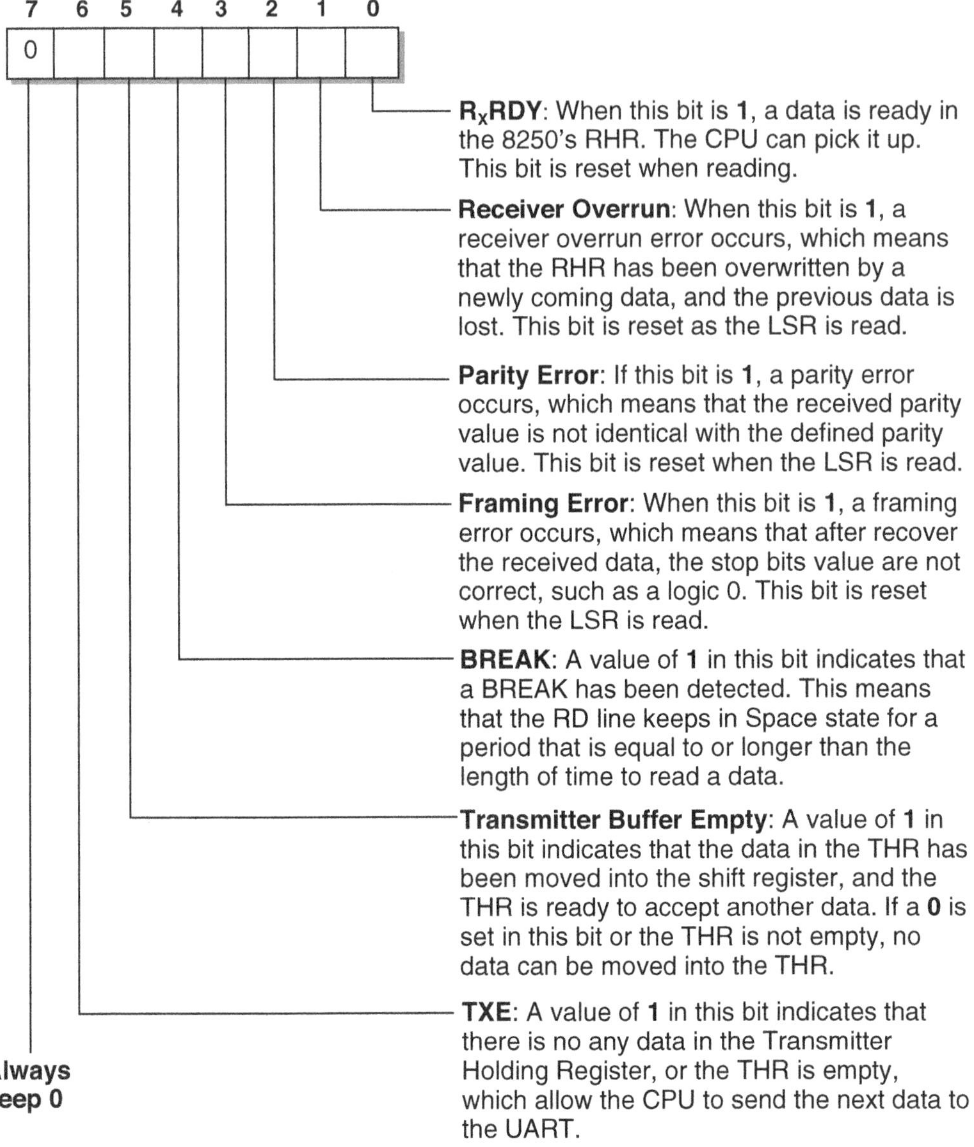

FIGURE 1.31 The 8250 line status register (LSR).

1.6.6.3.9 The Scratch Pad Register (SPR)

This register has no any functionality at all in early versions of the 8250 UART. You can consider it a byte of RAM and use it in the newer version of the 8250.

1.6.6.3.10 The Baud Rate LSB Divisor Latch Register and the Baud Rate MSB Divisor Latch Register

These two registers are used to store a 16-bit scalar factor that can be used to determine the baud rate used in data communication in the 8250 UART. The actual baud rate is determined based on the following two factors:

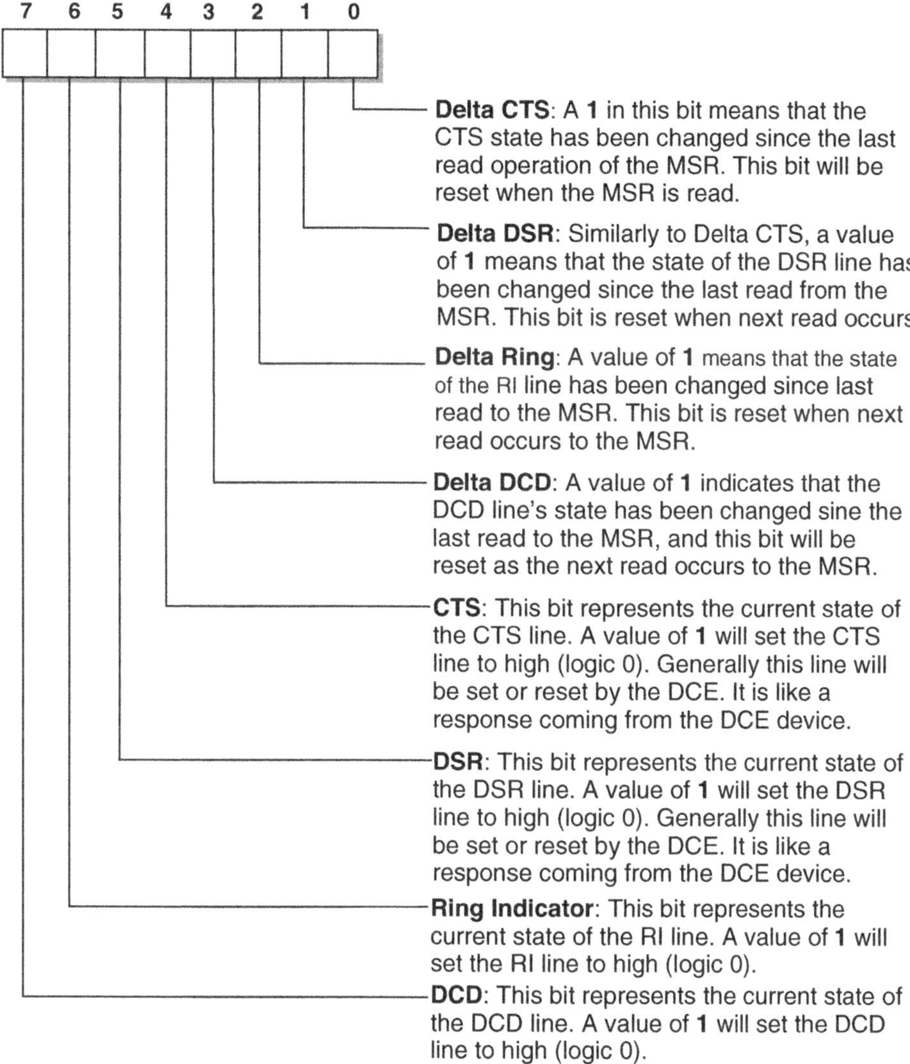

FIGURE 1.32 The 8250 modem status register (MSR).

- The 8250 internal reference clock frequency
- The 16-bit scalar factor stored in the baud rate LSB divisor latch register (BRDLR-LSB) and the baud rate MSB divisor latch register (BRDLR-MSB).

The high byte of this scalar factor is stored in the most-significant-byte in the BRDLR-MSB, and the low byte of the scalar factor is stored in the least-significant-byte in the BRDLR-LSB, respectively.

The calculation of the baud rate involves the formula given in Equation 1-2.

$$\frac{8250 \quad Internal \quad reference \quad clock \quad frequency}{16 \times Scalar \quad factor} \qquad \text{(Eq. 1-2)}$$

In equation 1-2, it can be seen that to calculate the actual baud rate, the 8250 internal reference clock frequency needs to be divided by both the 16-bit scalar factor and an integer of 16.

Generally, two internal reference clocks are utilized in the 8250 UART; the first clock frequency is 1.8432 MHz and the other available clock frequency is 3.072 MHz. Table 1-3 lists some often-used baud rates and the associated scalar factors for these two clock frequencies in hexadecimals. Notice that the high-byte (or left two digits) of the scalar factor should be placed in the baud rate MSB divisor latch register, and the low-byte (or right two digits) of the scalar factor should be placed in the baud rate LSB divisor latch register.

TABLE 1.3
The 8250 Baud Rate Divisor—LSB and MSB

	8250 clock 1.8432 MHz		8250 clock 3.072 MHZ	
Desired Baud Rate	**MSB**	**LSB**	**MSB**	**LSB**
50	09	00	0F	00
75	06	00	0A	00
110	04	17	06	D1
150	03	00	05	00
300	01	80	02	80
600	00	C0	01	40
1,200	00	60	00	A0
1,800	00	40	00	6B
2,000	00	3A	00	60
2,400	00	30	00	50
3,600	00	20	00	35
4,800	00	18	00	28
7,200	00	10	00	16
9,600	00	0C	00	14
19,200	00	06	00	0A
38,400	00	03	00	05
56,000	00	02	–	–

It can also be determined from the equation that after the 8250 internal reference clock has been selected, the only changeable parameter is the scalar factor, which means that by selection of a different scalar factor, a different baud rate from the previous equation can be obtained. To select a different scalar factor and place it into the baud rate MSB divisor latch register and the baud rate LSB divisor latch register, you need to have the following points in mind.

First, the baud rate LSB divisor latch register shares the same address, which is 03F8H for COM1, with the THR and RHR in 8250, and the baud rate MSB divisor latch register shares another common address, which is 03F9H for COM1, with the IER in 8250. To assign a scalar factor to the baud rate divisor LSB and the baud rate divisor MSB, you need to set a value of `1` to bit 7 of the line control register (LCR) to indicate that you want to use the baud rate divisor LSB and MSB. If bit 7 is reset to `0`, it means that you want to access the THR/RHR or IER.

Second, when calculating the baud rate, the division by 16 is automatically executed by the machine, and you do not need to take care of this operation at all.

For example, if you want to use a baud rate of 9,600 with an 8250 clock frequency of 1.8432 MHz for the COM1 port, you should perform the following steps:

1. Access the LCR by its address of 03FBH, and set a value of `1` on bit 7 of the LCR by writing a value of 80H to it.
2. Place the low byte of the scalar factor, which is 0C (based on Table 1-3), to the baud rate divisor LSB, whose address is 03F8H.
3. Place the high byte of the scalar factor, which is 00 based on Table 1-3, to the baud rate divisor MSB, whose address is 03F9H.
4. Reset bit 7 of the LCR to `0`.

At this point, the functionalities and configurations of all registers used in the 8250 UART have been introduced. In the next chapter, we will actually use the 8250; specifically, we will use these registers to develop some serial interfacing programs to practice what we have learned in this chapter.

We now need to discuss a very important idea used in serial data communications: the interrupt. This is a useful technique that is widely utilized in multitasking, especially in the real-time environment.

1.6.7 The 8250 UART Interrupt Operations

As previously mentioned, the 8250 has the ability to generate an interrupt request to the system when some event or task in the UART is finished. This interrupt operation is very useful for multitasking processes. By using the interrupt, the CPU does not need to spend time to wait for one of the data operations (for instance, when data is ready in the RHR) in 8250 to complete; the CPU can handle other more important jobs if the desired data operation is still going on in the UART. As soon as the desired data operation is completed, the UART can send an interrupt request to the CPU, and the CPU can temporarily stop executing jobs and respond to the UART's interrupt by turning the control to the UART interrupt service subroutine, which will process the data received from the RHR.

As seen in Figure 1.24, an INTRPT signal is used to produce an interrupt from the 8250 UART if the desired task is completed.

To correctly set up an 8250's interrupt mechanism and allow the UART to produce an interrupt when the desired job is finished, you need to perform the following steps:

1. Correctly set up the interrupt enable register (IER) to allow the desired task to produce an interrupt when that task is completed. For example, if we want an interrupt to be generated when the UART receives data (when the RHR is ready), we should set a value of `1` on bit 0 in the IER. On the other hand, we should set a value of `1` on bit 1 in the IER (refer to Figure 1.27) if we want an interrupt to be produced when data is sent out (which means that the THR is empty), from the 8250.
2. Properly set up the modem control register (MCR) to turn on all interrupts you've selected from the IER. To turn on the interrupts means that you allow the interrupt signal to be passed from the desired task, such as RHR, THR, or any error register to the `INTRPT` terminal in the 8250. To turn on all interrupts in the 8250, you should set a value of `1` on bit 3, which is the `Output2` signal, in the MCR (refer to Figure 1.30).

By completing the preceding two steps, you will correctly configure the UART to generate interrupts when the desired job is finished or the associated error is received. But another problem emerges: How does the CPU recognizes the interrupts generated by the 8250, and how does the CPU respond and process those interrupts if the CPU receives them? To answer these questions, you must have a basic understanding of the interrupt mechanism of 8088/80 × 86 computer systems.

In general microcomputer systems, especially in 8088/80 × 86 systems, all interrupts concerned with the internal subsystems, peripheral devices, and error mechanisms are controlled by a special interrupt processing unit or a microprocessor, which is called the *8259 peripheral interrupt controller* (PIC). The 8259 PIC works just as a coordinator between the interrupt sources and the CPU: It detects and organizes all interrupt sources and informs the CPU of how many interrupts are pending and which interrupt should be processed first according to their priority levels. If, when the CPU receives the interrupt information sent by the 8259, the priority level of the current interrupt request is higher than any other interrupt, the CPU will temporarily stop running the current task, reserve the associated working environment (such as the working registers and stack pointer register), and transfer control to the interrupt subroutine to process and execute the interrupt service subroutine. Figure 1.33 shows a typical structure of the interrupt system used in the most PCs.

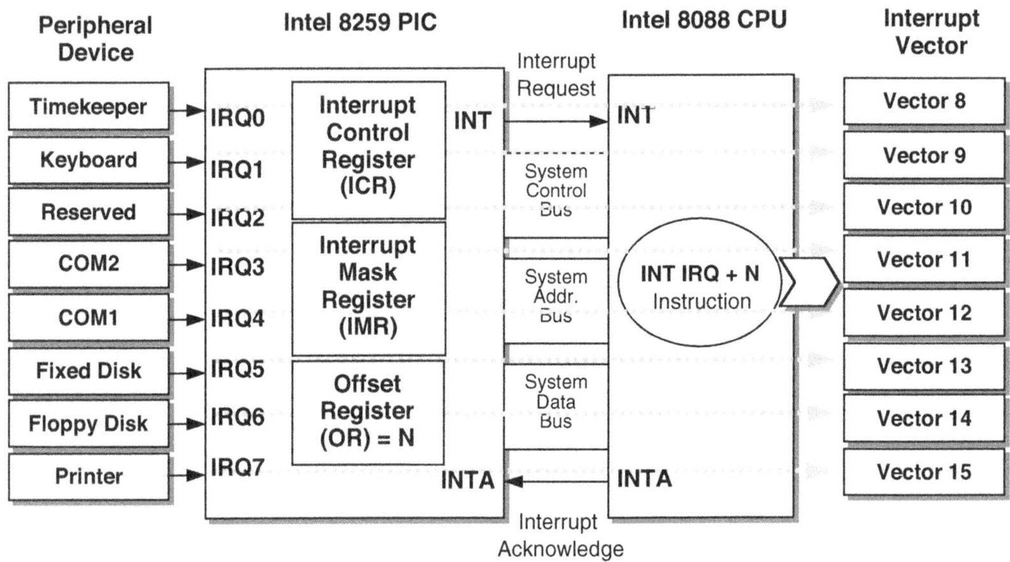

FIGURE 1.33 The configuration of interrupt process in PCs.

The 8259 PIC contains three important registers: the interrupt mask register (IMR) with an address of 21H, the interrupt control register (ICR) with an address of 20H, and the offset register.

The purpose of the IMR is to enable or disable the interrupts associated with peripheral devices, whereas the ICR is used to coordinate and control the interrupt's communication between the 8259 and the CPU. The offset register is used to store an offset, which is associated with an interrupt vector.

As shown in Figure 1.33, the 8259 can control a total of eight interrupt resources, and each interrupt source is assigned to a unique IRQ number (line), from IRQ0 to IRQ7. The IRQ line is activated when the associated interrupt occurs if that interrupt has been previously enabled by correct configuration of the IMR in the 8259.

TIP: Be sure to take care of the interrupt lines associated with COM1 and COM2 (the IRQ4 and IRQ3 interrupt lines, respectively). In PCs, COM1 and COM3 share one IRQ line (that is, IRQ4), and similarly, COM2 and COM4 share another interrupt line (that is, IRQ3). Take special care with these interrupt-sharing relationships among serial port communications. Try to avoid using an interrupt mechanism for COM1 and COM3 simultaneously. The same care should be taken for COM2 and COM4.

To enable and respond to an interrupt coming from a peripheral device, you must properly configure the IMR in the 8259 to allow the associated interrupt request to be passed into the associated IRQ line. Figure 1.34 shows a bit function and assignment of the IMR in the 8259.

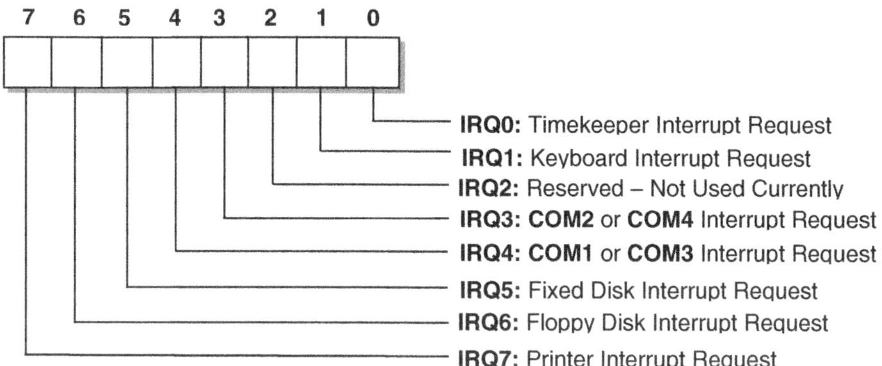

FIGURE 1.34 The 8259 interrupt mask register (IMR).

TIP: To enable an interrupt in the 8259, the associated bit in the IMR should be reset to 0 (unmasked), and to disable an interrupt, the associated bit should be set to `1` (masked). For example, to enable a COM1 interrupt only, a byte of `11101111` (0EFH) should be set on the IMR. A byte of `11100111` (0E7H) should be set on the IMR if both COM1 and COM2 interrupts are enabled.

After the IMR has been properly configured, the 8259 can correctly direct any interrupt request coming from the 8250 to the 8088 CPU. It does so by using the interrupt request line in the 8259 (INT), which is connected to the interrupt input of the 8088 CPU when the desired interrupts occur in the 8250. As the 8088 CPU receives this interrupt request, it will respond to the 8259 with an interrupt acknowledge signal as feedback to indicate to the 8259 that the CPU has received and recognized this interrupt request by using the INTA terminal.

Now we have answered the first part of the question we asked previously: How does the CPU recognize the interrupts generated by the 8250? To answer the second part (How does the CPU respond and process those interrupts if the CPU received them?), we need to understand the offset register and its purpose.

Notice in Figure 1.33 that each interrupt line in the 8259 is associated with an interrupt vector on the right side, and that these interrupt vectors are numbered from 8 to 15. As we know, when the CPU responds to an interrupt request, it should temporarily stop running the current program and transfer control to the associated interrupt service routine; the routine will then process the request if no higher interrupt request occurs. The CPU should perform the following steps in response to an interrupt request:

1. Identify the interrupt resource and find the correct entry address of the associated interrupt service routine (ISR).
2. Turn off the interrupt request line to mask (disable) all interrupts.
3. Reserve the elements of the working environment (such as the working registers, accumulators, stack pointer, and returning address) by pushing them into the stack.
4. Transfer control to the ISR by pushing the entry address of the ISR into the programmer counter.
5. Turn on the interrupt line to allow the higher-level interrupts to occur after entering the ISR.
6. Execute the ISR to finish processing the interrupt.
7. Turn off the interrupt line to disable all interrupts.
8. Recover the elements of the working environment (such as the working registers, accumulators, and stack pointer register) by popping them out of the stack.

9. Send the end-of-interrupt (EOI) command to the 8259 interrupt control register (ICR) to inform the 8088 CPU that the ISR has been completed.
10. Return to the original program by popping the returning address out of the stack and continuing to execute it.

From the steps listed here, it is obvious that each interrupt request needs an ISR to process it. In other words, the relationship between the interrupt request and the ISR is one to one. When an interrupt occurs, the associated ISR should be called and executed to process that interrupt. The next step is to identify the corresponding ISR for each interrupt request (`IRQi`). An interrupt vector can be used to identify the ISR. Figure 1.35 shows an interrupt vector and the entry address of the associated ISRs.

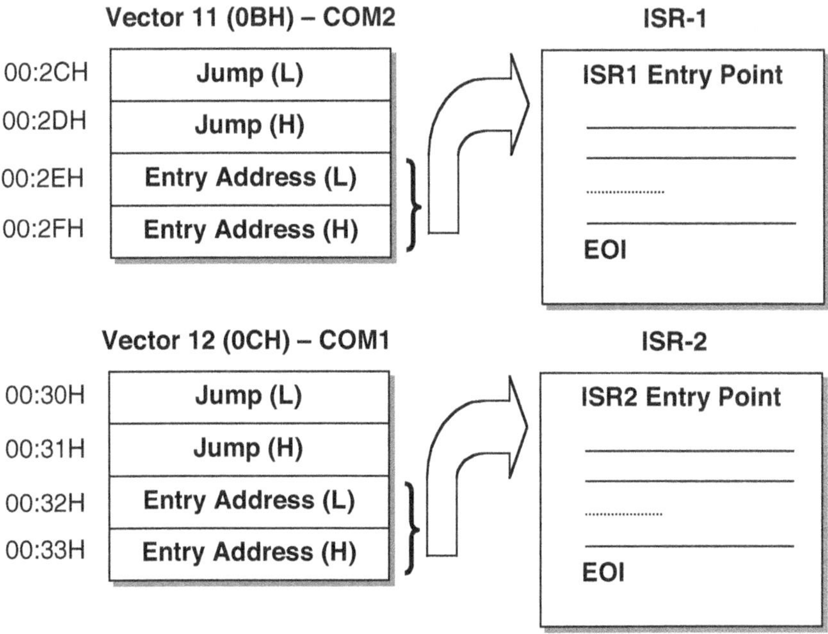

FIGURE 1.35 An example of interrupt vector.

TIP: The *interrupt vector* is simply an address index table, which means that each unit in the table stores the entry address of the associated ISR. Each vector has a four-byte memory space, and each vector is identified by a unique memory address. In Figure 1.33, the vector's starting address is 8. (also known as vector 8.) This is because the preceding vector addresses (from 0 to 7) are used by the system ISR to respond to and process the division-by-zero error.

Vector 11 (0BH) is associated with the interrupt request of COM2 and COM4, and vector 12 (0CH) is associated with the interrupt request of COM1 and COM3. Each interrupt vector contains a `JUMP` assembly language instruction, followed by the real entry address of the associated ISR, which requires four bytes of memory space. The address of vector 11 is from 00:2CH to 00:2FH (the first two bits are for the segment address), and vector 12 occupies an address between 00:30H and 00:33H. The real entry address (point) of the associated ISR is specified by the user during the programming development process. In Figure 1.33, the dash-line is used to connect each interrupt request with an associated interrupt vector.

Now we have a clear picture of the interrupt vector and its contents. How does the CPU set a connection between an interrupt request `IRQi` and its interrupt vector? The CPU identifies the interrupt request and the associated interrupt vector using the offset register, or OR.

Each `IRQi` line is mapped to an associated interrupt vector by an interrupt instruction, `INT N`, in the 8088 CPU system. The N is an offset that is equal to the sum of the IRQ number and the base offset in the 8088 CPU system.

The base offset in the 8088 system is equal to 8 (described previously), so the `INT N` instruction can be formed as

$$\text{INT N} = \text{INT IRQi} + 8 \quad \text{(Eq. 1-3)}$$

For example, the interrupt vector of the timekeeper is INT IRQ0 + 8 = INT 8, which is mapped to vector 8. The interrupt vector of COM1 is INT IRQ4 + 8 = INT 12 or `INT 0CH`, which is mapped to vector 12, and so on. In this way, the CPU establishes a one-to-one relationship between each interrupt request (`IRQi`) and its associated interrupt vector.

TIP: As previously mentioned, an EOI instruction must be inserted at the end of each ISR to indicate to the 8259 that the interrupt process has been completed. The CPU can then continue to execute the original program where the interrupt has occurred. Executing this EOI instruction is equivalent to sending a code of 20H to the interrupt control register (ICR) of the 8259 PIC, whose address is also 20H. After the 8259 receives this EOI information, it will inform the CPU to return from the interrupt ISR.

The 8259 will stop reporting further interrupts to the CPU if the 8259 does not receive the EOI information indicating that an interrupt has occurred and that the associated ISR is being executed, even if some interrupts have occurred. Upon receiving this EOI, the 8259 will continue to report any interrupts to the CPU. Remember to insert this EOI at the end of each ISR.

After this mapping is set up, whenever an interrupt occurs, the 8259 will provide a correct interrupt source to the 8088 CPU. Then the latter can identify the correct vector based on the interrupt source (`IRQi`) and direct the interrupt to the associated entry address of the ISR to further process the interrupt.

Summarily, the 8088 CPU responds and processes the interrupt request in the following sequence:

1. A peripheral device generates an interrupt to the 8259 PIC by activating the associated IRQ line.
2. The 8259 directs the interrupt request to the INT input of the 8088 CPU to generate an interrupt to the CPU if the IMR is configured properly.
3. The 8088 identifies the associated interrupt vector based on the IRQ number and the base address of the vector (stored in the offset register) by issuing and executing an `INT N` instruction (N = IRQ Number + 8).
4. By executing a `JUMP` instruction stored at each associated vector, the control is transferred to the ISR to finish processing the interrupt request.
5. At the end of the ISR, an EOI is executed, which will inform the 8259 PIC that the current interrupt is completed and the CPU can return to the original program to continue to execute it.

Chapter 2 of this book will present more detailed information about programming the 8250 UART.

1.6.8 The 16550 UART

As mentioned in section 1.6.2, the 16550 UART is identical to the 8250 UART except that the former has additional FIFO buffers that can hold up to 16 bytes of data. Specifically, the 16550 can be considered a pin-compatible copy of the 8250 UART. You will not find any difference between the 16550 and the 8250 if those additional FIFO buffers are not included in your data communication programming. Today, however, most PCs use the 16550 instead of the 8250 to meet the multitasking requirements of modern industrial and commercial applications. One of most important results of this replacement is the availability of high-speed data communication and processing.

The v.90 modem has a top baud rate of 56,000 bps (56kbps). With the addition of V.42bis data compression, this baud rate can be increased up to 224kbps. Operating at this baud rate, an RS-232 port will take about 45μs to pick up a character that is ready in the RHR; this means that the CPU must pick up the character quickly, before the next character enters the RHR. The potential is great for the CPU to lose data if the running speed of the system is not higher than the operating baud rate. One common problem is the CPU's switching time from protected mode to real mode, which is about 1ms for an 80286 CPU. Many characters can be lost with this kind of switching time.

The FIFO buffers designed in the 16550 prevent overrun errors from occurring when the UART works at this high speed. Both the 16550 transmitter and receiver have 16-byte FIFO buffers, but the receiver's FIFO buffers have a software-adjustable interrupt threshold. The FIFO buffers in the 16550 UART must be enabled by the associated software command if one wants to use them.

The following nine registers are identical in the 16550 and the 8250 UARTs:

- The transmitter holding register (THR)
- The interrupt enable register (IER)
- The interrupt identification register (IIR)
- The line control register (LCR)
- The modem control register (MCR)
- The modem status register (MSR)
- The scratch pad register (SPR)
- The baud rate LSB divisor latch register
- The baud rate MSB divisor latch register

Because of the similarity between the 16550 and the 8250 UARTs, only the registers that are different are discussed here. For detailed information about those registers that are identical in the 16550 and the 8250, refer to Section 1.6.6.

The following three registers in the 16550 UART differ from those in the 8250:

- The receiver buffer register (RBR), which roughly corresponds to the receiver holding register in the 8250
- The FIFO control register (FCR)
- The line status register (LSR)

We will discuss these three registers one by one in the following sections.

1.6.8.1 The Receiver Buffer Register (RBR)

The RBR is used by the 16550 UART to hold a received character or byte. Like the THR in the 8250, the RBR is the first register in the 16550 UART and has the same address as the port's base

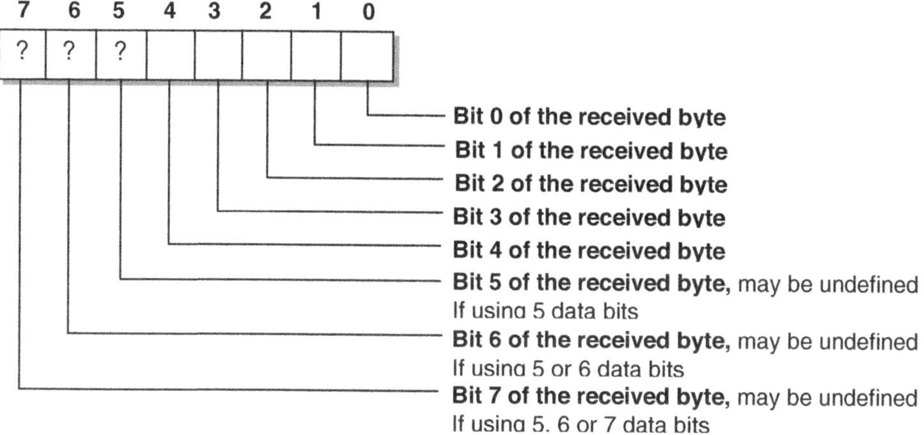

FIGURE 1.36 The 16550 receiver buffer register.

address. In COM1, this address is 03F8H. The RBR can be accessed via this address. Figure 1.36 shows the bit function and assignment for the receiver buffer register.

TIP: If you define fewer than eight data bits in the LCR, you should mask the unused bits to prevent unnecessary errors.

1.6.8.2 The FIFO Control Register (FCR)

The purpose of the FCR is to control and configure the FIFO buffers' status in the 16550 UART. You can access this register by adding 2 to the port's base address. In COM1, the FCR's address is 03FAH.

One of the most interesting features of the FCR register is its ability to configure the receiver threshold for the receiver FIFO buffers. Specifically, the receiver threshold is equivalent to the maximum number of bytes that can be placed in the FIFO buffers before a full RBR interrupt is generated. As soon as this interrupt is produced, the CPU needs to pick up the data from the RBR immediately. By specifying a different threshold number, you can change the size of the FIFO buffers. Figure 1.37 shows the bit function and configuration of the FCR.

1.6.8.3 The Line Status Register (LSR)

The purpose of the LSR is to report the status of the UART during its work. You can access this register by adding 5 to the port's base address. In COM1, this address is 03FDH.

The configuration of this register is nearly identical to that of the 8250 UART; the only difference is the bit function at bits 0, 1, and 7. Figure 1.38 shows the bit function and setup of the LSR in the 16550 UART.

A value of `1` in bit 0 means that new data is ready in the 16550's RBR. A value of `1` in bit 1 indicates a receiver overwrite error; this means that new data is coming but the receiver FIFO buffer is already full, so the new data is written into the FIFO and the previous data in the FIFO is lost. A value of `1` in bit 7 means that at least one error has occurred in the receiving FIFO buffer.

As previously mentioned, a significant difference between the 8250 and the 16550 is that the latter has FIFO buffers. These buffers allow data transmission speed can be greatly improved. Even so, the data transmission speed of a standard serial port is limited to a top speed of 115.2kbps by the PC's architecture. By using compression technology, however, you can achieve a transmission speed that exceeds this limitation, such as 56kbps.

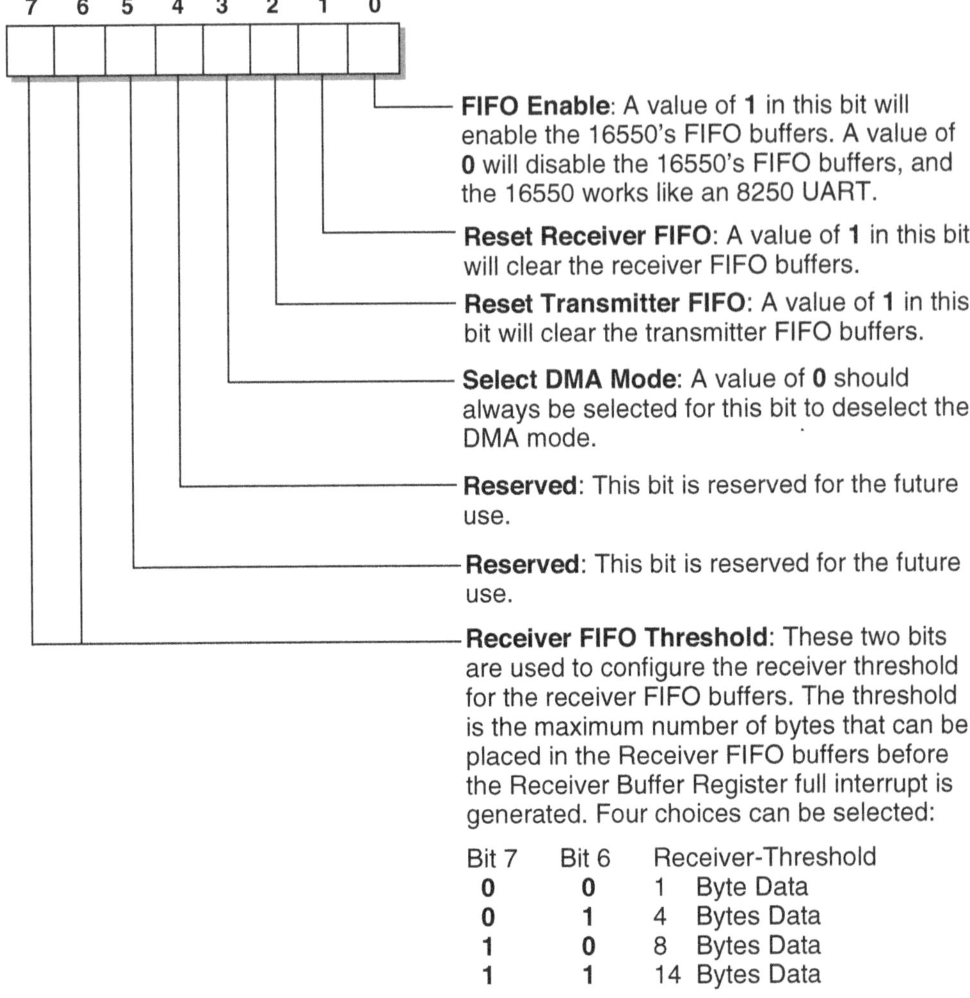

7 6 5 4 3 2 1 0
FIFO Enable: A value of 1 in this bit will enable the 16550's FIFO buffers. A value of 0 will disable the 16550's FIFO buffers, and the 16550 works like an 8250 UART.
Reset Receiver FIFO: A value of 1 in this bit will clear the receiver FIFO buffers.
Reset Transmitter FIFO: A value of 1 in this bit will clear the transmitter FIFO buffers.
Select DMA Mode: A value of 0 should always be selected for this bit to deselect the DMA mode.
Reserved: This bit is reserved for the future use.
Reserved: This bit is reserved for the future use.
Receiver FIFO Threshold: These two bits are used to configure the receiver threshold for the receiver FIFO buffers. The threshold is the maximum number of bytes that can be placed in the Receiver FIFO buffers before the Receiver Buffer Register full interrupt is generated. Four choices can be selected:
Bit 7 Bit 6 Receiver-Threshold
0 0 1 Byte Data
0 1 4 Bytes Data
1 0 8 Bytes Data
1 1 14 Bytes Data

FIGURE 1.37 The 16550 FIFO control register.

One way to improve transmission speed is to use the universal serial bus (USB), which has a transmission speed of millions of bits per second. Another solution is to use an internal modem, which we will discuss in the following section.

1.7 MODEMS AND FLOW CONTROL

Today almost every computer uses a modem as a DCE to transmit audio signals via telephone lines. PCs even use modems to connect to the Internet, so the modem plays an important role in today's data communications. But what is a modem?

1.7.1 Modem and Modem Control

A modem is a device that has the following two functions:

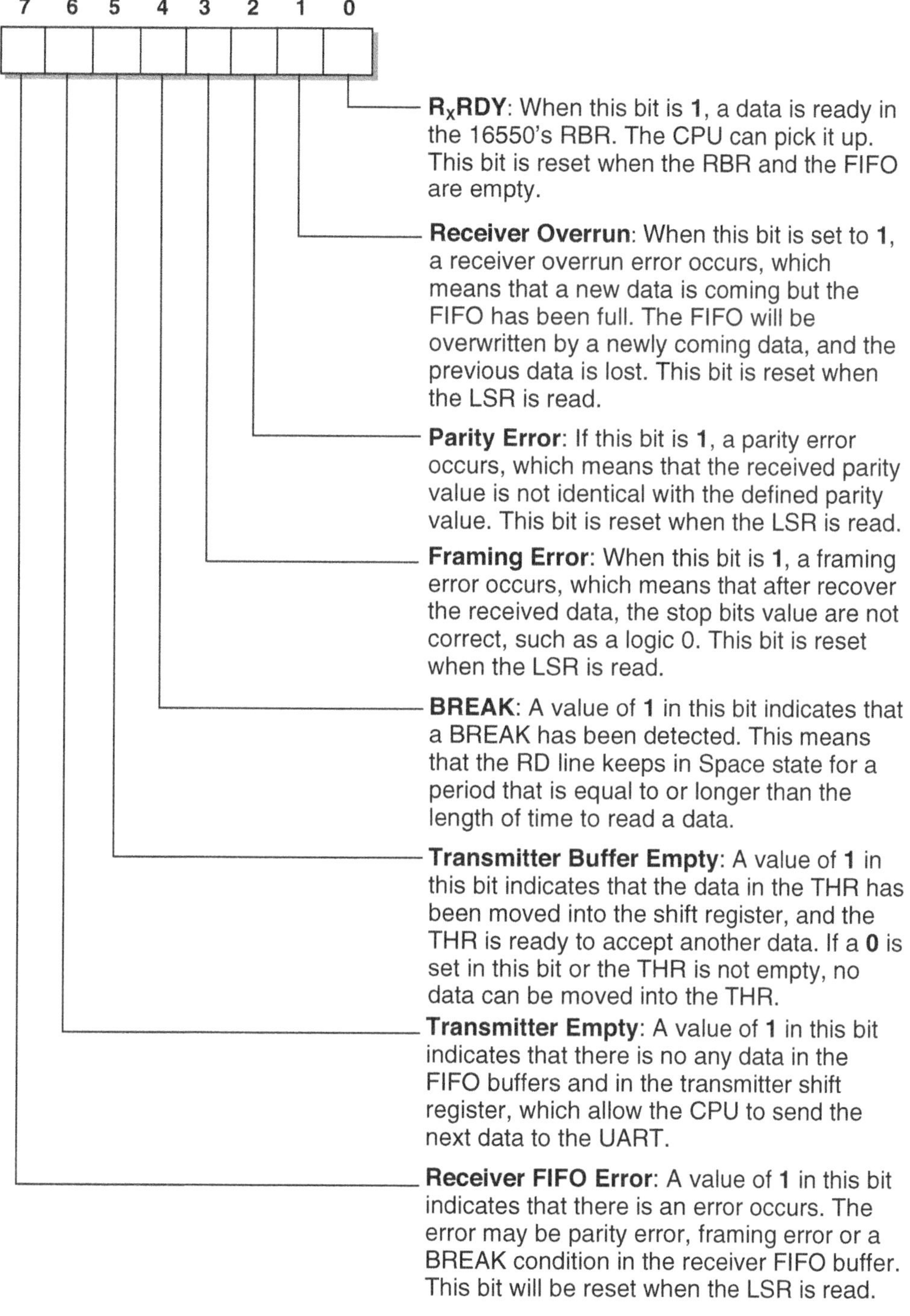

FIGURE 1.38 The 16550 line status tegister (LSR).

- It converts digital signals coming from PCs to analog signals or audio tones that can be transmitted over telephone lines.
- It converts analog signals or audio tones coming from telephone lines back to digital signals that can be processed by a PC.

These two conversions, called *modulation* and *demodulation,* respectively, are the real work of a modem. The devices used to perform these two processes are called the modulator and the demodulator.

1.7.1.1 Internal Modem and External Modem

The modems widely used in data communications can be divided into two categories: internal modems and external modems. Most internal modem cards include a built-in serial interface port, which can directly communicate with an 8250 or a 16550 UART. An external modem generally has its own power supply and a separate RS-232 serial port. The connection between an external modem and a PC is straightforward, and the RS-232 interface is the only way for the DTE and the DCE to be connected.

The advantage of the internal modem is that no additional RS-232 connection is needed because the serial port is built into the internal modem card. For this reason, the cost of an internal modem is relatively low compared with that of an external modem. On the other hand, the external modem has the advantage of flexibility, and it can be connected to any computer that has a serial port. Unlike internal modems that work only with IBM-compatible PCs, external modems can be used with different kinds of computers.

1.7.1.2 Modulation and Demodulation

Modulation is the process that converts digital signal to audio tones. Modulation can also be considered an encoding process in which digital signals, such as a sequence of square waveforms (binary bits), are encoded with another signal to form a sequence of analog signals. Demodulation, the inverse of modulation, is the process of extracting the original digital sequence from the analog signals. The simplest modulation method is *amplitude modulation.*

1.7.1.3 Amplitude Modulation

Amplitude modulation is also called *amplitude shift keying,* or ASK modulation. Amplitude modulation uses a fixed-frequency analog signal as the base signal, where the base signal is controlled by digital signals, or a sequence of binary bits. Figure 1.39 shows an example of ASK modulation.

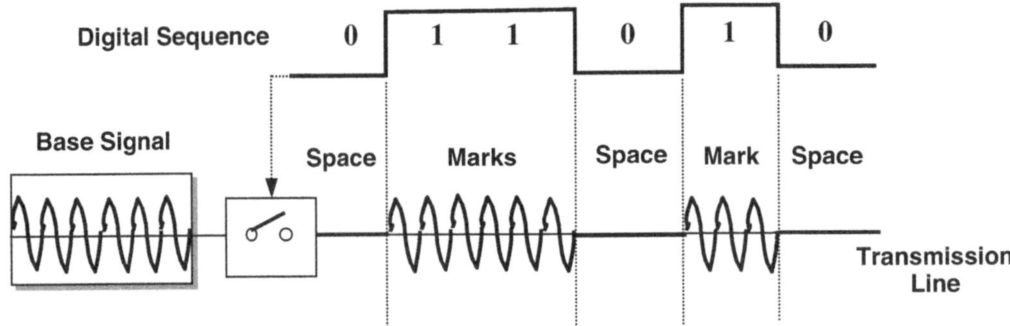

FIGURE 1.39 An example of the ASK modulation.

In Figure 1.39, a sinusoidal signal is used as the base signal. On the transmission line, the presence or absence of the base signal is under the control of the sequence of binary signals. A digital signal with a value of logical `1` is mapped to a Mark in the transmission line, which enables the base signal, and the sinusoidal signal is presented on the transmission line. A binary signal of logical `0` is associated with a Space level, which disables the base signal, causing it to disappear from the transmission line.

The digital sequence works just like a binary switch. A 1 turns the switch on and allows the base signal to be presented on the transmission line, and a 0 turns the switch off and blocks the base signal. The demodulator on the receiver side converts the base signal sequence back to the digital sequence according to the appearance and disappearance of the base signal sequence on the transmission line. A modem can be defined as a device that is used to perform the modulation and demodulation operations in data communications.

1.7.1.4 Frequency Modulation

Amplitude shift keying (ASK) is the simplest modulation method used in data communications, but it is not a robust process. In practice, because of the long transmission distance, the signals on transmission lines are affected by the noises and disturbances that exist around the lines. Most noises and disturbances have relatively high amplitudes, which are superimposed on the signals transmitted over the transmission lines and can thus cause data transmission errors.

To improve modulation and reduce the effects of noises and disturbances during data transmissions, *frequency shift keying* (FSK), which is a frequency modulation method, is preferable to ASK. One of the advantages of using FSK is that it is not easy to modify the frequency of a signal during its transmission.

The basic operation principle of FSK is as follows: The digital signals 0 and 1 are represented by two different audio tones with two different frequencies. Generally, the frequencies used for these two tones are 1,200 and 2,200 Hz. Figure 1.40 shows an example of FSK modulation.

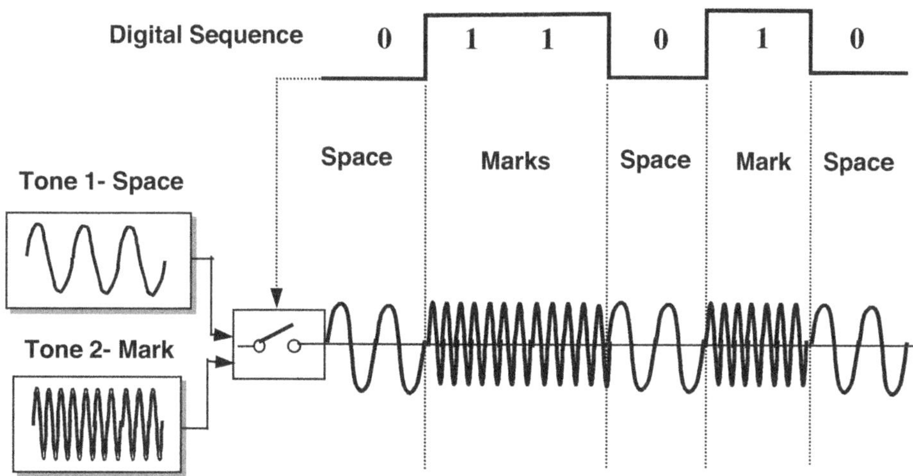

FIGURE 1.40 An example of the FSK modulation.

In FSK modulation, a binary signal works as a controller to turn a switch on and off between one tone with the higher-frequency tone and the lower-frequency tone; these tones are equivalent to the Mark and the Space levels on the transmission lines. On the receiver side, a demodulator is used to recover this digital sequence by distinguishing a logical 1 from a logical 0, based on the Mark and the Space it receives from the transmission line.

1.7.1.5 Phase Modulation

In Figure 1.40, it can be seen that frequency modulation encodes each binary bit into a single cycle of the modulated carrier. With the frequency limitation of the modulated carrier, the maximum available modulation cycle is limited to a certain number. This limitation lowers the maximum data transmission speed and, therefore, constricts the baud rate. To solve this problem, *phase modulation* can be adopted.

The operating principle of phase modulation is to try to encode more than 1 binary bit for each modulation cycle. This technique is called *phase shift keying* (PSK).

Figure 1.41 shows an example of PSK. Three waveforms are illustrated; all three have the same amplitude and the same frequency, but different phases. Waveform 1 can be considered a standard reference waveform. Waveform 2 is identical to waveform 1 and has the same phase. In other words, the phase difference between waveforms 1 and 2 is 0 degrees.

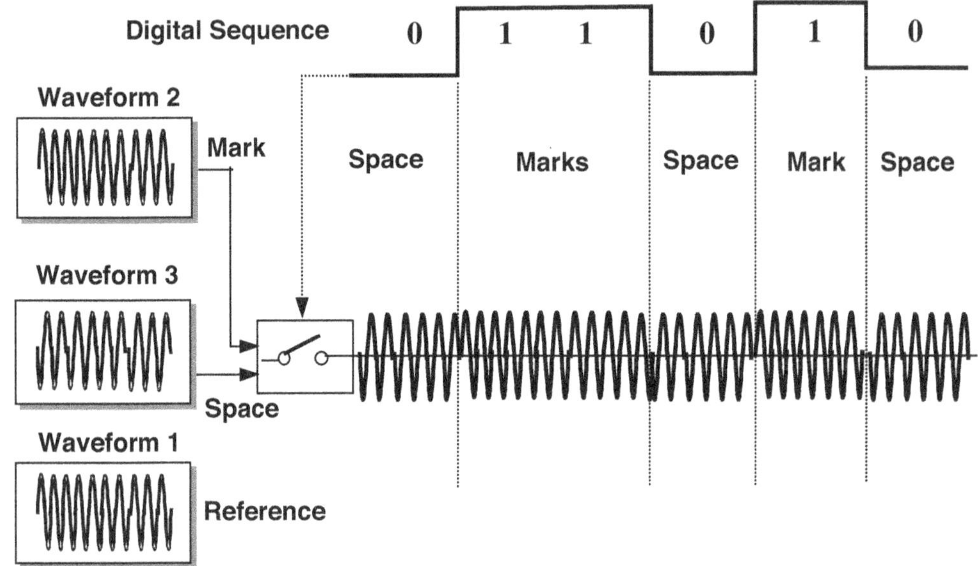

FIGURE 1.41 An example of the PSK.

Waveform 3 is also identical to waveform 1, except that its phase is 180 degrees behind waveform 1. In other words, the phase difference between waveforms 1 and 3 is 180 degrees.

During modulation, a digital value of `1` is associated with waveform 2 (in other words, a Mark is assigned to the transmission line), and a logical `0` is mapped to waveform 3 (assigning a Space to the transmission line). The binary sequence still works as a switch controller to turn data transmission on and off over waveforms 2 and 3, to output them to the transmission lines.

On the receiver side, a demodulator is used, and a copy of waveform 1 is available to this demodulator. To recover the original binary sequence, the demodulator performs an addition operation for the received waveform and the copy of waveform 1. If the received waveform is waveform 2, which is associated with the Mark, the result of the addition operation is nonzero because waveform 1 and waveform 2 are identical. However, if the received waveform is waveform 3, the addition result will be `0` because waveform 3 has a 180-degree phase difference from waveform 1. A result of `0` indicates that a Space is received.

1.7.1.6 Other Modulations

PSK uses an encoding method of one binary bit per modulation cycle. Some additional modulation methods are widely used in modems: *quadrature* PSK (a four-phase method, which uses two binary bits per modulation cycle), *differential phase shift keying* (DPSK), and *quadrature amplitude modulation* (QAM).

By using frequency modulation (FSK) and phase modulation (PSK) methods, data communication systems are able to reduce and suppress the noises and disturbances existing on the transmission lines, which greatly reduces the data transmission error rate. Quadrature amplitude modulation (QAM) is not as effective at reducing noise, although it does still improve transmission speed. In your real applications, you may have to choose between error reduction and maximum transmission speed.

1.7.1.7 Modem Control

Generally, a modem works in one of two modes: *online* mode or *command* mode. Online mode indicates that a modem has been successfully connected to the computer system and is ready to perform data communications. Command mode indicates that the modem is busying communicating with a DTE device.

As previously mentioned, the modem can be considered a DCE that can be connected with a computer system to perform data communications. By using a modem, a user can access the Internet from a PC via a telephone line. The most popular modem control method is the RS-232 serial protocol, where the modem is connected to the computer via an RS-232 port. Although no standard controlling command is set to control data transmission from the modem, the AT command set (developed by Hayes Microcomputer Products, Inc.) has become a standard for controlling modems.

The AT command set is composed of a sequence of control commands, and all commands are preceded with the keyword *AT* (the Attention command). Almost all modems used today recognize the AT command set.

When users issue different commands to the modem, a built-in unit in the modem card must be used to translate those RS-232 signals to AT commands that will be recognized by the modem.

1.7.2 Flow Control and File Transfer Control

Thus far, this chapter has reviewed the fundamentals knowledge of the RS-232 serial port protocol, its architecture, handshaking signals, the internal structures of the 8250 and 16550 UARTs, and modem control. We will now discuss how to control the flow of data between DTE and DCE devices.

Flow control is an important aspect of serial data communications. It is possible to lose data if the receiver's buffer is full or almost full but the sender keeps sending more data to the receiver. In this case, the receiver and sender need mutual communication to coordinate the data. In other words, the receiver needs to signal the sender when it is ready to receive more data and when it is not. If the receiver's buffer is close to the high mark on the buffer tank, the receiver should inform the sender to temporarily stop sending data. As previously mentioned, when two devices (the DTE and the DCE) are connected via an RS-232 cable to exchange information, certain steps should be taken to control the flow of data. There are two means of achieving this: hardware flow control and software flow control.

1.7.2.1 Hardware Flow Control

The most common method used for hardware flow control is RTS/CTS. To use this method, both the DTE and DCE must be connected via an RS-232 cable, and the handshaking signals (RTS and CTS) on both sides must be set up properly. A crossover connection should be made if a null modem cable is used for two DTE or DCE devices.

By using the RTS signal, the DTE device can control the starting or stopping of data transmission from the DTE to the DCE. Similarly, the DCE or the modem can control the starting or stopping of data from the DCE to the DTE by using the CTS signal.

The RTS and CTS just work together as a pair of signals. When the DTE is ready to begin a flow of data transmission, it initiates the transmission by activating the RTS line to inform the DCE device that a new flow of data is being sent. The DCE device alerts the DTE with a CTS signal if its receiver buffer is not full and it is ready to receive more data. When the receiver buffer of the DCE or the modem is close to the high mark, which means that the buffer is almost full, the modem will turn off the CTS line to the DTE to temporarily stop sending any data out. Finally, as the data stored in the receiver buffer is continuously moved out, the receiver buffer of the DCE or the modem will be nearly empty. Then the DCE or the modem can activate the CTS line to inform the DTE device to continue to send more data.

The reason that the DCE or modem turns the CTS line off before its buffer becomes completely empty is the time delay, which is the period of time required for the transmission of the feedback signal from the DCE or modem to the DTE. The DTE will continue to send out data even if the DCE has already turned the CTS line off. If the DCE does not turn off the CTS line until its buffer is empty, the DCE will definitely miss some of the data sent out by the DTE before the DTE receives the turned-off CTS signal because of this time delay. This will happen because the DCE has no more room to hold the data.

Generally, when we say that the receiver buffer is close to the high mark, it means that the buffer contains data occupying 75 percent of its volume. A buffer is considered close to empty when its capacity is at 25 percent of its volume.

The flow control between the DTE and DCE is similar to a handshaking control or a control signal exchange. As shown in Figure 1.42, RTS/CTS works as a pulse sequence. When the RTS signal is high, the transmission is initialized by the DTE, and the data begins to flow between the two devices. When the receiver's buffer of the DCE or the modem is nearly full, the CTS line is low, which prevents the DTE from sending more data. The data flow resumes when the CTS line returns to high.

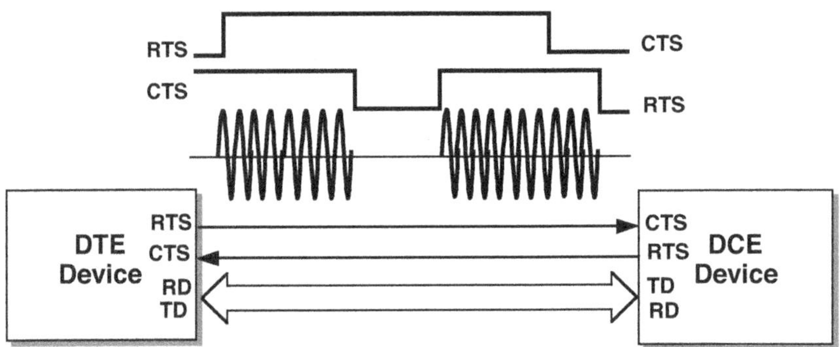

FIGURE 1.42 An illustration of the hardware flow control.

Although flow control is often used for exchanging data between two devices, in most implementations data transmission occurs in only a single direction. For example, a modem can be used to send a Web page from the server to the local machine. The local machine works as the DTE, and it will never turn off the RTS line to prevent the modem from sending back data (the Web page).

Besides RTS/CTS, several other handshaking signals, such as the DTR/DSR combination, can be used for flow control. As with the RTS/CTS signals, some devices use only one of these pairs to control data flow.

1.7.2.2 Software Flow Control

In some situations, hardware flow control is not possible. For example, Figure 1.16 shows the simplest null modem connection. In this connection, only three RS-232 signals (RD, TD, and ground lines) are used for the data exchanged between the two devices. To coordinate the flow control in this situation, a software flow control has to be utilized.

As in hardware flow control, software flow control uses a pair of control signals, XON and XOFF, which are associated with the characters 11H (decimal 17) and 13H (decimal 19), respectively. These two control signals are not connected via the communication lines, but they are transmitted as characters on the data lines (TD or RD) from both devices.

When two devices, such as the DTE and DCE or the modem, are connected via a simple three-line RS-232 cable, the flow of data is controlled by software flow control. As the receiving buffer on the modem side nears the high mark, an XOFF signal will be sent from the DCE back to the DTE device to inform the latter to stop sending out any data. As the data in the receiver buffer is continuously picked up, the buffer on the receiving side finally gets close to the low mark. Then an XON signal should be sent from the DCE or modem to the DTE device via the data line (TD). This signal informs the DTE that the modem is ready to pick up new data and allows the DTE to continue to send the data. The XON signal can be made with the key combination `Ctrl-Q`, and the XOFF signal can be created by pressing `Ctrl-S`. The user can issue these signals either from within a program or from the keyboard.

Compared with hardware flow control, software flow control has some disadvantages. For example, it has the tendency to confuse the DTE and DCE devices as data flows through the data lines. Also, when the receiver sends an XOFF signal back to the DTE device, it is possible for the DTE device to recognize those characters as normal data. The same thing happens to the DCE device.

1.7.2.3 File Transfer Control

In the preceding sections, we have discussed different methods used for controlling the data transmission between two devices. Next we will discuss a more complicated type of data transmission: blocks of data transmission.

Transmissions of blocks of data are also called *file transmissions* or file transfers. The purpose of using file transfer protocols (FTPs) when transmitting blocks of data is to make the file transmission error free, or as near perfect as possible.

A *protocol* is the equivalent of an agreement or a convention between devices, and each device should follow this agreement when perform data transmissions. For a block data transmission, some factors should be carefully considered to make sure the transmission is successful. One of these factors is the transmission header, which indicates that a block of data is to follow. Another factor is the number of bytes to be transmitted. The third is a mark that can be used for error checking of the file transmission.

Several protocols can be used for transferring blocks of data. In this section, we will discuss different FTPs. One of the simplest and most popular protocols is the XMODEM protocol.

1.7.2.4 The XMODEM Protocol

The XMODEM protocol was developed in 1977 and was one of the first FTPs. This protocol uses a byte (8 bits) of binary data as the data transmission unit, and no software handshaking signals are involved. A block of data is composed of 128-byte binary data, and each transmission processes at least a block of data between devices.

In the implementation, the XMODEM protocol is triggered by the receiver, which means that each block transmission is initialized and started on the receiving side. For this reason, the XMODEM protocol is also called a *receiver-driven* protocol. When the devices are ready for transmission of a block of data, the receiver sends a negative acknowledgment (NAK) signal (15H, decimal 21) to the transmitter to initiate the transfer. The block transmission will be formally started between the transmitter and receiver when the former receives the NAK signal from the receiver. Figure 1.43 shows a typical data transmission format in the XMODEM protocol.

SOH	Block Number	STX	Data Byte 1	......	Data Byte 128	ETX	CheckSum

FIGURE 1.43 A typical data transmission format in XMODEM.

- **SOH (start of header):** The binary code for this signal is 01H, which means the starting point of the transmission of a data block. Upon receiving this signal, the receiver recognizes that a block of data, or a packet of data, will come from the transmission side. The entire block contains 128 bytes of data.
- **Block number:** Also known as the packet sequence number, this is an 8-bit number used to indicate the location of the current block relative to the entire file transfer. The purpose of this block number is to confirm to the receiver that the received block of data is correct and expected. The first block is numbered 1, the second block is numbered 2, and so on. The final block, block 255, will be wrapped to 0.
- **STX (start of text):** This signal indicates the start of the textual data.
- **Data byte 1:** The first byte of data in the block.
- **Data byte 128:** The last byte of data in the block.
- **ETX (end of text):** This signal indicates the end of the data in the block. Note that this character is not a part of the body of data in the block.
- **CheckSum:** This is the least significant byte of the checksum value, which is a redundant byte and may be represented by an ASCII code.

During the file transfer, each time the receiver receives a byte of data, a checksum value is calculated on the receiving side. When the whole block of data is transmitted and 128 bytes of data have been received, the receiver will have a final checksum value. To confirm that the transmission process has been error-free, the final checksum value calculated by the receiver will be compared to the checksum value (`CheckSum`) sent by the transmitter. If the two checksum values are identical, it means that the transmission has been successful, and the receiver sends an ACK (06H) signal indicating this to the transmitter. The transmitter can then either send the next block of data or send an end of transmission (EOT–04H) signal to inform the receiver that the file transfer is complete. If the two checksum values are different, it means that some transmission errors have occurred during the file transfer. In this case, the receiver should send another NAK to the transmitter so that it will resend the block of data.

The checksum value used in this XMODEM protocol is the simplest one, and its length is only one byte (8 bits). To calculate the checksum each time the receiver receives a block of data, follow these steps:

1. Initially, reset the checksum value to 0.
2. When a byte of data is received, add that data to the checksum value, and shift the resulted checksum value left with 1 bit.
3. Continue the operation in the step 2 until the whole block of data is received. The final checksum result is obtained from the checksum value.

An important point to note is that if the transmitter cannot recognize the first NAK character sent by the receiver, the file transfer cannot be started, and the receiver will send the second NAK within one second. Similarly, the receiver will send the third NAK character to the transmitter within another second if the transmitter still cannot identify the NAK character. This situation will continue until one of the following two conditions occurs:

- The transmitter eventually recognizes the NAK character sent by the receiver, and the file transfer can be properly started.
- The receiver has continuously sent 10 NAK characters, each for 1 second, for a total time of 10 seconds. If this happens, a timeout error occurs, and the file transfer will be cancelled by the receiver.

Another point is that the files may not be evenly divided by 128. In that case, a sequence of EOF (end of file–1AH) characters should be padded to the last data block to achieve this length.

To terminate the file transfer, either the receiver or the transmitter can send a sequence of CAN (18H, decimal 24) characters to the transmission lines to inform the other device that it wants to abort the data transmission. Generally, two to five CAN characters are enough to complete the termination of a file transfer. XMODEM is a simple send-and-wait FTP and is widely used in data transfer blocks that have a fixed length.

1.7.2.5 The XMODEM-CRC Protocol

The XMODEM-CRC protocol is an improvement over the XMODEM protocol. As explained in the preceding section, the checksum value calculated in the XMODEM protocol is limited to a byte (8 bits) in length. It is probable that the checksum value calculated in XMODEM will miss some valuable data and therefore make that error-detection method invaluable. To improve the checksum calculation method, a CRC method is implemented. We will discuss the CRC method in detail in the next section.

Basically, the CRC method improves its credibility by using 16-bit (2-byte) binary data to calculate its checksum value. In practice, most programmers prefer to use a CRC table to perform the checksum calculation.

The implementation of an XMODEM-CRC protocol in a file transfer is similar to the XMODEM protocol except for the following differences:

- The receiver still initials a file transfer, but the initial character is a "C" rather than the NAK used in the XMODEM protocol.
- When the transmitter receives the "C" character, it starts the file transfer by sending a sequence of data, as shown in Figure 1.44.
- Each time the receiver receives data, it calculates the checksum value using the CRC method.
- As the whole file is transferred, the checksum value calculated by the receiver will be compared to the checksum value sent by the transmitter. If these values are identical, it means that the file transfer has been successful, and the receiver will either send an ACK signal back to the transmitter to allow it to send the next file or send an EOT to terminate the file transfer. If the checksum values are different, it means that errors have occurred during the file transfer, and the receiver will send an NAK to the transmitter to ask that the file should be resent.

SOH	Block Number	Complement Of Block	Data Byte 1	......	Data Byte 128	CRC CheckSum	
						H-Byte	L-Byte

FIGURE 1.44 A typical data transmission format in XMODEM-CRC.

As shown in Figure 1.44, some data formats are different in XMODEM-CRC from those used with the original XMODEM protocol. One difference is that both the STX and the ETX signals have disappeared. The second difference is that a complement of the block value is presented. The purpose of this value is to further strengthen error checking. The third difference is that the CRC checksum value, is now a 16-bit value with both high-byte and low-byte data. To remain compatible with the XMODEM protocol, the XMODEM-CRC protocol adopts the following method for a file transfer.

The start of the file transfer still occurs on the receiving end; the receiver sends a "C" character to the transmitter to indicate that the receiver is ready for the transfer. The transmitter then begins to send a block of data if the transmitter supports the XMODEM-CRC protocol. If the receiver does not receive a block of data after sending the "C" character, the receiver will continue to send another two "C" characters, each using 1 second of the time interval, to the transmitter. If the receiver still has not received any data after three "C" characters have been sent, the receiver will send the NAK characters to the transmitter instead of sending out more "C" characters. The receiver assumes that the transmitter does not support the XMODEM-CRC protocol, and it switches to XMODEM protocol to try to inform the transmitter to begin the file transfer.

The advantage of using XMODEM-CRC protocol for file transfer is to improve error-checking capability and make the transfer process more likely to succeed. The shortcoming is that this protocol makes error checking more complicated and therefore more time consuming.

1.7.2.6 The XMODEM-1K Protocol

The XMODEM-CRC protocol is an improvement over the XMODEM protocol's error checking. As the CPU running speed becomes faster and faster, the programs' sizes become bigger and bigger, which requires that file transfer sizes should also be increased. One problem that exists in both the XMODEM and the XMODEM-CRC protocols is the small size of the block during the file transfer. Only 128 bytes are allowed to be transferred for each block. This limitation greatly reduces file transfer speed. A solution to this problem is to use the XMODEM-1K protocol. Basically, no significant difference exists between the XMODEM-CRC and the XMODEM-1K protocols, and the only two minor differences are as follows:

- Each transferred block size in the XMODEM-1K protocol is increased from 128 bytes to 1,024 bytes (1 KB).
- The SOH is replaced by a new character, STX, which is a binary code of 02H and indicates the beginning of the text data.

A typical data format for the XMODEM-1K protocol is shown in Figure 1.45.

STX	Block Number	Complement Of Block	Data Byte 1	......	Data Byte 1024	CRC CheckSum	
						H-Byte	L-Byte

FIGURE 1.45 A typical data format of the XMODEM-1K protocol.

The XMODEM-1K protocol is compatible with the XMODEM-CRC protocol, which means that by using XMODEM-1K, the files can be transferred in blocks of either 128 or 1,024 bytes. A more interesting issue is that the XMODEM-1K can handle any combination of 128-byte and 1,024-byte data blocks.

1.7.2.7 The YMODEM Protocol

File transfers can be greatly improved in both transmission speed and transmission size by using the XMODEM-1K protocol, but it may be found at any time that only one file can be transferred using this protocol. To solve this problem and allow multiple (batch) files to be transferred simultaneously, another protocol, YMODEM, has been developed.

YMODEM is still a receiver-driven protocol. As with the XMODEM-1K protocol, the receiver initiates the file transfers by sending a "C" character to the transmitter. In order to transfer multiple files at a time, the YMODEM protocol contains an additional block called Block0. Figure 1.46 shows the structure of the Block0 used in the YMODEM protocol.

SOH	Block Number	Complement Of Block	File Name	File Size	Modification Date	File Mode	Serial Number	Nulls	CRC	
									H	L

FIGURE 1.46 The structure of a Block0 in the YMODEM protocol.

The Block0 contains some optional parameters that can be passed from the transmitter to the receiver. The meanings and functions of those parameters are listed here:

- **SOH:** This is a start bit that has a binary code of 01H, which is used to inform the receiver that a block of data will follow.
- **Block number:** This number is identical with that used in the XMODEM-1K protocol.
- **Complement of block:** This number is identical with that used in the XMODEM-1K protocol.
- **File name:** This string is used to indicate the name of the file that will be transferred. An 00H is attached at the end of this file name. If the string is a null string (" "), it indicates the end of the batch transfer.
- **File size:** This is a decimal string used to indicate the size of the file to be transferred. This parameter is optional.
- **Modification date:** This is an octal string used to indicate the date when the file is modified. This parameter is optional.
- **File mode:** This is also an octal string used to indicate the file mode. This parameter is optional.
- **Serial number:** This is an octal string used to indicate the serial number of the file. This parameter is optional.
- **Nulls:** This causes all unused spaces to be filled with 00H.
- **CRC:** This is a two-byte, error-checking value calculated via the CRC method.

Note that in Figure 1.46, many parameters contained in Block0 are optional. One point to remember is that if you want to set and pass one (current) parameter to the receiver, you must also set and pass all parameters located before the parameter you want to pass.

During the batch transfer, the receiver initiates a transfer by sending a "C" character to the transmitter. When the transmitter successfully receives this "C" character, it sends a Block0 signal to the receiver, as shown in Figure 1.46, as the first data. If the receiver receives this Block0, it sends an ACK signal to the transmitter to indicate that the batch transfer can be started. Upon receiving the ACK signal, the transmitter begins to transmit the files. The single file transfer will be terminated when the receiver receives an EOT character. To initiate another file transfer, the receiver sends another "C" character to the transmitter. When all files have been transferred, the transmitter sends another Block0 with a null string as the file name to inform the receiver that the batch transfer is completed.

1.7.2.8 The YMODEM-G Protocol

The YMODEM-G protocol is another improvement over the YMODEM protocol, especially in transmission speed. Basically, the YMODEM-G protocol is identical to YMODEM, but the two protocols have the following differences:

- The batch transfer in YMODEM-G is still started from the receiver side. When a batch transfer is ready to start, instead of sending a "C" character, the receiver sends a "G" character to initiate the file transfer.
- As soon as the transmitter receives this "G" character, the batch transfer is formally started. The transmitter continuously sends all blocks of data to the receiver without waiting for the receiver's acknowledgement feedback.
- When all blocks of data in a file are transferred, the transmitter sends an EOT character to the receiver and waits for feedback from the receiver.

As the batch transfer starts, the transmitter never waits for an ACK signal from the receiver between the block transmissions; instead, the transmitter continuously sends all blocks of data to the receiver. In other words, the receiver never sends an ACK signal to the transmitter during the block transmissions. In this way, transmission speed is greatly improved because numerous handshaking actions between the transmitter and the receiver have been eliminated.

However, the transmitter does send an EOT character; it then waits for the feedback from the receiver when all blocks of data in a file are transferred. This means that the handshaking functions between the transmitter and the receiver are activated and performed at the end of each file transfer, not at the end of each block.

One good thing is often balanced by a bad thing, and this is true for the YMODEM-G protocol. Because no handshaking function exists between the transmitter and the receiver during the blocks' transmissions in the YMODEM-G protocol, the receiver may miss some data or the received data contains errors. The receiver cannot ask the transmitter to resend all the blocks of data; some errors will occur during the blocks transmissions because of the speed of YMODEM-G. Figure 1.47 shows a block diagram of the batch transfer using the YMODEM-G protocol.

Generally, the receiver will terminate the batch transfer by sending a sequence of CAN characters to the transmitter if some errors occur or some bad blocks are received. The YMODEM-G protocol is also called an *error-correcting* protocol because it cannot retransmit blocks of data if some errors occur.

1.7.2.9 The ZMODEM Protocol

Both the XMODEM and YMODEM protocols can only work for a limited length of data, such as 8-bit data. Also, some handshaking signals, such as XON/XOFF, are not utilized in these two protocols. To improve these shortcomings, the ZMODEM protocol has been developed.

ZMODEM is similar to the YMODEM-G protocol, and as in YMODEM-G, the transmitter does not need to wait for an ACK from the receiver during the transfer of the blocks. The transmitter can send out all blocks of data continuously. The difference between the YMODEM-G and ZMODEM protocols is that the latter has an error-recovering capability, which means that the receiver can require that the transmitter retransmit the bad blocks if transmission errors occur. Another property of ZMODEM is that it utilizes certain handshaking signals, such as XON/XOFF, to enhance batch transmission and reduce the error rate. Finally, the ZMODEM protocol can transmit different lengths of data so it is suitable for working with packet-switched networks.

The shortcoming of using ZMODEM is that this protocol is very complex in real applications. Because of this disadvantage, ZMODEM has not been widely implemented for file transfers.

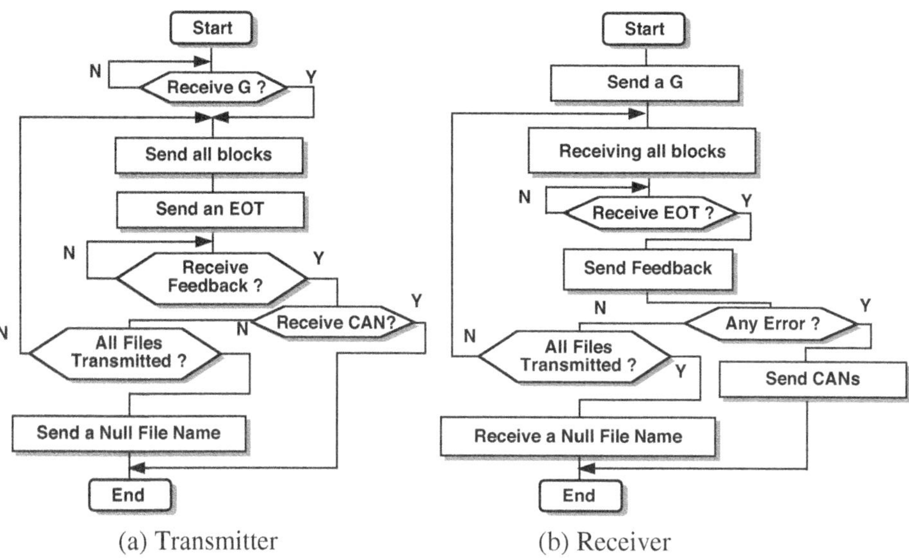

FIGURE 1.47 The block diagram of the YMODEM-G protocol.

1.7.2.10 The Kermit Protocol

The Kermit protocol was developed in 1981 by Frank Da Cruz and Bill Catching at Columbia University. The purpose of developing this protocol was to overcome some compatibility problems that existed in the XMODEM and the YMODEM protocols. Unlike XMODEM and YMODEM, the Kermit protocol can work on different platforms and allow file transfers and data exchanges between two devices on different operating systems. Another special point of the Kermit protocol is that it uses a packet, not a single character, as a handshaking signal for communications between the transmitter and the receiver.

Compared with the XMODEM and YMODEM protocols, Kermit has the following advantages:

- Kermit is a packet-oriented protocol, which means that all its handshaking signals are composed of packets. Unlike XMODEM and YMODEM, which each utilize a single character as the handshaking signal, Kermit uses packets to communicate between the sender and the receiver. This prevents confusion that might otherwise be introduced by the similarity between the data characters and handshaking characters, such as XON/XOFF, C, G, EOT, and so on.
- The operation sequence of the Kermit protocol is similar to that of the XMODEM protocol, but Kermit can transfer multiple files at a time. This is different than XMODEM, which can transfer only one file at a time.
- The packet's length can be modified based on each batch transfer requirement, and even the entire packet can be empty.
- The packet's contents can be extendible, which means that some new features can be added into a packet, and this addition will not affect the previous definition of the packet.

The batch transfer process in the Kermit protocol is similar to that in XMODEM. The beginning of the file transfer is triggered by the receiver, which sends an initial packet that includes a NAK character to the transmitter. As soon as the transmitter receives this starting packet, it sends out the whole block of data (the packet). When the receiver receives the data packet, it sends an ACK packet to request that the transmitter send the next block of data (the packet), or if errors are

MARK	LEN	SEQ	TYPE	DATA	CHECK-1	CHECK-2	CHECK-3

FIGURE 1.48 A typical Kermit packet format.

detected, the receiver sends a NAK packet asking that the transmitter resend the previous packet. Figure 1.48 shows a typical Kermit packet format.

The explanation for each field is listed here:

- `MARK`: This is the start mark of the packet, which is equivalent to an SOH byte.
- `LEN`: This indicates the total number of bytes in the packet. This number does not include the `LEN` itself or the MARK byte.
- `SEQ`: This is a modulo-64 sequence number. The sequence number starts with the first packet, the S packet. The range is between 0 and 63.
- `TYPE`: This is an ASCII character used to indicate which packet type is transmitted. The Kermit protocol has the following packet types:
  A—Attribute packet
  B—EOT packet
  D—Data packet
  E—Error packet
  F—File header packet
  N—NAK packet
  S—Send initiate or start packet
  T—Reserved and not currently used
  X—Display text on screen packet
  Y—ACK packet
  Z—EOF packet
- `DATA`: This field contains the real data values. The length and contents of the field vary according to the different packet types, and in some packet types, nothing exists in this field.
- `CHECK`: This is a checksum value used for error checking during packet transmission. Both the `LEN` and the `SEQ` fields are covered by the checksum calculations, but the `MARK` field is excluded. The default checksum value is a single byte, but it can be extended to double bytes or even three bytes, or 16-bit CRC values.

More detailed information for each of the packet types is listed here:

- **S packet:** The purpose of this packet is to inform the receiver that the transmitter will send some communication parameters with the packet. The sequence number of the S packet is 0. Its DATA field contains a total of 10 subfields, and each has a different functionality, such as the maximum packet size the receiver can receive, the maximum number of seconds to wait, the special character used to terminate a packet, and so on.
- **Y packet**: This packet is equivalent to an ACK packet; it is used by the receiver to indicate to the transmitter that a special packet, such as an S packet, has been received. This packet generally contains the following fields:
  SEQ (sequence number)
  LEN (length of bytes)
  CHECK
  DATA

The default DATA field in this Y-type packet is an empty field, but you can place feedback information in the field.

- **F packet:** This packet contains the name of the file to be transmitted. The file name is generally limited to digits or uppercase characters.
- **N packet:** This packet is equivalent to a NAK packet. When transmission errors are detected or a bad packet is received, the receiver will send a NAK packet back to the transmitter to ask that it resend the packet. This packet contains the following fields:
  SEQ
  LEN
  CHECK
  DATA
- The DATA field is generally empty.
- **D packet:** This is a DATA packet, and its DATA field contains the actual data to be transmitted.
- **B packet:** When the transmitter finishes all file transmissions, it sends a B (EOT) packet to the receiver to inform the latter that the transmission has been completed. The receiver can then feed back the transmitter with an ACK packet to indicate that the B packet is successfully received. Another packet the receiver can send is a NAK packet, which means that some errors occurred during the previous file transmission and that the receiver needs the transmitter to resend the packet.
- **Z packet:** When the transmitter finishes one file transmission, it sends a Z (EOF) packet to inform the receiver that the file has been transmitted. The receiver can respond to the transmitter with an ACK packet to indicate that the Z packet has been successfully received. Another packet the receiver can send is a NAK packet, which means that some errors occurred during the previous file transmission and that the receiver needs the transmitter to resend the packet.
- **E packet:** The E packet is used to transmit an error message from either one of the devices. This packet is sent if an error occurs during the packet transmission in either direction.
- **A packet:** This packet is used to transmit additional parameters, or attributes, for a file to be transmitted. These additional attributes are used to describe the properties of the file, such as its size, its contents, the date and time when it was created, the path where it is located, and any access information.

Relatively speaking, Kermit is a general-purpose protocol. This means that it can be utilized on any operating system with any platform. Because of its versatility, this protocol is more complicated in design and implementation than some of the other protocols discussed in this section. To determine which protocol is most suitable for your application, you need to consider the tradeoffs you'll make with each. For example, if your file-transferring tasks are small, and only a single file is usually transmitted, XMODEM-CRC is a good candidate. On the other hand, if you need to transfer numerous files of different sizes, the YMODEM-1K or the ZMODEM format would probably be a better choice. The Kermit protocol would be the most appropriate selection if you plan to transmit numerous files among different operating systems.

1.8 SERIAL COMMUNICATION ERRORS AND ERROR DETECTION

1.8.1 Block Redundancy—Checksum

The previously mentioned method for calculating block redundancy checksum values is the simplest of the checksum algorithms. It is only suitable for the 8-bit checksum calculation and is widely used in XMODEM protocol processing. The key point in applying this algorithm is cycling addition each received data. Figure 1.49 shows a block diagram of this algorithm.

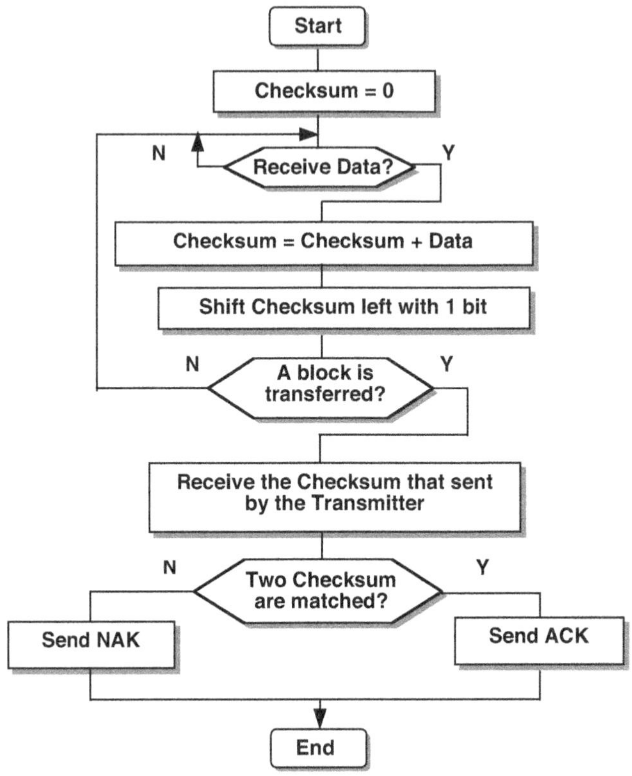

FIGURE 1.49 The block diagram of the checksum algorithm.

1.8.2 The Classical CRC Algorithm

The CRC is an error-checking algorithm widely used in data communications. Its full name, as stated earlier, is the cyclic redundancy check. The CRC algorithm is based on modulo-2 long division.

The received data can be considered a message, which is also called the *message polynomial.* The message should be divided by a divisor, which is also called a *generator polynomial.* This division process is performed in modulo-2 long division, which can be equivalent to a sequence of shifts in a shift register plus some exclusive OR (XOR) gates. After all the data has been processed in this modulo-2 long division, the value of the remainder is the CRC result, or the CRC remainder.

In contrast with traditional division, the CRC pays attention only to the remainder, not to the quotient. The CRC algorithm is defined as the remainder from modulo-2 division in which a number of 0 bits, equal to the number of bits in the remainder register, is appended to the message.

In normal binary division operations, the divisor is always subtracted from the remainder, and the quotient is set to 1 if the result of the subtraction is positive; otherwise, the quotient will be set to 0 if the result is less than 0. But in the CRC algorithm, an XOR logic operation is utilized to replace the subtraction operation. For example, suppose we subtract one binary number from another, as follows: $10011101 - 10001010 = 00010111$. The result of XORing these two binary numbers is $10011101 \oplus 10001010 = 00010111$. The result is identical for these two operations, and this is only a coincidental case. Generally, the subtraction results will differ from the XOR results.

Let us use another example to explain the algorithm further. Assume that we have received a message or some 32-bit binary data, and a divisor, which is 16-bit binary data with a value of 1021H. We want to perform a modulo-2 long division for these two numbers. This division can be exactly realized by using a shift register and some XOR gates, as shown in Figure 1.50.

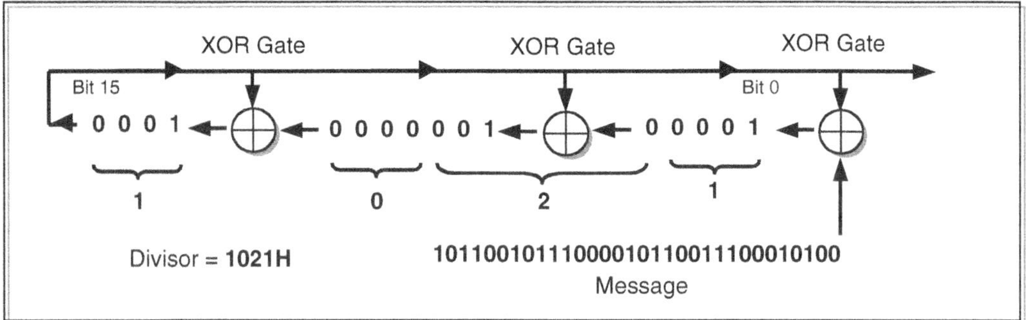

FIGURE 1.50 An example of modulo-2 division.

In Figure 1.50, three XOR gates are arranged in a special way; that is, each XOR gate is placed immediately to the right of a divisor bit with a value of 1. The message or data is shifted into the register, bit by bit, through the first XOR gate. The register simply works as a cycling chain from left to right.

The message is shifted bit by bit, from the LSB to the MSB, into the register. For each shifting, the shifted bit will be XORed with bit 15 (that is, bit 0 ⊕ bit 15, bit 4 ⊕ bit 15, bit 11 ⊕ bit 15, and so on). After the entire message has been shifted into the register, which means that the MSB of the message has been moved into the register, the contents in the register can be considered a CRC remainder. The additional 16 bits of 0 should be attached after this remainder.

The previous shifting process is exactly equivalent to a modulo-2 long division between the message and the divisor. If this process is represented by a polynomial, it can be expressed as follows:

(Message) $1x^{31}+0x^{30}+1x^{29}+1x^{28}+0x^{27}+0x^{26}+ \ldots\ldots +1x^{4}+0x^{3}+1x^{2}+0x+0x^{0}$

(Divisor) $1x^{16}+0x^{15}+0x^{14}+0x^{13}+1x^{12}+0x^{11}+ \ldots\ldots +1x^{5}+0x^{4}+0x^{3}+0x^{2}+0x+1x^{0}$

If only the nonzero coefficients are considered, we have

(Message) $x^{31}+x^{29}+x^{28}+x^{25}+x^{23}+x^{22}+x^{21}+x^{16}+x^{14}+x^{13}+x^{10}+x^{9}+x^{8}+x^{4}+x^{2}$

(Divisor) $x^{16}+x^{12}+x^{5}+1$

This polynomial division can also be expressed as a subroutine, which can be called by programs to calculate the CRC values for a given message or piece of data. (In practice, most programmers prefer to calculate the CRC value by using a table method).

During the data transmission, each time a block of data is received, the receiver calculates a CRC checksum using either the polynomial division method or the CRC table method. The block transmission is correct if the CRC result is identical to the CRC value sent from the transmitter. If these two values are different, it means that errors have occurred during the block transmission. In this case, the receiver should send a NAK signal to ask that the transmitter resend the block of data.

In some applications, after a block of data has been transferred, the receiver does not directly compare the CRC value calculated by the receiver with the CRC result from the transmitter. Instead, the receiver will consider the CRC value from the transmitter as part of the message and include that value in the CRC process. The receiver's CRC result will be 0 if both the received message and the calculated CRC are correct. The reason for this can be explained as follows.

For normal arithmetic division, we have

$$\text{Message} = (\text{Quotient} \times \text{Divisor}) + \text{Remainder} \quad \text{(Eq. 1-3)}$$

After adding the remainder to the two sides of Equation 1-3, we get

$$\text{Message} + \text{Remainder} = (\text{Quotient} \times \text{Divisor}) + \text{Remainder} + \text{Remainder} \quad \text{(Eq. 1-4)}$$

Remember, in modulo-2 division, the addition operation is equivalent to an XOR operation. By applying this translation, some items become

$$\text{Remainder} + \text{Remainder} = \text{Remainder} \oplus \text{Remainder} = 0 \quad \text{(Eq. 1-5)}$$

Recall that when any binary number is XORed with itself, the result should be 0. This is the result we obtained from Equation 1-5.

Applying this principle to Equation 1-4, we have

$$\text{Message} \oplus \text{Remainder} = (\text{Quotient} \times \text{Divisor}) \quad \text{(Eq. 1-6)}$$

Moving the divisor from the right side of Equation 1-6 to the left, we get

$$\frac{Message \;\oplus\; \mathrm{Re}\,mainder}{Divisor} = Quotient \quad \text{(Eq. 1-7)}$$

The physical meaning of Equation 1-7 is that when a message is XORed with the remainder, and then divided by the divisor, the remainder is 0.

The preceding method is identical with this analysis. When a block of data is accepted by the receiver, the next transmitted data should be the CRC values from the transmitter. If the receiver considers CRC as part of the message and places it into the CRC calculation in the receiving side, the remainder (the CRC values) should be 0 if both the message and the CRC values are error-free.

Figure 1.51 shows a CRC subroutine written in C code. The CRC subroutine is named `calCRC()`. The first argument, *msg,* is the received message, and the second argument, *uCRC,* is the intermediate CRC value, which is two bytes (16 bits) in length.

1.8.3 Variations of CRC

Several different variations of the CRC algorithm exist, such as the reversed CRC, the CRC-CCITT, and some other versions. An extensive discussion of these variations is beyond the scope of this book. Readers should refer to associated reference materials if more detailed knowledge on this issue is needed.

1.9 SERIAL COMMUNICATIONS WITH THE RS-422 AND RS-485

RS-232 serial communication is a popular protocol widely implemented in the industrial and commercial fields. As serial interface techniques are developed, more new devices and protocols are invented and applied in today's data communications field, including RS-422, RS-485, and

```
unsigned calCRC( int msg, unsigned  uCRC )
{
    int  index;
    for ( index = 8;  --index >= 0; )
    {
        if ( uCRC & 0x8000)
        {
            uCRC <<= 1;
            uCRC += ( (msg <= 1) & 0400 ) != 0 );
            uCRC ^= 0x1021;
        }
        else
        {
            uCRC <<= 1;
            uCRC += ( ( msg <<= 1 ) & 0400 ) != 0 );
        }
    }
    return uCRC;
}
```

FIGURE 1.51 A CRC calculation subroutine.

USB. In this section, we will discuss the fundamentals and operational principles of these new devices. The actual application examples of RS-485 are provided in Chapter 3.

In previous sections, we have discussed RS-232 serial port communication using some real examples. Generally speaking, RS-232 is an unbalanced data transmission system because both the transmitter (pin 3 in DB-9) and the receiver terminal (pin 2 in DB-9) have a voltage offset relative to the ground (pin 5 in DB-9). This voltage offset should be negative for both the transmitter and receiver terminal if no signal is being transmitted on the ports. If signals are being transmitted on the terminals, both the transmitter and receiver terminals will have alternate voltage offsets between +12 and -12 volts. An unbalanced RS-232 data transmission is shown in Figure 1.52.

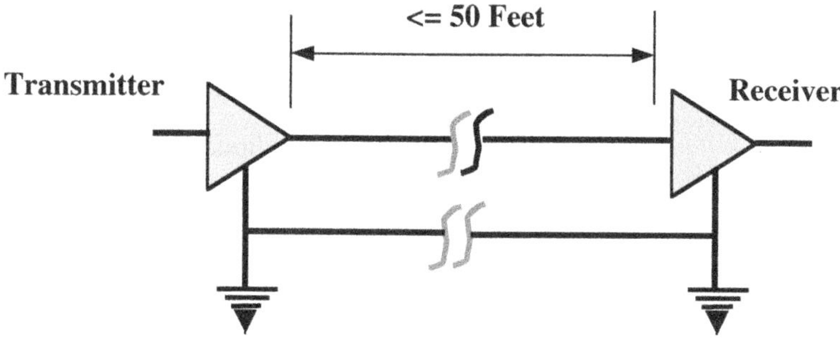

FIGURE 1.52 A serial RS-232 transmission mode.

The main problems involved with using an unbalanced RS-232 data transmission system are as follows:

- Low transmission rates (only up to hundreds of kbps)
- Short transmission distances (less than 50 feet)
- Little disturbance resistance on transmitted signals (so the error rate is relatively high)
- Point-to-point transmission (COM1 to COM2)

The RS-232 is most suitable for a single local device with low-transmission speed control.

As mentioned earlier, RS-422 and RS-485 have some advantages over RS-232, such as a longer transmission distance (up to 4,000 feet), a higher-transmission rate (up to 10 Mbps), and a better capability to resist disturbances. Another advantage of using RS-485 is that it is a multiple-point transmission system. This means that you can connect multiple ports with a single cable, and that each port can either send or receive signals to or from other multiple ports. This works like a tri-state control system, such as a microcomputer. The CPU, memory, and I/O ports are connected to a common bus, and each component can communicate with the others via the common bus by using a tri-state control system.

1.9.1 Basics of the RS-422 Standard

Both RS-422 and RS-485 utilize a balanced differential transmission structure, in which two transmission lines (A and B, for example) are used for each channel, and both lines are twisted together. If the port is idle and no signal is transmitted on the transmission lines, the voltage difference between line A and line B is negative (for instance, −5 volts). This voltage difference will be changed to positive (for instance, +5 volts) if the port is activated and a signal is transmitted over the lines.

The difference between RS-422 and RS-485 is that although RS-422 operates on the balanced differential transmission mode, it is still a point-to-point transmission system, and it can be considered an extension of the RS-232 system. One special point is that the RS-422 can extend the point-to-point interface up to 10 receivers with a single transmitter, as shown in Figure 1.53.

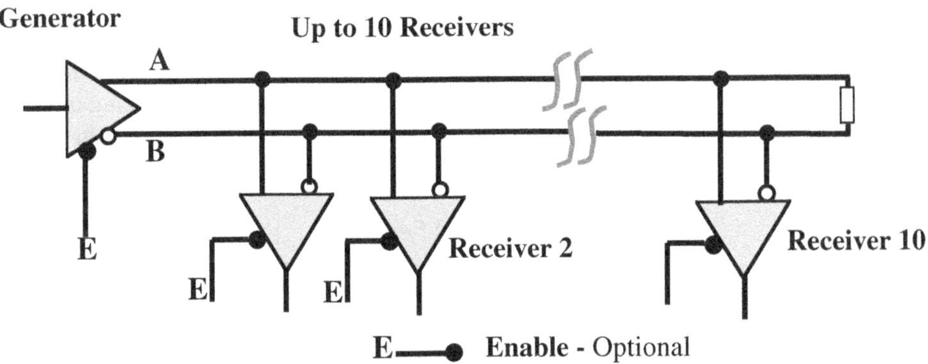

FIGURE 1.53 An RS-422 transmission mode.

If lines A and B are close together, they will be affected almost identically by external or environmental electromagnetic noise. If the lines are twisted together, then neither line is permanently closer to a noise source than the other. Hence, the well-known twisted pair is extremely effective for eliminating noise from the signals.

As mentioned earlier, to connect multiple ports on a single transmission cable, a tri-state structure is needed. This means that an `Enable` control signal is required for the RS-485 system. This is not necessary for the RS-422 system; in RS-422, the `Enable` control is optional.

Because of the balanced differential transmission structure, both the RS-422 and RS-485 transmission systems are better able to overcome the disturbance and interference than is the unbalanced RS-232 transmission system. The common-mode noise can be significantly reduced by using a balanced signal transmission.

1.9.2 Basics of the RS-485 Standard

The RS-485 enables multiple devices (up to 32) to communicate in half-duplex mode on a single pair of serial wires, with a ground reference wire, at distances up to 4,000 feet. Each device connected in the serial network is considered a node that is under the control of a tri-state control unit. Both the length of the network and the number of nodes can easily be extended using a variety of repeater products on the market.

In the RS-485 protocol, data is transmitted differentially on two wires twisted together (the twisted pair). The properties of differential signals provide high noise immunity and long-distance capabilities. An RS-485 network has two possible configurations: two-wire and four-wire. For a two-wire connection, the transmitter and receiver of each device are connected to a twisted pair. In a four-wire network, the master device has its transmitter connected to each of the slave receivers on one twisted pair. The slave transmitters are all connected to the master receiver on a second twisted pair. In both configurations, devices or nodes are addressable. As we previously mentioned, each node in the 485 network is controlled by a tri-state mechanism, which means that only one device can drive the twisted line at a time; therefore, drivers must be put into a high-impedance mode when they are not in use. The RS-485 device driver must be able to handle this high-impedance switch by using a signal line (if your RS-485 device is controlled via an RS-232 port, this is typically done with the RTS line).

A special issue in a two-wire communication over an RS-485 network is the turnaround delay. In a two-wire network, each time a device is selected to communicate with another one, both devices need to change their states from the high impedance to the active state. Both devices also need to change their states from active back to high impedance when the transmission is complete. The turnaround delay is the time period between the completion of the transmission and the point when both devices are changed back to a high-impedance state. This period of time is important in the two-wire network because during this time, no other devices can be active and no other transmission can be allowed to occur. A typical length of this turnaround delay is the transmission time of a character at the current baud rate.

A two-wire RS-485 network offers the advantage of low wiring costs and enables any two nodes to communicate easily. The disadvantage of using a two-wire network is that a half-duplex communication mode has to be adopted, and the turnaround delay must be handled carefully. A four-wire network enables the devices to work in full-duplex mode, which means that they can exchange information simultaneously. However, the price for this full-duplex operation is that only the master-slave communication mode is allowed to work this way. In this mode, the master device can receive information from any slave, but communication between slaves is prohibited. The RS-485 control software can handle addressing, turnaround delay, and the driver's tri-state functions.

Two wires in the RS-485 network are labeled A and B, according to the EIA RS-485 specifications. In some RS-485 products, these two wires are labeled + and −, respectively. Generally, the + is mapped to the B wire and the − is associated with the A wire. If these two wires are configured differently, it will not break the RS-485, but your network will not work properly.

1.9.3 The Operational Principle of the RS-485

Most RS-485 transmission systems use a master–slave control mode, and each slave unit has a unique address. The unit responds only to packets addressed to it, and the master, who periodically polls all connected slave units, creates these packets.

Unlike the RS-422 transmission system displayed in Figure 1.53, an RS-485 transmission system can have up to 32 generators and/or receivers working in half-duplex mode. A typical RS-485 transmission system with a two-wire multidrop network connection is shown in Figure 1.54. The master–slave transmission system needs a four-wire multidrop network connection.

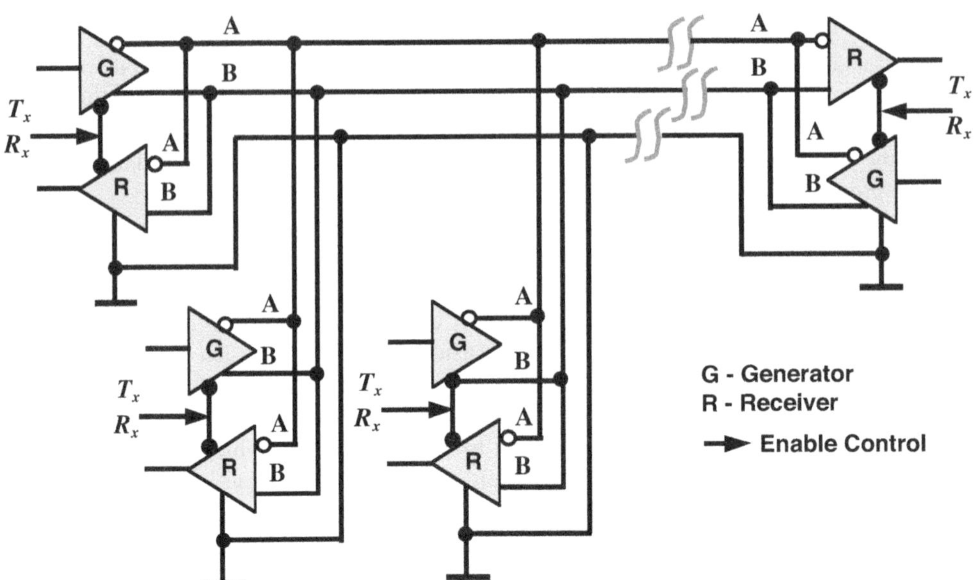

FIGURE 1.54 A typical RS-485 network.

For most applications, you can use the RTS control signal, which is available in the RS-232 transmission system, as the `Enable` control signal, and apply it in an RS-485 transmission system. Most serial transmission systems applied in the industrial and manufacturing fields are still RS-232 systems. If an RS-232 transmission system is replaced with an RS-485 system, a converter is needed to translate the control from the RS-232 to the RS-485 control system.

In Chapter 3, we will combine a real example to explore how to use an RS-485 transmission system to achieve real-time control of a motor speed control system. The original transmission system used in the motor speed control system is a traditional RS-232 system. In order to save development time, we just set a direct connection between an RS-485 port and an RS-232 port to create this transmission system interface.

1.10 SYSTEM SOFTWARE TOOLS FOR SERIAL COMMUNICATIONS

Computer manufactures provide serial software tools that are included with your computer. These tools help you test and check the functioning and performance of the serial ports installed on your computer. One of the most popular software tools is HyperTerminal, which can directly access and talk with your computer's serial ports. In this section, we will discuss two methods for testing the serial ports installed on your computer: the *loop-back* method and the *data exchange* method. The loop-back method connects TD and RD, which are two pins on a serial connector (refer to Figure 1.8), and this method only needs a single serial port. The connection is equivalent to connecting the sent-out data with the receiving terminal just like an internal loop, and the data sent out is immediately transported to the receiving buffer. The data exchange method involves connecting two computers via a null modem cable, as discussed in Section 1.5.2.

1.10.1 The Loop-Back Method for a Single Port

For RS-232 loop-back port testing, connect a standard serial connector, either a DB-9 or a DB-25, to the serial port you want to test on your computer. Refer to Figure 1.8, using a jump wire to connect the TD pin (pin 3 in DB-9, and pin 2 in the DB-25 connector) with the RD pin (pin 2 in DB-9, and pin 3 in the DB-25 connector) to get a loop connection.

For port testing on an RS-485 system, you should connect TXD+ and RXD+ together (pin 4 and pin 8 in the DB-9 connector), and TXD− and RXD− together (pin 5 and pin 9 in the DB-9 connector). Make sure your software is configured using a four-wire mode.

When the port is configured, follow these steps to perform this loop-back test:

1. Select `Start|Programs|Accessories|HyperTerminal` to start HyperTerminal. You can also double-click the `HyperTerminal` icon on your desktop if you already have a shortcut to open it.
2. If you are asked whether you would like to install a modem, select `No`.
3. In the next pop-up window, you are prompted to enter a name and select an icon for the connection. Enter `LoopBack` as the name and select the default icon, which is shown in Figure 1.55 (a). Then click `OK` to complete this step.
4. The following pop-up window asks whether you want to connect this port with a modem, a COM port, or a Transmission Control Protocol/Internet Protocol (TCP/IP) network. Select `Direct to COMx` from the `Connect using:` list box located at the bottom of the window. The `x` is the number of the COM port you want to test on your computer. For our application, we want to test port COM1, so `Direct to COM1` should be selected here, as shown in Figure 1.55 (b). Click `OK` to finish this step.
5. In the next pop-up window, which allows you to set up the serial port properties, change the baud rate to `9600` in the `Bits per second` text field. Also, select `None` from the `Flow control` list box. (We do not need any flow control for this test.) Keep all other settings unchanged. Your finished setup window should now match the one shown in Figure 1.56 (a). Click `OK` to continue.

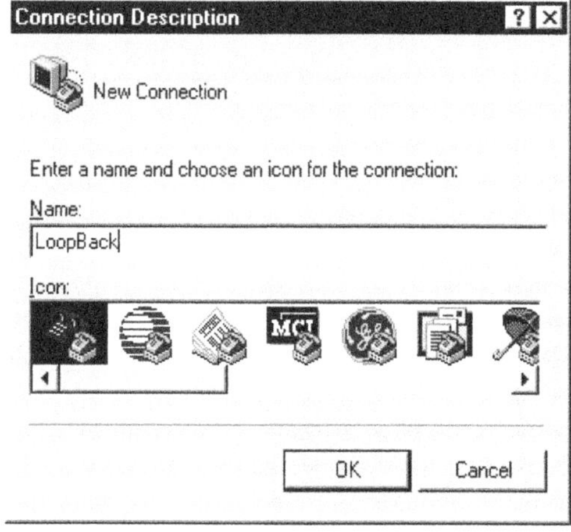

(a)

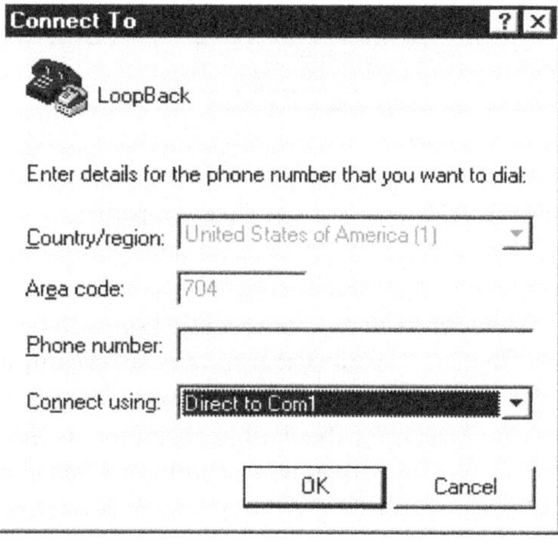

(b)

FIGURE 1.55 Open a new Hyperterminal.

6. Your HyperTerminal connection window opens. Before we can perform the test, we have one more thing to do, which is to set up the communication mode. Click `File|Properties` from the menu bar, and then click the `Settings` tab to open the `LoopBack`

`Properties` window. Check the `Play sound when connecting or disconnecting` checkbox, and click the `ASCII Setup . . .` button to set up the communication mode.

7. In the opened `ASCII` Setup window, which is shown in Figure 1.56 (b), check the following two checkboxes:
   - Echo typed characters locally
   - Append line feeds to incoming line ends

   Keep all other setups unchanged and click `OK` to close this window.
8. Click `OK` to close the `LoopBack Properties` window.

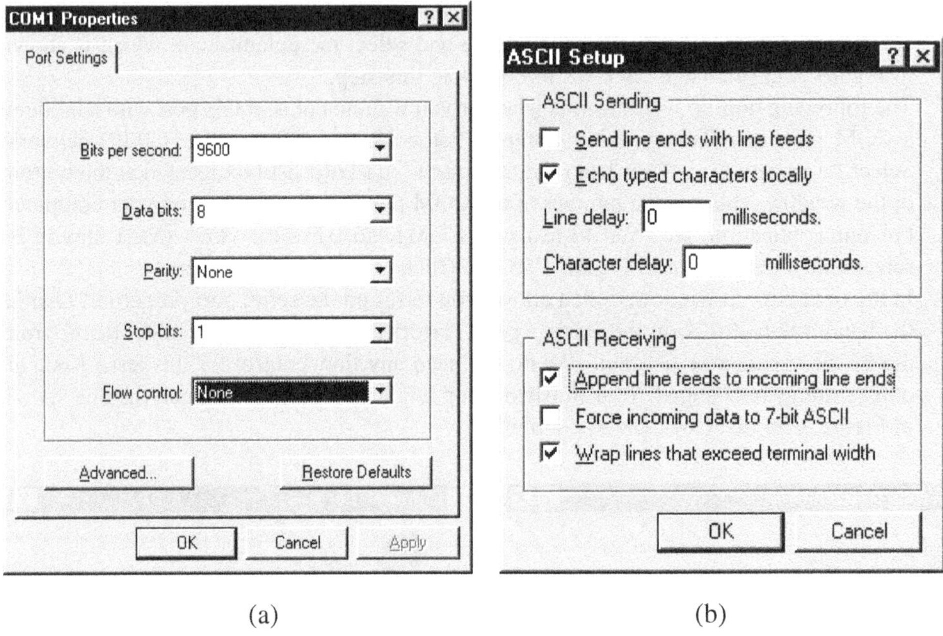

FIGURE 1.56 Setup of serial port properties.

Now let us begin the testing. Type something in the opened text area. For example, type "The Test Begins...." Your port testing is successful if you then see a sequence of double characters, such as "TThhee TTeesstt BBeeggiinnss...," in the window, as shown in Figure 1.57.

The reason for the double characters is that each time you type a character on the window, that character is immediately sent to the COM1 port. Because you have connected the TD and the RD pins together on your COM1 port, the sent-out character is immediately received by the port and displayed in the window. Because the `Echo typed characters` locally checkbox is checked, the typed or sent-out characters are also displayed in the window. For this reason, each character you type is doubled onscreen.

By using this HyperTerminal connection, you can easily test your serial port to confirm that it is operating correctly; you can also use it to perform serial data communications with other devices via the tested port.

Using this loop-back testing method, you can test only one port. To test two ports on a computer, or two ports located on two different computers, you need to use the null modem method described next.

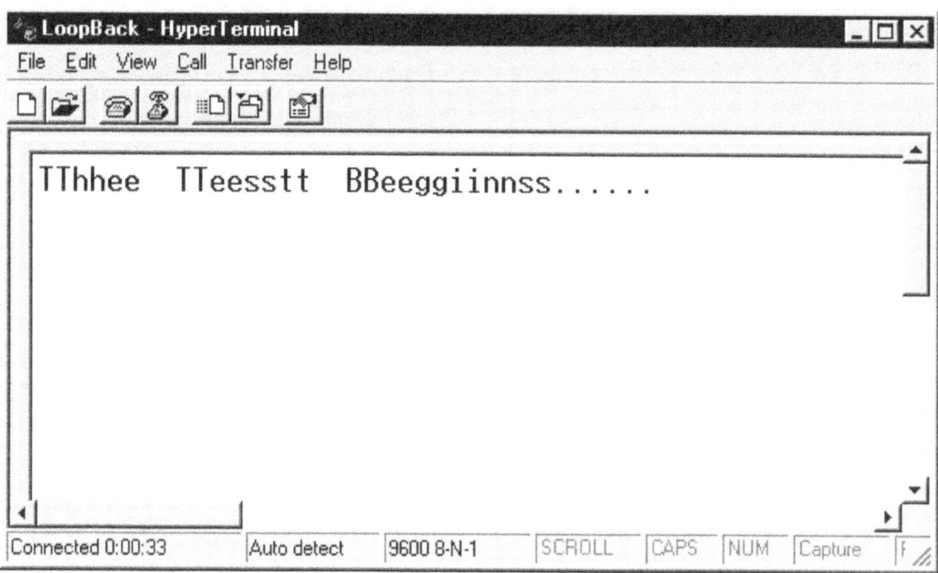

FIGURE 1.57 Testing results of the HyperTerminal.

1.10.2 The Null Modem Method for Testing Two Ports or Two Computers

This method uses a null modem cable for connecting two ports to test their operations with the HyperTerminal tool. Refer to Section 1.5.2 for a detailed description of the null modem connection.

Connect two ports using a null modem cable, either DB-9 or DB-25, depending on the ports you are using in your computer. It is highly recommended to use a shielded cable because the environmental noises and disturbances existing around the cable can be effectively reduced and even prevented by this kind of cable. You can obtain one of these cables from any electronics or computer shop, or you can order one online at www.digikey.com.

The following discussion assumes that we are using two ports installed on two different computers. Let us say that one port is on a computer whose operating system (OS) is Windows Me and the other one is on a computer using Windows 2000. The Windows Me computer works as a sender, and the Windows 2000 as a receiver, but you can select either computer as a sender or receiver. We want to perform some data communications between these two computers via the null cable.

1. After the cable is installed, open HyperTerminal on both computers. This time the setups and properties of the connection task will be a little different than those the last section.
2. In the opened HyperTerminal window, enter `NullModem` as the name of this connection for the two computers, and then click `OK` to continue.
3. In the next window, select the destination port you want to connect to from the `Connect using:` listbox. Select the COM number based on the port you are using. For our case, both computers use port COM1, so select `Direct to Com1` from the listbox and click `OK` to continue.
4. The next window is the `COM Port Properties` menu. Two properties need to be modified. One is the baud rate, with a default value of 2400, and the other one is the flow control mode. Change the baud rate from the default 2400 to 9600 (`Bits per second:`), and change the flow control to `software flow control`, or `XON/XOFF`, by selecting this mode from the `Flow control` listbox, shown in Figure 1.58 (a).

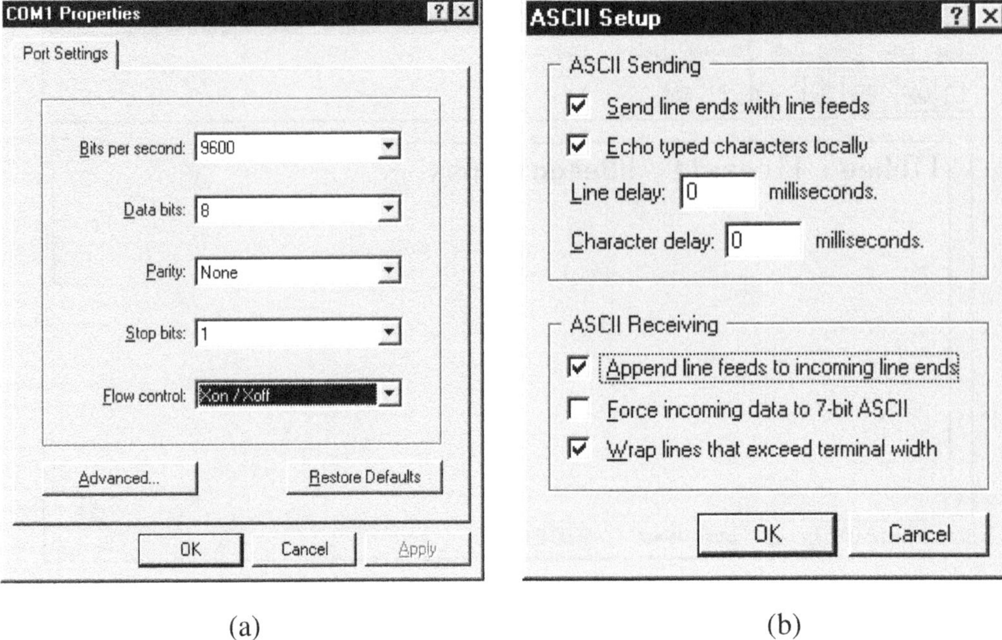

FIGURE 1.58 A null modem HyperTerminal connection.

5. Click `OK` to close the `COM1 Properties` window. The HyperTerminal connection window will be open. Select `File|Properties` from the menu bar to set up the properties of this NullModem connection.
6. In the opened window, click the `Settings` tab and click the `ASCII Setup ...` button to open the `ASCII Setup` window. Check the following checkboxes:
   - `Send line ends with line feeds`
   - `Echo typed characters locally`
   - `Append line feeds to incoming line ends`
7. Keep all other items unchanged, and then click `OK` to save these settings and close this window. Your finished ASCII Setup window should match the one shown in Figure 1.58(b).
8. The first checkbox is used to add a new line after each line of characters is sent. The second checkbox displays the sent character on the sender's screen, and the third checkbox is used to add another new line after receiving a line of characters at the receiver side. Finally, click `OK` to close the `NullModem` properties window.
9. In the opened HyperTerminal text area, type one line of characters and press `Enter` at the end of that line. For example, in our case, we typed, "Hello, this is a null modem test." This line of characters is immediately sent out via the null modem cable to the other computer after you press `Enter`. You can get this line from the opened HyperTerminal at the other computer.

You can continuously type as many lines of characters as you like in order to exchange the information with another computer. Figure 1.59 shows an example of this null modem data communication. It displays a situation on the sending side (Windows Me), and Figure 1.60 shows the situation on the receiving side (Windows 2000).

The reason we use the software flow control is because it is easier than hardware flow control. Also, in some simple null modem connections, only three lines are used (refer to Figure 1.16) and no hardware lines are available for the handshaking communications.

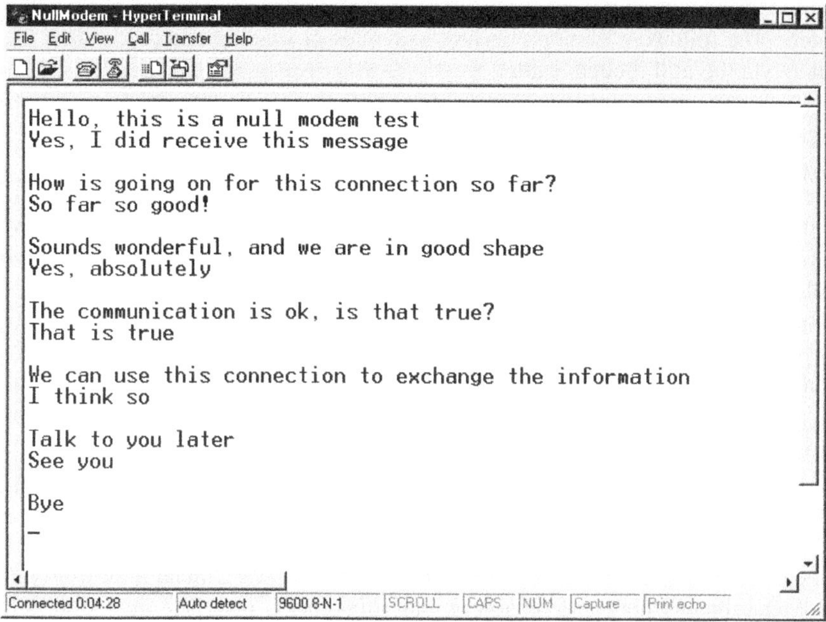

FIGURE 1.59 Sender side of a null modem data communication.

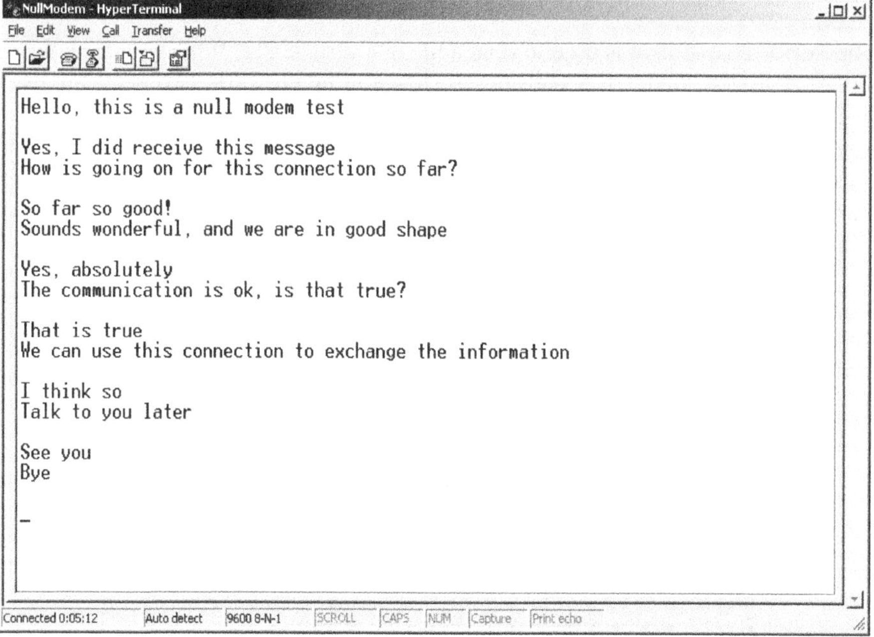

FIGURE 1.60 The receiver side of a null modem data communication.

By using this null modem connection with the help of HyperTerminal, you can easily connect and communicate with any other computer in your home, like a house network. You can "talk" with someone at another computer just as you can communicate with friends via the Internet using Instant Messenger. In some cases, you can use this connection to replace the local area network

(LAN) installed for your system. Using this connection you can easily send or receive files between two computers. The following section provides examples of sending and receiving a file between two computers via the null modem cable.

1.10.3 Exchange Files Between Two Computers via the Null Modem Method

By using a null modem connection and the HyperTerminal, we can perform a file transfer between two computers. The properties and setups of the ports and the HyperTerminal for two computers are identical with those we discussed in the preceding section.

If the HyperTerminal we opened in the last section is still open, you can continue to use it to perform the file transfer. If not, you need to open a new HyperTerminal connection and set up the port and connection as we did in the last section. We still assume that the Windows Me computer works as a sender and the Windows 2000 computer works as a receiver, but either computer can transmit or receive files to or from the other computer.

To send any kind of file from the sender to the receiver, you need to use the file transfer function from the current HyperTerminal connection.

1. In the opened HyperTerminal window, click the `Transfer` menu item from the menu bar. Four submenu items are displayed under this menu, and they are as follows:
   - `Send File`
   - `Receive File`
   - `Capture Text`
   - `Send Text File`
2. The `Send File` item is used to send a file in a certain FTP. When you click this item, a `Send File` dialog box pops up, as shown in Figure 1.61. Two fields are used for this file sending: `Filename` and `Protocol.`
3. The default sent file is located at C:\Program Files\Accessories\HyperTerminal. You can also select different files from the different folders on your computer by clicking the `Browse ...` button. You need to enter a valid file name to the `Filename:` field before you can send the file.
4. Seven popular FTPs can be selected for your file transmission. By clicking the `Protocol:` combox, you can find all of them (see Figure 1.61). Recall in Section 1.7.2.3, we discussed all eight different FTPs, such as the XMODEM, YMODEM, XMODEM-1K, YMODEM-G, and ZMODEM. You can find all those protocols in this protocol listbox. The default protocol is `ZMODEM With Crash Recovery`, which is identical to ZMODEM except it has the crash recovery capability.

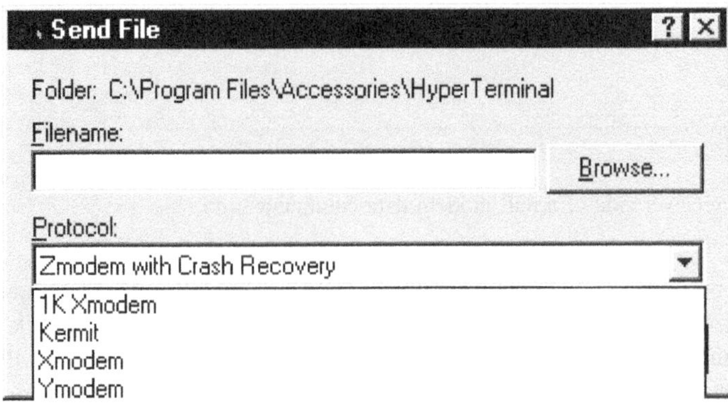

FIGURE 1.61 The send file.

5. The `Receive File` item is used to retrieve the file transmitted from the other computer via the serial port. Similar to the `Send File` item, the `Receive File` dialog box also includes two fields: the `Place received file in the following folder:` field and the `Use receiving protocol:` field (see Figure 1.62).

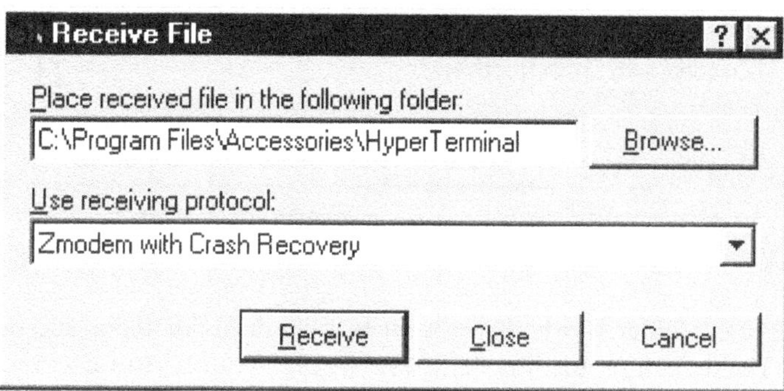

FIGURE 1.62 The receive file.

The default location for placing the received file is `C:\Program Files\Accessories\HyperTerminal`. You can place the received file in a different folder on your computer by clicking the `Browse` button to find the desired location. The default protocol is the `ZMODEM With Crash Recovery`. Of course, you can select any other protocol for the file transfer, but you need to pay attention to two points when you select the protocol for your file transmission:

- The protocol used in the Send file should be identical to the protocol in the Receive file.
- Using the XMODEM or XMODEM-1K protocol, the transferred file should be divided into a sequence of blocks of 128 bytes (XMODEM) or 1,024 bytes (XMODEM-1K).

`Capture Text` and `Send Text File` are similar to `Send File` and `Receive File` except that both are used to receive and send a text file.

After reviewing the menu items and their functionalities, it is time for us to perform some file transfers using HyperTerminal. First, we need to identify a file to be transmitted. In the following example, we will transfer a MS Word file named `LAB 0`, located in the `C:\1stBook` folder, from the sender (Windows Me computer) to the receiver (Windows 2000 computer). We want to save this file in the `C:\Book2` folder on the receiver computer.

TIP: One important point to note is that when you want to save a file in a specific folder on the receiver computer, you must first go to `Transfer|Receive File` and set up the file location and protocol for the receiver computer. You cannot begin a file transfer until you set up the properties of the receiver file on the receiving computer. If you begin the file transfer by setting up the Send file on the sending computer, the transferred file will be stored to the root directory (the `C:` folder) on the receiver computer. The `C:` folder is a default location for saving received files if the properties of the receiver file are not set up before the file transfer.

Now let's perform the file transfer. First, we need to set up the receiver file for the receiver computer.

1. In the opened HyperTerminal window on the Windows 2000 computer, click the `Transfer|Receive File` menu item from the menu bar and fill the file location and file protocol with the contents shown in Figure 1.63.

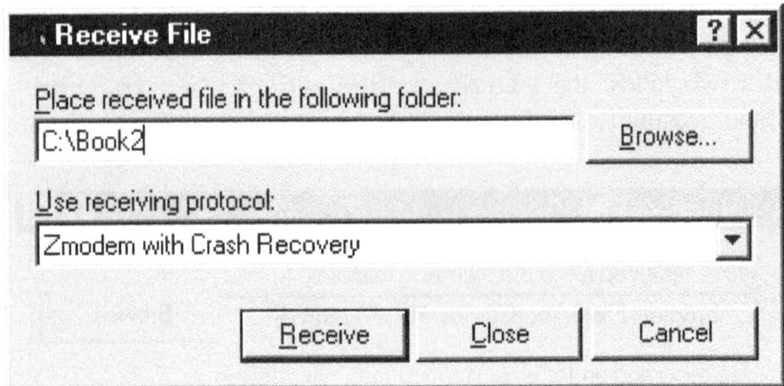

FIGURE 1.63 The setup of the receive file.

2. The `C:\Book2` folder is where we want to save the LAB 0.doc file on the receiver computer. The default protocol is `ZMODEM With Crash Recovery`, and we want to keep this protocol as our FTP. Click the `Receive` button when everything is done and we are ready to receive `LAB 0.doc` from the sender computer.
   As soon as you click the `Receive` button, a `Receive Processing` dialog box pops up. All fields in the dialog box are disabled (shown in a gray color) because currently no file has been sent out and the receiver is waiting for the file to be transferred.
3. Now go to the sender computer, Windows Me, and click the `Transfer|Send File` menu item from the menu bar at the opened HyperTerminal to open the Send File dialog box. Click the `Browse . . .` button to select the file, `LAB 0.doc`, which is located in the folder `C:\1stBook`. Keep the default protocol and click the `Send` button to begin to transmit this file. The `Send Processing` dialog box immediately pops up, as shown in Figure 1.64.

Zmodem with Crash Recovery file send for NullModem
Sending: C:\1stBOOK\LAB 0.doc
Last event: Sending Files: 1 of 1
Status: Sending Retries: 0
File: 48k of 397K
Elapsed: 00:00:24 Remaining: 00:02:57 Throughput: 2006 cps
Cancel cps/bps

FIGURE 1.64 The send processing dialog box.

The `Sending:` field contains the file name and location, which are supposed to be sent to the receiver. The `File:` processing bar is used to monitor and display the file transfer process, such as how many bytes of the file have been transmitted and the total size of the file. The `Elapsed:` field indicates how much time has been used and how much time is needed to finish this file transfer. After the `Send` button on the sender computer is pressed, the `Receive Processing` dialog box almost simultaneously becomes active, as shown in Figure 1.65.

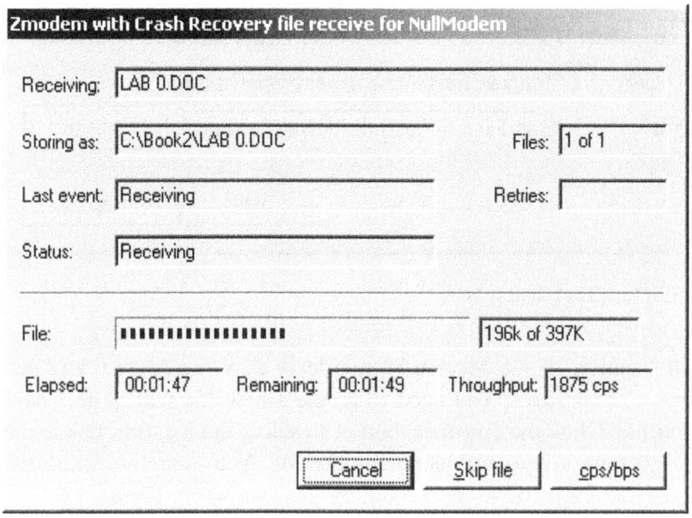

FIGURE 1.65 The receive processing dialog box.

The `Receiving:` field is used to display the name of the file currently being received. The `Storing as:` field indicates where this received file should be placed; in our case, it is the `C:\Book2` folder in the receiver computer. The `File:` field is similar to the `Send Processing` dialog box, which is used to indicate the receiving processing. The `Elapsed:` field is used to monitor the time spent for this file transfer and the total time needed to finish the transfer.

You can transfer any file of any size using this method since it is a convenient way to exchange data between two computers locally. Also, you can try to use different baud rates. We have tested rates of 19200, 38400, and even 115200, and all have been successful.

TIP: If you want to transfer a file but the receiver already has a file with the same name as the file to be transferred, the file will not be transmitted. In other words, the file cannot be updated after the file transfer to the receiver computer, and the file on the receiver computer will still be the original. So avoid using duplicate file names when performing file transfers.

Sometimes the HyperTerminal will display some characters or a sequence of characters, such as e**B000000023be50. This means the receiver still waits for the data to be transmitted.

1.10.4 Text File Transmission Between Two Computers

Before finishing this chapter, let us discuss how to exchange text files between two ports or two computers via the HyperTerminal. Basically, the exchange of text files is no different than that of general files. The only difference is that the transmitted text file can be displayed in the HyperTerminal text window when transmission is finished.

As an example, we will transmit a text file between a sending computer and a receiving computer. The file to be transferred is located in the `C:\Temp` folder on the sending computer, and the file name is **install_nidaq.txt**, which is a readme file developed by National Instrument Cooperation to help users install the NI-DAQ drivers.

1. Keep all setups and properties unchanged for the HyperTerminal, and on the receiving computer click the `Transfer|Capture Text` menu item from the menu bar to open the `Capture Text` dialog box, which is shown in Figure 1.66.

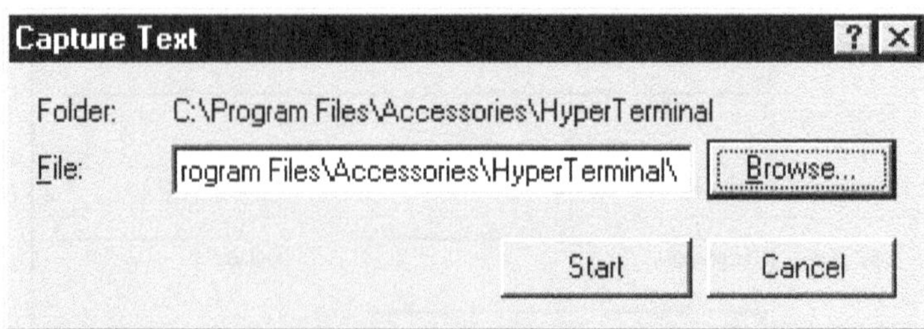

FIGURE 1.66 The Capture Text dialog box.

2. The default location of the received text file is `C:\Program Files\Accessories\HyperTerminal`. You need to create a new file with a new name to save the received text file. Click the `Browse` button to select the location where the text file will be stored, and type a new file name for the file. You complete these two jobs in the opened `Select Capture File` dialog box, shown in Figure 1.67.

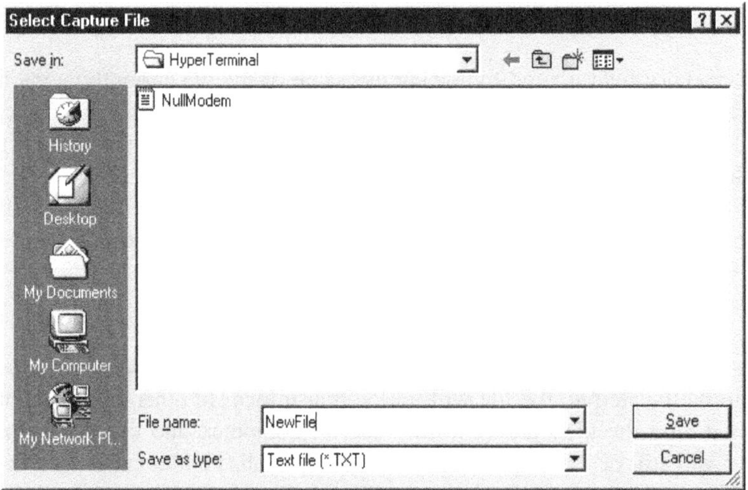

FIGURE 1.67 The Select Capture File dialog box.

3. We want to use the default folder to store the received text file. Type a new file name into the `File name:` field; in our case, it is `NewFile`. Click `Save` to save this new file name and close the dialog box.
4. Now click the `Start` button on the Capture Text dialog box, and wait for the text file to be transmitted from the sending computer.
5. Go to the sending computer and, in the HyperTerminal window, click the `Transfer|Send Text File` menu item from the menu bar to open the `Send Text File` dialog box, which is shown in Figure 1.68. Browse to the `C:\Temp` folder, select the desired file, `install_nidaq.txt`, and click `Open` to send the file.
6. Now go back to the receiving computer and you will find that some text has been displayed in the HyperTerminal window. Go to the `C:\Program Files\Accessories\HyperTerminal` folder to find the received text file `NewFile.txt` there. Double-click it to open the contents of this `readme` file, which is shown in Figure 1.69. Some nonprinted characters are represented by square blocks in the received text file.

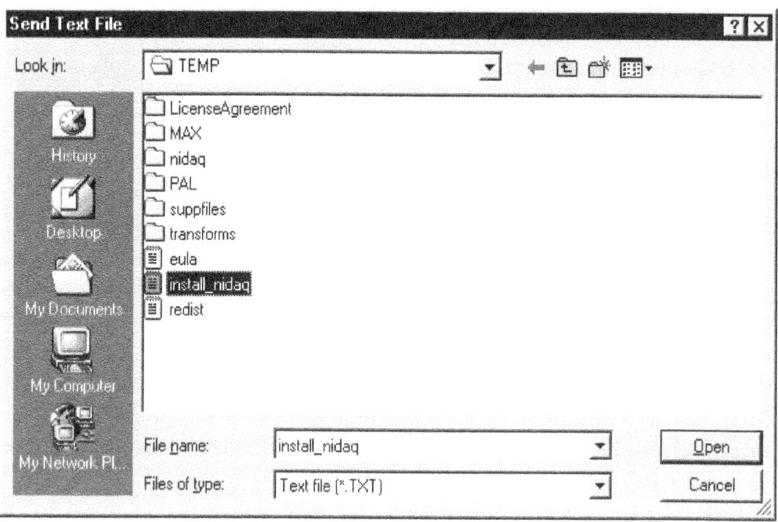

FIGURE 1.68 The Send Text File dialog box.

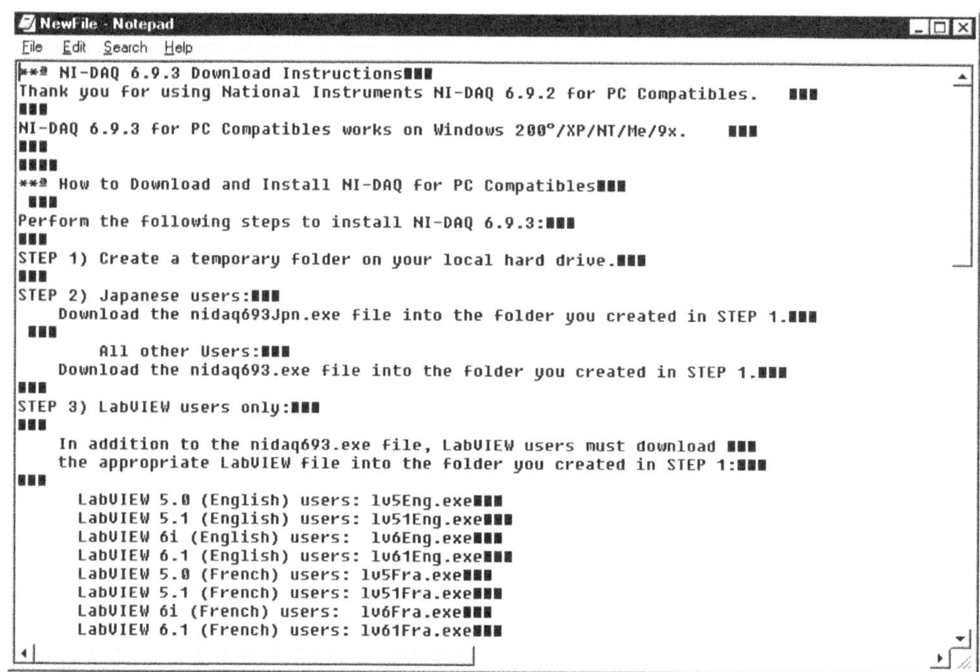

FIGURE 1.69 A transmitted text file example.

At this point, we have finished the discussion of data transmission and file transfer using HyperTerminal with a null modem cable that connects two serial ports or two computers. This method is very practical and convenient for local data communications, especially for two home computers. Of course, it is not as good as a real LAN, but it is an easy and cheap way to perform local data transmissions and file transfers. The transfer speed (baud rate) can be varied from 2,400 to 115200 based on your real system; also, the FTP can be selected by the user based on the size of the file to be transferred.

1.10.5 Summary of Using Different Protocols in the File Transfer

When using the HyperTerminal to perform the file transfer, different protocols can be utilized. The following is a summarization of different protocols to choose from:

- **XMODEM:** When using this protocol to perform the file transfer via HyperTerminal, you need to provide an additional name for the file to be received on the receiving computer, even if you've provided the file name on the sending side, because XMODEM cannot supply a name for the file to be received. In the `Receive File` dialog box, you must select or type a full name (including the path) for the file before the file transfer can be started.
  When you're working with this protocol, the file is transferred in blocks (each block occupies 128 bytes). You cannot "feel" any difference between these block transfers and the ZMODEM style during the data transmission.
  Note that the error-checking method used in the XMODEM protocol is a checksum value (8 bits), not a CRC value (16 bits).
- **XMODEM-1K:** The operation procedure for this protocol is identical to that of the XMODEM protocol, and you need to provide an additional file name for the file to be received on the receiving computer. The only difference between this protocol and the preceding one is that although the file is still transferred in blocks, each block occupies 1024 bytes.
- **YMODEM:** You do not need to provide any additional name for the file being received on the receiving computer when using this protocol to perform the file transfer. The file name is provided by you on the sending computer side in the `Sender File` dialog box. Note that the error-checking value used in this protocol is a CRC value, not a checksum value.
- **YMODEM-G:** When you're using this protocol, the file is transferred in packets, and the starting signal is a character G, not the C that is used in the preceding protocols. The error-checking value is a CRC value.
- **ZMODEM:** This protocol is similar to YMODEM-G, and the file is transferred in packets. The software flow control handshaking signal XON/XOFF is utilized for this protocol to coordinate the file transfer. Note that no error-checking value is used in this kind of file transfer because this protocol utilizes an error-recovering functionality to automatically recover errors during the file transfer. (Ask the sender to retransmit the packet if an error occurs during the packet's transmission.)
- **Kermit:** This protocol is similar to ZMODEM, with some exceptions. One of the most significant differences is that Kermit can be used to transfer files across different operating systems.

1.11 CHAPTER SUMMARY

This chapter has presented some fundamental information and terminology used in serial data communications. The following serial devices have been discussed:

- RS-232 serial ports
- RS-422 serial ports
- RS-485 serial ports
- Universal Serial Bus (USB) control
- Controller Area Network (CAN) control
- Firewire control

The fundamental concepts that have been explained in this chapter include:

- ASCII code
- RS-232 serial protocol
- The data terminal equipment (DTE) and the data communications equipment (DCE)
- Serial data formatting at the transistor-transistor-level (TTL) and at the transmission line level
- Transmission control parameters, such as the baud rate, parity value, stop bits, and data bits
- Handshaking signals and physical connectors
- RS-232 serial port connections, normal PC-to-modem connections, and null modem connections

The internal structure and operational principles of two basic serial interface components, the universal asynchronous receiver transmitters (UARTs) 8250 and 16550, have been introduced. In addition, the interrupt principle and the processing of the 8250 UART for a multiple-tasking environment have been presented and analyzed.

The modem and the control of modem operations have been discussed in detail in Section 1.7.1. The working principles of internal and external modems have been presented, along with the three popular signal modulation methods:

- Amplitude modulation (ASK)
- Frequency modulation (FSK)
- Phase modulation (PSK)

One of the most important issues in serial data transfer, flow control, has been presented and analyzed in Section 1.7.2. Two kinds of flow control, hardware and software flow control, are discussed in this section.

In Section 1.7.2.3, the file transfer control and protocol is introduced. Seven popular FTPs are discussed:

- XMODEM
- XMODEM-CRC
- XMODEM-1K
- YMODEM
- YMODEM-G
- ZMODEM
- Kermit

Errors and error detection in serial data communications are discussed in Section 1.8. Error processing is a very important and sensitive topic in relation to file transfers because it directly affects the success of the data transmission. Two error-checking methods, checksum and CRC, have been discussed in detail in this section.

More information about the RS-422 and RS-485 protocols has been presented in Section 1.9. The operational principles of these two protocols have been introduced in detail, complete with functional diagrams, in this section.

One of the most popular system serial software products, HyperTerminal, was introduced in Section 1.10. By using HyperTerminal with a suitable connection cable, you can test the functions of your system's serial ports. Two testing methods, the loop-back and null modem methods, were discussed, and several real-life examples were presented.

In Section 1.10.2, a real-time instant message exchange was shown step by step, using Hyper-Terminal along with a null modem cable connection between two computers. You can communicate between the computers using this method to create a home network.

By using HyperTerminal with a null modem cable, you can connect two computers to exchange the large files. Performing file transfers between two computers using different protocols was discussed in Section 1.10.3. The operating procedures of file transfer was illustrated step by step to show a clear and detailed picture of this kind of transmission.

In Section 1.10.4, the operation of text file transfer using the HyperTerminal between two computers was discussed. The detailed procedures were illustrated using a real-life example.

Finally, in Section 1.10.5, a quick summary was provided of all the popular protocols used for file transfer with HyperTerminal . Several important points were presented, including the similarities and differences between the different protocols during a file transfer procedure.

By using the HyperTerminal with a null modem serial cable, you can easily and conveniently exchange a file of any size between two computers. Also, by setting the different parameters, such as the baud rate and flow control method, you can modify the file transfer speed and transfer quality.

2 Serial Port Programming for MS-DOS in ANSI C and Assembly Languages

2.1 INTRODUCTION

2.1.1 VIRTUAL MACHINES

A *virtual machine* is an executable task consisting of an application, supporting software (such as ROM BIOS and MS-DOS), memory, and central processing unit (CPU) registers. The Virtual Memory Manager (VMM) can create multiple virtual machines. The first virtual machine created, called the *system virtual machine,* contains 16-bit Windows-based applications, Windows 32 applications, and threads created by Win32 applications. Other virtual machines are created for MS-DOS-based applications as they are started.

An MS-DOS-based application on a virtual machine runs in virtual 8086 mode (also called V86 mode). In V86 mode, applications run as if they were running on an Intel 8086 (or compatible) microprocessor. V86 mode provides the registers, instructions, and 1MB address space that real-mode applications are designed to use. This allows an MS-DOS-based application on a virtual machine to run successfully without modification. V86 mode also permits execution of protected-mode applications on virtual machines.

Each virtual machine has its own address space, input/output (I/O) port space, and interrupt vector table. The VMM maps ROM BIOS, MS-DOS, device drivers, and terminate and stay resident programs (TSRs) to the address space of the virtual machine so the application has access to MS-DOS system functions and ROM BIOS routines. A virtual machine running a protected-mode application also has its own local descriptor table (LDT).

Virtual machines provide memory protection, virtual memory, and privilege checking. If an application running on a virtual machine reads or writes memory addresses that have not been mapped into its virtual machine, or manipulates I/O ports to which it has not been allowed access, an *exception* (also called a *fault*) is generated, and the VMM regains control. The VMM and virtual devices can then provide the requested memory, carry out the intended I/O operation, or terminate the application. On a virtual machine, V86 mode applications run at privilege level 3. Protected-mode applications run at privilege level 1, 2, or 3.

2.1.2 MS-DOS-COMPATIBLE ANSI C PROGRAMMING

In this chapter, we will begin to discuss serial port programming in American National Standards Institute (ANSI) C and in assembly language. Serial port programming in the C/C++ environment can be divided into two categories, based on the operating system in which the program will be run:

- MS-DOS-compatible ANSI C programming
- Win32 application program interface (API) C/C++ programming

MS-DOS-compatible ANSI C programming can be used with the following operating systems:

- Windows 95
- Windows 98
- Windows Me

On IBM (or compatible) PCs, these three operating systems provide a virtual MS-DOS environment. On your own PC, you can access this environment directly by double-clicking the MS-DOS icon, which can usually be found in the `C:\Windows\Start\Programs\Accessories` directory. This icon starts a program called MS-DOS Prompt; it opens a window in which all MS-DOS programs can be run in virtual (V86) mode.

By using MS-DOS to run in virtual mode, C code and assembly code can access low-level serial hardware—such as the different registers in the 8250 or 16550 universal asynchronous receiver-transmitters (UARTs), as well as recommended standard-232 (RS-232) port registers—by means of standard I/O functions defined in the ANSI C libraries. Running in virtual mode is (roughly) the equivalent of running on an Intel 8086 or compatible microprocessor that has its own address space, I/O port space, and interrupt vector table.

Back when PCs still used Windows 3.*x* and older, non-Windows-based operating systems, user programs ran in true *real-time mode,* which meant that the operating system and the CPU would allow the programs to access the serial port directly, without executing any other programs stored on the computer. Unfortunately, real-time processing ended with those early operating systems. In Windows 95 and all subsequent multitasking releases, access to the serial port is controlled by the I/O manager. Components of the Windows product that have direct access to all aspects of the computer system are called *ring 0* programs. These are protected from *ring 3* programs, which are applications developed by users; thus, Windows users are prohibited from accessing any fundamental hardware controls. This restricted environment is called *protected mode.* Programmers for Windows 95/98/Me, however, do have the option of programming in V86 mode, in which the I/O manager controls and coordinates interfacing between user-designed applications and the low-level system resources.

TIP: Keep in mind that the V86 mode provided by Windows 95/98/Me is a *conditional* real-time mode. The operating system does allow the user's program to directly access a set of *virtual* low-level ports, but only for a predefined length of time. During this interval, the CPU transmits limited control to the user's program but also operates a timer and an error-detecting monitor to track the execution of the program. A timeout error will occur if the user's program remains inactive for a certain period of time (the length of which is defined by the system).

C/C++ programs developed with the Windows 32 API work in protected mode. In this kind of programming, it is absolutely prohibited for the user to access any low-level hardware directly. All of the Windows 95/98/Me and Windows NT/2000/XP operating systems can work in this mode. The difference between Windows 95/98/Me and Windows NT/2000/XP, however, is that the former systems can work in both V86 mode and protected mode, but the latter work only in protected mode. Windows NT/2000/XP provides only a virtual MS-DOS environment. The virtual MS-DOS icon can be found in the same location as in Windows 95/98/Me, `C:\Windows\Start\Programs\Accessories`. The virtual MS-DOS environment, called the MS-DOS Prompt in Windows 95/98/Me, is called Command Prompt in Windows NT/2000/XP, which indicates that MS-DOS cannot run in V86 mode under these operating systems.

Programs developed with the Windows 32 API or Visual C++ are compatible with the following operating systems:

- Windows NT
- Windows 2000
- Windows XP

TIP: Keep in mind that programs developed in ANSI C or assembly language can be run only on computers with Windows 95/98/Me operating systems in V86 mode, and that programs developed with Windows 32 API or Visual C++ will work only on computers with Windows NT/2000/XP operating systems in protected mode. Figure 2.1 illustrates this difference.

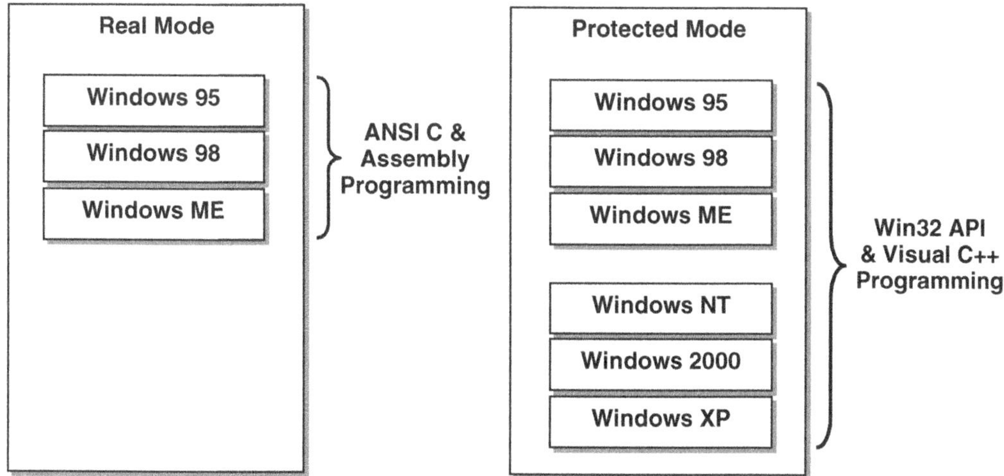

FIGURE 2.1 The different operation modes.

All programs developed in this chapter are MS-DOS compatible; they can be run only in V86 mode with Windows 95/98/ME operating system.

In this section, the programs developed to directly access the virtual low-level hardware will run and communicate with the registers defined in the 8250 or 16550 UARTs. As was explained in Chapter 1, the 8250 UART is a serial port controller, or an interface between the RS-232 ports and the CPU. Execution of a user program involves a communication process between the UART registers and the program, or more concisely, between the virtual CPU and the virtual UART, because the execution of the program is controlled by a virtual CPU.

The following sections will discuss serial port programming and present some real examples. The first sample program is a simple loopback testing program developed in ANSI C code. More sophisticated examples are presented later in this chapter.

2.2 A LOOPBACK SERIAL PORT TESTING PROGRAM DEVELOPED IN ANSI C

As mentioned earlier, the simplest serial port program is a loopback testing program. The term *loopback* indicates that the transmitted data (TD) pins and the received data (RD) pins in an RS-232 serial connector are connected to form a loop between the transmitting and receiving terminals. (Refer to Section 1.10.1 and Figure 1.8 in Chapter 1 for more detailed information on obtaining a loopback-compatible serial port connector.)

2.2.1 A Loopback Testing Program Developed in C

All programs developed in this chapter are compiled and built with Microsoft Visual C++ 6.0. To develop an MS-DOS-compatible program in the Windows 95/98/ME environment, it is necessary to use the *console* project format. Because of the simplicity of the following program, flow control and handshaking signals are not necessary. The only registers that must be accessed in this testing program are the transmitter holding register (THR) and the receiver holding register (RHR) in the 8250 or 16550 UART. To make this program as generic as possible, COM1 will be used as the testing port. The THR and the RHR will have the same address, 03F8H, which is the base address of COM1.

2.2.1.1 The `_outp()` and `_inp()` Functions

The key to testing a serial port using a console program developed in ANSI C is to directly communicate with the UART using two ANSI C functions, `_outp()` and `_inp()`, respectively. The `_outp()` function is used to send a byte to the THR, and the `_inp()` function is used to receive a byte from the RHR. The protocols of these two functions are shown in Figure 2.2.

```
int _outp( unsigned short port, int databyte );
int _inp( unsigned short port );
```

FIGURE 2.2 The protocols of `_outp()` and `_inp()` functions.

Both functions return an integer value. The `_outp()` function returns the integer that is sent out to the THR, and the `_inp()` function returns the data received from the RHR. The `_outp()` function has two arguments. The first argument is the port number, which is an unsigned short data type, and the second is the data value to be sent out. The `_inp()` function has only one argument, port, which is the port number from which the data will be retrieved.

Both of these functions are defined in the libc.lib system library in Visual C++ 6.0, and the system header file <conio.h>should be included when using these two functions.

2.2.1.2 The Detailed Program Code

The purpose of this loopback testing program is to repeatedly send a sequence of integers to the THR and, after a period of time, to pick up that integer sequence from the RHR. For testing purposes, the sequence of integers is selected from one to ten. The testing will be successful if the transmitted data matches the received data.

Now, let's begin to develop the loopback testing program. Launch Visual C++ 6.0 and open a new project with the following properties:

- Project type: Win32 Console Application
- Project name: `DirectCSPort`
- Project location: `C:\Chapter 2`

TIP: The project location is a folder where you want the project to be stored on your computer. Here we have used `C:\Chapter 2`, but you can select any valid folder on your computer as the location for storing your project.

In the open project, create a new C++ source file named `DirectCSPort.cpp`. (Due to its simplicity, this project needs no header file.)

Enter the code shown in Figure 2.3 into the `DirectCSPort.cpp` file.

```
/*****************************************************************************
 * NAME: DirectCSPort.cpp
 * DATE: July 1, 2003
 * PGMR: Y. Bai
 * DESC: Serial communication test program using C code directly access the serial port.
 *****************************************************************************/
  #include <stdio.h>
  #include <string.h>
  #include <stdlib.h>
A #include <conio.h>
  #include <ctype.h>
  #include <math.h>
  #include <dos.h>
B
  #define MAX     5000                        // max length of delay period of time
  #define COM1    (unsigned short)0x3F8       // serial port COM1
  #define COM2    (unsigned short)0x2F8       // serial port COM2
C int  TestSerial();
  void Delay(int num);
  void main(void)
  {
      int rc = 0;
      printf("\n");
D     rc = TestSerial();
E     if (rc != 0)
         printf("Error in TestSerial()!\n");
      else
         printf("Success in TestSerial()!\n");
      return;
  }
```

FIGURE 2.3 The main program of The Loopback test.

The purpose of each line of code is described here:

A: Useful header files are declared in this section. These header files contain the protocol definitions of the system functions. Among them, two header files are important. One is `stdio.h`, which provides the protocols for all standard I/O functions, such as `printf()` and `scanf()`, that are used in the system. The other is `conio.h`, which provides the protocols for the `_outp()` and `_inp()` functions.

B: Useful global constants are defined here. You can declare these constants as any data type by using the macro `#define` and by placing the associated cast operator in front of each constant. For example, `COM1` is defined as 03F8 preceded by an unsigned short casting operator, and `MAX` is defined as the maximum length of the delay. Once you declare the constants, they will be automatically translated to the associated data values when used in the program. For instance, `COM1` in the program is equivalent to a data value of 03F8.

C: Two user-defined functions are declared in this section. The `TestSerial()` function is used to call two I/O functions, `_outp()` and `_inp()`, to test the serial port COM1. The `delay()` function is used to delay the program until the data is stable on the THR. This function uses one argument, an integer representing the length of the delay interval.

D: In the body of the main function, the `TestSerial()` function is called to perform the serial port testing.

E: A return value, `rc`, is used to check the feedback of `TestSerial()`. A return value of `0` means the function call has been successful. If the return value is not `0`, an error has occurred during the function execution, and the error source will be printed on the screen.

Figure 2.4 shows the complete code of the user-defined `TestSerial()` function.

```
   /*****************************************************************************
    *        Subroutine to loop testing for the RS-232C port.                   *
    *****************************************************************************/
   int TestSerial()
   {
F     int index, value, result = 0;

      printf("Begin to execute outp() & inp()...\n");
G     for (index = 0; index < 10; index++)
      {
          printf("Data sent to COM1 is: %d\n", index);
          _outp(COM1, index);
H         Delay(500);
          value = _inp(COM1);
          printf("Data returned from COM1 is: %d\n", value);
          printf("\n");
I         if (value != index)
          {
               printf("Error in loop testing of the COM1!\n");
               result = -1;
               return result;
          }
      }
J     return result;
   }
```

FIGURE 2.4 The function body of `TestSerial()`.

F: Local variables are declared here. The variable `index` is used as a cycle variable in the `for` loop, and `value` is used to pick up the received data from the function call `_inp()`. `result` is a feedback variable that is returned to the main function to indicate whether or not the `_inp()` function has been successful.

G: A `for` loop is executed to obtain a sequence of integers and to send each integer to the COM1 port using the `_outp()` system function.

H: After each integer has been sent out, the `delay()` function is called to wait for a specified period of time. This time delay is necessary for stabilizing the data sent to the THR. After the delay, and once the data received in the RHR is stable, the `_inp()` function is called to pick up the received data. To display the testing result to the user in real time, the transmitted and received data is printed on the screen for each loop. The `delay()` function is shown in Figure 2.5.

This is not a standard time delay function; the standard time delay function would use the system clock as the timing standard and compare the current time with the timing standard to calculate the difference, or the elapsed time. The elapsed time would then be compared with the

```
/*****************************************************************************
 *          Delay subroutine to delay certain period of time                 *
 *****************************************************************************/
void Delay(int num)
{
      int m, n, cycle = MAX;

      for (m = 0; m <= num * cycle; m++)
          n = m - 1;
      return;
}
/******************************* End of Code *********************************/
```

FIGURE 2.5 Time delay function.

desired time period to determine whether the desired interval had been exceeded. However, for simplicity here, we'll use a nonstandard delay function.

I: To make sure that the transmitted data is identical to the received data, a comparison between them is performed. If the two are identical, the testing for the data transmission has been successful, and the program continues to test the next data. Otherwise, an error occurs and the error source is printed out. A value of `-1`, which indicates an error, is returned to the main function, and the program is terminated.

J: Finally, if no error has been encountered during the loop, a value of `0` is returned to the main function to indicate that the function call has been successful. In other words, the port testing process has worked successfully.

Compile and build the program, and then run it if no error is encountered. The results (if no errors occur) are shown in Figure 2.6.

Notice that in Figure 2.6 the transmitted and received data are identical, which means that the port testing has been successful.

You can modify the size of the sequence of the integers, by increasing the size to 1000 or greater. You can also define the maximum testing integer as a constant in the program. Then, each time you want to modify the size of the integer sequence, you need only modify that maximum number; you will not need to change any code in the program. You can find this program with the complete source code and executable code, as well as a project description file, in the folder `Chapter 2\DirectCSPort`, which is located on the CD included with this book.

2.3 EMBEDDING ASSEMBLY CODE INTO C PROGRAMMING

Sometimes it is more efficient to use assembly code than C code in a real-time programming environment. Assembly programming is more compatible with low-level code because assembly language is a low-level (or *machine-dependent*) language. On the positive side, low-level programming has a higher running speed and can use hardware resources more efficiently. However, one shortcoming is that because assembly code is a machine-specified language, every CPU has its own assembly language. In other words, programs developed in assembly language cannot be transported from one platform to another. Another drawback is that because assembly language is closer to machine code than C code is, assembly language is more difficult to learn and use. To successfully develop a program using assembly language, one needs to have solid knowledge of computer hardware (for example, the CPU structure, bus structure, and internal architecture). Even so, if we use inline assembly code, we do not need to have as thorough an understanding of the

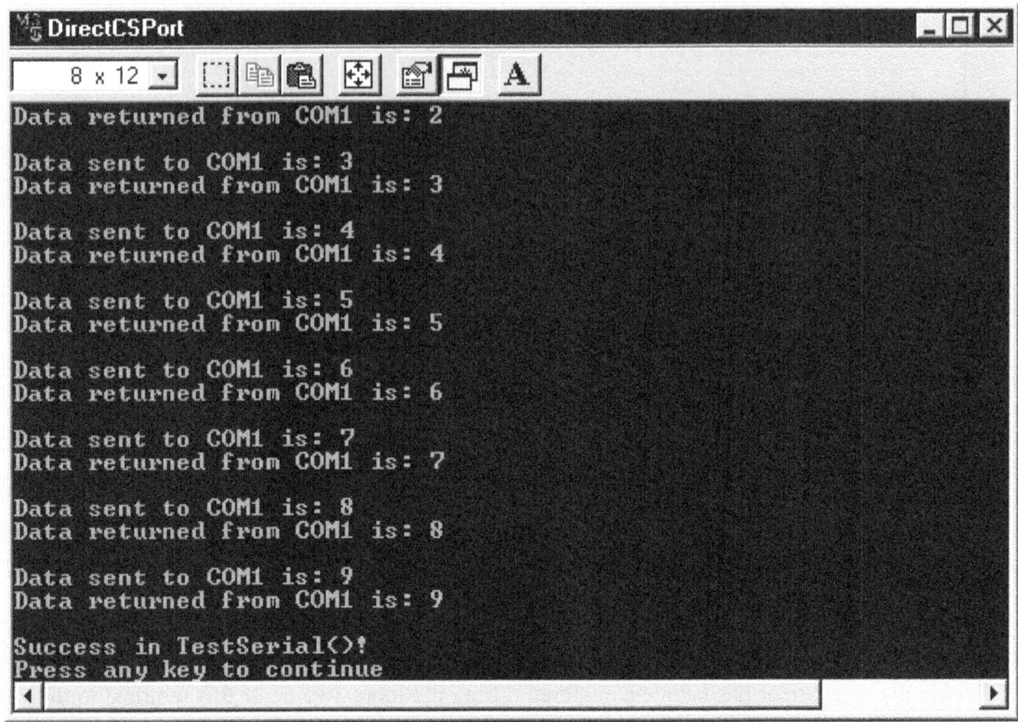

FIGURE 2.6 The running result of the DirectCSPort project.

computer's internal architecture, nor of the assembler's processes, but we can still improve our program's performance.

2.3.1 Inline Assembly Code

Because the inline assembler does not require separate assembly or link steps, it is more convenient than a separate assembler. Inline assembly code can use any C variable or function name that is in scope, so it can be easily integrated with your program's C code. Because assembly code can be mixed inline with C/C++ statements, it can perform tasks that are cumbersome or impossible in C/C++.

The uses of inline assembly code include the following:

- Writing functions in assembly language
- Spot-optimizing speed-critical sections of code
- Creating direct hardware access for device drivers
- Writing prolog and epilog code for naked calls

Inline assembly code is a special-purpose tool. As mentioned earlier, it is machine-dependent, which means that different platforms have different modules for processing assembly code. If you want to transport an application to different machine environments, you should definitely place machine-specific code in a separate module. However, because the inline assembler does not support all of Microsoft Macro Assembler's (MASM) macro and data directives, you may find it more suitable to use MASM for such modules.

None of the following MASM macro directives and macro operators are supported by the inline assembler:

- MACRO
- REPT
- IRC
- IRP
- ENDM
- <>, !, &,%, TYPE

Further, the LENGTH, SIZE, and TYPE operators have only limited meaning in inline assembly code. They cannot be used at all with the DUP operator because data cannot be defined with MASM directives or operators, but they can be used to find the sizes of C/C++ variables and types. Their use is summarized in this list:

- **LENGTH** returns the number of elements in an array. For all non-array variables, LENGTH returns a value of 1.
- **SIZE** returns the size of a C/C++ variable. (A variable's size is the product of its LENGTH and its TYPE.)
- **TYPE** returns the size of a C/C++ type or variable. If a variable consists of an array, TYPE will return the size of a single element in the array if the variable is an array.

For example, an eight-element integer array, int arry[8], can be operated by the above three operators. The results are shown in Table 2-1.

TABLE 2.1
Type and Variable Sizes in Inline Assembly Code

Inline Assembly Code	C Code	Real Size
LENGTH arry	sizeof(arry)/sizeof(arry[0])	8
SIZE arry	sizeof(arry)	16
TYPE arry	sizeof(arry[0])	2

The inline assembler supports the full instruction set of the Intel 486 processor. Additional instructions supported by the target processor can be created with the emit pseudoinstruction command.

2.3.2 The _asm Keyword

The _asm keyword invokes the inline assembler and can appear in any place where legal C/C++ statements are presented. This keyword must be followed by an assembly instruction, a group of instructions enclosed in braces, or at least an empty pair of braces. The term _asm *block* refers to any instruction or group of instructions, whether or not they appear in braces.

For example, the following _asm block codes, which are shown in Figure 2.7(a), are used to send a byte of data to the THR of COM1 (03F8). Alternatively, you can put the _asm keyword in front of each assembly instruction, as shown in Figure 2.7(b).

The _asm keyword is also equivalent to a statement separator, so you might choose to put all of the assembly instructions on the same line and separate them with by putting the _asm keyword, followed by a space, between each instruction.

All three of these style options generate the same output code, but the first style has several advantages. First, the braces clearly separate the assembly code from the C/C++ code and prevent needless repetition of the _asm keyword. In addition, braces can also prevent ambiguities. If you want to put a C/C++ statement on the same line as an _asm block, you must enclose the block in

```
__asm
{
    mov al, 01h
    mov dx, 3f8h
    out  al, dx
}
```
(a)

```
__asm  mov al, 01h
__asm  mov dx, 3f8h
__asm  out  al, dx
......
```
(b)

FIGURE 2.7 The inline assembly block.

braces; otherwise, the compiler will not know where assembly code ends and C/C++ code begins. Finally, because the text in braces has the same format as ordinary MASM text, you can easily cut and paste text from existing MASM source files.

TIP: Another important point is that unlike the braces used in C and C++, the braces enclosing an `_asm` block will not affect variable scope. You can also nest `_asm` blocks, which will not affect variable scope either.

2.3.3 Using C/C++ in _asm Blocks

Because inline assembly instructions can be mixed with C/C++ statements, they can refer to C and C++ variables by name, and use many other elements of those languages as well.

An `_asm` block can use the following language elements:

- **Symbols**, including labels, variable names, and function names
- **Constants**, including symbolic constants and `enum` members
- **Macros and preprocessor directives**, such as `#define`, `#ifdef` and so on
- **Comments**, such as `/* */` and `//`
- **Type names** (as long as the MASM type is legal)
- **`typedef` names**, which are generally used with operators (such as `PTR` and `TYPE`) or to specify structure or union members

Within an `_asm` block, you can specify integer constants with either C notation or assembler radix notation. For example, there is no difference between 0x3f8 and 3f8h inside the `_asm` block. This allows you to use a preprocessor, such as `#define`, to define a constant in C/C++ and use it in both C/C++ and assembly portions of the program. (An example using this kind of notation will be presented in section 2.3.10.) You can also specify constants in octal by preceding them with a 0. For example, 0888 specifies an octal constant.

2.3.4 Using Operators and Symbols in _asm Blocks

An `_asm` block cannot use C/C++ specific operators, such as the << operator. However, operators shared by C and MASM, such as the `*` operator, are interpreted as assembly language operators. For example, outside an `_asm` block, a pair of square brackets `[]` is interpreted as enclosing an array subscript, which C automatically scales to the size of an element in the array. Inside an `_asm` block, the pair is seen as the MASM index operator, which yields an unscaled byte offset from any data object or label.

An `_asm` block can refer to any C/C++ symbol that is in scope where the block appears. As previously mentioned, C and C++ symbols include variable names, function names, and labels. Symbolic constants and `enum` members are excluded. C++ member functions cannot be called.

The restrictions on using some C/C++ symbols are listed here:

- Each assembly language statement can contain only one C/C++ symbol. Multiple symbols can appear in the same assembly instruction only with LENGTH, TYPE and SIZE expressions.
- Functions referenced in an _asm block must be declared earlier in the program. Otherwise, the compiler cannot distinguish between the function names and labels.
- An _asm block cannot use any C/C++ symbols with the same spelling as MASM-reserved words. (MASM-reserved words include instruction names such as PUSH and register names such as AX.)
- Structure and union tags are not recognized in _asm blocks.

2.3.5 Accessing C/C++ Data in _asm Blocks

A significant advantage of using inline assembly code is the ability to refer to C/C++ variables by name. An _asm block can refer to all symbols, including variable names, in the scope where the block appears. For instance, in Figure 2.7(a), the port address of COM1, 3f8h, can be replaced by the symbol COM1 if COM1 has been defined before using a preprocessor such as #define COM1 3f8h. Like constants, variables can be referenced. For example, a variable with the name intVar can be referenced as:

```
_asm mov eax, intVar
```

This is equivalent to assigning the variable intVar to the EAX register pair.

If a class, structure, or union member has a unique name, an _asm block can refer to it using only the member name, without specifying the variable or typedef name before the period (.) operator. But if the member name is not unique, the period operator must be immediately preceded by a variable or typedef name. For example, the following structure types share same_name as their member name:

```
struct first_type          struct  second_type
{                          {
  char* weasel;            int   wonton;
  int    same_name;        long  same_name;
};                         };
```

If you declare variables with the types

```
struct first_type          hal;
struct second_type         oat;
```

All references to the member same_name must use the variable name because same_name is not unique. But the member weasel has a unique name, so it can be referred to by its member name:

```
_asm
{
  mov ebx, OFFSET hal
  mov ecx, [ebx]hal.same_name; must use 'hal'
  mov esi, [ebx].weasel; can omit 'hal'
}
```

Note that omitting the variable name is merely a coding convenience. The same assembly instructions are generated whether or not the variable name is present.

You can access data members in a class in C++ without regard to access restrictions. However, you cannot call member functions.

2.3.6 Using and Preserving Registers in Inline Assembly Code

In general, you should not assume that a register has a given value when an _asm block begins. Register values are not guaranteed to be preserved across separate _asm blocks. If you end a block of inline code and begin another, you cannot rely on the registers in the second block to retain their values from the first block. An _asm block inherits whatever register values result from the normal flow of control.

If you use the _fastcall calling convention, the compiler passes function arguments in registers instead of on the stack. This can create problems in functions with _asm blocks because a function will have no way of telling which parameter is in which register. If a function happens to receive a parameter in EAX and immediately stores something else in EAX, the original parameter is lost. In addition, the ECX register must be preserved in any function declared with _fastcall.

To avoid such register conflicts, do not use the _fastcall convention for functions that contain _asm blocks. If you specify the _fastcall convention globally with the /Gr compiler option, declare every function containing an _asm block with _cdecl or _stdcall. (The _cdecl attribute tells the compiler to use the C calling convention for that function.) If you are not compiling with /Gr, avoid declaring the function with the _fastcall attribute.

When using _asm to write assembly language in C/C++ functions, you do not need to preserve the EAX, EBX, ECX, EDX, ESI, or EDI registers. However, using these registers will affect code quality because the register allocator cannot use them to store values across _asm blocks. In addition, when encountering EBX, ESI or EDI in inline assembly code, the compiler is forced to save and restore those registers in the function prologue and epilogue.

You should preserve other registers you use (such as DS, SS, SP, BP, and flags registers) for the scope of the _asm block. You should preserve the ESP and EBP registers unless you have some reason to change them (for example, to switch stacks).

Note that if your inline assembly code uses the STD or CLD instructions to change the direction flag, you must restore the flag to its original value.

2.3.7 Jumping to Labels in _asm Blocks

Like an ordinary C/C++ label, a label in an _asm block has scope throughout the function in which it is defined (not only in the block). Both assembly instructions and goto statements can jump to labels inside or outside of the _asm block.

Labels defined in _asm blocks are not case sensitive; goto statements and assembly instructions can all refer to those labels without regard to case. C/C++ labels are case sensitive only when used by goto statements. Assembly instructions can jump to a C/C++ label without regard to its case.

The code in Figure 2.8 shows all the permutations.

Do not use C library function names as labels in _asm blocks. For instance, you might be tempted to use exit as a label, as shown in Figure 2.9.

Because exit is the name of a C library function, this code might cause a jump to the exit function instead of to the desired location.

As in MASM programs, the dollar symbol ($) serves as the current location counter in inline assembly code. It is a label for the instruction currently being assembled. In _asm blocks, its main use is to make long conditional jumps (Figure 2.10).

2.3.8 Calling C/C++ Functions in _asm Blocks

An _asm block can call only those global C++ functions that are not overloaded. If an overloaded global C++ function or a C++ member function is called, the compiler issues an error message.

You can also call any function declared with extern C linkage. This allows an _asm block within a C++ program to call the C library functions, because all the standard header files declare

```
void func( )
{
        goto C_Dest;          // legal: correct case
        goto c_dest;          // error: incorrect case

        goto A_Dest;          // legal: correct case
        goto a_dest;          // legal: incorrect case
        _asm
        {
            jmp C_Dest        ; legal: correct case
            jmp c_dest        ; legal: incorrect case

            jmp A_Dest        ; legal: correct case
            jmp a_dest        ; legal: incorrect case

        a_dest:               ; __asm label
        }
        C_Dest:               // C label
        return;
}
```

FIGURE 2.8 An example of using jump in inline assembly.

```
; BAD TECHNIQUE: using library function name as label
jne exit
  .
  .
  .
exit:
                    ; More __asm code follows
```

FIGURE 2.9 A bad use of jump in inline assembly.

```
jne $+5              ; next instruction is 5 bytes long
jmp farlabel
                     ; $+5
  .
  .
  .
farlabel:
```

FIGURE 2.10 A long jump using the $ sign.

the library functions to have `extern C` linkage. An `_asm` block can call C functions, including C library routines. For example, the block in Figure 2.11 calls the `printf` library routine.

Because function arguments are passed on the stack, you simply push the needed arguments—string pointers, in the previous example—before calling the function. The arguments are pushed in reverse order, so they will come off the stack in the desired order. To emulate the C statement `printf(format, hello, world)`, the example pushes pointers to `world`, `hello`, and `format`, in that order, and then calls `printf`.

```
#include <stdio.h>

char format[] = "%s %s\n";
char hello[] = "Hello";
char world[] = "world";
void main( )
{
  _asm
  {
    mov  eax, offset world
    push eax
    mov  eax, offset hello
    push eax
    mov  eax, offset format
    push eax
    call   printf
    //clean up the stack using unused register ebx so that main can exit cleanly
    pop  ebx
    pop  ebx
    pop  ebx
  }
}
```

FIGURE 2.11 An example of using Inline Assembly to Call C Functions.

2.3.9 Defining _asm Blocks as C Macros

C macros offer a convenient way to insert assembly code into source code, but this method requires extra care because each macro expands into a single logical line. To create trouble-free macros, follow these rules:

- Enclose the _asm block in braces.
- Put the _asm keyword in front of each assembly instruction.
- Use old-style C comments (designated with /* ... */ symbols) instead of assembly-style comments (designated with ;) or single-line C comments (designated with //).

To illustrate this, the following example defines a simple macro (Figure 2.12).

```
#define PORTIO _asm    \
/* Port output */       \
{                       \
  _asm mov al, 2        \
  _asm mov dx, 0xD007   \
  _asm out al, dx       \
}
```

FIGURE 2.12 A macro definition of Inline Assembly.

At first glance, the last three _asm keywords seem superfluous. They are needed, however, because the macro expands into this line:

```
_asm/* Port output */{ _asm mov al, 2 _asm mov dx, 0xD007 _asm out al, dx }
```

The third and fourth _asm keywords are needed as statement separators. The only statement separators recognized in _asm blocks are the newline character and the _asm keyword. Because a block defined as a macro is one logical line, you must separate each instruction with _asm.

The braces are essential as well. If they are omitted, the compiler can be confused by C/C++ statements to the right of the macro invocation on the same line. Without the closing brace, the compiler cannot tell where assembly code stops, and it interprets C/C++ statements after the _asm block as assembly instructions.

Assembly-style comments that start with a semicolon (;) continue to the end of the line. This causes problems in macros because the compiler ignores everything after the comment, all the way to the end of the logical line. The same is true of single-line C/C++ comments (//). To prevent errors, use old-style C comments (/* */) in _asm blocks defined as macros.

An _asm block written as a C macro can take arguments. Unlike an ordinary C macro, however, an _asm macro cannot return a value. Therefore, such macros cannot be used in C/C++ expressions.

Be careful not to invoke macros of this type indiscriminately. For instance, invoking an assembly-language macro in a function declared with the _fastcall convention may cause unexpected results.

At this point, we have finished discussing the use of inline assembly instructions in a C/C++ program. The following section will present several examples illustrating how to use inline assembly code. We will then embed that code into a C program very similar to the one we developed in Section 2.2.1, to improve the program's loopback testing of RS-232 data transmission.

2.3.10 Embedding Inline Assembly Code Within C Code

The program in this section is basically identical to our earlier loopback testing program. The only exception is that the low-level codes used to access the THR and RHR in the UART are replaced by inline assembly instructions. Another difference between the earlier program and this one is that here, instead of an integer sequence, a sequence of characters is used as the testing data that is sent to the THR in the UART.

Now, let's begin work on our improved loopback testing program.

Launch Visual C++ 6.0 and open a new project with the following properties:

- Project type: Win32 Console Application
- Project name: EmbedAssembly
- Project location: C:\Chapter 2

In the open project, create a new C++ source file named EmbedAssembly.cpp. Because of its simplicity, no header file is needed for this project. Enter the code shown in Figure 2.13 into the EmbedAssembly.cpp file.

The purpose of each line of code is described here:

A: Useful header files are declared in this section. These header files contain the protocol definitions of the system functions. Among them, one of the header files is very important. stdio.h provides the protocols for all standard I/O functions, such as the printf() and scanf(), that are used in the system. (Although the header conio.h is included here, we will not use the _outp() and _inp() functions in this program.)

B: Symbols and constants are declared here. Once these are defined in the header of the program, any type of code, such as C/C++ or inline assembly code, will be able to recognize them and use them without any problems. Most registers of COM1 in the 8250 UART are defined because they will be used during communication with the testing port. To keep the program simple, we'll again use COM1 as our testing port. Once we've defined the symbols and constants, we can use them in the program to directly access

```
/*****************************************************************************
 * NAME: EmbedAssembly.cpp
 * DATE: June 30, 2003
 * PGMR: Y. Bai - Copyright 2003-2007
 * DESC: Serial communication test program using embedded assembly language
 *         This program uses 8250 controller to loop-test a serial port.
 *****************************************************************************/
#include <stdio.h>
#include <string.h>
#include <stdlib.h>                                                                    A
#include <conio.h>
#include <ctype.h>
#include <math.h>
#include <dos.h>
#define  COM1      3f8h     // COM1 base address
#define  COM2      2f8h     // COM2 base address
#define  IER       3f9h     // COM1 Interrupt Enable Register                         B
#define  MCR       3fch     // COM1 Modem Control Register
#define  LCR       3fbh     // COM1 Line Control Register
#define  LSR       3fdh     // COM1 Line Status Register
#define  MSR       3feh     // COM1 Modem Status Register
void c_inial();             // Assembly subroutine used to initialize the UART
char reces();               // Assembly subroutine used to receive a byte (uchar)
char sends(char c);         // Assembly subroutine used to send out a byte             C
void delay(int num);        // Delay subroutine used to delay a period of time
void TestSerial();          // C-code subroutine used to test the serial port
void main(void)
{
    char cc;
    printf("\n********* WELCOME TO SERIAL LOOP TESTING ***********\n\n");           D
    printf("Do you want to begin the testing?  y/n\n");
    scanf("%c", &cc);
    if (cc == 'y' || cc == 'Y')                                                       E
      TestSerial();
    printf("************* TESTING END ***************\n");
    return;
}
```

FIGURE 2.13 The main program of Embedded Assembly Codes.

the associated registers without needing to remember each register's address. Each constant can be considered a symbol address for the desired register.

C: Some global functions are declared in this section. The first is an inline assembly subroutine used to initialize the COM1 port. The second is also an inline assembly subroutine and it is used to receive the looped-back character from the RHR in the 8250 UART. The third function, `sends()`, is an inline assembly function that is used to send a character to the THR in the UART. The final two functions are familiar to us because we used them in the previous example.

D: When the main program starts, the `printf()` and `scanf()` functions obtain the user's input from the keyboard. A key input of `y` indicates that the user wants to start the testing program.

E: Once a `y` is received, the `TestSerial()` function is called to begin testing of the serial port.

The body of the `TestSerial()` function is shown in Figure 2.14.

```
  /*****************************************************************************
   *         Subroutine to loop testing for the RS232C port.                       *
   *****************************************************************************/
   void TestSerial()
   {
      char sChar[] = {"abcdefghijklmnopqrstuvwxyz"};
F     char rc, rChar;
      int  index = 0;
G     c_inial();
H     while(!kbhit())
      {
I           rc =sends(sChar[index]);
J           rChar = reces();
            if (rChar != sChar[index])
            {
                printf("Error in receiving from the port!");
                return;
            }
K           else
            {
                printf("Sending  data is %c\n", sChar[index]);
                printf("Receiving data is %c\n", rChar);
            }
L           index++;
            if (index == 26)
               index = 0;
      }
      return;
   }
```

FIGURE 2.14 The function body of TestSerial().

F: Here a sequence of 26 characters is created; this sequence is the testing string that will be sent to the THR in the UART of the tested port. Several local variables are also generated, such as `rc`, which receives the feedback from calling the `sends()` function, and `rChar`, which receives the character returned when the `reces()` function is called. The `index` variable is used as a loop counter.

G: Next, a subroutine is called to initialize the serial port. This subroutine is a block of assembly instructions and it will be discussed later in this chapter.

H: A `while` loop is used here to continuously transmit and receive the character sequence for the tested port, COM1. The loop condition is a result of executing the function `kbhit()`. As long as this function returns a value of `false`, which means that no key has been pressed on the keyboard, the loop will continue its operation. To stop the testing, the user can press any key from the keyboard The `kbhit()` function will then return a value of `true`, which will stop the `while` loop and terminate the testing.

I: During the normal testing process, a testing character is sent out by a call to the `sends()` subroutine. This function returns a feedback value, `rc`. You can check this value to confirm whether or not the function call has been successful.

J: Once the testing character has been transmitted, the `reces()` function is called to receive the character from the RHR in the UART. A comparison is then performed between the transmitted character and the received characters. If the characters are identical, it means that testing has been successful. Otherwise, an error occurs. An error message is displayed on the screen, and testing is terminated.

K: If the characters are identical, both characters will be displayed on the screen to show the user that the test has been successful.

L: The `index` is incremented to continue to the next iteration. If the `index` value is greater than 26 (recall that we use 26 characters in the testing string), it is reset to 0.

Let us now examine the inline assembly code used in this program. First, let's take a look at the initialization function, `c_inial()`, which is shown in Figure 2.15.

```
/*****************************************************************************
 *         Initialization the 8250 communication port
 *****************************************************************************/
void c_inial()
{
  _asm
   {
M   mov dx, LCR        ; Select the Line Control Register to set up the comm. parameters.
    mov al, 80h        ; Bit7 = 1, 3f8h & 3f9h registers can access the baud rate divisor.
    out  dx, al        ; Nominal baud rate = 1843200/(baud rate*16).
N   mov dx, COM1       ;
    mov al, 60h        ; b7 - b0 = (60h) = (01100000b) -> 3f8h (baud rate low-byte)
    out  dx, al        ;
O   mov dx, IER        ;
    mov al, 00h        ; b7 - b0 = (00h) = (00000000b) -> 3f 9h (baud rate high-byte)
    out  dx, al        ; Set up the baud rate high & low bytes (0060h -> 1200 baud rate).
P   mov dx, LCR        ; Finish set up the Line Controller Register.
    mov al, 0bh        ; b7 - b0 = 0bh = (00001011b) -> odd parity, 1 stop bit, 8 data bits.
    out  dx, al        ; Set up LCR based on the above control parameters.
Q   mov dx, MCR        ; Set up Modem Control Register to set DTR & RTS to 1 (space or active).
    mov al, 03h        ; Self-test sub. if this line becomes "mov al,13h".
    out  dx, al        ; Finish set up the MCR.
R   mov dx, IER        ; Set up the Interrupt Enable Register.
    mov al, 0          ; No interrupt utilized.
    out  dx, al        ;
   }
}
```

FIGURE 2.15 The Initialize Function.

As with any general inline assembly block, this initialization block is enclosed by the `_asm` keyword, followed by a pair of braces. All inline assembly code should be covered by this pair of braces; you can write any assembly code inside the braces. This is a very easy way to embed assembly instructions within C/C++ code.

M: The first three instructions here are used to set the divisor latch access bit (DLAB) at the line control register (LCR) in the UART. This allows our program to access the least significant bit (LSB) and most significant bit (MSB), respectively, of the baud rate divisor. For more details, review to section 1.6.6.2 and Table 1-2 in Chapter 1; a section of Table 1-2 is shown again in Table 2-2.

For the COM1 port, it is clear that the THR and RHR use the same register address `(03F8H)` as the LSB register of the baud rate divisor, and that the interrupt enable register (IER) shares an address `(03F9H)` with the MSB register of the baud rate divisor. The only way to change this is to set a different bit value at bit 7 of the LCR. When bit 7 has a value of `1`, it means that the addresses `03F8H` and `03F9H` are used by the LSB and MSB, respectively, of the baud rate divisor, and not by the THR and RHR.

TABLE 2.2
A Segment of the 8250 Registers

Register	IN/OUT	COM1	COM2	Illustrations
Transmitter Hold Register	OUT	03F8H	02F8H	Bit 7 of Line Control Register = 0
Receiver Hold Register	IN	03F8H	02F8H	Bit 7 of Line Control Register = 0
Baud Rate Divisor (LSB)	OUT	03F8H	02F8H	Bit 7 of Line Control Register = 1
Baud Rate Divisor (MSB)	OUT	03F9H	02F9H	Bit 7 of Line Control Register = 1
Interrupt Enable Register	OUT	03F9H	02F9H	Bit 7 of Line Control Register = 0
Line Control Register	OUT	03FBH	02FBH	

A bit value of 1 at bit 7 is equivalent to a hexadecimal value of 80H. We use `dx` as the address register that stores the address of the LCR, which is `03FBH` for the COM1 port. It is important to note that this assembly block uses the constant LCR, defined at the beginning of this program, as the register address. We do not need to record the real register address in this style of inline assembly programming.

The block uses `al` as the data register that stores the data 80H, and uses the `out` assembly command to finish sending that data to the LCR in the UART.

N: In this section, the block stores the base address of COM1 (address `03F8H`, which is defined as a constant at the beginning of the program) to the `dx` register, and we store the LSB of the baud rate (60H) into the `al` register. The `out` is used to send this LSB to the baud rate divisor's LSB register because the base address, `03F8H`, points to the baud rate divisor's LSB register since bit 7 of the LCR has been set to 1 `(80H)`.

O: Here the block sets the MSB of the baud rate divisor to `00H.` The IER `(03F9H)` now points to the baud rate divisor's MSB register because bit 7 of the LCR has been set to 1. The complete baud rate is set to a 16-bit value, `0060H`, which is equivalent to a baud rate of 1200. You can set up different values for these two registers to obtain different baud rates. (Refer to Table 1-3 in Chapter 1 for more detailed information; a section of that table is shown again in Table 2-3.)

P: This section sets the data transmission format, including the parity value, the stop bits, and the number of data bits; we do this by configuring the LCR in the UART. (Refer to Figure 1-29 in Chapter 1 for the data format of the LCR; a similar diagram of this format appears in Figure 2.16.)
Here the LCR is set to `0BH (00001011).` This means that we will use eight data bits, one stop bit, and a parity value of `odd`. It is important to note that bit 7 of this register is now reset to 0; this means that all of the registers related to those elements that have a shared address (the THR and RHR, which normally share with the LSB of the baud rate divisor, as well as the LSB and IER, which normally share with the MSB of the baud rate divisor) have lost their sharing ability. Address `03F8H` is now mapped to either the THR or the RHR, and address `03F9H` is mapped only to the IER. Recall that the value in the DLAB is what enables and disables the sharing ability among these items.

Q: The block now sets up the modem control register (MCR) to properly control the communication mode of the modem. A value of `03H` is sent to this register to activate both the data terminal ready (DTR) line and the request to send (RTS) line; in other words, both lines are set to `space` state. Recall that these two signals are used for handshaking and hardware flow control. When the data terminal equipment (DTE) is ready to begin a data transmission, it activates these two signals to inform the data communication equipment (DCE) that a new data communication is ready to start. The

TABLE 2.3
A Segment of the 8250 Baud Rate Divisor—MSB and LSB

	8250 clock 1.8432 MHz		8250 clock 3.072 MHz	
Desired Baud Rate	**MSB**	**LSB**	**MSB**	**LSB**
50	09	00	0F	00
75	06	00	0A	00
110	04	17	06	D1
150	03	00	05	00
300	01	80	02	80
600	00	C0	01	40
1200	00	60	00	A0
1800	00	40	00	6B
2000	00	3A	00	60
2400	00	30	00	50
3600	00	20	00	35
4800	00	18	00	28
7200	00	10	00	16
9600	00	0C	00	14
19200	00	06	00	0A
38400	00	03	00	05

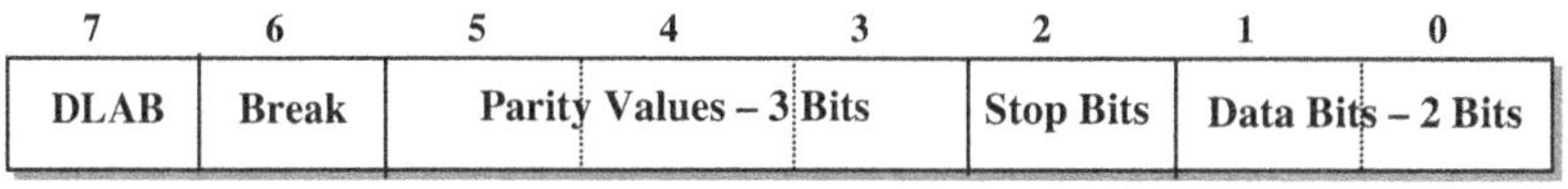

7	6	5 4 3	2	1 0
DLAB	Break	Parity Values – 3 Bits	Stop Bits	Data Bits – 2 Bits

FIGURE 2.16 The data format of the LCR.

DCE should reply to the DTE with another two associated signals, data send ready (DSR) and clear to send (CTS), to let the DTE know that the DCE is ready to receive the data.

R: Here a value of 0 is sent to the IER to indicate that no interruptions should be used in this data communication program. Remember that a decimal value of 0 here is equivalent to a hexadecimal value of `00H`. This data convention works as long as the decimal value of the data is less than `10`.

Now let's take a look at the sending inline assembly function, `sends()`, which is shown in Figure 2.17.

This function has an argument, `c`, which is the character to be sent to the THR in the UART. We will use this `c` variable directly in our inline assembly instructions.

S: A local character variable named `feedback` is declared here; it is used as a reply signal inform the calling function whether or not the inline function call has been successful. A returned question mark (`?`) character means that some error was encountered during the function's execution.

T: In this section the `_asm` keyword appears, followed by a pair of braces that enclose the inline assembly sequence. The first thing our block does here is to check the UART's state to make sure the THR is empty and the UART is ready to pick up new data. The line state register (LSR) in the UART is used to store the current status of the UART. We still use `dx` as the address register that stores the LSR's address, which is `03FDH`

```
/******************************************************************************
 *                     Send Data to the THR in the UART                       *
 ******************************************************************************/
char sends(char c)
{
S    char feedback;
     _asm
    {
T    done: mov  dx, LSR          ; Check the Line Status Register.
           in   al, dx           ; Inspect the state word.
           test al, 20h          ; THR is empty? (when b5 = 1: THR is empty).
           jz   done             ; No, continuing to check it and waiting.
U          mov  dx, COM1         ; THR is empty & ready to send the next character.
           mov  al, c            ; Assign character c to lower-byte in A register.
           mov  feedback, al     ; Return the sent-out character as a feedback.
           out  dx, al           ; Send the character to the 8250.
           jmp  end
V          mov  al, '?'          ; Error occurs, send '?' as a feedback.
           mov  feedback, al     ; Return the error information.
     end:  nop
    }
    return feedback;
}
```

FIGURE 2.17 The sending Inline Assembly Function.

for the COM1 port. Next, the block uses the assembly command `in` to retrieve the contents of the LSR and store that status message into the `al` register. By using a test operation (which is equivalent to an `AND` operation) to check the status stored in the `al`, our assembly code can inspect the value of bit 5 on the LSR to confirm its status. (Refer to Figure 1-31 in Chapter 1 to review the detailed formatting information for this register. A simplified format structure appears in Figure 2.18.)

7	6	5	4	3	2	1	0
0	TXE	THR Empty	Break	Framing Error	Parity Error	Receiver Overrun	R_XRDY

FIGURE 2.18 A simplified format of the LSR.

If the result of the `AND` 20H operation with the content of the LSR is 0 (which means that bit 5 of the LSR is 0), it means that the THR in the UART is not empty, and that our block cannot send any data to that register until bit 5 of the LSR is set to `1`. In this case, the block must perform a loop that will continue to check the bit's value until it is changed to `1`. A `jz done` instruction is used to turn the execution of the program back to a label `done`, wherein retrieval of LSR's bit 5 value is executed again with the `AND` operation.

U: If bit 5 of the LSR is set to 1, it means that the THR is empty. Our inline assembly code can then transfer the base address of COM1—`03F8H`, which is also the address of the THR in COM1—to the address register `dx`. The character to be transmitted, `c`, is also transferred to the data register `al`. Finally, the assembly command `out` is used to send this character to the THR.

The c character can also be transferred to the local variable feedback that is defined outside of this inline assembly block and is a C-type variable. The feedback character will be returned to the calling function when this inline assembly function ends.

V: This section of code performs error detection for the LSR. We did not use this error detection here. You can check all other bits in the LSR to confirm that the UART is operating properly. A question mark (?) character will be returned if any error is encountered.

Let us now discuss the reces() inline assembly function, which is used to receive a character from the RHR in the UART. The body of the function is shown in Figure 2.19.

```
/*****************************************************************************
 *          Receiving the character from the 8250 controller.               *
 *****************************************************************************/
  char reces()
  {
W    char dd;
     _asm
    {                       ; Line Status Register Bit Definition
X    done: mov dx, LSR      ; Check the Line Status Register  b0 = 1: Receive data is ready
           in   al, dx      ;                                 b1 = 1: Overrun error
           test al, 1eh     ; Detect any error happend?       b2 = 1: Parity error
           jnz  error       ; Yes, go to error processing.    b3 = 1: Framing error
           test al, 01h     ; The data is ready? (b0 = 1?)    b4 = 1: Break interrupt
           jz   done        ; No, continuing to check.        b5 = 1: THR is empty
                            ;                                       (ready to send data)
Y          mov  dx, COM1; Data is ready                       b6 = 1: Transmit Shift Register
                            ;                                       is empty
           in   al, dx      ; Get the character from the      b7     is always zero
                            ; receiver reg (3f8h_COM1).
           mov  dd, al      ; Returning the character received.
           jmp  end         ; RHR: Receiver Holding Register
Z   error: mov dx, COM1     ; Error occurs.
           in   al, dx      ;
           mov  al, '?'     ; Return a '?' as an indicator of the error
           mov  dd, al
     end:  nop
    }
    return dd;
  }
```

FIGURE 2.19 The Receiving Inline Assembly Function.

W: In this section, our block creates a local character variable, dd, which returns either the character received from the RHR in the UART if the function call is successful or the execution status if the function call fails.

X: Inside the _asm block, as with the sending function, we need to check the status of the RHR to make sure that a character is ready to be picked up. By using the AND function on the bit values of the LSR with the 1EH, our block determines whether or not an error has occurred in the UART. (Refer to Figure 2.18 for the detailed bit format of the LSR.) At this point, we are concerned only with the input status of the UART, so the higher bits, transmitter empty (TXE) and transmitter buffer empty (TBE) in bits 5 and 6, are masked by 0. Bit 7 of the LSR is always 0, so 1EH (00011110B) is used to check any possible errors. The AND 1EH operation should be 0 if no error occurs, otherwise it means that an error has happened. A jnz error assembly code is used to transfer the program to the error processing section if an error is detected. Here the `error` is a label used to indicate the starting point of the error processing section in the program.

If no error occurs, the next step necessary for receiving data is to check the status of the RHR in the UART. If bit 0 of the LSR has a value of `0`, it means that the RHR is still empty and no data is available. A `jz done` assembly instruction is used to transfer the program back to the entry point so it can continue checking the status of the LSR until bit 0 on the LSR is set to 1, which means that data is ready to be transferred from the RHR. Here, `done` is a label used to indicate the starting point of the program.

Y: If bit 0 on the LSR is set to 1, which means that a character is available in the RHR, our block uses the `dx` register to store the base address (03F8H) of port COM1 (which is also the address of the RHR in the UART), to pick up the character from the RHR, and to store it in the `al` register by using the assembly command `in`.

Finally, we assigns the received character to local variable `dd` (which has been created outside of this inline assembly block) and transfer the program to the exit point by using a `jmp end` assembly instruction. Here, `end` is another label used to provide a termination point for the program. At the end of this function, or at the outside of the inline assembly block, `dd` is returned to the calling function as the received character.

Z: If an error occurs, the program is transferred to the error processing section. A question mark `(?)` is sent to the `dd` variable, which is used to monitor the execution of the inline assembly block and will be returned to the calling function.

This completes our examination of the EmbedAssembly project.

Compile and build the program, and then run it. The running results (if no error occurs) are shown in Figure 2.20.

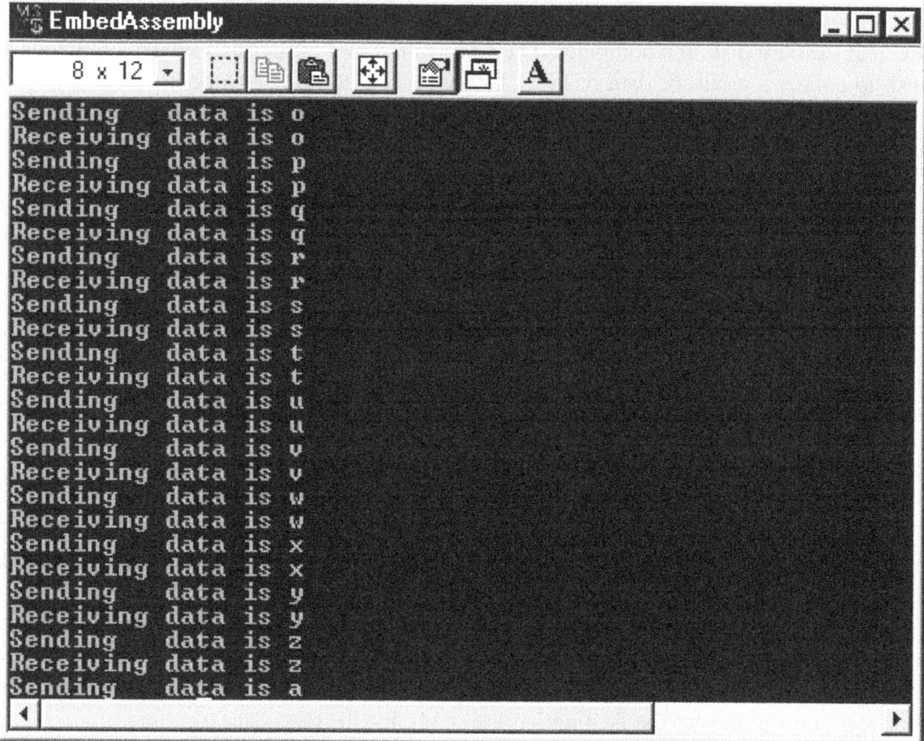

FIGURE 2.20 The running result of the program.

The program will run continuously if no error occurs, and both the transmitted and received data are shown on the screen. Because the program uses a while loop, the program can run in an infinite cycle until a key is pressed.

If the program keeps running on its own, implementation of the inline assembly code has been successful. Press the `spacebar` to stop the program. The implementation of the inline assembly code is successful.

The complete code for this project, including the source and the executable files, can be found in the folder `Chapter 2\EmbedAssembly` on the attached CD.

2.4 A SERIAL PORT COMMUNICATION PROGRAM DEVELOPED IN ANSI C

The first two sample applications in this chapter are both loopback programs that can be used to test a single port. In this section, we will discuss a data communication program implemented between two ports, or two computers.

In most computer data communication, one computer works as a master, and data communication is always started or triggered by this master computer. The master computer can be considered the DTE. The other computer, called the slave computer, waits for the trigger signals coming from the master computer, and replies with the requirements sent by the master. The slave computer can be considered the DCE. In real applications, most data communication between the DTE and the DCE is not mutual mode. This means that in most situations, one computer is used to control data communication, and the other computer is used to transmit the required data.

In the following example, we use two computers to perform serial data communication. One computer is considered the master computer, and the other is the slave computer. The master computer starts the data communication, and the slave computer needs to collect and transmit a sequence of data to the master computer. This situation is very similar to the one that exists between the CPU and the hard disk in a computer. The CPU works as a master and sends commands to the hard disk to collect a group of data or files. The hard disk controller works as a slave to provide and transmit the group of data or files required by the CPU. The difference between that situation and our case is that the data communication between the CPU and the hard disk happens in parallel mode, and ours happens in serial mode.

Two computers are connected via an RS-232 null modem cable. One computer is operating under Windows Me and the other uses Windows 98. This data communication program is developed in ANSI C for MS-DOS, so the operating systems on the computers must be one of the following:

- Windows 95
- Windows 98
- Windows Me

The functional block diagram of this data communication is shown in Figure 2.21.

When performing the data communication, either the hardware or software flow-control technique can be used to coordinate data transmission. In this example, the hardware flow control is used, which means that the `DTR/DSR` and the `RTS/CTS` signal lines are used for handshaking signals. The file transfer protocol (FTP) can also be used for this data communication. For simplicity, we do not use any protocol for this program. Synchronization between the master and the slave computers is performed by the `comm_start()` function, which means that before transmitting or receiving a character, both the master and the slave computer need to call this function to make sure that both the source and the destination are ready for the next data transfer.

Unlike those in some FTPs, this data exchange is started by sending a starting character `s` from the master computer to the slave computer. As shown in Figure 2.21, the `comm_start()` function

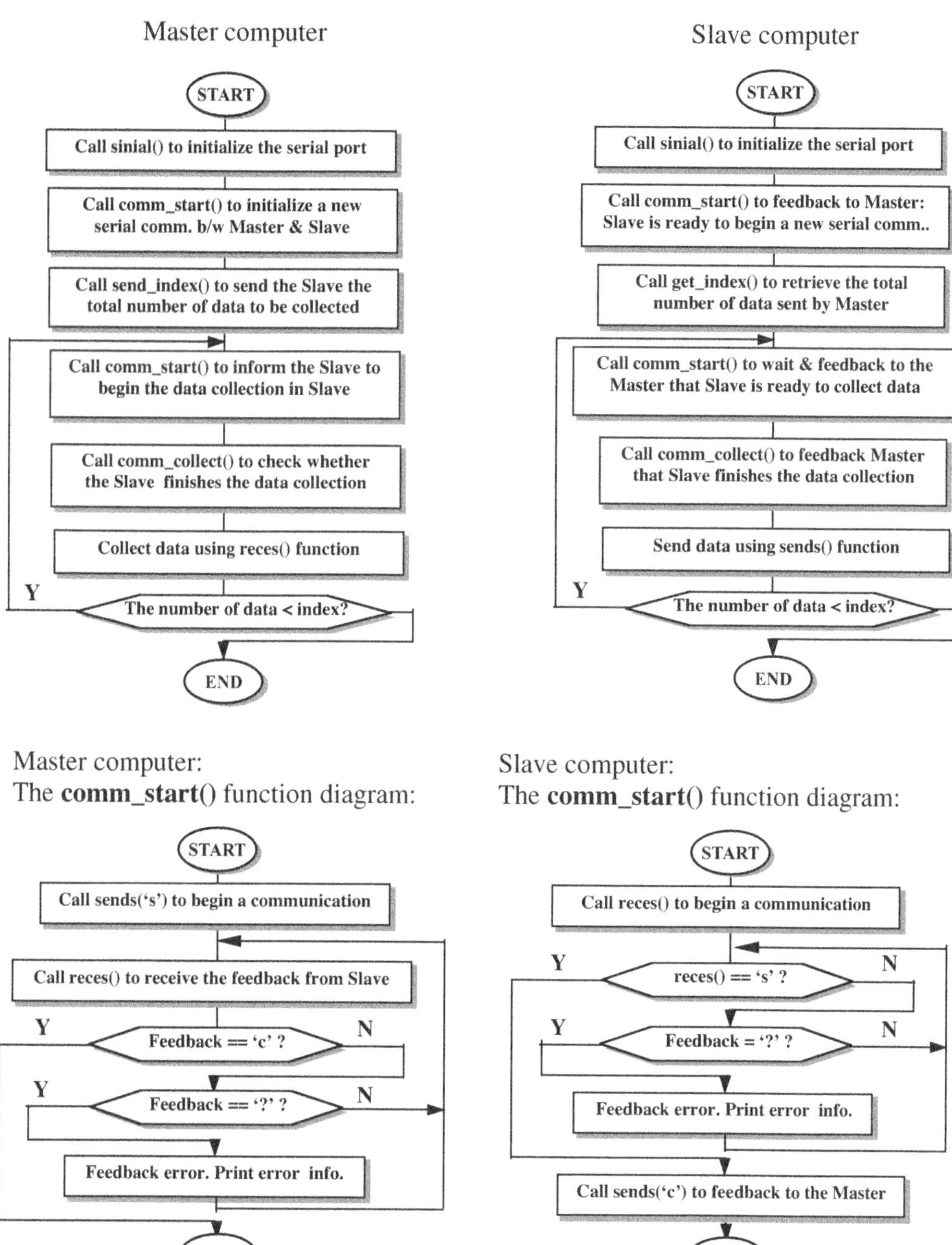

FIGURE 2.21 The block diagram of The Master-Slave Data Communications.

on the master side sends this `s` character to begin the data communication. The master will wait for feedback from the slave computer until the answering character `c` is received from the slave. If a question mark (`?`) is received, it means that an error has been encountered during transmission between the master and the slave; an error message will be printed and returned to the calling function to indicate that the function call has failed. The function returns a 0 if no error has occurred.

The slave computer will wait for the starting character `s` sent by the master, and it will reply to the master with the character `c` if it successfully receives the starting character. If an error occurs, it will be printed and returned to the calling function to terminate the program.

During the execution of the `comm_start()` function, the duration of the synchronization process between the master and the slave is limited by a timeout value. An error is generated if the synchronization period is longer than the timeout value.

The data exchange process between the master and the slave is similar. Both computers need to initialize the serial port by calling the `sinial()` function. Next, `comm_start()` is executed to synchronize the two computers. If this function call is successful, the master sends an index, which is the total amount of data to be transmitted from the slave to the master, by calling the function `send_index()`. If this index is successfully received by the slave, another synchronization process is executed between two computers to prepare the data exchange.

If the synchronization process is error-free, the `comm_collect()` function is called to begin the data transmission on both computers. This function is called in a loop format by the main function to repeat the data transfer until the loop number is equal to the `index`, which is the maximum amount of data to be transmitted from the slave to the master. A synchronization process is needed for each data transfer. Each data transfer consists of the slave sending data to the master and receiving feedback from the master.

A null modem cable needs to be installed between the master and the slave computers for this data transmission program.

2.4.1 The Serial Port Communication Program on the Master Side

Now let's take a look at the detailed code of this program. Because the program is somewhat complicated, a header file is needed to declare the function and constant protocols used in this program.

Launch Visual C++ 6.0 and create a new Win32 Console Application named `SerialComm`. Create a new C/C++ header file named `SerialComm.h`, and enter the code shown in Figure 2.22 into this header file.

A: The system header files used in the program are declared here. One system header file, `<time.h>`, is added because we need to use some system timing functions to calculate and monitor the timeout.

B: Variable types and global constants are declared in this section. Once these declarations are made, a short symbol can be used to represent the real variable type. For example, `USHORT` represents the unsigned short. These symbols make the program more concise.

C: The global constants used in the program are declared here. These constants are associated with the different addresses of the registers in the UART. (Refer to Tables 1-1 and 1-2 in Chapter 1 for a detailed list of addresses used in the different ports.) Some generally used port addresses are listed in Table 2-4.
An `elapsed` macro is defined here and is used to calculate the elapsed time based on a starting point. A system timing function `clock()` is used for this macro.

D: A data structure, `serialDATA`, is defined here because it will be needed in the data exchange process. In this example, data will be exchanged in a group, which means that each data set is composed of two items per group. The first is associated with a position, and the second is associated with an angle. This definition is based on one of our real projects that is used in the robot calibration and measurement processes. In that project, two computers work as two separate controllers to control two robots. But the data communication between these two robots needs to be in real time because the master robot needs the data collected by the slave robot, such as the current position and rotation angle of the slave robot, before it can determine the next movement of the slave robot.

```
/*****************************************************************************
 * NAME: SerialComm.h
 * DATE: 7/15/2003
 * PGMR: Y. Bai  Copyright 2003 - 2007
 * DESC:  Header file for the serial communication between two computers
 *****************************************************************************/
#include <stdio.h>
#include <stdlib.h>
#include <conio.h>
A  #include <string.h>
#include <math.h>
#include <time.h>

#define  MAXNUM       100                // Max data length
#define  BYTE         unsigned char      // Data type
B  #define  USHORT       unsigned short
#define  TIMEOUT      5                  // Time out code
#define  TMOUT        10                 // Time out value
#define  TMOUT1       1000               // Time out value for comm_start()
#define  NUMS         20                 // timeout number of sending/receiving data

USHORT      COM1  = 0x3f8;               // COM1 base address
C  USHORT      IER   = 0x3f9;               // COM1 Interrupt Enable Register
USHORT      LCR   = 0x3fb;               // COM1 Line Control Register
USHORT      MCR   = 0x3fc;               // COM1 Modem Control Register
USHORT      LSR   = 0x3fd;               // COM1 Line Status Register
USHORT      MSR   = 0x3fe;               // COM1 Modem Status Register

#define elapsed  ((clock() - start) / CLK_TCK)      // Calculate elapsed time

D  struct serialDATA
{
        char   pos[64];
        char   ang[64];
        double dpos;
        double dang;
};

void   sinial();
E  void   delay(int nums);
BYTE   sends(char  c, int  nums);
BYTE   reces(int  nums);
int    comm_start();
int    comm_collect(serialDATA*  res);
int    send_index(int  max);
```

FIGURE 2.22 The Header File of the Master Computer.

The string variables `pos` and `ang` are used in RS-232 data transmission. The variables `dpos` and `dang` are double variables that display their values on the master side when they are received from the slave computer.

E: The global functions used in this project are defined here. (Some of these functions have been discussed earlier in this section.) The `sends()` and `reces()` functions each have a `nums` argument, which is used to specify the maximum length of the timeout interval allowed as the function is executed. A timeout error will occur if the time period of execution of the function is longer than the `nums` value.

Now create a new C++ source file named `SerialComm.cpp`, and enter the codes that are shown in Figure 2.23 into this source file.

TABLE 2.4
Typical 8250 Registers

UART Register	IN/OUT	COM1	COM2	COM3	COM4
Transmitter Hold Register	OUT	03F8H	02F8H	03E8H	02E8H
Receiver Hold Register	IN	03F8H	02F8H	03E8H	02E8H
Baud Rate Divisor (LSB)	OUT	03F8H	02F8H	03E8H	02E8H
Baud Rate Divisor (MSB)	OUT	03F9H	02F9H	03E9H	02E9H
Interrupt Enable Register	OUT	03F9H	02F9H	03E9H	02E9H
Interrupt Identification Register	IN	03FAH	02FAH	03EAH	02EAH
Line Control Register	OUT	03FBH	02FBH	03EBH	02EBH
Modem Control Register	OUT	03FCH	02FCH	03ECH	02ECH
Line Status Register	IN	03FDH	02FDH	03EDH	02EDH
Modem Status Register	IN	03FEH	02FEH	03EEH	02EEH

F: The header file, `SerialComm.h`, should be included first in this main program to enable us to use any constant or function we defined in that header file.

G: Local variables are declared here. Two of them are important; one is the FILE pointer, `fp`, which is used to keep a handler for the opened file, and the other is the `serialDATA` structure. We use a file to store the data—in this case, the positions and angles received from the slave computer. The purpose of file is to let us check this data after the data communication and plot the data in graphic format. For the structure `serialDATA`, we must create a variable with data type `serialDATA`. When you create a structure, you must create a variable for it before you can use the structure.

H: When the program runs, the user must first enter an index, which is used to specify the maximum amount of data to be transmitted. A `scanf()` system I/O function is used to retrieve this user-entered index. Note that the second argument of the `scanf()` function is a pointer, so that argument must be preceded by the `&` address operator.

I: The `fopen()` system function is used here to create a new file. The first argument of this function is the path of the file to be created, and the second is the operation mode for the created file. The applied path of the file for this project is `C:\data`, and the file name is `serialCOM.dat`. We want to store the received data in this file, so a write mode, 'w', is used here. The `fopen()` function will return a file handler (pointer) if a new file is created successfully. A value of `NULL` will be returned if an error occurs when this function is executed. The program will be terminated if this error occurs.

J: In this section, a `malloc()` system function is called to allocate memory space for the pointer variable of the `sdata` structure. Remember, memory space must be allocated for this pointer-type variable in the heap area of the system memory—not on the stack—before this variable can legally be used in the program. A running error will occur if there is no memory assigned for the pointer-type variable. Because `sdata` is declared only as a pointer-type variable with no allocated memory space, `sdata` will point to nothing. As memory space is allocated for the pointer variable, `sdata` will point to the starting address of the structure variable.

K: Next, the `sinial()` function is called to initialize the serial port of the master computer.

L: In this section, the synchronization function, `comm_start()`, is executed on the master side to send the starting character `s` to the slave computer and wait for it to give feedback. If a `c` character is received from the slave computer, it means that synchronization has been successful and data communication can start. A nonzero value will be returned if this function call encounters any mistake. The error information will be printed and the program will be terminated.

```
/*****************************************************************************
 * NAME: SerialComm.cpp
 * DATE: 7/15/2003
 * PRGM: Y. Bai - Copyright 2003 - 2007
 * DESC: Use serial port communication between two computers. Two set of programs should
 *        be developed and installed in two computers: Master and Slave computers.
 *        This program is for the Master computer.
 *****************************************************************************/
F  #include "SerialComm.h"
   void main()
   {
G     FILE* fp;
      int     rc, num, index, repeat = 0;
      serialDATA* sdata;
H     printf("\n***** WELCOME TO SERIAL PORTS COMMUNICATION *****\n");
      printf("\nHow many data you want to process b/w computers? \n");
      printf("Enter an integer as the number of the data & press Enter key\n");
      scanf("%d", &index);
I     fp = fopen("C:\\data\\serialCOM.dat", "w");
      if (fp == NULL)
      {
          printf("File open error! program exit\n");
          return;
      }
J     sdata = (serialDATA* )malloc(sizeof(serialDATA));
K     sinial();
L     rc = comm_start();
      if (rc != 0) { printf("Error in comm_start()\n"); return; }
M     rc = send_index(index);
      if (rc != 0) { printf("Error in send_index()\n"); return; }
N     for (num = 0; num < index; num++)
      {
          rc = comm_start();
          if (rc != 0) { printf("Error in comm_start()\n"); return; }
          rc = comm_collect(sdata);
          printf("%d - Received pos =: %s\n", num, sdata ->pos);
          printf("%d - Received ang =: %s\n", num, sdata ->ang);
          fprintf(fp, "%.2f   %.2f\n", sdata->dpos, sdata->dang);
      }
O     fclose(fp);
      delete sdata;
      printf("\n************* END OF THE TEST **************\n\n");
   }
```

FIGURE 2.23 The main program in the Master Computer.

M: Following successful synchronization, the maximum amount of data to be transmitted between the master and slave computers is sent by calling the `send_index()` function from the master side. If any errors occur while this function is called, the error information will be printed out and the program will be terminated.

N: Here, a `for` loop is executed to repeat the data transmission between the two computers. The function `comm_collect()` is executed to retrieve the data from the slave side. Prior to executing each `comm_collect()` to retrieve a single group of data—position `pos` and angle `ang`, for example—the synchronization function of the master side, `comm_start()` must be called to make sure both computers are ready to exchange

the next data. The argument of the `comm_collect()` function is the `sdata variable`. This argument-passing format is called *passing by address,* and it allows any variable stored in a structure to be updated either inside or outside of a function. In other words, if any variable in this structure, such as `pos` or `ang`, is modified inside the `comm_collect()` function, the modification is reflected in all functions (including the main function) of the program. Consequently, the modified variable (`pos` or `ang`) can be picked up from the `structure` variable in the main function.
If no error occurs when the function is executed, the received or updated data, `pos` and `ang`, will be printed on the screen. The `fprintf()` system function will be called to store these data into the opened file. Because `sdata` is a pointer-type variable, a `->`operator is needed to access the real variables stored in the structure.

O: At this point, we need to close the file and clear the memory space allocated to the `sdata` variable. Note that no data can be written into the file until `fclose()` is executed to close the opened file.

Now that we've examined the body of the main function, we will discuss each function individually.

Still in the `SerialComm.cpp` source file, enter the following functions one by one after the main function. The first function is the synchronization function `comm_start()`, which is shown in Figure 2.24.

```
   int comm_start()
   {
P      BYTE signal;
       int     rc = 0;
Q      clock_t start;
       start  = clock();
R      signal = sends('s', NUMS);
S      while((reces(NUMS) != 'c') & !kbhit())
       {
            signal = sends('s', NUMS);
            if (signal == '?')
            {
                 printf("comm_start() error\n");
                 rc = -1;
                 break;
            }
T           if (elapsed >= TMOUT1)
            {
                 printf("time out occurs in comm_start()\n");
                 rc = TIMEOUT;
                 break;
            }
       }
       return rc;
   }
```

FIGURE 2.24 The Synchronization Function in the Master Computer.

P: Local variables are declared here. These variables are used to monitor the execution status of certain called functions. The variable `rc` is assigned a `0` value, which means there have been no errors.

Q: A `clock_t` system variable, `start`, is now created, and the `clock()` system function is called to track the time, based on the system timer.

R: Next, the function `sends()` is called to send the starting character `s` to the slave computer. The second argument of this function, `nums`, is the upper boundary of the timeout value, which is used to specify the length of time to be spent executing the function. A timeout error will be returned if executing the function takes longer than the specified interval.

S: After the first `sends()` function is executed, a `while` loop is run to repeatedly transmit the starting character `s` and wait for feedback from the slave computer. The `while` loop will continue its operation (sending out the starting character `s`) as long as both of the following conditions are true:

- The received feedback character from the slave computer is not a `c`.
- The user does not press a key.

The `while` loop will be terminated if one of the following situations occurs:

- A question mark `(?)` is returned when the `sends()` function is called to send the starting character. This would mean that an error has occurred during execution of the function.
- A timeout error occurs when the `sends()` function is called to send the starting character.

T: The function also checks the `elapsed time` value, which is calculated by comparing the current time and the start time. If the `elapsed` value is greater than the value of the argument `NUMS,` a timeout error occurs. The error information will be printed out and the program will be terminated. Finally, the `rc` variable is returned as feedback to the calling function.

TIP: In this program, the timeout limitation value is 20 seconds. You can modify this value in your own application, based on your situation.

Now we'll create the `send_index()` function. In the `SerialComm.cpp` source file, type in the code shown in Figure 2.25.

```
    int send_index(int max)
    {
        BYTE  rc;
        int   result = 0;
U       char* strIndex;
        char  buffer[8];
        short index, length;
V       strIndex = _itoa(max, buffer, 10);
        length  = strlen(buffer);
W       for (index = 0; index <= length; index++)
        {
            rc = sends(buffer[index], NUMS);
            if (rc == '?' || rc == '!')
            {
                printf("Error in sends()\n");
                result = -1;
                break;
            }
        }
        return result;
    }
```

FIGURE 2.25 The `send_index()` function in the master computer.

U: The local variables are declared here. `strIndex` is a string variable used to receive the running status of the function `_itoa()`. The **buffer** is an array that holds the translated characters obtained from the execution of `_itoa()`.

V: The `_itoa()` system function now translates the numeric value to the associated string variable. When the `sends()` function is executed to send out the index, the data to be sent out must be formatted as a sequence of characters. Each time `sends()` is executed, one character is transmitted. In other words, to send out a sequence of eight characters, you need to call and execute the `sends()` function eight times. The `itoa()` function translates the input argument max, which is equivalent to the maximum number of the data to be transmitted, from a numeric value to a string and stores the translated string result in the **buffer** array. The system function `strlen()` is called to obtain the length of the translated string variable, and this length information will be used in the `for` loop in the next step.

W: Here the `for` loop is performed to continuously transmit the translated sequence of characters. Each character can be identified by its position or index in the array (`buffer[index]`). If a transmission error or a timeout error occurs while the `sends()` function is running, the error information will be printed out and the program will be terminated. Finally, the execution status is returned to the calling function.

The next function we need to enter into the `SerialComm.cpp` source file is `comm_collect()`, which is shown in Figure 2.26.

```
    int comm_collect(serialDATA* res)
    {
X       BYTE signal;
        int index = 0, rc = 0;
Y       while ((signal = reces(NUMS))!= '\0')
        {
            if (signal == '?' || signal == '!')
            {
                printf("sends() error/port is not ready\n");
                return -1;
            }
Z           res->pos[index] = signal;
            index++;
        }
1       res ->pos[index] = '\0';
        index = 0;
2       while((signal = reces(NUMS)) != '\0')
        {
            if (signal == '?' || signal == '!')
            {
                printf("sends() error/port is not ready\n");
                return -1;
            }
3           res->ang[index] = signal;
            index++;
        }
4       res ->ang[index] = '\0';
5       res->dpos = atof(res->pos);
        res->dang = atof(res->ang);
        return rc;
    }
```

FIGURE 2.26 The `comm_collect()` function in the master computer.

X: Local variables are declared here. Both the index and the rc variables are reset to 0. The signal and rc variables are used to receive the running status of the reces() function and the comm_collect() function.

Y: Next, a while loop is continuously executed as long as the character returned by the reces() function is not equal to the null terminator (\0). (The null terminator indicates the end of the received string). In ANSI C, each string ends with a null character. This null character is automatically attached to the end of the string when any string operation function is called. In our program, when itoa() is called, the translated string is stored in the buffer array, and a null character is automatically added to the end of that string by the _itoa() function.

If an error is encountered during the execution of the reces() function, which is used to retrieve the character sent by the slave computer, the error information will be printed out and the program will be terminated

Z: If no error occurs, the received character is sent to the position string (pos[index]) in the serialDATA structure variable. The index variable specifies the position of the character in the pos[] array. As one character is received and stored, index is upgraded and the next loop begins.

1: If the reces() function returns a null character, we have reached the end of the string. The while loop is terminated because the loop condition is not satisfied, and a null character is attached to the end of the stored pos[] array to indicate that the received string is complete. The index variable is reset to 0 for the next while loop to be executed to retrieve the next data.

2: The next while loop performs a function similar to the previous while loop. It is used to retrieve the second string variable, angle or ang, sent by the slave computer.

3: Similar to the previous loop, each received character is stored in the ang[] array, and index is increased by 1 to indicate the next location of the string.

4: When the last character is received, a null character is attached to the end of the received string.

5: The system function atof() is called to translate the received strings to their associated numeric values and store them into the dpos and dang variables in the serialDATA structure variable.

Finally, the execution status of this function is returned to the function call.

It is important to note that the synchronization function comm_start() should be called before each comm_collect() can be executed. This will ensure that both computers are ready to properly exchange the next data.

The next function we need to discuss is sinial(), which is used to initialize the serial port. The body of the function is shown in Figure 2.27.

This initialization function is straightforward, and it is similar to the function c_inial() that was shown in Figure 2.15.

6: In this section, The MSB on the LCR is set to 1 (80H) to allow the user to access the LSB and MSB registers of the baud rate divisor to set up the baud rate by using the base address COM1 and the IER's address. The baud rate is set to 1200. You can set different baud rates by modifying this number based on your application..

7: Here an 0x0BH is sent to the LCR to set up the data transmission format. The format for this transmission is as follows: eight-bit data bits, odd parity, and one stop bit. The MCR is set to 0x03H to activate the DTR and the RTS lines. Finally the IER is set to 0, which means that no interrupt is used for this data communication.

```
/*****************************************************************************
 *              Initialization the 8250 communication port                   *
 *****************************************************************************/
void sinial()
{
6    _outp(LCR,  0x80);    // Select the LCR to set up the comm. parameters.
     _outp(COM1, 0x60);    // b7 - b0 = (60h) = (01100000b) -> 3f8h (baud rate low-byte)
     _outp(IER,  0);       // b7 - b0 = (00h) = (00000000b) -> 3f9h (baud rate high-byte)
                           // (0060h -> 1200 baud rate)
7    _outp(LCR,  0x0b);    // b7 - b0 = 0bh = (00001011) ->odd parity, 1 stop bit, 8 data bits.
     _outp(MCR,  0x03);    // Set up MCR to set DTR & RTS to 1 (space or active).
     _outp(IER,  0);       // Set up the Interupt Enable Register. No interrupt utilized.
}
```

FIGURE 2.27 The `sinial()` function in the master computer.

```
/*****************************************************************************
 *              Send handshaking signal to the slave computer              *
 *****************************************************************************/
BYTE sends(char c, int  nums)
{
8      int   rc = 0;
       char fdback;
9      clock_t start;
       start  = clock();
10     rc = _inp(LSR);
11     while ((rc & 0x20) == 0)                  // data is not ready, try nums times.
       {
           rc = _inp(LSR);
12         if (elapsed >= nums)
           {
                printf("THR is not ready/time out\n");
                fdback = '!';
                return fdback;
           }
       }
13     _outp(COM1, c);
       fdback = c;
       return  fdback;
}
```

FIGURE 2.28 The `sends()` function in the master computer.

The next function in the `SerialComm.cpp` source file is `sends()`, which is shown in Figure 2.28

8: Local variables are declared at the beginning of this function. The integer variable `rc` is used to monitor the running status of the system function `_inp()`, and `fdback` is used to hold the result of the function `sends()`. This execution result is returned to the calling function to indicate the running status of the function.

9: The `clock_t` variable `start` is used to mark the starting point of the time period for calculating the elapsed time of the function's execution. When `start = clock()` is executed, the current time is used as the starting point.

10: The `_inp()` system function is called to get the current running status of the UART.

11: A `while` loop is run to continuously check the status of the UART's registers, especially the fifth bit on the LSR. (Refer to Figure 2.18 for the definition on each bit on the LSR.) The fifth bit is named THR Empty, and is used to monitor whether or not the THR register is empty. A value of `1` in this bit indicates that the THR is empty; an `0` indicates that the THR still contains a character. When `rc & 0x20H ==0` is `true`, which means the THR is not empty and we cannot send any data to the UART, the `while` loop will continue to get the status of the LSR by using another `_inp()` function. This situation will continue until one of the following conditions exists:

`rc & 0x20H ==0` is false, which means that the fifth bit on the LSR is 1 and, therefore, the THR is empty.

A timeout error occurs, which means that repeatedly checking the status of the LSR has taken too long.

Either of these conditions can stop the `while` loop.

12: The elapsed time (`elapsed`) is compared with the desired interval of time (`nums`). If a timeout occurs, the error information will be printed out and the function will be terminated. The error code (`!`) will be returned to the function call to indicate that the `sends()` function has failed.

13: If the THR is empty, we can send out the next character to the THR by calling the `_outp()` system function. The transmitted character is also assigned to the feedback variable `fdback`, which is returned to the calling function.

The last function in our project is `reces()`, which is used to receive the data coming from the slave computer. The body of the function is shown in Figure 2.29.

14: Two local variables, `rc` and `dd`, are declared here; respectively, they indicate the returning status of the function `_inp()` and the character received.

15: The program starts the time counter by declaring the `start` variable and running the system function `clock()`.

16: We need to check the UART's status before we can pick up any data from the RHR in the UART. By using the `AND` operation on the LSR and the 0x1EH, we can check to see if an error has occurred during the last data transmission. (Refer to Figure 2.18 for the bit format and definition of the LSR.) The 0x1EH is binary data: 00011110. The unmasked bits (a 1 in the associated bit) responding to this 0x1EH are bit 4 (break), bit 3 (framing error), bit 2 (parity error) and bit 1 (receiver overrun). If the result of this `AND` operation is not equal to 0, it means that an error has occurred in the UART. The error message is printed out and a question mark (`?`) is returned to the function call to indicate that the function `reces()` has failed.

17: If the `AND` operation is equal to 0, it means that no error has occurred during the last data transmission. The program checks the UART status again by calling the system function `_inp()` to obtain the contents of the LSR.

18: Here the program checks bit 0 on the LSR to determine whether the data has been received in the RHR. (Refer to Figure 2.18.) Bit 0 in the LSR is controlled by a signal, R_XRDY. If this bit's value is `1`, it means that the data is in the RHR and ready to be picked up. If the bit's value is `0`, the RHR is still empty and no data is coming in. A

```
/*****************************************************************************
 *          Receiving the character from the 8250 controller.                *
 *****************************************************************************/
BYTE reces(int nums)
{
14      char dd;
        int  rc = 0;
15      clock_t start;
        start  = clock();
16      if ((_inp(LSR) & 0x1e) != 0)            // error occurs.
        {
            printf("serial error in reces()\n");
            dd = '?';
            return dd;
        }
17      rc = _inp(LSR);
18      while ((rc & 0x01) == 0)                // data is not ready, try nums times.
        {
            rc = _inp(LSR);
            if (elapsed >= nums)
            {
                printf("data is not ready/time out\n");
                dd = '!';
                return dd;
            }
        }
19      dd = _inp(COM1);                        // data is ready, get it in.

        return dd;
}
```

FIGURE 2.29 The `reces()` function in the master computer.

`while` loop is used here to continuously monitor bit 0 in the LSR until its value is `1`. This `while` loop will be terminated when one of the following conditions is true:

- Bit 0 on the LSR is equal to `1`, which means that the RHR has received valid data.
- A timeout error occurs, which means that checking bit 0 on the LSR has taken too long.

The `elapsed` macro is used here to calculate the elapsed time, based on a specific starting point. That time is compared with the desired interval, which is represented by the `nums` variable. The timeout error occurs if the actual time period is greater than the value of `nums`.

If a timeout error occurs, the error information will be printed out and an error code `(!)`, will be returned to the calling function.

19: If bit 0 on the LSR is equal to `1`, data is ready in the RHR of the UART. The `while` loop is terminated. and the system function `_inp()` is called to pick up the data. The address of the RHR is the base address of the COM1 port; this address has been defined as a constant `COM1` in the header file. The retrieved data is stored in the variable `dd`, and this variable is returned to the calling function as the received character.

Before finishing this project, we will examine a useful time delay function, even though it is not used in this project. Time delays are necessary in most data communication situations. Sometimes timing is a critical factor in serial data exchange, and in some situations, the serial data transmission cannot be properly completed if the time delay fails. (You can review this kind of problem in Section 2.7.)

A typical time delay function is shown in Figure 2.30.

```
/*****************************************************************************
*                    Time Delay Subroutine                                  *
*****************************************************************************/
void delay(int nums)
{
        clock_t start;
        start = clock();

        int ms = 0;
        if (nums <= 0)
            return;
        while(elapsed <= nums)
          ms += 1;

        return;
}
```

FIGURE 2.30 The time delay function.

This function is straightforward. The argument `nums` is used to determine the length of the time delay.

The complete code for this project, including the header file, the source file, and an executable file, can be found in the folder `Chapter 2\SerialComm`, which is located on the attached CD.

We now have both the header and source files ready. Compile and build the program by clicking `Build|Build SerialComm.exe` on the menu bar. The project is ready to run if no error is encountered during the building process. However, this is only half of the complete project; we now must develop a program on the slave computer.

2.4.2 The Serial Port Communication Program on the Slave Side

The preceding program was developed on the master computer, but to fulfill our data communication project, we need to use that program to communicate with another program developed on the slave computer. In this section, we will create that program.

Recall that the slave computer's tasks are to receive the index sent by the master, which is the maximum amount of the data to be transmitted from the slave computer to the master computer, and to transmit the data required by the master under the synchronization control of the two computers. The data needs to be transmitted to the master computer in groups, and each data item in the group consists of two elements, which, in our case, are the position and the angle of the robotic location. Therefore, in addition to fulfilling the tasks just described, the slave computer needs to generate a group of simulated data, each of which is composed of two elements, the position and the angle. To make data generation simple, we'll use the system functions `sin()` and `cos()` to simulate the real positions and angles of the robotic locations.

Now let's begin to develop the program for the slave side.

Launch Visual C++ 6.0 and create a new project with the following properties:

- Project type: Win32 Console Application
- Project name: `SerialComms`
- Project location: `C:\Chapter 2`

TIP: The project location is a folder where you want the project to be stored on your computer. Here we've used `C:\Chapter 2`, but you can select any valid folder on your computer as the location for storing your project.

In the open project, create a new C/C++ header file named `SerialComms.h` and enter the code shown in Figure 2.31.

```
/*****************************************************************************
 * NAME: SerialComms.h
 * DATE: 7/16/2003
 * PGMR: Y. Bai  Copyright 2003 - 2007
 * DESC:  Header file for the serial communication between two computers
 *****************************************************************************/
#include <stdio.h>
#include <stdlib.h>
#include <conio.h>
#include <string.h>
#include <math.h>
#include <time.h>
#define MAXNUM       100              // Max data length
#define BYTE         unsigned char    // Data type
#define USHORT       unsigned short
#define T            50               // Sine/cos signals period
A  #define A         10               // Sine/cos signal amplitude
#define TMOUT1       2000             // Time out value for comm_start()
#define NUMS         20               // Time out value
B  USHORT     COM2  = 0x2f8;         // COM2 base address
USHORT        IER   = 0x2f9;          // COM2 Interrupt Enable Register
USHORT        LCR   = 0x2fb;          // COM2 Line Control Register
USHORT        MCR   = 0x2fc;          // COM2 Modem Control Register
USHORT        LSR   = 0x2fd;          // COM2 Line Status Register
USHORT        MSR   = 0x2fe;          // COM2 Modem Status Register
#define elapsed ((clock() - start)/ CLK_TCK)
C  bool   cosFl = false;
double pi    = 3.14159265;
double ds    = 180/pi;
struct serialDATA
{
    char pos[64];
    char ang[64];
};
D  struct serialSIGNAL
{
    double pos[MAXNUM];
    double ang[MAXNUM];
};
void   sinial();
void   delay(int nums);
BYTE   sends(char c, int nums);
BYTE   reces(int nums);
int    comm_start();
int    comm_collect(serialDATA* res, double spos, double sang);
int    get_index();
E  void   gen_signal(serialSIGNAL* sgl);
```

FIGURE 2.31 The Header File of the project in the slave computer.

Because of the similarity between the master-side and slave-side programs, only the code that differs from the master-side program will be explained here. For detailed explanations of the code that is similar, refer back to Section 2.4.2.

A: The different global constants are declared in this header file. The constants `T` and `A` are the period and the amplitude of the robot's simulated sinusoidal elements, positions and angles. These constants are not fixed so you can modify them for your applications if you like.

B: Global serial port variables are declared here. Because we want to use COM2 as our serial port on the slave computer, a sequence of addresses for the registers associated with COM2 is defined. After this definition, all symbol variables are associated with the registers used by the COM2 port.

C: The Boolean variable `cosF1` is used to identify the second simulated elements, the phase angles of the robot. In the program, we have two ways to generate the second elements. One way is to generate a group of simulated linear phase angles and the other way is to produce a group of simulated cosine phase angles. A group of cosine phase angles will be generated if `cosF1` is true; otherwise, a group of linear phase angles is produced.

The variables `pi` and `ds` are two coefficients used in the generation of the simulated elements. `pi` is a mathematical constant, and `ds` is used to translate the angular degree to the radian degree to meet the calculation requirement for the simulated elements.

D: The structure `serialSIGNAL` is declared here; this structure is used to store the generated element arrays, `pos[]` and `ang[]`, respectively. Each element array is used to hold a sequence of elements. Currently, we use 100 as the maximum size of the array, but you can use a different size for these two arrays, based on your application. The data type for each element is a double floating point.

E: One more function is added for the slave-side part of the project. This is the data generation function that is used, in this case, to create a group of simulated data, positions, and angles of the robot. One argument of this function is a pointer to the structure `serialSIGNAL` that includes two double arrays. The reason we use a pointer-type structure is that the generated elements can be stored in this structure when the function is called and returned. We could not get this storage by using a pass-by-value structure.

The `main( )` function of the slave-side computer program is shown in Figure 2.32.

F: The local variables are declared at the heading of the main function. The `FILE-type` pointer variable `fp` is used to hold the file handler when the desired file is opened. The two pointer-type structure variables are `sdata` and `ssgl`, and their protocols are `serialDATA` and `serialSIGNAL` structures. We have to create these two structure variables before we can use them in our program.

G: The system function `fopen()` is called to create a data file in which we will store the generated simulated elements that will later be sent to the master computer. The file path is `C:\data`, the file name is `serialCOMs.dat`, and the operation mode is writing `(w)`. The `fopen()` function will return a file handler if the function call is successful, and a `NULL` if an error is encountered as the function is executed. If an error occurs, the error information will be printed out and the program will be terminated.

H: The `malloc()` system function is executed to allocate memory space for two pointer-type structure variables, `sdata` and `ssgl`. The `sizeof()` function is used to define the size of the associated structure.

```
/*****************************************************************************
 * NAME: SerialComms.cpp
 * DATE:  7/16/2003
 * PRGM: Y. Bai - Copyright 2003 - 2007
 * DESC:  Use serial port communication between two computers.
          This program is for the Slave computer.
 *****************************************************************************/
#include "SerialComms.h"

void main()
{
    FILE* fp;
    int     rc, num, index;
F   serialDATA*   sdata;
    serialSIGNAL* ssgl;

    printf("\n***** WELCOME TO SERIAL PORTS COMMUNICATION ******\n");
G   fp = fopen("C:\\data\\serialCOMs.dat", "w");
    if (fp == NULL)
    {
        printf("File open error! program exit\n");
        return;
    }
H   sdata = (serialDATA* )malloc(sizeof(serialDATA));
    ssgl  = (serialSIGNAL* )malloc(sizeof(serialSIGNAL));
I   sinial();
J   rc = comm_start();
    if (rc != 0) { printf("Error in comm_start()\n"); return; }
K   index = get_index();
L   gen_signal(ssgl);
M   for (num = 0; num < index; num++)
    {
        rc = comm_start();
        if (rc != 0) { printf("Error in comm_start()\n"); return; }
        rc = comm_collect(sdata,  ssgl->pos[num],  ssgl->ang[num]);
        if (rc != 0)
        {
            printf("comm_collect() error \n");
            break;
        }
N       printf("%d - Sending pos =: %s\n", num, sdata ->pos);
        printf("%d - Sending ang =: %s\n", num, sdata ->ang);
        fprintf(fp, "%s    %s\n", sdata ->pos,  sdata ->ang);
    }
O   fclose(fp);
    delete sdata;  delete ssgl;
    printf("\n************* END OF THE TEST **************\n\n");
}
```

FIGURE 2.32 The `main()` Function in the Slave Computer.

I: The `sinial()` function is called to initialize the serial port on the slave computer and make it ready to communicate with the master computer.

J: Next, the synchronization function `comm_start()` is executed to coordinate the master and the slave computers so they can begin the data communication task. An error will be returned if this synchronization function fails, and the program will be terminated.

K: If the synchronization function is executed successfully, the `get_index()` function, which is a partner of the `send_index()` function on the master side, should be called to retrieve the size of the data element to be transmitted from the slave to the master.

L: After the data size is obtained, the `gen_signal()` function is executed to create the simulated data. The argument for this function is used to store the generated elements.

M: A `for` loop is run to continuously transmit the generated data to the master computer one group at a time. Before the slave computer can send each group of data, which includes a simulated position and angle, the synchronization function `comm_start()` needs to be executed to make both master and slave computers ready to perform the data exchange. After `comm_start()` is executed successfully, `comm_collect()` is called to send two elements, represented by the arguments `ssgl->pos[num]` and `ssgl->ang[num]`, to the master computer via serial port COM2. If this function encounters any mistake, the error information will be printed out and the program will be terminated.

N: If the returned value of the function `comm_collect()` is error-free `(0)`, the sent out data—position and angle—will be printed out and stored in the data file that was opened at the beginning of the main program.

O: Finally, the system function `fclose(fp)` is called to close the opened file and write all data to that file. The memory spaces allocated for two pointer-type structure variables, `sdata` and `ssgl`, are cleaned up by a call to the system destructor.

The next function we need to discuss is the synchronization function `comm_start()`, which is shown in Figure 2.33.

```
    int comm_start()
    {
            BYTE signal;
            int      rc = 0;
            clock_t start;
            start = clock();
P           while((reces(NUMS) != 's') & (elapsed < TMOUT1))
            {
               signal = reces(NUMS);
               if (signal == '?')
               {
                    printf("comm_start() error\n");
                    rc = -1;
                    break;
               }
            }
Q           signal = sends('c', NUMS);
            if (signal == '?')
            {
               printf("Error in comm_start()\n");
               rc = -1;
            }
            return rc;
    }
```

FIGURE 2.33 The synchronization function in the slave computer.

The synchronization function for the slave computer is a little different from the one for the master computer.

P: When `comm_start()` begins, a `while` loop is run to continuously execute the function `reces()`, which gets the starting signal coming from the master computer. The `while` loop will be terminated if one of the following three conditions is satisfied:
A timeout error occurs.
A data communication error occurs.
The starting character `s` is received.

If a communication error occurs, the error information will be printed out and the program will be terminated.

Q: If the start character s is received, the `sends()` function is called to send the feedback character c to the master computer. If an error occurs, the error information will be printed and returned to the calling function.

The next function for the slave computer is `get_index()`. This function is a partner of the master computer function `send_index()`. It is used to retrieve the data length that will be transmitted from the slave computer to the master computer, and it is sent by `send_index()` from the master computer. The function is shown in Figure 2.34.

```
  int get_index()
  {
      BYTE rc;
R     int   result, index = 0;
      char  buffer[8];

S     while((rc = reces(NUMS)) != '\0')
      {
          buffer[index] = rc;
          index++;
      }
T     buffer[index] = '\0';
      result = atoi(buffer);
      printf("Received index =: %d\n", result);

      return result;
  }
```

FIGURE 2.34 The `get_index()` function in the slave computer.

R: Local variables are declared here. The `buffer[]` variable is a character array used to hold the received characters. The `index`, or the position of the data, is transmitted as a sequence of characters (ASCII codes) from the master side.

S: A `while` loop is used to continuously retrieve each character and store it into the `buffer[]` one character at a time. The `while` loop will be terminated when a null character `(\0)` is received, which means that we have reached the end of the data and that no more characters are attached in the sequence.

T: When the null character is detected, we need to attach a null character at the end of the `buffer[]` to make it a standard C-code string. Additionally, `atoi()`, a system string function, is called to convert the received data in the string to a numeric integer. Finally, the resulting integer is returned to the function call as the received index.

On the slave computer, we need to generate a group of simulated data segments that represents the positions and angles of the robot. This job is fulfilled by a call to the `gen_signal()` function, which is shown in Figure 2.35, from the slave computer.

The argument in this function is a pointer-type structure, `sgl`. By using this kind of variable, we ensure that the generated elements can be easily stored into the heap area of memory.

U: A `for` loop is used to generate a sequence of positions and angles and to store them into the `sgl` structure—more specifically, to store them into two double arrays, `pos[]` and `ang[]`, respectively. `MAXNUM` is used as the upper boundary for the size of the array, which in this case is a fixed number. This number can be replaced by the index

```
  void gen_signal(serialSIGNAL* sgl)
  {
        int index;
U       for (index = 0; index < MAXNUM; index++)
        {
            sgl -> pos[index] = A*sin((pi/T)*index);
V           if (cosFl)
                sgl -> ang[index] = A*cos((pi/T)*index);
            else
                sgl -> ang[index] = ds*((pi/T)*index);
        }
  }
```

FIGURE 2.35 The `gen_signal()` function in the slave computer.

received from the `get_index()` function discussed earlier. The program generates simulated data by executing the system function `sin()` with the constants `A` and `T`.

V: As was previously mentioned, `cosFl` is a Boolean variable. The simulated phase angles can be generated using the system function `cos()` if this Boolean variable is `true`. Otherwise, the phase angles are generated by means of a linear function.

The function `comm_collect()` for the slave computer, which is shown in Figure 2.36, is similar to the one for the master computer. Only the different codes are explained here.

```
  int comm_collect(serialDATA* res, double spos, double sang)
  {
        BYTE signal;
        int num = 0, nump, numa;
W       int lens1, lens2, rc = 0;
X       lens1 = sprintf(res->pos, "%.2f", spos);
        lens2 = sprintf(res->ang, "%.2f", sang);
Y       for (nump = 0; nump <= lens1; nump++)
        {
            signal = sends(res->pos[nump], NUMS);
            if (signal == '?' || signal == '!')
            {
                printf("Error in comm_collect()\n");
                return -1;
            }
        }
Z       for (numa = 0; numa <= lens2; numa++)
        {
            signal = sends(res->ang[numa], NUMS);
            if (signal == '?' || signal == '!')
            {
                printf("Error in comm_collect()\n");
                return -1;
            }
        }
        return rc;
  }
```

FIGURE 2.36 The `comm_collect()` function in the slave computer.

W: All local variables are declared here. The integer variables `lens1` and `lens2` are used to hold the returning value from the system function `sprintf()`, which converts numeric data to string data in a certain format. The `sprintf()` function returns an integer value that indicates the length of the converted string, including the terminating null character (`\0`) attached at the end of the string.

X: Next, two `sprintf()` functions are called to convert the simulated position and angle elements from double type to string type. Three arguments are used in `sprintf()`. The first is the destination variable, where the converted string will be stored. The second is a format string used to indicate the data format to which the converted string should be adapted. Here we want to convert the data elements `spos` and `sang` to the associated string and display them in double-data form. Do not confuse the string in the double format with the double data; the former is a string variable and the latter is a numeric variable. The third argument in the `sprintf()` function is the source data that needs to be converted to the associated string variable.

Y: A `for` loop is used to send out the position string, one character at a time, by a call to the `sends()` function. The `for` loop will be terminated when one of the following two conditions is true:

The upper boundary `lens1` is detected. Note that `lens1` is included inside the `for` loop, which means that the last null character should also be converted and attached at the end of the converted string.

A communication error is detected. The error information will be printed out and the program will be terminated if this occurs.

Z: Similar to sending out the position string, the phase angle is sent out by a call to the `sends()` function. It is important to note that when string is sent out, it proceeds the character by character via the RS-232 port. Therefore, a `for` loop is needed to fulfill the transmission of the whole string.

At this point, we have finished examining most of the functions used in the slave computer portion of our project. The remaining functions used on the slave side are `sinial()`, `sends()`, `reces()` and `delay()`. These functions are identical with those used in the master-side program.

2.4.3 Testing the Serial Port Communication Program Using Two Computers

After you have entered all of these functions into the source file, compile and build the target file for the project. Click the `Build|Build SerialComms.exe` menu item on the menu bar in the Visual C++ 6.0 workspace to build the project. If no error occurs, it is time to test the project.

Generally, the master and slave projects should be located on two different computers, and the two computers should be connected with a null modem cable via their serial ports. In our case, the master computer uses the COM1 serial port and the slave computer uses COM2. The master-side program should be located on the master computer, and the slave-side program on the slave computer. To test the serial data communication between the two computers, follow these steps:

- For the master computer:

  Click `Build|Execute SerialComm.exe` on the menu bar.

  Enter the amount of data to be transmitted when the running window pops up. In our case, enter `100`, which is the upper limit of data to be transmitted, and press the `Enter` key on the keyboard.

  The master program will wait for the signal coming from the slave computer.

- For the slave computer:
  Click `Build|Execute SerialComms.exe` on the menu bar.
  The slave program will send the feedback signal to the master computer, and the data communication will begin.

On the screen, you will see the data being exchanged between the master and slave computers. The test result on the master computer is shown in Figure 2.37.

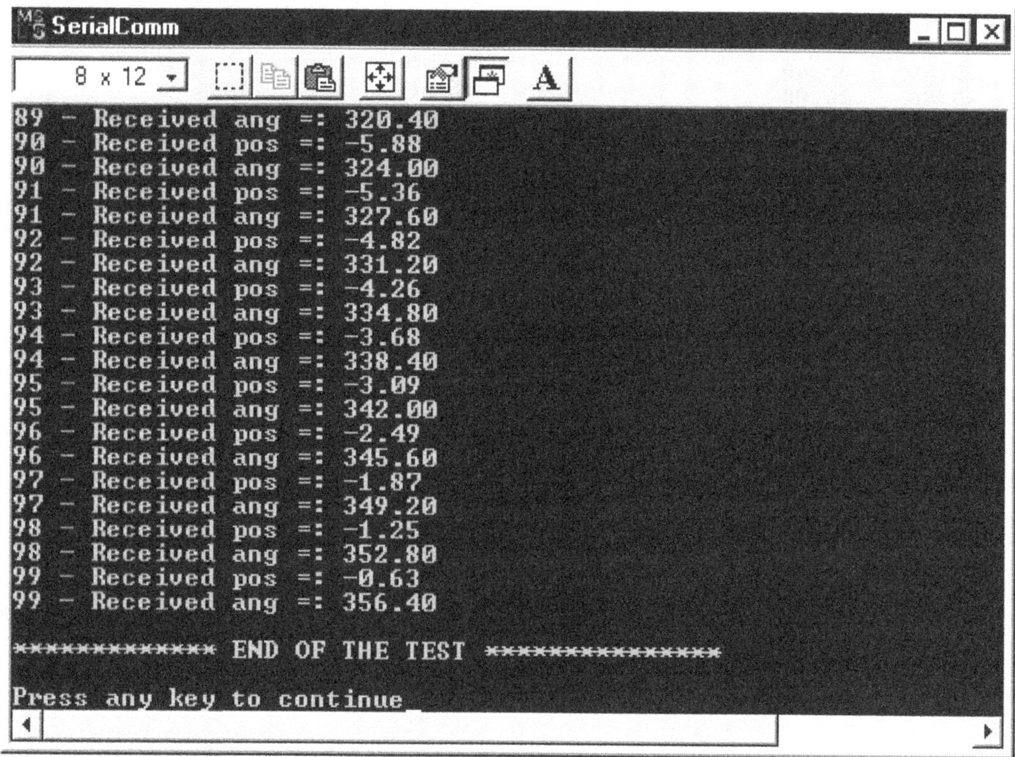

FIGURE 2.37 The test result of the serial communication on the master side.

When the test is finished, press any key, such as the `spacebar`, to terminate the program on both computers.

To confirm our test results, we can review the received data by opening the data file we stored during the data communication process; we can even plot the received data in graphic form to evaluate the data transmission.

The data file is located in the `C:\data` folder on the master computer, with the file name `serialCOM.dat`. You can review and plot the data from both computers. Here, we will try to evaluate the data communication for the master computer. Go to the data file folder and double-click the data file `serialCOM.dat` to open it. You will see that the received data is stored in two columns. The first column contains the positions, and the second contains the phase angles, as shown in Figure 2.38. (Note that the phase unit in Figure 2.38 is degrees, not radians).

To plot the data, we need to use the plot function in MATLAB. You can get a free 30-day evaluation of the MATLAB software by downloading it from the MATLAB home page. You will first need to complete a request form at the following Web site: http://www.mathworks.com/web_downloads/request.html. After downloading the MATLAB software, you will be ready to use the plot function to plot the test results.

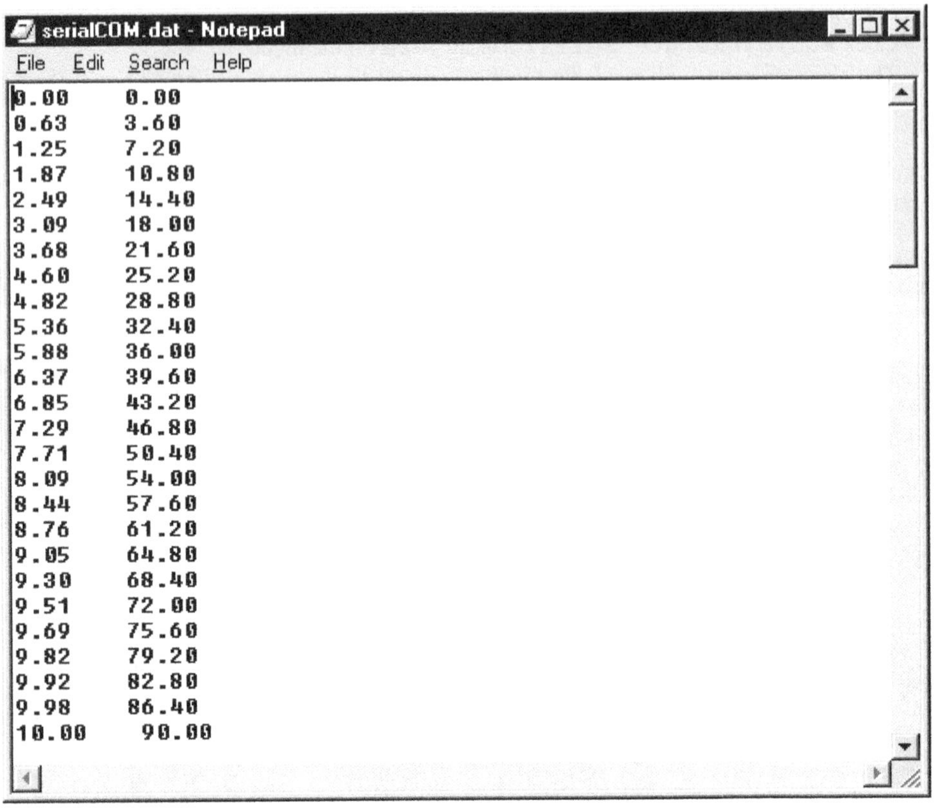

```
serialCOM.dat - Notepad
File  Edit  Search  Help
0.00    0.00
0.63    3.60
1.25    7.20
1.87    10.80
2.49    14.40
3.09    18.00
3.68    21.60
4.60    25.20
4.82    28.80
5.36    32.40
5.88    36.00
6.37    39.60
6.85    43.20
7.29    46.80
7.71    50.40
8.09    54.00
8.44    57.60
8.76    61.20
9.05    64.80
9.30    68.40
9.51    72.00
9.69    75.60
9.82    79.20
9.92    82.80
9.98    86.40
10.00    90.00
```

FIGURE 2.38 The result data file.

Open the MATLAB workspace and create a new M-file named `SerialCOM.m`; then enter the code shown in Figure 2.39.

A: The system function `fopen()` is used to open the data file, `serialCOM.dat`, which we created in the master program. Similar to a C-code function, this function returns a file handler `fid` if the file is successfully opened. The operation mode is read `(r)`.

B: Another system function, `fscanf()`, is called to retrieve the data from the data file smoothly. The first argument used in this function is the file handler obtained from the `fopen()` function previously discussed. The second argument is the format to which the destination data should adapt; Here we use the floating-point data format. The third argument is the amount of data to be picked up from the data file.

TIP: One point you must remember is that the original data file we created is a 100×2 array, which means that the data is stored in 100 rows and two columns. Each data item, which is composed of two elements, the position and the phase angle, occupies one row and two columns. To configure the function `fscanf()` to read out the data from this file correctly, you must transpose the dimension of the array from the original dimensions of 100×2 to the dimensions of 2×100 `([2, 100])`. This is a key point to remember when implementing the array in MATLAB. Without this step, an error will be encountered and the data readout will be not correct.

A new array variable `S` is used to hold the received data if `fscanf()` is executed successfully.

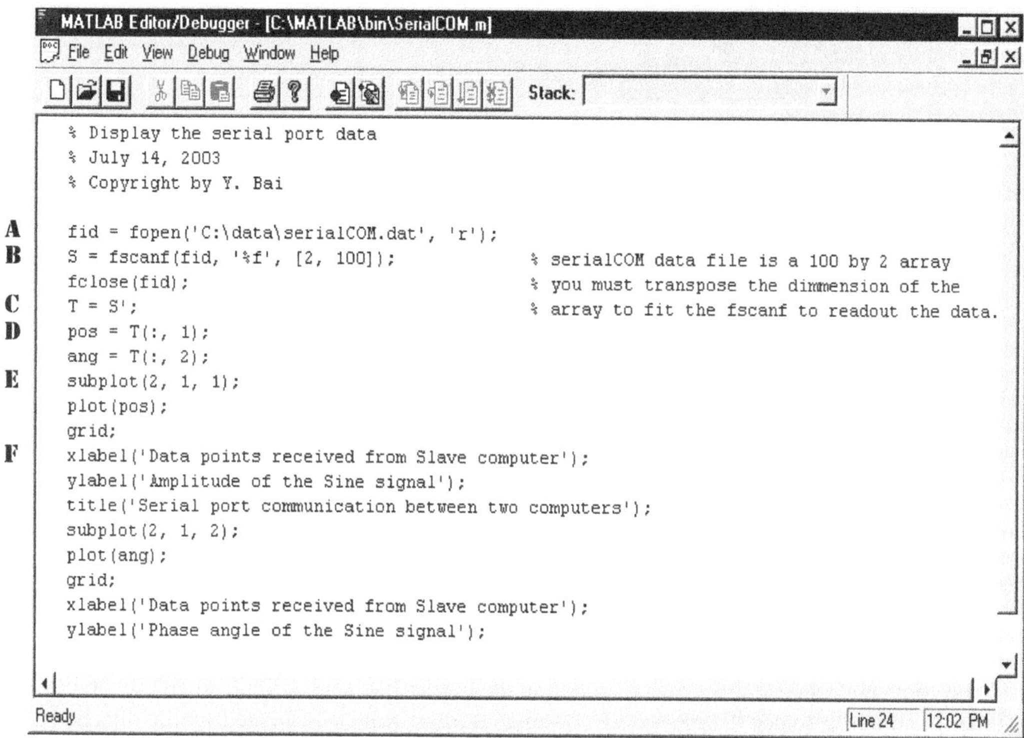

MATLAB Editor/Debugger - [C:\MATLAB\bin\SerialCOM.m]
File Edit View Debug Window Help
Stack:
% Display the serial port data
% July 14, 2003
% Copyright by Y. Bai
A fid = fopen('C:\data\serialCOM.dat', 'r');
B S = fscanf(fid, '%f', [2, 100]); % serialCOM data file is a 100 by 2 array
fclose(fid); % you must transpose the dimmension of the
C T = S'; % array to fit the fscanf to readout the data.
D pos = T(:, 1);
ang = T(:, 2);
E subplot(2, 1, 1);
plot(pos);
grid;
F xlabel('Data points received from Slave computer');
ylabel('Amplitude of the Sine signal');
title('Serial port communication between two computers');
subplot(2, 1, 2);
plot(ang);
grid;
xlabel('Data points received from Slave computer');
ylabel('Phase angle of the Sine signal');
Ready
Line 24
12:02 PM

FIGURE 2.39 The `serialCOM` plot function in MATLAB.

When the data is successfully obtained and stored in the array variable `S`, close the file by executing `fclose(fid)`.

C: Using a transposing operation, we return the data array to its original 100 × 2 format.

D: We can obtain two elements, position and angle, by picking up the column data separately. Each element is now an array with 100 × 1 elements.

E: The `subplot()` function in MATLAB is used to plot each element in a single graph. The first and second arguments represent the dimensions of the plot results. The numbers (2, 1) mean that the plot result is a graph 2 rows high and 1 column wide. The third argument is used to indicate which element is plotted. A 1 means that the first element is plotted at the top of the resulting plot. Following the `subplot()` function, the `plot()` function is executed to plot the position elements. The vertical axis represents the amplitude of the positions, and the horizontal axis represents the number of positions.

F: You can put labels on the plot to illustrate the functionality of the plotting by using MATLAB's `xlabel()`, `ylabel()`, and `title()` functions. Perform similar steps to plot the second element, angle, at the bottom of the resulting plot.

Save this file as `serialCOM.m` in the default MATLAB folder, `C:\MATLAB\bin`, on your master computer. (You can actually save this file in any searchable folder on your master computer, but to make the execution of this file easy, we selected the default folder.)

In the opened MATLAB workspace, type the file name `serialCOM` and press the `Enter` key. The MATLAB function `serialCOM.m` that is stored in the default folder will be executed immediately. The plot result is shown in Figure 2.40.

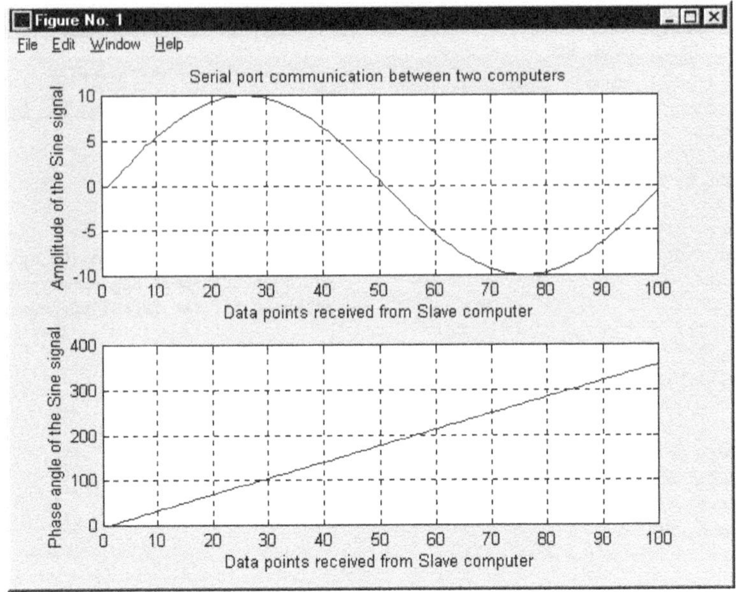

FIGURE 2.40 The plotting result of the received data.

The complete code for this project, including the header file, source file, and an executable file, can be found in the folder `Chapter 2\SerialComms`, which is located on the attached CD. The MATLAB file `serialCOM.m` is stored in both project folders, `Chapter 2\SerialComm` and `Chapter 2\SerialComms`, which correspond to the master and slave programs, respectively. To run these programs on your computer, you need to perform the following steps:

- Install the master project (`SerialComm`) on the master computer, and the slave project (`SerialComms`) on the slave computer.
- Connect two computers via their serial ports with a null modem cable. The header file will be modified based upon your port assignments. For example, if you use COM2 as the serial port of the master computer, you need to modify all constants associated with the serial port registers to match the base address of COM2. (That address is 0x2F8, not 0x3F8.) You will need to make similar modifications for the serial port of the slave computer if it uses COM2.
- Create a data file folder on the root drive to store the received data that will be plotted later. You can select any legal name for the data file folder, but in our case, `data` is used. All of the data files are stored in this folder, `C:\data`.

You will need to modify the code in your program if you have used a different data file folder on your computer.

In the next section, we will discuss how to embed inline assembly code into our ANSI C program and thus improve its serial data communications.

2.5 A SERIAL PORT COMMUNICATION PROGRAM DEVELOPED IN ANSI C AND INLINE ASSEMBLY CODE

To improve running speed, inline assembly instructions can be embedded into the C programs we developed in the last section. We can embed inline assembly code into both the master and the slave projects. The projects will operate more efficiently if we replace the original C instructions with assembly instructions for the lower-level subroutines, such as the `sinial()`, `sends()` and `reces()` functions. The main function and other functions used on the master and the slave computers are identical to those functions in the last section. First let's take a look at the master project.

2.5.1 Embedding Inline Assembly Code with the Master and the Slave Computers

Launch Visual C++ 6.0 and create a new project with the following properties:

- Project type: Win32 Console Application
- Project name: `SerialCommEmb`
- Project location: `C:\Chapter 2`

All of the functions in this project except the three low-level functions `sinial()`, `sends()`, and `reces()` are identical to those developed in the preceding section for the master computer. In the following sections, we will concentrate only on these three functions. Copy all of the functions from the last project, `SerialComm`, and modify the three functions `sinial()`, `sends()`, and `reces()`, as shown in Figures 2.41, 2.42, 2.43 and 2.44.

Figure 2.41 shows a part of the modified header file. The only changes in the file have been made to the functions `sends()` and `reces()`. The function `sends()` has only one argument, and the function `reces()` now has no argument.

```
......
struct serialDATA
{
      char   pos[64];
      char   ang[64];
      double dpos;
      double dang;
};
void    sinial();
BYTE sends(char c);
BYTE reces();
int     comm_start();
int     comm_collect(serialDATA* res);
int     send_index(int max);
```

FIGURE 2.41 A part of the modified header file.

Figure 2.42 shows the `sinial()` function, which is used to initialize the serial port before data communication can be started.

The workings of this piece of code are straightforward and require no explanation. Figures 2.43 and 2.44 show the `sends()` and `reces()` functions for the master side.

Both of these functions were discussed in Section 2.3.10. By compiling and building the project, we create an executable file, `SerialCommEmb.exe`.

The same modifications are performed for the slave computer. Create a new Win32 Console Application project named `SerialCommEmbs` on the slave computer; then copy all functions from the `SerialComms` program and paste them into the newly created project. Modify the header file and three functions as you have just done for the master computer project. A new project with embedded inline assembly instructions is generated. Compile and build the project. Now the project is ready to be run on both the master computer and the slave computer.

```
void sinial()
{
  _asm
  {
   mov dx, LCR          ; Select the Line Control Register to set up the comm. parameters.
   mov al, 80h          ; Bit7 = 1, 3f8h & 3f9h registers can access the baud rate divisor.
   out  dx, al          ; Nominal baud rate = 1843200/(baud rate*16).
   mov dx, COM1         ;
   mov al, 60h          ; b7 - b0 = (60h) = (01100000b) -> 3f8h (baud rate low-byte)
   out  dx, al          ;
   mov dx, IER          ;
   mov al, 00h          ; b7 - b0 = (00h) = (00000000b) -> 3f9h (baud rate high-byte)
   out  dx, al          ; Set up the baud rate high & low bytes (0060h -> 1200 baud rate).
   mov dx, LCR          ; Finish set up the Line Controller Register.
   mov al, 0bh          ; b7 - b0 = 0bh = (00001011b) -> odd parity, 1 stop bit, 8 data bits.
   out  dx, al          ; Set up LCR based on the above control parameters.
   mov dx, MCR          ; Set up MCR to set DTR & RTS to 1 (space or active).
   mov al, 03h          ; Self-test sub. if this line becomes "mov al,13h".
   out  dx, al          ; Finish set up the MCR.
   mov dx, IER          ; Set up the Interupt Enable Register.
   mov al, 0            ; No interrupt utilized.
   out  dx, al          ;
  }
}
```

FIGURE 2.42 The function `sinial()` in the master computer.

```
BYTE sends(char c)
{
   char feedback;
   _asm
   {
    done: mov    dx, LSR          ; Check the Line Status Register.
          in     al, dx           ; Inspect the state word.
          test   al, 20h          ; THR is empty? (when b5 = 1: THR is empty).
          jz     done             ; No, continuing to check it and waiting.
          mov    dx, COM1         ; THR is empty & ready to send the next character.
          mov    al, c            ; Assign character c to lower-byte in A register.
          mov    feedback, al     ; Return the sent-out character as a feedback
          out    dx, al           ; Send the character to the 8250.
          jmp    end
          mov    al, '?'          ; Error occurs, send '?' as a feedback
          mov    feedback, al     ; Return the error information.
     end: nop
   }
   return feedback;
}
```

FIGURE 2.43 The `sends()` function in the master computer.

After connecting the two computers with a null modem cable, run the program on the master computer by clicking `Build|Execute SerialCommEmb.exe` from the menu bar. After the master-side program has started, we can run the slave-side program. When prompted, enter `100` into the master computer for the size of the data segment to be transmitted. The two computers will yield similar results.

```
BYTE reces()
{
   char dd;
   _asm
   {                     ; Line Status Register Bit Definition
    done: mov dx, LSR    ; Check the Line Status Register   b0 = 1: Receive data is ready
          in   al, dx    ;                                   b1 = 1: Overrun error
          test al, 1eh   ; Detect any error happened?        b2 = 1: Parity error
          jnz  error     ; Yes, go to error processing.     b3 = 1: Framing error
          test al, 01h   ; The data is ready? (b0 = 1?)     b4 = 1: Break interrupt
          jz   done      ; No,continuing to check.          b5 = 1: THR is empty
          mov  dx, COM1; Data is ready                      b6 = 1: TSR is empty
          in   al, dx    ; Get the character from the       b7    is always zero
          mov  dd, al    ; Returning the character received.
          jmp  end       ;
   error:mov  dx, COM1 ; Error occurs.
          in   al, dx    ;
          mov  al, '?'   ; Return a '?' as an indicator of the error
          mov  dd, al
    end:  nop
   }
   return dd;
}
```

FIGURE 2.44 The `reces()` function in the master computer.

One of advantages of this project over the original serial port communication project we developed in Section 2.4 is that the execution speed is relatively faster because assembly code is used to replace the C code.

The complete code for this version of the master project, including the source file, header file, and executable file, can be found in the folder `Chapter 2\SerialCommEmb` located on the attached CD. The complete code, including the source file, header file, and executable file for the slave project can be found in `Chapter 2\SerialCommEmbs`.

2.6 AN INTERRUPT-DRIVEN SERIAL COMMUNICATIONS PROGRAM

In the previous sections, we discussed serial data communication in terms of a single port or double ports. The programs in those sections have a *polled I/O* operation style. While working in this style, the CPU is fully occupied by the serial interface program; it cannot perform any other tasks besides continuously looping and waiting for the THR to become empty (when sending data) or the RHR to become full (when receiving data). It is obvious that this style is inefficient due to the significant difference in the running speeds of the CPU and the serial peripheral devices. Today, most CPUs have running speeds as fast as 2 GHz, but most peripheral devices' running speeds are much slower. For example, the 56K modem has a baud rate of 56,000 bps. It can transmit about 7,000 bytes per second if this baud rate is used for serial data communication. For a 2 GHz CPU, its clock frequency is 2 GHz. Assuming its working clock frequency is 500 MHz (each working clock cycle contains four clock cycles), the processing speed of the data transmission is about 250 Mbps if two working clock cycles are needed to fulfill a single data operation from the internal bus. This results in a huge ratio between the working speeds of the CPU (250×10^6 bps) and the modem (7,000 bps). The CPU wastes a huge amount of time waiting to get its feedback from the terribly slow modem device. An efficient way to overcome this shortcoming in computer applications is to use interrupt operations.

2.6.1 The Interrupt Mechanism of the 8250 and 16550 UARTs

As we mentioned in section 1.6.7 of Chapter 1, the 8250 UART has an ability to generate an interrupt request for the system when some event or task in UART is finished, and this interrupt operation is very useful for the multitasking process. For example, when data is ready in the RHR, or the THR is empty, an associated interrupt can be generated by the 8250 UART and passed to the 8259 peripheral interrupt controller (PIC)— specifically, to the interrupt control register (ICR) in the 8259. The PIC can process the interrupt based on the interrupt vector and the content of the offset register to determine the interrupt request line (IRQ) number, and furthermore, to transfer control to the entry point of the interrupt service routine (ISR) to respond to the interrupt. (Review Figure 1.33 in Chapter 1 for a block diagram of the interrupt operation principle.)

Generally, you need to perform the following steps to make the 8250 UART and 8259 interrupt controller work together to enable, generate, and respond to an interrupt created by a peripheral device:

1. Correctly set up the interrupt enable register (IER) to allow the desired task to produce an interrupt once it has been completed. For example, if we want an interrupt to be generated when the UART receives data (meaning the RHR is ready), we should set a value of `1` on bit 0 in the IER. On the other side, we should set a value of `1` on bit 1 in the IER (refer to Figure 1-27 in Chapter 1) if we want an interrupt to be produced when data is sent out (which means the THR is empty) from the 8250 UART.
2. Properly set up the Modem Control Register (MCR) to turn on all interrupts you have selected from the IER. This will allow the interrupt signal to be passed from the desired device, such as the RHR, the THR, or any error register, to the INTRPT terminal in the 8250 UART. To turn on all interrupts in the 8250, you should set a value of `1` on bit 3, the `Output2` signal, in the MCR. (Refer to Figure 1-30 in Chapter 1.)
3. Properly set up the interrupt mask register (IMR) in the 8259 interrupt controller to enable the desired interrupt to occur. (Refer to Figure 1-34 in Chapter 1 for a detailed bit description of the IMR. For your convenience, this figure is redrawn as Figure 2.45.)

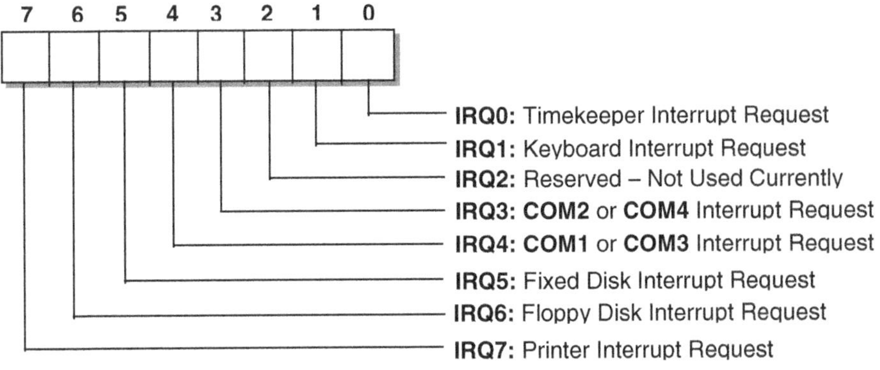

FIGURE 2.45 The 8259 Interrupt Mask Register (IMR).

To enable an interrupt, reset the associated IRQ bit to `0`. To disable an interrupt, set the associated IRQ bit to `1` to mask the interrupt. For example, to enable only a COM1 interrupt, set a byte of 11101111 (0EFH) on the IMR. A byte of 11100111 (0E7H) should be set on the IMR if both COM1 and COM2 interrupts are enabled.

4. Enter the correct entry address of the ISR into the associated IRQ interrupt vector. For example, if you want to use serial port COM1 as an interrupt source, you should enter the ISR entry address into interrupt vector 12 (refer to Figure 1-33 in Chapter 1), and if you want to use COM2 as the interrupt source you should put the ISR entry address into interrupt vector 11.

After you've completed these four steps, the computer is ready to handle and process the associated interrupts while your program runs.

Next, we will use a simple example to illustrate how to develop a program to enable, handle, and respond to the associated interrupts between the serial port, the keyboard, and the CPU.

2.6.2 A Sample Interrupt Program

This sample program consists of a main function and an interrupt subroutine. The serial port used for this program is COM1. The program performs the following functions:

- In the main function, a `do while` loop is used to continuously monitor whether a key is pressed on the keyboard by the user. If a key is pressed, the system function `getch()` is used to retrieve that character, and the `_outp()` function is called to send that character to COM1.
- The ISR is triggered by an interrupt source, which is the status of the RHR on COM1. As soon as data is received from COM1, its RHR will become full and the R_XRDY will be set to `1`. In the 16550 UART, this signal will not be triggered until the first-in-first-out (FIFO) buffer is nearly full, which means that there will be about 14 bytes of data stored in it. If the IMR is correctly configured, control will be transferred to the ISR, which will be executed when this interrupt is responded to.
- The ISR is also composed of a `do while` loop. As soon as a character is received, the ISR first checks the R_XRDY in the line state register (LSR) to confirm that data is available in the RHR. Next, the data is picked up and stored in a buffer. If all characters are collected, an end of instruction (EOI) notice is sent to the ICR in the 8259 to return the control from the ISR to the main function.
- When the ISR is complete and control has been returned to the main function, the character or character sequence stored in the buffer will be displayed on the screen inside the main function. The header file of this program is shown in Figure 2.46.

  A: Global constants and macros are declared and defined here. The macros `inportb` and `outportb` are used to represent the system functions `_inp()` and `_outp()`, respectively. The macros `getvect` and `setvect` represent the system functions `_dos_getvect` and `_dos_setvect`. ICR is the interrupt control register, addressed at `0x20`, and the IMR is the interrupt mask register, addressed at `0x21`. The constant `INTVECT (0x0C)` is the IRQ number of the serial port COM1.

  B: All registers used in the 8250 UART are defined as sequences of constants or symbols. The FIFO is the starting address of the first-in-first-out buffer. Both the THR and the RHR have the same address as the base address `(0x3F8)` of port COM1, so you can use COM1 to access either the THR or the RHR in the UART.

  C: Global variables are defined here. The `size` of the buffer is 1025. The variable `oldvect` is an unsigned long-type variable, and it is used to hold the default interrupt vector.

  D: The `oldvect()` function is a pointer function and `COM1INT()` is the interrupt handler program, or ISR, for COM1. If an interrupt is successfully captured by the

```
/*****************************************************************************
 * NAME: SerialInter.h
 * DATE:  7/18/2003
 * PGMR: Y. Bai  Copyright 2003 - 2007
 * DESC:   Header file for SerialInter.cpp.
 * NOTE:  This program can only be compiled by Microsoft C 6.0A or Turbo C++ 1.01.
 *****************************************************************************/
#include <dos.h>
#include <stdio.h>
#include <conio.h>
#include <stdlib.h>
#include <process.h>

#define       inportb       _inp
#define       outportb      _outp
#define       getvect       _dos_getvect
#define       setvect       _dos_setvect
#define       LENGTH        1025
A  #define    INTVECT       0x0C    /* Com Port's IRQ (Must change PIC setting) */

#define       USHORT        unsigned short
#define       BYTE          unsigned char
#define       ICR           0x20
#define       IMR           0x21

USHORT        COM1   = 0x3f8;          // COM1 base address
USHORT        IER    = 0x3f9;          // COM1 Interrupt Enable Register
USHORT        FIFO   = 0x3fa;          // COM1 FIFO buffer
B  USHORT     LCR    = 0x3fb;          // COM1 Line Control Register
USHORT        MCR    = 0x3fc;          // COM1 Modem Control Register
USHORT        LSR    = 0x3fd;          // COM1 Line Status Register
USHORT        MSR    = 0x3fe;          // COM1 Modem Status Register

C  int   bufferin  = 0;
int   bufferout = 0;
char rc;
char buffer[LENGTH];
unsigned long  oldvect;

D  void (_interrupt _far *oldvect)();
void (_interrupt _far COM1INT)();
```

FIGURE 2.46 The header file of the Interrupt Example Programs.

CPU, control will be transferred to this ISR and the interrupt request can be responded to inside the ISR. The interrupt service routine (ISR) is shown in Figure 2.47.

E: When the RHR or the FIFO is full, the R_XRDY in COM1 interrupt occurs. The control is transferred to `COM1INT()`, where the interrupt is processed and responded to. A `do while` loop is used to continuously check the status of bit 0 on the LSR in COM1 by reading the LSR.

F: If the value of bit 0 (R_XRDY) is `1`, which means that the RHR or the FIFO is full and data is ready to be picked up, the function `inportb()` is executed to retrieve the data and store it in the buffer. The data is picked up and stored in the buffer segment by segment, or character by character, and `bufferin` works as an index to define the location for each character stored in the buffer. This index will be reset to `0` if the size of the received data is more than 1,024 bits. This process will continue until the R_XRDY in the LSR is `0`, which means that all data has been collected and no more data exists in the RHR or the FIFO.

```
  /* Interrupt Service Routine (ISR) for COM1 */
  void (_interrupt _far COM1INT)()
  {
        BYTE c;
E       do {
              c = inportb(LSR);
              if (c & 1)
              {
F                 buffer[bufferin] = inportb(COM1);
                  bufferin++;
                  if (bufferin == LENGTH - 1)
                     bufferin = 0;
              }
         }while (c & 1);
G       outportb(ICR, 0x20);
  }
```

FIGURE 2.47 The Interrupt Service routine.

G: Before control can be transferred back the CPU and the ISR can be returned to the main function, an EOI notice should be sent to the interrupt control register in the 8259 interrupt controller to inform the controller that the ISR has been completed and control should be returned to the main function. The machine code of the EOI is, coincidentally, `0x20H`. When the controller receives this instruction, it will perform some postinterrupt tasks, such as cleaning up registers and memory spaces used for the interrupt, and will pop the content on the top of the stack to the programming counter to transfer control back to the main function. The main function is shown in Figure 2.48.

H: The first task the main function needs to perform is to turn off all interrupts on the COM1 serial port by sending a `0` to the IER in COM1 to mask all interrupt bits. The program must turn off all interrupts before the interrupt configuration to prevent any other possible interrupt from interfering. By executing the system functions `getvect()` and `setvect()`, we can pick up the old interrupt vector, store it into our temporary variable `oldvect`, and set up our new vector `COM1INT` in the system.

I: Next, we need to set up the COM1 serial port. We can configure the baud rate by setting bit 7 on the LCR, and now we can access the LSB and MSB registers of the baud rate divisor with the base addresses of COM1 `(03F8)` and IER `(03F9)`, respectively. The baud rate used in this program is 9600. The program sends the values `0x0C` and `0x00` to the baud rate divisor LSB and the MSB registers separately by executing the system function `outportb()` two times.

J: Now the data transmission format needs to be set up for this data communication. By sending `0x03` to the LCR, we set the data format as follows: eight-bit data bits, no parity, and one stop bit. We also enable the FIFO by setting the FIFO control register to `0xC7`. By sending `0x0B` to the MCR, we turn on the DTR, RTS, and OUT2 signals for COM1.

K: Now we need to select the interrupt sources by correctly setting up the IMR in COM1. (Refer to Figure 1-31 in Chapter 1.) By setting the IMR to 0xEF, we can unmask the interrupts coming from COM1 and COM3. But here, we only use COM1. Note that you can use either COM1 or COM3 for your port, not both, if you adapt the interrupt in your program. The computer will be confused if you used both ports in your program.

L: By sending `0x01` to the IER in COM1, we enable the R_XRDY to be the only interrupt source in this program. This means that as soon as data is received from COM1, its

```
/*****************************************************************************
 * NAME: SerialInter.cpp
 * DATE: 7/18/2003
 * PGMR: Y. Bai  Copyright 2003 - 2007
 * DESC:  Example interruption program.
 * NOTE: This program can only be compiled by Microsoft C 6.0A or Turbo C++ 1.01.
 *****************************************************************************/
#include "SerialInter.h"

void main(void)
{
     BYTE  c;
     outportb(IER, 0);                   /* Turn off interrupts - COM1 */
     oldvect = getvect(INTVECT);         /* Save old Interrupt Vector of later recovery */
H    setvect(INTVECT, COM1INT);          /* Set Interrupt Vector Entry */
                                         /* COM1, COM3 - 0x0C (Interrupt vector 12) */
                                         /* COM2, COM4 - 0x0B (Interrupt vector 11) */
// PORT 1 - Communication Settings
I    outportb(LCR, 0x80);                /* SET DLAB ON */
     outportb(COM1, 0x0C);               /* Set Baud rate - Divisor Latch Low Byte */
                                         /* Default 0x0C = 9,600 BPS */
     outportb(IER, 0x00);                /* Set Baud rate - Divisor Latch High Byte */
J    outportb(LCR, 0x03);                /* 8 Bits, No Parity, 1 Stop Bit */
     outportb(FIFO, 0xC7);               /* FIFO Control Register */
     outportb(MCR, 0x0B);                /* Turn on DTR, RTS, and OUT2 */
K    outportb(IMR,(inportb(IMR) & 0xEF)); /* Set Programmable Interrupt Controller */
                                         /* COM1, COM3 (IRQ4) - 0xEF */
                                         /* COM2, COM4 (IRQ3) - 0xF7 */
L    outportb(IER, 0x01);                /* Interrupt when data received – RxRDY */
M    printf("\nProgram running... Press ESC to quit \n");
     do{
           if (bufferin != bufferout)
           {
                rc = buffer[bufferout];
                bufferout++;
                if (bufferout == LENGTH - 1) { bufferout = 0; }
                printf(" %c", rc);
           }
N          if (kbhit())
           {
                c = getch();
                outportb(COM1, c);
           }
     }while (c != 27);                           /* 27 is equivalent to ESC */
O    outportb(IER, 0);                           /* Turn off interrupts - Port1 */
P    outportb(IMR, (inportb(IMR) | 0x10));       /* MASK IRQ using PIC */
                                                 /* COM1, COM3 (IRQ4) - 0x10 */
                                                 /* COM2, COM4 (IRQ3) - 0x08 */
Q    setvect(INTVECT, oldvect);                  /* Restore old interrupt vector */
     return;
}
```

FIGURE 2.48 The `main()` function body.

RHR will become full, the R_XRDY bit will be set to `1`, and an interrupt will be generated by the 8250 UART. This interrupt can be passed to the 8259 interrupt controller because we have already set up the IMR in the controller, and it can handle this interrupt (locate the IRQ) and pass it to the CPU to be further processed.

Next, the main function begins to perform a `do while` loop that will continuously monitor the status of the keyboard to see if a key has been pressed. To make this section clear, let's first take a look at section N.

N: Inside the `do while` loop, the system function `kbhit()` is used to determine whether a key has been pressed by the user. A `true` is returned if a key has been pressed. If this occurs, the pressed key or the character that is equivalent to the key is retrieved by another system function, `getch()`. Immediately, the received character is sent to COM1 to trigger an interrupt. As was previously mentioned, as soon as COM1 receives a character or the FIFO buffer is nearly full (which means that about 14 characters have been stored in it), an interrupt caused by the bit R_XRDY is generated. So it is equivalent to generate an interrupt when we send a character to COM1. (Refer to section F in Figure 2.47 for more details about the ISR.)
When a character is received by COM1 or the FIFO buffer is close to full and an interrupt occurs, that interrupt is transferred and processed by the interrupt service routine `COM1INT`. The routine's task is to pick up the received characters from COM1 and store them in the buffer one by one until the complete sequence of characters is processed. After the entire sequence of characters is stored, the ISR will be terminated and control will be returned to the main function so it can continue executing the instruction from which the interrupt (the instruction following the interrupted instruction) occurs.

M: As control is returned from the ISR to the `main()` function, the `main()` function is still continuously executed inside the `do while` loop. If the size of `bufferin` is not identical with that of `bufferout`, which means that a new character has been received and stored to the buffer by the ISR, the newly received character is picked up and displayed on the screen. This process will continue by increasing the index `bufferout` by one until all newly received characters are picked up and displayed on the screen. If the length of received character string is more then 1024, the next character will be wrapped to the beginning of the buffer. The `do while` loop, or the main function, is terminated as soon as the user presses the `ESC` key from the keyboard.

O: Before exiting the program, we need to turn off all the interrupts we previously turned on for COM1. We can do this by sending a 0 to the IER.

P: We now need to mask (inhibit) the interrupt of COM1 by masking bit 4 on the IMR, which is equivalent to sending a `0x10` to the IMR. (Refer to Figure 2.45.)

Q: Finally, we need to recover the original interrupt vector's content by executing the system function `setvect()`.

Note that this program must be compiled with one of the following compilers:

- Microsoft C 6.0A
- Turbo C++ 1.01

You cannot compile and run this program using Visual C++ 6.0. The source code and the header file for this project are provided in the folder `Chapter 2\SerialInter` on the attached CD.

2.7 PROGRAMMING THE INTERFACE BETWEEN PCS AND A/D CONVERTERS

This section covers the interface between serial ports and serial analog/digital (A/D) converters. With the continuing development of serial data communication and universal serial bus (USB) technology, more and more peripheral devices and equipment are being connected to and interfaced with computers using the serial mode. One of the most popular peripheral devices is the A/D converter. Any physical variables or signals existing in our real world—temperature, air pressure, humidity, the level of the liquid in a container, analog electronic current and voltage, the rotation speed of a motor, even a patients' blood pressure—must be converted to digital signals that can be accepted and processed by a computer. The signals can be either digital current or voltage. The implementation of A/D converters is a key in digital and computer control technology.

Developing interface programs to work with serial A/D converters is a good solution for items that exist in the real world. This discussion is divided into two major sections: the first section addresses the design and implementation of the interface program developed in ANSI C, and the second presents an interface program developed in ANSI C using inline assembly instructions. Two kinds of A/D converters are discussed here: one is the Texas Instruments™ TLC548, and the other is Maxim™ Integrated Products MAX187.

2.7.1 An Eight-Bit A/D Serial Interface Developed in ANSI C

The eight-bit A/D converter is a very popular converter and is applied in many industrial and commercial fields. In most applications, a special A/D interfacing card is needed to serve as a bridge between the computer and the A/D converter. In addition to the interfacing card, a specific device driver is also needed to drive the hardware of the A/D converter to communicate with the CPU and perform the data transfer and communication. It is obvious that these applications are neither economical nor simple in the real world.

When we use the RS-232 serial communication port and serial A/D converters, neither interfacing cards nor device drivers are needed. This option is not only low in cost, but it also simplifies the design and development of the A/D converting system.

2.7.1.1 The TLC548 Analog-to-Digital Converter

The TLC548 is a complementary metal oxide semiconductor (CMOS) analog-to-digital converter (ADC). It consists of integrated circuits built around an eight-bit switched-capacitor successive-approximation ADC. The TLC548 is designed for serial interface with a microprocessor or peripheral device through a three-state data output and one analog input. It uses the input/output clock (I/O clock) and the chip select (CS) inputs for data control. The maximum I/O clock input frequency of the TLC548 is 2.048 MHz.

The TLC548 operates under the control of the internal control logic unit and an internal system clock, and requires no external components. The on-chip system clock typically operates at 4MHz and allows internal device operation to proceed independently of serial I/O data timing, therefore permitting manipulation of the TLC548 as desired for a wide range of software and hardware requirements.

The I/O clock, along with the internal system clock, allows high-speed data transfer and conversion rates of 45500 conversions per second for the TLC548.

Additional TLC548 features include versatile control logic; an on-chip sample-and-hold circuit that can operate automatically or under microprocessor control; and a high-speed converter with differential high-impedance reference voltage inputs that ease radiometric conversion, scaling, and circuit isolation from logic and supply noises. The design of the totally switched-capacitor successive-approximation converter circuit allows conversion with a maximum total error of ±0.5 LSB in less than 17μs.

The block diagram of the internal structure of the TLC548 and an external top view of its package are shown in Figure 2.49 (a) and (b), respectively..

One of the most important features of the TLC548 is that it outputs data in serial format, so the digital output can be directly connected to a serial interface port, such as the RS-232 or RS-485, on a computer to perform many digital control tasks. In this program example, we develop an

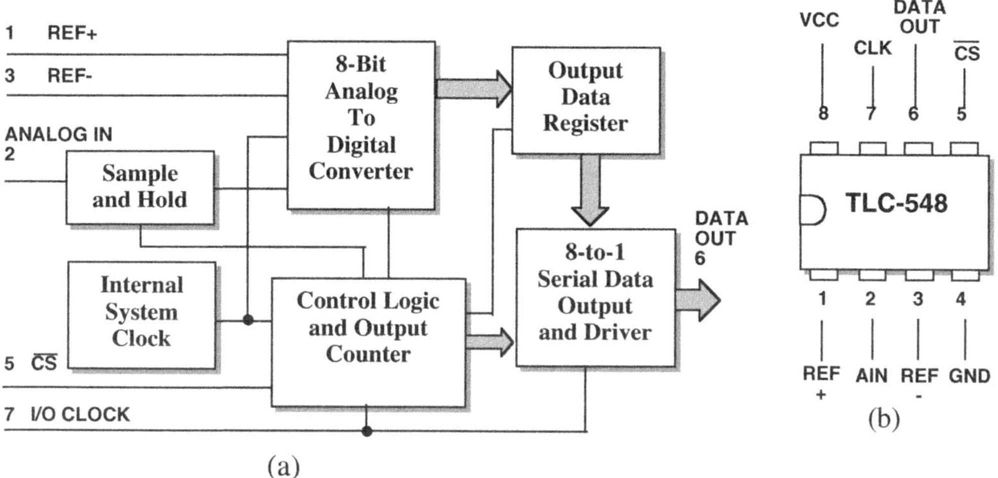

FIGURE 2.49 The structure of the TLC548.

interface between the computer and the TLC548 to collect the analog signals coming from the signal generator. You can replace the function generator with any actual physical signals in your applications. The functional block diagram of this project is shown in Figure 2.50.

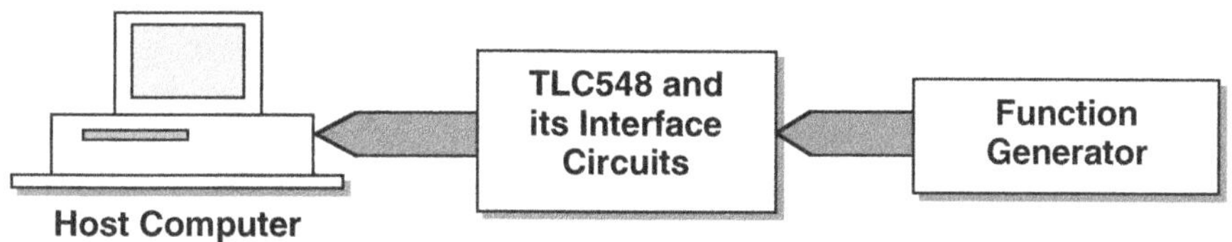

FIGURE 2.50 The functional block diagram of the interface.

A host computer is used as the controller to collect the digital output from the TLC548. The functional generator works as a simulated analog signal source or input to the TLC548. The interface program is located inside the host computer, where it can control and coordinate the data transfer between the ADC and the computer.

The operating system used in the host computer should be Windows 95/98/Me, because we will be developing our interface program in ANSI C for MS-DOS. The TLC 548 interface circuit is shown in Figure 2.51.

The elements parameters are listed in Table 2-5.

Make the hardware connection shown in Figure 2.51, based on the elements parameters in Table 2-5. Two advantages of this interface circuit are that it does not need an additional power supply, and that it is driven by the DTR signal in the RS-232 port. This DTR line can work as an enable signal, and the circuit will work properly as long as the DTR line outputs a value of `HIGH`, so we can use this line to activate or disable the circuit.

The RTS line works as the CS signal to select the TLC548 and let it begin to convert the analog input signal. As long as the power and the CS signal are activated, the TLC548 can immediately begin to convert the analog input automatically under the control of the internal control unit and the on-chip clock. To retrieve the converted result, the TLC548 needs an external I/O clock. Here the TD line is used as the I/O clock to serially transfer the converted result from the digital output (DOUT) of the TLC548, which is connected to the CTS line on the serial port, to the CTS transmission line. Therefore, the output rate is controlled by the frequency of the TD signal.

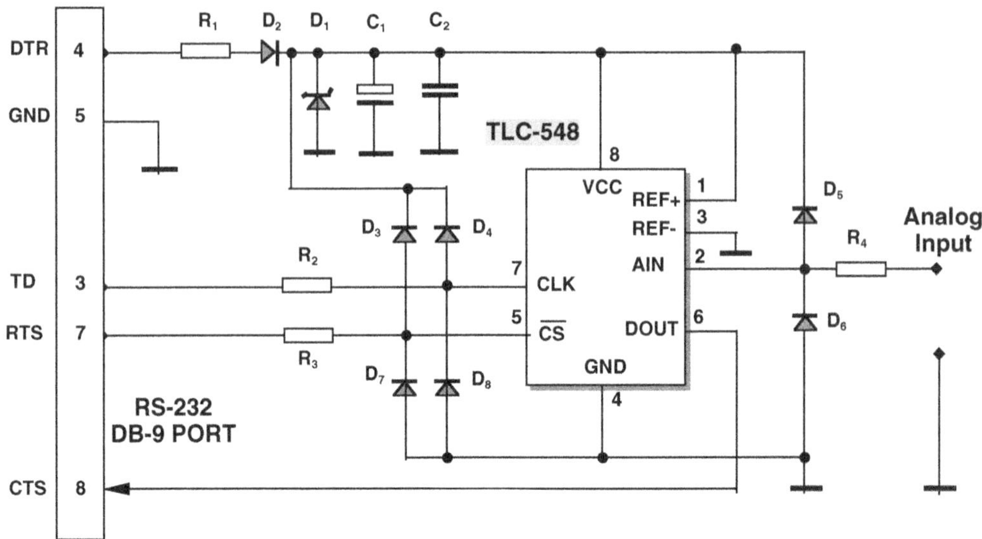

FIGURE 2.51 The TLC548 Interface Circuit. (The circuit diagram is reprinted by the permission of the author Tomi Engdahl at the site: http://www.hut.fi/Misc/Electronics/circuits/ad_serial.html.)

TABLE 2.5
Elements Parameters

Elements	Values	Comments
R_1	1 KΩ	Current-limited Resistor
R_2, R_3, R_4	30 KΩ	Current-limited Resistors
D_1	5.1 V	Zener Diode
$D_2 - D_8$	1N4148	Diodes
C_1	10 μF/15V	Electrolytic Capacitor
C_2	100 nF	Capacitor

Unlike traditional serial data communication, in which either hardware or software flow control is used, this data interface uses those signals as the control signals to drive the ADC and retrieve the converted result.

2.7.1.2 The TLC548 Serial Interface Program

Launch Visual C++ 6.0 and create a new project with the following properties:

- Project type: Win32 Console Application
- Project name: `SerialAD`
- Project location: `C:\Chapter 2`

Due to the simplicity of this program, no header file is necessary.

Create a new C++ source file named `SerialAD.cpp` and enter the body of the main function, shown in Figure 2.52, into the file.

A detailed explanation of the main function follows.

A: Global constants and the base address of the serial ports are defined as the associated symbols here. These symbols can be used to simplify your code by replacing them with

```
/*****************************************************************************
 * NAME: SerialAD.cpp
 * DATE: 7/3/2003
 * PRGR: Y. Bai - Copyright 2003 - 2007
 * DESC: Serial port interface program to communicate with a serial A/D converter
 *          (TLC-548) using C code
 *****************************************************************************/
#include <stdlib.h>
#include <stdio.h>
#include <dos.h>
#include <conio.h>
#include <string.h>

#define COM1          0x3F8
A #define COM2        0x2F8
#define BYTE          unsigned char
#define USHORT        unsigned short

void  Port_Init(USHORT c1, USHORT c2);
B BYTE Port_Read(USHORT r1, USHORT r2, USHORT r3);
void  delay(int num);

void main()
{
        FILE* fp;
C       BYTE  value[100];
        USHORT MCR, LCR, MSR;
        MCR = COM1 + 4; LCR = COM1 + 3; MSR = COM1 + 6;

        int index;

D       fp = fopen("C:\\SData\\Serial.dat", "w");
        if (fp == NULL)
        {
            printf("Error in open the file...\n");
            return;
        }
E       Port_Init(MCR, LCR);
F       for (index = 0; index < 100; index++)
        {
             value[index] = Port_Read(MCR, LCR, MSR);
             printf("The returned value is: %d\n", value[index]);
             fprintf(fp, "%d\n", value[index]);
        }
G       fclose(fp);
        Port_Init(MCR, LCR);

        return;
}
```

FIGURE 2.52 The main function body of the TLC548 Interface program.

the actual values in the program. For your convenience, both COM1 and COM2 are defined here in case you decide to use a different port for your application.

B: Three global functions are defined for this program. The `Port_Init()` function is used to initialize the selected serial port. The `Port_Read()` function is used to pick up the converted data from the TLC548 when the conversion is complete. The `delay()` function is used to delay for a certain period of time until the data on the transmission lines is stable.

C: Local variables are defined at the beginning of the main function. To make this example simple, we will try to collect a fixed set of data, 100 items, from the TLC548. The array value [] is used to hold this data. The FILE type variable fp is used to hold the handler of the opened file that will store the collected data, which we will use to plot a graph after the running the program. Unlike the header files we have developed in previous examples, in this program, we do not define each used register in the 8250 UART as a unique symbol. Instead, we use offsets and add the associated offset to the base address to obtain all other registers. The MCR, LCR, and MSR are defined in this way. Additionally, index is defined as the loop index to keep track of the position of each element we will retrieve from the TLC548.

D: The fopen() system function is executed to open a new data file that will store the collected data. The path of the data file is C:\Sdata, and its name is Serial.dat. If the file is successfully opened, the opened file handler is returned and stored to fp. Otherwise, a null value is returned to indicate that an error has occurred during the file-opening operation. The error information will be printed out, and the program will be terminated.

E: The function Port_Init() is called to initialize the selected serial port. Two arguments are passed in this function call. The first argument, MCR, is used to set the DTR line and the second argument, LCR, is used to reset the clock input to the TLC548.

F: A for loop is used to continuously retrieve the converted data from the TLC548. For each loop cycle, the Port_Read() function is executed to pick up converted data, and the retrieved data is stored into the array value[] one item at a time. The received data is also printed out on the screen and stored in the data file we opened at the beginning of the program. Note that the data is in integer format, which is equivalent to a sequence of raw data or an absolute integer sequence without any unit. You can modify this data type by multiplying it by a scalar factor that meets the requirement for your application.

G: When all data has been collected, the system function fclose() is called to close the data file and write all data to the file. The function Port_Init() is called again to clean up the environment of the interface circuit for the next conversion.

The Port_Init() and delay() functions are shown in Figure 2.53; both are straightforward.

```
/*****************************************************************************
 *                Initialize the serial port function                        *
 *****************************************************************************/
void Port_Init(USHORT c1, USHORT c2)
{
        printf("Initializing the port...\n");
H       _outp(c1, 3);                    // Set DTR to supply power/set CS to 1
        _outp(c2, 0);                    // Reset clock to 0 (LCR)
        return;
}
/*****************************************************************************
 *                Time delay function                                        *
 *****************************************************************************/
void delay(int num)
{
I       int nn, mm = 1000;
        for (nn = 0; nn < num * 100; nn++)
            mm = mm--;
        return;
}
```

FIGURE 2.53 The port initialization and time delay functions.

H: The task of the `Port_Init()` function is to set both the DTR and the RTS to `HIGH`. (Refer to Figure 1-30 in Chapter 1 for a description of the bit function of the MCR.) Bit 0 is associated with the DTR signal, and bit 1 is mapped to the RTS signal. A value of `1` in bit 0 means that the DTR line is activated and a `HIGH` value is present. This value works as the power supply for the TLC548 and should be kept unchanged during the ADC's working period. A value of `1` in bit 1 means that the RTS line is set to `HIGH`. Because the RTS line is connected to the CS in the TLC548 and the activated status of the CS is `LOW`, a `HIGH` in the CS is equivalent to disabling the CS, therefore the TLC548 is not selected.

Next, the LCR is reset to `0`. (Refer to Figure 1-29 in Chapter 1.) Bit 6 on the LCR is mapped to the `Break` signal. The TD line will output a `HIGH` value if bit 6 on the LCR is set to 1; it keeps its `LOW` value when bit 6 on the LCR is `0`. (Notice in Figure 2.51 that this TD line is connected to the `CLK` input on the TLC548, so the output of the TD line works as a clock signal to the TLC548.) Resetting the LCR to `0` is equivalent to resetting the TD output to `0` and indicates that there is no clock input for the TLC548.

I: The time delay function in this program is not a standard delay function. In a standard time delay function, the `clock()` system function would be adapted to mark the elapsed time and compare it with the desired time interval to determine the period to be delayed. Here, only an approximate time count is used. This time delay is not used in this program, but in some situations, it is a critical factor and can determine whether the A/D conversion is successful or not. An example of using the time delay is presented in the next section. The `Port_Read()` function is shown in Figure 2.54.

```
/*****************************************************************************
 *            Retrieve the converted result from the TLC548 function         *
 *****************************************************************************/
BYTE Port_Read(USHORT r1, USHORT r2, USHORT r3)
{
    int     index;
    BYTE value = 0, bValue;

J   _outp(r1, 1);                   //reset RTS to activate CS
K   for (index = 0; index < 8; index++)
    {
        value = value << 1;
L       _outp(r2, 0x40);            //clock high
M //     _outp(COM1, 0xff);          //sometimes you need this line to activate the TLC-548
N       bValue = _inp(r3);
        if (bValue & 0x10)
        {
            value++;
        }
O       _outp(r2, 0);               //clock low
    }
P   _outp(r1, 3);                   //CS high (deselect TLC-548)
    return value;
}
```

FIGURE 2.54 The `Port_Read()` function for the TLC548.

J: Three arguments are passed to this function and they are associated with three registers: MCR `(r1)`, LCR `(r2)` and MSR `(r3)`. The system function `_outp(r1, 1)` is executed to perform the following tasks on the MCR:
Keeping the DTR line output `HIGH` to provide the power to the TLC548 by setting bit 0 on the MCR
Resetting the RTS to `LOW` to activate the CS in the TLC548 to select the ADC by resetting bit 1 on the MCR to 0.

These functionalities are equivalent to setting the MCR to 1 (0x01).

K: A `for` loop is used to read back eight-bit data from the TLC548. Because the converted data of the TLC548 is serially transmitted bit by bit from the DOUT on the TLC548, eight clock cycles are needed to complete this eight-bit data transmission. The retrieved eight-bit data is stored in the variable `value`. Because the data is transmitted to `value` one bit at a time, a shift-left operation is needed. The starting bit is bit 0. Each time a bit is received, it should be added to the variable `value` from the LSB, then the variable `value` will be shifted one bit to the left. This process is continued until all eight bits of data are received.

L: The function `_outp(r2, 0x40)` is called to set bit 6 on the LCR to `1`. (Refer to Figure 1-29 in Chapter 1.) Setting a value of `1` to bit 6 on the LCR is equivalent to setting the `Break` signal, or setting the TD line to `HIGH`. Because the TD line is connected to the `CLK` input on the TLC548, this setting is equivalent to setting the `CLK` value to `HIGH` to direct the TLC548 to begin transmitting the first bit of converted data.

M: This line is very important in practical applications. In some cases, the TLC548 cannot be started properly, and you need to execute this line to send a `HIGH` to the TD line, and therefore to the `CLK` of the TLC548, to force the `CLK` to `HIGH`. Executing the function `_outp(COM1, 0xff)` is equivalent to sending a `HIGH` value to the TD line, and therefore to the `CLK`.

TIP: The author has often experienced this starting problem during experiments. If the received data from the TLC548 is either all 0 or all 0xff, you will need to activate this line in your program to trigger the TLC548 to start the data conversion. You may comment out this line once your system and your program work properly.

N: Once the `CLK` input is activated, data conversion on the TLC548 begins. The output data bit will be sent out serially from the DOUT on the TLC548. This DOUT output is connected to the CTS line on the serial port. By executing the function `_inp(r3)`, which is equivalent to inputting the status of the MSR, we can check whether the output bit value is `1` or `0`. (Refer to Figure 1-32 in Chapter 1.) Bit 4 on the MSR represents the current status of the CTS line. If this bit's value is `1` (0x10), it means that the received bit's value is `1` and therefore that the variable value should be increased by 1. Otherwise, a 0 is received, and the program need not do anything.

O: By executing the function `_outp(r2, 0)`, we reset the LCR and therefore reset the `CLK` on the TLC548 to `0`. The `for` loop will be continued to pick up and process the next bit if all eight bits have not been retrieved.

P: Finally after all eight bits of data have been received and stored, the function `_outp(r1, 3)` is called to reset the COM1 port. The received data stored in the variable `value` is one byte (eight bits), and is returned to the main function.

Now it is time to compile and build the entire program. From the menu bar in the Visual C++ 6.0 work environment, click the `Build|Build SerialAD.exe` menu item to compile and build the target program, if no compiling error occurs, click the `Build|Execute SerialAD.exe` menu item to run the program.

The results of running the program are shown in Figure 2.55.

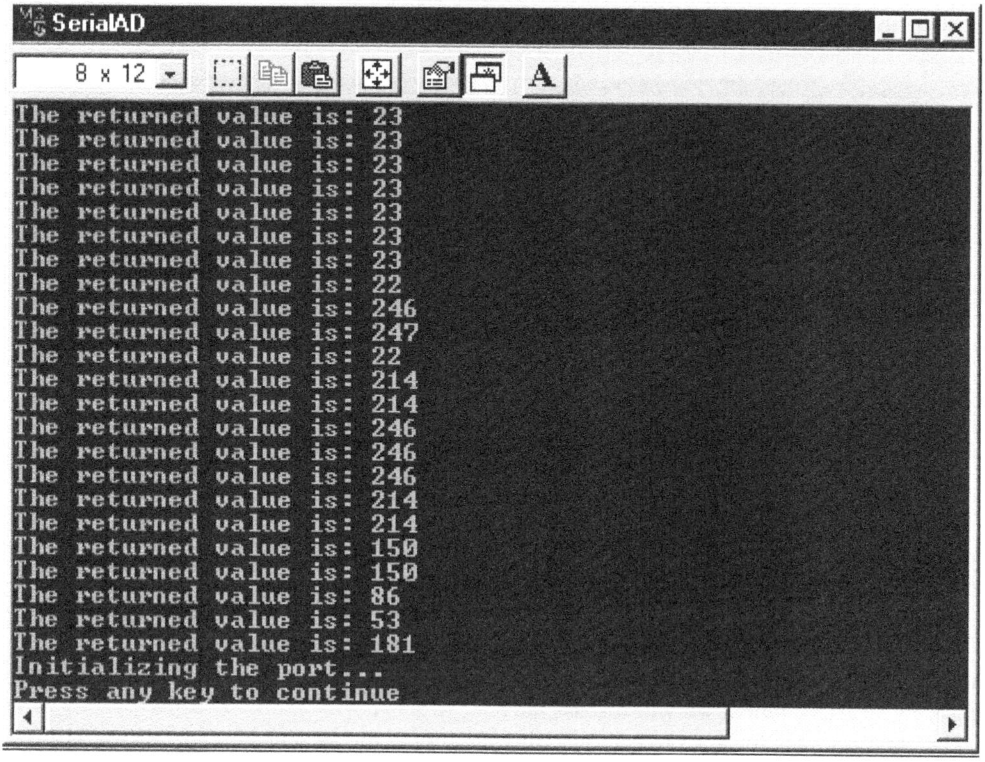

```
SerialAD
8 x 12
The returned value is: 23
The returned value is: 23
The returned value is: 23
The returned value is: 23
The returned value is: 23
The returned value is: 23
The returned value is: 23
The returned value is: 22
The returned value is: 246
The returned value is: 247
The returned value is: 22
The returned value is: 214
The returned value is: 214
The returned value is: 246
The returned value is: 246
The returned value is: 246
The returned value is: 214
The returned value is: 214
The returned value is: 150
The returned value is: 150
The returned value is: 86
The returned value is: 53
The returned value is: 181
Initializing the port...
Press any key to continue
```

FIGURE 2.55 The running result of the `SerialAD` project.

The input signal for the TLC548 is a sinusoidal waveform, with an amplitude of 5V and a frequency of 60Hz, which is comes from a function generator.

As with our preceding project, we can plot the received data using the `plot()` function in MATLAB to display the waveform. To do this, we need to develop a MATLAB M-file named `Serial.m`. Open the MATLAB workspace and create a new M-file; then enter the code shown in Figure 2.56.

```
% Display the serial port data retrieved from the TLC548
% July 3, 2003
% Copyright by Y. Bai

fid = fopen('C:/SData/Serial.dat', 'rt');
S = fscanf(fid, '%d');
plot(S);
grid;
fclose(fid);
```

FIGURE 2.56 Using MATLAB plot function to plot the A/D data.

The code is straightforward. The `fopen()` function is used to open the data file we created when running the C program. The operation mode is `rt`, which means that the data is read out in text format. You can use `rb` if you want to read the file in binary format.

Different waveforms, such as the sinusoidal, square, and triangle waveforms are input into the TLC548. Each waveform is plotted by the MATLAB `plot()` function on a separate graph. The collected sinusoidal and square waveforms are shown in Figure 2.57 (a) and (b).

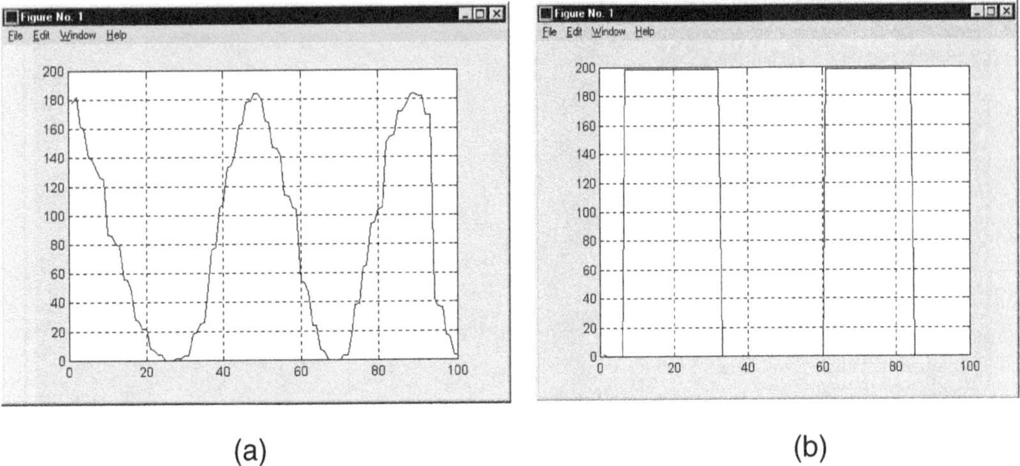

FIGURE 2.57 The Plot of the TLC548 Conversion Result.

Notice that the plotted waveforms in Figure 2.57 are not as smooth as we might have hoped. This is due to the resolution limitations of the eight-bit ADC. This resolution can be improved by using a 12-bit ADC, which we will discuss later.

The complete files for this project, including the source file, executable file, and the MATLAB M-file, are stored in the folder `Chapter 2\SerialAD`, which is located on the attached CD. To run this project, you need to create a path for the data file on your root drive (typically `C:\SData`).

Due to the limitations on the sampling rate using C code, the plot result is not smooth. One of the possible ways to improve the sampling rate is to speed up data collection during the data conversion process. As we know, when assembly code is used, the execution speed of a program can be significantly improved. In the next section, we will try to modify this A/D conversion program by adding inline assembly instructions to improve the sampling rate of the A/D conversion.

2.7.2 An Eight-Bit A/D Serial Interface Developed in ANSI C and Inline Assembly Code

In this section, we will discuss how to embed inline assembly instructions into the C code to improve the sampling rate on the eight-bit ADC. The difference between this project and the previous one is that the low-level instructions that access the serial port have been replaced by assembly codes.

The hardware in this project, including the TLC548 interface circuit and the interface connection, are identical with those in the previous project. Refer to Figure 2.51 to set up the hardware connection for this project. The serial port is still COM1. The analog input still comes from a function generator.

Launch Visual C++ 6.0 and create a new Win32 Console application named `SerialADEmbed`. Create a new header file named `SerialADEmbed.h`, and enter the code shown in Figure 2.58.

```
/*****************************************************************************
 * NAME: SerialADEmbed.h
 * DATE: 7/5/2003
 * PRGR: Y. Bai - Copyright 2003 - 2007
 * DESC: Header file for serial A/D converter testing program
 *****************************************************************************/
#include <stdio.h>
#include <stdlib.h>
#include <string.h>
#include <conio.h>

  #define  MAXNUM   100              // Max data length
  #define  BYTE     unsigned char    // Data type
A #define  USHORT   unsigned short
  #define  COM1     3f8h             // COM1 base address
  #define  IER      3f9h             // COM1 Interrupt Enable Register
  #define  LCR      3fbh             // COM1 Line Control Register
  #define  MCR      3fch             // COM1 Modem Control Register
  #define  LSR      3fdh             // COM1 Line Status Register
  #define  MSR      3feh             // COM1 Modem Status Register

B void  Port_Init();
  void  c_inial();
  BYTE  Port_Read();
  BYTE  c_getad();
```

FIGURE 2.58 The header file of the `SerialADEmbed` project.

A: The global constants and data types are declared in this header file. Most registers used in this project are mapped to the associated constant. The serial port connected to the TLC548 is COM1.

B: Four functions are used in this program. Besides `Port_Init()` and the `Port_Read()`, two additional functions, `c_inial()` and `c_getad()`, are added to this program. The inline assembly instructions are embedded in these two additional functions to improve the running speed of the program, as well as the actual data conversion. Figure 2.59 shows the main function of this program.

In the main function, the user header file `SerialADEmbed.h` is enclosed, which enables the main function to use the global constants and functions defined in the header file.

C: The local variables and data array are defined here. `fp` is the file pointer that is used to hold the returned file handler. `value[]` is a data array that stores the received data.

D: The system function `scanf()` is called to pick up the answer entered by the user to begin the program. Note that the second argument of this function is a pointer-type variable, not a regular variable, so the address operator `&` is applied in front of the character variable `cc`.

E: The `Port_Init()` function is executed to initialize the serial port COM1.

F: The `fopen()` function is called to open a new data file named `Serialad.dat`. This data file is located in the folder `C:\SData`, and the operation mode is write `(w)`. The file handler will be returned if this function call is successful; otherwise a `null` value is returned to indicate that an error has occurred during execution of the function. If an error occurs, the error information is printed out and the program is terminated.

G: A `for` loop is used to continuously collect the data coming from the TLC548. Each data segment is retrieved by a call to the `Port_Read()` function and is stored in the

```
/*****************************************************************************
 * NAME: SerialADEmbed.cpp
 * DATE: 7/5/2003
 * PRGR: Y. Bai - Copyright 2003 - 2007
 * DESC: Embedded assembly code (intel 8088/80x86) to communicate with a serial A/D
 *          converter (TLC-548) to get analog signal inputs from a RS-232 port
 *****************************************************************************/
#include "SerialADEmbed.h"
void main()
{
      FILE* fp;
      char    cc;
C     int     index;
      BYTE  value[100];
      printf("\n****** WELCOME TO SERIAL A/D CONVERTER TESTING *****\n");
      printf("\nBegin the A/D conversion? y/n\n");
D     scanf("%c", &cc);
      if (cc == 'y' || cc == 'Y')
      {
E           Port_Init();
F           fp = fopen("C:\\SData\\Serialad.dat", "w");
            if (fp == NULL)
            {
                  printf("File open error! program exit\n");
                  return;
            }
G           for (index = 0; index < MAXNUM; index++)
            {
                  value[index] = Port_Read();
                  printf("Received data =: %d\n", value[index]);
                  fprintf(fp, "%d\n", value[index]);
            }
H           fclose(fp);
      }
      printf("\n************* END OF THE TEST ***************\n\n");
}
```

FIGURE 2.59 The main function body of the `SerialADEmbed` project.

data array `value[]`. The received data is also printed out on the screen and stored in the opened data file `Serialad.dat`.

H: Finally the function `fclose()` is called to close the data file and write all data into the data file. The functions `Port_Init()` and `c_inial()` are shown in Figure 2.60.

I: The function `c_inial()` is an inline assembly function that is called by the `Port_Init()` function to initialize the port COM1.

J: The inline assembly code starts with the keyword `_asm`. The MCR's address, which is defined as a global constant, is sent to the address register `dx`, and a value of `0x03` is assigned to the `al` register. Executing the assembly instructions `out dx, al`, sends the `0x03` to the MCR in port COM1. This is equivalent to setting both the DTR and the RTS lines to `HIGH` to enable power for the TLC548 and to reset the CS signal on the TLC548 so that it deselects the A/D converter.

K: Resetting bit 6 (the `Break` signal) in LCR in port COM1 to `0`, the TD line in COM 1, which is connected to the `CLK` input on the TLC548, is therefore reset to `0`, and is thus disabled. Initialization of the serial port and the TLC548 is now complete. The functions `Port_Read()` and `c_getad()` are shown in Figure 2.61.

```
  void Port_Init()
  {
      printf("\nBegin to initialize the serial port...\n");
I     c_inial();
      return;
  }
  void c_inial()
  {
      _asm
J     {
         mov dx, MCR   ; Set up MCR to set DTR & RTS to 1 (space or active).
         mov al, 03h   ; Output power (DTR = 1) & disable CS of TLC548 (RTS = 1).
         out  dx, al   ; Finish set up the MCR.
K        mov dx, LCR   ; Select the Line Control Register to set up the clock of TLC548.
         mov al, 00h   ;
         out  dx, al   ; Disable the AD clock.
      }
  }
```

FIGURE 2.60 The `port Intialization` function.

L: The `c_getad()` function is an inline assembly function called by the `Port_Read()` function to retrieve the output of the TLC548. The returned result is stored to the variable `value`. The variable `value` is in turn stored to the data array `value[]` in the main function.

M: The inline assembly instructions start with the keyword `_asm`.

N: Setting a value of `0x01` to the MCR sets the DTR line to `HIGH` and resets the RTS line to `0`. These two lines are connected to the `VCC` and the CS, respectively, on the TLC548 A/D converter.. The consequences of this setup are that the power of the TLC548 is provided by the `HIGH` output of the DTR line, and the TLC548 is selected by resetting the RTS line to `LOW`. Refer to Figure 2.51 for the hardware connection. Now the TLC548 is ready to perform the data conversion.

O: The system register `cx` is used as a counter to monitor the data until eight bits is received. The program initializes this register by assigning it a constant value of `08h`. The system register `bl` is used to store the received data bit, so a `0` is assigned to this register to initialize it.

P: Executing the assembly instruction `shl bl, 1`, shifts the data stored in the `bl` register left by one bit. Because the received data is coming from the output of the TLC548, and the data is transmitted serially bit by bit, a shift operation is needed to move all eight bits of data into the `bl` register.

Q: Setting the 40h to the LCR assigns the `Break` signal bit a value of `1`. This signal will force the TD line to `HIGH`, and will also set the `CLK` on the TLC548 to `HIGH` to start the data conversion on the TLC548, because the `TD` line is connected to the `CLK` input on the TLC548.

R: These three lines of assembly codes are generally commented out, and if the TLC548 can be started properly, we do not need to use these three lines of codes at all. But as mentioned in the preceding section, in some cases the TLC548 cannot be triggered to work properly, so you may need to use these three lines of codes to start the TLC548. You can comment out these three lines of codes once the TLC548 is working properly.

These three lines are used to send a value of `08h` to the THR in the port COM1. When performing this operation, the TD line is also set to `HIGH` and this is equivalent to setting the `CLK` on the TLC548 to `HIGH` to start the A/D converter.

```
    BYTE Port_Read()
    {
        BYTE value;
L       value = c_getad();
        return value;
    }
    BYTE c_getad()
    {
        BYTE rc;
M       _asm
        {
N           mov  dx, MCR    ; Reset MCR - RTS to 0 (CS of TLC548 active - low).
            mov  al, 01h    ; Still keep output power (DTR = 1).
            out  dx, al     ; Finish set up the MCR.
O           mov  cx, 08h    ; Setup the counter of the reading loop
            mov  bl, 00h    ; Initialize the result (bl is used to store the result).
P     get: shl   bl, 1      ; Multiple result by 2 (equivalent to shift bl left with 1 bit).
            mov dx, LCR     ; Select the Line Control Register to active the clock of TLC548.
Q           mov al, 40h     ;
            out  dx, al     ; Enable the clock.
R   ;       mov al, 08h     ; You may need to add these three lines to start up the TLC548.
    ;       mov dx, COM1    ; new added
    ;       out  dx, al     ; new added
S           mov dx, MSR     ; Check the MSR b5 (when b5 = 1 -> CTS is set).
            in   al, dx     ; CTS is connected to output of the TLC548. CTS = 1 means that -
            test al, 10h    ; A binary value of 1 is obtained from TLC548 output.
            jz      done    ; b5 = 0, TLC548 outputs a binary 0. No operation is needed.
            inc  bl         ; b5 = 1, TLC548 outputs a binary 1. Increment result by 1.
T     done: mov dx, LCR     ; Select the Line Control Register to reset the clock of TLC548.
            mov al, 00h     ;
            out  dx, al     ; Disable the clock.
U           dec  cx         ; cx - 1 at each loop.
            jnz  get        ; Loop until all 8-bit output of TLC548 is done.
V           mov dx, MCR     ; Set up the MCR to set DTR & RTS to 1 (space or active).
            mov al, 03h     ; Output power (DTR = 1) & disable CS of TLC548 (RTS = 1).
            out  dx, al     ; Finish set up the MCR.
W           mov rc, bl      ; Reserve the result into rc.
        }
X       return rc;
    }
```

FIGURE 2.61 The port read function.

S: After the A/D starts to work, we need to check the value of bit 4 on the MSR, which is associated with the CTS line in the port COM1. The output of the TLC548 is connected to this CTS line. If a value of `00h` is received from the MSR, it means that the current output bit of the TLC548 is 0. We need to do nothing in this situation; the program will be transferred to the `label done` to perform the next bit operation. If a value of `10h` is received from the MSR, it means that the current output bit of the TLC548 is 1. We need to increase the `bl` register by 1 and the program will also be transferred to the `label done` to perform the next bit's operation.

T: From the beginning of the `label done,` the program will reset the `CLK` on the TLC548 by resetting the LCR in port COM1. As a result, we finish one clock cycle and get one bit from the TLC548.

U: Next, the program needs to check the status of the counter `cx` to determine whether it has gotten all eight bits of data. If the content of the register `cx` is not equal to 0 after it is decreased by 1, then we still have more bits to retrieve from the TLC548. The Program is transferred back to the `label get` where the `bl` register is shifted left by one bit, and the next bit's processing begins.

This process will continue until all eight bits of data are received.

V: Once all eight bits of data have been received, the MCR is set to `03h`. This is equivalent to the port initialization we did in the first step of this program. The DTR and RTS lines will be set to `HIGH` after this initialization.
W: The received data is assigned from the `bl` register to the variable `rc`.
X: Finally, the variable `rc` that stores the received data is returned to the `Port_Read()` function, and then returned to the main function.

We have finished our examination of this program, and it is the time to compile and build the program. In the Visual C++ 6.0 workspace, click the `Build|Build SerialADEmbed.exe` menu item from the menu bar to build the executable file. Then, if no error is encountered during the compiling and building processes, click `Build|Execute SerialADEmbed.exe` to run the program. The results are shown in Figure 2.62.

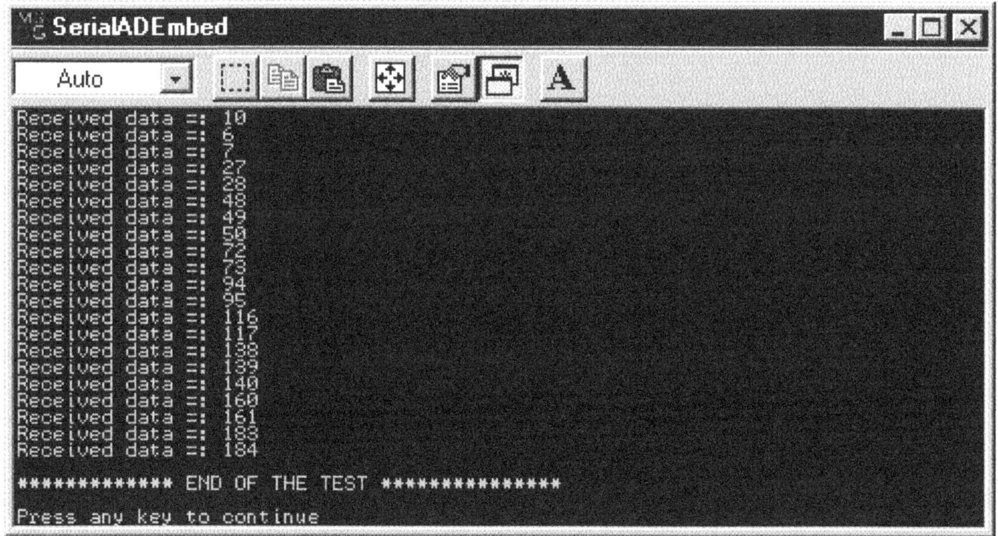

FIGURE 2.62 The running result of the `SerialADEmbed` project.

Next, we will develop a MATLAB program to plot the input waveform. Open the MATLAB workspace and create a new M-File named `Serialad.m`, and enter the code that is shown in Figure 2.63.

The results of running this MATLAB program is shown in Figure 2.64. Two waveforms, the sinusoidal and triangle waveforms, are tested and plotted here.

Notice that the results shown in Figure 2.64, which were obtained by using inline assembly instructions combined with C code, are smoother than those shown in Figure 2.57. Clearly, embedding inline assembly instructions within C code can improve the running speed of A/D conversion functions and improve the sampling rate.

The complete files for this project, including the header file, the source file, the executable file and the MATLAB plotting file, are stored in the folder `Chapter 2\SerialADEmbed`, which is located on the attached CD. To run this project on your computer, you will need to create a data

```
% Display the serial port data
% July 3, 2003
% Copyright by Y. Bai

fid = fopen('C:/SData/Serialad.dat','rt');
S = fscanf( fid,'%d');
plot(S);
grid;
fclose(fid);
```

FIGURE 2.63 The MATLAB plotting program.

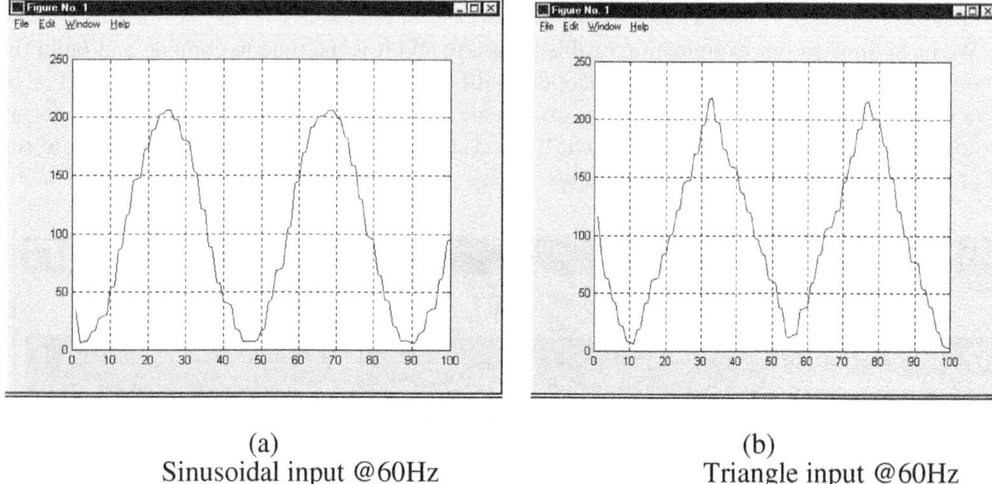

(a) Sinusoidal input @60Hz

(b) Triangle input @60Hz

FIGURE 2.64 The plotting results of the project `SerialADEmbed`.

file folder called `SData` on your root drive (typically, `C:\SData`) to store the data received from the TLC548.

2.7.3 A 12-Bit A/D Serial Interface Developed in ANSI C

The eight-bit A/D converter has limited resolution because of its data length. The default resolution of the TLC548 is about 10 mV (±0.5 LSB), and the accuracy is about 20 mV for the 0 ~ 5 V input analog voltages. It is obvious that this kind of A/D converter is not qualified for some higher accuracy measurement processes. To improve this resolution (and therefore the accuracy), a 12-bit A/D converter is introduced in this section.

2.7.3.1 The MAX187—12-Bit Serial A/D Converter

The 12-bit A/D converter we will discuss here is the product of Maxim Integrated Products™ Inc. The module is MAX187, which is a low-power, 12-bit serial A/D converter. The experimental interface circuit consists of the following elements:

- MAX187 12-bit serial A/D converter
- MAX220 multichannel RS-232 driver/receiver
- Some filter capacitors

Let's now take a look at the internal structure and working principles of the MAX187 and MAX189 A/D converters.

The MAX187/MAX189 serial 12-bit analog-to-digital converters (ADCs) operate from a single +5V power supply and accept a 0V-to-5V analog input. Both components feature an 8.5μs successive-approximation ADC, a fast track/hold (1.5μs), an on-chip clock, and a high-speed, three-wire serial interface.

The MAX187/MAX189 digitize signals at a 75ksps throughput rate. An external clock accesses data from the interface, which communicates without external hardware to most digital signal processors and microcontrollers. The interface is compatible with SPI™, QSPI™, and Microwire™.

The MAX187 has an on-chip buffered reference, and the MAX189 requires an external reference. Both the MAX187 and MAX189 save space with 8-pin DIP and 16-pin SO packages. Power consumption is 7.5mW and reduces to only 10μW in shutdown mode.

Excellent AC characteristics and very low power consumption, combined with ease of use and a small package size, make these converters ideal for remote DSP and sensor applications, or for circuits where low power consumption and space are crucial.

Some product specifications are listed here:

- 12-bit resolution
- ±1/2 LSB integral nonlinearity (MAX187A and MAX189A)
- Internal track and hold with a 75kHz sampling rate
- Single +5V operation
- Low power: 2μA shutdown current, 1.5mA operating current
- Internal 4.096V buffered reference (MAX187)
- Three-Wire serial interface, compatible with SPI, QSPI, and Wicrowire™
- Small-footprint 8-Pin DIP and 16-Pin SO

A functional diagram, as well as the pin configuration, of the MAX187 is shown in Figure 2.65 (a) and (b), respectively.

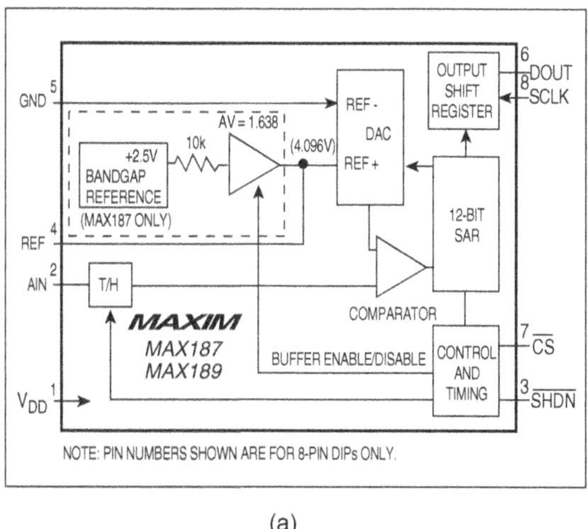

(a)

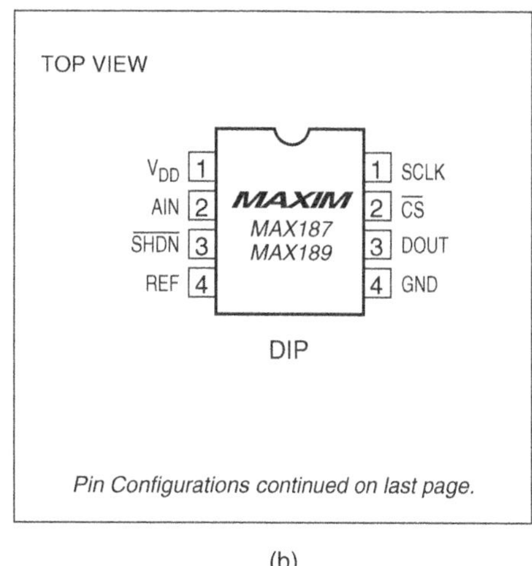

(b)

FIGURE 2.65 The functional diagram and pin configuration of MAX187. (Reprinted by the permission of Maxim Integrated Products, Inc. at http://pdfserv.maxim-ic.com/en/ds/MAX187-MAX189.pdf.)

2.7.3.2 The MAX220—Multichannel RS-232 Drivers and Receivers

Unlike the serial A/D converter TLC548 that we discussed in the preceding section, in which the A/D converter is directly connected to the RS-232 transmission lines, the MAX187 is connected to the RS-232 transmission lines via a line-level converter or a driver/receiver MAX220. As we discussed in Chapter 1, the voltage levels of serial data for the TTL and the RS-232 transmission lines are different (refer to Figure 1.6). Generally, you cannot directly connect a peripheral device that applies TTL signals to a DTE that applies RS-232 transmission signals because of the different voltage levels between those two signals. You need to apply a signal converter between the DTE and the DCE to transfer the voltage levels between those two signals. In this interface circuit, a multichannel RS-232 driver/receiver MAX220 is used to perform the conversion between the two different signals.

TIP: In some cases, even the TTL signals can be recognized by the RS-232 transmission lines. The TLC548 we discussed in the preceding section is an example of this kind of connection, which is economical and simple in practice although it is not a standard connection.

The internal structure and pin configuration of the MAX220 are shown in Figure 2.66.

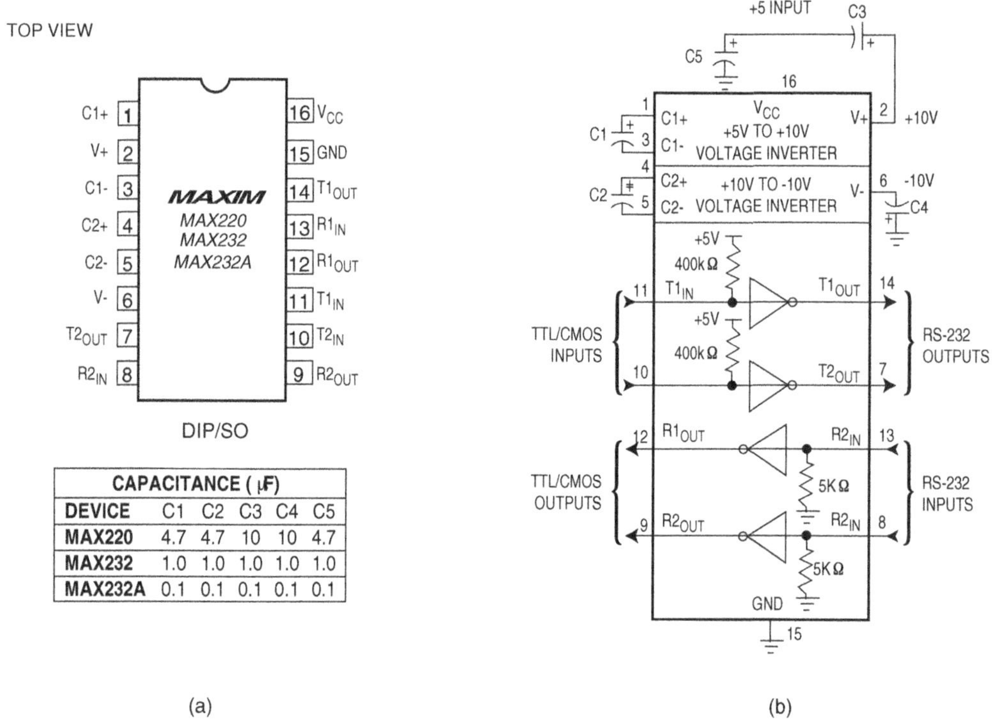

CAPACITANCE (μF)					
DEVICE	C1	C2	C3	C4	C5
MAX220	4.7	4.7	10	10	4.7
MAX232	1.0	1.0	1.0	1.0	1.0
MAX232A	0.1	0.1	0.1	0.1	0.1

FIGURE 2.66 . The pin configuration and the internal structure of MAX220. (Reprinted by the permission of Maxim Integrated Products, Inc. at http://pdfserv.maxim-ic.com/en/ds/MAX220-MAX249.pdf.)

The MAX220–MAX249 family of line drivers and receivers is intended for all EIA/TIA-232E and V.28/V.24 communications interfaces, particularly where ±12V is not available.

These components are especially useful in battery-powered systems because their low-power shutdown mode reduces power dissipation to less than 5μW. The MAX225, MAX233, MAX235, and MAX245/MAX246/MAX247 use no external components and are recommended for applications where printed circuit board space is critical.

Some specifications of the MAX220–MAX249 family are listed here:

- Operation from a single +5v power supply (+5V and +12V–MAX231 and MAX239)
- Low-power receive mode in shutdown (MAX223 and MAX242)
- Satisfaction of all EIA/TIA-232E and V.28 specifications
- Multiple drivers and receivers
- Three-state driver and receiver outputs
- Open-line Detection (MAX243)

Notice in Figure 2.66(b) that the MAX220 can be considered a multichannel (four-channel) level converter. Two channels are used for the conversion from the TTL/CMOS to the RS-232 level (transmit channels 1 and 2—T_1 and T_2), and another two channels are used for the conversion from the RS-232 to the TTL/CMOS level (receiver channels 1 and 2—R_1 and R_2).

TIP: One of the most important functions on the MAX220 is that the relationship between the input and the output is inverted. A NOT gate is connected between the input and the output for each channel in the MAX220. So the logic between the input signal and the output signal is equivalent to an inverter. This point must be remembered when applying the MAX220 in the interface circuits.

2.7.3.3 The 12-Bit Serial A/D Converter Interface Circuit

The 12-bit serial A/D converter interface circuit is shown in Figure 2.67.

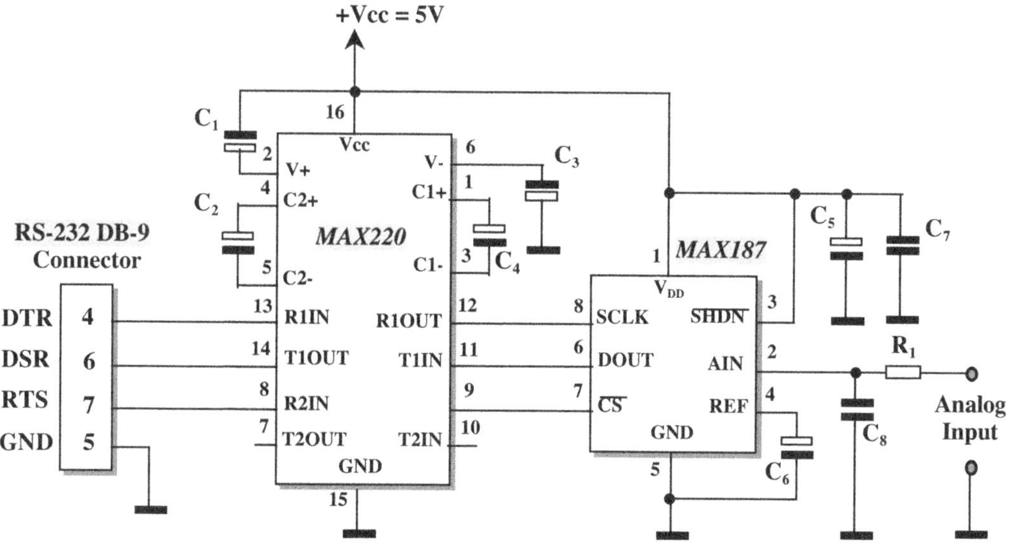

FIGURE 2.67 The interface circuit of the MAX187.

The elements parameters are listed in Table 2-6.

Notice in Figure 2.67 that two receiver channels, R_1 and R_2 on the MAX220, are used to convert and transmit the RTS and DTR signals from the RS-232 level to the TTL/CMOS level. The CS and SCLK lines are emulated by the RTS and DTR lines, respectively. Conversion data appears on the DSR line.

Interface to the PC is on a RS-232 port, rather than the transmission and reception lines of a UART. The port's RTS line provides a chip-select signal, and its DTR line provides a synchronous clock signal. A single-supply RS-232 interface chip (in the MAX220) converts these signals from

TABLE 2.6
Elements Parameters

Elements	Values	Comments
R_1	10 KΩ	Current-limited Resistor
$C_1 \sim C_4$	10 µF/25V	Electrolytic Capacitors
$C_5 \sim C_6$	4.7 µF/10V	Electrolytic Capacitors
$C_7 \sim C_8$	0.1 µF	Capacitors

RS-232 levels to CMOS-logic levels (and inverts them in the process). The converted data appears on the DSR line.

MAX187 is an eight-pin DIP that includes a twelve-bit ADC, voltage reference, track and hold capabilities, a serial interface, a clock generator, and a three-wire digital interface consisting of chip select (CS bar), serial clock (SCLK), and data out (DOUT) components. Conversions are initiated by a high-to-low transition on CS bar and take less than 8.5µs. The end of conversion, indicated by a high level on DOUT, leaves the 12-bit result stored in the converter's output shift register. The PC reads this result by clocking DTR while sampling the DSR 12 times. The conversion timing sequence of the MAX187 is shown in Figure 2.68.

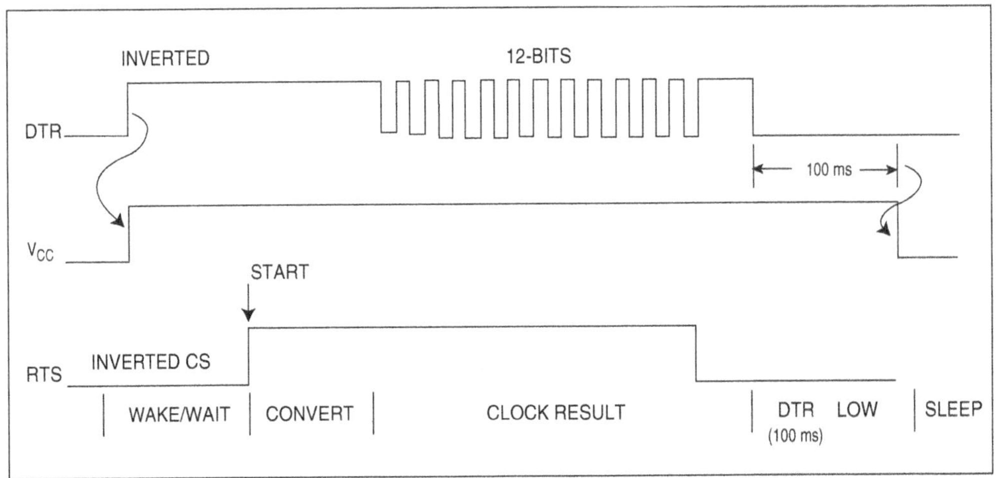

FIGURE 2.68 . The timing sequence of the data conversion on MAX187. (Reprinted by the permission of Maxim Integrated Products, Inc. at http://pdfserv.maxim-ic.com/appnotes.cfm/appnote_number/151)

The MAX187 begins converting data when its Chip Select (CS) has a HIGH-to-LOW transition, and this signal is connected to the RTS line that is converted from the RS-232 to the TTL/CMOS level by the MAX220 with an inverted logic. The MAX187 completes the 12-bit conversion using its own internal clock, and the end of conversion is marked by a HIGH level on the output DOUT. The PC retrieves the converted data from the DSR line (which is connected to the DOUT on the MAX187 via a logic-inverter MAX220) by sending a sequence of simulated clock data from the DTR line.

Once the data conversion has begun, the PC monitors the DSR line and waits until its state becomes HIGH, which means that the conversion is complete. Then the PC sends 12 simulated clock items via the DTR line that is connected to the SCLK (Serial CLK) on the MAX187, to serially move the converted data from the output shift register on the MAX187 to the DSR line. It picks up these items one by one by checking the value received on the DSR line.

Make the hardware connection according to Figure 2.67, and connect a function generator to the analog input terminal, which in Figure 2.67 appears as the analog signal source. Three different analog waveforms can be used as the input: sinusoidal, square and triangle signals.

Now it is time to configure our software to interface this A/D circuit and complete the data conversion.

2.7.3.4 The 12-Bit Serial A/D Converter Interface Program

The program in this section will be developed in C code. Launch Visual C++ 6.0 and create a new project with the following properties:

- Project type: Win32 Console Application
- Project name: `SerialMAX`
- Project location: `C:\Chapter 2`

In the open project, create a new header file named `SerialMAX.h;` in this file, enter the code shown in Figure 2.69.

```
/*****************************************************************************
 * NAME: SerialMAX.h
 * DATE: 7/10/2003
 * PGMR: Y. Bai  Copyright 2003 - 2007
 * DESC:  Header file for serial port interface to MAX - serial A/D
 *****************************************************************************/
#include <stdio.h>
#include <stdlib.h>
#include <string.h>
#include <conio.h>
#include <time.h>

    #define   MAXNUM    100              // Max data length
    #define   BYTE      unsigned char    // Data type
    #define   USHORT    unsigned short   //
A   #define   COM1      0x3f8            // COM1 base address
    #define   COM2      0x2f8            // COM2 base address
    #define   SCLK          1            // MCR bit1 = CLK for AD
    #define   CS            2            // MCR bit2 = CS of AD

    USHORT       IER  = 0x3f9;           // COM1 Interrupt Enable Register
    USHORT       LCR  = 0x3fb;           // COM1 Line Control Register
B   USHORT       MCR  = 0x3fc;           // COM1 Modem Control Register
    USHORT       LSR  = 0x3fd;           // COM1 Line Status Register
    USHORT       MSR  = 0x3fe;           // COM1 Modem Status Register

C   static clock_t  delts = 2;           // Delay 2 ms

D   void  Port_Init();
    int   Port_Read();
    void  sleepad();
    void  delay(clock_t ms);
```

FIGURE 2.69 The Header File of the `SerialMAX` Project.

A: The used global constants, such as the base addressed of serial ports COM1 and COM2, the length of the converted data array, and the command constants `SCLK` and `CS`, are defined at the beginning of this header file.
The COM1 serial port is used in this project. The command constants `SCLK` and `CS` are equivalent to the hexadecimals 0x01 and 0x02, respectively.

B: The addresses of all registers associated with COM1 are declared and represented by symbols. These symbols help simplify our program.

C: The `clock_t` variable `delts` is declared and initialized to a value of 2.

D: Four functions are defined and used in this program. The essential functions are `Port_Init()` and `Port_Read()`. The `delay()` function may not be used in some programs. The `sleepad()` function is equivalent to a `disable` function, and the purpose of this function is to disable the required signals and conditions to set the MAX187 to idle state for the data conversion.

Pay particular attention to the command constants `SCLK` and `CS`. These two signal terminals on the MAX187 are connected to the DTR and the RTS of RS-232, respectively, via a logic-inverter MAX220. The input and the output logic of the MAX220 are inverted. For example, to send a value of `HIGH` to the `SCLK`, you need to send a value of `LOW` to bit 0 on the MCR (refer to Figure 1.30 in Chapter 1), which will send an inverted logic signal to the DTR line, and vice versa.

In the open project, create a new C++ source file named SerialMAX.cpp; in this new file, enter the code shown in Figure 2.70.

In the main function body, the user-defined header file `SerialMAX.h` should be included first; once this is done, all constants and functions defined in the header file can be used by the main function.

E: The local variables are declared at the beginning of the main function. The `fp` variable is used to hold the opened file handler, and the data array `value[]` is used to store the received data coming from the MAX187 A/D converter. In this program, we want to collect a data total of 100. The `result` variable is used to store the converted data in a real physical unit, (in volts, for example).

F: The main function is initiated by an input character that is entered by the user. A `y` feedback character will start the main function.

G: The first function to be called is `Port_Init()`, which is used to initialize the MAX187 A/D converter and make it ready for the data conversion.

H: A data file named `serialmax.dat` is created by a call to the system function `fopen()`. In this program, the file path is `C:\SData`. The operation mode is write `(w)`. A `null` value will be returned if this function fails. If an error is encountered during the creation of the data file, the error information will be printed out and the program will be terminated.

I: A `for` loop is executed to continuously retrieve the converted data from serial port COM1. The loop is terminated when the size of the array is 100, which is the specified length of the array.

J: Inside the `for` loop, the `Port_Read()` function is repeatedly called to pick up each data segment transmitted from the MAX187, and the received data segments are assigned to the data array `value[]` one by one, based on the location of each. The received data is also printed on the screen to show the progression of the data process. First the data is printed out based on its original format (integer), and then the program converts the data to the double format by multiplying it with a scalar factor; finally, the converted data is also printed to the screen. For plotting purposes, the data is stored in the data file we opened at the beginning of the main function. This process will continue until the end of the `for` loop is reached.

K: Finally, before terminating the main function, the system function `fclose()` is executed to close the opened data file and write all data into the file.

The functions `Port_Init()`, `sleepad()` and `delay()` are shown in Figure 2.71.

```
/*****************************************************************************
 * NAME: SerialMAX.cpp
 * DATE:  7/10/2003
 * PRGR: Y. Bai - Copyright 2003 - 2007
 * DESC:  Use C/C++ code to communicate with a serial A/D converter (MAX-187)
          to get analog signal inputs from a RS-232 port
 *****************************************************************************/
#include "SerialMAX.h"

void main()
{
        FILE* fp;
        char    cc;
E       int     index, value[100];
        double result;

F       printf("\n**** WELCOME TO SERIAL A/D CONVERTER TESTING ****\n");
        printf("\nDo you want to begin the test?  y/n\n");
        scanf(" %c", &cc);
        if (cc == 'y' || cc == 'Y')
        {
G           Port_Init();
H           fp = fopen("C:\\SData\\serialmax.dat", "w");
            if (fp == NULL)
            {
                printf("File open error! program exit\n");
                return;
            }
I           for (index = 0; index < MAXNUM; index++)
            {
J               value[index] = Port_Read();
                printf("Received data (int) =: %d\n", value[index]);
//              fprintf(fp, "%d\n", value[index]);
                result = ((double)value[index]/4095.0)*5.0;
                printf("Received data (float) =: %.2f\n", result);
                fprintf(fp, "%.2f\n", result);
            }
K           fclose(fp);
        }
        printf("\n************* END OF THE TEST **************\n\n");
}
```

FIGURE 2.70 The main function of the `SerialMAX` project.

L: When the `Port_Init()` function is called, a comment is printed to show the user that the port initialization function is being executed. The function `_outp(MCR, SCLK)` is executed to send a value of `0x01` to the MCR. This operation has the following two results:

A value of `1` (`HIGH`) is set on the DTR line (refer to Figure 1.30 in Chapter 1). The `SCLK` input on the MAX187 is then reset to `0` because of the inversion operation of the MAX220 inverter.

A value of `0` (`LOW`) is set on the RTS line (refer to Figure 1.30 in Chapter 1). The CS signal on the MAX187 is then set to `1` because of the inversion operation of the MAX220 inverter. This logical `1` deselects the MAX187, and so the A/D does not start the data conversion operation at all.

M: When the `sleepad()` function is executed, the function `_outp(MCR, 0)` is called to send values of `0` to both the DTR and the RTS lines. The resulting inputs to the MAX187 are that the SCLK and the CS are set to 1, and the A/D converter is disabled.

```
  void Port_Init()
  {
      printf("\nBegin to initialize the serial port...\n");
L     _outp(MCR, SCLK);
      return;
  }
  void sleepad()
  {
M     _outp(MCR, 0);
  }
  void delay(clock_t ms)
  {
N     clock_t ms1, ms2, index;
O     if (!ms)
         return;
      if (ms <100)
      {
         do{
             for (index=0; index<10000; index++)
               ms -= 1;
           }while (ms>=0);
         return;
      }
      ms1 = ms + clock();
      do{
          ms2 = clock(); }while(ms2 < ms1);
  }
```

FIGURE 2.71 Some functions used in the `SerialMAX` project.

N: Certain local variables are defined at the beginning of the `delay()` function. Three variables, `ms1`, `ms2` and `index`, are all `clock_t` variables.

O: The function will return and do nothing if the input value is less than `0`. This means that the program needs to delay by `0` seconds. If the input argument is greater than `0` but smaller than `100`, a `do while` loop is used to create a delay. Following this loop, another `do while` loop is executed to extend the delay time to the specified interval. The last function, `Port_Read()`, is shown in Figure 2.72.

P: Certain local variables are defined at the entry point of the `Port_Read()` function. The integer variable `i` works as a loop counter for the `for` loop. The integer variable `result` contains the single converted data segment (12 bits). Because the converted data is 12 bits in length, an integer variable (not a byte) is used here. The `clock_t` variable `dlms`, which is the delay interval parameter, is initialized to `0x01`.

Q: The function `_outp(MCR, SCLK+CS)` is executed to send a decimal value of `3` (which is equivalent to a binary 00000011B), to the MCR. This function is equivalent to setting both the DTR and the RTS lines to logical `1`. The SCLK and the CS on the MAX187 are both reset to `0` because of the MAX220 inverter. Resetting CS to `0` selects and enables the MAX187, and thus causes the A/D to begin the data conversion under the control of the on-chip clock.

R: After the MAX187 starts its conversion, a `while` loop is executed to wait for the end of the data conversion. The completion of the data conversion is indicated by a `HIGH` value on the DOUT line (refer to Figure 2.68) of the MAX187; this DOUT is connected to the `DSR` line via the MAX220 logic inverter. Because of the `NOT` logic used in the MAX220, a logical `1` on the DOUT is inverted to a logical `0` (`LOW`) on the `DSR` line. When the `DSR` line becomes `LOW`, it means that the MAX187 has completed its data

```
  int Port_Read()
  {
       int    i, result = 0;
P      static clock_t d1ms = 0x1;              // Delay 1 ms
Q      _outp(MCR, SCLK+CS);                    // Send DTR to AD to begin conversion
R      while((_inp(MSR) & 32) !=0);            // Wait convert complete
S      for( i = 0;  i < 12;  i++)
       {
T          delay(d1ms);
           _outp(MCR, CS);                     // Set clock high
           delay(d1ms);
U          _outp(MCR, CS+SCLK);                // Set clock low
           delay(d1ms);
V          if ((_inp(MSR) & 32)==0)            // Received data '1'
              result += 1;
W          result = result << 1;
       }
X      _outp(MCR, SCLK);                       // Reset AD
Y      result = result >> 1;                  // Fix the final result
       return  result;
  }
```

FIGURE 2.72 The `Port_Read()` function in the `SerialMAX` project.

conversion and the data segments can be retrieved one by one and moved into the computer via the COM1 port. If the result of executing the instruction `_inp(MSR) & 32` is not equal to `0`, it means that the data conversion has not finished and the `while` loop will continue to run until the result is `0`. The decimal value 32 is equivalent to a binary value of 00100000B. If you refer to Figure 1.32 in Chapter 1, in which a detailed description of the bit configuration for the MSR is provided, you will find that the value of bit 5 is associated with the `DSR` status. A value of 1 on bit 5 indicates that a logical 1 has been received on the `DSR` line, and vice versa. The above `AND`ing operation will return `0` if the value on the `DSR` line (bit 5 on the MSR) becomes `0`.

S: After the data conversion is complete, a `for` loop is used to continuously pick up the data in 12 loop cycles (because the length of the converted data is 12 bits). The `delay()` function is executed first to wait for the converted data on the port. This time delay is very important, and the received data would be incorrect without it in most applications. We need to add this `delay()` function inside the `for` loop to make sure that the received data is error-free.

T: Now we need to send a sequence of simulated clocks to the SCLK terminal on the MAX187 to move the converted data from the converter's output shift register to the TSR line, and finally to the PC. The converted data is stored in the output shift register on the MAX187 once the data conversion is complete. To move the entire 12-bit data bit by bit to the `DSR` line, a `LOW`-to-`HIGH` transition is needed to apply on the serial clock input SCLK on the MAX187. By executing the function `_outp(MCR, CS)` (which is the equivalent of sending a binary value of 00000010 to the MCR. Refer to Figure 1.30 in Chapter 1, where bit 0 and bit 1 on the MCR are mapped to the DTR and the RTS lines, respectively. Refer also to Figure 2.67, where the DTR and the RTS lines are connected to the SCLK and the CS inputs on the MAX187, respectively. After executing the above `_outp()`, the DTR is reset to `0` and the RTS is set to `1`. Because of the MAX220 inverter, on the MAX187 side, the SCLK receives an `DTR` or a logical `1`, and the CS receives an `RTS` or a logical `0`, respectively. A `0` in the CS input keeps the MAX187 selected and enabled, and a `1` in the SCLK input lets the MAX187 move a bit of converted data out of its output shift register after a time delay is performed by instructing the MCR to wait for the transmitted data to be stable.

U: The function `_outp(MCR, SCLK+CS)` is called to send a decimal value of `3` (binary data 00000011B) to the MCR. Based on the analysis in Step T above, it can be found that this operation is equivalent to resetting both the SCLK and the CS values to `0` because of the MAX220 inverter. In other words, the purpose of this function call is to reset the serial clock SCLK to `0` because we have finished moving one bit out of the MAX187 and sending that bit to the `DSR` line. A time delay is needed to wait for the data on the transmission line.

V: Now we can pick up the data bit from the `DSR` line via RS-232 port COM1. This pickup is completed by checking the status of the `DSR` line without retrieving any data bits from the `DSR` line. As was mentioned, we use the integer variable `result` to store received data bit by bit. To check the status of the `DSR` line, the function `_inp(MSR) & 32` is executed. The result of this `AND` operation is `0` if the bit 5 on the MSR is `0`, which means that a logical `0` is received on the `DSR` line. A logical `0` on the `DSR` line means that a data bit with a value of `1` is received because of the inversion operation of the MAX220. The integer variable `result` is thus increased by 1 (which is equivalent to moving a 1 into the LSB on the `result`).

W: If the `AND` operation does not return a `0`, it means that a logical `1` has been received on the `DSR` line, and a data bit with a value of `0` is received. In this case, we do not need to add a 0 to the `result` variable. The only thing we need to do is shift the `result` left by one bit; this is equivalent to moving a 0 into the LSB on the `result`.

Now we have finished picking up one data bit from the output shift register on the MAX187. Next, we will repeat steps T, U, V and W in the `for` loop to pick up the next bit. This process will be continued until the entire 12-bit data segment is moved into the `result` variable.

X: After all 12 bits of data have been collected and stored to `result`, the function `_outp(MCR, SCLK)` is executed to reset the MAX187 A/D converter. The result of executing this function is to reset the SCLK to `0` and set the CS to `1` on the MAX187, which deselects the A/D converter. This operation is equivalent to executing the initialization function `Port_Init()` to initialize the MAX187.

Y: We need to totally shift the integer variable `result` 11 times to get the correct converted data because there are 12 data bits in each data segment, and the last bit LSB of `result` does not need to be shifted. Because the `result` variable has been shifted left by 12 times in the `for` loop, we have to make a modification on the final result by shifting the variable `result` right by one bit to fix the overshift problem. Finally, the converted result is returned to the main function.

Now it is time to compile and build the project. In the Visual C++ 6.0 workspace, click the `Build|Build SerialMAX.exe` menu item from the menu bar. If no errors occur, connect the function generator to the analog input on the MAX187 and set the waveform output to the square, then click `Build|Execute SerialMAX.exe` to run the project. The results are shown in Figure 2.73.

Next we will develop a MATLAB program to plot the acquired data to a graph. Open the MATLAB workspace and create a new M-File named `Serialmax.m`; then enter the code shown in Figure 2.74 into this M-file and save the file in the MATLAB default folder, `C\MATLAB\bin`.

The collected data is stored in the data file `serialmax.dat` while the project runs in the Visual C++ environment. In MATLAB, this data file is opened and the data is picked up to the data array `S`, and finally the array `S` is plotted in the MATLAB domain.

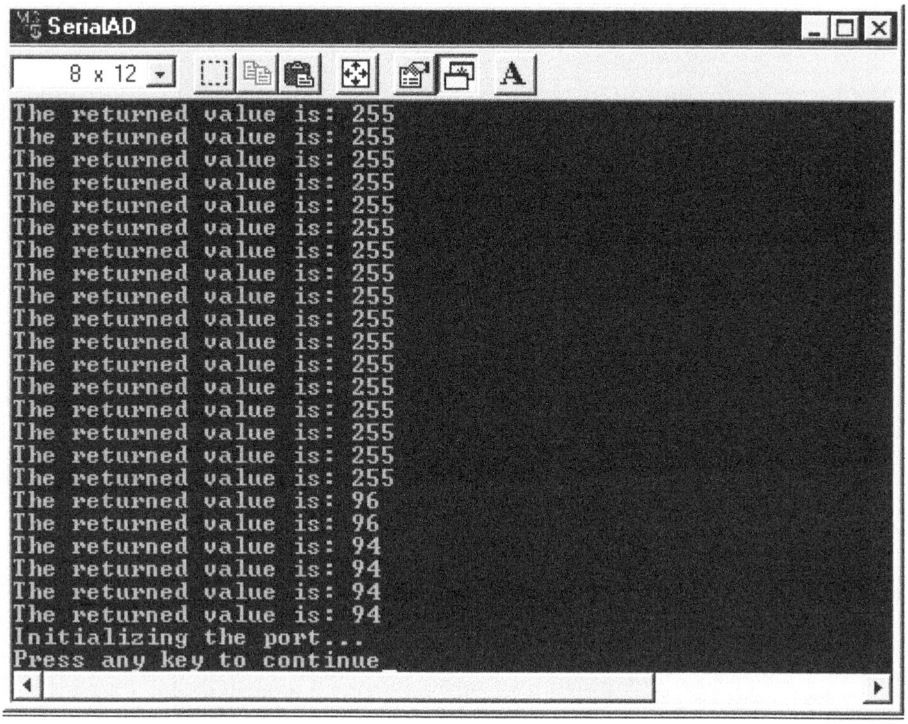

```
SerialAD
8 x 12
The returned value is: 255
The returned value is: 255
The returned value is: 255
The returned value is: 255
The returned value is: 255
The returned value is: 255
The returned value is: 255
The returned value is: 255
The returned value is: 255
The returned value is: 255
The returned value is: 255
The returned value is: 255
The returned value is: 255
The returned value is: 255
The returned value is: 255
The returned value is: 255
The returned value is: 255
The returned value is: 96
The returned value is: 96
The returned value is: 94
The returned value is: 94
The returned value is: 94
The returned value is: 94
Initializing the port...
Press any key to continue
```

FIGURE 2.73 The running result of the `SerialMAX` project.

```
% Display the serial port data
% July 3, 2003
% Copyright by Y. Bai

fid = fopen('C:/SData/serialmax.dat','rt');
S = fscanf(fid,'%f');
plot(S);
grid;
fclose(fid);
```

FIGURE 2.74 The MATLAB plot program `Serialmax.m`.

Three waveforms are tested here: sinusoidal, triangle and square waveforms. Connect the function generator with the input of the MAX187 and set up each of these three waveforms with the following parameters:

- Amplitude: 0 ~ 5 V
- Frequency: 20 Hz

Run the project in the Visual C++ environment for each waveform, and then open the MATLAB workspace and run the function `Serialmax.m` by typing the function name in the MATLAB workspace. The running result for each waveform is shown in Figure 2.75.

The vertical axis in Figure 2.75 represents the voltage of the waveform, and the unit is mV. The horizontal axis represents the sampling point of the waveforms. The sampling period is determined by the loop interval of the C code in the source file.

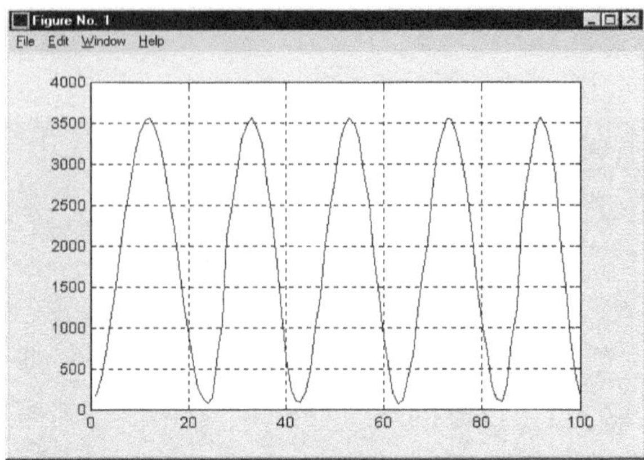

(a) Sinusoidal Waveform @20Hz

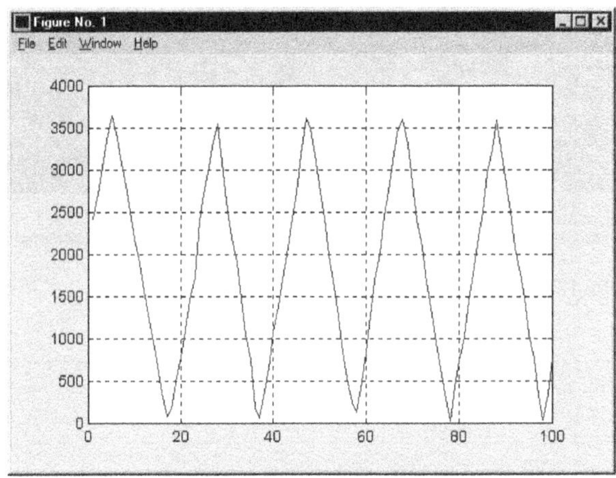

(b) Triangle Waveform @20Hz

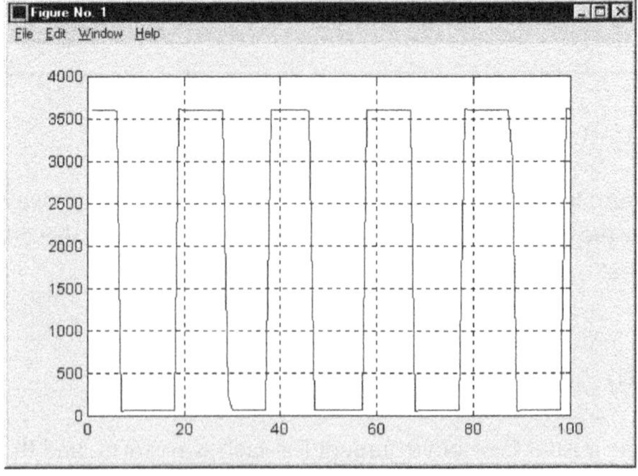

(c) Square Waveform @20Hz

FIGURE 2.75 The test results of three analog waveforms.

The complete files for this project, including the source file, the header file, the executable file, and the MATLAB file, are stored in the folder `Chapter 2\SerialMAX` on the attached CD. Before you can run this program on your computer, you need to create a data file folder at your root directory (typically `C:\SData`), to store the converted data. Copy the executable file and the MATLAB file to your computer and store them in the different directories; for example, store the executable file `SerialMAX.exe` in the root directory and the file `Serialmax.m` in the default MATLAB folder `C:\MATLAB\bin`. Then run the executable file and the `Serialmax.m` file so you can get the desired waveform output.

2.7.4 A 12-Bit A/D Serial Interface Developed in C and Inline Assembly Code

As we've learned, using inline assembly instructions can improve the sampling rate of the A/D converting functions. In this section, we examine how to embed inline assembly code within C code to improve the performance of the MAX187 A/D converter.

This project is similar to the preceding one, except that the low-level functions are replaced by inline assembly instructions, and that, in this project, the serial port COM2 is used.

Launch Visual C++ 6.0 and create a new project with the following properties:

- Project type: Win32 Console Application
- Project name: `SerialMAXEmbed`
- Project location: `C:\Chapter 2`

In the new project, create a new header file named `SerialMAXEmbed.h`; in this file, enter the code shown in Figure 2.76.

```
/*****************************************************************************
 * NAME: SerialMAXEmbed.h
 * DATE: 7/14/2003
 * PRGR: Y. Bai - Copyright 2003 - 2007
 * DESC: Header file for serial A/D converter testing program (MAX-187)
 *****************************************************************************/
  #include <stdio.h>
  #include <stdlib.h>
A #include <string.h>
  #include <conio.h>

  #define MAXNUM     100              // Max data length
  #define BYTE       unsigned char    // Data type
  #define COM2       2f8h             // COM2 base address
  #define IER        2f9h             // COM2 Interrupt Enable Register
B #define LCR        2fbh             // COM2 Line Control Register
  #define MCR        2fch             // COM2 Modem Control Register
  #define LSR        2fdh             // COM2 Line Status Register
  #define MSR        2feh             // COM2 Modem Status Register
  #define DT         0ffh             // Delay time for ADC
  #define SCLK         1              // MCR bit1 = SCLK for AD
  #define CS           2              // MCR bit2 = CS of AD

C void Port_Init();
  void c_inial();
  int  Port_Read();
  int  c_getad();
```

FIGURE 2.76 The header file of the `SerialMAXEmbed` project.

A: Some useful system header files are enclosed at the beginning of this header file. One of the most important header files in this program is `<conio.h>`, which provides low-level functions for accessing the serial port and its UART.

B: The global constants and user-defined data types are specified here. The SCLK and the CS are defined as decimal constants; however, they can both be recognized in the inline assembly instructions as hexadecimal numbers because their values are less than ten.

C: Four functions are declared and used in this program. Both the `c_inial()` and the `c_getad()` functions are inline assembly functions; they will be called by the functions `Port_Init()` and `Port_Read()`, respectively, during execution of the program.

Next we need to create a C++ source file named `SerialMAXEmbed.cpp`; in this file, enter the code shown in Figure 2.77.

```
/*****************************************************************************
 * NAME: SerialMAXEmbed.cpp
 * DATE:  7/14/2003
 * PRGR: Y. Bai - Copyright 2003 - 2007
 * DESC:  Embedded assembly code (intel 8088/80x86) to communicate with a serial A/D
          converter (MAX-187) to get analog signal inputs from a RS-232 port
 *****************************************************************************/
#include "SerialMAXEmbed.h"
void main()
{
      FILE*  fp;
      char     cc;
D     int       index, value[100];
      double  result;
      printf("\n**** WELCOME TO SERIAL A/D CONVERTER TESTING ****\n");
      printf("\nDo you want to begin the test?  y/n\n");
E     scanf(" %c", &cc);
F     if (cc == 'y' || cc == 'Y')
      {
G          Port_Init();
H          fp = fopen("C:\\SData\\serialmaxemb.dat", "w");
           if (fp == NULL)
           {
                printf("File open error! program exit\n");
                return;
           }
I          for (index = 0; index < MAXNUM; index++)
           {
                value[index] = Port_Read();
J               result = ((double)value[index]/4095.0)*5.0;
                printf("Received data =: %.2f\n", result);
K               fprintf(fp, "%.2f\n", result);
           }
L          fclose(fp);
      }
      printf("\n************ END OF THE TEST *************\n\n");
}
```

FIGURE 2.77 The main function of the `SerialMAXEmbed` project.

D: The local variables are defined at the beginning of the main function body. These variables include the `FILE` pointer variable `fp` that stores the handler of the opened file, the integer array `value[]` that stores the received data from the A/D converter, and the double variable **result** that is used to hold the converted data, display it in floating-point format, and then store the floating-point data in the data file.

E: The main function starts with an input character entered by the user. The system function `scanf()` is used to pick up that character. Note that the second argument of the function is a pointer-type variable, so an address operator `&` is preceded before the character variable `cc`.

F: The main function begins to run once a `y` or *Y* character has been received.

G: The `Port_Init()` function is called to initialize serial port COM2 and prepare it for the A/D conversion.

H: Before the data conversion starts, the data file, which is used to store the converted data, is opened by execution of the system function `fopen()`. The name of the data file is `serialmaxemb.dat`, and the path is `C:\SData`. A `null` value will be returned if any errors are encountered in opening this data file; the error information will printed on the screen and the program will be terminated.

I: If the data file is successfully opened, a `for` loop is executed by a call to the `Port_Read()` function to continuously pick up the converted data segments one by one from the MAX187. The retrieved data is moved into the integer array `value[]`.

J: To display the converted data in a real physical unit, the program uses a cast operator to convert the received data from integer form to double floating-point data. With the help of the scalar factor 4095 and the full-scaling voltage 5.0, the converted data is translated into real units (volts).

K: The converted data is now displayed on the screen so the user can track the process of the A/D conversion; and it also stored in the opened data file, which will be used later to plot the waveform of the received data.

L: Finally, before end of the main function, the system function `fclose()` is called to close the opened data file and to store all data into that file.

Next, we need to add the `Port_Init()` and `c_inial()` functions into the source file. These functions are shown in Figure 2.78.

```
    /*****************************************************************************
     *                 Initialize the serial port COM2                           *
     *****************************************************************************/
    void Port_Init()
    {
M       printf("\nBegin to initialize the serial port...\n");
        c_inial();

        return;
    }
    void c_inial()
    {
N       _asm
        {
            mov   dx, MCR      ; Set up MCR to set DTR & reset RTS (space or active).
O           mov   al, 01h      ; Enable MAX-187 (DTR = 1) & disable CS
                               ; (RTS = 0 is inverted by MAX-222 to 1).
            out   dx, al       ; Finish set up the MCR.
        }
    }
```

FIGURE 2.78 The initialization function of the `SerialMAXEmbed` project.

M: The Port_Init() function starts with a status display indicating that the port is being initialized. Then the inline assembly function c_inial() is called to begin execution of the port initialization.

N: The keyword _asm works as the starting point of the inline assembly instructions.

O: These three assembly codes are equivalent to one high-level C code, _outp(MCR, 01h). The functionality of these instructions is to send a value of 0x01 to the MCR, to assign a value of 1 to the DTR, and to reset the RTS to 0. Because of the MAX220 inverter, the SCLK, which is connected to the DTR line, is set to logical 0, and the CS bar, which is connected to the RTS line, is set to 1. Thus the SCLK is disabled and the MAX187 is deselected. The Port_Read() function is shown in Figure 2.79.

```
/*****************************************************************************
 *          Inline Assembly Function to Read Data From the Serial Port       *
 *****************************************************************************/
int Port_Read()
{
        int value;
P       value = c_getad();
        return value;
}
```

FIGURE 2.79 The Port_Read() function in the SerialMAXEmbed project.

P: The returned value of the Port_Read() function is an integer because the size of the converted data is 12 bits. The inline assembly function c_getad() is called to pick up the converted data from the MAX187. The inline assembly function c_getad() is shown in Figure 2.80.

Q: The short variable rc is used to store the received data. Because the converted data is 12 bits in length, a short type is used. In the Visual C++ 6.0 compiler, a short variable is equivalent to an integer variable, except that the length of the former is 16 bits and the length of the latter is 32 bits.

R: The keyword _asm indicates the beginning of the inline assembly code.

S: Setting the MCR with the function _outp(MCR, SCLK+CS) (to a decimal 3 or a binary 00000011b) causes both the DTR and the RTS lines to be set to 1. This setup is equivalent to resetting both the SCLK and the CS bar on the MAX187 to 0 because of the MAX220 inverter. After the CS bar is reset to 0, which is equivalent to enabling and selecting the A/D converter, the MAX187 begins to perform the data conversion. In short, the purpose of these three lines of instructions is to start the MAX187 so that it will perform the analog-to-digital conversion based on its own on-chip system clock.

T: Once the conversion has begun, our program needs to locate space to store the converted data and define the counter to monitor the number of converted binary bits. The register cx is selected as the counter. The maximum number of binary bits (which is 12) for each converted data segment is assigned to this register.

U: The register bx is selected for storing the converted data bit by bit; this register is initialized to 0.

V: Now we are ready to pick up the converted data from the MAX187. To identify whether the data conversion has been done, we need to check bit 5 on the MSR in the UART, because the DOUT on the MAX187 is connected to the DSR line that is mapped to bit 5 on the MSR. The DOUT outputs a logical 1 if the data conversion has been completed. Keep in mind the inversion relationship between the DOUT and the DSR line, because both of them are connected by a MAX220 inverter, So a logical 1 in the DOUT is the

```
/*****************************************************************************
 *          Inline Assembly Function to Read the Converted Data              *
 *****************************************************************************/
  int c_getad()
  {
Q     short rc;
R     _asm
      {
S          mov   dx, MCR        ; Set Modem Control Register - DTR=1 & RTS=1
           mov   al, SCLK+CS    ; Begin conversion (RTS inverted to 0 by MAX-220).
           out   dx, al         ; Finish set up the MCR.
T          mov   cx, 0ch        ; Setup the bit counter = 12 bit.
U          mov   bx, 00h        ; Setup result register bx=0000.
           mov   dx, MSR        ; Wait conversion complete
V   check: in    al, dx         ; Check if bit-5 of MSR=0, it connects to DOUT of AD.
           test  al, 20h        ; DOUT sends a 1 when conversion is done, but this is
                                ; inverted to 0 by the MAX220
           jnz   check          ; The bit-5 on MSR is not 0, means DOUT is not 1, wait.
W   again: mov   dx, DT         ; Conversion is finished. Delay a period.
    cycl1: dec   dx             ; Delay a short period of time
X          jnz   cycl1
           mov   dx, MCR        ;
           mov   al, CS         ; Set CLK of AD to high (DTR=0 RTS=1), both
           out   dx, al         ; DTR & RTS inverted to 1 & 0 (SCLK=1 CS=0 on AD).
           mov   dx, DT         ; Delay a short period of time
Y   cycl2: dec   dx             ;
           jnz   cycl2          ;
           mov   dx, MCR        ; Set CLK of AD to low
           mov   al, SCLK+CS    ; (DTR=RTS=1) DTR->SCLK, RTS->CS-bar.
Z          out   dx, al         ; SCLK=CS-bar=0 by MAX-220.
           mov   dx, DT         ; Delay a short period of time
1   cycl3: dec   dx             ;
           jnz   cycl3          ;
           mov   dx, MSR        ; Begin input 12-bit data bit-by-bit.
           in    al, dx         ; Check if the bit-5=1 on MSR (DOUT of AD).
2          test  al, 20h        ; If DOUT=1,which is inverted to 0 by MAX-220.
           jnz   done           ; So a 1 in bit-5 on MSR means a 0 in DOUT received.
           inc   bx             ; An 1 in DOUT is received, increase result bx by 1.
     done: shl   bx, 1          ; Shift result left by 1 bit.
3          dec   cx             ; 12-bit is completed?
           jnz   again          ; No, continuing on next bit
4          mov   dx, MCR        ;
           mov   al, SCLK       ; Reset MAX-187 AD converter.
           out   dx, al         ;
5          shr   bx, 1          ; Fix result by shifting bx right by 1 bit
           mov   rc, bx         ; Return the result.
      }
6     return rc;
  }
```

FIGURE 2.80 The inline assembly function `c_getad()`.

equivalent of a logical `0` in the DSR line, and vice versa. The instruction `test al, 20h` is used to determine whether bit 5 on the MSR is set to `0`. If the result of executing this instruction is a nonzero value, which means that a logical `1` has been received at bit 5 on the MSR, or a logical 0 received at the DOUT on the MAX187, it means that the data conversion has not been successfully completed. The instruction `jnz check` is used to direct the program back to the `label check` to continue inspecting the value of bit 5 until the received DOUT is `1`, which is equivalent to the received DSR being 0.

W: If the result of running the instruction `test al, 20h` is `0`, which means that the DOUT outputs a logical `1` and the received DSR line is reset to 0; it means that the data conversion has been successfully completed. A time delay is executed so that the program will wait for the converted data from the DSR line.

X: After the time delay, the converted data is stable on the DSR line, and the program can now pick up one bit of the data by sending out a clock to the SCLK terminal on the MAX187. The result of setting the CS (to a decimal `2` or a binary `00000010b`) on the MCR is to set a logical `1` on the RTS and a logical `0` on the DTR lines (refer to Figure 1.30. in Chapter 1), respectively. When this instruction is executed, it sets a logical `0` on the CS bar and a logical `1` on the SCLK terminals on the MAX187. This is equivalent to generating a `LOW`-to-`HIGH` transition on the SCLK (the CS bar setting is `0` to make the A/D selected), and therefore a converted data stored in the output shift register on the MAX187 is shifted one bit to the DSR line.

Y: Another time delay is performed so the system can wait for the data to arrive over the DSR line.

Z: By setting up the `SCLK+CS` on the MCR, which is equivalent to setting the MCR to binary byte 00000011b MCR, the DTR and RTS lines are set to logical `1`. (Refer to Figure 1.30 in Chapter 1.) Because of the MAX220 inverter, the SCLK and the CS bar on the MAX187 are reset to logical `0`. This means that the A/D converter is still selected, but the serial clock input is reset to 0 (meaning that SCLK is inactive). This operation is equivalent to resetting the clock, and is necessary because after the program finishes moving out one bit from the MAX187, we need to perform some preparations for the next bit transfer, and resetting the clock is one of those preparations.

1: Insert a time delay to stabilize the clock reset.

2: Now the program must move the data into the PC from the DSR line. Actually, it will not move any bits from the DSR line; instead it only checks each bit's value on the DSR line by inspecting bit 5 on the MSR. (Refer to Figure 1.32 in Chapter 1.) By executing the instruction `test al, 20h`, we can inspect the value of bit 5 on the MSR. A value of `1` in bit 5 means that a logical `1` is set on the DSR line, and a logical `0` is output from the DOUT on the MAX187 because of the MAX220 inverter. However, if bit 5 on the MSR is set to 0, it means that a logical `0` has been received on the DSR line and that, therefore, a logical `1` is output from the MAX187. If a logical 1 is inspected on bit 5 on the MSR, it means that a logical `0` has been output from the MAX187. In this case, we need do nothing to the storage register `bx` except to shift its contents left by one bit. We can do this by executing the instruction `jnz done`, which will transfer the program to label `done` to fulfill this shift. The shift includes a hiding operation, which will add a `0` to the LSB on the `bx` register because a logical `0` has been output from the DOUT on the MAX187. If a logical `0` is detected on the DSR line, a logical `1` will then be output from the DOUT on the MAX187, and the `bx` register will be increased by 1 on the LSB. This is equivalent to storing a value of `1` in the `bx`, because the MAX187 outputs a logical `1`. Following this addition, the `bx` is also shifted left by one bit to prepare it for the next bit input. In this way, our program finishes the collection and storage of one data bit, storing the partial result in the register `bx`.

3: Because the register `cx` is our counter, we can execute the instruction `dec cx` to determine whether we have collected and stored all 12 bits of data from the MAX187. If the result of executing this instruction is `0`, which means that all 12 bits of data have been collected, then we need to return the collected result to the calling function and exit the current inline assembly function. However, if the result is nonzero, it means that we need to collect the remaining bits from the MAX187. In this case, the program is transferred back to the `label` **again** and we need to repeat steps W, X, Y, Z, 1, and 2 to collect the next bit of data from the MAX187.

4: After all 12 bits of data have been collected and stored, we need to reset the MAX187. By sending the SCLK to the MCR, which is equivalent to setting the binary byte 00000001b to the MCR, we can set the SCLK and the CS-bar on the MAX187 logical 0 and logical 1, respectively. This is equivalent to resetting the serial clock on the MAX187 and deselecting the A/D converter.

5: We need to shift the result register `bx` left 11 times to get the correct data. But in steps W, X, Y, Z, 1 and 2, which together can be considered a loop operation, the `bx` is shifted 12 times. To correct this overshift error, we need to shift the `bx` right by `1`.

6: Finally, the collected result is assigned to the short variable `rc` that is returned to the calling function.

We have now examined all of the functions in this project. In the Visual C++ 6.0 workspace, click `Build|Build SerialMAXEmbed.exe` from the menu bar to compile and build the project. If no error occurs, click `Build|Execute SerialMAXEmbed.exe` to run the project. The input analog waveform to the MAX187 can be any of three waveforms: sinusoidal, square or triangular.

You can stop the program by pressing any key.

We can also develop a MATLAB plotting program to plot the collected results on the graph. To do this, open the MATLAB workspace and create a new M-File named `Serialmaxemb.m`; then enter the code shown in Figure 2.81 into the new file.

```
% Display the serial port data
% July 3, 2003
% Copyright by Y. Bai

fid = fopen('C:/SData/serialmaxemb.dat', 'rt');
S = fscanf(fid, '%f');
plot(S);
grid;
fclose(fid);
```

FIGURE 2.81 The MATLAB plot function.

Save this file in the MATLAB default folder (typically `C:\MATLAB\bin`).

To run the MATLAB program, type the name, `Serialmaxemb`, of this program in the MATLAB workspace. This will instruct the plot function to plot the collected data. The results are shown in Figure 2.82.

As previously mentioned, when compared with programs developed in C code, those written in inline assembly code have the advantage of running faster because assembly code is such a low-level language. In addition, programs that incorporate assembly language instructions can collect more converted data than can equivalent programs written purely in C. In other words, using inline assembly instructions yields a higher sample number of analog signals. This is illustrated in Figure 2.82. In the `SerialMAX` project we created in Section 2.7, the maximum frequency of the input analog signal is about 30 Hz. This frequency can be increased to 80 Hz using the enhanced project, `SerialMAXEmbed`.

The complete files for this project, including the source file, the header file, the executable file, and a MATLAB plot file, are stored in the folder `Chapter 2\SerialMAXEmbed`, which is located on the attached CD. To run this project on your computer, you need to create a new folder

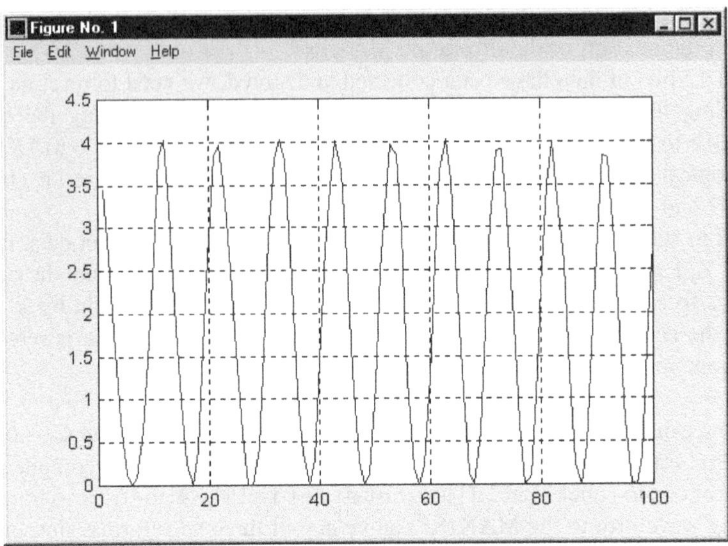

FIGURE 2.82 The running result of the `SerialMAXEmbed` project.

in which to store the converted data file. (Again, the most generic folder would be `C:\SData`.) To run the project on your computer, follow these steps:

1. Copy the executable file `SerialMAXEmbed.exe` and store it on the root drive on your computer.
2. Copy the MATLAB file `Serialmaxemb.m` and store it on your system in the default MATLAB folder (typically, `C:\MATLAB\bin`).
3. Run the executable file from your computer.
4. Finally, run the MATLAB file to plot the results of running the program.

2.8 CHAPTER SUMMARY

This chapter has presented a number of serial port interfacing projects developed in ANSI C for the MS-DOS environment. The concept of virtual machines was introduced in Section 2.1. Two categories of operating systems, Windows 95/98/Me and Windows NT/2000/XP, were also introduced, along with their associated virtual machines and running modes. When running MS-DOS-compatible ANSI C programs, the difference between these two categories is that Windows 95/98/Me provides a V86 mode, but Windows NT/2000/XP provides only a true protected mode.

In Section 2.2, a simple loopback test program, developed in ANSI C, demonstrated the use of low-level system functions to access serial ports.

Our discussion of inline assembly functions began in Section 2.3, and included detailed instructions on how to use them. Embedding assembly instructions into C code can greatly improve an entire program's running speed.

In section 2.4, we examined and created a practical serial port communication program. This sample program was designed to allow two computers (in our case, a master and a slave) to easily exchange data and files via the RS-232 serial ports. Step by step, both the master-side program and the slave-side program were discussed in detail.

We then improved the existing communication project by embedding the inline assembly instructions that we developed in section 2.5. This hands-on example illustrated the advantages of using inline assembly instructions within programs originally written purely in C.

In Section 2.6, our exploration deepened; here the interrupt mechanism and other functions of serial port communications were discussed and analyzed in detail as we examined an interrupt-driven serial port interfacing program.

The interfacing programs we analyzed in Section 2.7 were designed to facilitate communications between a PC and various A/D converters via the serial port. We tried out two commercial A/D converters, the TLC548 eight-bit serial converter and the MAX187 12-bit serial converter, and learned how they interface with the PC. These two A/D converters are very popular and widely implemented in the industrial and manufacturing fields. They are designed to greatly simplify the process of transferring data between PCs and A/D converters. With some simple hardware connections, an A/D converter and a PC can easily be configured to the communicate, and without the need for additional device drivers. This section included very detailed explanations and illustrations, and the supplemental CD at the back of this book provides you with the actual interface circuits for these two products. You also get the MATLAB plotting program, which we used in this section to plot the data we collected from our sample projects. Finally, we had some more practice with embedded assembly instructions that further improved the speed response of our original interface program.

3 Serial Port Interfaces Developed in VC++ 6.0

3.1 INTRODUCTION

This chapter examines serial port communication programs applied in the Windows NT/2000/XP operating systems (OSs). Serial port communication is widely applied in all industries, including commercial applications, manufacturing, and academic research and libraries. One of the most popular languages used for serial port programming is C/C++, which provides a good real-time environment for the serial communication applications.

The serial port driver is used for general-purpose functions. Any device applied to the serial transmission mode must follow the serial communication protocol without exception. A serial port driver therefore applies to any device that uses the serial port communication convention.

The driver provided by the manufacturers is a piece of software code, which works as a bridge to connect the program and the serial port to fulfill a serial communication between the computer and the device. A serial port interface configuration is shown in Figure 3.1.

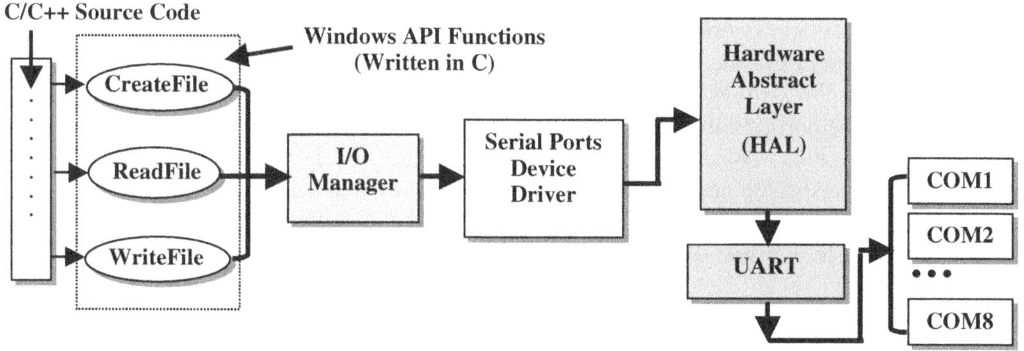

FIGURE 3.1 The configuration of the serial port interface.

When the program runs in protected mode, unlike the C programs discussed in Chapter 2, in which the low-level hardware is accessed by using a group of system *input/output* (I/O) functions such as `_inp()` and `_outp()`, all interfaces to the serial port here are performed by calling three Win32 applications programming interface (API) functions: `CreateFile()`, `ReadFile()`, and `WriteFile()`. These three Win32 API functions are mapped to the three C run-time functions `fopen()`, `fread()`, and `fwrite()`, respectively. These API functions provide paths to communicate with the serial port driver in order to access the serial port hardware. All Win32 API functions are written in C (not C++). Recall from Chapter 2 that these functions cannot directly access the serial driver from within functions themselves because the Window OS is a multiple-task mechanism. The I/O manager controls, from within the Windows OS, all processes that need to access hardware. Any function that needs to access the serial port will send a request to the I/O manager, which will talk directly to the serial port driver. Between the serial port driver and the actual port hardware is a Hardware Abstract Layer (HAL), which is a block of code that sets up mapping between the actual port controller (the UART) and the system memory. The HAL controls access to the hardware, while the Universal Asynchronous Receiver and Transmitter (UART) controls all serial ports.

Figure 3.1 illustrates the complications involved in processing a serial communication request in Windows NT/2000/XP. This complexity shouldn't be a cause of concern because the computer handles most jobs, and your concern is only certain interface functions need to be called to access the serial port. The process is similar to accessing a black box, and it isn't important to know too much about what is going on inside the black box if a function is called to communicate with the port.

Most computers have only one or two serial ports. Some specially designed computers provide up to four ports, and the use of interface cards can enable up to eight serial ports. In Section 3.4, we will discuss how to use an interface card, provided by LabVIEW, to add eight serial ports with interfacing mode RS-485.

Besides these interfacing functions, certain C/C++ functions are available for interfacing with serial ports. In this chapter, we will discuss these functions and examine a number of examples. In addition, we'll look at a detailed procedure that illustrates how to create, read, and write a serial port in C/C++, step by step.

The most popular methods for communicating with serial ports in C/C++ involve using Windows API functions. The most critical phase of programming for serial communications is configuring the port settings with the `DCB` structure. Erroneously initializing the `DCB` structure is a common problem. When a serial communication function does not produce the expected results, the `DCB` structure may be in error.

A call to the Windows API function `CreateFile()` opens a serial port with default port settings. Usually, the application needs to change the defaults. Typically, the `GetCommState()` function is used to retrieve the default settings of the port, and the `SetCommState()` function is used to set new port settings.

Configuring the ports involves using the `COMMTIMEOUTS` structure to set the timeout values for read/write operations. When a timeout error occurs, the `ReadFile()` or `WriteFile()` function returns the specific number of characters successfully transferred.

3.1.1 Configuring a Serial Port

To configure a serial port, our program should follow these steps:

1. Call the `CreateFile()` function to open a new serial port with the default settings.
2. Initialize the `DCBlength` member of the `DCB` structure to the size of the structure. This initialization is required before the program can pass `DCBlength` as a variable to any function.
3. Call the `GetCommState()` function to retrieve the default settings for the port opened with the `CreateFile()` function. To identify the port, specify it in the `hPort` parameter returned by `CreateFile()`.
4. Modify the `DCB` members as required. Figure 3.2 shows the `DCB` structure members that are most frequently modified.
5. Call the `SetCommState()` function to assign the new port settings.

To illustrate these steps, a piece of sample code is shown in Figure 3.2. Notice in this annotated code that all interfacing functions discussed thus far are highlighted.

The first step is to call the `CreateFile()` function to open a new port. Seven arguments are passed to this function.

The returned handler, `hPort`, is a key parameter for the opened serial port. This is a unique `ID` for the new port, and all following configurations for the serial port are based on this handler.

Next, a new port is opened, and the initialization to the `DCBlength` member of the `DCB` structure is executed, which is identical to step 2 we listed previously. Then a call to the

```
// Open the serial port.
hPort = CreateFile(lpszPortName,              // Pointer to the name of the port
        GENERIC_READ | GENERIC_WRITE,  // Access (read/write) mode
        0,                              // Share mode
        NULL,                           // Pointer to the security attribute
        OPEN_EXISTING,                  // How to open the serial port
        0,                              // Port attributes
        NULL);                          // Handle to port with attribute to copy
// If it fails to open the port, return error.
if ( hPort == INVALID_HANDLE_VALUE )
{
        CloseHandle(hPort);             // Could not open the port.
        LocalFree( lpMsgBuf );          // Free the buffer.
        return EC_FOPEN;
}
PortDCB.DCBlength = sizeof(DCB);
GetCommState(hPort, &PortDCB);                  // Get the default port setting information.
// Change the DCB structure settings.
PortDCB.BaudRate = 9600;                        // Current baud rate
PortDCB.fBinary = TRUE;                         // Binary mode; no EOF check
PortDCB.fParity = TRUE;                         // Enable parity checking.
PortDCB.fOutxCtsFlow = FALSE;                   // No CTS output flow control
PortDCB.fOutxDsrFlow = FALSE;                   // No DSR output flow control
PortDCB.fDtrControl = DTR_CONTROL_ENABLE; // DTR flow control type
PortDCB.fDsrSensitivity = FALSE;                // DSR sensitivity
PortDCB.fTXContinueOnXoff = TRUE;               // XOFF continues Tx
PortDCB.fOutX = FALSE;                          // No XON/XOFF out flow control
PortDCB.fInX = FALSE;                           // No XON/XOFF in flow control
PortDCB.fErrorChar = FALSE;                     // Disable error replacement.
PortDCB.fNull = FALSE;                          // Disable null stripping.
PortDCB.fRtsControl = RTS_CONTROL_ENABLE;  // RTS flow control
PortDCB.fAbortOnError = FALSE;                  // Do not abort reads/writes on error
PortDCB.ByteSize = 8;                           // Number of bits/bytes, 4-8
PortDCB.Parity = NOPARITY;                      // 0-4=no,odd,even,mark,space
PortDCB.StopBits = ONESTOPBIT;                  // 0,1,2 = 1, 1.5, 2
// Configure the port according to the specifications of the DCB structure.
if (!SetCommState (hPort, &PortDCB))
{
        printf("Unable to configure the port & Err Info. = %s\n", (LPCTSTR)lpMsgBuf);
        // Free the buffer.
        LocalFree( lpMsgBuf );
        return EC_INVAL_CONFIG;
}
// Retrieve the time-out parameters for all read and write operations on the port.
GetCommTimeouts(hPort, &CommTimeouts);

// Change the COMMTIMEOUTS structure settings.
CommTimeouts.ReadIntervalTimeout = MAXDWORD;
CommTimeouts.ReadTotalTimeoutMultiplier = 0;
CommTimeouts.ReadTotalTimeoutConstant = 0;
CommTimeouts.WriteTotalTimeoutMultiplier = 10;
CommTimeouts.WriteTotalTimeoutConstant = 1000;

// Set the time-out parameters for all read and write operations on the port.
if (!SetCommTimeouts (hPort, &CommTimeouts))
```

FIGURE 3.2 An example of the serial interface function. *(continued)*

```
{
        // Could not create the read thread.
        dwError = GetLastError();
        printf("Unable to set the time-out parameters & Err code = %ld\n", dwError);
        return EC_TIMEOUT_SET;
}
EscapeCommFunction(hPort, SETDTR);
EscapeCommFunction(hPort, SETRTS);
pCreate->h_Port = hPort;                    // reserve the port handle
```

FIGURE 3.2 An example of the serial interface function.

`GetCommState()` function is executed to retrieve the default settings for the newly opened port. After the default parameters have been modified, a call to `SetCommState()` is executed to set up these new settings.Similarly, the `GetCommTimeouts()` and `SetCommTimeouts()` functions are called to set up new parameters for the timeout structure. Finally, we need to save the port handler `hPort` to our user-defined data structure `pCreate` for future use.

By now, it may be apparent that for all function calls to access the port, either to retrieve or set up parameters for the opened serial port, the port handler `hPort` must be used as an identifier to access the port. That is why we need to store this handler in our data structure. This is the only way we can access that port. After configuring and initializing the serial port, we can access the port with either the `ReadFile()` or `WriteFile()` function.

3.1.2 Writing Data to the Serial Port

Typically, the `WriteFile()` function is used to access the port opened by the `CreateFile()` function and to send new data to the port. To be exact, send the new data to a memory location that is mapped to the writing buffer in the `UART`, and the latter will take charge of picking up that data and transmitting it to the port.

For a multiple-task OS, if we want to communicate to the port with an overlapping mode, we must create some threads in our application to transmit the data asynchronously between our machine and the port. For a simple task, we can call this function directly to communicate with the port.

To write to the serial port, our program should incorporate these steps:

1. Pass the port handler to the `WriteFile()` function in the `hPort` parameter. The `CreateFile()` function returns this handler when our program opens a new port.
2. Specify a pointer to the data to be written in `lpBuffer`. Typically, this will be binary data or a character array.
3. Specify the number of characters to write in `nNumberOfBytesToWrite`. For Windows CE–based devices, only one character is usually written, because the application must convert `Unicode` characters to `ASCII` characters to enable a text transfer to a device at the opposite end of a serial connection.
4. Specify in `lpNumberOfBytesWritten` a pointer to the number of bytes actually written. `WriteFile()` fills this variable so that our program can determine if the data has been transferred.
5. Be sure that the `lpOverlapped` parameter is set to NULL.

An example of `WriteFile()` is shown in Figure 3.3.

```
if (!WriteFile (hPort,                    // Port handle
                NumByte,                  // Number of bytes to write
                &dwNumBytesWritten,       // Pointer to the number of bytes written
                NULL))                    // Must be NULL for Windows CE
{
        // WriteFile failed. Report error.
        printf("Unable to write the port ...& Err Info. = %s", (LPCTSTR)lpMsgBuf);
        // Free the buffer.
        LocalFree( lpMsgBuf );
        .......
}
```

FIGURE 3.3 An example of `WriteFile()` function.

3.1.3 Reading Data from the Serial Port

Typically, a read operation is a separate thread that is always ready to process data arriving at a serial port (specifically, at the reading buffer of a `UART`). A communication event signals the read thread to indicate that there is data to be read at a serial port. The thread usually reads only one byte at a time—one `ReadFile()` call for one byte until all the data has been read. Then the read thread waits for another communication event.

To read data from a serial port, our program should incorporate these steps:

1. Pass the port handler to `ReadFile()` in the `hPort` parameter. The `CreateFile()` function returns this handler when a new port is created.
2. Specify a pointer to the data to be read in `lpBuffer`.
3. Specify the number of characters to read in `nNumberOfBytesToRead`.
4. Specify a pointer to the number of bytes actually read in the argument `lpNumberOfBytesRead`.
5. Be sure that `lpOverlapped` is set to NULL. Windows CE does not support the overlapped I/O.

Another important issue arises when dealing with reading data from a serial port, and that is how to handle the `WaitCommEvent()` function when interfacing to a serial port to read the data. In a Windows OS, some communication events are used to coordinate retrieving data from a serial port, such as `EV_RXCHAR`, `EV_CTS`, and `EV_RING`. These belong to system events and only apply to events of serial port communication (not synchronous events such as `Semaphores`, `Events`, `Mutex`, or `Critical Sections`). The problem is that if no event occurs when executing the `WaitCommEvent()` function to a serial port, that function will wait forever, which means that the program will enter a dead cycle and the computer will hang.

This is a serious problem for the system. To solve this dead-cycle problem when calling `WaitCommEvent()`, our program must create a separate thread for reading the data from a serial port. In addition, a timeout event must be added to monitor the `WaitCommEvent()` function. When executing a data-reading task, we first create a thread to execute the `WaitCommEvent()` and `ReadFile()` functions in that thread. Then we call the `WaitForSingleObject()` function to monitor the thread's running status. A timeout event will be signaled and returned from the thread if no serial event occurs when `WaitCommEvent()` is executed to wait for any kind of event in the thread. By configuring our program this way, we can avoid the dead cycle introduced by executing the `WaitCommEvent()` function when reading data from a serial port. Figure 3.4 shows a code example that uses a separate thread and a timeout event to read data from a serial port.

```
if (!(hThread = CreateThread(NULL,              // no security attributes
                0,                              // use default stack size
                (LPTHREAD_START_ROUTINE) ThreadFunc,
                (LPVOID)hCommPort,              // parameter to thread function
                CREATE_SUSPENDED,               // creation flag - suspended
                &IDThread) ) )                  // returns thread ID
{
        printf("Create Read Thread failed\n");
        return EC_CREATE_THREAD;
}
ResumeThread(hThread);                          // start thread function now
Ret = WaitForSingleObject(hThread, dTimeout);
if (Ret == WAIT_OBJECT_0)
{
        // data received & process it...
        // Need do nothing, the data has been stored in the hCommPort in Thread Func.
        // close thread handle
        CloseHandle(hThread);
}
else if (Ret == WAIT_TIMEOUT)
{
        // time out happened, warning & kill thread
        Ret = GetExitCodeThread(hThread, &ExitCode);
        if (ExitCode == STILL_ACTIVE)
        {
                printf("Time out happened!\n");         // debug purpose
                TerminateThread(hThread, ExitCode);
                CloseHandle(hThread);
                return EC_PORT_TIMEOUT;
        }
        else
        {
                printf("ERROR in GetExitCodeThread: != STILL_ACTIVE\n");
                ecStatus = EC_EXIT_CODE;
        }
}
else
{
        printf("ERROR in WaitFor SingleObject...\n");
        ecStatus = EC_WAIT_SINGLEOBJ;
}
......
```

FIGURE 3.4 An example of using the thread to handle the data reading and the timeout.

Here our program calls the `CreateThread()` function to create a new separate thread and process `WaitCommEvent()` in the thread function, `ThreadFunc`, which is shown in Figure 3.5. Once the thread function is running, we call the function `WaitForSingleObject()` to monitor the running status of the thread function. In actuality, we are monitoring the executing status of the `WaitCommEvent()` function. If a serial port event occurs, `WaitCommEvent()` will be signaled, and the `ReadFile()` function will be executed to read the data from the serial port. Once this has happened, the mission of the thread function has been accomplished; the thread function will be terminated and then returned to the `WaitForSingleObject() function`, and the latter will be signaled as it receives the returned thread handler `hThread`. These processes are illustrated in Figure 3.5.

If no serial event occurs during the execution of `WaitCommEvent()` in the thread function and the waiting period is over the timeout value set by `SetCommTimeouts()`, a timeout event

```
void WINAPI ThreadFunc(void* hCommPorts)
{
        ......
        // Specify a set of events to be monitored for the port.
        SetCommMask(CommPorts->handlePort, EV_RXCHAR | EV_CTS |
                                                    EV_DSR | EV_RLSD | EV_RING);

        // Wait for an event to occur for the port.
        WaitCommEvent(CommPorts->handlePort, &dwCommModemStatus, 0);

        // Re-specify the set of events to be monitored for the port.
        SetCommMask(CommPorts->handlePort, EV_RXCHAR | EV_CTS |
                                                    EV_DSR |EV_RLSD| EV_RING);

        if (dwCommModemStatus & EV_RXCHAR||dwCommModemStatus & EV_RLSD)
        {   // received the char_event
            // Read the data from the serial port.
            bResult = ReadFile(CommPorts->handlePort, &Byte, 1, &dwBytesTransferred, 0);

            if (!bResult)
            {
                printf("Unable to read the port ...& Err Info. = %s\n", (LPCTSTR)lpMsgBuf);
                LocalFree( lpMsgBuf );                // Free the buffer.
                printf("ERROR in PortRead - Timeout\n");
            }
            else
            {
                // store the data read.
                CommPorts->bByte = Byte;
                nTotRead++;
            }
        }

        return;
}
```

FIGURE 3.5 The thread function.

will occur. This timeout event will signal the `WaitForSingleObject()` function, which will terminate the execution of the function. In this case, a warning message will be sent to the system to indicate that a timeout has occurred.

Figure 3.5 shows the body of the thread function. A system function `SetCommMask()` is called to set the events that we want to monitor. These include `EV_RXCHAR` (the received character event), `EV_CTS` (CTS is signaled), `EV_DSR` (DSR is signaled), and `EV_RING` (the ring event). After that, the program calls `WaitCommEvent()` to wait the events as they occur.

If any of the desired events occur, `WaitCommEvent()` is activated. To ensure that the correct masks are used for the next reading process, `SetCommMask()` is called again to reset the desired masks for the serial events. Then after checking to confirm that it has received the correct event, the program reads the data by using the `ReadFile()` function. An error message will be displayed if any mistakes occur during the `ReadFile()` process.

At this point, we have finished reviewing the general functions used for serial port communications in C/C++. In the following section, we will give a more detailed description and present some actual examples.

TIP: All programs developed in this chapter can run in Windows NT/2000/XP or Windows 95/98/Me operating systems, but the running mode is different than the virtual (v86) mode we used in Chapter 2. These programs run in protected mode, which means that any access to the low-level hardware, such as the port or registers in the UART, is performed using Win32 API functions, not the system I/O functions as we did in Chapter 2.

3.2 A SINGLE-LOOP SERIAL PORT COMMUNICATION TEST IN C/C++

The first example in this chapter is a simple single-loop serial port test project developed in C/C++ (Win32 console mode). This program is similar to the project developed in Chapter 2, but different data structures and Win32 API functions are used here to access the low-level hardware. (Remember, this project is designed to run under the protected mode, not V86 mode as we used in Chapter 2.)

3.2.1 Hardware Installation

We'll need a DB-9 serial port for single-loop testing; the hardware installation is shown in Figure 3.6. Make the same connection with the serial port on your computer.

Pin-Number	Function
1	Not used
2	R_{XD}
3	T_{XD}
4	Not used
5	GND

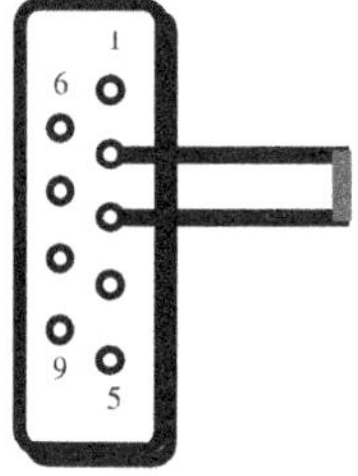

FIGURE 3.6 The loopback connection.

We first connect pin 2 with pin 3 on a DB-9 connector. This way, we form a single-loop structure. During testing, if the port is functioning correctly, all data sent to the port should be received from the same port. You can select either COM1 or COM2 for the testing port if multiple ports are available on your computer. (If only one port is available, it will usually be COM1). Be sure to turn off your computer before making this connection.

3.2.2 Developing a Console Application Testing Program

For this first simple example, we want to develop a `Win32 Console Application`, which is a C-code testing program that will be run in a DOS prompt window. Later on you can develop this program to a *dynamic link library* (DLL) or a Win32 Windows application if you like.

This example will perform a single-loop test for each serial port (from `COM1` to `COM8`) on our computer. For each test, a sequence of testing data (ASCII characters, from `0` through `9` and from `A` through `Z`) will be sent to each port. Then the sequence will be retrieved from each port, and a comparison will be made between the sent-out characters and the read-back characters to confirm that each port is correctly sending and reading data. The test will be successful if the sent-out and the read-back data sequences are identical. Otherwise, the test will be considered a failure, and an error message will be displayed on the screen.

First, create a new folder on your root drive and name it `C:\COMTest`. Then launch Visual C++ 6.0 and create a new project. Select `Win32 Console Application` from the `Projects` list. Enter `SimpleCOM` in the `Project name:` field, and make sure the content of the

`Location:` field is our user-defined project directory `C:\COMTest`. Click `OK` to open this new project.

Next we need to create two header files to declare the variables, structures, and functions used in this project. (The reason we'll use two header files is that the size of a single header file would be very large for this project.) From the menu, click `File|New`, and then select `C/C++ Header File` from the list that appears. Enter `SimpleCOM` in the `File name:` field, and then click `OK` to open the newly created header file, `SimpleCOM.h`. Enter the code shown in Figure 3.7 to this file.

```
/*****************************************************************************
 * NAME        : SimpleCOM.h
 * DESC        : Header file for SimpleCOM.cpp
 * DATE        : 7/15/2003
 * PGMR        : Y. Bai
 *****************************************************************************/
#ifndef SIMPLECOM_H_
#define SIMPLECOM_H_

#include <stdio.h>
#include <stdlib.h>
#include <string.h>
#include <windows.h>

#define MAX_MENU                    9
#define MAX_STRING                256
#define NOPARITY                    0
#define ONESTOPBIT                  0
#define RTS_CONTROL_DISABLE     0x00
A   #define RTS_CONTROL_ENABLE      0x01
#define DTR_CONTROL_DISABLE     0x00
#define DTR_CONTROL_ENABLE      0x01
#define  msg(info)   MessageBox(NULL, info, "", MB_OK)

typedef struct
{
  unsigned long  ulCtrlerID;
  char           cEcho;
B   char           cEORChar;
  long           lTimeout;
  long           lBaudRate;
  long           lDataBits;
  HANDLE         h_Port;
}SerialCreate, *pSerialCreate;
typedef struct
{
  char           *pcBuffer;
  BYTE           bByte;
C   int            iMaxChars;
  int            piNumRcvd;
  char           cTermChar;
  HANDLE         handlePort;
}CommPortClass;
```

FIGURE 3.7 The header file of the project SimpleCom. *(continued)*

```
D   typedef enum
    {
            OK                          = 0,            /* no error */
            EC_TIMEOUT,
            EC_FOPEN,
            EC_INVAL_CONFIG,
            EC_TIMEOUT_SET,
            EC_RECV_TIMEOUT,
            EC_EXIT_CODE,
            EC_WAIT_SINGLEOBJ,
            EC_INVALIDPORT,
            EC_WRITE_FAIL,
            EC_READ_FAIL,
            EC_TEST_FAIL,
            EC_CREATE_THREAD,
            EC_PORT_INITDONE,
            EC_UNKNOWNERROR
    }ERR_CODE;

    ERR_CODE PortInitialize(LPTSTR lpszPortName, pSerialCreate pCreate);
    ERR_CODE PortWrite(HANDLE handPort, BYTE bByte, int NumByte);
E   ERR_CODE PortRead(CommPortClass *hCommPort);
    void WINAPI ThreadFunc(void* hCommPorts);

    char* getMenuItem(unsigned char mPort);
    ERR_CODE SetupPort(char* cPort, int nPort);
    ERR_CODE TestPort(char* cPort, BOOL display);

    #endif
```

FIGURE 3.7 The header file of the project SimpleCom.

A: Some system constants are declared at the beginning of the file. All these constants are used to set up and configure the serial port to be tested. A simplified message box function is also declared here.

B: The data structure `SerialCreate` is declared here; it provides some parameters necessary for configuring and initializing the serial port.

C: The data structure `CommPortClass` is used to store the parameters necessary for the `PortRead()` function to receive data from the serial port.

D: The data structure `ERR_CODE` is next defined. It includes all errors that could possibly occur when the project is run. This structure is an `enum` type starting from `0`, which is defined as `OK` (no error); all elements having a values greater than `0` are mapped to different errors.
The advantage of using `enum` to define our error structure is to make the project clean. That is, integrating all errors within this structure will make it easy to check and modify all possible errors in the testing system. The `enum` structure also saves space by preventing us from having to write the values associated with all error constants.

E: All the functions that will be used in this project are declared here. The first four functions are used to directly communicate with the serial device driver and perform such interfacing tasks as initializing the port, writing to the port, and reading from the port. The thread function is used to handle the `PortRead()` function to avoid the dead cycle of the port when executing the `WaitCommEvent()` system function. The last three functions belong to the middle-layer functions that will call the four previous functions to access the serial port to fulfill the desired tasks.

Click the `File|New` menu item again to create the second header file, which should be named `Menu.h`. Enter the code shown in Figure 3.8 into this file.

```
  /*****************************************************************************
   * NAME        : Menu.h
   * DESC        : Header file for the menu input and menu display
   * PGMR        : Y. Bai
   *****************************************************************************/
  #define NUM_BYTE     1
  #define MAX_BYTE     90
  #define START_BYTE   48
  #define BAUD_RATE    9600
A #define NUM_BITS     8
  #define TIME_OUT     3000
  HANDLE         hPort;
B bool           TestPassed;
  bool           PortCreateflg[9];
C char* menuData[] =
  { {"A  Test Port COM 1\n"},
    {"B  Test Port COM 2\n"},
    {"C  Test Port COM 3\n"},
    {"D  Test Port COM 4\n"},
    {"E  Test Port COM 5\n"},
    {"F  Test Port COM 6\n"},
    {"G  Test Port COM 7\n"},
    {"H  Test Port COM 8\n"},
    {"X  EXIT\n\n"} };
  char* menuTitle[] =
D { {"SERIAL PORT TESTING  - Enter Selection > \n\n"}};
```

FIGURE 3.8 The header file Menu.h.

A: The remaining system constants are defined in this file. These parameters are used to set up the serial port and provide values for certain symbolic constants applied in the program.

B: Some global variables are declared here. The `hPort` variable is a handler used to reserve the returned handler when a new serial port is created. The Boolean variable `TestPassed` is used to keep and monitor the testing status of the ports. The Boolean array `PortCreateflg[]` is used to record the status of each port's initialization. An error will be encountered if the program tries to initialize a serial port that has already been initialized. By using this array, we can easily check the initialization status for each port, and thus avoid initialization duplication.

C: A pointer array is declared here; the elements of this array will be displayed on the screen as a test menu. In total, there are nine selections. Each of the upper eight selections, from `A` to `H`, is used to execute a routine that tests a separate serial port. The last selection, selection 9 (x), is used to exit the program.

D: The `menuTitle` variable is also a pointer array, which is used to display the menu title on the screen as the program runs.

Now let us create our source code. We will divide our source code into two files. One is called `SimpleCOM.cpp`, which is used to perform interactions with the user and pass parameters received from the keyboard to the interfacing functions to access the serial port. The other one is called `ComPortTest.cpp`, which is used to execute the interfacing functions to communicate with the port to fulfill the port test.

Let us now create the source file `SimpleCOM.cpp`. Click the `File|New` menu item, select `C++ Source File`, enter `SimpleCOM` into the `File name:` field, and then click `OK` to open this new source file. Enter the code shown in Figure 3.9 into this file.

```
/*****************************************************************************
 * NAME        : SimpleCOM.cpp
 * DESC        : Simple serial port test program - single loop
 * DATE        : 7/15/2003
 * PGMR        : Y. Bai
 *****************************************************************************/
#include "SimpleCOM.h"
#include "Menu.h"

void main()
{
     int     index;
     bool    select = TRUE;
     char    userInput[16];
A    char* comPort;
     ERR_CODE  ecRet = OK;
     unsigned char cPort;

     TestPassed = FALSE;
B    while(select)
     {
          printf("\n");
C         for (index = 0; index < MAX_MENU; index++)
          {
                 PortCreateflg[index] = FALSE;
                 printf(menuData[index]);
          }
          printf(menuTitle[0]);
          scanf("%s", userInput);
D         cPort = (unsigned char)userInput[0];
          comPort = getMenuItem(cPort);
          printf("select = %s\n", comPort);
          if (strcmp(comPort, "EXIT") == 0 || strcmp(comPort, "NULL") == 0)
             select = FALSE;
          else
          {
E                ecRet = SetupPort(comPort, (int)cPort);
                 if (ecRet)
                 {
                        select = FALSE;
                        break;
                 }
F                ecRet = TestPort(comPort, 1);
                 if (ecRet)
                 {
                        select = FALSE;
                        break;
                 }
G                if (TestPassed)
                    printf("\n**** %s TEST PASSED ***\n", comPort);
          }
     }
```

FIGURE 3.9 The major functions of the project SimpleCOM. *(continued)*

```
  ERR_CODE SetupPort(char* cPort, int nPort)
H {
          ERR_CODE ecRet = OK;
          pSerialCreate  pParam;

          pParam = new SerialCreate;

          pParam->lBaudRate = BAUD_RATE;
          pParam->lDataBits = NUM_BITS;
          pParam->lTimeout  = TIME_OUT;
I         if (PortCreateflg[nPort])
             return  ecRet;

J         ecRet = PortInitialize(cPort, pParam);
          if (ecRet != OK)
             printf("ERROR in PortInitialize()!\n");
          else
          {
               PortCreateflg[nPort] = TRUE;
               hPort = pParam->h_Port;
          }
K         delete pParam;

          return ecRet;
  }
L ERR_CODE TestPort(char* cPort, BOOL display)
  {
          BYTE   sByte;
          int       numByte = NUM_BYTE, MaxByte = MAX_BYTE;
          ERR_CODE ecRet = OK;
          CommPortClass* comPort = new CommPortClass;

          comPort->handlePort = hPort;
M         comPort->iMaxChars  = NUM_BYTE;

N         for (sByte = START_BYTE; sByte <= MaxByte; sByte++)
          {
               ecRet = PortWrite(hPort, sByte, numByte);
               if (ecRet)
               {
                    printf("PortWrite() is failed\n");
                    TestPassed = FALSE;
                    CloseHandle(hPort);
                    return EC_WRITE_FAIL;
               }
O              if (display)
                    printf("%s Port Sending: = %c\n", cPort, sByte);

P              ecRet = PortRead(comPort);
               if (ecRet)
               {
                    printf("PortRead() is failed\n");
                    TestPassed = FALSE;
                    CloseHandle(hPort);
                    return EC_READ_FAIL;
               }
```

FIGURE 3.9 The major functions of the project SimpleCOM. *(continued)*

```
Q                   if (display)
                       printf("%s Port Received: = %c\n", cPort, comPort->bByte);
R                   if (sByte != comPort->bByte)
                    {
                       TestPassed = FALSE;
                       return EC_TEST_FAIL;
                    }
               }
S              TestPassed = TRUE;
               delete comPort;
               return ecRet;
  }
T char* getMenuItem(unsigned char mPort)
  {
               char*    ret;
               switch (mPort)
               {
               case 'A':
               case 'a':  ret = "COM1";
                          break;
               case 'B':
               case 'b':  ret = "COM2";
                          break;
               case 'C':
               case 'c':  ret = "COM3";
                          break;
               case 'D':
               case 'd':  ret = "COM4";
                          break;
               case 'E':
               case 'e':  ret = "COM5";
                          break;
               case 'F':
               case 'f':  ret = "COM6";
                         break;
               case 'G':
               case 'g':  ret = "COM7";
                          break;
               case 'H':
               case 'h':  ret = "COM8";
                          break;
               case 'X':
               case 'x':  ret = "EXIT";
                          break;
               default: printf("Invalid Selection\n");
                         ret = "NULL";
               }
               return ret;
  }
```

FIGURE 3.9 The major functions of the project SimpleCOM.

The function of the coding is explained below:

A: The local variables are declared here. `select` is a Boolean variable used to control whether the `While` loop continues to run or stop. `userInput` is a C-string used to receive the user's selection. TestPassed is also a Boolean variable used to store and monitor the testing status for each port.

B: The port testing process begins with a While loop, which allows testing to continue as long as the process is free of errors.

C: At the beginning of the test, our program uses a for loop to initialize the PortCreateflg[] to False for each port, indicating that no port has yet been initialized. When using this for loop, we need to display the port test menu on the screen. The test menu is stored in a pointer array, and each pointer points to a string, so a loop is needed to display all the strings in that array.

D: The title of the test menu is displayed on the screen following the test menu. A message is displayed on the screen prompting you to select a port to be tested. The system function scanf() is used to receive the selection and translate it into an unsigned character. Then the program calls the GetMenuItem() function to translate our input, in string format, to the associated port. Next, the program checks our selection by calling the strcmp() function to determine whether we've selected EXIT or made an invalid selection. The variable **select** must be set to False for either of these situations; this will effectively terminate the While loop. Note that we use the string operation function strcmp() to compare two strings because the if condition operation—for example, if (comPort == "EXIT") or if (comPort == "NULL"), will not work properly in this context.

E: When we select a port for testing, the SetupPort() function is called to execute the initialization of that port. Our program resets the select Boolean variable to False here to exit the While loop if the function is not successful.

F: If SetupPort() proceeds without error, the initialization is fine, and the program can continue to perform the port test by calling the function TestPort() to send data to and read it back from the port. We set the second argument to 1 to indicate that we want to display each testing code on the screen. Also, our program will also reset the select Boolean variable and exit the While loop if the function returns an error.

G: If the TestPort() function has completed successfully and everything is fine, the program checks the status of the testing process by inspecting the Boolean variable TestPassed. If this variable is True, it means that testing has been successful; the program will display a message to show this result.

H: Now our program runs the SetupPort() function. The purposes of this function are to initialize the serial port we've selected and then to prepare the test to be run. The returned variable is initialized to OK, which means that no error has occurred. An object of the data structure pSerialCreate, pParam, is created and initialized with the default values.

I: Before the initialization process continues, our program checks the port we've selected to determine whether it has been initialized. If so, the program cannot duplicate initialization to that port, because the system won't allow us to reopen a port that has already been opened. In this case, the program returns an OK to the calling function, thus aborting the process.

J: If the port has not been initialized, the PortInitialize() function is called to perform the initialization of the port. If this function call is not successful, an error code is returned, and an error message is displayed on the screen. Otherwise, the Boolean variable PortCreateflg[] is set to True, to indicate that the selected port has been initialized.

K: Don't forget to delete the pointer variable pParam here. When creating this variable, we allocated memory space by using the new keyword. Our program must now clean that memory space by using the delete statement.

L: Now, enter the `TestPort()` function to begin the test of the selected port. Certain local variables are created here, as well as `comPort`, an object of the structure `CommPortClass`. The `new` keyword is used to allocate memory space for this object.

M: In this section, two important parameters of the `comPort` object, `handPort` and `iMaxChars`, are initialized with two values, `hPort` and `NUM_BYTE`. The first value is the handle of the opened serial port, and the second is the number of bytes that will be read from the port.

N: Here the program runs a `for` loop to do the actual testing of the port. The program periodically sends data to the port by calling the `PortWrite()` function, and also reads back that data from the same port by using the `PortRead()` function. The data string consists of `ASCII` code characters starting with the digit `0` (`48` in decimal) and continuing to the digit `9`, and then continuing with the characters `a` through `z` (`90` in decimal). If the `PortWrite()` function fails, the error information will be displayed on the screen. Our program will close the port handler and return an error code to the calling function.

O: If the call to the `PortWrite()` function has been successful, the program will check the Boolean `display` variable to determine whether the data that has been sent out should be displayed on the screen. If this variable is set, the data will appear on the screen, allowing us to monitor the testing process.

P: Following a successful execution of the function `PortWrite()`, our program calls the `PortRead()` function to pick up the data we've sent to test the port. If the function returns any error information, it is displayed on the screen. In this case, the program will close the port handler and return the error information to the calling function. In either case, when `PortWrite()` or `PortRead()` fails, the monitor variable `TestPassed` will be reset to `False` to inform the system that the test has failed.

Q: Just like the `PortWrite()` function, if the Boolean variable `display` is `True`, which means that the user wants to monitor each piece of data that is sent to and received from the tested port, the program will need to display the data on the screen.

R: If both `PortWrite()` and `PortRead()` functions are successful, our program must compare the sent-out data with the read-back data to determine whether the test results are identical. If the two are not identical, meaning that something has gone wrong on the tested port, the monitor Boolean variable `TestPassed` will be reset to `False`, and the error code will be returned to the calling function.

S: If the sent-out data and the read-back data sequences are identical, it means that the tested port has experienced no problems. In this case the monitoring variable, `TestPassed`, will be set to `True` to inform the system that the test has been successful. One thing we need to remember is to incorporate a `delete` statement at this point to clean up the memory space previously allocated for the `comPort` object.

T: This section covers the body of the function `getMenuItem()` function. The code for this function is straightforward and should pose no problem.

The `getMenuItem()` function is easy but takes too much space. Fortunately, We can simplify the function to make it smaller by inserting the `userInput = strlwr(userInput)` statement just after the step `D: scanf()`. In this way, we change the user's input to a lowercase character and can delete the section for checking the uppercase character from the `getMenuItem()` function. Now our program only needs to check the lowercase character to determine which port we have selected for testing.

Next let us create the second source file, `ComPortTest.cpp`, by clicking the `File|New` menu item and entering `ComPortTest` into the `File name:` field. Click `OK` to open this new source file, and then enter the code shown in Figure 3.10.

```
/*****************************************************************************
 * NAME: ComPortTest.cpp
 * DESC:   Support C++ file for SimpleCOM.cpp
 * DATE:   7/15/2003
 * PGMR: Y. Bai
 *****************************************************************************/
#include <stdio.h>
#include <stdlib.h>
#include "SimpleCOM.h"
ERR_CODE PortInitialize(LPTSTR lpszPortName, pSerialCreate pCreate)
{
    HANDLE  hPort;
    DWORD   dwError;
    DCB         PortDCB;
    ERR_CODE      ecStatus = OK;
    COMMTIMEOUTS   CommTimeouts;
    unsigned char  dBit;

    // Open the serial port.
    hPort = CreateFile(lpszPortName,                    // Pointer to the name of the port
            GENERIC_READ | GENERIC_WRITE,   // Access (read/write) mode
            0,                                          // Share mode
            NULL,                                       // Pointer to the security attribute
            OPEN_EXISTING,                              // How to open the serial port
            0,                                          // Port attributes
            NULL);                                      // Handle to port with attribute copy
     // If it fails to open the port, return error.
     if ( hPort == INVALID_HANDLE_VALUE )
     {
         // Could not open the port.
         dwError = GetLastError();
         msg("Unable to open the port");
         CloseHandle(hPort);
         return EC_FOPEN;
      }
     PortDCB.DCBlength = sizeof(DCB);
     // Get the default port setting information.
    GetCommState(hPort, &PortDCB);
    // Change the DCB structure settings.
    PortDCB.BaudRate = pCreate->lBaudRate;              // Current baud rate
    PortDCB.fBinary  = TRUE;                            // Binary mode; no EOF check
    PortDCB.fParity  = TRUE;                            // Enable parity checking.
    PortDCB.fOutxCtsFlow = FALSE;                       // No CTS output flow control
    PortDCB.fOutxDsrFlow = FALSE;                       // No DSR output flow control
    PortDCB.fDtrControl = DTR_CONTROL_ENABLE;  // DTR_CONTROL
    PortDCB.fDsrSensitivity = FALSE;                    // DSR sensitivity
    PortDCB.fTXContinueOnXoff = TRUE;                   // XOFF continues Tx
    PortDCB.fOutX = FALSE;                              // No XON/XOFF out flow control
    PortDCB.fInX  = FALSE;                              // No XON/XOFF in flow control
    PortDCB.fErrorChar = FALSE;                         // Disable error replacement.
    PortDCB.fNull = FALSE;                              // Disable null stripping.
```

FIGURE 3.10 The second source file of the project SimpleCOM. *(continued)*

```
        PortDCB.fRtsControl = RTS_CONTROL_ENABLE;    // RTS_CONTROL
        PortDCB.fAbortOnError = FALSE;               // Don't abort reads/writes error.
        dBit = (unsigned char)pCreate->lDataBits;
        PortDCB.ByteSize = dBit;                     // Number of bits/bytes, 4-8
        PortDCB.Parity = NOPARITY;                   // 0-4=no,odd,even,mark,space
        PortDCB.StopBits = ONESTOPBIT;               // 0,1,2 = 1, 1.5, 2
        // Configure the port according to the specifications of the DCB structure.
        if (!SetCommState (hPort, &PortDCB))
        {
            // Could not create the read thread.
            dwError = GetLastError();
            msg("Unable to configure the serial port");
            return EC_INVAL_CONFIG;
        }

        // Retrieve the time-out parameters for all read and write operations on the port.
        GetCommTimeouts(hPort, &CommTimeouts);

        // Change the COMMTIMEOUTS structure settings.
        CommTimeouts.ReadIntervalTimeout = MAXDWORD;
        CommTimeouts.ReadTotalTimeoutMultiplier = 0;
        CommTimeouts.ReadTotalTimeoutConstant = 0;
        CommTimeouts.WriteTotalTimeoutMultiplier = 10;
        CommTimeouts.WriteTotalTimeoutConstant = 1000;

        // Set the time-out parameters for all read and write operations on the port.
        if (!SetCommTimeouts (hPort, &CommTimeouts))
        {
            // Could not create the read thread.
            dwError = GetLastError();
            msg("Unable to set the time-out parameters");
            return EC_TIMEOUT_SET;
        }

        EscapeCommFunction(hPort, SETDTR);
        EscapeCommFunction(hPort, SETRTS);
        pCreate->h_Port = hPort;

        return ecStatus;
}
ERR_CODE PortWrite(HANDLE handPort, BYTE bByte, int NumByte)
{
    DWORD dwError;
    DWORD dwNumBytesWritten;
    ERR_CODE ecStatus = OK;

    if (!WriteFile (handPort,                     // Port handle
                   &bByte,                        // Pointer to the data to write
                   NumByte,                       // Number of bytes to write
                   &dwNumBytesWritten,            // Pointer to the number of bytes written
                   NULL))                         // Must be NULL for Windows CE
```

FIGURE 3.10 The second source file of the project SimpleCOM. *(continued)*

```
    {
        // WriteFile failed. Report error.
        dwError = GetLastError ();
        msg("ERROR in PortWrite ..");
        return EC_WRITE_FAIL;
    }
    return ecStatus;
}
ERR_CODE PortRead(CommPortClass *hCommPort)
{
    HANDLE  hThread;                          // handler for port read thread
    DWORD   IDThread;
    DWORD   Ret, ExitCode;
    DWORD   dTimeout = 5000;                  // define time out value: 5 sec.
    ERR_CODE ecStatus = OK;

    if (!(hThread = CreateThread(NULL,        // no security attributes
                  0,                          // use default stack size
                  (LPTHREAD_START_ROUTINE) ThreadFunc,
                  (LPVOID)hCommPort,          // parameter to thread funciton
                  CREATE_SUSPENDED,           // creation flag - suspended
                  &IDThread) ) )              // returns thread ID
    {
        msg("Create Read Thread failed");
        return EC_CREATE_THREAD;
    }

    ResumeThread(hThread);                    // start thread now
        Ret = WaitForSingleObject(hThread, dTimeout);
        if (Ret == WAIT_OBJECT_0)
        {
            // data received & process it... Need to do nothing
            // Because the data has been stored in the hCommPort in Thread Func.
            // close thread handle
            CloseHandle(hThread);
        }
        else if (Ret == WAIT_TIMEOUT)
        {
            // time out happened, warning & kill thread
            Ret = GetExitCodeThread(hThread, &ExitCode);
            msg("Time out happened in PortRead() ");
            if (ExitCode == STILL_ACTIVE)
            {
                TerminateThread(hThread, ExitCode);
                CloseHandle(hThread);
                return EC_RECV_TIMEOUT;
            }
            else
            {
                CloseHandle(hThread);
                msg("ERROR in GetExitCodeThread: != STILL_ACTIVE ");
                ecStatus = EC_EXIT_CODE;
```

FIGURE 3.10 The second source file of the project SimpleCOM. *(continued)*

```
            }
        }
        else
        {
            msg("ERROR in WaitFor SingleObject ");
            ecStatus = EC_WAIT_SINGLEOBJ;
        }
        return   ecStatus;
}
void WINAPI ThreadFunc(void* hCommPorts)
{
        BYTE      Byte;
        DWORD  dwError;
        BOOL     bResult;
        int          nTotRead = 0;
        DWORD  dwCommModemStatus, dwBytesTransferred;
        CommPortClass*  CommPorts;
        ERR_CODE ecStatus = OK;

        CommPorts = (CommPortClass* )hCommPorts;

        // Specify a set of events to be monitored for the port.
        SetCommMask(CommPorts->handlePort, EV_RXCHAR | EV_CTS | EV_DSR |
                                                                          EV_RLSD | EV_RING);
        // Wait for an event to occur for the port.
        WaitCommEvent(CommPorts->handlePort, &dwCommModemStatus, 0);
        // Re-specify the set of events to be monitored for the port.
        SetCommMask(CommPorts->handlePort, EV_RXCHAR | EV_CTS | EV_DSR
                                                                         | EV_RLSD| EV_RING);
        if (dwCommModemStatus & EV_RXCHAR||dwCommModemStatus & EV_RLSD)
        {
            // received the char_event
            // Read the data from the serial port.
            bResult = ReadFile(CommPorts->handlePort, &Byte, 1, &dwBytesTransferred, 0);

        if     (!bResult)
            {
                printf("Unable to read the port\n");
                switch (dwError = GetLastError())
                {
                    case ERROR_HANDLE_EOF:
                    printf("Serial Receive Failed\n");
                    break;
                }
            }
            else
            {
                // store the data read.
                CommPorts->bByte = Byte;
                nTotRead++;
            }
        }

        return;
}
```

FIGURE 3.10 The second source file of the project SimpleCOM.

The code in this source file may look familiar, because it first appeared in Sections 3.1.1 to 3.1.3 when we introduced the general process of serial port communications. All functions used in this file are interfacing functions that can directly access the serial port driver and the system I/O manager.

Three major functions, `PortInitialize()`, `PortWrite()`, and `PortRead()`, are skeleton functions in the body of this interfacing-level function, and all middle layer functions, such as `SetupPort()` and `TestPort()`, can communicate with these major interfacing functions to access the low-level serial device drivers.

We have thus far developed four files in this project, two header files and two source files. We can build our project right now by clicking the `Build|Build SimpleCOM.exe` menu item. We should not have any problems if our code is identical with the code in the preceding files.

Click the `Build|Execute SimpleCOM.exe` menu item to run the project. A DOS prompt window will open, as shown in Figure 3.11. The test menu and the test title are displayed on the screen.

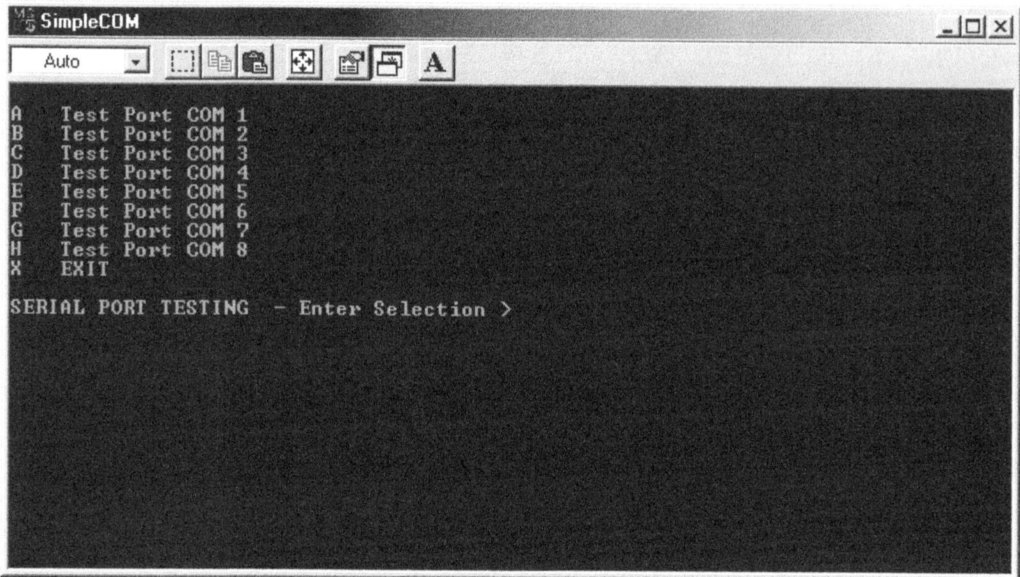

FIGURE 3.11 The starting window of running the project SimpleCOM.

In total, we can test eight serial ports, from `COM1` to `COM8`. On most computers, however, there are only one or two serial ports, typically `COM1` and `COM2`.

Make the selection by typing an `A`, which is used to test `COM1`, followed by pressing `Enter`. A sequence of testing characters will be displayed onscreen. Notice that these characters are displayed in pairs, which indicates that the test is proceeding successfully. The first character in each pair is the sent-out character, and the second is the read-back character. The test result

COM1 TEST PASSED

is displayed onscreen, as shown in Figure 3.12, once the test has been successfully completed.

Now try to make another selection, such as pressing `B` to see what happens. A message box with a text message will be displayed onscreen, as shown in Figure 3.13.

Notice from the error message in Figure 3.13 that the `COM2` port is not available on the computer. We can make inspect the value returned from the `PortInitialize()` function to get a clearer

```
SimpleCOM
COM1 Port Received: = V
COM1 Port Sending:  = W
COM1 Port Received: = W
COM1 Port Sending:  = X
COM1 Port Received: = X
COM1 Port Sending:  = Y
COM1 Port Received: = Y
COM1 Port Sending:  = Z
COM1 Port Received: = Z

**** COM1 TEST PASSED ***

A   Test Port COM 1
B   Test Port COM 2
C   Test Port COM 3
D   Test Port COM 4
E   Test Port COM 5
F   Test Port COM 6
G   Test Port COM 7
H   Test Port COM 8
X   EXIT

SERIAL PORT TESTING  - Enter Selection >
```

FIGURE 3.12 The running result of the project SimpleCOM.

FIGURE 3.13 The starting window of running the project SimpleCOM.

sense of the problem. By making any other selection, we will get the same error information, which means that only `COM1` is available at our current computer. At this point, however, our first serial port should have run successfully.

All files for this example project, including the source files, header files, and executable files, are stored in the folder `Chapter 3\SimpleCOM` on the attached CD-ROM. You can load these files onto your computer to test the project.

Note that this sample program was developed and executed on a computer with the Windows Me OS. It will not work on certain other operating systems, such as Windows 2000, until the following modifications are made:

- Incorporate the `new` keyword to dynamically create two character arrays, `userInput` and `comPort`, in the `main()` function of the `SimpleCOM.cpp` source file:

  ```
  userInput = new char[128]; comPort = new char[128];
  ```

- Clean up the memory space allocated for these two character arrays by using the `Delete` function before the program exits the `main()` function in the `SimpleCOM.cpp` source file:

  ```
  delete userInput; delete comPort;
  ```

- Change the `getMenuItem()` function to the following protocol:

  ```
  int getMenuItem (unsigned char mPort, char* ret);
  ```

  Once this is done, the program will pass and retrieve back the serial port name by using this `getMenuItem()` function. Originally, we asked this function to return a character array that included the serial port name, but this modified function is better than the original function. We need to change the protocol of this function in both the header file `SimpleCOM.h` and the source file `SimpleCOM.cpp`.
- The next modification changes the method of assigning the port name inside the `getMenuItem()` function. Originally, we directly used the assignment operator to assign the port name to a character array, such as `ret="COM1"`. This method will not "COM1". This method will not work in Windows 2000. To make it work, change this assignment to the following one:

  ```
  case 'a': strcpy(ret, "COM1");
  ```

We use the string operation function `strcpy()` to replace the original assignment operator. This will work much better than the original operation. Our modified `main()` and `getMenuItem()` functions are shown in Figures 3-14 and 3-15, respectively.

All the files for this modified project are located on the attached CD-ROM, in the folder `Chapter 3\SimpleCOM2`. You can load this project onto your computer to test it. First, however, be sure to designate a serial port to be tested.

All modified sections have been highlighted for both functions. We now must change the protocol of the `getMenuItem()` function in the header file `SimpleCOM.h` so that it matches the function implemented in the source file.

Once we've made these modifications, we can rebuild our project and run it on Windows 2000, and there should be no more problems.

3.2.3 A Serial Port Application in Visual C++

In this section, we'll develop a Microsoft Foundation Classes (MFC)-based testing program for the serial ports. This application will show you how to combine a static library with an MFC interface in order to make a testing project with a graphical user interface (GUI).

Launch Visual C++ 6.0 and create a new project by clicking the `File|New` menu item. Select `MFC AppWizard (exe)` under the `Projects` tab, and enter `mfcCOMTest` in the `Project name:` field. Make sure that the content of the `Location: field` is our user-defined project directory, `C:\CTCTest`. Click `OK` to go to the next page. Select `Single document` by clicking its radio button, and check the checkbox next to `Document/View Architecture support?` Click `Next` to continue to the next page. Click the `None` radio button for the database selection, and click `Next` again. For the following four pages, keep the default settings and click `Next` four times until you get to the last page. Click `Finish`, and then click `OK` to open the new project.

Click the `FileView` tab in the workspace to open all the created files. The following files have been created by the system:

- `MainFrm.cpp`
- `mfcCOMTest.cpp`
- `mfcCOMTestDoc.cpp`
- `mfcCOMTestView.cpp`
- `mfcCOMTest.rc`
- `StdAfx.cpp`

At this point, the header files associated with source files above have also been created.

```
void main()
{
        int  index;
        bool  select = TRUE;
        char* userInput;
        char* comPort;
        ERR_CODE  ecRet = OK;
        unsigned char cPort;

        userInput = new char[128];
        comPort   = new char[128];

        TestPassed = FALSE;
        while(select)
        {
                printf("\n");
                for (index = 0; index < MAX_MENU; index++)
                {
                     PortCreateflg[index] = FALSE;
                     printf(menuData[index]);
                }

                printf(menuTitle[0]);
                scanf("%s", userInput);
                userInput = strlwr(userInput);
                cPort = (unsigned char)userInput[0];
                getMenuItem(cPort, comPort);
                printf("select = %s\n", comPort);
                if (strcmp(comPort, "EXIT") == 0 || strcmp(comPort, "NULL") == 0)
                   select = FALSE;
                else
                {
                   ecRet = SetupPort(comPort, (int)cPort);
                   if (ecRet)
                   {
                         select = FALSE;
                         break;
                   }
                   ecRet = TestPort(comPort, 1);
                   if (ecRet)
                   {
                         select = FALSE;
                         break;
                   }
                   if (TestPassed)
                      printf("\n**** %s TEST PASSED ***\n", comPort);
                 }
        }
        delete  userInput;
        delete  comPort;

        return;
}
```

FIGURE 3.14 The Modified Function `getMenuItem`.

`MainFrm.cpp` is a main window file used to create a window frame for our application and to handle all window messages. `mfcCOMTest.cpp` is our main application program; it is also the main thread in this project. This application is the main controller for our project, and it creates three

```
int getMenuItem(unsigned char mPort, char* ret)
{
        switch (mPort)
        {
        case 'a': strcpy(ret, "COM1");
                  break;
        case 'b': strcpy(ret, "COM2");
                  break;
        case 'c': strcpy(ret, "COM3");
                  break;
        case 'd': strcpy(ret, "COM4");
                  break;
        case 'e': strcpy(ret, "COM5");
                  break;
        case 'f': strcpy(ret, "COM6");
                  break;
        case 'g': strcpy(ret, "COM7");
                  break;
        case 'h': strcpy(ret, "COM8");
                  break;
        case 'x': strcpy(ret, "EXIT");
                  break;
        default: printf("Invalid Selection\n");
                  strcpy(ret, "NULL");
        }
        return 0;
}
```

FIGURE 3.15 The Modified Main Function Body.

class objects: `MainFrm`, `mfcCOMTestDoc`, and `mfcCOMTestView`. The `mfcCOMTestDoc` class is used to store and handle all program data in our project. The `mfcCOMTestView` class is a child of the `MainFrm` class and provides a client area of the frame window in our application. The `mfcCOMTest.rc` is a resource file that provides all the resources for our project. `StdAfx.cpp` is a source file that includes the standard header files applied in our project.

Two class objects play important roles as our project runs; one is the document class `mfcCOMTestDoc`, and the other one is the client area of the frame window `mfcCOMTestView`. These two class objects will communicate with each other to process and display the program data between the `Document` and `View` classes.

Because this project is relatively large, we will divide the development process into the following subsections:

- Developing the `Document` class, `mfcCOMTestDoc`. In this class, we save and process all the data for the project, including the program data, user data, and interface data.
- Developing the `View` class, `mfcCOMTestView`. In this class, we develop some routines and add functions that will communicate with our `Document` class to receive the data we input and then display the processing results on the GUI (a dialog box that will be developed later).
- Developing two dialog box classes, `COMDLG` and `LoopDlg`. The first class is used as a main GUI to interface with our input. Among other tasks, it reads the input and displays the testing results on the GUI. The second class is used as a support GUI to pick up the

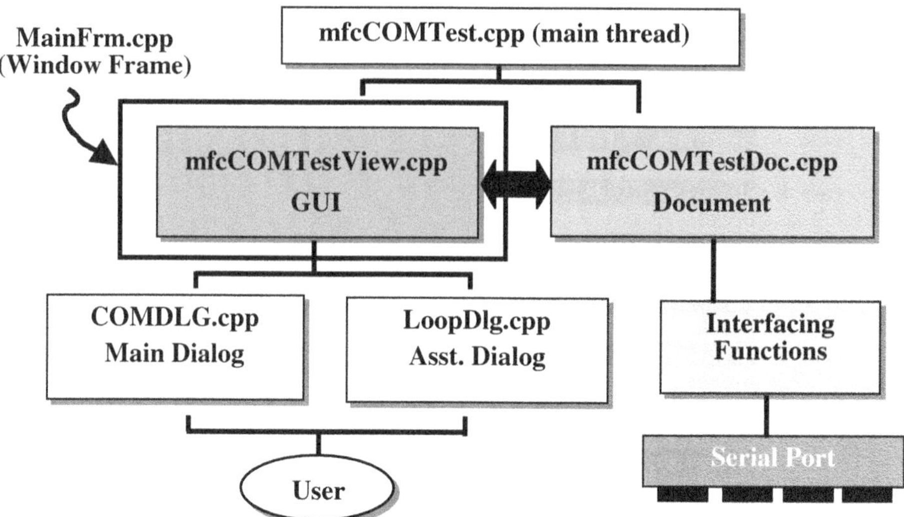

FIGURE 3.16 The program structure.

loop number we enter when we wish to perform loop testing on the serial port. The functional block diagram of this project is shown in Figure 3.16.

Notice in this figure that the top block is our main thread, `mfcCOMTest.cpp`, which is the main controller of our project. This thread controls and coordinates two subclasses, `mfcCOMTest-Doc.cpp` and `mfcCOMTestView.cpp`, to make our project work properly.

The class `mfcCOMTestView.cpp` makes up the GUI of our project, which means that it takes charge of interfacing with the keyboard and displaying the test results on the GUI. The `Document` class `mfcCOMTestDoc.cpp`, is used to store and process the program data as our project runs. This processing needs to communicate with the `View` class, `mfcCOMTestView.cpp`, to obtain all necessary keyboard input and to send the processing results back to the `View` class, which will display them on the GUI.

Our `MainFrm.cpp` only provides a window frame for our project, which processes all window messages. This main window frame is necessary for our project and is a parent for all our child windows, such as the `View` class, `mfcCOMTestView.cpp`, `COMDLG.cpp`, and `LoopDlg.cpp` windows, which will be discussed next.

Two dialog box classes are used in this project to allow the `View` class to pick up keyboard or menu input. The default view client area is a initially blank, so we can add the windows to use as our GUI. `COMDLG` is our main dialog box, and it will handle all user input. `LoopDlg` is only an assistant window; it obtains the loop number when we choose to perform loop testing.

In this project, all interfacing functions are assigned to the `Document` class, and these functions can be used to access the serial port device driver. In Figure 3.16, a direct connection appears between the interfacing functions and the serial port, which is not true. The interfacing functions cannot directly access the serial port hardware; instead, interfacing happens via the serial driver. It is absent in the picture in order to save space.

In this application, we use the same functions that we developed in our preceding sample project. We put the middle-layer functions, such as `SetupPort()` and `TestPort()`, in the `View` class, and we put all interfacing functions in the `Document` class. In this way, we can evenly locate the functions in both classes. Of course, we can put our functions in any class, but for *object-oriented programming* (OOP), we should put the associated functions near their related classes to make things clear and simple. Now let us take a look at our `Document` class.

3.2.3.1 Developing the `Document` Class

Because the `Document` class will contain our program data, we need to add the most data, including the variables and structures, to the header file of this class.

Open the `Document` class header file `mfcCOMTestDoc.h` and just before the class declaration, add the structures shown in Figure 3.17.

```
// mfcCOMTestDoc.h : interface of the CMfcCOMTestDoc class
//
/////////////////////////////////////////////////////////////////////////////
#if !defined(AFX_MFCCOMTESTDOC_H__32EB7F5E_AFC6_4429_BE2C_637C2160A902__
INCLUDED_)
#define AFX_MFCCOMTESTDOC_H__32EB7F5E_AFC6_4429_BE2C_637C2160A902__
INCLUDED_
#if _MSC_VER > 1000
#pragma once
#endif // _MSC_VER > 1000

#define NUM_BYTE                    1
#define MAX_BYTE                    90
#define START_BYTE                  48
#define  BAUD_RATE                  9600
#define  NUM_BITS                   8
#define  TIME_OUT                   3000
#define MAX_MENU                    9
#define MAX_STRING                  256
#define NOPARITY                    0
#define ONESTOPBIT                  0
#define RTS_CONTROL_DISABLE       0x00
#define RTS_CONTROL_ENABLE        0x01
#define DTR_CONTROL_DISABLE       0x00
#define DTR_CONTROL_ENABLE        0x01
 #define msg(info)  AfxMessageBox(info)
 typedef struct
 {
   unsigned long  ulCtrlerID;
    char          cEcho;
    char          cEORChar;
    long          lTimeout;
    long          lBaudRate;
    long          lDataBits;
    HANDLE        h_Port;
 }SerialCreate, *pSerialCreate;
 typedef struct
 {
    char          *pcBuffer;
    BYTE          bByte;
    int           iMaxChars;
    int           piNumRcvd;
    char          cTermChar;
    HANDLE        handlePort;
    }CommPortClass;
    typedef enum
    {
```

FIGURE 3.17 The document class. *(continued)*

```
        OK                          = 0,            /* no error */
        EC_TIMEOUT,
        EC_FOPEN,
        EC_INVAL_CONFIG,
        EC_TIMEOUT_SET,
        EC_RECV_TIMEOUT,
        EC_EXIT_CODE,
        EC_WAIT_SINGLEOBJ,
        EC_INVALIDPORT,
        EC_WRITE_FAIL,
        EC_READ_FAIL,
        EC_TEST_FAIL,
        EC_CREATE_THREAD,
        EC_PORT_INITDONE,
        EC_UNKNOWNERROR
}ERR_CODE;

class CMfcCOMTestDoc : public CDocument
{
protected: // create from serialization only
        CMfcCOMTestDoc();
        DECLARE_DYNCREATE(CMfcCOMTestDoc)

// Attributes
public:

// Operations
public:
......
```

FIGURE 3.17 The document class.

In Figure 3.17, notice that some codes are already in the opened `Document` class header file. Visual C++ 6.0 automatically wrote that code when we created the project. This is similar to a professional planner, who would devise a rough outline of events, leaving us to fill in the details. In our program, Visual C++ 6.0 is the planner, and it has already written some skeleton code for us. All we need to do is to plug some actual project code into the skeleton. Sounds easy, doesn't it? It actually is not, but it is still convenient. We cannot enjoy this convenience until we have a clear picture about the overall plan.

We added all the symbolic constants and three structures into this `Document` file. One point we need to pay attention to is the macro definition, `msg(info)`. In the MFC environment, we should use the MFC-based message box function, `AfxMessageBox()`, to replace the Win32 message box function `MessageBox()`.

Now, we must add our three interfacing functions, `PortInitialize()`, `PortWrite()`, and `PortRead()`, to this `Document` class. We use a new method to add these functions to the class, as follows.

In the Visual C++ 6.0 workspace, click the `ClassView` tab to open the class view for this project. All classes in this project are listed here. Find our `Document` class, `CMfcCOMTestDoc`. (Note that our file name has been modified by the system; it is now preceded by a capital `C`, and the first character `m` has been changed from lowercase to uppercase.) Don't worry about the modification of the file name. Just use it as is for now. After finding this file, right-click the file icon. From the popup menu that appears onscreen, select the `Add Member Function...` item to open the dialog box shown in Figure 3.18.

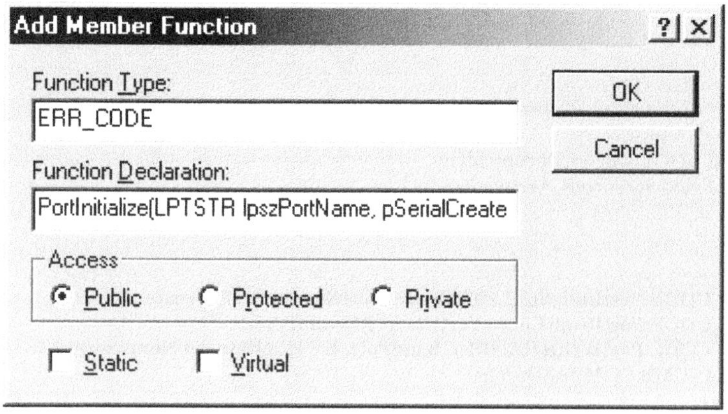

FIGURE 3.18 The add member function dialog.

Type `ERR_CODE` in the `Function Type:` field, and type the protocol of the function in the `Function Declaration:` field. Our finished dialog box should match the one shown in Figure 3.18. Click `OK` to save this addition. In the same way, finish adding the other interfacing functions (PortWrite() and PortRead()) to the `Document` class.

The advantage of using this method to add functions is that Visual C++ 6.0 will automatically add the functions to both the header file (`.h`) and the implementation file (`.cpp`). We are not required to type the function protocol or the scope resolution operator into the implementation file. Later on, we will explain why a scope resolution operator (::) should be used in the function implementation.

Now reopen the header file for this document, shown in Figure 3.19. In order to save space, we only display the interfacing functions added. Figure 3.19 shows the section that follows Figure 3.17.

We can also open the source file of this document, `mfcCOMTestDoc.cpp`, and find that the protocols of the three interfacing functions have been inserted there. We need to add the protocol of our thread function, `ThreadFunc()`, to the top the `Document` file, which is shown in Figure 3.20.

Copy the body of each interfacing function from the last project to each function in the document file. To save space, we do not want to duplicate these functions here, as they are exactly identical to the code in our preceding project. Copy the body of the thread function, `ThreadFunc()`, from the preceding example to this document file.

One thing we want to mention about this source file is the function protocol in the implementation file. For example, the function `PortRead()` is defined as follows in the implementation file:

```
ERR_CODE CMfcCOMTestDoc::PortRead(CommPortClass *hCommPorts)
```

Between the function returned type (`ERR_CODE`) and the function name (`PortRead`) is a class name, `CMfcCOMTestDoc`, followed by a double colon (`::`). This double colon is an OOP requirement called the *scope resolution operator.* The class name followed by the double colon indicates that the function only belongs to the class, and that this function's scope is within the class the function is defined by. Any other class or user who wants to use this function has to place its class name in front of the function to indicate the function's scope. Otherwise, nobody will be able to access the function. All other interfacing functions have the same definitions. All class functions must follow this law without exception.

```
// Attributes
public:
// Operations
public:
// Overrides
        // ClassWizard generated virtual function overrides
        //{{AFX_VIRTUAL(CMfcCOMTestDoc)
        public:
        virtual BOOL OnNewDocument();
        virtual void Serialize(CArchive& ar);
        //}}AFX_VIRTUAL
// Implementation
public:
        ERR_CODE PortInitialize(LPTSTR lpszPortName, pSerialCreate pCreate);
        ERR_CODE PortRead(CommPortClass* hCommPorts);
        ERR_CODE PortWrite(HANDLE handPort, BYTE bByte, int NumByte);
        virtual ~CMfcCOMTestDoc();
#ifdef _DEBUG
        virtual void AssertValid() const;
        virtual void Dump(CDumpContext& dc) const;
#endif
......
```

FIGURE 3.19 The document class header file.

```
// mfcCOMTestDoc.cpp : implementation of the CMfcCOMTestDoc class
//
#include "stdafx.h"
#include "mfcCOMTest.h"
#include "mfcCOMTestDoc.h"
#ifdef _DEBUG
#define new DEBUG_NEW
#undef THIS_FILE
static char THIS_FILE[] = __FILE__;
#endif
void WINAPI ThreadFunc(void* hCommPorts);
/////////////////////////////////////////////////////////////////////////////
// CMfcCOMTestDoc
```

FIGURE 3.20 The protocol of the thread function.

3.2.3.2 Developing the `View` Class

The development of the `View` class is not as easy as the development of the `Document` class because the `View` class interfaces to different class objects, such as the `Document` class object and `Dialog box` class object. Let us take a look at this issue.

Open the `View` class header file, `mfcCOMTestView.h`, and add the following variables into this header file:

- **HANDLE hPort:** The file handler of the serial port
- **bool TestPassed:** The Boolean variable used to keep and monitor the test result

- **bool PortFlag[9]:** The Boolean array used to keep and monitor the initialization status of each port
- **`COMDLG* comDlg`:** The private pointer of dialog box `COMDLG` class

Your finished `View` class header file should match the one shown in Figure 3.21.

```
    // mfcCOMTestView.h : interface of the CMfcCOMTestView class
    //
    /////////////////////////////////////////////////////////////////////////////
    #if !defined(AFX_MFCCOMTESTVIEW_H__C2EF8627_5369_4401_9700_40AA6BF75642
    __INCLUDED_)
    #define AFX_MFCCOMTESTVIEW_H__C2EF8627_5369_4401_9700_40AA6BF75642__
    INCLUDED_
    #if _MSC_VER > 1000
    #pragma once
    #endif // _MSC_VER > 1000
A   class COMDLG;
    class CMfcCOMTestView : public CView
    {
    protected: // create from serialization only
        CMfcCOMTestView();
        DECLARE_DYNCREATE(CMfcCOMTestView)
    // Attributes
    public:
        CMfcCOMTestDoc* GetDocument();
        HANDLE hPort;
B       bool TestPassed;
        bool PortFlg[9];
    // Operations
    public:
    // Overrides
    .......
    private:
C       COMDLG* comDlg;
    };
```

FIGURE 3.21 The view class header file.

Let us now add three variables, `hPort`, `TestPassed`, and `PortFlg[9]`, to the class. Similar to adding the interfacing functions to the `Document` class, we add these variables to the `View` class. Click the `ClassView` tab in the Visual C++ 6.0 workspace, find our `View` class `CMfcCOMTestView` on the list, and right-click it to open a popup menu. Click the `Add Member Variable...` item to open the dialog box shown in Figure 3.22.

Enter `HANDLE` in the `Variable Type:` field and `hPort` in the `Variable Name:` field, as shown in Figure 3.22. Make sure the `Public` radio button is selected, and click `OK` to add this variable to the `View` class. In this way, we add a `Public` variable `hPort` to the class. The `Public` button means that any other class or object can access this variable without any limitations. Next, add another two variables, `TestPassed` and `PortFlg[9]`, to this class. At this point, we have finished task B (shown in Figure 3.21).

Some explanation should be given about tasks A and C shown in Figure 3.21. First, let us take a look at C. `COMDLG` is a dialog box that we will create and add to this project later. It will serve as a main GUI, which will allow for user input as the project runs. Because we will be adding

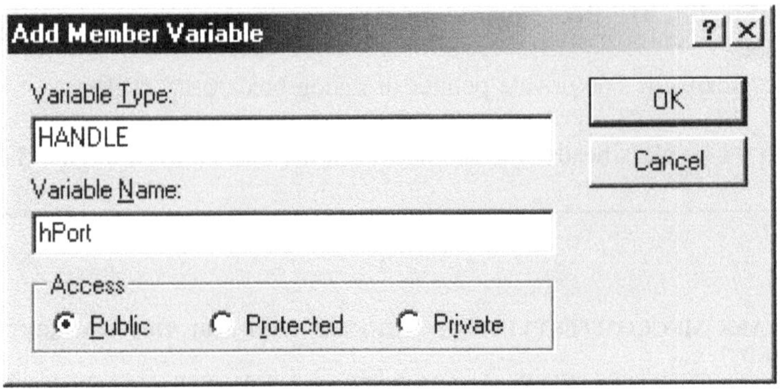

Add Member Variable
Variable Type: HANDLE
Variable Name: hPort
Access: Public (selected), Protected, Private

FIGURE 3.22 The add member variable dialog.

middle-layer functions (such as SetupPort() and TestPort()) to this View class later, we need to set up a connection between the components in the main GUI (the COMDLG dialog box) and those middle-layer functions so that we can click the components in the COMDLG dialog box to access those middle-layer functions in the View class. To add a pointer from the main dialog box class to this View class, we must create this connection. Later on, the View class will be able to access the main dialog box by using this pointer.

To add the pointer to the View class, right-click the View class from the ClassView list. Then click the Add Member Variable... item to open the dialog box. Enter COMDLG* in the Variable Type: field and comDlg in the Variable Name: field, as shown in Figure 3.23. Make sure that the Private radio button is selected because we want to add this pointer as a private type, and we don't want any other class or object to be able to access this pointer.

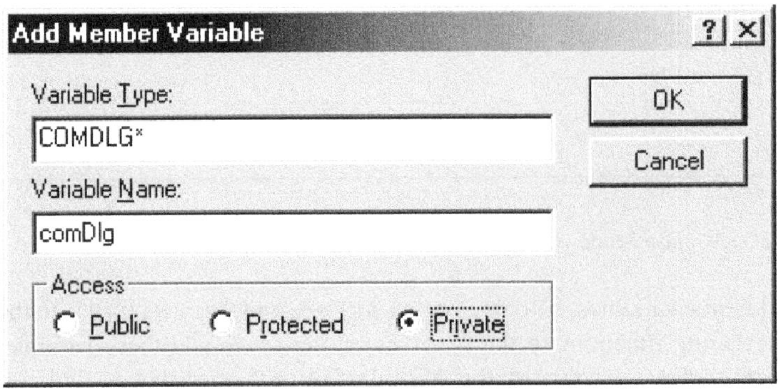

Add Member Variable
Variable Type: COMDLG*
Variable Name: comDlg
Access: Public, Protected, Private (selected)

FIGURE 3.23 The add member variable dialog—2.

Finally, let us take a look at part A in Figure 3.21. Because the View class mfcCOMTestView knows nothing about the dialog box class COMDLG, we would encounter an error if we compiled our project right now since the compiler does not have any knowledge about the COMDLG class. We must declare that class and let the View class know that we have a COMDLG class in the project. To do that, we can use a method called *predeclaring* a class in the View header file by using the keyword class followed by the class name to add the class COMDLG at the top of the View class header file. Then the View class will know that the project includes another class named COMDLG, and the compiler will know about the class when we compile the project.

One question some readers may have is, why do we add these variables in the View class file, but not in the Document class file? We can choose either method, and these variables are closer to the View class because they will be applied in the View class later on.

Now, we need to take care of the middle-layer functions applied in the View class. Two functions, SetupPort() and TestPort(), must be added to the View class. Click the ClassView tab in the Visual C++ 6.0 workspace, find our View class, CMfcCOMTestView, and right-click it. In the opened popup menu, click the Add Member Function... item to open the dialog box. In the opened dialog box, enter ERR_CODE in the Function Type: field, enter SetupPort(int nPort, int nBaud) in the Function Declaration: field, and make sure that the Public radio button is selected. The finished dialog box should match the one shown in Figure 3.24. Click OK to close the dialog box and add the new SetupPort() function to the View class. In the same manner, add the second function, TestPort(), to the View class.

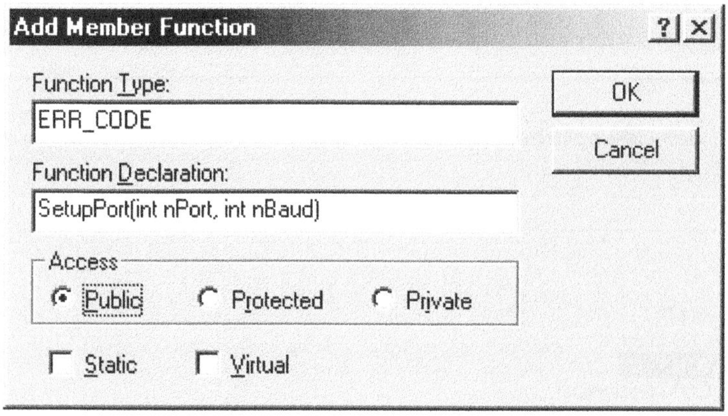

FIGURE 3.24 The add member function dialog.

A modification has been made to the arguments in the SetupPort() function. Originally, the first argument was a character array that represented the serial port name. However, in this case, an integer is used to replace that character array. By using this integer, we simplify both the user input and the COM port selection process that we will see later on in the program source file, mfcCOMTestView.cpp. Similarly, the second argument is added and is used to represent the baud rate parameter that will be entered from the main dialog box as the program runs.

Now open the View class header file again. Notice that these two middle-layer functions have been added into the Implementation section of the View class, as shown in Figure 3.25.

Now we have finished the coding for the View class header file. Next, we will enter the coding for the View class implementation file.

Click the FileView tab in the Visual C++ 6.0 workspace. Then double-click the file named mfcCOMTestView.cpp to open the View class implementation file. We now need to include the header file of the main dialog box to define the protocols of the dialog box class COMDLG in the View class because the View class will access and communicate with the main dialog box class as the program runs. At the top of the opened View class file, type #include "COMDLG.h" to include this header file to the View class. (See Figure 3.26.)

We now need to declare a character pointer array comPORT[], which is used to store all possible COM port names. Add this declaration at the top of the View class file, as shown in Figure 3.26. In the figure, the newly added sections have been highlighted.

The advantage of using this character pointer array is that we can save space when transferring the menu selection to the port name. In the preceding example, we used a function, getMenuItem(),

```
// Overrides
        // ClassWizard generated virtual function overrides
        //{{AFX_VIRTUAL(CMfcCOMTestView)
        public:
        virtual void OnDraw(CDC* pDC); // overridden to draw this view
        virtual BOOL PreCreateWindow(CREATESTRUCT& cs);
        protected:
        virtual BOOL OnPreparePrinting(CPrintInfo* pInfo);
        virtual void OnBeginPrinting(CDC* pDC, CPrintInfo* pInfo);
        virtual void OnEndPrinting(CDC* pDC, CPrintInfo* pInfo);
        //}}AFX_VIRTUAL
// Implementation
public:
        ERR_CODE TestPort(int cPort);
        ERR_CODE SetupPort(int nPort, int nBaud);
        virtual ~CMfcCOMTestView();
#ifdef _DEBUG
......
```

FIGURE 3.25 The view class header file.

```
// mfcCOMTestView.cpp : implementation of the CMfcCOMTestView class
//

#include "stdafx.h"
#include "mfcCOMTest.h"
#include "COMDLG.h"
#include "mfcCOMTestDoc.h"
#include "mfcCOMTestView.h"

#ifdef _DEBUG
#define new DEBUG_NEW
#undef THIS_FILE
static char THIS_FILE[] = __FILE__;
#endif

char* comPORT[] = { {"COM1"}, {"COM2"}, {"COM3"}, {"COM4"}, {"COM5"},
            {"COM6"}, {"COM7"}, {"COM8"}, {"COM9"}};
/////////////////////////////////////////////////////////////////////////////
// CMfcCOMTestView
```

FIGURE 3.26 The modified header file of the view class.

to fulfill this translation. Because we've used the character pointer array, we won't need to use that function again. We can directly use the index, which is the port number entered by the user when the program runs, to locate the port name from this character pointer array. For example, `comPORT[0]` means that `COM1` has been selected from the menu.

Still in the `View` class implementation file, click the scroll bar and browse down until we find the function `SetupPort()`, which we previously added. Enter the code shown in Figure 3.27 into the body of the function.

A: Some local variables are declared at the beginning of this function. The `pParam` is an object of the structure `pSerialCreate` defined in the `Document` class header file. Then a `new` keyword is used to dynamically allocate memory space for the newly created object `pParam`. The variable `portNum` is assigned with a value equal to `nPort-1`.

```
////////////////////////////////////////////////////////////////////////////
// CMfcCOMTestView message handlers
ERR_CODE CMfcCOMTestView::SetupPort(int nPort, int nBaud)
{
        int portNum;
A       ERR_CODE ecRet = OK;
        pSerialCreate  pParam;

        pParam = new SerialCreate;
        portNum = nPort - 1;

B       pParam->lBaudRate = nBaud;
        pParam->lDataBits = NUM_BITS;
        pParam->lTimeout  = TIME_OUT;

        CMfcCOMTestDoc* pDoc = GetDocument();
C       ASSERT_VALID(pDoc);
D       if (PortFlg[portNum])
           return ecRet;
E       ecRet = pDoc->PortInitialize(comPORT[portNum], pParam);
        if (ecRet != OK)
           msg("ERROR in PortInitialize()!");
        else
        {
F           PortFlg[portNum] = TRUE;          // set port init flag as true
            hPort = pParam->h_Port;           // reserve the port handler
        }
G       delete pParam;

        return ecRet;
}
```

FIGURE 3.27 The function `SetupPort()`.

The minimum value of the port number entered from the keyboard is `1`, and the minimum index of the character pointer array is `0`. In order to match this relationship, the `nPort` should be `1` less. The `portNum` is used as the index for the character pointer array to locate a port name.

B: Here we need to assign setup parameters to the newly created structure object `pParam`. Later on, these setup parameters will be passed into the `PortInitialize()` interfacing function with the structure object `pParam` to initialize the serial port. These parameters include the baud rate, the number of bits, and the timeout value.

C: At this point, a key operation appears. As we already know, while the program runs, the communication between the `View` class and the `Document` class is necessary because the keyboard or menu input and the resulting data need to be processed and displayed in these two separate classes. Microsoft provides a communication method, or bridge, between the `View` and `Document` classes, called `GetDocument()`, and we can find the definition of this method in the `View` class implementation file. This method returns a pointer to the current `Document` class object. Our application must access the interfacing functions to initialize the serial port, write data to the port, and read data from the port. All these interfacing functions are declared and implemented in our `Document` class file. In order to access these functions, we must use this `GetDocument()` method defined in our `View` class. Of course, we can define other objects and use other methods to communicate between these two classes if we like. Here we want to use this method, which is provided by the system, to communicate between these two classes.

In order to do this, we first need to dynamically create a new instance pointer, pDoc, which points to our current Document class object, and assign the method, GetDocument(), to this newly created instance pointer which is an equivalent method of using pDoc in the program to call the method GetDocument() to obtain the address of the current Document class object. After obtaining a pointer of the current Document class object, we use a system debug macro, ASSERT_VALID(), to make sure we have obtained a valid pointer of the current Document class object.

D: Before our program can call the interfacing function PortInitialize() to set up the serial port, it must check the Boolean flag array PortFlg[] to make sure that the port has not been initialized. It may get an error if it reinitializes a port—specifically, if it tries to reopen a port that has already been opened, because Windows does not allow us to do that. If the port has been initialized, just return the control to the calling function without any other action.

E: If the port has not been initialized, our program calls the interfacing function PortInitialize() located in our Document class to set up the serial port. It accesses this interfacing function by using the Document pointer, pDoc, which it obtained earlier, in this form:

```
ecRet = pDoc->PortInitialize(comPORT[portNum], pParam);
```

Because the pDoc is a pointer, our program uses an arrow operator to access the function. The first argument of this function is a character string that represents the port name. An index is used to locate the desired port name from the character pointer array. If the interfacing function encounters any errors, an error message will be displayed on the screen.

F: If the function calling is successful, the Boolean flag is set to True, indicating that this port has been initialized. We reserve the returned handler of the opened port to the variable hPort, which is defined in our View class, for further use later.

G: Before exiting the function, our program must use the delete to clean up the memory space allocated for the pParam structure object. A memory leakage error may occur if this space is not cleaned up.

Now the coding for the SetupPort() function is done. Next, we need to code for another middle-layer function, TestPort().

Still in the View class implementation file, browse to find the TestPort() function. Enter the code shown in Figure 3.28 into the body of this function.

A: Some local variables are declared at the beginning of this function. sData[] and rData[] are two null-terminated character arrays. These two character arrays will be used to store the data sent out and read back from the serial port, and to display the data in two text boxes in the main dialog box. We create a structure object pointer, comPort, by using the new keyword. This structure object is used to store the necessary parameters for the reading operation when the interfacing function PortRead() is executed.

B: As with the SetupPort() function discussed earlier, we need to create an instance pointer that points to our current Document class. Once this is done, our program can access the interfacing functions defined in the Document class from the View class.

C: Before our application can execute either of the write or read operations, it must check the Boolean flag to make sure that the port has been initialized. If it has not, an error message will be displayed onscreen, and the program will return to the calling function without any action.

D: If the port has been initialized, our program assigns the necessary reading parameters to the comPort structure object to initialize the object. These parameters are used to

```
  ERR_CODE CMfcCOMTestView::TestPort(int cPort)
  {
          BYTE    sByte;
A         char    sData[16], rData[16];
          int     numByte = NUM_BYTE;
          ERR_CODE ecRet = OK;
          CommPortClass* comPort = new CommPortClass;

B         CMfcCOMTestDoc* pDoc = GetDocument();
          ASSERT_VALID(pDoc);

C         if (!PortFlg[cPort - 1])
          {
                  msg("Port not Initialized!");
                  return ecRet;
          }
D         comPort->handlePort = hPort;
          comPort->iMaxChars  = NUM_BYTE;

E         for (sByte = START_BYTE; sByte <= MAX_BYTE; sByte++)
          {
F                 ecRet = pDoc->PortWrite(hPort, sByte, numByte);
                  if (ecRet)
                  {
                          msg("PortWrite() is failed");
G                         TestPassed = FALSE;
                          return EC_WRITE_FAIL;
                  }
H                 sprintf(sData, "%c", sByte);
                  comDlg->m_sendData.SetWindowText(sData);
                  comDlg->m_sendData.UpdateWindow();
I                 ecRet = pDoc->PortRead(comPort);
J                 if (ecRet)
                  {
                          msg("PortRead() is failed");
                          TestPassed = FALSE;
                          return EC_READ_FAIL;
                  }
K                 sprintf(rData, "%c", comPort->bByte);
                  comDlg->m_readData.SetWindowText(rData);
                  comDlg->m_readData.UpdateWindow();
L                 if (sByte != comPort->bByte)
                  {
                          TestPassed = FALSE;
                          return EC_TEST_FAIL;
                  }
          }
M         TestPassed = TRUE;
N         delete comPort;

          return ecRet;
  }
```

FIGURE 3.28 The function `TestPort()`.

support the execution of the `PortRead()` interfacing function to retrieve the data from the serial port. Here, two major parameters are assigned: the opened port handler and the number of the bytes to be read.

E: A `for` loop is used for port testing. During testing, our program sends a sequence of ASCII characters to the serial port, and then reads back this sequence data from the same port. The sequence starts from the numeric value of `0` (48 in ASCII code) and ends at the character `Z` (90 in ASCII code). The loop condition variable is `sByte`.

F: During the loop testing, the interfacing function `PortWrite()` is called to write new data to the port. Note that we have to use the instance pointer of the `Document` class `pDoc` to access the interfacing functions defined in that class.

G: If the function calling fails, an error message will be displayed on the screen. Also, the Boolean flag `TestPassed` will be reset to `False`, which indicates that the port testing was not successful. The program returns to the calling function with an error status.

H: If the function is successful, the sent data will be displayed as a string in the text box in the main dialog box. First, the program uses the `sprintf()` function to convert the data from a byte to a character. Then it uses one of the member variables of the main dialog box class (`comDlg`), `m_sendData`, to display this character in the text box within the main dialog box. We perform communications between the main dialog box and the `View` class by using the object pointer `comDlg`, which will be discussed later. After the character is sent to the text box in the main dialog box, the program calls the `UpdateWindow()` system function to refresh the main dialog box and display the character on the screen.

I: After writing data to the port, the program must read the data back from the same port by calling another interfacing function `PortRead()`.

J: If this function calling fails, an error message will be displayed onscreen. The Boolean flag `TestPassed` will be reset to `False` to indicate to the system that the testing was not successful, and the program will return to the calling function with an error status.

K: If the function calling is successful, our application converts the received data to a character by using the `sprintf()` function and then accesses the member variable `m_readData`, which is defined in the main dialog box class `COMDLG`, to display this character in the text box. Then an `UpdateWindow()` system function is called to make the character visible onscreen.

L: To check the testing result, we need to compare the data we sent with the data read back. The testing is successful if both are identical. Otherwise, the test is a failure. In that case, the Boolean flag `TestPassed` will be reset to `False`, and the program will return to the calling function with an error status.

M: If the testing is successful, the Boolean flag `TestPassed` is set to `True`.

N: Finally, the program must clean up the memory space we allocated for the structure object `comPort` before we assigned the reading parameters to this structure.

We are almost finished coding the `View` class, but we cannot finish it right now, because we need to add some code in both the constructor and the destructor of the View class. It is easy to be confused if we add the code right now, because the code is closely related to the main dialog box that we will discuss in the next section. For now, we will reserve some space for that code.

3.2.3.3 Developing the Dialog Box Classes

We have two dialog boxes left to be developed. One is the main dialog box and the other is the loop number input dialog box. First, let us develop the main dialog box.

The main dialog box, as mentioned earlier, is the main GUI in this project. The `View` class provides only a blank area, but we can add many GUI components to that area to personalize our GUI. In this application, we want to use a dialog box as our GUI.

Of course, we can directly create a dialog-based MFC project when we create a new MFC project by selecting the `Dialog based` radio button on the second project page. In our application, we select `Single document` style. The reason we make this selection is that we want to familiarize ourselves with the `Document-View` class idea and design method because no `Doc-`

ument-View class structure will be available if we create a Dialog-based application. The Dialog-based applications are relatively easier compared to the Document-View applications.

The first step in developing a dialog box GUI is to add a dialog box into our project. To do that, click the ResourceView tab in the Visual C++ 6.0 workspace to open the resource files. In the opened resource file list, click the plus sign next to the resource file folder mfcCOMTest resources, and all default resource files in this project will be displayed. To show all the dialog boxes that exist in this project, click the plus sign next to the Dialog folder. Currently, only one default dialog box, IDD_ABOUTBOX, is included there.

Right-click the Dialog folder; on the popup menu that appears, click the Insert Dialog item. A default dialog box with the editor is displayed onscreen.

Right-click the dialog box and select the Properties item from the popup menu to open the Dialog Properties dialog box, shown in Figure 3.29. Enter IDD_COMTESTDLG in the ID: field, and COM Test Dialog in the Caption: field, as shown in Figure 3.29. Click the Close button, located in the upper-right corner of the dialog box, to close it.

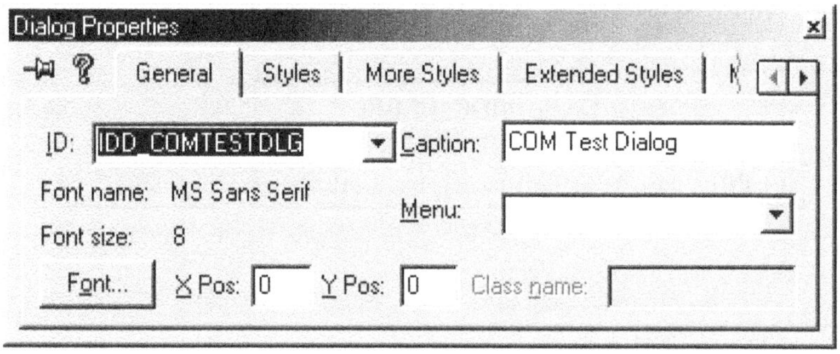

FIGURE 3.29 The dialog properties.

Enlarge the dialog box and right-click it. In the popup menu that appears, click the ClassWizard... item. The Adding a class dialog box appears with a prompt to select a class to hold this dialog box. The default selection is Create a new class. Keep this default selection and click OK to open the New Class dialog box. In the opened dialog box, enter COMDLG in the Name: field and click OK to open its MFC ClassWizard dialog box. Just click the OK to close this dialog box at this moment.

On the dialog page, add the following components to this dialog:

- Static Text: ID: IDC_STATIC Caption: Welcome to MFC Serial Port Testing
- Group Box: ID: IDC_STATIC Caption: Port Settings
- Static Text: ID: IDC_STATIC Caption: COM Port
- Edit Box: ID: IDC_PORT_EDIT
- Static Text: ID: IDC_STATIC Caption: Baud Rate
- Edit Box: ID: IDC_BAUD_EDIT
- Group Box: ID: IDC_STATIC Caption: Testing Data
- Static Text: ID: IDC_STATIC Caption: Send Data
- Edit Box: ID: IDC_SEND_EDIT
- Static Text: ID: IDC_STATIC Caption: Read Rate
- Edit Box: ID: IDC_READ_EDIT
- Button: ID: IDINIT Caption: INIT
- Button: ID: IDTEST Caption: TEST

- Button: ID: `IDLOOP` Caption: `LOOP`
- Button: ID: `IDEXIT` Caption: `EXIT`
- Static Text: ID: `IDC_LABEL` Caption:

The finished dialog box should match the one shown in Figure 3.30.

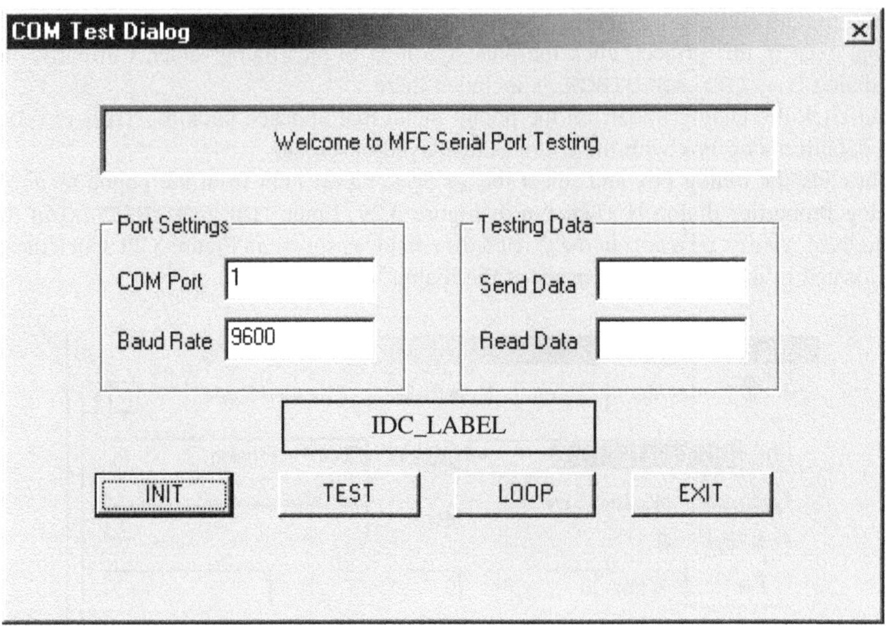

FIGURE 3.30 The GUI of the project SimpleCOM.

The last Static Text (`IDC_LABEL`) cannot be seen right now because we haven't yet set a caption there. This Static Text is used to display the testing status as the program runs, for example, "the initialization is finished" or "testing is successful."

Don't pay too much attention to the two numbers currently displayed in the `COM Port` and `Baud Rate` boxes; we will explain them later on.

Now we have finished creating a new dialog box with a new class named `COMDLG`. If we open the files window by clicking the `FileView` tab, we will find that a new class named `COMDLG`, including header `COMDLG.h` and source files `COMDLG.cpp`, has been added to our project.

We need to set up the connection between the components in our GUI and the event-processing functions. This means that when we activate a component from the GUI, by means of clicking a button or typing something into a text box, an event should be created to respond to this component's activation. This event is generated by the Windows system. What we need to do is set a connection between the event and an event procedure, and add some code into that event procedure to process the event. To set this connection, we need to use the `ClassWizard` tool provided by Microsoft Visual C++ 6.0.

In Visual Basic, when we add a new component to the GUI, the protocol of an event procedure associated with that component is automatically created in the program file. When we double-click that component from the GUI, the event procedure associated with that component will be automatically opened, and we can directly add any code into that event procedure to finish processing that event as necessary. But in Visual C++ 6.0, we have to add and set up this connection ourselves.

Now we will demonstrate how to use the `ClassWizard` to add the event procedure and set up the connection between the components in our GUI (the main dialog box) and the event procedure we've added.

In this application, we don't need to add event procedures for all the components in our main dialog box. We only need to add the event procedure and set up the connections between the components and event procedures for the following components:

- Edit Box: ID: `IDC_PORT_EDIT`
- Edit Box: ID: `IDC_BAUD_EDIT`
- Edit Box: ID: `IDC_SEND_EDIT`
- Edit Box: ID: `IDC_READ_EDIT`
- Button: ID: `IDINIT` Caption: `INIT`
- Button: ID: `IDTEST` Caption: `TEST`
- Button: ID: `IDLOOP` Caption: `LOOP`
- Button: ID: `IDEXIT` Caption: `EXIT`
- Static Text: ID: `IDC_LABEL` Caption:

The first two edit boxes are used to receive the user's input from the keyboard, such as the serial port number and the baud rate. These parameters will be passed into the `PortInitialize()` interfacing function to set up and initialize the serial port. The next two edit boxes are used to display the data sent out to and data read back from the serial port. Four command buttons are used to activate the associated event functions to execute the desired testing jobs. The last static text component is used to display the testing status of the serial port, such as the initialization messages, the data written, and the data read status.

For the first four edit boxes, we don't need to create any event procedures because these components are only used to receive user data or display the testing data. Thus, we can consider these components as member variables of the class `COMDLG`.

To create a member variable for our dialog box class by using the ClassWizard tool, follow these steps:

1. Select the component.
2. Right-click that component to open a popup menu.
3. Select the `ClassWizard...` item to open the `MFC ClassWizard` dialog box.
4. Use the `Message Maps` or `Member Variables` tab to create either event functions or member variables.
5. Click either the `Add Function` or the `Add Variable` button to add the member function or member variable into our program's main dialog box class.

Now let us follow the previous steps to add member variables to our dialog box class. First, let us add a member variable for the edit box `IDC_PORT_EDIT`:

1. Click the dialog box `IDD_COMTESTDLG` to open our dialog box. Select the edit box `IDC_PORT_EDIT` by clicking it.
2. Right-click this edit box, and select `ClassWizard...` item to open the `MFC ClassWizard` dialog box.
3. In the opened dialog box, select the `Member Variables` tab to open the member variable page.
4. In the opened member variable page, select the edit box `IDC_PORT_EDIT`. Then click the `Add Variable...` button to open the `Add Member Variable` dialog box.
5. Select `int` from the `Variable type:` field, and type `comPort` after the default value: `m_` in the `Member variable name:` field. Our finished member variable dialog box should match the one shown in Figure 3.31
6. Click `OK` to save this member variable in the dialog box class `COMDLG`.

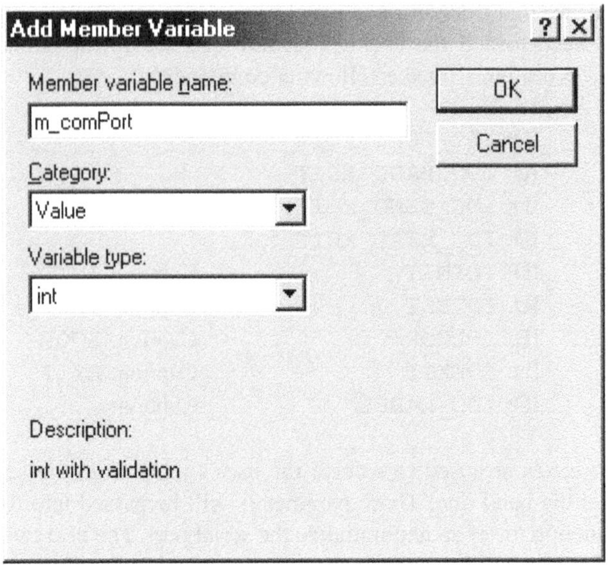

FIGURE 3.31 The add member variable dialog.

TABLE 3.1
Member Variables

Component ID	Value Type	Category	Member Variable Name
IDC_BAUD_EDIT	int	Value	m_baudRate
IDC_SEND_EDIT	CEdit	Control	m_sendData
IDC_READ_EDIT	CEdit	Control	m_readData
IDC_LABEL	CStatic	Control	m_resLabel

In the same way, add the following member variables to our dialog box class (see Table 3-1)

When we set a member variable, we can define it as either a value or a component by selecting the `Value type` property. By defining a member variable as a value, we can directly access that variable and pick up the value of that variable while the program runs. By defining the member variable as an object, (such as an object with the `CEdit` type), we can access the object and all methods associated with it. For example, suppose that we want to use `IDC_READ_EDIT` and `IDC_SEND_EDIT` components to display the sending out and reading back data from a serial port. We need to set up these two member variables as two components of type `CEdit` class. In this way, we can access these two components and use all the associated methods provided by the class `CEdit`. When we display the sending out or reading back data using these two components, we can use the `SetWindowText()` method to set the data that will be displayed in each component.

Next, we need to add the event functions to our `COMDLG` dialog box. The dialog box class holds our dialog box GUI. In other words, this class controls and responds to the components of the GUI. In this application, we need to create four event functions, and each one is associated with a command button. To add an event function to our dialog box class, follow these steps:

1. In the dialog box panel, right-click the component for which we want to add an event function.
2. From the popup menu that appears, select the `ClassWizard...` menu item to open the `MFC ClassWizard` dialog box.

3. Click the Message Maps tab to open the Message Maps page.
4. Select a component, such as IDINIT, from the Object IDs: list.
5. Select BN_CLICKED from the Messages: field. (Alternatively, we could select BN_DOUBLECLICKED if we wanted the action type to be a double-click of the mouse button.)
6. Click the Add Function... button.
7. Click OK to add the event function to the dialog box class.

Next we must add four event functions to our dialog box class; these functions are listed in Table 3-2.

TABLE 3.2
Event Functions

Component ID	Message	Function Name
IDINIT	BN_CLICKED	OnInit
IDTEST	BN_CLICKED	OnTest
IDLOOP	BN_CLICKED	OnLoop
IDEXIT	BN_CLICKED	OnExit

We also need to add a system initialization function for the dialog box OnInitDialog(). This function is created by the system based on a window message, WM_INITDIALOG.

To add this system function to the dialog box class, select COMDLG from the Object IDs: field, and select WM_INITDIALOG from the Messages: field. Click the Add Function button to add this function to our class.

Now, when we open the source file, COMDLG.cpp, we will find that all four of these member functions and a system function have been added to the file.

Recall that in Section 3.2.3.2 when we developed our View class, we mentioned that we couldn't finish the coding for that class source file until we developed the main dialog box COMDLG. It is now time for us to solve this problem and finish that section.

We need to set a connection between the View class and the main dialog box class COMDLG to perform the accessing or calling of the middle-layer functions defined in the View class from the main dialog box. When we activate a component from the main dialog box (by clicking the INIT button, for example), an event or a message will be generated by the system. To respond to this event or message, we need to call the SetupPort() function to initialize the serial port to make it ready for the subsequent port testing. However, the function SetupPort() is defined in the View class, so we need to make a connection between the main dialog box and the View class to make the function SetupPort() that is defined in the View class available or accessible for the main dialog box class COMDLG. Recall that on line C in Figure 3.21, we added an object pointer of the class COMDLG to the View class, and we mentioned that this pointer could be used as a connection between the class objects in COMDLG and View.

In order to make a connection between two classes, we need to use an *active-passive* class structure. In this class structure, we need to define one of two class objects as an active class object and the other one as a passive class object. The active class will be created first when the program is run, and then it will create the passive class. To access or communicate between the active and passive classes, each class has to reserve an address of the other class, no matter what kind of class it is. This means that we should reserve a passive class object pointer in the active class object and an active class object pointer in the passive class object. In our application, the View class is an active class object and the main dialog box class COMDLG is a passive class object.

Because the View class is an active class object, we must add and reserve a pointer of the passive class COMDLG into the active class mfcCOMTestView. We have already added this pointer in the last section. (Refer to line C in Figure 3.21.) Now we need to add the active class pointer (a pointer of class mfcCOMTestView) into our passive class COMDLG. Follow these steps to fulfill this addition:

1. Click the ClassView tab in the Visual C++ 6.0 workspace to open all the classes that we have installed into our project.
2. Find our passive class, COMDLG, from the list, and right-click this class file. On the popup menu that appears, click the Add Member Variable... menu item to open the Add Member Variable dialog box, shown in Figure 3.32.
3. Type CMfcCOMTestView* in the **Variable Type:** field, and sView in the Variable Name: field. (See Figure 3.32.)
4. Make sure the Private radio button is selected. (This will prevent any other class or object from accessing our active class.)
5. Click OK to add this active class pointer to our passive class COMDLG.

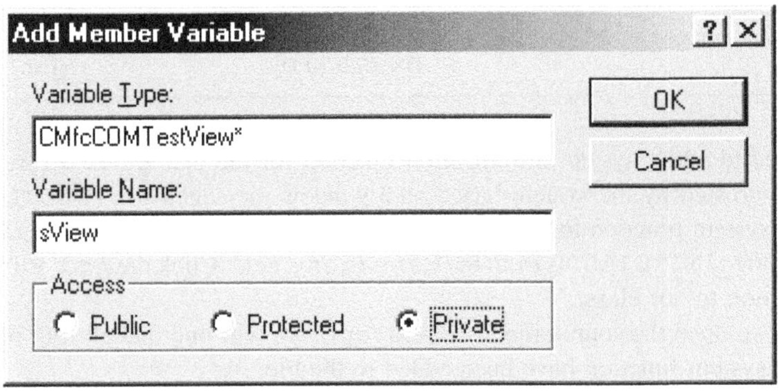

FIGURE 3.32 The add member variable dialog.

Right now each of our classes, active and passive, has the address of the other class. But how do they communicate with each other? The active class should generate the passive class object based on the reserved pointer holding the address of the passive class within the active class. After the passive class object is generated, the active class should also set and pass an address of the active class itself to the passive class object. In this way, the passive class object can access the active class by using this address. How does the passive class object do this? We need to add two more member functions to the passive class COMDLG to allow this access.

The first member function we need to add into the passive class is called the *setter*:

```
void setComView(CMfcCOMTestView* comView);
```

The argument type of this member function is a pointer of the active class, CMfcCOMTestView*.

The second member function we need to add is called a *getter*:

```
CMfcCOMTestView* getComView();
```

This member function returns a pointer to the active class. Using the examples shown above as guidelines, add these two member functions into our passive class COMDLG.

By using the *setter*, the active class can set and pass its address to the passive class. By using the *getter*, the passive class can retrieve the active class's address from the passive class to access the active class object.

Now we can add another member variable, `InitFlg`, which is a Boolean variable used to monitor and store the initialization status of the serial port.

After finishing these steps, click the `FileView` tab in the Visual C++ 6.0 workspace, and click `COMDLG.h` to open the header file of our passive class, which is shown in Figure 3.33.

```
   #if
   !defined(AFX_COMDLG_H__F5283D11_BC10_493C_BF02_5392BC20CE3B__INCLUDED_)
   #define AFX_COMDLG_H__F5283D11_BC10_493C_BF02_5392BC20CE3B__INCLUDED_

   #if _MSC_VER > 1000
   #pragma once
   #endif // _MSC_VER > 1000
   // COMDLG.h : header file
   //
A  class CMfcCOMTestView;                    // very important - 7/17/2002 - Y. Bai
   /////////////////////////////////////////////////////////////////////////////
   // COMDLG dialog

   class COMDLG : public CDialog
   {
   // Construction
   public:
        bool InitFlg;
B      CMfcCOMTestView* getComView();
C       void setComView(CMfcCOMTestView* comView);
       COMDLG(CWnd* pParent = NULL);  // standard constructor

   // Dialog Data
        //{{AFX_DATA(COMDLG)
        enum { IDD = IDD_COMTESTDLG };
       Cstatic     m_resLabel;
D      CEdit       m_readData;
       CEdit       m_sendData;
        int        m_comPort;
        int        m_baudRate;
        //}}AFX_DATA

   // Overrides
       // ClassWizard generated virtual function overrides
       //{{AFX_VIRTUAL(COMDLG)
       protected:
       virtual void DoDataExchange(CDataExchange* pDX);    // DDX/DDV support
       //}}AFX_VIRTUAL

   // Implementation
   protected:
       // Generated message map functions
       //{{AFX_MSG(COMDLG)
       afx_msg void OnInit();
       afx_msg void OnExit();
E      afx_msg void OnTest();
       afx_msg void OnLoop();
       virtual BOOL OnInitDialog();
       //}}AFX_MSG
       DECLARE_MESSAGE_MAP()
   private:
F      CMfcCOMTestView* sView;
   };
   .......
```

FIGURE 3.33 The header file `COMDLG.h`.

On lines B and C, notice that one member variable, `InitFlg`, and the two member functions we added above have been included. On lines D and E, you'll see that all class member variables and member functions added into the class `COMDLG` by using the `ClassWizard` tool are listed under the `Dialog Data` and `Message Map` catalogs in the header file. On line F the active class pointer `sView`, which is the address of the active class `CMfcCOMTestView` and was added earlier, is located under the `Private` variable catalog in this header file.

Pay particular attention to line A. This line is very important for both the header file and active class source file. The main dialog box class `COMDLG` has no knowledge about our `View` class `mfcCOMTestView`, and neither does the compiler. An error message will be displayed if we compile our program without line A, because the compiler will not recognize the `mfcCOMTestView` class, as opposed to the main dialog box class `COMDLG`. We must use this predeclared class definition to inform the compiler that we have a `View` class in this project, and to release this class information to the compiler. Then compiler will recognize the `View` class and will give us no problems when we compile our main dialog box class.

Now that the main dialog box class header file is ready, we can finish the tail section of the `View` class source file. The `View` class object is an active class object in our project; it will create the passive class object `COMDLG` and pass itself as an address argument to that object. This address will be used as a connection by the passive class to access the active class. The best place to create a passive class object from the active class object is inside the constructor of the active class.

Now open our `View` class source file `mfcCOMTestView.cpp`, and move the cursor to the line `CMfcCOMTestView construction/destruction` to locate the constructor and destructor sections of the file. In the constructor section, enter the code shown in Figure 3.34.

```
    ///////////////////////////////////////////////////////////////////////////
    // CMfcCOMTestView construction/destruction

    CMfcCOMTestView::CMfcCOMTestView()
    {
            // TODO: add construction code here
A           comDlg = new COMDLG;

B           hPort = 0;
            TestPassed = FALSE;
            for (int i = 0; i < MAX_MENU; i++)
            PortFlg[i] = false;

C           comDlg->setComView(this);
            if (comDlg->DoModal() == IDOK)
               exit (0);
    }

    CMfcCOMTestView::~CMfcCOMTestView()
    {
D           delete  comDlg;
    }
```

FIGURE 3.34 The view class constructor and destructor.

In line A, we use the pointer of the passive class object `comDlg` (which we added to this active class in the last section) to dynamically create a new object of the class `COMDLG` by using the keyword `new`.

In line C, after this new object of the passive class is created, the active class (`View`) calls the method `setComView()`, (the *setter* that was added into the passive class above). `setComView()` passes and sets a `this` pointer to the newly created passive class object `comDlg`. In this way, the active class or the View class sets an address that points to the active class itself in the passive class comDlg. The this pointer represents the current class object mfcCOMTestView.

After setting this address, the active class (View class) continues to call the DoModal() method to display the main dialog box in a modal mode and release control from the current class to the passive class comDlg, which is our main dialog box class object. If the main dialog box returns an IDOK message, it means that the Exit button has been clicked. The active class will then call the exit(0) system method to terminate the program. An argument of 0 means that the termination is error free.

In line B, some initializations are performed inside the constructor. This includes resetting the TestPassed flag and the port status flag array PortFlg[], as well as initializing the port handler to 0.

Finally, on line D, we clean up the memory space allocated for the new passive class object comDlg by using the delete command. At this point, we have finished the coding of the View class in our project.

To provide a clear picture of how the passive class object retrieves the active class address, which is passed by the active class in line C in Figure 3.34, we need to continue to code for our passive class object source file COMDLG.cpp. Open this source file by clicking the FileView tab in the Visual C++ 6.0 workspace and double-clicking COMDLG.cpp. In Figure 3.35, notice that all the member functions we've included have been automatically added to the file by the computer.

```
......
void COMDLG::setComView(CMfcCOMTestView* comView)
{
        sView = comView;
}

CMfcCOMTestView* COMDLG::getComView()
{
        return sView;
}
```

FIGURE 3.35 The portion source file of the COMDLG class.

Currently, we only need to take care of the two member functions we've added, which are the *setter*, setComView(), and the *getter*, getComView(). Browse our source file to locate these two function bodies, as shown in Figure 3.35.

The role of the *setter*, setComView(), is simple. It assigns the passed address of the active class to the reserved pointer of the active class, sView. The *getter*, getComView(), simply returns the reserved pointer of the active class. With these two member functions, the passive class object COMDLG can easily access any component defined in the active class object.

Now we will look at the complete source code for this passive class. First, we need to include two header files in the source file. Enter the commands shown in Figure 3.36 at the top of the source file. Once these two header files are included, the main dialog box class will be aware of the two class objects.

```
#include "mfcCOMTestDoc.h"
#include "mfcCOMTestView.h"
```

FIGURE 3.36 Two header files on the COMDLG class.

```
//////////////////////////////////////////////////////////////////////////////
// COMDLG dialog
COMDLG::COMDLG(CWnd* pParent /*=NULL*/)
        : CDialog(COMDLG::IDD, pParent)
{
    //{{AFX_DATA_INIT(COMDLG)
    m_comPort = 1;                  // modify this port number as default - Bai.
    m_baudRate = 9600;              // modify this as default baud rate - Bai.
    //}}AFX_DATA_INIT
}
```

FIGURE 3.37 The constructor of the class COMDLG.

Next let us take a look at the constructor, shown in Figure 3.37. Two member variables, `m_comPort` and `m_baudRate`, are initialized here. The original values for these two variables are both `0`. For our application, we will set these two member variables with definite initial values, such as `1` for COM Port (`COM1`) and `9600` for the baud rate. Modify these two variables' initial values as shown in Figure 3.37.

Let us now modify the system initialization function, `OnInitDialog()`, which we've added as a system member function using the previous steps. Enter the code shown in Figure 3.38 into this function.

```
BOOL COMDLG::OnInitDialog()
{
    CDialog::OnInitDialog();
    // TODO: Add extra initialization here
    InitFlg = false;
    return TRUE;        // return TRUE unless you set the focus to a control
                        // EXCEPTION: OCX Property Pages should return FALSE
}
```

FIGURE 3.38 The dialog initialization function.

Only one command is applied for this function to reset the initialization status of the serial port to `False`. Some readers may argue about the usefulness of this if we have already defined the initialization status flag for each port in the `View` class (`PortFlg[]`). These flags belong to different levels and have different purposes. The `InitFlg` used here works only for the main dialog box. Although it looks as though this flag duplicates the job of the `PortFlg[]` class, we prefer this style because it makes our program safer.

Let us continue by finishing all the source code for this class, which is shown in Figure 3.39.

A: When the `INIT` button is clicked in the main dialog box, an event will be created by the system, and that event will be passed into the `OnInit()` member function to be processed. Some local variables will be generated at the beginning of this function. One of the most important variables is `comView`, which is a pointer to the active class or `View` class object in our project. This pointer can be obtained by calling the member function `getComView()`, which is also called a *getter*, from the passive class `COMDLG`. After the program obtains this pointer, it calls a system macro `ASSERT_VALID` to confirm that we have received a valid address of the active class `mfcCOMTestView`. After obtaining this pointer, the program can use it to access and call any member variable or member function defined in the active class (our `View` class). This step is the key to

```
    void COMDLG::OnInit()
    {
            // TODO: Add your control notification handler code here
            ERR_CODE  ecRet = OK;
A           CMfcCOMTestView*  comView = getComView();
            ASSERT_VALID(comView);

B           UpdateData(TRUE);
C           ecRet = comView->SetupPort(m_comPort, m_baudRate);
            if (ecRet)
            {
                msg("ERROR in INIT");
                return;
            }
D           InitFlg = true;
            m_resLabel.SetWindowText("The Port has been Initialized");
    }

    void COMDLG::OnTest()
    {
            // TODO: Add your control notification handler code here
            ERR_CODE  ecRet = OK;
E           CMfcCOMTestView*  comView = getComView();

F           if (!InitFlg)
            {
                msg("No Initialization !");
                return;
            }
G           m_resLabel.SetWindowText("");
            UpdateData(TRUE);
H           ecRet = comView->TestPort(m_comPort);
            if (ecRet)
              msg("ERROR in TEST");

I           if (comView->TestPassed)
              m_resLabel.SetWindowText("Testing is Successful!");
    }
    void COMDLG::OnExit()
    {
        // TODO: Add your control notification handler code here
J       CMfcCOMTestView*  comView = getComView();

        InitFlg = false;
        CloseHandle(comView->hPort);
K       CDialog::OnOK();
    }

    void COMDLG::setComView(CMfcCOMTestView *comView)
    {
        sView = comView;
    }

    CMfcCOMTestView* COMDLG::getComView()
    {
        return  sView;
    }
```

FIGURE 3.39 The functions in the COMDLG.

access any middle-layer function defined in the View class to perform serial port operations.

B: Next, our program must call the system function UpdateData() to update all the numeric values defined in the main dialog box window. Before clicking the INIT button, one should have finished entering the serial port number and baud rate in the two edit boxes, IDC_PORT_EDIT and IDC_BAUD_EDIT, respectively. The purpose of executing the UpdateData() system function is to make these two numeric values available to our program. In other words, after we execute this UpdateData() function, two member variables, m_comPort and m_baudRate, should be updated with the current numeric values entered from the keyboard. Our program uses these two member variables as arguments and passes them to the middle-layer function to set up the serial port. These two member variables would be zeros if we didn't execute this UpdateData() system function before we called a middle-layer function.

C: After following the previous steps, the program can now access and call the middle-layer function, SetupPort(), which is defined in our View class (or active class), by the pointer of the View class, comView, which was created and obtained in step A. The program uses an arrow operator to access the SetupPort() function because comView is an address. Two member variables, m_comPort and m_baudRate, are passed as arguments to the middle-layer function. An error message will be displayed onscreen if this function call fails. Otherwise, the program will continue to the next step.

D: If the function call is successful, the initialization status flag InitFlg is set to True to inform the system that the initialization has been performed. The message "The Port has been Initialized" will be displayed by m_resLabel as static text so that the program's execution status is displayed on the screen. Because the Static Text m_resLabel is defined as a CEdit control object, we can call one of the CEdit class methods, SetWindowText(), to display this message in the main dialog box.

E: If the TEST button is clicked in the main dialog box, an associated event will be created, and this event will be passed to the member function, OnTest(), to be processed. As in step A, we must first create a local pointer variable, comView, and obtain the address of the View class mfcCOMTestView by executing the member function getComView(). After this address is obtained, the program can use it to access any variable or member function defined in the View class.

F: Before calling the middle-layer function TestPort() to test the serial port, the program must check the initialization status flag InitFlg to confirm that the serial port has been initialized. If the port has not been initialized, a message will be displayed on the screen prompting us to initialize the port; the program will then return to the calling function without any further operation.

G: If the port has been initialized, the program will execute one of the member functions of the Static Text object m_resLabel, SetWindowText(), to clean up the old display content of this object and make it ready to display a new message. As in step B, an UpdateData() system function is executed to refresh all numeric values defined in the main dialog box, including the com port number, m_comPort, which is entered from the keyboard by the user.

H: Next, the program calls the middle-layer function TestPort(), which is defined in our View class mfcCOMTestView. It does so by using the class object pointer comView (obtained in step E above) to test the serial port whose port number is defined by the argument m_comPort. An arrow operator is used to access this middle-layer function because comView is an address (a pointer) of our View class object. An error message will be displayed if this middle-function call fails.

I: Finally, the program checks the testing status flag TestPassed, which is defined in our View class mfcCOMTestView. If this flag is True, which means that the testing for the current port has been successful, we refresh the Static Text object m_resLabel by calling its member function SetWindowText() with the message "Testing is successful!"

J: When EXIT button is clicked in the main dialog box (indicating that the program should be terminated), an associated event will be created and passed to the member function OnExit() to be processed further. As in steps A and E above, the program first needs to obtain the address of the View class object, comView, by calling the member function getComView(). The reason for this is that the program needs to close the port handler before it terminates, and the port handler hPort is defined in the View class. After this address is obtained, the program resets the initialization status flag InitFlg to False and then executes the CloseHandle() system function with our port handler, comView->hPort, as an argument to close the port.

K: When the main dialog box class object terminates and returns to the calling function, the default returning function CDialog::OnOK() should be executed to smoothly exit the dialog class object and return to our View class object. In this application, the dialog box object is called from our View class's constructor (see Figure 3.34, step C), so the dialog box should be returned to our View class's constructor. It is important to use this default returning function when exiting a dialog box that returns to the calling function. Otherwise, the program would encounter errors.

The following two functions are the *setter* and *getter*. We have another member function to be coded, called OnLoop(). The purpose of this member function is to repeatedly test a serial port in a certain loop number. (We will discuss this function issue later on, after we finish our first version of the project.)

At this point, we have finished developing all the classes in the project. It is now time to build the project. Click the Build|Set Active Configuration... menu item and select mfcCOMTest–Win32 Release from the Project configurations: list. Then click OK to save this setting and close this dialog box.

To build the project, click the Build|Build mfcCOMTest.exe menu item. If everything is OK, click the Build|Execute mfcCOMTest.exe menu item to run the project. The main dialog box will be displayed onscreen, as shown in Figure 3.40.

The default COM Port number is 1, which is mapped to COM1, and the baud rate is 9600. Click INIT button to initialize the serial port with these two default parameters. The message "The port has been initialized" is displayed by the Static Text object.

Then click the TEST button to test the selected serial port. The data sent out and read back will be displayed in the Send Data and Read Data edit boxes, respectively. If the testing is successful, the message "Testing is successful!" is displayed by the Static Text object, which is shown in Figure 3.41.

Now try to change the COM port number by entering a different number, such as 2, in the COM Port edit box. Then click the INIT button again to try to initialize the serial port. A message box will be displayed, as shown in Figure 3.42 (a), with the message " Unable to open the port". This means that the system cannot find the selected port. In other words, the port we've selected is not available on the current computer system. Click OK to close this message box.

For now, keep the number 2 in the COM Port edit box and click the TEST button. See what happens? Another message box, with the message "Port not Initialized" is displayed onscreen, as shown in Figure 3.42 (b). Click OK to close this message box.

Now let us test another aspect of our project. Restart the project, but this time don't click INIT first; instead click TEST. This indicates that we want to test the serial port without first initializing the port. What happens as a result of this action? A message box with the message "No Initialization" is displayed, as shown in Figure 3.42 (c). This means that we cannot execute testing for any serial port without initializing the port first. Our project is successful.

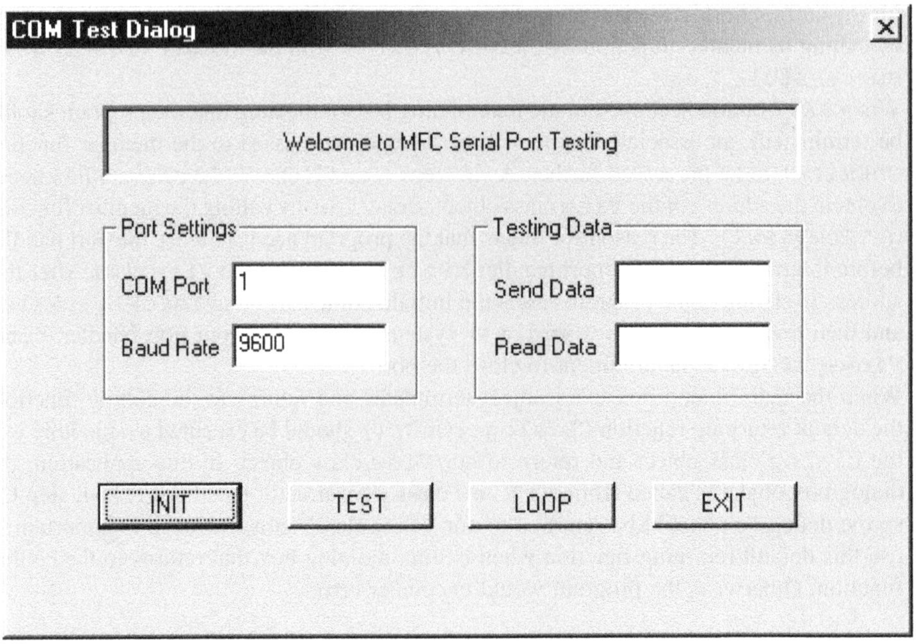

FIGURE 3.40 The main dialog box.

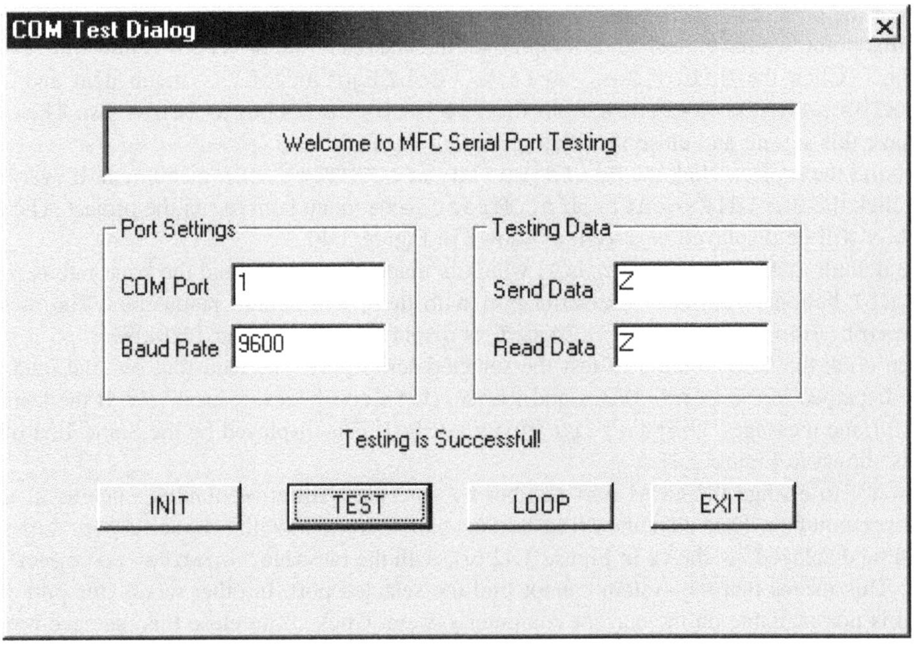

FIGURE 3.41 The running result of the project SimpleCOM.

TIP: In the current program, the testing process is relatively fast because we haven't included any delay subroutines in the testing loop. One issue we should emphasize is the delay method. If we were to insert `Sleep()` functions into the body of the testing loop, our testing program would not work. This is because the `Sleep()` function would release

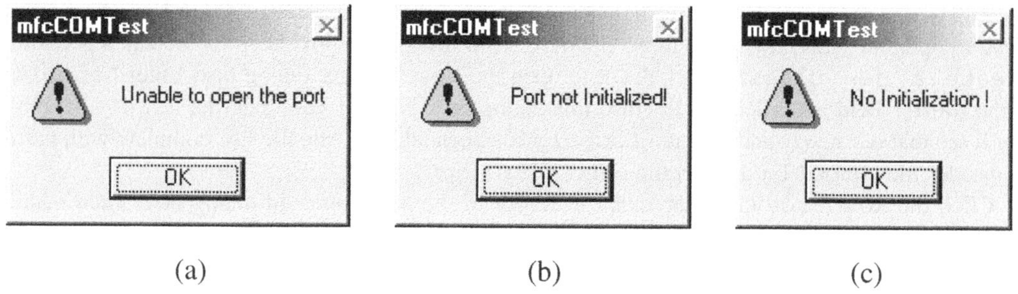

FIGURE 3.42 The error and message boxes.

> control to the CPU and enable processes with a higher priority to take over the control. The problem is that control might not return to our testing loop body when the Sleep time is up. If this happened, our program would appear to be deadlocked and would no longer respond. Always be careful when using the `Sleep()` function to handle the delay issue in a program. Of course, we can develop other routines to make a time delay in the testing loop without releasing control to the CPU.

We will now add one more procedure to our project: loop testing. Sometimes we need to test a serial port for a relatively long period of time. To meet this requirement, we can develop a loop-testing mode, which will let us select different loop numbers and allow the testing program to be executed multiple times until the specified number of loops have finished.

We need to add one more dialog box to our project so that when it runs, we can select the loop number. Click the `ResourceView` tab in the Visual C++ 6.0 workspace to open the resource list. Click the plus sign next to the `Dialog` folder to display all the dialog boxes developed for the project thus far. Currently, two dialog boxes are used in our project: One is the default dialog box `IDD_ABOUTBOX`, and the other one is our main dialog box, `IDD_COMTESTDLG`. We will now add the loop number selection dialog box.

Right-click the `Dialog` folder and click the `Insert Dialog` item from the popup menu. A default dialog box platform and an edit toolbox will appear onscreen. Right-click the default dialog box platform, and click the `Properties` item on the popup menu to open the `Dialog Properties` dialog box, shown in Figure 3.43.

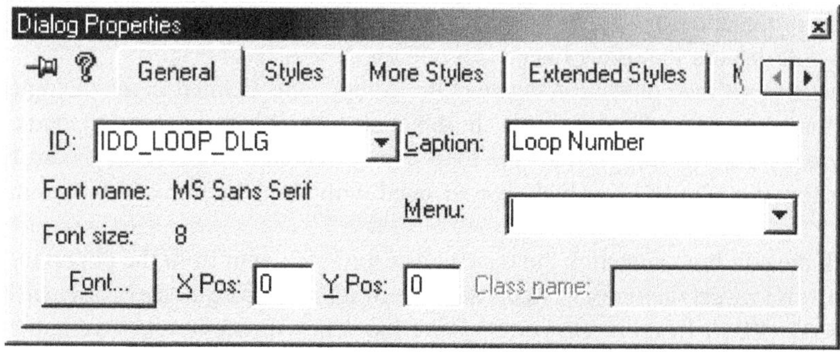

FIGURE 3.43 The dialog properties.

Enter `IDD_LOOP_DLG` in the `ID:` field and add `Loop Number` in the `Caption:` field, as shown in Figure 3.43. Click the Close button located on the upper-right corner of the dialog box to save these settings and close the box.

Right-click the dialog box platform again. Click the `ClassWizard...` item from the popup menu to open the `Adding a Class` dialog box. In this dialog box, keep the default selection, `Create a new class`, and click `OK` to open the `New Class` dialog box. Enter `LoopDlg` in the `Name:` field and click `OK` to close this dialog box. Now, if you click the `FileView` tab, you'll see that our newly added class, `LoopDlg` has been added to the file list, complete with both the header file (`LoopDlg.h`) and the source file (`LoopDlg.cpp`).

Click the `ResourceView` tab again to return to the newly created dialog box. Then make the following modifications:

- Delete the default `Cancel` button.
- Move the `OK` button to the bottom.
- Add some static text with the following properties:

  ID: `IDC_STATIC` Caption: `Enter the Loop Number`

- Add one edit box with the following properties:

  ID: `IDC_LOOP_EDIT`

The finished dialog box should match the one shown in Figure 3.44.

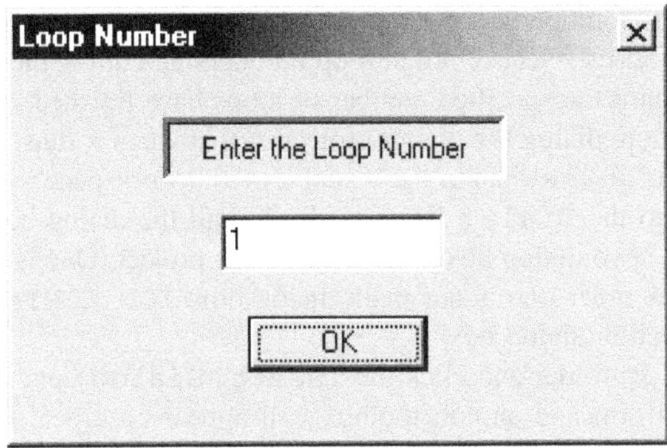

FIGURE 3.44 The loop number dialog.

The content of the edit box should be `Edit` in our application. Don't worry about the number right now. We will discuss this issue later.

Now we need to set the connection between the components defined in the dialog box and the member functions defined in the source file. In this dialog box class, we need to create a member variable, `m_loopNum`, which represents the loop number entered from the keyboard by the user, and a member function, `OnOK()`, which is associated with the `OK` command button in the dialog box.

Right-click the edit box, and click the `ClassWizard...` item from the popup menu to open the `MFC ClassWizard` dialog box. Keep the default tab, `Message maps`, selected, and then select `IDC_LOOP_EDIT` from the `Object IDs:` list. Click the `Member Variables` tab and click the `Add Variable...` button to open the `Add Member Variable` dialog box, which is shown in Figure 3.45.

Select `int` from the `Variable type:` list, and type `loopNum` after the character `m_` in the `Member variable name:` field, as shown in Figure 3.45. Leave the `Value` selection unchanged in the `Category:` field, and click `OK` to save this setting.

Click the `Message Maps` tab again to return to the message page. Try to find and select the ID of our `OK` button, `IDOK`, on the `Object IDs:` list. Click the `BN_CLICKED` item on the

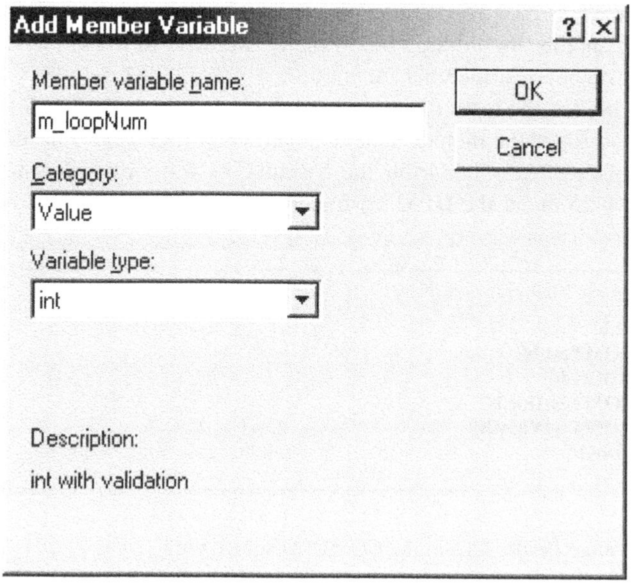

Add Member Variable
Member variable name:
m_loopNum
OK
Cancel
Category:
Value
Variable type:
int
Description:
int with validation

FIGURE 3.45 The add member variable dialog.

`Messages:` list, and then click the `Add Function...` button to add the member function `OnOK()` to the `LoopDlg` class. Click `OK` to save these settings and to close the `MFC ClassWizard` dialog box.

Now click the `FileView` tab in the workspace to open our file list. Nothing need be done to the header file of our newly added dialog box, `LoopDlg.h`, but we do need to make a minor modification to our source file, `LoopDlg.cpp`. Double-click this file folder to open the source file and move the cursor to the dialog box constructor, shown in Figure 3.46.

```
......
/////////////////////////////////////////////////////////////////////////////
// LoopDlg dialog
LoopDlg::LoopDlg(CWnd* pParent /*=NULL*/)
        : CDialog(LoopDlg::IDD, pParent)
{
    //{{AFX_DATA_INIT(LoopDlg)
    m_loopNum = 1;                  // modify this as the default loop number
    //}}AFX_DATA_INIT
}
......
```

FIGURE 3.46 The constructor of the LoopDlg class.

Notice that in the dialog box constructor, the default value for our edit box `m_loopNum` is `0`. Change this default value to `1`. Now the loop test will be executed at least once.

That is all the new coding needed for the loop dialog box. Looks very easy, doesn't it? We need, however, to do some interface coding in our main dialog box class, `COMDLG`, to set a connection between the main dialog box and the `loop` number dialog box class. Once this connection is established, the loop number entered by the user in the loop number dialog box can be passed to the main dialog box, and a loop test can be executed by the main dialog box.

We must also add an `include` statement in the source file of our `COMDLG` dialog box to let it know that we have another loop dialog box. Finally, we need to finish the coding for the main dialog box by adding a loop test member function.

Open the source file for the main dialog box by double-clicking the file folder `COMDLG.cpp` on the `FileView` list. Enter the include statement shown in Figure 3.47 at the top of this source file. Click the `ResourceView` tab from the Visual C++ 6.0 workspace and click the folder `IDD_COMTESTDLG` item under the `Dialog` folder to open our main dialog box platform.

```
// COMDLG.cpp : implementation file
#include "stdafx.h"
#include "mfcCOMTest.h"
#include "COMDLG.h"
#include "mfcCOMTestDoc.h"
#include "mfcCOMTestView.h"
#include "LoopDlg.h"                        // add this include statement
```

FIGURE 3.47 Include more header files in the COMDLG source file.

Next, right-click the `LOOP` command button. Then click `ClassWizard...` to open the `MFC ClassWizard` dialog box. With the default tab `Message Maps` selected, click `IDLOOP` on the `Object IDs:` list. Click the `BN_CLICKED` item on the `Messages:` list, and click the `Add Function...` button to add the member function `OnLoop()` into our main dialog box class source file.

Click the `FileView` tab again to return to the file list, and double-click our main dialog source folder `COMDLG.cpp` to open it. Browse to the member function `OnLoop()`, which was added earlier, and enter the code shown in Figure 3.48 into this function.

A: Local variables are declared at the beginning of this member function. The `comView` is an important pointer variable that represents a pointer to our `View` class `mfcCOMTestView`. It works as a connection between the `View` class and our main dialog box class. By calling the `getComView()` member function, we can obtain this pointer variable and assign it to `comView`.

B: Before we can run the loop test for the serial port, we need to check the initialization status flag `InitFlg` to make sure the port to be tested has been properly initialized. An error message will be displayed onscreen if the port has not been initialized, and the program will return to the calling function without any further action.

C: If the port has been initialized, the program will clean up the content of the Static Text object `m_resLabel` by calling its member function `SetWindowText()`. This function will display updated information based on the testing jobs and results.

TIP: The program will create an instance of the loop number dialog box class, `lpDlg`, which is much like creating a new loop number dialog box. An `UpdateData()` member function is called to refresh all variable values in our main dialog box and make the value in `m_comPort` updated to our program. Don't be confused about this `UpdateData()` function; it belongs to our main dialog box, not to the loop number dialog box. Without execution of this update function, the value in the edit box object, `m_comPort`, may be incorrect.

```
  ......
  void COMDLG::OnLoop()
  {
        // TODO: Add your control notification handler code here
A       int Numloop;
        ERR_CODE ecRet = OK;
        CMfcCOMTestView* comView = getComView();
B       if (!InitFlg)
        {
            msg("No Initialization !");
            return;
        }
C       m_resLabel.SetWindowText("");
        LoopDlg lpDlg;
        UpdateData(TRUE);
D       if (lpDlg.DoModal() == IDOK)
        {
E           lpDlg.UpdateWindow();
F           for (Numloop = 0; Numloop < lpDlg.m_loopNum; Numloop++)
            {
                ecRet = comView->TestPort(m_comPort);
                if (ecRet)
                    msg("ERROR in TEST");
            }
G           m_resLabel.SetWindowText("Loop Testing is Successful!");
        }
  }
  ......
```

FIGURE 3.48 The `OnLoop()` function in the COMDLG class.

D: Here, the program calls a member function of the loop number dialog box class, `DoModal()`, to display the box onscreen. After the loop number dialog box is displayed, the controllability of the system is transferred from the current main dialog box to the loop number dialog box because the loop number dialog is a model dialog box. The main dialog box waits until an `IDOK` system message is received, which means that the user has finished entering the loop number and pressed `OK` in the loop number dialog box.

E: After the `IDOK` message has been received, the program calls a member function of the loop number dialog box, `UpdateWindow()`, to refresh the variable values in the dialog box. This step is important because when the `IDOK` message is received, the program assumes that a number has been entered in the `m_loopNum` edit box. In order to pick up that loop number and make it available, we should execute this `UpdateWindow()` member function. Otherwise, the value in the `m_loopNum` may be incorrect.

F: A `for` loop is used for the loop testing. The loop number is determined by the value stored in the edit box object, `m_loopNum`, which is defined in the loop number dialog box. The program repeatedly calls a middle-layer function, `TestPort()`, using the argument `m_comPort`, until the maximum loop number is hit. `TestPort()` is defined in our `View` class, and `m_comPort` is the port number. If the `TestPort()` function fails, an error message will be displayed. We can add one `return` or `break` statement here to exit the loop testing if any mistake is encountered.

G: If everything is fine and the loop testing is completed successfully, the program will set a message, Loop testing is successful!, in the edit box object m_resLabel by calling its SetWindowText() member function. At this point, we have finished the coding for this project.

Now click the Build|Build mfcCOMTest.exe menu item from the menu bar to build our project. If everything is fine, click the Build|Execute mfcCOMTest.exe menu item to run the project. The main dialog box is displayed as the program runs. Click INIT to initialize the serial port COM1 with the default baud rate 9600. Then click LOOP to perform the loop testing of the port. The loop number dialog box is displayed onscreen, as shown in Figure 3.49.

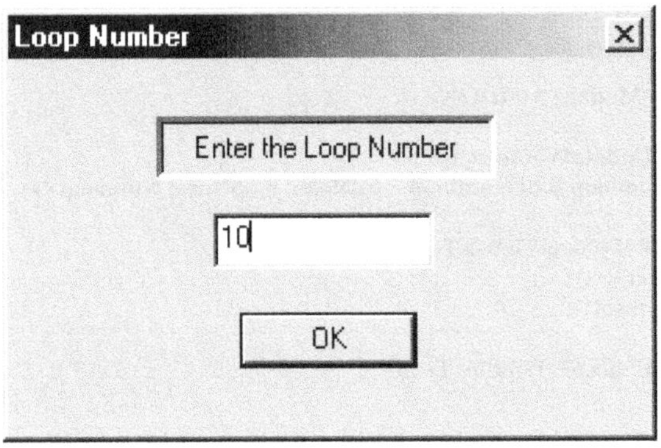

FIGURE 3.49 The loop number dialog.

Enter 10 in the edit box and click OK. This will instruct the project to perform ten rounds of loop testing for serial port COM1.

The loop testing will begin as soon as OK has been clicked. The data sent out and read back is displayed in the two edit boxes. Finally, if the loop testing is successful, the message, Loop testing is successful!, will be displayed in the Static Text object m_resLabel, as shown in Figure 3.50.

Now modify the baud rate from the current default, 9600, to 19200, and click INIT to reinitialize the COM1 serial port. Click the TEST button to test the port again at this new baud rate.

Click LOOP and enter 30 in the loop number edit box within the loop number dialog box. Click OK in the loop number dialog box to begin the loop test at the new baud rate. The loop test should be successful. Click the EXIT button to terminate the project.

Before we can finish this section, we must discuss how to access the About dialog box, which is a default project dialog box. It is created by the system automatically when a new MFC project is created in the Visual C++ 6.0 environment. Recall that earlier, when we added two dialog boxes to our project, a default dialog box IDD_ABOUTBOX was already in existence. This dialog box and the associated components are created by the system, and the class that holds the dialog box is created in the main thread file, mfcCOMTest.cpp. The class name of this dialog box is CAboutDlg, indicating that it is a child of the CDialog class. A member function of this class is called OnAppAbout(); it is created and defined in the main thread file as well.

If we open the main thread source file mfcCOMTest.cpp and browse down to the bottom of the file, we will find this member function implementation, as shown in Figure 3.51.

Inside the body of the function, a new instance of the class CAboutDlg, aboutDlg, is created, and a member function, DoModal() is called to display this dialog box on the screen.

If we want to use the existing About dialog class and the member function provided by the main thread, we need to perform the following tasks:

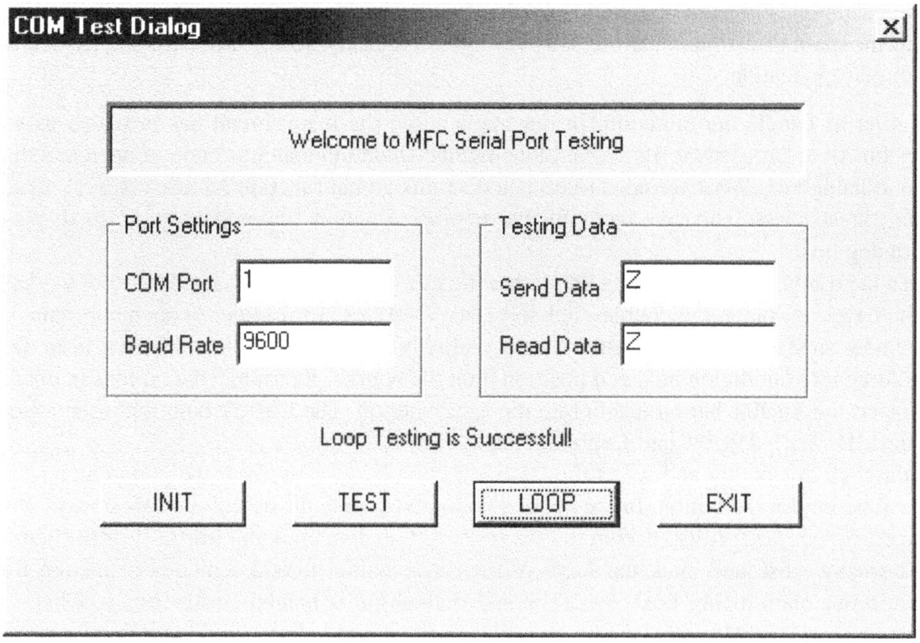

FIGURE 3.50 The running result of the loop number test.

```
// App command to run the dialog
void CMfcCOMTestApp::OnAppAbout()
{
        CAboutDlg aboutDlg;
        aboutDlg.DoModal();
}
/////////////////////////////////////////////////////////////////////////////
// CMfcCOMTestApp message handlers
```

FIGURE 3.51 The about dialog.

- Adding a new command button to our main dialog box with the caption `ABOUT`
- Setting a new member function for that button, such as `OnAbout()`
- When the user clicks the `ABOUT` button, directing the click event to the main thread to execute the member function `OnAppAbout()`

Now that we know what we should display in the `About` dialog box, we need to know how to display the `About` dialog in our project.

TIP: The MFC in Visual C++ provides a common place from which we can access any class object defined in our project. In this application, this common place is our main thread application class, `mfcCOMTest`. A global function, `AfxGetApp()`, is provided by the system, and by using this global function, any class object defined in our project can access the main thread application `mfcCOMTest`. If we want to access any other class object defined in our project from one class object, we need to reserve all pointers of desired class objects in the main thread application. When we want to access any other class object, we can use the global function `AfxGetApp()` to first access the main thread application and then find the desired class object by accessing the pointer reserved in the main thread application. This way, we can easily access any class object defined in our application.

Now let us handle our situation. In our application, the main thread has provided us with a member function, `OnAppAbout()`, and this member function contains code to open and display the About dialog box. What we need to do is to use this global function `AfxGetApp()` to access the main thread class. Then we can call the member function `OnAppAbout()` to display the About dialog box.

Open the resource list by clicking the `ResourceView` tab from the Visual C++ 6.0 workspace. Click the `Dialog` folder and double-click the `IDD_COMTESTDLG` folder to open our main dialog box. We now must add one more button to the dialog box. Select a command button from the edit toolbox, drag it to our dialog box, and position it on the bottom. Rearrange the buttons in the dialog box to insert the `ABOUT` button just before the `EXIT` button. The `ABOUT` button has the following properties: ID: `IDC_ABOUT` and Caption: `ABOUT`.

Right-click this button and select the `ClassWizard...` item from the popup menu to set a member function for the button. In the opened dialog box, keep the default tab, `Message Maps`, unchanged. Select `IDC_ABOUT` from the `Object IDs:` list, click the `BN_CLICKED` item from the `Messages:` list, and click the `Add Function` button to add a member function for the button into our main dialog box class. The added function is named `OnAbout()`. Click `OK` to close the `MFC classWizard` dialog box. The finished dialog box should match the one shown in Figure 3.52.

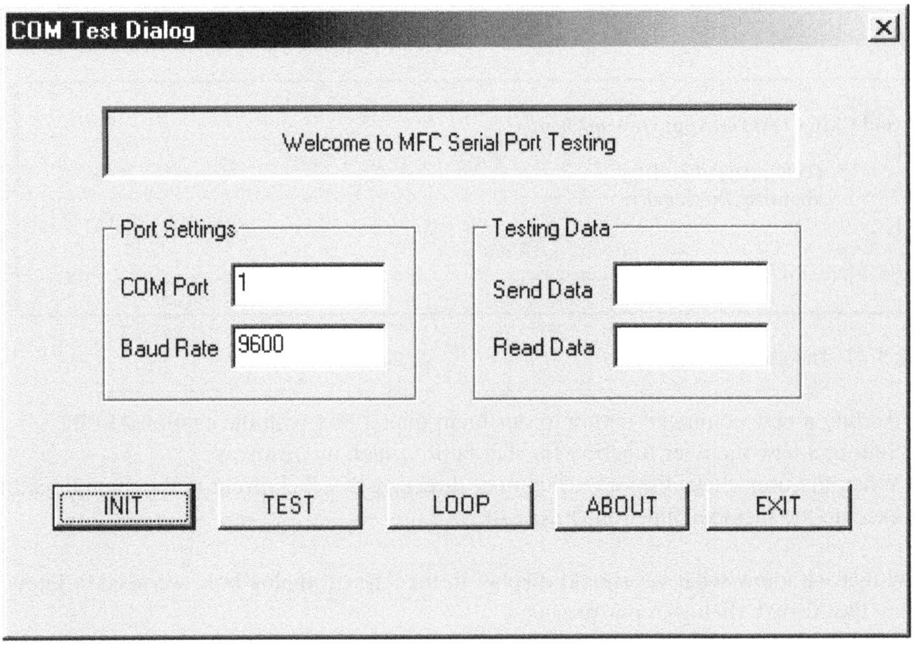

FIGURE 3.52 The modified COM test dialog.

Now open the source file for the main dialog box to finish the coding for this file. Click the `FileView` tab from the workspace and double-click our main dialog box source file folder, `COMDLG.cpp`, to open its source file. Notice that the newly added member function, `OnAbout()`, has been included. Browse to this function and enter the code shown in Figure 3.53 into the body of this function.

```
void COMDLG::OnAbout()
{
    // TODO: Add your control notification handler code here
    CMfcCOMTestApp* mfcCOMApp = (CMfcCOMTestApp*) AfxGetApp();
    mfcCOMApp->OnAppAbout();
}
```

FIGURE 3.53 The `OnAbout` function.

By default, the global function `AfxGetApp()` will return a pointer that points to a class object with the `CWinApp` class type. Our main thread class object, `mfcCOMTest`, is also a subclass of the class `CWinApp`, so a cast (`CMfcCOMTestApp*`) is needed to transfer the returned pointer to our main thread class object type. After this translation, the returned pointer is assigned to the newly created pointer variable `mfcCOMApp`, as shown in Figure 3.53. Then we can call the member function `OnAppAbout()` by using the obtained pointer, which is the address of our main thread class object, to display the About dialog box on the screen.

Click the `Build|Build mfcCOMTest.exe` menu item again to rebuild our project. Choose the `Build|Execute mfcCOMTest.exe` menu item to run the project.

When the main dialog box appears, click `ABOUT`. The default About dialog box will be displayed at the top of the main dialog box, which is shown in Figure 3.54.

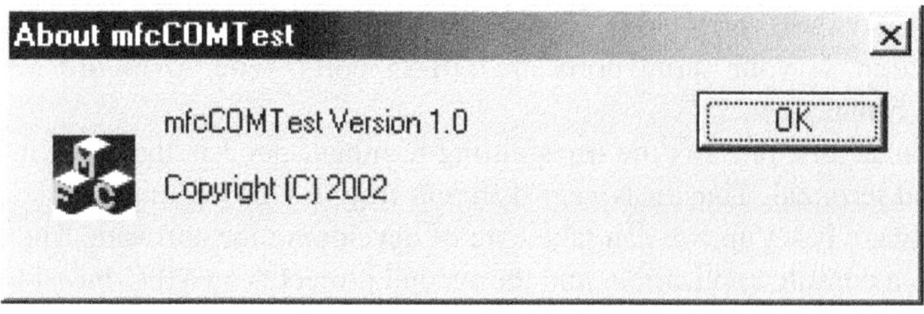

FIGURE 3.54 The running result of the about dialog.

Everything looks fine for our project, so click `OK` to close the About dialog box. Our project is now finished.

All the files for this project, including the header files, source files, and executable files, are located on the attached CD-ROM, in the `Chapter 3\mfcCOMTest` folder. As always, you can copy all these files and test the project on your own computer. Don't forget to install the serial port before running this project. Good luck!

3.3 A DOUBLE-LOOP SERIAL PORT TEST IN VISUAL C++

In this section, we will discuss how to communicate between two serial ports with a null-modem configuration, thereby testing two serial ports simultaneously.

3.3.1 Hardware Connection

In the last section, we tested a serial port using a single-loop method. To test two serial ports with a null-modem strategy, we need to use the double-loop testing method. The null-modem connects pin 2 in the first port to pin 3 in the second port, and pin 3 in the first port to pin 2 in the second port, as shown in Figure 3.55.

Pin-Number	Function
1	Not used
2	R_{XD}
3	T_{XD}
4	Not used
5	GND

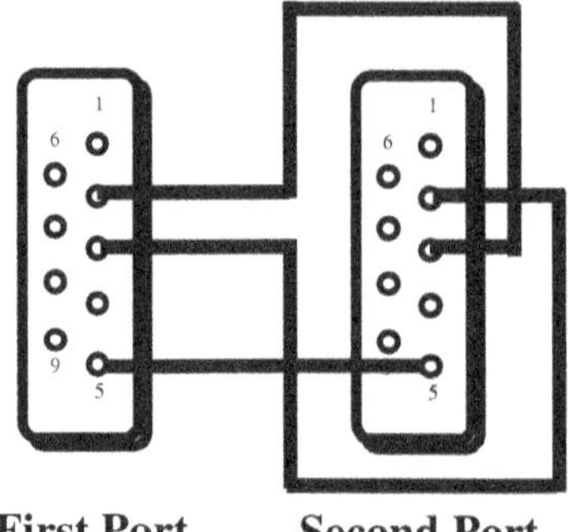

FIGURE 3.55 The double loop connection for the DB-9 connector.

In this null-modem connection, pin 2 in the first port is the receiving terminal, and pin 3 in the second port is the transmitting terminal. If data is sent from the second port via pin 3, ideally this data should be received by the first port via pin 2. The same goes for pin 3 in the first port and pin 2 in the second port. In this way, we can test two ports by sending data from one port and receiving this data from another port.

To make this double-loop test, make sure two serial ports are available on the computer. `COM1` and `COM2` are the two default serial ports for most computers if two ports are available to the user. Make a connection for these two `DB-9` connectors, as shown in Figure 3.55, and connect the two connectors to the associated serial ports on our computer. Make sure the power is off before you make this connection. If your serial ports are DB-25 ports, refer to Figure 3.56 for the port configuration and connection.

For DB-25 connectors, pin 2 is the transmitting terminal, pin 3 is the receiving terminal, and pin 7 is the ground terminal. Thus, it is very different from a DB-9 connector.

After the hardware is set up, we can take care of developing the software. The first project we want to develop is a console application, and the second project is an MFC-based testing program.

Pin-Number	Function
1	Not used
2	T_{XD}
3	R_{XD}
4	Not used
5	
6	
7	GND
8	
.	
.	
25	

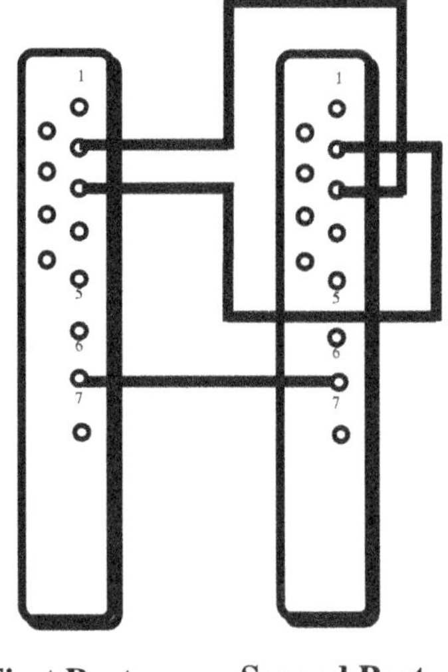

FIGURE 3.56 The double loop connection for the DB-25 connector.

3.3.2 A Console-Based Double-Loop Serial-Port-Testing Project

Launch Visual C++ 6.0 and create a new project, and select `Win32 Console Application` from the Projects list. Enter `DoublePorts` in the `Project name:` field, and make sure the content of the `Location:` field is our user-defined project folder `C:\CTCTest`. Click `OK` to open this new project.

First, we need to create three header files:

- Menu.h declares the variables and structures of the testing menu.
- Error.h declares the variables and structures of the error information.
- DoublePorts.h declares the variables and functions of the testing process.

Click `File|New` to create these three header files, and enter the code from Figures 3-57, 3-58, and 3-59 into these three header files.

Two port handlers, `hsPort` and `hrPort`, are declared here because we need to communicate with two serial ports to perform the double-loop testing. The `hsPort` handler is used for the sending port, and the `hrPort` handler is used for the receiving port.

Two menu character pointer arrays are used to display the testing menu and testing title, as in the first example in this chapter. Two flags, `sPortFlg` and `rPortFlg`, are used to reserve the initialization status of the two ports. Some symbolic constants are also declared in this menu header file (refer to Figure 3.57).

```
/*****************************************************************************
 * NAME        : Menu.h
 * DESC        : Header file for the menu input and menu display
 * DATE        : 7/16/2003
 * PGMR        : Y. Bai
 *****************************************************************************/
#define NUM_BYTE     1
#define MAX_BYTE     90
#define START_BYTE   48
#define BAUD_RATE    9600
#define NUM_BITS     8
#define TIME_OUT     3000

HANDLE hsPort;
HANDLE hrPort;
bool  TestPassed;
bool  sPortFlg;
bool  rPortFlg;

char* menuData[] =
{ {"A  Create Ports\n"},
  {"B  Test Ports\n"},
  {"C  Kill Ports\n"},
  {"X  Exit\n\n"}
};

char* menuTitle[] =
{ {"SERIAL PORT TESTING  - Enter Selection > \n\n"}
};
```

FIGURE 3.57 The header file menu.h.

```
/*****************************************************************************
 * NAME        : Error.h
 * DESC        : Header file for Error definition
 * DATE        : 7/15/2003
 * PGMR        : Y. Bai
 *****************************************************************************/
typedef enum
{
  OK                          = 0,             /* no error */
  EC_TIMEOUT,
  EC_FOPEN,
  EC_INVAL_CONFIG,
  EC_TIMEOUT_SET,
  EC_RECV_TIMEOUT,
  EC_EXIT_CODE,
  EC_WAIT_SINGLEOBJ,
  EC_INVALIDPORT,
  EC_WRITE_FAIL,
  EC_CREATE_THREAD,
  EC_UNKNOWNERROR
}ERR_CODE;
```

FIGURE 3.58 The header file Error.h.

Figure 3.58 shows an error message structure, which represents all the possible errors that could be encountered while our project is running. This error message structure is identical to the one we used in the preceding example.

Figure 3.59 shows the variables and functions used in this testing project. The interfacing functions are identical with those we used in the last example, but some middle-layer functions have been modified based on the different requirements for this application.

A new function, `startPort()`, has been added to this file. During the initialization stage, we need to initialize our two ports separately and reserve each port handler when a new port is created. We use a `PortName` structure to reserve the handlers for these two ports. Another modification is the `TestPort()` function. Two character pointer variables, used to reserve the two ports' names, are used as the arguments and passed to this function.

As we did in the last example, we need to develop two source files to hold our source code because this source code is relatively large. The first source file, `DoublePorts.cpp`, is used to hold the middle-layer functions, which interface directly with the user and connect the actions of the user to the low-level or interfacing functions located in the second source file, `ComPort-Test.cpp`, in order to perform the serial port testing. Figure 3.60 shows the first source file, `DoublePorts.cpp`.

A: The testing program starts from the `main()` function, which is the entry point for the `Console Application` project. All local variables are declared at the beginning of this function. The integer variable `index` is used as the loop variable, and the Boolean variable `select` is used as the loop condition variable for the `While` loop.

B: Here we dynamically create two character arrays and a data structure object with the `new` keyword. `comPort` and `userInput` are used to receive the COM port name and the user input. `portName` is a structure object used to reserve the opened port names because we have two ports now.

C: Three flags are initialized to `False`. The `TestPassed` flag stores the testing status. The `sPortFlg` and `rPortFlg` are used to keep the initialization status of each of the two serial ports, respectively. A `True` setting for either of these flags means that the associated port has been initialized.

```
/*****************************************************************************
 * NAME        : DoublePorts.h
 * DESC        : Header file for DoublePorts.cpp
 * DATE        : 7/24/2003
 * PGMR        : Y. Bai
 *****************************************************************************/
#ifndef DOUBLEPORTS_H_
#define DOUBLEPORTS_H_

#include <windows.h>
#include <stdio.h>
#include <stdlib.h>
#include <string.h>
#include <malloc.h>
#include "Error.h"

#define MAX_MENU                    4
#define MAX_STRING                256
#define NOPARITY                    0
#define ONESTOPBIT                  0
#define RTS_CONTROL_DISABLE    0x00
#define RTS_CONTROL_ENABLE     0x01
#define DTR_CONTROL_DISABLE    0x00
#define DTR_CONTROL_ENABLE     0x01

#define msg(info)   MessageBox(NULL, info, "", MB_OK)

typedef struct
{
   unsigned long   ulCtrlerID;
   char          cEcho;
   char          cEORChar;
   long          lTimeout;
   long          lBaudRate;
   long          lDataBits;
  HANDLE   hPort;
}SerialCreate, *pSerialCreate;

typedef struct
{
   char    *pcBuffer;
   BYTE   bByte;
   int       iMaxChars;
   int       piNumRcvd;
   char     cTermChar;
   HANDLE handlePort;
}CommPortClass;

typedef struct
{
    char   sComPort[16];
    char   rComPort[16];
```

FIGURE 3.59 The header file `DoublePorts.h`. *(continued)*

```
}PortName, *pPortName;

ERR_CODE PortInitialize(LPTSTR lpszPortName, pSerialCreate pCreate);
ERR_CODE PortWrite(HANDLE handPort, BYTE bByte, int NumByte);
ERR_CODE PortRead(CommPortClass *hCommPort);
void WINAPI ThreadFunc(void* hCommPorts);

ERR_CODE SetupPort(char* cPort, int pFlg);
ERR_CODE TestPort(char* sPort, char* rPort,  BOOL display);
ERR_CODE startPort(pPortName pName);
int getMenuItem(unsigned char mPort,  char* ret);
#endif
```

FIGURE 3.59 The header file `DoublePorts.h`.

D: A `While` loop is used to perform the main testing process. As long as the loop condition variable `select` is `True`, the code inside the loop will be continually executed until `select` becomes `False` or a `break` is encountered. When the program is run, it will continuously display the testing menu, prompt us to make selections, and show the testing results until we select `Exit` from the menu.

E: A `for` loop is used to display the main testing menu and the prompt message onscreen. The `menuData[]` variable is a character pointer array, and each index of this array is mapped to a menu item (a character array). In total, we have four items, so `MAX_MENU` has a value of `4`.

F: The `scanf()` system function is used to pick up user input after the prompt message is displayed. Another system function, `strlwr()`, is used to convert the input to lowercase, and this lowercase string is in turn converted to an unsigned character variable, which can be operated later on by the `switch` statement in the `getMenuItem()` function.

G: Next, the converted user input is passed into the `getMenuItem()` function as an argument, and that function returns a character array associated with our menu selection. For instance, `COM1` is associated with an input of the character `1`. Note that we have modified this function to accommodate a broad range of user input.

H: If we select `x` or make an invalid selection from the menu, an `EXIT` or a `NULL` will be returned by the `getMenuItem()` function. In this case, we need to jump out of the `While` loop and terminate the program. We can perform this operation by setting the Boolean `select` variable to `False`.

I: If we select `a`, which is associated with the character array `INIT`, the program will call the `startPort()` function to initialize the serial ports. The argument of this function is a pointer of the structure object, `portName`, which contains two character arrays, each of which holds the name of one port. We need this structure to store the ports' names when executing the `startPort()` function to open the serial ports because we will use these ports' names next when we execute the `TestPort()` function to test the ports.
If the `startPort()` function fails, an error message will be displayed onscreen, and the program will exit the `While` loop and be terminated.

J: If we select `b`, which is mapped to a character array `TEST`, the program will call the `TestPort()` function to execute the testing process on the ports. Here the data structure object `portName` is used to pass the two ports' names to the testing function. The `portName->sComPort` and `portName->rComPort` statements represent the sending port and receiving port, respectively. If the `TestPort()` function fails, an error message will be displayed, and the program will exit the `While` loop and be terminated.

```
  /*****************************************************************************
   * NAME        : DoublePorts.cpp
   * DESC        : Test double serial ports program - double loop
   * DATE        : 7/24/2003
   * PGMR        : Y. Bai
   *****************************************************************************/
  #include "DoublePorts.h"
  #include "Menu.h"

  void main()
  {
        int     index;
A       bool    select = TRUE;
        char* userInput;
        char* comPort;
        ERR_CODE    ecRet = OK;
        unsigned char  cPort;

        comPort   = new char[128];
B       userInput = new char[128];
        pPortName portName = new PortName;

        TestPassed = FALSE;
C       sPortFlg   = FALSE;
        rPortFlg   = FALSE;

D       while(select)
        {
            printf("\n");
E           for (index = 0; index < MAX_MENU; index++)
                printf(menuData[index]);

            printf(menuTitle[0]);
F           scanf("%s", userInput);
            userInput = strlwr(userInput);
            cPort = (unsigned char)userInput[0];
G           getMenuItem(cPort, comPort);
H           if (strcmp(comPort, "EXIT") == 0 || strcmp(comPort, "NULL") == 0)
                select = FALSE;

I           else if (strcmp(comPort, "INIT") == 0)
            {
                ecRet = startPort(portName);
                if (ecRet != OK)
                {
                      printf("ERROR in startPort\n");
                      break;
                }
            }
J           else if (strcmp(comPort, "TEST") == 0)
            {
                ecRet = TestPort(portName->sComPort, portName->rComPort, 1);
```

FIGURE 3.60 The source file `Double Ports.cpp`. *(continued)*

```
                if (ecRet)
                {
                    printf("ERROR in TestPort\n");
                    break;
                }
            }
K           else if (strcmp(comPort, "KILL") == 0)
                printf("\n");
            if (TestPassed)
                printf("\n**** TEST PASSED ***\n");
        }
        delete  userInput;
L       delete  comPort;
        delete  portName;

        return;
}
M   ERR_CODE startPort(pPortName pName)
{
        ERR_CODE  ecRet = OK;
        char*           comPort;
        unsigned char  sendComm = '1',  recvComm = '2';
        unsigned char  userInput[MAX_STRING];

        comPort   = new char[128];

N       printf("Defaults Ports - send: COM %c  recv: COM %c\n", sendComm, recvComm);

        printf("\nChange Default Ports [N]?");
        scanf("%s", userInput);
O       if (userInput[0] == 'y'|| userInput[0] == 'Y')
        {
            printf("Enter send COM Port [%c]: ", sendComm);
            scanf("%s", userInput);
            if(userInput[0] != 0)
                sendComm = userInput[0];
            printf( "Enter recv COM Port [%c]: ", recvComm);
            scanf("%s", userInput);
            if(userInput[0] != 0)
                recvComm = userInput[0];
        }
P       getMenuItem(sendComm, comPort);
        printf("select send port: %s\n",  comPort);
        strcpy(pName->sComPort,  comPort);
        ecRet = SetupPort(comPort,  1);
        if (ecRet)
        {
            delete comPort;
            return ecRet;
        }
Q       getMenuItem(recvComm, comPort);
        printf("select recv port: %s\n",  comPort);
        strcpy(pName->rComPort,  comPort);

        ecRet = SetupPort(comPort,  2);
        if (ecRet)
        {
            delete   comPort;
            return  ecRet;
        }
```

FIGURE 3.60 The source file `Double Ports.cpp`. *(continued)*

```
R           delete  comPort;
            return ecRet;
    }
S   ERR_CODE SetupPort(char* cPort,  int pFlg)
    {
            ERR_CODE    ecRet = OK;
            pSerialCreate  pParam;

            pParam = new SerialCreate;

            pParam->lBaudRate = BAUD_RATE;
            pParam->lDataBits   = NUM_BITS;
            pParam->lTimeout    = TIME_OUT;

            if (sPortFlg && pFlg == 1)
T              return  ecRet;
            if (rPortFlg && pFlg == 2)
               return  ecRet;

U           ecRet = PortInitialize(cPort,  pParam);
            if (ecRet != OK)
               printf("ERROR in PortInitialize()!\n");
            else
            {
                if (pFlg == 1)
V               {
                    sPortFlg = true;
                    hsPort = pParam->hPort;
                }
                else
                {
                    rPortFlg = true;
                    hrPort = pParam->hPort;
                }
            }
            delete  pParam;
W           return  ecRet;
    }
```

FIGURE 3.60 The source file `Double Ports.cpp`.

K: If we select `c`, which is mapped to a character array `KILL`, the program will not need to do anything because at this point, the program will close the ports' handlers if any error is encountered during the testing process. Thus, a blank line is printed for this choice. If the status of the testing flag is `True`, meaning that testing has been successful, an associated message will appear onscreen.

L: Before exiting the main function, the program uses the `delete` command to clean up the memory space allocated for the character pointer arrays and structure object.

TIP: Notice the character array operations in this function. From steps H, J, and K, it may already be apparent that the string operation function `strcmp()` is used to check the returned character array from the function `getMenuItem()` to detect any menu selection. Generally, string operating functions are useful for performing string operations because in some cases, using the equal operator will not work.

M: Certain local variables are declared at the beginning of the `startPort()` function. Two unsigned character variables, `sendComm` and `recvComm`, are used for storing the default COM port numbers. The unsigned character array `userInput[]` is used to receive our input as the program runs. The character array comPort reserves the returned string result associated with our selection.

N: Two printf() functions are used to display the default COM port numbers and the prompt that instructs us to select the COM ports. The scanf() function is used to pick up our selection.

O: Entering a y would indicate that we don't want to use the default ports, but prefer instead to input new port numbers. The scanf() functions are used to pick up the new port numbers entered from the keyboard, and these port numbers are assigned to the local variables sendComm and recvComm, which will be used in the next step.

P: Next, the program calls the getMenuItem() function to convert the unsigned characters sendComm and recvComm to the associated COM port strings (typically COM1 and COM2). Then we call the string operating function strcpy() to reserve the converted sending port name to the portName structure, which will be returned to the calling function (the main() function) for further use. The SetupPort() function is then executed to initialize the sending serial port. If the function fails, our program must delete the memory space allocated for the comPort character array, and the program returns the error status to the calling function.

Q: As in step P, the getMenuItem() function is called to get the mapped receiving port name, reserve this name to the portName structure, and call the SetupPort() function to initialize the receiving serial port.

R: Before exiting this function, our program must use delete to clean up the memory space allocated for the comPort character array.

S: To execute the SetupPort() function to initialize the serial port, the program uses a flag, pFlg, to indicate to the system which port should be initialized. A value of 1 on the flag means that the current port is the sending port, and a value of 2 on the flag means that the current port is the receiving port. Some local variables are declared at the beginning of this function.

T: Before we can call the function PortInitialize() to initialize the ports, the program must confirm that the port has not been initialized. By checking the initialization status flag sPortFlg and the flag pFlg, we can easily identify whether the sending port or the receiving port has been initialized. Notice that a && operator is used to make sure that both conditions are satisfied. If the port has been initialized, we just return an OK status without any other action.

U: If the port has not been initialized, the PortInitialize() function is called to initialize the port. An error message will be displayed if this function calling fails.

V: If the function call is successful, our program identifies the opened sending port and receiving port separately. For the sending port, we set the initialization status flag, sPortFlg, to True, which means that the port has been initialized and doesn't need to be initialized again. Also, we reserve the opened port handler to the global sending handler variable hsPort. Similarly, we set the initialization status flag, rPortFlg, to True and reserve the opened receiving port handler to the global receiving handler variable hrPort.

W: Finally, we use the delete command to clean up the memory space allocated for the structure SerialCreate.

The second source file, ComPortTest.cpp, is nearly identical to the one developed in the last example, although a minor modification has been made to this source file, as shown in Figure 3.61.

```
/*****************************************************************************
 * NAME        : ComPortTest.cpp
 * DESC        : Support C++ file for SimpleCOM.cpp
 * DATE        : 7/24/2003
 * PGMR        : Y. Bai
 *****************************************************************************/
#include "DoublePorts.h"

ERR_CODE PortInitialize(LPTSTR lpszPortName, pSerialCreate pCreate)
{
        HANDLE          hPort;
        DWORD           dwError;
        DCB             PortDCB;
        unsigned char   dBit;
        ERR_CODE        ecStatus = OK;
        COMMTIMEOUTS    CommTimeouts;

        // Open the serial port.
        hPort = CreateFile(lpszPortName,              // Pointer to the name of the port
                GENERIC_READ | GENERIC_WRITE,        // Access (read/write) mode
                0,                                   // Share mode
                NULL,                                // Pointer to the security attribute
                OPEN_EXISTING,                       // How to open the serial port
                0,                                   // Port attributes
                NULL);                       // Handle to port with attribute to copy

        // If it fails to open the port, return error.
        if ( hPort == INVALID_HANDLE_VALUE )
        {
            // Could not open the port.
            dwError = GetLastError();
            msg("Unable to open the port");
            CloseHandle(hPort);
             return EC_FOPEN;
        }
        PortDCB.DCBlength = sizeof(DCB);

        // Get the default port setting information.
        GetCommState(hPort, &PortDCB);
        // Change the DCB structure settings.
        PortDCB.BaudRate = pCreate->lBaudRate;          // Current baud rate
        PortDCB.fBinary  = TRUE;                        // Binary mode; no EOF check
        PortDCB.fParity  = TRUE;                        // Enable parity checking.
        PortDCB.fOutxCtsFlow = FALSE;                   // No CTS output flow control
        PortDCB.fOutxDsrFlow = FALSE;                   // No DSR output flow control
        PortDCB.fDtrControl = DTR_CONTROL_ENABLE;   // DTR flow control type
        PortDCB.fDsrSensitivity = FALSE;                // DSR sensitivity
        PortDCB.fTXContinueOnXoff = TRUE;               // XOFF continues Tx TRUE
        PortDCB.fOutX = FALSE;                          // No XON/XOFF out flow control
        PortDCB.fInX  = FALSE;                          // No XON/XOFF in flow control
        PortDCB.fErrorChar = FALSE;                     // Disable error replacement.
        PortDCB.fNull = FALSE;                          // Disable null stripping.
```

FIGURE 3.61 The source file `ComPortTest.cpp`. *(continued)*

```
        PortDCB.fRtsControl = RTS_CONTROL_ENABLE; // RTS flow control
        PortDCB.fAbortOnError = FALSE;               // Don't abort reads/writes on error.
        dBit = (unsigned char)pCreate->lDataBits;
        PortDCB.ByteSize = dBit;                     // Number of bits/bytes, 4-8
        PortDCB.Parity = NOPARITY;                   // 0-4=no odd even mark space
        PortDCB.StopBits = ONESTOPBIT;               // 0, 1, 2 = 1, 1.5, 2 stop bit

        // Configure the port according to the specifications of the DCB structure.
        if (!SetCommState (hPort, &PortDCB))
        {
                // Could not create the read thread.
                dwError = GetLastError();
                msg("Unable to configure the serial port");
                return EC_INVAL_CONFIG;
        }
        // Retrieve the time-out parameters for all read and write operations on the port.
        GetCommTimeouts(hPort, &CommTimeouts);

        // Change the COMMTIMEOUTS structure settings.
        CommTimeouts.ReadIntervalTimeout = MAXDWORD;
        CommTimeouts.ReadTotalTimeoutMultiplier = 0;
        CommTimeouts.ReadTotalTimeoutConstant = 0;
        CommTimeouts.WriteTotalTimeoutMultiplier = 10;
        CommTimeouts.WriteTotalTimeoutConstant = 1000;

        // Set the time-out parameters for all read and write operations on the port.
        if (!SetCommTimeouts (hPort, &CommTimeouts))
        {
                // Could not create the read thread.
                dwError = GetLastError();
                msg("Unable to set the time-out parameters");
                return EC_TIMEOUT_SET;
        }

        EscapeCommFunction(hPort, SETDTR);
        EscapeCommFunction(hPort, SETRTS);
        pCreate->hPort = hPort;

        return  ecStatus;
}

ERR_CODE PortWrite(HANDLE handPort, BYTE bByte, int NumByte)
{
    DWORD dwError;
    DWORD dwNumBytesWritten;
    ERR_CODE ecStatus = OK;

    if (!WriteFile (handPort,              // Port handle
                    &bByte,                // Pointer to the data to write
                    NumByte,               // Number of bytes to write
                    &dwNumBytesWritten,    // Pointer to the number of bytes written
                    NULL))                 // Must be NULL for Windows CE
    {
        // WriteFile failed. Report error.
```

FIGURE 3.61 The source file `ComPortTest.cpp`. *(continued)*

```
            dwError = GetLastError ();
            msg("ERROR in PortWrite ..");
            return EC_WRITE_FAIL;
        }
        return ecStatus;
}
ERR_CODE PortRead(CommPortClass *hCommPort)
{
        HANDLE hThread;                              // handler for port read thread
        DWORD  IDThread;
        DWORD  Ret, ExitCode;
        DWORD  dTimeout = 5000;                      // define time out value: 5 sec.
        ERR_CODE ecStatus = OK;

        if (!(hThread = CreateThread(NULL,           // no security attributes
                        0,                           // use default stack size
                        (LPTHREAD_START_ROUTINE) ThreadFunc,
                        (LPVOID)hCommPort,           // parameter to thread function
                        CREATE_SUSPENDED,            // creation flag - suspended
                        &IDThread) ) )               // returns thread ID
        {
            msg("Create Read Thread failed");
            return EC_CREATE_THREAD;
        }
        ResumeThread(hThread);                       // start thread now
        Ret = WaitForSingleObject(hThread, dTimeout);
        if (Ret == WAIT_OBJECT_0)
        {
            // data received & process it... Need to do nothing
            // because the data has been stored in the hCommPort in Thread Func.
            // close thread handle
            CloseHandle(hThread);
        }
        else if (Ret == WAIT_TIMEOUT)
        {
            // time out happened, warning & kill thread
            Ret = GetExitCodeThread(hThread, &ExitCode);
            msg("Time out happened in PortRead() ");
            if (ExitCode == STILL_ACTIVE)
            {
                TerminateThread(hThread, ExitCode);
                CloseHandle(hThread);
                return EC_RECV_TIMEOUT;
            }
            else
            {
                CloseHandle(hThread);
                msg("ERROR in GetExitCodeThread: != STILL_ACTIVE ");
                ecStatus = EC_EXIT_CODE;
            }
        }
```

FIGURE 3.61 The source file `ComPortTest.cpp`. *(continued)*

```
    else
    {
        msg("ERROR in WaitFor SingleObject ");
        ecStatus = EC_WAIT_SINGLEOBJ;
    }
    return  ecStatus;
}

void WINAPI ThreadFunc(void* hCommPorts)
{
    BYTE      Byte;
    DWORD  dwError;
    BOOL     bResult;
    int          nTotRead = 0;
    DWORD  dwCommModemStatus, dwBytesTransferred;
    CommPortClass*  CommPorts;
    ERR_CODE ecStatus = OK;

    CommPorts = (CommPortClass* )hCommPorts;

    // Specify a set of events to be monitored for the port.
    SetCommMask(CommPorts->handlePort, EV_RXCHAR | EV_CTS | EV_DSR |
                                                                      EV_RLSD | EV_RING);

    // Wait for an event to occur for the port.
    WaitCommEvent(CommPorts->handlePort, &dwCommModemStatus, 0);

    // Re-specify the set of events to be monitored for the port.
    SetCommMask(CommPorts->handlePort, EV_RXCHAR | EV_CTS | EV_DSR
                                                                      |EV_RLSD| EV_RING);

    if (dwCommModemStatus & EV_RXCHAR||dwCommModemStatus & EV_RLSD)
    // received the char_event
    {
        // Read the data from the serial port.
        bResult = ReadFile(CommPorts->handlePort, &Byte, 1, &dwBytesTransferred, 0);

     if     (!bResult)
        {
            printf("Unable to read the port\n");
              switch (dwError = GetLastError())
              {
                  case ERROR_HANDLE_EOF:
                        printf("Serial Receive Failed\n");
                        break;
              }
          }
          else
         {
              // store the data read.
              CommPorts->bByte = Byte;
              nTotRead++;
          }
    }

    return;
}
```

FIGURE 3.61 The source file `ComPortTest.cpp`.

The modification is the header file included in this source file. In the preceding example, this source file included the header file `Error.h`, which declares protocols of all possible error messages for this project. In this example, however, we include that header file in our main header file, `DoublePorts.h`. In this way, `Error.h` can be removed from this source file, and only the main header file `DoublePorts.h` is still included.

That is all the coding for this project. You can now build the project by clicking the `Build|Build DoublePorts.exe` menu item. You can set the building configuration to the `Release` mode if you want to save space. If no errors occur, you can run the project. Start by clicking the `Build|Execute DoublePorts.exe` menu item. A DOS-like window is opened onscreen and the testing menu is displayed, as shown in Figure 3.62.

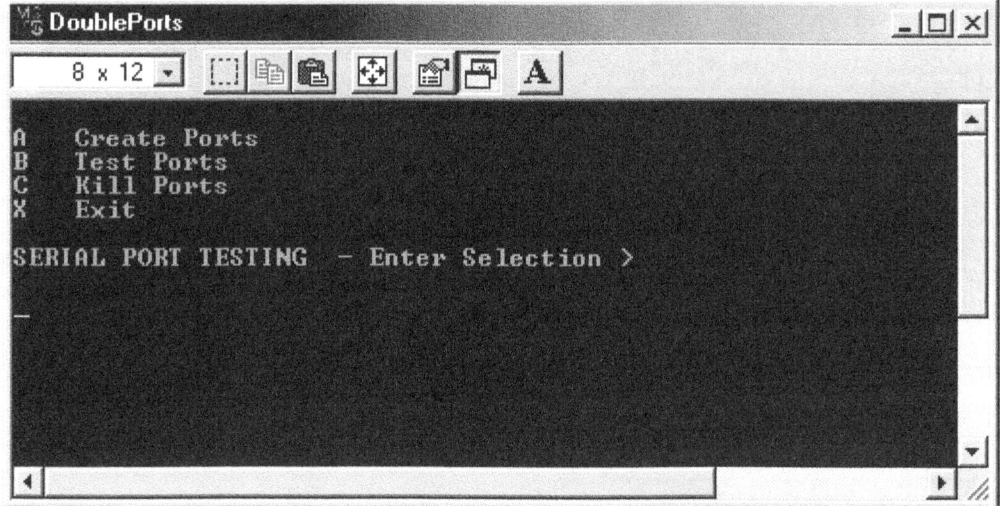

FIGURE 3.62 The running head of the project doublePorts.

Enter an `A` from the keyboard and press `Enter`. A prompt will appear, asking you to select the testing ports. The two default-testing ports in this project are COM1 and COM2, as shown in Figure 3.63.

Enter `y` to answer the prompt "`Change Default Ports [N]?`" because the two ports on our current machine are COM5 and COM6. Enter `5` and `6` for the following prompts to tell the system that we want to change the ports to COM5 and COM6, using COM5 as the sending port and COM6 as the receiving port. As you can see in Figure 3.63, the selected ports will be echoed onscreen:

```
select send port: COM5
select recv port: COM6
```

If no error message is displayed, our initialization has been successful. Now we need to test the serial ports by sending data from the sending port, and by receiving the same data from the receiving port. Press `b` to start the testing. A sequence of testing data (ASCII codes `0` to `9` and `A` to `Z`) is displayed onscreen. As shown in Figure 3.64, the displayed data is marked by the labels

```
COM5 Port Sending:
COM6 Port Received:
```

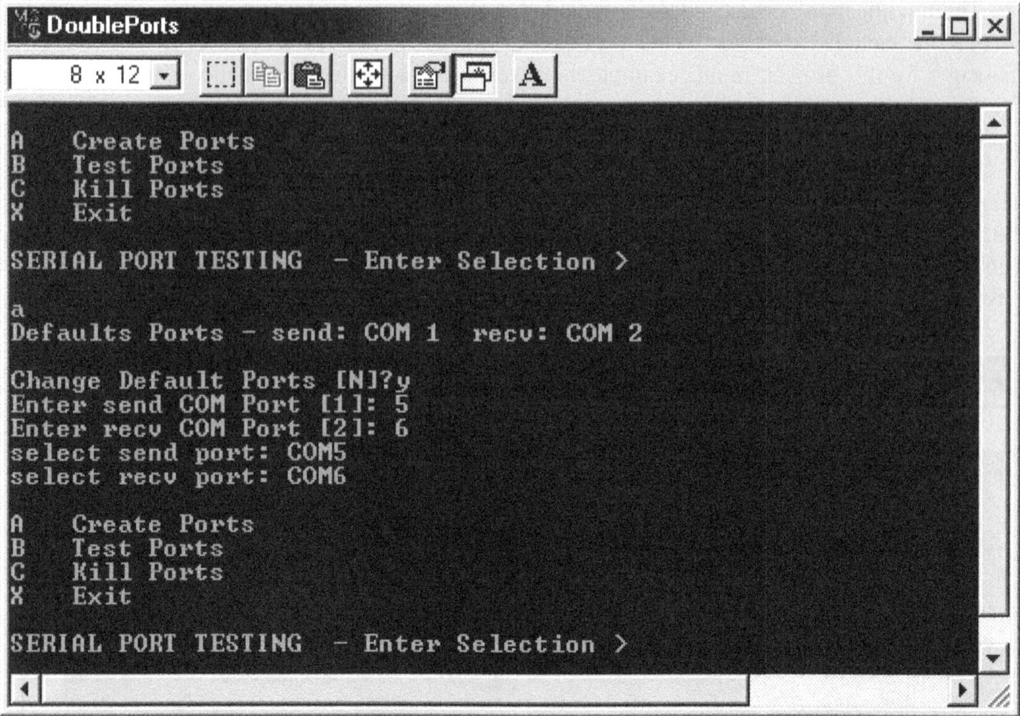

FIGURE 3.63 The running menu of the project DoublePorts.

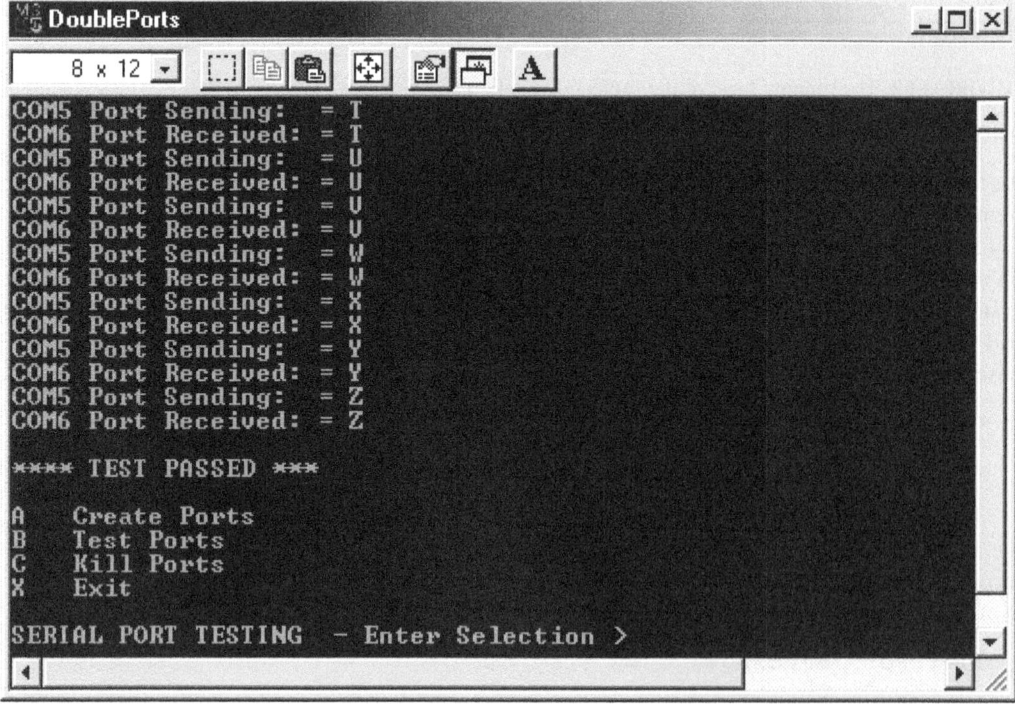

FIGURE 3.64 The running result of the project DoublePorts.

If the whole sequence of testing data sent from the sending port is identical to the sequence of data received by the receiving port, it means that our testing has been successful because all the data sent from the sending port has been correctly received by the receiving port. In this case, a `***TEST PASSED***` message will be displayed, as shown in Figure 3.64. Press `x` to end the project.

All of the files used for this project are stored on the attached CD-ROM, in the folder `Chapter 3\DoublePorts`. You can copy these files to your machine and test the actual serial ports on your own computer. Be sure to install and configure the serial port connectors on your machine before running this testing project.

In some cases, this project may not work properly. The possible reasons for this are as follows:

- The port connectors are connected incorrectly. Make sure to connect the two DB-9 (or DB-25) connectors exactly as we did in Figures 3-55 and 3-56.
- The port configuration is incorrect. You can address this problem by following these steps:
    1. Open the `Control Panel` window.
    2. Double-click the `System` icon to open it.
    3. Click the `Device Manager` tab.
    4. Find the icon labeled `Ports (COM & LPT)`.
    5. Click the plus sign next to the `Ports (COM & LPT)` icon.
    6. Make sure that the desired ports are listed.
    7. If the ports are installed, double-click each one to open its properties window, and confirm that the settings are correct. The settings should match those shown in Figure 3.65.

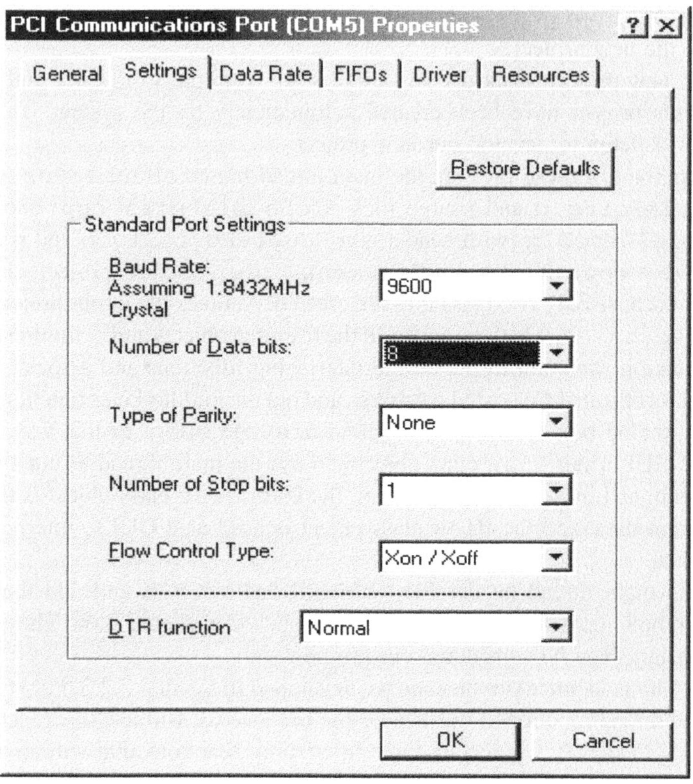

FIGURE 3.65 The default serial port settings.

8. If a port still has problems, double-click the name of that port to open its properties window again. You may need to update the drivers for the port.
9. Click the `Driver` tab, and then click the `Update Driver...` button. Put the floppy disk or CD that contains the updated driver into the floppy disk drive or CD-ROM drive to update the drivers for your serial ports. If you don't have an updated driver available on hand, one can usually be downloaded from the manufacturer's Web site.

- The ports are disabled. On some Windows 95 and 98 machines, the Basic Input/Output System (BIOS) can be used to set up your hardware. You'll need to confirm that your serial ports are set to `Enable` in the BIOS setup file. (Sometimes a port may be set to `Disabled`.) Check this by entering the BIOS, and enable the port if it is disabled.

3.3.3 A Double-Loop Serial-Port-Testing Project Using MFC

In this section, we want to add a GUI to the port-testing program we developed in the preceding section. We will use the `ClassWizard` provided by Visual C++ 6.0 MFC as a tool for developing an MFC-based testing project.

Launch Visual C++ 6.0 and create a new project, and select `MFC AppWizard (exe)` from the **Projects** list. Enter `mfcDoublePorts` in the `Project name:` field as the name for the new project. Make sure the content of the `Location:` field is our user-defined project folder `C:\CTCTest`. Click `OK` to go to the next page.

Select the `Dialog-based` radio button from the second page because we want to demonstrate how to develop a Dialog-based project. We have already learned how to develop an MFC-based single document project (a `Document-View` structure project) in Section 3.2.3. Keep clicking `Next` for the following two pages without touching any of the default settings, and finally click `Finish` to open the new project.

In the opened new project, click the `FileView` tab from the workspace and we can see that all the files for this project have been created automatically by the system. These project files provide us with a skeleton to develop our new project.

The most important of these files are the main thread file `mfcDoublePorts` (including the header `mfcDoublePorts.h` and source files `mfcDoublePorts.cpp`) and our main GUI dialog `mfcDoublePortsDlg` (with header `mfcDoublePortsDlg.h` and source files `mfc-DoublePortsDlg.cpp`). Unlike the `Document-View` structure project, the Dialog-based project is simpler because only two class files are created. Another file in our project is the resource file `mfcDoublePorts.rc`, which provides all the resource objects and definitions for this project.

For our application, we want to put all the interfacing functions and associated variables into the main thread class object, `mfcDoublePorts`, and put the middle-layer functions and associated variables into the dialog box class object `mfcDoublePortsDlg`. In this way, we can use the dialog box as our GUI or our `View` class object and use the main thread as our `Document` class object. As we mentioned in Section 3.2.3 earlier, the `Document` class object is used to store and operate our program data, and the `View` class object is used as a GUI to interface with the user and display the data.

Now open the main thread header file `mfcDoublePorts.h` and add the following data structures and symbolic constants to this header file, shown in Figure 3.66. These data structures and symbolic constants can be considered our program data.

The program data is identical to the code we developed in Section 3.2.3. For step A, we declare the protocol of the thread function at this header file because we will use this function in this main thread class object. In step `B`, we declare three interfacing functions that will also be used in this `Document`-like class object file.

Now open our `View`-like class object header file, `mfcDoublePortsDlg.h`, and add the following variables and functions to this file, as shown in Figure 3.67.

```
// mfcDoublePorts.h : main header file for the MFCDOUBLEPORTS application
//
#if !defined(AFX_MFCDOUBLEPORTS_H__B760A554_4DB1_4101_A061_0CCBAE319D95
                                                              __INCLUDED_)
#define AFX_MFCDOUBLEPORTS_H__B760A554_4DB1_4101_A061_0CCBAE319D95
                                                              __INCLUDED_
#if _MSC_VER > 1000
#pragma once
#endif // _MSC_VER > 1000

#ifndef __AFXWIN_H__
        #error include 'stdafx.h' before including this file for PCH
#endif

#include "resource.h"            // main symbols

A   void WINAPI ThreadFunc(void* hCommPorts);

/////////////////////////////////////////////////////////////////////////////
// CMfcDoublePortsApp:
// See mfcDoublePorts.cpp for the implementation of this class
//

#define NUM_BYTE                        1
#define MAX_BYTE                        90
#define START_BYTE                      48
#define  BAUD_RATE                      9600
#define  NUM_BITS                       8
#define  TIME_OUT                       3000
#define MAX_MENU                        4
#define MAX_STRING                      256
#define NOPARITY                        0
#define ONESTOPBIT                      0
#define RTS_CONTROL_DISABLE             0x00
#define RTS_CONTROL_ENABLE              0x01
#define DTR_CONTROL_DISABLE             0x00
#define DTR_CONTROL_ENABLE              0x01

#define  msg(info)   AfxMessageBox(info)
typedef struct
{
   unsigned long ulCtrlerID;
   char          cEcho;
   char          cEORChar;
   long          lTimeout;
   long          lBaudRate;
   long          lDataBits;
   HANDLE        hPort;
}SerialCreate, *pSerialCreate;

typedef struct
{
   char*         pcBuffer;
   BYTE          bByte;
```

FIGURE 3.66 The header file `mfcDoublePorts.h`. *(continued)*

```
   int          iMaxChars;
   int          piNumRcvd;
   char         cTermChar;
   HANDLE       handlePort;
}CommPortClass;

typedef enum
{
   OK                        = 0,          /* no error */
   EC_TIMEOUT,
   EC_FOPEN,
   EC_INVAL_CONFIG,
   EC_TIMEOUT_SET,
   EC_RECV_TIMEOUT,
   EC_EXIT_CODE,
   EC_WAIT_SINGLEOBJ,
   EC_INVALIDPORT,
   EC_WRITE_FAIL,
   EC_CREATE_THREAD,
   EC_READ_FAIL,
   EC_TEST_FAIL,
   EC_UNKNOWNERROR
}ERR_CODE;

class CMfcDoublePortsApp : public CWinApp
{
public:
    ERR_CODE PortRead(CommPortClass* hCommPort);
B   ERR_CODE PortWrite(HANDLE handPort, BYTE bByte, int NumByte);
    ERR_CODE PortInitialize(LPTSTR lpszPortName, pSerialCreate pCreate);
    CMfcDoublePortsApp();

// Overrides
    // ClassWizard generated virtual function overrides
    //{{AFX_VIRTUAL(CMfcDoublePortsApp)
    public:
    virtual BOOL InitInstance();
    //}}AFX_VIRTUAL
// Implementation

     //{{AFX_MSG(CMfcDoublePortsApp)
          // NOTE - the ClassWizard will add and remove member functions here.
          // DO NOT EDIT what you see in these blocks of generated code !
     //}}AFX_MSG
     DECLARE_MESSAGE_MAP()
};

/////////////////////////////////////////////////////////////////////////////

//{{AFX_INSERT_LOCATION}}
// Microsoft Visual C++ will insert additional declarations immediately before the previous
line.

#endif //
!defined(AFX_MFCDOUBLEPORTS_H__B760A554_4DB1_4101_A061_0CCBAE319D95__
                                                                    INCLUDED_)
```

FIGURE 3.66 The header file `mfcDoublePorts.h`.

```
// mfcDoublePortsDlg.h : header file
//

#include "mfcDoublePorts.h"          // Added by ClassView
#if
!defined(AFX_MFCDOUBLEPORTSDLG_H__A9D5B7B0_D88A_4754_AA53_807116603C8A
                                                            __INCLUDED_)
#define
AFX_MFCDOUBLEPORTSDLG_H__A9D5B7B0_D88A_4754_AA53_807116603C8A__
                                                            INCLUDED_

#if _MSC_VER > 1000
#pragma once
#endif // _MSC_VER > 1000

/////////////////////////////////////////////////////////////////////////////
// CMfcDoublePortsDlg dialog

typedef struct
{
A       char   sComPort[16];
        char   rComPort[16];
}PortName, *pPortName;

class CMfcDoublePortsDlg : public CDialog
{
// Construction
public:
        HANDLE   hrPort;
        HANDLE   hsPort;
B       bool     rPortFlg;
        bool     sPortFlg;
        bool     TestPassed;

        ERR_CODE startPort();
C       ERR_CODE SetupPort(char* cPort, int bRate, int pFlg);
        ERR_CODE TestPort(char* sPort, char* rPort, BOOL display);
        CMfcDoublePortsDlg(CWnd* pParent = NULL);     // standard constructor

// Dialog Data
        //{{AFX_DATA(CMfcDoublePortsDlg)
        enum { IDD = IDD_MFCDOUBLEPORTS_DIALOG };
        CStatic     m_label;
        CEdit       m_readData;
D       CEdit       m_sendData;
        int         m_sendPort;
        int         m_recvPort;
        int         m_baudRate;
        //}}AFX_DATA

        // ClassWizard generated virtual function overrides
        //{{AFX_VIRTUAL(CMfcDoublePortsDlg)
        protected:
        virtual void DoDataExchange(CDataExchange* pDX);      // DDX/DDV support
        //}}AFX_VIRTUAL
// Implementation
protected:
```

FIGURE 3.67 The header file `mfcDoublePortsDlg.h`. *(continued)*

```
    HICON m_hIcon;

    // Generated message map functions
    //{{AFX_MSG(CMfcDoublePortsDlg)
    virtual BOOL OnInitDialog();
    afx_msg void OnSysCommand(UINT nID, LPARAM lParam);
    afx_msg void OnPaint();
    afx_msg HCURSOR OnQueryDragIcon();
E   afx_msg void OnInit();
    afx_msg void OnTest();
    afx_msg void OnLoop();
    afx_msg void OnAbout();
    afx_msg void OnExit();
    //}}AFX_MSG
    DECLARE_MESSAGE_MAP()
};
```

FIGURE 3.67 The header file mfcDoublePortsDlg.h.

We added some variables that will be used in this class object. Strictly speaking, we should add these variables to our Document-like class object, or our main thread class object, and access these variables from our View-like class object by using a connection between the two class objects. Because we want to save some space and make the program convenient, we added these variables to this class object. We can add them in the main thread class object if necessary.

A: A PortName data structure is declared in this header file because this structure will be used in this class object file. The purpose of this structure is to reserve the opened port names for further use in the program.

B: Five variables (also called attributes) are also declared in this header file. Two port handlers are used to reserve the handlers of the opened ports because these two port handlers will be used throughout the program. hsPort and hrPort are used to reserve the sending port and receiving port handlers, respectively. Two Boolean variables, sPortFlg and rPortFlg, are used to hold the initialization status of the two ports. A True value for any previously mentioned Boolean variable means that the port has been initialized. The TestPassed Boolean variable is used to store the testing status of the program, and a True value for this flag means that the testing has been successful.

C: Three middle-layer functions are declared in this class object. The startPort() is a medium function, and it sets the connection between the INIT event activated by the keyboard and the execution of the initialization function for the ports. The SetupPort() and TestPort() functions were discussed in Section 3.2.3. The former is used to initialize and set up the serial ports, and the latter is used to test the initialized ports.

D: We will add these six components to the dialog box GUI later and use them to interface to the testing program as the program runs.

E: Five member functions, OnInit(), OnTest(), OnLoop(), OnAbout(), and OnExit(), are used to execute the associated actions to perform the testing tasks on the ports. They will be added into the dialog box GUI in the next step.

Before we can continue to develop the code for the two source files, let us first develop our dialog box GUI object. Click the ResourceView tab from the workspace to open the resource files for this project. Right-click the Dialog icon and select the Insert Dialog item from the popup menu to open a default dialog box window.

Drag the opened default dialog box to enlarge it, and then right-click it. Select the `Properties` item from the popup menu. Enter `DOUBLE PORTS TESTING` in the `Caption:` field and enter `IDD_MFCDOUBLEPORTS_DIALOG` in the `ID:` field. Click the Close button to save these settings. Add the following components to the dialog box. The finished dialog box should match the one shown in Figure 3.68:

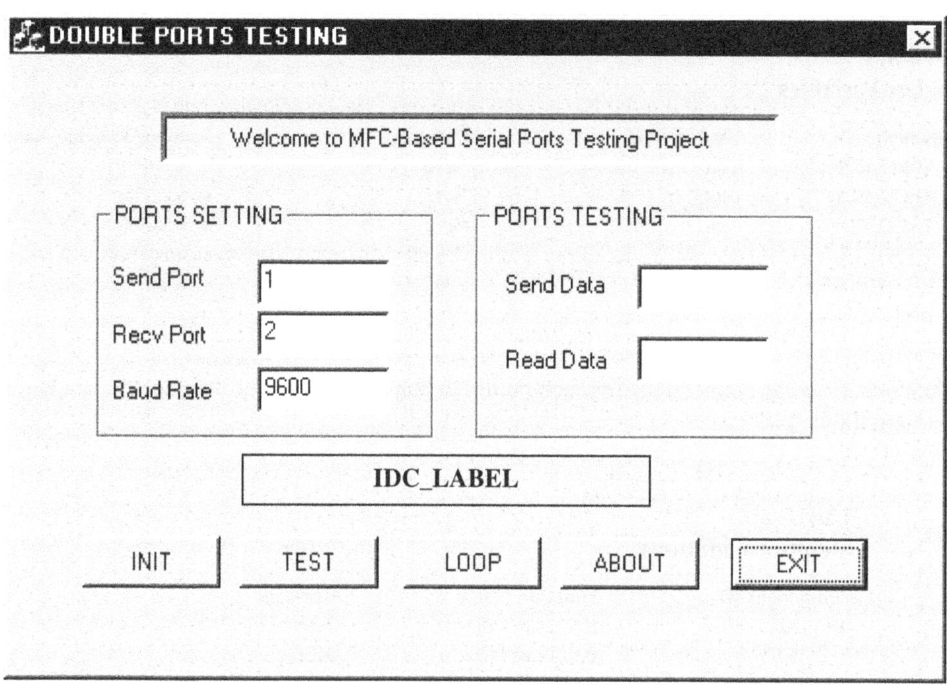

FIGURE 3.68 The GUI of the project mfcDoublePorts.

- Static Text: ID: `IDC_STATIC` Caption: `Welcome to MFC-Based Serial Port Testing Project`
- Group Box: ID: `IDC_STATIC` Caption: `PORTS SETTING`
- Static Text: ID: `IDC_STATIC` Caption: `Send Port`
- Edit Box: ID: `IDC_SEND_EDIT`
- Static Text: ID: `IDC_STATIC` Caption: `Recv Port`
- Edit Box: ID: `IDC_RECV_EDIT`
- Static Text: ID: `IDC_STATIC` Caption: `Baud Rate`
- Edit Box: ID: `IDC_BAUD_EDIT`
- Group Box: ID: `IDC_STATIC` Caption: `PORTS TESTING`
- Static Text: ID: `IDC_STATIC` Caption: `Send Data`
- Edit Box: ID: `IDC_WRITE_EDIT`
- Static Text: ID: `IDC_STATIC` Caption: `Read Data`
- Edit Box: ID: `IDC_READ_EDIT`
- Static Text: ID: `IDC_LABEL` Caption:
- Button: ID: `IDC_INIT` Caption: `INIT`
- Button: ID: `IDC_TEST` Caption: `TEST`
- Button: ID: `IDC_LOOP` Caption: `LOOP`
- Button: ID: `IDC_ABOUT` Caption: `ABOUT`
- Button: ID: `IDC_EXIT` Caption: `EXIT`

Don't worry about the numbers in the edit boxes; we will talk about this issue later.

Let us now set the connection between each component in the dialog box and each member variable in the class file `mfcDoublePortsDlg`. Right-click each component and select the `ClassWizard...` item from the popup menu to open the `MFC ClassWizard` dialog box. Set the connection for each component in the dialog box as shown in Table 3-3.

TABLE 3.3
Member Variables

Component ID	Value type	Category	Member Variable Name
IDC_SEND_EDIT	int	Value	m_sendPort
IDC_RECV_EDIT	int	Value	m_recvPort
IDC_BAUD_EDIT	int	Value	m_baudRate
IDC_WRITE_EDIT	CEdit	Control	m_sendData
IDC_READ_EDIT	CEdit	Control	m_readData
IDC_label	CStatic	Control	m_label

Continue to set the connections for each button in our dialog box to a message in the class file, as shown in Table 3-4.

TABLE 3.4
Member Functions

Component ID	Function Name	Messages
IDC_INIT	BN_CLICKED	OnInit
IDC_TEST	BN_CLICKED	OnTest
IDC_LOOP	BN_CLICKED	OnLoop
IDC_ABOUT	BN_CLICKED	OnAbout
IDEXIT	BN_CLICKED	OnExit

Now click `OK` in the `MFC ClassWizard` dialog box to close the dialog box.

The dialog box is contained by the class `mfcDoublePortsDlg` in our project. Click the `FileView` tab to open the source files, and double-click our dialog box class header file `mfc-DoublePortsDlg.h`. We will find that all member variables and functions added above have been installed in this header file, as mentioned at steps `D` and `E` earlier.

This completes the work on our main GUI window. Now let us finish developing our source code for our two class object files.

First, we will finish the coding of our main thread class file, `mfcDoublePorts.cpp`. The complete source file of the main thread class is shown in Figure 3.69. Move the cursor to find the three interfacing functions we added earlier. Add the following code into each interfacing function as shown in Figure 3.69.

Now let us take a look at this source file. The code between steps `A` and `E` is created by the system automatically when we create this project. We can consider these codes as a skeleton or frame that we can fill with code to fulfill our program's functionalities. The code between steps `F` and `K` was developed by us and is basically the interfacing functions. They are similar to those we developed in the previous examples.

```
    // mfcDoublePorts.cpp : Defines the class behaviors for the application.
    //
    #include "stdafx.h"
    #include "mfcDoublePorts.h"
    #include "mfcDoublePortsDlg.h"

    #ifdef _DEBUG
    #define new DEBUG_NEW
    #undef THIS_FILE
    static char THIS_FILE[] = __FILE__;
    #endif

    /////////////////////////////////////////////////////////////////////////////
    // CMfcDoublePortsApp
A   BEGIN_MESSAGE_MAP(CMfcDoublePortsApp, CWinApp)
            //{{AFX_MSG_MAP(CMfcDoublePortsApp)
                    // NOTE - the ClassWizard will add and remove mapping macros here.
                    // DO NOT EDIT what you see in these blocks of generated code!
            //}}AFX_MSG
            ON_COMMAND(ID_HELP, CWinApp::OnHelp)
    END_MESSAGE_MAP()

    /////////////////////////////////////////////////////////////////////////////
    // CMfcDoublePortsApp construction

B   CMfcDoublePortsApp::CMfcDoublePortsApp()
    {
            // TODO: add construction code here,
            // Place all significant initialization in InitInstance
    }
    /////////////////////////////////////////////////////////////////////////////
    // The one and only CMfcDoublePortsApp object
C   CMfcDoublePortsApp theApp;
    /////////////////////////////////////////////////////////////////////////////
    // CMfcDoublePortsApp initialization
    BOOL CMfcDoublePortsApp::InitInstance()
    {
            AfxEnableControlContainer();

            // Standard initialization
            // If you are not using these features and wish to reduce the size
            //  of your final executable, you should remove from the following
            //  the specific initialization routines you do not need.

    #ifdef _AFXDLL
            Enable3dControls();               // Call this when using MFC in a shared DLL
    #else
            Enable3dControlsStatic();         // Call this when linking to MFC statically
    #endif

D           CMfcDoublePortsDlg dlg;
            m_pMainWnd = &dlg;
            int nResponse = dlg.DoModal();
```

FIGURE 3.69 The source file `mfcDoublePorts.cpp`. *(continued)*

```
E          if (nResponse == IDOK)
           {
                // TODO: Place code here to handle when the dialog is
                //  dismissed with OK
           }
           else if (nResponse == IDCANCEL)
           {
                // TODO: Place code here to handle when the dialog is
                //  dismissed with Cancel
           }
           // Since the dialog has been closed, return FALSE so that we exit the
           //  application, rather than start the application's message pump.
           return FALSE;
   }
F  ERR_CODE CMfcDoublePortsApp::PortInitialize(LPTSTR lpszPortName, pSerialCreate
                                                                         pCreate)
   {
           HANDLE          hPort;
           DWORD           dwError;
           DCB             PortDCB;
           unsigned char   dBit;
           ERR_CODE        ecStatus = OK;
           COMMTIMEOUTS    CommTimeouts;

           // Open the serial port.
           hPort = CreateFile(lpszPortName,  // Pointer to the name of the port
                   GENERIC_READ | GENERIC_WRITE,  // Access (read/write) mode
                   0,                       // Share mode
                   NULL,                    // Pointer to the security attribute
                   OPEN_EXISTING,           // How to open the serial port
                   0,                       // Port attributes
                   NULL);                   // Handle to port with attribute to copy

           // If it fails to open the port, return error.
           if ( hPort == INVALID_HANDLE_VALUE )
           {
                dwError = GetLastError();                 // Could not open the port.
                msg("Unable to open the port");
                CloseHandle(hPort);
                return EC_FOPEN;
           }
           PortDCB.DCBlength = sizeof(DCB);

           // Get the default port setting information.
           GetCommState(hPort, &PortDCB);

           // Change the DCB structure settings.
           PortDCB.BaudRate = pCreate->lBaudRate;          // Current baud rate
           PortDCB.fBinary  = TRUE;                        // Binary mode; no EOF check
           PortDCB.fParity  = TRUE;                        // Enable parity checking.
           PortDCB.fOutxCtsFlow = FALSE;                   // No CTS output flow control
           PortDCB.fOutxDsrFlow = FALSE;                   // No DSR output flow control
           PortDCB.fDtrControl = DTR_CONTROL_ENABLE;// DTR_CONTROL_ENABLE
```

FIGURE 3.69 The source file `mfcDoublePorts.cpp`. *(continued)*

```
        PortDCB.fDsrSensitivity = FALSE;                    // DSR sensitivity
        PortDCB.fTXContinueOnXoff = TRUE;                   // XOFF continues Tx TRUE
        PortDCB.fOutX = FALSE;                              // No XON/XOFF out flow control
        PortDCB.fInX  = FALSE;                              // No XON/XOFF in flow control
        PortDCB.fErrorChar = FALSE;                         // Disable error replacement.
        PortDCB.fNull = FALSE;                              // Disable null stripping.
        PortDCB.fRtsControl = RTS_CONTROL_ENABLE;    // RTS flow control
        PortDCB.fAbortOnError = FALSE;                      // Don't abort reads/writes on error.
        dBit = (unsigned char)pCreate->lDataBits;
        PortDCB.ByteSize = dBit;                            // Number of bits/bytes, 4-8
        PortDCB.Parity = NOPARITY;                          // 0-4=no,odd,even,mark,space
        PortDCB.StopBits = ONESTOPBIT;                      // 0,1,2 = 1, 1.5, 2
        // Configure the port according to the specifications of the DCB structure.
        if (!SetCommState (hPort, &PortDCB))
        {
            // Could not create the read thread.
            dwError = GetLastError();
            msg("Unable to configure the serial port");
            return EC_INVAL_CONFIG;
        }
        // Retrieve the time-out parameters for all read and write operations on the port.
        GetCommTimeouts(hPort, &CommTimeouts);
        // Change the COMMTIMEOUTS structure settings.
        CommTimeouts.ReadIntervalTimeout = MAXDWORD;
        CommTimeouts.ReadTotalTimeoutMultiplier = 0;
        CommTimeouts.ReadTotalTimeoutConstant = 0;
        CommTimeouts.WriteTotalTimeoutMultiplier = 10;
        CommTimeouts.WriteTotalTimeoutConstant = 1000;
        // Set the time-out parameters for all read and write operations on the port.
        if (!SetCommTimeouts (hPort, &CommTimeouts))
        {
            // Could not create the read thread.
            dwError = GetLastError();
            msg("Unable to set the time-out parameters");
            return EC_TIMEOUT_SET;
        }

        EscapeCommFunction(hPort, SETDTR);
        EscapeCommFunction(hPort, SETRTS);
        pCreate->hPort = hPort;
        return  ecStatus;
}
```

G

```
ERR_CODE CMfcDoublePortsApp::PortWrite(HANDLE handPort, BYTE bByte, int NumByte)
{
        DWORD dwError;
        DWORD dwNumBytesWritten;
        ERR_CODE ecStatus = OK;
```

FIGURE 3.69 The source file `mfcDoublePorts.cpp`. *(continued)*

```
        if (!WriteFile (handPort,                   // Port handle
                        &bByte,                     // Pointer to the data to write
                        NumByte,                    // Number of bytes to write
                        &dwNumBytesWritten,         // Pointer to the number of bytes written
                        NULL))                      // Must be NULL for Windows CE
        {
              // WriteFile failed. Report error.
              dwError = GetLastError ();
              msg("ERROR in PortWrite ..");
              return EC_WRITE_FAIL;
        }
        return ecStatus;
}
H  ERR_CODE CMfcDoublePortsApp::PortRead(CommPortClass *hCommPort)
{
        HANDLE hThread;                             // handler for port read thread
        DWORD  IDThread;
        DWORD  Ret, ExitCode;
        DWORD  dTimeout = 5000;                     // define time out value: 5 sec.
        ERR_CODE ecStatus = OK;
I       if (!(hThread = ::CreateThread(NULL,                // no security attributes
                        0,                                  // use default stack size
                        (LPTHREAD_START_ROUTINE)ThreadFunc,
                        (LPVOID)hCommPort,                  // parameter to thread function
                        CREATE_SUSPENDED,                   // creation flag - suspended
                        &IDThread)))                        // returns thread ID
        {
              msg("Create Read Thread failed");
           return     EC_CREATE_THREAD;
        }
J       ::ResumeThread(hThread);                            // start thread now
        Ret = WaitForSingleObject(hThread, dTimeout);
        if (Ret == WAIT_OBJECT_0)
        {
              // data received & process it...Need to do nothing
              // because the data has been stored in the hCommPort in Thread Func.
              // close thread handle
              CloseHandle(hThread);
        }
        else if (Ret == WAIT_TIMEOUT)
        {
              // time out happened, warning & kill thread
              Ret = GetExitCodeThread(hThread, &ExitCode);
              msg("Time out happened in PortRead() ");
              if (ExitCode == STILL_ACTIVE)
              {
                     TerminateThread(hThread, ExitCode);
                     CloseHandle(hThread);
                     return EC_RECV_TIMEOUT;
              }
```

FIGURE 3.69 The source file `mfcDoublePorts.cpp`. *(continued)*

```
                else
                {
                        CloseHandle(hThread);
                        msg("ERROR in GetExitCodeThread: != STILL_ACTIVE ");
                        ecStatus = EC_EXIT_CODE;
                }
        }
        else
        {
                msg("ERROR in WaitFor SingleObject ");
                ecStatus = EC_WAIT_SINGLEOBJ;
        }
        return ecStatus;
}
K void WINAPI ThreadFunc(void* hCommPorts)
{
        BYTE            Byte;
        DWORD           dwError;
        BOOL            bResult;
        int             nTotRead = 0;
        DWORD           dwCommModemStatus, dwBytesTransferred;
        CommPortClass*  CommPorts;
        ERR_CODE        ecStatus = OK;

        CommPorts = (CommPortClass* )hCommPorts;

        // Specify a set of events to be monitored for the port.
        SetCommMask(CommPorts->handlePort, EV_RXCHAR | EV_CTS | EV_DSR |
                                                        EV_RLSD | EV_RING);
        // Wait for an event to occur for the port.
        WaitCommEvent(CommPorts->handlePort, &dwCommModemStatus, 0);

        // Re-specify the set of events to be monitored for the port.
        SetCommMask(CommPorts->handlePort, EV_RXCHAR | EV_CTS | EV_DSR|
                                                        EV_RLSD| EV_RING);
        if (dwCommModemStatus & EV_RXCHAR||dwCommModemStatus & EV_RLSD)
        {
            // Received the char_event & read the data from the serial port.
            bResult = ReadFile(CommPorts->handlePort, &Byte, 1, &dwBytesTransferred, 0);
            if (!bResult)
            {
                msg("Unable to read the port");
                if ( (dwError = GetLastError()) == ERROR_HANDLE_EOF)
                    msg("Serial Receive Failed");
            }
            else
            {
                // store the data read.
                CommPorts->bByte = Byte;
                nTotRead++;
            }
        }

        return;
}
```

FIGURE 3.69 The source file `mfcDoublePorts.cpp`.

A: This section is used by the system to add messages and is called the message map section, to the project. The system will add a message macro to the project if necessary. The message will be passed down from the parent class object `CWinApp`, so we should not edit this section ourselves.

B: This section is the constructor section of our main thread class object, and most of the time the initialization code should be added to this section by the system. All significant project initialization codes should be added into the `InitInstance()` member function in this class object.

C: In this step, the system creates an object of our main thread class, `theApp`. This is the only object created by the system and used in our project. We must have only one of these objects created because all other class objects developed in our project are controlled by this main thread class object. That is why this class object is called the main thread object in our project.

D: The `InitInstance()` is an important member function, and the most important system initialization jobs are processed in this function. Besides some other initialization procedures, our main dialog box is created from here. The command

```
CMfcDoublePortsDlg dlg;
```

is used to create a new instance of our dialog box, `dlg`. The handler of this dialog box is reserved in the system variable `m_pMainWnd`, which can be used to access our dialog box from the main thread object. Next, the member function `DoModal()` is called to display our dialog box onscreen. Our dialog box is a Modal dialog box because it is issued and displayed by using the `DoModal()` function.

E: After the dialog box is created and displayed, the main thread will wait for feedback by monitoring the returning value of the `DoModal()` member function. The default returning values of the `DoModal()` function are either `IDOK` or `IDCANCEL`, which are associated with two default buttons, `OK` and `Cancel`, in the dialog box window. When either value is received, the main thread should destroy the dialog box and clean up the environment installed for the dialog box. All these functionalities should be taken care of by the main thread object, or in reality, by the system itself. So currently we cannot find any code in these two cases. Finally, a `False` is returned to the system to indicate that the project will be terminated.

F: At the beginning of section `F`, our user-developed interfacing functions are provided. The first one is the `PortInitialize()` function, which is used to set up and initialize the serial ports to be tested. This function is identical to the one we developed in the previous example, so we don't need to duplicate the explanation again for this function.

G: The `PortWrite()` interfacing function is provided in this section. It is also identical to the one we developed earlier.

H: The `PortRead()` interfacing function is provided in this section. Two small modifications have been made to the function we developed previously.

I: The first modification is the `CreateThread()` system function. In some cases, when we compile a project that contains some system API functions, such as the `Create Thread()` API function in our case, the compiler may give an error message such as "`CreateThread() function does not take 6 arguments.`" But if we check the protocol of the system function `CreateThread()` using the MSDN library, we will find that `CreateThread()` does take `6` arguments. What is wrong? The problem is that the `CreateThread()` system function is called from within the member function `PortRead()`, which belongs to the class `mfcDoublePorts` in our current project. The class name `mfcDoublePorts` is placed before the function name `PortRead()`, and a scope resolution operator :: is used to connect the class object and the function together. This format will tell the compiler that the function `PortRead()` belongs to the class `mfcDoublePorts`.

When we compile our program, the compiler will have not any knowledge about the scope of the system function `CreateThread()`. Because we put this system function inside the body of the `PortRead()` function, the compiler would consider that this system function also belongs to the class `mfcDoublePorts` since no scope resolution operator precedes this system function. MFC also provides a member function `CreateThread()`, but this function belongs to the class `CWinThread` and it only has three arguments. Our compiler would consider that we are using the `CreateThread()` function, which belongs to the class `CWinThread` if no scope resolution operator precedes the function.

To solve this problem, place a scope resolution operator :: in front of the system function `CreateThread()`, as we did previously. The purpose of this scope resolution operator is to tell the compiler that this system function does not belong to the current class, but that it is a global (or general-purpose) Win32 API function. In this way, our program can be compiled with no problem.

J: Similar to the system function `CreateThread()`, we add a scope resolution operator before the system function `ResumeThread()`. This is done to tell the compiler that this function does not belong to the current class and is a general-purpose Win32 API function.

K: Our thread function `ThreadFunc()` is provided in this section. It is identical to the one we developed earlier.

At this point, we have finished developing our main thread class object. Now let us develop the source code for our main dialog box class file. Go to the `FileView` and double-click our dialog box class file `mfcDoublePortsDlg.cpp` to open it. Then add the following code to this source file, which is shown in Figure 3.70.

Because of space limitations, we don't want to display all the source code in this file. Some of the code has no direct relationship to our application, so we will only show the codes that are closely related to our application (refer to the files in the attached CD for these complete codes).

A: This included header file is used to define the protocols of the variables and functions in the loop dialog box that we will develop later. Don't be worried about this header file right now, as we will discuss this in the next section.

B: A character pointer array `comPORT[]` is declared in this source file and is used to define the port names based on the index. By using this pointer array, we can get the port name directly, based on the position index, and can ignore the `getMenuItem()` function. We can define this pointer array in any file, but we prefer to define it in this source file because it will be used in this file only.

C: A default `About` dialog box is declared in this section. This dialog box is created by the system automatically when we create the project. This dialog box is inherited from the `CDialog` class and has all the properties the `CDialog` class has.

D: Inside the constructor of our main dialog box `mfcDoublePortsDlg`, the three member variables we added are initialized here. Originally, all these variables are initialized to 0. We have modified these three variables to the values shown in Figure 3.70. We set our default sending port to `COM1`, the receiving port as `COM2`, and the baud rate as `9600`. You can select other initial values for these variables based on your application.

E: In the Data Map area, we can find all the member variables we added into the project earlier. In total, there are six variables, five edit box variables, and one label variable.

```
// mfcDoublePortsDlg.cpp : implementation file
//
#include "stdafx.h"
#include "mfcDoublePorts.h"
#include "mfcDoublePortsDlg.h"
A #include "LoopDlg.h"                                    // don't forget to add this header file
#ifdef _DEBUG
#define new DEBUG_NEW
#undef THIS_FILE
static char THIS_FILE[] = __FILE__;
#endif
B char* comPORT[] = { {"COM1"}, {"COM2"}, {"COM3"}, {"COM4"}, {"COM5"},
                                        {"COM6"}, {"COM7"}, {"COM8"}, {"COM9"}};
/////////////////////////////////////////////////////////////////////////////
// CAboutDlg dialog used for App About
C class CAboutDlg : public CDialog
{
public:
        CAboutDlg();
// Dialog Data
        //{{AFX_DATA(CAboutDlg)
        enum { IDD = IDD_ABOUTBOX };
        //}}AFX_DATA
        // ClassWizard generated virtual function overrides
        //{{AFX_VIRTUAL(CAboutDlg)
        protected:
        virtual void DoDataExchange(CDataExchange* pDX);    // DDX/DDV support
        //}}AFX_VIRTUAL
// Implementation
protected:
        //{{AFX_MSG(CAboutDlg)
        //}}AFX_MSG
        DECLARE_MESSAGE_MAP()
};
......
/////////////////////////////////////////////////////////////////////////////
// CMfcDoublePortsDlg dialog

CMfcDoublePortsDlg::CMfcDoublePortsDlg(CWnd* pParent /*=NULL*/)
        : CDialog(CMfcDoublePortsDlg::IDD, pParent)
{
        //{{AFX_DATA_INIT(CMfcDoublePortsDlg)
        m_sendPort = 1;                         // set default send port _Bai
D       m_recvPort = 2;                         // set default recv port _Bai
        m_baudRate = 9600;                      // set default baud rate _Bai
        //}}AFX_DATA_INIT
        // Note that LoadIcon does not require a subsequent DestroyIcon in Win32
        m_hIcon = AfxGetApp()->LoadIcon(IDR_MAINFRAME);
}

void CMfcDoublePortsDlg::DoDataExchange(CDataExchange* pDX)
{
```

FIGURE 3.70 The source file `mfcDoublePortsDlg.cpp`. *(continued)*

```
E       CDialog::DoDataExchange(pDX);
        //{{AFX_DATA_MAP(CMfcDoublePortsDlg)
        DDX_Control(pDX, IDC_LABEL, m_label);
        DDX_Control(pDX, IDC_READ_EDIT, m_readData);
        DDX_Control(pDX, IDC_WRITE_EDIT, m_sendData);
        DDX_Text(pDX, IDC_SEND_EDIT, m_sendPort);
        DDX_Text(pDX, IDC_RECV_EDIT, m_recvPort);
        DDX_Text(pDX, IDC_BAUD_EDIT, m_baudRate);
        //}}AFX_DATA_MAP
}

BEGIN_MESSAGE_MAP(CMfcDoublePortsDlg, CDialog)
        //{{AFX_MSG_MAP(CMfcDoublePortsDlg)
        ON_WM_SYSCOMMAND()
        ON_WM_PAINT()
        ON_WM_QUERYDRAGICON()
F       ON_BN_CLICKED(IDC_INIT, OnInit)
        ON_BN_CLICKED(IDC_TEST, OnTest)
        ON_BN_CLICKED(IDC_LOOP, OnLoop)
        ON_BN_CLICKED(IDC_ABOUT, OnAbout)
        ON_BN_CLICKED(IDEXIT, OnExit)
        //}}AFX_MSG_MAP
END_MESSAGE_MAP()

/////////////////////////////////////////////////////////////////////////////
// CMfcDoublePortsDlg message handlers
G BOOL CMfcDoublePortsDlg::OnInitDialog()
{
        CDialog::OnInitDialog();
        // Add "About..." menu item to system menu.
        // IDM_ABOUTBOX must be in the system command range.
        ASSERT((IDM_ABOUTBOX & 0xFFF0) == IDM_ABOUTBOX);
        ASSERT(IDM_ABOUTBOX < 0xF000);
        CMenu* pSysMenu = GetSystemMenu(FALSE);

  if (pSysMenu != NULL)
  {
        CString strAboutMenu;
         strAboutMenu.LoadString(IDS_ABOUTBOX);
         if (!strAboutMenu.IsEmpty())
        {
            pSysMenu->AppendMenu(MF_SEPARATOR);
            pSysMenu->AppendMenu(MF_STRING, IDM_ABOUTBOX, strAboutMenu);
        }
  }
  // Set the icon for this dialog.  The framework does this automatically
  //  when the application's main window is not a dialog
  SetIcon(m_hIcon, TRUE);                  // Set big icon
  SetIcon(m_hIcon, FALSE);                 // Set small icon
```

FIGURE 3.70 The source file `mfcDoublePortsDlg.cpp`. *(continued)*

```
        // TODO: Add extra initialization here
        rPortFlg   = FALSE;
H       sPortFlg   = FALSE;
        TestPassed = FALSE;
        return TRUE;  // return TRUE  unless you set the focus to a control
    }
    void CMfcDoublePortsDlg::OnSysCommand(UINT nID, LPARAM lParam)
    {
        if ((nID & 0xFFF0) == IDM_ABOUTBOX)
        {
            CAboutDlg dlgAbout;
I           dlgAbout.DoModal();
        }
        else
        {
            CDialog::OnSysCommand(nID, lParam);
        }
    }
    ......
J   void CMfcDoublePortsDlg::OnInit()
    {
        // TODO: Add your control notification handler code here
        ERR_CODE  ecRet = OK;

        ecRet = startPort();
        if (ecRet)
        {
                msg("ERROR in INIT");
                return;
        }
K       m_label.SetWindowText("The Ports have been Initialized");
    }
L   ERR_CODE CMfcDoublePortsDlg::startPort()
    {
        int      portNum;
        ERR_CODE  ecRet = OK;
M       UpdateData(TRUE);
        portNum = m_sendPort - 1;
N       ecRet = SetupPort(comPORT[portNum],  m_baudRate,  1);
        if (ecRet)
        {
            msg("ERROR in SetupPort() - Sending Port");
            return ecRet;
        }
O       portNum = m_recvPort - 1;
```

FIGURE 3.70 The source file `mfcDoublePortsDlg.cpp`. *(continued)*

```
            ecRet = SetupPort(comPORT[portNum], m_baudRate, 2);
            if (ecRet)
                msg("ERROR in SetupPort() - Recving Port");
            return ecRet;
    }
    ERR_CODE CMfcDoublePortsDlg::SetupPort(char *cPort, int bRate, int pFlg)
    {
            ERR_CODE      ecRet = OK;
P           pSerialCreate pParam;
            pPortName     pName;
            CMfcDoublePortsApp* mfcDoubleApp = (CMfcDoublePortsApp*) AfxGetApp();
            pParam = new SerialCreate;
            pName  = new PortName;
            pParam->lBaudRate = bRate;
            pParam->lDataBits = NUM_BITS;
            pParam->lTimeout  = TIME_OUT;
            if (sPortFlg && pFlg == 1)
Q               return ecRet;
            if (rPortFlg && pFlg == 2)
                return ecRet;
R           ecRet = mfcDoubleApp->PortInitialize(cPort, pParam);
            if (ecRet != OK)
                msg("ERROR in PortInitialize()!");
            else
            {
S               if (pFlg == 1)
                {
                    sPortFlg = true;                     // set init flag for send port
                    hsPort = pParam->hPort;              // reserve the send port handler
                    strcpy(pName->sComPort, cPort);      // reserve the send port name
                }
T               else
                {
                    rPortFlg = true;                     // set init flag for recv port
                    hrPort = pParam->hPort;              // reserve the recv port handler


                    strcpy(pName->rComPort, cPort);      // reserve the recv port name
                }
            }
            delete pParam;
U           delete pName;
            return ecRet;
    }
    void CMfcDoublePortsDlg::OnTest()
    {
            // TODO: Add your control notification handler code here
            ERR_CODE  ecRet = OK;
V           if (!sPortFlg || !rPortFlg)
            {
```

FIGURE 3.70 The source file `mfcDoublePortsDlg.cpp`. *(continued)*

```
            msg("No Initialization !");
            return;
        }
        pPortName pName  = new PortName;
        m_label.SetWindowText("");
W       ecRet = TestPort(pName->sComPort, pName->rComPort, 1);
        if (ecRet)
           msg("ERROR in TestPort()");
X       if (TestPassed)
           m_label.SetWindowText("Testing is Successful!");
Y       delete pName;
}
ERR_CODE CMfcDoublePortsDlg::TestPort(char *sPort, char *rPort, BOOL display)
{
        BYTE   sByte;
a       char   sData[16], rData[16];
        int    numByte = NUM_BYTE;
        ERR_CODE ecRet = OK;
b       CMfcDoublePortsApp* mfcDoubleApp = (CMfcDoublePortsApp*) AfxGetApp();
        CommPortClass* comPort = new CommPortClass;
c       comPort->handlePort = hrPort;
        comPort->iMaxChars  = NUM_BYTE;
d       for (sByte = START_BYTE; sByte <= MAX_BYTE; sByte++)
        {
            ecRet = mfcDoubleApp->PortWrite(hsPort, sByte, numByte);
            if (ecRet)
            {
                msg("PortWrite() is failed");
                TestPassed = FALSE;
                return EC_WRITE_FAIL;
            }
            sprintf(sData, "%c", sByte);
e           m_sendData.SetWindowText(sData);
            m_sendData.UpdateWindow();

f            ecRet = mfcDoubleApp->PortRead(comPort);
             if (ecRet)
             {
                 msg("PortRead() is failed");
                 TestPassed = FALSE;
                 return EC_READ_FAIL;
             }
g            sprintf(rData, "%c", comPort->bByte);
            m_readData.SetWindowText(rData);
            m_readData.UpdateWindow();

h           if (sByte != comPort->bByte)
            {
```

FIGURE 3.70 The source file `mfcDoublePortsDlg.cpp`. *(continued)*

```
                    TestPassed = FALSE;
                    return EC_TEST_FAIL;
               }
          }
i         TestPassed = TRUE;

          delete comPort;
          return ecRet;
}
j    void CMfcDoublePortsDlg::OnAbout()
     {
          // TODO: Add your control notification handler code here
          OnSysCommand(IDM_ABOUTBOX, NULL);
     }
     void CMfcDoublePortsDlg::OnExit()
     {
          // TODO: Add your control notification handler code here
          rPortFlg   = FALSE;
k         sPortFlg   = FALSE;
          TestPassed = FALSE;

l         if (sPortFlg && rPortFlg)
          {
               CloseHandle(hsPort);
               CloseHandle(hrPort);
          }
m         CDialog::OnOK();
     }
```

FIGURE 3.70 The source file `mfcDoublePortsDlg.cpp`.

F: The five member functions we added to this project are displayed in this message map area. Each member function is associated with a message that will activate the associated member function while the program is running.

G: `OnInitDialog()` is an important system initialization function in this source file. All significant initialization jobs should be processed under this function. This includes loading the system menu, loading the `About` dialog box menu, and setting the system icons.

H: This is where we take care of our initialization codes. We initialize three Boolean variables in this section. `sPortFlg` and `rPortFlg` represent the initialization status of our sending port and receiving port, respectively. The `TestPassed` flag is used to keep the testing status. All these variables are initialized to `False` at the beginning of the program.

I: The member function `OnSysCommand()` is used to display the default `About` dialog box. This function is provided by the system itself. If the function received a message with a message ID equal to `IDM_ABOUTBOX`, the system will call the member function `DoModal()` to run and display the default `About` dialog box. The reason we mention this here is that we will use this system function to display this default `About` dialog box in the next section.

J: Now let us discuss our user-defined member function. The first one is the `OnInit()` member function we added. To initialize the serial ports, the program calls a medium function, `startPort()`, to execute the setup for the serial ports. An error message will be displayed onscreen if this function encounters any mistakes, and the program will return to the calling function without any further action.

K: If the function startPort() is successful, a member function of the edit box control m_label, SetWindowText(), will be executed to display a label to show this initialization result in the dialog box.

L: Now we will enter the startPort() function. An integer variable portNum is declared under this function and is used to hold the port number entered from the keyboard. This portNum will be used as a position index for the character pointer array comPORT[] to obtain the port name associated.

M: A system function, UpdateData(), is executed to refresh all numeric values in the dialog box and make them available to the program. The program picks up the value that was entered from the keyboard as the sending port number in the Send Port edit box. The program then assigns this port number to the portNum we declared earlier. We subtract 1 from that value because the minimum port number entered from the keyboard is 1, but the minimum index of the character pointer array comPORT[] is 0.

N: Then the program calls the SetupPort() function to initialize the sending serial port. This function has three arguments. The first one is the port name, which we can obtain from the character pointer array comPORT[] based on the index portNum as we did in the previous step. The second argument is the baud rate, which we can directly obtain from the value of the Baud Rate edit box m_baudRate. The third argument is an integer flag used to indicate which port is being initialized. A value of 1 on that flag means the current port is the sending port, and a value of 2 means the current port is the receiving port. An error message will be displayed if this function call fails, and the program will return to the calling function without any further action.

O: Similar to the last step, the program picks up the receiving port number from the Recv Port edit box m_recvPort. To correctly obtain the associated port name from the character pointer array comPORT[], we subtract 1. This time the third argument of the function SetupPort() should be 2, which indicates that the current port to be initialized is the receiving port. An error message will be displayed onscreen if this function call fails, and the program will return to the calling function.

P: At the beginning of the SetupPort() function, some local variables and structure pointers are declared. The structure pointer pParam, which will be passed into the PortInitialize() function, is used to store the initialization information for the port to be initialized. Also, this structure will be used to reserve the opened port handler as the initialization is successfully completed and returned. The pName is used to reserve the initialized port name, and this port name will be used in the following steps. The SetupPort() function needs to call the interfacing function PortInitialize(), located in our main thread class file mfcDoublePorts.cpp, to perform the initialization job to the serial port. In order for us to access that interfacing function, we need to call the global function AfxGetApp() to obtain a pointer that points to our main thread class file. The following command fulfills this functionality:

```
CMfcDoublePortsApp* mfcDoubleApp = (CMfcDoublePortsApp*) AfxGetApp();
```

The global function AfxGetApp() will return an object with a type of CWinApp, so a cast is needed to convert the default object to our main thread object.

Q: Before we can call the interfacing function PortInitialize() to set up the port, we first need to check if the port has already been initialized. By checking the initialization status flag sPortFlg, which is the status of the sending port, and the integer flag pFlg, which indicates which port is being initialized, we can identify whether the sending port has been initialized. If both flags are True, meaning the sending port has already been initialized, we return the control to the calling function without any operation.

We use the same method to check whether the receiving port has been initialized, and return the control to the calling function if the initialization has taken place.

R: If any of the ports have not been initialized, we call the interfacing function `PortInitialize()` by using the object pointer `mfcDoubleApp` we obtained earlier to set up the port. An error message will be displayed if this initialization fails.

S: If the port initialization is successful, we must reserve the initialized port information. We identify the initialized port by using the integer flag `pFlg`. The initialized port should be the sending port if the value of that flag is `1`; otherwise, the initialized port is the receiving port. For the sending port, we need to reserve the initialization status of that port by setting the flag `sPortFlg` to `True`. Also, we must pick up the initialized sending port handler from the structure `pParam` (`pParam->hPort`) and assign it to the member variable `hsPort`. Finally, we need to copy the initialized sending port name to the structure `pName` to reserve this port name.

T: For the receiving port, we execute similar procedures to reserve the receiving port information.

U: Before exiting this function, we need to use the `delete` to clean up the memory spaces allocated for the two structures `pParam` and `pName`.

V: If we click the `TEST` button in the dialog box while the program is running, a message will be created and that message will be passed to the member function `OnTest()` for further processing. The first thing our program must do is to confirm that both serial ports have been successfully initialized. It does this by checking the initialization status flags `sPortFlg` and `rPortFlg`. If any of the ports have not been initialized, a message will be displayed onscreen reminding us to initialize the port. A port name structure `pName` is then generated and used to pass the port names to the `TestPort()` function. A member function `SetWindowText()` is called to clean up the label displayed by the Static Text object `m_label`, making it ready to display the next new label.

W: The `TestPort()` function is called to begin the process of testing the serial ports. This function needs three arguments. The first one is the sending port name, the second one is the receiving port name, and the last one is a Boolean flag used to indicate whether the testing result should be displayed in the dialog box. Because we have reserved both sending port and receiving port names in the structure `pName` (in the steps S and T), we can pick up both port names from this structure and pass them to the `TestPort()` function. We use a `1` as the value of the last argument to tell the system that we want to display the testing result. An error message will be displayed if this function calling fails.

X: If the test is successful, the testing status flag `TestPassed` should be `True`. In this case, we need to update the label to "`Testing is successful!`"

Y: Before exiting this function, our program must execute the `delete` to clean up the memory space allocated for the structure `pName`.

Now let us take a closer look at the `TestPort()` function. This is the core function in this project, so we will discuss it step by step (refer to Figure 3.70):

a: Local variables are declared at the beginning of this function. The `sData[]` and `rData[]` variables are character arrays, and they are used to store the converted sent and received data in a character format because this format is easy to display in the edit control of the dialog box.

b: In the `TestPort()` function, our program needs to call the interfacing functions `PortWrite()` and `PortRead()` to perform the testing of the serial ports. However, these two functions are defined in our main thread class file `mfcDoublePorts.cpp`. In order to access the functions, as we did before, we must first obtain a pointer that points to our main thread object. By calling the global function AfxGetApp(), our program can get that pointer, mfcDoubleApp. We also need to create a structure pointer, comPort, which will hold the port information for the receiving port.

c: After the structure pointer comPort is generated, the program can reserve the receiving port information, such as the receiving port handler and the maximum receiving bytes, to this structure. Later on, the program can pass this structure into the PortRead() function, and the latter can pick up the port information from the structure and use it easily.

d: A for loop is used for this testing function. The program will send a sequence of ASCII data to the sending port, and then the same data will be picked up from the receiving port. If the sent and received data sequences are identical, meaning that the test has been successful, a testing success message will be displayed on the label object. The ASCII sequence is from 0 to 9, and from A to Z. First, the PortWrite() interfacing function is called by the pointer mfcDoubleApp we obtained earlier. The port handler, hsPort, is mapped to the sending port handler. If this function fails, an error message will be displayed onscreen, and the testing status flag, TestPassed, will be reset to False. The program will then return to the calling function.

e: If the function calling is successful, our program must execute the system function sprintf() to convert the sent data from a byte to a character. The member function SetWindowText() must then be called to display this data on the edit control object m_sendData. Sometimes a call to the member function UpdateWindow() is necessary to make sure the data will be properly displayed on the edit control object.

f: After the data has been successfully sent from the sending port, the program must pick up that data from the receiving port by executing another interfacing function, PortRead(). This function has only one argument, the data structure pointer comPort, which was created earlier. We have already reserved the receiving port handler and other port information in this structure, so our program can pass it to the PortRead() function, and the latter can obtain the necessary information from this structure. An error message will appear onscreen if this function fails, and the testing status flag, TestPassed, will be reset to False. In this case, the program will return to the calling function without further action.

g: If the function is successful, our program must pick up the returned data from the data structure comPort, convert it to the character variable, and finally display it on the Read Data edit control m_readData by calling the member function SetWindowText(). A call to the member function UpdateWindow() is necessary to make sure the data is displayed on the edit control object correctly.

h: If the data sent out is not identical to the data received, the TestPassed flag will be reset to False, which means that the testing has failed. In this case, an error message will be returned to the calling function.

i: If there is no error, then the test has been successful, and the testing status flag TestPassed will be set to True. Before exiting this function, our program must use the Delete command to clean up the memory space allocated for the comPort data structure.

j: If we click the ABOUT button from the dialog box when the program is running, a message will be created by the system and be passed to the function OnAbout() to be processed further. As we mentioned in step I, a default About dialog box is provided by the system when we create this project. A member function, OnSysCommand(), is used to activate and display this About dialog box. It is easy to call this function because it is defined in the current dialog box class file. When calling this function, the first argument should have the message ID, IDM_ABOUTBOX, and the second argument can be NULL because we don't have any other system parameters to pass to the function.

k: To execute the OnExit() function, our program must reset all the flags used in the project.

l: The program must now close all the port handlers it has opened. An error message will occur if we try to close the handler of an unopened port, so the program must first check each port to see whether it has been opened. The program inspects the port initialization status flags, sPortFlg and rPortFlg, respectively. If no port has been opened, the program simply returns control to the calling function. If any of the ports have been opened, the CloseHandle() function is called to close it.

m: Finally, we place CDialog::OnOK() at the end of the OnExit() function. This is very important, and we may encounter an error if we don't include this statement here. It tells the system that we want to exit the project, and the system will then handle all other cleanup jobs necessary for a smooth exit.

It has been a long journey, but we have finally finished writing the code for our source files. Click the Build|Build mfcDoublePorts.exe item to build the project. If no error occurs, click Build|Execute mfcDoublePorts.exe to run the project. The main dialog box will be displayed onscreen, as shown in Figure 3.71.

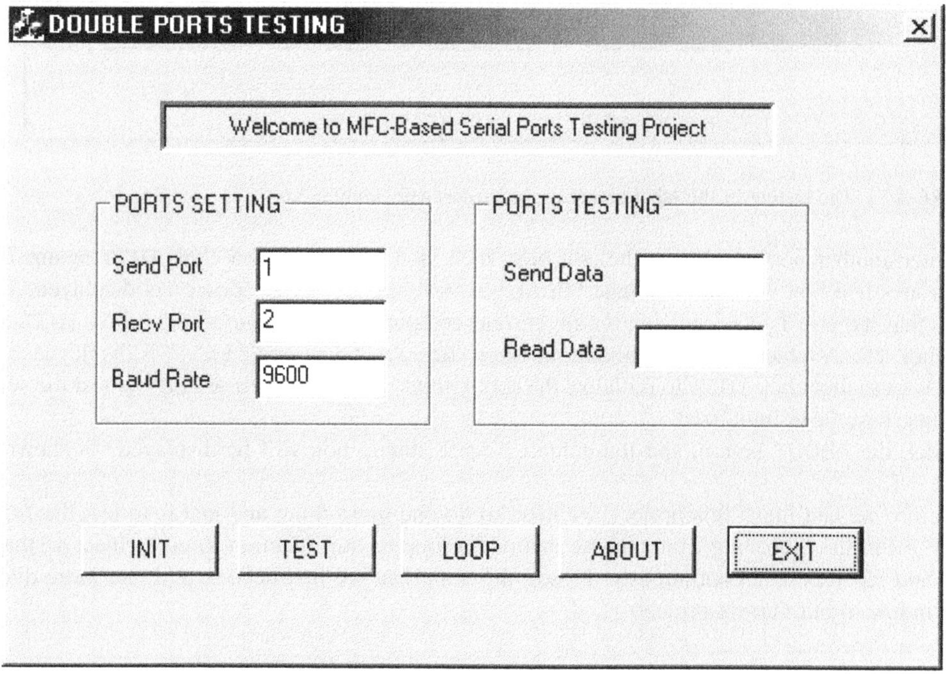

FIGURE 3.71 The running dialog of the project mfcDoublePorts.

The default ports are COM1 and COM2, which are mapped to the sending and receiving ports, respectively. The default baud rate is 9600. Enter 5 in the Send Port edit box and 6 in the Recv Port edit box, because on our machine the two available serial ports are COM5 and COM6.

Click INIT to initialize the serial ports. If the initialization is successful, the message "The ports have been initialized" will be displayed on the m_label object, which is located just above the Command buttons. Then click TEST to test these two ports. The sent and received data will be displayed in two edit boxes, `Send Data` and `Read Data`. If the testing is successful, the message "`Testing is successful!`" will be displayed on the label, as shown in Figure 3.72.

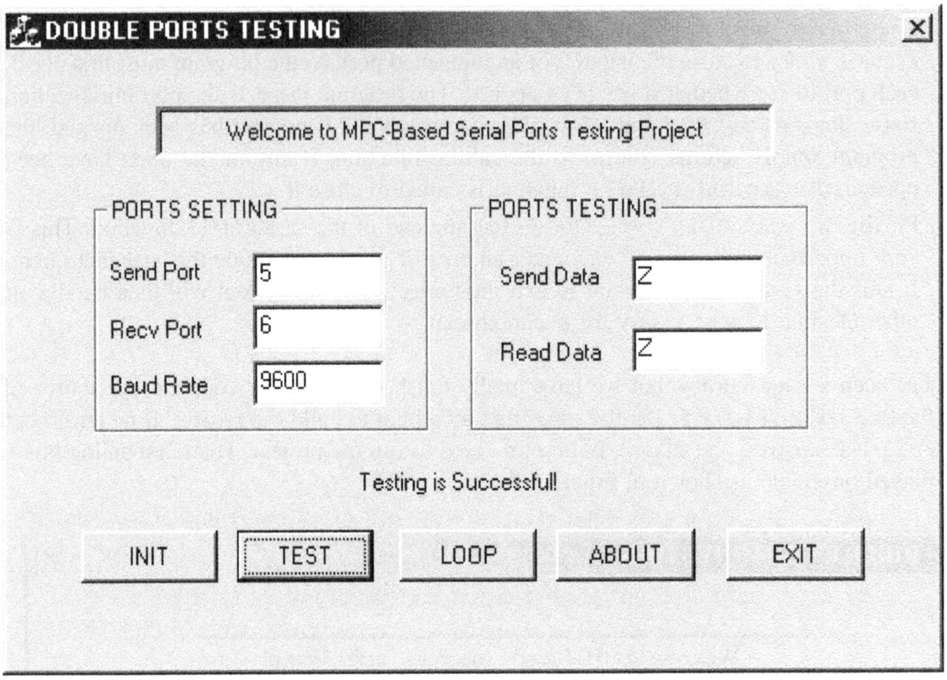

FIGURE 3.72 The testing of the label object in the project mfcDoublePorts.

Enter another port number in the edit box, such as `3` or `4`, and then click `INIT` again. This time a message box with the message "`Unable to open the port`" is displayed. This means that the port is not available on the current computer. If we forget to first click `INIT` and then click `TEST`, a message box with the message "`No Initialization!`" is displayed. This reminds us to first click `INIT` to initialize the serial ports; we can then click `TEST` to test the serial ports that have been initialized.

Click the `ABOUT` button, and the default `About` dialog box will be displayed, as shown in Figure 3.73.

Before we can finish this project, we need to do one more thing and that is to test the `LOOP` button. As in the preceding example, we can add a loop-testing function to our project so that it sends and receives data continuously. To add this function, we first need to add one more dialog box window to our current project.

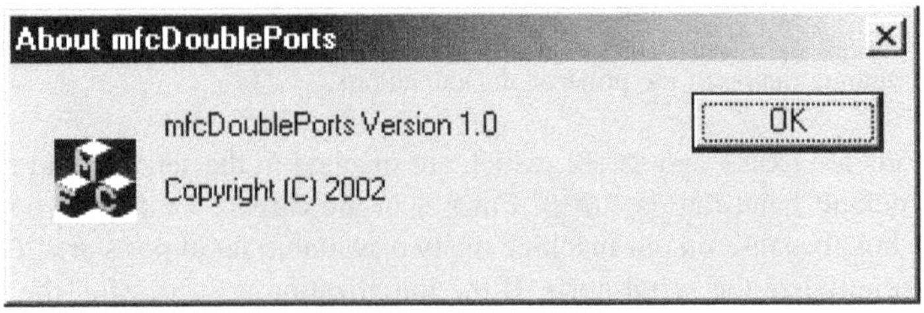

FIGURE 3.73 The about dialog in the project mfcDoublePorts.

Click the ResourceView tab in the workspace and right-click the Dialog icon. Select the Insert Dialog item from the popup menu to open a default dialog box window. Delete the default Cancel button and move the OK button to the bottom of the dialog box. Then make the following modifications:

- Right-click the dialog box, and select the Properties item from the popup menu to open its Dialog Properties box.
- Enter IDD_LOOP_DLG in the ID: field, and enter LOOP DIALOG in the Caption: field.
- Click the Close button located at the upper-right corner of the dialog box to close the box.
- Right-click the dialog box again, and select the ClassWizard... item from the popup menu to open the Adding a Class dialog box.
- In the opened dialog box, keep the default selection Create a new class unchanged, and click OK to open the New Class dialog box.
- Enter LoopDlg in the Name: field, and then click OK to save this newly created class and close the dialog box.

Now a new class file, LoopDlg.h and LoopDlg.cpp, has been created and added to our current project. In addition, let us include the following components to our loop dialog box:

- Static Text: ID: IDC_STATIC Caption: Enter the Loop Number
- Edit Box: ID: IDC_LOOP_EDIT

Right-click the edit box, and select the ClassWizard... item from the popup menu to open the MFC ClassWizard dialog box. Select the edit box we've just added by clicking its ID IDC_LOOP_EDIT from the Control IDs: list. Then click the Member Variables tab and hit the Add Variable... button to open a dialog box. In the opened dialog box, select int from the Variable type: box, and type loopNum in the Member variable name: field after the m_ character, as shown in Figure 3.74. Click OK to close this dialog box, and do the same to close the MFC ClassWizard dialog box.

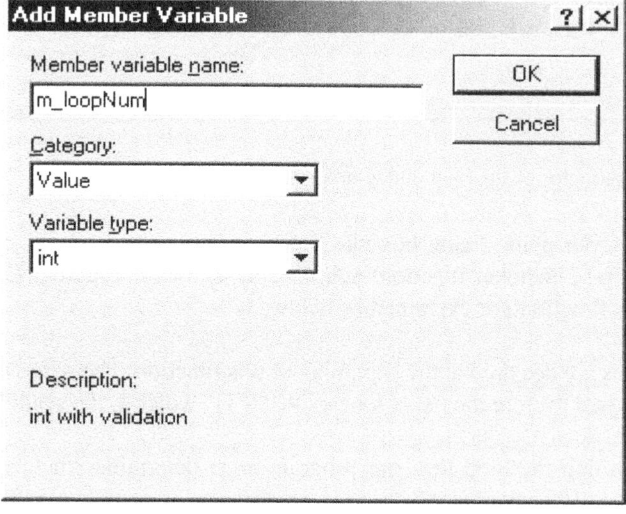

FIGURE 3.74 The add member variables dialog.

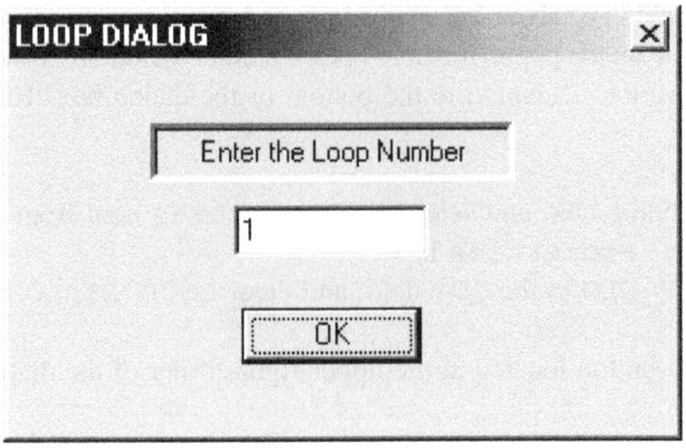

LOOP DIALOG

Enter the Loop Number

1

OK

FIGURE 3.75 The loop input dialog box.

Our finished dialog box should match the one shown in Figure 3.75. Don't be worried about the number in the edit box now.

Now click the `FileView` tab in the workspace to open our source files. Notice that the newly added classes (`LoopDlg.h` and `LoopDlg.cpp`) have been added to our project. We won't need to edit these files much because we will only use this dialog box to pick up user input, which is represented by the loop number.

However, we do need to slightly modify the source file `LoopDlg.cpp` to change the default value of the loop number. Double-click the file `LoopDlg.cpp` to open it, browse to the constructor of this class file, and change the default loop number `m_loopNum` from `0` to `1`. This means that loop testing will be executed at least once. The code in this section is shown in Figure 3.76.

```
/////////////////////////////////////////////////////////////////////////////
// LoopDlg dialog

LoopDlg::LoopDlg(CWnd* pParent /*=NULL*/)
        : CDialog(LoopDlg::IDD, pParent)
{
        //{{AFX_DATA_INIT(LoopDlg)
        m_loopNum = 1;                          // set the default loop number
        //}}AFX_DATA_INIT
}
......
```

FIGURE 3.76 The constructor of the loop dialog box.

Now double-click our main dialog box class object file, `mfcDoublePortsDlg.cpp`, and browse to the `OnLoop()` member function. Add the code shown in Figure 3.77 into this function.

The codes in this function are explained as below:

A: Local variables are declared at the beginning of this function. The `snPort` and `rnPort` variables are used to store the index for `comPORT[]`, which is the sending and receiving port name arrays.

B: Before performing the loop test, our program must determine whether the ports have been initialized. When we run the program, an error message will be displayed reminding us to initialize and set up any of the ports that have not been initialized.

C: The label object `m_label` is cleaned up and ready to display the next new label.

```
  void CMfcDoublePortsDlg::OnLoop()
  {
          // TODO: Add your control notification handler code here
          int  Numloop;
A         int  snPort, rnPort;
          ERR_CODE  ecRet = OK;
B         if (!sPortFlg || !rPortFlg)
          {
               msg("No Initialization !");
               return;
          }
C         m_label.SetWindowText("");
D         LoopDlg  lpDlg;
          UpdateData(TRUE);
          snPort = m_sendPort - 1;
          rnPort = m_recvPort - 1;
E         if (lpDlg.DoModal() == IDOK)
          {
               lpDlg.UpdateWindow();
F              for (Numloop = 0; Numloop < lpDlg.m_loopNum; Numloop++)
               {
                   ecRet = TestPort(comPORT[snPort], comPORT[rnPort], 1);
                   if (ecRet)
                      msg("ERROR in TEST");
               }
G              m_label.SetWindowText("Loop Testing is Successful!");
          }
  }
```

FIGURE 3.77 The OnLoop() member function.

D: Here we create a new object of the `LoopDlg` class, `lpDlg`. The member function `UpdateData()` is executed to refresh all numeric values in our main dialog box, such as the port numbers on `m_sendPort` and `m_recvPort`, and make them available to the program. The numeric values of the two edit boxes, `m_sendPort` and `m_recvPort`, are picked up and assigned to the two local variables `snPort` and `rnPort`, respectively. Subtraction is necessary to match the port number and the index in the port name character array.

E: A `DoModal()` member function is called to install and display our loop dialog box. When we run the program, this function will wait until we click `OK` in the dialog box. Then an `UpdateWindow()` member function will be called to update all numeric values in the dialog box (including the loop number we enter, which will be stored in `m_loopNum`).

F: Next, a `for` loop is used to repeatedly send and receive data from the ports. The maximum loop number is determined by the loop number `m_loopNum` that we entered in the loop dialog box as the program is running. Inside the loop, the `TestPort()` function is called to perform the actual testing of the serial ports. An error message will be displayed if this function fails.

G: If each testing loop is successful, a message, "`Testing is successful!`," will be displayed on the label object `m_label`.

One more thing we need to confirm is the header file of this loop dialog box, `LoopDlg.h`. As we mentioned in step A in Figure 3.70, we must include this header file in our main dialog box class file, `mfcDoublePortsDlg.cpp`. Otherwise, the compiler will not have any knowledge about our loop dialog box. Thus, we should include this header file at the top of our main dialog box class file (as shown in step A in Figure 3.70), to make the compiler aware that we have a loop dialog box available in this project.

Now let us rebuild our project and then run it. Press `Ctrl+F5` on the keyboard. When the main dialog box appears, enter `6` in the `Send Port` edit box, and enter `5` in the `Recv Port` edit box. Click `INIT` to initialize these two serial ports. A message will be displayed on the label to indicate if the initialization has been successful.

Continue to click `TEST` to test these two serial ports. A message will also display on the label to indicate whether our testing is successful or not.

Now click `LOOP`, and our loop dialog box will be displayed at the top of our main dialog box, as shown in Figure 3.78. The default loop number is `1`, not `0`, because we modified this default value in the constructor of our loop dialog box. Enter `10` in the edit box, and click `OK` in the loop dialog box to close it. We will find that the sending and receiving data will be alternatively displayed in two edit boxes, `Send Data` and `Read Data`, within our main dialog box. Finally, if no errors have occurred, a message will be displayed on the label to indicate that the test has been successful.

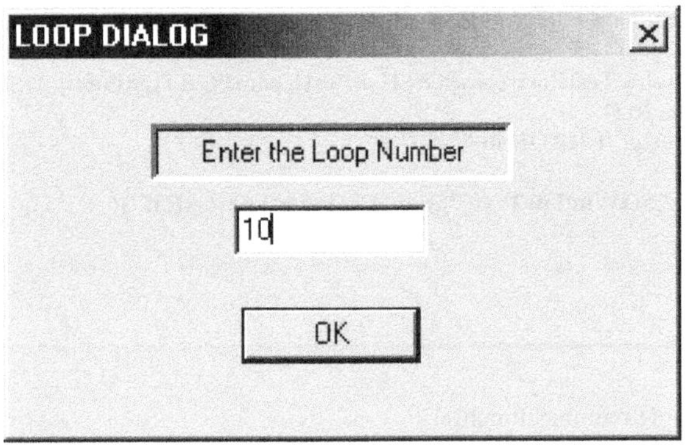

FIGURE 3.78 The running status of the loop dialog box.

We can make modifications to our testing program as needed. For example, we can switch the sending and receiving ports after one loop is finished. To do this, we would change the receiving port from port `6` to port `5`, change the sending port from port `5` to port `6`, and test both ports again.

The source files and executable files for this project are stored on the attached CD, in the `Chapter 3\mfcDoublePorts` folder. You can load these files to your own machine to test them. Remember to install the hardware properly on your computer before attempting to test this project.

3.4 RS-485 SERIAL PORT COMMUNICATION

A RS-485 serial port communication program is discussed in this section.

3.4.1 OVERVIEW

In Section 1.9 in Chapter 1, we discussed RS-485 serial port communications. As we mentioned, RS-232 is an unbalanced data transmission system because both the transmitter (pin 3 in DB-9) and receiver terminals (pin 2 in DB-9) have a voltage offset relative to the ground (pin 5 in DB-9). This voltage offset should be negative for both the transmitting and receiving terminals if no signal is being transmitted on the ports. If signals are being transmitted on the terminals, both terminals will have alternate voltage offsets between positive 12 volts and negative 12 volts.

Recall that RS-485 is a so-called balanced communication system. In this communication protocol, the transmitted data is presented on the transmission lines in the differential mode. (This is unlike RS-232, in which an offset voltage exists between the signal and the reference line.) The RS-485 can therefore effectively eliminate the affects of common noises and disturbances around the transmission lines. In the following section, we discuss RS-485 serial communications and supply a sample application.

3.4.2 An RS-485 Application for Real-Time Control

This section describes how to use an RS-485 transmission system, incorporating a sequence of DC motors, to control the speed of fluid flow. The hardware in this example is the `LabVIEW` NI-485 Serial Interface Card Module, manufactured by National Instruments Corporation. The advantages of using this module is that the overhead of RS-232 serial communication can be effectively avoided and that multiple asynchronous communication channels can be realized simultaneously. By using NI-485, we can significantly improve the communication rate and increase the distance over which we can perform the data communications.

The NI-485 module, `PCI-485/4`, is used in this testing platform. Four ports are available on the PCI-485/4 interface card. Figure 3.79 shows the basic structure of this card.

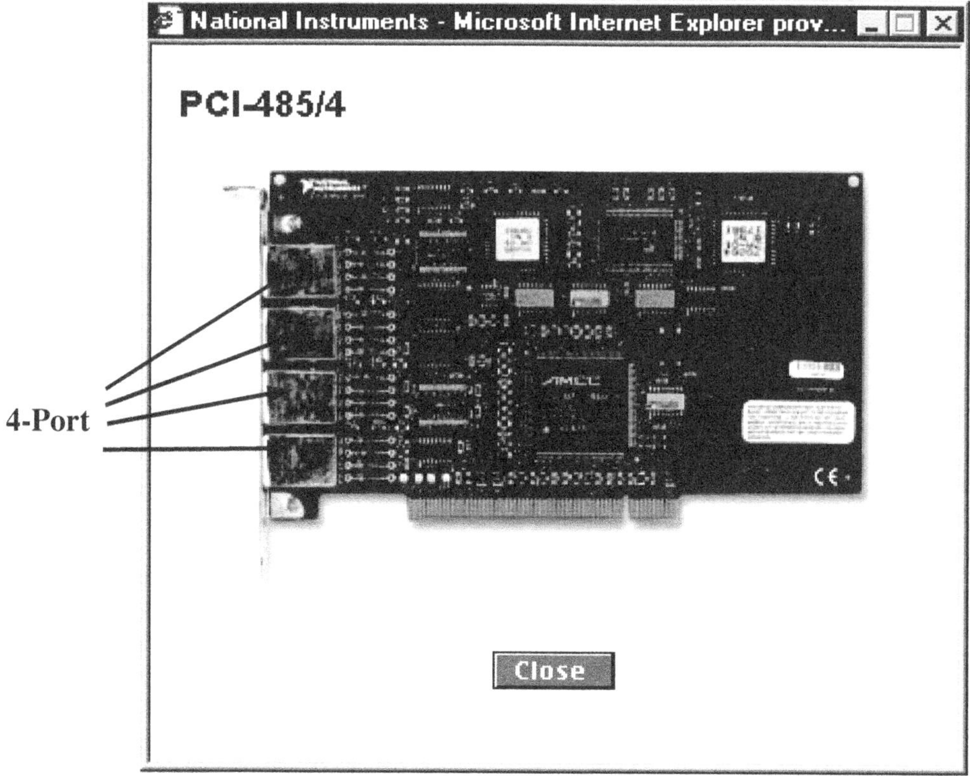

FIGURE 3.79 The NI PCI-485 card.

Four nonisolated converter cables are needed to connect to the four ports on the interface card, and these cables can be connected to the control units. The output of each converter is a standard DB-9 serial port in RS-485 communication mode. We need another converter cable (home-made shown in Figure 3.83) to connect to the port of the motor speed control board and achieve real-time control of the motor's speed, which will be discussed in the following section.

National Instruments provides both the hardware and the installation software for this NI-485 interface card, and the software includes the standard Win32 serial drivers for all the ports installed on this NI-485 card. When developing the application, remember to use the standard Microsoft Windows serial communication functions to access these drivers and ports. We need to develop the application code to communicate with the NI-485 card and set up normal communication with the outside world.

Let us begin this project with the setup and installation of the RS-485 transmission system provided by National Instruments. The installation sequence is as follows:

1. Install the installation software (including the driver) for the NI-485 transmission system.
2. Install the interface card in a free peripheral component interface (PCI) slot on our computer.
3. Identify and run the diagnostic test for the NI-485 card installed.

We must follow this installation sequence exactly to properly install the NI-485 transmission system. It is crucial to install the software first and then the hardware (the NI-485 interface card). Errors or abnormal performances may occur if the installation is not performed in this sequence.

3.4.2.1 Installing and Setting Up the NI-485

Insert the CD provided by NI into your CD-ROM drive, and follow these instructions to finish the installation of the software:

1. Select `Start|Settings|Control Panel` to open the Control Panel.
2. Double-click the `Add/Remove Programs` icon in the Control Panel to launch the `Add/Remove Programs` dialog box. The `Add/Remove Programs` dialog box appears.
3. Click the `Install` or `Add New Programs` button.
4. When prompted, click the `Next` or (CD or Floppy) button to proceed. The software installation wizard appears.
5. The setup wizard will guides you through the necessary steps to install the NI-485 serial software. You can go back and change values where appropriate by clicking the `Back` button. When you've finished, you can exit the setup wizard by clicking the `Cancel` button.

When the software is successfully installed, you can install the `PCI-485/4` interface card on your computer. Be sure to turn off and unplug your computer first; then insert the interface card into a free PCI slot. Finally, start the computer and follow these steps to perform the diagnostic test provided on the CD:

1. Click `Start|Programs|National Instruments|NI-Serial|Diagnostic`.
2. Click the `Start` button and the testing results will be displayed in a dialog box, as shown in Figure 3.80
3. Click `Exit` to end the diagnostic test.

The installed ports are port 5 through port 8, which are the default ports installed on the machine by the NI installation software.

Now let us set up the control mode for each port:

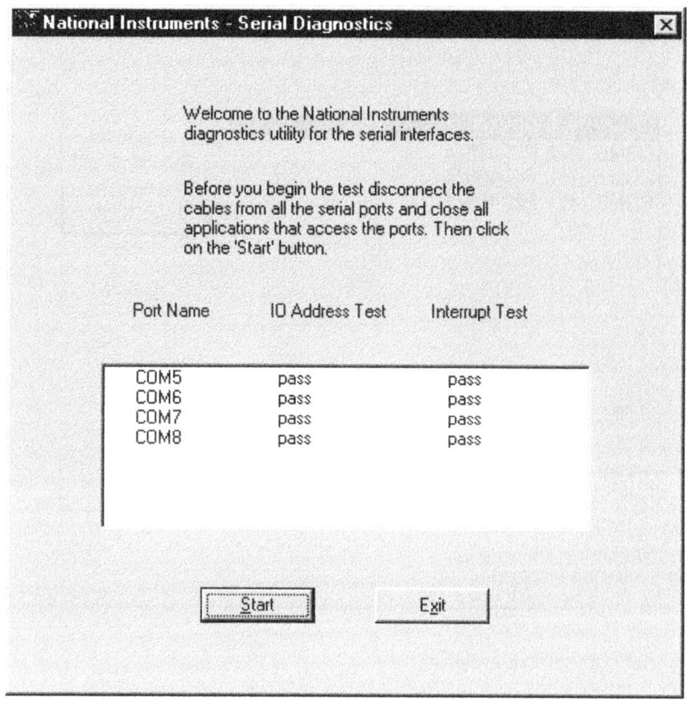

FIGURE 3.80 The NI diagnostics utility dialog.

1. Click `Start|Settings|Control Panel` to open the Control Panel.
2. Double-click the `NI Port` icon on the Control Panel. A dialog box will be displayed, as shown in Figure 3.81.
3. Highlight one of the ports, such as COM5, and click the `Settings...` button. Another dialog box will pop up, as shown in Figure 3.82.
4. Click the `Transceiver Mode:` list box and select `2 Wire TxRdy Auto` mode from the list. (See Figure 3.82.)

This completes the mode setup for one port; all of the other ports (COM6, COM7, and COM8) will need to be set up the same way. The reason we select this communication mode is because the current port and cable in the motor control system operates in two-wire mode. After this setup, you need to reboot your computer to activate the settings you've made for the card.

3.4.2.2 NI-485 Serial Port Setup and Installation

On our old motor speed control system, the original data transmission system is an RS-232 with a two-wire mode. We must now set up a connection between the RS-232 port and our RS-485 port to establish an interface between the old system and the new one. We need to connect the positive transmitter terminal (pin 8 on a DB-9) with the positive receiver terminal (pin 4 on a DB-9) on the RS-485 DB-9 port (A). We also must connect the negative transmitter terminal (pin 9) with the negative receiver terminal (pin 5) on the RS-485 DB-9 port (B). We can consider the first connection terminal A, and the second connection terminal B; these can be mapped to a typical RS-485 two-wire mode connection. Then we can connect terminal A to the transmitting terminal (pin 3), and terminal B to the receiving terminal (pin 2) on a standard RS-232 DB-9 port, which is shown in Figure 3.83.

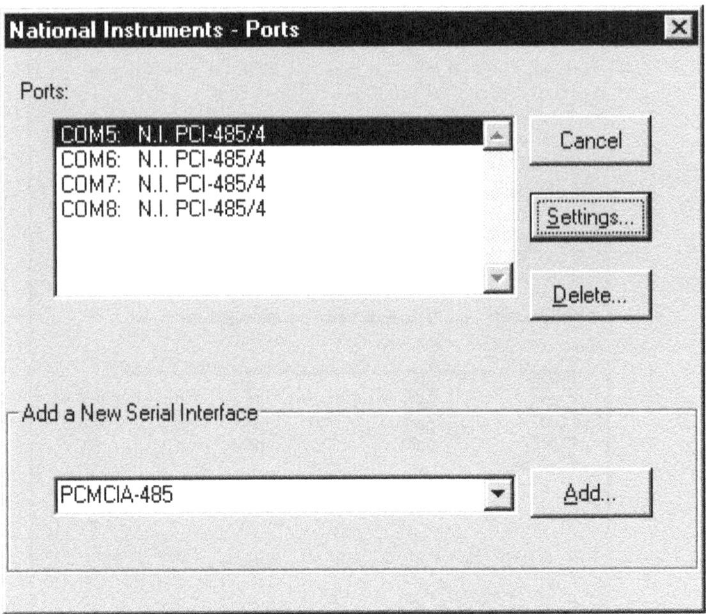

FIGURE 3.81 The serial port selection dialog.

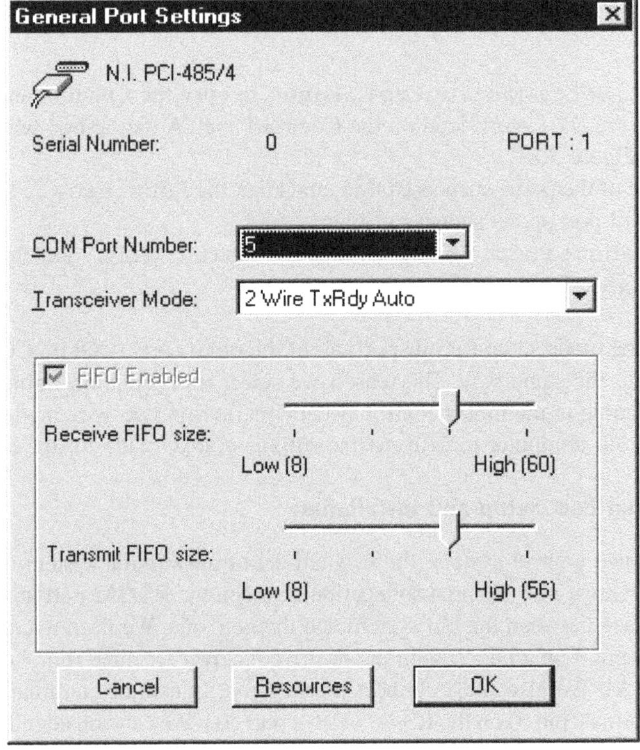

FIGURE 3.82 The serial port mode settings dialog.

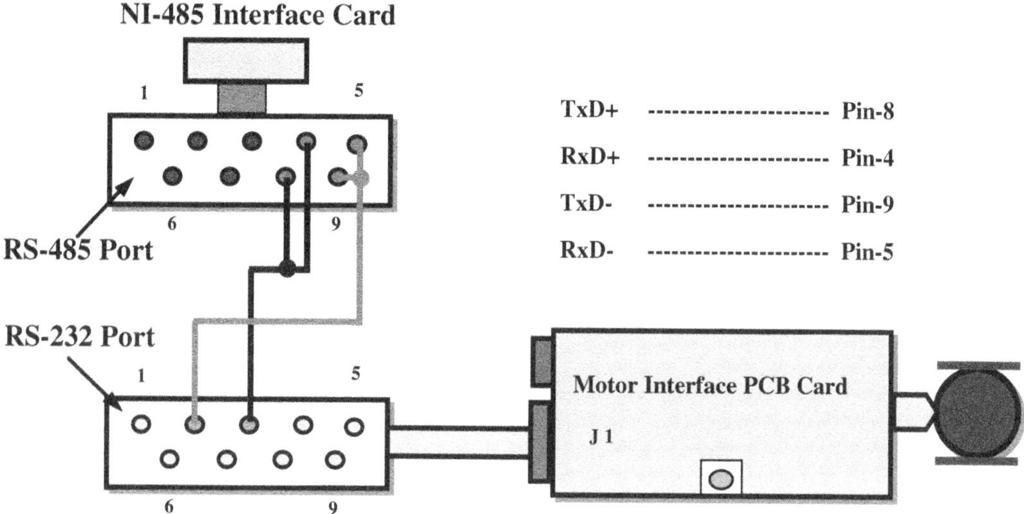

FIGURE 3.83 The RS-485 hardware connection.

The connection shown in Figure 3.83 is called `2-Wire TxRdy Auto` mode for the RS-485 communication protocol. At this point, we have finished the installation of the NI-485 module `PCI-485/4` transmission system.

3.4.2.3 Software Implementation with the NI-485

After the installation of the NI-485 module, we can implement any project source code we've developed in this chapter, such as `SimpleCOM`, `mfcCOMTest`, `SimpleCOM2`, `DoublePorts`, and `mfcDoublePorts`. All these source code files are compatible with the NI-485 transmission system.

3.5 CHAPTER SUMMARY

The serial interfaces implemented in the Visual C++ 6.0 environment have been discussed in detail in this chapter. These serial interfaces are designed to run in protected mode so they can work in multitasking operating systems. First, a single-loop serial port testing program was developed to show readers how to communicate with and test a serial port in the Visual C++ 6.0 environment. A more complicated example, a double-loop serial port testing program, was discussed and developed following the single-loop testing program. An MFC-based serial port testing program was also developed to illustrate how to use the `Document-View` class models to develop an example of OOP serial data communications. The RS-485 serial port communication was discussed in Section 3.4. Finally, an actual example of the RS-485 communication mode, interfacing with a smart motor control system, was provided to show readers how to actually implement the RS-485 mode to communicate with the peripheral devices via the serial port.

4 Serial Port Programming in Visual BASIC

4.1 INTRODUCTION

Visual Basic is a very popular high-level programming language that has been widely implemented in all fields of our society because of its simplicity. Visual Basic is one of the easiest languages to learn and use, especially for people who do not have much programming experience.

Visual Basic is also a powerful language that can be implemented both in high-level commercial applications, such as database applications and Internet developments, and in real-time control applications, such as data acquisitions and feedback controls.

In the early days, Visual Basic was not considered a good candidate for real-time control or data acquisition applications because of its relatively slow processing and running speed compared with that of C/C++. This situation has been significantly changed with development of the more advanced semiconductor technologies and high-speed processors applied in today's computer and computer control systems. Compared with a 200 MHz CPU, a 4 GHz processor implemented in one of today's computers can significantly improve the performance of programs developed in Visual Basic. For relatively simple applications developed in Visual Basic, real-time control ability has become almost identical to the performance of equivalent programs developed in C/C++. Today, more and more data acquisition programs and real-time control applications are written in Visual Basic. Of course, for more complicated application programs, C/C++ is still a good candidate for high-speed and real-time control objectives.

Visual Basic itself has no ability to access low-level hardware. The purpose of developing Visual Basic was to improve the performance of programs originally developed in BASIC, which is an old *procedure-oriented* programming language. Visual Basic is an *object-oriented, event-driven* programming language, and as such it provides much better graphics and control than does the old BASIC programming language. The main application fields of Visual Basic include tools for developing data management, database access, and Internet applications. Many Visual Basic applications are developed and implemented in the commercial, hospital, and service fields. The designers of Visual Basic did not intend to develop a powerful language to access and control low-level hardware in real time, and thus, by itself, Visual Basic can neither access nor control low-level hardware. However, by using certain external interfaces, Visual Basic can easily and efficiently access and control low-level hardware.

In this chapter, we will concentrate on using Visual Basic programming to control serial ports. Visual Basic can access low-level hardware in the following three ways:

- Calling the Windows application program interfaces (Win32 APIs)
- Implementing the Active-X control, `MSComm`
- Calling the dynamic link libraries (DLLs) developed in C/C++

All of these methods depend on the Windows API functions.

To access the serial ports, a Visual Basic program needs to access and interface the UARTs that work as local controllers of the ports. In Chapter 2, we discussed accessing and interfacing the UARTs by using MS-DOS-compatible I/O system functions. The functions are stored in the system libraries and can easily be called by developers who want to access serial ports in a DOS environment. Recall that DOS is a single-task operating system (meaning that it can handle only one task at any moment), so under DOS, our programs can directly access and control low-level hardware by using system I/O functions. In a Windows environment, however, programs are prohibited from directly accessing and controlling the serial ports (as our programs were able to do in the DOS environment in Chapter 2), because the Windows operating system is a multitasking system. In Windows, all access to low-level hardware (such as the UART) is under the control of a special component, the I/O manager. Figure 4.1 shows a functional diagram of Visual Basic interfacing with low-level hardware—in this case, the serial ports.

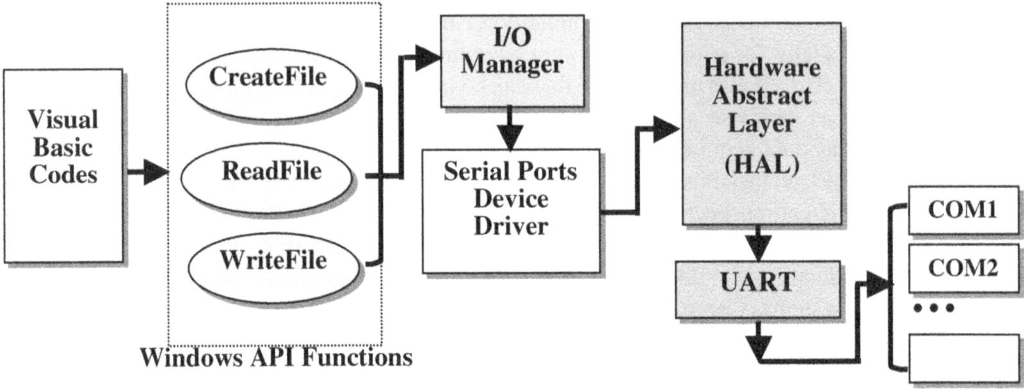

FIGURE 4.1 Functional diagram of the serial port interface.

To access the UART and serial ports, Visual Basic calls the Windows API functions. Each API function call is passed to the I/O manager and then translated to the associated serial port device driver (developed by the manufacturer of the serial device). Device driver are software applications that perform the interfacing between the API functions and their associated low-level hardware devices. In the Windows NT/2000/XP operating systems, the serial device driver needs to access the UART via another piece of software called the *Hardware Abstract Layer* (HAL), which is shown in Figure 4.1.

In the early days of programming, BASIC was an interpreter-executing programming language, which meant that the instructions in early BASIC programs were interpreted and executed line by line. First the instruction was interpreted from the high-level BASIC language to the low-level binary code; then that interpreted instruction was executed by the CPU. When the first instruction was completed, the CPU would interpret and execute the next instruction, line-by-line, until the entire program had run. This running mode is still available in Visual Basic today. In the Professional or Enterprise edition of Visual Basic 6.0, developers have the choice of compiling their programs to either of two destination formats:

- Standard Visual Basic P-Code (pseudo code) format
- Visual Basic Executable (native code) format

The P-Code format is an intermediate step between the high-level instructions in a Visual Basic program and the low-level native code executed by the computer's processor. At run time, Visual Basic translates each P-Code statement to native code and executes it line-by-line, as the old BASIC language did. However, by compiling directly to the Visual Basic Executable format, you can eliminate the intermediate P-Code step.

P-Code is a machine-independent format (and is very similar to the bytecode in the Java programming language). The advantage of translating a Visual Basic program to the P-Code format is that it can be portable to different operating systems and can be run on different machines. However, Visual Basic needs a separate tool to convert the P-Code to binary code (which is machine-dependent language) and then to run that binary code on a machine. This tool, called the *execution engine*, is a dynamic link library (`MSVBVM60.DLL`) that performs the conversion between the P-Code and machine code, and then executes the resulting machine code. One disadvantage of translating to P-Code is its slow execution speed. It takes a longer period of time to first translate the high-level code into P-Code, then interpret that P-Code to binary code, and finally execute the machine code. Keep in mind, too, that every single instruction in the program will be processed in this way, line-by-line, until the entire program has run.

Compiling a program to Visual Basic Executable format rather than P-code means that the program will be fully translated to the native instructions of the processor chip. This process is very similar to the compiling process in C/C++ and Visual C++ programming. Direct translation to native code will greatly speed up loops and mathematical calculations, and may also speed up calls to services provided by the execution engine `MSVBVM60.DLL`. As a result, the execution speed of the program can be significantly improved, even if it still needs the execution engine. (The services provided by this DLL include startup and shutdown code for the application, processing of forms and intrinsic controls, and such run-time functions as `Format` and `CLng`.) The performance of programs developed in Visual Basic is greatly improved by compilation; as mentioned earlier, for simple programs, execution speed can be matched to that of similar programs developed in C/C++ or Visual C++.

From the point of view of applications, Visual Basic is a very good language. Besides being useful for database applications, GUI designs, ActiveX controls, and OLE, COM, and DCOM applications, Visual Basic provides a wonderful user interface and excellent event handling explicitly because it is an object-oriented and event-driven language. In this chapter, we will use these advantages of Visual Basic in some real-time control systems to make things easier. Specifically, we will develop applications for serial port communications, data acquisitions, and testing that call the Win32 API functions to handle some high-speed operations.

This chapter is organized in the following format:

- We'll begin with a discussion of calling Windows APIs from within Visual Basic to access the serial ports. To illustrate these principles, we'll examine some real examples that use serial ports to perform data communications and data acquisitions.
- We'll discuss an Active-X control, `MSComm`, which is a popular serial ports tool applied in Visual Basic. The working principles of this tool will be illustrated in detail by several actual projects, which will perform interfacing to the 8-bit and 12-bit serial A/D converters for data acquisitions, serial data communications between two computers, and file transmission between master and slave computer systems.
- Finally we'll examine the interface between Visual Basic and the dynamic link libraries (DLLs), and develop some actual examples that incorporate these libraries.

4.2 CALLING WINDOWS API FUNCTIONS TO INTERFACE THE SERIAL PORTS

The first method used by Visual Basic to access the serial ports is to call the Win32 API functions. The other two methods are also based on the Win32 API functions, and we'll discuss these methods in the following sections.

4.2.1 Windows API Functions

Microsoft has developed a group of interface functions to help users conveniently access low-level hardware devices, such as the UART and serial ports; recall from Chapters 2 and 3 that these are the application program interface (API) functions. There are thousands of API functions defined in the Windows environment, and they are stored in various associated Dynamic Link Libraries that are part of the Windows operating system.

The Windows API contains thousands of functions, subroutines, types, and system constants that can be used in Visual Basic applications. In order to access and use any Windows API function, you must first declare the prototype of that function in Visual Basic format; this declaration will define a mapping relationship between the variables and components in Visual Basic and those in the C programming language.

Basically speaking, calling Windows API functions is very similar to calling the DLL functions developed in C/C++, because the Windows API itself is a collection of DLLs and all of the functions in the Window API DLLs are written in C language (albeit, not in C++).

As mentioned earlier, the Windows API provides thousands of functions, subroutines, and constants, that can be accessed and called within Visual Basic applications. Those functions and subroutines can be divided into the following categories:

- Standard API applications
- Window system information
- Graphics
- Interaction with the system registry

Windows system information is generally used to control and manage the system and keep it working properly. Icons and other graphics are used to help the user access the system input and output devices. In this chapter, we will concentrate on the first topic on the list, standard API applications, which allow the Visual Basic developer to access low-level hardware by using general-purpose API functions and subroutines from within the Visual Basic domain. The standard Dynamic Link Libraries (DLLs) that contain the API functions are listed in Table 4.1.

TABLE 4.1
The Standard Dynamic Link Libraries

Windows API DLL	Description
kernel32.dll	Windows 32 core base API library
gdi32.dll	Graphics Device Interface API library
user32.dll	User interface library
version.dll	Version control library
advapi32.dll	Advanced API libraries supporting numerous APIs
comdlg32.dll	Common dialog API library
shell32.dll	Windows 32 Shell API library
winmm.dll	Windows multimedia library
winspool.drv	Print spooler interface that contains the print spooler API calls

The top three DLLs in Table 4.1 contain the most popular or the core Windows API functions. Most API functions we will discuss and use in this chapter are located in these DLLs.

Incorporating a Windows API function in a program involves two steps: You first must declare the prototype of the API function in Visual Basic format, and then you can call the API function. Let us now take a look at the mapping relationship between the data types in Visual Basic programming language and those in the C programming language; this relationship is detailed in Table 4.2.

The first column lists the definitions of variables in the C/C++ domain. The second column shows the associated variable declarations in the Visual Basic domain. (`var` represents the nominal

TABLE 4.2
The Mapping Relationship Between Data Types in Visual Basic and C/C++

Visual Basic Data Type	VB Argument Type	C/C++ Data Type
ByVal *var* As String	ByVal	char (LPSTR)
ByVal *var* As Long	ByVal	Handle
ByVal *var* As Byte	ByVal	BYTE
ByVal *var* As Integer	ByVal	int, UINT
ByVal *var* As Long	ByVal	Long
var As Long	ByRef	Integer Pointer (LPINT)
ByVal *var* As Integer	ByVal	Short
ByVal *var* As Double	ByVal	Double
Sub procedure	N/A	Void
ByVal *var* As Integer	ByVal	WORD
ByVal *var* As Long	ByVal	DWORD
As Any or ByVal *var* As Long	ByRef	NULL
var As Any	ByRef	Void Pointer (LPVOID)
var As Integer	ByRef	LPWORD
ByVal *var* As Long	ByRef	LRESULT

name for that variable in the Visual Basic domain.) The third column is the data argument type. By default, this argument type is `ByRef`, which means that the argument is a reference or a pointer.

The prototype declaration of a Windows API function is generally identical to the declaration of a DLL function in Visual Basic. The formats for declaring a subroutine and a function are shown in Figure 4.2.

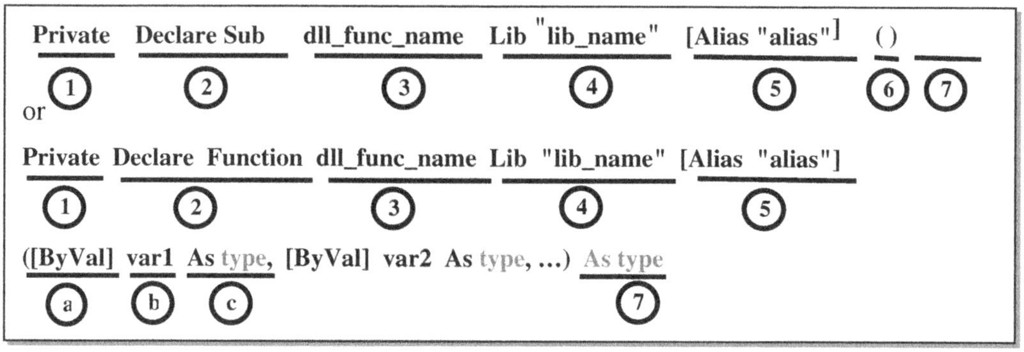

Private **Declare Sub** **dll_func_name** **Lib "lib_name"** **[Alias "alias"]** **( )**
① ② ③ ④ ⑤ ⑥ ⑦
or
Private **Declare Function** **dll_func_name** **Lib "lib_name"** **[Alias "alias"]**
① ② ③ ④ ⑤
([ByVal] var1 As type, [ByVal] var2 As type, ...) As type
ⓐ ⓑ ⓒ ⑦

FIGURE 4.2 Declaration formats for the Windows API functions.

The API DLL functions can be divided into two categories, based on their returned values when they mapped into the Visual Basic domain. If a function has no returned value (or if it returns a void), the function should be mapped to a Subroutine (`Sub`) in the Visual Basic domain. If a function does have a returned value (including `NULL`) the function should be mapped to a `Function`. The declarations of two functions are shown In Figure 4.2. The upper function has no returned value, so it is mapped to a `Sub` when it is declared in Visual Basic domain. (Notice that field 7 is blank; this is the location the data type of the returned value is defined.)

The lower function has a returned value, so it is mapped to a `Function` in the Visual Basic domain. Again, field 7 is used to define the returned data type. Let us now explore this function declaration process in detail.

4.2.1.1 Mapping to a Subroutine

The definition of subroutine formats for the Windows API functions are described below:

1: Private

This is a scope definition for the DLL function that will be used in the Visual Basic program. (Examine the upper function in Figure 4.2.) The `Private` keyword indicates that the declared DLL function can be used only by the event procedures in the current form. Event procedures defined in other forms cannot use this DLL function directly. In general, all DLL functions should be defined by this `Private` keyword. (You can use the code module to declare a `Public` DLL function, which will be accessible by all event procedures.)

2: Declare Sub

This is the function declaration keyword. Because this DLL function returns nothing, it should be declared a `Sub`.

3: dll_func_name

The original name of the DLL function should be placed here. For instance, `GetSystemTime` should be placed at this location for an API DLL function named `GetSystemTime()`.

4: Lib "libname"

The keyword `Lib` is used to indicate that the declared DLL function is located in a library. The library's name should followed the `Lib` keyword and be enclosed in a pair of quotation marks. For instance, the DLL function `GetSystemTime()` is located at the `kernel.dll` library, so in Figure 4.2 the name "`kernel`" should be placed after the `Lib` keyword. Generally, the entry here should includes both the library's name and the path where the library is located.

5: Alias "alias"

When working with Windows API functions that use Strings, you need to add an `Alias` clause to the function declaration to specify the correct format for the function. (This clause is necessary because some Windows API functions have different formats to meet requirements for different applications.) For example, the function `SetWindowText` has two formats: `SetWindowTextA` and `SetWindowTextW`. The former is used for the ANSI version of the function, and the latter is used for the Unicode version. There is no DLL function named `SetWindowText` in the Windows API DLLs; you will, however, find either `SetWindowTextA` or `SetWindowTextW`, depending on the code you're using. Thus, you have to use the `Alias` clause to specify the correct format for the function you wish to declare. Following are the two possible declarations for `SetWindowText`:

```
Private Declare Function SetWindowText Lib "user32" Alias
"SetWindowTextA" (ByVal..)

Private Declare Function SetWindowText Lib "user32" Alias
"SetWindowTextW" (ByVal..)
```

The upper declaration here is used for the ANSI version of the function, and the lower declaration is used for the Unicode version.

The `alias` string following the keyword `Alias` is a case-sensitive name, which means that the function name must exactly match the name of the original function.

A pair of square brackets would mean that an item is optional in some cases. For instance, most Windows API functions have only one format; when declaring one of these functions, you do not need to include the `Alias` clause.

6: ()

The parentheses are used to enclose all arguments of the DLL function.

7: (returned value type)

Because this is a Sub and has no any returned value, this field is left blank.

4.2.1.2 Mapping to a Function

The lower function in Figure 4.2 is declared in much the same way as the upper one. The only difference is that this function has a returned value, so it is declared a Function, not a Sub. Notice that field 7 is not blank here; it contains the returned value type of the function.

- **a:** In Visual Basic, when declaring an external function, we must explicitly indicate the method by which the argument is to be passed (for example, whether it will be passed by argument or by reference). This method is called the passing mode. Most functions are passed by value. Note that in some cases, this field is optional.
- **b:** This section contains the variable's name. (Note that this is simply a placeholder name; it will be replaced by the actual variable name in the program code.)
- **c:** This field is used to define the variable's type. (Refer to Table 4.2 for details on the type conversions between the Visual Basic and C/C++ domains.)

4.2.2 The API Viewer

Visual Basic provides a tool, the API Viewer, that allows developers to view and scan all the Windows API DLL functions. You can use the API Viewer to browse the declarations (API function protocols), constants, and subroutines included in any text file or Microsoft Jet database. You can also select any DLL function from the API Viewer and insert it into your application. To use this tool, you must first load the API Viewer into your Visual Basic project workspace. The API Viewer can be loaded into each of your Visual Basic projects and used for only that project. If you want the API Viewer to be loaded automatically when you generate new projects, you can develop a template and load the API Viewer into that template. You can save the template as a default project, and then later on, you can open and save it under different names for your specific projects.

Before you can load the API Viewer, you must open a Visual Basic project. In the newly opened Visual Basic project, click the Add-Ins|Add-In Manager menu item from the menu bar to open the Add-In Manager dialog box, which is shown in Figure 4.3.

In this dialog box, select VB 6 API Viewer from the Available Add-Ins list, and check both the Loaded/Unloaded and Load on Startup checkboxes from the Load Behavior information box, which is located in the lower-right corner of the Add-In Manager dialog box. Then click the OK button to load the API Viewer and close the dialog box.

Now we have loaded the API Viewer. Click the Add-Ins menu item again from the menu bar and you will find that the API Viewer has been added to this menu. Click it to open the API Viewer dialog box, which is shown in Figure 4.4.

When you open the API Viewer, notice that all control fields and buttons except for one text field: API Type. This field allows us to select different API components and add them into a Visual Basic project after the API functions are loaded. Three components are available from the API Type text field:

- **Constants:** If we select this component, we can select and add any API constants defined in the API library.
- **Declarations:** If we select this component, we can select and add any functions defined in the API library.
- **Types:** If we select this component, we can select and add any structure defined in the API library.

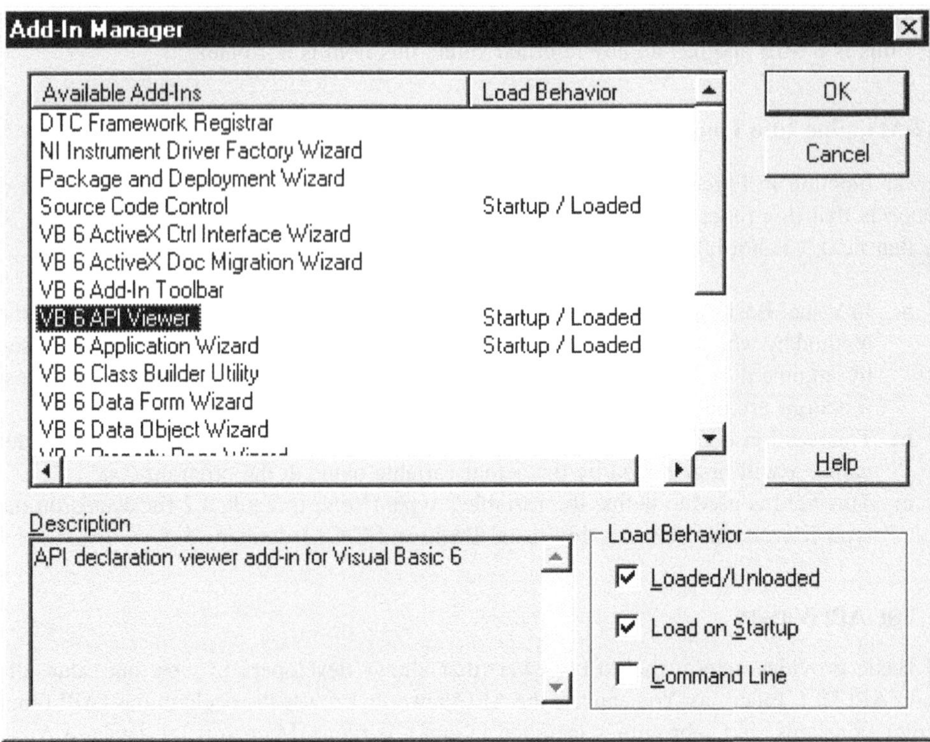

FIGURE 4.3 The API Viewer's `Add-In Manager` dialog box.

Now we need to load the API functions. Select the `File|Load Text File...` item from the menu bar in the API Viewer. Another dialog box is displayed, and you are asked to select one file from the following three files:

- APILOAD.TXT
- MAPI32.TXT
- Win32API.TXT

We are only concerned with the `Win32API.TXT` file, because it contains all the API DLL functions, in text format. Select this item and click the `Open` button to load the file. All DLL API functions are now loaded and displayed in alphabetical sequence on the `Available Items list`.

Now, select any API function, constant, or structure type from the list by clicking the item; then click the `Add` button to add the item to the `Selected` Items list box. You must also select a scope for the selected item by checking either the `Public` or `Private` radio button in the `Declare Scope` frame box. The `Public` keyword indicates that the scope of the selected item is public, which means that it can be used by all event procedures and all forms in the current Visual Basic project. The `Private` keyword means that the selected item can be used only by all event procedures in the form that the items are added to.

The item you've added into the `Selected` Items list box has not yet been incorporated in the Visual Basic project. Click the `Insert` button to add the selected item into your project, exactly into a form on your project. A dialog box pops up as you click the `Insert` button to confirm whether you wish to insert the item (see Figure 4.5). Click `Yes` to add the selected item into our Visual Basic project.

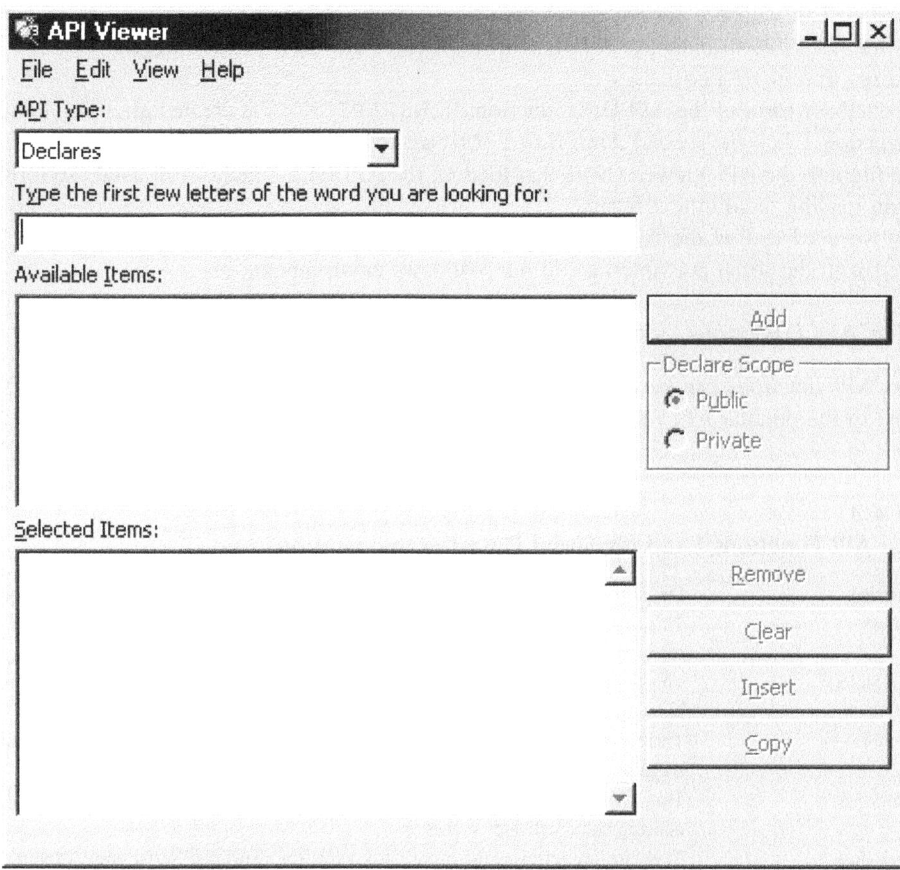

FIGURE 4.4 The API Viewer.

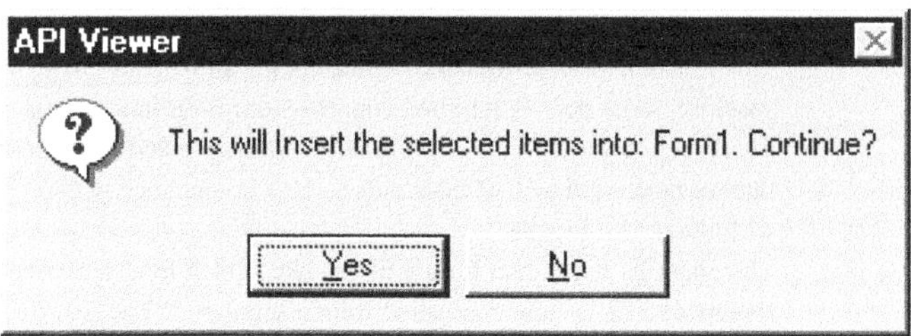

FIGURE 4.5 The `Confirmation` dialog box.

When you load the API DLL functions from the `API Viewer` by clicking the `File` menu item, there are three submenu items on the `File` list:

- Load Text File...
- Load Database File
- Convert Text to Database

Recall that we used the first item earlier to load the `Win32API.TXT` file after we installed the API Viewer. A quicker, and more convenient way to load the Win32 API functions is to load the Win32 API in database format rather than text format. To do this, we must first convert the `Win32API.TXT` file to database (MDB) format. Select the third item, `Convert Text to Database`, from the `File` list:

The database form of the API DLL function, `WIN32API.MDB`, is created after you complete this conversion. Click the second item, `Load Database File`, to load the `WIN32API.MDB` database file into the API Viewer. (Note that loading the API DLL functions in database format is faster than loading them in text format.)

Now we need to find the API DLL functions, data structures, and system constants that are associated with the serial port interface in our Windows environment.

4.2.3 The API Functions, Structures and Constants in Serial Communications

Windows API functions can be divided into different groups based on their purposes. Table 4.3 lists some of the popular API functions used for serial data communications.

TABLE 4.3
Popular API Functions Used for Serial Data Communications

API Function	Description
CreateFile()	This function creates a handle to a communications resource, such as a serial port. A returned value of `-1` means that an error has occurred.
SetCommState()	This function configures a serial port according to the specifications in a device-control block (a `DCB` structure). A returned nonzero value indicates success.
GetCommState()	This function returns the current control settings (with a `DCB` structure) for a specified serial port. A returned nonzero value indicates success.
SetCommMask()	This function specifies a set of events to be monitored for a serial port. A returned nonzero value indicates success.
GetCommMask()	This function retrieves the event mask value for a specified serial port. A returned nonzero value indicates success. The `GetCommMask()` function uses a 32-bit mask variable to indicate the set of events that can be monitored for a particular serial port.
GetCommTimeouts()	This function retrieves the timeout parameters for all read and write operations on a specified serial port.
SetCommTimeouts()	This function sets the timeout parameters for all read and write operations on a specified serial port. A returned nonzero value indicates success.
WaitCommEvent()	This function waits for an event to occur for a specified serial port. The set of events that are monitored by `WaitCommEvent()` is contained in the event mask associated with the device handle.
ReadFile()	This function reads data from a file handle, which must have been created by a `CreateFile()` function called from a serial port. The `ReadFile()` function returns when either the number of bytes requested has been read or an error has occurred. A returned nonzero value indicates success.
WriteFile()	This function writes data to a file by using the file handle, which must have been created with a `CreateFile()` function from a serial port. Returned a nonzero indicates success.
CloseHandle()	This function closes an open object handle. Use `CloseHandle()` to close handles returned by calls to the CreateFile() function.
EscapeCommFunction()	This function provides additional control of a serial port.

Tables 4.4, 4.5, and 4.6 list some most useful data structures used for serial data communications.

The *device control block* (`DCB`) is a useful data structure that is used to configure the serial port to perform serial data communications. The parameters defined in the `DCB` structure are listed in Table 4.4.

TABLE 4.4
The `DCB` Data Structure

Data Field	Type	Description
DCBlength	Long	The length or size of the `DCB` data structure.
BaudRate	Long	The data transfer rate in bits per second.
ByteSize	Byte	The number of bits in a character
EofChar	Byte	The character that is used to indicate the end of a data stream.
ErrorChar	Byte	The value of the character used to replace bytes received with a parity error.
EvtChar	Byte	The specified character used to indicate an event.
fBitFields	Long	Flag bits used to control various aspects of the serial driver.
Parity	Byte	The byte value used to indicate the parity method.
StopBits	Byte	Specifies the number of stop bits to be used. It is one of the following values: • ONESTOPBIT (1 stop bit) • ONE5STOPBITS (1.5 stop bits) • TWOSTOPBITS (2 stop bits)
wReserved	Integer	Reserved for future use.
wReserved1	Integer	Reserved for future use.
XoffChar	Byte	Specifies the value of the `XOFF` character for both transmission and reception.
XonChar	Byte	Specifies the value of the `XON` character for both transmission and reception.
XoffLim	Integer	Specifies the maximum number of bytes accepted in the input buffer before the `XOFF` character is sent. The maximum number of bytes accepted is calculated by subtracting this value from the size, in bytes, of the input buffer.
XonLim	Integer	Specifies the minimum number of bytes accepted in the input buffer before the `XON` character is sent.

During the initialization and configuration of a serial port, the API function `SetCommState()` is always used to set up the port. This function uses the `DCB` structure as an argument that contains all configured parameters necessary for initializing and setting up the port. This setup determines the working parameters of the serial port, such as the baud rate, the size of a transmitted data string, the number of stop bits, the parity method, the termination character, and the event character.

TIP: Generally, when you use the API function `SetCommState()` to configure a serial port, you do not need to define all parameters in the `DCB` structure. Some of parameters can be left at their default values. You can first use the `GetCommState()` API function to get those default values, then modify some of them based on your program's requirements, and finally set those parameters to the serial port by calling the `SetCommState()` function.

The `COMMTIMEOUTS` structure is used with the `SetCommTimeouts()` and `GetCommTimeouts()` functions to set and query the timeout parameters for a communication device. The parameters determine the behavior of the `ReadFile()` and `WriteFile()` function operations on the device. The parameters included in the `COMMTIMEOUTS` structure are listed in Table 4.5.

Reading from and writing to serial communication ports in 32-bit Windows is significantly different from reading from and writing to serial ports in 16-bit Windows. When performing serial data communications in a Windows 32 environment, two data communication styles can be used: `nonoverlapped` I/O and `overlapped` I/O.

4.2.3.1 Nonoverlapped I/O

Nonoverlapped I/O is very straightforward, though it has limitations. In nonoverlapped I/O, the calling thread is blocked when an operation takes place. Once the operation is complete, the block is lifted and the thread can continue its work. This type of I/O is useful for multithreaded applications because while one thread is blocked on an I/O operation, other thread can still perform work. It is

TABLE 4.5
The COMMTIMEOUTS Data Structure

Data Field	Type	Description
ReadIntervalTimeout	Long	Specifies the maximum acceptable time, in milliseconds, to elapse between the arrival of two characters on the communication line. During a `ReadFile()` operation, the time period begins when the first character is received. If the interval between the arrival of any two characters exceeds this amount, the `ReadFile()` operation is completed and any buffered data is returned. A value of `0` indicates that interval timeouts are not used.
ReadTotalTimeoutConstant	Long	Specifies the constant, in milliseconds, used to calculate the total timeout period for read operations. For each read operation, this value is added to the product of the `ReadTotalTimeoutMultiplier` member and the requested number of bytes. Values of `0` for both `ReadTotalTimeoutMultiplier` and `ReadTotalTimeoutConstant` members indicates that total timeouts are not used for read operations.
ReadTotalTimeoutMultiplier	Long	Specifies the multiplier, in milliseconds, used to calculate the total timeout period for read operations. For each read operation, this value is multiplied by the requested number of bytes to be read.
WriteTotalTimeoutConstant	Long	Specifies the constant, in milliseconds, used to calculate the total timeout period for write operations. For each write operation, this value is added to the product of the WriteTotalTimeoutMultiplier member and the number of bytes to be written. Value of `0` for both `WriteTotalTimeoutMultiplier` and `WriteTotalTimeoutConstant` indicate that total timeouts are not used for write operations.
WriteTotaltimeoutMultiplier	Long	Specifies the multiplier, in milliseconds, used to calculate the total timeout period for write operations. For each write operation, this value is multiplied by the number of bytes to be written.

the responsibility of the application to correctly serialize access to the port. If one thread is blocked and waiting to complete its I/O operation, all other threads that subsequently call a communication API will be blocked until the original operation is completed. For instance, if one thread is waiting for a `ReadFile()` function to return, any other thread that issues a `WriteFile()` function will be blocked.

One of the many factors to consider when choosing between nonoverlapped and overlapped operations is portability. Overlapped I/O is not a good choice when portability is desired because most operating systems do not support it. However, most operating systems support some form of multithreading, so multithreaded nonoverlapped I/O is usually the best choice.

4.2.3.2 Overlapped I/O

Overlapped I/O is not as straightforward as nonoverlapped I/O, but it allows more flexibility and efficiency. A port opened for overlapped operations allows multiple threads to perform I/O operations at the same time, and to perform other work while the I/O operations are pending. The behavior of overlapped operations also allows a single thread to issue many different requests and do work in the background while the operations are pending.

In both single-threaded and multithreaded applications, some synchronization must take place between the issuing of requests and the processing of results. Each thread must be blocked until the result of its operation is available. The advantage is that overlapped I/O allows a thread to do some work between the time of the request and its completion. If no work can be done, then the only case for overlapped I/O is that it allows for better user response.

Overlapped I/O is the type of operation that the MTTTY sample uses. It creates a thread that is responsible for reading the port's data and reading the port's status. It also performs periodic background work. The program creates another thread exclusively for writing data out the port.

To use overlapped I/O for performing data communications, you must use the OVERLAPPED structure as an argument when opening the serial port with the CreateFile() API function. The parameters defined for the OVERLAPPED data structure are listed in Table 4.6.

TABLE 4.6
The OVERLAPPED Data Structure

Data Field	Type	Description
hEvent	Long	Handle to an event set to the signaled state when the operation has been completed. The calling process must set this member either to 0 or a valid event handle before calling any overlapped functions. To create an event object, use the CreateEvent() function.
Internal	Long	Reserved for operating system use.
InternalHigh	Long	Reserved for operating system use.
Offset	Long	Specifies a file position at which to start the transfer. The file position is a byte offset from the start of the file. The calling process sets this member before calling the Readfile() or WriteFile() function. This member is ignored when reading from or writing to named pipes and communications devices and should be 0.
OffsetHigh	Long	Specifies the high word of the byte offset at which to start the transfer. This member is ignored when reading from or writing to named pipes and communications devices and should be 0.

There are other Win32 API functions that can be used for the serial data communications; these include OpenComm(), ReadComm(), WriteCom(), and CloseCom(). The readers can refer to the associated materials in MSDN Library to get information about applications of those functions.

In addition to being familiar with API functions and data structures, you also need to understand the API constants associated with serial device communications. Most parameters contained in the API data structures are defined by using these API constants. All API data structures and constants are defined in the Win32API.TXT file (which we loaded in Section 4.2.2). Figure 4.6 shows an example of an opened Win32API.TXT file.

The most popular API constants used in data communications are listed in Table 4.7. Most of those API constants are 32 bits long and are depicted in hexadecimal format.

TIP: When these API constants are used in a Visual Basic program, they must be redeclared. This is very different from the data structures and constants defined in header files in the C/C++ programming environments; in C/C++, you need only include the header files in your C/C++ applications, and then in your program, you can use any data structure or constant defined in the associated header file. In Visual Basic, however, you must redeclare the constants and data structures defined in the Win32API.TXT file before you can use any of them.

Now let's use the Win32 API functions, data structures and constants we've discussed here to develop an actual Visual Basic example program for performing serial data communications.

4.2.4 A Visual Basic Program Using Win32 API Functions

This example is a loopback testing program used to test the performance of serial port and COM1 is used in this example. Refer to Figure 3.6 in Chapter 3 to configure the hardware connection for the COM1 port.

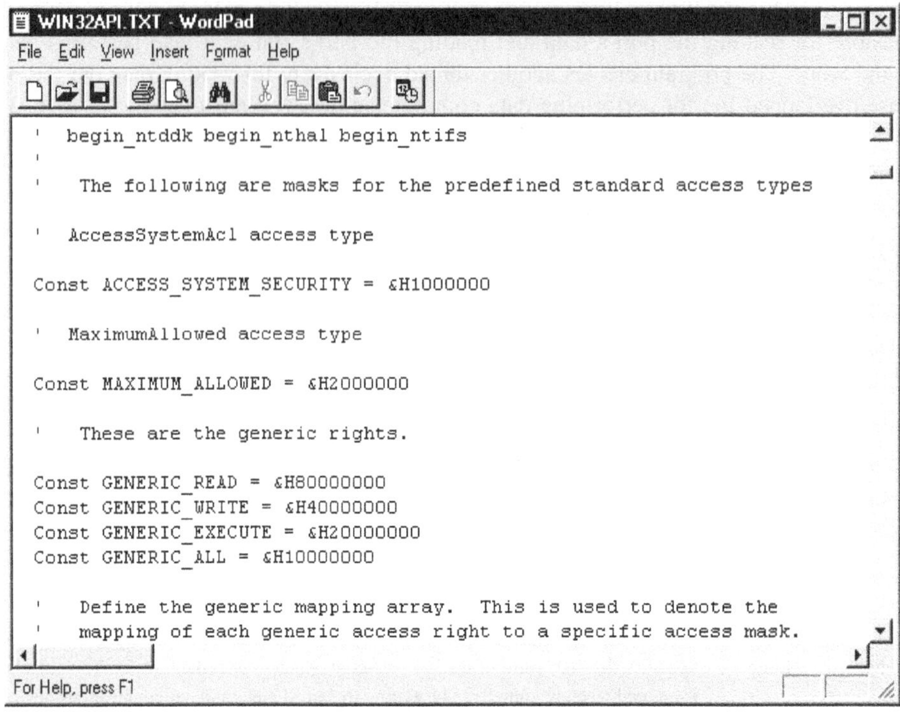


```
'  begin_ntddk begin_nthal begin_ntifs
'
'   The following are masks for the predefined standard access types

'  AccessSystemAcl access type

Const ACCESS_SYSTEM_SECURITY = &H1000000

'  MaximumAllowed access type

Const MAXIMUM_ALLOWED = &H2000000

'   These are the generic rights.

Const GENERIC_READ = &H80000000
Const GENERIC_WRITE = &H40000000
Const GENERIC_EXECUTE = &H20000000
Const GENERIC_ALL = &H10000000

'   Define the generic mapping array.  This is used to denote the
'   mapping of each generic access right to a specific access mask.
```

FIGURE 4.6 An example of the `Win32API.TXT` file.

TABLE 4.7
The Most Popular API Constants Used in Serial Communications

API Constant	Associated Function or Data Structure
GENERIC_READ = &H80000000	CreateFile()
GENERIC_WRITE = &H40000000	CreateFile()
FILE_ATTRIBUTE_NORMAL = &H80	CreateFile()
CREATE_ALWAYS = 2	CreateFile()
OPEN_ALWAYS = 4	CreateFile()
OPEN_EXISTING = 3	CreateFile()
INVALID_HANDLE_VALUE = -1	CreateFile()
MAXDWORD = &HFFFF	COMMTIMEOUTS
EV_RXCHAR = &H1	SetCommMask()
EV_RXFLAG = &H2	SetCommMask()
EV_TXEMPTY = &H4	SetCommMask()
EV_CTS = &H8	SetCommMask()
EV_DSR = &H10	SetCommMask()
EV_RLSD = &H20	SetCommMask()
EV_BREAK = &H40	SetCommMask()
EV_ERR = &H80	SetCommMask()
EV_RING = &H100	SetCommMask()
EV_PERR = &H200	SetCommMask()

Launch Visual Basic 6.0 or Microsoft Visual Basic.NET to create a new project named VBAP-ISerial.vbp. Two forms are used in this program. One form is used to receive the setup parameters that we will enter at run time to configure the serial port COM1, and the other form is used to the perform the actual testing of the serial port.

4.2.4.1 Developing Two Graphical User Interfaces

Click the Project|Add Form item on the Visual Basic menu bar. From the dialog box that appears, click the Open button to add a new form, and name the form Setup. On this form, add the components that are listed in Table 4.8.

TABLE 4.8
Components of the Setup Form

Object Type	Properties	Values
Form	Name	Setup
	Caption	VB Setup
Label	Name	Label1
	Caption	Enter Setup Parameters for Serial Port
Label	Name	Label2
	Caption	Port Number
Text box	Name	txtPort
	Text	
Label	Name	Label3
	Caption	Baud Rate
Text box	Name	txtBaudRate
	Text	
CommandButton	Name	cmdOK
	Caption	OK

Set the BackColor property of the form to yellow. The finished Setup form should now match the form shown in Figure 4.7.

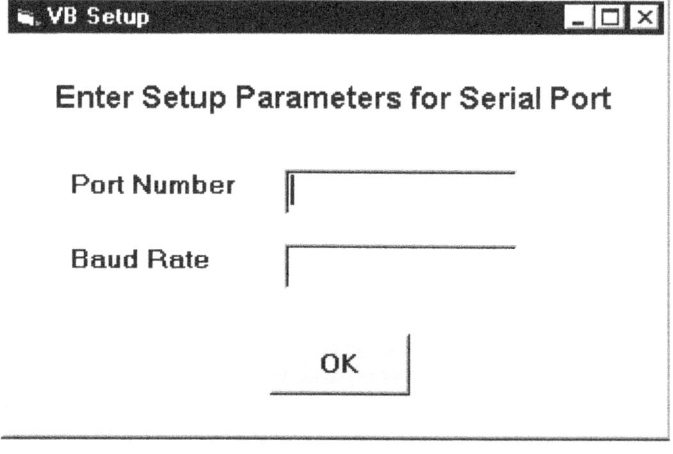

FIGURE 4.7 The Setup form.

When the program is run, two text boxes on the `Setup` form, `Port Number` and `Baud Rate`, will allow us to enter the port number and the desired baud rate.

Click the `Project|Add Form` item again on the Visual Basic menu bar. Click the `Open` button in the opened dialog box to add another new form, and then name the form `frmSerial`. On this form, add the components and objects that are listed in Table 4.9.

TABLE 4.9
Components of the `frmSerial` Form

Object Type	Properties	Values
Form	Name	frmSerial
	Caption	Serial Form
Label	Name	Label1
	Caption	Welcome to The VB API Serial Port Project
Frame	Name	Frame1
	Caption	Port Setup
Label	Name	Label2
	Caption	COM Port
Label	Name	lblComPort
	BackColor	Yellow
Label	Name	Label3
	Caption	Baud Rate
Label	Name	lblBaud Rate
	BackColor	Yellow
Frame	Name	Frame2
	Caption	Testing Data
Label	Name	Label4
	Caption	Sending Data
Text box	Name	txtWdata
	Text	
Label	Name	Label5
	Caption	Reading Data
Text Box	Name	txtRdata
	Text	
CommandButton	Name	cmdSetup
	Caption	Setup
CommandButton	Name	cmdWrite
	Caption	Write
CommandButton	Name	cmdRead
	Caption	Read
CommandButton	Name	cmdLoop
	Caption	Loop
CommandButton	Name	cmdExit
	Caption	Exit

Your completed form, `frmSerial`, should match the one shown in Figure 4.8.

The two labels, `COM Port` and `Baud Rate`, will indicate the serial port and the baud rate selected when the program is run. Two text boxes, `txtWdata` and `txtRdata`, will display the data sent to and received from the tested port. The `Setup` button will be used to configure the serial port based on the COM Port and Baud Rate settings that we enter on the `Setup` form. The `Write` button will allow us to send a data item to the port, and the `Read` button to receive a data

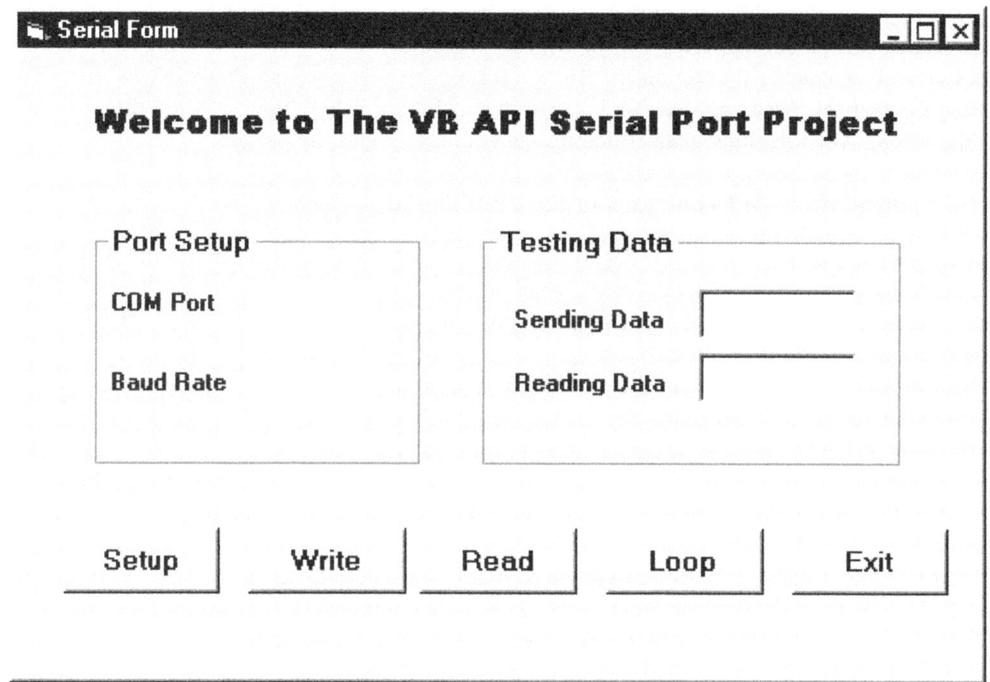

FIGURE 4.8 The completed `frmSerial` form.

item from the same port. We'll use the `Loop` button to continuously send and receive data to and from the selected port. Finally, we'll use the `Exit` button to terminate the program.

Now that the graphical user interfaces are complete, we can begin coding the program. The first step is to add the API functions into the project because we want to use the Win32 API functions to access the serial port and transfer data through it. Before we can load the API functions, however, we need to add a module into our project to contain them. We need this module because our program will need to use those added API functions, data structures, and constants in all event procedures and forms in the current project. This means that we need to declare those API functions, data structures, and constants as global format, and in Visual Basic, a module must be created to store all global functions, variables, and constants.

To create a module for the current project, follow these steps:

- Select `Project|Add Module` from the menu bar.
- In the opened Add Module dialog box, make sure that the default tab, `New`, is selected; then click the `Open` button to add a new module into the project.
- Change the name of the newly added module from the default, `Module1`, to `VBAPI-Module`.
- In the `Project Explorer` window, click the newly added module, `VBAPIModule`, to select it.

Before we can add the desired API functions, data structures, and constants into our module, we need fine-tune the way it will process user entry.

Type `Options Explicit` in the top text area of the `VBAPIModule` module. This command will keep the error-warning system working as we continue coding our program, thus preventing us from misusing or misspelling the names of the objects.

Next we need to declare two global variables, comPort and baudRate, in the VBAPIModule. These two global variables will be used as temporary buffers to store the COM Port and Baud Rate values that we'll enter on the Setup form at run time. Using Public Keyword and set the type for both of these variables to long (refer to Figure 4.11). Now it is the time for us to load the Win32 API functions, data structures, and constants into the project.

4.2.4.2 Adding Win32 API Functions to the VBAPISerial Project

As mentioned in Section 4.2.2, in order to load the API functions, you must add the API Viewer into your VB project. In our opened VBAPISerial project, click the Add-Ins|Add-In Manager menu item to open the Add-In Manager dialog box. Select the VB 6 API Viewer item and make sure that the two checkboxes Loaded/Unloaded and Load on Startup are checked; then click OK to add the API Viewer into the project and close the Add-In Manager.

Now click the Add-Ins menu item again, and you'll see that the API Viewer has been added into the project. Click the API Viewer item to open the API Viewer dialog box (which was shown in Figure 4.4). Click the File |Load Text File... menu item in the API Viewer dialog box, then select WIN32API.TXT and click the Open button to load the API functions into the project.

Next we need to add the API constants into the module VBAPIModule. Make sure that the VBAPIModule is selected in the Project Explorer window in the current project.

In the opened API Viewer dialog box, select Constants from the API Type: list box. In the text box labeled Type the first few letters of the word you are looking for:, type in the keyword Generic. A sequence of API constants appears in the Available Items: list box. Select the GENERIC_READ = &H80000000 constant from the list, and make sure that the Public radio button in the Declare Scope box is checked; Then click the Add button to add this constant to the Selected Items list box, which is shown in Figure 4.9. To add this API constant into our new module, click the Insert button. A message box appears to confirm that you want to add this constant to VBAPIModule, which is shown in Figure 4.10. Click Yes. Now open the module VBAPIModule, and you'll find that the constant has been added.

In the same way, we need to add all the constants listed in Table 4.7. To select each of these constants, you can either type its first few letters in the second text box labeled Type the first few letters of the word you are looking for: or select it from the Available Items: list box. Pay particular attention to the Public radio button located in the Declare Scope box. You must check this button before you can add any constants into our VB project because the Public keyword means that the constant you add will be a global constant. Otherwise the constant you add will be a private constant, and it will be unavailable for use by different forms in the current VB project. Our half-finished module, VBAPIModule, should match the one shown in Figure 4.11.

The first six API constants are used to open a new serial port that appears as a file in the Windows 32 environment. The GENERIC_READ and GENERIC_WRITE constants are used in the second argument (access-mode) in the API CreateFile() function to indicate that the opened port can be operated in both read mode and write mode. The FILE_ATTRIBUTE_NORMAL constant works as the sixth argument in the API CreateFile() function to present the file's attribute and flag, and indicate that the opened file (port) has no other attributes. By using this attribute argument, you can set the additional operation mode for the opened port, such as read only, archive, hide or write only modes. The followed three constants are used as the fifth argument in the CreateFile() function to indicate the creation mode of the file or port. CREATE_ALWAYS is used to create a new file, and OPEN_ALWAYS is used to open an existing file (unless the file doesn't exist, in which case it is created). Because the serial port that works as a file in Win32 has been created by the manufacturer, we do not need to create a new serial port file. Here the constant

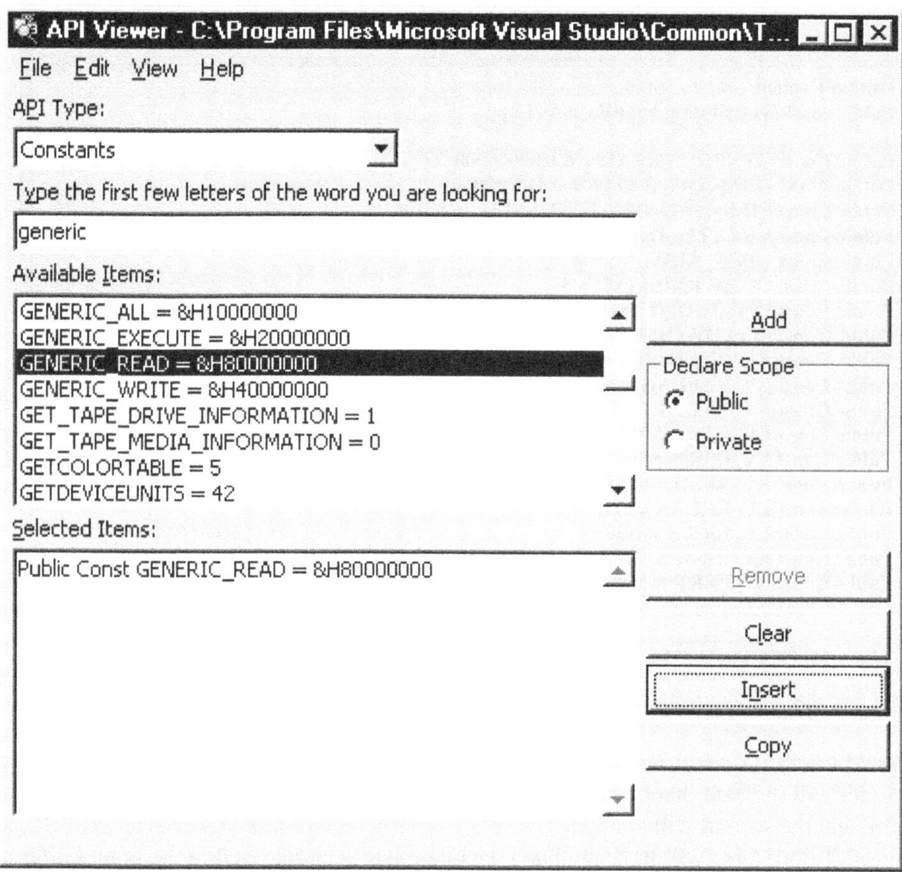

FIGURE 4.9 The opened `API Viewer` dialog box.

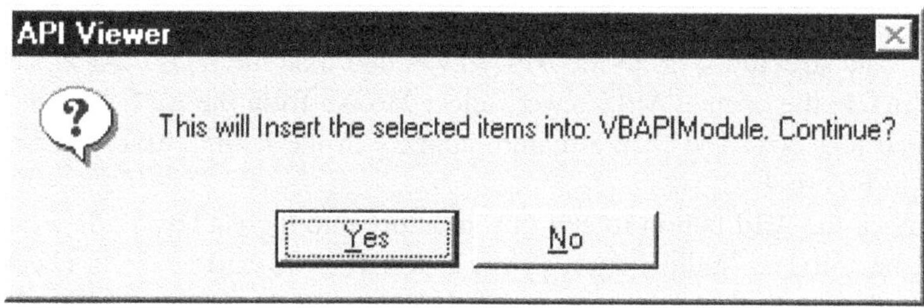

FIGURE 4.10 The `Confirmation` message box.

`OPEN_EXISTING` is used to indicate that we want to open an existing file as the medium for the serial port.

The constant `INVALID_HANDLE_VALUE` is used to hold the returned value from the call to the API function `CreateFile()`. A value of `-1` will mean that the function call has failed. The `MAXDWORD` constant works as the upper boundary of the timeout period during which our program can access the serial port.

The last ten constants are used in the second argument of the API function `SetCommMask()`, which is used to set the communication events to be monitored to indicate which event or which events combination should be monitored during the serial data communications. Among these

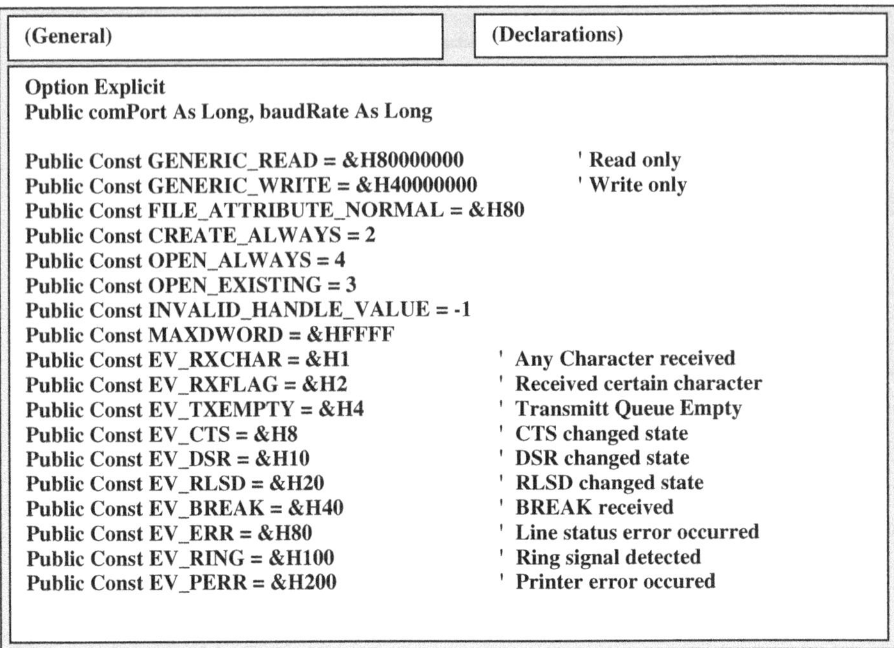

```
(General)                                   (Declarations)

Option Explicit
Public comPort As Long, baudRate As Long

Public Const GENERIC_READ = &H80000000           ' Read only
Public Const GENERIC_WRITE = &H40000000          ' Write only
Public Const FILE_ATTRIBUTE_NORMAL = &H80
Public Const CREATE_ALWAYS = 2
Public Const OPEN_ALWAYS = 4
Public Const OPEN_EXISTING = 3
Public Const INVALID_HANDLE_VALUE = -1
Public Const MAXDWORD = &HFFFF
Public Const EV_RXCHAR = &H1              ' Any Character received
Public Const EV_RXFLAG = &H2              ' Received certain character
Public Const EV_TXEMPTY = &H4             ' Transmitt Queue Empty
Public Const EV_CTS = &H8                 ' CTS changed state
Public Const EV_DSR = &H10                ' DSR changed state
Public Const EV_RLSD = &H20               ' RLSD changed state
Public Const EV_BREAK = &H40              ' BREAK received
Public Const EV_ERR = &H80                ' Line status error occurred
Public Const EV_RING = &H100              ' Ring signal detected
Public Const EV_PERR = &H200              ' Printer error occured
```

FIGURE 4.11 API constants added to the Visual Basic project.

constants, `EV_RXCHAR` and `EV_RLSD` are most important for our application. At run time, the first constant will indicate that a character has been received and placed in the input buffer on the serial port, and the second will show that the status of the *receive line signal detect* (`RLSD`) signal has changed. Both events will indicate that a data item has been received in the input buffer on the tested serial port. Certain other events, such as `EV_DSR`, `EV_CTS` and `EV_ERR`, are used to indicate the current states of the handshaking lines and the running status of the serial port.

Next we need to add the API data structures to the project. Three data structures are needed for our application: the *device control block* (`DCB`), the `COMMTIMEOUTS` and the `OVERLAPPED` structures.

To add these data structures, go to the API Viewer and load the `Win32API.TXT` file (if it is not already loaded). In the opened API Viewer, select `Types` from the `API Type:` box and type `DCB` in the second text box. The `DCB` structure appears in the `Available Items:` list box, which is shown in Figure 4.12.

Before you click the `Add` button to add this structure into the `Selected Items:` list box, make sure that the `Public` radio button in the `Declare Scope` box is checked. Now the structure can be added into the project as a global data structure. Open the Visual Basic project VBAPISerial (if it is not already opened), and click to select the module `VBAPIModule` from the `Project Explorer` window; we want to insert the `DCB` data structure into this module. Return to the API Viewer and click the `Insert` button to add this structure to the module. Click the `Yes` button in the confirmation message box to confirm this addition and close the box. In a similar way, we can add the other two data structures, `COMMTIMEOUTS` and `OVERLAPPED`.

After adding these three data structures, our module should look like the one shown in Figure 4.13. (The functionality of each data item in these three data structures was described in detail in Tables 4.4, 4.5 and 4.6, respectively.)

Finally we need to add the API functions into our project. Go to the API Viewer and load the `Win32API.TXT` file (if it is not already loaded). Select the `Declares` item from the `API Type:`

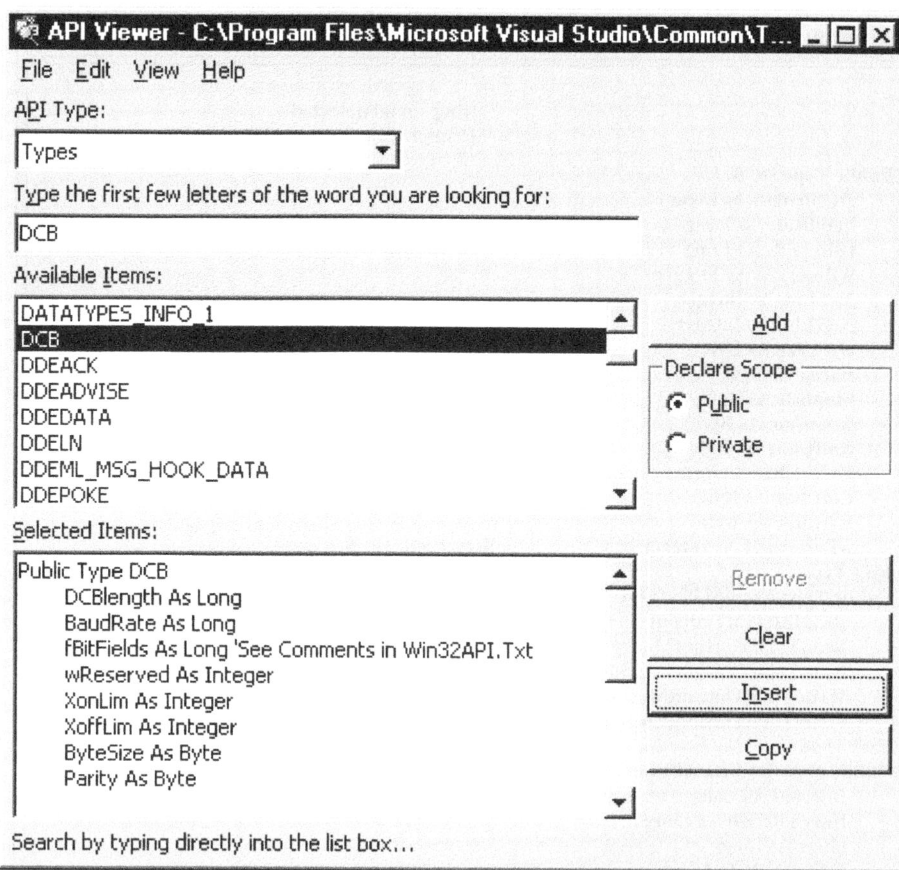

FIGURE 4.12 API data structures for the Visual Basic project.

list box, and all available API functions will appear in the `Available Items:` list box. We need to add all the API functions listed in Table 4.3 except for two, `GetCommMask()` and `EscapeCommFunction()`; we do not need these two functions in our current application.

In the API Viewer, type the `CreateFile` keyword in the text box labeled `Type the first few letters of the word you are looking for:` or select the `CreateFile` from the `Available Items:` list box. Make sure that the `Public` radio button in the `Declare Scope` box is checked, and then click the `Add` button to add the function to the `Selected Items:` list box, which is shown in Figure 4.14.

Make sure the module file `VBAPIModule` that we've added to our project is selected in the `Project Explorer` window in the Visual Basic environment. Then click the `Insert` button, and click `Yes` to confirm that we want to insert the `CreateFile` function into the module. In a similar way, we can add all the other desired API functions into `VBAPIModule`.

One more API function we need to add to our project is `timeGetTime()`, which is used to pick up the current system time. This function can be used to delay serial data communication for a certain period of time in some situations.

After the API functions have been added into the module, it should match the one in Figure 4.15.

Now all required API constants, data structures, and functions have been added into our project, and we are ready to develop our serial port loopback testing program. We'll begin by finish the code for the two forms we developed at the beginning of the project.

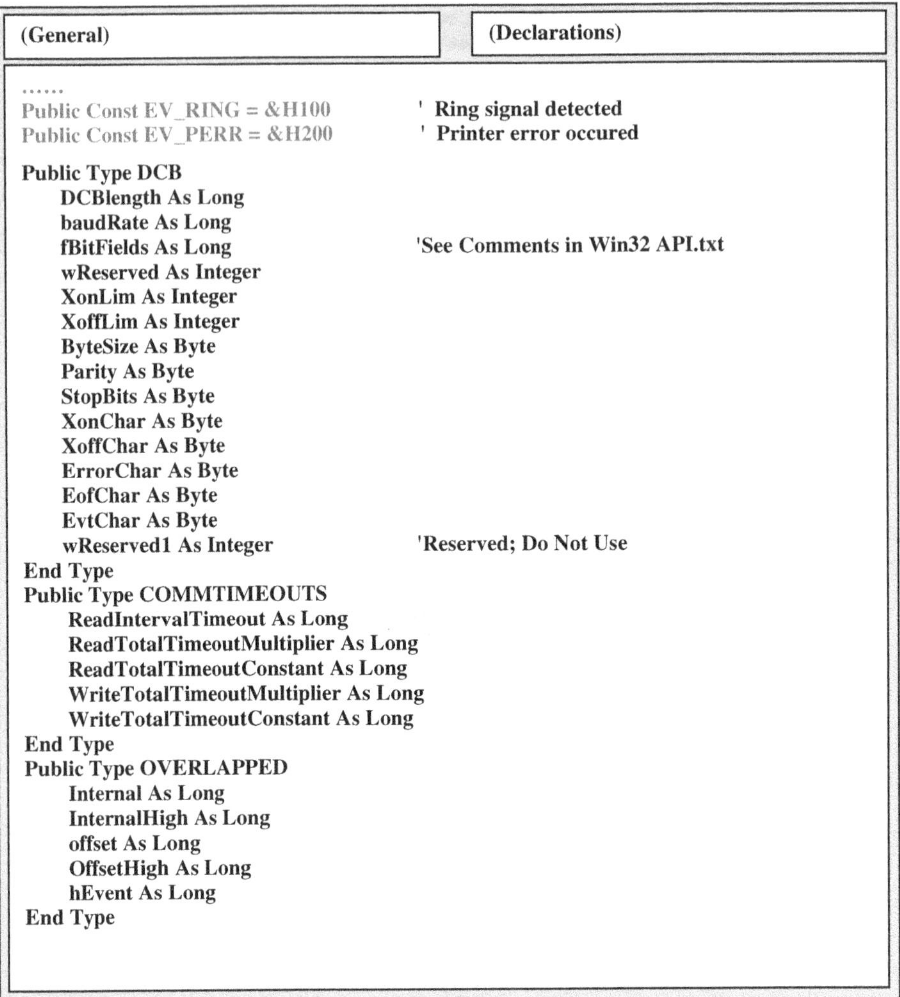


```
......
Public Const EV_RING = &H100          ' Ring signal detected
Public Const EV_PERR = &H200          ' Printer error occured

Public Type DCB
    DCBlength As Long
    baudRate As Long
    fBitFields As Long                'See Comments in Win32 API.txt
    wReserved As Integer
    XonLim As Integer
    XoffLim As Integer
    ByteSize As Byte
    Parity As Byte
    StopBits As Byte
    XonChar As Byte
    XoffChar As Byte
    ErrorChar As Byte
    EofChar As Byte
    EvtChar As Byte
    wReserved1 As Integer             'Reserved; Do Not Use
End Type
Public Type COMMTIMEOUTS
    ReadIntervalTimeout As Long
    ReadTotalTimeoutMultiplier As Long
    ReadTotalTimeoutConstant As Long
    WriteTotalTimeoutMultiplier As Long
    WriteTotalTimeoutConstant As Long
End Type
Public Type OVERLAPPED
    Internal As Long
    InternalHigh As Long
    offset As Long
    OffsetHigh As Long
    hEvent As Long
End Type
```

FIGURE 4.13 The added data structures.

4.2.4.3 Developing the `Setup` Form

Referring back to Figure 4.7, notice that the `Setup` form contains two text boxes and one command button. Recall that this form will be used to store the serial port number and the baud rate we enter to configure the port we wish to test. This form should be the first form to be executed when the project is running. To make this happen, click the `Project|VBAPISerial Properties...` menu item from the Visual Basic menu bar to open the `Project Properties` dialog box, which is shown in Figure 4.16. Then select the `Setup` form from the `Startup Object:` text box (shown in Figure 4.16) and click the `OK` button to make the selection effective. Now `Setup` will be the first form to be called and executed when our project runs.

Now select the `Setup` form from the `Project Explorer` window in the Visual Basic environment, and click the `View Code` button to open the `Setup` form's code window. In this window, enter the code that is shown in Figure 4.17.

A: As in the code module `VBAPIModule`, we first need to type the statement `Option Explicit` at the top of the code window. Recall that this statement will allow the error-

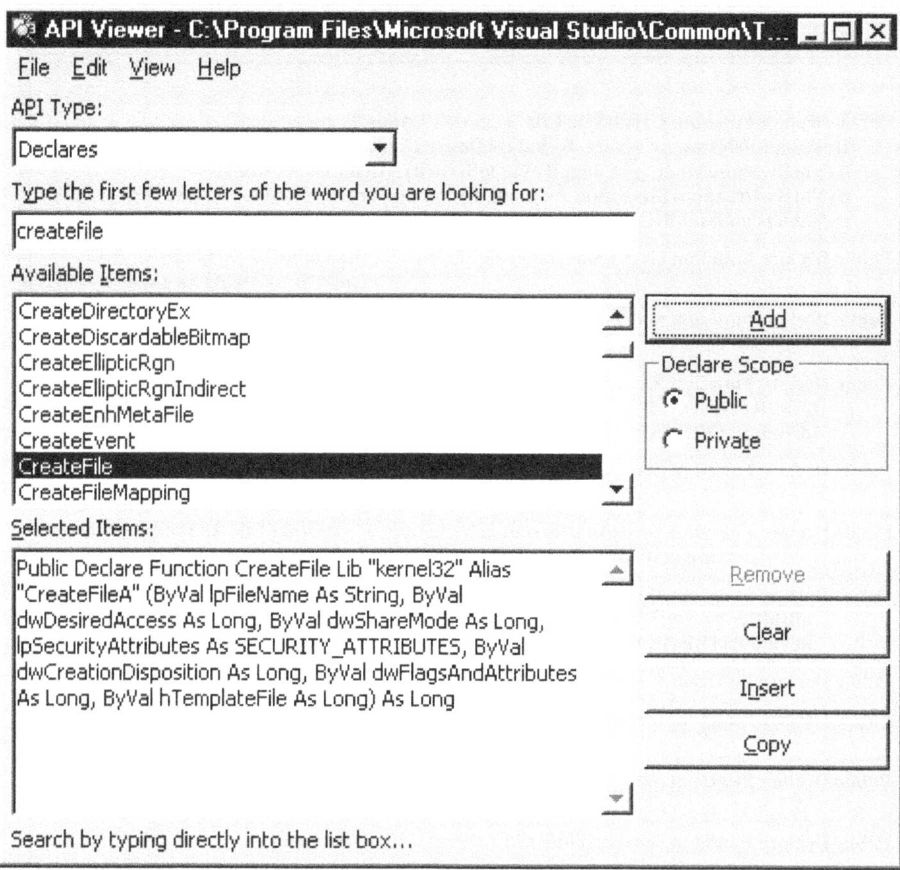

FIGURE 4.14 API functions added to the Visual Basic project.

detecting system in Visual Basic to work properly, thus protecting us from misusing or misspelling the objects we declare in this form.

B: In the first event procedure, `Form_Load()`, we define the form's location on the screen window in pixels. The horizontal and vertical coordinates of the upper-left corner should both be set to 2500 pixels. These settings will position the `Setup` form at the approximate center of the screen. `Me` is the default name of the `Setup` form object, so to represent the form here you can use either the actual name of the form, `Setup`, or the default name `Me`.

C: This is the starting point of the event procedure `cmdOK`, and it will be triggered as we click the command button `OK` at run time. When this button is clicked, our program must check two text boxes, `txtPort` and `txtBaudRate`, to make sure that they contain a valid port number and baud rate, respectively. If either of these text boxes is empty, a message box will appear, warning us to enter the appropriate data. The program will then exit from this subroutine and allow us to enter the new data.

D: Next our program must determine whether the port number we've entered is a valid number. In this application, we limit the port numbers from 1 to 4 (representing COM1 through COM4). In your own applications, you can modify this range if your system has more than four serial ports. If the port number entered at run time is beyond the specified range, a message box will appear instructing us to enter the correct data, and the program will exit from this event procedure, waiting for us to reenter the valid data.

```
(General)                                    (Declarations)

......
Public Declare Function CreateFile Lib "kernel32" Alias "CreateFileA" _
    (ByVal lpFileName As String, ByVal dwDesiredAccess As Long, _
     ByVal dwShareMode As Long, ByVal lpSecurityAttributes As Long, _
     ByVal dwCreationDisposition As Long, ByVal dwFlagsAndAttributes As Long, _
     ByVal hTemplateFile As Long) As Long
Public Declare Function GetCommState Lib "kernel32" (ByVal nCid As Long, _
                                                      lpDCB As DCB) As Long
Public Declare Function SetCommState Lib "kernel32" (ByVal hCommDev As Long, _
                                                      lpDCB As DCB) As Long
Public Declare Function ReadFile Lib "kernel32" (ByVal hFile As Long, _
        lpBuffer As Any, ByVal nNumberOfBytesToRead As Long, _
        lpNumberOfBytesRead As Long, lpOverlapped As OVERLAPPED) As Long
Public Declare Function SetCommMask Lib "kernel32" (ByVal hFile As Long, _
                                         ByVal dwEvtMask As Long) As Long
Public Declare Function WaitCommEvent Lib "kernel32" (ByVal hFile As Long, _
                   lpEvtMask As Long, lpOverlapped As OVERLAPPED) As Long
Public Declare Function WriteFile Lib "kernel32" (ByVal hFile As Long, _
        lpBuffer As Any, ByVal nNumberOfBytesToWrite As Long, _
        lpNumberOfBytesWritten As Long, lpOverlapped As OVERLAPPED) As Long
Public Declare Function CloseHandle Lib "kernel32" (ByVal hObject As Long) As Long
Public Declare Function GetCommTimeouts Lib "kernel32" (ByVal hFile As Long, _
                                lpCommTimeouts As COMMTIMEOUTS) As Long
Public Declare Function SetCommTimeouts Lib "kernel32" (ByVal hFile As Long, _
                                lpCommTimeouts As COMMTIMEOUTS) As Long
Public Declare Function timeGetTime Lib "winmm.dll" () As Long
```

FIGURE 4.15 Added API functions in the Visual Basic project.

E: If both the port number and the baud rate are valid, a `Val()` function is called to convert the port number and the baud rate from text form to their associated numeric values. These values are then stored in two global variables—`comPort` and `baudRate`, respectively—which will be used later by another form, `frmSerial`, to configure the serial port for testing.

F: Before exiting this event procedure, our program must hide the current `Setup` form and display the `frmSerial` form to continue testing the serial port. Two methods, `Show` and `Hide`, are used to perform this task.

At this point, we have finished creating the code for the `Setup` form.

4.2.4.4 Developing the `frmSerial` Form

Now click and select the `frmSerial` form from the `Project Explorer` window in Visual Basic environment, and click the `View Code` button to open the form's code window. In this window, enter the code that is shown in Figure 4.18.

VBAPISerial - Project Properties

General | Make | Compile | Component | Debugging

Project Type: Standard EXE

Startup Object: Setup

Project Name: VBAPISerial

Help File Name:

Project Help Context ID: 0

Project Description:

Unattended Execution

Upgrade ActiveX Controls

Require License Key

Retained In Memory

Threading Model

Thread per Object

Thread Pool 1 threads

OK Cancel Help

FIGURE 4.16 The `Project Properties` dialog box.

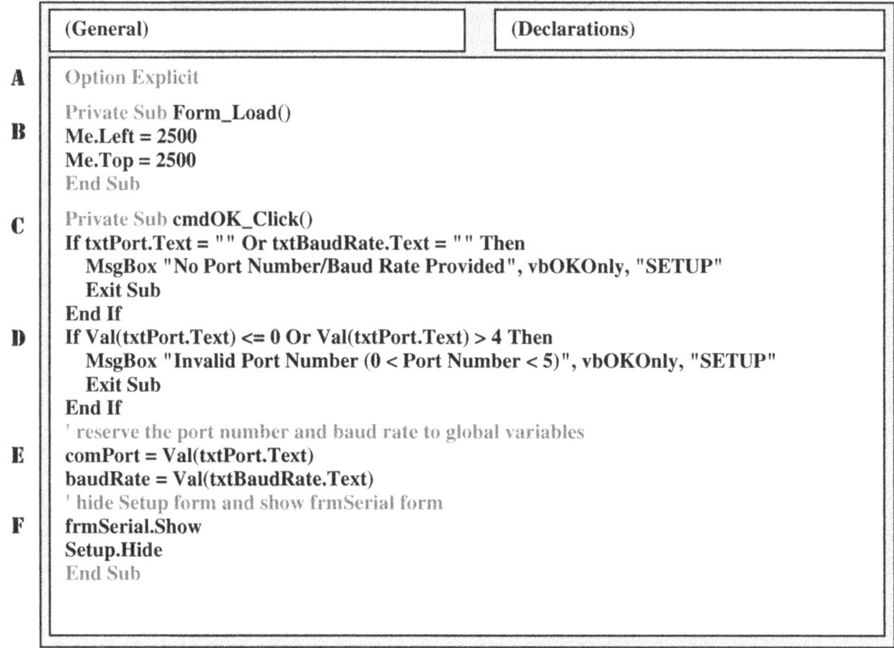

```
   (General)                          (Declarations)
A  Option Explicit
   Private Sub Form_Load()
B  Me.Left = 2500
   Me.Top = 2500
   End Sub
C  Private Sub cmdOK_Click()
   If txtPort.Text = "" Or txtBaudRate.Text = "" Then
      MsgBox "No Port Number/Baud Rate Provided", vbOKOnly, "SETUP"
      Exit Sub
   End If
D  If Val(txtPort.Text) <= 0 Or Val(txtPort.Text) > 4 Then
      MsgBox "Invalid Port Number (0 < Port Number < 5)", vbOKOnly, "SETUP"
      Exit Sub
   End If
   ' reserve the port number and baud rate to global variables
E  comPort = Val(txtPort.Text)
   baudRate = Val(txtBaudRate.Text)
   ' hide Setup form and show frmSerial form
F  frmSerial.Show
   Setup.Hide
   End Sub
```

FIGURE 4.17 Code for the Setup form.

```
   (General)                                  (Declarations)

G  Option Explicit
H  Dim comDCB As DCB, comTMOut As COMMTIMEOUTS, comOverlap As OVERLAPPED
   Dim sLoop As Boolean, setFlg As Boolean, hPort As Long, openSuccess As Long

I  Private Sub Form_Load()
   Dim rc As Boolean
J  Me.Left = 2000
   Me.Top = 2000
K  sLoop = False
   setFlg = False
L  lblComPort.Caption = comPort
   lblBaudRate.Caption = baudRate
   End Sub
```

FIGURE 4.18 Code for the `frmSerial` form.

Each section of this code is explained in this list:

G: As we did for the `Setup` form, we need to use the `Option Explicit` statement to avoid misusing and misspelling the objects and variables in this form.

H: Some *form-level* variables are declared at the beginning of this form. Form-level variables can be accessed and used by all event procedures in the current form. The first three variables are data structure variables, and they are associated with the three data structures `DCB`, `COMMTIMEOUTS`, and `OVERLAPPED`. At run time, the Boolean variables `sLoop` and `setFlg` will be used to store the status of the program and the flag of the setup procedure, respectively. A `True` value for `sLoop` will indicate that the program is running at the loop read/write mode, and a `True` value for `setFlag` will indicate that the `Setup` event procedure has been executed and the serial port has been properly configured. The `hPort` and `openSuccess` variables store the values returned from call to the API functions such as to `CreateFile()`, `GetCommState()`, `WriteFile()`, and `ReadFile()`.

I: This is the starting point of the first event procedure, `Form_Load()`.

J: Here we define the form's location on the screen window, in pixels. The horizontal and vertical coordinates of the upper-left corner should both be set to 2000 pixels. These settings will position the `frmSerial` form at the approximate center of the screen.

K: Next we need to initialize both Boolean variables, `sLoop` and `setFlg`, to `False` to make them ready for use in the testing program.

L: Here the program will display two serial port setup parameters, `COM Port` and `Baud Rate`, which we create by assigning the two global variables `comPort` and `baudRate` to the two labels—specifically, to the labels' `Caption` properties, `lblComPort` and `lblBaudRate`, respectively.

Now click the `View Object` button in the `Project Explorer` window to open the form window for our `frmSerial` form. We need to create the code for the `Setup` command button. The task of this button is to configure the correct communication parameters for the serial port. Double-click this button to open its event procedure window, and in this window, enter the code that is shown in Figure 4.19.

Each section of this code is described here:

M: Two local variables, `rc` and `cPort`, are declared first. `rc` is a Boolean variable that will store the running status of the API functions as our program is run. `cPort` is a

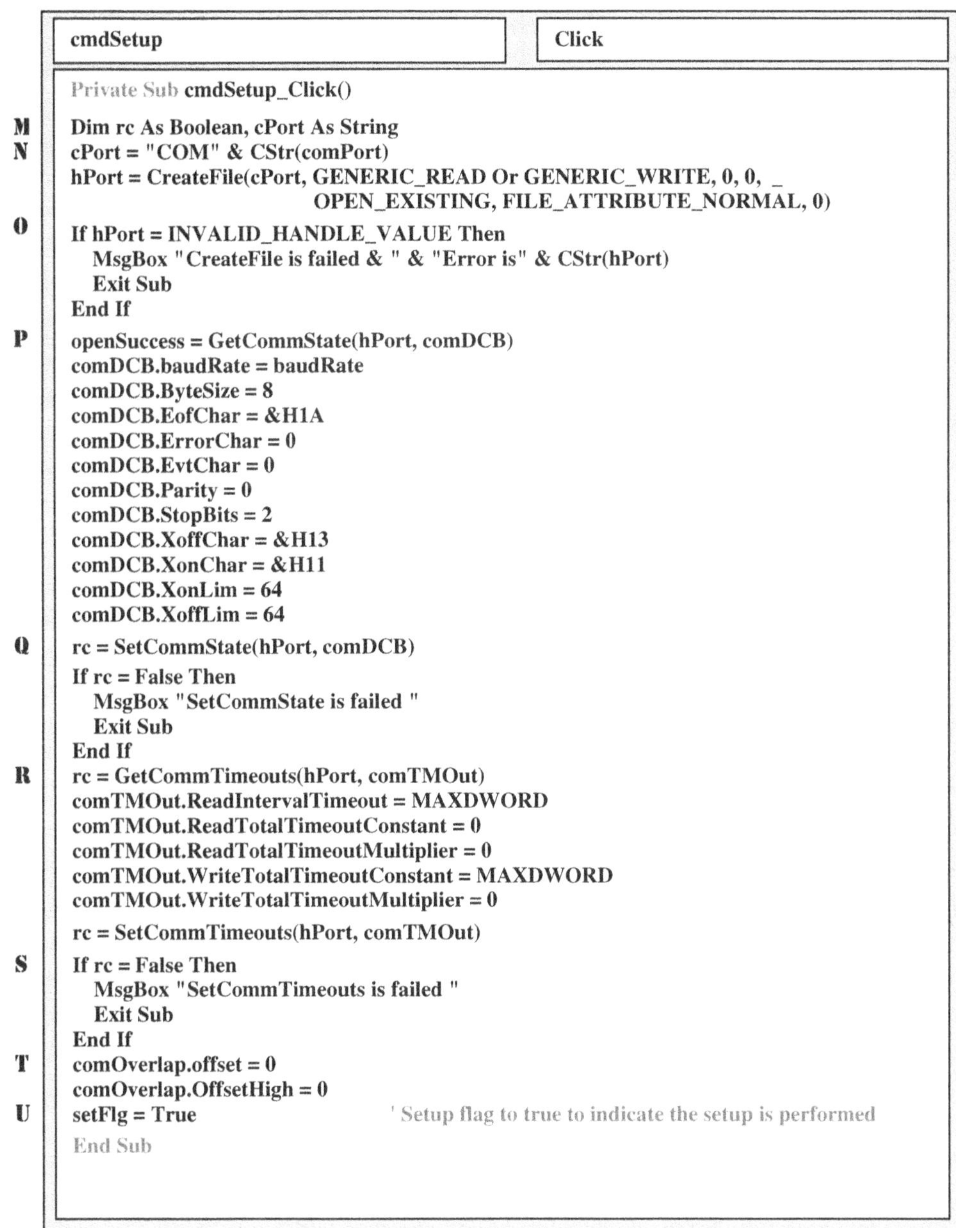

```
cmdSetup                                   Click

  Private Sub cmdSetup_Click()
M Dim rc As Boolean, cPort As String
N cPort = "COM" & CStr(comPort)
  hPort = CreateFile(cPort, GENERIC_READ Or GENERIC_WRITE, 0, 0, _
                     OPEN_EXISTING, FILE_ATTRIBUTE_NORMAL, 0)
O If hPort = INVALID_HANDLE_VALUE Then
    MsgBox "CreateFile is failed & " & "Error is" & CStr(hPort)
    Exit Sub
  End If
P openSuccess = GetCommState(hPort, comDCB)
  comDCB.baudRate = baudRate
  comDCB.ByteSize = 8
  comDCB.EofChar = &H1A
  comDCB.ErrorChar = 0
  comDCB.EvtChar = 0
  comDCB.Parity = 0
  comDCB.StopBits = 2
  comDCB.XoffChar = &H13
  comDCB.XonChar = &H11
  comDCB.XonLim = 64
  comDCB.XoffLim = 64
Q rc = SetCommState(hPort, comDCB)
  If rc = False Then
    MsgBox "SetCommState is failed "
    Exit Sub
  End If
R rc = GetCommTimeouts(hPort, comTMOut)
  comTMOut.ReadIntervalTimeout = MAXDWORD
  comTMOut.ReadTotalTimeoutConstant = 0
  comTMOut.ReadTotalTimeoutMultiplier = 0
  comTMOut.WriteTotalTimeoutConstant = MAXDWORD
  comTMOut.WriteTotalTimeoutMultiplier = 0
  rc = SetCommTimeouts(hPort, comTMOut)
S If rc = False Then
    MsgBox "SetCommTimeouts is failed "
    Exit Sub
  End If
T comOverlap.offset = 0
  comOverlap.OffsetHigh = 0
U setFlg = True              ' Setup flag to true to indicate the setup is performed
  End Sub
```

FIGURE 4.19 Code for the `Setup` command button.

string variable that composes a string containing the serial port name "COM," followed by the port number we entered at run time.

N: The `&` operator and the built-in function `CStr()` will compose the string to be stored in the string variable `cPort`. The format of the string is important because the first argument in the API `CreateFile()` function must be in this format. Once the string is composed, the `CreateFile()` is called to open an existing serial port as the file with the specified port's name. The first argument of the `CreateFile()` function is the serial port `cPort`, which consists of the port's name and number. An `Or` operator is used for the second argument, `GENERIC_READ Or GENERIC_WRITE`, which indicates that the opened file can be read from and written to. The fifth argument, OPEN_EXISTING, specifies that the function can open only an existing serial port as the file handle. This function will return an error message if the existing port is not available or cannot be opened. The sixth argument, FILE_ATTRIBUTE_NORMAL, indicates that no other file attributes are needed for opening the file. The third, fourth and seventh arguments are set to 0 because they are not used in this application.

O: At this point, before the program can continue running, it must check the value returned by the API function call to determine whether the call has been successful. An error message will appear if the returned value is -1, which means that the file has failed to open. In this case, the program will exit the current procedure.

P: If the file has been opened successfully, our program will continue to configure the serial port by calling another API function, SetCommState(). To correctly and easily configure the serial port with this API function, we must first obtain the device control block (DCB) by calling the API function GetCommState(). Two arguments are included in this function call. The first is the file handle hPort, which is created and returned by the call to the CreateFile() function in step N (if this function call has been successful). The file handle behaves like an identifier that represents the entry point of the opened file. Our program must use this file handle each time it accesses the opened file to read data from it or write data to it. The second argument is the data structure comDCB, which contains the default configuration parameters for the serial port. After executing the function GetCommState() with two arguments, the program will obtain the current data structure from the comDCB argument. Here we select some important parameters from the obtained data structure and modify them according to our application. In this program we use only three of these parameters: the baud rate, data bits, and stop bits. Our program will modify these three parameters according to the baudRate value we enter at run time, and with values of 8 for data bits and 2 for stop bits.

The EofChar, XonChar, and XoffChar variables can be assigned their default values, which are &H1A, &H11 and &H13, respectively.

Q: After the modification of the serial port parameters, our program will use the DCB data structure to call the SetCommState() function, which will configure the serial port. A returned False value indicates that the function call has failed; in this case, an error message will appear on the screen and the program will exit the procedure.

R: Here we set up the timeout parameters for the serial port. First our program must call the GetCommTimeouts() function to obtain the default timeout parameters from the comTMOut data structure. Next we can make some modifications to those parameters based on our application, and finally, by executing the SetCommTimeouts() function, we can successfully set the modified timeout parameters to the serial port. Two of these parameters are especially significant. One is ReadIntervalTimeout and the other is WriteTotalTimeoutConstant. Both of these parameters are assigned to the upper boundary of the timeout constant MAXDWORD.

S: A returned value of False will indicate that the execution of the SetCommTimeouts() function has failed; in this case, an error message will appear, and the program will exit the current procedure.

T: Next we need to set up the overlapped data structure. Only two parameters in this structure are important to us; these are the offset and OffsetHigh parameters. (Refer to Table 4.6.) Both of these parameters should be reset to 0 to ensure that the serial port works properly.

U: Before we can finish coding this event procedure, we need to set the setFlg flag to True to indicate that the Setup event procedure has been successfully completed and the serial port has been correctly configured. This flag is very important, because an error may be encountered if the program tries to send or read data to or from the serial port without first configuring the port by executing the `Setup` event procedure. To avoid this error, we use `setFlg` to indicate whether or not the `Setup` event procedure has been performed successfully.

Next we must create code for the data writing event procedure that will be triggered by a click of the `Write` command button.

Click the View Object button in the `Project Explorer` window in the Visual Basic workspace. When the `frmSerial` form window opens, double-click the `Write` command button to open its event procedure, and enter the code that is shown in Figure 4.20.

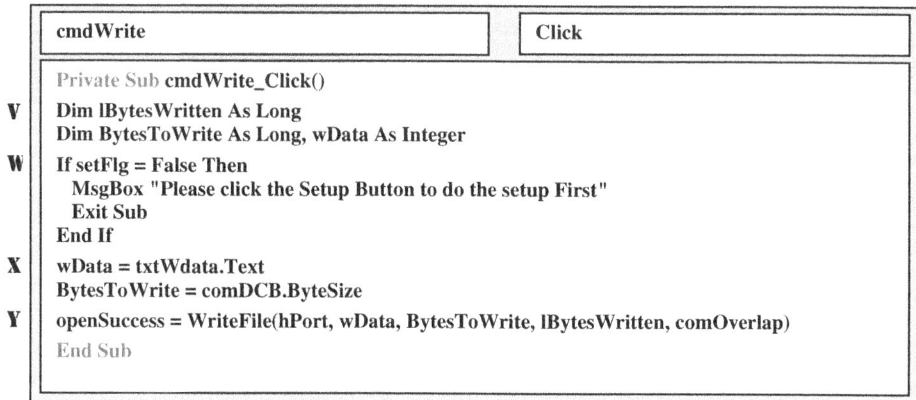

cmdWrite
Click
Private Sub cmdWrite_Click()
V Dim lBytesWritten As Long
Dim BytesToWrite As Long, wData As Integer
W If setFlg = False Then
MsgBox "Please click the Setup Button to do the setup First"
Exit Sub
End If
X wData = txtWdata.Text
BytesToWrite = comDCB.ByteSize
Y openSuccess = WriteFile(hPort, wData, BytesToWrite, lBytesWritten, comOverlap)
End Sub

FIGURE 4.20 Code for the `Write` event procedure.

Each section of this code is explained in the following list.

V: Three local variables are declared at the beginning of this procedure. The first variable, `lBytesWritten`, is the starting address that will store the data written to the serial port. The `BytesToWrite` variable will store the number of bytes to be written to the port, and the `wData` variable will store the single byte of data to be written to the port.

W: Before our program can issue the `Write` command that will call the API function `WriteFile()` to send data to the serial port, it must execute the `Setup` event procedure to ensure that the port has been successfully configured. It determines the status of the port by checking the status of the Boolean variable `setFlg`. A value of `False` indicates that the `Setup` event procedure has not been executed and thus, that the port has not been configured. In this case, a message box will appear reminding us to set up the port.

X: If the port has been configured and `setFlg` has a value of `True`, the data to be sent to the port will be picked up from the `Sending Data` text box, `txtWdata`, and then sent out by a call to the API `WriteFile()` function after the value `BytesToWrite` is assigned by the `ByteSize` element in the data structure `DCB`.

Y: After calling the API `WriteFile()` function, our program can write the data to the serial port—specifically, to the output buffer of the UART.

We can now finish the coding the data reading event procedure. Click the `View Object` button in the `Project Explorer` window to open the `frmSerial` form window, and then double-click the `Read` command button on the form to open its `event procedure` window. In this window, enter the code that is shown in Figure 4.21.

```
cmdRead                                  Click

   Private Sub cmdRead_Click()
Z  Dim lBytesRead As Long
   Dim BytesToRead As Long, rData As Integer
1  If setFlg = False Then
     MsgBox "Please click the Setup Button to do the setup First"
     Exit Sub
   End If
2  BytesToRead = comDCB.ByteSize
   openSuccess = ReadFile(hPort, rData, BytesToRead, lBytesRead, comOverlap)
3  txtRdata.Text = CStr(rData)
   End Sub
```

FIGURE 4.21 Code for the `Read` event procedure.

Each section of this code is explained in the following list.

Z: As in the `Write` event procedure, we must first declare three local variables. The `lBytesRead` variable is the starting address that will store the data read from the port. The `BytesToRead` variable will indicate the number of bytes to be read from the serial port. The `rData` variable will store the value of the data to be read from the port.

1: Here we need to check the Boolean variable `setFlg` to make sure that the `Setup` event procedure has been successfully executed and that the port has been configured based on our desired parameters. A value of `False` indicates that the `Setup` event procedure has not been executed and thus, that the port has not been configured. In this case, a message box will appear reminding us to set up the port.

2: If the port has been configured and `setFlg` has a value of `True`, it means that the port has been configured. In this case, the value of `BytesToWrite` will be assigned by the `ByteSize` element in the data structure `DCB`, and the API `ReadFile()` function will be called to read the data from the port.

3: Using the built-in function `CStr()`, our program converts the returned data from a numeric value to a string and then displays the result in the `Reading Data` text box.

Now we have another two command buttons to be coded. We'll use the `Loop` button to trigger the `cmdLoop_Click` event procedure, which will continuously send and receive data to and from the selected port. Finally, we'll use the `Exit` button to terminate the project.

In order to test the serial port by using the `Loop` command, our program will continuously send a sequence of random data to the serial port, and read it back from the same port. The range of the random data is from `1` to `100`. By comparing the data that is sent out with the data that is read back, our program can test the working status of the serial port.

Click the View Object button from the Project Explorer window in Visual Basic workspace to open the `frmSerial` form window, and double-click the `Loop` button to open its event procedure window. Enter the code that is shown in Figure 4.22.

Each section of this code is explained in the following list.

4: Several local variables are declared here. `rc` is a Boolean variable that will store the running status of the API functions as our program is run. The `randNum` variable will store the generated random number to be sent to the port for this procedure. The `evtMask` variable will store the returned current event masks as they are received from the tested serial port.

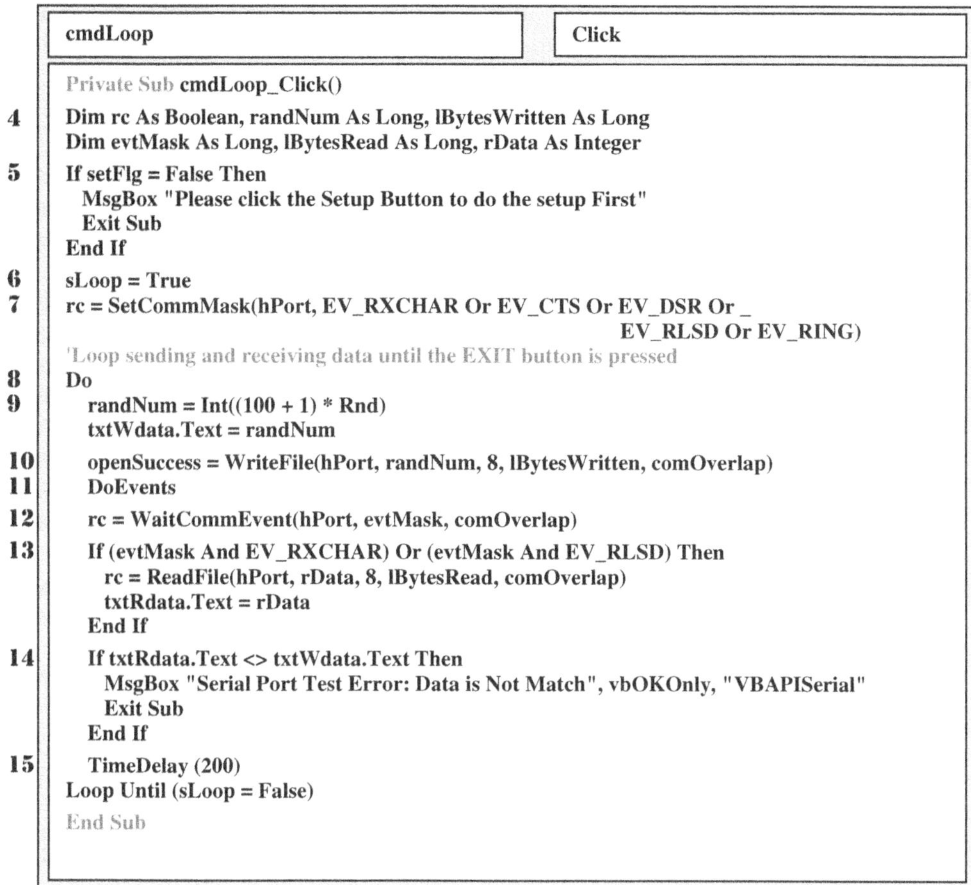

```
cmdLoop                                   Click

Private Sub cmdLoop_Click()
4   Dim rc As Boolean, randNum As Long, lBytesWritten As Long
    Dim evtMask As Long, lBytesRead As Long, rData As Integer
5   If setFlg = False Then
      MsgBox "Please click the Setup Button to do the setup First"
      Exit Sub
    End If
6   sLoop = True
7   rc = SetCommMask(hPort, EV_RXCHAR Or EV_CTS Or EV_DSR Or _
                                                EV_RLSD Or EV_RING)
    'Loop sending and receiving data until the EXIT button is pressed
8   Do
9     randNum = Int((100 + 1) * Rnd)
      txtWdata.Text = randNum
10    openSuccess = WriteFile(hPort, randNum, 8, lBytesWritten, comOverlap)
11    DoEvents
12    rc = WaitCommEvent(hPort, evtMask, comOverlap)
13    If (evtMask And EV_RXCHAR) Or (evtMask And EV_RLSD) Then
        rc = ReadFile(hPort, rData, 8, lBytesRead, comOverlap)
        txtRdata.Text = rData
      End If
14    If txtRdata.Text <> txtWdata.Text Then
        MsgBox "Serial Port Test Error: Data is Not Match", vbOKOnly, "VBAPISerial"
        Exit Sub
      End If
15    TimeDelay (200)
    Loop Until (sLoop = False)
End Sub
```

FIGURE 4.22 Code for the Loop event procedure.

5: As in both the Read and Write event procedures, our program must check the Boolean variable setFlg to determine whether the Setup event procedure has been performed to configure the port. A value of False indicates that the Setup event procedure has not been executed and thus, that the port has not been configured. In this case, a message box will appear reminding us to set up the port.

6: By setting the Boolean variable sLoop to True, we indicate to the program that it should run in Loop testing format.

7: To read back data from the serial port, we need to setup and monitor a sequence of events. When the serial port performs an action, such as sending out or receiving data, the status of the port is changed, and this status change will be reflected on the buffers and transmission lines of the associated port. (Refer to Section 1.6.6.2 in Chapter 1 for a more detail explanation of this issue.) By calling the API function SetCommMask(), we can specify a set of events to be monitored for the serial port. Here we setup and monitor five events, but only two of them are important to us: EV_RXCHAR and EV_RLSD. At run time, the first constant will indicate that a character has been received and placed in the input buffer on the serial port, and the second will show that the status of the receive line signal detect (RLSD) has changed. Both events indicate that a data item has been received and is available to be picked up from the serial port being tested.

8: Here the program uses a Do-Until loop structure to repeatedly send out data and receive it back via the tested port, and this loop will not be terminated until a False value is received from the Boolean variable `sLoop`, which will be reset in the `Exit` event procedure when triggered by the `cmdExit_Click` event. We can initiate this event at run time by clicking the `Exit` command button.

9: Inside the loop, our program will generate a random number by calling the built-in function `Rnd()`. The upper and lower boundaries of this random sequence are `100` and `1`, respectively. By using another built-in function `Int()`, the program can convert the generated random data from the double to the integer type. (Note that the default data type of the `Rnd()` function is double.) The random data will then be assigned to the local `randNum` variable and displayed in the `txtWdata` text box.

10: By calling the API function `WriteFile()`, our program will send the random number `randNum` to the serial port. This function includes five arguments. The first argument is the file handle, created by a call to the `CreateFile()` function. If the execution of that function is successful, it returns a file handle that is equivalent to an ID for the opened port file. The second argument is `randNum`, the data to be sent to the port. The third argument indicates the size of the data to be transmitted; a value of 8 (`8-bits`) is used here. The fourth and the fifth arguments specify the size of the data that has been written and the overlapped data structure that is used to indicate whether this write operation should be nonoverlapped or overlapped.

11: Here the `DoEvents` command is inserted inside the loop; this command is very important to a multitasking environment. `DoEvents` will prevent the dead cycle of the `Do-Until` loop and allow control to temporarily leave the loop when it has no important tasks to execute so that higher-priority system tasks can be performed. This will gives the CPU flexibility and allow it to take care of all tasks (including our project) according to their priority levels. If the `DoEvents` statement is not included in the loop, then if no any action is occurring inside the `Do-Until` loop (for example, if the program is waiting for valid events to be returned by the `WaitCommEvent()` function), then the CPU simply remains in idle status and cannot process other important tasks. The `DoEvents` statement greatly improved the dynamic performance of the computer systems and allows the multiple tasks to be processed simultaneously.

12: Once the `DoEvents` statement is inserted in the loop, our program can call the API `WaitCommEvent()` function to wait for data receiving events to occur. Three arguments are included in this call. The first specifies the file handle that works as an ID for the opened file. The second argument is an event mask that contains all the events we want to monitor from the tested port. The third argument is an overlapped data structure that is indicates whether this function should work in non-overlapped or overlapped I/O mode.

13: If an event is detected and returned by the `WaitCommEvent()` function, our program will use the `And` and `Or` operators to determine whether the returned event is an `EV_RXCHAR` or an `EV_RLSD` constant. When data is received and stored in the input buffer of the serial port, the API `ReadFile()` function will be called to pick up the data from the input buffer. The retrieved data will then be displayed in the `txtRdata` text box.

14: To test the performance of the port, our program will compare the sent out data with the retrieved data. The test will be successful if the data units are identical; otherwise, the program will exit the data transmission loop, and a message box will appear to show us that a mismatch error has occurred.

15: To enhance the running speed of our program, we use a customer-built delay function, `TimeDelay()` (which will be discussed later in more detail), to delay each transmission of data by 200 milliseconds. You can modify this delay period if you want a higher processing speed in your own applications.

This Do-Until loop will not be terminated until the Boolean variable sLoop is reset to False; this reset process will occur in the Exit event procedure when we clicks the Exit command button at run time.

Now we must code the Exit event procedure. The purpose of this procedure is to terminate the program and clean up the environment that we've set for the program.

Click the View Object button from the Project Explorer window in the Visual Basic workspace. When the frmSerial form window appears, double-click the Exit command button to open its event procedure window, and then enter the code that is shown in Figure 4.23.

cmdExit	Click

```
   Private Sub cmdExit_Click()
16 sLoop = False
17 openSuccess = CloseHandle(hPort)
18 End
   End Sub
```

FIGURE 4.23 Code for the Exit event procedure.

16: In the Exit event procedure, we need to reset the Boolean variable sLoop to False to inform the Do-Until loop located in the Loop event procedure that we want to terminate the program.

17: The API CloseHandle() function will be called to close the opened file. This function will include one argument, hPort, which specifies the ID for the opened file that represents the serial port. (Note that whenever you use the CreateFile() function to open any file in your program, you must use the CloseHandle() function to close the opened file. Otherwise, you may encounter an error if you try to run your program a second time because the file will still be opened. You cannot open a file if it is already opened.)

18: By executing the End statement, Visual Basic will terminate our program.

Before we can test and run our project, we need to add the customer-built function, TimeDelay(). With the program still in code window status, click the Tools|Add Procedure... item from the menu bar in the Visual Basic workspace to open the Add Procedure dialog box. Check the Sub radio button in the Type box and the Private radio button in the Scope box. Enter the function name, TimeDelay, into the Name box, as shown in Figure 4.24. Click OK to add this function into the project and close the Add Procedure dialog box.

Recall that in Visual Basic, all procedures are divided into two categories: subroutines and functions. A procedure with no returned value is called a subroutine, and a procedure with a returned value is called function. Our TimeDelay() function will have no returned value, so it is a subroutine. (This is why we had to check the Sub radio button in the Add Procedure dialog box when adding this function.) The Private keyword is used to indicate that the added subroutine belongs only to the current form, frmSerial, and that it cannot be accessed by any object or event procedure located on any other forms in the project.

Notice in the code window that the TimeDelay() subroutine has been added to our form. In this event procedure, enter the code that is shown in Figure 4.25.

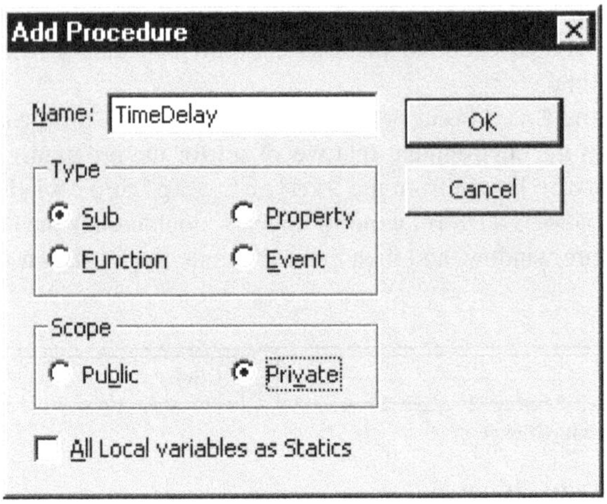

Add Procedure

Name: TimeDelay

Type: Sub / Function / Property / Event

Scope: Public / Private

All Local variables as Statics

OK Cancel

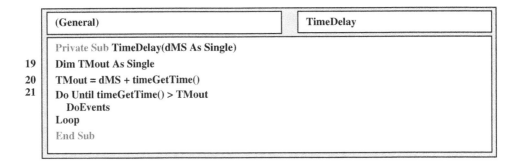

FIGURE 4.24 The Add Procedure dialog box.

```
(General)                                TimeDelay

   Private Sub TimeDelay(dMS As Single)
19 Dim TMout As Single
20 TMout = dMS + timeGetTime()
21 Do Until timeGetTime() > TMout
     DoEvents
   Loop
   End Sub
```

FIGURE 4.25 The customer-built `TimeDelay()` subroutine.

19: A local variable `TMout` is declared at the beginning of the procedure. This variable will store the elapsed time.

20: The API `timeGetTime()` function will be called to get the current system time; this obtained time value will then be added with the specified delay time value. The sum will be stored in the local `TMout` variable.

21: A `Do-Until` loop will track whether the system time obtained by calling the `timeGetTime()` function is greater than the value stored in the local `TMout` variable. This loop will be terminated once this condition is `True`, which will indicate that the desired delay time is up. The `DoEvents` statement here will allow the CPU to handle more important jobs when no action is occurring inside the loop.

Now that we have finished creating all the code for our project, the time has come to test and run the project.

4.2.5 Testing and Running the VBAPISerial Project

Recall that we specified the `Setup` form as our startup window in the `Project|VBAPISerial Properties` dialog box, which means that the `Setup` form will be called and executed first as the project runs. Now click the `Start` button from the standard toolbar in the Visual Basic workspace to run the project. As expected, the `Setup` form is displayed first. In the two text boxes, enter the port number you wish to test and the baud rate you wish to use; in Figure 4.26, we've specified port COM1 and a baud rate of 9600.

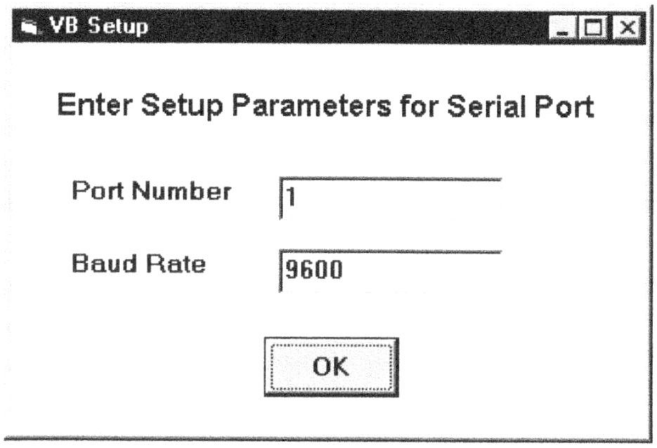

FIGURE 4.26 Running status of the `Setup` form.

Click the `OK` button once you've finished setting up the program. The second form, `frmSerial`, will appear, as shown in Figure 4.27. The port number and the baud rate you entered on the `Setup`

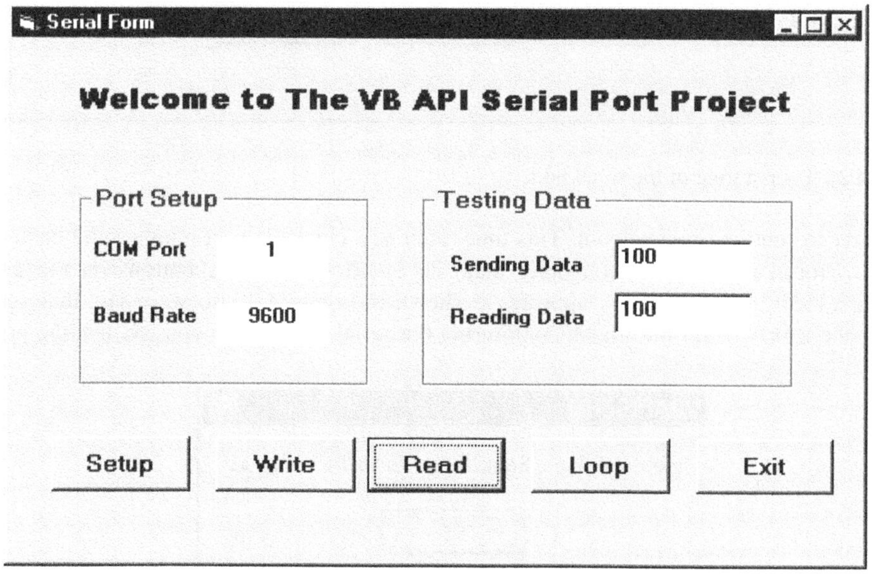

FIGURE 4.27 Running Status of the `frmSerial` form.

form are displayed in the `COM Port` and the `Baud Rate` boxes. Click the `Setup` button to configure the selected serial port using the existing `Port Number` and `Baud Rate` selections. Type some data (`100` in our case) into the `Sending Data` text box and click the `Write` button to send the data out to the serial port. To confirm that the port works properly, click the `Read` button, and the received data will be displayed in the `Reading Data` text box, as shown in Figure 4.27.

If the data received is identical with the that was sent out, it means that the serial port works very well and is error-free. If the received data does not match the sent out data, an error message will appear indicating that port testing has failed for this data transmission.

Now click the `Loop` button to continuously send out and receive back a sequence of random data. This time, the sent out and received data is periodically displayed in the Sending Data and Reading Data text boxes, respectively, which are shown in Figure 4.28. The interval between displaying sent out and received data is dependent on the time delay period controlled by the `TimeDelay()` subroutine. Click the `Exit` button to terminate the program.

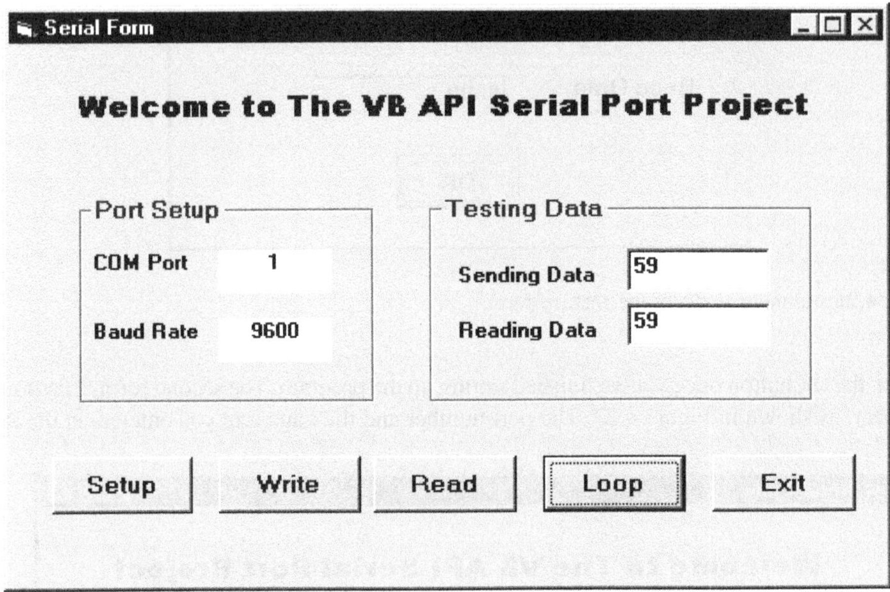

FIGURE 4.28 Loop testing of the serial port.

Now try to run the project again. This time, after you enter the port number and baud rate on the `Setup` form, click any button other than the `Setup` and `Exit` buttons on the `frmSerial.frm` form. A message box appears, as shown in Figure 4.29, to warn you that you must first click the `Setup` button to finish configuring the serial port before you can test the port.

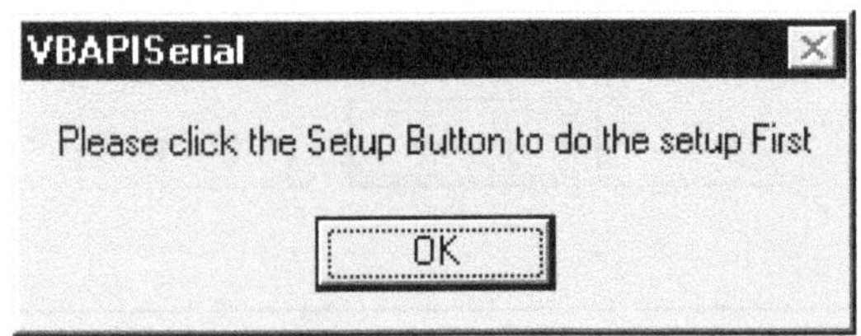

FIGURE 4.29 The `Setup Warning` message box.

This is the effect of the Boolean `setFlg` variable that we added to the project. Click `OK` in the message box, and then click the `Setup` button to finish configuring the serial port. Now you can continue to test the serial port by either sending out or reading back data as described earlier. Our project is very successful.

The complete project files, including the two forms, `Setup.frm` and `frmSerial.frm`, one module `VBAPIModule.bas` and an executable file `VBAPISerial.exe`, are stored in the folder

`Chapter 4\VBAPISerial` on the attached CD. You can load those programs and run them on your computer.

4.3 USING THE ACTIVE-X MSCOMM CONTROL TO INTERFACE WITH THE SERIAL PORTS

In this section, we discuss a very popular serial port interfacing tool, an Active-X control named MSComm, which is designed specially to let Visual Basic interface with the serial port to perform serial data communications in the Windows environment.

4.3.1 Overview of the Active-X MSComm Control

MSComm has been developed as an Active-X control, and it can be embedded into the Visual Basic environment to perform serial port control and data communications. MSComm allows you to add both simple and advanced serial port communication features to your applications to create a full-featured, event-driven communication tool.

MSComm provides an interface to a standard set of communications commands. It allows you to establish a connection to a serial port, connect to another communication device (a modem, for instance), issue commands, exchange data, and monitor and respond to various events and errors that may be encountered during a serial connection. The utilization of MSComm to interface to the serial port can be divided into different layers, as shown in Figure 4.30.

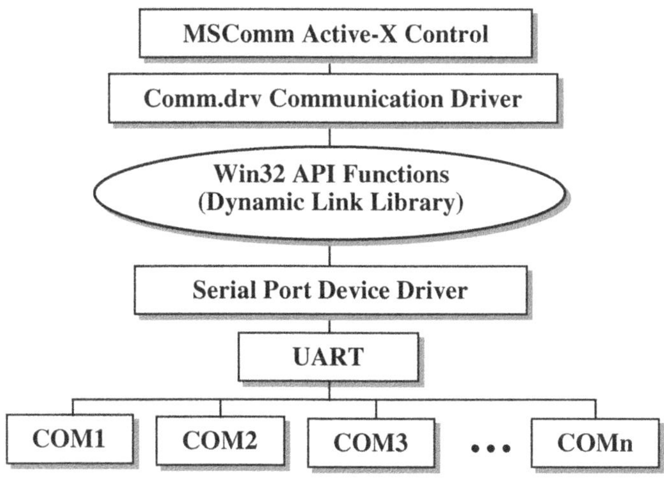

FIGURE 4.30 Block diagram of the MSComm control.

MSComm can be considered the top layer that resides beyond the communication driver `Comm.drv`, which is composed of a collection of Windows API library functions. By using the Win32 API functions contained in the Win32 DLLs (refer to Table 4.1), the `Comm.drv` driver can translate the instructions included in the MSComm layer and pass them to the serial device drivers developed by different serial device manufacturers to provide access to the serial ports.

When you use MSComm as an interface to communicate with the serial ports, you access serial hardware via the Win32 API functions. MSComm can be thought of as a collection of subroutines that can call different Win32 API functions to complete the associated data communication operations. The subroutines can be written in different languages and can be embedded and linked into different working environment.

When you install Microsoft Visual Basic Professional and Enterprise Editions, the Active-X control for the MSComm tool is automatically installed on your computer, in a file named either MSComm16.OCX (for 16-bit computers) or MSComm32.OCX (for 32-bit computers). To activate this Active-X control from your computer, you must open a new Visual Basic project and add that component from the `Project|Components` dialog box.

All interface operations of MSComm are performed using a collection of a properties that belong to that Active-X control. Keep in mind that in MSComm, no function is available for interfacing with the serial port for the data communications. All interfacing operations between MSComm and the serial devices are realized using the Active-X control properties. The properties of the MSComm control can be divided into four categories, according to their purposes:

- Port configuration
- Data transfer
- Handshaking
- Identification of the control

We will now discuss these properties in detail.

4.3.1.1 Configuration Properties for the ActiveX MSComm Control

Table 4.10 lists the ActiveX properties used for configuring serial ports.

TABLE 4.10
Port Configuration Properties for the ActiveX MSComm Control

Property	Description
CommID	Returns a handle that identifies an opened port
CommPort	Indicates the current opened port number
InBufferSize	Indicates the current input buffer's size in bytes
InputLen	Indicates the length of the character string to be read by the input property
InputMode	Indicates the type of data transfer (text or binary)
NullDiscard	Indicates whether the Null character (`0`) should be transferred or neglected
OutBufferSize	Indicates the output buffer's size in bytes
ParityReplace	Indicates the character that replaces an invalid character in the event of a parity error
PortOpen	Sets or checks the port status (`True` = opened, `False` = closed)
RThreshold	Indicates the number of characters to be received in the input buffer before triggering the event comEvReceive
Settings	Indicates the port configuration parameters such as the baud rate, data bits, parity and stop bits.
SThreshold	Indicates the number of characters stored in the output buffer before triggering the event comEvSend

The most popular properties used in the serial data communications are:

- CommPort
- Settings
- InBufferSize
- InputLen
- InputMode
- OutBufferSize
- PortOpen

- RThreshold
- SThreshold

To configure a port, you must assign its COM number to the `CommPort` property, and use the `Settings` property to set values for the baud rate, parity, data bits and stop bits. The `RThreshold` and the `SThreshold` properties are used to define the number of characters stored in the input/output buffers before the receiving event `comEvReceive` or sending event `comEvSend` can be triggered. The `PortOpen` property is used to open and close the port. Set this property to `True` in order to open a port and `False` to close the port. You can also check this property to determine the current port's status. The `InBufferSize` and `OutBufferSize` properties are used to define the volume in which the input and output buffers can hold the number of characters in bytes.

4.3.1.2 Data Transfer Properties for the ActiveX MSComm Control

Table 4.11 lists the ActiveX properties used for performing data transfer operations.

TABLE 4.11
Data Transfer Properties for the ActiveX MSComm Control

Property	Description
CommEvent	A constant indicating the most recent communication event
EOFEnable	Indicates whether the input should stop when receiving the EOF character (`True` = yes, `False` = no)
InBufferCount	Indicates the number of characters that have been received in the input buffer
Input	Identifies data read from the input buffer
Output	Identifies data sent to the output buffer
OutBufferCount	Indicates the number of characters that are stored in the output buffer

4.3.1.3 Handshaking Properties for the ActiveX MSComm Control

The third category of ActiveX properties includes handshaking signals. These handshaking signals can be further divided into two groups:

- Setup signals
- Feedback signals

Table 4.12 lists the handshaking signals used with the MSComm control.

TABLE 4.12
Handshaking Signals for the ActiveX MSComm Control

Signal	Description
Break	Sets or clears a break signal on the transmission line
DTREnable	Sets or clears the DTR line (`True` = set, `False` = clear)
RTSEnable	Sets or clears the RTS line (`True` = set, `False` = clear)
CDHolding	Returns the current status of the CD line
CTSHolding	Returns the current status of the CTS line
DSRHolding	Returns the current status of the DSR line
Handshaking	Sets the current handshaking protocol to the port

In Table 4.12, the upper three properties belong to the Setup signals group, and the lower four properties belong to the Feedback signals group. You can use the properties in the Setup signals group to set or clear the associated transmission line, and you can also check the status of those transmission lines by reading back the signals in the Feedback signals group. For example, in most cases, we use the DTR and RTS lines on the DTE side to issue the starting signal that informs the DCE that the DTE wants to initiate a data communication task. On the DCE side, the program checks the status of the DSR and CTS lines to determine when the data communication task should be started.

In a serial interface program that incorporates the MSComm control, the status of the DSR and CTS transmission lines can be automatically reported by the associated events. All events in the MSComm control can be represented by different event constants, and they all belong to an `OnComm` event object. Whenever a change in a transmission line occurs, the change will trigger an associated event that belongs to the `OnComm` object. The triggered event can be identified by reading the associated constant from the `CommEvent` property. In other words, when the status of a transmission line is changed, the change triggers an associated event, and the `CommEvent` property of the MSComm control changes its value to a constant that indicates the event. Table 4.13 lists some commonly used `CommEvent` constants.

TABLE 4.13
Commonly Used `CommEvent` Constants

Constant	Meaning
comEvCTS	The status of the CTS line has been changed.
comEvDSR	The status of the DSR line has been changed.
comEvCD	The status of the CD line has been changed.
comEvFof	The EOF character has been received (1AH) – <Ctl-Z>.
comEventRing	A Ring signal has been detected at R1.
comEventBreak	A Break signal has been received.
comEvSend	There are fewer characters than `SThreshold` number of characters in the output buffer, which means that the output buffer is almost empty and that more characters can be sent to the transmit buffer.
comEvReceive	There are `Rthreshold` number of characters in the input buffer, which means that the input buffer is almost full and that the program must pick up the received data immediately.

The trigger for the `comEvSend` and `comEvReceive` constants is determined by the value you set for the `SThreshold` and the `RThreshold` properties, respectively. For example, if you set both `SThreshold` and `RThreshold` to `10`, the `comEvSend` will be triggered when the number of characters stored in the output buffer is equal to or less than ten, and the `comEvReceive` will be triggered when the number of characters stored in the input buffer is equal to or more than ten.

You can disable the `comEvSend` event by setting the `SThreshold` property to `0`, and disable the `comEvReceive` event by setting the `RThreshold` property to `0`.

We should now discuss in detail the `Handshaking` signal listed in Table 4.12. `Handshaking` is the process of metering the flow of information over an RS-232 connection. The MSComm Active-X control supports the following handshaking options:

- Hardware handshaking
- Software handshaking
- No handshaking

To select a handshaking option, you can set the `Handshaking` property in Table 4.12 to one of constants that are listed in Table 4.14.

TABLE 4.14
MSComm Handshaking Constants

Constant	Meaning
comNone	Use no handshaking. (This is the default constant.)
comXOnXOff	Use XON/XOFF software handshaking.
comRTS	Use RTS/CTS hardware handshaking.
comRTSXOnXOff	Use both RTS/CTS hardware and XON/XOFF software handshaking.

In addition to the normal handshaking events in the Handshaking signal group, MSComm provides a sequence of error events used to report exceptions and mistakes that occurred during data communication. Table 4.15 lists some popular error events used with RS-232 data communications.

TABLE 4.15
MSComm Error Event Constants for RS-232

Constant	Meaning
comEventFrame	The receiver is not able to detect a Stop bit. This error occurs if the transmitting node quits before sending a complete data, or if the bit rates or number of bits in the settings don't match.
comEventParity	The received parity value does not match the expected one.
comEventOverrun	More characters have arrived when any of buffers on the UART is full.
comEventRxOver	More characters have arrived when the input buffer on the UART is full.,
comEventTxOver	More characters have been written to the output buffer when it is already full.

Typically, the `comEvReceive` event should be triggered when the number of characters received and stored in the input buffer is equal to or greater than the `RThreshold` value you set up as you configure the port with the MSComm properties. In the extreme situation that characters are still coming even though the input buffer is full, an error event, `comEventRxOver`, is triggered and reported to the system to indicate that an overrun error has occurred on the receiver side. Similarly, a `comEventTxOver` error event is triggered if more data is being written to the output or transmit buffer if that buffer is already full.

During communications, both the sender and the receiver should be configured with the same transmission parameters (such as the baud rate, data bits, stop bits and parity values). On the receiving side, whenever new data is received, the receiver needs to check the parity value that arrives with the received data and compare it with the setup parity value to make sure that the two are identical. If these parity values are not the same, a `comEventParity` error event is triggered to notify the system that a mismatch error in parity value has occurred.

4.3.1.4 Identification Properties for the ActiveX MSComm Control

The final group of properties for the ActiveX MSComm Control contains the identification properties. Identification properties are used to indicate values for the current opened port number, port name, port as an object, port parent and port tag settings. Table 4.16 shows the popular identification properties used with the MSComm control.

4.3.1.5 The Operation of the MSComm Control

The ActiveX MSComm control can be used to simplify the sending out and reception of data over an RS-232 serial connection.

TABLE 4.16
Common Identification Properties for the ActiveX MSComm Control

Property	Description
Index	A number used to indicate the current port (MSComm) if there are multiple ports used and those ports are considered as a port collection
Name	Identifies the current port (MSComm)
Object	Indicates that the port is considered as an object (MSComm)
Parent	Indicates the form, object or collection that contains the port (MSComm)
Tag	Indicates an expression defined by the user

4.3.1.5.1 Sending and Receiving Data with the MSComm Control

To send data to a serial port, set the `Output` property of the MSComm control to the data to be sent. To receive data from the serial port, assign a variable to the `Input` property of the MSComm control to pick up the data received. If your system will be receiving text data, a string variable can be used. If your system will be receiving binary data, you can use a variable of the `Variant` type and then reassign the `Variant` variable to a byte array variable. After the value of `Input` is assigned to a variable, `Input` is automatically cleared. When there is nothing available to be read from the serial port, `Input` returns an empty string.

Both text and binary data can be transmitted with MSComm, and transmission can be controlled with the `InputMode` property. To send and receive text data, set the `InputMode` to `comInput-ModeText`. To send and receive binary data, set the `InputMode` to `comInputModeBinary`.

It is convenient to be able to determine how many data characters are waiting to be read from the input buffer without actually pulling them out of the buffer. The `InBufferCount` property of the MSComm control is a good indicator because this property returns the number of characters waiting in the input buffer. If all data waiting in the input buffer is read out, the input buffer is empty, and the `InBufferCount` property goes to `0`. When using the handshaking signal to trigger the `comEvReceive` event, your program can use the `InBufferCount` property to determine whether all data has been read from the input buffer (`InBufferCount = 0`). If you assign a value to the `RThreshold` property, your program can determine the number of characters that have arrived in the input buffer before the `comEvReceive` event can be triggered. Similarly, by setting the `SThreshold` property, you can let your program know how many characters can be written into the transmit buffer before the `comEvSend` event will be triggered.

4.3.1.5.2 Using Handshaking Signals and Events in Serial Data Communications

If you incorporate the MSComm handshaking signals in your application, it will trigger the associated data communication events automatically whenever the status of the transmission lines changes. For example, when the handshaking signal `comRTS` is used for a data transmission, the `comEvCTS` event on the receiving side will be automatically triggered if the `RTSEnable` property on the transmitter side is set to `True`.

Another advantage of using the handshaking signals and events is that the status of the input and output buffer can be automatically reported when a desired situation occurs. For example, the `comEvReceive` event can be triggered automatically when the number of characters waiting in the input buffer is equal to or greater than the `RThreshold` value. Similarly, the `comEvSend` event can be triggered when the number of characters written in the transmit buffer is equal to or greater than the `SThreshold` value.

Another benefit of using the handshaking signals and events is that any data communication error can be automatically reported, so no special subroutine is needed to periodically check those errors.

When you incorporate the MSComm handshaking signals and events in your application, the event object `OnComm`, which works as the entry point of the event procedure to respond to all events, is used to respond to various events. When any event occurs, the application automatically sets an associated event constant (review Table 4.13) to the `CommEvent` property and jumps to the control's `OnComm` subroutine. Inside the event subroutine, a `Select Case` structure is used to determine what kind of action should be taken.

One special event is the device control block (`DCB`) structure error. If any error occurs in the `DCB` structure, a `comEventDCB` event is triggered, and the associated error-processing procedure is then called to handle the situation.

At this point, we have spent a quite a bit of space discussing the use of the Active-X MSComm control to streamline data communications within the Visual Basic environment. We will now use some actual sample programs to illustrate the use of MSComm in real applications.

4.3.2 A Serial Port Communication Program Developed with MSComm

Our first project will use MSComm to perform data transmission over a RS-232 null modem cable between two ports that are located on two different computers. Two programs are developed for this example. One program is developed on a master computer, and the other is developed on a slave computer. Both the master-side and slave-side programs can send and receive data to and from each other. Both programs incorporate a loop feature; on the master side, the loop initiates a data communication task. On the slave side, the loop sends a continuous block of data to the master. The checksum value is attached to the last data bit on the stream and is used to make sure that the data communication is error-free. For simplicity, this project uses the polling data transfer method and handshaking signals to send and receive data. Both the handshaking and the `OnComm` events are used in this project to make the data transmission more efficient. The functions of the master and slave programs are listed here:

- The COM port and the baud rate can be selected dynamically by the user when the programs run.
- Both the master and slave program can send or receive a single data.
- In loop mode, any data transmission task is initialed by the master program, and the slave program feeds data back to the master program by sending a `C` character to start the data transmission.
- Both the master and slave programs use hardware handshaking signals. The master issues an RTS enable command to activate the RTS line to initial a data transfer task. The slave program also issues an RTS enable command and then sends back a `C` character to indicate that it is ready for data transmission. This process is included in a function called `CommStart()`.
- Each time the slave sends data out, it then waits for feedback from the master. If the feedback from the master program is an `ACK` signal, it means that the master has successfully received the data sent by the slave. In response, the slave sends the next data unit. If the feedback from the master program is a `NAK` signal, it means either that an error has occurred during data transmission or that a timeout has occurred on the master computer. In this case, the slave program resends the data until a timeout error occurs to let the slave know that a serious error has occurred in the system and that data transmission must be stopped immediately.
- Each time the master receives data from the slave, it will respond with either an `ACK` signal (if the data is received successfully) or a `NAK` signal (if an error or a timeout has occurred). The master will continue to wait for the slave to resend the data until a timeout error occurs again to let the master know that a serious error has occurred in the system and that data transmission must be stopped immediately.

- After the last data segment has been transferred, a checksum value is sent from the slave computer to the master computer. The master program uses this value to determine whether or not the block of data has been transmitted successfully.

Figure 4.31 presents a functional block diagram of data transmission in loop mode. Let us now develop the master program for our data transmission project.

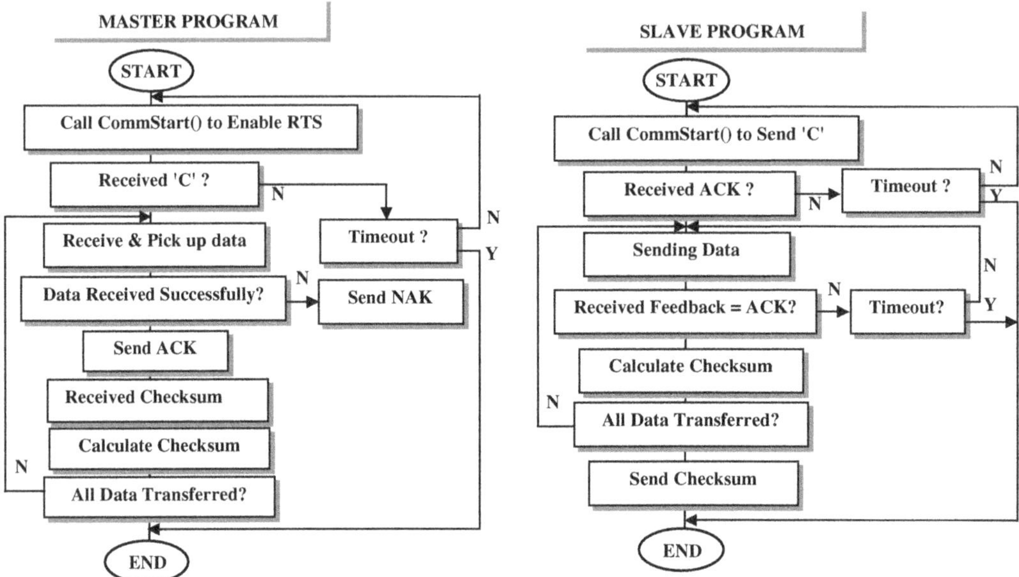

FIGURE 4.31 Block diagram of the `Loop` mode.

4.3.2.1 The Serial Interface Program for the Master Computer

The operations of the master program are illustrated in Figure 4.31. Two forms are used in this program. The first form is used to receive the COM port number and the baud rate that we will enter at run time to configure the serial port, and the second form is used to the perform the actual testing of the serial port. This project also incorporates a code module that will declare and store most of the global constants and variables used in this project.

4.3.2.1.1 Developing the Graphical User Interfaces

To use the Active-X MSComm control in Visual Basic, we need to create a new project and activate the `Microsoft Comm Control 6.0` Communications class. Launch Visual Basic and open a new `Standard.EXE` project. In the opened project window, click the `Project|Components...` item from the menu bar to open the Components dialog box, which is shown in Figure 4.32.

Keep the default `Controls` tab selected and browse down until you find the `Microsoft Comm Control 6.0` option. Check this option to activate the Active-X control in our new project. (See Figure 4.32.) Click the `OK` button to close this dialog box. Immediately, you can see that the `MSComm` icon, which resembles a telephone, has been added to the toolbox window in our project.

Now click the `View Object` button to open the form window. Change the name of the form to `Setup` and add the controls that are listed in Table 4.17.

The finished `Setup` form should look like the one shown in Figure 4.33.

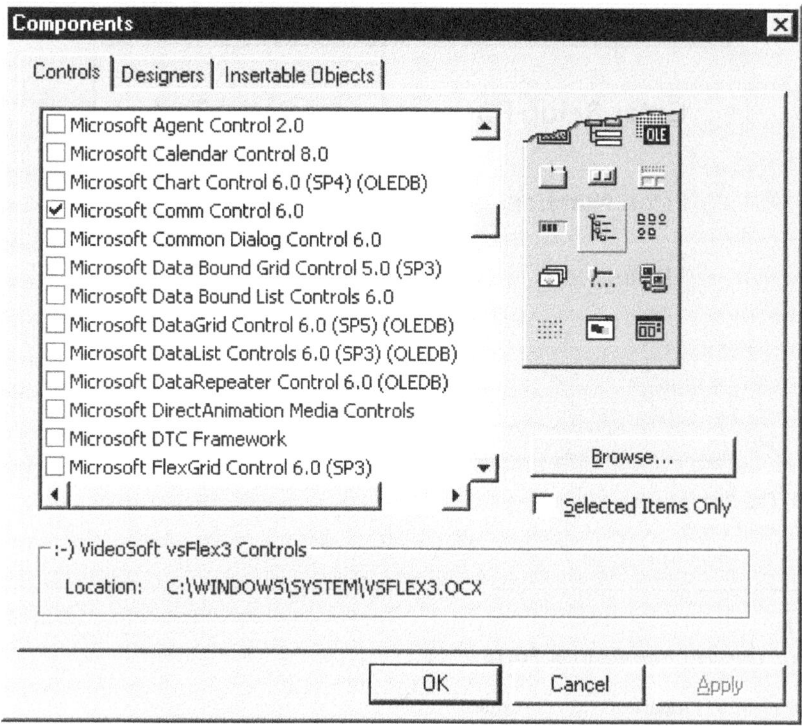

FIGURE 4.32 The `Components` dialog box in Visual Basic.

TABLE 4.17
Controls for the `Setup` Form

Control Type	Properties	Values	Control Type	Properties	Values
Label	Name	Label2	Text box	Name	txtBaudRate
	Caption	Port Number		Text	
Text box	Name	txtPort	CommandButton	Name	CmdSetup
	Text			Caption	Setup
Label	Name	Label3	Label	Name	Label1
	Caption	Baud Rate		Caption	Enter Setup
				Parameters for Serial Port	

The caption for `label1` is `Enter Setup Parameters for Serial Port`, as shown in Figure 4.33. Before we can create the code for this form window, we need to add another form to perform the actual data transmission.

Select the `Project|Add Form` menu item from the menu bar in the Visual Basic workspace to add a new form; name this form `VBCommPorts`. On the newly added form, add the controls that are listed in Table 4.18.

In addition to the controls listed in Table 4.18, we must add the MSComm control to the form. Go to the `Toolbox` window, click the `MSComm` icon that we added earlier, and place it on the lower-left corner of the form. The default name for this MSComm control is `MSComm1`. Keep this name unchanged. We must also need to add a timer to monitor the timeout value. Go to the Toolbox

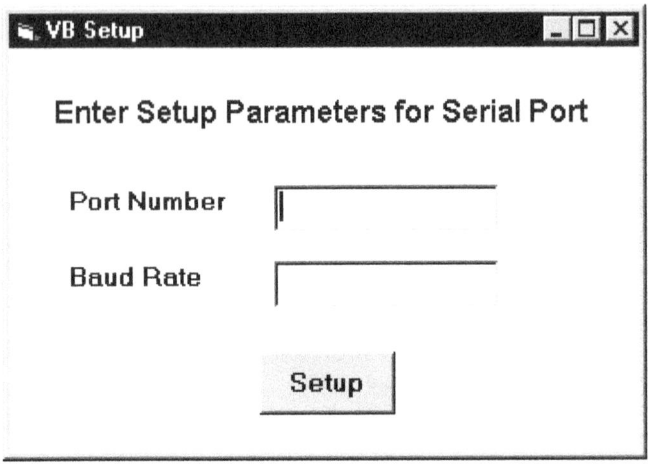

FIGURE 4.33 The `Setup` form Window.

TABLE 4.18
Controls for the `VBCommPorts` Form

Control Type	Properties	Values
Label	Name	Label1
	Caption	Welcome to the Serial Ports Communication Test
Frame	Name	Frame1
	Caption	Port Setup
Label	Name	Label2
	Caption	COM Port
Label	Name	lblComPort
	Caption	Yellow
Label	Name	Label3
	Caption	Baud Rate
Label	Name	lblBaudRate
	Caption	Yellow
Frame	Name	Frame2
	Caption	Testing Data
Label	Name	Label4
	Caption	Sending Data
Text box	Name	txtWdata
	Text	
Label	Name	Label5
	Caption	Readintg Data
Text box	Name	txtRdata
	Caption	
CommandButton	Name	cmd Send
	Caption	Send
CommandButton	Name	CmdReceive
	Caption	Receive
CommandButton	Name	cmdLoop
	Caption	Loop_Receive
CommandButton	Name	cmdExit
	Caption	Exit

window, select the timer, and place it on the low-right corner of the form. Set the properties for the timer control that are listed in Table 4.19.

TABLE 4.19
Properties for the `VBTimer` Control

Property	Value
Name	VBTimer
Enabled	`False`
Interval	6000 (ms)

Notice that the time interval will be measured in milliseconds, and that we use six seconds as the timeout interval value. You can modify this value based on your actual applications. The finished `VBCommPorts` form should match the one shown in Figure 4.34.

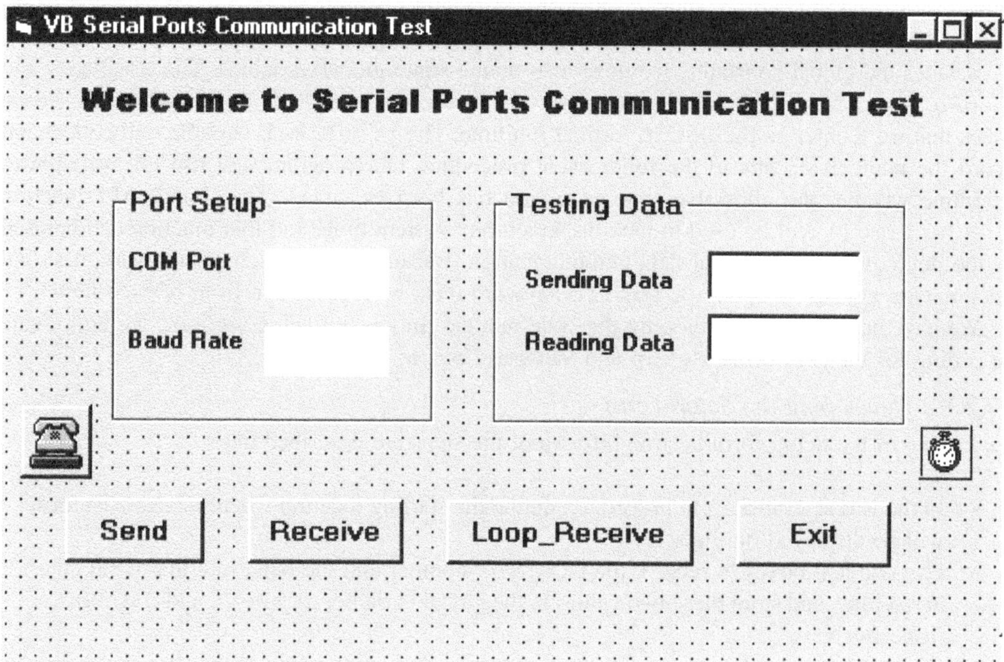

FIGURE 4.34 The `VBCommPorts` form.

To declare and apply the global constants and variables, we need to add a code module to our project. Click the `Project|Add Module` item from the menu bar, and click `Open` in the Add Module dialog box to add a new module to the project. Name the module `VBCommLoop`. Now that we have finished designing the graphical user interface for our master-side program, we can begin the coding process for each form.

4.3.2.1.2 Developing the Code Module

We must now declare all global constants and variables to be used in this program in the code module `VBCommLoop`. Double-click the code module to open its code window, and then enter the code that is shown in Figure 4.35.

```
(General)                                    (Declarations)

Option Explicit
Public Const ACK = &H6
Public Const NAK = &H15
Public Const EOF = -&H1A
Public Const NO_C_RECEIVED = -1
Public Const TIME_OUT = 1
Public Const SUCCESS = 0
Public Const FAIL = -2
Public comPort As Long, baudRate As Long, timeLimit As Integer
Public Declare Function timeGetTime Lib "winmm.dll" () As Long
```

FIGURE 4.35 The coding of the code module.

The first three constants in the code module are system constants, which means that they are defined by the system and are standard handshaking signals, widely used in serial data communications. The next four constants are user-defined constants, specially designed for this project.

Besides the global constants, we must also define some global variables. The `comPort` and `baudRate` variables will be used as temporary buffers to hold the `COM Port` and `Baud Rate` values that we'll enter on the `Setup` form at run time. The `timeLimit` variable will collect and record the number of calls to the timer event procedure. Our program will use this variable to determine whether the allowable timeout period has been exceeded. The Win32 API function `timeGetTime()` will be used to pick up the current system time, and this function can be used for the delay purpose for serial data communication. Because all these constants, variables, and functions are globally scoped, the `Public` keyword must be preceded in front of each item.

We have now finished developing the code module. In the following sections, we will create the coding for the two forms, `Setup` and `VBCommPorts`.

4.3.2.1.3 Developing the Setup Form

The coding of the Setup form is straightforward; the steps are described here:

- In the `Form_Load` event procedure, define the starting location where the `Setup` form will be displayed on the screen.
- Use two text boxes to receive the COM Port number and the baud rate that we'll enter at run time, and store these two values in the global variables `comPort` and `baudRate`, respectively.
- When the `Setup` button is clicked at run time, determine whether the data that we've entered is correct. If not, display a message box prompting us to enter the correct data.
- Hide the `Setup` form and display the `VBCommPorts` form to continue the data transmission task.

From the `Project Explorer` window in the Visual Basic workspace, click the `View Code` button to open the `Setup` form's code window. In this window, enter the code that is shown in Figure 4.36.

Each section of this code is explained in the following list.

A: We first need to type the statement `Option Explicit` at the top of the code window. Recall that this statement will allow the error-detecting system in Visual Basic to work properly, thus protecting us from misusing or misspelling the objects we declare in this form.

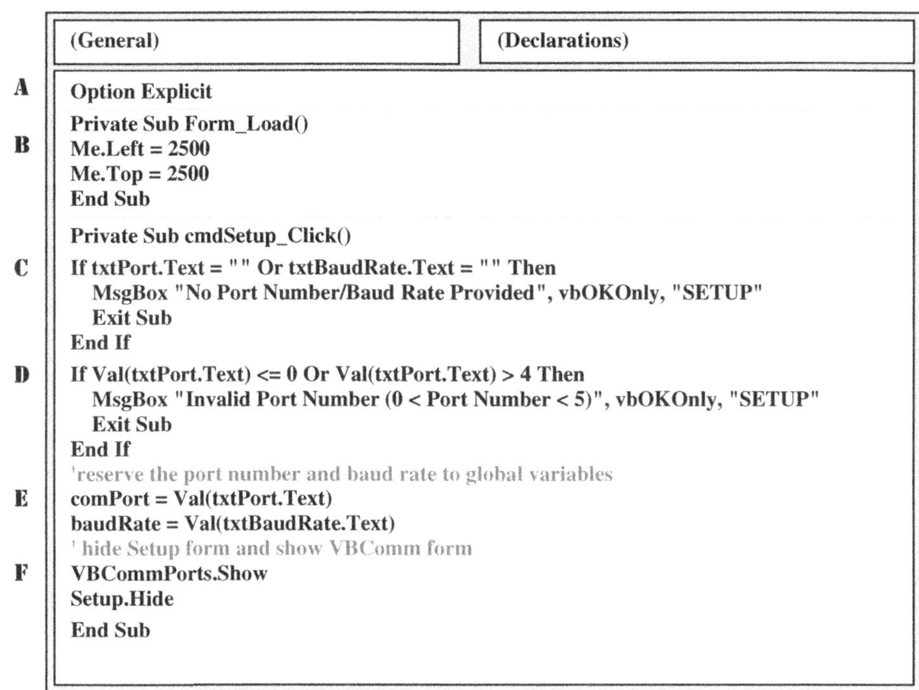

```
(General)                                (Declarations)
A  Option Explicit
   Private Sub Form_Load()
B  Me.Left = 2500
   Me.Top = 2500
   End Sub
   Private Sub cmdSetup_Click()
C  If txtPort.Text = "" Or txtBaudRate.Text = "" Then
      MsgBox "No Port Number/Baud Rate Provided", vbOKOnly, "SETUP"
      Exit Sub
   End If
D  If Val(txtPort.Text) <= 0 Or Val(txtPort.Text) > 4 Then
      MsgBox "Invalid Port Number (0 < Port Number < 5)", vbOKOnly, "SETUP"
      Exit Sub
   End If
   'reserve the port number and baud rate to global variables
E  comPort = Val(txtPort.Text)
   baudRate = Val(txtBaudRate.Text)
   ' hide Setup form and show VBComm form
F  VBCommPorts.Show
   Setup.Hide
   End Sub
```

FIGURE 4.36 Code for the `Setup` form.

B: In the first event procedure, `Form_Load()`, we define the form's location on the screen window in pixels. The horizontal and vertical coordinates of the upper-left corner should both be set to 2500 pixels. These settings will position the `Setup` form at the approximate center of the screen. `Me` is the default name of the `Setup` form object, so to represent the form here you can use either the actual name of the form, `Setup`, or the default name `Me`.

C: The coding of the `Setup` event will be started by checking two text boxes, `Port Number` and `Baud Rate`. This check is necessary because at run time, the program must ensure that the values we entered in these text boxes are valid. If it is not valid, the program will display a message box prompting us to enter the valid data.

D: Our program must now perform another check to ensure that the port number we enter is a valid value. In this application, the range of the port numbers is from 1 to 4. If the port number entered at run time is beyond the specified range, a message box will appear instructing us to enter the correct data. (In your own applications, you can modify this range if your system has more than four serial ports.)

E: If both the port number and the baud rate are valid, a `Val()` function will be called to convert the port number and the baud rate from text form to their associated numeric values. These values will then be stored in two global variables—`comPort` and `baudRate`, respectively—which will be used later by the `VBCommPorts` form.

F: Now the `Setup` form has completed its mission. Two system methods, `Hide` and `Show`, respectively, will be called to hide the `Setup` form and display the `VBCommPorts` form. Most of our data communication work will be performed by the `VBCommPorts` form.

At this point, we have finished coding the `Setup` form for this program.

4.3.2.1.4 Developing the VBCommPorts Form

The operations of this form are described here:

- During the execution of the `Form_Load` event procedure, port configuration will be performed based on the `Port Number` and `Baud Rate` values we enter on the `Setup form` at run time. The form's initial screen location is also defined in this procedure.
- The `Send` button will use hardware handshaking signals to send a single character to the serial port of the slave computer. A timeout monitor will ensure that the data is sent out successfully within a given period of time.
- The `Receive` button will use hardware handshaking signals to receive a single character from the serial port of the slave computer. A timeout monitor will ensure that the data is received successfully within a given period of time.
- When the `Loop_Receive` button is clicked at run time, the master program will receive a continuous block of data sent by the slave program. The hardware handshaking signals, timeout monitor, and checksum methods are used for this data transmission. The received data will be stored in a data file that can be used in the future. (For example, we may wish to plot and analyze the data later on.)
- During the sending and receiving processes, the sent and received data will be displayed in real time, in two text boxes on the `VBCommPorts` form. This feedback will let us monitor the operation of the serial port.

Now we'll code the `Form_Load` event procedure and declare the form-level variables. From the `Project Explorer` window in the Visual Basic workspace, click the `View Code` button and open the code window for the `VBCommPorts` form. In this window, enter the codes that are shown in Figure 4.37.

Each section of this code is explained in the following list.

G: As we did in the `Setup` form, we must type the statement `Option Explicit` at the top of the code window. Recall that this statement will allow the error-detecting system in Visual Basic to work properly, thus protecting us from misusing or misspelling the objects we declare in this form. A form-level `TimeOut` variable is also declared here. The purpose of this Boolean variable is to monitor the current timeout status. A `True` value for this variable will indicate that a timeout has occurred during data transmission. This variable can only be used on this `VBCommPorts` form because we define it as a form-level variable.

H: In the `Form_Load` event procedure, we first define the form's location on the screen window in pixels. The horizontal and vertical coordinates of the upper-left corner should both be set to 2000 pixels. These settings will position the `VBCommPorts` form at the approximate center of the screen. `Me` is the default name of the form object, so to represent the form here you can use either the actual name of the form, `Setup`, or the default name `Me`. Next we should initialize some global and form-level variables. The global `timeLimit` variable and the form-level `TimeOut` variable are initialized to `0` and `False`, respectively.

I: Next our program uses the MSComm control to initialize and configure the serial port. First we need to disable the RTS transmission line by resetting the `RTSEnable` handshaking signal to `False`. Later, we can initialize a data communication job by setting the `RTSEnable` handshaking signal to `True`.

J: Now the program will use two labels, `lblComPort` and `lblBaudRate`, to display the `Port Number` and `Baud Rate` values. The program assigns two global variables,

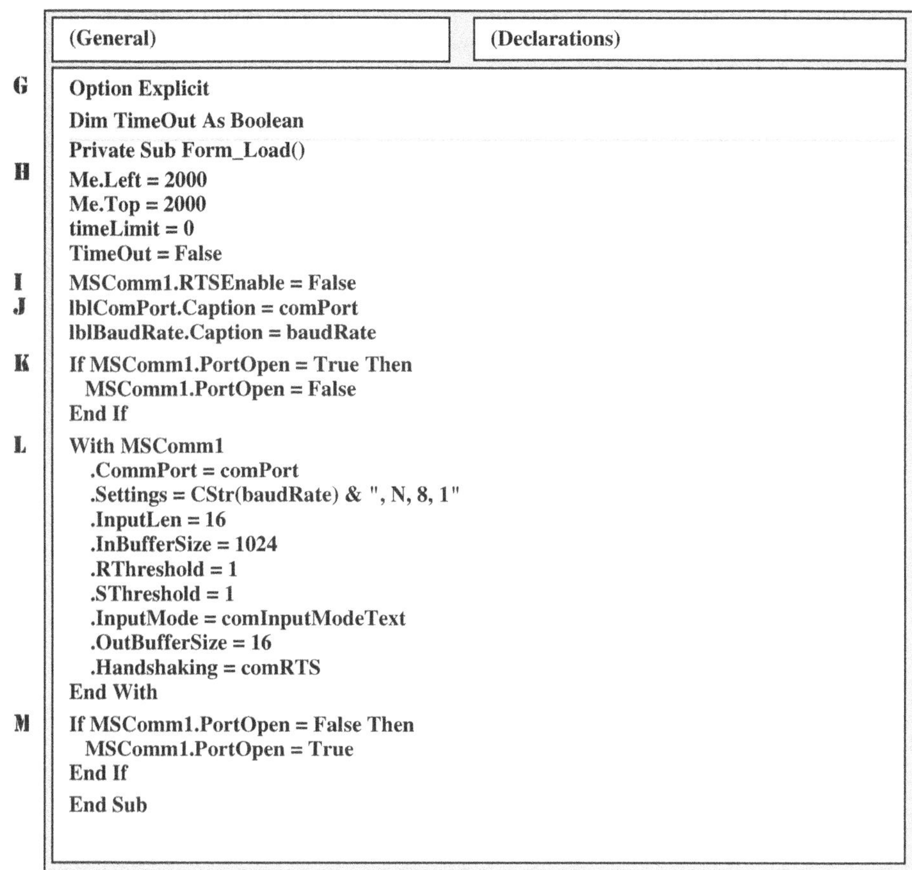

```
(General)                              (Declarations)

G  Option Explicit
   Dim TimeOut As Boolean
   Private Sub Form_Load()
H  Me.Left = 2000
   Me.Top = 2000
   timeLimit = 0
   TimeOut = False
I  MSComm1.RTSEnable = False
J  lblComPort.Caption = comPort
   lblBaudRate.Caption = baudRate
K  If MSComm1.PortOpen = True Then
     MSComm1.PortOpen = False
   End If
L  With MSComm1
     .CommPort = comPort
     .Settings = CStr(baudRate) & ", N, 8, 1"
     .InputLen = 16
     .InBufferSize = 1024
     .RThreshold = 1
     .SThreshold = 1
     .InputMode = comInputModeText
     .OutBufferSize = 16
     .Handshaking = comRTS
   End With
M  If MSComm1.PortOpen = False Then
     MSComm1.PortOpen = True
   End If
   End Sub
```

FIGURE 4.37 Code for the `VBCommPorts` form.

`comPort` and `baudRate`, to the `Caption` property of these two labels. The global variables will be used as temporary buffers to store the Port Number and Baud Rate values that we entered on the `Setup` form at run time.

K: Before we can configure the serial port with the MSComm control, we have to make sure that the port is closed. Our program uses the `PortOpen` property of the MSComm control to check the port status and reset it to `False` (to close it) if the port is opened.

L: Now we can begin to configure the port by using the properties of the MSComm control. To make this configuration simple, we'll use the `With` statement provided by Visual Basic. The configuration is performed in the following sequence:

The global variable `comPort` that contains the serial port number entered by the user is assigned to the `CommPort` property as the current port number.

The `Settings` property is used to configure the serial port based on the port parameters selected by the user. This property is represented as a string with four fields in the following order: baud_rate, parity value, data bits and stop bits. Each field is separated by a comma. In our case, a built-in function, `CStr()`, is used to convert the global variable `baudRate` that contains the baud rate entered by the user from a numeric value to a string variable. The concatenation operator `&` is then used to combine the baud rate with the other three fields (No parity, 8 data bits and 1 stop bit), and to assign the combined values to the Settings property.

The `InputLen` property is used to indicate how many characters should be read from the input buffer during the each reading period. A value of `16` is assigned to this property, which means that during each cycle we want to read 16 characters.

The `InBufferSize` property was illustrated in Table 4.10. This property is used to indicate the total number of characters, in bytes, that can be stored in the current input buffer. In our case, a value of 1024 is used.

The `RThreshold` property is used to set the number of characters received in the input buffer before the `comEvReceive` event is fired. The `SThreshold` property is used to set the number of characters stored in the output buffer before the `comEvSend` event is fired. For our program, we set both properties to 1 to indicate that both events should be triggered as soon as one character is received in the input buffer or one character is written into the transmit buffer.

The `InputMode` property is used to determine what kind of data will be transmitted during the data transfer task. We will transfer only text data, so here the `comInput-ModeText` constant is assigned to this property. (We needn't make any changes here because the default transfer mode is text data.)

Similar to `InBufferSize`, the `OutBufferSize` property is used to define the number of characters that can be stored in the transmit buffer. In our case, a value of 16 is used.

The `Handshaking` property is used to define the handshaking type used for data transmission. Our program will use the hardware handshaking method, so a `comRTS` is assigned to this property.

Don't forget to attach the `End With` statement to the end point of the `With` block.

M: After the port has been configured, we can open the port to make it ready for data communications. After checking the `PortOpen` property, our program can assign a suitable Boolean value to that property to open the port.

Now let's continue the coding for our remaining controls. First we need to create the code for the `Send` command button. The purpose of the `Send` button is to send a single data unit to the serial port of the slave computer.

In the form window `VBCommPorts`, double-click the `Send` command button to open its event procedure window. In this window, enter the code that is shown in Figure 4.38.

N: Before we can send any data to the port, we need to set the hardware handshaking signal. By setting the property `RTSEnable` to `True`, we set the RTS transmission line to active state. This RTS status initials a new data communication task. The slave program can response to this initial state with a feedback of `C` to inform the master computer that the slave computer is ready for a data transmission task. We also enable the `VBTimer` here by setting its `Enabled` property to `True`. We use this timer to monitor the timeout value and set the `TimeOut` Boolean variable to indicate when the interval set for the timer has been exceeded, which will mean that a timeout has occurred during a data transmission.

O: Next a `Do-Until` loop structure is used to pause processing until either the `CTS-Holding` property is set to `True`, which means that the slave has received the RTS signal sent by the master, and has responded with an active CTS signal to indicate that the slave computer is ready for data communication, or the `TimeOut` Boolean variable is set to `True`, which means that a timeout has occurred.

P: Inside the `Do-Until` loop, where the program will periodically check the status of the CTS line, all CPU time is occupied by the program and the CPU cannot handle any other task, even if that task has higher priority. This situation is called a dead cycle and

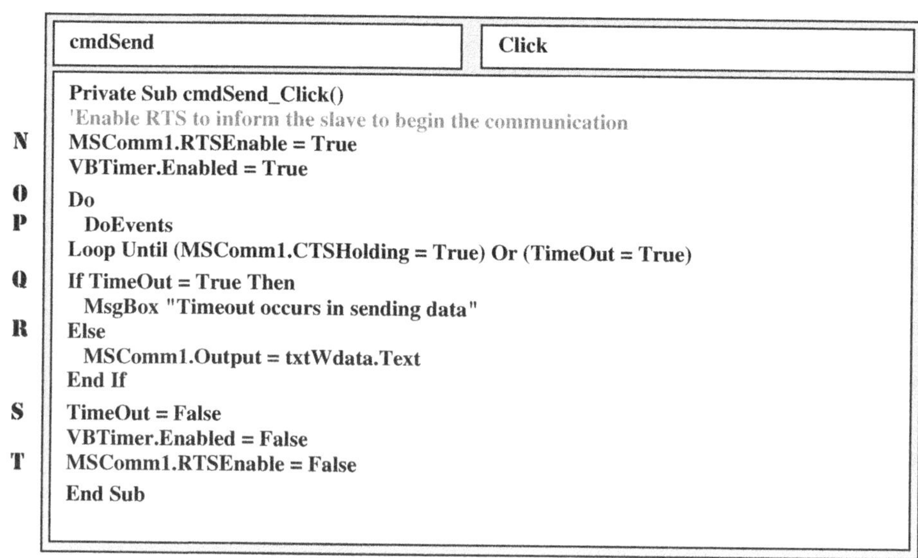

```
  cmdSend                     Click

  Private Sub cmdSend_Click()
  'Enable RTS to inform the slave to begin the communication
N MSComm1.RTSEnable = True
  VBTimer.Enabled = True
O Do
P   DoEvents
  Loop Until (MSComm1.CTSHolding = True) Or (TimeOut = True)
Q If TimeOut = True Then
    MsgBox "Timeout occurs in sending data"
R Else
    MSComm1.Output = txtWdata.Text
  End If
S TimeOut = False
  VBTimer.Enabled = False
T MSComm1.RTSEnable = False
  End Sub
```

FIGURE 4.38 Code for the `Send` Command button.

is no good for a multitasking environment. We insert a `DoEvents` statement into the `Do-Until` loop to prevent this situation. The `DoEvents` statement enables the control to be periodically transferred from the current program to the CPU and allows the CPU to process other tasks if the current program is in idle status. This transfer is periodical and allows multiple tasks to be processed in parallel.

Q: If the `Do-Until` loop is terminated by a timeout situation, it means that either the CTS line has not been activated by the slave computer or the master computer cannot receive an activated signal from its CTS line. A message box will appear to display the error information, and the program will return the error information to the Visual Basic platform.

R: Otherwise, if the `Do-Until` loop is terminated by a `CTSHolding` ⊕`=True`, which means that the slave computer has received the RTS signal and is ready for the data transmission. After sending the data (which we enter at run time) that is stored in the text box `txtWdata` to the `Output` property of the MSComm control, our program can write the data to the serial port of the slave computer. Because we will be transferring text data, the `Text` property of the text box is directly assigned to the `Output` property of the MSComm control without any conversion.

S: At this point, a single data transmission task has been completed, successfully or not. We need to reset the Boolean `TimeOut` variable to make it ready for the future use. We also must disable `VBTimer` to stop it from running.

T: Finally we need to reset the `RTSEnable` property to disable the RTS signal.

The purpose of the `Receive` command button is to receive a single data item sent by the slave computer. In the opened code window, select the `cmdReceive` item from the object box to open its event procedure, and enter the code that is shown in Figure 4.39.

U: To receive data using the hardware handshaking method, our program must activate the RTS transmission line by setting the `RTSEnable` property of the MSComm control to `True`. This signal is the equivalent of responding to the sender, which now is the slave computer, to indicate that the master computer is ready to receive data. Our program

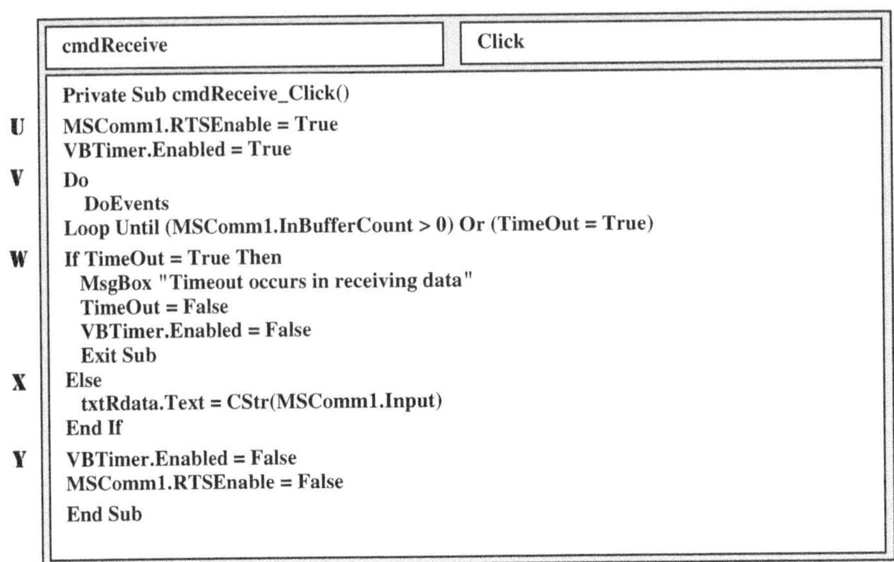

```
cmdReceive                    Click

  Private Sub cmdReceive_Click()
U MSComm1.RTSEnable = True
  VBTimer.Enabled = True
V Do
    DoEvents
  Loop Until (MSComm1.InBufferCount > 0) Or (TimeOut = True)
W If TimeOut = True Then
    MsgBox "Timeout occurs in receiving data"
    TimeOut = False
    VBTimer.Enabled = False
    Exit Sub
X Else
    txtRdata.Text = CStr(MSComm1.Input)
  End If
Y VBTimer.Enabled = False
  MSComm1.RTSEnable = False
  End Sub
```

FIGURE 4.39 Code for the `Receive` Command button.

enables the `VBTimer` here by setting its `Enabled` property to `True` and thus begin monitoring the time period spent by the data transmission.

V: As in the `Send` event procedure, a `Do-Until` loop is used here to wait for one of two events: either a timeout error or a data arrival in the input buffer. By checking the `InBufferCount` property, our program can determine whether any data has arrived in the input buffer. A `DoEvents` statement is inserted inside this loop to prevent the dead cycle.

W: If the timeout event occurs, it will be identified by a `True` value in the Boolean `TimeOut` variable, and a message box will be displayed to show us this error. The `TimeOut` variable will then be reset, and the `VBTimer` will be disabled to stop the function of the timer. The program will return the error state to the Visual Basic platform.

X: If the `Do-Until` loop is terminated by the `InBufferCount>0` event, it means that the data has been successfully received by the input buffer. The `Input` property of the MSComm control will be used to pick up the data and assign it to the text box `txtRdata` to display the received data.

Y: After the data transmission is completed, we need to reset the `VBTimer` and the RTS transmission line by resetting the `Enabled` property of the `VBTimer` and the `RTSEnable` property of the MSComm control, respectively.

Both the Send and the Receive event procedures need the `VBTimer` to monitor and report any timeout errors that occur during the data transmission process. The `VBTimer` operates according to its event procedure, `VBTimer_Timer()`. The coding of this event procedure is shown in Figure 4.40.

Z: The `VBTimer` event procedure is called whenever the time interval has been exceeded. In our case, this time interval is set to `6000` (six seconds, because the interval is measured in milliseconds). If no data is received or the status of the `CTSHolding` signal is kept unchanged during the period of six seconds, a timeout error will occur and the `VBTimer` event procedure will be called. Once the program enters this event procedure, the global variable `timeLimit` will increase by 1 and the Boolean `TimeOut` variable will be set to `True` to indicate that a timeout error has occurred.

VBTimer	Timer

Z
```
Private Sub VBTimer_Timer()
timeLimit = timeLimit + 1
TimeOut = True
End Sub
```

FIGURE 4.40 Code for the `VBTimer`.

The global variable `timeLimit` records the times at which the timeout occurs. (In different applications, the timeout period is different, so this value depends on the developer and the actual implementations.) During the initial state of the data transmission, the sender and the receiver need a synchronization process, which means that they need to share a convention for the starting point of that data transmission. The period of this synchronization process generally needs a little longer time to complete than does a data transmission process. The `timeLimit` variable is used to allow the `VBTimer` event procedure to be called multiple times; a longer timeout period can be obtained as long as the value of the `timeLimit` is smaller than a preferred value defined by the user.

Now let's take a look at the `Loop_Receive` event procedure, which will be triggered by a click of the `Loop_Receive` command button. The purpose of this event procedure is to continuously receive a block of data sent by the slave program from the slave computer.

The operations of this event procedure are described here:

- As previously mentioned, before the master computer can receive a continuous block of data from the slave computer, the master and the slave computer need to complete a synchronization process. This process is performed by a call to the `CommStart()` function. An argument included in this function is used to set the upper boundary of the timeout period.
- When the `CommStart()` function is executed and the executing status is returned, we need to monitor the running status of the function. If a `NO_C_RECEIVED` error is returned, it means that a problem exists on the serial communication hardware. An error message will be displayed and the program will be terminated. If a timeout error has occurred, call the `CommStart()` to repeat the synchronization process. If, after this process, a timeout error is encountered again, it means that the problem is unusually serious; in this case, the error information will be displayed and the program will be terminated. If the function returns a `SUCCESS` signal, it means that the master computer has successfully sent out the initial character and received the feedback (here, a `C` character) from the slave program. The synchronization process has been successful, and both the master and the slave computer are ready for the data communication task.
- A data file will be opened to store the received data. This data file can be used in the future (if, for example, we wish to plot and analyze the data later on).
- A receiving loop will be executed to continuously pick up the block of data sent by the slave computer. Inside the loop, the `CommRecv()` function is called to pick up each data unit sent by the slave program. If a timeout occurs during the execution of this function, the function is called again so that the program can retry receiving the data. If, after the second time, the function still encounters a timeout error, the error information will be displayed and the program will be terminated.
- If the `CommRecv()` function has executed successfully, the received data will be assigned to the `txtRdata` text box to be displayed on the screen.
- The checksum value is calculated using the current received data.

- The loop will continue until the end of file character (EOF) is received from the slave computer, which means that data transmission has been completed.
- A function named recvChkSum() will be called to receive the checksum value sent by the slave computer.
- The calculated checksum value will be compared with the checksum value received from the slave computer. If the values are identical, a SUCCESS message is displayed, which means that the block of data has been successfully transmitted; otherwise an error message will appear.

Now let us complete the coding for the Loop_Receive event procedure, and then examine in detail each function that it incorporates. In the code window, select cmdLoop from the object list to open its event procedure, enter the code that is shown in Figure 4.41.

1: Four local variables are declared at the beginning of this procedure. The rc variable stores the returned status of the running function. The Index variable is used as a loop counter for the Do-Until loop. The rcArray() variable is a two-dimensional integer array that picks up the returned status and the value of the calling function. The chkSum variable is an integer that stores the checksum value calculated in the master-side program based on the received data.

2: The chkSum variable is initialized to 0. Each time this event procedure is triggered and executed, the chkSum variable must be initialized to 0 to ensure that the calculation of the checksum value is correct.

3: The CommStart() function is called to perform the synchronization process between the master and the slave programs. An argument with a value of 100 is passed into this function. As previously explained, this argument stores the upper boundary of the timeout period for this function. The VBTimer interval is set to 6000 (six seconds, because the interval is measured in milliseconds); this means that the VBTimer event procedure is called for each period of six seconds if no data is received or no change is detected in the CTS line during that period of time. Inside the event procedure, the timeLimit is increased by 1 and the Timeout is set to True. The argument with a value of 100 is the upper boundary of the timeLimit, so CommStart() will be continuously called if the timeLimit has a value less than 100 when the timeout occurs. This means that the CommStart() function will be repeatedly called 100 times after the timeout error occurs, for a total time period of 600 seconds. (This argument can be modified to suit your actual implementations.)

4: After the CommStart() function is executed, we need to check its returned status to determine our next step. Normally, a C character will be received as feedback from the slave computer, which means that the slave computer has received the RTS signal and is ready for data transmission. If a NO_C_RECEIVED error is received, it means that a hardware problem exists between the master and the slave computer. An error message will be displayed and the program will be terminated.

5: If a timeout error is returned, the CommStart() function will be called again to retry the synchronization process another 100 times.

6: If, after the second call, the function still returns a timeout error or a NO_C_RECEIVED error, it means that a serious hardware problem exists between the master and the slave computer. An error message will be displayed and the program will be terminated. In this case, we must fix the hardware problem before the program can be run again.

7: If the function returns a SUCCESS signal, it means that a C character has been received from the slave computer and that both computers are ready to perform data transmission. In this case, a data file will be opened with a default file number of 1. This data file is used to store the received data for future use.

cmdLoop	Click

```
   Private Sub cmdLoop_Click()
1  Dim rc As Integer, index As Integer, rcArray() As Integer, chkSum As Integer
2  chkSum = 0
3  rc = CommStart(100)
4  If rc = NO_C_RECEIVED Then
      MsgBox "Time Out occurs, no C received from the Slave"
      Exit Sub
5  ElseIf rc = TIME_OUT Then
      rc = CommStart(100)
6     If (rc = TIME_OUT) Or (rc = NO_C_RECEIVED) Then
         MsgBox "Second time CommStart() failed...exit"
         Exit Sub
      End If
7  ElseIf rc = SUCCESS Then
     Open "C:\data\VBCOM2Ports.dat" For Output As #1
8    Do
9       rcArray() = CommRecv()
        If rcArray(1) = TIME_OUT Then
           rcArray() = CommRecv()                    ' Re-Receive the data
10         If rcArray(1) = TIME_OUT Then
              MsgBox "Second times CommRecv() failed....exit"
              Exit Sub
           End If
11      ElseIf rcArray(1) = SUCCESS Then
           txtRdata.Text = rcArray(2)
12         On Error GoTo chkSumHandler
           chkSum = (rcArray(2) + chkSum) * 2
13         Print #1, CStr(rcArray(2))
        End If
     Loop Until (rcArray(2) = EOF)
14   Close #1
15   rcArray() = recvChkSum()
     If rcArray(1) = SUCCESS Then
        Print rcArray(2)
        If rcArray(2) = chkSum Then
           MsgBox "The program is completed successfully"
        Else
           MsgBox "Checksum is mismatched"
        End If
     Else
        MsgBox "Receiving the chksum is failed"
     End If
   End If
16 Exit Sub
17 chkSumHandler:
     Resume Next
   End Sub
```

FIGURE 4.41 Code for the `Loop Receive` event procedure.

8: Following the opening of the data file, a `Do-Until` loop will be executed to continuously receive a block of data sent by the slave computer. (You can add a `DoEvents` statement into this loop to make it more suitable for a multitasking environment.)

9: The `CommRecv()` function will be called to pick up the single data item received and stored in the input buffer. This function will return an integer array `rcArray()`. The first element in the array is the execution status of this function, and the second element is the received data value from the input buffer.

TIP: When calling a function that returns an array in Visual Basic, you cannot clearly define the dimension for that array when you declare the array variable. Consequently, you declare a dynamic array whose dimension is undetermined. Inside the function that is supposed to return the array, you must declare a local array with the definite dimension, and then assign and return that array before the function exits.

You may have found that in step 1 above, the `rcArray()` has no dimension when it is declared. This is an example of how to use a function that returns an array.

By checking the first element of the returned array `rcArray(1)`, we can inspect the running status of the `CommRecv()` function. If the returned element is a timeout error, we need to call that function and try again to pick up the data from the input buffer.

10: If, after the second call, the `CommRecv()` function still returns a timeout error, it means that a problem exists in the serial hardware between the two computers. The error information will be displayed in a message box, and the program will be terminated so that we can fix the hardware problem.

11: If the `CommRecv()` function returns a `SUCCESS` signal, it means that the data has been successfully retrieved from the input buffer. The data value that is stored in the second element in the array `rcArray(2)` is assigned to the text box `txtRdata` to be displayed on screen.

12: The system statement `On Error Go To` is used here to avoid the overflow error warning made by the Visual Basic platform. As you know, `chkSum` is defined as an integer variable. In Visual Basic, an integer is a 16-bit binary data. During the checksum calculation, the partial result needs to shift a number of bits to the left, and the number of this shift is equal to the number of data bits received. In other words, one shift left is performed for each received data bit. It is obvious that an overflow will occur for this 16-bit variable. The calculation of the checksum value never prevents this overflow, and it is not an error for our checksum calculation. Therefore, in order to avoid the overflow error warning issued by Visual Basic and to keep our program running, we use the `On Error Go To` statement to transfer the program to a position where it can handle this warning. A symbolic address, `chkSumHandler`, is used to direct the warning to jump to the address where the warning can be handled. The checksum calculation is straightforward: Each time a new data unit is received, it is added to the partial result, and the addition result is then shifted left by 1 bit. Because there is no shift command available in Visual Basic, we use multiplication to replace it. Multiplying the result by 2 is equivalent to shifting left by one bit.

13: The received data that is stored in the returned array `rcArray(2)` will be converted to a text string by the built-in function `CStr()` and then written into the data file with a file number of 1. The codes between step 8 and step 13 will be repeatedly executed until the `EOF` character is received, which means that all data has been transmitted and that the data transmission is completed.
Note that the `EOF` character is received and returned by the second element in the array `rcArray(2)`, not the first element; this is because the first one is used to store the running status of the `CommRecv()` function.

14: After all data has been transferred and written into the data file, a `Close #1` statement will be used to close the data file. This step is very important; if we fail to include it, no data can be written into the data file, and our data file will be blank. In addition, our data file will be still opened, and our program will encounter an error the next time we try to run it.

15: Now we need to pick up the checksum value transmitted from the slave computer. During data transmission, both the master and the slave program need to calculate their checksum values separately. After the data transmission task has been completed, these two checksum values need to be compared. The checksum calculated by the master computer is stored in the `chkSum` variable, and the checksum calculated by the slave computer is received and stored in the second element of the `rcArray(2)` array. By comparing these two checksum values, our program can determine whether the data transmission has been successful. If the two values are identical, it means that data transmission has been successful; otherwise the transmission has failed.

16: After the program has finished comparing the checksum values, the `cmdLoop_Click` procedure should finish and should exit. In our program, however, we have a symbolic `chkSumhandler` address immediately following the checksum comparison. An `Exit Sub` must be used here to direct the function to exit without touching that symbolic address. If the program did not use this `Exit Sub` command, the event procedure would continue to execute the instruction under the symbolic address `chkSumHandler` and an error would be encountered. Because the codes between steps 13 and 15 have nothing to do with the overflow, the procedure would continue to execute the instructions under the symbolic `chkSumHandler` address. In Visual Basic, an error will be encountered warning us not to perform the overflow error protection for this segment of code because it is impossible to have an overflow occur.

TIP: When using the `On Error Go To` statement in a function, you should always place the `symbolic_address` variable in the last line of the function. Remember also to use an `Exit Sub` command before the `symbolic_address` variable to direct the function to exit without touching the instruction under the `symbolic_address`. Otherwise, your program will encounter an error issued by Visual Basic platform.

17: Under the symbolic address `chkSumHandler`, we place one instruction, `Resume Next`, to handle overflow errors for the checksum calculation. If an overflow error is encountered, this instruction will allow the function to execute the instruction that immediately follows the one that has caused the error.

The coding of the `Loop_Receive` event procedure is complete. Now let's discuss each of the functions used by this event procedure. The first function is the synchronization process `CommStart()`. The operation of this function is described here:

- The RTS transmission line on the master computer is activated to initiate a data transmission task. The timer `VBTimer` is enabled to monitor the time period spent by the data transmission.
- A `Do-Until` loop is used to pause processing until one of the following conditions occurs:

  The CTS transmission line is active and data has arrived in the input buffer. This means that the slave computer has received the RTS signal and responded with the CTS signal, and sent a `C` character back to the master computer to indicate that the slave computer is ready for data transmission.

  A timeout error has occurred, but the value of `timeLimit` is less than the value of the upper boundary we've set for this function.

- If the timeout error has occurred and the value of timeLimit is greater than the value of the upper boundary we've set, it means that multiple timeouts have occurred and that a hardware problem exists on the serial communication lines. In this case, the CommStart() function returns a NO_C_RECEIVED error, indicating that the error cannot be overcome by multiple executions of the function; in this case, the program must be terminated.
- If no error occurs, the Do-Until loop is terminated by an event indicating that the CTS transmission line has been signaled and that data has arrived in the input buffer. The Input property of the MSComm control is used to pick up the data stored in the input buffer. If the received data is a C, it means that the slave computer is ready for data transmission. An ACK character should be sent back to the slave program from the master to inform it that the C character has been successfully received by the master computer, and the data transmission can begin. The CommStart() function returns a SUCCESS signal to the calling event procedure. If the received data is not a C , the master program sends a NAK character back to the slave computer to indicate that the feedback character C has not been received and that the slave program needs to resend that character. Then the function returns a timeout error to the calling event procedure.
- Before the program can exit the CommStart() function, the RTS line needs to be reset to inactive status. The VBTimer must also be disabled to stop it from running, and the Boolean TimeOut variable should be reset to False to prepare it for the next timeout monitoring period.

Now we need to add a new user-defined CommStart() function into our project.

TIP: When adding a user-defined procedure into the project, you must be very careful because in Visual Basic, user-defined procedures are divided into functions and subroutines. If your new procedure has no returned value, it should be defined as a subroutine in Visual Basic. If the new procedure must return something, it should be defined as a function. This arrangement is totally different from that of the functions used in other programming languages.

Because our CommStart() procedure needs to return an integer variable, it is devised as a function in the Visual Basic environment.

From the Project Explorer window in the Visual Basic workspace, click the View Code button. Select the Tools|Add Procedure... item from the menu bar to open the Add Procedure dialog box, which is shown in Figure 4.42.

In the Add Procedure dialog box, enter CommStart into the Name: text box as the name for this function. Click the Function radio button to tell Visual Basic that we'll be adding a function, not a subroutine. Select the Private radio button to limit the function's scope to this form only. The Add Procedure dialog box should now match the one shown in Figure 4.42.

Before we can write any code into this function, we need to finish defining it. The CommStart() function has an integer argument and needs to return an integer; we now must manually add that argument, along with the returned variable type. To add these components, type waitTime as Integer into the parentheses following the function name, and attach As Integer to the end of the function header. Now enter the code that is shown in Figure 4.43.

Each section of this code is explained in the following list.

18: A local variable, startData, is declared at the beginning of the CommStart() function. This is a string variable that will store the received data from the slave computer. Following this local variable definition, some other initializations are performed. The timeout flag TimeOut is set to False, and the RTSEnable property of the MSComm

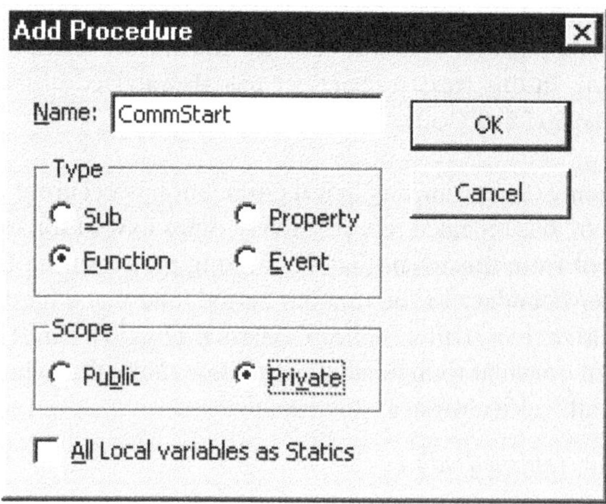

FIGURE 4.42 The `Add Procedure` dialog box.

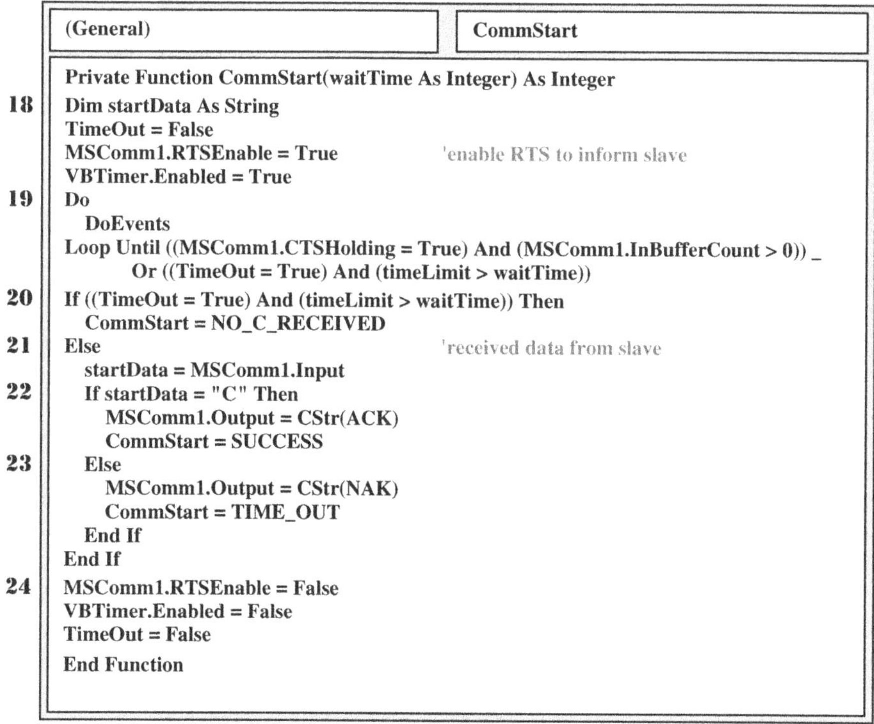

```
(General)                                  CommStart

   Private Function CommStart(waitTime As Integer) As Integer
18 Dim startData As String
   TimeOut = False
   MSComm1.RTSEnable = True               'enable RTS to inform slave
   VBTimer.Enabled = True
19 Do
      DoEvents
   Loop Until ((MSComm1.CTSHolding = True) And (MSComm1.InBufferCount > 0)) _
         Or ((TimeOut = True) And (timeLimit > waitTime))
20 If ((TimeOut = True) And (timeLimit > waitTime)) Then
      CommStart = NO_C_RECEIVED
21 Else                                   'received data from slave
      startData = MSComm1.Input
22    If startData = "C" Then
         MSComm1.Output = CStr(ACK)
         CommStart = SUCCESS
23    Else
         MSComm1.Output = CStr(NAK)
         CommStart = TIME_OUT
      End If
   End If
24 MSComm1.RTSEnable = False
   VBTimer.Enabled = False
   TimeOut = False
   End Function
```

FIGURE 4.43 The user-defined `CommStart()` function.

control is set to `True` to activate the RTS transmission line. The timer `VBTimer` is also enabled so that it can monitor the time period spent by the data transmission.

19: A `Do-Until` loop will be used to pause execution until one of the following two conditions occurs:

A timeout error occurs, and the value of the `timeLimit` variable is greater than the upper boundary (`waitTime`) that we set when this function is called.

The CTS transmission line is signaled (`CTSHolding = True`), which means that the slave computer has received the RTS signal sent by the master computer and returned an activated CTS signal. In this case, a character has also arrived in the input buffer of the master computer (`InBufferCount >0`).

20: If the first condition is true, it means that the timeout has occurred many times and that the `Do-Until` loop has repeated its cycle many times to wait for some event to happen. It can be concluded from this event that the waiting period of the `Do-Until` loop has exceeded the upper boundary of the timeout period, and that a hardware problem exists on the communication lines. The `CommStart()` function will return a `NO_C_RECEIVED` constant to indicate this problem. Note that when a value is returned from a function call in Visual Basic, the protocol is

function name = returned value

21: If the second condition is true, it means that a character has arrived in the input buffer of the master computer. The `Input` property of the MSComm control will be used to pick up that character and assign it to the local variable `startData`.
22: If the received character is a `C`, it means that the slave computer is ready to receive data transmission. The master computer should send back an `ACK` character to inform the slave computer that it has successfully received the `C` character. If `CommStart()` function is completed successfully, it will return a `SUCCESS` signal to the calling event.
23: If the received data is not a `C`, it means that something has gone wrong during the data transmission process between the master and slave. In this case, the master program will send a `NAK` character back to the slave computer to ask it resend the `C` character. The function will return a timeout error to the calling event procedure to ask the event procedure to call the function again to try to pick up the `C` character.
24: Before exiting the function, our program must clean up the initializations. The RTS transmission line should be reset to inactive by the `RTSEnable` property of the MSComm control. The timer `VBTimer` should be disabled to stop it from running, and the `TimeOut` flag should be reset to `False` to prepare it for future use.

The `CommStart()` function is terminated by the `End Function` statement. Compare this statement with the `End Sub` statement used to terminate subroutines. This is one of the differences between the function and the subroutine used in Visual Basic programming environment.

The next function is `CommRecv()`, which is used to receive each data unit sent by the slave computer. The operations of this function are explained here:

- A local integer array with two elements is declared because the function will return an array. The first element indicates the status of the function's execution, and the second element is used to hold the received data.
- The `RTSEnable` property of the MSComm control is enabled to activate the RTS transmission line, and the `VBTimer` is enabled to begin monitoring the time period spent by the data transmission. The `TimeOut` flag is reset to `False`.
- A `Do-Until` loop is executed until either a single data unit arrives in the input buffer of the master computer or A timeout error occurs.
- The RTS transmission line and `VBTimer` are disabled
- If the `Do-Until` loop is terminated by the timeout error, so the data sent by the slave computer is not received by the master computer. The `TimeOut` is reset, and a `NAK` character is sent to the slave computer requesting that it resend the data. The `CommRecv()` function returns the timeout error to the calling event procedure.

- If the data is received successfully. An `ACK` character is sent back from the master to the slave computer. The received data is returned to the calling event procedure by the `CommRecv()` function.

Because `CommRecv()` needs to return an integer array, it is defined as a function in the Visual Basic environment.

Following the previous steps as we add the function `CommStart()`, add the `CommRecv()` function into master-side program. The properties of the function are listed in Table 4.20.

TABLE 4.20
Properties for the `CommRecv()` Function

Property	Value
Name	CommRecv
Type	Function
Scope	Private

Type `As Integer()` at the end of the newly added function. Enter the code that is shown in Figure 4.44 into the function. Your finished code should match that shown in Figure 4.44.

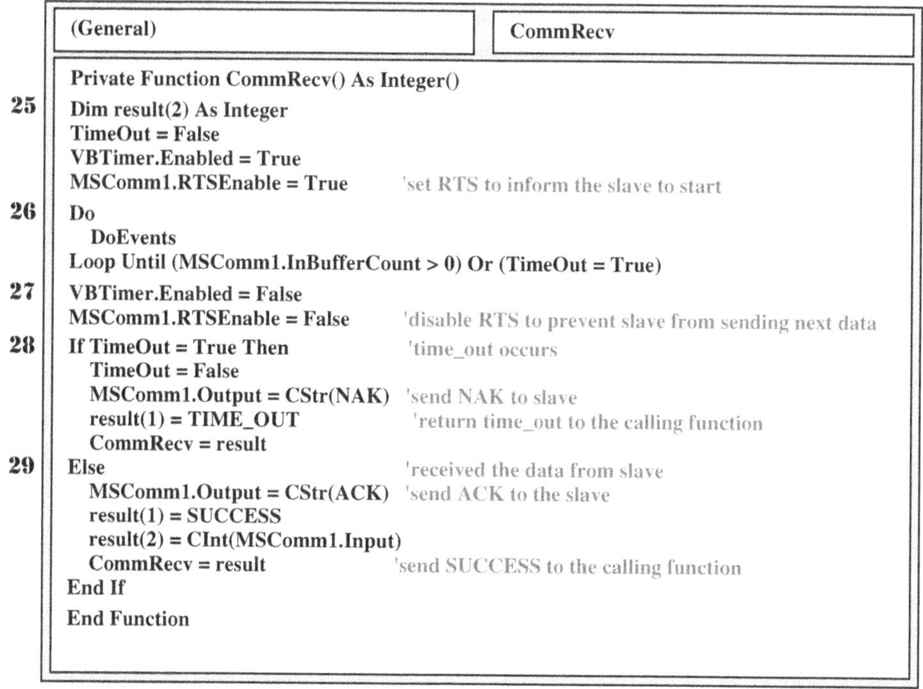

FIGURE 4.44 Code for the `CommRecv()` function.

Each section of this code is explained in the following list.

25: A local integer array, `result(2)`, with two elements will be declared at the beginning of this function. This declaration is necessary because the function needs to return an array. This array cannot be declared with a definite dimension in the function declaration;

in other words, the array must be declared as a dynamic array. But inside the function, you should declare this array with the definite dimension (here the dimension is 2), and this array would work as the returned array when the function returned to the calling event procedure.

Besides the declaration of the local array, some initializations are completed following that declaration. The flag `TimeOut` is reset to `False`. The `VBTimer` and the RTS lines are enabled to prepare for data transmission between the two computers.

26: A `Do-Until` loop will be executed until one of two conditions exists:

A data unit arrives in the input buffer on the master computer (`InBufferCount >0`).
A timeout error occurs (`TimeOut = True`).

27: The RTS line and the `VBTimer` will be disabled, because one data transmission has been completed.

28: If a timeout error occurs, the program resets the `TimeOut` flag and uses the `Output` property to send a `NAK` character to the slave computer requesting that it to resend the last data segment. The `CommRecv()` function returns the timeout error to the calling event procedure.

29: If the data arrives successfully, the program will use the `Output` property to send an `ACK` character back to the slave computer. The `Input` property of the MSComm control will then be used to pick up the received data from the input buffer and assign the data to the second element of the returned array `result(2)`. The `SUCCESS` constant is assigned to the first element of the returned array `result(1)`. Finally the function returns the `result` array to the calling event procedure.

The last function, `recvChkSum()`, is used to retrieve the checksum value sent by the slave computer. The operations of this function are described here:

- This function returns an integer array with two elements. The first element represents the running status of the function, and the second element stores the received checksum value.
- The `CommRecv()` function is called to retrieve the received checksum value.
- If a timeout error occurs, `CommRecv()` is called again to retry receiving the checksum value.
- If, after the second call, `CommRecv()` still returns a timeout error, it means that a hardware problem exists between the two computers. The function returns a timeout error to the calling event procedure.
- If the `CommRecv()` function returns a `SUCCESS` signal, it means that the checksum value has been received successfully. The function will then return the checksum value to the calling event procedure.

Now add this new user-defined function to the program, incorporating the properties that are listed in Table 4.21.

Type `As Integer()` at the end of the function declaration to indicate that the function will return an integer array. Then enter the code that is shown in Figure 4.45. The body of the finished function should match that shown in Figure 4.45.

This function works by calling the `CommRecv()` function that we added earlier. In fact, you can combine the `recvChkSum()` function with `CommRecv()` to get one function. Here, in order to make things clear, we will develop these two functions separately.

TABLE 4.21
Properties for the `recvChkSum()` Function

Property	Value
Name	recvChkSum
Type	Function
Scope	Private

```
(General)                                   recvChkSum

   Private Function recvChkSum() As Integer()
30 Dim rcArray() As Integer
31 rcArray() = CommRecv()
32 If rcArray(1) = TIME_OUT Then
      rcArray() = CommRecv()                    're-receive the data
      If rcArray(1) = TIME_OUT Then
         recvChkSum = rcArray
         Exit Function
      End If
33 ElseIf rcArray(1) = SUCCESS Then
      recvChkSum = rcArray
   End If
   End Function
```

FIGURE 4.45 Code for the `recvChkSum()` function.

Each section of this code is described in the following list.

30: A local integer array `rcArray()` is declared at the beginning of this function. This array will store the running status and the received checksum value returned by the `CommRecv()` function. This array will also be returned by the `recvChkSum()` function to the calling event procedure. Because this array is used to receive the returned data from a function, it must be declared as a dynamic array (one with no definite dimension).

31: The `CommRecv()` function will be called to retrieve the checksum value sent by the slave computer. The local integer array `rcArray()` will store and reserve the returned running status and the checksum value.

32: If the `CommRecv()` function returns a timeout error, we need to call that function again to try retrieving the checksum value. If, after the second calling, the function still returns a timeout error, it means that a hardware problem exists on the data communication lines. The function will return this error by assigning the returned array `rcArray()` to the function itself. The function will be terminated and exited.

33: If the `CommRecv()` function returns a `SUCCESS` signal, it means that the checksum value has been retrieved successfully. The program will return the status and the checksum value to the calling event procedure by assigning the `rcArray()` array to the function itself.

At this point, we have completed the coding for all user-defined functions in our master-side program. Before we can finish this project, however, we need to complete the coding for the last event, an exit event that will be triggered by a click of the `Exit` command button.

From the Project Explorer window in Visual Basic workspace, click the View Object button and double-click the Exit command button to open its event procedure. Enter the code that is shown in Figure 4.46 into this event procedure.

cmdExit	Click

```
Private Sub cmdExit_Click()
MSComm1.PortOpen = False
End
End Sub
```

FIGURE 4.46 Code for the Exit event procedure.

The operation of this event procedure is simple and straightforward: It closes the opened serial port and terminates the program. We must close any opened port before we can terminate the program; otherwise the port will be remained opened and we will not be able to open it again the next time we run this program. The PortOpen property of the MSComm control is used to close the opened port (by setting it to False). In Visual Basic, the program is terminated by an End command.

Now the project is completed. However, we cannot yet run or test it because we need the slave-side program to communicate with this master program to perform the data transmission task. Our next job is to develop the program that runs on the slave computer.

4.3.2.2 The Serial Interface Program for the Slave Computer

There are a quite a few similarities between the master and the slave programs. For example, both programs need to perform the following tasks to complete the data transmission:

- Initializing and configuring the serial port
- Calling the CommStart() function to perform the synchronization process
- Calling the cmdSend event procedure to send a single data character
- Calling the cmdReceive event procedure to receive the single data character
- Using VBTimer timer to monitor the timeout period and report the timeout error by setting the TimeOut flag
- Calling the cmdLoop event procedure to send or receive a block of data
- Calling the cmdExit event procedure to terminate the program

In spite of these similarities, there are some differences between the two programs. These differences are listed in Table 4.22.

4.3.2.2.1 Developing the Graphical User Interfaces

Like the master-side program, the slave-side program includes two forms and one code module. The design of the two forms for the slave program is nearly identical with the design of those forms in the master program. The two forms' names are Setup and VBCommPorts, and they have the same controls, including the MSComm Active-X control and timer, as do the two forms developed in the master program. Refer back to the instructions in Sections 4.3.2.1.3 and 4.3.2.1.4 to develop these forms for the slave-side program. The Loop_Receive is changed to Loop_Send in the slave side. The finished forms are similar to the forms shown in Figures 4.33 and 4.34.

The code module for the slave project is slightly different than the code module for the master project. Open a new Visual Basic project and name it VBCOMMPort_Slave.vbp. Add two forms

TABLE 4.22
Differences Between the Master-Side and Slave-Side Applications

Program Type	Function or Event	Difference
Master	CommStart()	Initializes the data transmission task by setting the RTS line
Slave	CommStart()	Receives the CTS signal and sends back a `C`
Master	cmdLoop	Continuously receives a block of data sent by the slave
Slave	cmdLoop	Continuously sends a block of data to the master
Master	CommRecv()	Receives a single data character sent by the slave
Slave	CommSend()	Sends a single data character to master
Master	recvChkSum()	Receives the checksum value sent by the slave
Slave	sendChkSum()	Sends the checksum value to the master
Slave	GetData()	Generates a block of data to be sent to the master

and design them exactly as you did the two forms for the master project. Make sure you include the MSComm control and the timer.

4.3.2.2.2 Developing the Code Module

Add a new code module, name it `VBComm`, enter the code shown in Figure 4.47 into this code module.

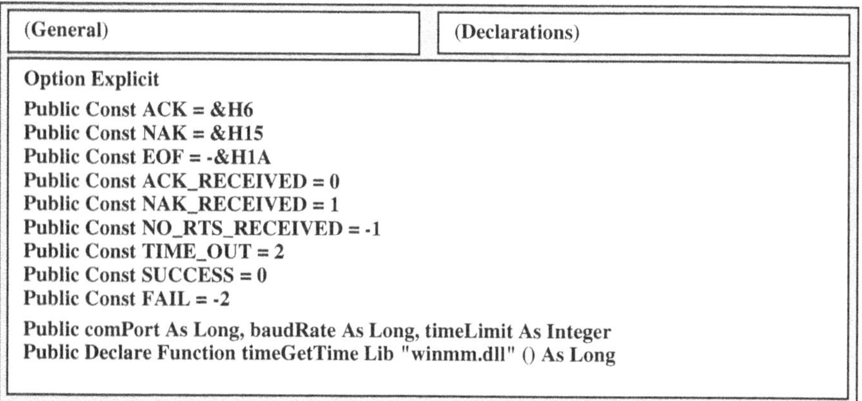

```
(General)                    (Declarations)

Option Explicit
Public Const ACK = &H6
Public Const NAK = &H15
Public Const EOF = -&H1A
Public Const ACK_RECEIVED = 0
Public Const NAK_RECEIVED = 1
Public Const NO_RTS_RECEIVED = -1
Public Const TIME_OUT = 2
Public Const SUCCESS = 0
Public Const FAIL = -2
Public comPort As Long, baudRate As Long, timeLimit As Integer
Public Declare Function timeGetTime Lib "winmm.dll" () As Long
```

FIGURE 4.47 Code module for the slave-side program.

The first three global constants in the code module are system constants, which means that they are defined by the system according to standard serial communication conventions. The next six global constants are user-defined constants, specially designed for this project.

Besides the global constants, we must also define some global variables. The `comPort` and `baudRate` variables will be used as temporary buffers to hold the `COM Port` and `Baud Rate` values that we'll enter on the `Setup` form at run time. The `timeLimit` variable will collect and record the number of calls to the timer event procedure. Our program will use this variable to determine whether the allowable timeout period has been exceeded. The Win32 API function `timeGetTime()` will be used to pick up the current system time. This function can be used in a time delay function to delay a certain period of time for the data communication task.

We have now finished configuring the two forms and the code module. Now we need to create the coding for the two forms. (Although here, we will detail only the coding for the form `VBCommPorts` form. Again, the code for the `Setup` form is identical to that of the `Setup` form in the master project.)

4.3.2.2.3 Coding of the VBCommPorts Form

The functions of the `VBCommPorts` form in the slave-side project are detailed here:

- During the execution of the `Form_Load` event procedure, the port initialization and configuration will be performed based on the `Port Number` and `Baud Rate` values we entered on the `Setup form` at run time. The form's initial screen location is also defined in this procedure. The communication setup parameters for the port on the slave computer should be identical with those parameters used for the port on the master computer. Some key parameters are `baud rate`, `parity value`, `data bits`, and `stop bits`, and these parameters must be identical with the corresponding port parameters set in the master-side program.
- The `Send` button will use hardware handshaking signals to send a single character from the slave computer to the serial port of the master computer.
- The `Receive` button will use hardware handshaking signals to receive a single character from the serial port of the master computer. The received data will be displayed in the `Reading Data` text box.
- When the `Loop_Send` button is clicked at run time, a block of data generated on the slave computer will be sent to the master computer. The slave program will calculate the checksum value based on the values of the sent out data, and this checksum value will be sent to the master program when the data block is transmitted.
- When the `Exit` button is clicked, the slave-side program will be terminated.

As mentioned previously, some of the event procedures and functions developed for both the master and slave programs are identical. In this section, we will discuss only those event procedures and functions that are different than those developed for the master-side program. Refer to Table 4.22, which lists all different functions and event procedures between the master and the slave programs. We'll be creating code for only these items.

Notice in Table 4.22 that all the different functions between two programs are included in the `cmdLoop` event procedure. This event procedure is used to send a block of data from the slave program to the master program, along with the checksum inspection. This is the only event procedure that differs between the two programs. All other event procedures, including `Form_Load`, `cmdSend`, `cmdReceive` and `cmdExit`, are exactly identical on both computers. As we create the code for the `VBCommPorts` form in the slave-side program, we will focus primarily on the `cmdLoop` event procedure.

The operation of this event procedure is described here:

- The `CommStart()` function is called to perform the synchronization process between the slave and the master computers.
- If a `NO_RTS_RECEIVED` error is returned from the `CommStart()` function, it means that the master has not issued a signal to start a data transmission task. In this case, the event procedure will be exited and the program will be terminated
- If `CommStart()` returns a timeout error or a `NAK` character, it means that the master program has issued an `RTS` signal to try to start data transmission but it has not received a `C` feedback character from the slave program. In this case, the slave program will call the `CommStart()` function to try the synchronization process again.
- If the second call to `CommStart()` still returns either a timeout error or a `NAK` character, it means that the serial transmission between two computers has encountered some hardware problems. The event procedure will be exited and the program will be terminated.
- If the `CommStart()` function successfully completes the synchronization process and returns an `ACK_RECEIVED` signal, the slave program will call the `GetData()` function

to generate a block of data. A `for` loop will be used and the `CommSend()` function will be called to send a single data character to the master computer.

- The sent out data is displayed in the `Sending Data` text box.
- If the `CommSend()` function returns a timeout error or a `NAK` character, it means that the master program has failed to receive the data item sent by the slave program; in this case, `CommSend()` is called again to resend the data. If, after the second call, the `CommSend()` function still returns either a timeout error or a `NAK` feedback character, it means that a hardware problem exists on the transmission lines between the two computers. In this case, the event procedure will be exited and the program will be terminated.
- If the data has been successfully sent out by the slave program and received by the master computer, the checksum value is calculated.
- The **for** loop will continue to send data until the entire block of data has been sent.
- After all data is sent, the `sendChkSum()` function is executed to send the calculated checksum from the slave program to the master program. The master program uses this checksum to confirm whether or not the data transmission task has been successful.
- A `SUCCESS` message will be displayed if the checksum value has been successfully sent out by the slave program and received by the master program. Otherwise an error message will be displayed to indicate that the function has failed.

Now let's develop the code for this event procedure. Select the `VBCommPorts` form and click the View Object button from the Project Explorer window in Visual Basic workspace to open the `VBCommPorts` form window. Double-click the `Loop_Send` command button to open its event procedure window. In this window, enter the code, that is shown in Figure 4.48. Each section of this code is explained in the following list.

A: Some local variables and arrays are declared at the beginning of this event procedure. `rc` is a Boolean variable that will store the returned running status of the `CommStart()`, `CommSend()`, and `sendChkSum()` functions. The array `dArray()` will be used to retrieve and reserve the generated data block to be sent to the master program. The `Index` variable will work as a loop counter for the `for` loop, and the `chkSum` variable will store the checksum value calculated by the slave-side program.
The `chkSum` variable is initialized to `0` because it works as an accumulator to store the checksum value in this event procedure.

B: The `CommStart()` function will be called first to perform the synchronization process between the slave and master programs. This function will check the status of the CTS line and return a `C` to the master program if the CTS line has been activated by the master program. An argument with a value of `100` is passed into this function, which means that it will be executed 100 times, In other words, the program will pause for up to 600 seconds (10 minutes) if the CTS line is not active. If the function returns a `NO_RTS_RECEIVED` error, it means that some problems exist on the transmission lines between two computers. In this case, the event procedure will be exited and the program will be terminated. A message box will appear to display the error information on the screen.

C: If the function returns a timeout error or a `NAK_RECEIVED` error, it means that an activated CTS signal has been detected and received by the slave computer, but after sending a `C` character back to the master program, the slave program has received no response or a `NAK` character from the master computer. In this case, we need to call the `CommStart()` function again to perform the synchronization process once more.

D: If, after the second calling, `CommStart()` still returns either timeout error or NAK_RECEIVED error, the event procedure will be exited and the program will be terminated.

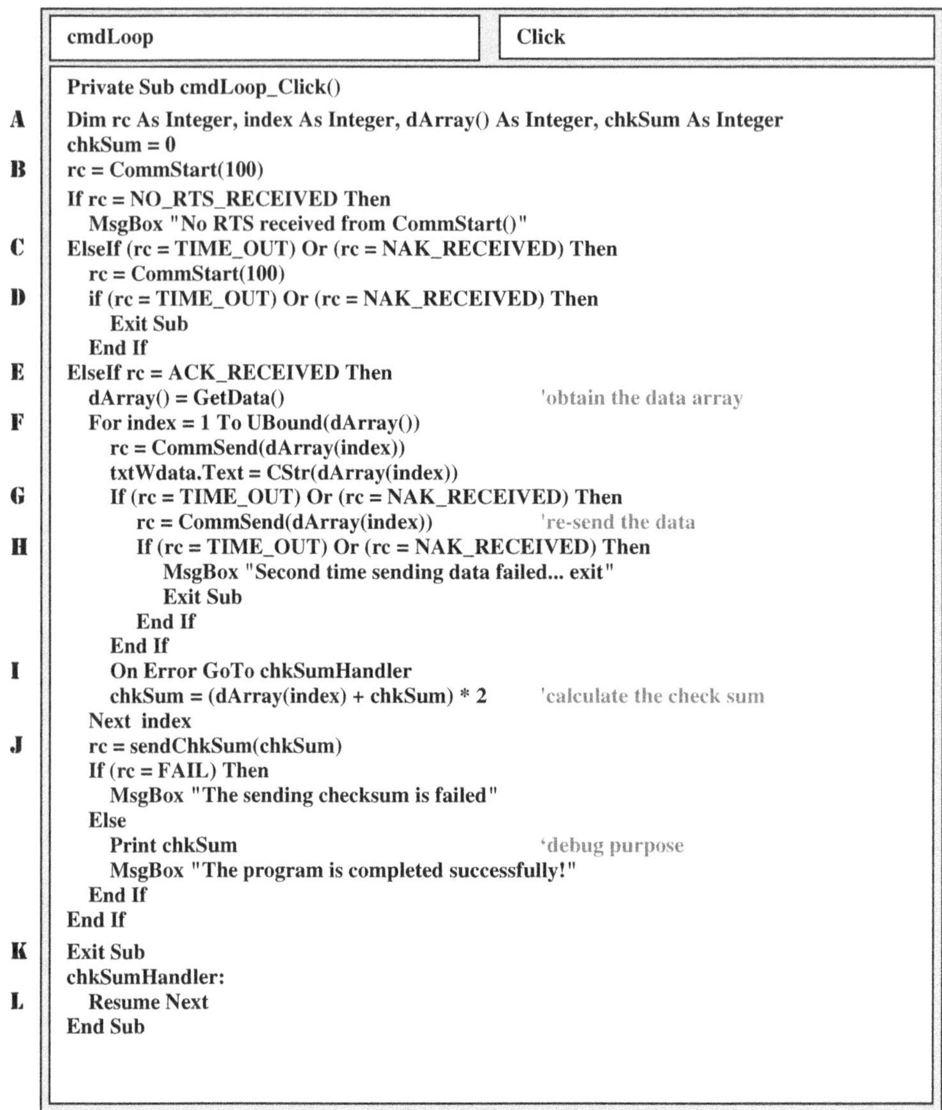

```
cmdLoop                         Click

  Private Sub cmdLoop_Click()
A Dim rc As Integer, index As Integer, dArray() As Integer, chkSum As Integer
  chkSum = 0
B rc = CommStart(100)
  If rc = NO_RTS_RECEIVED Then
    MsgBox "No RTS received from CommStart()"
C ElseIf (rc = TIME_OUT) Or (rc = NAK_RECEIVED) Then
    rc = CommStart(100)
D   if (rc = TIME_OUT) Or (rc = NAK_RECEIVED) Then
      Exit Sub
    End If
E ElseIf rc = ACK_RECEIVED Then
    dArray() = GetData()                          'obtain the data array
F   For index = 1 To UBound(dArray())
      rc = CommSend(dArray(index))
      txtWdata.Text = CStr(dArray(index))
G     If (rc = TIME_OUT) Or (rc = NAK_RECEIVED) Then
        rc = CommSend(dArray(index))              're-send the data
H       If (rc = TIME_OUT) Or (rc = NAK_RECEIVED) Then
          MsgBox "Second time sending data failed... exit"
          Exit Sub
        End If
      End If
I     On Error GoTo chkSumHandler
      chkSum = (dArray(index) + chkSum) * 2       'calculate the check sum
    Next index
J   rc = sendChkSum(chkSum)
    If (rc = FAIL) Then
      MsgBox "The sending checksum is failed"
    Else
      Print chkSum                                'debug purpose
      MsgBox "The program is completed successfully!"
    End If
  End If
K Exit Sub
  chkSumHandler:
L   Resume Next
  End Sub
```

FIGURE 4.48 Code for the `cmdLoop` event procedure.

E: If the returned result from the `CommStart()` function is `ACK_RECEIVED`, it means that the synchronization process is successful and an `ACK` feedback has been received from the master program. The data transmission task can be started because both computers are ready. The function `GetData()` will be executed to generate a block of data, which will be stored in the data array `dArray()`.

F: A `for` loop is used to continuously send each data segment from the slave to the master program. A built-in function, `UBound()`, is used to determine the upper boundary of the data block array. Inside the loop, the `CommSend()` function is called to send each data segment stored in the data array `dArray(Index)` to the serial port, and finally to the master program. The `Index` loop counter works as a position index for the data array to indicate which data should be sent out. The sent out data is displayed on the screen in the text box `txtWdata`.

G: If the CommSend() function returns a timeout error or a NAK_RECEIVED error, we need to call this function again to request that it resend the last data segment.

H: If, after the second call, the function still returns either a timeout error or a NAK_RECEIVED error, it means that some problem exists on the communication hardware. In this case, the program will be terminated and the error information will be displayed on the screen.

I: If the data has been sent out successfully, our program must calculate the checksum value. (Review Section 1.8 and Figure 1-49 in Chapter 1 for detailed information about the checksum calculation.) The checksum variable chkSum is defined as an integer (16 bits in Visual Basic), which means that variable can store a maximum unsigned integer of 65535. But during the checksum calculation, the chkSum needs to be shifted left by one bit each time a data segment is sent out, so the total shifting number of chkSum variable equals the total number of bits waiting to be sent in the data block. For a large data block, it is obvious that an overflow of the variable chkSum will occur for this kind of calculation. To avoid this situation, we need to use the On Error Go To ErrHandler statement, which is a system error processing tool provided by Visual Basic. Once we incorporate this statement, if an overflow or any other error occurs, then the program will be transferred to the symbolic address Errhandler where the error will be processed. The ErrHandler name is chkSumHandler in this application. Following this statement, we can perform the checksum calculation.

J: After the whole data block has been transmitted, the sendChkSum() function will be called to send the calculated checksum from the slave-side program to the master-side program. The master program also performs a checksum calculation based on the data it receives. Finally, to determine whether the data transmission has been successful or not, the master program will compare its own checksum value with the checksum value it has received from the slave program. If the two values are identical, it means that the data transmission has been successful.

If the sendChkSum() function is successful, the checksum value will be printed and a SUCCESS message will appear on the screen. Otherwise, an error message will appear to indicate that the function has failed.

K: Before the event procedure can be exited, an Exit Sub statement must be inserted before the overflowing error handler. This will allow the program to exit the event procedure without executing the overflow error process. If our program does not contain the Exit Sub statement, it will encounter an error when it tries to exit the procedure.

L: For the overflowing error handler, one final statement, Resume Next, is executed. This statement instructs the program to execute the instruction that immediately follows the instruction that has caused the overflow error to occur. In our case, the program will jump to execute the Next index instruction, which is located just below the checksum calculation instruction.

Now let's take a closer look at the functions we've used here. Four functions are used in this event procedure: CommStart(), GetData(), CommSend(), and sendChkSum(). First let's discuss the CommStart() function.

The CommStart() function used in the slave-side program is different than that used in the master-side program. (Recall that these details were listed in Table 4.22.) The operation of this function is described here:

- A string variable is created and is assigned a C character.
- The VBTimer is enabled and begins monitoring the time period spent by the data transmission.

- A Do-Until loop is used to pause processing until one of the following conditions occurs:

  The CTSHolding signal is detected.
  A timeout error occurs and the timeLimit value is greater than the upper boundary of the timeout value set by the user.

- If the CTSHolding signal is detected, it means that the master program issued this signal and is ready for data transmission. A C character is sent back from the slave to the master program to inform the latter that the slave computer is ready for data transmission. The VBTimer is also disabled and the timeLimit is reset to 0.
- If a timeout error occurs and the timeLimit value is beyond the upper boundary of the timeout period, the CommStart() function returns an error signal, NO_RTS_RECEIVED, to the calling event procedure to indicate that during the given period of time (10 minutes), no CTS activated signal has been detected. Then the VBTimer is disabled and the program exits the function.
- After the C character is sent out, the function needs to get the feedback from the master program to confirm that the latter has received that character. The VBTimer is enabled and begins monitoring the time period spent by the data transmission. Another Do-Until loop is used to pause processing until one of the two following conditions exists:

  A timeout error has occurred.
  InBufferCount is greater than 0, which means that a character has arrived in the input buffer of the slave computer.

- If a timeout error has occurred, the CommStart() function returns a TIME_OUT error message to the calling event procedure.
- If a character has arrived in the input buffer, the Input property of the MSComm control is used to pick up the character. The RTS signal in the slave side is then disabled to prevent the master program from sending another character.
- If the received character is ACK, the function returns an ACK_RECEIVED signal to the calling event procedure; otherwise it returns a NAK_RECEIVED signal.
- The setting for the handshaking signals and timer are reset and cleaned up.

Now, from the Visual Basic code window, click the Tools|Add Procedure item on the menu bar to open the Add Procedure dialog box. Select the parameters that are listed in Table 4.23 to add the CommStart() function into our slave-side program.

TABLE 4.23
CommStart() Parameters for the Slave-Side Program

Parameter	Value
Name	CommStart
Type	Function
Scope	Private

Type the argument waitTime As Integer inside the parentheses of this function, and attach a returning type of As Integer at the tail of the function. Finally, enter the code that is shown in Figure 4.49 into the function. The body of the finished CommStart() function should match the one shown in Figure 4.49.

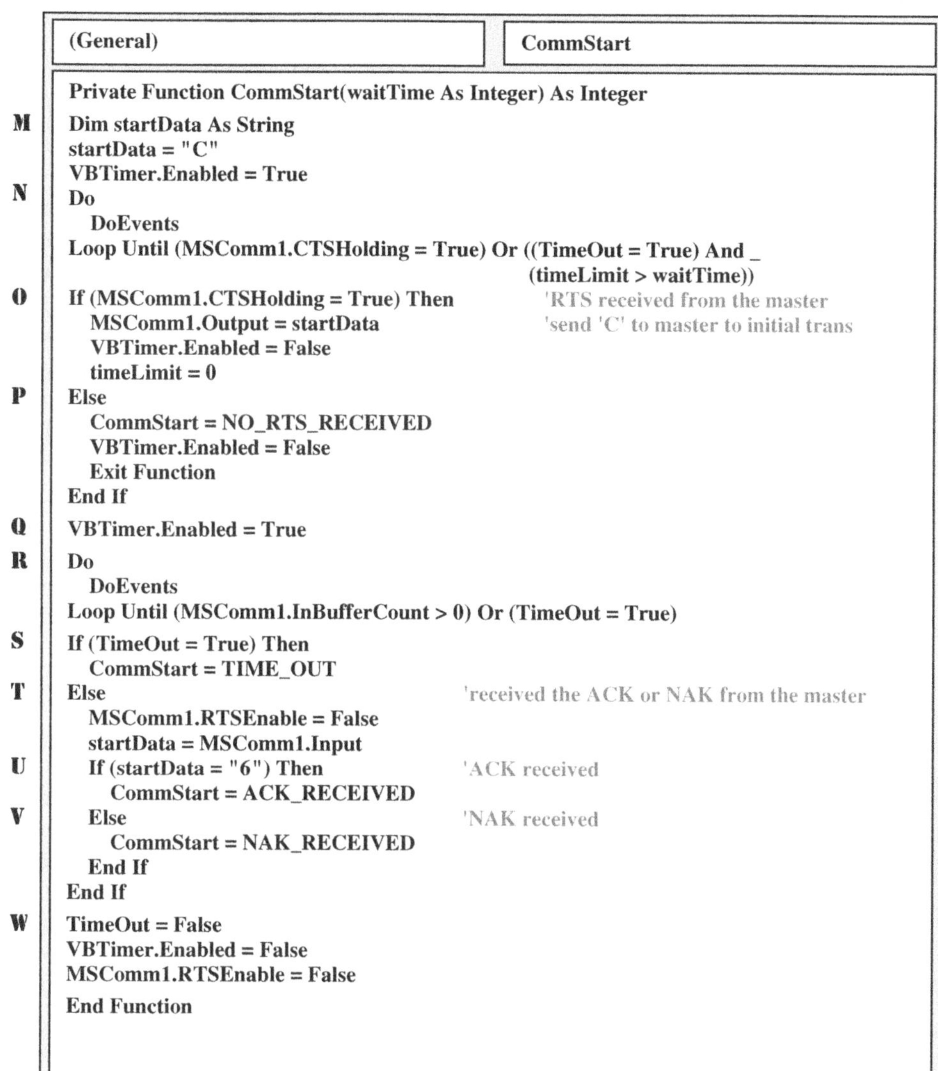

```
(General)                                   CommStart

   Private Function CommStart(waitTime As Integer) As Integer
M  Dim startData As String
   startData = "C"
   VBTimer.Enabled = True
N  Do
     DoEvents
   Loop Until (MSComm1.CTSHolding = True) Or ((TimeOut = True) And _
                                         (timeLimit > waitTime))
O  If (MSComm1.CTSHolding = True) Then        'RTS received from the master
     MSComm1.Output = startData                'send 'C' to master to initial trans
     VBTimer.Enabled = False
     timeLimit = 0
P  Else
     CommStart = NO_RTS_RECEIVED
     VBTimer.Enabled = False
     Exit Function
   End If
Q  VBTimer.Enabled = True
R  Do
     DoEvents
   Loop Until (MSComm1.InBufferCount > 0) Or (TimeOut = True)
S  If (TimeOut = True) Then
     CommStart = TIME_OUT
T  Else                                'received the ACK or NAK from the master
     MSComm1.RTSEnable = False
     startData = MSComm1.Input
U    If (startData = "6") Then         'ACK received
       CommStart = ACK_RECEIVED
V    Else                              'NAK received
       CommStart = NAK_RECEIVED
     End If
   End If
W  TimeOut = False
   VBTimer.Enabled = False
   MSComm1.RTSEnable = False
   End Function
```

FIGURE 4.49 Code for the `CommStart()` `function` in the slave-side program.

Each section of this code is explained in the following list.

M: A string variable `startData` is declared, and the character `C` is assigned to this string variable. At run time, this string variable will work as the feedback character sent to the master program by the slave program. The `VBTimer` will be enabled so that it can track the time period spent by the data transmission.

N: A `Do-Until` loop will be used to pause processing until one of the following two conditions occurs:

A `CTSHolding` signal is detected, which means that the master program has issued the RTS signal and is ready to begin a data transmission task.

A timeout error occurs and the `timeLimit` value is greater than the upper boundary of the timeout period (which is set by the user). This means that the slave program has continuously checked the CTS signal for ten minutes, but the signal is still inactive.

In this case, a hardware problem exists on the transmission lines between the two computers.

O: If an activated CTS signal is detected, the `Output` property of the MSComm control will be used to send out the character `C` as feedback to the master program. The `VBTimer` will be disabled and the `timeLimit` reset to `0`.
P: If a timeout error is received and the `timeLimit` value is greater than the upper boundary of the timeout period (`waitTime`), the function will return a `NO_RTS_RECEIVED` error to the calling event procedure. The `VBTimer` will be disabled, and the program will exit the function.
Q: If the `CTSHolding` handshaking signal has been successfully detected and the feedback character `C` has been sent out by the slave program, the slave program will wait for a response from the master program. If the slave program receives an `ACK` character, it means that the master is ready for the data transmission task. The `VBTimer` will be enabled and begin monitoring the time period spent by the data transmission.
R: Another `Do-Until` loop will be used to pause processing until one of the following two conditions exists:

A timeout error occurs.
`InBufferCount` is greater than `0`, which means that a character has arrived in the input buffer of the slave computer.

S: If a timeout error occurs, the function will return a `TIME_OUT` error message to the calling event procedure.
T: If the `InBufferCount` is greater than `0`, the `Input` property of the MSComm control will pick up the character. The RTS line is disabled to prevent the master program from sending any additional data. (The RTS in the slave is connected to CTS in the master.)
U: If the received character is `ACK` (6), it means that the master program has successfully received the `C` character sent by the slave program and is ready for the data communication. In this case, the function will return an `ACK_RECEIVED` constant to the calling event procedure.
V: If the character `NAK` has been received, the function will return a `NAK_RECEIVED` constant to the calling event procedure.
W: Finally, before exiting the function, the program will clean up the handshaking signal and the `VBTimer`. Both the `VBTimer` and the RTS signal will be disabled, and the flag `TimeOut` will be reset to `False`.

The next function is the `GetData()` function. The purpose of this function is to generate a block of data, and assign that block of data to an integer array that is used as a sequence of data to be sent to the master program later.

To make things simple, our block of data is a sequence of integers from 1 to 99. The last character is the `EOF` message, which indicates the end of the file to be transmitted.

Click the `Tools|Add Procedure` item from the menu bar to open the `Add Procedure` dialog box. Add the `GetData()` function to the slave side program, and then enter the code shown in Figure 4.50 into this function.

Keep in mind that because this function returns an array, you must attach `As Integer()` at the end of the function header. You must also declare a local integer array, `sendArray(100)` inside the function; here, the definite dimension is `100`, which means totaly there are 100 data to be returned to the calling event procedure.

Now let's discuss the `CommSend()` function. This function is used to send data to the master program and wait for a valid response. If an `ACK` character is returned, it means that the master program has successfully received the data sent by the slave program, and that the slave program

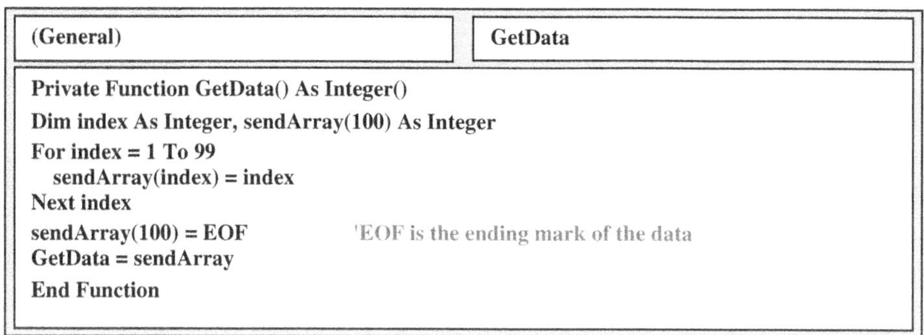

```
(General)                                      GetData

Private Function GetData() As Integer()
Dim index As Integer, sendArray(100) As Integer
For index = 1 To 99
   sendArray(index) = index
Next index
sendArray(100) = EOF          'EOF is the ending mark of the data
GetData = sendArray
End Function
```

FIGURE 4.50 Code for the `GetData()` function.

can send the next data. A feedback of the `NAK` indicates that the data was not received by the master program and that the slave program needs to resend it. The operations of this function are listed here:

- The timer `VBTimer` is enabled to monitor the time period spent by the data transmission.
- A `Do-Until` loop is used to pause processing until one of the following conditions occurs:

  An active `CTSHolding` signal is detected
  A timeout error occurs

- The timeout flag is reset, and the `VBTimer` is disabled.
- If a timeout error occurs, the function returns a `TIME_OUT` error message.
- The `Output` property of the MSComm control is used to send the data out to the serial port and then to the master program.
- The VBTimer is activated to specify how long the slave-side program should wait for a response from the master program.
- If a timeout error occurs, the function returns a `TIME_OUT` error message to the calling event procedure.
- If a character is received by the input buffer, the `Input` property picks it up.
- If an `ACK` is received, data transmission has been successful, and the function returns an `ACK_RECEIVED` constant to the calling event procedure.
- If a timeout or other error has occurred, the function returns a `NAK_RECEIVED` constant to the calling event procedure.

Now, click the `Tools|Add Procedure` menu item to open the `Add Procedure` dialog box, and enter the parameters that are listed in Table 4.24 to add a new `CommSend()` function into our project.

TABLE 4.24
`CommSend()` Parameters for the Slave-Side Program

Property	Value
Name	CommSend
Type	Function
Scope	Private

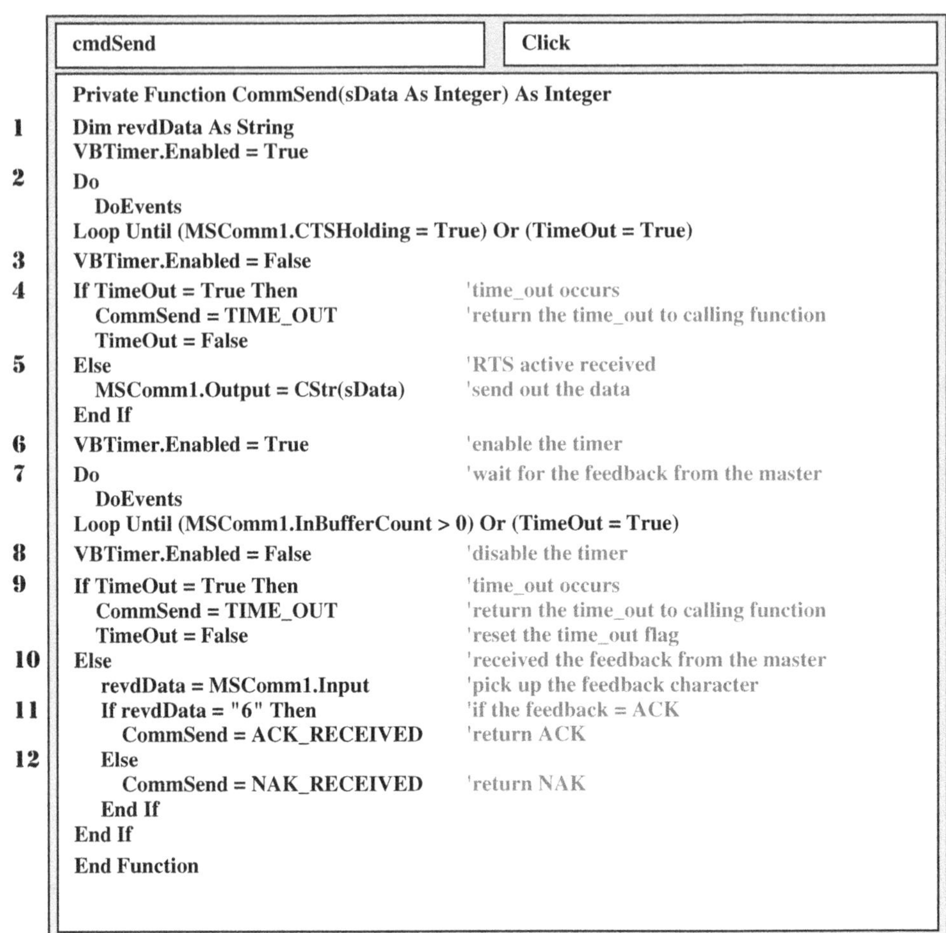

```
cmdSend                                   Click

   Private Function CommSend(sData As Integer) As Integer
1  Dim revdData As String
   VBTimer.Enabled = True
2  Do
     DoEvents
   Loop Until (MSComm1.CTSHolding = True) Or (TimeOut = True)
3  VBTimer.Enabled = False
4  If TimeOut = True Then               'time_out occurs
     CommSend = TIME_OUT                'return the time_out to calling function
     TimeOut = False
5  Else                                 'RTS active received
     MSComm1.Output = CStr(sData)       'send out the data
   End If
6  VBTimer.Enabled = True               'enable the timer
7  Do                                   'wait for the feedback from the master
     DoEvents
   Loop Until (MSComm1.InBufferCount > 0) Or (TimeOut = True)
8  VBTimer.Enabled = False              'disable the timer
9  If TimeOut = True Then               'time_out occurs
     CommSend = TIME_OUT                'return the time_out to calling function
     TimeOut = False                    'reset the time_out flag
10 Else                                 'received the feedback from the master
      revdData = MSComm1.Input          'pick up the feedback character
11    If revdData = "6" Then            'if the feedback = ACK
        CommSend = ACK_RECEIVED         'return ACK
12    Else
        CommSend = NAK_RECEIVED         'return NAK
      End If
   End If
   End Function
```

FIGURE 4.51 Code for the `CommSend()` function in the slave-side program.

Enter the code that is shown in Figure 4.51 into this new function. Do not forget to enter the `sData As Integer` argument into the parentheses of the function and the `As Integer` argument at the end of the function header, as shown in Figure 4.51. Each section of this code is explained in the following list.

1: A local string variable, `revdData`, is declared at the beginning of this function. This variable will retrieve and store the response character coming from the master program after the data is sent out by the slave program. The `VBTimer` will be enabled so that it can track the time period spent by the data transmission.

2: A `Do-Until` loop is used to pause processing until one of two following conditions exists:

   An activated `CTSHolding` signal is detected.
   A timeout error occurs.

3: If either of these events occurs, the `VBTimer` is first disabled to prevent it from setting the `TimeOut` flag.

4: If a timeout error happened, the function returns to the calling event procedure with a `TIME_OUT` constant. The `TimeOut` flag is also reset to `False`.

5: If an activated `CTSHolding` signal is detected, the `Output` property of the MSComm control is used to send the data `sData` out to the master program.
6: Then we need to wait for the response from the master program to confirm whether the data is received by the master program successfully. Enable the VBTimer again to start another `Do-Until` waiting process.
7: A `Do-Until` loop is executed and this loop is continued until one of the following two conditions exists:

A character has arrived in the input buffer on the slave computer.
A timeout error happened.

8: If either event occurs, the `VBTimer` is first disabled to prevent it from setting the flag TimeOut.
9: If a timeout error happened, the function returns to the calling event procedure with a TIME_OUT constant. The `TimeOut` flag is also reset to `False`.
10: Otherwise, a character has arrived in the input buffer. The `Input` property of the MSComm is used to pick up that character and store it into the local variable `revdData`.
11: If the received character is an `ACK` (6) constant, it means that the master program has successfully received the data sent by the slave program, the function returns to the calling event procedure with an `ACK_RECEIVED` constant.
12: Otherwise, a `NAK` character is received, which means that the data is not received by the master program, the function returns to the calling event procedure with a NAK_RECEIVED constant to indicate that the slave program needs to re-send the last data again.

Now we come to the last function developed in the slave-side program, which is the `sendChkSum()` function. This function is straightforward; it needs to call the `CommSend()` function we discussed above to send the checksum value calculated by the slave program to the master program. The master program needs this checksum to confirm the success of the data transmission.

Add a new function with the parameters that are listed in Table 4.25.

TABLE 4.25
`sendChkSum()` Parameters for the Slave-Side Program

Property	Value
Name	sendChkSum
Type	Function
Scope	Private

Enter the `cSum As Integer` argument into the parentheses of the function and the `As Integer` at the end of the function. Enter the code that is shown in Figure 4.52 into this new function. Your finished function should match the one shown in Figure 4.52.

13: A local variable `rc` is defined first, and this variable will retrieve and store the executing status of the `CommSend()` function that is called inside this function.
14: The `CommSend()` function is called to try to send out the checksum value that is an argument passed to the `sendChkSum()` function. Exactly you can combine the `sendChkSum()` and `CommSend()` functions together to get one. Here in order to make things simple and clear, we separate these two functions.
If `CommSend()` returns either a timeout error or a `NAK` signal, it means that the checksum value is not received by the master program successfully, so we need to re-send that value by calling the `CommSend()` function again.

```
sendChkSum                                   Click

   Private Function sendChkSum(cSum As Integer) As Integer
13 Dim rc As Integer
14 rc = CommSend(cSum)
   If (rc = TIME_OUT) Or (rc = NAK_RECEIVED) Then
      rc = CommSend(cSum)                                    're-send the checksum
15    If (rc = TIME_OUT) Or (rc = NAK_RECEIVED) Then
         rc = FAIL
         sendChkSum = rc
         Exit Function
      End If
16 ElseIf (rc = ACK_RECEIVED) Then
      rc = SUCCESS
      sendChkSum = rc
   End If
   End Function
```

FIGURE 4.52 Code for the `SendChkSum()` function in the slave-side program.

15: If, after the second calling, the `CommSend()` function still returns the same error signals, this means that a hardware problem exists on the transmission lines between two computers. The function returns to the calling event procedure with a `FAIL` constant to indicate that the communication architecture should be checked and the problem should be fixed before the program can be executed.

16: Otherwise if an `ACK` signal is received from the master program, which means that the checksum value has been successfully received by the master computer. A `SUCCESS` signal is returned to the calling event procedure to indicate that the data transmission task can be terminated.

Before we can finish this project, we need to confirm one more thing. That is to configure the startup object or the first form to be executed as the project runs. In both master and slave project, two forms are developed and the `Setup` form, which can be considered the startup object, should always be executed first when the project runs. To set the `Setup` form as the startup object, go to the `Project|VBCOMMPort_Slave Properties...` menu item to open the Project Property dialog box. Select `Setup` from the `Startup Object` box, and click `OK` to save the setup.

Now we have finished the coding for all event procedures and functions, and it is the time for us to run and test our projects that are developed on the master computer and on the slave computer.

Connect two serial ports that are located at two computers with a Null Modem cable. (Refer to Section 1.5.2 and to Figures 1-16 and 1-17 in Chapter 1 to complete this connection). In our application, COM1 is selected for both ports. Define one computer as the master computer in which the master project, `VBCOMMPort_Master`, is installed and another one as the slave computer in which the slave project, `VBCOMMPort_Slave`, is installed.

When the program runs, if we choose not to use the mouse to access each control, such as the text box, to input the serial port parameters, we can use the `Tab` key on the keyboard to complete this job. To do this, we need to set up the `TabIndex` property for each control. Open the `Setup` form windows for both the master and slave projects and enter the values that are listed in Table 4.26 into the `TabIndex` property for the different controls on the `Setup` form .

Now click the `Start` button on both project to run the master and the slave project on two computers. The order in which to run the master and the slave project is not important, either project can be run first or second and it does not matter.

TABLE 4.26
TabIndex Values

Control Name	Caption/Text	TabIndex Value
Label2	Port Number	0
txtPort		1
Label3	Baud Rate	2
txtBaudRate		3
cmdSetup	Setup	4

As the project runs, both Setup form are displayed. You can find that the focus is set on the first text box marked by Port Number label, and you can directly enter the desired port number in that box. Enter 1 as our port number (because we used COM1 on two computers), and then press the Tab key from the keyboard to move the focus to the next text box, which is labeled as Baud Rate. Enter 9600 as our baud rate and press the Tab key again to move the focus to the Setup command button (Figure 4.53), press the Enter key from the keyboard to finish this setup. Perform this setup for both projects on two computers. Again, the order in which to complete this setup is not important.

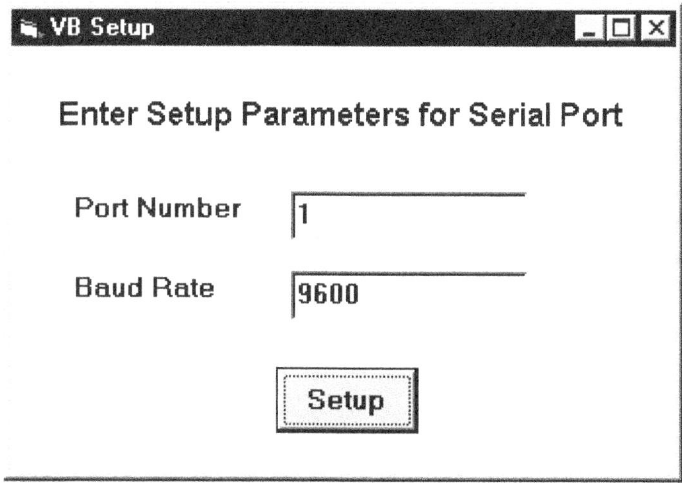

FIGURE 4.53 The running Setup form for two projects.

Now the second form, VBCommPorts, is displayed. In the master computer, type a number into the Sending Data text box, for instance, enter 1000, and then click the Send button to send the data out. In the slave computer, click the Receive button and you can find that the data sent by the master is received and displayed in the Reading Data text box on the slave computer. You can perform the sending and receiving data functions on either the master or the slave computer because each form has both Send and Receive buttons. If one computer is used to send the data, another computer must be used to receive the data.

Let's test the loop send and loop receive functions between two computers. Click the Loop_Receive button from the master computer, and then click the Loop_Send button from the slave computer. Immediately you will see that the number displayed in the Reading Data text box on the master computer begins to change; the same change can be found in the Sending Data text box on the slave computer. This means that the block of data is being transmitted between the master and the slave computers via the serial port COM1. These situations are shown in Figures 4.54 and 4.55.

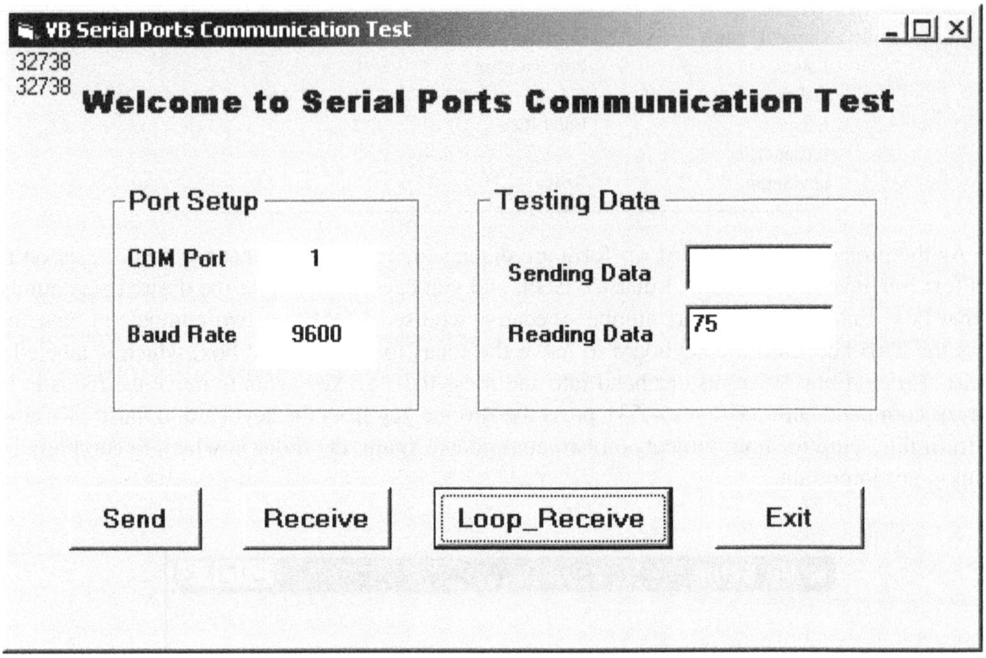

FIGURE 4.54 The master computer.

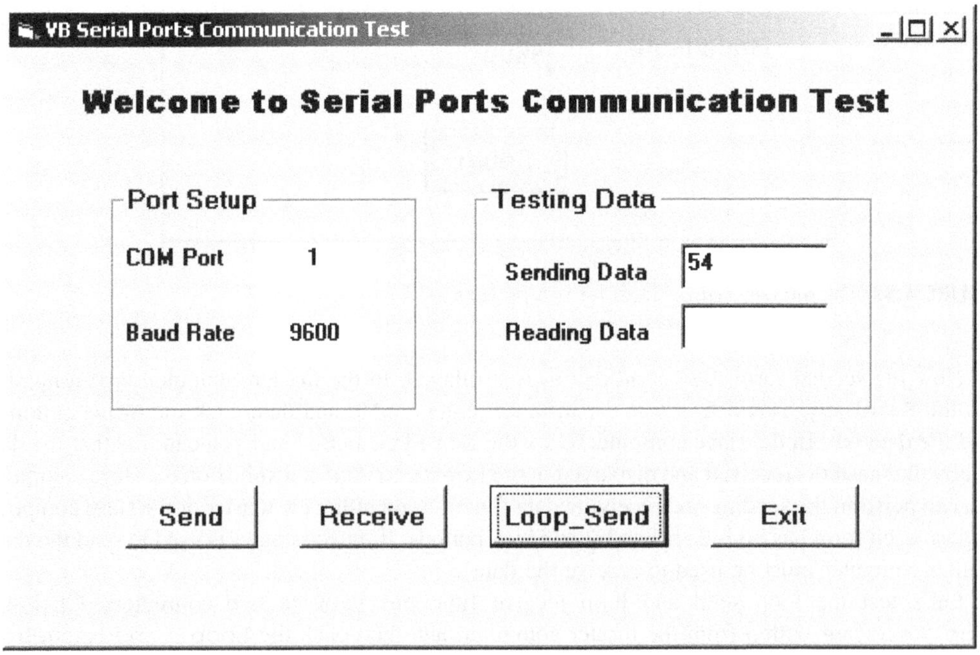

FIGURE 4.55 The slave computer.

Figure 4.54 shows the situation on the master computer that is receiving the block of data transmitted from the slave computer. Figure 4.55 shows the situation happened on the slave computer that is sending the block of data to the master computer.

This loop sending and receiving is terminated by an EOF character. This means an EOF character is sent out from the slave computer when all data in the block is sent, and the same EOF character is received by the master computer to indicate the ending of the data transmission.

From the master computer, you can find that the checksum value 32738 is displayed on the upper-left corner of the form. This is for the debug purpose and you can hide this display in the real applications.

Finally when the EOF character is sent out from the slave computer and received by the master computer, a message box will be displayed to indicate whether this block of data transmission has been successful or not. If both checksums are identical, the data transmission has been successful and a successful message will be displayed. Otherwise an error message will be displayed. The last data displayed in both `Sending Data` on the slave computer and `Reading Data` on the master computer are –26, which is the EOF character. Figure 4.56 shows the successful message displayed on the message box. The (a) is for the master computer and the (b) is for the slave computer.

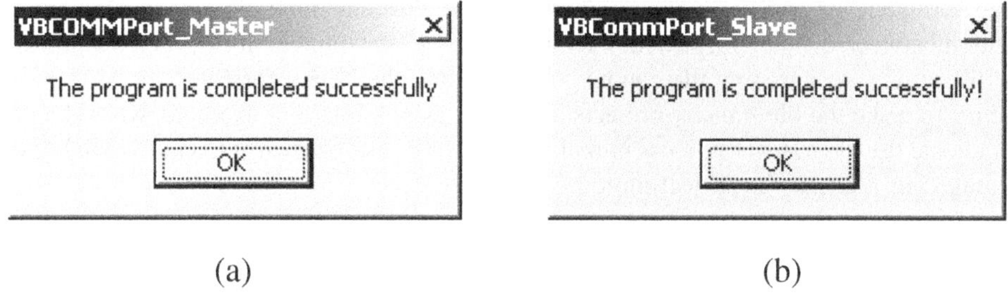

FIGURE 4.56 The message boxes for both the master-side and slave-side programs.

It does not matter either the `Loop_Send` button on the slave computer is clicked first or the `Loop_Receive` button on the master computer is clicked first. Any of two buttons can be clicked first but the preference is that the `Loop_Receive` button on the master computer should be clicked first because it is located at the master computer and a data transmission task should be issued by the master computer.

You can test this data transmission task by using different baud rates, such as 19200, 38400 or even 115200. These two projects work fine for all baud rates. Click the `Exit` button to terminate both projects at two computers. Our project is successful.

The complete project files, including the project on the master computer and on the slave computer, are stored at two folders: `VBComm2Ports_Mst` and `VBComm2Ports_Slv`, which are located in the `Chapter 4` folder in the attached CD.

The project developed in both master computer and the slave computer can be used to perform some data transmission tasks between two computers. There is a limitation existed for these projects, that is: the data must be text or string and the size of the data file is relatively small. In the next example, we try to develop a project that can be used to transfer binary data file with a large size.

The communication events in the MSComm control are used in the next example to improve the efficiency of data transmission between the two computers. The project developed in the next example can be used for file transfer methods that use the file flow control strategy.

4.3.3 A Serial Interface for the File Flow Control Between Two Computers

In this section, we try to develop some projects used to transfer data files between computers. As you know, one of the most important properties of using the serial communication between computers is the files transfer, which allows different computers share the file via serial interfaces. This is an easy and convenient method for a group of computer users to form a Local Area Network (LAN) via serial ports to share the information they need. Although some commercial LAN available in the market, most of them are relatively complicated in the structure and expensive in the cost. To make a LAN using the serial interface to share data files is a simple and cheap way.

We try to develop two projects in this section, one is located on the master computer and the other one is located on the slave computer. Basically there is no significant difference between these two projects, either the master or the slave computer can transmit binary files or receive binary files.

In order to make things simple, currently the master project is designed to send the file only, and the slave project is to receive the file only although both send and receive button is added into both project. You can copy the codes of the send event procedure in the master project and paste them into the send event procedure in the slave project, and do the same thing for the receive event procedure in the slave and the master project. In this way, both project can send and receive files.

The advantage of transmission of binary files is that any kind of file or program can be transmitted between computers, such as executable files (.exe), image files (.jpeg), batch files (.bat) and dll files (.dll), because any file can be converted into the binary format.

We try to make the file transfer projects as perfect as possible. For example, we add a progress bar to indicate the file transfer process in real time. We also use Microsoft Common Dialog Control 6.0 to make our file transfer project more professional.

4.3.3.1 The File Transfer Program for the Master Computer

The purpose of the master project is to send the file to the slave computer. As we previous mentioned, currently the master project can only be used to send the file. But you can copy the codes from the receive event procedure in the slave project and paste them into the receive event procedure in the master project, therefore the master project can both send and receive the file.

Two forms are used in this project: `Setup` and `VBCommFile`.

The `Setup` form is used to collect the serial port configuration parameters that we enter at run time to set up the serial port. The `VBCommFile` is to perform the file transmission task between two computers.

The operation of this program is described here:

- The `Setup` form is used to collect the serial port configuration parameters, such as the port number and the baud rate used for the file transmission.
- The configuration parameters entered at run time are checked to make sure that the parameters are valid values.
- The `VBCommFile` form appears. The properties of the MSComm control are used to initialize and configure the serial port
- When the `Send` command button is clicked by the user, a file selection dialog box will be displayed to allow the user to select the desired file to be transferred.
- Then the file is transmitted to the serial port, eventually to the slave computer.
- The checksum value is calculated after each byte is transmitted.
- During the file transmission, a progress bar is used to display the progress of the file transmission in real time.

- When the whole file is transmitted, the calculated checksum is compared with the received checksum sent by the slave project to confirm whether the file transmission has been successful.
- Finally the file transmission result will be displayed.

Now let's begin to develop this master project in the following steps.

4.3.3.1.1 Designing Two Forms for the Graphical User Interface

Two forms are developed for this project, the `Setup` form and the `VBCommFile` form. Launch Visual Basic 6.0 to open a new `Standard.EXE` project, and name the project `VBFile_Master.vbp`.

Before we can develop the graphical user interfaces, we need first to add the following components and Active-X control to the new project because we want to use them.

- Microsoft Comm Control 6.0
- Microsoft Common Dialog Control 6.0
- Microsoft Windows Common Controls 6.0 (SP4)

In the newly opened project, click the `Project|Components` menu item to open the Components dialog box, which is shown in Figure 4.57.

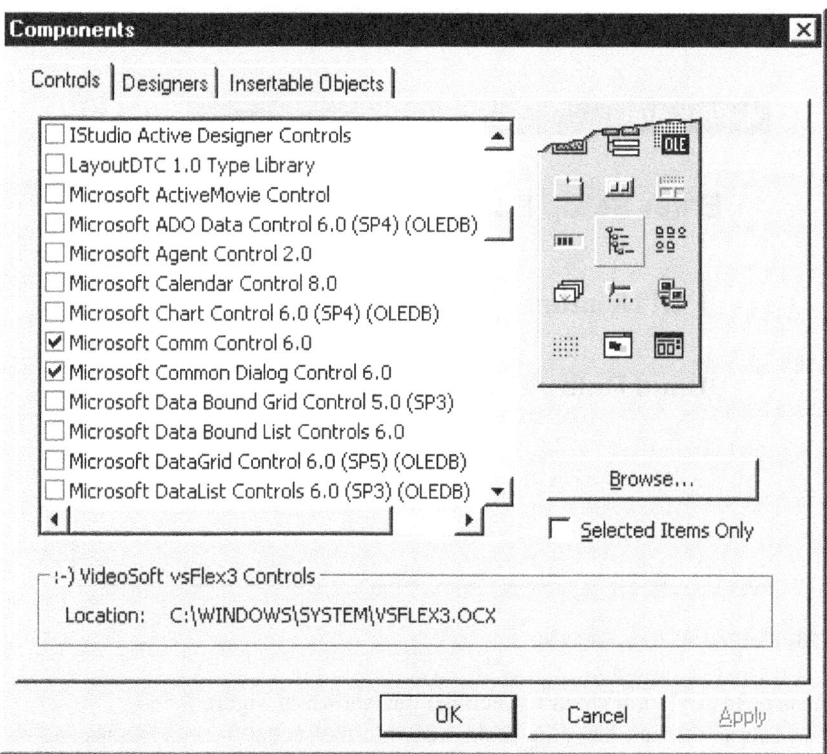

FIGURE 4.57 The `Components` dialog box.

Keeping the default tab `Controls` selected, browse the controls from the control list until you find the three items listed above; then check the associated checkbox to select them (Figure 4.57), and click the `OK` button to add them into the project.

Immediately you can find that the selected components have been added into the toolbox window on the project.

Microsoft Comm Control 6.0 is the Active-X control MSComm. Microsoft Common Dialog Control 6.0 is used to help the user select the file to be transmitted from the current computer. Microsoft Windows Common Controls 6.0 include a group of special components used in Visual Basic projects, such as the ProgressBar, StatusBar, TreeView, Slider, and ImageList.

Now let's begin to develop our graphical user interface for this project.

Add two forms into this new project. Name the first form `Setup` and the second one `VBCommFile`. Add the controls that are listed in Table 4.27 into the first form, `Setup`.

TABLE 4.27
Controls for the `Setup` Form

Control Type	Properties	Values	Control Type	Properties	Values
Label	Name	Label2	Text box	Name	txtBaudRate
	Caption	Port Number		Text	
Text box	Name	txtPort	CommandButton	Name	CmdSetup
	Text			Caption	Setup
Label	Name	Label3	Label	Name	Label1
	Caption	Baud Rate		Caption*	

*The caption property for the Control `Label1` is: Enter setup parameters for Serial Port.

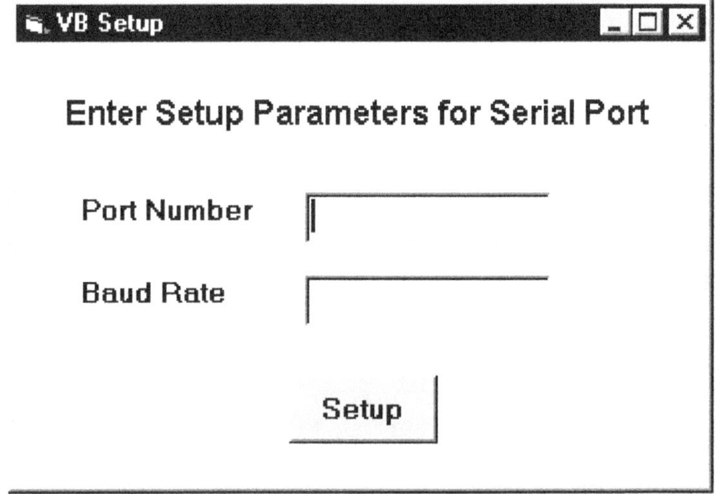

FIGURE 4.58 The `Setup` form window.

Our finished `Setup` form should match the one shown in Figure 4.58

Add the controls that are listed in Table 4.28 into the second form `VBCommFile`. Note that besides the normal controls, we need to add the following components into this project to help and improve the data transmission efficiency:

- MSComm control (Name: `MSComm1`)
- Common dialog control (Name: `dlgFile`)
- ProgressBar control (Name: `Progress`)

TABLE 4.28
Controls for the `VBCommFile` Form

Control Type	Properties	Values
Label	Name	Label1
	Caption	Welcome to Serial Ports Communication Test
Frame	Name	Frame1
	Caption	Port Setup
Label	Name	Label2
	Caption	COM Port
Label	Name	lblComPort
	Caption	
	BackColor	Yellow
Frame	Name	Frame2
	Caption	Testing Data
Label	Name	Label4
	Caption	Sending Data
Text box	Name	txtWdata
	Text	
Label	Name	Label5
	Caption	Reading Data
Text box	Name	txtRdata
	Text	
CommandButton	Name	cmdSendFile
	Caption	Send File
CommandButton	Name	cmdRecvFile
	Caption	Receive File
Command Button	Name	cmdExit
	Caption	Exit

- Timer control 1 (Name: `VBTimer`—monitor the timeout error)
- Timer control 2 (Name: `ProgressTimer`—monitor the progress bar)

Your finished form `VBCommFile` should match the one shown in Figure 4.59.

Add the properties listed in Table 4.29 into the first timer control, `VBTimer`.

Add the properties that are listed in Table 4.30 to the second timer control, `ProgressTimer`, as well.

Our two forms are now complete. Now we need to add a new code module to hold some global constants and variables used in this project. Click the `Project|Add Module` menu item from the menu bar in Visual Basic workspace to add a new module. Name that module as `VBComm.bas`.

4.3.3.1.2 The Coding of the Code Module

Double-click the new added code module, and enter the code that is shown in Figure 4.60 into this module.

This code is straightforward. The statement `Option Explicit` is used to prevent us from misusing or misspelling the names of the variables or objects used in the project. All global constants are declared in this module and those constants can be accessed and used by all event procedures on all forms for the current project. Some often-used variables are declared in this module as the global variables, such as the `comPort`, `baudRate`, `timeLimit`, `FileLength`, and `FileIndex`. The `FileLength` is used to hold the length of the file to be transmitted and it can be used as a denominator in calculating of the percentage of the file that has been transmitted and it can be displayed on the `ProgressBar`. The `FileIndex` works as an index to indicate how many

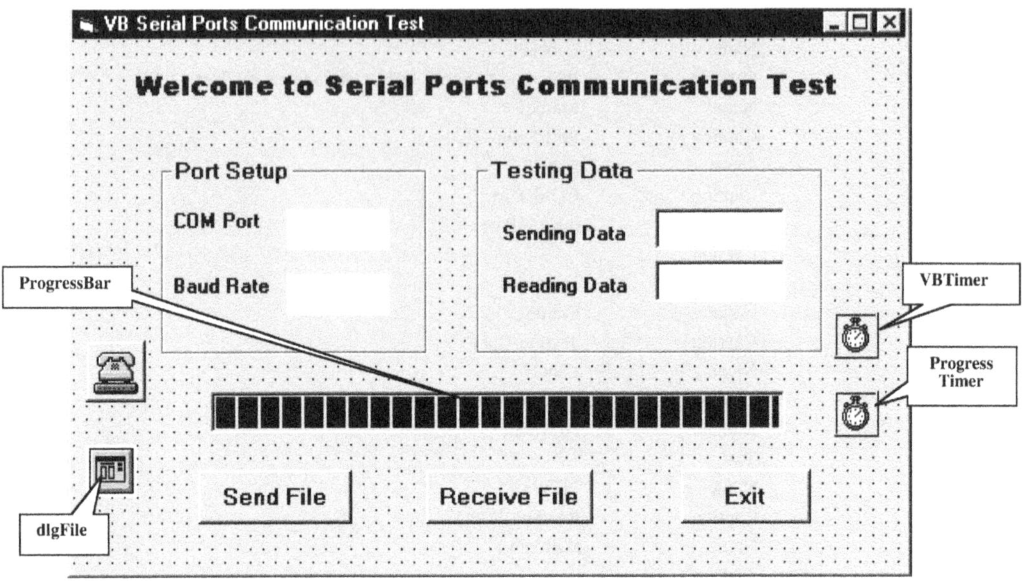

FIGURE 4.59 The `VBCommFile` form window.

TABLE 4.29
Properties for the `VBTimer` control

Control Type	Properties	Values
Timer	Name	VBTimer
	Enabled	`False`
	Interval	10000 (ms)

TABLE 4.30
Properties for the `ProgressTimer` Control

Control Type	Properties	Values
Timer	Name	ProgressTimer
	Enabled	`False`
	Interval	10 (ms)

(General)	(Declarations)

```
Option Explicit
Public Const ACK = &H6
Public Const NAK = &H15
Public Const EOF = -&H1A
Public Const ACK_RECEIVED = 0
Public Const NAK_RECEIVED = 1
Public Const NO_RTS_RECEIVED = -1
Public Const TIME_OUT = 2
Public Const SUCCESS = 0
Public Const FAIL = -2
Public comPort As Long, baudRate As Long, timeLimit As Integer
Public FileLength As Long, FileIndex As Long
Public Declare Function timeGetTime Lib "winmm.dll" () As Long
```

FIGURE 4.60 The coding of the code module

bytes has been transmitted, and it is used as a numerator in calculating of the percentage of the file that has been transmitted.

The `timeGetTime()` function is a Win32 API function that is included in the Win32 dynamic link library `winmm.dll`; it can be used to pick up the current system time. This function may be used in a time delay function to delay a period of time for some actions executed in the project. Although it is not used in the current project, here we still keep this function to be used in the future.

The first three constants, ACK, NAK and EOF, belong to the system constants and those constants are defined by the serial communication convention. The system constants can be used by any project without any modification. The followed six constants belong to user-defined constants and are specially used for the current project. The values of those constants can be modified based on the actual applications.

At this point, we finished the coding of the code module.

4.3.3.1.3 The Coding of the Setup Form

The coding of the Setup form can be divided into two sections. The first section is the coding of the `Form_Load` event procedure in which all initializations should be performed for this form. The second section is the coding of the command button `Setup`, in which the serial port configuration parameters should be reserved and checked.

Select the `Setup` form and click the `View Code` button from the `Project Explorer` window in Visual Basic to open its code window. Enter the code that is shown in Figure 4.61 into this code window.

A: In the `Form_Load` event procedure, the default name of the form `Me` is used, and two properties, `Left` and `Top`, are used to define the starting position of the form as the project runs. Both coordinates are initialized to 2500 pixels and this make the form positioned at the center of the screen.

B: At beginning of the `Setup` command button event procedure, we need to determine whether both text boxes, `txtPort` and `txtBaudRate`, has been entered the port number and the baud rate. If both text boxes are empty, a message will be displayed prompting us to enter both a valid port number and a baud rate to make the program continue to the next step.

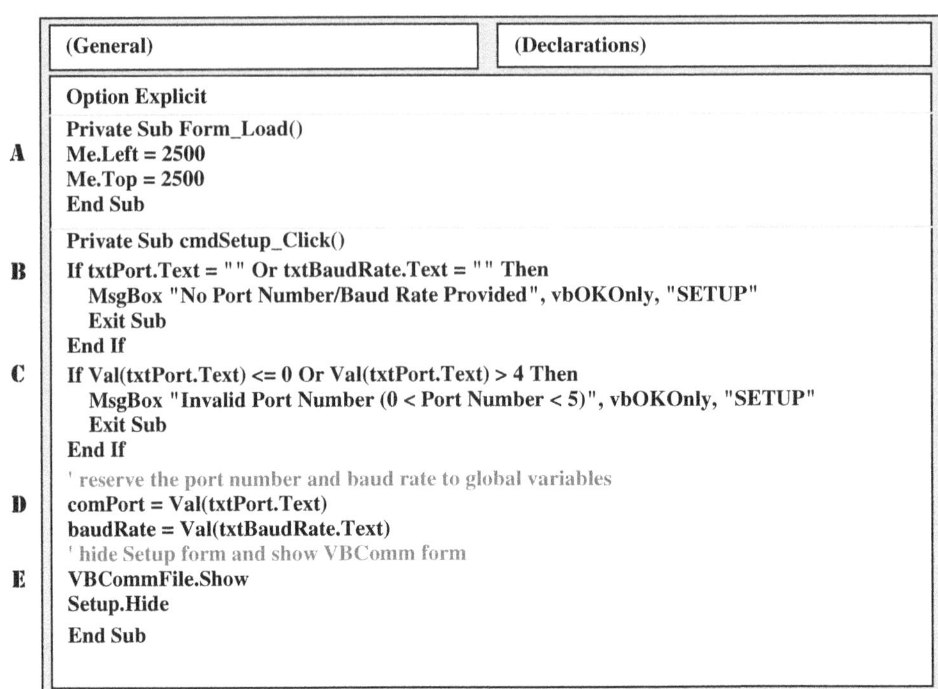

```
(General)                    (Declarations)

Option Explicit
Private Sub Form_Load()
A   Me.Left = 2500
    Me.Top = 2500
    End Sub
    Private Sub cmdSetup_Click()
B   If txtPort.Text = "" Or txtBaudRate.Text = "" Then
       MsgBox "No Port Number/Baud Rate Provided", vbOKOnly, "SETUP"
       Exit Sub
    End If
C   If Val(txtPort.Text) <= 0 Or Val(txtPort.Text) > 4 Then
       MsgBox "Invalid Port Number (0 < Port Number < 5)", vbOKOnly, "SETUP"
       Exit Sub
    End If
    ' reserve the port number and baud rate to global variables
D   comPort = Val(txtPort.Text)
    baudRate = Val(txtBaudRate.Text)
    ' hide Setup form and show VBComm form
E   VBCommFile.Show
    Setup.Hide
    End Sub
```

FIGURE 4.61 Code for the `Setup` form.

C: If both text boxes include port number and baud rate, next we need to check if those are valid values for our current application. For this application, we defined the range of the valid serial ports is from COM1 to COM4. If the value entered at run time is not within that range, a message will be displayed prompting us to enter a valid value for the port number.

D: If both values are valid, two global variables, `comPort` and `baudRate`, are used to reserve the entered port number and baud rate because both of these parameters is used in the next form to configure the serial port. A built-in `Val()` function is used to convert two values from the text format to the numeric format.

E: Two built-in methods, `Show` and `Hide`, are used to display the second form `VBCommFile` and hide the first form `Setup` because the mission of the first form has completed.

The real configuration is performed in the second form `VBCommFile` by using the MSComm control, and the `Setup` form is only used to collect the valid parameters.

4.3.3.1.4 The Coding of the VBCommFile Form

The coding of the `VBCommFile` form can be divided into several sections. The first section is the coding of the Form_Load event procedure. This coding includes the initialization and configuration of the serial port using properties of the MSComm control. The second section is the coding of the command button `cmdSendFile` event procedure. The purpose of this event procedure is to perform sending data file to the serial port and checking the feedback from the slave computer to make sure that the file is transmitted successfully. The third section is the coding of functions used in the `cmdSendFile` event procedure, such as the `CommStart()`, `CommSend()` and `getFileName()` functions. The last section is the coding for some other event procedures, such as the `VBTimer`, `ProgressTimer` and `cmdExit` event procedures.

4.3.3.1.4.1 Developing the `Form_Load` Event Procedure

Before we can start the coding of the first section, we need to declare a form-level variable, `TimeOut`. This is a Boolean variable that works as a flag to indicate the current timeout status of the running program.

Select the `VBCommFile` form from the Project Explorer window in Visual Basic and click the `View Code` button to open its code window. Type `Option Explicit` on the first line of the window, and then enter `Dim TimeOut As Boolean` on the next line. Press the `Enter` key and a form-level variable is generated, as shown in Figure 4.62.

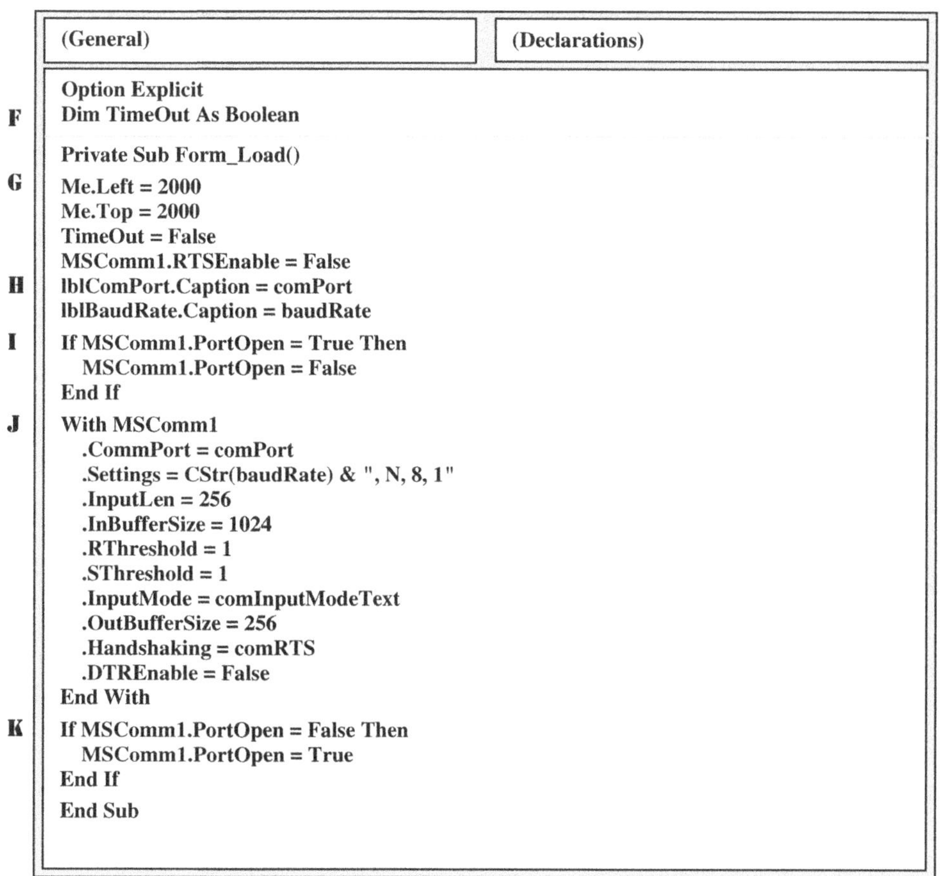

```
   (General)                                   (Declarations)

   Option Explicit
F  Dim TimeOut As Boolean

   Private Sub Form_Load()
G  Me.Left = 2000
   Me.Top = 2000
   TimeOut = False
   MSComm1.RTSEnable = False
H  lblComPort.Caption = comPort
   lblBaudRate.Caption = baudRate
I  If MSComm1.PortOpen = True Then
     MSComm1.PortOpen = False
   End If
J  With MSComm1
     .CommPort = comPort
     .Settings = CStr(baudRate) & ", N, 8, 1"
     .InputLen = 256
     .InBufferSize = 1024
     .RThreshold = 1
     .SThreshold = 1
     .InputMode = comInputModeText
     .OutBufferSize = 256
     .Handshaking = comRTS
     .DTREnable = False
   End With
K  If MSComm1.PortOpen = False Then
     MSComm1.PortOpen = True
   End If
   End Sub
```

FIGURE 4.62 Code for the `Form_Load` event procedure.

Now let's begin with the first section, the `Form_Load` event procedure. Still in the code window, go to the Object list and select the `Form` object. The `Form_Load` event procedure is opened. Enter the code that is shown in Figure 4.62 into this opened event procedure.

F: The form level's `TimeOut` variable is declared here. This variable can only be accessed and used by all event procedures in the current form `VBCommFile`. If some other forms want to use this variable, the form's name `VBCommFile` must be placed in front of this variable, such as `VBCommFile.TimeOut`.

G: The default name of the form `Me` is used to set up the initial location of the form as the project runs. `Both Left` and `Top` coordinates are assigned with a value of 2000 pixels. This make the form displayed at the center of the screen when the form is loaded and displayed. Initializations are performed for some variables and properties of the MSComm control. The form level's `TimeOut` variable is reset to `False`, and the `RTSEnable` property of the MSComm control is disabled.

H: The global variables, `comPort` and `baudRate`, which store the port number and the baud rate entered on the `Setup` form, are assigned to two labels `lblComPort` and `lblBaudRate`, respectively. In this way, the port number and the baud rate can be displayed in those labels.

I: In order to setup and configure the serial port using the properties of the MSComm control, the associated port must be closed. The `PortOpen` property is used to determine whether the port is open or not. If the port is open, close it by assigning a `False` to the `PortOpen` property. This check and operation is very important.

TIP: When configuring a serial port using the properties of the MSComm control, the port must be in the close status. You cannot perform a valid configuration to the serial port if the port is in open status.

J: The `With` statement is used to configure and set up the serial port using properties of the MSComm control. The advantage of using the `With` statement is that we do not need to precede the object name `MSComm1` for each property to assign the associated value to it.

The port number stored in the global variable `comPort` is assigned to the `CommPort` property as the port ID that is used for the data transmission task.

The baud rate stored in the global variable `baudRate` is converted to a string value and assigned to the `Settings` property of the MSComm control with the `parity`, `data bits` and `stop bits` because the `Settings` property needs a string variable.

The `InputLen` property is used to determine the number of characters each time we use the `Input` property to read from the input buffer. A value of 256 is assigned to that property here, which means that we want to read out totally 256 characters for each reading operation.

For both `RThreshold` and `SThreshold` properties, a value of 1 is assigned. This means that the events `comEvSend` or `comEvReceive` will be triggered either when a character is written into the transmit buffer or when a character has arrived in the input buffer.

For the `InputMode`, we still use the text format. Some readers may argue that why we did not use the binary format if we decide to transmit the file in the binary format. That is True, but the problem of using the binary format in the MSComm control is that it makes the program more complicated. Because the received data cannot be directly stored in a normal variable type, and you must store the received data in a `Variant` variable and then convert it into a string, and finally may be you need convert it into a certain numeric values for your special requirement in your application. This process is both time-consuming and complex in real-world programming, so here we still use the text format property; and later on we can convert the text string into binary bytes and then send those bytes over the transmission lines.

For the `Handshaking` signal, we use the hardware handshaking method by assigning a `cmdRTS` to the `Handshaking` property.

The `DTREnable` property is reset to `False`. The purpose of using this property in this application is that we want to use this signal to inform the slave computer that the file transmission is complete. Of course, one can use the `EOF` to do this, but in real world, the byte you are transferring in the file maybe coincidentally has a value (−26

= EOF) that is identical to this EOF character. In that way, the file transfer may encounter some mistakes. In order to avoid those identity possibilities, we prefer to use the DTR signal to perform this operation.

K: Now after the port has been initialized and configured, the port can be opened. By setting the PortOpen property to True, we open the port.

4.3.3.1.4.2 The Coding of the cmdSendFile Event Procedure

The operation of this event procedure is described here:

- Initialize local variables and properties of the MSComm control to make them ready to be used by this event procedure to perform the file transmission.
- Obtain the name of the file that is to be transferred using the getFileName() function.
- Get the file length that can be used for the ProgressBar.
- Enable the ProgressBar to begin to monitor and display the progress of the file transfer process.
- Call the CommStart() function to perform the synchronization process between the master and the slave program.
- Call the CommSend() function to send the file length to the slave program via serial port. This step is necessary because the slave program needs this information to calculate the percentage of the file received on the slave side and display this percentage on the ProgressBar on the slave computer.
- A for loop is used to repeatedly call the CommSend() function to send each byte of the file to the slave program via the serial port.
- The sent out byte is also displayed in the text box txtWdata.
- The checksum value is calculated after each byte is sent out.
- When the whole file is transferred, the DTREnable signal is activated and sent out to inform the slave program that the file transfer is complete, and the checksum value will be sent.
- Call the CommSend() function to send out the checksum value.
- The ProgressBar is disabled.
- The DTREnable signal is inactivated.

Now click the VBCommFile form from the Project Explorer window to select it, and then click the View Object button to open its form window. Double-click the Send File command button to open its event procedure. Enter the code that is shown in Figure 4.63 into this event procedure.

Each section of this code is explained in the following list.

L: Some local variables are declared here. The variable rc is used to reserve the running status of some calling functions, such as the CommStart() and CommSend(). The chkSum is used to reserve the checksum value calculated at master program. The FileName is used to store the file name selected at run time, which is a string variable. The FileData is a byte variable that is used to reserve each byte of the file read by using the Get method from an opened binary file.

M: The variables' initializations are performed at the beginning of this event procedure. Two of them are important. One of them is the initial value of the ProgressBar and it should be reset to 0. The other one is the DTREnable property that is used to signal the slave program that the file is transferred, and the checksum value will be sent out. This property should be reset to False at the beginning of the program.

cmdSendFile	Click

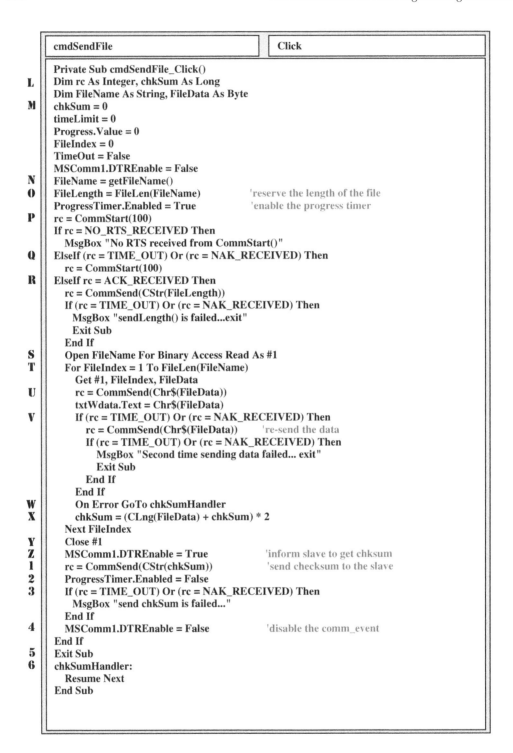

```
  Private Sub cmdSendFile_Click()
L Dim rc As Integer, chkSum As Long
  Dim FileName As String, FileData As Byte
M chkSum = 0
  timeLimit = 0
  Progress.Value = 0
  FileIndex = 0
  TimeOut = False
  MSComm1.DTREnable = False
N FileName = getFileName()
O FileLength = FileLen(FileName)          'reserve the length of the file
  ProgressTimer.Enabled = True            'enable the progress timer
P rc = CommStart(100)
  If rc = NO_RTS_RECEIVED Then
    MsgBox "No RTS received from CommStart()"
Q ElseIf (rc = TIME_OUT) Or (rc = NAK_RECEIVED) Then
    rc = CommStart(100)
R ElseIf rc = ACK_RECEIVED Then
    rc = CommSend(CStr(FileLength))
    If (rc = TIME_OUT) Or (rc = NAK_RECEIVED) Then
      MsgBox "sendLength() is failed...exit"
      Exit Sub
    End If
S   Open FileName For Binary Access Read As #1
T   For FileIndex = 1 To FileLen(FileName)
      Get #1, FileIndex, FileData
U     rc = CommSend(Chr$(FileData))
      txtWdata.Text = Chr$(FileData)
V     If (rc = TIME_OUT) Or (rc = NAK_RECEIVED) Then
        rc = CommSend(Chr$(FileData))       're-send the data
        If (rc = TIME_OUT) Or (rc = NAK_RECEIVED) Then
          MsgBox "Second time sending data failed... exit"
          Exit Sub
        End If
      End If
W     On Error GoTo chkSumHandler
X     chkSum = (CLng(FileData) + chkSum) * 2
    Next FileIndex
Y   Close #1
Z   MSComm1.DTREnable = True               'inform slave to get chksum
1   rc = CommSend(CStr(chkSum))            'send checksum to the slave
2   ProgressTimer.Enabled = False
3   If (rc = TIME_OUT) Or (rc = NAK_RECEIVED) Then
      MsgBox "send chkSum is failed..."
    End If
4   MSComm1.DTREnable = False              'disable the comm_event
  End If
5 Exit Sub
6 chkSumHandler:
    Resume Next
  End Sub
```

FIGURE 4.63 Code for the `cmdSendFile` event procedure.

N: The getFileName() function is called to pick up the file selected at run time from the Microsoft Common Dialog Control tool. This function returns a complete file name including the drive, path and file name.

O: The built-in FileLen() function is called to get the file length. This function needs an argument, FileName, to compute the file length. This parameter is very important because we need this one to calculate the percentage of the transmitted file and display it on the ProgressBar control. This parameter must be sent to the slave program for the same purpose. To use the ProgressBar to periodically display the percentage value of the transferred file, we need another timer to handle this job. That timer is named ProgressTimer, which should be enabled at this point.

P: The CommStart() function is called to perform the synchronization process between the master and the slave programs. An argument of 100 is passed into that function to indicate that the function will try to wait for about 17 minutes for the RTSEnable signal to be activated by the slave program (The time interval of the VBTimer is 10 seconds). This function waits for an activated RTSEnable signal triggered by the slave program, and send a C character to inform the slave program that the master program is ready to transfer the file. If a NO_RTS_RECEIVED status is returned from this function, which means that the slave does not trigger the RTS line and it is not ready for this file transmission, an error message will be displayed and the function is returned with that error information.

Q: If the function returns either TIME_OUT or NAK_RECEIVED error, it means that the slave program has activated the RTSEnable signal and the master program has received this signal. The master program has sent back a C character to the slave program to inform the latter that the master program is ready for file transfer. But the slave computer did not return an ACK to the master program to acknowledge that it did receive that C character. This situation may also be caused by the master program, which means that the slave program did send back an ACK but the master program cannot receive that feedback because of some errors occurred on the master computer. In either case, the CommStart() function is called again to retry to complete this synchronization process. You can add some codes followed this second function call to direct the program to exit this event procedure if the function still returns a either TIME_OUT or NAK_RECEIVED error.

R: If the CommStart() function returns ACK_RECEIVED, which means that the synchronization process has been successful and both computers are ready for this file transfer. The CommSend() function is called to send the file length to the slave program. If the function returns either a TIME_OUT or a NAK_RECEIVED error, which means that the file length is sent out but the slave program did not return a desired feedback, the error message will be displayed and the event procedure is exited.

S: If the file length is sent out successfully, the data file to be transferred is opened with the binary format. The default file number is #1 if this is the first file that has been opened in the project.

T: A for loop is used to repeatedly send out each byte of the file. The upper boundary of this loop is determined by a built-in FileLen() function that returns the total number of bytes stored in the file to be transferred. The statement: Get #1, FileIndex, FileData is used to pick up each byte from the file based on the FileIndex, and the retrieved byte is stored in the variable FileData.

U: The CommSend() function is called to send out each retrieved byte in the text format. The built-in Chr$() function is used to convert the data from the binary to the text format because the InputMode property of the MSComm control is defined as comInputModeText, which is a text format. The sent out data is also sent and displayed in the txtWdata text box.

V: If the CommSend() function return either a TIME_OUT or a NAK_RECEIVED error, which means that the sent out data is not successfully received by the slave program, the function is executed again to retry to send the last data. If, after the second calling, the function still returns the same error, which means that there are some serious problems existed on the transmission lines between two computers, the error message will be displayed and the event procedure is exited.

W: The On Error Go To ErrHandler statement is used here to prevent the overflow error from occurring during the checksum calculation process. Because the chkSum is defined as an integer variable (16-bit) and during the checksum calculation, each time when a data is sent out, that data value should be added into the chkSum, and then a shift-left operation is applied to the chkSum, which is equivalent to multiplying the chkSum value by 2. The number of this shift-left operation depends on the number of bytes stored in the file to be transmitted. When transferring a large size file, it is obvious that an overflow error will occur because the number of the shift-left operation is a huge one. To prevent this overflow error from stopping our program running, we use the On Error Go To ErrHandler statement to transfer the program to the specified handler to handle this error. We have another method to avoid this overflow error occurring and that method will be discussed below when we make this project as an executable file.

X: The checksum value is calculated after each data is sent out. Because the possible overflow error has been handled by the ErrHandler (chkSumHandler), no overflow error occurs during this calculation. The data will be sent out one by one in this for loop until all data in the file is sent out.

Y: After all data is sent out, the file must be closed by calling the statement Close #1. This step is very important, and if you missed this step, you cannot open this file again and your program will encounter an Open File error next time as you run this project.

Z: When the file is transferred, we need to send the calculated checksum to the slave program. The DTREnable signal is activated by assigning a True to the DTREnable property of the MSComm control. This signal informs the slave program that the file transfer is done and the checksum value is to be sent.

1: Then the CommSend() function is executed again to send out this checksum value.

2: The ProgressTimer is disabled.

3: If the CommSend() function returns either a TIME_OUT or a NAK_RECEIVED error, which means that the checksum value is not received by the slave program, the error message will be displayed and the event procedure returns.

4: The DTREnable signal is inactivated by assigning a False to the DTREnable property of the MSComm control.

5: An Exit Sub statement must be inserted in this event procedure at this position to direct the event procedure to exit from here. The event procedure would encounter an error without this statement at this position. Because the overflow error handler, chk-SumHandler, is located below and it is used to handle any overflow. If no overflow occurs, the event procedure does not need to execute this handler. An error would occur if the event procedure executes this handler but without an overflow occurring. To avoid this situation happening, this Exit Sub statement is necessary.

6: The function of the chkSumHandler just throws the overflow error and resume the program from the next line. This means that if an overflow error occurs, the program will be transferred to this chkSumHandler. The chkSumHandler does not take care of this error and only executes the instruction that is just located below the instruction that causes the overflow error. In our case, this instruction is Next FileIndex, which is just below the chkSum calculation instruction.

Now let's take a look at some functions used in this event procedure.

4.3.3.1.4.3 The Coding of the CommStart() Function

The operation of this function is described here:

- Enable the `VBTimer` to watch the timeout error.
- Using the `Do-Until` loop to wait for one of following two conditions occurs:

  An activated `CTSHolding` signal is received, which means that the CTS line is activated by the slave computer and the master computer has detected this signal.

  A timeout error occurs and the `timeLimit` value is greater than the upper boundary set by the user. This means that the program has waited about 17 minutes for an activated `CTSHolding` signal, but still this signal is not activated by the slave computer.

- If an activated `CTSHolding` signal is received, a `C` character is sent back to the slave program to inform latter that the master program is ready for this file transfer. The `VBTimer` and the `TimeOut` flag are reset to `False`.
- If a timeout occurs with a `timeLimit` value that is greater than the upper boundary of the timeout period, a `NO_RTS_RECEIVED` constant is returned to the calling event procedure and the program will exit the function.
- If an activated `CTSHolding` signal is received and the master program sent back a `C` character to the slave program. The next step is to wait for the feedback from the slave program to confirm that the latter did receive that character. The `VBTimer` is enabled to monitor the timeout error.
- A `Do-Until` loop is used again to wait for one of the following two conditions exists:

  A timeout error occurs.

  A character has arrived in the input buffer on the master computer.

- If a timeout error occurs, the function returns to the event procedure with a `TIME_OUT` constant.
- If a character arrives in the input buffer, we need to pick up that character and determine whether the character is an ACK.
- If the received character is `110`, which is equal to ACK, the function returns to the calling event procedure with an `ACK_RECEIVED` constant to indicate that the successful feedback signal coming from the slave program is received.
- Otherwise the function returns a `NAK_RECEIVED` constant to the calling event procedure, indicating that the feedback sent by the slave program is invalid.
- Some clean up work is performed before the program exits the function.

Add a new function into the current form `VBCommFile` by clicking the `Tools|Add Procedure` menu bar from the code window in Visual Basic workspace. Enter the parameters that are listed in Table 4.31 into the open dialog box to add this new function.

TABLE 4.31
Properties for the `CommStart()` Function

Property	Value
Name	CommStart
Type	Function
Scope	Private

On the new added function header, enter the argument `waitTime As Integer` into the parentheses and type `As Integer` at the end of this function as the returned type. Then enter the code that is shown in Figure 4.64 into this new added function. Your finished function body should match the one shown in Figure 4.64.

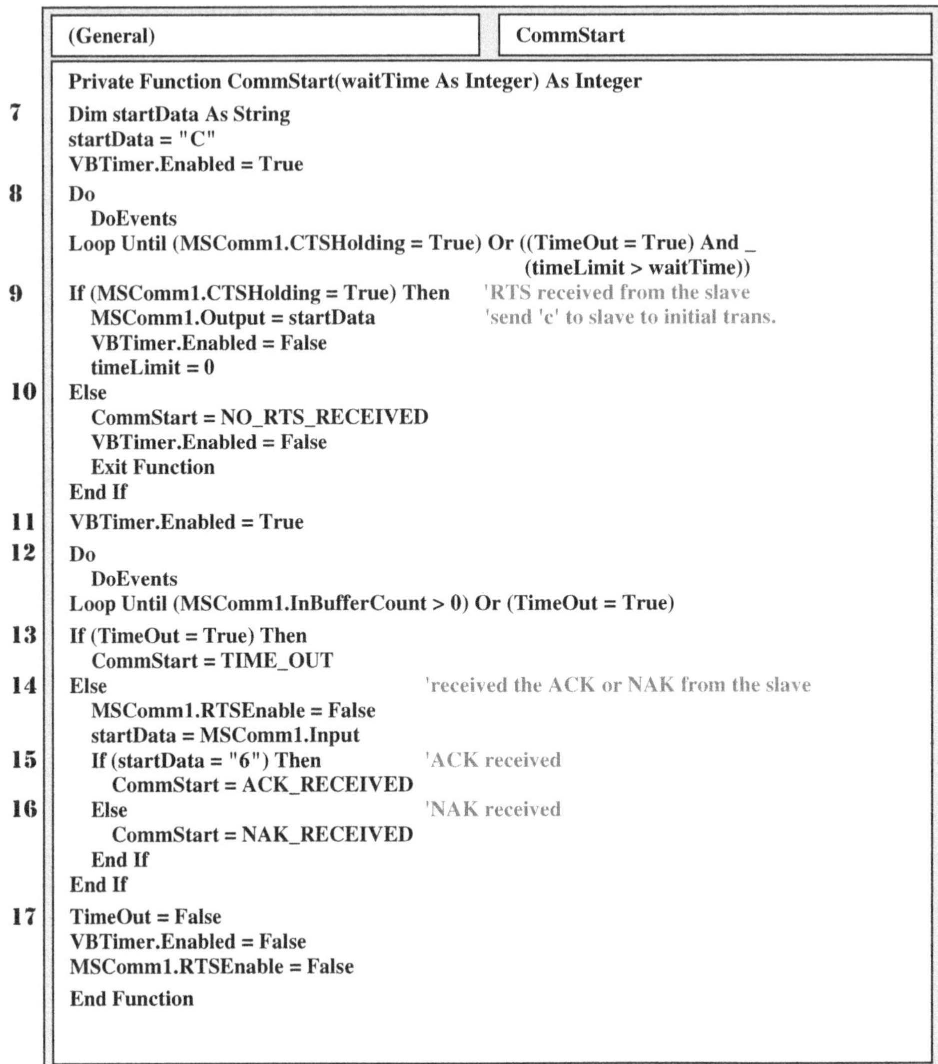

```
(General)                                   CommStart

   Private Function CommStart(waitTime As Integer) As Integer
7  Dim startData As String
   startData = "C"
   VBTimer.Enabled = True
8  Do
     DoEvents
   Loop Until (MSComm1.CTSHolding = True) Or ((TimeOut = True) And _
                                     (timeLimit > waitTime))
9  If (MSComm1.CTSHolding = True) Then     'RTS received from the slave
     MSComm1.Output = startData            'send 'c' to slave to initial trans.
     VBTimer.Enabled = False
     timeLimit = 0
10 Else
     CommStart = NO_RTS_RECEIVED
     VBTimer.Enabled = False
     Exit Function
   End If
11 VBTimer.Enabled = True
12 Do
     DoEvents
   Loop Until (MSComm1.InBufferCount > 0) Or (TimeOut = True)
13 If (TimeOut = True) Then
     CommStart = TIME_OUT
14 Else                                 'received the ACK or NAK from the slave
     MSComm1.RTSEnable = False
     startData = MSComm1.Input
15   If (startData = "6") Then          'ACK received
       CommStart = ACK_RECEIVED
16   Else                               'NAK received
       CommStart = NAK_RECEIVED
     End If
   End If
17 TimeOut = False
   VBTimer.Enabled = False
   MSComm1.RTSEnable = False
   End Function
```

FIGURE 4.64 Code for the `CommStart()` function.

Each section of this code is explained in the following list.

7: A string local variable `startData` is declared and the character `C` is assigned to this variable. This variable is used as a feedback to the slave computer to indicate that the master program is ready for the file transfer. The `VBTimer` will be enabled so that it can track the time period spent by the data transmission.

8: A `Do-Until` loop is used to wait for either an activated `CTSHolding` signal is detected or a timeout error occurs.

9: If an activated CTSHolding signal is detected, which means that the slave program has activated this signal to try to start a file transfer, and this signal has been detected by the master program. To response to this signal, the master program needs to send back a C character to inform the slave program. The Output property of the MSComm control is used to send this character to the slave program. Both the VBTimer and the TimeOut flag are reset to prevent the program from continuing to monitor the timeout error.
Note that a data transmission or a file transfer task is always issued or started by the receiver-side program; the sender program always responses a C character to the receiver to indicate that the sender is ready for that data transmission or file transfer task.

TIP: When you perform a data transmission or a file transfer task between two computers, the beginning of the task is always issued by the Receiver Computer by means of either a hardware or software handshaking signal. The Sender Computer always response to this handshaking with a C character to inform the Receiver Computer that the Sender Computer is ready for the transmission task. It does not matter which one is master or slave computer.

10: If the timeout error occurs and the timeLimit value is greater than the upper boundary waitTime, which means that the program has waited for about 17 minutes and no activated CTS line is detected, the function returns to the calling event procedure with a NO_RTS_RECEIVED constant to indicate this situation. The VBTimer is also disabled. Note that the RTS signal is activated by the slave program on the slave computer, and this line is equivalent to the CTS line on the master computer. (Refer to Figure 1.17 in Chapter 1 for more detailed information about the Null Modem connection.)
11: If an activated CTSHolding signal is detected and a C character has been sent out by the master program, we need to wait and get the response from the slave program. The VBTimer will be enabled and begins monitoring the time period spent by the data transmission because we need to use another Do-Until loop to wait for this response.
12: A Do-Until loop is used to wait for the response from the slave program.
13: If a timeout error occurs, which means that during a period of 10 seconds (the time interval of the VBTimer is 10000 milliseconds), the program did not receive the response from the slave program, the function returns to the calling event program with a TIME_OUT constant to indicate this situation.
14: Otherwise the event MSComm1.InBufferCount >0 occurs, which means that a data has arrived in the input buffer on the master computer. The Input property of the MSComm control is used to pick up that data. The RTSEnable signal is also reset.
15: If the received character is ACK, the function returns to the calling event procedure with an ACK_RECEIVED constant to indicate that the synchronization process has been successful and both computers are ready to the file transfer task.
16: Otherwise the function returns a NAK_RECEIVED constant.
17: Finally the clean up is performed before the program exits the function. Both VBTimer and RTSEnable are disabled, and the TimeOut flag is reset to False.

The next function we need to discuss is CommSend() function.

4.3.3.1.4.4 The Coding of the CommSend() Function

The operation of this function is described here:

- The VBTimer is enabled to begin to watch the possible timeout error.
- A Do-Until loop is used to wait for an activated CTS signal that is triggered by the slave computer.

- If that loop is terminated by a timeout error, which means that during a period of 10 seconds no activated CTS signal is detected, the function returns with a `TIME_OUT` constant.
- If an activated CTS signal is detected during that loop period, which means that the slave computer is ready to receive a new data, the `Output` property of the MSComm control is used to send the data out.
- Another `Do-Until` loop is used to wait for the response from the slave program to confirm that the data is received successfully by the slave computer.
- If a timeout error occurs during that waiting period, the function returns to the calling event procedure with a `TIME_OUT` constant.
- If the loop is terminated by the event `MSComm1.InBufferCount >0`, it means that a character has arrived in the input buffer of the master computer. The `Input` property of the MSComm control is used to pick up that character from the input buffer.
- If the received character is an `ACK`, the function returns an `ACK_RECEIVED` to the event procedure to indicate that the data transfer has been successful.
- Otherwise the function returns a `NAK_RECEIVED` constant to the calling event procedure.

Open the code window for the form `VBCommFile` and add a new `CommSend()` function into this form, and assign it with the parameters that are listed in Table 4.32.

TABLE 4.32
Properties for the `CommSend()` Function

Property	Value
Name	CommSend
Type	Function
Scope	Private

Enter an argument `sData As String` into the parentheses of the new added function header, and type `As Integer` at the end of the function (Figure 4.65). Enter the code that is shown in Figure 4.65 into this new added function. Your finished function body should match the one shown in Figure 4.65.

Each section of this code is explained in the following list.

18: A string local variable `revdData` is declared at the beginning of this function, and this variable will retrieve and store the feedback character from the slave computer after the master program sent out a data. The `VBTimer` will be enabled so that it can track the time period spent by the data transmission.

19: A `Do-Until` loop is used to wait for either an activated `CTSHolding` signal is detected, which is set by the slave program, or a timeout error occurs.

20: If the loop is terminated by either case, the `VBTimer` is disabled to prevent it from continuing to issue a timeout error.

21: If a timeout terminates the loop, which means that during a period of 10 seconds, no activated `CTSHolding` signal is detected, the function returns to the calling event procedure with a TIME_OUT constant. The `TimeOut` flag is also disabled.

22: Otherwise the loop is terminated by receiving an activated `CTSHolding` signal. The `Output` property of the MSComm control is used to send the data to the slave program via the serial transmission line.

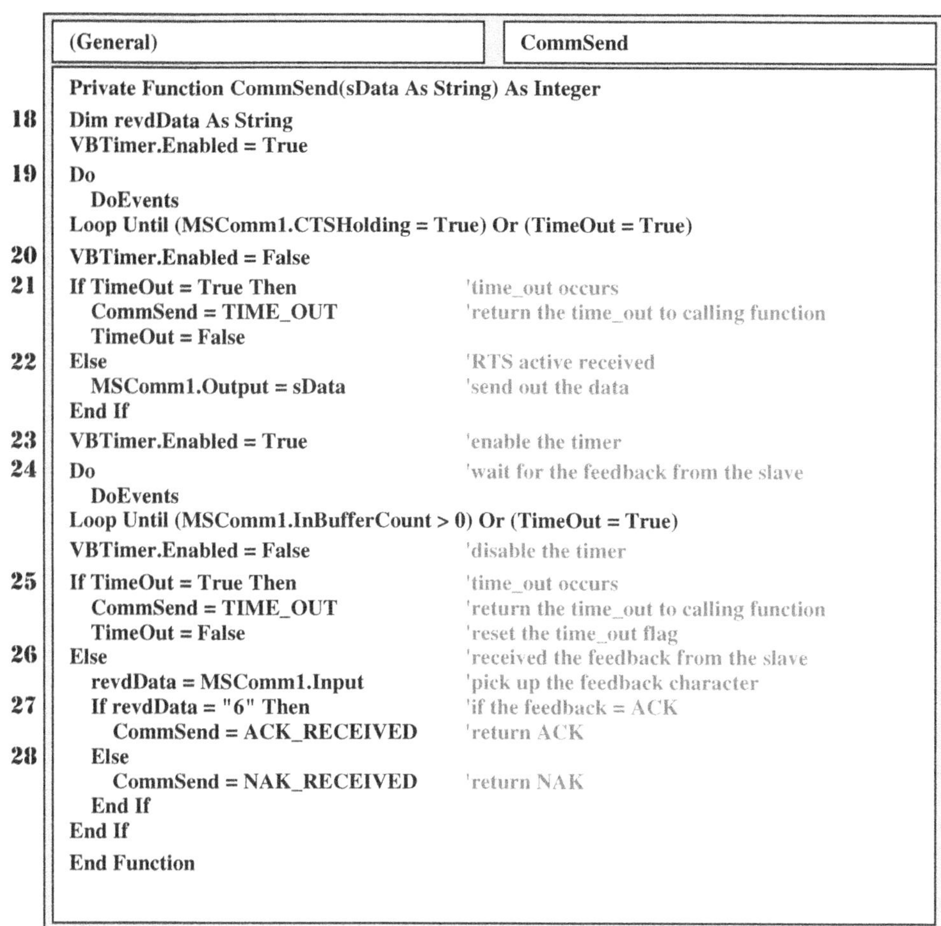

```
(General)                                   CommSend

   Private Function CommSend(sData As String) As Integer
18 Dim revdData As String
   VBTimer.Enabled = True
19 Do
     DoEvents
   Loop Until (MSComm1.CTSHolding = True) Or (TimeOut = True)
20 VBTimer.Enabled = False
21 If TimeOut = True Then                   'time_out occurs
     CommSend = TIME_OUT                    'return the time_out to calling function
     TimeOut = False
22 Else                                     'RTS active received
     MSComm1.Output = sData                 'send out the data
   End If
23 VBTimer.Enabled = True                   'enable the timer
24 Do                                       'wait for the feedback from the slave
     DoEvents
   Loop Until (MSComm1.InBufferCount > 0) Or (TimeOut = True)
   VBTimer.Enabled = False                  'disable the timer
25 If TimeOut = True Then                   'time_out occurs
     CommSend = TIME_OUT                    'return the time_out to calling function
     TimeOut = False                        'reset the time_out flag
26 Else                                     'received the feedback from the slave
     revdData = MSComm1.Input               'pick up the feedback character
27   If revdData = "6" Then                 'if the feedback = ACK
       CommSend = ACK_RECEIVED              'return ACK
28   Else
       CommSend = NAK_RECEIVED              'return NAK
     End If
   End If
   End Function
```

FIGURE 4.65 Code for the `CommSend()` function.

23: After the data is sent out, we need to wait for the feedback from the slave program to confirm that the slave computer did receive that data. To make this waiting start, we enable the `VBTimer` to monitor the possible timeout error.

24: Another `Do-Until` loop is used to wait for one of two conditions exists: either the feedback from the slave program or a timeout error. When that loop is terminated by either event, the `VBTimer` should be disabled to prevent any additional timeout errors from being reported.

25: If a timeout error occurs, the function returns to the calling event procedure with a TIME_OUT constant to indicate this situation. The `TimeOut` flag is reset to `0` (`False`) to indicate that the timeout error has been responded.

26: Otherwise it means that a character has arrived in the input buffer on the master computer. The `Input` property of the MSComm control is used to pick up that character. The received character is then stored in the local variable `revdData`.

27: If the received character is "6" (`ACK`), which means that the slave program has successfully received the data sent by the master program, the function returns to the calling event procedure with an `ACK`_RECEIVED constant to indicate this situation to the event procedure.

28: Otherwise it means that a NAK character is received. The function returns to the calling event procedure with a NAK_RECEIVED constant. The program needs to re-send that data if this situation is really occurred.

The last function we need to coding is the `getFileName()` function.

4.3.3.1.4.5 The Coding of the getFileName() Function

The purpose of this function is to allow the user to select the desired file to be transmitted from the files stored in the local derives on the master computer. Microsoft Common Dialog Control 6.0 is used to accomplish this. In Section 4.3.3.1.1, we illustrated how to add this component to our current project. This component provides a sequence of properties and allows us to modify this dialog control as we desired. Four properties are very important to us, which are

- DialogTitle
- Filter
- FileName
- ShowOpen

and we want to use them in the current project.

The `DialogTitle` is used to display the title of the dialog control when it is opened. The `Filter` is used to select the desired type of the default files, and the `ShowOpen` property is used to display the dialog control when it is opened. The `FileName` is used to store the file name selected by the user at run time. Now we add a new function into this Visual Basic project by clicking the `Tools|Add Procedure` menu item. Assign the new function the parameters that are listed in Table 4.33.

TABLE 4.33
Properties for the `getFileName()` Function

Property	Value
Name	getFileName
Type	Function
Scope	Private

Type `As String` at the end of this new added function because this function needs to return the selected file name that is a string variable. Enter the code that is shown in Figure 4.66 into this function. Your finished function body should match the one shown in Figure 4.66.

Each section of this code is explained in the following list.

29: The `With` statement is used to assign the values to the properties of the Microsoft Common Dialog Control 6.0, `dlgFile`, which is the name of the dialog control we assigned when we add that control to our project. The usage of `With` statement can save the time and space when assigning the value to each property of the control. For example, we do not need to precede the control name `dlgFile` for each property to assign its value. The property `Filter` is assigned by "All Files (*.*)|*.*" value to display all files in the current folder. The property `ShowOpen` is to indicate to the dialog control that this dialog needs to be displayed when it is opened. The `End With` statement is needed to complete the using of the `With` statement.

30: A `Do-Until` loop is used to pause processing until the `FileName` property of the `dlgFile` control is filled by a certain file name selected by the user at run time.

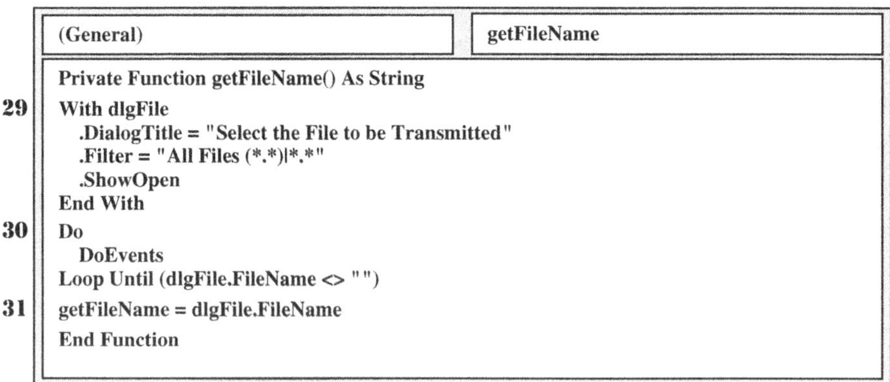

```
(General)                                   getFileName

   Private Function getFileName() As String
29 With dlgFile
     .DialogTitle = "Select the File to be Transmitted"
     .Filter = "All Files (*.*)|*.*"
     .ShowOpen
   End With
30 Do
     DoEvents
   Loop Until (dlgFile.FileName <> "")
31 getFileName = dlgFile.FileName
   End Function
```

FIGURE 4.66 Code for the `getFileName()` function.

31: After the file name is selected, the function returns to the calling event procedure with this selected file name.

Now we have finished the coding for all functions used in the `cmdSendFile` event procedure. Next let's take a look at the rest of the event procedures used in this project.

We have three more event procedures to take care of, which are: `VBTimer` event procedure, `ProgressTimer` event procedure and `Exit` command button event procedure.

4.3.3.1.4.6 The Coding of the Other Event Procedures

The purpose of the `VBTimer` is to trigger the `TimeOut` flag to report a timeout error when its time interval is up. The task of the `ProgressTimer` is to periodically calculate and display the percentage of the file that has been transmitted. The `Exit` command button triggers an event procedure that cleans up the working environment and terminates the project. The coding for these three event procedures is shown in Figure 4.67.

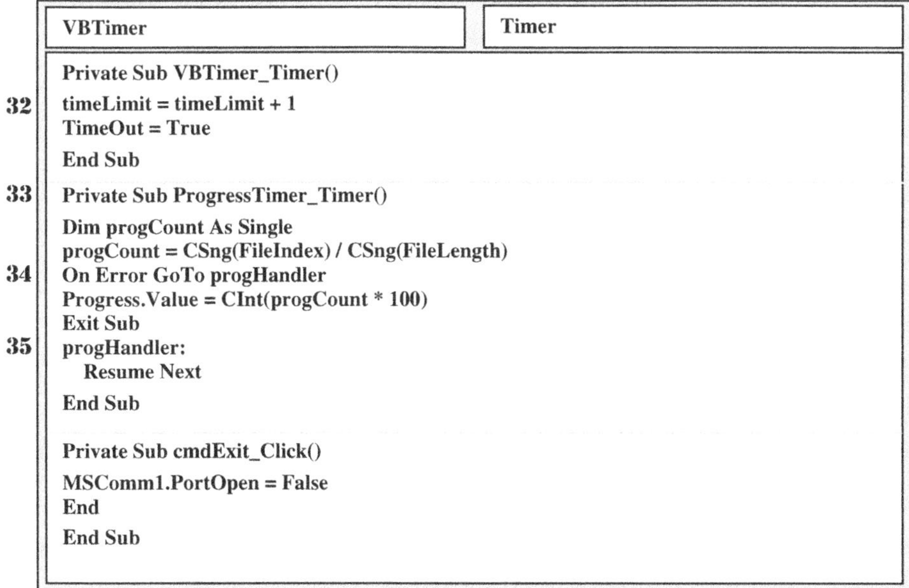

```
VBTimer                                     Timer

   Private Sub VBTimer_Timer()
32 timeLimit = timeLimit + 1
   TimeOut = True
   End Sub
33 Private Sub ProgressTimer_Timer()
   Dim progCount As Single
   progCount = CSng(FileIndex) / CSng(FileLength)
34 On Error GoTo progHandler
   Progress.Value = CInt(progCount * 100)
   Exit Sub
35 progHandler:
     Resume Next
   End Sub

   Private Sub cmdExit_Click()
   MSComm1.PortOpen = False
   End
   End Sub
```

FIGURE 4.67 Code for the remaining event procedures.

32: The timeLimit is increased by 1 as soon as the VBTimer's interval is up. This variable is used to accumulate the times of the timeout error occurs, and this variable is also used to compare with the upper boundary set by the user to determine the maximum possible length of the waiting time for the CTS signal. The TimeOut flag is set to True whenever the VBTimer interval is up. This TimeOut flag setting is used to inform the system that a timeout error occurs.

33: The purpose of the ProgressTimer is to periodically calculate and display the percentage of the file that has been transmitted. A local single variable progCount is declared and it is used to reserve the intermediate result of the division of FileIndex and FileLength. Note that both the FileIndex and the FileLength are long type global variable, a cast operation CSng() is needed to convert both data to the single type data.

34: A system error processing method On Error Go To progHandler is used here to avoid the possible error in the multiplication operations. In our case, a very small result is obtained from the division, and therefore a possible error occurs when convert the product of that small result with the 100 into the integer by using the built-in function CInt() in the next step. To prevent this kind of error from occurring, we branch the program to the symbolic address progHandler to handle that error. Another point is that the Value property of the ProgressTimer can only be assigned an integer, the CInt() is used to match that property.

35: In the label progHandler, the program does not do anything except branching the program to continue to execute the next instruction (Exit Sub), which followed the multiplication operation, by using the statement Resume Next. The Exit event procedure is used to clean up the setup of the serial port and terminate the program. The PortOpen property of the MSComm control is used to close the opened port. The End statement is to terminate the project.

At this point, we complete all coding for this master project. Recall that in Section 4.3.3.1.4.2, when we provided explanations for the cmdSendFile event procedure, at step W we mentioned that we have another method to prevent the overflow error from occurring when we make this project as an executable file. That is True. We can avoid the overflow error without using the On Error Go To ErrHandler statement in our program. To do that, we need to make our project as an executable file.

As you know, in the early days, Visual Basic runs the program in the interpreter mode. This means that Visual Basic can only use the interpreter to convert one line code in the program into the machine code and execute that code. In this way, Visual Basic can finish running your entire program line by line. It is obvious that this mode is low efficiency in running the program.

Later on, in order to make the Visual Basic program compatible with different operating systems or platforms, Visual Basic first convert the source code into the so-called P-code. This P-code can be considered as a common code and it can be recognized by different machines with different platforms. This P-code can be installed in the different platform and can be converted into the associated machine code by a so-called virtual machine (interpreter) that is only compatible with that platform.

Today, Visual Basic provides a more efficient way for us to convert and run the source code, which is the compiler. By using the compiler, the Visual Basic source code can be entirely converted to the machine code and that compiled code can be run immediately at that machine. But this method can only be used in certain platform or certain operating system, and it cannot be used in the cross-platform situation. This method is to make Visual Basic an executable file.

Why the overflow error can be avoided when make the project an executable file? The answer is that Visual Basic provides a sequence of options when converting the source code into the executable file, and these options are located in the Project Properties dialog box.

Now let's take a look at how to use the compiler to avoid the overflow error. Click the `Project|VBFile_Master Properties...` menu item from the Visual Basic menu bar to open the `Project Properties` dialog box, then select the `Compile` tab, which is shown in Figure 4.68.

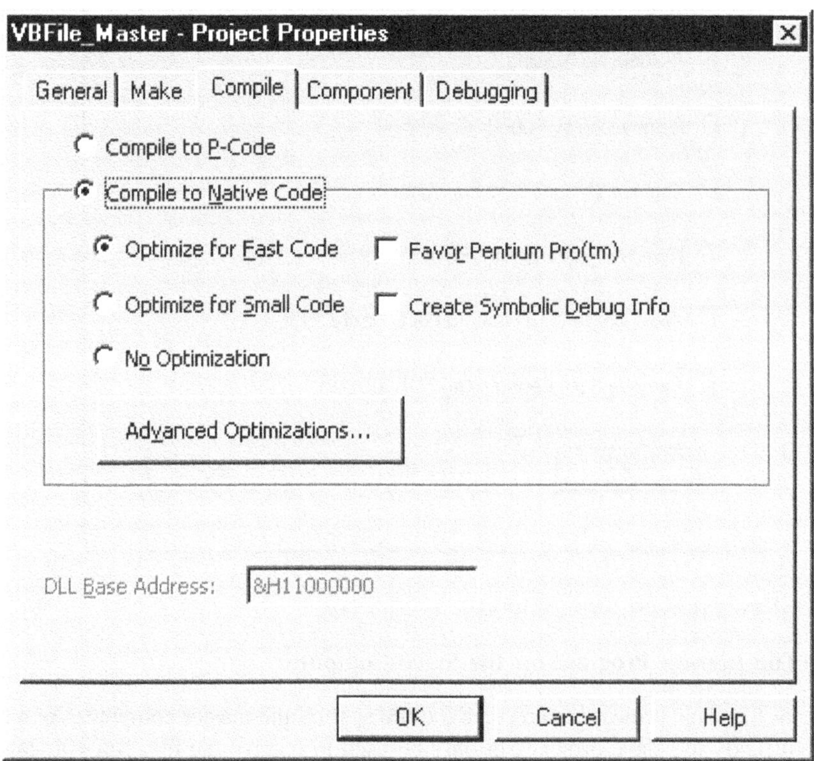

FIGURE 4.68 The `Project Properties` dialog box.

Check the `Compile to Native Code` radio button, which means that we want to use the compiler to convert the entire source code into the machine code. Check the `Optimize for Fast Code` radio button to enhance the running speed of our converted program. Then click the `Advanced Optimizations` button to open the `Advanced Optimizations` dialog box, which is shown in Figure 4.69.

In the `Advanced Optimizations` dialog box, check the checkbox of `Remove Integer Overflow Checks` to select this item. Click the `OK` button for both opened dialog boxes to close them. Now we have selected to compile our program to the machine code without checking the overflow error.

Click the `File |Make VBFile_Master.exe...` menu item from the Visual Basic menu bar to compile the program to the executable file. This compiled file has no any overflow checking ability as it runs later.

When using this method, You should be very careful to avoid disabling the system error-checking methods in your program. Your program will crash if you try to avoid some possible errors by disabling certain error-checking methods in your program, but your program did encounter that kind of error in some other locations where you did not pay attention. You must find the exact location of the possible error in your program before you can use this method.

We have completed the development of the serial file transfer program in the master side. We now need to develop the associated file transfer program for the slave side to test our program.

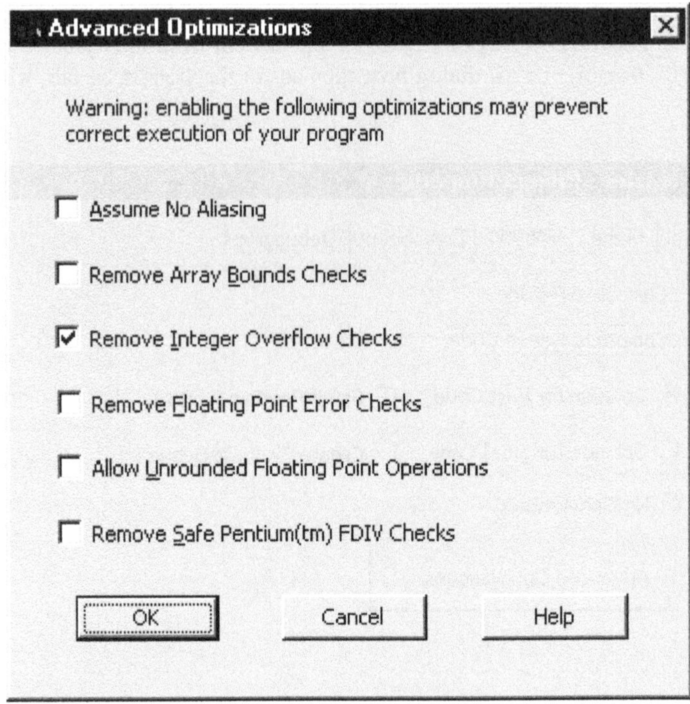

FIGURE 4.69 The `Advanced Optimizations` dialog box.

4.3.3.2 The File Transfer Program for the Slave Computer

The purpose of the slave project is to receive the file sent by the master computer. As we previous mentioned, currently the slave project can only be used to receive the file. But you can copy the code from the send event procedure in the master project and paste them into the send event procedure in the slave project, therefore the slave project can both send and receive the file.

Basically, the slave project is very similar to the master project. Still two forms are used in this project: `Setup` and `VBCommFile`. Both forms are identical with those developed in the master project. The `Setup` form is used to collect the serial port configuration parameters entered by the user to set up the serial port. The `VBCommFile` is to perform the receiving file between two computers.

Launch Visual Basic 6.0 to open a new `Standard.EXE` project, name the project as `VBFile_Slave.vbp`. Add two forms `Setup` and `VBCommFile` into this new project. Design these two forms exactly as we did for those two forms developed in the master project.

Add the following components and Active-X control to the new project by clicking the `Project|Components` menu item:

- Microsoft Comm Control 6.0
- Microsoft Common Dialog Control 6.0
- Microsoft Windows Common Controls 6.0 (SP4)

As we did for the master project, add the following controls into the second form, `VBCommFile`. Besides the normal controls, two timers are also added.

- MSComm control (Name: `MSComm1`)
- Common dialog control (Name: `dlgFile`)

- ProgressBar control (Name: `Progress`)
- Timer control 1 (Name: `VBTimer`—monitor the timeout error)
- Timer control 2 (Name: `ProgressTimer`—monitor the progress bar)

Besides add these controls and components, we also need to add a code module to store the global constants and variables used in the slave project. Click the `Project|Add Module` menu item to add a new module into this project and name this module as `VBComm.bas`.

All graphical user interfaces in the slave project are identical with those developed in the master project. (Refer to Section 4.3.3.1.1 to complete the design of these forms.) Now we begin to coding for each form and module.

4.3.3.2.1 The Coding of the Code Module

Double-click the new added code module, and enter the code that is shown in Figure 4.70.

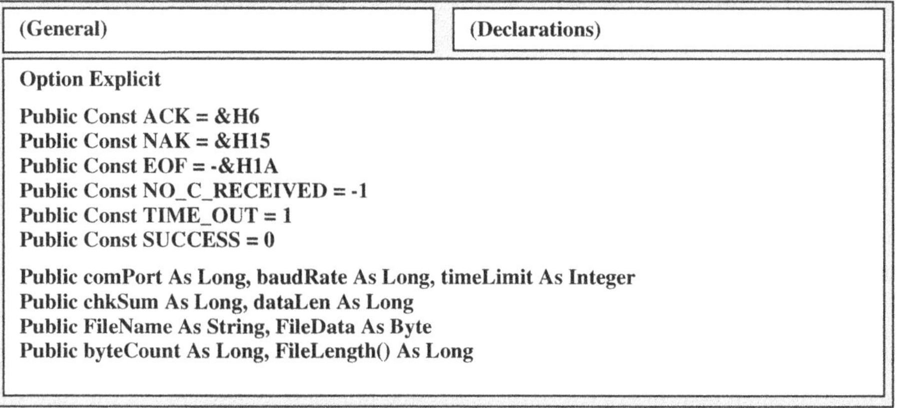

```
(General)                         (Declarations)

Option Explicit

Public Const ACK = &H6
Public Const NAK = &H15
Public Const EOF = -&H1A
Public Const NO_C_RECEIVED = -1
Public Const TIME_OUT = 1
Public Const SUCCESS = 0

Public comPort As Long, baudRate As Long, timeLimit As Integer
Public chkSum As Long, dataLen As Long
Public FileName As String, FileData As Byte
Public byteCount As Long, FileLength() As Long
```

FIGURE 4.70 The code module.

This coding is straightforward and is similar to the coding of the module in the master project. The statement `Option Explicit` is used to prevent user from using variables without declaring them, misusing or misspelling the names of the variables or objects used in the project. All global constants are declared in this module and those constants can be accessed and used by all event procedures on all forms for the current project. The often-used variables are declared in this module as the global variables. These variables are described in the following list:

- comPort: Reserves the `Port Number` value entered at run time
- baudRate: Reserves the `Baud Rate` value entered at run time
- timeLimit: Stores the times when the timeout error occurs
- chkSum: Stores the checksum value
- dataLen: Stores the number of converted bytes from the received data string
- FileName: Stores the name of the file selected at run time
- FileData: Reserves the byte value converted from the received data string

The `FileLength()` is an array and it is used to hold the received file length from the master program. It can be used as a denominator in calculating of the percentage of the file that has been received and it can be displayed on the `ProgressBar`. The `FileData` is used to reserve the byte value converted from the received data string because the received data is in the text format and a conversion is needed to translate the string to a sequence of bytes. The `dataLen` is used to hold the number of converted bytes from the received data string.

The first three constants, ACK, NAK, and EOF, belong to the system constants and those constants are defined by the serial communication convention. The system constants can be used by any project without any modification. The followed three constants belong to user-defined constants and are specially used for the current project. The values of those constants can be modified based on the actual applications.

At this point, we finished the coding of the code module. The coding of the Setup form is identical to the coding of the Setup form in the master project. (Refer to Section 4.3.3.1.3 to complete the coding of the Setup form.)

4.3.3.2.2 The Coding of the VBCommFile Form

The coding of the VBCommFile form can be divided into several sections. The first section is the coding of the Form_Load event procedure. This coding is identical to the coding of the Form_Load event procedure in the master-side program. (Refer to Section 4.3.3.1.4.1 in this Chapter to finish this coding.) The second section is the coding of the command button cmdRecvFile event procedure. The purpose of this event procedure is to receive the data file from the master program and checking the feedback from the master computer to make sure that the file is transmitted successfully. The third section is the coding of functions used in the cmdRecvFile event procedure, such as the CommStart(), CommRecv(), and getFileName() functions. The last section is the coding for some other event procedures, such as the VBTimer, ProgressTimer and cmdExit event procedures.

For the functions and event procedures used in the VBCommFile form, some of them are identical to those developed in the master-side program, such as the getFileName() function, VBTimer and cmdExit event procedures. To make things simple and save time, these functions and event procedures will not be repeated here again. (Refer to Section 4.3.3.1.4.2 to complete the coding for these items.)

Another important difference between the slave and the master program is that the OnComm event of the MSComm control is used in the slave-side program to take care of the receiving the file transmitted from the master computer. The advantage of using this OnComm event is that the CPU can spend most of its time on running other tasks. In other words, the CPU does not need to repeatedly check the status of the input buffer to determine whether a data has arrived on the slave computer without performing any other tasks. This is a typical Object-Oriented/Event Driven programming style and it is very efficient in running multiple-task in the multi-task environment. The OnComm event can be automatically triggered as a data has arrived in the input buffer.

In the following sections, we concentrate on the functions and event procedures that are different with those developed in the master-side program. These include the following event procedures and functions:

- cmdRecvFile
- OnComm
- ProgressTimer
- CommStart()
- CommRecv()

Before we can begin the coding for any event procedure or function in the VBCommFile form, we need to add two form level's variables: the Boolean flag TimeOut and the Boolean variable evtEOF. The latter is used as an indicator of receiving the EOF character during the file transfer process.

Open the code window of the form VBCommFile, enter the Option Explicit statement in the form's General Declaration section, and then declare two form-level variables, TimeOut and evtEOF.

4.3.3.2.2.1 The Coding of the cmdReceiveFile Event Procedure

The operation of this event procedure is described here:

The `getFileName()` function is called to obtain a full name that contains both the file name and the complete path. This full name is used to hold and reserve the received file transmitted by the master program, and it can be considered as a destination file.

TIP: When receiving a file via file transfer method in the serial format, you must indicate the destination file name that will hold the received file. No matter whether you are using a Hyper-terminal or a user-developed software to perform this file transfer.

- The `CommStart()` function is called to perform the synchronization process between the slave and the master program.
- If the function returns a `NO_C_RECEIVED` error, which means that the `C` character sent by the master program is not received by the slave program during the maximum timeout period, the error message will be displayed and the event procedure is exited.
- If a timeout error is returned, the `CommStart()` function is called again to retry to synchronize the starting point between the two programs. If, after the second calling, the function still returns a timeout error or `NO_C_RECEIVED` error, this means that there are some problems existed on the transmission line between two computers. This error message will be displayed and the event procedure is exited.
- If the function returns a `SUCCESS` signal, it means that the synchronization process has been successful and a feedback character `C` has been received in the input buffer on the slave computer.
- After the synchronization process has been successfully completed, next the function `CommRecv()` is executed to try to pick up the file length sent by the master program.
- If the function returns a timeout error, the error message will be displayed and the event procedure is exited.
- If the file length parameter is received successfully, the destination file is opened to be ready to store the received file.
- The `OnComm` event procedure is activated to begin to monitor the `comEvReceive` event. This event will be automatically triggered if a data has arrived in the input buffer on the slave computer.
- A `Do-Until` loop is used to wait until the `evtEOF` flag is set, which means that the whole file has been transmitted and the `EOF` character is received at the end of the file. This flag is set by the event `comEvDSR` in the `OnComm` event procedure. Because we use the DTR as the end signal of transmitted file in the master side, and that signal is equivalent to the DSR on the slave side. As an activated DSR signal is detected on the slave computer, the `comEvDSR` event is generated and the flag `evtEOF` is set to inform the slave program that the `EOF` is received.
- After the `EOF` is received, the destination file is closed because the whole file has been received.
- Then the function `CommRecv()` is executed to pick up the checksum value sent by the master program.
- If the function returns a timeout, which means that the checksum value is not received successfully, the error message will be displayed and the event procedure is exited.
- Otherwise if the checksum value is received successfully, the received checksum is compared with the calculated checksum made in the slave-side program. If both checksum are identical, this file transfer has been successful. The success message will be displayed. If the checksum values are different, it means that the file transfer has failed; in this case, an error message will appear.
- Reset the `ProgressTimer` and `Progress` value.

Now open the `VBCommFile` form window and double-click the `Receive File` button to open its event procedure. Enter the code that is shown in Figure 4.71 into this procedure.

```
   cmdRecvFile                          Click

   Private Sub cmdRecvFile_Click()
A  Dim rc As Integer, checkSum() As Long
   byteCount = 0
   timeLimit = 0
   chkSum = 0
B  FileName = getFileName()             'get the file name to store the received file
C  rc = CommStart(100)
   If rc = NO_C_RECEIVED Then
     MsgBox "Time Out occurs, no C received from the Slave"
     Exit Sub
D  ElseIf rc = TIME_OUT Then
     rc = CommStart(100)
     If (rc = TIME_OUT) Or (rc = NO_C_RECEIVED) Then
       MsgBox "Second time CommStart() failed...exit"
       Exit Sub
     End If
E  ElseIf rc = SUCCESS Then
     FileLength = CommRecv()
F    If FileLength(0) = TIME_OUT Then
       MsgBox "Timeout occurs in getLength()...exit"
       Exit Sub
     End If
G    Open FileName For Binary Access Write As #1
H    MSComm1.RThreshold = 1             'enable comm_event
     MSComm1.SThreshold = 1             'enable comm_event
     Do
I      DoEvents
     Loop Until (evtEOF = True)
J    evtEOF = False
     Close #1
K    checkSum = CommRecv()
     If checkSum(0) = TIME_OUT Then
       MsgBox "received checksum is failed...exit"
       Exit Sub
L    ElseIf checkSum(0) = SUCCESS Then
       If checkSum(1) = chkSum Then
         MsgBox "The program is completed successfully"
       Else
         MsgBox "Check Sum is not matched"
       End If
     End If
M    ProgressTimer.Enabled = False
     Progress.Value = 0
   End If
   End Sub
```

FIGURE 4.71 Code for the `cmdRecvFile` event procedure.

Each section of this code is explained in the following list.

A: Two local variables are declared here. The `rc` variable is used to store the running status of some calling functions, such as the `CommStart()` function. The `checkSum()` is an array that is used to pick up and store the received checksum value sent by the master program. Followed this declaration, the initializations are performed for some variables. The global variable byteCount is used as a counter to count how many bytes of the file have been received on the slave computer. Another global variable checkSum is used to reserve the checksum value calculated in the slave-side program as each data is received. Do not be confused between the local array variable checkSum() and the global variable chkSum. The former is used to reserve the received checksum value that is calculated and sent by the master program, and the latter is used to reserve the checksum value calculated by the slave program as each data is received. These two checksum values should be identical if the file transmission has been successful.

B: The getFileName() function is called to obtain the destination file name. You must select a destination file name and use that destination file to reserve the received file data, and that file is the destination for the file to be transferred.

C: Next the CommStart() function is called to perform the synchronization process between the slave and the master program. The purpose of this synchronization process is to make both programs begin to transfer data in step. If that function returns a NO_C_RECEIVED error, which means that the slave program cannot receive the feedback character C sent by the master program, the error message will be displayed and the event procedure is exited.

D: If that function returns a TIME_OUT error, which means that the slave program did receive a feedback character sent by the master program, but that character is not C. The event procedure will call the CommStart() function again to re-execute that synchronization process. If, after the second calling, the function still returns either a TIME_OUT or a NO_C_RECEIVED error, it means that a hardware problem exists between the master and the slave computer. An error message will be displayed and the event procedure is terminated.

E: Otherwise, if the function returns a SUCCESS signal, it means that the synchronization process has been successful and both programs are ready to start the file transfer task. The function CommRecv() is executed to pick up the file length parameter that is supposed to be sent by the master program.

F: If the function returns a timeout error, it means that the slave program cannot receive this file length parameter successfully from the master program, the error message will be displayed and the event procedure is exited.

G: Otherwise, the file length parameter is received successfully by the slave program, and the slave program can start to pick up the data transmitted from the master program. The destination file is opened to be ready to reserve the received file. The #1 indicates the opened file is the first file in the slave-side program if no file is opened before.

H: By setting the RThreshold and SThreshold property of the MSComm control to 1, we can start the OnComm event monitor to begin to detect and response the associated events occurred in the serial port. In this application, we only take care of the following two events:

comEvReceive
comEvDSR

The first event is used to detect and response to a data that has arrived in the input buffer on the slave computer. The second event is used to detect the EOF character that should be sent by the master program and should be received by the slave program at the end of the file transfer. You can disable the OnComm event procedure by setting both RThreshold and SThreshold to 0.

I: After the OnComm event procedure is enabled, all data receiving jobs is handled by the coding in the comEvReceive event case automatically and we do not need to take care of it in this event procedure at all. (We will discuss that coding later on in this section.) Another `Do-Until` loop is used to pause processing until the file transfer task is completed, which is reported by the event `comEvDSR`. As soon as an activated DSR signal is detected, which is activated by the master program by setting the DTR line in the master side at the end of the file transfer, the flag `evtEOF` is set to `True`.

J: When the flag `evtEOF` is set, the `Do-Until` loop is terminated because the file transfer job is done. To avoid any confusion, this flag is reset to `False` immediately after it is set. The opened destination file is closed to reserve the received file data.

K: Next we need to pick up the received checksum value sent by the master program by calling the function `CommRecv()`. If the function returns a timeout error, the error message will be displayed and the event procedure is exited.

L: Otherwise if the function returns a `SUCCESS` signal, it means that the slave program successfully received the checksum value sent by the master program. This received checksum value needs to be compared with the calculated checksum value made by the slave program. If both values are identical, which means that this file transfer has been successful, the success message will be displayed. Otherwise it means that some error is encountered during this file transfer, and the mismatch message is also displayed.

M: Finally the `ProgressTimer` is disabled and its `Value` property is reset to `0`.

The coding of the event procedure `cmdRecvFile` is completed.

4.3.3.2.2.2 The Coding of the OnComm Event Procedure

This event procedure picks up and stores the received file data by using the event provided by MSComm Control. Both the pick up and the storage can be significantly improved by using this event style to receive the file data. A `While` loop is used in this event case to repeatedly pick up each byte of data until all data is received. Go to the form window by selecting the `VBCommFile` form object from the `Project Explorer` window and clicking the View Object button, then double-click the `MSComm` icon on the form to open its event procedure. Enter the code that is shown in Figure 4.72 into this event procedure.

Each section of this code is explained in the following list.

N: Two local variables are declared here. The `index` is a long type variable and it works as an index in the `for` loop to select each byte from the received text data. The `TmpData` is a string variable and it is used to store the received text data temporarily. The `String*1` means that this string is defined as a single-character string and it can only be used to store a single-byte data even it is declared as a string variable.

O: The `Select Case` structure is used to select the suitable event from the event constant `CommEvent`.

P: If the event `comEvReceive` occurs, a `While` loop is used to continuously pick up each data from the input buffer until the buffer is empty, which means that no data is left in there. The `Input` property of the MSComm control is used to get each data and assign that data to the `TmpData`. The received data is also displayed in the text box `txtRdata`.

Q: The data is originally obtained in the master-side program by opening the data file in the binary format, then the binary format data is converted to the text format data and transmitted to the slave computer. In order to recover the data back to the binary format, some steps are needed. First we need to get the data length by using the built-in function `Len()` and assign that data length to the global variable `dataLen`.

R: A `for` loop is used to repeatedly get each character using the built-in function `Mid()`. Each character is first converted to the ASCII code and then converted to the `Byte` type value in Visual Basic before the `Mid()` is applied. The coefficient `1` at the end of the function indicates that each time only one character is converted. The converted character

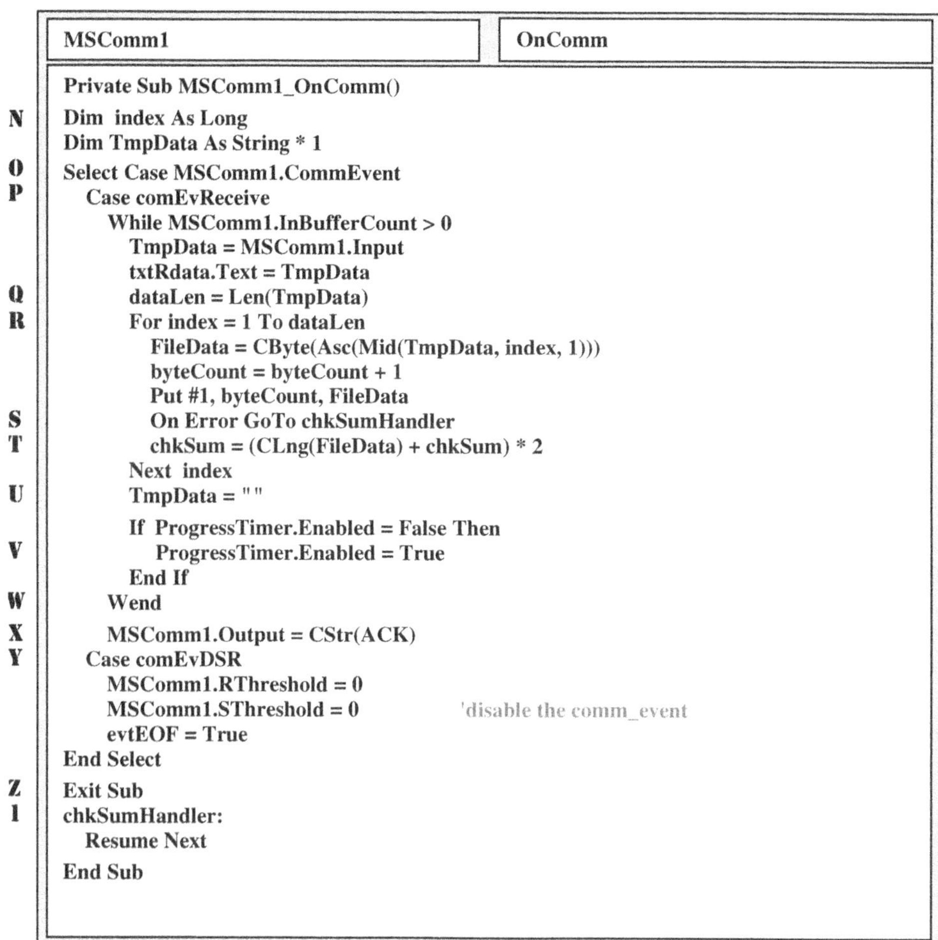

```
  MSComm1                                OnComm

  Private Sub MSComm1_OnComm()
N Dim index As Long
  Dim TmpData As String * 1
O Select Case MSComm1.CommEvent
P   Case comEvReceive
      While MSComm1.InBufferCount > 0
        TmpData = MSComm1.Input
        txtRdata.Text = TmpData
Q       dataLen = Len(TmpData)
R       For index = 1 To dataLen
          FileData = CByte(Asc(Mid(TmpData, index, 1)))
          byteCount = byteCount + 1
          Put #1, byteCount, FileData
S         On Error GoTo chkSumHandler
T         chkSum = (CLng(FileData) + chkSum) * 2
        Next index
U       TmpData = ""
        If ProgressTimer.Enabled = False Then
V          ProgressTimer.Enabled = True
        End If
W     Wend
X     MSComm1.Output = CStr(ACK)
Y   Case comEvDSR
      MSComm1.RThreshold = 0
      MSComm1.SThreshold = 0          'disable the comm_event
      evtEOF = True
  End Select
Z Exit Sub
1 chkSumHandler:
    Resume Next
  End Sub
```

FIGURE 4.72 Code for the `OnComm` event procedure.

is assigned to the global variable `FileData`, which is then written into the destination file by using the `Put #1` statement. The `byteCount` works as a position index to define the position of the data to be written into the file.

S: After one byte of data is received and stored, we need to calculate the checksum value. An `On Error Go To chkSumHandler` statement is inserted before the calculation of the checksum value to prevent the overflow error from occurring.

T: Then the checksum is computed. The `FileData` needs to be converted to the Long data type before the calculation because it is defined as a `Byte` type in the code module. Each byte of data is processed in this way until a complete data is done.

U: After a data is stored, the temporary variable `TmpData` is reset to an empty string to make it ready for the next data.

V: Enable the `ProgressTimer` to display the percentage of the file received on the `Progress` bar on the slave computer.

W: This process will continue until all data is received and processed. The `Wend` is used to terminate the `While` loop.

X: When all data received, an `ACK` feedback is sent to the master program to inform the latter that the data is received successfully. The `Output` property of the MSComm control is used to perform this job.

Y: If the event `comEvDSR` is signaled, which means that the DTR line has been activated by the master computer, it is equivalent for the slave to have received an `EOF` character sent by the master. This marks the end of the file transfer. The flag `evtEOF` is set to `True` to inform the slave program that situation.

Z: The `Exit Sub` statement must be inserted here to allow this event procedure to terminate and exit at this point. Otherwise the event procedure would continue to execute the instructions that that follow the label `chkSumHandler`. Your program may encounter an error if this situation occurs. To prevent such errors, this statement is necessary.

1: The label `chkSumHandler` directs the program to continue to execute the next instruction, `Resume Next`, which follows the instruction that caused the overflow error.

The next coding is for the `ProgressTimer` event procedure.

4.3.3.2.2.3 The Coding of the ProgressTimer Event Procedure

The objective of this event procedure is to periodically display the percentage of the file that has been received on the slave computer in the progress bar. Refer to Table 4.30, which lists the parameters of the `ProgressTimer` in the master-side program, the time interval of this timer is 10 milliseconds. In the slave program, the same timer and parameters are used. Click the `VBCommFile` object from the `Project Explorer` window and click the `View Object` button, then double-click the `ProgressTimer` to open its event procedure. Enter the code that is shown in Figure 4.73 into this event procedure.

```
ProgressTimer                                   Timer

  Private Sub ProgressTimer_Timer()
2 Dim count As Single
3 count = CSng(byteCount) / CSng(FileLength(1))
4 Progress.Value = CInt(count * 100)
  End Sub
```

FIGURE 4.73 Code for the `ProgressTimer` event procedure.

2: A local variable `count` is declared here and it is used to store the calculation result of the percentage between the received bytes and the total bytes in the file.

3: The `byteCount` indicates the current number of the bytes received and the `FileLength(1)` represents the total number of bytes in the transmitted file. Both of these data items need to be converted into the Single data type before they can be performed the division operation because both of them are `Long` data type global variables declared in the code module file.

4: The divided result is a fractional data, and it needs to be multiplied by a factor of 100 and converted into the Integer before it can be assigned to the `Value` property of the `ProgressTimer`. The `Value` property of the timer is used to display the part of the percentage of the file to be received on the progress bar.

Now we have finished the coding for all event procedures and functions used in the slave-side program.

We are ready to test our projects by transmitting data files between the master and the slave computers now. To do that, you need to connect two serial ports that are located at two different computers with a null modem cable. (Refer to Section 1.5.2, Figure 1-17 in Chapter 1 to get more detailed information about the null modem cable and complete this connection.)

In both the master and the slave computers, run the associated project by clicking the `Start` button or pressing the `F5` key. The `Setup` form is displayed first, as shown in Figure 4.74. Enter the serial communication parameters, such as `1`, for the port number and 115200 for the baud rate, and click the `Setup` button to complete this setup.

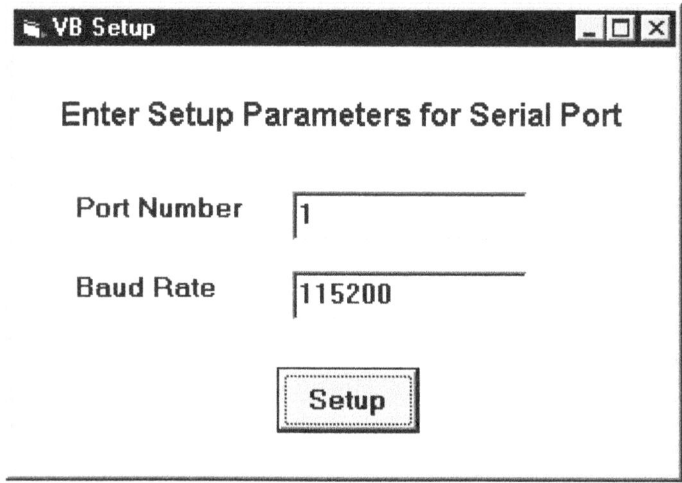

FIGURE 4.74 The `Setup` form.

You can also use the `Tab` key on the keyboard to sequentially access each object, such as the `Port Number` text box, the `Baud Rate` text box and the `Setup` button, by using the `TabIndex` property we set in Table 4.26. Press the `Enter` key to finish this step.

The reason we select `115200` as the baud rate is that the file can be transferred at a high speed by using this high baud rate. You may wish to use some other baud rate, such as 9600, 19200, or 38400.

The second form `VBCommFile` is displayed. You can now click either the `Send File` or the `Receive File` button on either the master or the slave computer to begin this file transfer project. But we prefer to first click the `Receive File` button on the slave computer because the actual file transfer is started from the slave program by responding a `C` character to the master computer.

First click the `Receive File` button from the `VBCommFile` form. Immediately the `Common` dialog box will be displayed to allow us to select the name and the path for the file to be received by the slave program. In this application, we selected this project folder as the file path, `VBCommFile_Slave`, and enter the `vFile.doc` into the `File name:` box as the name for this file since we will transfer a document file, as shown in Figure 4.75.

Click the `Open` button to begin this file transfer (file receiving). The `VBCommFile` form is now waiting for the file to be transferred, as shown in Figure 4.76.

Now go to the master computer and run the master project by clicking the Start button on the master program. Enter the same serial communication parameters, such as `1` for the port number and `115200` for the baud rate, and click the `Setup` button to complete this setup.

Click the `Send File` button on the `VBCommFile` form on the master computer to try to send a file to the slave computer. A `Common` dialog box appears to allow us to select the file to be transmitted. In this application, we selected a Microsoft Word file named `CHAPTER 1.doc`

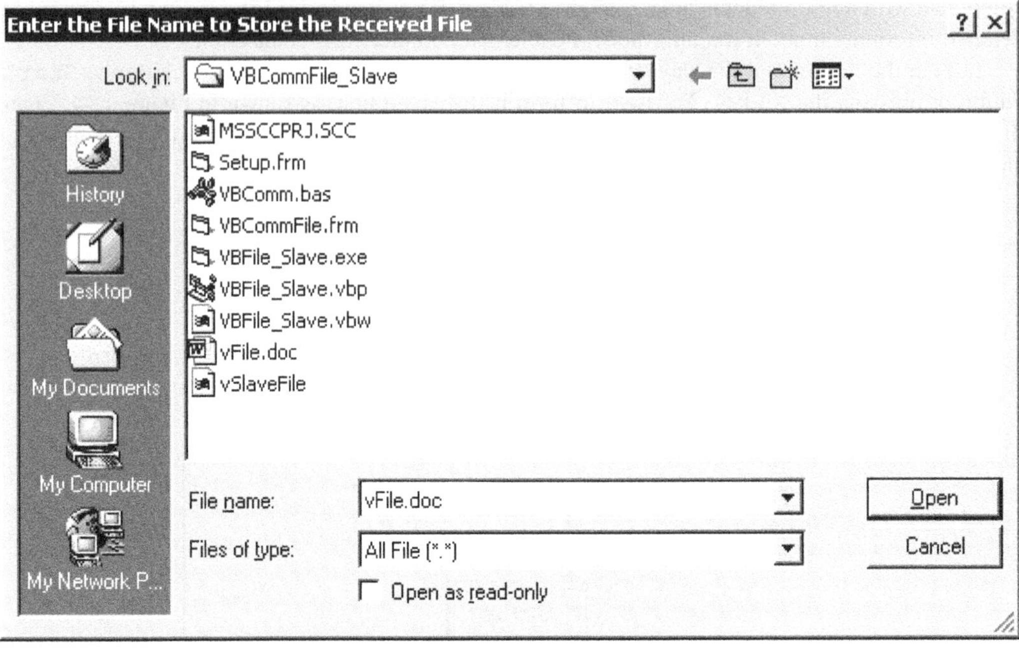

FIGURE 4.75 The `Common` dialog box for the slave-side program.

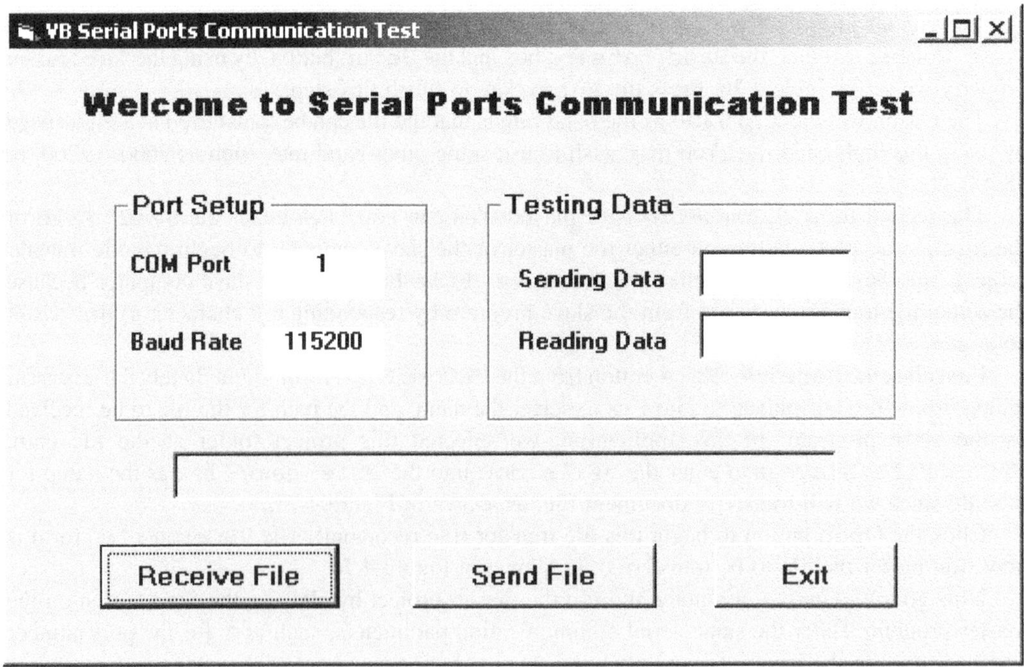

FIGURE 4.76 The `VBCommFile` form for the slave-side program.

that is a 50KB file to send to the slave computer. You can try to send any file stored in your system. Select this file as shown in Figure 4.77, and click the Open button to begin the file transfer.

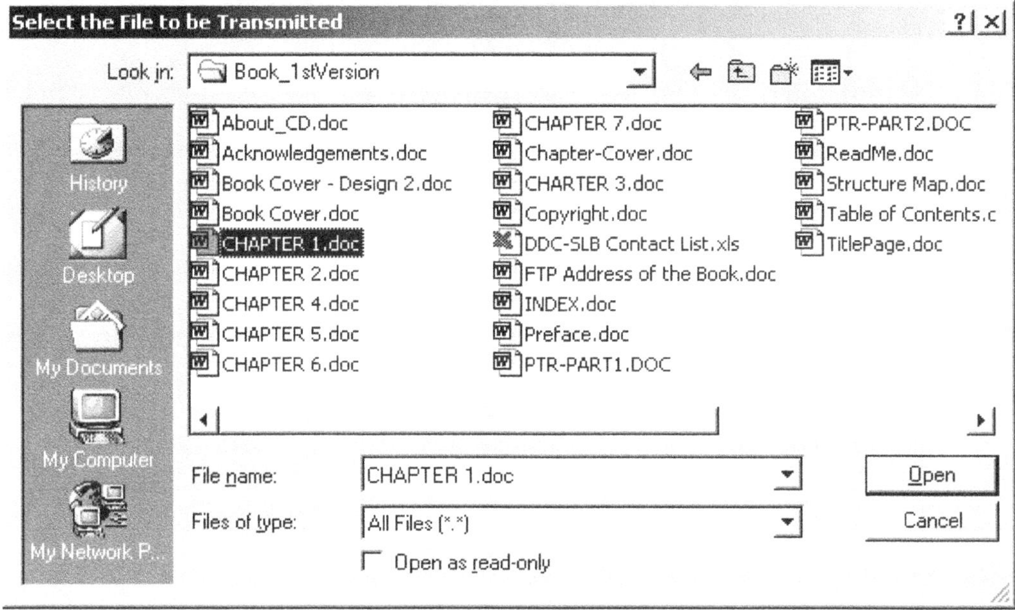

FIGURE 4.77 The Common dialog box for the master-side program.

Now back to the slave computer, and you can find that the percentage of the file that has been received is displayed in the progress bar, which is shown in Figure 4.78. The received byte is displayed in the Reading Data text box. Note that some of the bytes are noncharacter bytes and cannot be displayed in the normal character.

On the master side, the progress of the sending file is also displayed in the progress bar on the master computer, which is shown in Figure 4.79. The sending data is displayed in the Sending Data text box.

When this file is transmitted successfully, a successful message is displayed on both the master and the slave computer, as shown in Figures 4.80 (a) and (b), respectively.

The total time period of transferring this 50KB file is about 1 minute. You can open this transmitted file from the slave computer to confirm the correctness of this file transfer.

The advantage of using this project to perform the file transfer is that it can transfer any kind of file, which means that this project can be used to transfer files with different formats, since the file is transferred in the binary format.

We tested this project by transferring some popular formats, such as the .com file, .exe file, .dll file, .ocx file, .jpg file, .pdf file and .doc file, and all file transfers are successful.

This file transfer project can be used in the real file transfer applications. To transfer files between two computers, you need to install the master and the slave project on the different computers, and connect both computers with a null modem cable on the available ports on two computers.

The completed project files, including the master and the slave project, are located on the attached CD. The master project files are located in the folder

```
Chapter 4\VBCommFile_Master
```

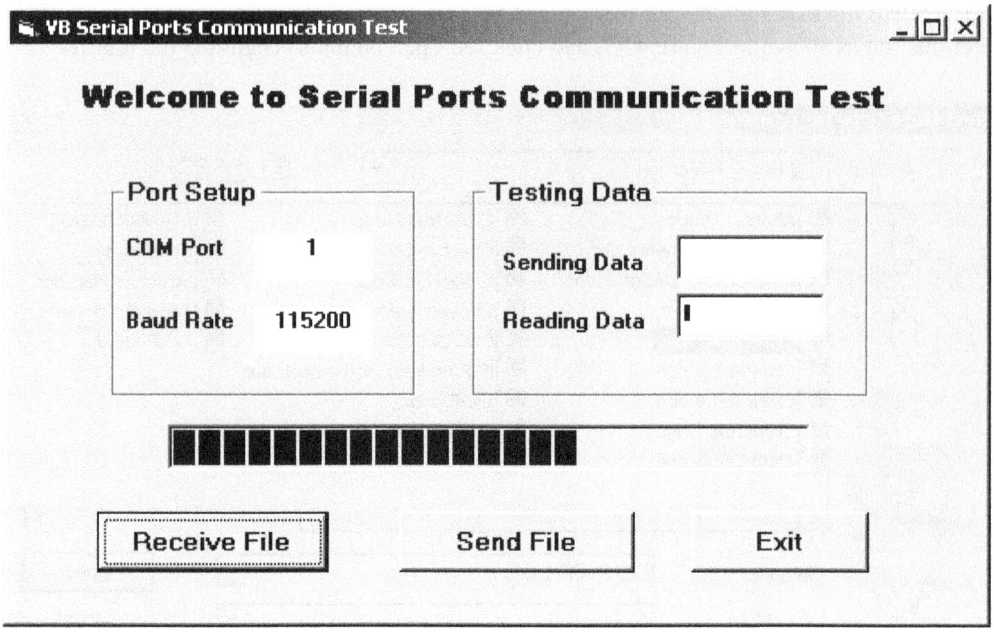

FIGURE 4.78 The progress bar for the slave computer.

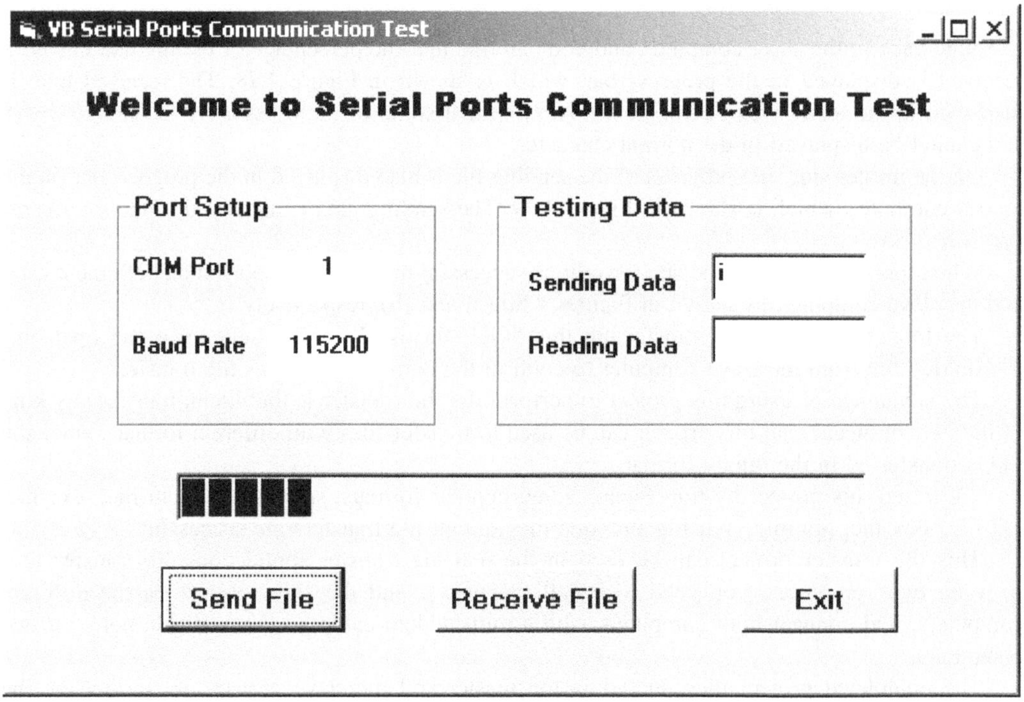

FIGURE 4.79 The progress bar for the master computer.

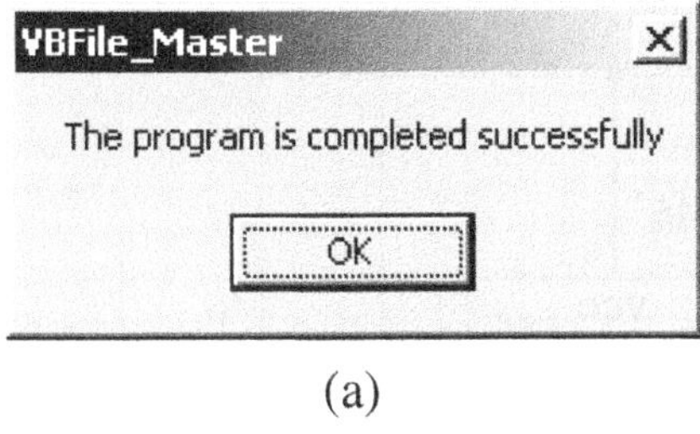

(a)

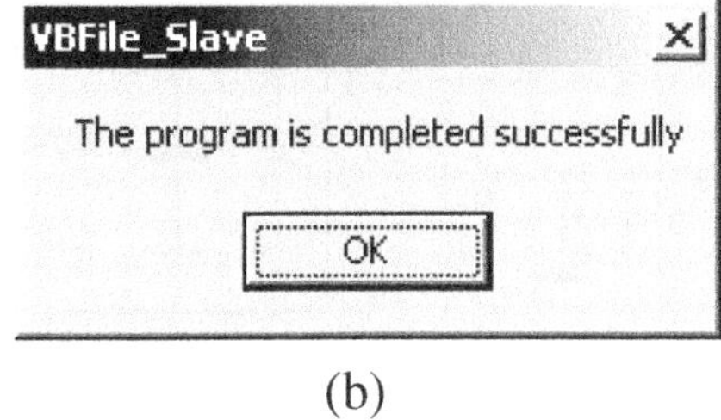

(b)

FIGURE 4.80 The successful message boxes.

The slave project files are located in the folder

```
Chapter 4\VBCommFile_Slave
```

You can load those projects and run them to perform the file transfers between two of your computers.

Our file transfer projects are very successful.

In the following two sections of this Chapter, we will discuss two interesting serial A/D converter interfaces using the MSComm control. One is for 8-bit A/D converter and the other is for the 12-bit serial A/D converter.

4.3.4 Developing a Serial Interface for the TLC548 8-Bit A/D Converter

Generally, you'll need to implement a special interface card to perform the A/D conversion. You'll also need to install the associated device drivers to coordinate the operation of the interface cards and complete the A/D conversions. This used to be a popular working mode for real-time data acquisition via parallel interfaces. Today, however, as the running speed of the CPU becomes faster and faster, the serial interface becomes more and more important in the connection between the computer and the peripheral equipment. One of the most important advantages of using the serial interface for A/D conversion is that you do not need to install any interface cards or associated device drivers on your computer. The serial ports on the computer work as the interface card, and the serial driver has been installed by the manufacturer before you buy your computer. Everything is on your computer and you do not need to install anything new. It is ready for the A/D conversion.

Our first example will be a serial interface for an 8-bit serial A/D converter, TLC548, which is an 8-pin DIP integrated circuit. (Refer to Section 2.7.1.1 and Figure 2-49 in Chapter 2 to get more detailed information about the TLC548 A/D converter.)

4.3.4.1 The Interface Circuit of the 8-Bit Serial A/D Converter

For your convenience, the interface circuit is redrawn here, as shown in Figure 4.81. Table 4.34 lists the component values used in the circuit.

One of advantages of this circuit is that this interface circuit does not need any additional power supply, and the circuit is driven by the DTR signal in the RS-232 port. This DTR line can work as an enable signal and the circuit can work properly as long as the DTR line outputs a signal of `HIGH`; we can use this line to activate or disable the circuit.

The RTS line works as the Chip Select (CS) signal to select and enable the TLC548 to begin to convert the analog input signal. As long as the power and the CS signal are activated, the TLC548 can immediately begin to convert the analog input automatically under the control of the internal control unit and the on-chip clock. To retrieve the converted result, an external I/O clock is needed. Here the TD line is used as the I/O clock to serially transfer the converted result to the DOUT of

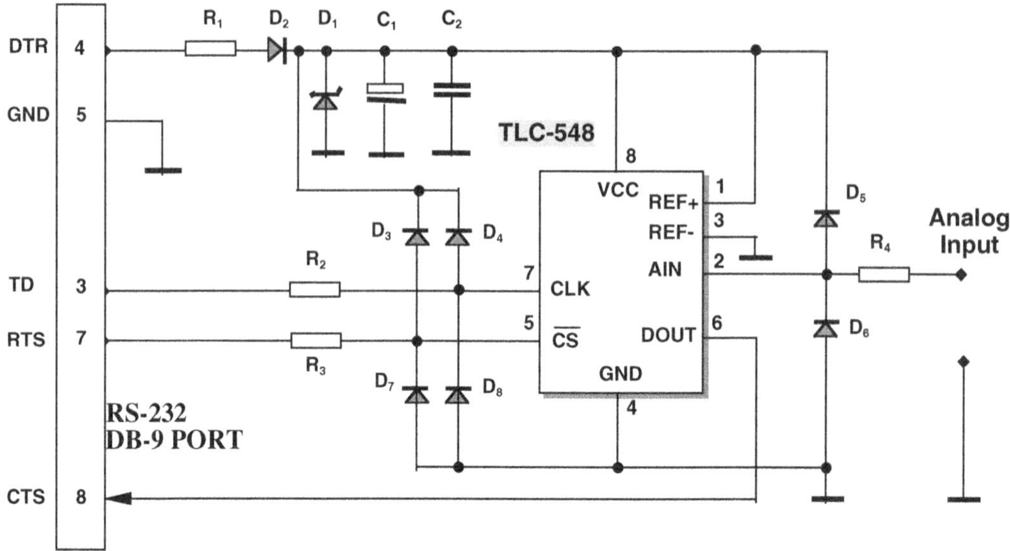

FIGURE 4.81 The TLC548 Interface Circuit.

TABLE 4.34
The Elements Parameters

Elements	Values	Comments
R_1	1 KΩ	Current-limited Resistor
R_2, R_3, R_4	30 KΩ	Current-limited Resistors
D_1	5.1 V	Zener Diode
D_2 – D_8	1N4148	Diodes
C_1	10 μF/15 V	Electrolytic Capacitor
C_2	100 nF	Capacitor

the TLC548, which is connected to the CTS line on the serial port. The output rate is controlled by the frequency of the TD signal.

Unlike the traditional serial data communications, in which either the hardware or the software flow control is used, this interface uses those signals as the control signals to drive the A/D converter and retrieve the converted result.

4.3.4.2 The Interface Program Design

This interface program sends control commands to the A/D converter and coordinates with it to perform the A/D conversion. The command sequence for converting and retrieving one byte of data is described here:

1. During the initialization, enable the DTR line to provide the power to the TLC548, and enable the RTS line to inactive the CS-bar signal on the TLC548 (the CS-bar active signal is `LOW`). Send a `0` to the TD line to inactive the CLK on the TLC548.
2. When the A/D conversion is ready to start, reset the RTS line to `LOW` to activate the CS-bar signal on the TLC548 to enable the A/D chip.

3. Then send a signal of HIGH to the TD line as a rising edge for the CLK on the TLC548 to begin to perform the first bit conversion.
4. By checking the status of the CTS line, we can determine whether the converted result of the first bit is a logical 1 (CTS = HIGH) or a logical 0 (CTS = LOW) because the DOUT on the TLC548 is connected to the CTS line.
5. A variable used to store the retrieved result is increased by 1 if a logical 1 is detected on the CTS line, otherwise a 0 is added into that variable. Then the variable is shifted left by one bit to make it ready for the next converted bit.
6. After the first bit is converted and stored, the TD line is reset to 0 to make the CLK on the TLC548 inactive.
7. Continue to go to steps 3, 4, 5 and 6 to retrieve the next converted bit, and in this way, we can convert and retrieve all 8-bit converted result and store it into the variable.
8. After one-byte data is converted, the RTS line is enabled to deselect the CS-bar on the TLC548 to disable the A/D chip.

You can develop the sequence above as a subroutine, and call it to perform multiple bytes data conversion and storage. Let us now begin developing our interface program. This program needs two forms as the graphical user interfaces and one code module to store the global variables and functions.

4.3.4.2.1 Designing Two Graphical User Interfaces

Launch Visual Basic 6.0 to open a new Standard.EXE project, name the project as VBSerial-ADTLC.vbp. Click Project|Add Form menu bar in the Visual Basic workspace to add two forms. Name them as Setup and VBComm, respectively. Click the Project|Add Module menu item to add a new code module. Name the module as VBSerialAD.bas. Open the new added form Setup, add the components that are listed in Table 4.35 into this form.

TABLE 4.35
Controls for the Setup Form

Control Type	Properties	Values	Control Type	Properties	Values
Label	Name	Label2	Text box	Name	txtBaudrate
	Caption	Port Number		Text	
Text box	Name	txtPort	CommandButton	Name	CmdOK
	Text			Caption	OK
Label	Name	Label3	Label	Name	Label1
	Caption	Baud Rate		Caption*	

*The Caption property for the control Label1 is: Enter Setup Parameters for Serial Port.

Your finished form Setup should match the one shown in Figure 4.82.

Add the controls listed in Table 4.36 into the second form, VBComm. Besides the normal controls, we need to add the following components into this project to help and improve the data transmission efficiency:

MSComm control (Name: MSComm1)

Click the Project|Components menu item from Visual Basic menu bar to open the Components dialog box and add Microsoft Comm Control 6.0 (MSComm control) into the toolbox window for this new project (refer to Figure 4.57 to complete this component addition). Then click that MSComm control from the toolbox window, drag it into the form VBComm and place it on

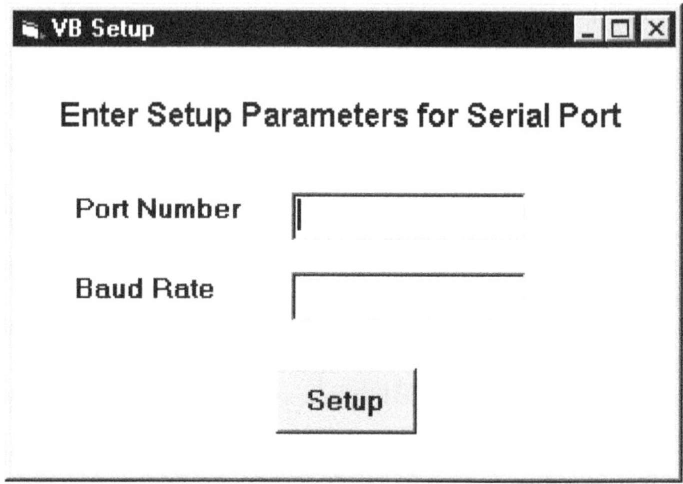

FIGURE 4.82 The `Setup` form window.

the lower-left corner. (Refer to Figure 4.83.) Your finished form `VBComm` should match the one shown in Figure 4.83.

4.3.4.2.2 The Coding of the Code Module

Open the code module `VBSerialAD.bas` and add the code that is shown in Figure 4.84 into this new module.

Two global variables are declared here, one is the `comPort`, which is used to store the port number entered at run time, and the other is the `baudRate`, which is used to store the baud rate selected at run time. The global function `timeGetTime()` is a Win32 API DLL function and it is used to retrieve the current system time. This function can be used in a time delay function to pick up the system time.

4.3.4.2.3 The Coding of the Setup Form

This form dynamically receives two serial communication parameters, `COM Port` and `Baud Rate`, from the user as the project runs. Two parameters are input from two text boxes, `txtPort` and `txtBaudRate`, respectively. The form needs to determine whether the input parameters are valid values.

Click the `Setup` form from the `Project Explorer` window to select it and click the `View Code` button to open its code window. Enter the code that is shown in Figure 4.85 into this code window.

Each section of this code is explained in the following list.

A: The default name of the form `Me` is used to locate the `Setup` form at the center of the screen as the project runs. Both the `Left` and the `Top` properties are assigned 2500 pixels to define the origin of the form.

B: When the `OK` command button is clicked, the form needs to check and confirm that the communication parameters entered at run time are valid values. First the form checks if both text boxes are filled with some values. If not, an error message will be displayed to warn the user to enter valid values.

C: Next the form needs to determine whether these two parameters are within the valid range. Currently we define the range of the serial ports used in this application are from COM1 to COM4. The built-in function `Val()` is used to convert two parameters from

TABLE 4.36
Controls for the `VBComm` Form

Control Type	Properties	Values
Label	Name	Label1
	Caption	Welcome to Serial Port ADC Testing
Frame	Name	Frame1
	Caption	Port Setup
Label	Name	Label2
	Caption	COM Port
Label	Name	lblComPort
	Caption	
	BackColor	Yellow
Label	Name	Label3
	Caption	Baud Rate
Label	Name	lblBaudRate
	Caption	
	BackColor	Yellow
Frame	Name	Frame2
	Caption	Testing Data
Label	Name	Label4
	Caption	Data Index
Text box	Name	txtIndex
	Text	
Label	Name	Label5
	Caption	Received Data
Text box	Name	txtRdata
	Text	
CommandButton	Name	cmdSetup
	Caption	Setup
CommandButton	Name	cmdReceive
	Caption	Receive
CommandButton	Name	cmdPlot
	Caption	Plot
		cmdExit
CommandButton	Name	cmdExit
	Caption	Exit

the text format to the numeric values. An error message will be displayed to ask the user to re-enter the valid parameters if any of parameters is beyond the range we defined above.

D: If both parameters are error-free, these two parameters are assigned to the global variable `comPort` and `baudRate` and they are used later by the next form.

E: Finally the `Setup` form finished its mission and it is removed by using the `Hide` method. The next form `VBComm` will be displayed by using the `Show` method. Note that although the `Setup` form is hidden from the screen, it is still available in this project.

The `Setup` form is the first form that should be called and run as the project is executed because two serial communication parameters, `comPort` and `baudRate`, are needed to perform the serial communication between the computer and the TLC548 serial A/D converter. These two parameters need to be entered first as the project runs.

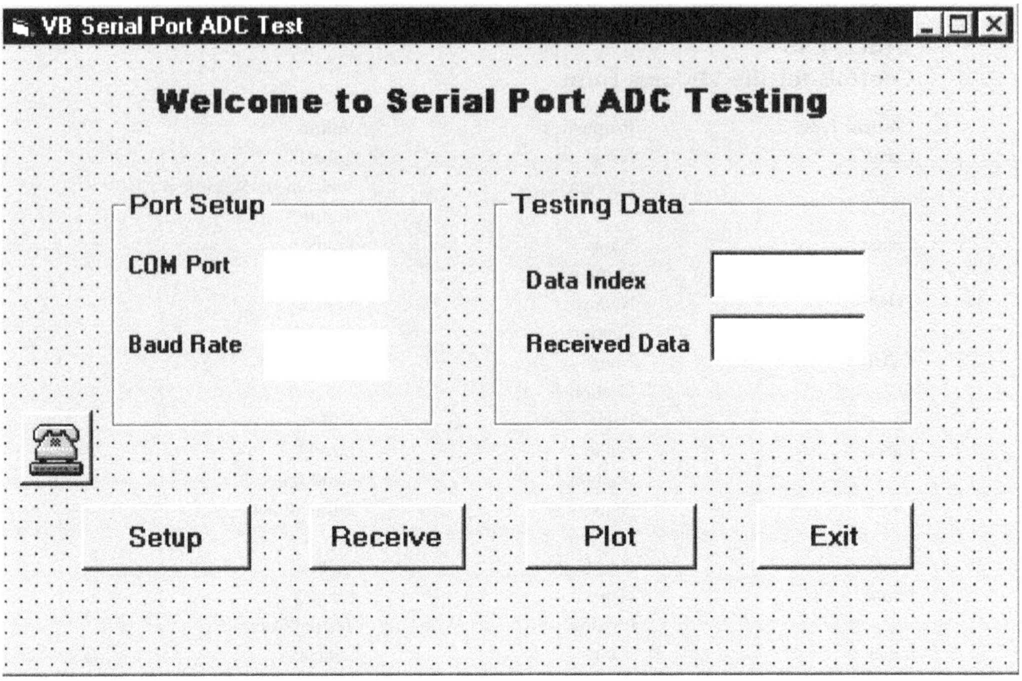

FIGURE 4.83 The `VBComm` form.

```
(General)                      (Declarations)

Option Explicit
Public comPort As Long, baudRate As Long
Public Declare Function timeGetTime Lib "winmm.dll" () As Long
```

FIGURE 4.84 The code module.

4.3.4.2.4 The Coding of the VBComm Form

There are four command buttons are located on this form, `Setup`, `Receive`, `Plot`, and `Exit`. The `Setup` button is used to set up the serial communication parameters on the specified serial port (in this application, we selected the COM1 as our serial port). The `Receive` button is used to begin to collect the data coming from the TLC548 A/D converter. The received data is stored in a data file that can be used later. The `Plot` button is used to plot the received data in the MATLAB domain by using the Active-X control. The `Exit` button is to terminate the project.

The operation of the coding in this form is described here:

- During the form loading period, the serial port is initialized and configured by using the properties of the MSComm control.
- The `Setup` command is used to set the initial conditions for the TLC548, and make it ready for the data conversion.
- The `Receive` command is used to continuously collect 100 converted data from the TLC548. The received data is also displayed in the text box `txtRdata` and stored into a data file that can be used later.
- The `Plot` command is used to plot the received data that is stored in a data file.

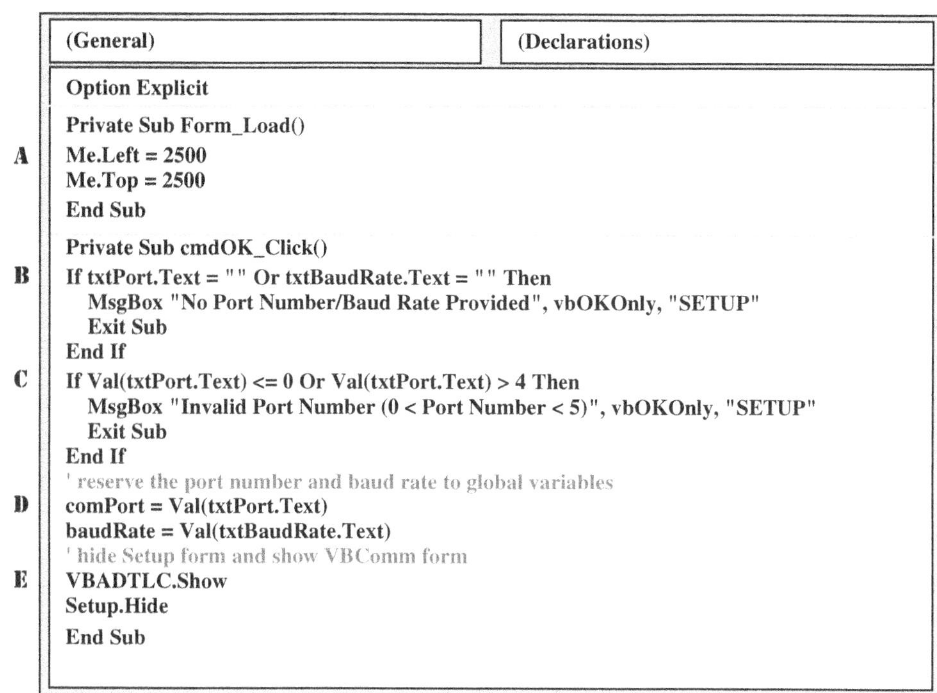

```
(General)                                   (Declarations)

  Option Explicit
  Private Sub Form_Load()
A Me.Left = 2500
  Me.Top = 2500
  End Sub
  Private Sub cmdOK_Click()
B If txtPort.Text = "" Or txtBaudRate.Text = "" Then
    MsgBox "No Port Number/Baud Rate Provided", vbOKOnly, "SETUP"
    Exit Sub
  End If
C If Val(txtPort.Text) <= 0 Or Val(txtPort.Text) > 4 Then
    MsgBox "Invalid Port Number (0 < Port Number < 5)", vbOKOnly, "SETUP"
    Exit Sub
  End If
  ' reserve the port number and baud rate to global variables
D comPort = Val(txtPort.Text)
  baudRate = Val(txtBaudRate.Text)
  ' hide Setup form and show VBComm form
E VBADTLC.Show
  Setup.Hide
  End Sub
```

FIGURE 4.85 Code for the `Setup` form.

Three functions are used in this project to support the performance of the A/D conversion.

- **GetAD_Data():** This function provides the detail operation steps to complete the control of the A/D converter and the collection of the converted data using the hardware handshaking signals.
- **SaveDataFile():** This function is used to store the received data into a data file, and that data file can be used later.
- **TimeDelay():** This function provides a certain period of time delay for the project. This time delay is very useful in some situation and it makes the A/D conversion more flexible and reliable.

Now open the code window of the form `VBComm`, declare a form-level variable and enter the code that is shown in Figure 4.86 into the `Form_Load` event procedure to initialize and configure the serial port.

Each section of this code is explained in the following list. First we need to enter the `Option Explicit` statement in the Form's General Declaration section to prevent the user from using some variables without declaring them or misspelling them.

F: A form-level variable `Matlab` is declared here and it is an Object type variable. This variable is used to access the MATLAB Active-X control from the Visual Basic domain to call a MATLAB M-File to perform the plotting in the MATLAB domain. By using MATLAB, we can display the received A/D converted data in a 2D format.

G: Still the default name of the form `Me` is used to define the initial position of the `VBComm` form window. Both horizontal and vertical coordinates of the origin are 2000 pixels, and this makes the form window on the center of the screen as the project runs.

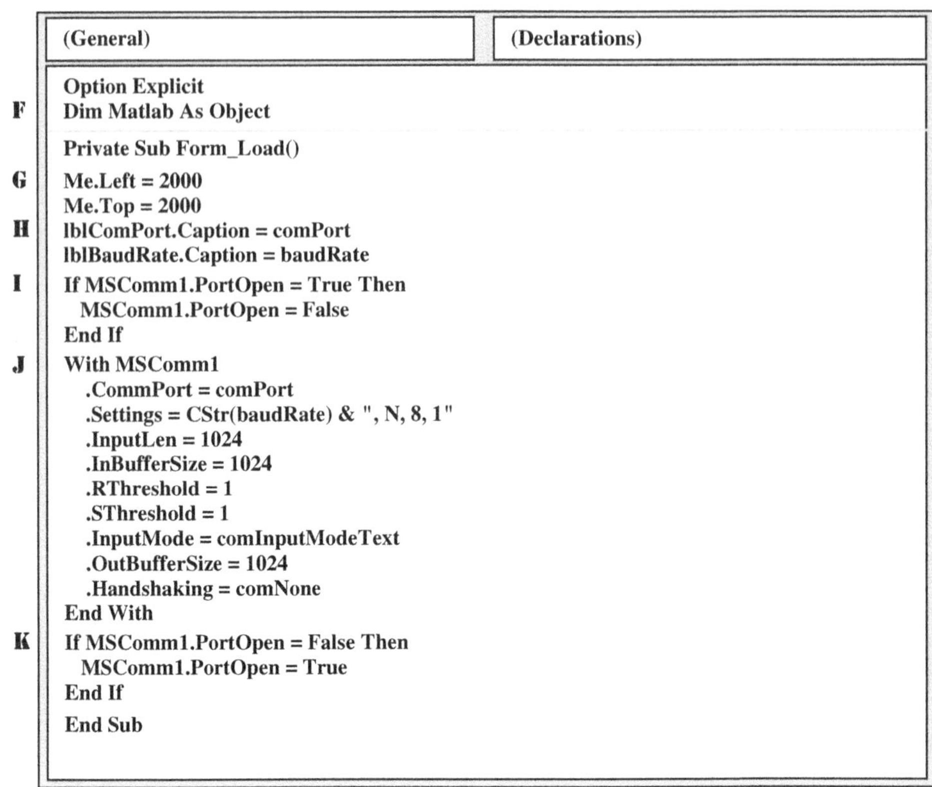

```
  (General)                          (Declarations)

  Option Explicit
F Dim Matlab As Object
  Private Sub Form_Load()
G Me.Left = 2000
  Me.Top = 2000
H lblComPort.Caption = comPort
  lblBaudRate.Caption = baudRate
I If MSComm1.PortOpen = True Then
    MSComm1.PortOpen = False
  End If
J With MSComm1
    .CommPort = comPort
    .Settings = CStr(baudRate) & ", N, 8, 1"
    .InputLen = 1024
    .InBufferSize = 1024
    .RThreshold = 1
    .SThreshold = 1
    .InputMode = comInputModeText
    .OutBufferSize = 1024
    .Handshaking = comNone
  End With
K If MSComm1.PortOpen = False Then
    MSComm1.PortOpen = True
  End If
  End Sub
```

FIGURE 4.86 Code for the `form_Load` event procedure on VBComm form.

H: Two global variables, `comPort` and `baudRate`, in which the port number and the baud rate are stored, are assigned to the two associated labels to be displayed in there.

I: Before we can use the properties of the MSComm control to configure the serial port, we must make sure that the port is not opened. By checking the `PortOpen` property, we can close the port if it is opened.

J: We use `With` statement to configure the port by assigning initialization values to the associated properties of the MSComm control. The global variable `comPort` is assigned to the `CommPort` property as the port number used in the serial data communications. The `Settings` property is a string variable, and therefore the `baudRate` needs to be converted to a string by using the built-in function `CStr()`. The converted baud rate is concatenated with other parameters by using the ampersand operator `&`. Both the `RThreshold` and the `SThreshold` are set to 1, which means that the `comEvReceive` and `comEvSend` events are triggered when one character has arrived in the input buffer or a character is sent to the transmit buffer. The data transmission mode is the text format by setting the `InputMode` property to `comInputModeText`. The `Handshaking` property is set to `comNone`, which means that we do not use any handshaking signal in this project. Recall that the TLC548 A/D converter is a serial A/D converter and all control terminals on the TLC548 are connected to the hardware handshaking lines in the serial port. Because the handshaking signals are used to control the operations of the TLC548, we cannot use any of them to perform serial data communications.

K: After the port is configured, we can open the serial port and make it ready for the data conversion.

In the following, we perform our coding based on each command button that is associated with each event procedure: `Setup`, `Receive`, `Plot`, and `Exit`. We'll discuss the coding of those three functions in the last step.

Click the `VBComm` form from the Project Explorer window and click the View Object button to open its form window, and then double-click the `Setup` button to open its event procedure. Enter the code that is shown in Figure 4.87 into this event procedure.

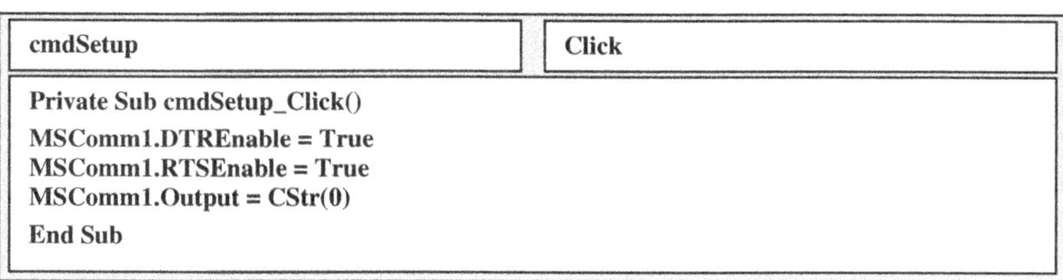

cmdSetup	Click

```
Private Sub cmdSetup_Click()
MSComm1.DTREnable = True
MSComm1.RTSEnable = True
MSComm1.Output = CStr(0)
End Sub
```

FIGURE 4.87 Code for the `Setup` event procedure.

The `Setup` event procedure activates the TLC548 A/D converter and ensures that it is ready for the data conversion. Both the DTR and the RTS lines are set to `True` to activate both signals. The DTR line is connected to the Vcc on the TLC548 (refer to Figure 4.81). When it is active, a signal of `HIGH` is applied on the Vcc to provide the power for the A/D converter. The RTS line is connected to the Chip Selected (CS-bar) on the TLC548. A signal of `HIGH` on this line disables the CS-bar because its active status is a `LOW` logic level. The TD line is connected to the CLK input of the ADC. To disable this CLK input, a `0` is sent to the TD line using the `Output` property of the MSComm control. Because the `Output` property can only access the text data, the built-in function `CStr()` is used to convert the numeric `0` to a text string `"0"`.

The next button is the `Receive` button. Double-click this button on the `VBComm` form window to open its event procedure. Enter the code that is shown in Figure 4.88 into this event procedure.

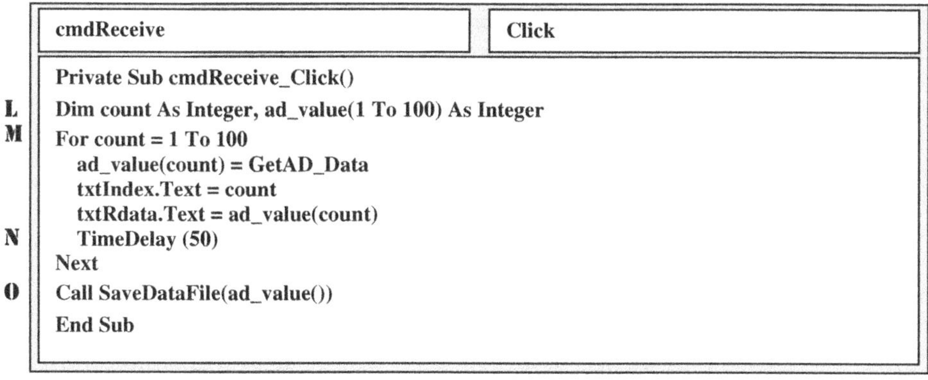

cmdReceive	Click

```
  Private Sub cmdReceive_Click()
L Dim count As Integer, ad_value(1 To 100) As Integer
M For count = 1 To 100
     ad_value(count) = GetAD_Data
     txtIndex.Text = count
     txtRdata.Text = ad_value(count)
N    TimeDelay (50)
  Next
O Call SaveDataFile(ad_value())
  End Sub
```

FIGURE 4.88 Code for the `Receive` event procedure.

Each section of this code is explained in the following list.

L: A local variable `count` is declared here, and this variable works as an loop counter in a `for` loop to continuously pick up the converted data by calling the function

`GetAD_Data()`. An integer array `ad_value()` is also declared here, and this array is used to store the received data from the TLC548 A/D converter.

M: A `for` loop is used to repeatedly retrieve 100 converted data from the A/D converter. Each time when the function `GetAD_Data()` is called, an byte of data (8-bit) is converted and received from the TLC548. The `count` will be displayed in the text box `txtIndex`, and the received data will be displayed in the text box `txtRdata`.

N: The `TimeDelay()` function is executed to wait for the TLC548 to complete its conversion and to make the data stable on the transmission line before the data can be retrieved. Currently a 50-millisecond delay is applied in this project.

O: Finally the subroutine `SaveDataFile()` is executed to save the received data into a data file.

The `Plot` button event procedure calls the MATLAB M-File to plot the received data in the MATLAB domain. The advantage of using this `Plot` button is that you do not need to switch to the MATLAB domain to perform this plot, and you can directly do that in Visual Basic domain. This is very convenient.

Open the `VBComm` form window and double-click the `Plot` button to open its event procedure. Enter the code that is shown Figure 4.89.

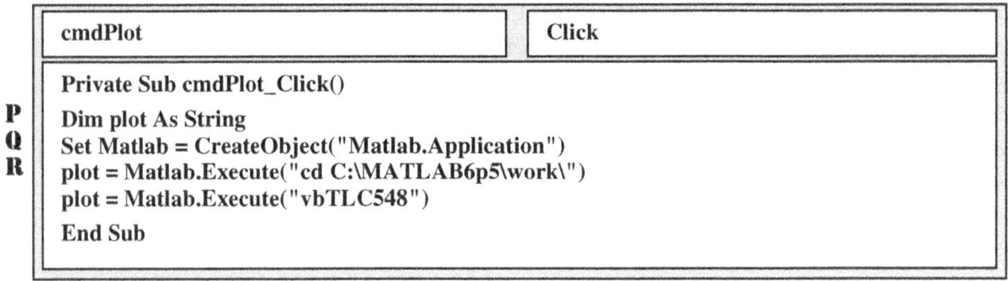

cmdPlot	Click

```
  Private Sub cmdPlot_Click()
P Dim plot As String
Q Set Matlab = CreateObject("Matlab.Application")
R plot = Matlab.Execute("cd C:\MATLAB6p5\work\")
  plot = Matlab.Execute("vbTLC548")
  End Sub
```

FIGURE 4.89 Code for the `Plot` event procedure.

This event procedure uses the MATLAB Active-X control to access the M-File developed in the MATLAB domain to plot the data that is stored in the data file. To use this Active-X control, the following requirements are needed.

1. You must have installed the MATLAB 6.0 or higher in your computer. In our case, we install and use MATLAB 6.5 Release 13.
2. A M-File that is used to plot a 2D graph based on the data file has been developed in the MATLAB domain.
3. The M-File is named vbTLC548.m and it is stored in the folder C:\MATLAB6p5\work.
4. The converted data has been stored in a data file named vbTLC548.dat and it is stored in the folder C:\data.

The step 2, 3 and 4 will be detailed in the following sections. Let's first finish our discussion of the `Plot` event procedure.

P: A local variable `plot` is declared here, which is used to store the returned value of the MATLAB method `Execute()`.

Q: An MATLAB object is created by calling the `CreateObject()` method. The argument is Matlab.Application, which indicates that the created object is an MATLAB Application. The created object is returned to the form-level variable `Matlab` we declared before.

R: First the `Execute()` method of the object `Matlab` is called to set up the work directory, which is the directory under which the M-File is stored. In this application, we store our M-File in the directory `C:\MATLAB6p5\work`. Then the `Execute()` method is called again to run our M-File to plot the 2D graph for the collected data stored in the data file. The M-File is named `vbTLC548.m` in this application.

TIP: When calling a MATLAB M-File by using the Active-X control from Visual Basic applications, you must perform the `Execute()` method two times. The first call is used to set the work directory or the path for the M-File, and the second call is to run the actual M-File.

Now let's take care of the step 2, 3, and 4. First we need to develop a M-File named `vbTLC548.m`. This file is used to plot a 2D graph of the received data stored in a data file named `vbTLC548.dat`. Launch MATLAB 6.5 and create a new M-File. Name the newly created M-File `vbTLC548.m`, and enter the code that is shown in Figure 4.90.

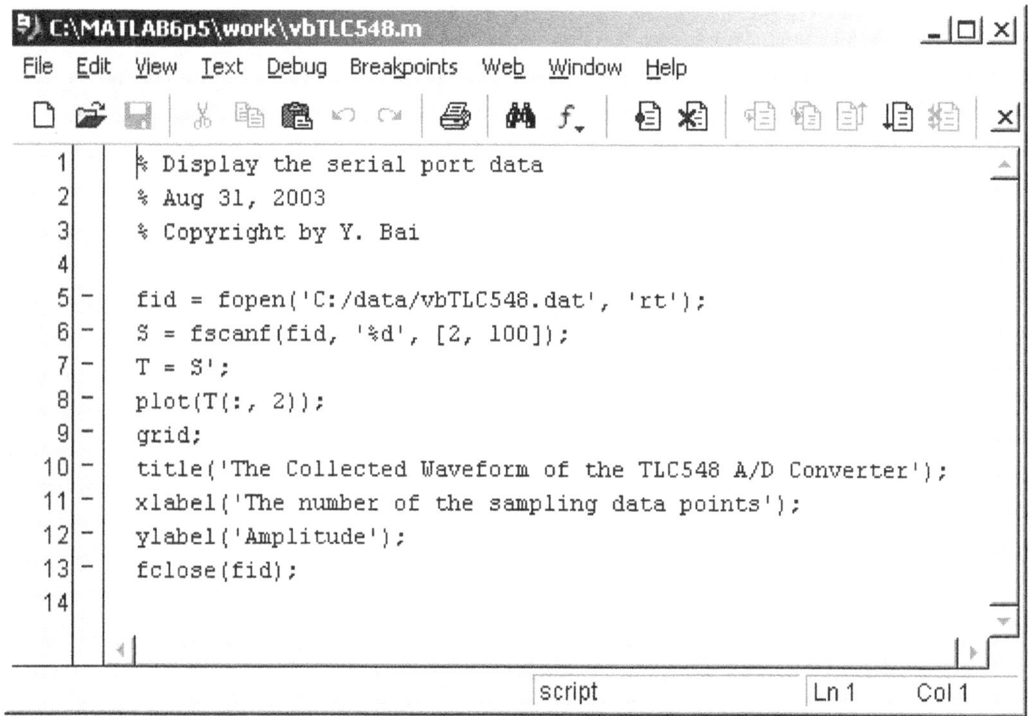
C:\MATLAB6p5\work\vbTLC548.m
File Edit View Text Debug Breakpoints Web Window Help
% Display the serial port data
% Aug 31, 2003
% Copyright by Y. Bai
fid = fopen('C:/data/vbTLC548.dat', 'rt');
S = fscanf(fid, '%d', [2, 100]);
T = S';
plot(T(:, 2));
grid;
title('The Collected Waveform of the TLC548 A/D Converter');
xlabel('The number of the sampling data points');
ylabel('Amplitude');
fclose(fid);
script
Ln 1
Col 1

FIGURE 4.90 The M-File `vbTLC548.m`.

The code in this M-File is straightforward. Before executing this M-File, the converted data has been stored in the data file (VbTLC548.dat) and that data file is stored in the directory `C:\data` (we will discuss this storage later).

First the `fopen()` function is executed to open that data file. The operation mode is `rt`, which means that the data is read out in the text format. The opened file returns a file handler and assigns it to the `fid`. Then the `fscanf()` is called to read out the data in a 2 by 100 array format. Note that the data stored into the data file is a 100 by 2 array when we save the collected data. You must transpose this array (to 2 by 100) when you read it out by using the `fscanf()` function. Otherwise you may encounter an operation error.

After the data is read out, you must transpose it again to recover the original dimension of the array. The `plot()` function is called to plot the second columns' elements in the array. Note that the first column of the array is the index and the second column is the data.

Finally, call the function `fclose()` to close the opened data file. Save this M-File to the folder `C:\MATLAB6p5\work`. The last event procedure is the `Exit`. Figure 4.91 shows the coding for this event procedure.

cmdExit	Click

```
Private Sub cmdExit_Click()
MSComm1.PortOpen = False
End
End Sub
```

FIGURE 4.91 Code for the `Exit` event procedure.

The meaning of each coding of this event procedure is easy to be understood. Now let's handle the three functions used in this project. The first one is the function `GetAD_Data()`. This is a very important function used in this project, and this function provides the real interface between the TLC548 A/D converter and the computer.

In the code window, click the `Tools|Add Procedure` menu item to open the `Add Procedure` dialog box. Add the parameters that are listed in Table 4.37 into this dialog box to add a new function.

TABLE 4.37
Properties of the `GetAD_Data()` Function

Property	Value
Name	GetAD_Data
Type	Function
Scope	Private

Type `As Integer` at the end of the newly added function `GetAD_Data()`, and enter the code that is shown in Figure 4.92. The finished function should match the one shown in Figure 4.92.

Each section of this code is explained in the following list.

S: Two integer local variables are declared here. The `index` works as a loop counter to repeatedly pick up 1 byte or all 8-bit data from the TLC548 A/D converter. The `value` works as a temporary buffer to reserve the received data. Initially the `value` is reset to `0`.

T: The RTS line is disabled to obtain a logical `0` to select the TLC548 chip because the RTS line is connected to the CS-bar on the A/D converter. The TLC548 is ready to convert the data when this CS-bar is activated. Notice that the CS-bar signal is activated when it receives a logical `0`.

U: A `for` loop is used to repeatedly retrieve 8-bit data from the CTS line. Refer to Figure 4.81, the DOUT on the TLC548, which is the output buffer of the A/D converter, is connected to the CTS line of the serial port. All converted data is transmitted to the port via this CTS line. First the temporary buffer `value` is multiplied by 2, which is equivalent to shifting the `value` left by one bit. Because the data is moved into the `value` buffer

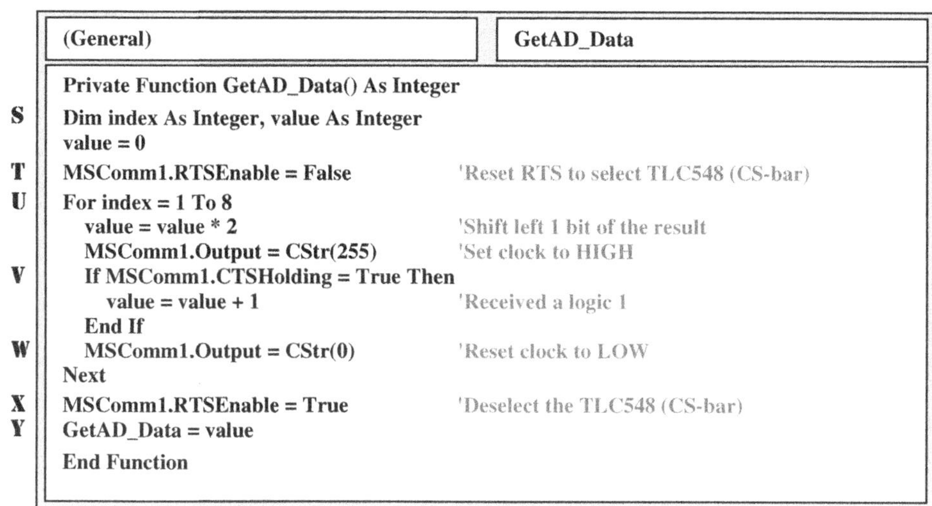

```
  (General)                              GetAD_Data

  Private Function GetAD_Data() As Integer
S Dim index As Integer, value As Integer
  value = 0
T MSComm1.RTSEnable = False              'Reset RTS to select TLC548 (CS-bar)
U For index = 1 To 8
     value = value * 2                   'Shift left 1 bit of the result
     MSComm1.Output = CStr(255)          'Set clock to HIGH
V    If MSComm1.CTSHolding = True Then
        value = value + 1                'Received a logic 1
     End If
W    MSComm1.Output = CStr(0)            'Reset clock to LOW
  Next
X MSComm1.RTSEnable = True               'Deselect the TLC548 (CS-bar)
Y GetAD_Data = value
  End Function
```

FIGURE 4.92 Code for the `GetAD_Data()` function.

bit-by-bit in the serial format, so this shift is necessary to reserve a space for each bit. Then the TD line is set to `HIGH` by output a 255 to the port to enable the CLK on the TLC548 to begin the data conversion.

V: After the data conversion is complete, we need to check the CTS line to determine the converted result for each bit because only one bit can be transmitted on the CTS line at a moment. If a signal of `TRUE` is detected, which means that a logical `1` is received, the buffer `value` is increased by 1. Otherwise no action is needed because the buffer `value` has nothing to do with a logical `0`. This addition is equivalent to set a value of `1` on the associated bit of the buffer `value` and this set up is dependent on the logic value on the CTS line.

W: The TD line is reset to `0`, and therefore the CLK on the TLC548 is reset to `0`, by sending a `CStr(0)` to the `Output` property of the MSComm control after one bit is converted and stored. This process is continued until all 8-bit data is converted.

X: After one byte data is converted, the RTS line is set to `HIGH` again to deselect the TLC548 chip and to stop its conversion.

Y: The converted one-byte data is returned to the calling event procedure by assigning the `value` buffer to the function `GetAD_Data`.

The next function is the `SaveDataFile()`. The purpose of this function is to save the received data into a data file that can be used later. In Visual Basic, a function is defined as a subroutine if that function has no returned value. The function `SaveDataFile()` does not need to return any value, so it is a subroutine here.

In the code window, click the `Tools|Add Procedure` menu item to open the `Add Procedure` dialog box. Enter the parameters that are listed in Table 4.38 into this dialog box to add a new subroutine.

Inside the parentheses of the new added subroutine `SaveDataFile()`, type `dArray() As Integer` because this subroutine has an array as the argument. Enter the code that is shown in Figure 4.93 into the subroutine. Your finished subroutine body should match the one shown in Figure 4.93.

Z: A local integer variable `index` is declared here, and it works as a loop counter to pick up all data stored in the data array and write it into the data file one by one.

TABLE 4.38
Properties of the `SaveDataFile` Subroutine

Property	Value
Name	SaveDataFile
Type	Sub
Scope	Private

```
(General)                    SaveDataFile

  Private Sub SaveDataFile(dArray() As Integer)
Z Dim index As Integer
1 Open "C:\data\vbTLC548.dat" For Output As #1
2 For index = 1 To UBound(dArray())
     Print #1, Str(index) & "    " & dArray(index)
  Next index
3 Close #1
  End Sub
```

FIGURE 4.93 Code for the `SaveDataFile()` subroutine.

1: The full name of the data file is `C:\data\vbTLC548.dat`. An `Open` instruction is used to open this file for the `Output` operation, which means the write mode. Because no any other file is opened in this project, this is the `#1` file.
2: A `for` loop is used to repeatedly write each byte of data into the file. The built-in function `UBound()` is used to determine the upper boundary of the data array. Two elements are written into the file for each data: the data index and the data value. The ampersand operator '&' is used to concatenate these two elements together. You do not have to convert the `index` to the string when writing the elements into the data file and the `Print` can do that automatically.
3: Finally, close the data file by using the `Close` command after the data is stored to the file.

The last function is the `TimeDelay()`. Similar to the subroutine `SaveDataFile()`, this function also belongs to the subroutine because it has no returned value.

In the code window, click the `Tools|Add Procedure` menu item to open the `Add Procedure` dialog box. Enter the parameters that are listed in Table 4.39 into this dialog box to add a new subroutine.

TABLE 4.39
Properties of the `TimeDelay()` Subroutine

Property	Value
Name	TimeDelay
Type	Sub
Scope	Private

Inside the parentheses of the new added subroutine `TimeDelay()`, type `dMS As Single` because this subroutine has a single data as the argument. Enter the code that is shown in Figure 4.94 into this subroutine. Your finished subroutine body should match the one shown in Figure 4.94.

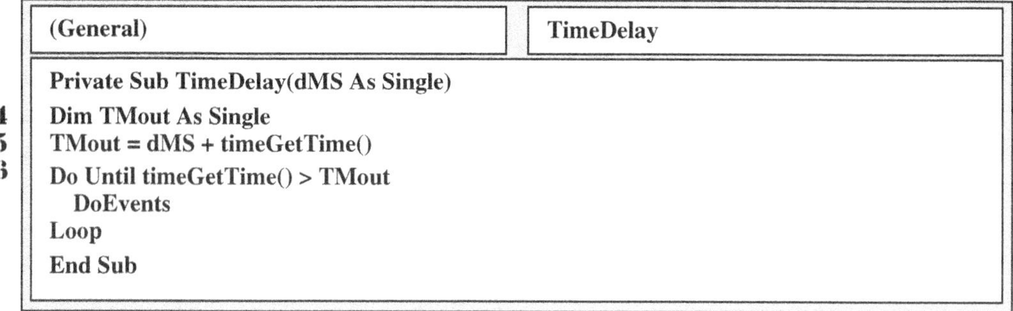

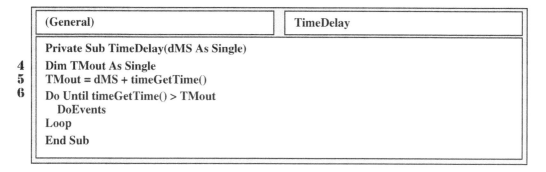

```
(General)                          TimeDelay

  Private Sub TimeDelay(dMS As Single)
4 Dim TMout As Single
5 TMout = dMS + timeGetTime()
6 Do Until timeGetTime() > TMout
    DoEvents
  Loop
  End Sub
```

FIGURE 4.94 Code for the `TimeDelay()` subroutine.

This subroutine pauses processing for a period of time based on the input argument. The delay time is measured in milliseconds.

4: A local variable `TMout` is declared here and it works as an accumulator to summarize the argument and the current system time.
5: The input argument `dMS` can be considered as an offset, and this offset is added with the current time obtained using the Win32 API function `timeGetTime()` together as a time block. This time block is equivalent to a time-leading moment that will occur in the future.
6: A `Do-Until` loop is used to pause processing until the current time is greater than the time block we obtained earlier. This means that the desired time period is elapsed and the time is up. Do not forget to insert the `DoEvents` inside the `Do-Until` loop to allow the CPU to handle some other more important jobs in your computer if the elapsed time period is not complete.

Now we have finished all coding for this project. Because we have two forms developed in this project, we need to indicate to Visual Basic which form should be executed first as the project runs. In this application, we want the `Setup` form to be executed first because two serial communication parameters, `comPort` and `baudRate`, are obtained from this form. These two parameters are entered as the project runs.

To make this happen, click the `Project|VBSerialADTLC Properties` menu item from the Visual Basic menu bar to open the `Project Property` dialog box. Keep the default tab `General` selected, and select the `Setup` from the `Startup Object:` box. Click OK to save this setup. Now we are ready to test and run our project.

4.3.4.3 Implementation of the Serial Interface for the 8-Bit Serial A/D Converter

Make the circuit connection as shown in Figure 4.81. Currently we use a DB-9 RS-232 serial port. The analog input signal is coming from a function generator. Three waveforms can be selected for that function generator, sinusoidal, square and triangle. Remember to turn off your computer before you connect this circuit to the serial port on your computer; otherwise you may encounter hardware problems as you run this project.

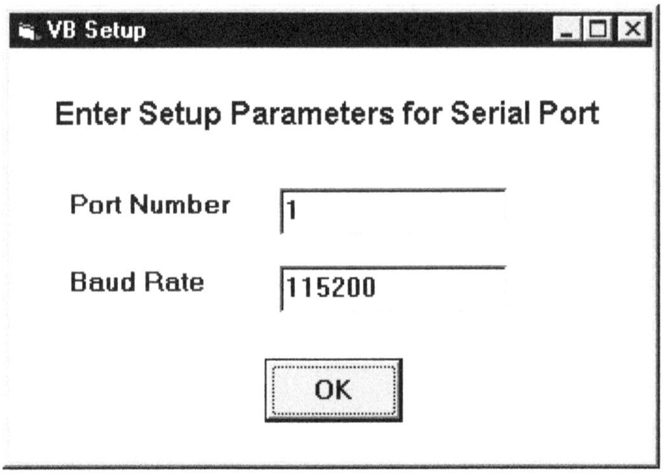

FIGURE 4.95 Running status of the `Setup` form.

Run the project after you finish connecting the interface circuit to the computer via the serial port. The `Setup` form appears, as shown in Figure 4.95. Enter the port number and baud rate to the associated text boxes. In our case, we use the COM1 and 115200 baud rate. Enter 1 to the port number text box and 115200 to the baud rate text box, and then click `OK` to finish this setup.

Immediately, the second form `VBComm` appears with the port number and baud rate displayed on the `COM Port` and the `Baud Rate` labels, as shown in Figure 4.96.

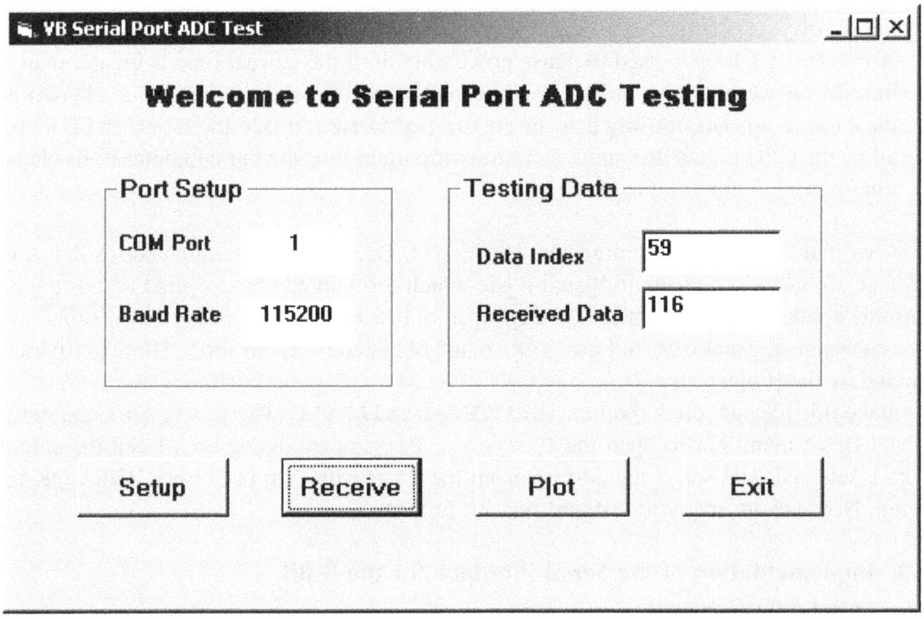

FIGURE 4.96 Running status of the `VBComm` form.

Click the `Setup` button to finish the configuration of the serial port, and then click the `Receive` button to start the TLC548 A/D conversion and collect the converted data. The data index and the converted data are displayed in the `Data Index` and the `Received Data` text boxes in real time, as shown in Figure 4.96. The collected data is also stored into a data file.

When the data conversion is complete, click the `Plot` button to plot the received data. The MATLAB Figure workspace is opened and the converted data is plotted in the MATLAB domain. The waveform we used is square waveform. Figure 4.97 shows the plotting result for this square input.

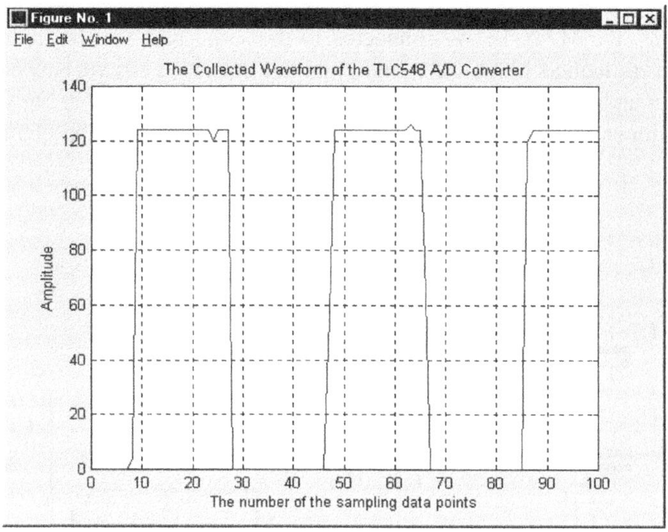

FIGURE 4.97 The square waveform @20 Hz (TLC548).

The amplitude of the waveform is the raw data and the range of the amplitude is 0 ~ 255. You can obtain the real amplitude by multiplying the raw data with a scalar factor. The formula for calculating the value of the scalar factor is shown here:

$$Scalar\ \ Factor = \frac{Raw\ \ data\ \ value}{255} \times Max\ \ output\ \ amplitude\ \ of\ \ the\ \ Function\ \ Generator$$

Click the `Exit` button to end the project. Our project is very successful!

The complete project files, including the form files, executable file and MATLAB M-File, are included in the folder `Chapter 4\VBSerialAD` on the attached CD.

By using this serial A/D converter interface, we can easily to measure and acquire analog signals in real time via the serial port without installing additional interface cards and device drivers on the computer. It is both economical and convenient to perform the data collection and analysis in real time with real data.

One potential problem existed in this interface is the low accuracy. For an 8-bit A/D converter with a 5.0 V full measuring scale, the accuracy is about (1/255)*5.0 = 20 mV. For a two-polarity input, such as –5.0 ~ 5.0 V, the accuracy is about 40 mV. To improve this resolution and the accuracy, a 12-bit A/D converter is a solution. In the next section, a 12-bit A/D converter MAX187 is discussed.

4.3.5 Developing a Serial Interface for the MAX187 12-Bit A/D Converter

The MAX-187 is a low power 12-bit serial A/D converter produced by Maxim Integrated Products, Inc. This A/D converter operates under a single +5V supply and accepts a 0V to 5V analog input. It features an 8.5μs successive-approximation ADC, a fast track/hold (1.5μs), an on-chip clock, and a high-speed 3-wire serial interface. (Refer to Section 2.7.3 and Figure 2-65 in Chapter 2 to get more detailed information about the MAX-187).

4.3.5.1 The Interface Circuit of the MAX-187 A/D Converter

In most applications, the MAX-187 is connected to the serial port via the multiple-channel RS-232 Drivers/Receivers named MAX-220. The complete interface circuit between the MAX-187 serial A/D converter and the serial port is shown in Figure 2-67 in Chapter 2. For your convenience, this diagram is redrawn in Figure 4.98. Table 4.40 lists the values of the elements used in this interface circuit.

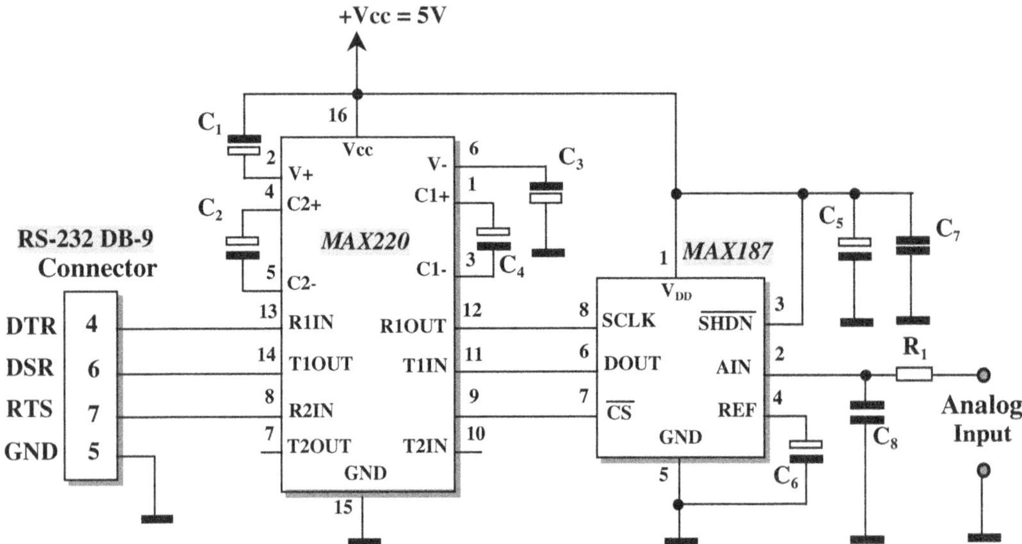

FIGURE 4.98 The interface circuit of the MAX187.

TABLE 4.40
The Elements Parameters

Elements	Values	Comments
R_1	10 KΩ	Current-limited Resistor
$C_1 \sim C_4$	10 µF/25V	Electrolytic Capacitors
$C_5 \sim C_6$	4.7 µF/10V	Electrolytic Capacitors
$C_7 \sim C_8$	0.1 µF	Capacitors

The MAX-187 has its own internal clock, internal buffer reference and the output buffer. The conversion is triggered by the CS-bar signal, which means that as long as the CS-bar receives a signal of `LOW`, the conversion is started with the help of the internal clock without the external assistance. After the conversion is complete, the converted data stored in the output buffer can be shifted out by the external clock signal SCLK. So relatively speaking, the MAX-187 is more suitable for the high-speed A/D conversion because the data conversion is controlled by the internal clock, not the external clock control signal.

Three transmission lines, DTR, DSR and RTS, are used as the control and data signals between the MAX-187 and the serial port. The DTR works as an external clock to shift the converted data out from the output buffer on the MAX-187 when the conversion is complete. The DSR line works as a data line to serially receive the converted data driven by the SCLK signal. The RTS line works as the Chip Selected (CS) signal to enable/disable the MAX-187 to perform the data conversion.

The MAX-220 provides level translating between the TTL/CMOS signal and the formal transmission signals applied on the RS-232 serial convention. Refer to Figure 1-6 in Chapter 1 to get a clear picture for the transmission signal levels.

The serial port we used for this application is a DB-9 RS-232 port. Make the circuit connection as shown in Figure 4.98 and connect this interface to the serial port on the computer. In our case, we still use the COM1 as the serial port.

4.3.5.2 Designing the Graphical User Interfaces

Two forms are designed in this project: `Setup` and `VBCommMAX` forms. Similar to the last project, the `Setup` form is used to collect the serial port communication parameters, such as the port number and the baud rate, and the `VBCommMAX` form is used to perform the data conversion, data storage and data plotting. The plotting application used in this project is Microsoft Chart Control 6.0.

Microsoft Chart Control 6.0 is an Active-X control that helps the user to perform some 2D or 3D graphics plotting in the Visual Basic domain. You can plot different kinds of graphics by using this control. It is a convenient tool to help the user to represent the collecting data or running results on 2D graph in Visual Basic domain.

Launch Visual Basic 6.0 and open a new `Standard.EXE` project. Name the project as `VBMAX.vbp`.

Click the `Project|Components` menu item to add the following components and Active-X controls into this new project:

- Microsoft Comm Control 6.0 (Name: MSComm1)
- Microsoft Chart Control 6.0 (SP4) (OLEDB) (Name: MSChart1)

4.3.5.2.1 The Setup Form Design

The `Setup` form collects the serial port parameters. Two text boxes and one command button are designed for this purpose. On the new opened project, click the `Project|Add Form` menu item from the Visual Basic menu bar to add a new form named `Setup`. Enter the controls and parameters listed in Table 4.41 into this form.

TABLE 4.41
Controls for the `Setup` Form

Control Type	Properties	Values	Control Type	Properties	Values
Label	Name	Label2	Text box	Name	txtBaudRate
	Caption	Port Number		Text	
Text box	Name	txtPort	CommandButton	Name	CmdOK
	Text			Caption	OK
Label	Name	Label3	Label	Name	Label1
	Caption	Baud Rate		Caption*	

*The Caption property for the control `Label1` is: Enter Setup Parameters for Serial Port.

Your finished form `Setup` should match the one shown in Figure 4.99.

4.3.5.2.2 The VBCommMAX Form Design

Click the `Project|Add Form` menu item to add the second form `VBCommMAX`. Add components and controls listed in Table 4.42 into this form.

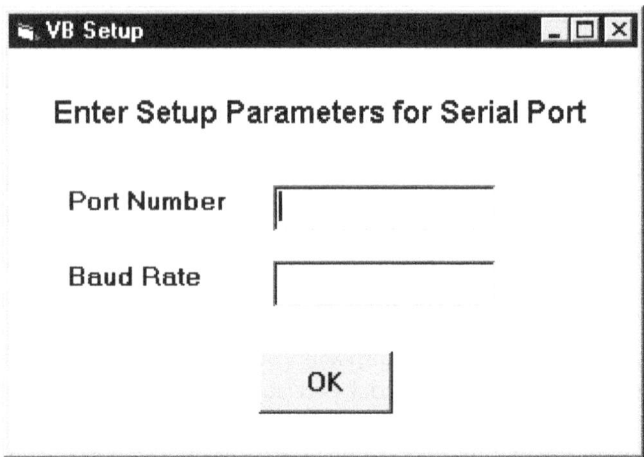

FIGURE 4.99 Design of the setup form.

Besides the normal controls and components listed in Table 4.42, we also need to add the following controls into this form.

- Microsoft Comm Control 6.0 (Name: MSComm1)
- Microsoft Chart Control 6.0 (SP4) (OLEDB) (Name: MSChart1)
- Timer control (Name: VBMAXTimer)

Go to the tools window and click these three controls one by one, and drag them into the form. (Refer to Figure 4.100.) The finished `VBCommMax` form should match the one shown in Figure 4.100.

4.3.5.3 Coding the Project

We divide the coding process into three sections: Coding for the code module, coding for the `Setup` form and coding for the `VBCommMAX` form.

4.3.5.3.1 The Coding of the Code Module

The code module is used to store some global variables and functions used in this project. Click the `Project|Add Module` menu item to add a new module named `VBSerialMAX.bas` into this project. Your finished code module `VBSerialMAX` should match the one shown in Figure 4.101.

A: A global constant GETAD_TIMEOUT is declared here. This constant is used to indicate that a timeout error occurs during the retrieving the converted data.

B: Two global variables are declared, `comPort` and `baudRate`. Both variables are used to store the serial communication parameters, such as the port number and baud rate, entered by the user as the project runs.

C: A Win32 API function `timeGetTime()` is declared here, and this function is used to get the current system time that can be used in the time delay function in the project.

4.3.5.3.2 The Coding of the Setup Form

The purpose of the `Setup` form is to collect the serial parameters entered by the user, and check the correctness of those parameters. Click the `Setup` form to select it from the Project Explorer window, and click the `View Code` button to open its code window. In this window, enter the code that is shown in Figure 4.102.

On the top line (Form's General Declaration section), type `Option Explicit`. This statement will prevent the user from using variables or controls without declaring them first.

TABLE 4.42
Controls for the `VBCommMAX` Form

Control Type	Properties	Values
Label	Name	Label1
	Caption	Welcome to Serial Port ADC Testing
Frame	Name	Frame1
	Caption	Port Setup
Label	Name	Label2
	Caption	COM Port
Label	Name	lblComPort
	Caption	
	BackColor	Yellow
Label	Name	Label3
	Caption	Baud Rate
Label	Name	lblBaudRate
	Caption	
	BackColor	Yellow
Frame	Name	Frame2
	Caption	Testing Data
Label	Name	Label4
	Caption	Data Indesx
Text box	Name	txtIndex
	Text	
Label	Name	Label5
	Caption	Received Data
Text box	Name	txtRdata
	Text	
CommandButton	Name	cmdSetup
	Caption	Setup
CommandButton	Name	cmdReceive
	Caption	Receive
CommandButton	Name	cmdPlot
	Caption	Plot
CommandButton	Name	cmdExit
	Caption	Exit

D: The default name of the form `Me` is used to locate the `Setup` form around the center of the screen by setting its origin at 2500 pixels in both horizontal and vertical coordinates.

E: Next the form needs to determine whether the user enters two valid parameters on two text boxes, `txtPort` and `txtBaudRate`. A warning message will be displayed to reminder the user to enter those parameters if an empty result is detected for any of text boxes.

F: In this application, we defined that a valid port number should be between 1 and 4. By checking the `Text` property of both text boxes, we can identify whether the port number entered at run time is a valid value (within the range of 1 and 4). An error message will be displayed to ask the user to re-enter that value if an invalid value is encountered.

G: The valid port number and baud rate are assigned to the associated global variables `comPort` and `baudRate`. Those values will be used later in the second form.

H: The mission of the `Setup` form is complete, so the `Hide` method is called to remove that form from the screen, and the `Show` method is executed to display the second form `VBCommMAX`.

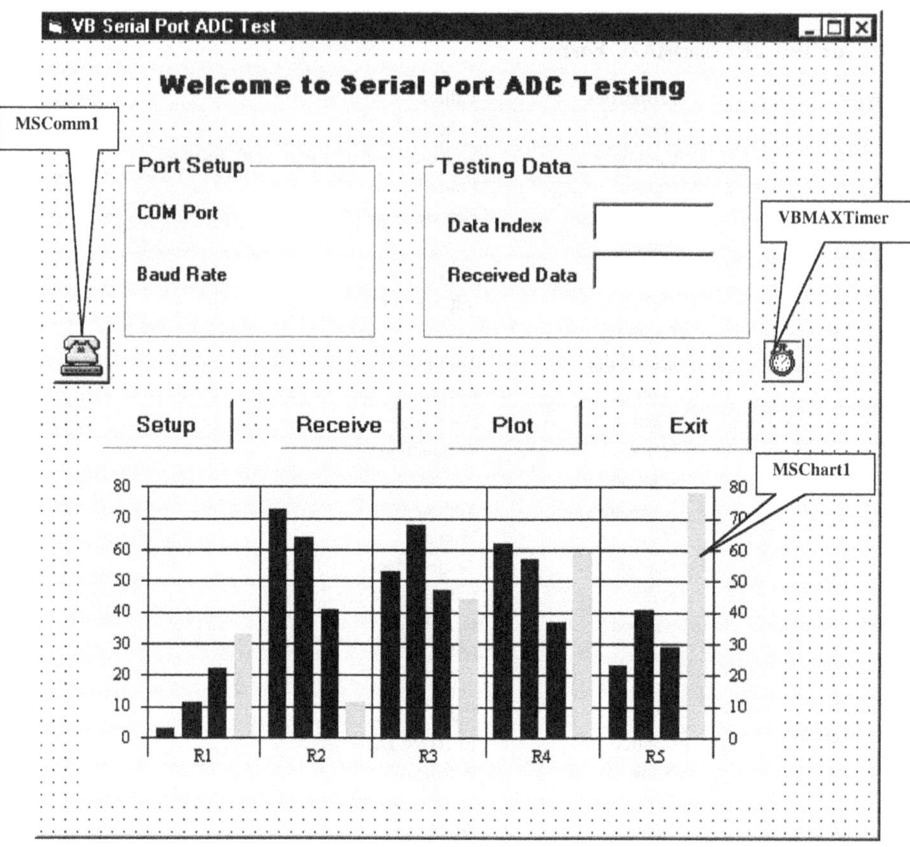

FIGURE 4.100 Design of the `VBCommMAX` form.

(General)	(Declarations)

```
  Option Explicit
A Public Const GETAD_TIMEOUT = -1
B Public comPort As Long, baudRate As Long
C Public Declare Function timeGetTime Lib "winmm.dll" () As Long
```

FIGURE 4.101 The Coding of the `Code` module.

4.3.5.3.3 The Coding of the VBCommMAX Form

This form starts the MAX-187 A/D converter, collects the converted data, stores the data into a data file, and plots the received data in a Microsoft Chart graph. Five event procedures, `Setup`, `Receive`, `Plot`, `Exit`, and `VBMAXTimer`, are used to coordinate with the form to complete these tasks. Three functions, `GetAD_Data()`, `SaveDataFile()`, and `TimeDelay()`, are also used by the event procedures to perform some special tasks.

We'll first concentrate on these five event procedures, and then give a detailed discussion of those three functions. First we need to create a form-level variable, `TimeOut`, which is a Boolean variable. This variable works as a flag to monitor the timeout error. Type the `Option Explicit`

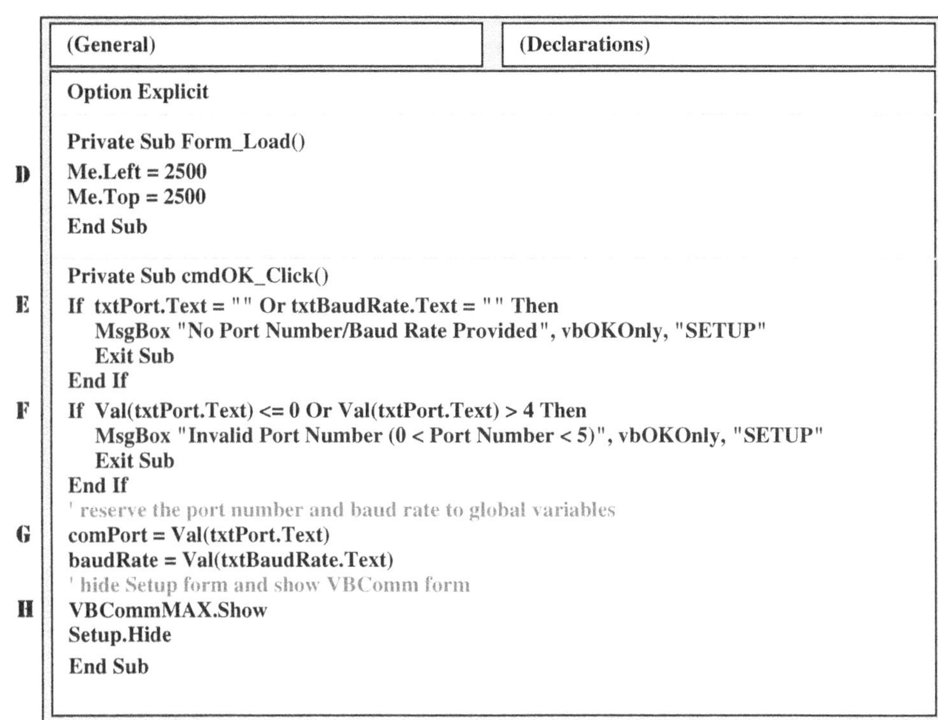

```
  (General)                          (Declarations)

  Option Explicit

  Private Sub Form_Load()
D Me.Left = 2500
  Me.Top = 2500
  End Sub

  Private Sub cmdOK_Click()
E If txtPort.Text = "" Or txtBaudRate.Text = "" Then
     MsgBox "No Port Number/Baud Rate Provided", vbOKOnly, "SETUP"
     Exit Sub
  End If
F If Val(txtPort.Text) <= 0 Or Val(txtPort.Text) > 4 Then
     MsgBox "Invalid Port Number (0 < Port Number < 5)", vbOKOnly, "SETUP"
     Exit Sub
  End If
  ' reserve the port number and baud rate to global variables
G comPort = Val(txtPort.Text)
  baudRate = Val(txtBaudRate.Text)
  ' hide Setup form and show VBComm form
H VBCommMAX.Show
  Setup.Hide
  End Sub
```

FIGURE 4.102 Code for the `Setup` form.

statement in the Form's General Declaration section, and then declare that Boolean `TimeOut` variable. Refer to Figure 4.103 to finish this declaration.

The `Form_Load` event procedure is the first procedure to be executed when this form is loaded. The purpose of this event procedure is to initialize and configure the serial port using the parameters entered by the user and the properties of the MSComm control. Select the `VBCommMAX` form and click the `View Code` button from the `Project Explorer` window in Visual Basic workspace to open its code window. Select the `Form` from the object list to open the `Form_Load` event procedure. Enter the code that is shown in Figure 4.103. Your finished event procedure body should match the one shown in Figure 4.103.

Each section of this code is explained in the following list.

- I: The default name of the form `Me` is used to locate the position of the form `VBCommMAX`. By assigning the `Left` and the `Top` property with 2000 pixels, the form is supposed to be positioned at the center of the screen as the form is loaded and displayed.
- J: Some initializations are performed at the beginning of this event procedure. The form-level `TimeOut` variable is reset to `False`, and the `VBMAXTimer` is disabled. Two global variables, `comPort` and `baudRate`, are assigned to the associated labels to be displayed in there.
- K: Before we can use the properties of the MSComm control to configure the serial port, we must make sure that the port is not opened. By checking the `PortOpen` property, we can detect and close the port if it is opened.
- L: We use the `With` statement to configure the port by assigning initialization values to the associated properties of the MSComm control. The global variable `comPort` is assigned to the `CommPort` property as the port number used in the serial data communications. The `Settings` property is a string variable, and therefore the `baudRate`

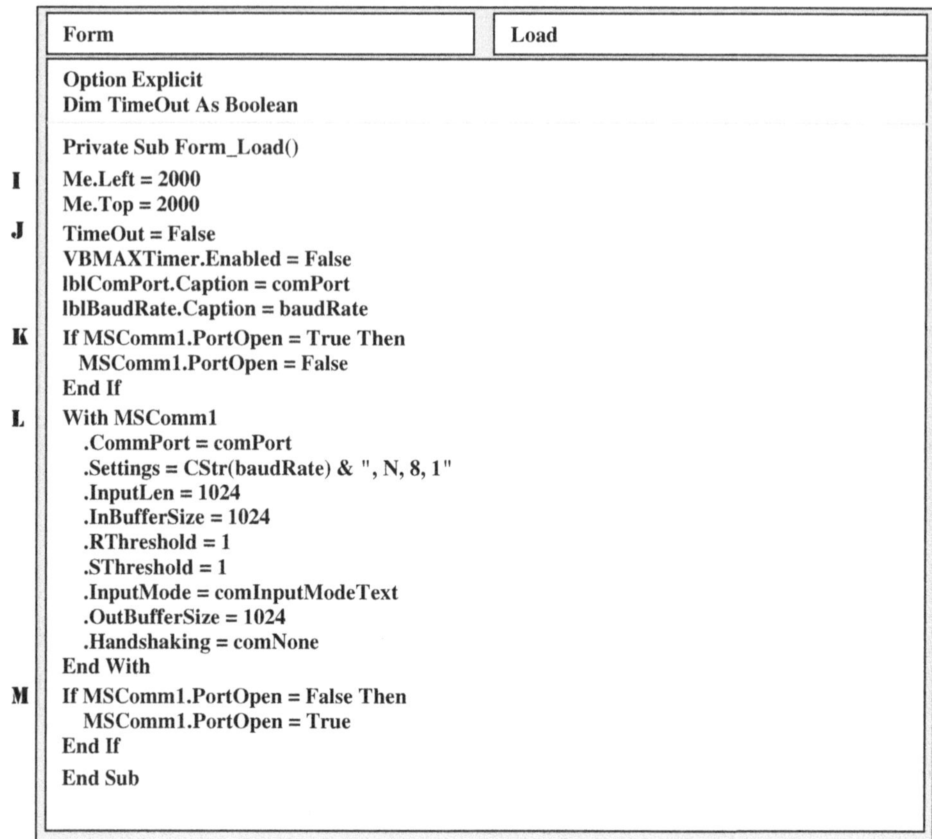

```
Form                                    Load

   Option Explicit
   Dim TimeOut As Boolean

   Private Sub Form_Load()
I  Me.Left = 2000
   Me.Top = 2000
J  TimeOut = False
   VBMAXTimer.Enabled = False
   lblComPort.Caption = comPort
   lblBaudRate.Caption = baudRate
K  If MSComm1.PortOpen = True Then
     MSComm1.PortOpen = False
   End If
L  With MSComm1
     .CommPort = comPort
     .Settings = CStr(baudRate) & ", N, 8, 1"
     .InputLen = 1024
     .InBufferSize = 1024
     .RThreshold = 1
     .SThreshold = 1
     .InputMode = comInputModeText
     .OutBufferSize = 1024
     .Handshaking = comNone
   End With
M  If MSComm1.PortOpen = False Then
     MSComm1.PortOpen = True
   End If
   End Sub
```

FIGURE 4.103 Code for the `Form_Load` event procedure.

needs to be converted to a string by using the built-in function `CStr()`. The converted baud rate is concatenated with other parameters by using the ampersand operator '&'. Both the `RThreshold` and the `SThreshold` are set to 1, which means that the `comEvReceive` and `comEvSend` events are triggered when one character has arrived in the input buffer or a character is sent to the transmit buffer. The data transmission mode is the text format by setting the `InputMode` property to `comInputModeText`. The `Handshaking` property is set to `comNone`, which means that we do not use any handshaking signal in this project. Recall that the MAX-187 A/D converter is a serial A/D converter and all control terminals on the MAX-187 are connected to the hardware handshaking lines in the serial port. Because the handshaking signals are used to control the operations of the MAX-187, we cannot use any of them to perform serial data handshaking operations.

M: After the port is configured, we can open the serial port and make it ready for the data conversion.

In the following, we perform our coding based on five event procedures, `Setup`, `Receive`, `Plot`, `Exit`, and `VBMAXTimer`. We'll discuss the coding of the three functions `GetAD_Data()`, `SaveDataFile()`, and `TimeDelay()` in the last step.

Click the `VBCommMAX` form from the `Project Explorer` window and click the `View Object` button to open its form window, and then double-click the `Setup` button to open its event procedure. Enter the code that is shown in Figure 4.104 into this event procedure.

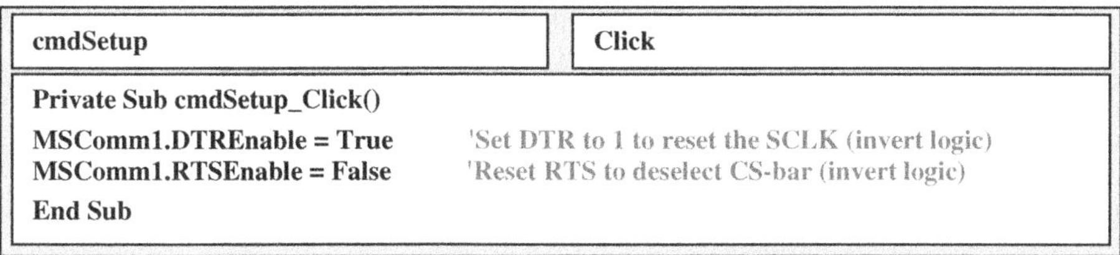

```
cmdSetup                                  Click

Private Sub cmdSetup_Click()
MSComm1.DTREnable = True       'Set DTR to 1 to reset the SCLK (invert logic)
MSComm1.RTSEnable = False      'Reset RTS to deselect CS-bar (invert logic)
End Sub
```

FIGURE 4.104 Code for the `Setup` event procedure.

The DTR line is connected to the SCLK input on the MAX-187 via the MAX-220, and the RTS is connected to the CS-bar input of the MAX-187 via the MAX-220, too. Keep in mind that the MAX-220 is an inverting driver. This means that all signals input to the MAX-220 are inverted at the output of the MAX-220. This concludes that we have to apply a negative logic signal for both DTR and the RTS lines in order to get the correct control signal applied on the MAX-187. So when a `True` is applied on the DTR line, a signal of `LOW` is obtained at the signal SCLK on the MAX-187 side, and a `False` applied on the RTS line will create a signal of `HIGH` at the signal CS-bar to deselect the MAX-187.

The next event procedure is the `Receive`. Double-click the `Receive` button on the `VBCommMAX` form window to open its event procedure. In this window, enter the code that is shown in Figure 4.105.

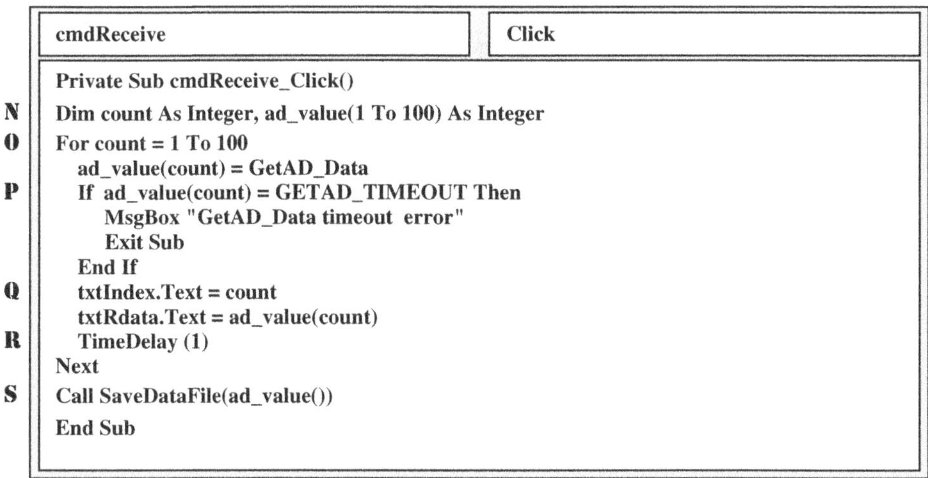

```
   cmdReceive                                  Click

   Private Sub cmdReceive_Click()
N  Dim count As Integer, ad_value(1 To 100) As Integer
O  For count = 1 To 100
      ad_value(count) = GetAD_Data
P     If ad_value(count) = GETAD_TIMEOUT Then
          MsgBox "GetAD_Data timeout  error"
          Exit Sub
      End If
Q     txtIndex.Text = count
      txtRdata.Text = ad_value(count)
R     TimeDelay (1)
   Next
S  Call SaveDataFile(ad_value())
   End Sub
```

FIGURE 4.105 Code for the `Receive` event procedure.

Each section of this code is explained in the following list.

N: A local variable `count` is declared here, and this variable works as an loop counter in a `for` loop to continuously pick up the converted data by calling the function `GetAD_Data()`. An integer array `ad_value()` is also declared here, and this array is used to store the received data from the MAX-187 A/D converter.

O: A `for` loop is used to repeatedly retrieve 100 converted data from the A/D converter. Each time when the function `GetAD_Data()` is called, a data (12-bit) is converted and received from the MAX-187.

P: If a timeout error occurs, the error message will be displayed and the event procedure is exited.

Q: The `count` will be displayed in the text box `txtIndex`, and the received data will be displayed in the text box `txtRdata`.

R: The `TimeDelay()` function is executed to wait for the MAX-187 to complete its conversion and to make the data stable on the transmission line before the data can be retrieved. Currently a 1 millisecond delay is applied in this project.

S: Finally the subroutine `SaveDataFile()` is executed to save the received data into a data file.

The `Plot` event procedure plots the received data that stored in a data file in a 2D graphic format using Microsoft Chart Control. Click the `VBCommMAX` form from the `Project Explorer` window and click the `View Object` button to open its form window. Then double-click the `Plot` button to open its event procedure window. In this window, enter the code that is shown in Figure 4.106.

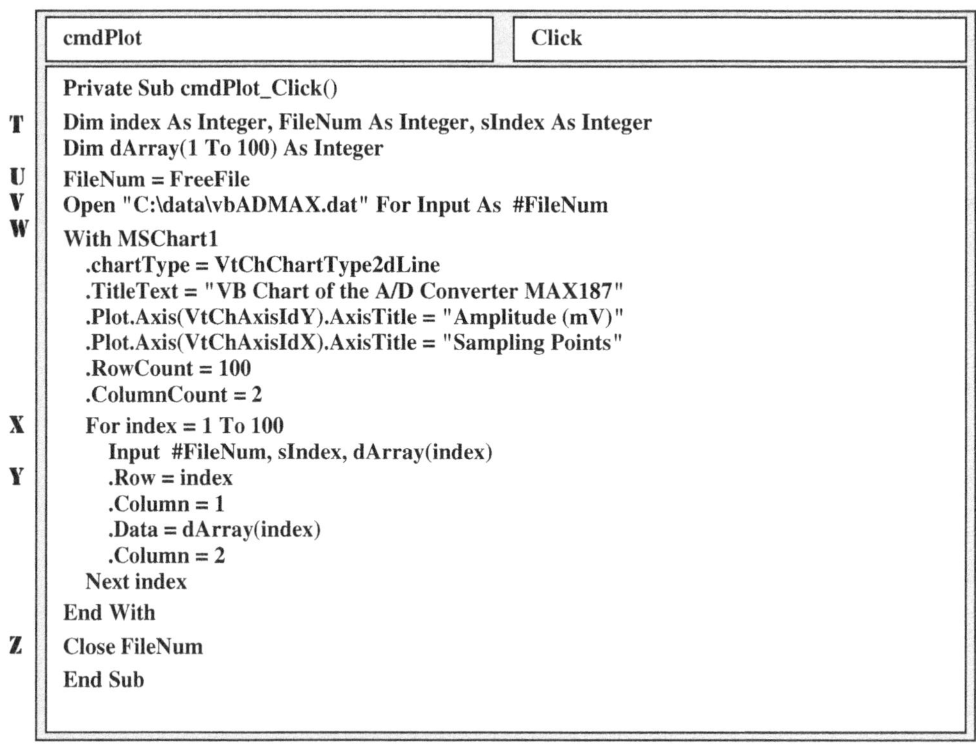

```
cmdPlot                                   Click

  Private Sub cmdPlot_Click()
T Dim index As Integer, FileNum As Integer, sIndex As Integer
  Dim dArray(1 To 100) As Integer
U FileNum = FreeFile
V Open "C:\data\vbADMAX.dat" For Input As #FileNum
W With MSChart1
     .chartType = VtChChartType2dLine
     .TitleText = "VB Chart of the A/D Converter MAX187"
     .Plot.Axis(VtChAxisIdY).AxisTitle = "Amplitude (mV)"
     .Plot.Axis(VtChAxisIdX).AxisTitle = "Sampling Points"
     .RowCount = 100
     .ColumnCount = 2
X    For index = 1 To 100
        Input #FileNum, sIndex, dArray(index)
Y       .Row = index
        .Column = 1
        .Data = dArray(index)
        .Column = 2
     Next index
  End With
Z Close FileNum
  End Sub
```

FIGURE 4.106 Code for the `Plot` event procedure.

Each section of this code is explained in the following list.

T: Some local variables are declared here. The `index` is used as a loop counter to repeatedly read out 100 data stored in the data file. The `FileNum` works as the file number or the file ID that has been opened in the project. The `sIndex` is a virtual variable and its purpose is to store the index read out from the first column of the data file. Recall that when we store the data into the data file, two columns are stored. The first column is the index of the data and the second column is the data. This variable is not actually used in this project and it is only used to match the format of the data read out from the data file. The `dArray` is an integer array with 100 elements, and it is used to store the data read out from the data file.

U: The statement `FreeFile` is a system command and it is used to identify a file number that has not been used by the system. The identified file number is assigned to the `FileNum`, and this `FileNum` can be identified by the system as a new file ID.

V: The data file that stored the converted data is opened by using the `Open` command with the `FileNum` as an identifier. In this application, the data file is stored by the full name `C:\data\vbADMAX.dat`.

W: The `With` statement is used to assign all properties of the MSChart1 control with associated values to plot the chart. Each property is illustrated as follows:

chartType = VtChartType2dLine: defines the chart type is 2D with line style.
TitleText: used to display the title of the chart.
Plot.Axis(VtChAxisIdY).AxisTitle: used to display the title in the Y axis.
Plot.Axis(VtChAxisIdX).AxisTitle: used to display the title in the X axis.
RowCount = 100: the data array has 100 rows.
ColumnCount = 2: the data array has 2 columns.

X: A `for` loop is used to repeatedly read out each data and index from the data file. Each index and data is considered as a point (x, y) to be plotted on the chart.

Y: The `index` is assigned to the property `Row`, which works as column 1. The data `dArray(index)` is assigned to the property `Data`, which works as column 2. After this assignment, each time, when a group of data that includes both the data and the associated index is read out from the data file, the `Row` and `Data` properties are executed to plot that group of data as one point on the chart. This process is continued until 100 data is plotted.

Z: Finally the `Close` command is executed to close the opened data file.

This data plotting is different with that in the last project in which a MATLAB M-File is called from within the Visual Basic environment. The actual data plotting occurs in the MATLAB domain and the MATLAB is treated as an Active-X control with a late binding process in the Visual Basic workspace. Comparably speaking, it is a little faster to perform the data plotting by using Microsoft Chart Control directly in the Visual Basic domain.

The last two event procedures are the `Exit` and the `VBMAXTimer`.

The purpose of the `Exit` event procedure is to clean up the port setup and terminate the project. The `VBMAXTimer` monitors the time being spent on data transmission and triggers the timeout signal when the desired time period is over. Both event procedures are straightforward and easy to understand. Figure 4.107 lists these two event procedures' body.

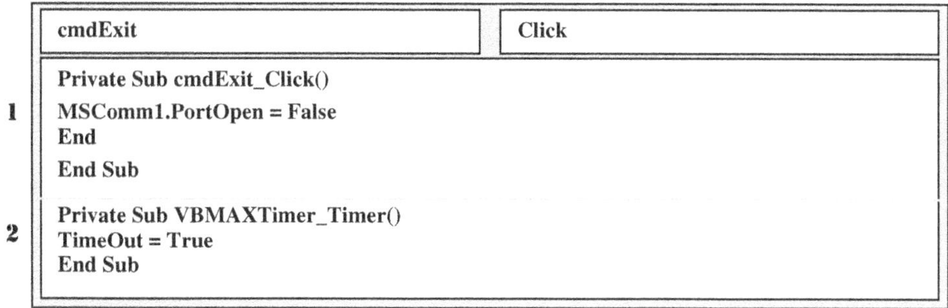

FIGURE 4.107 Code for two event procedures.

1: As soon as the Exit event procedure is executed, the PortOpen property of the MSComm control is reset to False to close the opened port. The End statement is then used to terminate the project.
2: When the time interval of the VBMAXTimer is up (5000-millisecond interval is used here), the Boolean flag TimeOut is set to True to inform the system that a timeout error occurs.

Following we discuss three functions used by the event procedure Receive. These three functions are GetAD_Data(), SaveDataFile() and TimeDelay().

The function GetAD_Data() is used to send the associated control commands to the MAX-187 serial A/D converter, check its working status and pick up the converted data from the MAX-187 if the data conversion is complete. The communications between the MAX-187 and the computer is accomplished by transmission lines. Refer to Figure 4.98, you can better understand the operating principles of this function, which are described here:

- Enable the VBMAXTimer and the RTS transmission line. The former is used to track the time period spent by the data transmission, and the latter is to select the MAX-187 A/D converter to make it begin to perform the data conversion.
- Refer to Figure 4.98, the DSR line is connected to the DOUT terminal of the MAX-187 via the MAX-220. A level of HIGH on the DOUT indicates that the data conversion is complete. Because of the inverting logic of the MAX-220, a signal of HIGH on the DOUT becomes a signal of LOW on the DSR line if the DOUT on the MAX-187 is HIGH, which means that the data conversion is done. By monitoring the status of the DSR line, the function can determine if the data conversion is complete. A LOW level on the DSR line means that the data conversion is done.
- If a timeout error occurs, the function returns with this error information.
- If the data conversion has been successfully completed and the DOUT signal is detected, the DTR transmission line is periodically triggered to HIGH and LOW to provide a sequence of clock input to move the converted data from the output buffer of the MAX-187 into the serial port via the DSR line. Then the received data is stored into a data buffer.
- After all 12-bit data is received and stored, the DTR and the RTS lines are disabled to reset the SCLK and the CS-bar signal on the MAX-187 to make the latter idle.
- The function returns the converted result to the calling event procedure.
- The VBMAXTimer and the timeout flag are reset to 0.

Each section of this code is explained in the following list (see Figure 4-108).

3: Two local variables are declared here. The index works as the loop counter to repeatedly pick up all 12 bits converted data from the MAX-187. The value works as a temporary buffer to store each converted data. Notice that because the MAX-187 is a 12-bit ADC, an integer type variable (16-bit in VB) is used here. The buffer is first reset to 0.
4: Because the RTS line is connected to the CS-bar on the MAX-187 via the inverter MAX-220, we have to use the negative logic signal to communicate with the MAX-187. To set the property RTSEnable to True, it is equivalent to send a signal of LOW or logical 0 to the CS-bar on the MAX-187. In this way, we enable the MAX-187 to begin the data conversion and this conversion operation is under the control of the internal clock provided by the MAX-187 itself. The VBMAXTimer is also enabled to begin to monitor the possible timeout error.

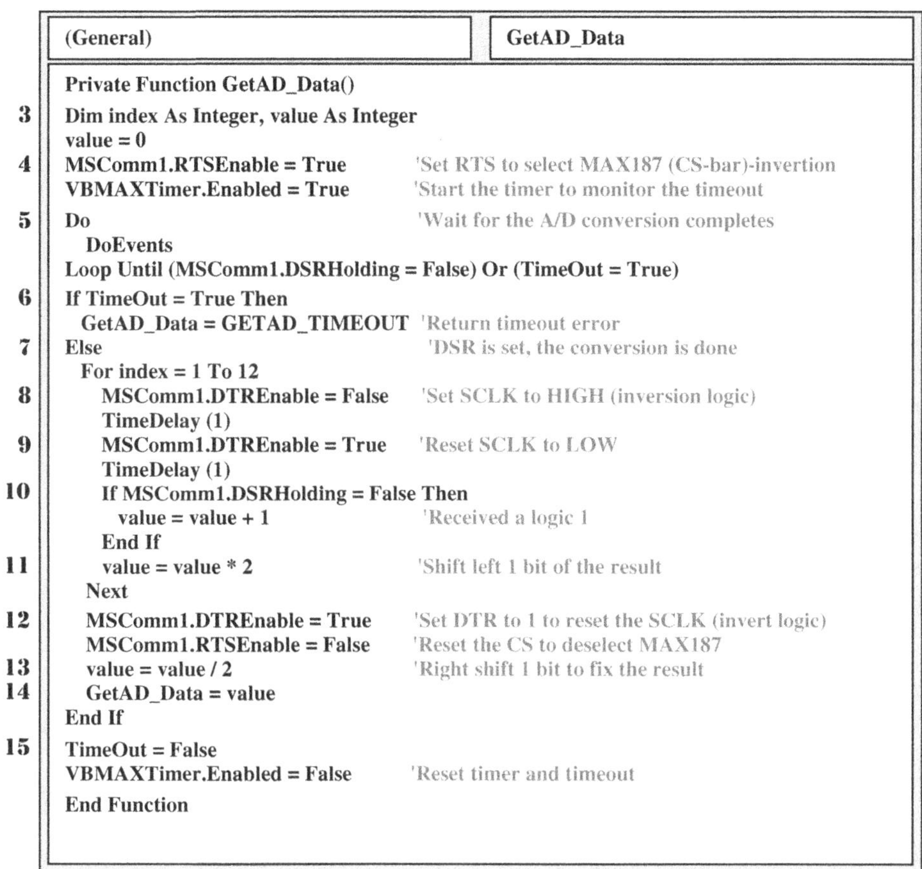

```
(General)                                   GetAD_Data

   Private Function GetAD_Data()
3  Dim index As Integer, value As Integer
   value = 0
4  MSComm1.RTSEnable = True          'Set RTS to select MAX187 (CS-bar)-invertion
   VBMAXTimer.Enabled = True         'Start the timer to monitor the timeout
5  Do                                'Wait for the A/D conversion completes
     DoEvents
   Loop Until (MSComm1.DSRHolding = False) Or (TimeOut = True)
6  If TimeOut = True Then
     GetAD_Data = GETAD_TIMEOUT      'Return timeout error
7  Else                              'DSR is set, the conversion is done
     For index = 1 To 12
8      MSComm1.DTREnable = False     'Set SCLK to HIGH (inversion logic)
       TimeDelay (1)
9      MSComm1.DTREnable = True      'Reset SCLK to LOW
       TimeDelay (1)
10     If MSComm1.DSRHolding = False Then
         value = value + 1           'Received a logic 1
       End If
11     value = value * 2             'Shift left 1 bit of the result
     Next
12   MSComm1.DTREnable = True        'Set DTR to 1 to reset the SCLK (invert logic)
     MSComm1.RTSEnable = False       'Reset the CS to deselect MAX187
13   value = value / 2               'Right shift 1 bit to fix the result
14   GetAD_Data = value
   End If
15 TimeOut = False
   VBMAXTimer.Enabled = False        'Reset timer and timeout
   End Function
```

FIGURE 4.108 Code for the `GetAD_Data()` function.

5: A `Do-Until` loop is used to pause processing until either a timeout error or a logical `0` on the DSR line has been detected. Do not forget to insert the `DoEvents` statement in the loop to avoid entering a dead cycle.

6: If a timeout occurs, which means that a logical `0` is not detected on the DSR line during the desired time period, the error message `GETAD_TIMEOUT` is returned to the calling event procedure.

7: Otherwise a logical `0` is detected on the DSR line. Refer to Figures 4.98, the DSR line is connected to the DOUT output terminal on the MAX-187 via the inverter MAX-220. When the MAX-187 completes one data conversion, the DOUT terminal outputs a signal of `HIGH` with a certain period of time (refer to Figure 2.68 in Chapter 2). This signal of `HIGH` is inverted to a signal of `LOW` or logical `0` on the DSR line via the inverter MAX-220. By detecting the status of the DSR line, we can identify whether the data conversion is complete or not. If a logical `0` is detected on the DSR line, which means that the DOUT terminal on the MAX-187 is set to `HIGH`, and therefore the MAX-187 has completed one data conversion. A `for` loop is used to repeatedly read out 12-bit data from the DSR line.

8: Refer to Figure 4.98, the DTR line is connected to the SCLK terminal on the MAX-187. This SCLK works as an external clock input to serially shift the converted data from the

DOUT output to the DSR line. Because of the inverter MAX-220, to apply a signal of `LOW` on the DTR line is equivalent to applying a signal of `HIGH` on the SCLK terminal. By resetting the `DTREnable` property to `False`, we can set a signal of `HIGH` on the SCLK terminal.

9: After a time delay, we set the DTR line to `HIGH` to reset the clock on the SCLK terminal on the MAX-187. In this way, we finished sending a clock cycle to the SCLK. Therefore, one bit of converted data should be moved out from the DOUT to the DSR line under the driving of this clock cycle. A time delay is needed to wait that moved bit stable.

10: By detecting the status of the DSR line, we can identify whether a logical `0` or `1` is received. If a `False` is detected on the DSR line, which means that a logical `1` is received because of the inverting operation of the MAX-220. The receiving buffer `value` should be increased by 1 on the associated bit. Otherwise a logical `0` is received. No action is needed for receiving a logical `0`.

11: To make each converted bit move into the receiving buffer in order, the buffer must be shifted left by one bit after receiving one bit data. This shift is equivalent to a multiplication of 2 to the buffer.

Repeat steps 8, 9, 10 and 11, we can pick up all 12 bits of converted data. The result is stored in the receiving buffer `value`.

12: After all 12 bits of data is received, we need to reset the SCLK and CS-bar on the MAX-187 to make it ready for the next conversion. This can be finished by setting the DTR line to True (`HIGH`) and resetting the RTS line to False (`LOW`).

13: During the left-shifting operation in step 11, one more shift is performed at the last bit. We need to fix that by performing a shift right operation. A division by 2 of the result is equivalent to that operation.

14: The final result, which is stored in the `value` buffer, is returned to the calling event procedure.

15: Before we can exit the function, we need to reset the `VBMAXTimer` and the timeout flag `TimeOut`.

TIP: Some careful reader may have a question for the function header: This function has no defined returning data type. That is ok for this special case. In Visual Basic, if a `function` missed the returned data type, VB can add one for that function automatically and the added data type is `Variant`. Although this is an auto-step, the execution speed of this function would be slow compared with a definite data type.

The next function is the `SaveDataFile()`. As we mentioned in the last project, this function is defined as a subroutine in Visual Basic because no returned value is applied for this function.

In the code window, click the `Tools|Add Procedure` menu item to open the `Add Procedure` dialog box. Enter the parameters that are listed in Table 4.43 into this dialog box to add a new subroutine.

TABLE 4.43
Properties of the `SaveDataFile()` Subroutine

Property	Value
Name	SaveDataFile
Type	Sub
Scope	Private

Inside the parentheses of the new added subroutine `SaveDataFile()`, type `dArray() As Integer` because this subroutine has an array as the argument. Enter the code that is shown in Figure 4.109 into this subroutine. Your finished subroutine body should match the one shown in Figure 4.109.

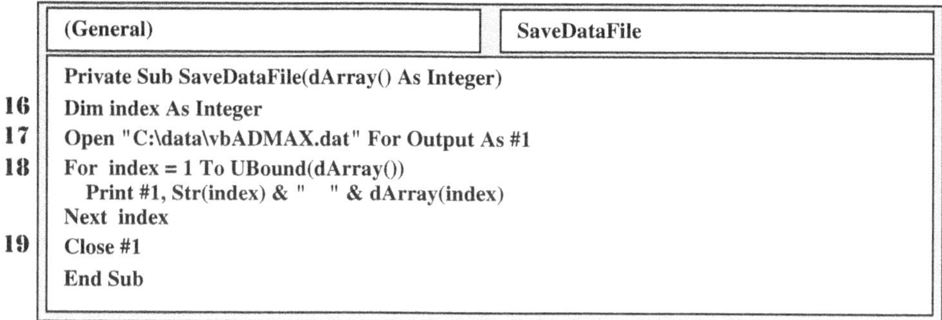

```
(General)                                   SaveDataFile

   Private Sub SaveDataFile(dArray() As Integer)
16 Dim index As Integer
17 Open "C:\data\vbADMAX.dat" For Output As #1
18 For index = 1 To UBound(dArray())
     Print #1, Str(index) & "    " & dArray(index)
   Next index
19 Close #1
   End Sub
```

FIGURE 4.109 Code for the `SaveDataFile()` subroutine.

16: A local integer variable `index` is declared here, and it works as a loop counter to pick up all data stored in the data array and write it into the data file one-by-one.

17: The full name of the data file is `C:\data\vbADMAX.dat`. An `Open` instruction is used to open this file for the `Output` operation, which means the write mode. Because no any other file is opened in this project, this is the `#1` file.

18: A `for` loop is used to repeatedly write each byte of data into the file. The built-in function `UBound()` is used to determine the upper boundary of the data array. Two elements are written into the file for each data: the data index and the data value. The ampersand operator '&' is used to concatenate these two elements together. You do not have to convert the `index` to the string when writing the elements into the data file and the `Print` can do that automatically.

19: Finally, close the data file by using the `Close` command after the data is stored to the file.

The last function is the `TimeDelay()`. This function is also defined as a subroutine in Visual Basic.

In the code window, click the `Tools|Add Procedure` menu item to open the `Add Procedure` dialog box. Enter the parameters that are listed in Table 4.44 into this dialog box to add a new subroutine.

TABLE 4.44
Properties for the `TimeDelay()` Subroutine

Property	Value
Name	TimeDelay
Type	Sub
Scope	Private

Inside the parentheses of the new added subroutine `TimeDelay()`, type `dMS As Single` because this subroutine has a single data as the argument. Enter the code that is shown in Figure 4.110 into this subroutine. Your finished subroutine body should match the one shown in Figure 4.110.

```
(General)                                    TimeDelay

Private Sub TimeDelay(dMS As Single)
20 Dim TMout As Single
21 TMout = dMS + timeGetTime()
22 Do Until timeGetTime() > TMout
     DoEvents
   Loop
   End Sub
```

FIGURE 4.110 Code for the `TimeDelay()` subroutine.

This subroutine pauses processing for a period of time based on the input argument. The delay time is measured in milliseconds.

20: A local variable `TMout` is declared here and it works as an accumulator to summarize the argument and the current system time.

21: The input argument `dMS` can be considered as an offset, and this offset is added with the current time obtained using the Win32 API function `timeGetTime()` together as a time block. This time block is equivalent to a time-leading moment that will occur in the future.

22: A `Do-Until` loop is used to pause processing until the current time is greater than the time block we obtained earlier. This means that the desired time period is elapsed and the time is up. Do not forget to insert the `DoEvents` inside the `Do-Until` loop to allow the CPU to handle some other more important jobs in your computer if the elapsed time period is not complete.

Now we have finished all coding for this project. Because we have two forms developed in this project, we need to indicate to Visual Basic which form should be executed first as the project runs. In this application, we want the `Setup` form to be executed first because two serial communication parameters, `comPort` and `baudRate`, are obtained from this form. These two parameters are entered by the user as the project runs.

To make this happen, click the `Project|VBMAX Properties` menu item from the Visual Basic menu bar to open the `Project Property` dialog box. Keep the default tab `General` selected, and select the `Setup` from the `Startup Object:` box. Click OK to save this setup. Now we are ready to test and run our project.

4.3.5.4 Implementation of the Serial Interface for a 12-Bit Serial A/D Converter

Make the circuit connection as shown in Figure 4.98. Currently we use a DB-9 RS-232 serial port. The analog input signal is coming from a function generator. Three waveforms can be selected for that function generator, sinusoidal, square, and triangle. Be sure to turn off your computer before connecting this circuit to the serial port located on your computer; otherwise you may encounter hardware problems when you run the project.

Run the project after you finish connecting the interface circuit to the computer via the serial port. The `Setup` form appears, as shown in Figure 4.111. Enter the port number and baud rate to the associated text boxes. In our case, we use the COM1 and 9600 baud rate. Enter 1 to the port number text box and 9600 to the baud rate text box, and then click `OK` to finish this setup.

Immediately the second form `VBCommMAX` appears with the port number and baud rate displayed on the `COM Port` and the `Baud Rate` labels, as shown in Figure 4.112.

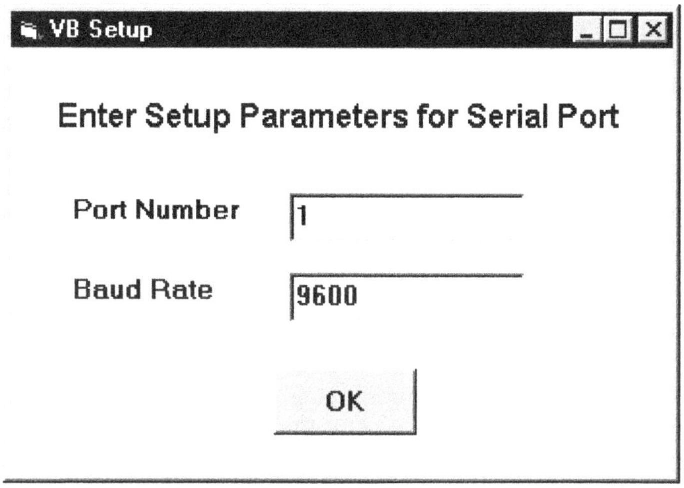

VB Setup

Enter Setup Parameters for Serial Port

Port Number 1

Baud Rate 9600

OK

FIGURE 4.111 Running status of the `Setup` form.

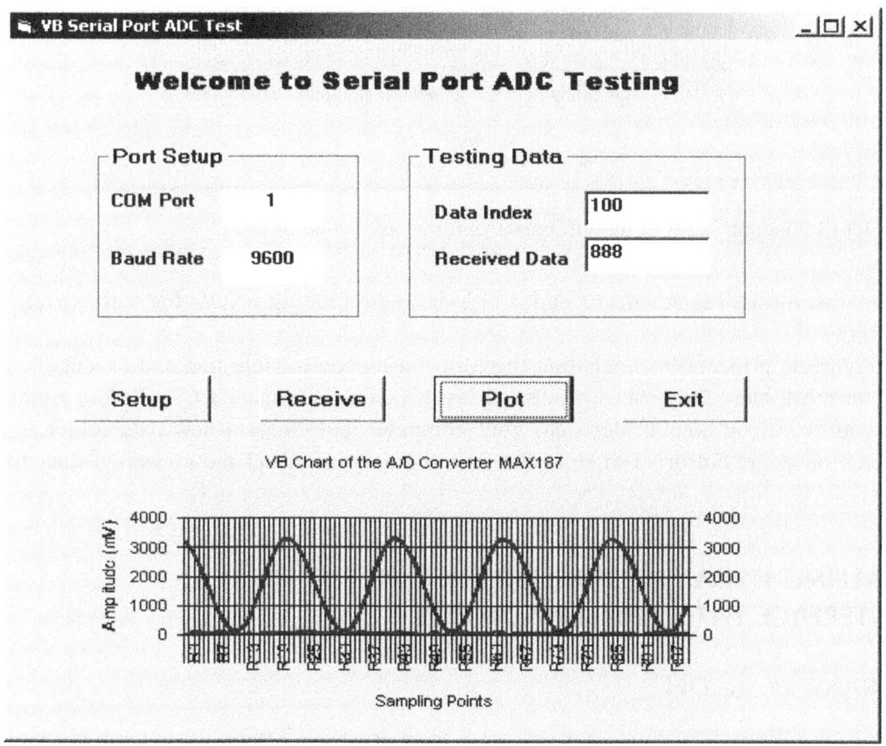

FIGURE 4.112 Running status of the `VBCommMAX` form—sinusoidal input.

Click the `Setup` button to finish the configuration of the serial port, and then click the `Receive` button to start the MAX-187 A/D conversion and collect the converted data. The data index and the converted data are displayed in the `Data Index` and the `Received Data` text boxes in real time, as shown in Figure 4.113. The collected data is also stored into a data file.

When the data conversion is complete, click the `Plot` button to plot the received data. In this application, two waveforms that come from the function generator are tested, sinusoidal and

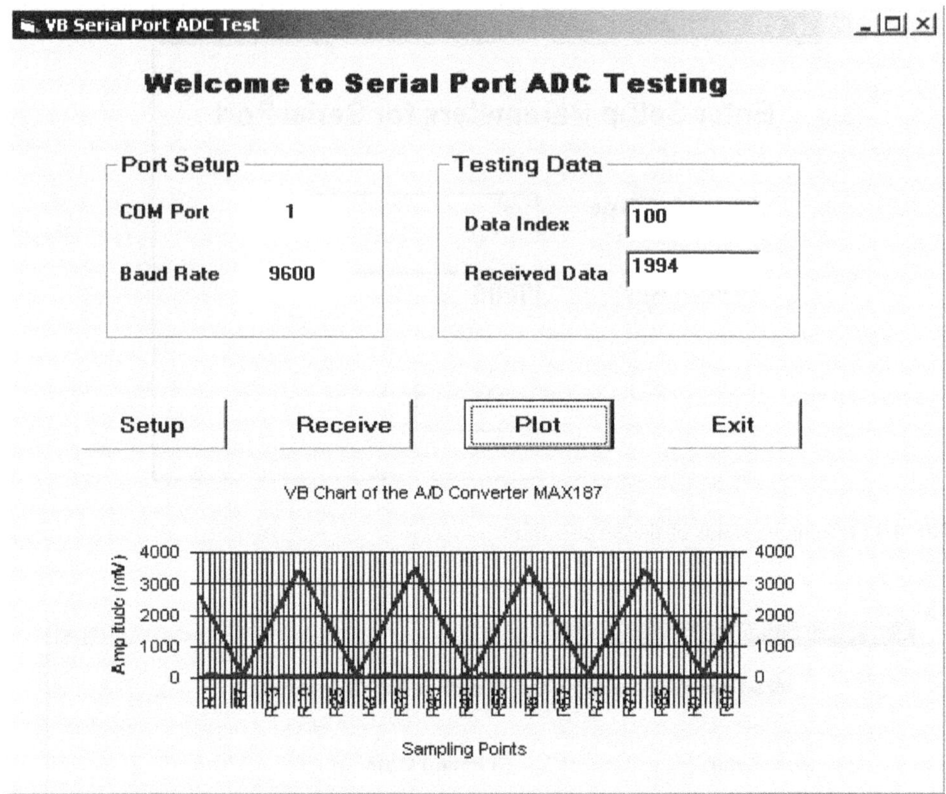

FIGURE 4.113 Running status of the `VBCommMAX` form—triangular input.

triangular waveforms. Figures 4.112 and 4.113 show the plotting results for both waveforms on the `MSChart1`.

The complete project files, including the form files, code module file, and executable file are included in the folder `Chapter 4\VBSerialMAX` on the attached CD. Before running this project, you must load all the files onto your computer and create a new data folder (typically `C:\data`) on your root drive to store the data file as you collect the converted data from the MAX-187.

4.4 CALLING DYNAMIC LINK LIBRARY PROCEDURES TO INTERFACE WITH THE SERIAL PORTS

4.4.1 Review of the DLL

Dynamic Link Library (DLL) is a powerful tool to interface to different programming languages. Any programming language can call a subroutine or a function, or a collection of functions developed in the different languages via the DLL. The role of the DLL just likes a bridge that set a path between the different programming language users.

Unlike the compiler, which uses the static link or early binding, the DLL belongs to the late binding process. This is the reason why it is called the dynamic link library. During the compiling process, the compiler will assign and reserve the space for the DLL and assign the starting address of the DLL to a dynamic table. As the project runs, the program platform or the operating system can dynamically load the DLL into the memory and execute it immediately.

It is obvious that one of the advantages of using the DLL is that it can save memory space. Another advantage is that the DLL can be developed in any programming language, and it can be called and executed by any other third party programming language.

In Section 4.1, we discussed the Win32 API functions. Exactly all Win32 API functions are stored in the different dynamic link libraries (refer to Table 4.1). All DLL files are extended with the .dll keyword.

Although the DLL can be developed by using the different languages, the popular language that is used to develop the DLL is C/C++. As you know, C/C++ is a very popular programming language and widely implemented in industrial, commercial, and manufacturing fields. In this section, we will concentrate on developing the DLL using the C/C++ programming language.

Generally, the DLL can be divided into two categories: Win32 general purpose DLL and MFC-based DLL. The former can be developed in either C environment or in Visual C++ environment, but the latter can only be developed in Visual C++ environment. The Win32 general-purpose DLL has a relatively wider range of implementations, and it can be called by most third-party programs, such as Visual Basic, Java, Perl, and Smalltalk. The MFC-based DLL can only be accessed by limited languages, such as Visual C++ and Visual Basic. But the MFC-based DLL has an advantage compared with the Win32 general purpose DLL, which is that the former can access objects and classes defined in the MFC library.

In order to meet the needs of general-purpose applications, in this section we concentrate on the development of the Win32 general-purpose DLL. The DLL developed in this section is called User-Defined DLL, which is different with the Win32 API DLL that is developed by the system.

To implement a Win32 general-purpose DLL, which is similar to call a Windows API DLL as we discussed in Section 4.2, you must first declare the DLL function prototype. This declaration is similar to the declarations in Section 4.2, but it is not exactly the same. Besides the declaration, you also need to develop a user-defined DLL and make connection between Visual Basic and the DLL developed in Visual C++. We will discuss this issue in detail at next section.

4.4.2 General Requirement for Calling a User-Defined DLL

To successfully call a user-defined DLL from within Visual Basic program, you must perform the following tasks:

- Develop a user-defined DLL in Visual C++ domain
- Declare and map the DLL functions in Visual Basic domain

Let us take a look at these two issues separately. First let's see the requirement of developing a Win32 general-purpose DLL. In order to develop a Win32 general purpose DLL, you need the following files:

- Source Files:
  Define and develop the source code for the DLL. This source code contains all DLL functions and local functions, as well as all features of the DLL.

- Header Files:
  Declare the prototypes for all DLL functions, local functions and other components, such as structures, structure pointers. These header files are necessary if the DLL functions would be accessed by some programs developed in C/C++. You must place these header files into the calling programs to provide prototypes for all DLL functions.

- DEF File:
  DEF file is called definition file. This file is used to export all DLL functions developed

in the source files to the outside world. The third-party programs cannot access any DLL function without this definition file. Based on this DEF file, the third-party programs can easily identify any DLL function developed in either C or Visual C++. For some calling programs developed in C/C++, they don't even need this DEF file and they can still find the DLL functions they need.

- LIB File:
  LIB file is called library file. This file is used to provide a path for the calling program to locate the DLL file when the calling program is compiled. Without this library file, the compiler cannot recognize any DLL function as it compiles the calling program. This library file must be inserted into the calling program and linked with the calling program together to obtain the target file if the calling program is developed in C/C++.

- DLL File:
  Basically, a DLL file is similar to an executable file (`.exe`) but it cannot run by itself. You need a calling program to call that DLL file to access and run DLL functions that located in that DLL file. This DLL file (`.dll`) can be placed in the current calling program folder, or a searchable path at your machine, such as in `C:\WINDOWS\SYSTEM`. In this way, the computer can automatically find that DLL file and dynamically connect it with your calling program together. You can also define a user-defined DLL directory and save the DLL file under that directory. But you must make that user-defined DLL directory as a searchable directory at your system. Otherwise your computer cannot know where to find that DLL file, and a `Cannot find the DLL` error would be displayed on the screen as your project runs.

In order to declare and map DLL functions in Visual Basic domain, you need:

- *Declare the prototype of DLL functions*—This declaration is similar to the declarations in Section 4.2 when calling a Windows API DLL function. One difference is that the library's name clause. You should place a full name of the library, which includes the completed path and the library's name, in this clause. For example, you developed a DLL file named `SerialDLL.dll` and save this file in the directory `C:\stdll`. Then you need to place the full name of that library, `C:\stdll\SerialDLL.dll`, in the library's name clause.

We want to develop a simple serial test example project to begin our discussion. The example is a loop-back test program used to test the serial port.

4.4.3 An Example of Calling DLL to Interface the Serial Port

In this project, each testing command is sent from within the Visual Basic domain and passed to the associated DLL function developed in Visual C++. The DLL works as a device drive to test the serial port according to the command sent by Visual Basic. The commands sent from within Visual Basic are:

- **Setup:** Sends out a setup command to initialize a serial port
- **Write:** Sends out a value to a serial port
- **Read:** Picks up a value from a serial port
- **Close:** Terminates the DLL and Visual Basic application

Associated with commands defined in Visual Basic domain, the following four interface functions should be contained in the dynamic link library:

- int Setup(int cPort, int bRate).
- int Write(int sdata).
- unsigned char Read().
- int Close().

First let's take a look at the hardware configuration for this loop-back test.

4.4.3.1 Configuring the Hardware for the Loop-Back Test

The simplest serial port test program is a loopback testing program. The loopback means that the TD and the RD pins in a RS-232 serial connector are connected together to form a loop between the sending out and receiving in terminals. Refer to Figure 1.8 and Section 1.10.1 in Chapter 1 to get more detail information about the loopback connection. For your convenience, the loopback connection for a DB-9 serial port is redrawn in Figure 4.114.

Pin-number	Function
1	Not used
2	R_{XD}
3	T_{XD}
4	Not used
5	Ground

FIGURE 4.114 Loopback connection of the serial port.

Make the connection as Figure 4.114 for the serial port on your computer. The connection is identical if you are using a DB-25 serial port because the only difference between the pin-2 and pin-3 on DB-9 and DB-25 is the switch between the transmit and the receive terminals.

4.4.3.2 Developing a Dynamic Link Library in Visual C++

Now let's handle to develop a DLL to perform the loopback test for the serial port in Visual C++ domain.

4.4.3.2.1 Definition of the Data Structure and Constants in Header File

We need to define the following constants and macro that are shown in Figure 4.115 for this DLL program.

```
#define MAX_STRING                  256
#define NOPARITY                      0
#define ONESTOPBIT                    0
#define RTS_CONTROL_DISABLE        0x00
#define RTS_CONTROL_ENABLE         0x01
#define DTR_CONTROL_DISABLE        0x00
#define DTR_CONTROL_ENABLE         0x01
#define msg(info)    MessageBox(NULL, info, "", MB_OK)
```

FIGURE 4.115 Definition of the constants and macro.

The top three constants are used as the protocol settings of the serial port communication. The following constants are used as the switches settings of the serial port structure. The macro, `msg(info)`, is used to simplify the message box function used in the program.

```
typedef struct
{
    char  *pcBuffer;        /* Buffer to store the received data */
    int   iMaxChars;        /* Max number of characters to be received */
    int   piNumRcvd;        /* Actual number of characters received */
    char  cTermChar;        /* Terminal character */
} CommPortClass;

typedef struct
{
    unsigned long  ulCtrlerID;   // serial port ID
    char           cEcho;        // echo character
    char           cEORChar;     // end of character
    long           lTimeout;     // time out value
    long           lBaudRate;    // baud rate
    long           lDataBits;    // data bits
} SerialCreate, *pSerialCreate;

typedef enum
{
    OK     = 0,              // no error
    EC_TIMEOUT,              // system time out error
    EC_FOPEN,                // file open error
    EC_INVAL_CONFIG,         // invalid configuration error
    EC_TIMEOUT_SET,          // set structure time out error
    EC_RECV_TIMEOUT,         // receiver time out error
    EC_EXIT_CODE,            // get exit code error
    EC_WAIT_SINGLEOBJ,       // WaitForSingleObject function error
    EC_INVALIDPORT,          // invalid port error
    EC_WRITE_FAIL,           // write function error
    EC_CREATE_THREAD,        // create thread error
    EC_UNKNOWNERROR          // unknown error
} ERR_CODE;
```

FIGURE 4.116 Definition of the structures.

We also need to define the following structures for the local functions used in the DLL file, which are shown in Figure 4.116. The `enum` structure is used to keep the error code clear, because we have a quite few error conditions to be handled.

The following are the definitions for the global variables used in this DLL file:

```
HANDLE  hPort;
char*   sPortName;
bool    PortCreateflg = false;
```

The `hPort` is the handle variable, which is used to reserve the newly created file handle. The `sPortName` is used to store the port name in a string format. The `PortCreateflg` is a Boolean variable, which is used to record the status of the port creation (if a port has been created or not).

The following are the definitions for the local functions used in this DLL file:

```
ERR_CODE PortInitialize(LPTSTR lpszPortName, pSerialCreate pCreate);
ERR_CODE PortWrite(char* bByte, int NumByte);
```

```
ERR_CODE PortRead(CommPortClass* hCommPort);
void WINAPI ThreadFunc(void* hCommPorts);
```

These functions are used only inside the DLL and have no connection with the outside functions, so they are called local functions. These local functions call the serial port drives and set the connection between the interface functions and the serial port I/O functions.

- **PortInitialize()**: Initialize and configure the serial port based on the port name and baud rate arguments.
- **PortWrite():** Calls the serial port drive to write the data byte (bByte) to the serial port. The number of bytes written is determined by the argument `NumByte`.
- **PortRead():** Calls the serial port drive to read back the data written to the port. The argument is a structure pointer, which contains the necessary data buffer and character structure.
- **ThreadFunc():** Because the dead cycle may happen when the `PortRead()` function is called to read back the data from the port, it is a good idea to use a thread to handle this issue.

The definition of the interface functions used in this DLL file is shown in Figure 4.117.

```
/*-----------------------------------------------------------------------------------------*/
#define DllExport    __declspec( dllexport )
/*-----------------------------------------------------------------------------------------*/

DllExport int Setup(int cPort, int bRate);
DllExport int Read();
DllExport int Write(int sdata);
DllExport int Close();
```

FIGURE 4.117 Definition of the interface functions.

The declaration `declspec(dllexport)` is a popular one for the general-purpose DLL call, so we define it as a macro (`DllExport`) to convenience the programming. Following this definition, four interface functions are defined; these functions will call the local functions defined earlier to contact the serial port I/O functions and complete the testing. A functional block diagram of this serial port test program is shown in Figure 4.118.

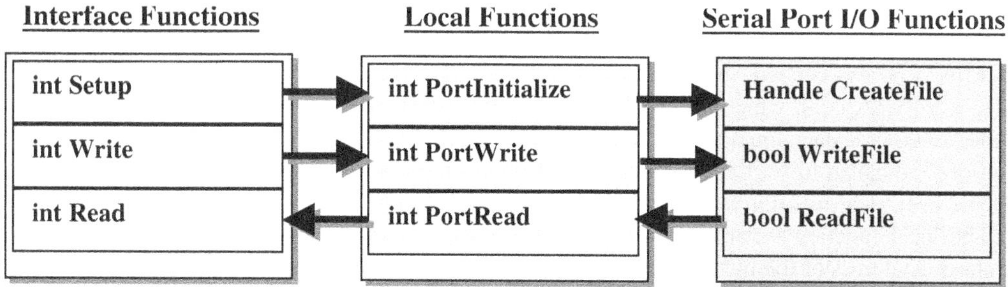

FIGURE 4.118 Functional block diagram of the serial port test program.

This test is divided into three levels in software design. The interface functions will work as an interface between the Visual Basic and Visual C++ dynamic link library, which can be considered as level 1. The local functions belong to level 2, and they set a connection between the interface functions and the serial port I/O functions. The local functions also perform some initialization and preparation works before they calling the serial port I/O functions. The port I/O functions are considered as level 3, and they will talk to the I/O manager and furthermore, to the port hardware to perform the port testing. All these function definitions are integrated into the header file of this DLL program, which is named `SerialDLL.h`.

Launch Visual C++ 6.0 and create a new project with the type of `Win32 Dynamic-Link Library`, enter `SerialDLL` to the `Project name:` input field as the name for this project. Click `OK` to open this new project. Open the Windows Explorer, create a new folder in the root directory, in our case it is `C:\stdll`, which is used to store the developed DLL file. Create a new header file named `SerialDLL.h` and enter all the definitions displayed earlier into this header file. The completed header file is shown in Figure 4.119.

4.4.3.2.2 Coding of the Interface Function

Create a new C++ source file by clicking `File|New` menu item from the Visual C++ 6.0 workspace, select the `Files` tab and click the `C++ Source File` from the list. Enter `SerialDLL` to the `File name:` input field as this source file name, and click `OK` to open the newly created source file. Enter the code that is shown in Figure 4.120 into this file.

Each interface function will call its associated local function to perform the desired task. Each interface function also performs some necessary data and structure initializations and assignments based on the arguments passed from the Visual Basic domain.

In this application, the range of the valid serial ports is from COM1 to COM4. You can modify this range if you have different port configuration in your machine. The `new` keyword is used to create a new structure or structure pointer and to allocate the memory space for it. You must use the `delete` keyword to clean the memory space you allocated for that structure when it is no longer to be used. The `new` and `delete` keywords can be considered as a partner.

A macro `msg`, which is a simplified definition of the messagebox function, is used to display a warning message if the program encounters any error, and this method is very convenient for the programmer to debug the code.

4.4.3.2.3 Coding of the Local Function Body

The next step is to develop the local functions. The local functions are used to contact the serial port drive, so it is a little complicated. Four local functions are developed in this DLL file. The first one is `PortInitialize()`, which is used to initialize the serial port to be tested. The body of this function is shown in Figure 4.121.

At the beginning of this function, some data structures are declared and the function checks if the port has been created or not. A port is created by using the function `CreateFile()` if no port has been generated, and the handle is returned and stored in the variable `hPort` if the port is created successfully.

After a port is created, the serial communication data structures are generated, such as `DCB` and `COMMTIMEOUTS`, which are used to set the serial data structures. Then the current `DCB` and `COMMTIMEOUTS` data structures are retrieved and modified based on our application. Finally two functions are called to set the DTR and the RTS transmission lines in the RS-232 port.

The next local function is `PortWrite()`, whose coding is shown in Figure 4.122.

The local function `PortWrite()` has two arguments, `*bByte` and `NumByte`, which are the starting address of the bytes to be written to the port and the number of the bytes to be written. The `WriteFile()` function is called to interface to the low-level drive to write bytes into the port. A message box with a piece of warning information will be displayed if this calling encounters any error.

```
/*****************************************************************************
 * NAME          : SerialDLL.h
 * DESC.         : Header file for SerialDLL.cpp
 *****************************************************************************/
#ifndef _SERIALDLL_H_
#define _SERIALDLL_H_
#define MAX_STRING                   256
#define NOPARITY                       0
#define ONESTOPBIT                     0
#define RTS_CONTROL_DISABLE         0x00
#define RTS_CONTROL_ENABLE          0x01
#define DTR_CONTROL_DISABLE         0x00
#define DTR_CONTROL_ENABLE          0x01
#define msg(info)      MessageBox(NULL, info, "", MB_OK)
```

```
typedef struct
{
   unsigned long  ulCtrlerID;     // serial port ID
   char           cEcho;          // echo character
   char           cEORChar;       // end of character
   long           lTimeout;       // time out value
   long           lBaudRate;      // baud rate
   long           lDataBits;      // data bits
} SerialCreate, *pSerialCreate;
typedef struct
{
   char   pcBuffer[100];          /* Buffer to store the received data */
   int    iMaxChars;              /* Max number of characters to be received */
   int    piNumRcvd;              /* Actual number of characters received */
   char   cTermChar;              /* Terminal character */
} CommPortClass;
typedef enum
{
   OK        = 0,                 // no error
   EC_TIMEOUT,                    // system time out error
   EC_FOPEN,                      // file open error
   EC_INVAL_CONFIG,               // invalid configuration error
   EC_TIMEOUT_SET,                // set structure time out error
   EC_RECV_TIMEOUT,               // receiver time out error
   EC_EXIT_CODE,                  // get exit code error
   EC_WAIT_SINGLEOBJ,             // WaitForSingleObject function error
   EC_INVALIDPORT,                // invalid port error
   EC_WRITE_FAIL,                 // write function error
   EC_CREATE_THREAD,              // create thread error
   EC_UNKNOWNERROR                // unknown error
} ERR_CODE;
HANDLE   hPort;
char*      sPortName;
bool       PortCreateflg = false;
ERR_CODE PortInitialize(LPTSTR lpszPortName, pSerialCreate pCreate);
ERR_CODE PortWrite(char* bByte, int NumByte);
ERR_CODE PortRead(CommPortClass *hCommPort);
void WINAPI ThreadFunc(void* hCommPorts);
#define DllExport    __declspec( dllexport )
DllExport int Setup(int  cPort, int  bRate);
DllExport int Read();
DllExport int Write(int  sdata);
DllExport int Close();
#endif
```

FIGURE 4.119 Header file for the DLL.

```
/*****************************************************************************
 * NAME       : SerialDLL.cpp
 * DESC.      : DLL functions to interface to rs-232 serial port, called by Visual Basic.
 * PRGMER.    : Y. Bai
 *****************************************************************************/
#include <stdio.h>
#include <windows.h>
#include <stdlib.h>
#include <string.h>
#include "SerialDLL.h"

DllExport int Setup(int cPort, int bRate)
{
        ERR_CODE  rc = OK;
        pSerialCreate  pParam;

        pParam = new SerialCreate;             // create a new pointer structure
        pParam->lBaudRate = bRate;             // assign values to variables in structure
        pParam->lDataBits = 8;
        pParam->lTimeout  = 3000;

        switch(cPort)                          // check the port number
        {
        case 1:
                sPortName = "COM1";            // port is COM1
                break;
        case 2:
                sPortName = "COM2";            // port is COM2
                break;
        case 3:
                sPortName = "COM3";            // port is COM3
                break;
        case 4:
                sPortName = "COM4";            // port is COM4
                break;
        default:
                return EC_INVALIDPORT;
        }
        if (PortCreateflg)                     // port flag is true means port was set
        {
                msg("Port has been Setup ");
                return rc;
        }
        rc = PortInitialize(sPortName, pParam); // call local func. to configure port
        if (rc != 0)
           msg("ERROR in PortInitialize()!");
        delete pParam;                         // clean pointer structure
        PortCreateflg = true;                  // set port creation flag

        return rc;
}

DllExport int Write(int sdata)
{
        int  numByte = 1;                      // define written length as 1 byte
        char sByte[8];
        ERR_CODE rc = OK;
```

FIGURE 4.120 Code for the interface functions. *(continued)*

```
        sprintf(sByte, "%c", sdata);            // convert integer to character
        rc = PortWrite(sByte, numByte);         // call local func. to write the character
        if (rc != 0)
           msg("ERROR in PortWrite() !");
        return rc;
}
DllExport int Read()
{
        int idata;
        char cdata[8];
        ERR_CODE rc = OK;
        CommPortClass* commClass;
        commClass = new CommPortClass;          // create a new pointer structure
        commClass->iMaxChars = 1;               // assign value to the variable in structure

        rc = PortRead(commClass);               // call local func. to read back the data
        if (rc != 0)
           msg("ERROR in PortRead()! ");

        sprintf(cdata, "%d", commClass->pcBuffer[0]);
        idata = atoi(cdata);                    // convert the character to integer
        delete commClass;                       // clean up structure
        return idata;
}
DllExport int Close()
{
        ERR_CODE rc = OK;

        if (PortCreateflg)
            CloseHandle(hPort);                 // clean up the port handler
        PortCreateflg = false;                  // reset the port creation flag
        return rc;
}
```

FIGURE 4.120 Code for the interface functions.

The local function `PortRead()` needs to call a thread to retrieve the data written to the port. The purpose of using a thread to handle retrieving data is to avoid the program to enter a dead cycle if no any event occurs to the serial port. The coding of the function `PortRead()` is shown in Figure 4.123.

The `PortRead()` function has one argument, `*hCommPort`, which is a structure pointer. This structure pointer will be passed into the thread as a null pointer parameter later on when the `PortRead()` creates that thread. After the thread is created, the thread function is suspended by one of arguments CREATE_SUSPENDED. The thread function will not start to execute until a `ResumeThread()` function is called. The newly created thread returns a handler `hThread`, which will be used by all other components to access the thread.

After the function `ResumeThread()` is executed, the thread function starts to run. Because this thread function is a little complex, we leave the detailed discussion of that thread function to the next section. The thread function retrieves the data written to the serial port and stores the data in a buffer defined in the `hCommPort` structure for further processing.

```
ERR_CODE PortInitialize(LPTSTR lpszPortName, pSerialCreate pCreate)
{
    DWORD               dwError;
    DCB                 PortDCB;
    ERR_CODE            ecStatus = OK;
    COMMTIMEOUTS        CommTimeouts;
    unsigned char       dBit;

    // check if the port has been created...
    if (PortCreateflg)
    {
        msg("Port has been initialized!");
        return  ecStatus;
    }
    // Open the serial port.
    hPort = CreateFile(lpszPortName,  // Pointer to the name of the port
                GENERIC_READ | GENERIC_WRITE,
                                      // Access (read/write) mode
                0,                    // Share mode
                NULL,                 // Pointer to the security attribute
                OPEN_EXISTING,        // How to open the serial port
                0,                    // Port attributes
                NULL);                // Handle to port with attribute to copy

    // If it fails to open the port, return error.
    if ( hPort == INVALID_HANDLE_VALUE )
    {
        // Could not open the port.
        dwError = GetLastError();
        msg("Unable to open the port");
        CloseHandle(hPort);
        return  EC_FOPEN;
    }

    PortCreateflg = TRUE;
    PortDCB.DCBlength = sizeof(DCB);

    // Get the default port setting information.
    GetCommState(hPort, &PortDCB);

    // Change the DCB structure settings.
    PortDCB.BaudRate = pCreate->lBaudRate;      // Current baud rate
    PortDCB.fBinary  = TRUE;                    // Binary mode; no EOF check
    PortDCB.fParity  = TRUE;                    // Enable parity checking.
    PortDCB.fOutxCtsFlow = FALSE;               // No CTS output flow control
    PortDCB.fOutxDsrFlow = FALSE;               // No DSR output flow control
    PortDCB.fDtrControl = DTR_CONTROL_ENABLE; //DTR flow control type
    PortDCB.fDsrSensitivity = FALSE;            // DSR sensitivity
    PortDCB.fTXContinueOnXoff = TRUE;           // XOFF continues Tx
    PortDCB.fOutX = FALSE;                      // No XON/XOFF out flow control
    PortDCB.fInX  = FALSE;                      // No XON/XOFF in flow control
    PortDCB.fErrorChar = FALSE;                 // Disable error replacement.
    PortDCB.fNull = FALSE;                      // Disable null stripping.
```

FIGURE 4.121 Code for the `PortInitialize()` function. *(continued)*

```
    PortDCB.fRtsControl = RTS_CONTROL_ENABLE;  // RTS flow control
    PortDCB.fAbortOnError = FALSE;             // Do not abort reads/writes on error.
    dBit = (unsigned char)pCreate->lDataBits;
    PortDCB.ByteSize = dBit;                   // Number of bits/bytes, 4-8
    PortDCB.Parity = NOPARITY;                 // 0-4=no,odd,even,mark,space
    PortDCB.StopBits = ONESTOPBIT;             // 0,1,2 = 1, 1.5, 2

    // Configure the port according to the specifications of the DCB structure.
    if (!SetCommState (hPort, &PortDCB))
    {
        // Could not create the read thread.
        dwError = GetLastError();
        msg("Unable to configure the serial port");
        return  EC_INVAL_CONFIG;
    }
    // Retrieve the time-out parameters for all read and write operations on the port.
    GetCommTimeouts(hPort, &CommTimeouts);

    // Change the COMMTIMEOUTS structure settings.
    CommTimeouts.ReadIntervalTimeout = MAXDWORD;
    CommTimeouts.ReadTotalTimeoutMultiplier = 0;
    CommTimeouts.ReadTotalTimeoutConstant = 0;
    CommTimeouts.WriteTotalTimeoutMultiplier = 10;
    CommTimeouts.WriteTotalTimeoutConstant = 1000;

    // Set the time-out parameters for all read and write operations on the port.
    if (!SetCommTimeouts (hPort, &CommTimeouts))
    {
        // Could not create the read thread.
        dwError = GetLastError();
        msg("Unable to set the time-out parameters");
        return  EC_TIMEOUT_SET;
    }
    EscapeCommFunction(hPort, SETDTR);
    EscapeCommFunction(hPort, SETRTS);

    return  ecStatus;
}
```

FIGURE 4.121 Code for the `PortInitialize()` function.

A `WaitForSingleObject()` function is called after the thread runs. This function is used to monitor and wait for one of two events (components) occurs: the running thread completion event that is associated with the WAIT_OBJECT_0. This event occurs when the thread function is normally completed and terminated. The other one is the timeout event, which is associated with the event WAIT_TIMEOUT. This event occurs if the program enters a dead cycle. If the first event occurs (WAIT_OBJECT_0), which means that the thread has successfully obtained the data written to the serial port and the data has been stored into the buffer defined in the `hCommPort` data structure, the function `PortRead()` will close the thread handler and exit the program because the data has been obtained. If the second event occurs (WAIT_TIMEOUT), which means that the

```
/*****************************************************************************
 * NAME         : PortWrite()
 * DESC.        : Write data to the port
 * DATE         : 11/9/03
 * PRGMER.      : Y. Bai
*****************************************************************************/
ERR_CODE PortWrite(char* bByte, int NumByte)
{
    DWORD dwError;
    DWORD dwNumBytesWritten;
    ERR_CODE ecStatus = OK;

    if (!WriteFile (hPort,                 // Port handle
                    bByte,                 // Pointer to the data to write
                    NumByte,               // Number of bytes to write
                    &dwNumBytesWritten,    // Pointer to the number of bytes written
                    NULL))                 // Must be NULL for Windows CE
    {
        // WriteFile failed. Report error.
        dwError = GetLastError ();
        msg("ERROR in PortWrite ..");
        return EC_WRITE_FAIL;
    }

    return ecStatus;
}
```

FIGURE 4.122 Code for the local `PortWrite()` function.

program enters a dead cycle and no event to trigger the serial port. In that case, the `PortRead()` function also terminates the thread function and close the thread handler, but returns a timeout error to the calling function. In any other case, an error status is returned to the calling function to indicate that an error is encountered when executing this `PortRead()` function.

4.4.3.2.4 Coding of the Thread Reading Function

The thread function is the real body of the thread, which executes the task assigned to the thread. In our application, we use a thread to check and retrieve the data written to the port and store the data into a buffer defined in the data structure.The advantage of using a thread to handle this job is to avoid the dead cycle, which would happened if no any event triggers the port. The complete coding of the thread function is shown in Figure 4.124.

The thread has an argument `hCommPorts`, whose type is a null pointer. This means that this argument can be adopted and converted to hold any kind of data. This argument is passed into the thread by the `CreateThread()` function and it is exactly a data structure whose values has been initialized by the interface function `Read()` before the `PortRead()` local function is called.

After declare some local variables and data structures at the beginning of the thread function, we need to convert the null pointer parameter, `hCommPorts`, to the destination data structure, `CommPortClass`.

Next we need to assign a set of event masks to the serial port controller (UART) by using `SetCommMask()` system function. We combine a sequence of event masks by using the `or` operator to allow the multiple events to trigger the port. Such as received a char, the DSR or the CTS line is activated, or a ring is received. If any of those events happened, the UART can immediately response to that event by executing the associated command.

Next we use a `while` loop and a system function `WaitCommEvent()` to continuously monitor those events and process the event if any of events happened. Please note that this function

```
/*****************************************************************************
 * NAME        : PortRead()
 * DESC.       : Read data from the serial port
 *****************************************************************************/
ERR_CODE PortRead(CommPortClass *hCommPort)
{
    HANDLE  hThread;                          // handler for port read thread
    DWORD   IDThread;
    DWORD   Ret, ExitCode;
    DWORD   dTimeout = 5000;                  // define time out value: 5 sec.
    ERR_CODE ecStatus = OK;
     if (!(hThread = CreateThread(NULL,          // no security attributes
                           0,                  // use default stack size
                           (LPTHREAD_START_ROUTINE) ThreadFunc,
                           (LPVOID)hCommPort,   // parameter to thread function
                           CREATE_SUSPENDED, // creation flag - suspended
                           &IDThread) ) )        // returns thread ID
     {
         msg("Create Read Thread failed");
         return  EC_CREATE_THREAD;
     }
     ResumeThread(hThread);                   // start thread now
     Ret = WaitForSingleObject(hThread, dTimeout);
     if (Ret == WAIT_OBJECT_0)
     {
         // Data received & process it... need to do nothing because the data is stored in the
         // hCommPort  in the Thread Function.  The only thing is to close thread handle
         CloseHandle(hThread);
     }
     else if (Ret == WAIT_TIMEOUT)              // Time out happened
    {                                          // Warning & kill thread
         Ret = GetExitCodeThread(hThread, &ExitCode);
         msg("Time out happened in PortRead() ");
         if (ExitCode == STILL_ACTIVE)
         {
             TerminateThread(hThread, ExitCode);
             CloseHandle(hThread);
              return  EC_RECV_TIMEOUT;
         }
         else
         {
              CloseHandle(hThread);
              msg("ERROR in GetExitCodeThread: != STILL_ACTIVE ");
              ecStatus = EC_EXIT_CODE;
         }
     }
     else
    {
         msg("ERROR in WaitFor SingleObject ");
         ecStatus = EC_WAIT_SINGLEOBJ;
    }
    return  ecStatus;
}
```

FIGURE 4.123 Code for the `PortRead()` function.

only monitors the serial communication events, not synchronous events. If a received-a-char event happened, we call `ReadFile()` to read back this character and store it in the buffer by using: `CommPorts->pcBuffer[nTotRead] = Byte`.

The buffer is defined inside the data structure `CommPorts`, and the local variable `nTotRead` represents the total number of bytes read.

```
/*****************************************************************************
* NAME    : ThreadFunc()
* DESC.   : The reason to use this thread is to overcome the hung up introduced by the
*         : WaitCommEvent() function which waits for only the comm. event, not synchro-
*         : nition event. The program will be dead-cycle without this thread.
* PRMR.   : Y. Bai
*****************************************************************************/
void WINAPI ThreadFunc(void* hCommPorts)
{
    char  Byte;
    BOOL  bResult, fDone;
    int   nTotRead = 0;
    DWORD dwCommModemStatus, dwBytesTransferred;
    CommPortClass*  CommPorts;
    ERR_CODE ecStatus = OK;
    CommPorts = (CommPortClass* )hCommPorts;
    // Specify a set of events to be monitored for the port.
    SetCommMask(hPort, EV_RXCHAR | EV_CTS | EV_DSR | EV_RLSD | EV_RING);
    fDone = FALSE;
    while (!fDone)
    {
      // Wait for an event to occur for the port.
      WaitCommEvent(hPort, &dwCommModemStatus, 0);
      // Re-specify the set of events to be monitored for the port.
      SetCommMask(hPort, EV_RXCHAR | EV_CTS | EV_DSR |EV_RLSD| EV_RING);
      if (dwCommModemStatus & EV_RXCHAR||dwCommModemStatus & EV_RLSD)
      {
          //  received the char_event & loop to wait for the data.
          do
          {
              // Read the data from the serial port.
              bResult = ReadFile(hPort, &Byte, 1, &dwBytesTransferred, 0);
   if           (!bResult)
              {
                      msg("ERROR in ReadFile !");
                      fDone = TRUE;
                      break;
              }
                else
                {
                      // Display the data read.
                      if (dwBytesTransferred == 1)
                      {
                          if (Byte == 0x0D ||Byte == 0x0A)       // null char or LF
                          {
                              CommPorts->piNumRcvd = nTotRead;
                              fDone = TRUE;
                              break;
                          }
                          CommPorts->pcBuffer[nTotRead] = Byte;
                          nTotRead++;
                          if (nTotRead == CommPorts->iMaxChars)
```

FIGURE 4.124 Code for the `Read Thread` function. *(continued)*

```
                        {
                            fDone = TRUE;
                            break;
                        }
                    }
                    else
                    {
                        if (Byte == 0x0D ||Byte == 0x0A)        // null char or CR
                        {
                            msg("Received null character ");
                            fDone = TRUE;
                            break;
                        }
                    }
                }
            }while (dwBytesTransferred == 1); //while (nTotRead < pRecv->iMaxChars);
        }  // if
    }      // while
    return;
}
```

FIGURE 4.124 Code for the `Read Thread` function.

Next we need to check if we reach the maximum number of characters we suppose to read. If it is, we should set the `while` loop condition flag and exit the loop. Besides to check the maximum number of characters, we also need to check if we received the `null` or `CR` character. In some applications, the terminal string is marked by a `null` or `CR` character. The `while` loop will also be terminated if either case happened.

After we stored the received character into the buffer, we can terminate the `while` loop, and furthermore, to end the thread. An associated event WAIT_OBJECT_0 will be sent to the `WaitForSingleObject()` function in the `PortRead()` local function to inform the function that the reading thread has been successfully completed and the data has been obtained and stored in the buffer. The `PortRead()` will return an `OK` status to the interface function `Read()` to indicate that the `PortRead()` function has been successfully completed. The interface function will pick up the data stored in the buffer and convert it into a suitable format and return it to the Visual Basic domain.

4.4.3.2.5 Coding of the Definition File

Before we can finish our dynamic link library, we need to generate a definition file for this DLL. The purpose of the definition file is to export all interface functions to the public and any guy can "see" the interface functions by using the definition file. The definition file for this DLL is shown in Figure 4.125.

The first line is used to declare the name of the dynamic link library. Following the keyword `EXPORTS`, all our four interface functions are listed. In this way, all interface functions can be exported to the third party and can be seen by the public.

TIP: This definition file is important in the interface between Visual Basic and the DLL developed in Visual C++. Without it, Visual Basic may not identify the interface functions

```
LIBRARY SerialDLL.dll
EXPORTS
Setup
Read
Write
Close
```

FIGURE 4.125 Code for the definition file.

defined in the DLL as your program runs. This potential bug is difficult to find in some situations, so be careful when you develop a DLL and try to use it to interface to Visual Basic.

4.4.3.2.6 Build and Install the Complete DLL File

Now click the Build|Build SerialDLL.dll menu item from the Visual C++ 6.0 workspace to build our dynamic link library. No error would be encountered if everything is fine. The SerialDLL.dll file will be generated in the Debug folder (you can change the Configurations by clicking Build|Set Active Configurations menu item to the Release version if you like).

In the Visual C++ domain, click the File |Open menu item to open the Open dialog box. Make sure that the project name SerialDLL is in the Look in: input field. Double-click the Debug folder from the list, and click the down-arrow from the Files of type: input field on the bottom, go all the way down until you hit the last item, All Files (*.*). Click this item and you will find the resulting DLL file SerialDLL.dll from the list. Right-click on this DLL file and click Copy from the pop up menu, and then click Cancel button to close the Open dialog box.

Open the Windows Explorer, find the newly created folder C:\stdll as we did in section 4.4.3.2.1 (You need to create this new folder in the root drive on your machine if you have not), and click this folder. Then click Edit|Paste menu item to paste the DLL file SerialDLL.dll to this folder. Now we finished building the DLL file and installing it on our newly created folder C:\stdll.

Finally, set this new folder to your system path and make it as a new system path variable to your machine. In this way, the computer can locate this DLL file when it is used by your system as your program runs. You can also save that DLL file SerialDLL.dll directly into your default system path, such as C:\WINDOWS\SYSTEM in Windows Me or C:\WINNT\System in Windows 2000. If you saved your DLL file in that way, you don't need to take care of the path and the computer can automatically locate that DLL file for you as your program runs.

Our DLL file is completed, and next we need to develop a Visual Basic project to call this DLL to interface to the serial port to finish the testing jobs.

4.4.3.3 Developing a Visual Basic Testing Project

Let us switch to Visual Basic domain to develop our Visual Basic project to call that DLL to test the serial port. In this Visual Basic project, we plan to create two forms, one is used to get the user's inputs for the COM port setup parameters, such as COM port number and baud rate, and another one is used to send commands to test the serial port.

4.4.3.3.1 Developing the Graphical User Interfaces and the Code Module

Launch Visual Basic 6.0 and create a new Standard EXE project. On the opened project, change the default form's Name from Form1 to VBSerialDLL, and set the Caption property to VB Serial Port Test DLL.

Click Project1 icon on the Project Explorer window, and enter `VBSerial` to the `Name` property of this project to change the project's name to `VBSerial.vbp`.

Now click `Project|Add Form` menu item to add another form, `Setup`, and add the controls that are listed in Table 4.45 to this form.

TABLE 4.45
Controls for the `Setup` Form

Control Type	Properties	Values	Control Type	Properties	Values
Label	Name	Label2	Text box	Name	txtBaudRate
	Caption	Port Number		Text	
Text box	Name	txtPort	CommandButton	Name	CmdOK
	Text			Caption	OK
Label	Name	Label3	Label	Name	Label1
	Caption	Baud Rate		Caption*	

*The Caption property for the control `Label1` is: Enter Setup Parameters for Serial Port.

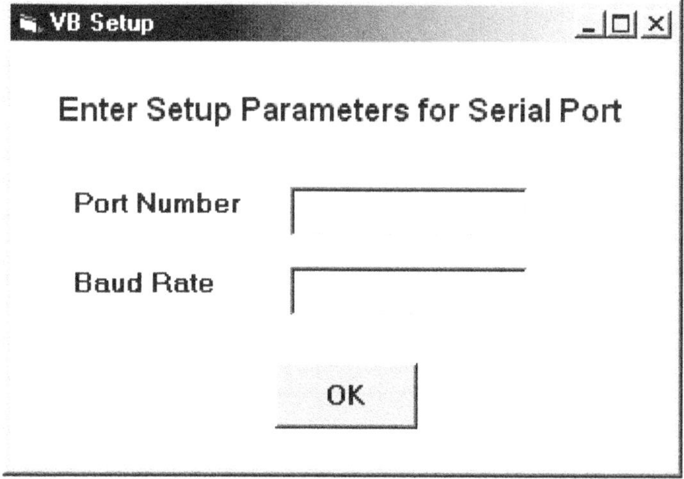

FIGURE 4.126 The `Setup` form.

Set the Form's `BackColor` property to `Yellow`. Your finished Form should match the one shown in Figure 4.126.

Besides two forms, we need to add a code module to this project. Click `Project|Add Module` menu item to add a new module named `VBSerial.bas` into this project.

Click the first form `VBSerialDLL` to select it and add the controls that are listed in Table 4.46 into this form.

Besides the controls listed in Table 4.46, we need add a timer into this form. Add a timer with the properties that are listed in Table 4.47 into the form.

Your finished form VBSerialDLL should match the one shown in Figure 4.127.

Now we have finished designing our forms. Next we need to coding for each form and code module.

TABLE 4.46
Controls for the `VBSerialDLL` Form

Control Type	Properties	Values
Label	Name	Label1
	Caption	Welcome to The Serial Port Testing DDL Project
Frame	Name	Frame1
	Caption	Port Setup
Label	Name	Label2
	Caption	COM Port
Label	Name	lblComPort
	Caption	
	BackColor	Yellow
Label	Name	Label3
	Caption	Baud Rate
Label	Name	lblBaudRate
	Caption	
	BackColor	Yellow
Frame	Name	Frame2
	Caption	Testing Data
Label	Name	Label4
	Caption	Sending Data
Text box	Name	txtWdata
	Text	
Label	Name	Label5
	Caption	Reading Data
Text box	Name	txtRdata
	Text	
CommandButton	Name	cmdSetup
	Caption	Setup
CommandButton	Name	cmdText
	Caption	Test
CommandButton	Name	cmdExit
	Caption	Exit

TABLE 4.47
Controls for the `VBSerialTimer`

Control Type	Properties	Values
Timer	Name	VBSerialTimer
	Enabled	`True`
	Interval	5000 (ms)

4.4.3.3.2 Coding of the Code Module

Open the new added code module `VBSerial` and enter the code that is shown in Figure 4.128 into this module.

Two global variables are declared in this module, `comPort` and `baudRate`. These two variables are used to hold the port number and the baud rate entered by the user on the `Setup` form as the project runs. These two parameters will be used later by another form `VBSerialDLL` to configure the serial port to be tested.

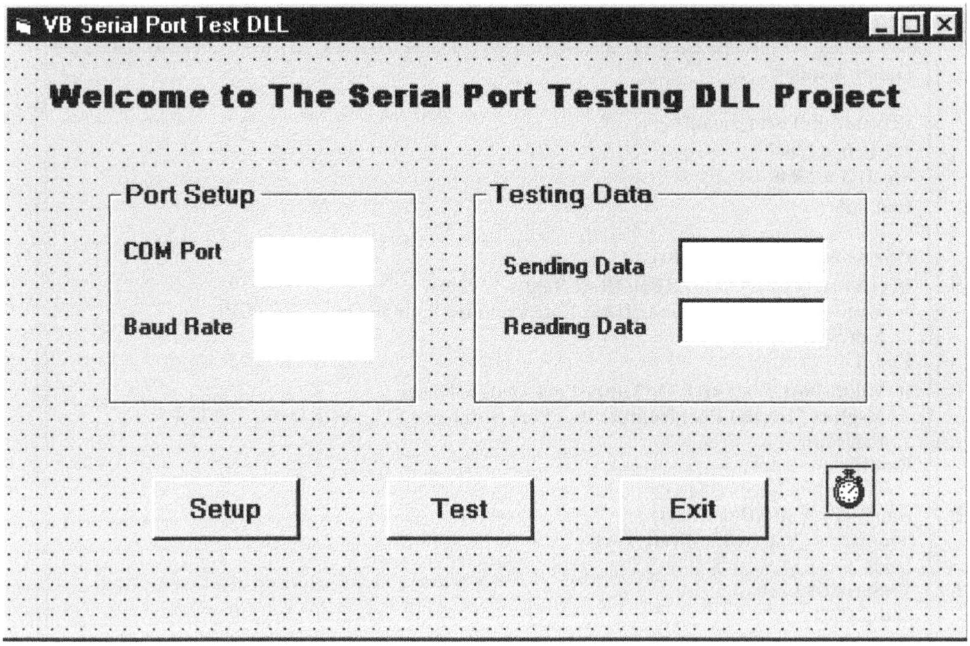

FIGURE 4.127 The `VBSerialDLL` form.

(General)	(Declarations)
Option Explicit **Public comPort As Long, baudRate As Long**	

FIGURE 4.128 The code module.

4.4.3.3.3 Coding of the Setup Form

The purpose of the `Setup` form is to collect the serial parameters entered by the user at run time and to check the correctness of those parameters. Click the `Setup` form to select it from the Project Explorer window, and click the `View Code` button to open its code window. Enter the code that is shown in Figure 4.129 into this window.

On the top line (Form's General Declaration section), type `Option Explicit`. This statement will prevent the user from using variables or controls without declaring them first.

A: The default name of the form `Me` is used to locate the `Setup` form around the center of the screen by setting its origin at 2500 pixels in both horizontal and vertical coordinates.

B: Next the form needs to determine whether the user enters two valid parameters on two text boxes, `txtPort` and `txtBaudRate`. A warning message will be displayed to reminder the user to enter those parameters if an empty result is detected for any of text boxes.

C: In this application, we defined that a valid port number should be between 1 and 4. By checking the `Text` property of both text boxes, we can identify whether the port number

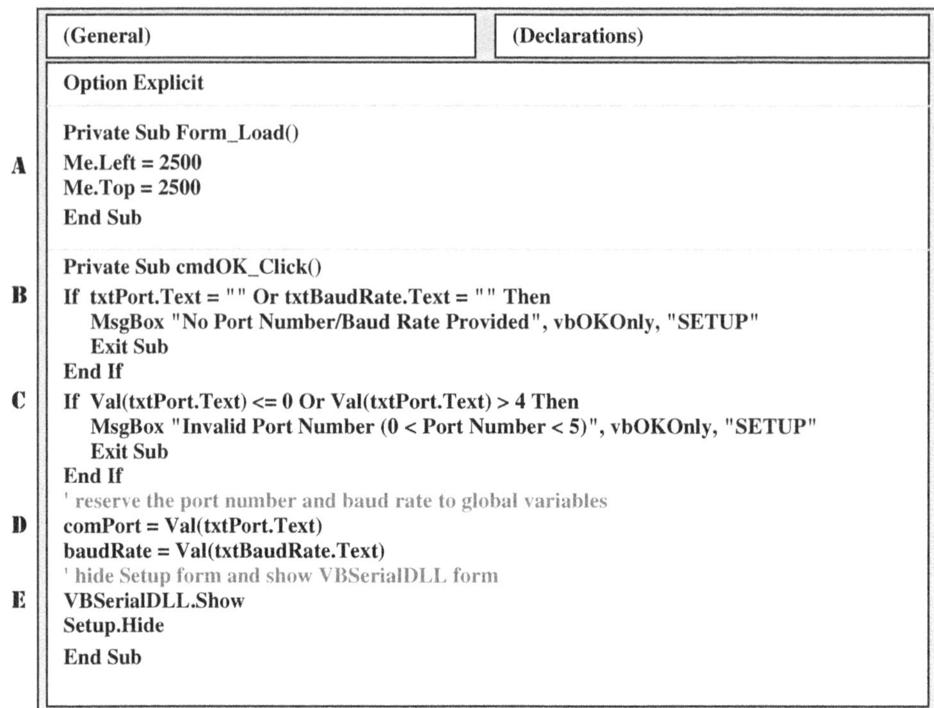

```
(General)                                  (Declarations)

Option Explicit

Private Sub Form_Load()
A  Me.Left = 2500
Me.Top = 2500
End Sub

Private Sub cmdOK_Click()
B  If txtPort.Text = "" Or txtBaudRate.Text = "" Then
     MsgBox "No Port Number/Baud Rate Provided", vbOKOnly, "SETUP"
     Exit Sub
End If
C  If Val(txtPort.Text) <= 0 Or Val(txtPort.Text) > 4 Then
     MsgBox "Invalid Port Number (0 < Port Number < 5)", vbOKOnly, "SETUP"
     Exit Sub
End If
' reserve the port number and baud rate to global variables
D  comPort = Val(txtPort.Text)
baudRate = Val(txtBaudRate.Text)
' hide Setup form and show VBSerialDLL form
E  VBSerialDLL.Show
Setup.Hide
End Sub
```

FIGURE 4.129 Code for the `Setup` form.

entered by the user is a valid value (within the range of 1 and 4). An error message will be displayed to ask the user to re-enter that value if an invalid value is encountered.

D: The valid port number and baud rate are assigned to the associated global variables `comPort` and `baudRate`. Those values will be used later in another form.

E: The mission of the `Setup` form is complete, so the `Hide` method is called to remove that form from the screen, and the `Show` method is executed to display another form, `VBSerialDLL`.

4.4.3.3.4 Coding of the VBSerialDLL Form

The `VBSerialDLL` form will send control commands to the DLL developed in Visual C++ and interface with the I/O port functions to communicate with the serial port to be tested. The interface functions developed in Visual Basic are directly connected to associated functions developed in the DLL. By using these interface functions, Visual Basic can control the low-level serial port via UART, send control commands and test data to the port, and retrieve the data from the port.

From the point of view of the functional diagram, Visual Basic just likes a headquarter that send commands to the branch departments that work as the associated functions developed in the DLL, each command issued by Visual Basic in the Visual Basic domain is exactly equivalent to a subroutine developed in the Visual C++ domain. The actual interface between the program and serial port occurs in the Visual C++ domain. Visual Basic works just as a graphical user interface and center controller that issues all different commands based on the user's inputs.

To efficiently interface or call those branch departments from the Visual Basic domain, one of the most important steps is to correctly define the interface functions developed in the Visual C++ domain in the Visual Basic domain. Because all those interface functions are used in the form `VBSerialDLL`, we can define those functions as the form-level functions in the form's `General Declaration` section. Click the `VBSerialDLL` form from the `Project Explorer` window

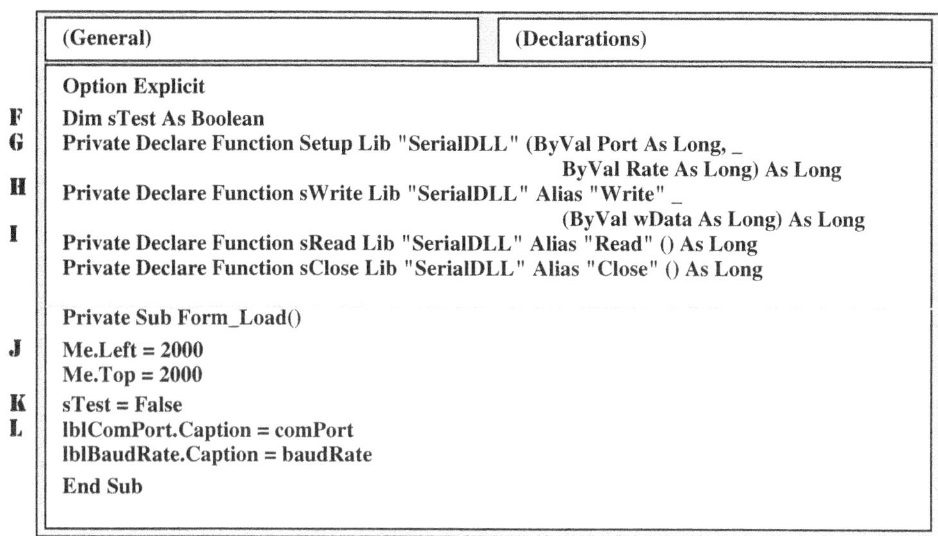

```
(General)                    (Declarations)

  Option Explicit
F Dim sTest As Boolean
G Private Declare Function Setup Lib "SerialDLL" (ByVal Port As Long, _
                                   ByVal Rate As Long) As Long
H Private Declare Function sWrite Lib "SerialDLL" Alias "Write" _
                                   (ByVal wData As Long) As Long
I Private Declare Function sRead Lib "SerialDLL" Alias "Read" () As Long
  Private Declare Function sClose Lib "SerialDLL" Alias "Close" () As Long

  Private Sub Form_Load()
J Me.Left = 2000
  Me.Top = 2000
K sTest = False
L lblComPort.Caption = comPort
  lblBaudRate.Caption = baudRate
  End Sub
```

FIGURE 4.130 Code for the `Form_Load` event procedure.

in the Visual Basic workspace, and click the `View Code` button to open its code window. Select the `(General)` item from the `Object` list to open its Form's General declaration section. Enter the code that is shown in Figure 4.130 into this section. Then select the `Form` item from the `Object` list to open its `Form_Load` event procedure. Enter the initialization codes into this `Form_Load` event procedure. Because the initialization codes are relatively simple, we coding this event procedure with the general declaration section together. Your finished coding for these two sections should match the one shown in Figure 4.130.

F: In the Form's General Declaration section, we declare a Boolean variable `sTest`, which will be used as a flag or a monitor to store the status of the current project. This flag should be reset (`False`) at the beginning of the project and should be set (`True`) if the `Test` command button is clicked at run time, which means that the project is under the testing status. Refer to Table 4.47, the `Enabled` property of the `VBSerialTimer` is set to `True`, which means that this timer is in working status as soon as the project runs. The Boolean variable `sTest` works as an indicator inside the `VBSerialTimer` event procedure to enable the timer to periodically display the sending out and receiving in data on two text boxes. Although the timer will be enabled during the whole period that the project runs, its working status is controlled by the Boolean variable `sTest`. This means that the timer can display both sending out and receiving in data only when the `sTest` is set to `True`.

G: Following the declaration the Form-level variable, four user-defined DLL functions are declared. Refer to Figure 4.2 to obtain a clear picture in declaring a DLL function in Visual Basic applications.

All DLL functions used in this project are located at a DLL file named `SerialDLL.dll`, which is developed in Visual C++ domain in the last section. The first function is `Setup()`, which is used to initialize the serial port with two major parameters, port number and the baud rate. Both parameters are integer values in Visual C++ domain, so we pass them by value and the data type is mapped to `Long` in the Visual Basic domain. This function returns an integer value (in C/C++ domain) to feedback the running status of that function to the system. A mapping of data type `Long` is applied to this returned variable, too, because the definition of the integer is 32-bit in Visual C++ and 16-bit in Visual Basic domain.

H: The second function is `Write()` function, which is used to pass an integer to the DLL function, and the latter sends the data to the serial port, exactly to the transmit buffer of the UART. The argument `wData` is mapped to a `Long` in Visual Basic. One point we want to emphasize is the function's name. Because the `Write` is a reserved keyword in Visual Basic and a system function with the same name has been defined in Visual Basic, we cannot use the same name to declare our user's function. An `Alias` clause is used here to indicate that our real function name is `Write`, but in order to avoid to conflict with the system function, a pseudo-name, `sWrite` is used to represent that real function in the program. An error message "`Expected Identifier`" will be displayed if you insist on using the real function name in this declaration.

TIP: When declaration of the DLL function in Visual Basic domain, you cannot directly use any name that has been used by Visual Basic as a reserved word or as a system function name as your function's name. You should use a `pseudo name` as your function's name with an `Alias` clause to indicate the actual name of your function if your function's name conflicts with any reserved word or name used by Visual Basic.

This function also returns an integer as the feedback to the system to show the executing result of this function call. A returned `0` means successful.

I: The next DLL function is `Read()`, which is used to read back the data from the serial port. Similarly to the `Write()` function, `Read` is also a reserved keyword in Visual Basic, so an `Alias` clause is used here, too. Our program must call the `sRead()` function in the program to access this `Read()` function to pick up the data from the serial port. A running status of this function can be returned from the calling function to the system to show the running result of that function. A returned `0` means successful. The final DLL function is `Close()`, which is used to clean up the environment setup for testing the serial port. The clean up job includes closing the reading thread. This function also needs an `Alias` clause because the `Close` is a reserved keyword in Visual Basic. A returned value is used to show the running result of this function. A returned `0` means successful.

Some readers maybe have found that the DLLs' names don't have the extension (`.dll`). That is ok if you have copied that DLL file to a searchable or a system DLL directory at your machine. Computer can automatically recognize and locate your DLL without problem.

TIP: You do not need to clearly indicate the DLL library name with the .dll extension if that DLL file has been copied into a searchable path or the system path at your machine when you declare the DLL function in Visual Basic domain.

J: The `Form_Load` event procedure is loaded and executed first when this Form is executed. Any initialization job should be performed here. We still use `Me` object (The Form itself) and its position properties (`Left` and `Top`) to set up the initial location of this Form window on the screen as it will be displayed on the system. A 2000-pixel is assigned to both horizontal and vertical coordinates of the origin to make the form locate around the center on the screen.

K: Another initialization job is to reset the flag `sTest`, to indicate to the system that the current status of the program is idle.

L: Following we need to display the current settings of the serial port with two parameters, comPort and baudRate, which are global variables. The values of those two global variables are obtained from the first Form Setup and entered by the user at run time. Later on we need these two parameters to configure the serial port by calling a DLL function Setup(). We assign these two parameters to two labels to display them on the Form.

Totally there are four event procedures applied in this project: Setup, Test, VBSerialTimer and Exit. Each of them is associated with a command button except the VBSerialTimer. We'd like to code our project based on this sequence. First let's handle the Setup event procedure.

This event procedure calls a DLL function to initialize the serial port with two parameters, comPort and baudRate. The procedure also needs to check the returned status of that DLL function to make sure that the DLL function is executed successfully. An error message should be displayed on the screen to warn the user if this function encountered any mistake, which is indicated with a nonzero returned value.

Click the cmdSetup item from the Object list to open the Setup event procedure, and enter the code that is shown in Figure 4.131.

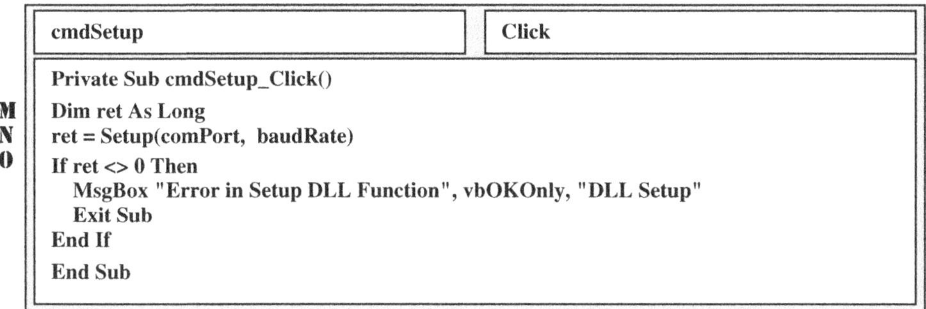

```
cmdSetup                    Click

  Private Sub cmdSetup_Click()
M Dim ret As Long
N ret = Setup(comPort, baudRate)
O If ret <> 0 Then
     MsgBox "Error in Setup DLL Function", vbOKOnly, "DLL Setup"
     Exit Sub
  End If
  End Sub
```

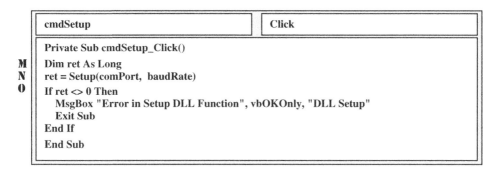

FIGURE 4.131 Code for the Setup event procedure.

M: A local variable, ret, is declared at the beginning of this procedure, which is used to store and reserve the returned status of executing the DLL function. The variable type is Long, which is to match the definition of integers in Visual C++.

N: Then the DLL Setup() function is called with two global variables to initialize the serial port.

O: When the function returns, we need to check its returned status to make sure the correctness of executing that function. A 0 will be returned if this calling has been successful, otherwise an error message would be displayed on the screen and the program would exit the event procedure.

The coding for the Test command button event procedure is very simple. When the Test command button is clicked at run time, the sTest flag should be set, and this informs the system that the current program's status is testing. Click the cmdTest item from the Object list to open its event procedure, and enter the code that is shown in Figure 4.132 into this procedure.

The set of the flag sTest is used to inform the Timer VBSerialTimer to begin to periodically execute the DLL functions Write() and Read() to test the serial port. The body of the VBSerialTimer event procedure is shown in Figure 4.133.

P: Two local variables, ret and randNum, are declared at the beginning of this procedure. The first variable is used to store and reserve the returned status of the DLL functions,

cmdTest	Click

```
Private Sub cmdTest_Click()
sTest = True
End Sub
```

FIGURE 4.132 Code for the `Test` event procedure.

VBSerialTimer	Timer

```
  Private Sub VBSerialTimer_Timer()
P Dim ret As Long, randNum As Long
  ' create a random number with a range of 0 ~ 100
Q randNum = Int((100 + 1) * Rnd)
R If sTest = True Then
      txtWdata.Text = randNum
      ret = sWrite(randNum)
S     If ret <> 0 Then
         MsgBox "Error in Write DLL Function", vbOKOnly, "DLL Write"
         Exit Sub
     End If
T    ret = sRead()
     txtRdata.Text = ret
U    If ret <> randNum Then
        MsgBox "Serial Port Test Error: Data is Not Match", vbOKOnly, "DLL Read"
        Exit Sub
     End If
  End If
  End Sub
```

FIGURE 4.133 Code for the `VBSerialTimer` event procedure.

and the second one is used to store a random data that is created by calling the `Rnd` function defined in Visual Basic. Both variables are integers in C/C++, a `Long` type is used here to map them to the integers in Visual Basic domain.

Q: We want to use a sequence of random numbers to test the serial port, so we create this random sequence by calling the `Rnd` system function. The `Rnd` creates a random number in a double type, and therefore we need to use a built-in function `Int()` to cast and convert it to an integer value. The range of this random sequence is between 0 and 100. Of course you can make your selection for this range based on your applications.

R: After a random data is created, the Timer needs to check the current status of the program by inspecting the flag `sTest`. As mentioned earlier, this flag should be set if the user clicked the `Test` command button, which means that the current program is in testing status.

If this flag has been set, the Timer will begin to execute the test task. First the random number is sent to the text box `txtWdata` to be displayed on that text box. Then the DLL function `sWrite()` is called and the random number is passed into the DLL, in which the random data is finally sent to the serial port by a driver function defined in the DLL.

S: Next the Timer should check the status of executing that DLL function by inspecting the returned value `ret`. A `0` will be returned if the function call has been successful, otherwise an error message will be displayed on the screen and the program exits the procedure.

T: If everything is normal, the Timer calls the DLL function `sRead()` to read back the random data sent to the serial port. The returned data will be displayed on screen in the `txtRdata` text box.

U: Finally, the Timer needs to check the testing result by comparing the sent out data and the read back data. If the data strings are identical, it means that the test has been successful; otherwise, the testing has failed. In this case, an error message will appear onscreen and the program will exit the procedure.

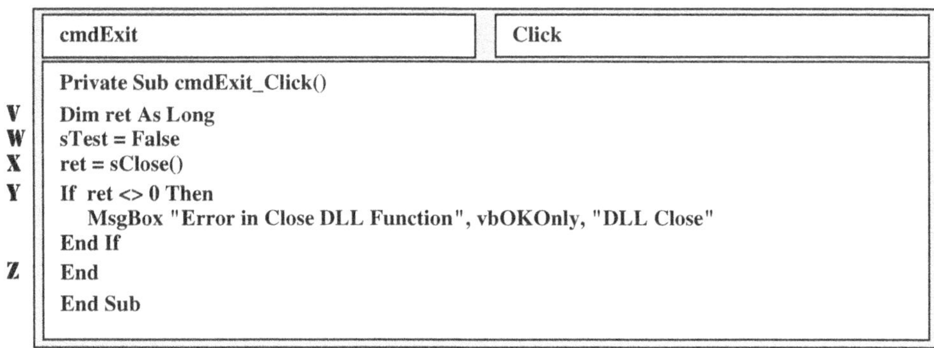

```
cmdExit                                   Click

  Private Sub cmdExit_Click()
V Dim ret As Long
W sTest = False
X ret = sClose()
Y If  ret <> 0 Then
     MsgBox "Error in Close DLL Function", vbOKOnly, "DLL Close"
  End If
Z End
  End Sub
```

FIGURE 4.134 Code for the `Exit` event procedure.

The last event procedure we need to code is the `Exit`. This procedure cleans up the settings of the serial port by executing the DLL function `sClose()`. Open this event procedure and enter the code that is shown in Figure 4.134 into this procedure.

V: A local variable `ret` is declared first. This variable is used to store the running status of the DLL function `sClose()`.

W: Then the program's flag sTest is reset. This is a very important step. Without this step, the flag would be still in set status, and therefore the timer would continue to call DLL functions to send out and read back data from the serial port. In other words, the timer event procedure will continue to run even the user clicked the `Exit` command button and wants to stop the testing program. After this flag is reset, the timer will be informed that the testing is done and the timer event procedure should be terminated.

X: After the timer event procedure is terminated, a DLL function `sClose()` is called to clean up the environment setup made by the DLL functions during the testing process in Visual C++ domain. Similarly to other DLL function calls, a check of the returned status is performed to make sure that the function call has been successful.

Y: If the `sClose()` function call has been unsuccessful, an error message will be displayed on the screen.

Z: The `End` statement is used to terminate the project.

At this point, we finished developing the Visual Basic serial port test project.

Before we can run this project to test the serial port, we have to make sure that the DLL file is correctly installed on the machine at the correct location. You have three ways to do that: You can install the DLL file in a searchable path, or in the system DLL path on your machine, or you can directly copy the DLL file onto your current project folder. In our application, we install our DLL file on one of searchable paths, `C:\stdll`, in our computer. Make sure that you do this job correctly before you can run this project, otherwise you may encounter some potential problems as your project runs.

4.4.3.3.5 Test and Implementation of the Project

Now let us test our project by pressing `F5` key from the keyboard. As your project runs, the first form `Setup` is displayed on the screen. Enter the setup parameters, 1 for the `comPort` and 9600 for the `baudRate`, to the associated text boxes, which is shown in Figure 4.135.

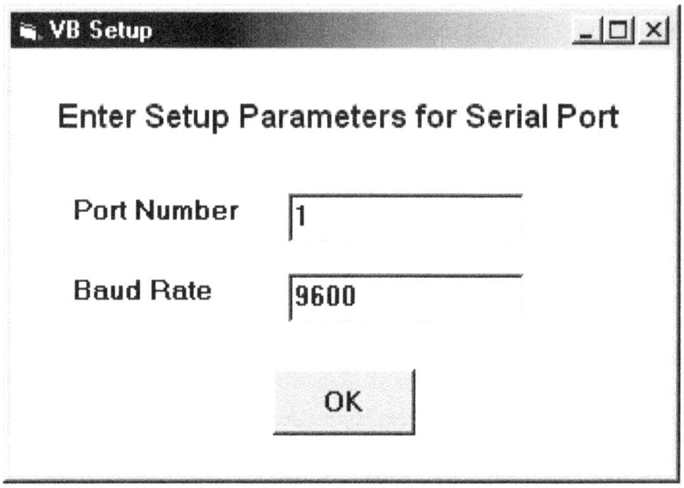

FIGURE 4.135 Running status of the `Setup` form.

In our application, the available port is `COM1` and the baud rate we selected is `9600`. You can select different parameters based on your system. Click the `OK` button to continue the project.

The second form in our project, `VBSerialDLL`, is displayed on the screen, which is shown in Figure 4.136.

Notice that two parameters we entered on the last form have been displayed on two labels in the `Port Setup` information box. Click the `Setup` command button to call the DLL function `Setup()` to initialize the serial port with these two parameters. Then click `Test` button to begin the testing.

As the test begins, random data is created and sent to the serial port. The data is displayed in the text box with a label of `Sending Data`. The read back data is displayed on the bottom text box labeled with `Reading Data`. The interval between displaying these two data is about 500 milliseconds, or maybe a little longer. You can find that the sending out data is exactly identical to the reading back data, which means that the serial port works fine and our testing has been successful. The running result is shown in Figure 4.137.

Occasionally an error message may be displayed to indicate that the port testing has not been successful, and that is understandable. Because the chance for a real error occurring in the serial port application did exist in the real world. Sometimes an error doesn't mean that the error comes from the serial port itself, and it may be introduced by some disturbances or magnetic field around the computer system. Anyway, the chance of that kind of error is very small.

All files of this project, including the DLL source files, header file, DEF file and DLL file, Visual Basic source files, Code Module and executable file, are located at the attached CD ROM in the folder `Chapter 4\VBSerialDLL`. The DLL file `SerialDLL.dll` and its associated source files are

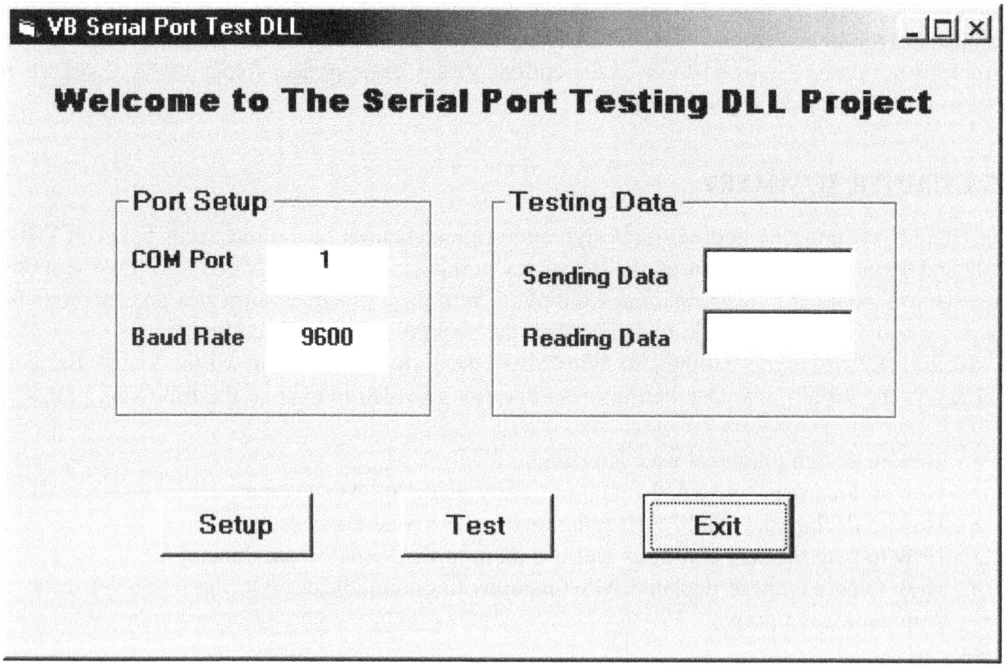

FIGURE 4.136 Running status of the `VBSerialDLL` form.

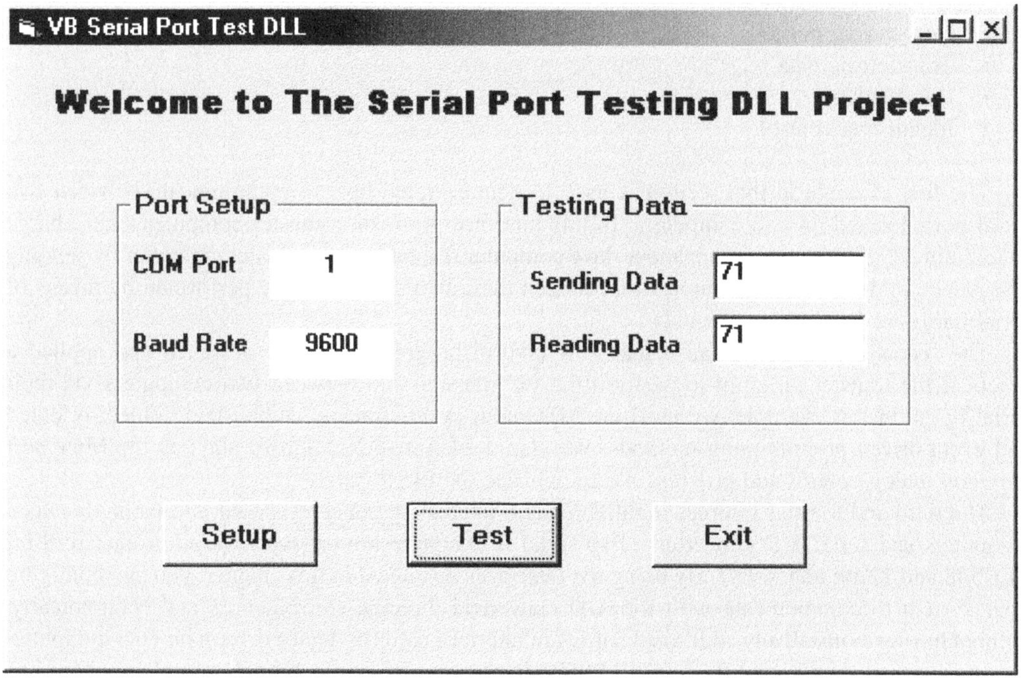

FIGURE 4.137 Running status of the `VBSerialDLL` form.

stored in the folder `SerialDLL` that is under this folder. You can copy these files to your local machine and run it. You should copy the DLL file `SerialDLL.dll` to a searchable folder at your system (in our case, `C:\stdll`) or to the current Visual Basic project folder `VBSerialDLL` in order to run this project on your computer.

4.5 CHAPTER SUMMARY

This chapter has concentrated on the design and implementation of the interfaces between Visual Basic and serial communication ports. The topics in this chapter were divided into three sections. Each section included at least one real example to introduce practical strategies and methods for designing and applying the code to accomplish the desired serial interface functions.

Section 4.2 discussed calling the Win32 API DLL functions from within Visual Basic to interface to the serial ports. Detailed information was provided to explain the following points:

- How to design graphical user interfaces
- How to load the Win32 API function library using the API Viewer
- How to declare the Win32 API functions in the Visual Basic domain
- How to map the API constants and use them in the Visual Basic domain
- How to access those declared API functions to communicate with the low-level serial communication ports

Section 4.3 introduced an Active-X control, MSComm, and presented four examples. The features and properties of the MSComm control were explained, and our discussion focused on four main procedures:

- Configuring ports
- Transferring data
- Handshaking
- Identifying control

The first example in this section is used to demonstrated how to communicate between two serial ports located on two computers. In this interface protocol, a master computer takes charge of initiating data communication, and a slave computer responds to the master computer by sending a sequence of data. The communication between these two computers are performed by means of serial hardware handshaking signals.

The second example was an actual flow control program. Here we designed and applied a practical file transfer program to perform the file transmission between two computers via their serial ports. In this example, we used the MSComm event strategy, emphasizing object-oriented and event-driven programming methods. We also used Active-X controls, such as the Microsoft common dialog control and progress bar to enhance the file transfer.

The third and fourth examples highlighted two interesting concepts: serial interfacing between computers and serial A/D converters. Two serial A/D conversion products were introduced: 8-bit TLC548 and 12-bit MAX-187. By using the interfaces discussed in this chapter, you can configure your system to communicate with the A/D converters directly, conveniently, and economically, without having to install any additional hardware interface cards or device drivers on your computer. An interface between Visual Basic and MATLAB was presented in our third example to show you how to plot the collected data in the MATLAB domain by calling an Active-X control from your Visual Basic applications. Another Active-X control, Microsoft Chart Control, was introduced in the fourth example to show you how to plot the collected data in the Visual Basic domain.

Section 4.4 introduced another way to access the serial port from within the Visual Basic domain: the Dynamic Link Library, or DLL. By calling the interface functions developed in the

DLL, Visual Basic can access the low-level serial hardware. This method provides a convenient way to perform real-time data acquisition and measurement from within the Visual Basic domain. The real-time work is accomplished by the DLL functions in the Visual C++ domain, and Visual Basic provides a very professional and friendly graphical user interface. All example codes have been tested and debugged, and you can directly load those programs and test them on your machine.

5 Serial Port Programming in LabVIEW

5.1 INTRODUCTION

LabVIEW is a powerful tool for implementing real-time testing and measurement in academic and industrial applications. Serial data communication is crucial in these and many other fields, and serial devices are now standard components of almost every PC. Most computers include two RS-232-based serial ports. Serial communication is also commonly used for instrumentation; numerous GPIB-compatible devices also come with RS-232 ports. Serial communication is often used for data acquisition in conjunction with a remote sampling device.

In the early days, the LabVIEW product used some traditional VIs to perform serial port interfacing and communications; these included `Open Serial Driver.vi`, which was used to open serial ports, `Serial Port Read.vi`, which was used to read a sequence of data from an open serial port, and the `Serial Port Write.vi`, which was used to write data to an open serial port. Today, most of those VIs have been removed and replaced by a new standard called *virtual instrument software architecture* (VISA). VISA is a single interface library for controlling VXI, GPIB, RS-232, and other types of instruments on all LabVIEW platforms. VISA is a standard endorsed by the Plug and Play Systems Alliance, which includes more than 35 of the largest instrumentation companies in the industry. The VISA standard has unified the industry to make software interpretable and reusable over time, regardless of instrument I/O operations.

LabVIEW provides different levels of VI designed to simplify serial interfaces and applications in the real world. The fundamental VIs are used to make interfacing programs easy to write and use. The advanced serial VIs enable developers to select more control options, thus making interface program design more flexible.

In this chapter, we'll concentrate on the VISA standard and discuss the design and application of the serial port interface, using the examples developed with VIs that belong to the VISA library.

In Section 5.2, a basic VISA serial interface example is introduced. The example project is a loopback serial port testing program, and some basic VISA VIs are used for this example. Advanced serial port interface programs are discussed in Section 5.3. Two examples are provided in this section to illustrate the serial communications between the serial A/D converters and the RS-232 port. The first example is an 8-bit serial A/D converter, TLC548, and the second one is a 12-bit serial A/D converter, MAX187. In Section 5.4, we'll explore how to perform serial port interfacing by calling the control program written in external programming language. Such calling methods are divided into two categories: Calling the shared DLL, which is described in Section 5.4, and calling the Code Interface Node from within the LabVIEW domain, which is described in Section 5.5. Section 5.6 discusses some other methods for interfacing with the serial ports from LabVIEW.

5.2 A BASIC SERIAL PORT INTERFACE FOR WRITING AND READING DATA

In this section, a basic serial port interface program is discussed. The project is a loopback testing program and it is used to test and confirm that the serial port installed at your computer works fine.

The hardware connection is simple, which is to connect the TD terminal (pin 3) and the RD terminal (pin 2) together on a DB-9 serial connector. For the DB-25 connector, the similar connection is needed. In this way, the data transmission terminal is connected back to the data reception terminal, and the sent-out data should be identical with the received data if the serial port is errorfree during the testing process.

Connect pin 2 and pin 3 together on either a DB-9 or a DB-25 serial connector to make our testing ready. We need to develop a LabVIEW program to perform this loopback test.

5.2.1 Designing the Front Panel for the Loopback Testing Program

The front panel is divided into three sections:

- The serial port setup section, which includes the port configuration parameters and the testing success and failure LED indicators.
- The data writing section, which includes the write-out switch controller, the number of written data units, the value of the written data, and the writing progress indicator (indicates the percentage of data that has been sent).
- The data reading section, which includes the read-in switch controller, the number of bytes to be read, the received data, and the reading progress indicator.

These three sections will be embedded into three raised boxes on the front panel. Now we will set up the LabVIEW development environment.

Launch LabVIEW 7.0 Express and open a new VI. On the new opened VI, click the `Window|Show Tools Palette` item to display the Tools Palette dialog box (Figure 5.1(c)). Then click the `Window|Show Block Diagram` item to open its block diagram window.

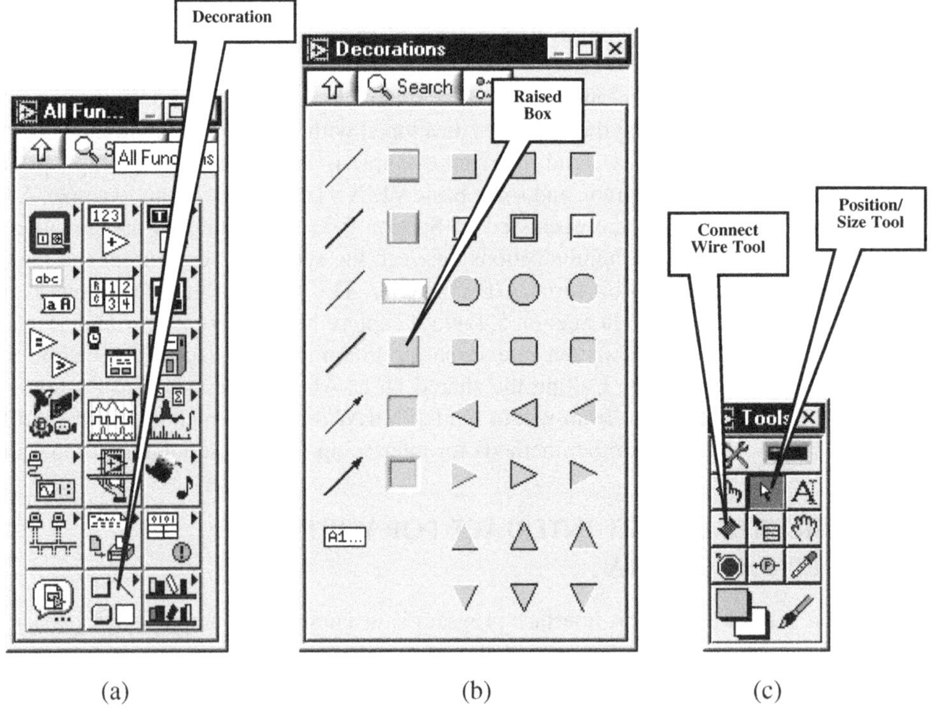

FIGURE 5.1 The Controls and Tools Palette.

Similarly, click the Window|Show Functions Palette from the Block Diagram window to open the Function Palette, which is shown in Figure 5.1(a). Now we have five windows/dialog boxes opened and we did need them to develop our LabVIEW example program.

Select Raised Box from the Decorations dialog box (see Figure 5.1), and drag it into the panel. You need to add three raised boxes as background container to hold three sections we discussed earlier. At run time, the first raised box will be used to configure the serial ports. Add the following controls to the first raised box:

- A VISA serial name input box (to display the serial port ID)
- Four numeric controls (for setting serial port configuration parameters)
- Two Round LED indicators (to indicate success or failure of the test)

At run time, the second raised box will control the data writing process. Add the following controls into the second raised box:

- A vertical toggle switch (to start or stop data writing)
- A numeric control (for setting the number of data to be written to the port)
- A numeric indicator (for displaying the value of data to be written)
- A horizontal graduated bar (to indicate the progress of data transmission)

At run time, the third raised box will control the data reading process. Add the following controls to the third raised box:

- A vertical toggle switch (to start or stop data reading)
- A numeric control (for setting the number of bytes to be received from the port)
- A numeric indicator (for displaying the value of data to be received)
- A horizontal graduated bar (to indicate the progress of data reception)

The finished front panel for this project should match one that is shown in Figure 5.2. The default setup parameters are shown in Figure 5.2. Modify all the labels in your own front panel to match those shown here.

Click the File|Save menu item in the front panel to save this project as BasicSerial.vi. Next we need to develop the programming codes for this project. In LabVIEW, the programming codes are represented by a sequence of block diagram because LabVIEW is a graphical programming language. The coding process is to design the block diagram in the Block Diagram Window.

5.2.2 Designing a Block Diagram for the Loopback Testing Program

Open the Block Diagram window by clicking the Window|Show Block Diagram menu item from the front panel. Recall that this program will repeatedly send a sequence of random numbers to the port's transmitting buffer, and at the same time, read the data back from the port's receiving buffer. (For this program, the transmission terminal is connected to the reception). The test will be successful if the sent and receivd data segments are identical.

The completed block diagram for this project is shown in Figure 5.3.

A For loop is used to repeatedly send a sequence of random numbers to the transmit buffer. The numeric control # of Data is used to define the cycle times of the loop, which is connected to the loop upper bound N. A VISA Configure Serial Port VI is used to accept the port setup parameters entered by the user, and to configure the serial port. The output of that VISA Configure Serial Port VI is the duplicate VISA resource name that works as a serial port ID. This serial port ID can be used by all other controls in this project to identify that port.

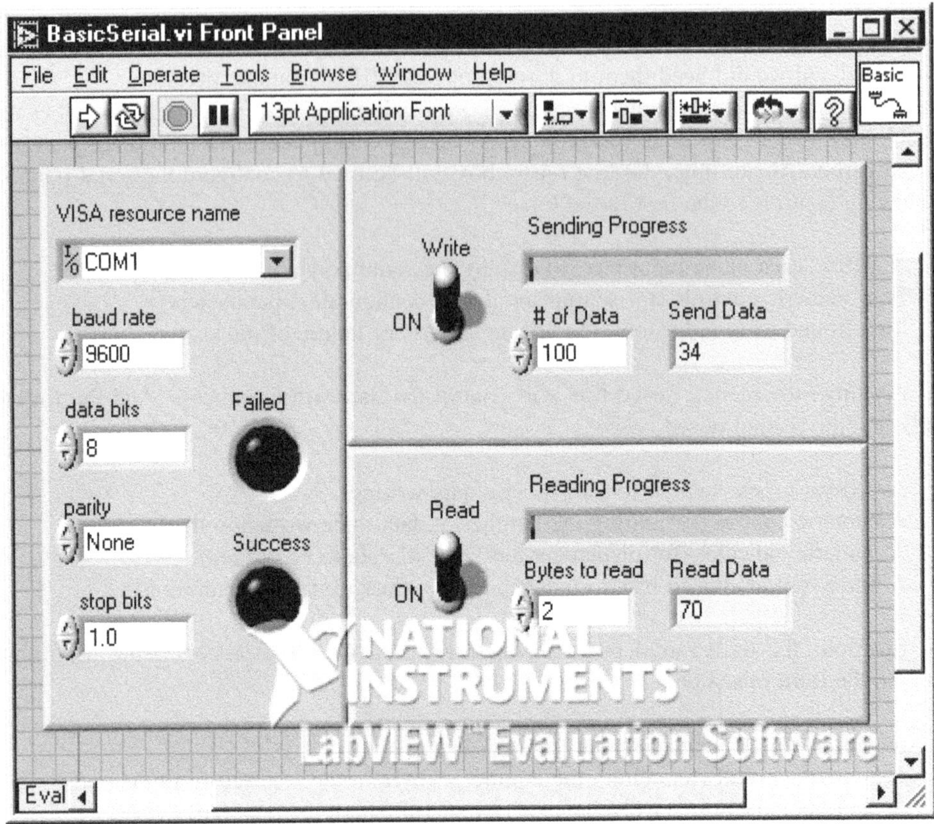

FIGURE 5.2 The finished front panel of the project.

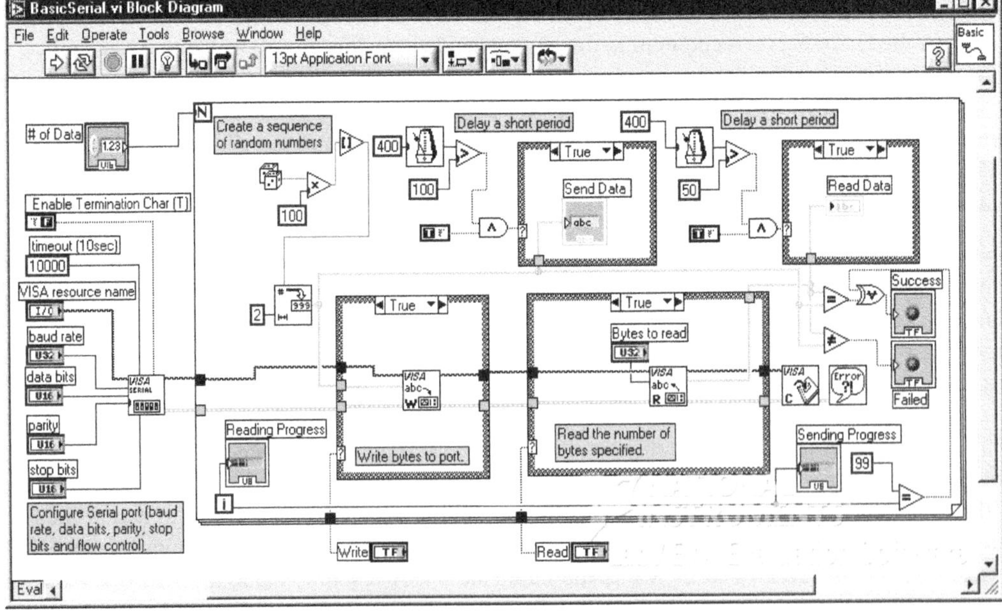

FIGURE 5.3 The completed block diagram of the project.

Inside the For loop, four case structures are used. The two lower case structures are controlled by two vertical toggle switches, Write and Read. If the switches are set to True, a VISA Write VI is used in the first structure to write the data produced by the random number generator to the serial port. The input of this VISA Write VI is coming from the output of the previous VI, VISA Configure Serial Port, which provides a valid serial port ID. This serial port ID is translated to the next VI, VISA Read in the second Case Structure, as the input to that VI. The VISA Read VI repeatedly reads back the data from the serial port. Each time the length of the data to be read is controlled by the numeric control Bytes to read in the reading section in the front panel. Currently the value of this Bytes to read is set to 2 because the range of the random numbers we created is between 1 and 100, which is a two-digit number.

When data is sent to the port, a numeric indicator named Send Data is used to display the data in real time. Similarly, when data is read back from the port, another numeric indicator named Read Data is used to display the received data in real time. Both numeric indicators are programmed inside two case structures. the reason for that is because of the timing issue. In the block diagram, the program order is: first the data is sent out, and then the data is read back. But in the real situation, especially when the program runs, the write and read operation does not always follow this order. In order to solve this order problem, two Wait Until Next ms Multiple VIs are used to delay processing by a certain period of time. The upper boundary of the delay time is used to control two case structures in which the numeric indicators Send Data and the Read Data are embedded. If the sending delay time is up, the Send Data case structure is set to True, and the sending data is displayed in that indicator. Similarly, if the reading delay time is up, the Read Data case structure is set to True and the read data is displayed in the associated indicator. A comparator is used to compare the upper boundary and the lower boundary of the time delay value.

A Random Number (0-1) VI is used to create a sequence of random numbers for this testing. The default VI can only create a sequence of random numbers between 0 and 1. In order to obtain a sequence of random number with a range of between 1 and 100 (2-digit), the default sequence is multiplied by a constant 100 using a multiplier. This random number sequence is a floating-point type, so a Round To Nearest VI is used to convert that floating-point sequence to the integer random number sequence because we want to send an integer sequence to the serial port.

The VISA Write VI can only accept the string input, so a Number To Decimal String VI is used to convert that integer random sequence to the string random sequence. The width input on the Number To Decimal String VI should be 2 because each element in the random sequence is a 2-digit integer.

After each data segment is sent out and read back, we need to compare both data to confirm whether the test is successful or not. An Equal? and a Not Equal? VI is used to perform these comparisons. The comparison result is connected to Success and Failed LED, respectively. If both data is identical, the Equal? comparator outputs a True, which activates the Success LED, otherwise, the Failed LED is on, which means that both data is not equal and the test is failed.

Maybe you have found that there is a problem for the Success LED. If the test is successful, this LED is set to on and this on will be kept even the project is complete. This situation will continue until the next time when you run the project again for another testing. This is no good for a real testing project because nobody wants to keep that LED on forever. To solve that problem, an Exclusive Or VI is added. One of inputs to that Exclusive Or VI is coming from an Equal? comparator that is used to compare the loop counter with a constant 99 which is the upper boundary of the For loop. If the upper boundary is reached, which means that all 100 random data units (0-99) have been sent out and read back, the Equal? tool outputs a True. If the test result is successful, its Equal? comparator will also output a True. Both True makes the Exclusive Or VI output a False. This False turns the Success LED off.

The testing progress can be expressed by two Horizontal Graduated Bar VIs, Sending Progress and Reading Progress. These two VIs are connected to the For loop counter i.

During the testing process, these two VIs can display the percentage of data that has been sent and the data has been read.

After all data is sent to the port and read back from the port, a VISA `Close` VI is used to close the opened serial port. A `Simple Error Handler.vi` is also used to monitor and process any possible error occurred during the testing process.

You can modify the `# of Data` value, the time delay value, and the serial port setup parameters to match the requirements for your applications.

At this point, the coding for this testing project is complete. We are ready to run and test the project.

5.2.3 Running and Testing the Loopback Testing Program

Go to the front panel of the project, and click the `Run` button to start the project. The running status of this project is shown in Figure 5.4.

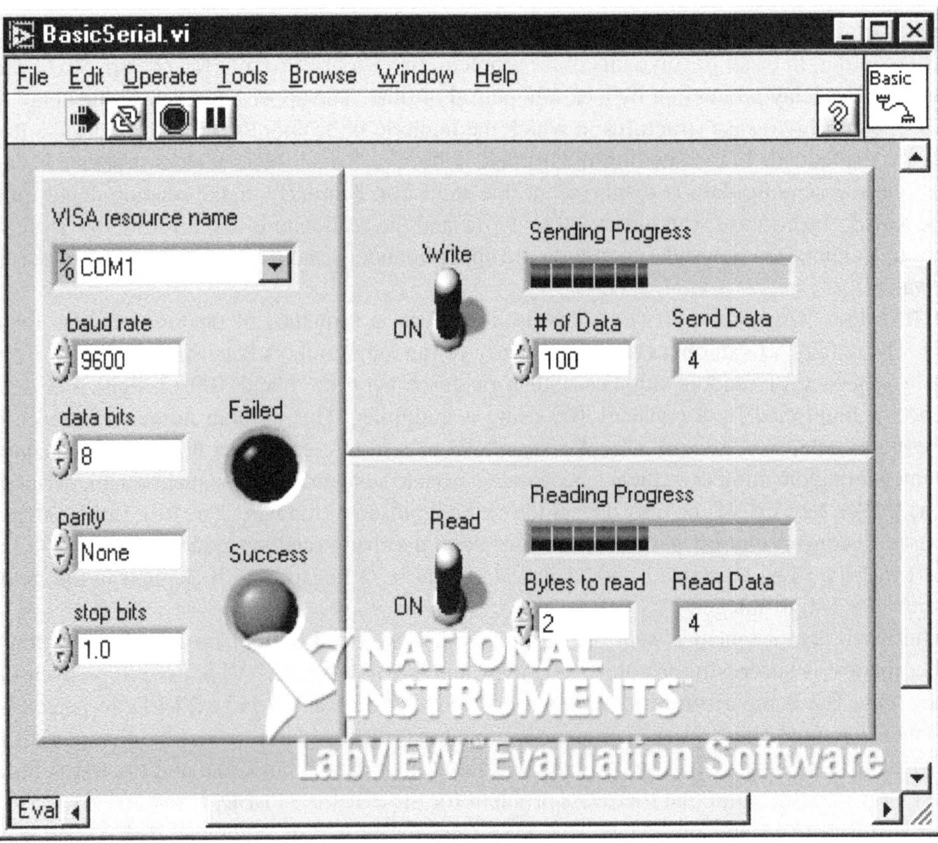

FIGURE 5.4 Results of running the loopback testing project.

As the project runs, the sent-out data is displayed in the `Send Data` indicator and the received data is displayed in the `Read Data` indicator. Both the `Sending Progress` and the `Reading Progress` bars display the percentage of data that has been sent and has been received. If the send-out data is identical with the read-back data, the `Success` LED is set to on, as shown in Figure 5.4.

Our first project is successful.

The complete project files, including the front panel and the block diagram files, are stored on the attached CD under the folder `Chapter 5\BasicSerial`. You can download this project and test it on your computer. You need first to install the serial connector on your computer and make it as a loopback test mode.

5.3 ADVANCED SERIAL PORT INTERFACES

In this section, we discuss two kinds of serial A/D converters that can be interfaced to the RS-232 port using the LabVIEW programming language.

5.3.1 Using VISA to Interface with an 8-Bit Serial A/D Converter, TLC548

Unlike the example we discussed in the last section, which used the basic VISA components to perform the serial data communications, this one will use the advanced VISA components to control serial data transfer between the computer and the A/D converter. Interface programming for the advanced or high-level components is associated with the different VIs used for each component. Typically, high-level programming is easier than low-level programming. LabVIEW programming is divided into different levels. Each level is determined by the VI level you are using in your program. For example, in the `Instrument I/O|VISA` library, a sequence of simple VISA VIs is provided for the users to help you perform basic serial I/O operations, such as VISA `Read`, VISA `Write`, and VISA `Clear`. Besides those simple VISA VIs, LabVIEW provides an additional VI library named VISA `Advanced`, shown in Figure 5.5(a).

The VISA `Advanced` library provides additional VIs that supports more complicated interface designs and applications, such as VISA `Open`, VISA `Close`, VISA `Find Resource`, VISA `Configure Serial Port`, VISA `Bytes` at `Serial Port`, and VISA `Serial Break`. Most of these advanced VIs are listed in Figure 5.5.

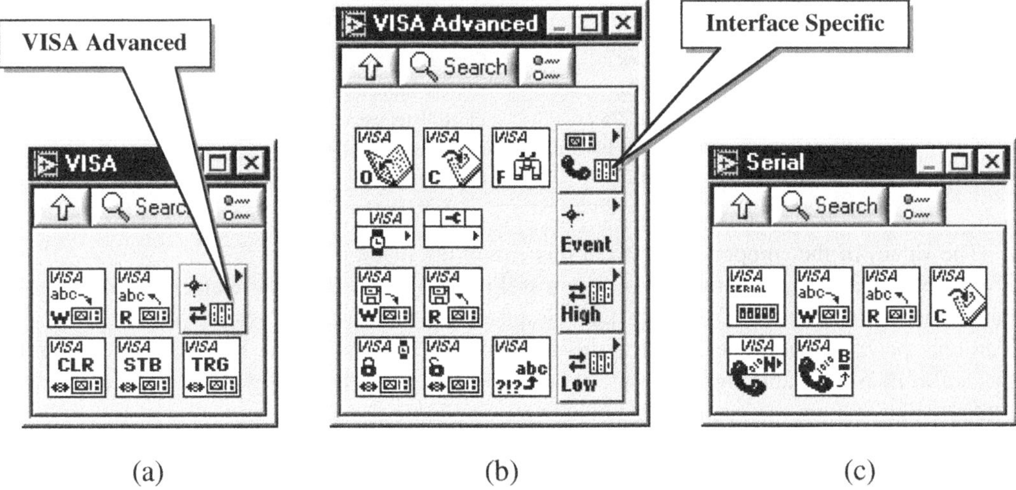

FIGURE 5.5 The basic and advanced VISA VIs.

The difference between the basic and advanced level VISA VIs is that for the basic level VISA VIs, only limited terminals or interfaces are provided to the user, and most low-level funtions are controlled or selected by the system by using the default parameters. But for the advanced level VISA VIs, most terminals and interfaces are released to the user to let us make direct control selections. This arrangement gives us maximum control over the low-level components and, therefore, provides the ability to design sophisticated interface applications.

The serial A/D converter we used in this section is an eight-bit serial A/D converter TLC548. (Refer to Section 2.7.1.1 and Figures 2.49 and 2.51 in Chapter 2 to get more detailed information about the TLC548 A/D converter). For your convenience, the interface circuit is redrawn in Figure 5.6.

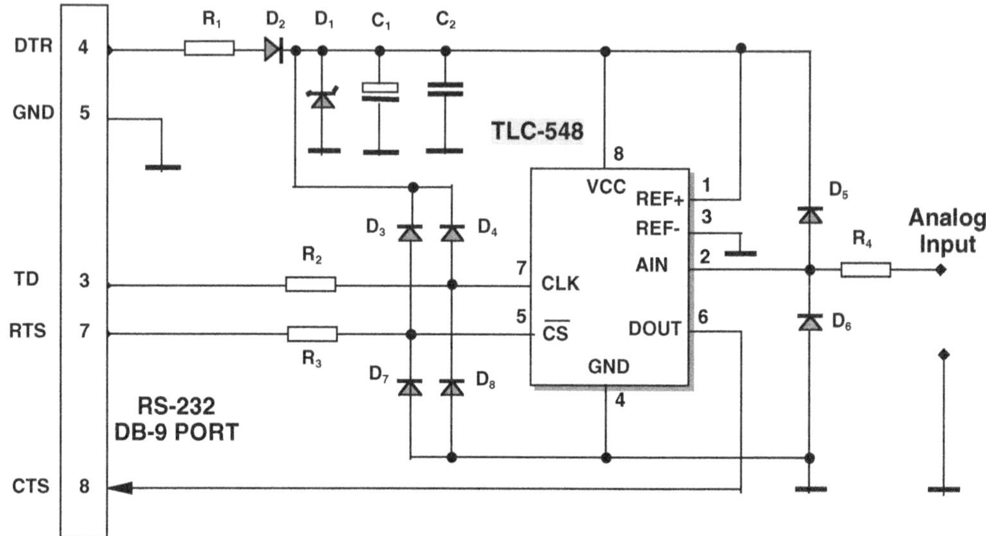

FIGURE 5.6 Interface circuit of the TLC548 A/D converter.

TABLE 5.1
The Elements Parameters

Elements	Values	Comments
R_1	10 KΩ	Current-limited resistor
$C_1 \sim C_4$	10 μF/25V	Electrolytic capacitors
$C_5 \sim C_6$	4.7 μF/10V	Electrolytic capacitors
$C_7 \sim C_8$	0.1 μF	Capacitors

The values of the components used in this circuit are listed in Table 5.1.

Make the hardware connection as shown in Figure 5.6 based on the elements parameters in Table 5.1. One advantage of this interface circuit is that this interface circuit does not need any additional power supply. The circuit is driven by the DTR signal in the RS-232 port. This DTR line can work as an enable signal and the circuit can work properly as long as the DTR line outputs a `HIGH` value. So we can use this line to activate or disable the circuit.

The RTS line works as the Chip Select (CS) signal to select and enable the TLC548 to begin to convert the analog input signal. As long as the power and the CS signal are activated, the TLC548 can immediately begin to convert the analog input automatically under the control of the internal control unit and the on-chip clock. To retrieve the converted result, an external I/O clock is needed. Here the TD line is used as the I/O clock to serially transfer the converted result from the DOUT of the TLC548, which is connected to the CTS line on the serial port, to the CTS transmission line of the RS-232 serial port. So the output rate is controlled by the frequency of the TD signal.

Now let's begin to develop this example program. We divide this program into two sections, the main program and the data collection subroutine, and each section is associated to a VI. The main program is used to manage and keep the whole project working properly, and the data collection subroutine is used to collect the converted data from the serial A/D converter TLC548.

First we need to design the graphic user interface that is equivalent to the panel in the LabVIEW environment.

5.3.1.1 Designing a Front Panel for the Main Program

Launch LabVIEW 7.0 Express and create a new project by completing the following steps:

- Double-click the `LabVIEW 7.0` icon on the desktop
- Click the `Start Using LabVIEW` item that is located at the lower-right corner of the LabVIEW startup window
- Click the `New...` button
- Click the `OK` button that is located at the lower-right corner of the `New` dialog box

A new LabVIEW project is created.

We need to add the following items into this panel:

1. One lowered rounded box for the label
2. Two raised boxes to be used as background containers
3. Six numeric control boxes that will store the serial communication parameters
4. Two text arrays that will hold the serial I/O port ID and the collected data
5. One waveform chart control that will display the collected data

Now let's add each component to the panel, one by one.

First from the opened `Controls Palette` shown in Figure 5.7 (a), select `Decorations|Lowered Rounded Box`, shown in Figure 5.7 (b), and drag the new box to the top of the panel. Click the `Position/Size` tool from the `Tools Palette` shown in Figure 5.7 (c), and click the `Rounded Box` option. Then, from the background color pad on the `Tools Palette` shown in Figure 5.7 (c) select `yellow` as the background color for the rounded box. Select the `Edit Text` tool from the `Tools Palette`, and enter the following text to label the rounded box:

Serial A/D Converter Testing—TLC548 8-Bit A/D Converter

Next select `Raised Box` from the `Decorations` dialog box shown in Figure 5.7 (b) and drag it into the panel. You need to add two of these boxes because we'll need two background containers.

Select the `Numeric Control` option from the `Control Palette`. We need a total of six numeric controls, so you need to add them one by one.

Next you need to add two text arrays into the panel. The first one is used to select and reserve the serial I/O port ID, and the second is used to reserve the collected data from the TLC548.

Finally you need to add a waveform chart control to the panel; this control will display the collected data.

Your finished panel should match one that is shown in Figure 5.8.

The label for each numeric and text box is shown in Figure 5.8. You should modify all labels to make them identical with those displayed in the figure. For the X-axis scale of the waveform chart, you need to set the `Minimum` and the `Maximum` properties to `0` and `6`, respectively. To do this, right-click the waveform chart and select the `X Scale|Formatting` item from the pop-up menu; this will open the `Chart Properties` dialog box. Select the `Scale` tab and the `Time (X-Axis)` item from the upper textbox, and type `0` and `6` into the `Minimum` and the `Maximum` textboxes, respectively. The purpose of changing this scale is to match the waveform of the collected data to allow the waveform to be displayed in a good format.

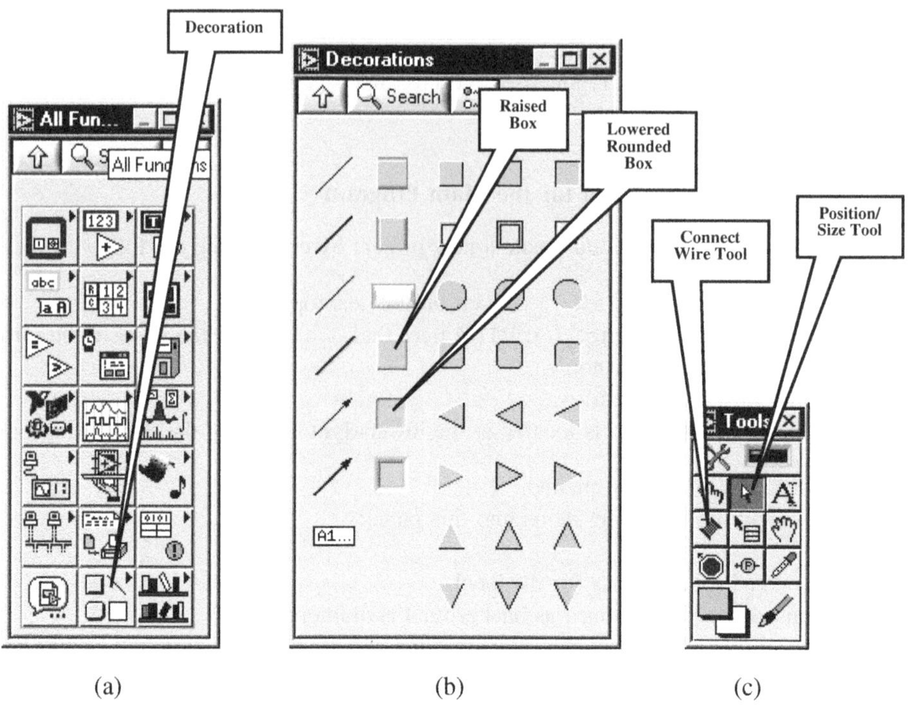

FIGURE 5.7 The Controls and Tools Palette.

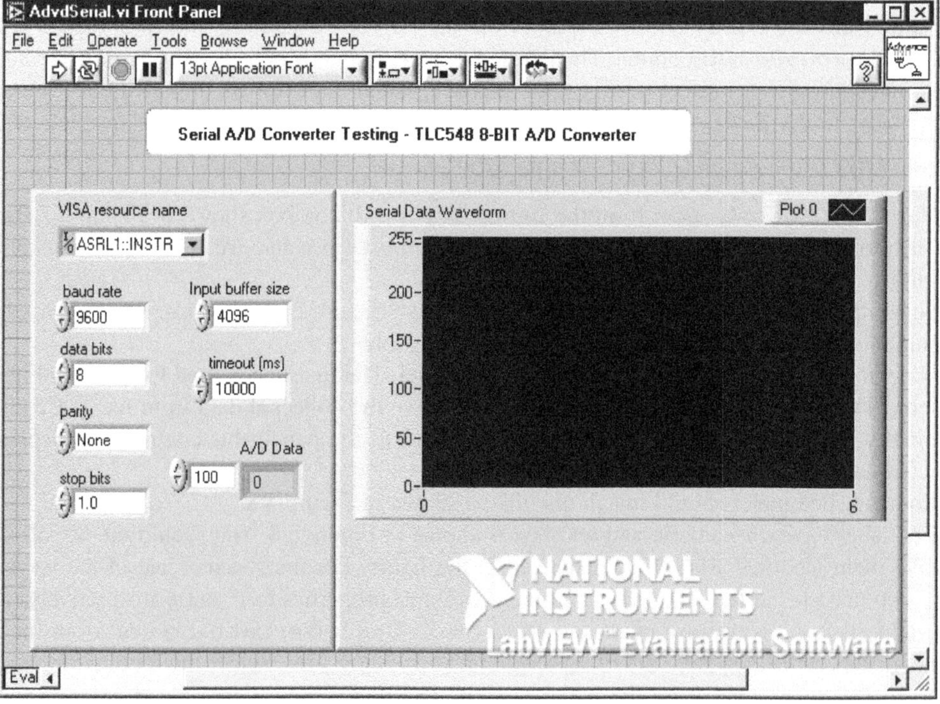

FIGURE 5.8 Front panel for the main program.

Another issue we want to emphasize is the data array. To add a data array, you need to first select and add a general array, as shown in Figure 5.9 (a), and then select a numeric indicator from the Control Palette and add it into the space of the general array, as shown in Figure 5.9 (b). You can select the array size by typing the desired size into the dimension box. In this example, a size of 5 is selected, which means that this is a one-dimensional array with five elements in it.

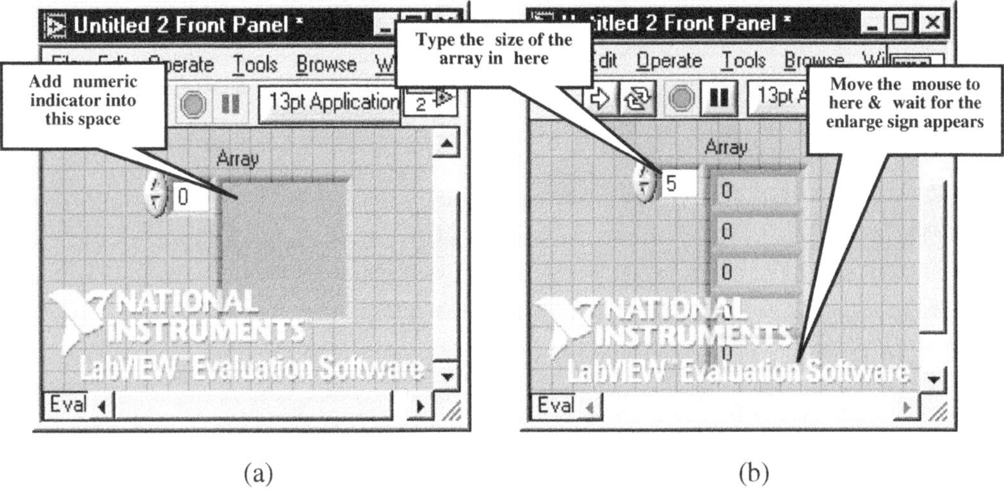

FIGURE 5.9 Creation of an array.

You can enlarge the array to view all five elements on the array by moving the mouse to the lower-right corner of the array and waiting until the enlarge sign is displayed; and then you can drag down the array to view all five elements, as shown in Figure 5.5 (b). All of these operations are performed by using the Position/Size tools on the Tools Palette.

In this application, the size for the data array is 100.

The parameters displayed on each box in Figure 5.8 are real parameters used in this project. The VISA resource name ASRL1::INSTR is equivalent to the serial port ID COM1. The serial communication parameters are standard values. The timeout value is 10 seconds (10000 ms).

Save this new project as AdvdSerial.vi.

5.3.1.2 Develop a Block Diagram for the Main Program

Now let's develop the codes for our main program.

Click the Window|Show Block Diagram item from the panel of the project AdvdSerial.vi to open the code window. A finished block diagram of this project is shown in Figure 5.10.

We divide this block diagram into two sections to discuss: The first section is from the input/output control to the While loop, and the second section consists of the codes inside the While loop.

Figure 5.11 shows the block diagram of the first section.

Before we can continue to develop the block diagram for the main program, we need first to list procedures of the main program. (Refer to Section 2.7.1.2 in Chapter 2 to review the procedures of the main program used to control data communication between the computer and the TLC548.)

The operations of the main program are listed here:

1. During the initialization, the DTR line is enabled to provide the power to the TLC548, and the RTS line is triggered to deactive the CS-bar signal on the TLC548. (The CS-bar

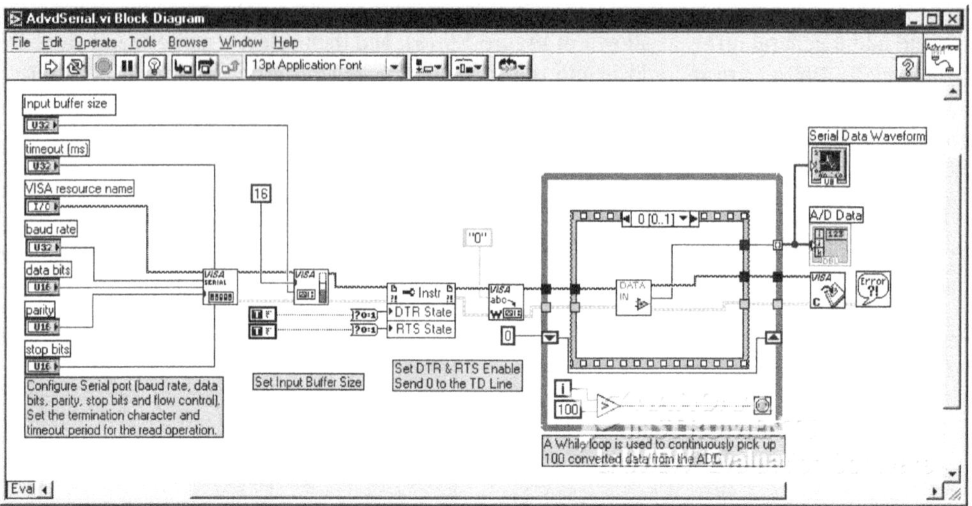

FIGURE 5.10 Block diagram for the AdvdSerial.vi project.

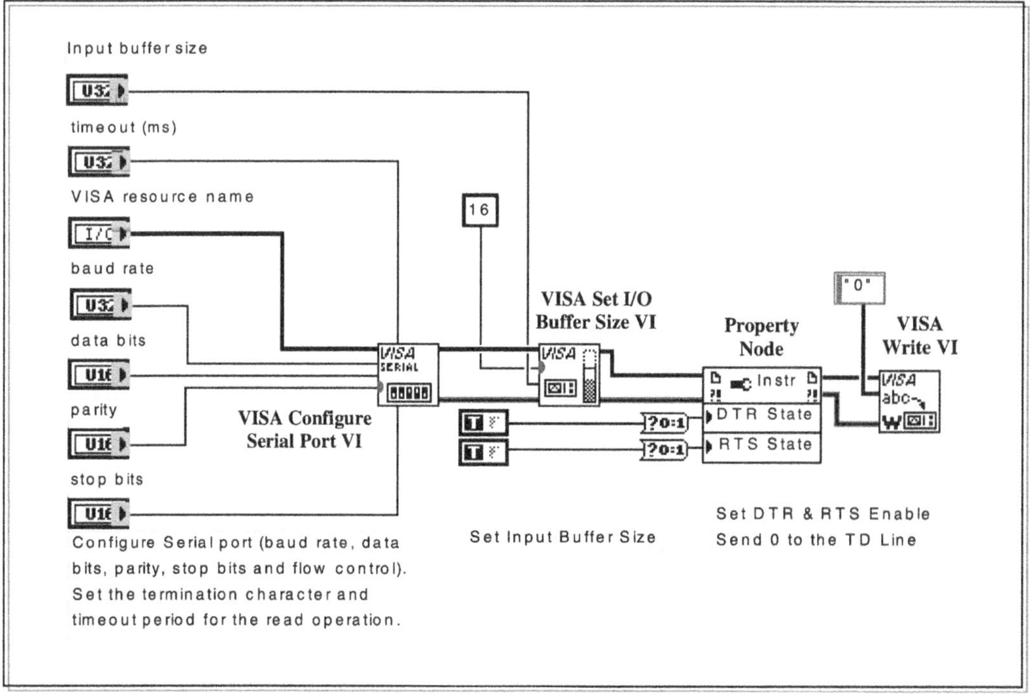

FIGURE 5.11 Block diagram for the main program (first section).

active signal is `LOW`.) A value of `0` is sent to the TD line to deactive the CLK on the TLC548.

2. The main program uses a `While` loop to continuously call the subroutine that will be developed next to get each byte of converted data from the TLC548, and store the received data into a data array.
3. The converted data is plotted on the waveform chart control.

These tasks can be completed via the block diagram shown in Figure 5.11.

An advanced VI, VISA `Configure Serial Port` (VISA serial), is used here to configure and initialize the serial port according to the serial parameters entered by the user at run time.

After this configuration and initialization, the serial port COM1 is ready to perform the data communication with the serial A/D converter. The input control VISA resource name is used to identify the configured serial port (here is COM1). This ID will be used by all associated components in this project later to identify the opened and configured port.

Following the VISA `Configure Serial Port` VI, a VISA `Set I/O Buffer Size` VI is used to initialize and set up the input buffer size for the UART. The serial port ID is passed from the VISA `Configure Serial Port` VI to this VI. The mask value 16 is used to indicate that the current size is defined for the input buffer. A value of 32 of the mask indicates that the current size is used to define the output buffer on the UART. In this application, a size of 4096 is used for the input buffer.

Next an `Instrument Property Node` is used to enable the DTR and the RTS transmission lines. The serial port ID is input to the `Property Node` as a reference, and the `Property Node` can automatically adapt to the class of the object you referenced by the port ID. The `Property Node` works just like a virtual function and it can be pre-configured to access a group of different VISA properties and Active-X properties. The most often-used VISA properties applied in the serial port interfaces are: DTR state, DSR state, RTS state, CTS state, DCD state, RI state and Break state. All of these states can be enabled or disabled by setting a `1` (asserted) or a `0` (unasserted) for the associated property. To enable the DTR and the RTS states, a `Boolean To (0,1)` converter is used to translate the Boolean variable `True` to 1, and assign it to both the DTR and the RTS states.

Finally a VISA `Write` VI is used to write a `0` to the TD line to disable the CLK input on the TLC548 A/D converter. You need to note that the data written into the serial port is in the format of a string, not a number. A "`0`" string is used here to represent a numeric 0 to be written into the transmit buffer of the serial port.

All of these VIs should be connected with the `error in` and `error out` VI terminals and this makes sure that each of them works properly.

Programming in the LabVIEW domain is very similar to programming done in any high-level programming language such as C/C++ or Visual Basic. All VIs are connected with each other one by one, from left to right, in a sequence. This is a typical sequence programming structure.

The second section of the main block diagram is shown in Figure 5.12.

After a "`0`" is written to the transmit buffer to disable the CLK on the TLC548, the main program uses a limited `While` loop (cycled 100 times) to call a subroutine named `DATA IN` to continuously collect 100 converted data from the TLC548. A `Stacked Sequence` structure is used to cover another sequence operations. Each subroutine is defined as a `SubVI` in the LabVIEW domain.

Each time, when the `SubVI DATA IN` is called, a byte (eight bits) of converted data is collected by that SubVI and feedback to the main program. After each `SubVI` calling, the main program needs to delay a period of time (10 milliseconds in this application) to make the collected data stable and safely stored in the data array. A `Wait Until Next ms Multiple` VI is used to perform that time delay, as shown in Figure 5.12 (b).

The block diagrams enclosed by the dash line belong to the first section.

Finally the VISA `Close` VI is used to close the opened serial port because the data communication is complete. The received data is sent to the data array and to the waveform chart to be displayed there.

The `While` loop will be terminated if the cycle repeats over 100 times. This program compares the loop index `i` with a constant of `100` to track the number of cycles. The `While` loop is initialized to `0` at the beginning of each loop by a constant of `0` that is assigned to the shift register.

At this point, we have completed the coding for our main program. Next we need to code the collect data subroutine (or `SubVI` in LabVIEW terminology).

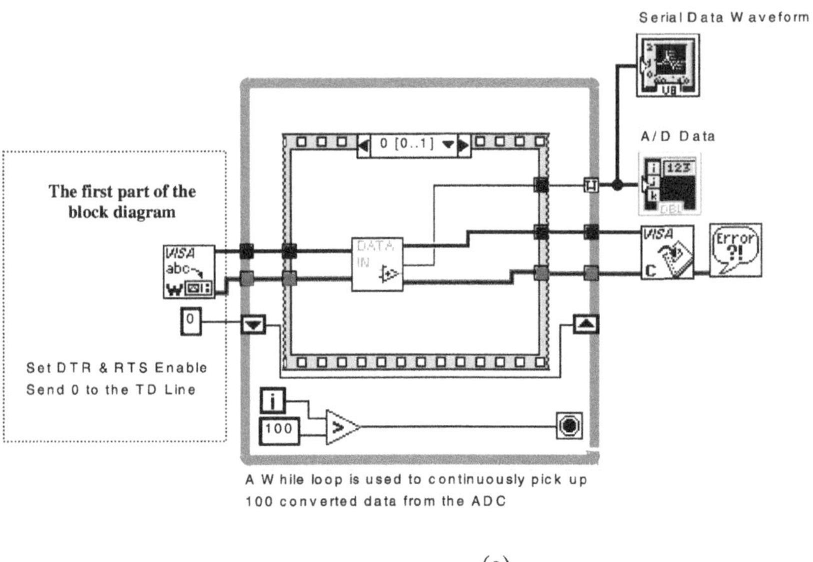

(a)

(b)

FIGURE 5.12 Block diagram for the main program (second section).

5.3.1.3 Designing a Front Panel for the Data Collection SubVI

The data collection subroutine is considered a SubVI in the LabVIEW environment. Because the block diagram of the data collection is a little complicated, we divide this as the second section for this project.

The operations of this SubVI are described here:

1. When the A/D conversion is ready to start, reset the RTS line to `LOW` to activate the CS-bar signal on the TLC548 to enable the A/D chip.
2. Then send a `HIGH` to the TD line as a rising edge for the CLK on the TLC548 to begin to perform a new bit conversion.
3. By checking the status of the CTS line, we can determine whether the converted result of the data bit is a logical `1` (CTS = `HIGH`) or a logical `0` (CTS = `LOW`) because the DOUT on the TLC548 is connected to the CTS line.
4. A variable used to store the retrieved result is increased by 1 if a logical `1` is detected on the CTS line, otherwise a `0` is added into that variable. Then the variable is shifted left by one bit to make it ready for the next converted bit.
5. After the data bit is converted and stored, the TD line is reset to `0` to make the CLK on the TLC548 inactive.
6. Continue to steps 2, 3, 4, and 5 to retrieve the converted bit, and repeat the process until all eight bits of converted data have been stored in the variable.
7. After one-byte data is converted, the RTS line is enabled to deselect the CS-bar on the TLC548 to disable the A/D chip.

Based on the functions of this SubVI, the number of input and output controls is limited. The following is a list of the input and output controls used in this SubVI:

- The serial port ID (input)
- The error in control (input)
- The converted data—1 byte (output)
- The returned serial port ID (output)
- The error out control (output)

A local Boolean indicator `CTS State` is used to monitor and display the state of the CTS transmission line. Another Boolean constant is used to reset the RTS line as the A/D conversion starts. Both variables are only used for this SubVI.

The input controls `serial port ID` and `error in` are coming from the outputs of the second section block diagram in the main program, exactly from the VISA `Write` VI, as shown in Figure 5.12 (a).

Open a new VI and enter the following controls into the front panel, as shown in Figure 5.13. Save this panel as `GetAD_Data.vi`. This is our SubVI that will collect the converted data from the TLC548, bit by bit. This SubVI returns an eight bits (one byte) of converted data to the main program using the converted data output terminal when it finishes the one-byte data conversion.

Your finished front panel of the `GetAD_Data` VI should match one that is shown in Figure 5.13.

Modify all labels and set the default values for all textboxes and LED indicator based on the values displayed in Figure 5.13. The VISA `resource name` and the VISA `destination name` are corresponding to input serial ID and the output serial port ID, respectively. For the `error in` and `out` cluster controls, you can get them easily by coping those controls from some example front panels and paste them into this panel. Otherwise you have to create it by using the cluster control yourself.

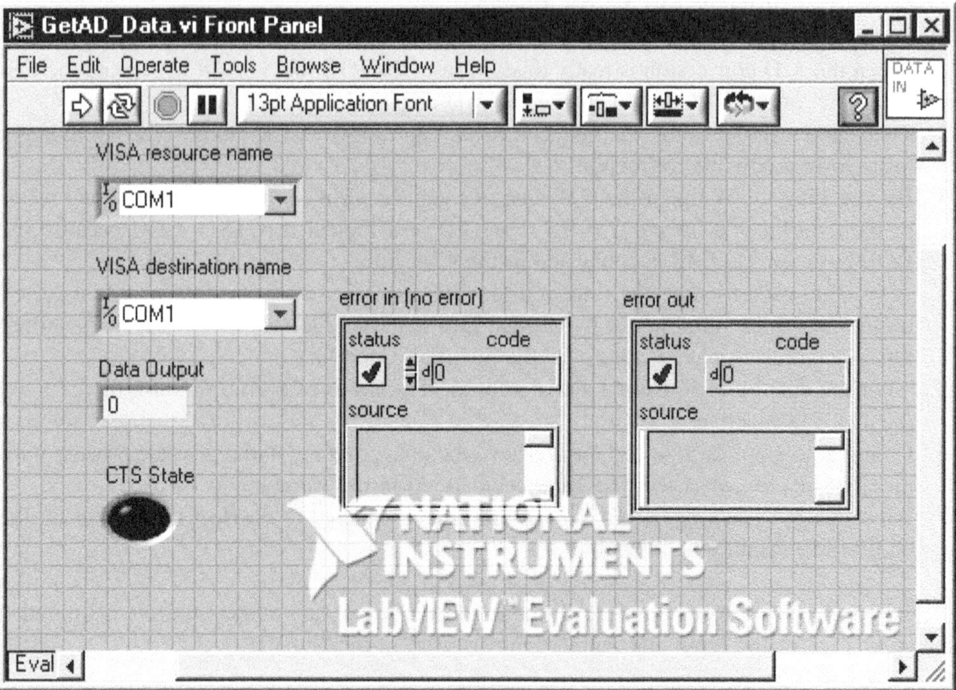

FIGURE 5.13 Front panel for the `GetAD_Data` SubVI.

5.3.1.4 Developing a Block Diagram for the Data Collection SubVI

We can develop the block diagram of this SubVI as shown in Figure 5.14.

At the beginning of this SubVI, two `Property Nodes` are used to perform steps 1 and 3 to reset the RTS line to `LOW` and thus enable the CS-bar signal on the TLC548 to select the A/D converter and to monitor the state of the CTS line to pick up the converted data. A Boolean constant is used to reset the RTS line. The `Property Node` control can be obtained from the `Function Palette` in the following sequence:

Instrument I/O|`VISA`|`VISA Advanced`. The location of the `Property Node` control on the `Function Palette` is shown in Figure 5.15 (a).

A limited `While` loop is used to repeatedly pick up the converted data bit by bit from the TLC548. The loop is terminated as the cycle number is greater than 8, which means that a complete data unit (eight bits) has been collected from the A/D converter. The `While` loop is initialized by a numeric constant `0` with the data type of `unsigned 8-bit`, or `U8`. This numeric constant can be considered as a variable to store the converted data and is also passed into the first sequence as the initial value of the converted data using the shift register of the `While` loop.

Inside the `While` loop, a sequence structure is used to perform a sequence of operations to complete the data collection. This operation sequence proceeds as follows:

1. The converted data that has a data type of unsigned 8-bit (U8) is first shifted left by one bit. This operation is equivalent to multiply the converted data by 2. This step is necessary because each converted bit needs one space to store its value, therefore the shift left makes space for the next converted bit on the converted data.
2. Then we need to send a `HIGH` ("255") to the TD line as a rising edge for the CLK on the TLC548 to begin to perform a new bit conversion. This `HIGH` should be transmitted to the output buffer on the UART by using the VISA `Write` VI with an input string of "255."

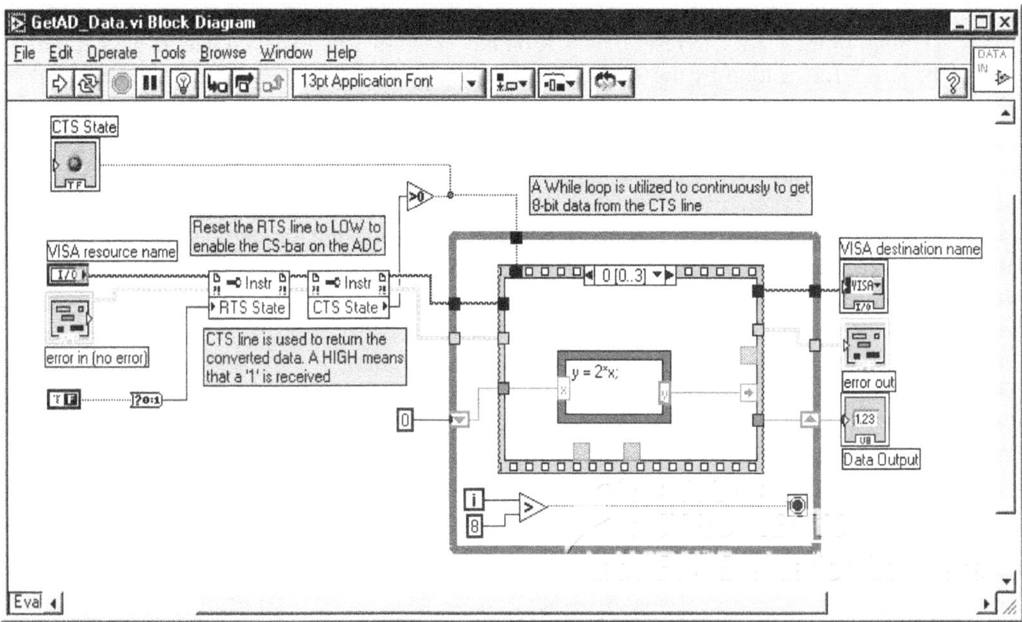

FIGURE 5.14 Block diagram for the `GetAD_Data` SubVI.

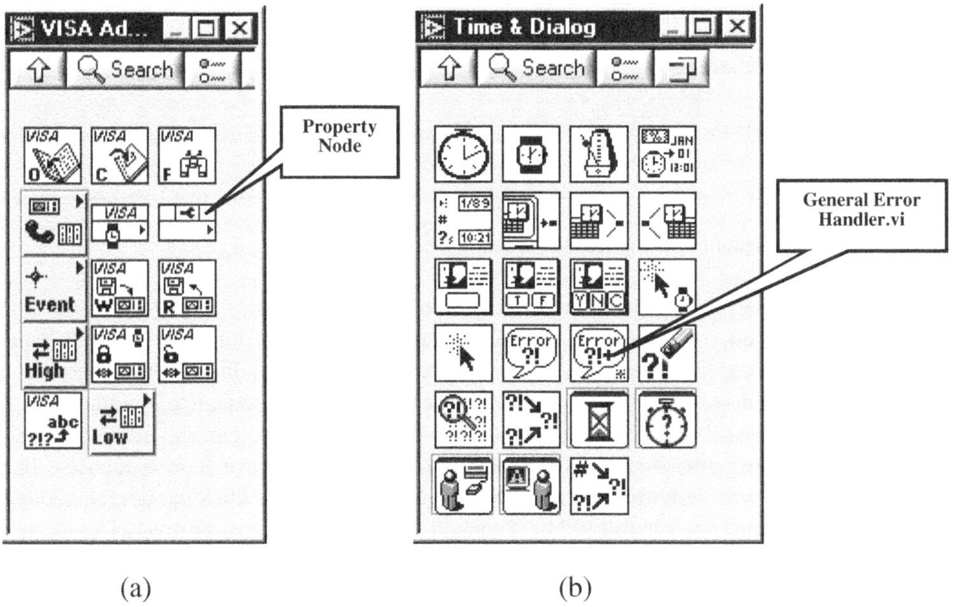

FIGURE 5.15 Locations of the `Property Node` and `Error Handler` VIs.

3. By checking the status of the CTS line, we can determine whether the converted bit is a logical `1` (CTS = `HIGH`) or a logical `0` (CTS = `LOW`) because the DOUT on the TLC548 is connected to the CTS line. If a `HIGH` is detected on the CTS line, which means that a logical `1` is received, the associated converted bit is increased by 1.
4. Otherwise no operation is needed for this converted bit, which is equivalent to adding a `0` to the associated converted bit.

5. After one bit is received, a LOW (0) is sent to the transmit buffer (and ultimately to the TD line) of the UART to reset the CLK on the TLC548. The received data is passed into the next While loop by the shift register to be continued for the next received bit until all eight bits have been received.
6. The complete received data is sent to the output data indicator (Data Output) that is returned to the main program.

Now let's follow the operation sequence above to develop our block diagram step by step. (Refer to Figure 5.14.) All of these sequence operations are performed inside the While loop, so we will concentrate on the block diagrams inside the While loop. The block diagram of step 1, which is equivalent to sequence 0, is shown in Figure 5.16.

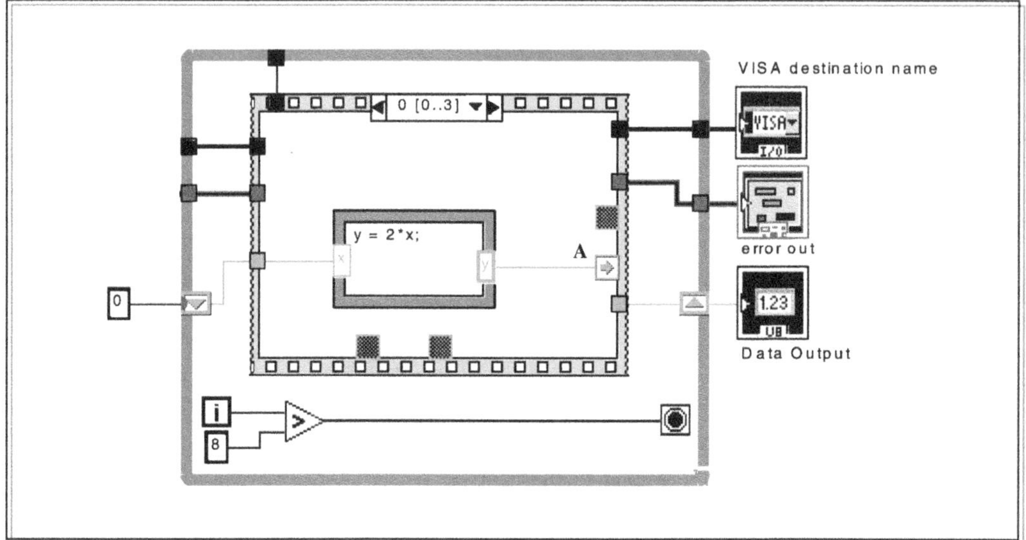

FIGURE 5.16 Block diagram for step 1 of the GetAD_Data SubVI.

The Stacked Sequence structure is located in the Structures directory on the Function Palette. When you select and add this structure to the block diagram, a default sequence structure is used. You can add more frames (cases) based on this default structure. The first case starts from 0. To add more frames, right-click on the border of the sequence structure and click the Add Frame After item, You can also add a frame before the current frame by selecting the Add Frame Before item. In this application, we need to use four sequences that are corresponding to four programming instructions. So add three frames after the default sequence.

To multiply the converted data by 2, a Formula Node structure is used. The Formula Node structure is located in the Structures directory on the Function Palette. Add a new Formula Node structure to the Sequence 0 structure, and then add one input and one output node to the newly added Formula Node structure by right-clicking on its border. Select Add Input and Add Output from the pop-up menu. Type *x* and *y* in the added input and output nodes, respectively, to name them. Then wire the input node to the left shift register of the While loop, and the output node to the sequence node that is created next. In order to transmit the converted data from one sequence to another one, we need to create several sequence local nodes. Each sequence local node corresponds to one sequence structure. To create a new sequence local node for the current sequence structure, right-click on its border and select Add Sequence Local from the pop-up menu. A new sequence local node is added on the border of the current sequence structure. Wire the output *y* to the newly added sequence local node A, as shown in

Figure 5.16, and the node becomes an arrow that points out. Type the equation `y = 2*x;` inside the `Formula Node` structure to complete this multiplication operation. Note that the semicolon must be attached at the end of the equation.

The block diagram of step 2 (sequence 1) is shown in Figure 5.17.

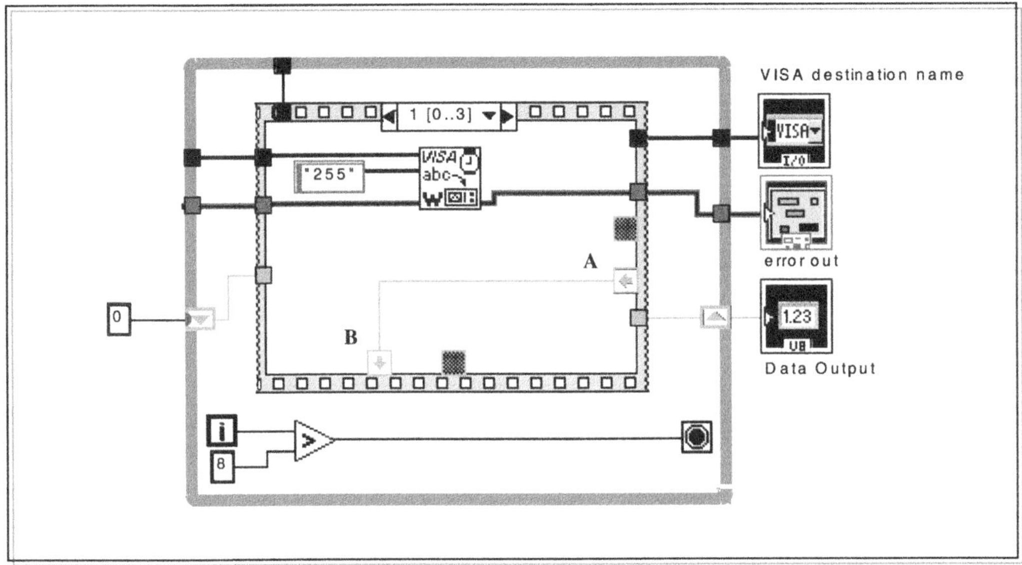

FIGURE 5.17 Block diagram for step 2 of the `GetAD_Data` SubVI.

A VISA `Write` VI is used here to output a `HIGH` to the serial port, and this `HIGH` must be represented by a string constant of "255" that is written into the write buffer on the VISA `Write` VI. In order to transmit the converted data from the current sequence to the next sequence, we need to create another `Sequence Local Node` structure for this sequence structure. Right-click on the border of the current sequence structure (sequence structure 1), and select the `Add Sequence Local` item from the pop-up menu to create a new sequence local node `B`. Wire from the last sequence local node `A` to the new added sequence local node `B`, as shown in Figure 5.17. In this way, the value of the converted data can be translated from the current sequence structure to the next one.

The `serial port ID` and the `error in` inputs of the `VISA Write` VI are obtained from the corresponding outputs of the Property Node (refer to Figure 5.14) in the `GetAD_Data` SubVI.

The `error out` output of the VISA `Write` VI is connected to the `error out` cluster to display any possible error during the processing of that VI.

The Block Diagram of Step 3 in the `GetAD_Date` SubVI is shown in Figure 5.18.

In this sequence structure (sequence 2), the associated bit of the converted data needs to be increased by 1 if a logical `1` is detected on the CTS line because the CTS transmission line is connected to the DOUT terminal on the TLC548 A/D converter. A logical `1` corresponds to a `HIGH` in the CTS line. A case structure is used here to work as a decision-making structure. Add a new `Case` structure that is located the `Structures` directory on the `Function Palette` into this sequence structure. To perform the increment of the associated bit of converted data, a `Formula Node` structure is added into this `True` case structure. Add one input and one output to this structure, and name them x and y, respectively. Connect the last Sequence Local Node `B` to the input x of the `Formula Node` structure as shown in Figure 5.18. Type the equation $y = x + 1$; inside the `Formula Node` structure to complete this increment operation for the converted data bit. To pass the converted data to the next sequence, we need to create another Sequence Local node `C`. Connect

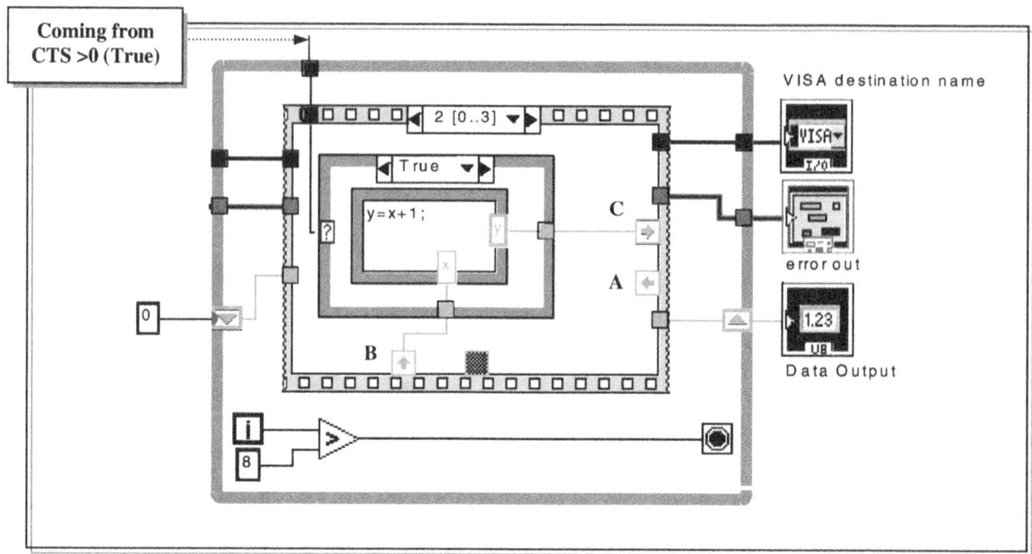

FIGURE 5.18 Block diagram for step 3 of the `GetAD_Data` SubVI.

the output *y* of the `Formula Node` structure to the newly added local node `C` to pass the data to the next sequence.

The Block Diagram of Step 4 in the `GetAD_Data` SubVI is shown in Figure 5.19.

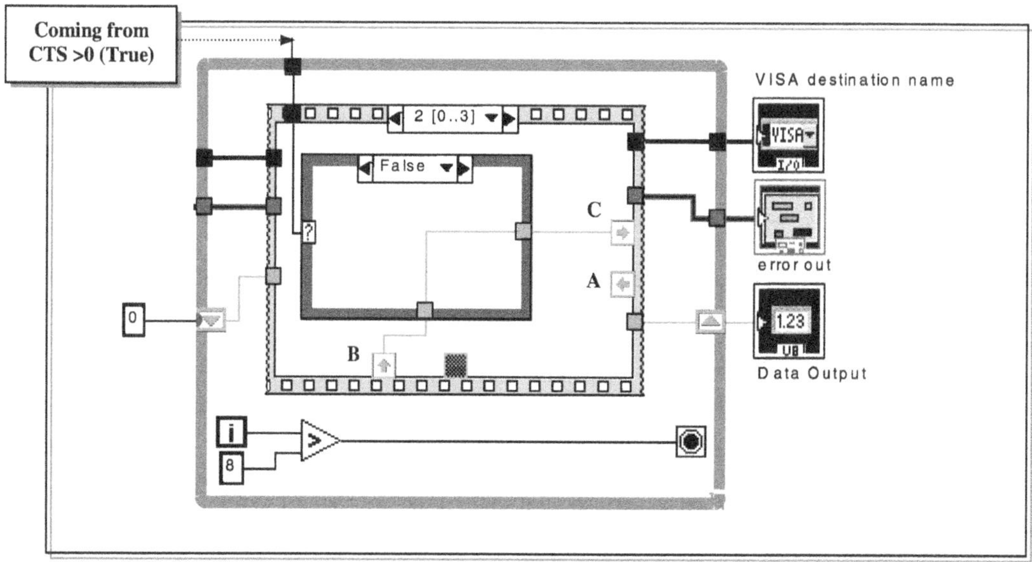

FIGURE 5.19 Block diagram for step 4 of the `GetAD_Data` SubVI.

If a `LOW` value is detected in the CTS line, which means that a logical `0` has been received from the TLC548 A/D converter, this situation can be expressed by a `False` case structure, as shown in Figure 5.19. No action is needed for this situation and it is equivalent to add a 0 to the associated bit on the converted data. We can then directly transmit the converted data to the next sequence structure. This operation is equivalent to connect nodes B and C together.

The block diagram of steps 5 and 6 in the `GetAD_Data` SubVI is shown in Figure 5.20.

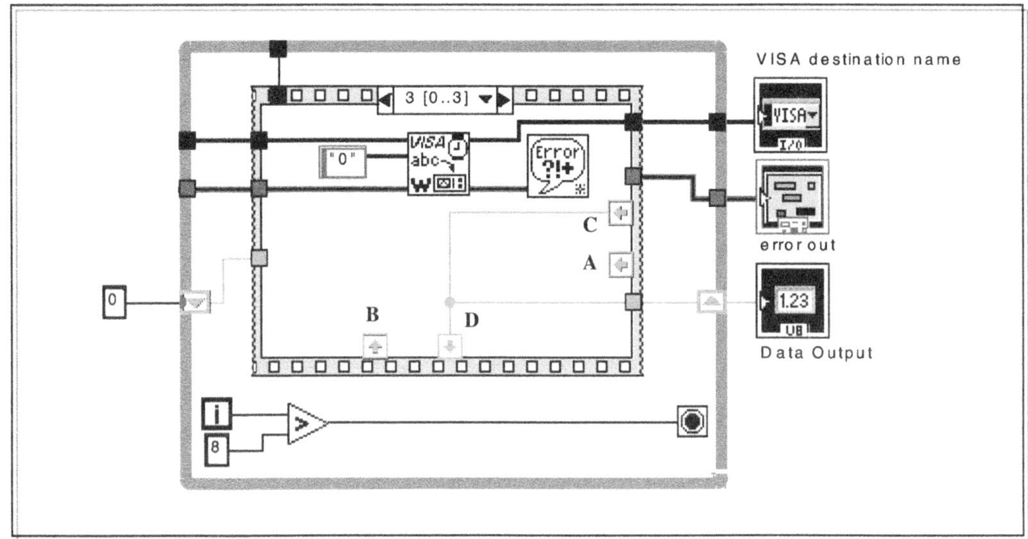

FIGURE 5.20 Block diagram for Steps 5 and 6 of the `GetAD_Data` SubVI.

After one bit of data is received, a logical `0` is written to the TD line to reset the CLK on the TLC548 A/D converter because the TD transmission line of the serial port is connected to the CLK input on the TLC548. This operation is performed by sending a string "`0`" to the `VISA Write` VI in the final sequence structure, sequence 3. The serial port ID and the error output are sent to the indicator VISA `destination name` and the `error out` cluster, as shown in Figure 5.20. Those indicators work as the outputs of this SubVI and will be returned to the main program.

A `General Error Handler` VI is added at the end of the VISA `Write` VI to monitor and process any possible error occurred during that write operation. The `General Error Handler` VI is located in the `Time & Dialog` directory on the `Function Palette`, which is shown in Figure 5.15 (b).

We can add another Sequence Local node `D` to this sequence structure if the converted data needs to be passed into the next structure. The data unit passed to the local node is `C`, which is an unsigned eight-bit variable stored the converted data, should be translated to the shift register on the `While` loop to receive the next bit of data in the next cycle of the `While` loop. A wire is connected between the node `C` and the shift register of the `While` loop to complete this operation. The complete eight-bit data string should be returned to the main program if all eight bits of data have been received. This can be done by assigning the converted data to the `Data Output` indicator.

We'll now outline the tasks necessary for making this VI a SubVI and allowing the main program to call it.

5.3.1.4.1 Making the `GetAD_Data VI` a SubVI

Our first task is to make this VI a SubVI. Follow these steps:

1. Edit the Icon.

In the block diagram window, click the `Window|Show Front Panel` item to open its front panel.

In the `Tools Palette`, click the `Connect Wire` tool to select it. Move the cursor onto the `VI` icon that is located in the upper-right corner (see Figure 5.21), and right-click on that icon to open its pop-up menu, then select the `Edit Icon` item to open the Icon Editor. (See Figure 5.22.) Delete the old stuff (except the graphic in the lower-right corner) and click the text editor A to type `DATA IN` inside the icon, as shown in Figure 5.22. Click `OK` to save these changes.

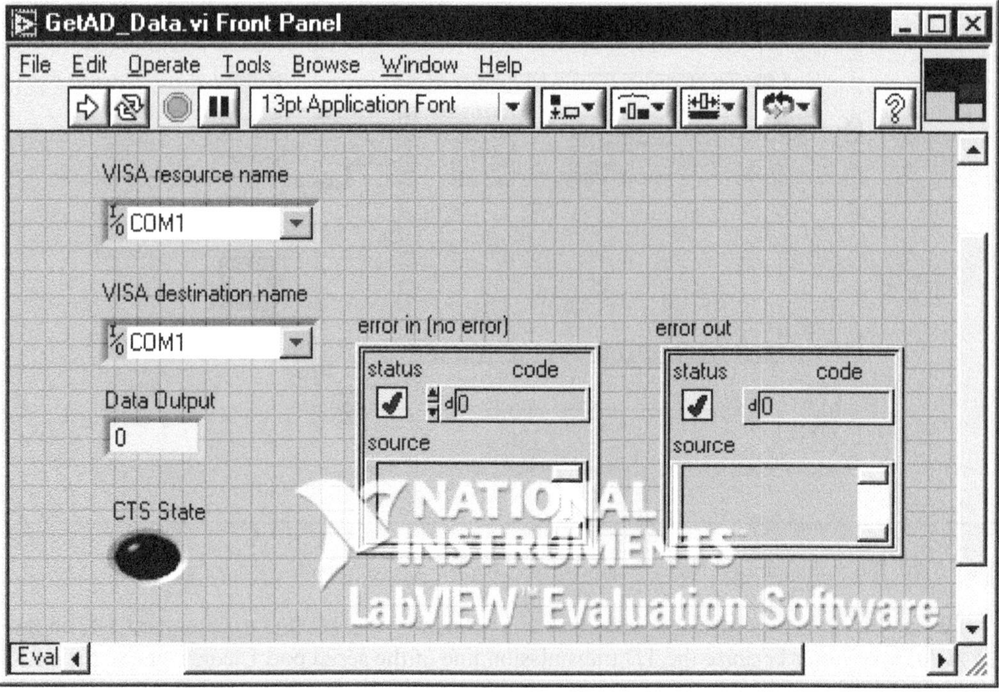

FIGURE 5.21 The edit of the `VI` icon.

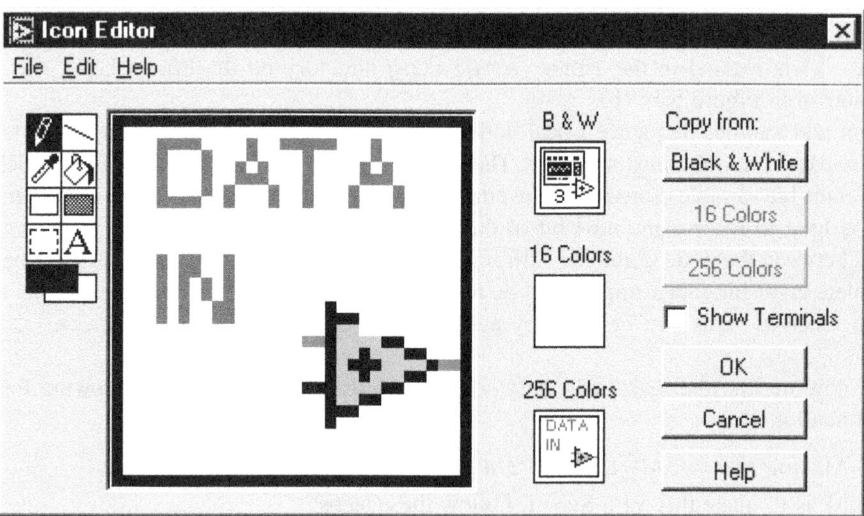

FIGURE 5.22 The `Icon Editor` window.

2. Set the connection between each connector and each control on the panel.

The next step is to select the terminal pattern for the SubVI. The terminal pattern is a graphic representation for each SubVI, and you can define how many connectors or terminals can be installed on the SubVI by using the `Show Connector` menu item. Those connectors or terminals can be considered as the input/output nodes that make the connection between this SubVI and the external VIs. Right-click the SubVI icon that is located in the upper-right corner, and select the Show Connector item from the pop-up menu. Immediately, the default connector pattern is displayed. Right-click on that VI icon and select the Patterns item from the pop-up menu to display a collection of available patterns. You can select different patterns according to the number of input and output controls on the current SubVI. In our case, we have six controls on the front panel of this SubVI (refer to Figure 5.13), but only five of them work as input and output. (The CTS State control is a local control, used only for this SubVI). Therefore, we need five connectors or terminals on the pattern. The input and output controls of this SubVI are listed here:

- VISA resource name—Serial port ID (input)
- Error in cluster (input)
- VISA destination name—Serial port ID (output)
- Error out cluster (output)
- Data Output—U8 indicator (output)

We select a pattern that has two input connectors on the left side and three output connectors on the right side as our pattern.

3. Set the connections between the connectors on the selected pattern and the controls on the front panel of the SubVI.

Go to the Tools Palette and select the Connect Wire tool. Go to the front panel, click the VISA resource name control to select it, and then go to the upper-left connector on the pattern that is located in the upper-right corner of the front panel. Click on that upper-left connector and immediately it will be highlighted, which means that a connection between the connector and the selected control (VISA resource name) has been set up. In the same way, click error in cluster on the front panel to select it, and then click the lower-left connector on the pattern; this connector is highlighted, which means that a connection between that lower-left connector and the error in cluster setting has been installed. Continue setting the connections between the connectors, located on the righthand side of the pattern, and the output controls on the front panel.

Now we have made the VI as a SubVI. Click the File|Save menu item to save this SubVI as GetAD_Data.vi.

5.3.1.4.2 Calling the GetAD_Data SubVI from the Main Program

To call the GetAD_Data SubVI developed in the preceding section, we need first to add that SubVI into the block diagram of the main program.

Open the block diagram of the main program. Click the Select a VI... control from the Functions Palette, which is shown in Figure 5.23 (a). In the opened dialog box, browse and find our SubVI, GetAD_Data.vi, and click the Open button to add it into our main program, as shown in Figure 5.23 (b). Immediately, the SubVI icon is displayed on our main program block diagram. Move it into the Case 0 sequence under the While loop in the main program, and finish the wire connection for this SubVI. (Refer back to Figure 5.12a.)

That is all! We are ready to call this SubVI from the main program.

5.3.1.5 Testing and Running the Project

Save both the main program and the SubVI onto the computer. Now we can test and run this project.

From the front panel of the main program AdvdSerial.vi, click the Run button on the toolbar, and the program will begin to run. The waveform we are testing is the triangle that is coming from the function generator. The running results are displayed on the waveform chart control, which is shown in Figure 5.24.

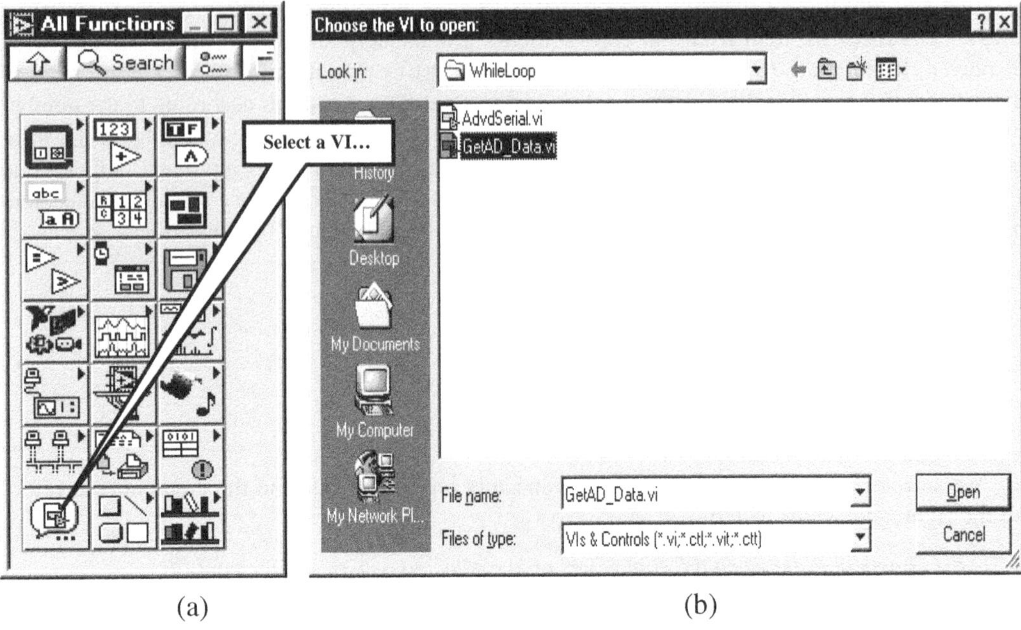

FIGURE 5.23 The `Select VI` control and its dialog box.

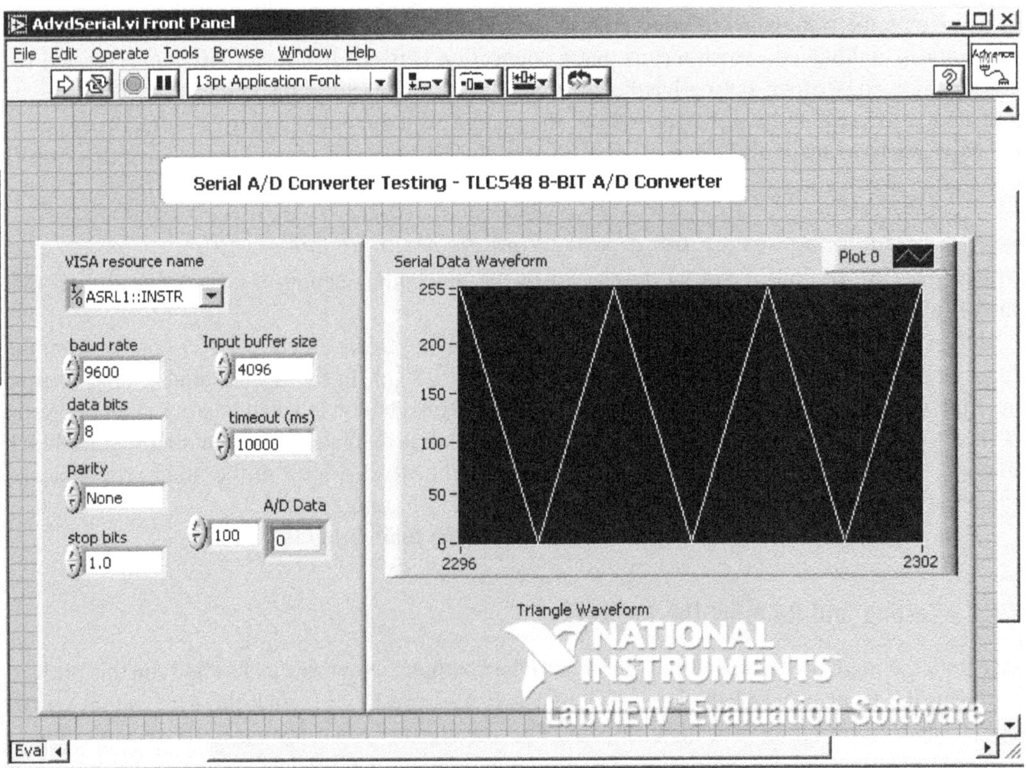

FIGURE 5.24 Results of running the main program.

During the main program running, you can open the front panel of the SubVI, GetAD_Data.vi. Each received data can be displayed in the Data Output indicator in real time, and the CTS state can be reflected in the CTS State LED in real time, which is shown in Figure 5.25. It is very interesting to watch this real-time processing!

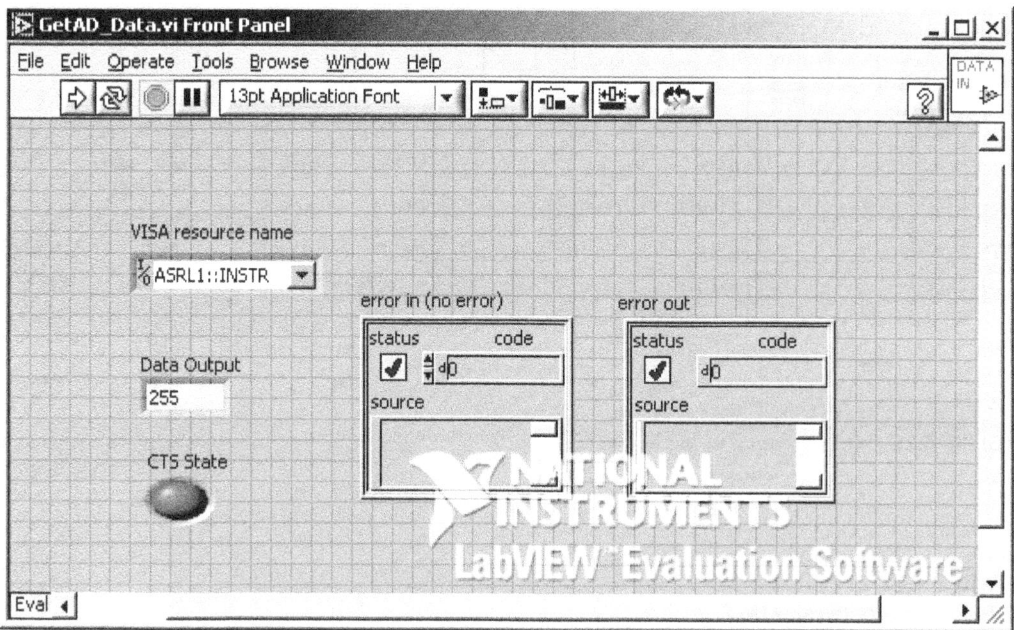

FIGURE 5.25 Results of running the GetAD_Data SubVI.

The completed files for this project are located on the attached CD, in the folder Chapter 5\AdvdSerial\TLC548\WhileLoop. A similar project that is developed with a For Loop structure is located in the folder Chapter 5\AdvdSerial\TLC548\ForLoop.

You can download those projects into your computer to test them.

5.3.2 Using VISA to Interface with a 12-Bit Serial A/D Converter MAX187

In this section we discuss how to use the VISA to communicate with a 12-bit serial A/D converter MAX187. The MAX187 is a product of the Maxim Integrated and it is a 12-bit A/D converter with a serial output buffer. Refer to Figures 2-65, 2-66 in Chapter 2 for more detailed information about the MAX187 and MAX220.

The interface connection between the RS-232 serial port and the MAX187 is shown in Figure 2-67 in Chapter 2. For your convenience, we re-draw the interface circuit here in Figure 5.26.

The elements parameters are shown in Table 5.2.

Compared with the 8-bit A/D converter discussed in the last section, the 12-bit A/D converter has more resolution and accuracy. Make the circuit connection as shown in Figure 5.26, and connect the circuit to the serial port on your computer. The input signal comes from a function generator that can output three different waveforms: sinusoidal, square, and trianglular waveforms.

One point you need to pay attention to is the serial driver/translator MAX-220. This component provides an inverting logical between the input and the output. Instead of sending a logical HIGH, you should send a logical LOW to the MAX-220 if you want to send a HIGH to one of terminals on the MAX-187 because the MAX-220 inverted that logical signal.

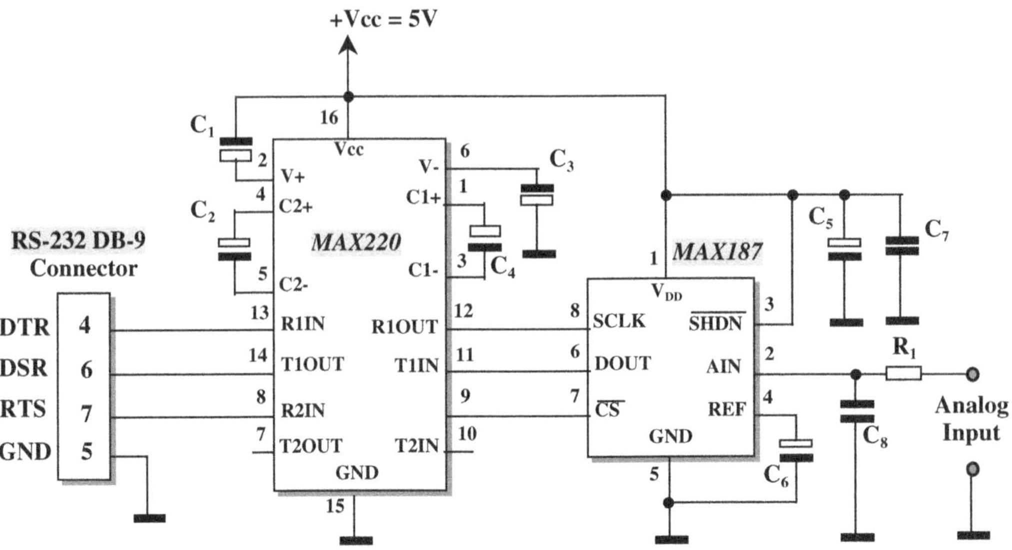

FIGURE 5.26 Interface circuit of the MAX187.

TABLE 5.2
The Elements Parameters

Elements	Value	Comments
R_1	1 KΩ	Current-limited resistor
R_2, R_3, R_4	30 KΩ	Current-limited resistors
D_1	5.1 V	Zener diode
D_2–D_8	1N4148	Diodes
C_1	10 μF/15 V	Electrolytic capacitor
C_2	100 nF	Capacitor

The MAX187 begins the data conversion when its Chip Select (CS) has a `HIGH`-to-`LOW` transition, and this signal is connected to the RTS line that is converted from the RS-232 to the TTL/CMOS level by the MAX220 with an inverted logical setting. The MAX187 completes the 12-bit conversion using its own internal clock, and the end of conversion is marked by a `HIGH` value on the output DOUT. The PC retrieves the converted data from the DSR line, which is connected to the DOUT on the MAX187 via a logical inverter MAX220, by sending a sequence of simulated clock from the DTR line.

After the data conversion starts, the PC monitors the DSR line and waits until its state becomes to `HIGH`, which means that a data conversion is complete. The PC sends 12 simulated clocks via the DTR line that is connected to the SCLK (Serial CLK) on the MAX187, to serially move the converted data from the output shift register on the MAX187 to the DSR line, and picks up them one by one by checking the value received on the DSR line.

Similar to the last example, two VIs are used in this project; one is the main program that controls and coordinates the A/D converter, data collection, error monitoring, and data displaying. The other one is a data collection subroutine that is specially used for the data collection from the A/D converter. So the development of this project is divided into two sections; the first section is to develop the main program and the second section is to develop the data collection subroutine.

5.3.2.1 Designing a Front Panel for the Main Program

Launch LabVIEW 7.0 Express and create a new project named `MAXSerial.vi` by completing the following steps:

- Double click the LabVIEW 7.0 icon on the desktop
- Click the `Start Using LabVIEW` item that is located at the lower-right corner of the LabVIEW startup window
- Click the `New...` button
- And following a click on the `OK` button that is located at the lower-right corner of the New dialog box

A new LabVIEW project is created.
We need to add the following items into this panel:

1. One lowered rounded box for the label
2. Two raised boxes to be used as background containers
3. Six numeric control boxes that will store the serial communication parameters
4. Two text arrays that will hold the serial I/O port ID and the collected data
5. One waveform chart control that will display the collected data

First from the opened `Controls Palette`, select the `Decorations|Lowered Rounded Box`, then drag and size it into the top of the panel. Click the `Position/Size` tool on the `Tools Palette` and click the `Rounded Box` option to select it. Then select yellow color as the background color for this rounded box by clicking the background color pad from the `Tools Palette`. Select the `Edit Text` tool from the `Tools Palette` to type the following letters as the label into the rounded box:

Serial A/D Converter Testing—MAX187 12-BIT A/D Converter

Next select the `Raised Box` from the `Decorations` dialog box and drag it into the panel. You need to add two of this kind of boxes because we use both of them as the background container.

Third you need to select the Numeric control from the `Control Palette` and add it into the panel. Totally we need six of them, so you need to add them one by one.

Fourth you need to add two text arrays into the panel. The first one is used to select and reserve the serial I/O port ID, and the second one is used to reserve the collected data from the MAX187.

Finally you need to add a waveform chart into the panel; this chart will display the collected data.

Your finished panel should match the one that is shown in Figure 5.27.

The label for each numeric and text box is shown in Figure 5.27. You should follow the figure to modify each label and make them identical with those displayed in the figure. The parameters displayed in Figure 5.27 are default parameters as this project runs. Those default parameters are highly recommended to be used for this project.

In this project, we want to display a real-time relationship between the collected data and the sampling periods. To do that, you need to set the `x` scale of the waveform chart to the relative time mode. Follow these steps to finish the configuration.

- Select the `Position/Size/Select` tool from the `Tools Palette`.
- Right-click on the waveform chart, and select `X Scale|Formatting...` menu item from the pop-up menu to open the `Chart Properties` dialog box, which is shown in Figure 5.28.
- In the opened dialog box, select the `Format and Precision` tab.
- In the upper textbox, select the `Time (X-Axis)` item.
- Select `Relative time` from the bottom line of the list box that is located just under the upper textbox.

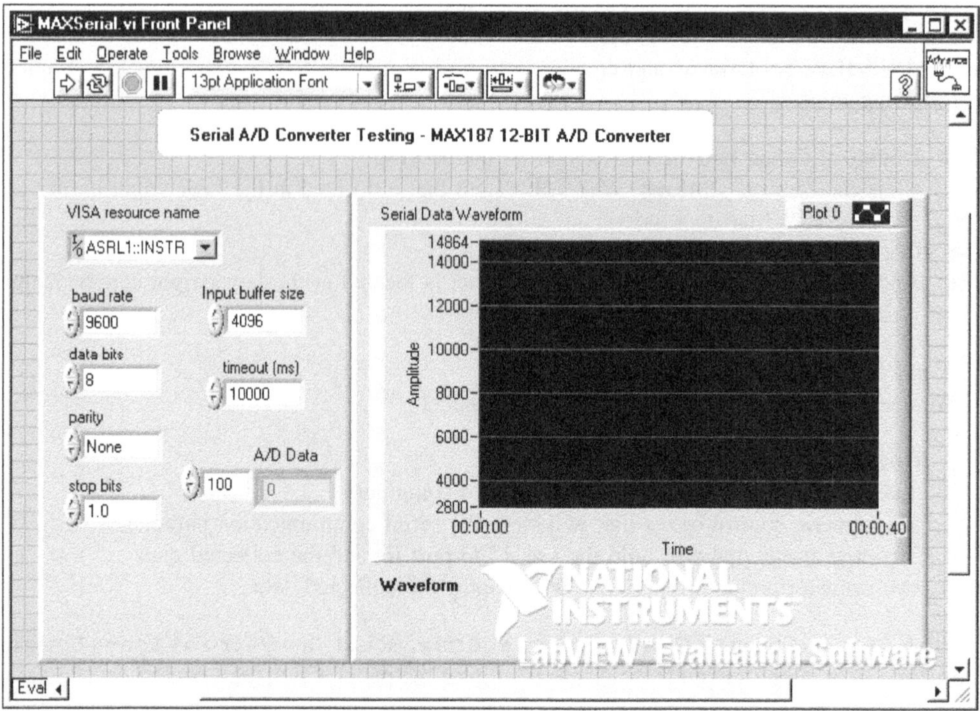

FIGURE 5.27 Front panel for the main program.

- Select the HH:MM:SS radio button.
- Click the OK button to save these settings.

The VISA resource name ASRL1::INSTR is equivalent to the serial port ID COM1. The serial communication parameters are standard values. The timeout value is ten seconds (10000 ms). The size of the data array is 100, which means that we want to collect 100 converted data and display them on the waveform chart. Once we set up the Visible Scale Label property on both the X-axis and the Y-axis of the waveform chart control, the labels Amplitude (for the vertical axis) and Time (for the horizontal axis) can be displayed on the chart.

5.3.2.2 Developing a Block Diagram for the Main Program

Click the Window|Show Block Diagram item from the front panel of the project MAXSerial.vi to open the code window. A finished block diagram for this project is shown in Figure 5.29.

You can configure the transmission lines, such as the DTR and the RTS, by using the Property Nodes of the VISA class. The data collection is performed by using a While loop with a limited cycle number of 100. A subroutine VI named DATA IN, which is used to pick up each 12-bit converted data from the MAX-187 A/D converter, is included inside the While loop to finish the data collection job.

We can divide this block diagram into two sections to discuss: The first section is from the control input/output to the While loop, and the second section is the codes inside the While loop.

Figure 5.30 shows the block diagram of the first section.

An advanced VI, VISA Configure Serial Port (VISA serial), is used here to configure and initialize the serial port based on the serial parameters entered by the user.

After this configuration and initialization, the serial port COM1 is ready to perform the data communication with the serial A/D converter. The input control VISA resource name is used

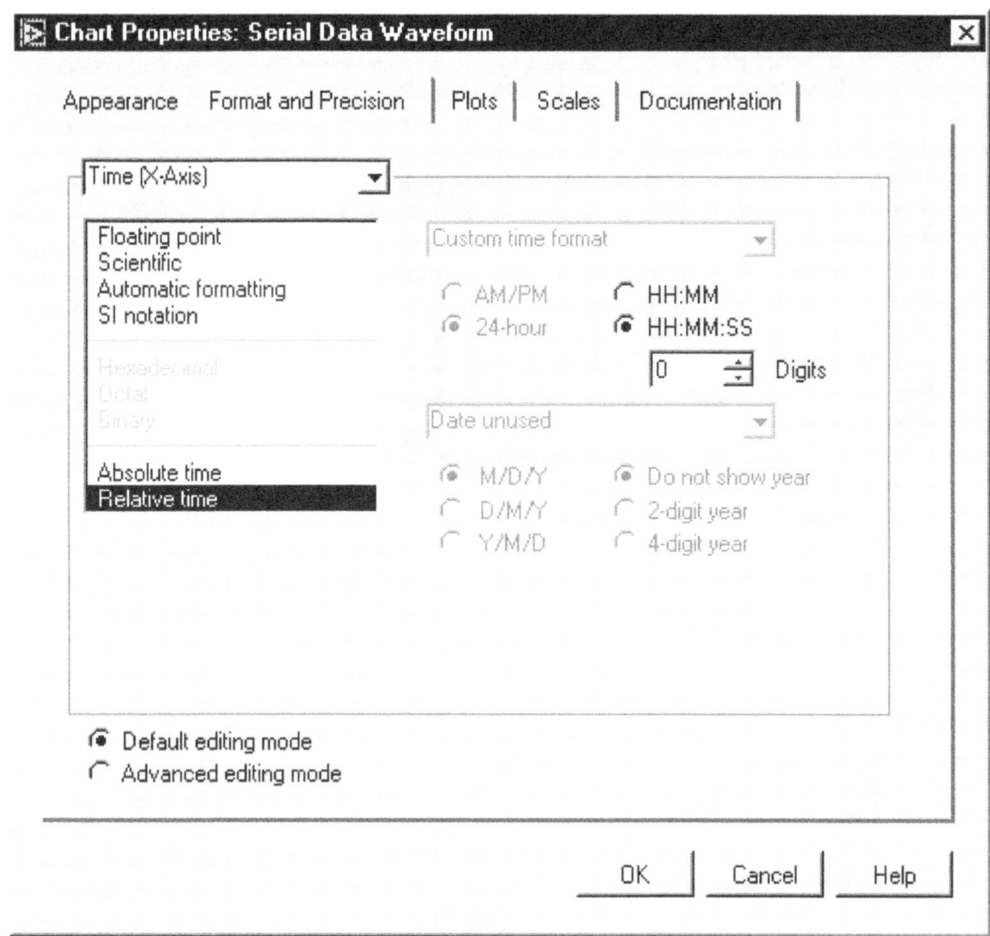

FIGURE 5.28 The setup of the relative time property for the X scale.

to identify the configured serial port (here is COM1). This ID will be used by all associated components in this project later to identify the opened and configured port.

Following the VISA `Configure Serial Port` VI, a VISA `Set I/O Buffer Size` VI is used to initialize and set up the input buffer size for the UART. The serial port ID is passed from the VISA `Configure Serial Port` VI to this VI. The mask value `16` is used to indicate that the current size is defined for the input buffer. A value of `32` for the mask indicates that the current size is used to define the output buffer on the UART. In this application, a size of `4096` will be used for the input buffer.

Next an `Instrument Property Node` is used to enable the DTR and disable the RTS transmission lines. The serial port ID is input to the `Property Node` as a reference, and the `Property Node` can automatically adapt to the class of the object you referenced by the port ID. The `Property Node` works just like a virtual function, and it can be preconfigured to access a group of different VISA properties and Active-X properties. The most often-used VISA properties applied in the serial port interfaces are: DTR state, DSR state, RTS state, CTS state, DCD state, RI state, and Break state. All of these states can be enabled or disabled by setting a `1` (asserted) or a `0` (unasserted) on the associated property. To enable the DTR line, a `Boolean To (0,1)` converter is used to translate the Boolean variable `True` to `1`, and assign it to the DTR state. Similarly to the DTR line, to disable the RTS line, a `Boolean To (0,1)` is used to convert the `False` to 0 and assign it to the RTS line.

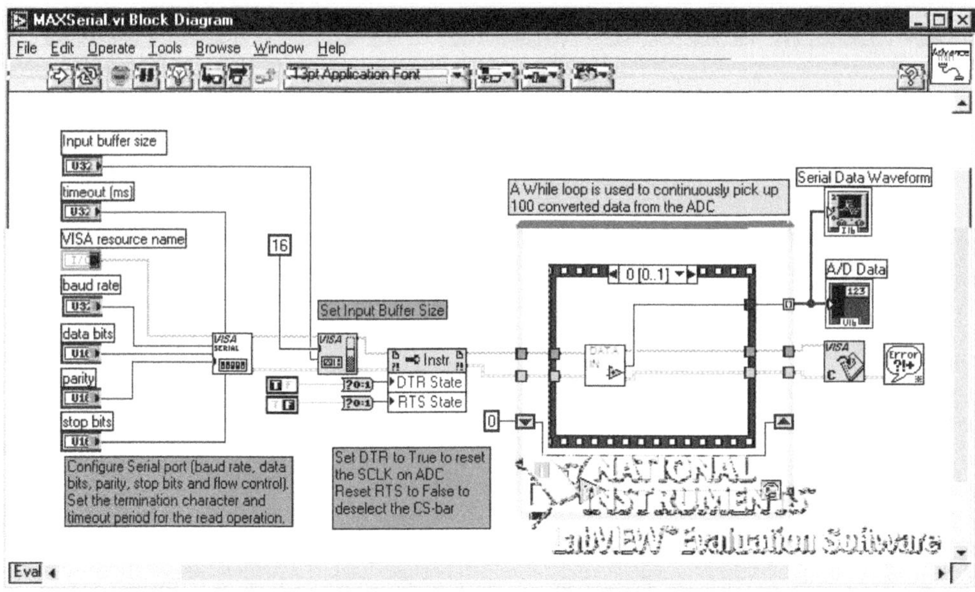

FIGURE 5.29 Block diagram for the main program.

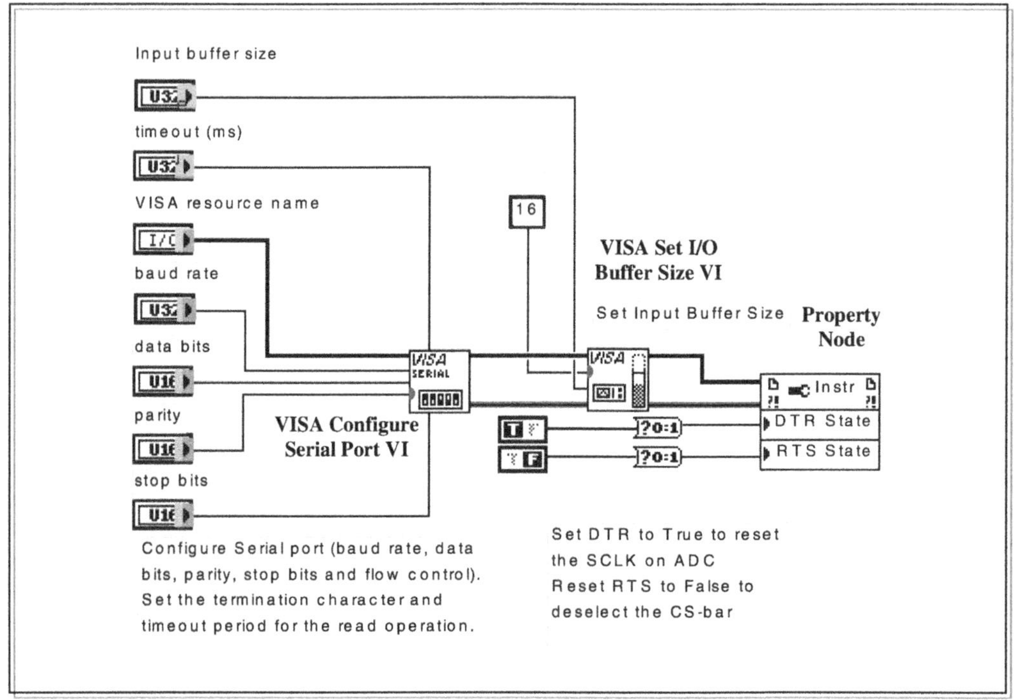

FIGURE 5.30 Block diagram for the main program (first section).

The reason why the DTR line is enabled and the RTS line is disabled is because of the MAX-220 inverter. During the initialization state, a `HIGH` value should be sent to the CS-bar on the MAX-187 to deselect the chip, and a `LOW` value should be sent to the SCLK input of the MAX-187 to disable the Shift clock signal on the chip. (Refer to the circuit shown in Figure 5.26.) The

DTR line is connected to the SCLK input on the MAX-187 via the MAX-220, and the RTS line is connected to the CS-bar input on the MAX-187 via the MAX-220. Because of the inverting logical provided by the MAX-220, if a `HIGH` value is needed in the CS-bar input, a `LOW` signal should be sent to the RTS line to disable it. Similarly, if a `LOW` value is needed in the SCLK input, a `HIGH` signal should be sent to the DTR line, which will enable the DTR.

For the detailed information about the operation principle of the MAX-187 and the MAX-220, refer to Section 2.7.3.3 in Chapter 2.

The second section of the main block diagram is shown in Figure 5.31.

After the DTR line is enabled and the RTS line is disabled, the main program uses a limited `While` loop (cycled 100 times) to call a subroutine named DATA IN to continuously collect 100 converted data from the MAX-187. A `Stacked Sequence` Structure is used to cover another instruction sequence operations. Each time, when the `SubVI` DATA IN is called, a 12-bit converted data is collected by that `SubVI` and feedback to the main program. After each `SubVI` calling, the main program must be delayed for a period of time (one millisecond in this application) to ensure that the collected data is stable and safely stored in the data array. A `Wait Until Next ms Multiple` VI is used to perform this time delay, as shown in Figure 5.31(b).

Finally the VISA `Close` VI is used to close the opened serial port because the data communication is complete. The received data is sent to the data array and displayed on the waveform chart.

A `General Error Handler.vi` is used to process any possible error occurred during the A/D conversion and displaying.

The `While` loop will be terminated if the cycle runs over 100 times. The system compares the loop index `i` with a constant of `100`. The `While` loop is also initialized to `0` at the beginning of each loop by using a constant of `0` that is assigned to the `Shift Register`.

At this point, we complete the coding of the main program of this project. Next we need to complete the coding for the collect data subroutine, or `SubVI`, in the LabVIEW environment.

5.3.2.3 Designing a Front Panel for the `GetMAXData SubVI`

This SubVI will collect 12 bits of converted data from the MAX-187 and feed it back to the main program. The following input/output controls are needed for this SubVI:

- A serial port ID reference number coming from the main program (input)
- A serial port ID reference number returning to the main program (output)
- A 12-bit converted data indicator returned from this SubVI to the main program (output)
- An error in cluster control (input)
- An error out cluster control (output)
- A timeout upper boundary (input)
- A DSR state monitor (local)

We need three input controls and three output controls for this SubVI, and totally we should add six input/output controls and a local DSR control to the panel.

Open a new VI and add these seven controls to the front panel; these are shown in Figure 5.32. Save this panel as `GetMAXData.vi` and this is our SubVI that is used to specially collect the converted data from the MAX-187 bit by bit. This SubVI returns a 12-bit converted data segment to the main program using the converted data output terminal when it finishes the data conversion.

The VISA `resource name` and the VISA `destination name` are the input serial port ID and the output serial port ID references. The default parameters for both references are COM1. Don't worry about this default value and these values would be replaced by the actual input parameters (`ASRL1::INSTR`) coming from the main program as the project runs. The `Data Output` is a signed 16-bit indicator that is used to return the converted 12-bit data to the main program. The timeout upper boundary is 5 *seconds* for this application. The `DSR State` LED

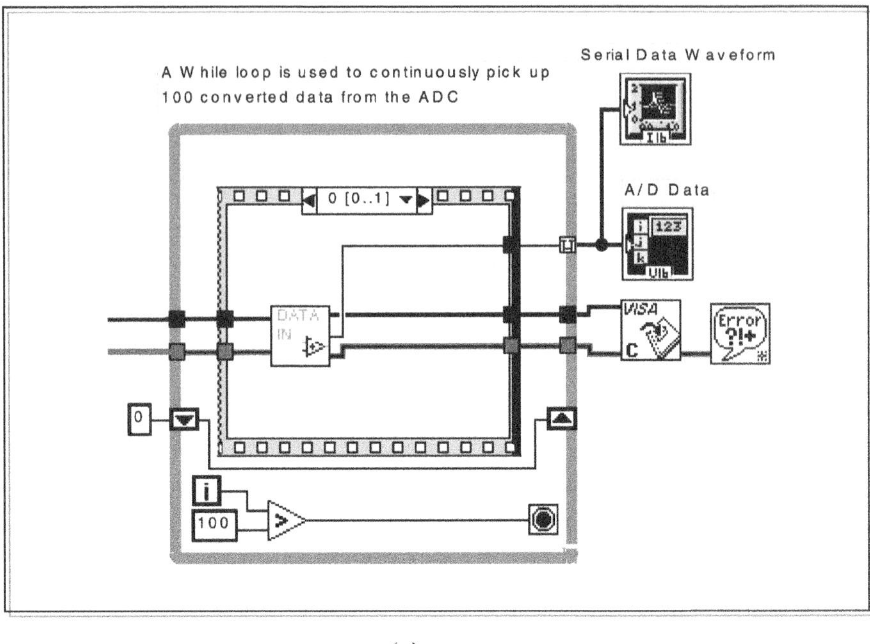

(a)

(b)

FIGURE 5.31 Block diagram for the main program (second section).

indicator is only used in this SubVI and it works as an indicator to display the state of the DSR line during the project runs. For the `error in` and `error out` cluster controls, you can get them easily by coping those controls from some example front panels and paste them into this panel. Otherwise you have to create it by using the cluster control yourself.

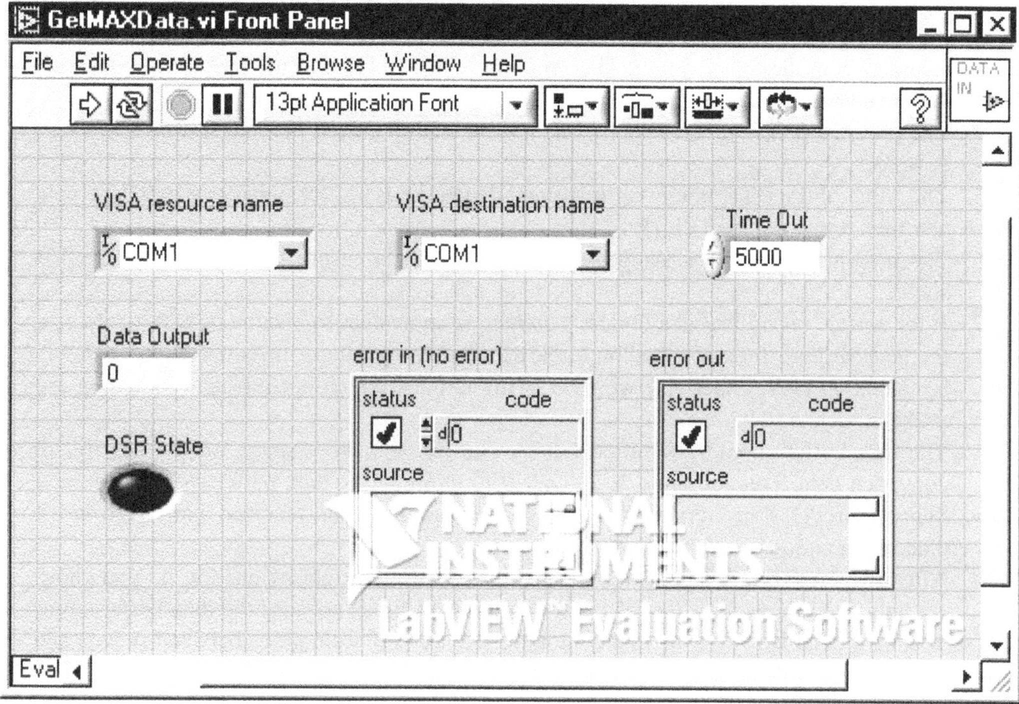

FIGURE 5.32 Front panel for the `GetMAXData.vi` SubVI.

The front panel of this SubVI is completed, next let's take a look at the block diagram of this SubVI.

5.3.2.4 Developing a Block Diagram for the `GetMAXData` SubVI

The MAX187 begins its data conversion when its Chip Select (CS) has a `HIGH`-to-`LOW` transition, and this signal is connected to the RTS line that is converted from the RS-232 to the TTL/CMOS level by the MAX220 inverter. The MAX187 completes the 12-bit conversion using its own internal clock, and the end of conversion is marked by a `HIGH` on the output terminal DOUT on the MAX187. The PC retrieves the converted data from the DSR line, which is connected to the DOUT on the MAX187 via a logical inverter MAX220, by sending a sequence of simulated clocks from the DTR line.

After the data conversion starts, the PC monitors the DSR line and waits until its state becomes `HIGH`, which means that a data conversion is complete, then the PC sends 12 continuous simulated clocks via the DTR line that is connected to the SCLK (Serial CLK) on the MAX187, to serially move the converted data from the output shift register on the MAX187 to the DSR line, and picks up them one by one by checking the value received on the DSR line.

The operation sequence of this process is as follows:

1. The program must set the RTS line to `True` (to enable the RTS state) which will activate the CS-bar input that instructs the MAX187 to begin the data conversion.
2. After the data conversion starts, the system uses a timeout mechanism to monitor the state of the DSR line. If a timeout error occurs, a warning message will be displayed on the screen.
3. If a `LOW` value is detected on the DSR line, it means that a 12-bit data conversion has been completed. Next we need to send a sequence of simulated clocks to the SCLK input

on the MAX187 to shift the converted 12-bit data, bit by bit, from the DOUT buffer to the serial port. To do this, first reset the DTR line to `False` to provide a `LOW-to-HIGH` transaction in the SCLK input. The program will then retrieve the first bit of converted data from the DOUT terminal.

4. The program delays processing by one millisecond to ensure that the shifted bit of data is stable.
5. The value of the DTR line is set to `True`, which sends a `LOW` signal to the SCLK input and thus resets the shift clock.
6. The program delays processing by one millisecond to ensure that the SCLK signal is stable.
7. If the shifted bit of data is a logical `1`, which is equivalent to a value of `LOW` or `False` on the DSR line, the associated bit in the data buffer that stores the converted data should be increased by 1. Otherwise we need to do nothing, which is equivalent to adding a `0` to the associated bit.
8. The data buffer should be shifted left by one bit to make a space for the next bit of converted data. This left-shift is equivalent to multiply the data buffer by 2.
9. Steps 3 through 8 are repeated until all 12-bit data has been received and stored in the data buffer.
10. After all 12-bit data is received, the data buffer is shifted right by one bit. As you know, we only need to perform the left-shift operation 11 times because the data buffer stores 12 bits of data. However, there are a total of 12 left-shift operations between steps 3 and 8. This right-shift effectively divides the data buffer by 2, and is necessary to prevent a leftward overshift.
11. After all 12-bit data is received and stored in the data buffer, the DTR line is set to `True` to reset the SCLK input on the MAX187, and the RTS line is reset to `False` to deselect the CS-bar signal. The received data should be sent to the `Data Output` indicator, which will be returned to the main program.

This sequence can be expressed by the following Visual Basic codes. Figure 5.33 compares those Visual Basic codes with the SubVI we created earlier. By doing that, you should have a clear picture of how this SubVI works.

Now let's develop the block diagram for this SubVI. The block diagram, which is mapped to steps 1 through 3, is shown in Figure 5.34.

Set the RTS state to `True` by using the `Property Node` VI. A `Case` structure is used to detect the state of the DSR line. The `True` case is selected if a `LOW` (`False`) is detected on the DSR line. Inside the `Case` structure, a `Stacked Sequence` structure is used to divide the data collection job into two stages. The first stage is to pick up and store all 12-bit converted data into a data buffer, and the second stage is to right-shift the resulting data buffer with one bit to fix the overshift problem.

A limited `While` loop (this one cycles only 12 times) is embedded inside the `Stacked Sequence` structure to collect and store each shifted bit of data with the help of another `Stacked Sequence` structure. The second structure has six sequences, which are equivalent to six instructions in a text programming language. In the first case (case 0), the DTR line is reset to `False` to transmit a `HIGH` signal to the SCLK input on the MAX187; the program is ready to shift the first bit of converted data from the MAX187 to the DSR line.

An I16 constant is input to the `Shift Register` of the `While` loop to initialize the data buffer to `0`. This I16 constant can be considered the initial value of the data buffer.

The block diagram for step 4 is shown in Figure 5.35.

A `Wait Until Next ms Multiple` VI is used inside the case 1 structure to delay SubVI by one millisecond. A U8 constant with a value of `1` is input to the `Wait Until Next ms Multiple` VI as the upper boundary of the delay time.

```
   (General)                                   GetAD_Data

   Private Function GetAD_Data()
   Dim index As Integer, value As Integer
   value = 0
1  MSComm1.RTSEnable = True          'Set RTS to select MAX187 (CS-bar)-invertion
   VBMAXTimer.Enabled = True         'Start the timer to monitor the timeout
2  Do                                'Wait for the A/D conversion completes
     DoEvents
   Loop Until (MSComm1.DSRHolding = False) Or (TimeOut = True)
   If TimeOut = True Then
     GetAD_Data = GETAD_TIMEOUT 'Return timeout error
   Else                                'DSR is set, the conversion is done
3    For index = 1 To 12
       MSComm1.DTREnable = False     'Set SCLK to HIGH (inversion logic)
4      TimeDelay (1)
5      MSComm1.DTREnable = True      'Reset SCLK to LOW
6      TimeDelay (1)
7      If MSComm1.DSRHolding = False Then
         value = value + 1             'Received a logic 1
       End If
8      value = value * 2             'Shift left 1 bit of the result
9    Next
     MSComm1.DTREnable = True        'Set DTR to 1 to reset the SCLK (invert logic)
     MSComm1.RTSEnable = False       'Reset the CS to deselect MAX187
10   value = value / 2               'Right shift 1 bit to fix the result
     GetAD_Data = value
   End If
11 TimeOut = False
   VBMAXTimer.Enabled = False        'Reset timer and timeout
   End Function
```

FIGURE 5.33 Comparison of Visual Basic and SubVI codes.

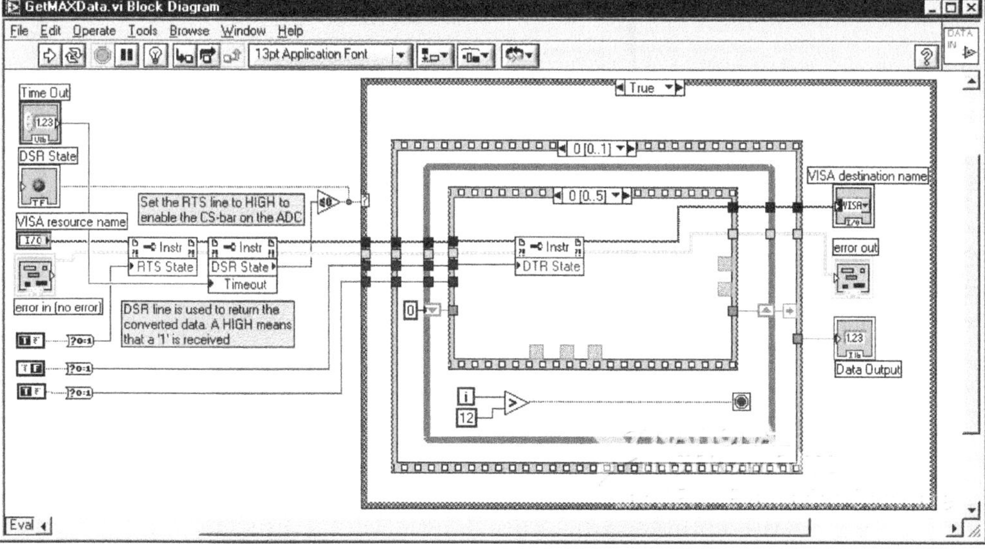

FIGURE 5.34 Block diagram for steps 1 through 3.

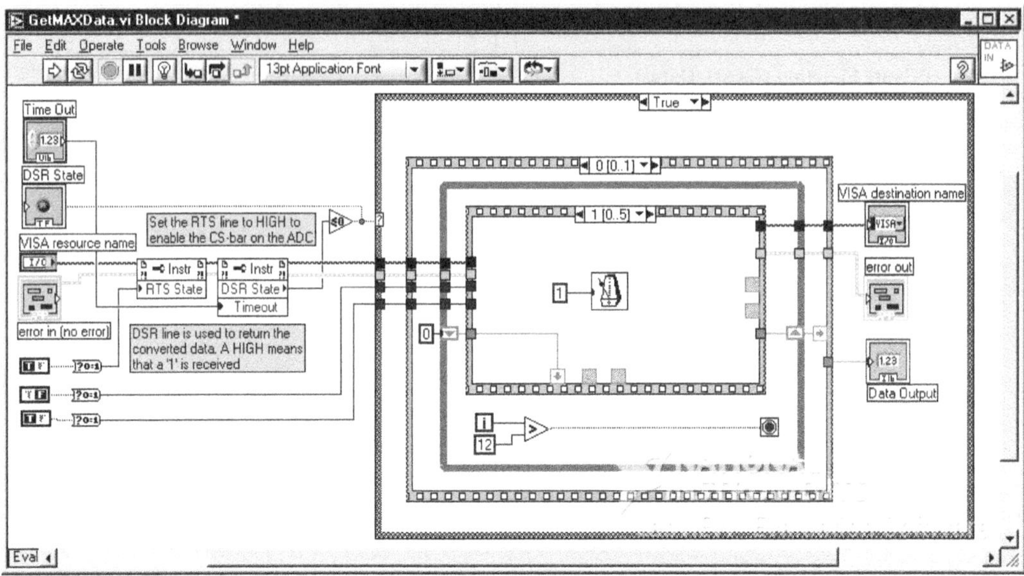

FIGURE 5.35 Block diagram for step 4.

In order to pass the data buffer from one sequence to the next one, we need to create one `Sequence Local` node on the `Stacked Sequence` structure for each case. Right-click on the border of the current `Stacked Sequence` structure (case 1), and select the `Add Sequence Local` item from the pop-up menu to add the first `Sequence Local node` on this case structure (Figure 5.35). Then wire from the I16 constant to the newly created `Sequence Local node` to pass the initial value of the data buffer to the next sequence structure.

The block diagram for step 5 is shown in Figure 5.36.

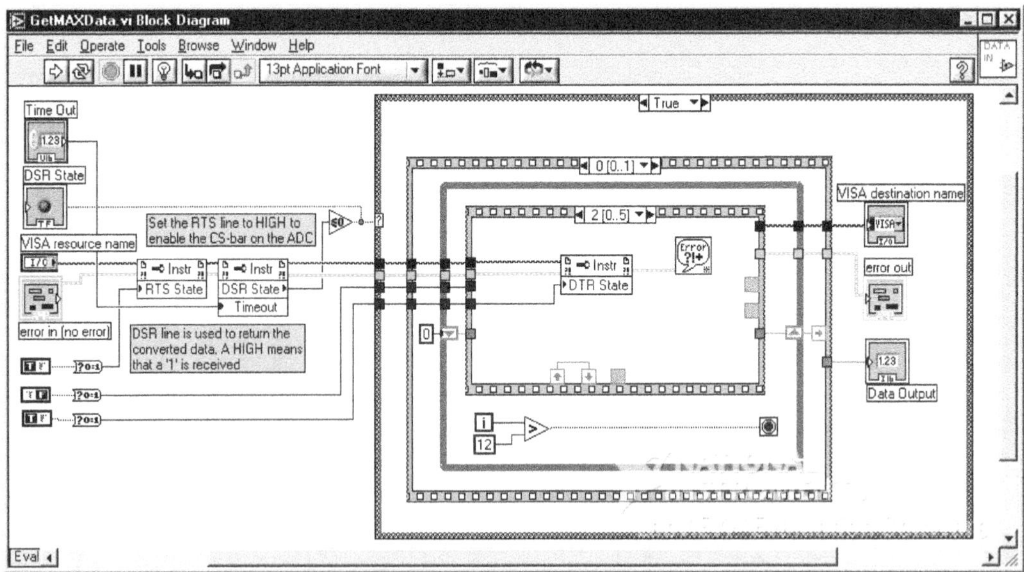

FIGURE 5.36 Block diagram for step 5.

In this step, the DTR line is set to `True` to reset the SCLK input on the MAX187. Combining steps 3, 4 and 5, a complete clock cycle is provided to the SCLK terminal on the MAX187 by setting the different states to the DTR line.

In order to pass the data buffer to the next sequence, another `Sequence Local node` is created and a wire is connected between the first `Sequence Local node` and the newly created `Sequence Local node.`

The block diagram for step 6 is shown in Figure 5.37.

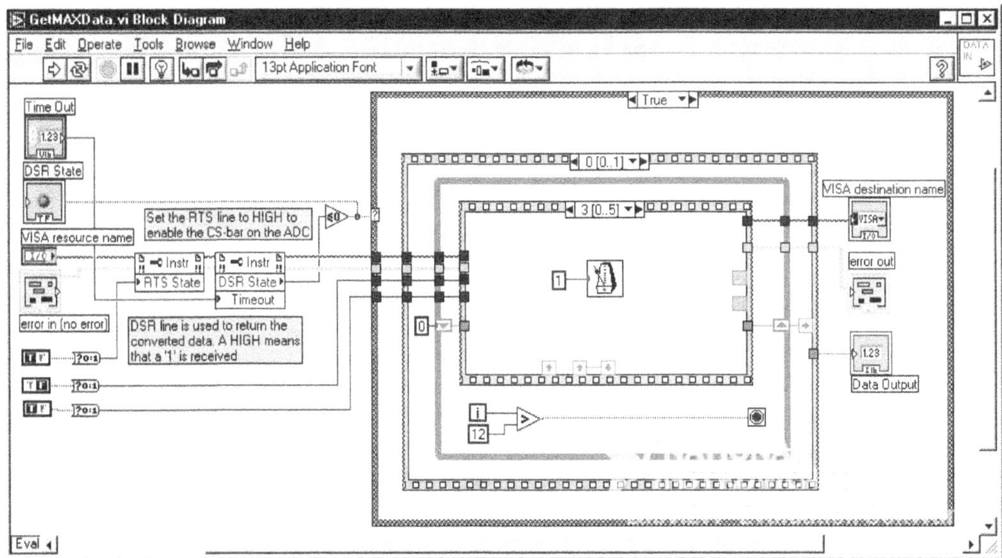

FIGURE 5.37 Block diagram for step 6.

There is nothing new in this block diagram. The only thing you need to note is that in order to pass the data buffer to the next sequence structure, a new `Sequence Local node` or the third `Sequence Local node` must be created, and a connection between the second `Sequence Local node` created at step 5 and the newly created `Sequence Local node` should be made. Refer to Figure 5.37, this connection is at the bottom of the `Stacked Sequence Structure` (Case 3).

A block diagram of step 7 is shown in Figure 5.38.

In this step, we need first to check the state of the DSR line. A `LOW` or `False` value on the DSR line means that a logical `1` on the converted bit is received from the MAX187. The corresponding bit of the received data that is stored in the data buffer should be increased by one. A `Case` Structure and a `Formula Node` structure are used to meet this situation. An input and an output node are added into the `Formula Node` structure. The input data is coming from the third `Sequence Local node` we created at the last step. Similarly, in order to pass this resulted data to the next sequence structure, we need to create another new `Sequence Local node` or the fourth `Sequence Local node`. Type $y = x + 1$; inside the `Formula Node` structure to complete this increment operation, and connect the output y to the fourth `Sequence Local node` we've just created to pass the resulted data to the next sequence.

A block diagram of step 8 is shown in Figure 5.39.

If a `HIGH` or `True` value is detected on the DSR line, it means that a logical `0` has been received from the MAX187. We need only perform one operation, which is to connect the data coming from the Input node of the `Formula Node` to the fourth `Sequence Local node`. This allows the data to be passed into the next sequence structure.

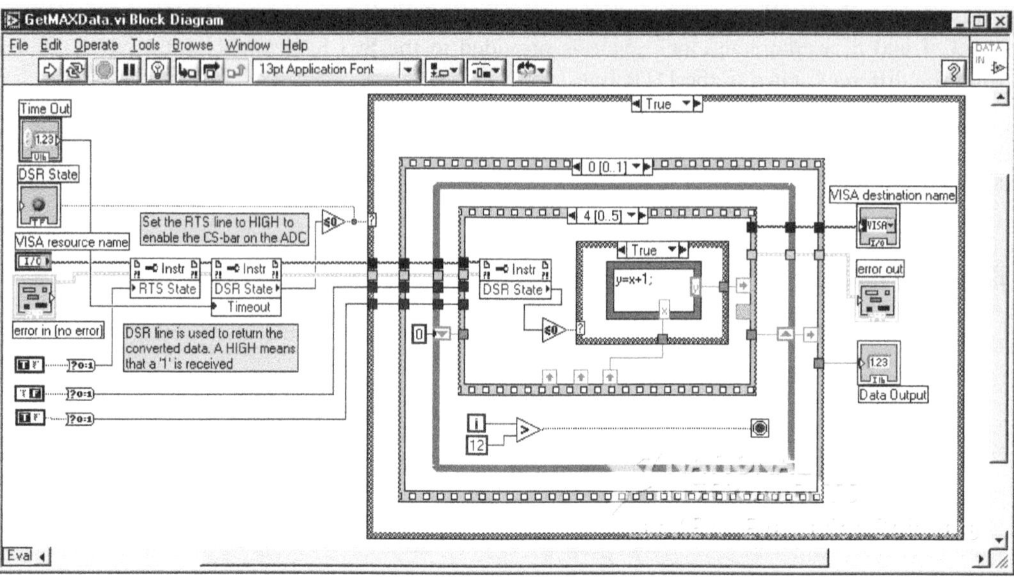

FIGURE 5.38 Block diagram for step 7.

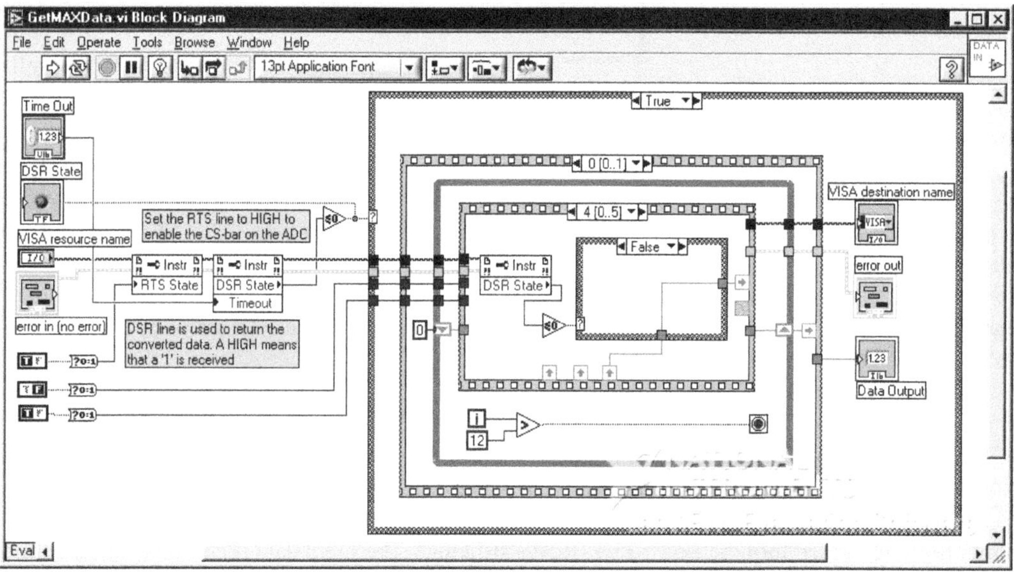

FIGURE 5.39 Block diagram for step 8.

A block diagram of steps 9 and 10 is shown in Figure 5.40.

A `Formula Node` structure is used to perform this multiplication operation. An input and an output node are added into this `Formula Node` structure. The input node is connected to the fourth `Sequence Local node` we created at step 8 and that node contains the converted data passed from the previous sequences. To pass this multiplication result to the next sequence structure, we need to create another new or the fifth `Sequence Local node`. Connect the output of this Formula Node structure *y* to the fifth `Sequence Local node`, and therefore to pass the result

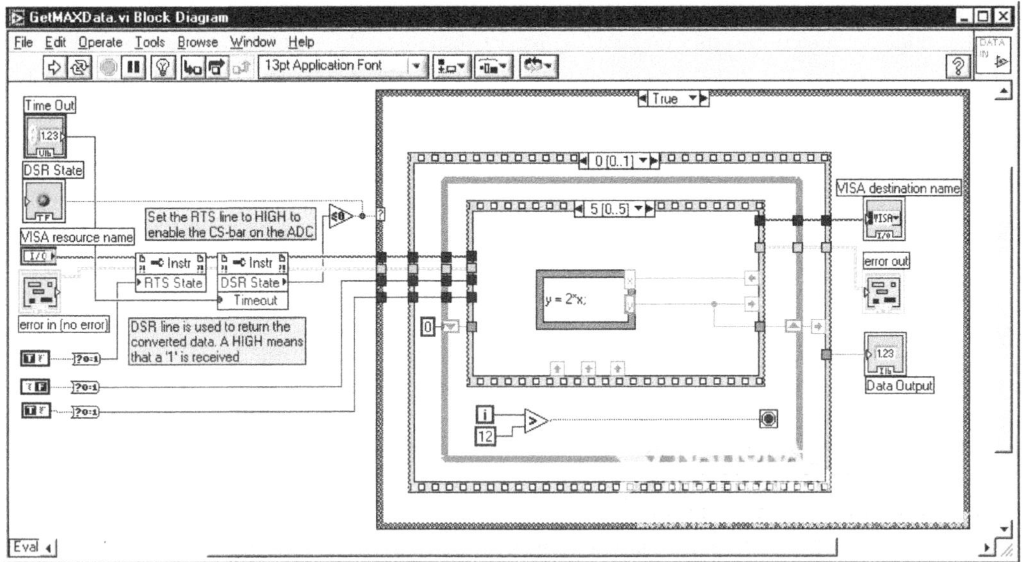

FIGURE 5.40 Block diagram for steps 9 and 10.

to the next sequence structure. Pass this result to the `Shift Register` in the `While` loop and allow the data buffer to continue to receive the next converted bit value from the MAX187 in the following loops.

Repeat steps 3 to 9 until all 12 bits of data have been received. Finally, a shift-right operation is needed to fix the over-shift problem. To perform that operation, the result needs to be passed to the next `Case Structure` that is located just outside of the `While` loop. Add a new `Sequence Local node` on that `Stacked Sequence` structure and connect the wire from the `Shift Register` on the `While` loop to this new added `Sequence Local node`, as shown in Figure 5.40.

The block diagram of steps 11 and 12 is shown in Figure 5.41.

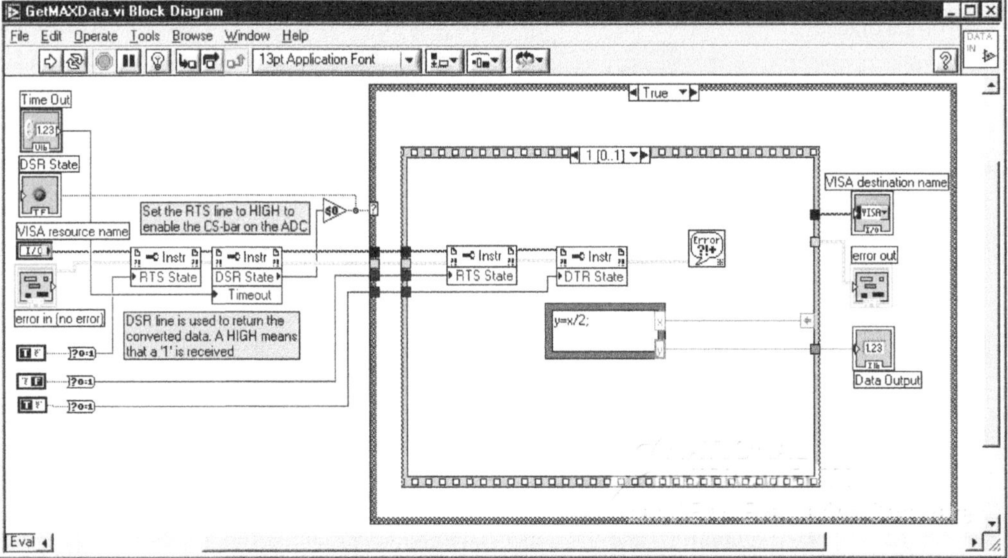

FIGURE 5.41 Block diagram for steps 11 and 12.

A Formula Node structure is used to complete this division operation. An input x and an output y node are added into this Formula Node structure. The input node is connected to the Sequence Local node we created at the last steps, steps 9 and 10. The previous data result is passed into that node. The output y is connected to the Data Output indicator that returns the converted result to the main program.

After all 12 bits of data have been received and passed to the main program, the DTR line is set to True to disable or send a LOW to the SCLK input on the MAX187 A/D converter. The RTS line is reset to False to deselect the MAX187 by sending a HIGH to the CS-bar input on the MAX187.

A General Error Handler.vi is used here to handle any possible error occurred during these operations.

5.3.2.5 Configuring the GetMAXData VI as a SubVI

Referring to Section 5.3.1.4.1, we can perform similar steps to make this LabVIEW program GetMAXData VI as a SubVI and call it from within the main program later. Select the Connect Wire tool from the Tools Palette and open the Front Panel of this SubVI, right-click the icon that is located in the upper-right corner of the panel. Select the Show Connector item from the pop-up menu to select the pattern for this icon. Still we use five connectors for this SubVI, which is shown in Figure 5.42, and these five connectors are associated with five input/output controls that are also shown in Figure 5.42.

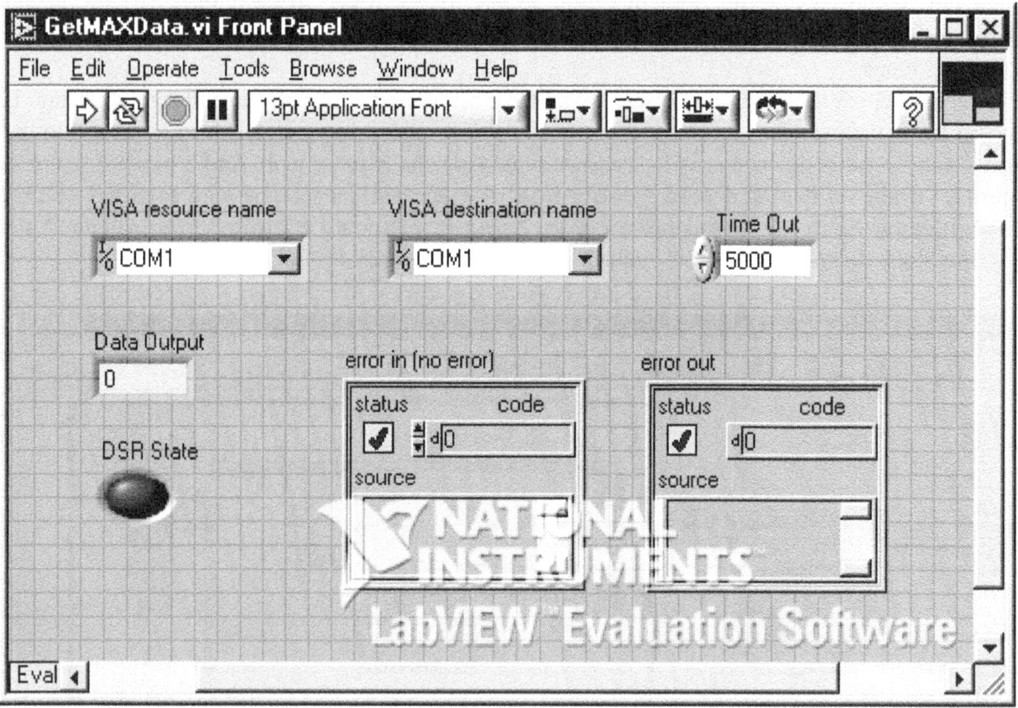

FIGURE 5.42 The SubVI icon and connectors.

In the icon, the upper-left and lower-left connectors are corresponding to the VISA resource name and the error in controls, and the upper-right and lower connectors are connected to the VISA destination name and the error out controls. The middle-right connector is connected to the Data Output indicator that is used to return the received converted data to the main program.

After the pattern and connectors on the SubVI are completed, click `File|Save` item to save this SubVI.

Now we need to add this SubVI into the main program. Open the block diagram of the main program `MAXSerial.vi`, click the `Select a VI` item from the `Functions Palette`, and choose the `GetMAXData.vi` from the opened dialog box. Click the Open button to add this SubVI into our main program. Make the connections for this SubVI as shown in Figure 5.29.

Now we are ready to run and test this project.

5.3.2.6 Testing and Running the Project

Open the front panel of the main program `MAXSerial.vi`, and click the Run button to start running the project. The baud rate we use here is 19200, but of course you can select a different rate for your applications. The analog waveforms we used are a sinusoidal waveform, a square waveform, and triangular waveform, and these are created by a function generator. The output of these three waveforms is shown in Figures 5.43, 5.44, and 5.45, respectively.

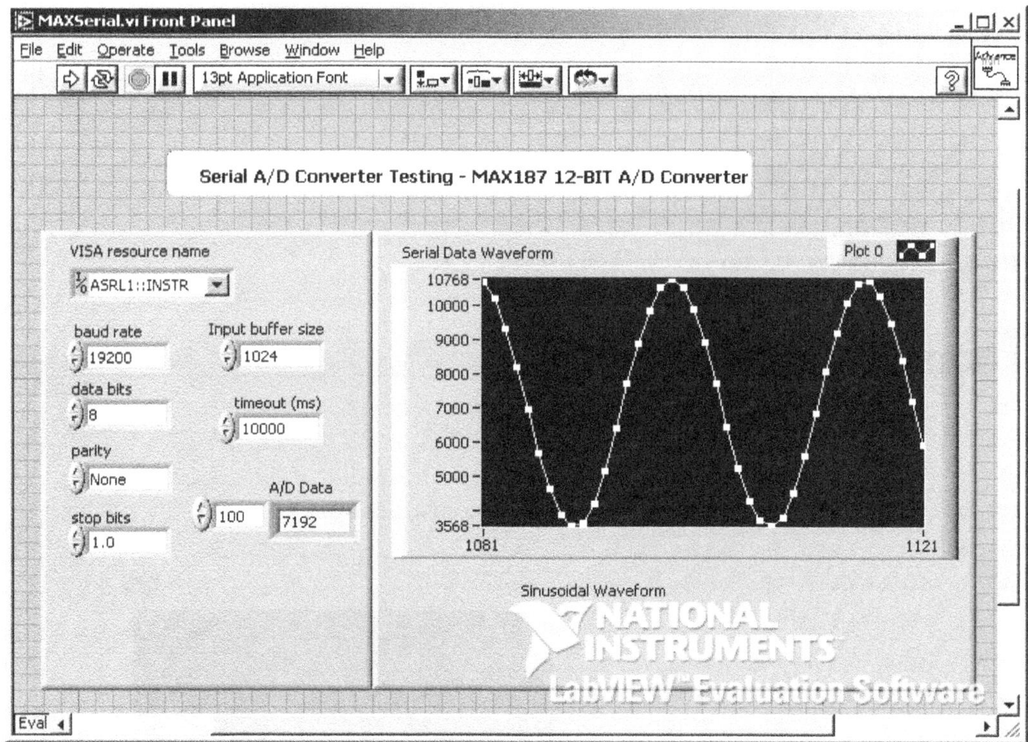

FIGURE 5.43 Running `MAXSerial.vi` with a sinusoidal waveform.

The amplitude of the waveforms is represented by the I16 numbers. The number at the horizontal axis represents the number of sampling points.

The files for this project, including the main program block diagram, its front panel, the SubVI block diagram, and its front panel, are located on the attached CD in the folder `Chapter 5\AdvdSerial\MAX187\MAX187`.

You can modify this program to display the real time (in HH:MM:SS format) on the horizontal axis and the real measurement units (volts, for instance) on the vertical axis. A sample project named `MAXSerialReal` has these features; it is located on the attached CD in the folder `Chapter 5\AdvdSerial\MAX187\MAX187Real`.

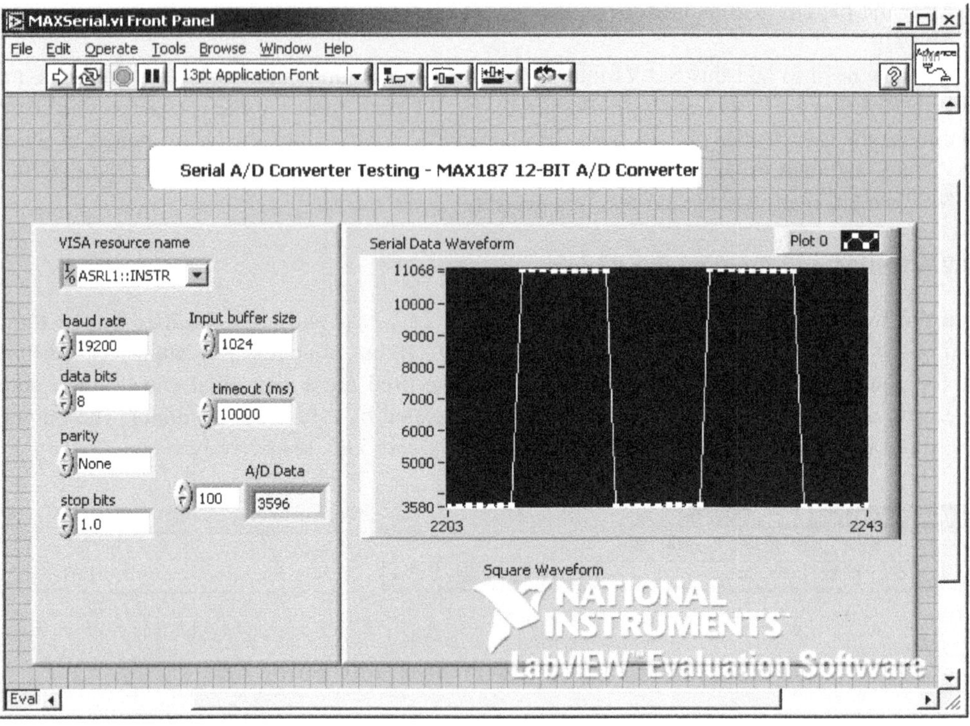

FIGURE 5.44 Running `MAXSerial.vi` with a square waveform.

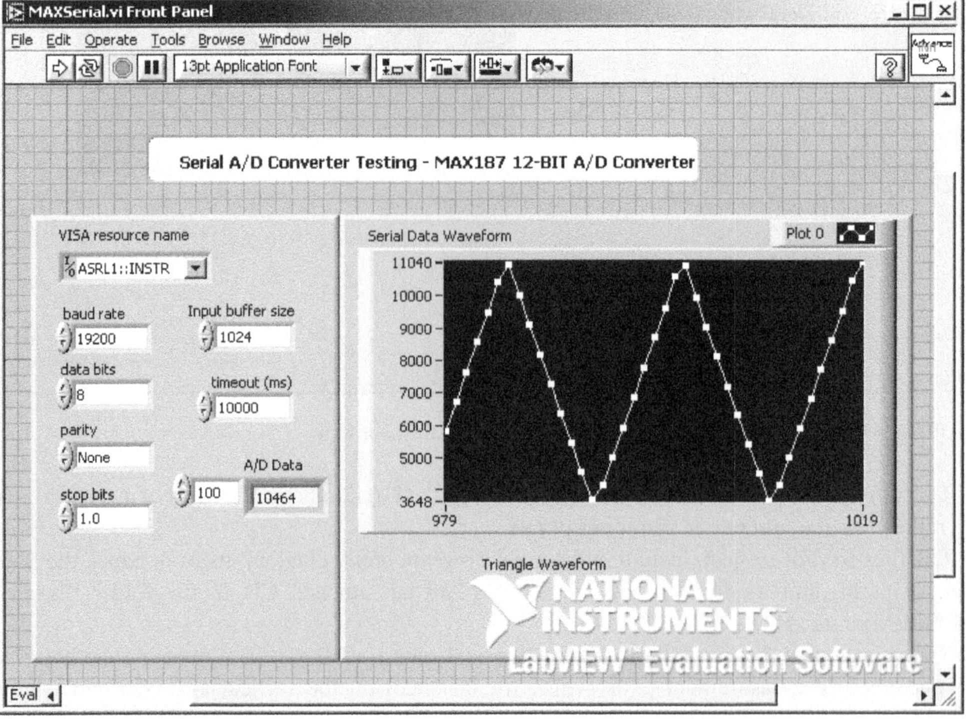

FIGURE 5.45 Running `MAXSerial.vi` with a triangular waveform.

5.4 CALLING THE DLL FROM LABVIEW TO INTERFACE WITH THE SERIAL PORT

In this section, we discuss how to call the shared DLL developed in third-party languages from within LabVIEW to perform some special functionalities.

5.4.1 Using Call Library Function and the Code Interface Node

In LabVIEW, two interface tools, Call Library Function and the Code Interface Node (CIN), are used to control communications between the block diagram of the LabVIEW and the components developed in third-party languages. These two tools can be used to develop block diagram objects designed to link LabVIEW with source code written in other conventional programming languages. They appear on the block diagram as icons with input and output terminals. Linking external code to LabVIEW includes the following steps:

1. You compile the source code and link it to form executable code. (If you already have a compiled DLL, this step is not necessary.)
2. LabVIEW calls the executable code when the node executes.
3. LabVIEW passes input data from the block diagram to the executable code.
4. LabVIEW returns data from the executable code to the block diagram.

The LabVIEW compiler can generate code fast enough for most programming tasks. You can call CINs and shared libraries from LabVIEW to accomplish tasks that a text-based language can accomplish more easily, such as time-critical tasks. You can also use CINs and shared libraries for tasks you cannot perform directly from the block diagram, such as calling system routines for which no corresponding LabVIEW functions exist. CINs and shared libraries can link existing code to LabVIEW, although you might need to modify the code so it uses the correct LabVIEW data types.

CINs and shared libraries execute synchronously, so LabVIEW cannot use the execution thread used by these objects for any other tasks. When a VI runs, LabVIEW monitors the user interface, including the menus and keyboard. In multithreaded applications, LabVIEW uses a separate thread for user interface tasks. In single-threaded applications, LabVIEW switches between user interface tasks and running VIs.

When CIN or shared library object code executes, it takes control of its execution thread. If an application has only a single thread of control, the application waits until the object code returns. In single-threaded operating systems such as Macintosh, these objects even prevent other applications from running.

LabVIEW cannot interrupt object code that is running, so you cannot reset a VI that is running a CIN or shared library until execution completes. If you want to write a CIN or shared library that performs a long task, be aware that LabVIEW cannot perform other tasks in the same thread while these objects executes.

5.4.2 Using the Call Library Function to Access DLLs

You can call most standard shared libraries with Call Library Function. In Windows these libraries are Dynamic Link Libraries. Call Library Function includes a large number of data types and calling conventions. You can use it to call functions from most standard and custom-made libraries.

Call Library Function is most appropriate when you have existing code you want to call, or if you are familiar with the process of creating standard shared libraries. Because a library uses a format standard among several development environments, you can use almost any development environment to create a library that LabVIEW can call. Refer to the documentation for your compiler to determine whether you can create standard shared libraries.

Use Call Library Function to call a 32-bit Windows DLL, a Macintosh Code Fragment, or a UNIX Shared Library function directly.

To access and add a Call Library Function, go to the `Functions»Advanced` palette and click the Call Library Function icon, as shown in Figure 5.46.

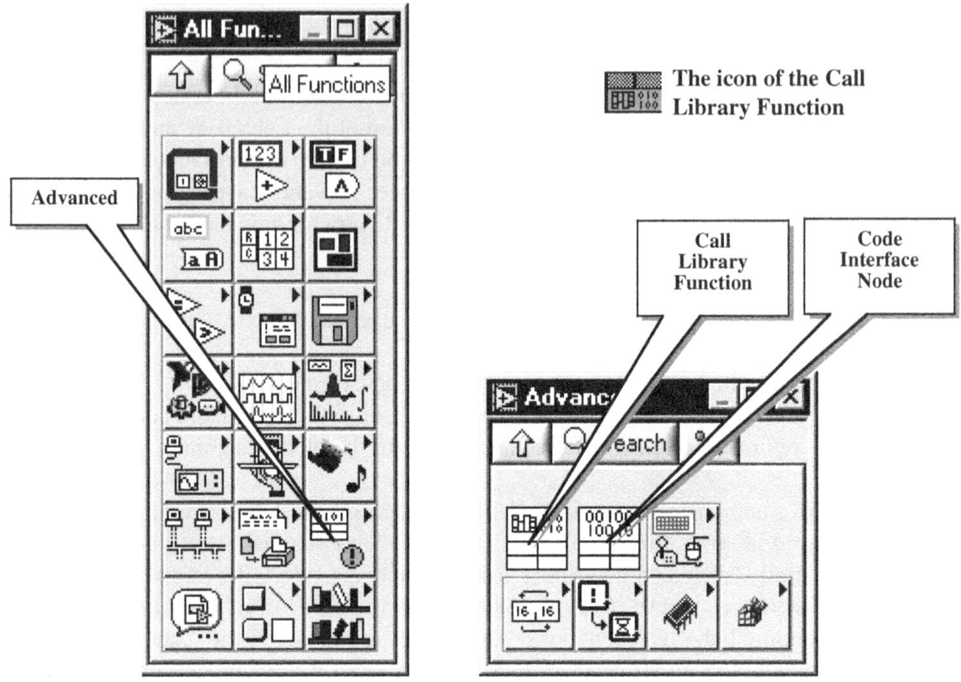

FIGURE 5.46 Using the Call Library Function and the Code Interface Node.

When you click the Call Library Function tool from the Advanced sub-palette, an icon of the Call Library Function, which is shown in Figure 5.46, can be added into the block diagram on the LabVIEW project.

Call Library Function provides a group of properties that can be used to configure and set up the function to perform the desired tasks. By right-clicking on the icon of the Call Library Function, all properties are displayed on a pop-up menu. Two of them are important to us: `Configure` and `Create.c File`.

To set up a connection between Call Library Function and the external codes, you need first to configure the diagram of the Call Library Function by using the `Configure` property. The following setup features are included inside the `Configure` property (Figure 5.47):

- Library Name or Path
- Function Name
- Calling Conventions
- Parameters
- Type
- Data Type
- Browse Button
- Add Parameters Before
- Add Parameters After
- Delete this Parameter

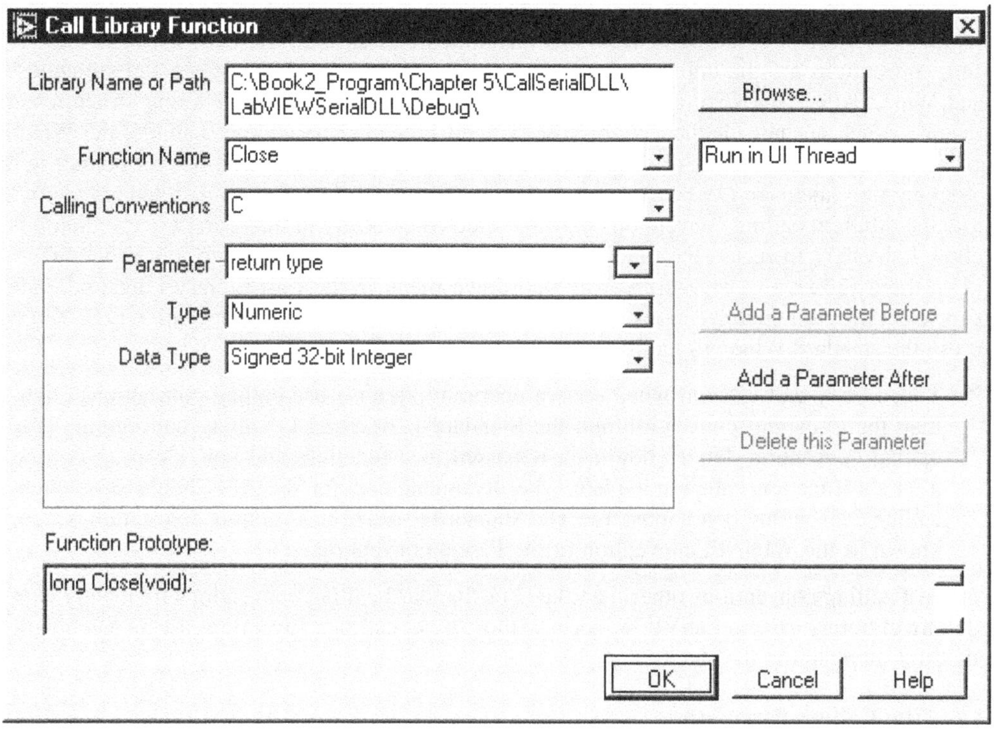

FIGURE 5.47 An example of the `Configure` property dialog box.

Figure 5.47 shows an example of the `Configure` property dialog box. The location of the DLL file is determined by the contents of the `Library Name or Path`, which can be selected by clicking the `Browse` button to find this DLL file. The DLL function name is `Close` in this example.

5.4.2.1 The Calling Conventions

In order to meet different requirements, different systems use different calling conventions. The most popular calling conventions are: `_asm`, `_fastcall`, `_based`, `_inline`, `_cdecl`, and `_stdcall`.

The `_cdecl` is the default calling convention for C and C++ programs. Because the stack is cleaned up by the caller, it can do `vararg` functions. The `_cdecl` calling convention creates larger executables than `_stdcall`, because it requires each function call to include stack cleanup code.

The `_stdcall` calling convention is used to call Win32 API functions. For both `_cdecl` and `_stdcall` calling conventions, the arguments that passed to the procedure are pushed into the stack in the right-to-left order.

The `_fastcall` calling convention specifies that arguments to functions are to be passed in registers, not in stack.

The `_based` keyword specifies that a pointer is a 32-bit offset from a 32-bit pointer base. The `_inline` keywords allow the compiler to insert a copy of the function body into each place the function is called. The insertion occurs only if the compiler's cost/benefit analysis shows it to be profitable. The `_asm` keyword invokes the inline assembler and can appear wherever a C or C++ statement is legal. It cannot appear by itself. It must be followed by an assembly instruction, a group of instructions enclosed in braces, or, at the very least, an empty pair of braces. The term "`_asm` block" here refers to any instruction or group of instructions, whether or not in braces.

Here we only concentrate on the _cdecl and _stdcall calling conventions. Besides the differences of these two calling conventions mentioned earlier, the difference between these two calling conventions are the definitions of variables, functions, system constants and structures in C and Win32 APIs. The C programming language defines its own programming structures and functions, which are not identical with those defined in Win32 APIs. For example, the Window Handler defined in the Win32 APIs is HWND, but it is equivalent to a double-integer pointer in the C programming language (int**). Depends on what kinds of functions and structures you want to use, the different calling conventions must be selected correctly in this Configure dialog box to allow LabVIEW to access the functions and structures you've selected for your program.

Use the Calling Conventions pull-down menu in the Call Library Function dialog box to select the calling conventions for the function. The default calling convention is C. You can also use the standard Windows calling convention, _stdcall.

TIP: Your library call can fail when certain operating systems use calling conventions other than the C calling convention and the Standard (_stdcall) calling convention. The calling convention defines how data is passed to a function, and how clean up occurs after the function call is complete. The documentation for the API should say which calling convention(s) you must use. The Standard (_stdcall) calling convention is also known as the WINAPI convention or the Pascal convention.

Use of calling conventions other than the C or Standard calling conventions frequently causes the failure of library calls in LabVIEW, because those other calling conventions use an incompatible method for maintaining the stack.

5.4.2.2 The Calling Parameters

Initially, Call Library Function has no parameters and has a return value of Void. To add parameters to the function, click the Add a Parameter Before or After button. To remove a parameter, click the Delete this Parameter button.

Use the Parameter pull-down menu to select different parameters or the return value. You may wish to edit the Parameter name to something more descriptive, thus making it easier to switch between parameters. The parameter name does not affect the call, but it is propagated to output wires.

Use the Type pull-down menu to indicate the type of each parameter. The return type can be Void (meaning that the function will not return a value), Numeric, or String.

For parameters, you can select Numeric, Array, String, Waveform, ActiveX, or Adapt to Type.

After you select an item from the Type pull-down menu, you'll see more items that you can use to indicate details about the data type and about how to pass the data to the library function. The call library function has a number of different items for data types, because of the variety of data types required by different libraries. Refer to the documentation for the library you call to determine which data types to use.

Following is a list of most-often used type:

- Void Accepted only for the return value. This value is not available for parameters. If your function will not return any values, set the return value parameter to Void.
- Numerics For numeric data types, you must indicate the exact numeric type using the Data Type pull-down menu. Valid types include the following:

  Signed and unsigned 8-bit, 16-bit, and 32-bit integers
  Four-byte, single-precision numbers
  Eight-byte, double-precision numbers

You cannot use extended-precision numbers or complex numbers. (Standard libraries generally do not use these.)

You also must use the `Pass` pull-down menu to indicate whether you want to pass the value or a pointer to the value.

- `Arrays` Indicates the data type of an array (using the same items as for numeric data types), the number of dimensions, and the format to use for passing the array. Use the `Array Format` pull-down menu to make one of the following choices:

  `Array Data Pointer` Passes a pointer to the array data
  `Array Handle` Passes a pointer to a pointer to a four-byte value for each dimension, followed by the data
  `Array Handle Pointer` Passes a pointer to an array handle

- `Strings` Indicates the string format for strings. Valid values for String
- `Format` includes CString Pointer, Pascal String Pointer, String Handle, or String Handle Pointer —Select a string format that the library function expects. Most standard libraries expect either a C string (a string followed by a Null character) or a Pascal string (a string preceded by a length byte). If the library function you are calling is written for LabVIEW, you might want to use the `String Handle` format, which is a pointer to a pointer to four bytes for length information, followed by string data.
- `Waveform` For waveform data types, you indicate the dimension, and then use the `Data Type` pull-down menu to indicate the exact numeric type.
- `ActiveX` For ActiveX objects, you select one of the following items from the `Data Type` pull-down menu:

  `ActiveX Variant Pointer`—Passes a pointer to ActiveX data.
  `IDispatch* Pointer`—Passes a pointer to the `IDispatch` interface of an ActiveX Automation server.
  `IUnknown Pointer`—Passes a pointer to the `IUnknown` interface of an ActiveX Automation server.

- `Adapt to Type` Passes arbitrary LabVIEW data types to DLLs in the same way that they are passed to a CIN, as follows:

  Scalars are passed by reference. A pointer to the scalar is passed to the library.
  Arrays and **strings** are passed as handles (pointers to pointers to the data).
  Clusters are passed by reference.
  Scalar elements in arrays or clusters are passed in a sequence. For example, a cluster containing a numeric value is passed as a pointer to a structure containing a numeric value.
  Cluster within arrays are passed in a sequence.
  Strings and arrays within clusters are referenced by handles.

TIP: Do not attempt to resize an array with system functions such as `realloc`, because they might crash your system. Instead, use one of the CIN manager functions, such as `NumericArrayResize`.

5.4.2.3 Calling Functions That Expect Other Data Types

You might encounter a function that expects a data type LabVIEW does not use. For example, you cannot use Call Library Function to pass an arbitrary cluster or array of non-numeric data. If you need to call a function that expects other data types, use one of the following methods:

- Depending on the data type, you might be able to pass the data by creating a string or array of bytes that contains a binary image of the data you want to send. You can create binary data by typecasting data elements to strings and concatenating them.
- You can write a library function that accepts data types that LabVIEW does use, and specify parameters to build the data structures the library function expects, and then call the library function.

5.4.2.4 The `Create.c` File

Another feature provided by the Call Library Function is the `Create.c` file. This file is used to create the protocol for the DLL function to be called in the DLL library, based on the calling convention you selected from the preceding property. After you finish configuring the DLL function (using the `Configure` property), you can select `Create.c` File to create an empty function body. The default name for this protocol file is `code.c`. You'll need to add the function body and then make the necessary modifications based on the compiler you are using. You can also move the body of this function, or combine it with other functions together to form an integrated DLL file.

This property is very important and you should perform this step to generate the function protocol. Although it is possible for you to directly develop the DLL file with the same name and signatures as those of the function defined by using the `Configure` property, it is highly recommended that you use this property to generate the function protocol and copy it into the DLL file to fulfill the development of the target DLL file.

Another point you need to note is that you can develop a C convention calling function in the C++ environment with some modifications to the function body generated by the `Create.c File` property. We will use a real example to show how to do this in the following section.

5.4.2.5 Multiple Calls to the Shared DLL Function

In a multithreaded operating system, you can make multiple calls simultaneously to a DLL or a shared library. By default, all call library objects run in the user interface thread. The control below the `Browse` button in the `Call Library Function` dialog box reflects your selection of `Run in UI Thread` or `Reentrant`.

Run in UI Thread is a popular running method for most DLL functions. For a multitasking or a multithreading operating system, such as Windows 95/98/NT/2000/XP, when a VI (such as a Call Library Function) is run, LabVIEW opens a separate thread to handle that VI and monitor its running status. After a new thread that is used to run the VI is generated, LabVIEW transfers control to that thread itself, and LabVIEW then cannot interrupt the thread until it is done running. Unlike the `Run in UI Thread` mode, `Reentrant` allows multiple different threads to access and call a DLL function simultaneously. Before you configure a Call Library Function object to be reentrant, make sure that multiple threads can call the function(s) simultaneously. The following list shows the basic characteristics of thread-safe code in a shared library.

- It stores no global data (no global variables or files on disk, for example); it does not access any hardware (in other words, it does not contain register-level programming); it makes no calls to any functions, shared libraries, or drivers that are not thread safe.
- It uses semaphores or mutexes to protect access to global resources.
- It is called by only one non-reentrant VI.

Now you should have a relatively clear picture of the properties and features of the Call Library Function used in LabVIEW. In the following section, we'll develop a sample program that applies this tool to develop a project that calls external code to interface with the serial port. The example developed in this section is similar to the one developed in Section 5.3.1. We'll develop a shared DLL and call it from within LabVIEW to communicate with a serial A/D converter, via an RS-232 port.

5.4.3 Using the Call Library Function to Interface with the TLC548 Serial A/D Converter

The project is developed in the following sequence:

1. We create a new LabVIEW project with Call Library Function VI as the interface between the external codes and LabVIEW.
2. We configure the DLL functions, based on the desired function protocol, using the `Configure` property provided in the `Call Library Function` dialog box.
3. We use the `Create.c File` property to generate the DLL function protocols.
4. We develop a DLL target file that includes the DLL functions defined in steps 2 and 3.
5. We use the `Browse` button in the `Call Library Function` dialog box to locate and connect the DLL target file with LabVIEW.
6. We run a LabVIEW project that calls DLL functions to interface with the TLC548 serial A/D converter and thus collect data via the serial port.

Now let's develop our project.

5.4.3.1 Interface Circuit of the TLC548 Serial A/D Converter

The hardware connection and interface circuit between the computer and the serial A/D converter TLC548 is detailed in Section 5.3.1 and illustrated here in Figure 5.48.

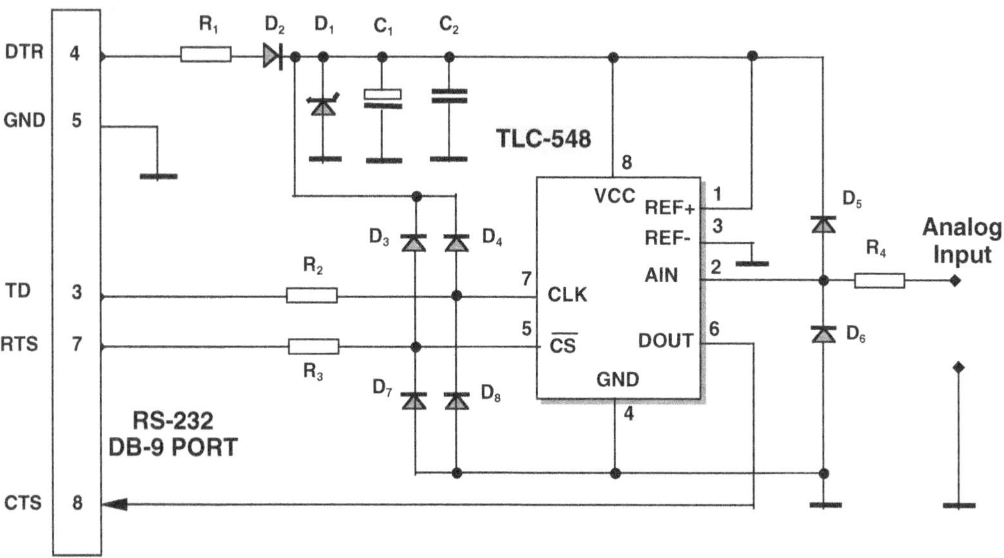

FIGURE 5.48 Interface circuit of the TLC548 A/D converter

The values of the components used in this circuit are listed in Table 5.3.

Make the hardware connection as shown in Figure 5.48 based on the elements parameters in Table 5.3. The serial port used in this project is still COM1.

TABLE 5.3
The Elements Parameters

Elements	Values	Comments
R_1	1 KΩ	Current-limited resistor
R_2, R_3, R_4	30 KΩ	Current-limited resistors
D_1	5.1 V	Zener riode
D_2–D_8	1N4148	Diodes
C_1	10 μF/15 V	Electrolytic capacitor
C_2	100 nF	Capacitor

5.4.3.2 Building the Function Protocol in LabVIEW

Launch LabVIEW 7.0 Express and create a new project named `CallSerialDLL.vi`. Add the following components into the front panel of this new project:

- An array control, `Port Settings`, which includes six elements. This array stores values for the serial port configuration parameters (the port number, baud rate, parity, data bits, stop bits, and timeout).
- A numeric control, `# of Data`, that is used to store the number of data to be collected from the A/D converter.
- A numeric indicator, `Data Output`, that is used to display each received data from the TLC548 in real time.
- A horizontal graduated bar, `Progress`, that is used to display the data collection progress in real time.
- Two square LEDs, `Setup Error` and `Close Error`, are used to monitor and display possible errors during the setup and close operations.
- A waveform chart, `A/D Data Waveform`, is used to display the collected data in real time.

The finished front panel of the project should match the one shown in Figure 5.49.

Modify all labels that are associated to each component on the front panel to match those that displayed in Figure 5.49.

Open the `Block Diagram` of this project and perform the following steps to complete the design of this block diagram.

- Add a `Stacked Sequence` Structure into this block diagram. Add another two additional frames to this `Stacked Sequence` Structure by right-clicking on this structure and select the `Add Frame After` item from the pop-up menu.
- Add a `While` loop into the second frame (frame 1) on the new added `Stacked Sequence` Structure we did in the last step.
- Add three call library function nodes into three `Stacked Sequence` structures, exactly each call library function node into each `Stacked Sequence` structure. For the second call library function node, it should be inserted into the `While` loop.
- Go to the first call library function node that is added into the first frame (frame 0), right-click on that node and select the `Configure` item from the pop-up menu to open its Call Library Function dialog box. Finish the setting up of the first part for this Call Library Function by entering the parameters that are shown in Figure 5.50.
- The returned data is a signed 32-bit integer that is used to indicate whether this function calling is successful or not. The function name is `Setup` and the calling convention is

CallSerialDLL.vi Front Panel
File Edit Operate Tools Browse Window Help
13pt Application Font
A/D Data Waveform
Plot 0
Port Settings
0
1
9600
8
1
0
5000
# of Data
100
Data Output
0
Setup Error
Close Error
Progress
255
200
150
100
50
1
Amplitude
00:00:00
00:01:41
Time
NATIONAL INSTRUMENTS
LabVIEW Evaluation Software
Eval

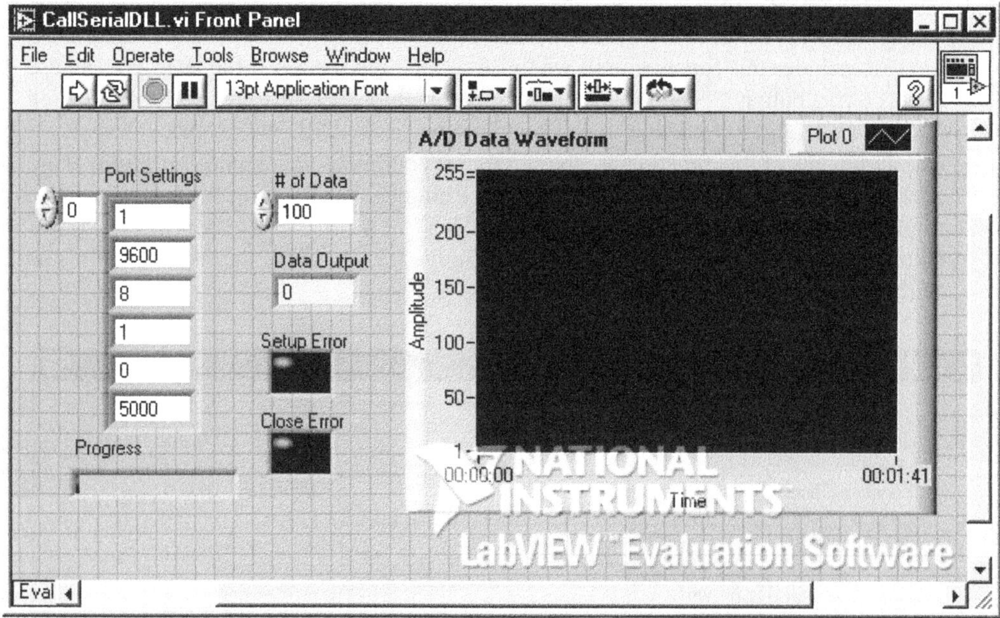

FIGURE 5.49 Front panel for the `CallSerialDLL.vi` project.

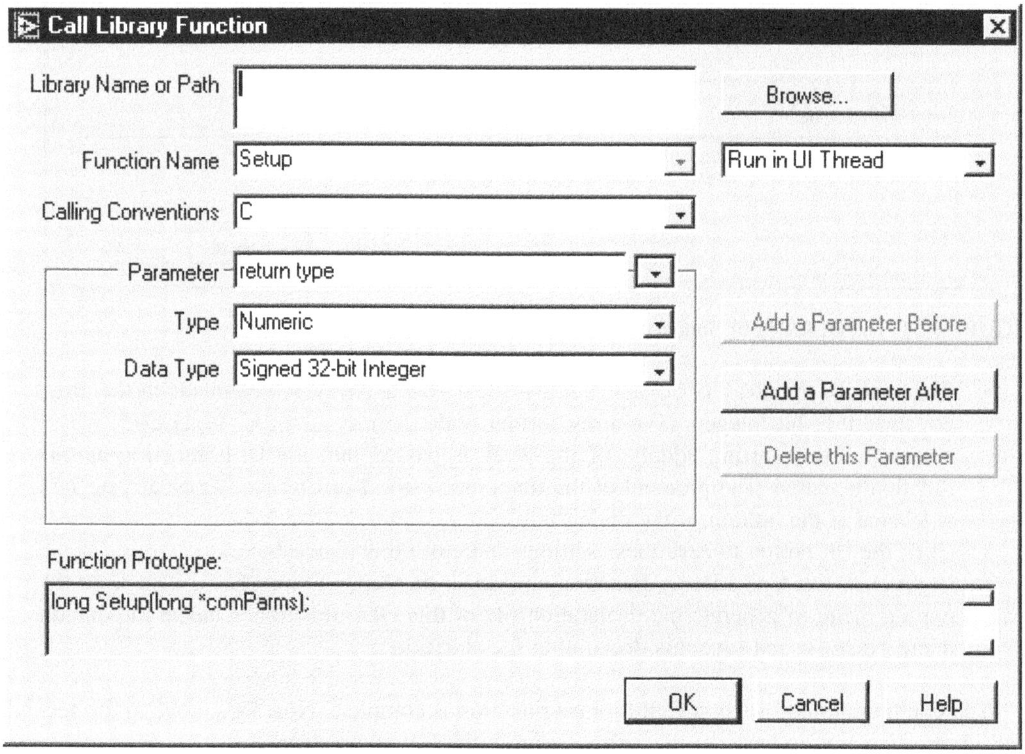

Call Library Function
Library Name or Path
Browse...
Function Name
Setup
Run in UI Thread
Calling Conventions
C
Parameter
return type
Type
Numeric
Data Type
Signed 32-bit Integer
Add a Parameter Before
Add a Parameter After
Delete this Parameter
Function Prototype:
long Setup(long *comParms);
OK
Cancel
Help

FIGURE 5.50 The `DLL Setup` function (part 1).

the default one, C convention. For the `Library Name or Path` box, keep it blank at this moment. Because we cannot determine the location and path of the target DLL file that includes this function until we finish developing that DLL file later. We can use the `Browse` button to find the location and the path of that DLL and add that location into the Call Library Function dialog box later when the DLL file is built.

- The arguments of this function are the serial port configuration parameters. Totally there are six parameters we need to enter from the front panel as the project runs and we like to place those six parameters into an array. Click the `Add a Parameter After` button to add this array, which is shown in Figure 5.51, to finish the second part of the setting up.

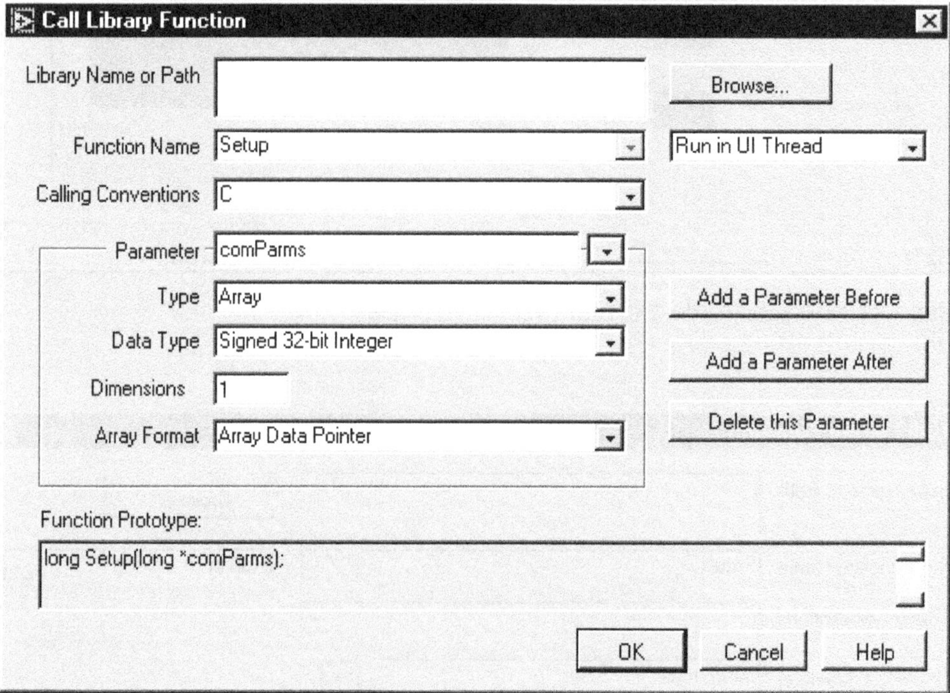

FIGURE 5.51 The DLL `Setup` function (part 2).

- The name of the array is `comParms` and the `Type` is Array. All elements in the array are signed 32-bit integers. The array format is the `Array Data Pointer`, which means that the starting address of the array is passed into the DLL function as this function is called. The protocol of the function for the `Function Prototype` box is located at the bottom of the dialog box.
- Click the `OK` button to save these settings and close this dialog box.
- Right-click this Call Library Function and select the `Create.c File` item from the pop-up menu to generate the declaration file of this DLL function. Change the default name `code.c` and save this declaration file as `code1.c`.

The configuration of the first Call Library Function is complete. Now let's move to the second Call library Function to perform its configuration in the following steps.

- Go to the second call library function node that is added into the second frame (frame 1), right-click on that node and select the `Configure` item from the pop-up menu to open

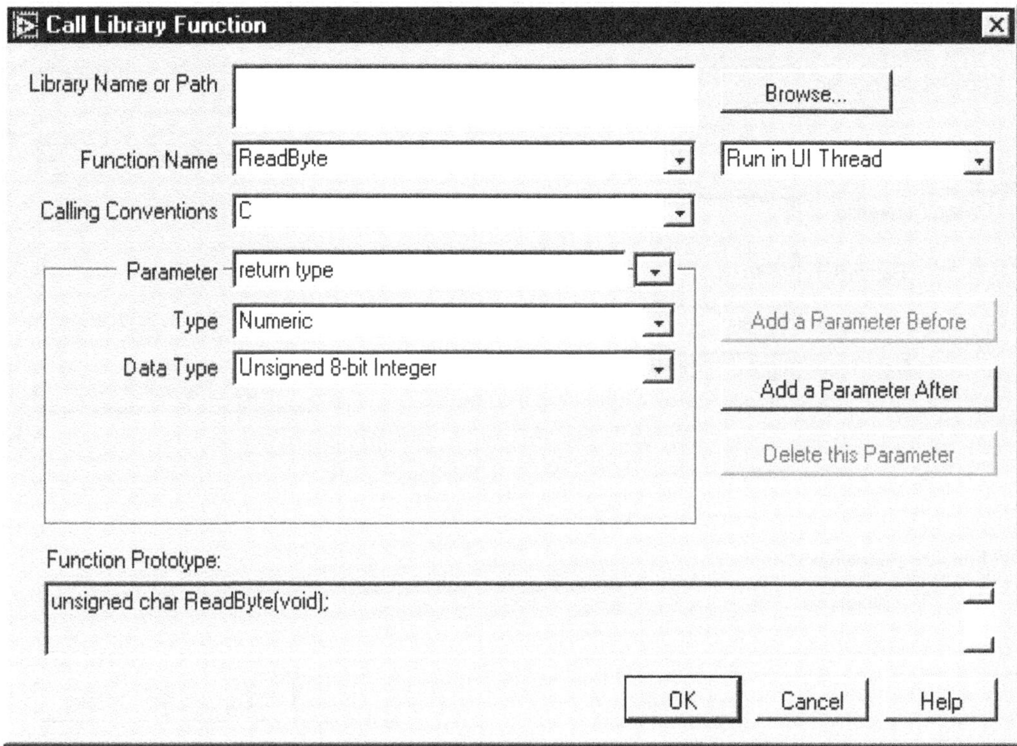

FIGURE 5.52 The DLL `ReadByte` function.

its Call Library Function dialog box. Finish the setting up of this Call Library Function by entering the parameters that are shown in Figure 5.52.

- The function name is `ReadByte`, and the returned data type is an unsigned eight-bit integer. This integer corresponds to the collected data from the TLC548 A/D converter. There is no argument for this function. Click the `OK` button to save this setting and close this dialog box.
- Right-click on this Call Library Function and select the `Create.c File` item from the pop-up menu to generate the declaration file of this DLL function. Change the default file name `code.c` and save this declaration file as `code2.c`.

For the third Call Library Function, perform the following steps to finish the setup.

- Go to the third Call Library Function node that we've added into the third frame (frame 2), right-click on that node and select the `Configure` item from the pop-up menu to open the `Call Library Function` dialog box. Finish configuring this Call Library Function by entering the parameters that are shown in Figure 5.53.
- The function name is `Close` and the returned data type is a signed 32-bit integer. This 32-bit integer corresponds to the running status of the `Close` function. There is no argument for this function. Click the `OK` button to save this setting and close the dialog box.
- Right-click on the Call Library Function and select the `Create.c File` item from the pop-up menu to generate the declaration file of this DLL function. Replace the default name `code.c` and save this declaration file as `code3.c`.

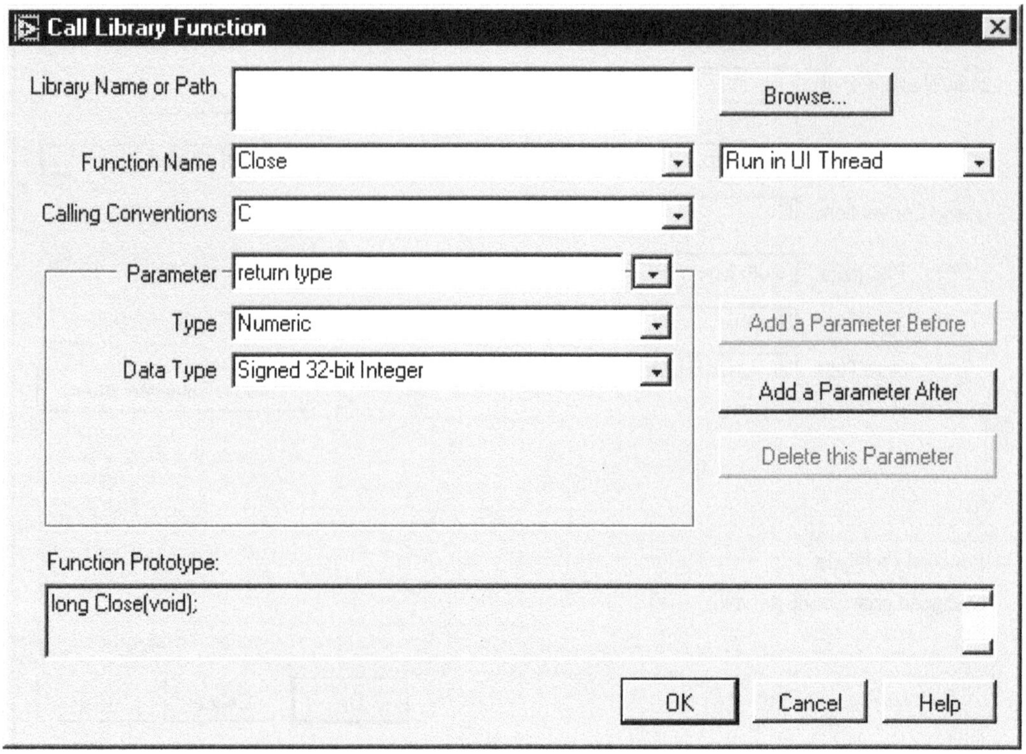

FIGURE 5.53 The DLL `Close` function.

5.4.3.3 Building the Block Diagram in LabVIEW

Now let's finish the block diagram of this project in LabVIEW domain.

The first step to interface with the DLL functions to communicate with the serial A/D converter is to correctly configure the serial port and the TLC548 A/D converter. The detailed configurations are performed in the DLL function `Setup`, and the programming in the LabVIEW domain just likes a high-level design.

Open the `Block Diagram` window of this project, go to the first frame (frame 0), and complete the wiring for this diagram, as shown in Figure 5.54.

The `Port Settings` array, which contains six port configuration parameters, is connected to the `comParms` input on the `Setup` call library function node as the input. The returned value (`0` means success) that is a signed 32-bit integer is converted to a Boolean value by using a `Not Equal To 0?` VI. This converted Boolean value is assigned to the `Setup Error` LED to determine whether any error has occurred (≠ 0) during the `Setup` process.

The programming of the second frame (frame 1) is shown in Figure 5.55.

The `ReadByte` Call Library Function returns an eight-bit unsigned integer that corresponds to a byte of collected data from the A/D converter. This returned data is sent to the `Data Output` indicator to display the received result in real time. This data is also sent to the Waveform Chart control to show the complete waveform of the collected data.

You may encounter a wiring error if you directly connect the returned data of the `ReadByte` Call Library Function to the waveform chart control because the latter can only accept a data array input, but the returned data is a single byte of data. To solve this problem, you can first replace the `While` loop control with a `For` loop control and finish the connection between the returned data and the waveform chart control. Then you can recover back to the `While` loop control.

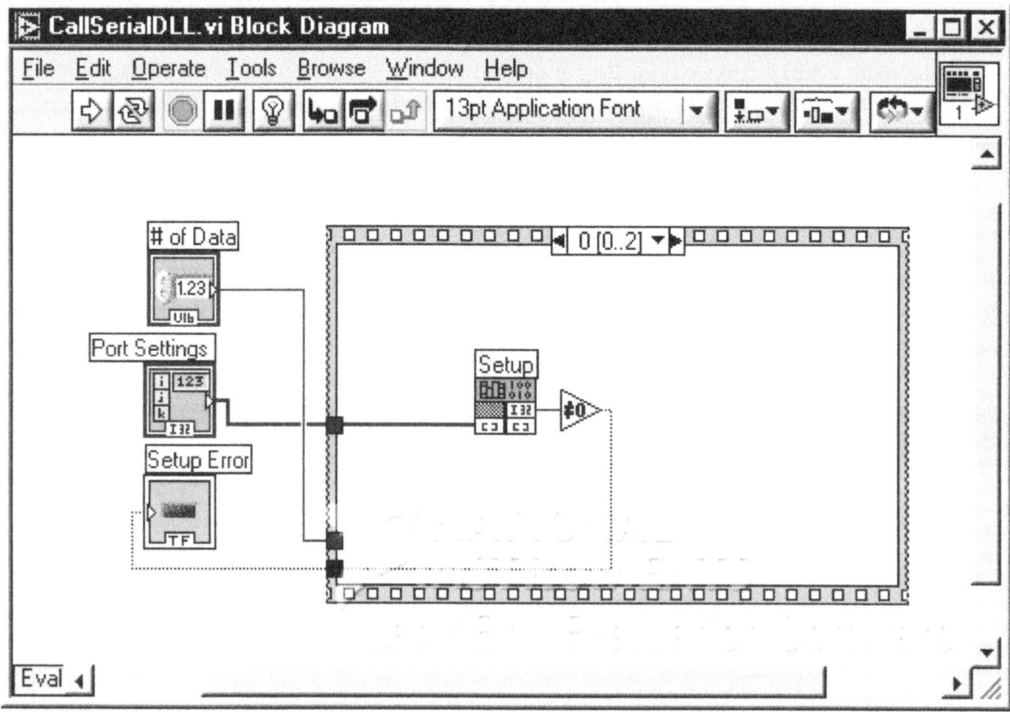

FIGURE 5.54 Block diagram for frame 0.

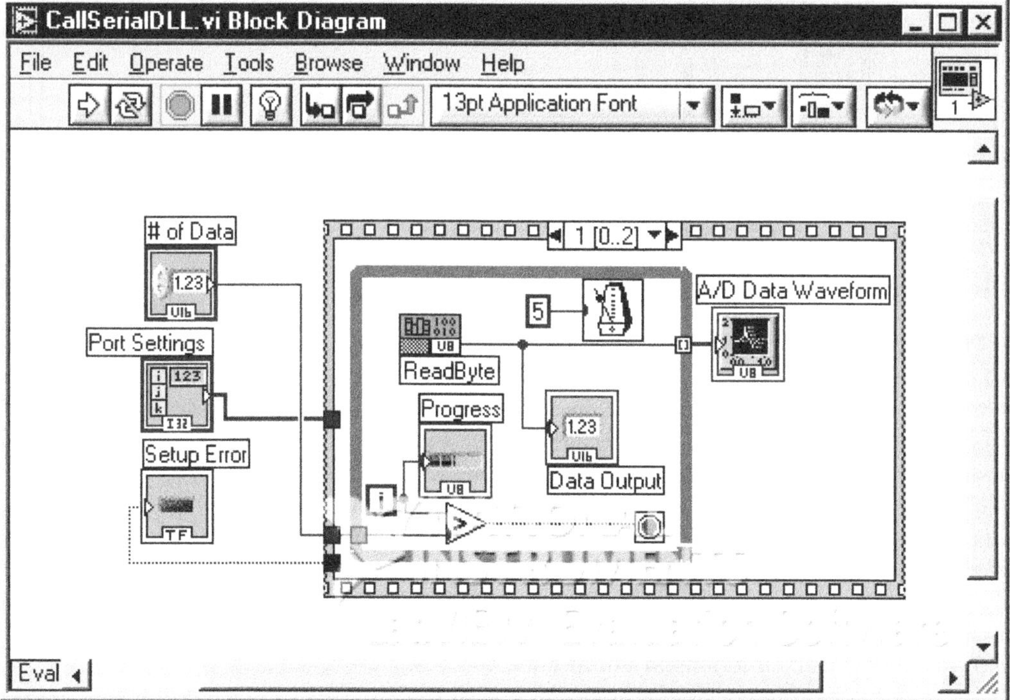

FIGURE 5.55 Block diagram for frame 1.

TIP: You cannot directly connect a single data unit with the Waveform Chart control inside a `While` loop because the Waveform Chart needs a data array input. You can temporarily replace the `While` loop with a `For` loop and finish the connection between the single data and the Waveform Chart control inside the `For` loop. Then recover the `While` loop.

The `# of Data` is compared with the cycle index `i` of the `While` loop, and the `While` loop is terminated when the `i` is greater than the `# of Data` (it is 100 in this application). This is equivalent to loop 100 times to collect 100 converted data from the TLC548 A/D converter. The `Progress` indicator is also connected to the cycle index `i` to monitor and display the progress of the data collection process. A `Wait Until Next ms Multiple` VI is used in this loop to delay each data collection cycle by five milliseconds.

The programming of the third frame (frame 2) is shown in Figure 5.56.

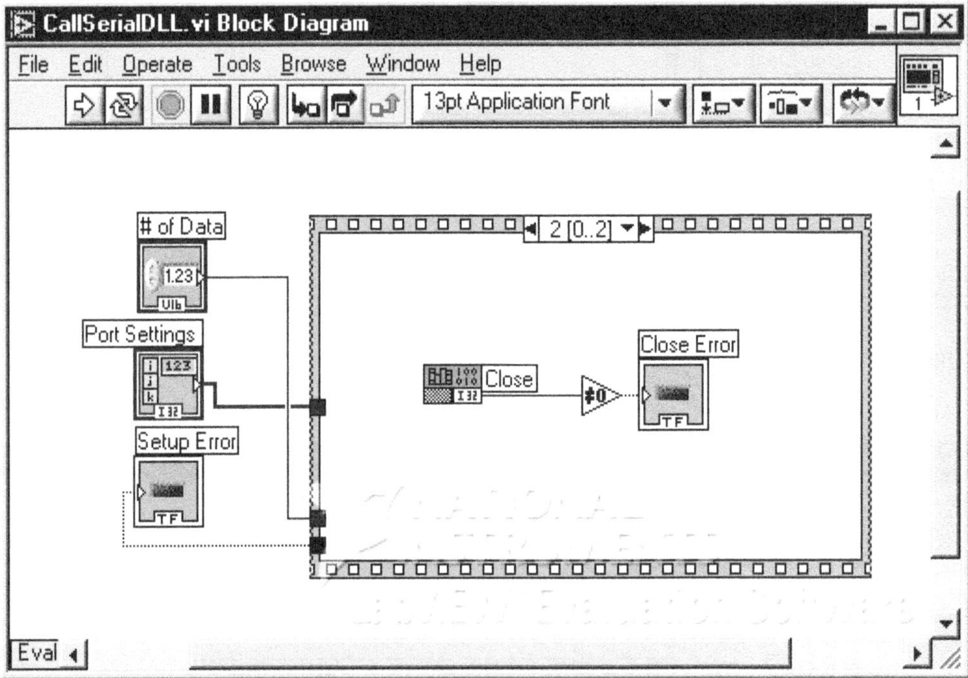

FIGURE 5.56 Block diagram for frame 2.

The block diagram of this frame is very simple. When all data is received from the TLC548 A/D converter, the DLL `Close` function needs to clean up the working environment set for this serial data communication and close the opened serial port. This function returns a signed 32-bit integer to indicate whether this function calling is successful or not. A returned `0` means that the `Close` function is successful. Otherwise an error has been encountered.

Now we have finished all block diagrams of this project. We need to develop a DLL file that contains all three functions, `Setup`, `ReadByte`, and `Close`, to interface those call library function nodes we developed in the LabVIEW domain to complete the data communication between LabVIEW and the TLC548 A/D converter via the serial port.

5.4.3.4 Building DLL Functions in Visual C++

Refer to Figure 5.48, which shows the interface circuit and connections between the TLC548 serial A/D converter and the RS-232 serial port. Four transmission lines are used for transferring data between the port and the A/D converter. The DTR line is used to provide the power for the converter, and the RTS line is used to provide the CS-bar selection signal on the TLC548. The TD line is used to transmit a sequence of clock cycles to the CLK input of the converter to move the transmitted data out of the output buffer of the converter. The output data is moved to the CTS line on the serial port bit by bit, and the moving rate depends on the rate of the clock cycle specified on the CLK input.

5.4.3.4.1 The Functionalities of the DLL Functions

The functionalities of the DLL functions can be categorized into the following three sections:

- **Configuring the serial port:** The DLL `Setup` function can be used to perform this task. During the configuration stage, the serial port COM1 is opened, the port settings parameters are transferred to the COM1 to configure the port, and both the DTR and the RTS lines are set to `HIGH` to enable the power for the TLC548 and disable the CS-bar selection signal to deselect the A/D converter. A `LOW` signal is sent to the TD line to inactivate the CLK input on the A/D converter.
- **Convert and collect each converted data from the A/D converter:** The DLL function `ReadByte` works for these tasks. A `For` loop is used inside a local function `PortRead()` to continuously convert and pick up one byte (eight bits) of converted data from the TLC548. To convert and receive each byte of data, the associated transmission lines should be properly enabled or disabled so that they provide the proper transmission signals to the TLC548. Each received data byte is stored into a temporary variable, and finally returned to the call library function node `ReadByte`.
- **Clean up and close the opened port:** When all data is converted and received, the setup environment of the serial port should be clean up and the opened port should be closed. The DLL function `Close` is supposed to handle this job.

5.4.3.4.2 Characteristics of TLC548 Serial Port Communications

In the normal serial data communications, transmission lines are used and controlled by the communication driver. Each transmission line performs its associated task to coordinate the data transmitting and receiving between the DTE and the DCE. But in this application, the transmission lines are not used to perform the same functions as those used in normal data communications. Because of this specialty, some special Win32 system functions are used to allow the user to directly access and modify the status of transmission lines. The following functions and steps must be adapted to meet the requirements of this special interface circuit.

- To use the transmission lines as the special purposes and allow the user to directly access the transmission lines, one must first use the DCB structure to configure the transmission signals with the correct properties (values) during the configuration stage.
- To access and control the different transmission lines, the extended system functions `EscapeCommFunction()` must be used. This function directs a communication driver to perform an extended setting or resetting for a selected transmission line. In other words, this function allows the user to directly access and control the specific transmission line in the Windows multi-task environment.
- To check the current status of the specific transmission line, two methods are generally used. The first is to set an event mask that causes notification of the application when the desired events occur. The `SetCommMask()` function sets this event mask, and the `WaitCommEvent()` function waits for the desired events to occur. The second method for retrieving the status of the serial port is to use some Win32 system functions, such as the function `GetCommModemStatus()`. This function retrieves the actual state of

transmission lines by returning a bit mask for each line, a 0 for LOW or no voltage and 1 for HIGH voltage. In this application, the second method is adapted.

Keeping these points in mind, we can now develop the DLL file for this application.

5.4.3.4.3 Developing the DLL Project

Launch Visual C++ 6.0 to create a new project with the following properties:

- Project name: LabVIEWSerialDLL
- Project type: Win32 Dynamic Link Library
- Location: C:\Book2_Program\Chapter 5\CallSerialDLL

A new project folder, LabVIEWSerialDLL, is generated. Before we can continue, we need to copy the following header files into this folder because the project need them. Open the Windows Explorer and copy the following header files from the folder C:\Program Files\National Instruments\LabVIEW 7.0 Evaluation\cintools into the new project folder LabVIEWSerialDLL:

- extcode.h
- fundtypes.h
- platdefines.h

You'll need also copy the library file labview.lib from this folder if you want to use some LabVIEW manager functions to do any of the following:

- Allocate, free, or resize arrays, strings, or other data structures that are passed into or out of your library from LabVIEW
- Work with LabVIEW Path data types
- Work with file refnums inside your library
- Use any of the Support Manager functions

In this application, we do not use any LabVIEW manager function; only those three header files are needed.

In the newly generated project, create a new header file named LabVIEWSerialDLL.h and a C++ source file named LabVIEWSerialDLL.cpp.

Now click the menu item Project|Add To Project|Files... to add the three header files, extcode.h, fundtypes.h, and platdefines.h, into this project.

Recall that in Section 5.3.3.2, we created three C-type declaration files named code1.c, code2.c, and code3.c, and these declaration files are associated with three different Call Library Functions in LabVIEW. Open each of these three files by double-clicking them from within Visual C++ workspace and copy the prototype of each function into the newly created header file and source file as shown in Figure 5.57.

To make thing simple, we show these three declaration files together in one file. You need to copy the #include "extcode.h" and three function declarations that have been highlighted and paste them into the project header file LabVIEWSerialDLL.h. Copy three function body that currently are empty and paste them into the project source file LabVIEWSerialDLL.cpp.

Now we are ready to develop each DLL function one-by-one in this project. First let's take a look at the header file of this project.

5.4.3.4.4 Designing the Header File

Besides the function declarations we copied earlier, there are some other declarations, such as the global variables, system constants, structures and local functions used in this project. Another

```
/* Call Library source file ---- code1.c */
#include "extcode.h"
long Setup(long comParms[]);          // Function declaration
long Setup(long comParms[])           // Function body
{
   /* Insert code here */
}
/* Call Library source file ---- code2.c */
#include "extcode.h"
unsigned char ReadByte(void);         // Function declaration
unsigned char ReadByte(void)          // Function body
{
   /* Insert code here */
}
/* Call Library source file ---- code3.c */
#include "extcode.h"
long Close(void);                     // Function declaration
long Close(void)                      // Function body
{
   /* Insert code here */
}
```

FIGURE 5.57 Three function declarations defined in LabVIEW.

important issue is that you must explicitly export each DLL function to make it available to LabVIEW. In this application, you must use the `_declspec (dllexport)` keyword to export all three DLL functions in this project to LabVIEW. To make things simple, we can define a constant to represent this keyword and use that constant in the program to simplify this definition.

The complete header file of this project is shown in Figure 5.58. Each section of this code is explained in the following list.

A: The system header file `Windows.h` is included first in this header file because this system header file provides all object definitions applied in the Windows environment. As an example, the `MessageBox()` function is defined in that system header file.

B: To avoid multiple including of this header file, the system macro `#ifndef` is used here. The purpose of this macro is to allow the other source file to include this header file if this header file has not been included before by that source file. In C/C++ programming, it is illegal to include a header multiple times by any source file in the project. To avoid that situation occur, the macro `#ifndef` and `#define` are used. You need to attach a `#endif` at the end of this header file if you used this macro.

C: Some constants are defined here and most of them are serial communication related parameters, such as NOPARITY, ONESTOPBIT, and RTS_CONTROL_ENABLE or _DISABLE. As previous mentioned, the transmission lines used in this project are not normal format, it is necessary for us to set and reset each transmission line by using the function `EscapeCommFunction()`. You must set the transmission lines to either `CONTROL_ENABLE` or `CONTROL_DISABLE` state during the configuration stage in order to use that extended function to access and set/reset any transmission line.

D: To make our program simple and clear, two data types, unsigned char and unsigned long, are redefined using the macro `#define` as UCHAR and ULONG, respectively. After this re-definition, we can use these two re-defined data type to save the time and the space in the declaration of variables and functions that use this data type. Another

```
  /*****************************************************************************
   * NAME          : LabVIEWSerialDLL.h
   * DESC.         : Header file for LabVIEWSerialDLL.cpp
   *****************************************************************************/
A  #include <Windows.h>
B  #ifndef _LABVIEWSERIALDLL_H_
   #define _LABVIEWSERIALDLL_H_
C  #define MAX_STRING                256
   #define NOPARITY                    0
   #define ONESTOPBIT                  0
   #define RTS_CONTROL_DISABLE      0x00
   #define RTS_CONTROL_ENABLE       0x01
   #define DTR_CONTROL_DISABLE      0x00
   #define DTR_CONTROL_ENABLE       0x01
D  #define UCHAR          unsigned char
   #define ULONG          unsigned long
   #define msg(info)      MessageBox(NULL, info, "", MB_OK)
E  #ifdef __cplusplus
   extern "C" {
   #endif                        /* __cplusplus */
F  typedef struct
   {
     ULONG  ulCtrlID;            // Port ID
     char   cEcho;               // Echo character
     char   cEORChar;            // EOR character
     long   lTimeout;            // Time out value
     long   lBaudRate;           // Baud rate
     long   lDataBits;           // Data bits
   } SerialCreate, *pSerialCreate;
G  typedef struct
   {
     UCHAR pcBuffer;             /* Store the received byte of data */
     int      iMaxChars;         /* The number of maximum received characters */
     int      iMaxBits;          /* The maximum bits */
     int      piNumRcvd;         /* The number of data received */
     char     cTermChar;         /* The terminate character */
   } CommPortClass;
H  typedef enum
   {
     OK        = 0,              /* no error */
     EC_TIMEOUT,
     EC_FOPEN,
     EC_INVAL_CONFIG,
     EC_TIMEOUT_SET,
     EC_RECV_TIMEOUT,
     EC_EXIT_CODE,
     EC_INVALIDPORT,
     EC_WRITE_FAIL,
     EC_GETMODSTATUS,
     EC_UNKNOWNERROR
   } ERR_CODE;
```

FIGURE 5.58 The completed header file. *(continued)*

```
I  FILE*  fp;
   HANDLE hPort;
   char*     sPortName;
   bool      PortCreateflg = false;
   /* Local Functions */
J  ERR_CODE PortInitialize(char* lpszPortName, pSerialCreate pCreate);
   ERR_CODE PortRead(CommPortClass *hCommPort);
   ERR_CODE PortWrite(char* bByte, int NumByte);
   /*-----------------------------------------------------------------*/
K  #define DllExport  __declspec( dllexport )
   /*-----------------------------------------------------------------*/
L  DllExport long Setup(long comParms[]);
   DllExport UCHAR ReadByte(void);
   DllExport long Close();
   #ifdef __cplusplus
   }
M  #endif                /* __cplusplus */
   #endif                /* #ifndef     */
```

FIGURE 5.58 The completed header file.

simplification is to re-define the `MessageBox()` function by using the macro `#define`. After this re-definition, the length of the function `MessageBox()` can be greatly shorten and it is very easy to be placed in the program by using the `msg()` with a text string as the information.

E: When you build shared libraries for C++, you must prevent the C++ compiler from decorating the function names in the final object code. To do this, wrap the function declaration in an extern “C” clause, `extern "C" { ....}`. The codes included inside the opening and ending braces are considered as the C codes and the compiler converts them to the C object codes, not C++ object codes. One point you need to note is that if you disable C++ decoration of a function, the compiler cannot create polymorphic versions of the function.

F: Two structures are defined here to convenience to the port configurations. The first structure is the `SerialCreate` that contains useful port communication parameters, such as the baud rate, data bits, timeout value and other parameters used to check and indicate the communication status.

G: The second structure is the `CommPortClass` that is used to hold parameters to perform receiving the data from the port correctly.

H: An `enum` structure `ERR_CODE` is declared to define the numeric error value that is associated with each possible error occurred during the project runs. We can save much time by using this kind of definition, in which each error code is sequenced from the integer `0` to the maximum integer value.

I: Global variables are declared in this section. The purpose of these global variables is to simplify the program and allow different source files to share some common variables. Although the global style is not recommended in the object-oriented programming environment, it can really simplify and speed up the process for application programs that need the high-speed and the real-time responses. The `fp` is a `FILE` pointer variable and it is used to open a new data file that can be used to store the collected data during the program runs. This data file can be read later and can be plotted as a waveform in any programming environment. The `hPort` is used to reserve the file handle that represents the opened port. Any code can use this `hPort` to access the opened serial port in the program. `PortCreateflg` is a Boolean variable and it works as a flag to monitor the port configuration process and indicate whether it succeeds or fails. This variable is set to `True` if the port configuration is successfully processed. The `sPortName` is a string variable and it is used to reserve the port name in the text format because the port initialization function needs the port name as the text format.

J: Three local functions are declared here. The purposes of these functions is to coordinate the DLL functions to perform data communications between the serial port and the computer. The DLL functions work as interface functions, and the local functions work as executive functions to communicate directly with the low-level system routines. The `PortInitialize()` function is used to configure the serial port; this function has two arguments. The first one is the port name, entered in text format, and the second is a pointer of the data structure `SerialCreate`, which is the starting address in which the configuration parameters are stored. The `PortRead()` and the `PortWrite()` are used to directly access the low-level system routines that perform data transmission and reception.

K: The macro `#define` is used to define the keyword `_declspec (dllexport)` as a user-defined constant, `DllExport`. After this definition, this keyword can be easily replaced by the constant.

L: In this section, three DLL function declarations are presented. These function declarations are copied from three declaration functions `code1.c`, `code2.c`, and `code3.c`, which are generated in three Call Library Functions in LabVIEW domain. You need to precede the user-defined constant `DllExport` for each of these function declarations to export them to LabVIEW. Don't forget to attach the ending brace for the `extern "C" {` clause we've added to the header file earlier.

M: Attach the ending brace for the macro `#ifndef`.

Next let's develop three DLL functions one-by-one. The first one is the `Setup` function.

5.4.3.4.5 The DLL `Setup` Function

Open the project source file `LabVIEWSerialDLL.cpp` and enter the code shown in Figure 5.59. Each section of this code is explained in the following list.

N: The project header file `LabVIEWSerialDLL,h` is included first because all definitions and prototypes of variables, functions and constants used in this project are declared in that header file. You must include those definitions if you want to use those items defined in the header file.

O: As we did for the header file, a `DllExport` constant is preceded before the function `Setup` to export this function to LabVIEW. Inside the `Setup` function body, some local variables are declared at the beginning of this function. The returned variable `rc` is defined as the `enum` structure `ERR_CODE` and an `OK` is assigned to that variable to initialize it to `0`.

P: The system function `fopen()` is called to open a new data file named `data.dat`. The returned file handler is assigned to the FILE pointer `fp`. This data file is used to store the collected data from the TLC548 A/D converter later during the program runs.

Q: A `SerialCreate` structure variable `pParam` is generated by using the `new` keyword. The `new` keyword is used to create a new structure variable and allocate the memory space for that structure variable. The `new` returns the starting address in which the structure variable `pParam` is stored. The variables defined inside the structure `SerialCreate` are initialized using the values of elements stored in the argument array that

```
/*****************************************************************************
 * NAME        : LabVIEWSerialDLL.cpp
 * DESC.       : DLL functions to interface to RS-232 serial port, called by LabVIEW.
 * PRGMER.     : Y. Bai
 * DATE        : 10/30/2003
 *****************************************************************************/
   #include <stdio.h>
   #include <stdlib.h>
   #include <string.h>
N  #include "LabVIEWSerialDLL.h"
   DllExport long Setup(long comParms[])          //comParms[0] = port_number
   {                                              //comParms[1] = baud_rate
O      ERR_CODE  rc = OK;                         //comParms[2] = data_bits
P      fp = fopen("data.dat", "w");               //comParms[3] = stop_bit
Q      pParam = new SerialCreate;                 //comParms[4] = parity
       pParam->lBaudRate = comParms[1];           //comParms[5] = timeout_value
       pParam->lDataBits = comParms[2];
       pParam->lTimeout  = comParms[5];
R      switch((int)comParms[0])
       {
          case 1:
               sPortName = "COM1";
               break;
          case 2:
               sPortName = "COM2";
               break;
          case 3:
               sPortName = "COM3";
               break;
          case 4:
               sPortName = "COM4";
               break;
          default:
               return EC_INVALIDPORT;
       }
S      if (PortCreateflg)
       {
            msg("Port has been Setup ");
            return rc;
       }
T      rc = PortInitialize(sPortName, pParam);
       if (rc != 0)
          msg("ERROR in PortInitialize()!");
U      delete pParam;
V      PortCreateflg = true;
W      return rc;
   }
```

FIGURE 5.59 Coding of the DLL function `Setup`.

is passed from the LabVIEW domain when executing the Call Library Functions in LabVIEW. Each element's position and its definition are clearly explained in the comment statements. Only four elements' values are used in this application.

R: A switch structure is used to identify the desired port number. The condition variable for this switch structure is the first element stored in the argument array `comParms[0]` that corresponds to the desired port number. The string variable `sPortName` is assigned by the associated port name based on the port number that is the first element stored in the argument array `comParms[0]`. This translation from the port number to the port name is necessary because the `PortInitialize()` function needs this port name as the string format to open and configure the serial port. In this application, the range of the valid port number is between 1 and 4. You can decide your range based on your applications.

S: If the Boolean variable `PortCreateflg` is already set to `True`, which means that the port has been opened and configured, a message is displayed to remind the user and the program returns to the calling function without performing any configuration.

T: Otherwise, the local function `PortInitialize()` is called to perform the opening and configuring of the port operations. Two arguments are passed into that function, the port name `sPortName` that is a string variable and the configuration parameters stored in the `SerialCreate` structure variable `pParam`. The function returns a `0` if it is successful; otherwise a nonzero value is returned to indicate that the function call has failed. In the latter situation, an error massage is displayed.

U: Because the `new` keyword is used to create a data structure variable `pParam`, the `delete` command must be also used to clean up the memory space allocated by the `new` keyword for that data structure when it is no longer being used.

V: After the port is successfully opened and configured, the Boolean variable `PortCreateflg` should be set to `True` to indicate that the port has been opened and configured. We do not need to reopen the port if the port has been opened. In fact, our program may encounter an opening error if you attempt to open a port that is already opened. By using this Boolean variable as a flag, you can avoid this possible error.

W: Finally, the running status of this function is returned to the calling function.

It can be found from this `Setup` coding that the actual initialization and configuration job is performed inside the local function `PortInitialize()`. The coding for that local function is shown in Figure 5.60.

```
  ERR_CODE PortInitialize(char* lpszPortName, pSerialCreate pCreate)
  {
X     DWORD dwError;
      DCB       PortDCB;
      ERR_CODE ecStatus = OK;
      COMMTIMEOUTS  CommTimeouts;
      UCHAR dBit;
Y     if (PortCreateflg)                         // check if the port has been created...
      {
          msg("Port has been initialized!");
          return ecStatus;
      }
Z     hPort = CreateFile(lpszPortName,           // Pointer to the name of the port
                         GENERIC_READ | GENERIC_WRITE, // Access (read/write) mode
                         0,                      // Share mode
                         NULL,                   // Pointer to the security attribute
                         OPEN_EXISTING,          // How to open the serial port
                         0,                      // Port attributes
                         NULL);                  // Handle to port with attribute to copy
```

FIGURE 5.60 Coding for the local function `PortInitialize()`. *(continued)*

```
   // If it fails to open the port, return error.
1  if ( hPort == INVALID_HANDLE_VALUE )
   {
       // Could not open the port.
       dwError = GetLastError();
       msg("Unable to open the port");
       CloseHandle(hPort);
       return EC_FOPEN;
   }
2  PortCreateflg = TRUE;
   PortDCB.DCBlength = sizeof(DCB);
   // Get the default port setting information.
3  GetCommState(hPort, &PortDCB);
   // Change the DCB structure settings.
4  PortDCB.BaudRate = pCreate->lBaudRate;     // Current baud
   PortDCB.fBinary = TRUE;                    // Binary mode; no EOF check
   PortDCB.fParity = FALSE;                   // Disable parity checking.
   PortDCB.fOutxCtsFlow = FALSE;              // No CTS output flow control
   PortDCB.fOutxDsrFlow = FALSE;              // No DSR output flow control
5  PortDCB.fDtrControl = DTR_CONTROL_ENABLE; // DTR flow control type
   PortDCB.fDsrSensitivity = FALSE;           // DSR sensitivity
   PortDCB.fTXContinueOnXoff = FALSE;        // XOFF continues Tx
   PortDCB.fOutX = FALSE;                     // No XON/XOFF out flow control
   PortDCB.fInX = FALSE;                      // No XON/XOFF in flow control
   PortDCB.fErrorChar = FALSE;                // Disable error replacement.
   PortDCB.fNull = FALSE;                     // Disable null stripping.
6  PortDCB.fRtsControl = RTS_CONTROL_ENABLE; // RTS flow control
   PortDCB.fAbortOnError = FALSE;             // Do not abort reads/writes on error.
7  dBit = (UCHAR)pCreate->lDataBits;          // Assign data bits
   PortDCB.ByteSize = dBit;                   // Number of bits/bytes, 4-8
   PortDCB.Parity = NOPARITY;                 // 0-4=no,odd,even,mark,space
   PortDCB.StopBits = ONESTOPBIT;             // 0,1,2 = 1, 1.5, 2
   // Configure the port according to the specifications of the DCB structure.
8  if (!SetCommState (hPort, &PortDCB))
   {
       // Could not set the timeout parameter.
       dwError = GetLastError();
       msg("Unable to configure the serial port");
       return EC_INVAL_CONFIG;
   }
   // Retrieve the time-out parameters for all read and write operations on the port.
9  GetCommTimeouts(hPort, &CommTimeouts);

   // Change the COMMTIMEOUTS structure settings.
10 CommTimeouts.ReadIntervalTimeout = MAXDWORD;
   CommTimeouts.ReadTotalTimeoutMultiplier = 0;
   CommTimeouts.ReadTotalTimeoutConstant = 0;
   CommTimeouts.WriteTotalTimeoutMultiplier = 10;
   CommTimeouts.WriteTotalTimeoutConstant = 1000;
```

FIGURE 5.60 Coding for the local function `PortInitialize()`. *(continued)*

```
      // Set the time-out parameters for all read and write operations on the port.
11    if (!SetCommTimeouts (hPort, &CommTimeouts))
      {
         // Could not set the port timeout parameter.
         dwError = GetLastError();
         msg("Unable to set the time-out parameters");
         return EC_TIMEOUT_SET;
      }
12    EscapeCommFunction(hPort, SETDTR);    //Set DTR
      EscapeCommFunction(hPort, SETRTS);    //Set RTS
13    ecStatus = PortWrite("0", 1);         //Output 0 to the TD line to make CLK LOW.
      if (ecStatus != 0)
         msg("ERROR in PortWrite()...Setup !");
14    return ecStatus;
   }
```

FIGURE 5.60 Coding for the local function `PortInitialize()`.

Each section of this code is explained in the following list.

X: Some local variables are declared at the beginning of this function. The variable `dwError` is a double word integer and it is used to hold the returned error code for the system function calling. The DCB (Device Control Block) structure is a very useful data structure used in the control settings and configurations of the serial port. (Refer to Section 4.2.2 and Table 4-4 in Chapter 4 for a more detailed description of this structure). All configurations of the serial devices are performed by using this structure. A variable of this structure `PortDCB` is declared here in order to use this structure in this function. The `ecStatus` is a variable of `enum` structure ERR_CODE and it is used to hold the returned status of the user-defined function calling. An initial value `OK` is assigned to that variable. The COMMTIMEOUTS is another useful data structure widely used for serial data communications and it is used to set the timeout values for serial devices. The variable `dBit` is used to temporarily store the value of the data bit.

Y: Similarly as we did in the last function, first we need to check whether the port has been opened and configured. The function needs to do nothing except returning to the calling function if the port has been configured. This check can be finished by inspecting the status of the Boolean variable `PortCreateflg`. The reason why we make this check in two times is that we do not want to cause any error for this port opening issue.

Z: If the port has not been opened, the system function `CreateFile()` is called to try to open a new port. Seven arguments are included in this function calling. The first one is the port name in the text format such as "COM1." The second parameter is used to indicate the open mode of the port. The GENERIC_READ|GENERIC_WRITE means that this port can perform read and write operations. The third parameter is the share mode. A `0` means that this port cannot be shared with other threads. The fourth argument is used to indicate the security attribute and it can be used to determine whether the returned port handle can be inherited by child processes. If this parameter is NULL, which means that the handle cannot be inherited. The next parameter is the creating mode that is used to indicate which action to take on files that exist, and which action to take when files do not exist. The opened file is mapped to the associated serial port or device. The parameter OPEN_EXISTING means that the opening is failed if the file (port) does not exist. The sixth parameter is used to indicate whether this opening has additional attributes. A 0 means that there is no additional attributes for this file opening. The last parameter specifies a handle with GENERIC_READ access to a template file. The template file supplies file attributes and extended attributes for the file being created.

1: If the system function CreateFile() is successful, an opened file handler should be returned and this handler works as unique ID for the opened port. Otherwise an INVALID_HANDLE_VALUE returned to indicate that the function calling is failed. To get the exact error code, the GetLastError() system function is executed, and the error message is displayed. The CloseHandle() system function may be called to make the opened port closed if it was opened by chance. The user-defined error code EC_FOPEN is returned to the calling function to indicate that error.

2: The Boolean variable PortCreateflg is set to True if the port opening is successful. Next we need to configure the port with the DCB structure. The DCBLength parameter needs to be filled first and the sizeof operator is used to get the length of the DCB structure.

3: To use the DCB structure to configure the serial port, you need first to obtain the default DCB structure by calling the system function GetCommState(). Two parameters are included in this function calling. The first one is the port handler obtained from the CreateFile() and the second is the DCB structure variable PortDCB that returns the default DCB structure.

4: After the default DCB structure is obtained, we can assign new values to the elements on that structure based on our applications. The baud rate is assigned to the BaudRate element in the DCB. Other assignments have been explained by the associated comments. Two elements are important to us: one is the fDtrControl and the other is the fRtsControl. Because the serial port interface applied in this project is not normal serial communication mode, the handshaking signals cannot be used as the normal interfacing signals as the traditional serial port did. So those handshaking signals should be set to DTR_CONTROL_ENABLE and RTS_CONTROL_ENABLE, respectively. In this way, we can use the extended system function EscapeCommFunction() to set or reset those lines directly. These two settings are indicated by the explanation steps 5 and 6 in the coding.

7: The temporary variable dBit is used to pick up and reserve the data bit's size from the SerialCreate structure variable pCreate. This value is assigned to the ByteSize element in the DCB structure.

8: The system function SetCommState() is called to configure the port by using the completed DCB structure. If this function returns a False, which means that the function calling is failed, the error message is displayed and a user-defined error code EC_INVAL_CONFIG is returned to the calling function.

9: Next we need to set the timeout values for the port by using the system function SetCommTimeouts(). We must first to get the default timeout structure CommTimeouts by using the system function GetCommTimeouts().

10: After the default timeout structure is obtained, we can use SetCommTimeouts() to set the desired timeout values for the port.

11: If the function SetCommTimeouts() is failed, an error message is displayed and a user-defined error code EC_TIMEOUT_SET is returned to the calling function to indicate this error situation.

12: Now we need to set two transmission lines, DTR and RTS, to provide the power to the TLC548 A/D converter and deselect the chip. To do that, we must use the extended function EscapeCommFunction(). Two arguments are passed into that function. The first one is the opened port ID, and the second one is the function code. Both SETDTR and SETRTS are system constants that are used to perform setting certain transmission line on the serial port.

13: In order to disable the CLK signal on the TLC548, we need to reset the TD line because this line is connected to the CLK on the TLC548 (refer to Figure 5.48). By calling the function `PortWrite("0", 1)`, we can send a `0` to the TD line. An error message is displayed if this function calling fails.

14: Finally the running status of this function is returned to the calling function.

The coding for another local function, `PortWrite()`, is shown in Figure 5.61.

```
/*****************************************************************************
 * NAME:    PortWrite()
 * DESC.:   Write data to the port
 * DATE:    11/9/03
 * PGMR.:  Y. Bai
 *****************************************************************************/
ERR_CODE PortWrite(char* bByte, int NumByte)
{
    DWORD dwError;
    DWORD dwNumBytesWritten;
    ERR_CODE ecStatus = OK;
    if (!WriteFile (hPort,                  // Port handle
                    bByte,                  // Pointer to the data to write
                    NumByte,                // Number of bytes to write
                    &dwNumBytesWritten,     // Pointer to the number of bytes written
                    NULL))                  // Must be NULL for Windows CE
    {
        // WriteFile failed, report error.
        dwError = GetLastError ();
        return EC_WRITE_FAIL;
    }
    return  ecStatus;
}
```

FIGURE 5.61 The local function `PortWrite()`.

5.4.3.4.6 The DLL `ReadByte()` Function

An empty function body, `ReadByte()`, has been added into the source file in Section 5.3.3.4.3 (refer to Figure 5.57). Enter the keyword `DllExport` in front of the function header, and enter the code shown in Figure 5.62 into the function body.

15: Some local variables are declared here. The `ad_data` can be considered as a buffer and it is used to reserve the received data from the serial port, or from the TLC548 A/D converter. The `rc` variable stores the returned running status of the calling function. `commClass` is a pointer variable of the data structure `CommPortClass`, defined in the header file.

16: The `new` keyword is used to allocate memory space for the pointer variable `commClass` and return the starting address of that variable. Two setup parameters are assigned to the elements of the structure variable `commClass`, `iMaxChars` and `iMaxBits`.

17: A local function `PortRead()` is called to retrieve the converted data from the TLC548 A/D converter via the serial port. An error message is displayed if the function calling is failed.

```
   DllExport UCHAR ReadByte(void)
   {
15     UCHAR ad_data;
       ERR_CODE rc = OK;
       CommPortClass* commClass;
16     commClass = new CommPortClass;
       commClass->iMaxChars = 1;
       commClass->iMaxBits  = 8;
17     rc = PortRead(commClass);
       if (rc != 0)
           msg("ERROR in PortRead()! ");
18     fprintf(fp, "%d\n", commClass->pcBuffer);     //Reserve the data into a file
       ad_data = commClass->pcBuffer;
19     delete commClass;
20     return ad_data;
   }
```

FIGURE 5.62 Coding for the second DLL function `ReadByte()`.

18: The received data is also written into a data file by using the system function `fprintf()`. The `fp` is the opened file handler obtained from the `Setup()` DLL function. The received data (1-byte) is stored into the data buffer `ad_data`.
19: After the data is stored into the buffer, the `commClass` must be removed by using the `delete` command. In this way, the memory space of the `commClass`, which is allocated by using the keyword `new`, can be cleaned up.
20: Finally the data buffer is returned to the calling function as the received data.

The coding of the local function `PortRead()` is shown in Figure 5.63.

21: Local variables are declared at the beginning of this function. The `dwModemStatus` is a double word variable that is used to hold the running status of the transmission lines in the modem. The `index` works as the loop counter for the `For` loop structure to get each bit of converted data from the A/D converter. The `ad_data` works as a buffer to store the received data. The `CommPorts` is a pointer variable of the data structure `CommPortClass` and it contains all definitions of the parameters that are used to define the standards for the data collection. The `ecStatus` is a variable of the `enum` structure and it is used to hold the running status of the calling function.
22: A force conversion is used to convert the input argument `hCommPort` to the structure `CommPortClass` and assign the input argument to the local variable `CommPorts`. This conversion is necessary and it makes sure that the input argument can be passed and assigned to the local variable defined inside the function.
23: The extended function `EscapeCommFunction()` is called to reset the RTS line and enable the TLC548 A/D converter to begin to perform the data conversion.
24: A `For` loop structure is used to continuously pick up each bit of converted data from the A/D converter via the serial port (until all 8 bits of data are received).
25: The data buffer `ad_data` is shifted left by one bit to reserve one space for the next bit of data.
26: The `PortWrite()` function is called to set the TD line and sets a `HIGH` on the CLK input on the TLC548. This is equivalent to provide a `LOW-TO-HIGH` transaction on the CLK input and triggering the A/D to begin to perform the data conversion. An error

```
/*****************************************************************************
 * NAME:     PortRead()
 * DESC:     Read data from serial port
 * PGRMR:  Y. Bai
 * DATE:     10/31/03
 *****************************************************************************/
ERR_CODE PortRead(CommPortClass *hCommPort)
{
21      DWORD  dwModemStatus;
        int   index;
        UCHAR  ad_data = 0;
        CommPortClass*  CommPorts;
        ERR_CODE ecStatus = OK;
22      CommPorts = (CommPortClass* )hCommPort;
23      EscapeCommFunction(hPort, CLRRTS);        // Reset RTS to LOW to enable the CS-bar
24      for (index = 0; index < CommPorts->iMaxBits; index++)
        {
25          ad_data = ad_data << 1;
26          ecStatus = PortWrite("255", 1);   //Output 0 to the TD line to make CLK LOW.
            if (ecStatus != 0)
            {
                msg("ERROR in PortWrite()...HIGH !");
                return  ecStatus;
            }
27          if (!GetCommModemStatus(hPort, &dwModemStatus))
            {
                msg("ERROR in GetModemStatus()!");
                return  EC_GETMODSTATUS;
            }
28          if (MS_CTS_ON & dwModemStatus)        // Get the CTS status.
               ad_data++;
29          ecStatus = PortWrite("0", 1);       //Output 1 to the TD line to make CLK HIGH.
            if (ecStatus != 0)
            {
                msg("ERROR in PortWrite()...LOW !");
                return  ecStatus;
            }
        }
30      EscapeCommFunction(hPort, SETRTS);        // Set RTS to HIGH to disable the CS-bar
31      CommPorts->pcBuffer = ad_data;
32      return  ecStatus;
}
```

FIGURE 5.63 Coding for the local function `PortRead()`.

message is displayed if the function calling has failed, and the error status is returned to the calling function.

27: After the TLC548 begin to conversion, we need to monitor and check the output of the A/D, which is connected to the CTS line. To do that, the system function `GetCommModemStatus()` is used. This function returns a long pointer to a 32-bit variable that specifies the current state of the modem control-register values. This value can be a combination of multiple values of the control registers. To distinguish the desired status of the control register or transmission line, a group of system constants can be used by performing an AND operation.

28: We need to check the status of the CTS line by performing an AND operation between the system constant MS_CTS_ON and the combination of statuses that are stored in `dwModemStatus`. The result of this operation is `True` if the CTS line is `HIGH`, which means that a logical `1` is detected from the output of the A/D converter. In this case, the data buffer `ad_data` is increased by 1.

29: If the CTS line is `LOW`, no action is needed. A `LOW` value is written to the TD line to reset the CLK signal on the TLC548. An error message is displayed and the error status is returned to the calling function if this writing operation is failed. At this point, we've finished one bit of data collection. Continue in this way, until we have collected all eight bits of data.

30: After a data byte is collected, the extended function `EscapeCommFunction()` is called again to set the RTS line to `HIGH` to deselect the A/D converter by sending a logical `1` to the CS-bar input on the TLC548.

31: The received data is reserved to one of elements `pcBuffer`, which belongs to the data structure `CommPorts` that is returned to the calling function.

32: The running status of this function is returned to the calling function to indicate the running result to the calling function.

5.4.3.4.7 The DLL `Close` Function

The last DLL function is `Close`, which cleans up the configuration of the serial port and then closes the port. An empty function body for this function has been added into the source file. Enter the keyword `DllExport` in front of the function header, and enter the code shown in Figure 5.64 into the function body.

```
DllExport long Close()
{
    ERR_CODE  rc = OK;
    if (PortCreateflg)
      CloseHandle(hPort);
    PortCreateflg = false;
    fclose(fp);
    return  rc;
}
```

FIGURE 5.64 Code for the DLL function `Close`.

We need to check the Boolean variable `PortCreateflg` to make sure whether the port has been opened or not. An error message is displayed if you want to close a port but no port has been opened. The system function `CloseHandle()` with the port ID as the argument is executed if the port is opened and configured (`PortCreateflg` is `True`). The following clean up jobs include the reset of the `PortCreateflg` and close of the data file. The running status of this function is returned to the calling function.

TIP: Do not attempt to close a serial port or a file if that port or file has never been opened. You may encounter an error if you try to do that. You can perform closing a port or a file only when that port or file has been opened.

At this point, we have finished the coding of this DLL file.

Click the `Build|Build LabVIEWSerialDLL.dll` menu item from Visual C++ 6.0 workspace to create the target DLL file. You can generate the target DLL file in one of two modes: `Debug` or `Release` mode. In our case, we select the `Release` mode because this mode needs less memory space. The target DLL file `LabVIEWSerialDLL.dll` is stored at the following folder: `C:\Book2_Program\Chapter 5\CallSerialDLL\LabVIEWSerialDLL\Release`. You can select different folder to store your DLL file based on your application.

5.4.3.4.8 Testing and Running the Project in the LabVIEW Domain

Before we can test and run this project in LabVIEW domain, we need first to connect the target DLL file with the Call Library Functions defined for the LabVIEW domain in Section 5.4.3.2.

Open the project `CallSerialDLL.vi` and open its `Block Diagram` window. Perform the following steps to connect the target DLL file to each call library function node.

- Right-click the first node, `Setup`, in frame 0 and select the `Configure` item from the pop-up menu to open its `Call Library Function` dialog box. Click the `Browse` button to locate the target DLL file, which is shown in Figure 5.65, and click `OK` button to finish this connection. The target DLL file is displayed in the `Library Name or Path` box.
- Repeat the preceding steps to connect the target DLL file with the other nodes `ReadByte` and `Close`, respectively.

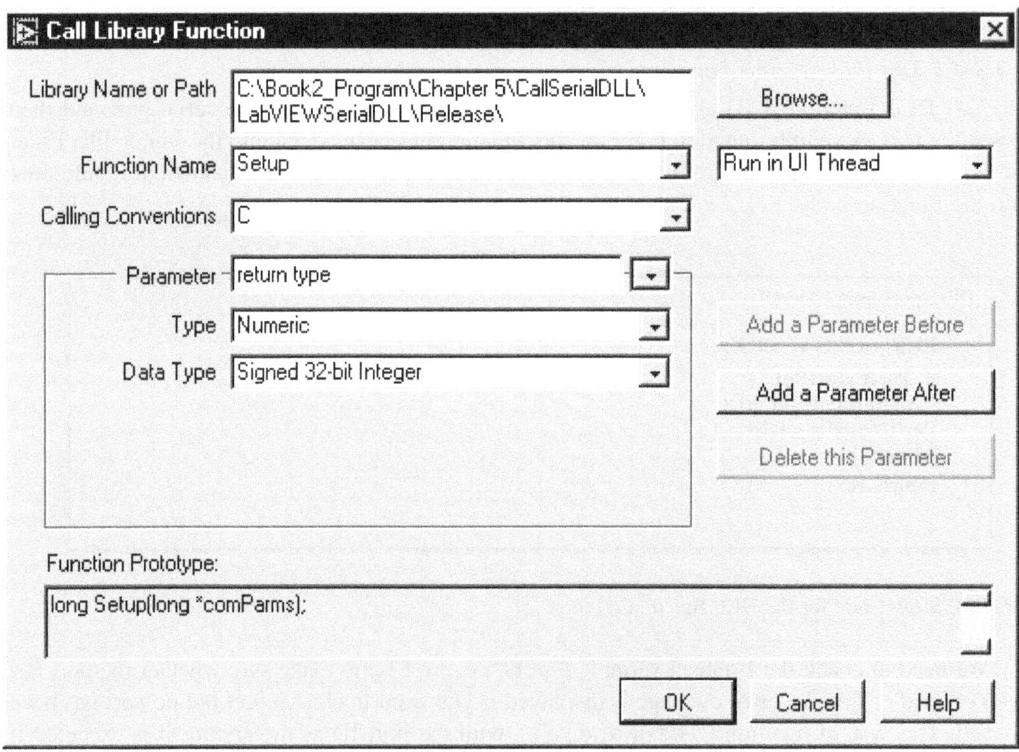

FIGURE 5.65 Connection of the target DLL file.

Connect the input of the TLC548 A/D converter with a functional generator. The input waveform can be sinusoidal, triangular or square. In our case, we select the square waveform. Set the output amplitude of the waveform between 0 and 5 volts, with a frequency of 20 Hz.

Now we are ready to run and test this project.

Click the `Run` button from the `Front Panel` window in LabVIEW domain to run the project. The TLC548 begins to convert the data and the converted data is displayed in the `Data Output` indicator in real time, the progress bar displays the percentage of received data, and the received data is displayed in the `Waveform Chart` Control, which is shown in Figure 5.66.

The `Setup Error` or `Close Error` LED would be on if an error was encountered during the setup or closing process. You can set the horizontal axis of the waveform as the relative time to get the real-time output of the A/D converter.

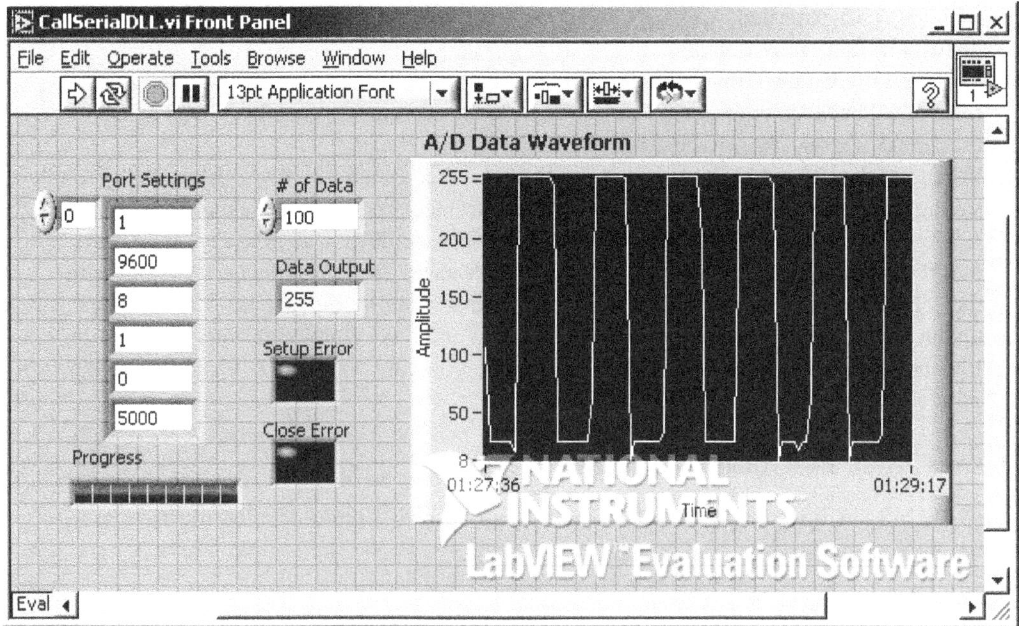

FIGURE 5.66 Running the `CallSerialDLL.vi` project.

The complete project files, including the LabVIEW Front Panel file, Block Diagram file, data file, DLL source files and DLL target file, are stored on the attached CD on the folder: `Charter 5\CallSerialDLL`.

5.5 CALLING THE CIN FROM LABVIEW TO INTERFACE WITH THE SERIAL PORT

Besides the `Call Library Function` we discussed in the last section, LabVIEW provides another way to interface to the routines developed in the third-party language or so-called external codes. Similar to the call library function node, this method also uses a node called the `code interface node` (CIN) to communicate with the external codes. The CIN can be considered as a block diagram node that links C/C++ source code to LabVIEW.

The interface for CINs supports a variety of compilers, although not all compilers can create code in the correct executable format. External code must be compiled as a form of executable appropriate for a specific platform. The code must be relocatable, because LabVIEW loads external code into the same memory space as the main application.

To call a CIN to interface to the external codes includes the following steps.

1. Create a CIN by inserting a CIN VI into the block diagram in LabVIEW.
2. Create the associated CIN source code by right-clicking CIN VI on the block diagram; then select the `Create.c File` item from the pop-up menu. This `.c` file works as a template that lets you enter your user-specific codes into the CIN function to complete the desired jobs.
3. After the CIN source file is completed, you need to compile it into a format LabVIEW can recognize and can use. There are different methods can be used to fulfill this compiling job depends on the platform and the language you are using. In this book we concentrate on the Microsoft Windows platform and Visual C++ 6.0 language. The output of the compiler is the CIN object code and it is represented by a LabVIEW subroutine

with the `.lsb` extension. This CIN object code can be recognized and used by LabVIEW and run in LabVIEW domain.

4. You need to load the CIN object code to the memory and links the code with the current front panel or block diagram in LabVIEW by right-clicking on the CIN VI and selecting the `Load Code Resource` item from the pop-up menu.
5. When run the VI, you have two choices. One is to directly run the current project without saving VI. In that case, LabVIEW calls the CIN object code and passes any data wired to the CIN, and receives the feedback from the CIN. Another way is to save the VI first before running that VI. If you did that, LabVIEW saves the CIN object code along with the VI so LabVIEW no longer needs the original code to execute the CIN. You can update your CIN object code with new version at any time. But you need to perform the loading of the updated CIN object code before you can run the VI if you want your project updated.

5.5.1 The Calling Procedure of the CIN

Based on the introduction provided in the last section, we give a more detailed illustration about the calling CIN in this section.

5.5.1.1 Creating a CIN

To create a CIN, you need first to add the CIN VI into the block diagram of your LabVIEW project. From the `Functions»Advanced` palette, access the `code interface node` and place it on a block diagram. A CIN has terminals with which you can indicate which data passes to and from a CIN. Initially, the CIN has one set of terminals, and you can pass a single value to and from the CIN. To add additional terminals, resize the node, then right-click the node and select `Add Parameter`.

Figure 5.67 shows how to resize the node to add parameters. Each pair of terminals corresponds to a parameter LabVIEW passes to the CIN. The two types of terminal pairs are input-output and output-only.

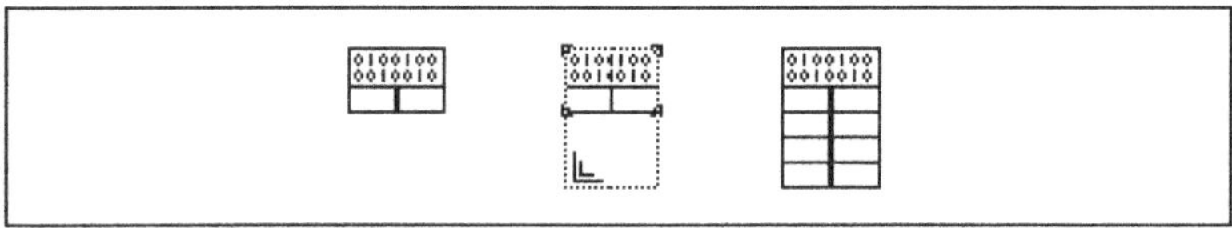

FIGURE 5.67 Adding parameters in CIN. "Using External Code in LabVIEW," Part Number 370109A-01, p. 3-4. (Reprinted with the permission of National Instruments Corporation)

By default, a terminal pair is input-output; the left terminal is the input terminal, and the right terminal is the output terminal. For example, consider a CIN that has a single terminal pair. A 32-bit integer control is wired to the input terminal and a 32-bit integer indicator is wired to the output terminal, as shown in Figure 5.68.

When the VI calls the CIN, the only argument LabVIEW passes to the CIN object code is a pointer to the value of the 32-bit integer input. When the CIN completes, LabVIEW then passes the value referenced by the pointer to the 32-bit integer indicator. When you wire controls and indicators to the input and the output terminals of a terminal pair, LabVIEW assumes that the CIN can modify the data passed. If another node on the block diagram needs the input value, LabVIEW might have to copy the input data before passing it to the CIN.

Consider the same CIN, but with no indicator wired to the output terminal, as shown in Figure 5.69.

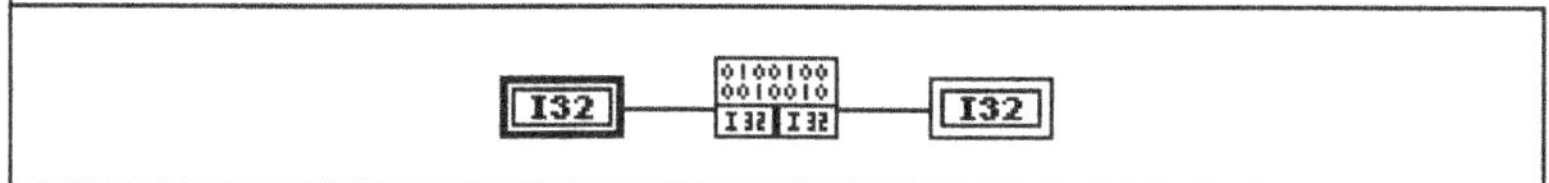

FIGURE 5.68 The input-output pair of a CIN VI. "Using External Code in LabVIEW," Part Number 370109A-01, p. 3-4, 3-5. (Reprinted with the permission of National Instruments Corporation)

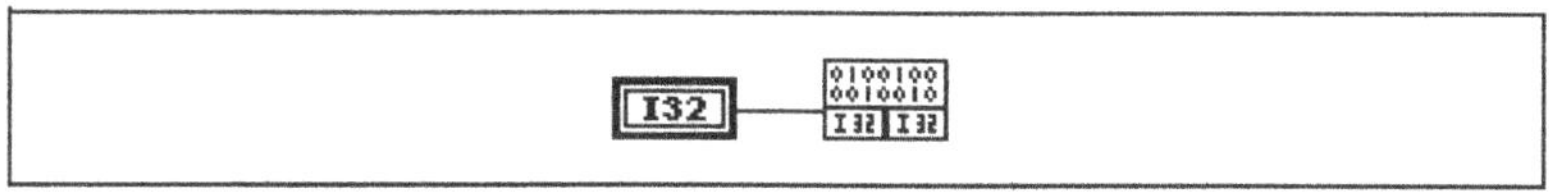

FIGURE 5.69 A CIN without output. "Using External Code in LabVIEW," Part Number 370109A-01, p. 3-4, 3-5. (Reprinted with the permission of National Instruments Corporation)

If you do not wire an indicator to the output terminal of a terminal pair, LabVIEW assumes that the CIN will not modify the value you pass to it. If another node on the block diagram uses the input data, LabVIEW does not copy the data. The source code should not modify the value passed into the input terminal of a terminal pair if you do not wire the output terminal.

If the CIN does modify the input value, nodes connected to the input terminal wire may receive the modified data.

If you use a terminal pair only to return a value, make it an output-only terminal pair by resizing the node then right-clicking the node and selecting `Output Only`. If a terminal pair is output-only, the input terminal is gray, as shown in Figure 5.70.

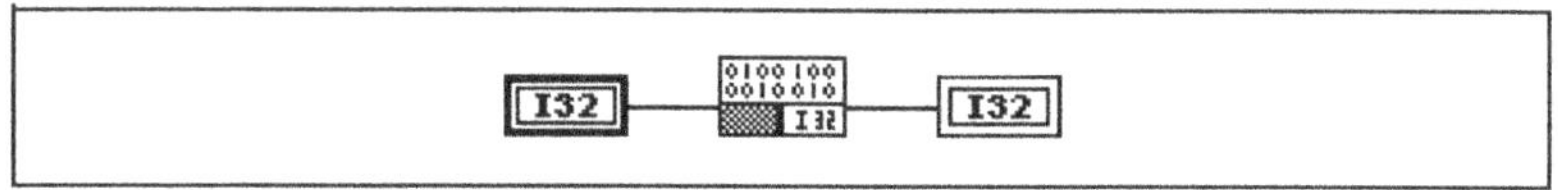

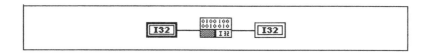

FIGURE 5.70 An Output Only CIN. "Using External Code in LabVIEW," Part Number 370109A-01, p. 3-5. (Reprinted with the permission of National Instruments Corporation)

For output-only terminals, LabVIEW creates storage space for a return value and passes the value by reference to the CIN the same way it passes values for input-output terminal pairs. If you do not wire a control to the left terminal, LabVIEW determines the type of the output parameter by checking the type of the indicator wired to the output terminal. This can be ambiguous if you wire the output to two destinations that have different data types. To solve this problem, wire a control to the left (input) terminal of the terminal pair as shown in the previous illustration. In this case, the output terminal takes on the same data type as the input terminal. LabVIEW uses the input type only to determine the data type for the output terminal; the CIN does not use or affect the data of the input wire.

To remove a pair of terminals from a CIN, right-click the terminal you want to remove and select `Remove Terminal`. LabVIEW disconnects wires connected to the deleted terminal pair. Wires connected to terminal pairs below the deleted pair remain attached to those terminals and stretch to adjust to the terminals' new positions.

Connect wires to all the terminal pairs on the CIN to specify the data you want to pass to the CIN, and the data you want to receive from the CIN. The order of terminal pairs on the CIN corresponds to the order in which parameters are passed to the code. You can use any LabVIEW data types as CIN parameters, so you can pass arbitrarily complex hierarchical data structures, such as arrays containing clusters that can in turn contain other arrays or clusters to a CIN.

5.5.1.2 Creating a .c File

Right-click the node and select `Create.c File` to create a .c file in the style of the C programming language. The .c file describes the routines you must write and the data types for parameters that pass to the CIN. For example, consider the following call to a CIN shown in Figure 5.71, which takes a 32-bit integer as an input and returns a 32-bit integer as an output.

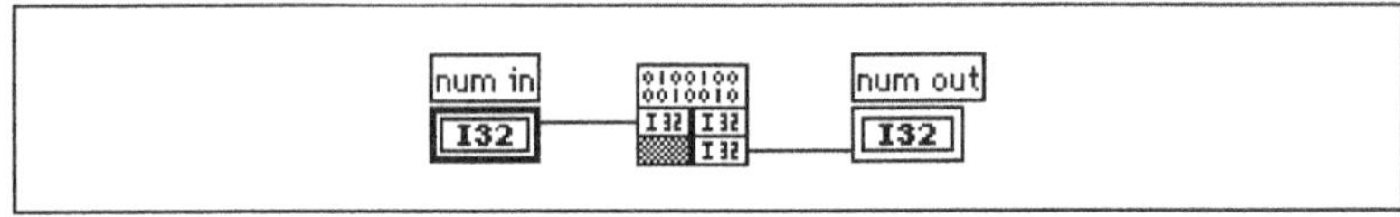

FIGURE 5.71 Creating a .c file. "Using External Code in LabVIEW," Part Number 370109A-01, p. 3-6. (Reprinted with the permission of National Instruments Corporation)

The following code excerpt is the initial .c file for this node. You can write eight routines for the CIN. The `CINRun` routine is required and the others are optional. If an optional routine is not present, LabVIEW uses a default routine when building the CIN.

```
/* CIN source file
*/
#include "extcode.h"
CIN MgErr CINRun(int32 *num_in, int32 *num_out);
CIN MgErr CINRun(int32 *num_in, int32 *num_out) {
/* ENTER YOUR CODE HERE */
return noErr;
}
```

This .c file is a template in which you must write C code. The `extcode.h` header file is automatically included, because it defines basic data types and a number of routines that can be used by CINs. The `extcode.h` also defines some constants and types whose definitions may conflict with the definitions of system header files. The `cintools` directory also contains `host-type.h`, which resolves these differences. This header file also includes many of the common header files for a given platform.

Always use `#include "extcode.h"` at the beginning of your source code. If your code needs to make system calls, also use `#include "hosttype.h"` immediately after `#include "extcode.h,"` and then include your system header files. The `hosttype.h` includes only a subset of the .h files for a given operating system. If the .h file you need is not included by `hosttype.h`, you can include it in the .c file for your CIN after you include `hosttype.h`.

LabVIEW calls the `CINRun` routine when it is time for the node to execute. `CINRun` receives the input and output values as parameters. The other routines (`CINLoad, CINSave, CINUn-load, CINAbort, CINInit, CINDispose`, and `CINProperties`) are housekeeping routines, called at specific times so you can take care of specialized tasks with your CIN. For example, LabVIEW calls `CINLoad` when it first loads a VI. If you need to accomplish a special task when your VI loads, put the code for that task in the `CINLoad` routine. To do so, write your `CINLoad` routine as follows:

```
CIN MgErr CINLoad(RsrcFile reserved) {
Unused (reserved);
/* ENTER YOUR CODE HERE */
return noErr;
}
```

The `MgErr` data type is a LabVIEW data type corresponding to a set of error codes the manager routines return. If you call a manager routine that returns an error, you can either handle the error or return the error so LabVIEW can handle it. If you can handle the errors that occur, return the error code `noErr`.

After calling a CIN routine, LabVIEW checks the `MgErr` value to determine whether an error occurred. If an error occurs, LabVIEW aborts the VI containing the CIN. If the VI is a subVI, LabVIEW aborts the VI containing the subVI. This behavior enables LabVIEW to handle conditions when a VI runs out of memory. By aborting the running VI, LabVIEW can possibly free enough memory to continue running correctly.

In general, you only need to write the `CINRun` routine. Use the other routines when you have special initialization needs, such as when your CIN must maintain some information across calls, and you want to preallocate or initialize global state information. The following code shows an example of how to fill out the `CINRun` routine from the previously shown LabVIEW-generated `.c` file to multiply a number by two.

```
CIN MgErr CINRun(int32 *num_in, int32 *num_out) {
*num_out = *num_in * 2;
return noErr;
}
```

5.5.1.3 Using the Visual C++ IDE to Compile the CIN Source Code

You must compile the source code for the CIN as a LabVIEW subroutine (`.lsb`) file. After you compile your C/C++ code in one of the compilers that LabVIEW supports, you use a LabVIEW utility that puts the object code into the `.lsb` format.

Because the compiling process is often complex, LabVIEW includes utilities that simplify the process. These utilities take a simple specification for a CIN and create object code you can load into LabVIEW. These tools vary depending on the platform and compiler you use.

In this section, we limit our discussion on the Microsoft Visual C++ IDE applied in Windows platform.

To build CINs using the Visual C++ Integrated Development Environment, complete the following steps.

1. Create a new DLL project. Select `File|New` and select `Win32 Dynamic-Link Library` as the project type. You can name your project whatever you want.
2. Add CIN objects and libraries to the project. Select `Project|Add To Project|Files` and select `cin.obj, labview.lib, lvsb.lib`, and `lvsbmain.def` from the `Cintools` subdirectory. You need these files to build a CIN.
3. Add `Cintools` to the include path. Select the `Tools|Options` menu item and select Directories tab. Add the path to your `Cintools` directory at the last line in the `Directories:` box.
4. Set alignment to `1 byte`. Select the `Project|Settings`, select the C/C++ tab and set the `Category` to `Code Generation`. Select the `Struct member alignment` tab and select `1 byte`.
5. Choose a run-time library. Select the `Project|Settings`, select the `C/C++` tab and set the `Category` to `Code Generation`. Select `Multithreaded DLL` in the `Use run-time library` control.

6. Make a custom build command to run `lvsbutil`. Select the `Project|Settings`, and select the `Custom Build` tab, change the `Commands` field as follows; (this code should appear on a single line):

```
"<your path to cintools>\lvsbutil" $(TargetName) -d "$(WkspDir)\$(OutDir)"
```

Change `Outputs` file fields to $(OutDir)$(TargetName)`.lsb`.

5.5.1.4 Loading the CIN Object Code

To load the code resource, right-click the node and select `Load Code Resource`. Select the `.lsb` file you created in step 4.

LabVIEW loads your object code into memory and links the code to the current front panel or block diagram. After you save the VI, the file containing the object code does not need to be resident on the computer running LabVIEW for the VI to run.

If you modify the source code, you can load the new version of the object code using the `Load Code Resource` option. The file containing the object code for the CIN must have an extension of `.lsb`.

There is no limit to the number of CINs per block diagram.

Following we use a real example to illustrate this procedure. This example uses the CIN to interface a serial A/D converter via serial port. The A/D converter used in this section (introduced in Section 5.3.2) is a 12-bit converter MAX187 manufactured by Maxim Integrated Products.

5.5.2 Using CIN to Interface with a Serial A/D Converter

Generally, the designing and building of a CIN interface is more complicated than a shared DLL. You should use a shared DLL to call the external code if your application allows you to do that unless your project includes some complicated data structures. The advantages of using the CIN is to allow you to apply some LabVIEW data structures to interface to the third-party routines, to modify the data and array size and transfer multi-dimension arrays between two domains. Any advantage definitely brings some disadvantages, that is `True` for the CIN. More flexibilities result in more complex in the design and applications of CIN. I do not mean that the CIN is no good compared with the DLL, but what I mean is that you must spend more time and energy to design your application if the CIN is involved.

Because each CIN corresponds to one `.c` source file with the name `CINRun()`, you cannot compile and build the target (`.lsb`) file that contains more than one `CINRun()` function in the third-party environment. In our case, the Visual C++ 6.0 IDE only allows you to build a target file extended with `.lsb` with the source file that contains only one `CINRun()` function.

5.5.2.1 The Hardware Interface Circuit

The interface circuit of the MAX187 A/D converter is shown in Figure 5.26. For your convenience, we redraw that circuit in Figure 5.72.

The elements parameters are shown in Table 5.4.

The DTR and the RTS lines are used as the inputs to the MAX187 to provide the SCLK and CS-bar control signals. The DSR line is used to receive the output of the A/D converter, and the converted data can be transmitted serially from the output buffer of the MAX187 to the serial port via this DSR transmission line. All of these transmission lines work in an extended style, so no handshaking procedures should be used on those lines in this application.

Make the circuit connection as shown in Figure 5.72. The serial port used in this project is a DB-9 port and the port number is COM1.

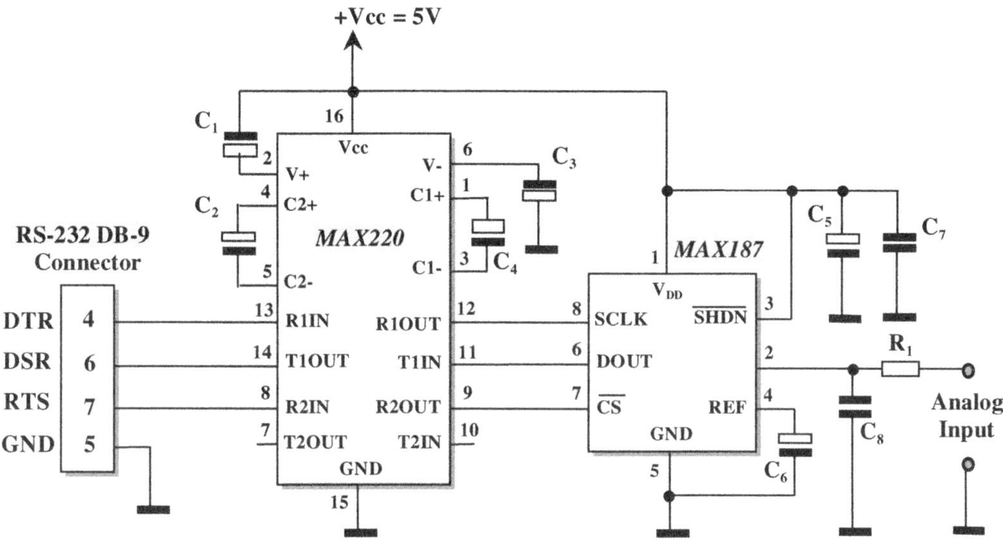

FIGURE 5.72 Interface circuit of the MAX187.

TABLE 5.4
The Elements Parameters

Elements	Values	Comments
R_1	10 KΩ	Current-limited resistor
$C_1 \sim C_4$	10 μF/25V	Electrolytic capacitors
$C_5 \sim C_6$	4.7 μF/10V	Electrolytic capacitors
$C_7 \sim C_8$	0.1 μF	Capacitors

5.5.2.2 Designing of a Front Panel for the Project

The front panel of this project is very similar with one used in the last project. Refer to Figure 5.49 to design this front panel.

Launch LabVIEW 7.0 Express and open a new project named `CallSerialCIN`. Your finished panel should match one that is shown in Figure 5.73.

The difference between this panel and the last one is that one numeric indicator, `Port Handle`, is added into this panel. This indicator is used to display the port handler that is associated with an opened port. One more LED is also provided to monitor and display the running result of the data collecting subroutine. Another difference is the displaying unit of the data waveform. The unit of the output is transferred to real voltage units by multiplying a scalar factor in the LabVIEW domain.

Modify all labels and make them identical to those in Figure 5.73. All serial port setup parameters are practical and should be saved as the default parameters.

5.5.2.3 Using CIN to Develop a Block Diagram

The block diagram of this project is similar to that developed in the last project. Three sequence structures are used to finish the serial port configuration, data collection, and the serial port closing. For each sequence structure, the key component is the `Code Interface node` that works as an interface between the LabVIEW and the subroutines developed in the external codes.

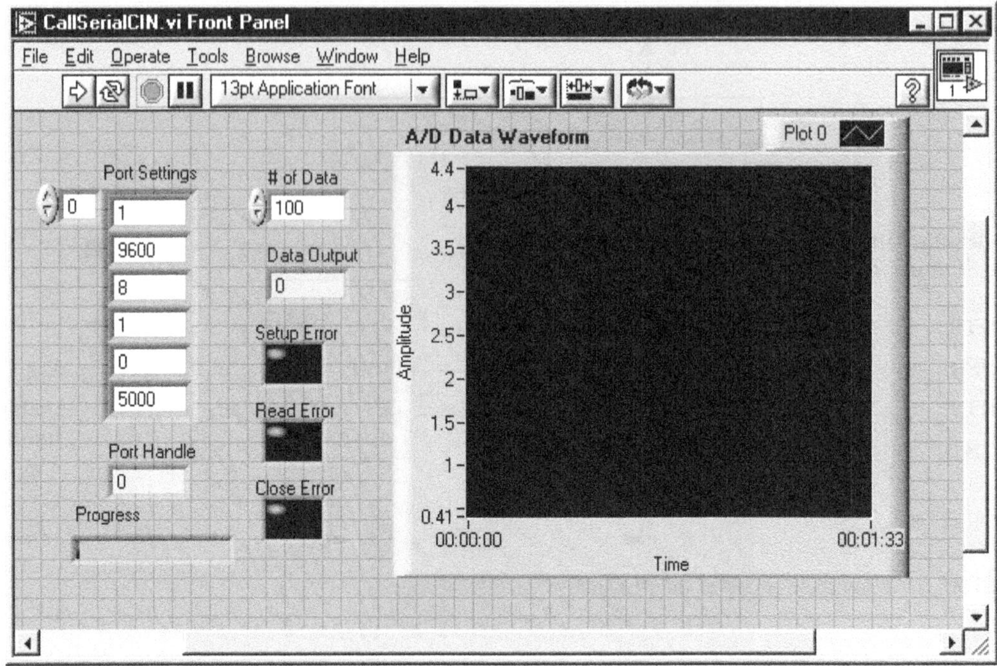

FIGURE 5.73 Front panel for the CallSerialCIN.vi project.

5.5.2.3.1 Developing a Block Diagram for the Port Setup

Open the `Block Diagram` window and add the following VIs that are shown in Figure 5.74 into the first sequence structure.

The key component in the first sequence structure is a `Code Interface Node` VI named `CINSetup`. This node initializes and configures the serial port, based on the setup parameters obtained from the LabVIEW panel, and returns the port handler for the opened serial port.

Pick up the `Code Interface Node` VI from the `Functions|Advanced` icon and drag it down to get three input-output pairs. All terminals on the left hand side are inputs and the outputs are for the terminals on the right hand side. The first input-output pair is used as the input terminal that passes the setup parameters to the serial port via the external codes. Connect the top input of the `CINSetup` node with the numeric array control `Port Settings` that provide an array of serial port setup parameters, and this array is an argument to the `CINSetup()` function and works as an input to that function.

This `CINSetup()` function should return two parameters after it is executed: the port handler, if the port is successfully opened and configured, and the running status of the function.

For the first returned parameter port handler, set the second input-output pair as an `Output Only` terminal by right-clicking on the `CINSetup` node and select the `Output Only` item from the pop-up menu. Connect the output terminal of that `Output Only` to the `Port Handle` numeric indicator. This `Port Handle` should be passed into the next sequence structure as the input to the next `Code Interface node, CINReadData`. To do this, right-click on the border of the sequence structure and select the `Add Sequence Local` item from the pop-up menu to add a sequence local terminal, and wire this terminal with the output terminal of the `Output Only` on the `CINSetup` node.

The second returned parameter is a 32-bit signed integer that is used to indicate the running status of the `CINSetup()` function. A `Not Equal To 0?` VI is used to translate the returned integer into a Boolean value to trigger the `Setup Error` LED. Connect the output terminal of the third input-output pair of the `CINSetup` node to the input of the `Not Equal To 0?` VI.

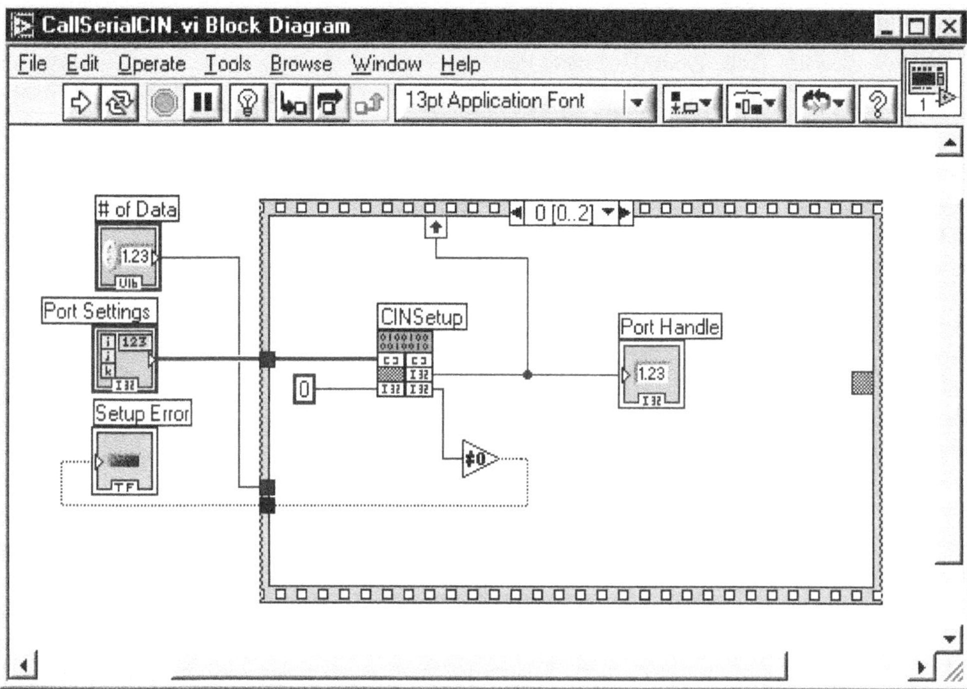

FIGURE 5.74 Block diagram for the first sequence structure: `Setup`.

Does it work? No. You may encounter a connection error. The reason for this is that you did not explicitly indicate the output type for that output terminal, so LabVIEW is confused about this connection. A solution for this kind of connection error is to first connect a Numeric constant that has the same data type as the output to the input terminal of the third input-output pair. In this way, you make LabVIEW clear what kind of data you want to output.

TIP: Do *not* attempt to connect any ambiguous output of a `Code Interface Node` to any VIs. A good habit is: Always explicitly indicate the output data type by setting the same data type at the input terminal on the input-output pair.

Finally connect the output of the `Not Equal To` 0? VI to the `Setup Error` LED.

5.5.2.3.2 Developing a Block Diagram for the Data Collection

The second sequence structure is used to collect the converted data from the MAX187 A/D converter via the `CINReadData` node. This block diagram repeatedly collects 100 converted data (12-bit binary data) using a `While` loop from the MAX187 via the `CINReadData` interface node. Each loop needs to call the `CINReadData` node to obtain one 12-bit converted data segment. The received data is converted to the real voltage unit and displayed in both the `Data Output` indicator and the waveform chart. the data collection progress is represented by a `Progress Bar` VI in real time.

The completed block diagram of this sequence structure is shown in Figure 5.75.

First add a `Code Interface node` into this sequence and name it as `CINReadData`. Enlarge this node to obtain four input-output pairs. The first input-output pair is an `Output Only` terminal and it is used to return a 12-bit converted data from the A/D converter. The data type of this output is an `int16` in the LabVIEW domain and it is equivalent to a `Short` data type in Visual C++ 6.0. To make this output data type explicit to LabVIEW, connect a Numeric Constant to the input terminal even it is an `Output Only` terminal. Then wire the output terminal of this first input-output pair to the input of a `Multiply` VI. The purpose of multiplying the collected

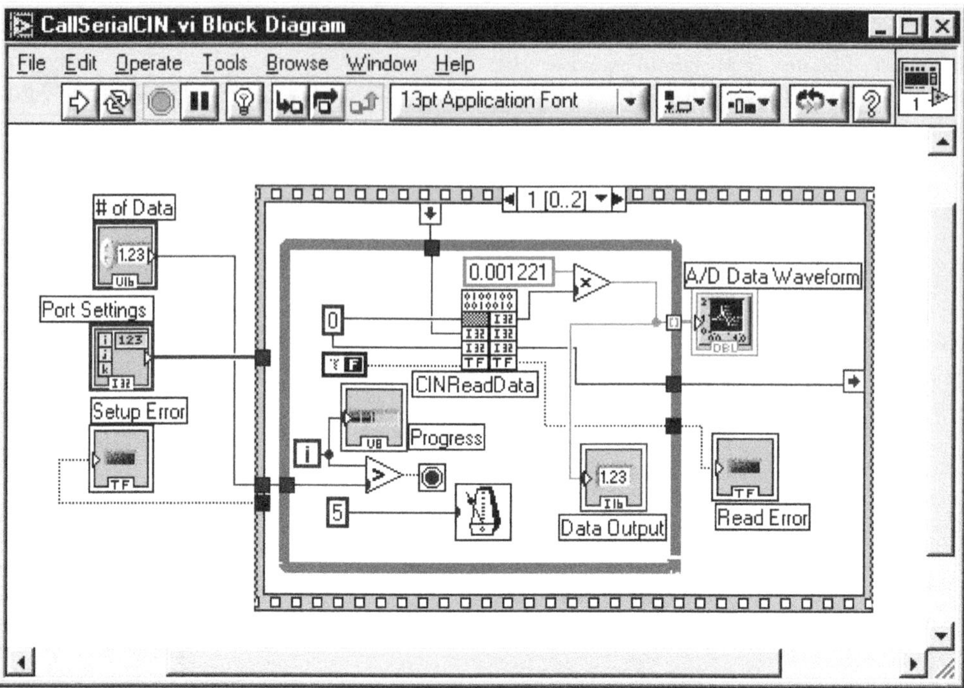

FIGURE 5.75 Block diagram for the second sequence structure: `Read Data`.

data by a constant 0.001221 that is equal to 5.0 ÷ 4095 is to convert the received data to the real voltage unit. The maximum input voltage to the MAX187 is 5.0 V and the A/D is a 12-bit converter. The output of the `Multiply` VI is connected to both the Waveform Chart to display the collected data in a waveform format and the `Data Output` indicator to display that data in real time. You may encounter a connection error if you did not connect a Numeric Constant to the input terminal of the first input-output pair.

The second input-output pair is used as an input terminal that receives the `Port Handle` passed from the previous sequence structure. As the serial port is opened and configured by the first sequence structure, the `Port Handle` is a key for any other routines to access that port. So we need to reserve this `Port Handle` and pass it to all the following sequences where they need it. Connect the input terminal of the second input-output pair with the `Sequence Local` item together to receive the `Port Handle` passed from the first sequence structure.

The third input-output pair works as an output to pass the `Port Handle` to the next sequence structure because the `Port Handle` is also needed for the next `Code Interface node`, `CINClose`, which is located in the next sequence structure and is used to close the port. We now need to pass it to the next structure. Right-click on the border of the current sequence structure and select the `Add Sequence Local` item from the pop-up menu to add the second `Sequence Local` item, and wire the output terminal to the newly added `Sequence Local` item. Similarly, you may encounter a connection error when you do that connection. To solve this problem, connect the input terminal of the third input-output pair to the `Numeric` constant too. Now both the first and the third input terminals are connected to the same Numeric constant. That does not matter because we only use this constant as an indicator to LabVIEW and thus prevent ambiguity on the associated output terminals.

The fourth input-output pair works as an output of this node to return the running status of this CIN function `CINReadData()`. Before connecting the output terminal of the fourth input-output pair to the `Read Error` LED, you need first to connect the input terminal to a `False` Constant

VI. In this way, you explicitly indicate to LabVIEW that the output terminal is a Boolean variable that can be directly connected to a LED.

The `While` loop counter `i` is connected to the `Progress` VI to display the progress of receiving the converted data as the program runs. This counter is also compared with a numeric control, `# of Data`, to monitor the end point of the data conversion. A `True` value is sent to the `Stop` control of the `While` loop to stop the loop if the counter's value is greater than the value of `# of Data`.

A `Wait Until Next ms Multiple` VI is used to delay each loop by five milliseconds. This delay is optional and depends on your application. The smaller the delay time, the higher the frequency of the analog signal that can be detected.

5.5.2.3.3 Developing a Block Diagram for the Port Closing

The last sequence structure is used to close the serial port. The interface between the LabVIEW and the external codes is made of another `Code Interface Node, CINClose`, which is located at the third sequence structure. This node is simply to close the opened serial port. The completed block diagram of this sequence structure is shown in Figure 5.76.

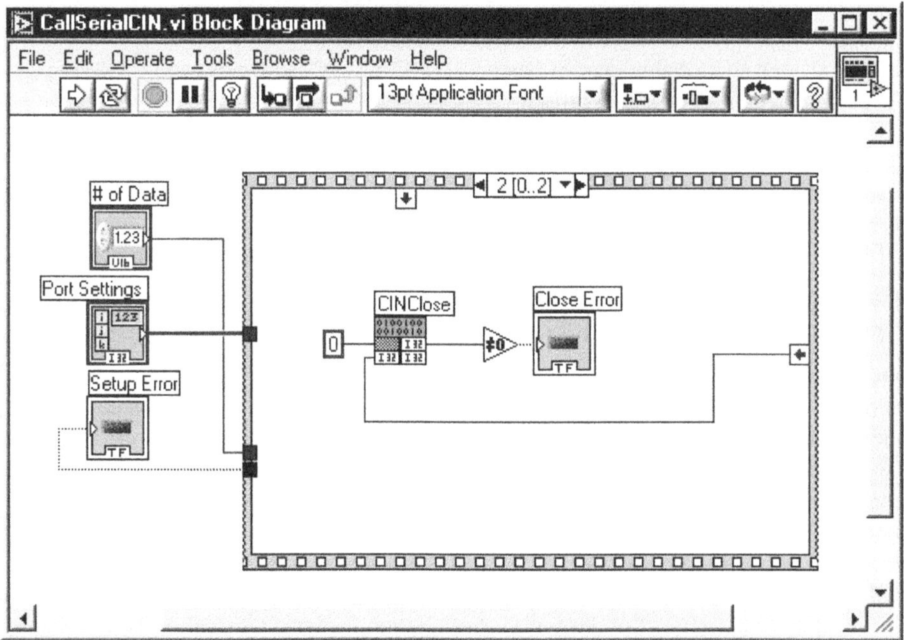

FIGURE 5.76 Block diagram for the third sequence structure: `Close Port`.

Add a `Code Interface node` into this sequence structure and enlarge it to get two input-output pairs. The top input-output pair is used as an output terminal to return the running status of this CIN function `CINClose()`. First make this pair as an `Output Only` terminal, and then connect a `Numeric` constant to the top input terminal to indicate to LabVIEW explicitly that this output terminal has an `int32` data type. After you finish this connection, you can directly connect this output to a `Not Equal To 0?` VI.

The bottom input-output pair works as an input terminal to receive the `Port Handle` value passed from the preceding sequence structure. Connect this input terminal with the `Sequence Local` item to get this input.

Note that there is a difference between the colors on these three `Code Interface nodes`. Both the `CINSetup` and `CINClose` nodes have an orange color, but the `CINReadData` node has a yellow color. What does this color difference mean? The orange color means that the CIN is not a thread-safe node, which means that it cannot be called or run in a multiple-threads environment. To make it a thread-safe node, you need to add the `CINProperties` function into the `.c` file. We will look at an example of the thread-safe node in the following compiling section.

The `CINProperties` function only labels your CIN as being safe to run from multiple threads. Whether the CIN is actually thread safe depends entirely upon the C code that has been written. (You can consult your C code documentation for information about running C code simultaneously from multiple threads). The following list presents basic answers to the question, *Is my CIN code thread safe?*

- CIN code is thread safe when it stores no unprotected global data (no global variables or files on disk, for example); it does not access any hardware (in other words, it does not contain register-level programming); it makes no calls to any functions, shared libraries, or drivers that are not thread safe.
- CIN code is thread safe when it uses semaphores or mutexes to protect access to global resources.
- A CIN call is thread safe when only one non-reentrant VI calls the CIN, and when the code accesses no global resources (such as `CINInit`, `CINAbort`, and `CINDispose`) through CIN housekeeping routines.

Note that `CINReadData` is a thread-safe node, but `CINSetup` and `CINClose` are not.

At this point, we have finished coding our project in the LabVIEW domain. Before we can continue, we need to create a `.c` file that is associated with each CIN to produce the prototype of each CIN function, because we need to write our routine inside those CIN functions with the third-party language.

5.5.2.3.4 Generating the CIN Source Files

Go to the first sequence structure and right-click on the `CINSetup node`, and select the `Create.c File` item from the pop-up menu. Enter `CINSetup.c` in the `File name:` box within the opened dialog box, which is shown in Figure 5.77, and click the `Save` button to save this file to our project folder, `CallSerialCIN`..

Perform the similar steps to create another two CIN source file, `CINReadData.c` and `CINClose.c`, respectively. An example of this kind of CIN source file, `CINSetup.c`, is shown in Figure 5.78

Note that the `Code Interface Nodes` only provide an interface frame between the LabVIEW and the external codes; you need to design your programming tasks by writing the associated code inside those CIN functions. Finally you also need to compile the external codes contained in the associated CINs into a format that can be recognized and run by LabVIEW. You cannot run this project until you finish compiling and loading these external codes to an `.lsb` format that can be read by the LabVIEW domain. To make the external codes that are located in the associated CIN functions recognizable by LabVIEW, you need to use different tools or compilers to finish the job. In this book, we concentrate on the Visual C++ 6.0 compiler. We will now discuss how to compile the external codes that are written in the CINs to the format that LabVIEW can recognize and use.

TIP: You need to write your interface routine with a third-party language inside the .c file generated with the associated `Code Interface Node` inside the CIN function. You also need to compile the interface routine written in an external language into a target file that can be recognized and used by LabVIEW by using any suitable compiler. The

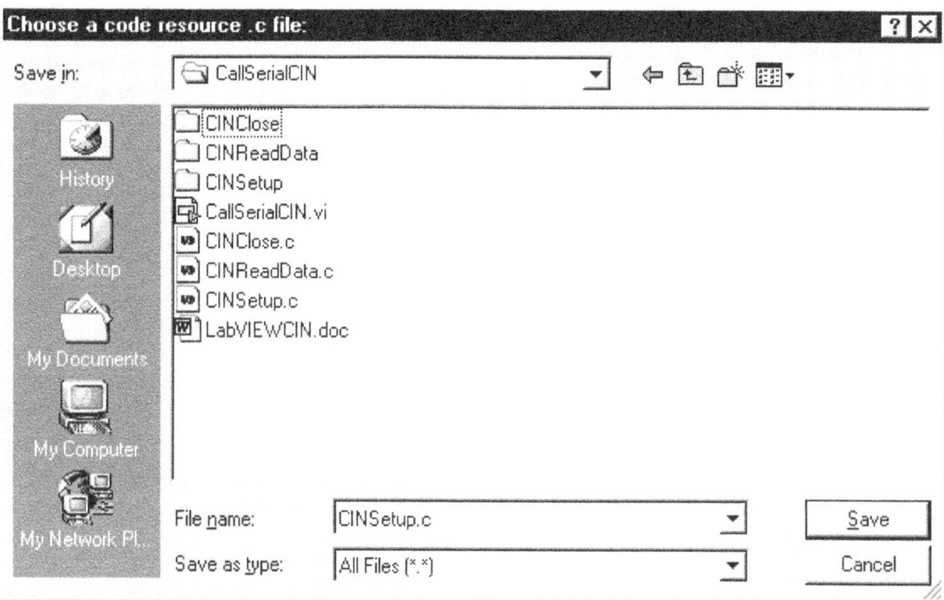

FIGURE 5.77 The `Create.c File` dialog box.

```
/* CIN source file */
#include "extcode.h"
/* Typedefs */
typedef struct {
    int32 dimSize;
    int32 COM[1];
} TD1;
typedef TD1 **TD1Hdl;
MgErr CINRun(TD1Hdl *PortSettings, int32 *PortHandle, int32 *arg1);
MgErr CINRun(TD1Hdl *PortSettings, int32 *PortHandle, int32 *arg1)
{
      /* Insert code here */
      return noErr;
}
```

CIN Structure and Function Declarations

CIN Function Definition

FIGURE 5.78 An example of the `CIN` source file.

target file is extended with the extension `.lsb`. You cannot run your LabVIEW program that contains the CINs until you load the target file into the LabVIEW domain.

Following we use Visual C++ 6.0 IDE to develop our interface routines and compile them into the target file with the Visual C++ 6.0 compiler.

5.5.2.4 Using the Visual C++ 6.0 IDE to Develop the CIN Object Code

As we previous mentioned at the beginning of this section, each CIN source file (`.c` file) must be compiled and built to a single target library file (`.lsb`) that can be recognized and loaded by LabVIEW before the program that contains the CINs can be executed. In the following sections, we use three CINs generated at the last section to discuss how to finish the coding and compiling of those target files that can be recognized and used by the LabVIEW.

5.5.2.4.1 The DLL `CINSetup` Function

From right now, we design and build our CIN functions inside the Visual C++ 6.0 domain.

First let's develop the first CIN function `CINSetup`.

Launch Visual C++ 6.0 and create a new project with the following properties:

- Project name: `CINSetup`.
- Project type: `Win32 Dynamic-Link Library`.
- Location: `C:\Book2_Program\Chapter 5\CallSerialCIN`.

In the newly created project, create a header file named `CINSetup.h` and a source file named `CINSetup.cpp`. Before we can continue, we need copy the following files into our current project folder. You can skip this step and directly add these files into the current project by using the `Project|Add To Project|Files` menu items. But the project developed in this way is not portable because the files you added into this project are still located at the original folders. Open the Windows Explorer to copy the following files into our current project folder `C:\Book2_Program\Chapter 5\CallSerialCIN\CINSetup`:

- cin.obj
- labview.lib
- lvsb.lib
- lvsbmain.def
- extcode.h
- fundtypes.h
- hosttype.h
- platdefines.h

The top four files are used to coordinate the environment and program variables between the LabVIEW and the Visual C++ 6.0, and the bottom four header files provide the prototypes and mappings of the data types, structures and functions between the LabVIEW and C/C++. All of these files are located at the default installation folder of the LabVIEW 7.0 software. In our case, the folder is `C:\Program Files\National Instruments\ LabVIEW 7.0\cintools`.

In Visual C++ 6.0 workspace, select the `Project|Add To Project|Files` menu item to add those copied files into our current project `CINSetup`.

5.5.2.4.1.1 Header File for the CIN Function `CINSetup`

In Visual C++ 6.0, open the `CINSetup.c` file we generated at the LabVIEW domain in Section 5.5.2.3.4. An example of this opened `CINSetup.c` file is shown in Figure 5.78. Refer to Figure 5.78, copy the CIN structure and function declarations into the header file `CINSetup.h` that we created earlier, and copy the CIN function definition into the source file `CINSetup.cpp`, respectively.

On the opened `CINSetup.h` header file, add the following codes that are shown in Figure 5.79 into this header file.

A: The system header file `Windows.h` is included first in this header file because this system header file provides all object definitions applied in the Windows environment. As an example, the `MessageBox()` function is defined in that system header file. The `#include "extcode.h"` is copied from the `CINSetup.c` file as we did earlier.

```
  /****************************************************************************
   * NAME:      CINSetup.h
   * DESC:      Header file for the CINSetup.cpp
   ****************************************************************************/
A #include <Windows.h>
  #include "extcode.h"
B #ifndef _CINSETUP_H_
  #define _CINSETUP_H_
C #define MAX_STRING                256
  #define NOPARITY                    0
  #define ONESTOPBIT                  0
  #define RTS_CONTROL_DISABLE      0x00
  #define RTS_CONTROL_ENABLE       0x01
  #define DTR_CONTROL_DISABLE      0x00
  #define DTR_CONTROL_ENABLE       0x01
D #define UCHAR          unsigned char
  #define ULONG          unsigned long
  #define msg(info)      MessageBox(NULL, info, "", MB_OK)
E #ifdef __cplusplus
  extern "C" {
  #endif /* __cplusplus */
F typedef struct
  {
    ULONG  ulCtrlID;
    char   cEcho;
    char   cEORChar;
    long   lTimeout;
    long   lBaudRate;
    long   lDataBits;
  } SerialCreate, *pSerialCreate;
G typedef enum
  {
    OK      = 0,           /* no error */
    EC_TIMEOUT,
    EC_FOPEN,
    EC_INVAL_CONFIG,
    EC_TIMEOUT_SET,
    EC_RECV_TIMEOUT,
    EC_EXIT_CODE,
    EC_WAIT_SINGLEOBJ,
    EC_INVALIDPORT,
    EC_WRITE_FAIL,
    EC_CREATE_THREAD,
    EC_GETMODSTATUS,
    EC_UNKNOWNERROR
  } ERR_CODE;
  // Generated by CIN in LabVIEW (CIN Source File .c)
H typedef struct
  {
      int dimSize;            // array dimension
      int COM[1];             // array elements
  } TD1;
  typedef TD1 **TD1Hdl;
```

FIGURE 5.79 Header file for the `CINSetup` function. *(continued)*

```
I   HANDLE  hPort;
    char*   sPortName;
    /* local functions */
J   ERR_CODE PortInitialize(char* lpszPortName, pSerialCreate pCreate);
    //CINSetup() CIN Function
K   MgErr CINRun(TD1Hdl PortSettings, int32 *PortHandle, int32 *flg);
    #ifdef __cplusplus
    }
L   #endif  /* __cplusplus */
    #endif
```

FIGURE 5.79 Header file for the `CINSetup` function.

B: To avoid multiple including of this header file, the system macro `#ifndef` is used here. The purpose of this macro is to allow the other source file to include this header file if this header file has not been included before by that source file. In C/C++ programming, it is illegal to include a header multiple times by any source file in the project. To avoid that situation occur, the macro `#ifndef` and `#define` are used. You need to attach a `#endif` at the end of this header file if you used this macro.

C: Some constants are defined here and most of them are serial communication related parameters, such as `NOPARITY`, `ONESTOPBIT`, `RTS_CONTROL_ENABLE` and `RTS_CONTROL_DISABLE`. As we previous mentioned, the transmission lines used in this project are not normal format, it is necessary for us to set and reset each transmission line by using the function `EscapeCommFunction()`. You must set the transmission lines to either the `CONTROL_ENABLE` or `CONTROL_DISABLE` state during the configuration stage in order to use that extended function to access and set/reset any transmission line.

D: To make the program simple and clear, two data types, unsigned char and unsigned long, are redefined using the macro `#define` as UCHAR and ULONG, respectively. After this re-definition, we can use these two re-defined data type to save the time and the space in the declaration of variables and functions that use this data type. Another simplification is to re-define the `MessageBox()` function by using the macro `#define`. After this re-definition, the length of the function `MessageBox()` can be greatly shorten and it is very easy to be placed in the program by using the `msg()` with a text string as the information.

E: When you build shared libraries for C++, you must prevent the C++ compiler from decorating the function names in the final object code. To do this, wrap the function declaration in an extern "C" clause, `extern "C" { ....}`. The codes included inside the opening and ending braces are considered as the C codes and the compiler converts them to the C object codes, not C++ object codes. One point you need to note is that if you disable C++ decoration of a function, the compiler cannot create polymorphic versions of the function.

F: A data structure is defined here to convenience to the port configurations. The structure is named `SerialCreate` that contains useful port communication parameters, such as the baud rate, data bits, timeout value and other parameters used to check and indicate the communication status.

G: An enum structure ERR_CODE is declared to define the numeric error value that is associated with each possible error occurred during the project runs. Space can be greatly saved by using this kind of definition and each error code is sequenced from the integer 0 to the maximum integer value.

H: The data structure TD1 is generated by LabVIEW when we create the CIN source file CINSetup.c, and this structure is copied from that source file. This structure defined the array that contains the serial port configuration parameters located in LabVIEW domain. The first element of this structure is an integer dimSize that indicates the size or the length of the array, and the second element COM[1] is the array that stores the real array elements. The index 1 means that all elements in the array are arranged to a 1-dimensional array. For example, a 2 × 3 array is arranged to a 1-dimensional array that contains 6 elements from the first one [0] to the last one [5]. In our case, the array is a one-dimension array with 1 × 6 elements.

I: Global variables are declared in this section. The purpose of these global variables is to simplify the program and allow different source files to share some common variables. Although the global style is not recommended in the Object-Oriented-Programming environment, it can really simplify and speed up the process for the application programs that need the high-speed and the real-time responses. The hPort is used to reserve the file handle that represents the opened port. Any code can use this hPort to access the opened serial port in the program. The sPortName is a string variable and it is used to reserve the port name in the text format because the port initialization function needs the port name as the text format.

J: A local function is declared here. The purpose of this function is to coordinate the CIN function to perform the data communications between the serial port and the computer. The CIN functions work as the interface functions and the local function works as the executive functions to directly communicate with the low-level system routines to complete the data processing tasks. The PortInitialize() function is used to configure the serial port and this function has two arguments. The first one is the port name represented by the text format, and the second is a pointer of the data structure SerialCreate, which is the starting address in which the configuration parameters are stored.

K: The declaration of the CIN function CINSetup() is placed in this header file to provide the function prototype that is used later by the source file. This function declaration is copied from the CINSetup.c file as we did in the beginning on this section. You need to note that we have modified this function to meet the requirement of our application. Refer to Figure 5.78, the first nominal argument of this function, PortSettings, is a pointer to the structure TD1Hdl. Note that the TD1Hdl itself is a double pointer to the data structure TD1 that is defined by LabVIEW. So this argument now is a triple pointer to the structure TD1. To make thing simple and practical, we prefer to remove the pointer operator in front of this nominal argument PortSettings to make it a double pointer. The third nominal argument of the original function generated in LabVIEW is *arg1. We modify this argument to *flg to indicate that this argument is a flag and it is used to return the running status of this function. A returned nonzero value, or a False value, means that an error has occurred.

L: Attach two ending braces for the macros #ifndef_CINSETUP_H_ and #ifdef _cplusplus.

Now let's take a look at the coding of the source file.

5.5.2.4.1.2 Source File for the CINSetup Function

Open the created source file CINSetup.cpp and enter the following codes that are shown in Figure 5.80 into this source file.

```
   /*****************************************************************************
    * NAME:       CINSetup.cpp
    * DESC:       Interface program to MAX187 Serial A/D converter
    * PGMR:       Y. Bai
    * DATE:       11/6/2003
    *****************************************************************************/
   #include <stdio.h>
   #include <stdlib.h>
   #include <string.h>
M  #include "CINSetup.h"
N  MgErr CINRun(TD1Hdl PortSettings, int32 *PortHandle, int32 *flg)
   {
      /* Insert code here */
O     ERR_CODE  rc = OK;               //COM[0] = port number, COM[1] = baud_rate,
      pSerialCreate  pParam;           //COM[2] = data_bits,  COM[3] = stop_bit
      pParam = new SerialCreate;       //COM[4] = parity,     COM[5] = timeout_value
P     pParam->lBaudRate = (*PortSettings)->COM[1];
      pParam->lDataBits = (*PortSettings)->COM[2];
      pParam->lTimeout  = (*PortSettings)->COM[5];
Q     switch((int)(*PortSettings)->COM[0])
      {
         case 1:
            sPortName = "COM1";
            break;
         case 2:
            sPortName = "COM2";
            break;
         case 3:
            sPortName = "COM3";
            break;
         case 4:
            sPortName = "COM4";
            break;
         default:
            *flg = EC_INVALIDPORT;
      }
R     rc = PortInitialize(sPortName, pParam);
      if (rc != 0)
            msg("ERROR in PortInitialize()!");
S     delete pParam;
T     *flg = 0;
      *PortHandle = (long)hPort;
U      return noErr;
   }
```

FIGURE 5.80 Code for the `CINSetup` source file.

Each section of this code is explained in the following list.

M: The header file `CINSetup.h` is included at the top of this source file because the prototypes of the variables and functions used in this source file are declared in that header file. Some other system header files are also included here.

N: The definition of the CIN function `CINSetup()` is placed here. You need to note that all CIN functions are named `CINRun()` no matter what kind of actual name you used in the CIN source file. This is one reason why you cannot compile a single target file that includes more than one CIN functions, because the Visual C++ 6.0 compiler does not allow different functions to have the same function name in one source file. You need to note that the nominal arguments of this function have been modified (the first argument `PortSettings` and the third `*flg`). Refer to step K to get detailed instructions for these modifications.

TIP: All CIN functions generated by LabVIEW have a unique name `CINRun()` no matter what kind of real name you declared in the `Code Interface Node`. You cannot modify this name and LabVIEW identify the CIN source file and target file based on this name. For this reason, each CIN source file must be developed as a single project and compiled to a single target file by Visual C++ IDE.

O: Inside this function, some local variables are declared. The `rc` is an `enum` structure variable and it is used to hold the running status of local functions. `pParam` is a pointer variable of the structure `SerialCreate`. The `new` keyword is used to create a new pointer variable and allocate the memory space for that variable `pParam`.

P: The serial port configuration parameters stored in the array `PortSettings` are assigned to the elements of the structure variable `pParam`. The purpose of this assignment is to pass those parameters to the local function `PortInitialize()` to configure the serial port later. To make this passing simple, we need to integrate all elements into that structure variable and only pass the latter into the local function. Special attention should be paid to the sequence of this assignment. In LabVIEW, the elements stored in an array are in one-dimensional format. For example, if you have a 2×3 array with 6 elements and the array name is `A[]`, all these 6 elements are arranged into the array in a one-dimension format, starting from the first element `A[0]` continue until the last element `A[5]` in one row.

TIP: In LabVIEW, all elements stored in an array are arranged into the array in one-dimension format, starting from the first element and ending at the last element. An m $\times$ `n array A[ ]` (`m` = number of rows, `n` = number of columns) is arranged as A[0], A[1], ... A[m $\times$ `n` −1]. If you want to pick up the element at row `i` and column `j` from this m $\times$ n array, use A[i*n + j]. Note both `i` and `j` starts from 0. For an element located at first row, use 0 as i. Same thing to the column number.

In our case, we used a 1×6 array. The 6 elements are arranged as `COM[0]`, `COM[1]`, ... `COM[5]`. Another point you need to note is the casting operation. Because the `PortSettings` is a double pointer structure variable, you need to precede a pointer operator (`*`) in front of this variable to make it a single-pointer variable, then use a → operator to access the associated element stored in the array `COM[1]`. Parentheses must be used to contain the whole pointer variable `*PortSettings` to make it a valid address. Each element's position and its meaning is illustrated in the comment section.

Q: The element `(*PortSettings)->COM[0]` is the port number. Here we use this port number to identify the associated port selected by the user. An `int` casting is used to convert this port number to an integer that is used in the switch-case structure. The purpose of using this structure is to convert the port number to the port name represented by a text string because the local function `PortInitialize()` needs this port name to configure the port later.

R: After the serial port configuration parameters are obtained, the local function `Port-Initialize()` is called to execute the initialization and configuration of the serial port. Two arguments are passed to that function. The first one is the port name represented in the text format, and the second is the pointer variable that points to the structure

SerialCreate and all configuration parameters are stored in that structure. An error message is displayed if this function calling is failed.

S: After the configuration and initialization are completed, the variable pParam is not needed. The built-in function delete is used to clean up the memory space allocated for that structure variable.

T: The *flg = 0 is returned to the CIN to inform the LabVIEW that the function calling is successful. Because the *PortHandle is a returned variable that contains the port handle of the opened and configured serial port, the global variable hPort that contains the valid port handle is assigned to the *PortHandle as the returned handle. A (long) casting is necessary for this assignment.

U: A return noErr is used to return this function to the LabVIEW domain. This return format is a popular style and widely used in the CIN.

The coding of the local function PortInitialize() is shown in Figure 5.81. Each section of this code is explained in the following list.

V: Some local variables are declared at the beginning of this function. The variable dwError is a double word integer and it is used to hold the returned error code for the system function calling. The DCB (Device Control Block) structure is a very useful data structure used in the control settings and configurations of the serial port. (Refer to Section 4.2.2 and Table 4-4 in Chapter 4 for more detailed description of this structure.) Configuration of the serial devices is performed with this structure. A variable of this structure PortDCB is declared here in order to use this structure in this function. The ecStatus is a variable of the enum structure ERR_CODE and it is used to hold the returned status of the user-defined function calling. An initial value OK is assigned to that variable. COMMTIMEOUTS is another useful data structure widely used for serial data communications and it is used to set the timeout values for serial devices. The variable dBit is used to temporarily store the data bits value.

W: The system function CreateFile() to try to open a new port. Seven arguments are included in this function calling. The first one is the port name in the text format such as "COM1." The second parameter is used to indicate the open mode of the port. The GENERIC_READ|GENERIC_WRITE means that this port can perform read and write operations. The third parameter is the share mode. A 0 means that this port cannot be shared with other threads. The fourth argument is used to indicate the security attribute and it can be used to determine whether the returned port handle can be inherited by child processes. If this parameter is NULL, which means that the handle cannot be inherited. The next parameter is the creating mode that is used to indicate which action to take on files that exist, and which action to take when files do not exist. The opened file is mapped to the associated serial port or device. The parameter OPEN_EXISTING means that the opening is failed if the file (port) does not exist. The sixth parameter is used to indicate whether this opening has additional attributes. A 0 means that there is no additional attributes for this file opening. The last parameter specifies a handle with GENERIC_READ access to a template file. The template file supplies file attributes and extended attributes for the file being created.

X: If the system function CreateFile() is successful, an opened file handler should be returned and this handler works as unique ID for the opened port. Otherwise an INVALID_HANDLE_VALUE returned to indicate that the function calling is failed. To get the exact error code, the GetLastError() system function is executed, and the error message is displayed. The CloseHandle() system function may be called to make the opened port closed if it was opened by chance. The user-defined error code EC_FOPEN is returned to the calling function to indicate that error.

```
ERR_CODE PortInitialize(char* lpszPortName, pSerialCreate  pCreate)
{
V       DWORD  dwError;
        DCB         PortDCB;
        ERR_CODE   ecStatus = OK;
        COMMTIMEOUTS  CommTimeouts;
        UCHAR  dBit;
        // Open the serial port.
W       hPort = CreateFile(lpszPortName,                  // Pointer to the name of the port
                           GENERIC_READ | GENERIC_WRITE, // Access (read/write) mode
                           0,                            // Share mode
                           NULL,                         // Pointer to the security attribute
                           OPEN_EXISTING,                // How to open the serial port
                           0,                            // Port attributes
                           NULL);                        // Handle to port with attribute to copy
        // If it fails to open the port, return error.
X       if ( hPort == INVALID_HANDLE_VALUE )
        {
          // Could not open the port.
          dwError = GetLastError();
          msg("Unable to open the port");
          CloseHandle(hPort);
          return EC_FOPEN;
        }
        PortDCB.DCBlength = sizeof(DCB);
        // Get the default port setting information.
Y       GetCommState(hPort, &PortDCB);
        // Change the DCB structure settings.
Z       PortDCB.BaudRate = pCreate->lBaudRate;   // Current baud
        PortDCB.fBinary  = TRUE;                 // Binary mode; no EOF check
        PortDCB.fParity  = FALSE;                // Enable parity checking.
        PortDCB.fOutxCtsFlow = FALSE;            // No CTS output flow control
        PortDCB.fOutxDsrFlow = FALSE;            // No DSR output flow control
        PortDCB.fDtrControl = DTR_CONTROL_ENABLE; // DTR flow control type
        PortDCB.fDsrSensitivity = FALSE;         // DSR sensitivity
        PortDCB.fTXContinueOnXoff = FALSE;       // XOFF continues Tx
        PortDCB.fOutX = FALSE;                   // No XON/XOFF out flow control
        PortDCB.fInX  = FALSE;                   // No XON/XOFF in flow control
        PortDCB.fErrorChar = FALSE;              // Disable error replacement.
        PortDCB.fNull = FALSE;                   // Disable null stripping.
        PortDCB.fRtsControl = RTS_CONTROL_ENABLE; // RTS flow control
        PortDCB.fAbortOnError = FALSE;           // Do not abort reads/writes on error.
        dBit = (UCHAR)pCreate->lDataBits;        // Assign data bits
        PortDCB.ByteSize = dBit;                 // Number of bits/bytes, 4-8
        PortDCB.Parity = NOPARITY;               // 0-4=no,odd,even,mark,space
        PortDCB.StopBits = ONESTOPBIT;           // 0,1,2 = 1, 1.5, 2

       // Configure the port according to the specifications of the DCB structure.
1      if (!SetCommState(hPort, &PortDCB))
       {
         // Could not create the read thread.
         dwError = GetLastError();
```

FIGURE 5.81 Code for the local function `PortInitialize()`. *(continued)*

```
        msg("Unable to configure the serial port");
        return EC_INVAL_CONFIG;
    }
    // Retrieve the time-out parameters for all read and write operations on the port.
2   GetCommTimeouts(hPort, &CommTimeouts);
    // Change the COMMTIMEOUTS structure settings.
3   CommTimeouts.ReadIntervalTimeout = MAXDWORD;
    CommTimeouts.ReadTotalTimeoutMultiplier = 0;
    CommTimeouts.ReadTotalTimeoutConstant = 0;
    CommTimeouts.WriteTotalTimeoutMultiplier = 10;
    CommTimeouts.WriteTotalTimeoutConstant = 1000;
    // Set the time-out parameters for all read and write operations on the port.
4   if (!SetCommTimeouts (hPort, &CommTimeouts))
    {
        // Could not set the port timeout parameter.
        dwError = GetLastError();
        msg("Unable to set the time-out parameters");
        return EC_TIMEOUT_SET;
    }
5   return ecStatus;
}
```

FIGURE 5.81 Code for the local function `PortInitialize()`.

Y: To use the DCB structure to configure the serial port, you need first to obtain the default DCB structure by calling the system function `GetCommState()`. Two parameters are included in this function calling. The first one is the port handler obtained from the `CreateFile()` and the second is the DCB structure variable `PortDCB` that returns the default DCB structure.

Z: After the default DCB structure is obtained, we can assign new values to the elements on that structure based on our applications. The baud rate is assigned to the `BaudRate` element in the DCB. Other assignments have been explained by the associated comments. Two elements are important to us: one is the `fDtrControl` and the other is the `fRtsControl`. Because the serial port interface applied in this project is not normal serial communication mode, the handshaking signals cannot be used as the normal interfacing signals as the traditional serial port did. So those handshaking signals should be set to DTR_CONTROL_ENABLE and RTS_CONTROL_ENABLE, respectively. In this way, we can use the extended system function `EscapeCommFunction()` to set or reset those lines directly. The temporary variable `dBit` is used to pick up and reserve the data bits value from the `SerialCreate` structure variable `pCreate`. This data bits value is assigned to the `ByteSize` element in the DCB structure.

1: The system function `SetCommState()` is called to configure the port by using the completed DCB structure. If this function returns a `False`, which means that the function calling has failed. An error message is displayed, and a user-defined error code, `EC_INVAL_CONFIG`, is returned to the calling function.

2: Next we need to set the timeout values for the port by using the system function `SetCommTimeouts()`. We must first get the default timeout structure `CommTimeouts` by using the system function `GetCommTimeouts()`.

3: By using the `CommTimeouts` structure, which is obtained from the system function `GetCommTimeouts()`, we can set the desired timeout values based on our application.

4: After the default timeout structure is configured with our desired parameters, we can use SetCommTimeouts() to set the timeout values for the port.

If the function SetCommTimeouts() has failed, an error message is displayed, and a user-defined error code EC_TIMEOUT_SET is returned to the calling function.

5: Finally, the running status of the function is returned to the calling function.

Now it is the time for us to compile and build the target file for our CIN function.

5.5.2.4.1.3 Compiling and Building the CINSetup.lsb Target File

To compile and build the target file CINSetup.lsb, follow these steps:

- Select the Project|Settings menu item from the menu bar on Visual C++ 6.0, and click the C/C++ tab. Select the Code Generation from the Category box.
- Still inside the C/C++ page, select the Multithreaded DLL from the User run-time library box and select 1 Byte from the Struct member alignment box.
- Still inside the Project|Settings dialog box, click the Custom Build tab and type "C:\Program Files\National Instruments\LabVIEW 7.0\cintools\lvsbutil" $(TargetName) -d "$(WkspDir)\$(OutDir)" into the Commands list box. (This is a one-line command, and the quotation marks are included.) Type: $(OutDir)$(TargetName).lsb into the Outputs list box that is just below the Commands list box. You can use the Directory and the Files button to help you finish this typing.

By using these parameters, we selected the target file builder lvsbutil that is located at the cintools directory and defined the target file name as CINSetup.lsb. The built target file is located at the Debug folder. Of course, you can change this folder by selecting the Release folder from the Build|Set Active Configuration item.

Now click the Build|Build CINSetup.dll menu item to build our target file. Both CINSetup.dll and the target file, CINSetup.lsb, are generated in the Debug folder if this building is error-free.

You can load this target file from the Debug folder to the CINSetup node in LabVIEW domain. But we prefer to do this later with other two target files together.

5.5.2.4.2 The DLL CINReadData Function

Launch Visual C++ 6.0 and create a new project with the following properties:

- Project name: CINReadData.
- Project type: Win32 Dynamic-Link Library.
- Location: C:\Book2_Program\Chapter 5\CallSerialCIN.

In the newly created project, create a header file named CINReadData.h and a source file named CINReadData.cpp. Before we can continue, we need copy the following files into our current project folder. You can skip this step and directly add these files into the current project by using the Project|Add To Project|Files menu items. But the project developed in this way is not portable because the files you added into this project are still located at the original folders. Open the Windows Explorer to copy the following files to our current project folder C:\Book2_Program\Chapter 5\CallSerialCIN\CINReadData:

- cin.obj
- labview.lib

- lvsb.lib
- lvsbmain.def
- extcode.h
- fundtypes.h
- hosttype.h
- platdefines.h

All of these files are located at the default installation folder of the LabVIEW 7.0 software. In our case, the folder is `C:\Program Files\National Instruments\LabVIEW 7.0\cintools`.

From the Visual C++ 6.0 workspace, select the `Project|Add To Project|Files` menu item to add those copied files into our `CINReadData` project.

5.5.2.4.2.1 Header File for the `CINReadData` Function

In Visual C++ 6.0, open the `CINReadData.c` file we generated in the LabVIEW domain in Section 5.5.2.3.4. Copy the CIN function declarations into the header file `CINReadData.h` we created earlier, and copy the CIN function definition into the source file `CINReadData.cpp`, respectively.

Open the `CINReadData.h` header file, add the following codes that are shown in Figure 5.82 into this header file.

Each section of the code for the header file is explained in the following list.

A: The system header file `Windows.h` is included first in this header file because this system header file provides all object definitions applied in the Windows environment. As an example, the `MessageBox()` function is defined in that system header file. The `#include "extcode.h"` is copied from the `CINReadData.c` file as we did earlier.

B: To avoid multiple including of this header file, the system macro `#ifndef` is used here. The purpose of this macro is to allow the other source file to include this header file if this header file has not been included before by that source file. In C/C++ programming, it is illegal to include a header multiple times by any source file in the project. To avoid that situation occur, the macro `#ifndef` and `#define` are used. You need to attach a `#endif` at the end of this header file if you used this macro.

C: Some constants are defined here. The `MAX_BYTE` and `MAX_BITS` constants are used to define the maximum bytes and bits for the collected data from the serial port. In this application, we need only one byte of data for each reading, and 12 bits of collected data.

D: When you build shared libraries for C++, you must prevent the C++ compiler from decorating the function names in the final object code. To do this, wrap the function declaration in an extern "C" clause, `extern "C" { ....}`. The codes included inside the opening and ending braces are considered as the C codes and the compiler converts them to the C object codes, not C++ object codes. One point you need to note is that if you disable C++ decoration of a function, the compiler cannot create polymorphic versions of the function.

E: A data structure is defined here to convenience the data collection. The structure is named `CommPortClass` that contains useful data collection definitions, such as the data buffer, maximum characters and bits.

F: An `enum` structure `ERR_CODE` is declared to define the numeric error value that is associated with each possible error occurred during the project runs. Space can be greatly saved by using this kind of definition and each error code is sequenced from the integer 0 to the maximum integer value.

G: A global variables `hPort` is declared in this section. The purpose of this global variable is to simplify the program and allow different source files to share some common

```
  /*****************************************************************************
   * NAME:        CINReadData.h
   * PGMR:        Y. Bai
   *****************************************************************************/
A #include <Windows.h>
  #include "extcode.h"
B #ifndef _CINREADDATA_H_
  #define _CINREADDATA_H_
C #define MAX_BYTE      1
  #define MAX_BITS      12
  #define msg(info)     MessageBox(NULL, info, "", MB_OK)
D #ifdef __cplusplus
  extern "C" {
  #endif  /* __cplusplus */
E typedef  struct
  {
     short pcBuffer;            /* store the received 12-bit A/D data */
     int    iMaxChars;          /* number of the maximum characters  */
     int    iMaxBits;           /* number of the maximum bits of a data */
     int    piNumRcvd;          /* number of data received */
     char  cTermChar;           /* termination character */
  } CommPortClass;
F typedef  enum
  {
     OK        = 0,             /* no error */
     EC_TIMEOUT,
     EC_FOPEN,
     EC_INVAL_CONFIG,
     EC_TIMEOUT_SET,
     EC_RECV_TIMEOUT,
     EC_EXIT_CODE,
     EC_WAIT_SINGLEOBJ,
     EC_INVALIDPORT,
     EC_WRITE_FAIL,
     EC_CREATE_THREAD,
     EC_GETMODSTATUS,
     EC_UNKNOWNERROR
  } ERR_CODE;
G HANDLE        hPort;
  /* local functions */
H ERR_CODE PortRead(CommPortClass *hCommPort);
  void WINAPI ThreadFunc(void* hCommPorts);
  void Delay(int num);
  //CINReadData() CIN Function
I MgErr CINRun(int16 *DataOutput, int32 *hPortIn, int32 *hPortOut, LVBoolean *flg);
J MgErr CINProperties(int32 prop, void *data);
  #ifdef __cplusplus
  }
K #endif  /* __cplusplus */
  #endif
```

FIGURE 5.82 Header file for the `CINReadData` function.

variables. Although the global style is not recommended in the Object-Oriented-Programming environment, it can really simplify and speed up the process for the application programs that need the high-speed and the real-time responses. The `hPort` is used to reserve the file handle that represents the opened port. Any code can use this `hPort` to access the opened serial port in the program.

H: Three local functions are declared here. The purpose of these functions is to coordinate the CIN function to perform the data collection between the serial port and the computer. The CIN functions work as the interface functions and the local function works as the executive functions to directly communicate with the low-level system routines to complete the data collection tasks. The `PortRead()` function is used to retrieve the converted data from the MAX187 via the serial port. The argument of this function is a pointer structure variable that contains the data collection definitions. The thread function `ThreadFunc()` is used to check the status of the serial port and pick up the data from the MAX187 A/D converter. You need to note that this thread function is the core of the thread we create later in this project. By using this thread function, we can prevent possible dead cycles caused when no serial communication event occurs to the port. In most applications, this infinite waiting causes the computer to hang up forever if no further action is taken. The function `Delay()` is a user-defined time delay function and its purpose is to delay a certain period of time during the program runs.

I: The declaration of the CIN function `CINReadData()` is placed in this header file to provide the function prototype that is used later by the source file. This function declaration is copied from the `CINReadData.c` file as we did in the beginning on this section. You need to note that we have modified this function to meet the requirement of our application. The second argument `*PortHandle` has been modified to `*hPortIn`, which means that this is an input port handle. The third argument, `*arg1`, is modified to `*hPortOut`, which means that this is an output port handle. The fourth argument, `*arg2` is modified to `*flg` to represent a Boolean variable. This Boolean variable will be returned to the LabVIEW domain to indicate the running status of the function.

J: A `CINProperties()` system function is declared here, and this function is used to make our function `CINReadData` as a thread-safe function.

K: Attach two ending braces for the macros `#ifndef _CINREADDATA_H_` and `#ifdef _cplusplus`.

5.5.2.4.2.2 Source File for the `CINReadData` Function

For general port writing operations, you can directly access the port and execute the write operations. W must be very careful with port reading operations, however, because the data can be read only when it is ready, or when a desired condition or event is triggered by certain communication conditions. Theoretically speaking, an event should definitely occur if data is ready or certain conditions are met, but in the real world this is untrue. Many situations exist in which no event occurs, even when the data is ready and all conditions are met. When such conflicts occur, the computer will hang up indefinitely.

To solve this problem, we can use a reading thread specially designed to execute port reading operations. A timeout monitor or flag can be used to check the running status of the thread. A timeout error can be generated if the thread has no response after a certain period of time. In this way, we can prevent dead cycles during port reading operations.

Open the source file `CINReadData.cpp` and enter the code shown in Figure 5.83.

Each section of this code is explained in the following list.

L: The system and user-defined header files are declared at the beginning of this source file. The header file "`CINReadData.h`" is a user-defined header file and must be included here because all variables and functions used in this function are defined in that file.

M: The system function `CINProperties()` is used to define this CIN function a thread safe function and it can be called by multiple threads simultaneously in this project.

```
/*****************************************************************************
 * NAME:       CINReadData.cpp
 * DESC:       Interface program to MAX187 Serial A/D converter
 * PGMR:       Y. Bai
 *****************************************************************************/
#include <stdio.h>
#include <stdlib.h>
#include <string.h>
L  #include "CINReadData.h"
M  MgErr  CINProperties(int32  prop,  void *data)
{
    switch (prop)
    {
        case kCINIsReentrant:
        *(Bool32 *)data = TRUE;
        return  noErr;
    }
    return  mgNotSupported;
}
N  MgErr CINRun(int16 *DataOutput,  int32 *hPortIn,  int32 *hPortOut,  LVBoolean *flg)
{
    /* Insert code here */
O   ERR_CODE rc = OK;
    short ad_data;
    CommPortClass* commClass;
    hPort = (HANDLE)(*hPortIn);
    *hPortOut = *hPortIn;
P   commClass = new CommPortClass;
    commClass->iMaxChars = MAX_BYTE;
    commClass->iMaxBits  = MAX_BITS;
Q   EscapeCommFunction(hPort, SETDTR);        //Set DTR to disable the SCLK
    EscapeCommFunction(hPort, CLRRTS);        //Reset RTS to disable the CS-bar
R   rc = PortRead(commClass);
    if (rc != 0)
       *flg = LVTRUE;
    else
       *flg = LVFALSE;
S   ad_data = commClass->pcBuffer;
    delete  commClass;
T   *DataOutput = ad_data;
U   return  noErr;
}
ERR_CODE PortRead(CommPortClass *hCommPort)
{
V   HANDLE hThread;                    // handler for port read thread
    DWORD  IDThread;
    DWORD  Ret, ExitCode;
    DWORD  dTimeout = 500;             // define time out value: 500 ms.
    ERR_CODE ecStatus = OK;
```

FIGURE 5.83 Source file for the `CINReadData` function. *(continued)*

```
W       if (!(hThread = CreateThread(NULL,                    // no security attributes
                        0,                                    // use default stack size
                        (LPTHREAD_START_ROUTINE) ThreadFunc,
                        (LPVOID)hCommPort,                    // parameter to thread function
                        CREATE_SUSPENDED,                     // creation flag - suspended
                        &IDThread) ) )                        // returns thread ID
        {
            msg("Create Read Thread failed");
            return EC_CREATE_THREAD;
        }
X       ResumeThread(hThread);                                // start thread now
Y       Ret = WaitForSingleObject(hThread, dTimeout);
        if (Ret == WAIT_OBJECT_0)
        {
            // data received & process it...need to do nothing because the data
            // has been stored in the hCommPort in Thread Func. Close thread handle
            CloseHandle(hThread);
        }
Z       else if (Ret == WAIT_TIMEOUT)
        {
            // time out happened, warning & kill thread
            Ret = GetExitCodeThread(hThread, &ExitCode);
            if (ExitCode == STILL_ACTIVE)
            {
                TerminateThread(hThread, ExitCode);
                CloseHandle(hThread);
                return EC_RECV_TIMEOUT;
            }
            else
            {
                CloseHandle(hThread);
                msg("ERROR in GetExitCodeThread: != STILL_ACTIVE ");
                ecStatus = EC_EXIT_CODE;
            }
        }
1       else
        {
            msg("ERROR in WaitFor SingleObject ");
            ecStatus = EC_WAIT_SINGLEOBJ;
        }
2       return  ecStatus;
    }
3   void WINAPI ThreadFunc(void* hCommPorts)
    {
4       BOOL   fDone;
        short   ad_data = 0;
        DWORD  dwModemStatus;
        int   index, nTotRead = 0;
        DWORD  dwCommModemStatus;
        CommPortClass*  CommPorts;
        ERR_CODE ecStatus = OK;
```

FIGURE 5.83 Source file for the `CINReadData` function. *(continued)*

```
5     CommPorts = (CommPortClass* )hCommPorts;
6     EscapeCommFunction(hPort, SETRTS);  // Set RTS to enable the CS-bar to start A/D
      // Specify a set of events to be monitored for the port.
7     SetCommMask(hPort, EV_DSR);
8     fDone = FALSE;
9     while (!fDone)
      {
          // Wait for an event to occur for the port.
10        WaitCommEvent(hPort, &dwCommModemStatus, 0);
11        if (dwCommModemStatus & EV_DSR)          // received the DSR event
          {
12            for (index = 0; index < CommPorts->iMaxBits; index++)
              {
13                EscapeCommFunction(hPort, CLRDTR);  //Reset DTR (HIGH in SCLK)
                  Delay(10);
14                EscapeCommFunction(hPort, SETDTR);  //Set DTR (LOW in SCLK)
                  Delay(10);
15                if (!GetCommModemStatus(hPort, &dwModemStatus))
                  {
                      msg("ERROR in GetModemStatus()!");
                      fDone = TRUE;
                      break;
                  }
16                if (MS_DSR_ON & dwModemStatus)       //DSR status is HIGH.
                      ad_data = ad_data + 0;
17                else                                 //DSR status is LOW
                      ad_data++;
18                ad_data = ad_data << 1;
              }
19            EscapeCommFunction(hPort, SETDTR);       //Set DTR (LOW in SCLK)
              EscapeCommFunction(hPort, CLRRTS);       //Reset CS to deselect A/D
20            ad_data = ad_data >> 1;
21            CommPorts->pcBuffer = ad_data;
              fDone = TRUE;
              break;
          }
      } // end of while loop
  }
  void Delay(int  num)
  {
22    int k, m, n = 100*num;
23    for (m = 0; m < n; m++)
          k++;
  }
```

FIGURE 5.83 Source file for the `CINReadData` function.

After this function is executed and loaded to the node in the LabVIEW domain, the color of the node should be changed from the orange to the yellow, which means that this is a thread safe node. You need to note that the real thread safe property depends on the CIN function, not only depends on this system function.

N: The CIN function `CINReadData()` is defined here. The arguments of this function have been modified, such as the second, the third and fourth argument has been modified to new name, respectively. Refer to step `I` in the last section to get more information for these modifications.

O: The local variables are defined at the beginning of this function. The rc is a variable of structure enum and it is used to hold running status of some local functions such as PortRead(). The variable ad_data is a short type of integer (16 bits in Visual C++) that works as a buffer to store the collected data received from the MAX187 A/D converter. The commClass is a pointer variable of the structure CommPortClass and it is used to reserve the data collection definitions such as the maximum bytes, maximum bits, and termination character of the collected data. A casting operation (HANDLE) is needed to convert the argument *hPortIn from the int32 to the HANDLE type variable and assign it to the global variable hPort. This conversion is very important, and the input port handle *hPortIn that is passed from the last CIN function CIN-Setup can be used by this function to access the opened serial port and perform the data collection. This input port handle is directly assigned to the output port handle *hPortOut and passed to the next CIN function CINClose().

P: The new keyword is used to create a pointer variable of the structure CommPortClass, commClass. The starting address of this pointer variable is returned and assigned to that variable. Two data collection definitions, MAX_BYTE and MAX_BITS, are assigned to the associated variables of the structure pointer variable. This structure pointer variable will be passed as an argument to the function PortRead() to coordinate the data collection later.

Q: The extended function EscapeCommFunction() is called to set the DTR and reset the RTS lines, respectively. Using these set and reset procedures is equivalent to disable the SCLK input and deselect the CS-bar on the MAX187 because both lines are connected to those two inputs on the MAX187 via an inverter MAX220. Note that the status of the transmission line is the opposite of the input signals on the MAX187 due to the inverting logical of the MAX220.

R: The local function PortRead() is called with the argument commClass to perform the data collection from the MAX187 via the serial port. If the returned status rc is not 0, which means that some error is encountered during this function execution, the output variable *flg is assigned with the LVTRUE to indicate to the LabVIEW that this function calling is failed. Otherwise a LVFALSE is returned to the LabVIEW to inform the latter that the function calling is successful.

S: If the PortRead() is successful, the received data (12-bit) is reserved to the data buffer ad_data. Then the structure pointer variable commClass is removed and its memory space is cleaned by using the delete instruction because its mission is finished.

T: Then the received data is assigned from the data buffer ad_data to the output argument *DataOutput and returned to the node CINReadData in the LabVIEW domain.

U: A noErr is returned to the LabVIEW to indicate that the function calling is error-free.

V: Some local variables are declared inside the local function PortRead(). The hThread is a HANDLE that is used to hold the thread handle when a new thread is created. The IDThread is a double word integer that is used to reserve the thread ID as a new thread is opened. The Ret holds the running status of some system function such as WaitForSingleObject(), and the ExitCode is used to hold the exit code when a thread or an object is terminated. The dTimeout is a double word integer that is used to hold the timeout value.

W: The system function CreateThread() is called to create a new thread that is used to handle the port reading process. If this calling is successful, the returned thread's handle is assigned to the hThread. A returned value of False means that this function calling is failed, an error message is displayed and the function returns this error information to the calling function. The third argument of this function calling is the thread function named ThreadFunc. This thread function is a real body to execute the thread. The thread only provides a frame of the thread and the actual thread job is performed inside the thread function. The fourth argument of this function, hCommPort that is a pointer variable of the structure CommPortClass, is very important to this application because it contains all data collection definitions. To pass this structure variable into the thread function, one must place it in this position and in this format. The fifth argument is a system constant that indicates the running status of the thread when it is created. The CREATE_SUSPENDED means that the created thread is suspended, and will not run until the ResumeThread() function is executed.

X: A ResumeThread() function is called to begin to run the thread function.

Y: The system function WaitForSingleObject() is called to monitor and wait for the thread function until it is completed. This function returns when the specified object (thread function) is in the signaled state or when the time-out interval elapses. Two arguments are passed into this function, hThread that is the thread handle and the dTimeout that is the upper boundary value of the timeout. If the function returns WAIT_OBJECT_0, which is the thread handle, it means that the thread function is executed successfully, the data is collected and the thread function is terminated automatically as it is completed. No other action is needed for this situation except closing the thread by using CloseHandle() system function.

Z: If the function returns WAIT_TIMEOUT, which means that a timeout error occurs and the data collection is failed (no event is signaled). Two steps are needed for this situation. First we need to retrieve the exit code of the thread function by calling the system function GetExitCodeThread(). If the exit code indicates that the thread function still runs (STILL_ACTIVE), the function TerminateThread() is executed to stop the thread function, and then to close the thread by calling the function CloseHandle(). Another choice is that if the exit code of the thread is not equal to STILL_ACTIVE, which means that the thread function has been terminated, we can directly close the thread by calling the function CloseHandle().

1: If the function returns other values, which means that some error occurs when calling this function, an error message is displayed and the function returns this error to the calling function.

2: The running status of this function ecStatus is returned to the calling function.

3: The coding of the thread function ThreadFunc() starts from here. The argument hCommPorts contains the data collection definitions.

4: All local variables are declared at the beginning of this function. The Boolean variable fDone works as a condition variable for the While loop that waits for communication events to occur during the data collection process. The ad_data works as a data buffer to store a single collected data. The double word variable dwModemStatus works as an argument to be passed into the system function GetCommModemStatus(), and the returned status of the associated transmission line is stored in this argument. The variable dwCommModemStatus works a similar way as the variable dwModemStatus did, and it returns the associated event status as the function WaitCommEvent() is called.

5: A casting operation (CommPortClass*) is performed to convert the argument hCommPorts that has a void* data type into the CommPortClass* structure type. This cast is very important and it is necessary because the argument hCommPorts is a void* data type. Any argument included in a thread function must be in a void* data type without any exception. In order to use that structure, one must uses a cast operator to convert that argument to the desired data type.

TIP: To pass an argument with different data type into a `thread function`, the data type of the passed argument must be `void*`. Inside the `thread function`, in order to use that argument, one has to use a cast operator to convert that argument back to the desired data type.

6: The extended system function `EscapeCommFunction()` is called to set the RTS line to `HIGH` to enable the MAX187 to begin the data conversion. Refer to Figure 5.72, the RTS line is connected to the CS-bar input on the MAX187 via the inverter MAX220. A `HIGH` in RTS produces a `LOW` at the CS-bar on the MAX187.

7: After the data conversion starts, we need to monitor the status of the DSR line because this line is connected to the output buffer (DOUT) of the MAX187. The converted data will be transmitted from the output buffer to the serial port serially via this DSR line (refer to Figure 5.72). In order to do that, one must use the system function `SetCommMask()` to select and mask the desired transmission line. An event will be generated as the status of the DSR line is changed; this event can be detected by the function `WaitCommEvent()`. The functions `SetCommMask()` and `WaitCommEvent()` work together to complete the configuration and detection of the status of a transmission line.

8: The Boolean variable `fDone` is reset to `False` to be ready to start the `While` loop.

9: A `While` loop is used to wait for the event that is associated with the desired or masked transmission line to occur (in our case, it is DSR).

10: The system function `WaitCommEvent()` is executed to detect the possible event to occur. If you use this function without an associated thread function, a dead cycle may be occur, causing your system to be hung up indefinitely. A timeout error occurs when this function is included inside the thread function if no event has been signaled during the waiting process.

11: The function `WaitCommEvent()` will be terminated if the desired event occurs. The returned status of the associated transmission line is stored in the argument `dwCommModemStatus`. An `AND` operation is used to check if the desired event EV_DSR is detected.

12: If the EV_DSR is received, a `For` loop is used to repeatedly collect 12 bits of converted data. To retrieve each bit of data, a simulated or an external clock must be provided. This clock is generated using a sequence of instructions.

13: Here the function `EscapeCommFunction()` is called to reset the DTR line. This reset operation is equivalent to provide a `HIGH` for the SCLK input on the MAX187. (Refer to Figure 5.72.) A user-defined function, `Delay()`, is executed to make this simulated clock stable and accepted by the SCLK input.

14: Another `EscapeCommFunction()` is called after this delay to set the DTR line to `HIGH`, which is equivalent to a `LOW` setting in the SCLK input. Following this set, another delay is inserted. In this way, a completed simulated clock cycle is generated to the SCLK input on the MAX187, and one bit of converted data can be shifted from the output buffer on the MAX187 to the serial port via the DSR line.

15: Now we need to check the level or status of the DSR line to determine whether a logical `1` or a logical `0` is received. To do that, you need to call the system function `GetCommModemStatus()`. This function can return the current status of the desired transmission line. An error message would be displayed if this function calling encountered any mistake. The function is terminated and returned to the calling function after the error message is displayed.

16: By using the operation MS_DSR_ON & `dwModemStatus`, we can detect whether the DSR line is set to `HIGH` or `LOW`. You need to note that a `HIGH` (ON) in the DSR line is associated with a logical 0 because of the inverter MAX220. In that case, only a 0 is added into the data buffer `ad_data`.

17: If a `LOW` value is detected on the DSR line, which is equivalent to a logical `1` in the converted bit, the data buffer in the LSB should be increased by 1.

18: The data buffer `ad_data` is shifted left by one bit to reserve the space for the next bit of data. This process (from step 12 to this step) will be continued until all 12 bits of data is converted and received.

19: Once all 12 bits are received, the system function `EscapeCommFunction()` is called to set the DTR line to `HIGH`, which is equivalent to resetting the SCLK input on the MAX187. Set the RTS line to `LOW`; this is equivalent to provide a `HIGH` setting on the CS-bar on the MAX187 to deselect the latter. `SETDTR` and `CLRRTS` are two system constants used in the transmission line configuration.

20: During the data collection process, the data buffer is totally shifted left by 12 bits. But for a 12-bit data segment, shifting left 11 times is enough because the last bit does not need to shift. So a compensation is needed to make this data correct. This compensation can be accomplished by shifting the final result right by one bit.

21: The final result is assigned to the `pcBuffer` that is an element of the data structure `CommPortClass` to be returned to the calling function. The Boolean condition variable `fDone` is set to `True` to stop the `While` loop. The instruction `break` is unnecessary in stopping the loop, but we use it here to make thing more reliable.

22: The function `Delay()` is a simple user-defined function that will halt processing for a designated period of time. Three local variables are declared here; all are integer variables.

23: A `For` loop is used to repeatedly increase the variable k by 1 until `n = m`.

5.5.2.4.2.3 Compiling and Building the `CINReadData.lsb` Target File

To compile and build the `CINReadData.lsb` target file, follow these steps:

- Select the `Project|Settings` menu item from the menu bar on Visual C++ 6.0, and click the `C/C++` tab. Select `Code Generation` from the `Category` box.
- Inside the C/C++ page, select the `Multithreaded DLL` from the `User run-time library` box and select `1 Byte` from the `Struct member alignment` box.
- Still inside the `Project|Settings` dialog box, click the `Custom Build` tab and type: `"C:\Program Files\National Instruments\LabVIEW 7.0\cintools\lvsbutil" $(TargetName) -d "$(WkspDir)\$(OutDir)"` into the `Commands` list box. (This should be a one-line command, and the quotation marks are included.) Next, type: `$(OutDir)$(TargetName).lsb` into the `Outputs` list box that is just below the `Commands` list box. You can use the `Directory` and `Files` buttons to help you finish this typing.

By using these parameters, we select the target file builder `lvsbutil` that is located at the `cintools` directory and define the target file name as `CINReadData.lsb`. The built target file is located in the `Debug` folder. Of course, you can change this folder by clicking `Build|Set Active Configuration` and selecting the `Release` folder item.

Now click the `Build|Build CINReadData.dll` menu item to build our target file. Both `CINReadData.dll` and the target file, `CINReadData.lsb`, are generated in the `Debug` folder if the process is error free.

You can load this target file from the `Debug` folder to `CINReadData` node in the LabVIEW domain. We will do this later.

5.5.2.4.3 The DLL `CINClose` Function

The `CINClose` function closes the opened serial port.

Launch Visual C++ 6.0 and create a new project with the following properties:

- Project name: `CINClose`.
- Project type: `Win32 Dynamic-Link Library`.
- Location: `C:\Book2_Program\Chapter 5\CallSerialCIN`.

In the newly created project, create a header file named `CINClose.h` and a source file named `CINClose.cpp`. Before we can continue, we need copy the following files into our current project folder. You can skip this step and directly add these files into the current project by using the `Project|Add To Project|Files` menu items. But the project developed in this way is not portable because the files you added into this project are still located at the original folders. Open the Windows Explorer to copy the following files into our current project folder, `C:\Book2_Program\Chapter 5\CallSerialCIN\CINClose`:

- cin.obj
- labview.lib
- lvsb.lib
- lvsbmain.def
- extcode.h
- fundtypes.h
- hosttype.h
- platdefines.h

All of these files are located at the default installation folder of the LabVIEW 7.0 software. In our case, the folder is `C:\Program Files\National Instruments\LabVIEW 7.0\cintools`.

In Visual C++ 6.0 workspace, select the `Project|Add To Project|Files` menu item to add those copied files into our current project `CINClose`.

5.5.2.4.3.1 Header File for the `CINClose` Function

In Visual C++ 6.0, open the `CINClose.c` file we generated in Section 5.5.2.3.4. Copy the CIN function declaration into the header file `CINClose.h` we created earlier, and copy the CIN function definition into the source file `CINClose.cpp`.

Open the `CINClose.h` header file and enter the code that is shown in Figure 5.84.

A: The system header file `Windows.h` is included first in this header file because this file provides all object definitions applied in the Windows environment. As an example, the `MessageBox()` function is defined in that system header file. The `#include "extcode.h"` is copied from the `CINClose.c` file .

B: To prevent multiple inclusions of this header file, the system macro `#ifndef` is used here. The purpose of this macro is to allow the other source files to include this header file if the file has not been previously included in the source file. In C/C++ programming, it is illegal to include a header multiple times by any source file in the project. To prevent this from occurring, we use the `#ifndef` and `#define` macros. We need to attach a `#endif` at the end of this header file if these macro have been used.

C: To simplify the program, we redefine the `MessageBox()` function by using the `#define` macro. The length of the `MessageBox()` function can then be greatly shortened and easily placed in the program by means of the `msg()` macro.

D: When you build shared libraries for C++, you must prevent the C++ compiler from decorating the function name in the final object code. To do this, wrap the function

```
  /*****************************************************************************
   * NAME:        CINClose.h
   * DESC:        Header file for the CINClose.cpp
   * PGMR:        Y. Bai
   *****************************************************************************/
  #include <Windows.h>
A #include "extcode.h"
B #ifndef _CINCLOSE_H_
  #define _CINCLOSE_H_
C #define msg(info)          MessageBox(NULL, info, "", MB_OK)
D #ifdef __cplusplus
  extern "C" {
  #endif    /* __cplusplus */
E typedef enum
  {
    OK        = 0,           /* no error */
    EC_TIMEOUT,
    EC_FOPEN,
    EC_INVAL_CONFIG,
    EC_TIMEOUT_SET,
    EC_RECV_TIMEOUT,
    EC_EXIT_CODE,
    EC_WAIT_SINGLEOBJ,
    EC_INVALIDPORT,
    EC_WRITE_FAIL,
    EC_CREATE_THREAD,
    EC_GETMODSTATUS,
    EC_UNKNOWNERROR
  } ERR_CODE;
  //CINClose() CIN Function
F MgErr CINRun(int32 *flg, int32 *PortHandle);
  #ifdef __cplusplus
  }
G #endif   /* __cplusplus */
  #endif
```

FIGURE 5.84 Header file for the `CINClose` function.

declaration in an external C clause, `extern "C" { ....}`. The code inside the opening and ending braces is considered C code, and the compiler converts it to C object code (not C++ object code). Note that if you disable C++ decoration of a function, the compiler cannot create polymorphic versions of the function.

E: An `enum` structure `ERR_CODE` is declared to define the numeric error value that is associated with each error that migh occur when the project runs. Space can be greatly saved by using this kind of definition. Each error code is sequenced from the integer 0 to the maximum integer value.

F: The declaration of the CIN function `CINClose()` is placed in this header file to provide the function prototype that is used later by the source file. This function declaration is copied from the `CINClose.c` file, as described in the previous section. Note that we have modified this function to meet the requirement of our application. The first nominal argument of this function, `*arg1`, has been replaced by `*flg` that works as a returned flag to the node in the LabVIEW domain. The second argument is unchanged; it works as an input port handle.

G: Attach two ending braces for the macros `#ifndef _CINCLOSE_H_` and `#ifdef _cplusplus`.

```
  /*****************************************************************************
   * NAME:      CINClose.cpp
   * DESC:      Interface program to MAX187 Serial A/D converter
   * PGMR:      Y. Bai
   * DATE:      11/6/2003
   *****************************************************************************/
  #include <stdio.h>
  #include <stdlib.h>
  #include <string.h>
H #include "CINClose.h"
I MgErr CINRun(int32 *flg, int32 *PortHandle)
  {
      /* Insert code here */
J     CloseHandle((HANDLE)(*PortHandle));
K     *flg = 0;
L     return noErr;
  }
```

FIGURE 5.85 Coding of the `CINClose` source file.

5.5.2.4.3.2 Source File for the `CINClose` Function

Open the created source file `CINClose.cpp` and enter the codes that is shown in Figure 5.85. Each section of this code is explained in the following list.

H: The header file `CINClose.h` is included at the top of this source file because the prototypes of the variables and functions used in this source file are declared in that header file. Some other system header files are also included here.

I: The definition of the CIN function `CINClose()` is placed here. You need to note that all CIN functions are named `CINRun()` no matter what kind of actual name you used in the CIN source file. You also need to note that the first nominal argument of this function have been modified from `*arg1` to the `*flg`.

J: The system function `CloseHandle()` is called to close the opened port handle. One point you need to note is the casting operation. You must use the (HANDLE) to cast the `*PortHandle` and convert it into the `HANDLE` data type (`void**`).

K: The `*flg` flag is assigned a `0` and then returned to the node in the LabVIEW domain to indicate to the latter that the function calling has been successful.

L: Finally, a system status variable `noErr` is returned to the LabVIEW domain.

At this point, we can complete the coding of all three CIN functions. These three CIN functions, including the header files, source files, and target files, are stored on the attached CD in the following three folders:

- Chapter 5\CallSerialCIN\CINSetup
- Chapter 5\CallSerialCIN\CINReadData
- Chapter 5\CallSerialCIN\CINClose

You can copy those files and load them on your own computer to test them.

5.5.2.5 Loading the CIN Object Code and Running the Project

Now it is time for us to connect the nodes we defined in LabVIEW domain with the CIN target files together. You can keep three CIN projects developed in Visual C++ 6.0 open. Launch and open the LabVIEW project named `CallSerialCIN` we developed in Section 5.5.2.3. Perform the necessary steps to connect the target file with each Code Interface node. For example, to connect the target file `CINSetup.lsb` with the code interface node in LabVIEW, follow these steps:

- Open the `Block Diagram` that contains the `CINSetup` node (inside frame 0), right-click on the `CINSetup` node and select the `Load Code Resource` item from the pop-up menu.
- On the opened dialog box, browse to the location where the target file `CINSetup.lsb` is located. In our case, this file is located at `C:\Book2_Program\Chapter 5\CallSerialCIN\CINSetup\Debug`.
- Select the target file and click the `Open` button to load the file into `CINSetup` node in LabVIEW.

Perform similar steps to load the other two target files, `CINReadData.lsb` and `CINClose.lsb`, into the associated nodes `CINReadData`, and `CINClose` in LabVIEW domain, respectively.

After the connection has been made between each node and its associated target file, we can run the project to test our coding. Make sure that the hardware connection is complete. (Refer to Figure 5.72). Then click the `Run` button in the project `CallSerialCIN.vi` to start the LabVIEW project. Three analog signals are used for this project: sinusoidal, triangular and square waveforms. Set the frequency on the function generator to 20 through 40 Hz, and the amplitude to 4.0 through 5.0 volts. (This value must be less than 5.0 volts because that is the maximum voltage allowed for the MAX187.) The first signal to be tested is the sinusoidal waveform.

When the `Run` button is clicked and the project started, the collected data is displayed in the `Data Output` textbox and the `A/D Data waveform` chart, which is shown in Figure 5.86. The progress of the data collection is displayed on the `Progress` bar. The port handle is displayed in the `Port Handle` textbox in real time.

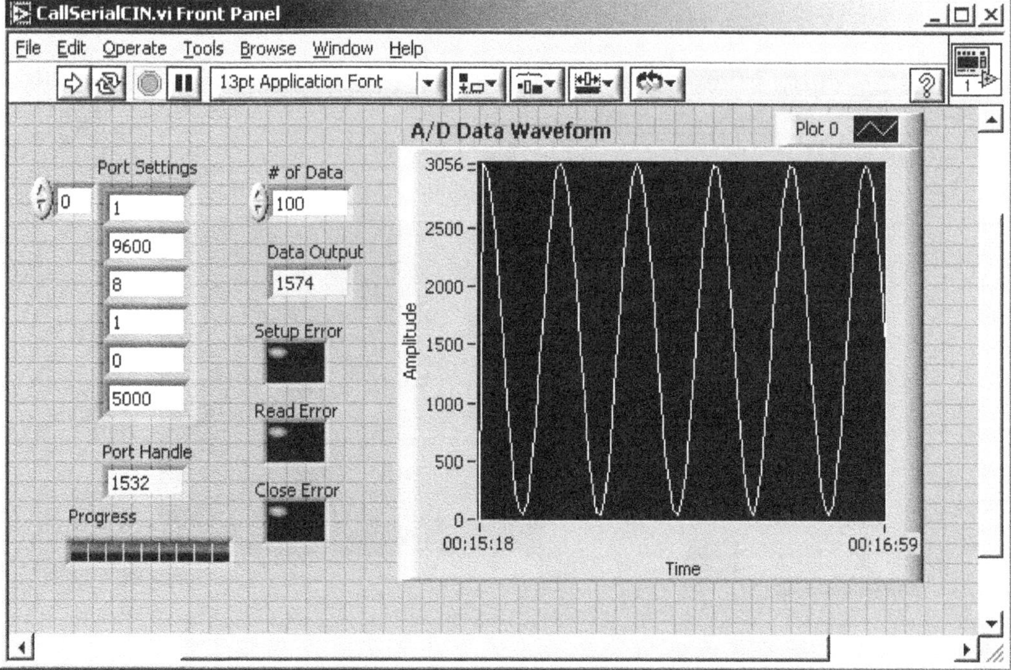

FIGURE 5.86 Testing the sinusoidal waveform.

Each time as you start the project, a different port handle is selected. This port handle is determined by the computer when the port is opened.

The result of testing the triangular waveform is shown in Figure 5.87, and the result for square waveform is shown in Figure 5.88.

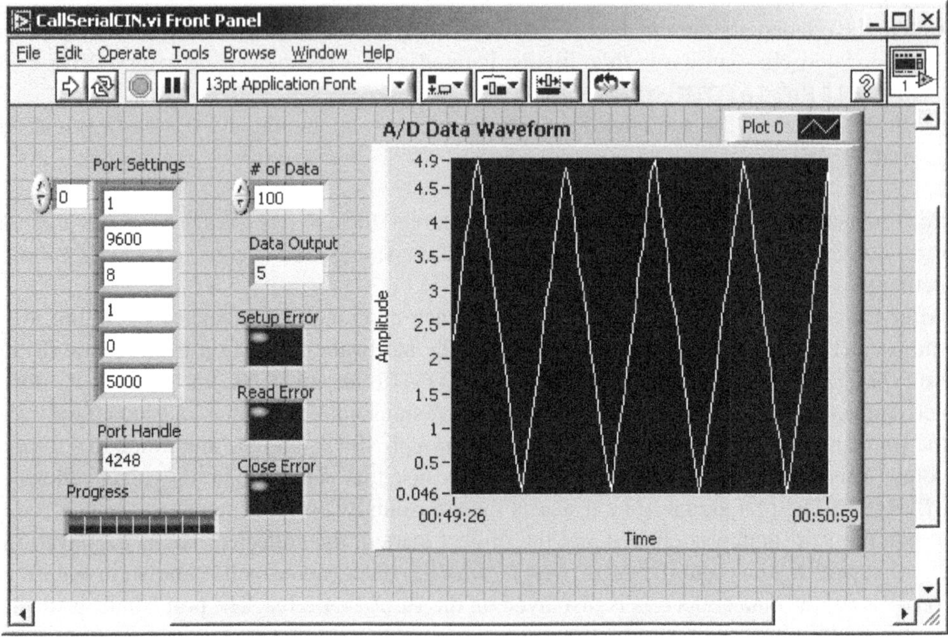

FIGURE 5.87 Testing the triangular waveform.

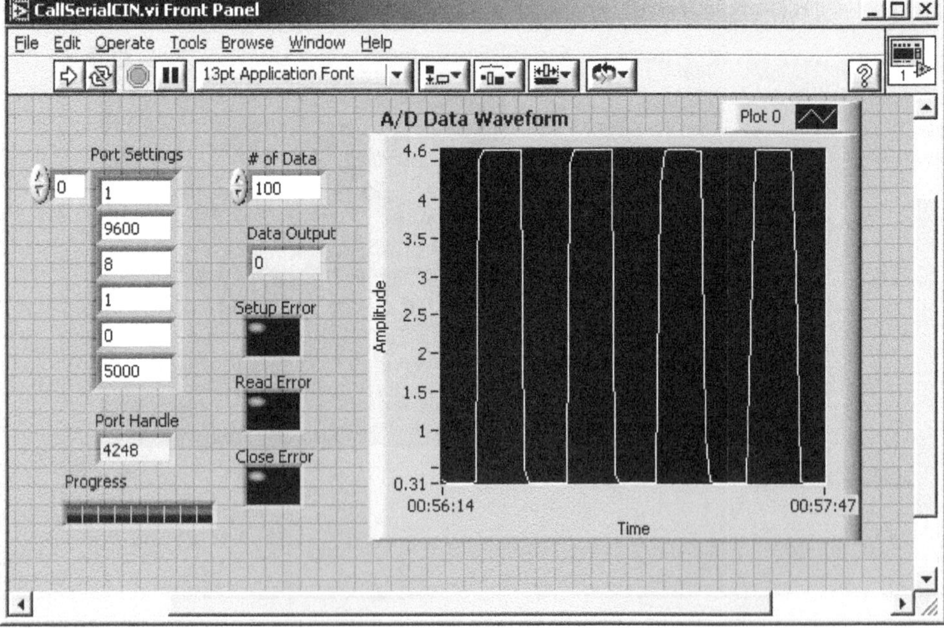

FIGURE 5.88 Testing the square waveform.

Notice that in the waveform charts displayed in Figures 5.87 and 5.88, the real unit of the collected data is used and displayed. For the waveform chart displayed in Figure 5.86, we still use the raw data without scaling it into the real unit.

Compared with those waveforms obtained from the TLC548 8-bit A/D converter in Section 5.4.3, more accurate results can be obtained by using the 12-bit A/D converter.

The complete project, including the front panel and block diagram, is located on the attached CD in the folder `Chapter 5\CallSerialCIN`. The original C files generated by each `Code Interface Node`, such as `CINSetup`, `CINReadData` and `CINClose`, are also included in this folder.

5.6 OTHER METHODS FOR INTERFACING WITH THE SERIAL PORT

Besides the methods discussed thus far, LabVIEW provides other tools for interfacing with serial ports, such as LabWindows/CVI, Measurement Studio for Visual Basic, and Measurement Studio for Visual C++. Most of those methods use either Active-X controls or the VISA class to access the serial ports and transmit data between the LabVIEW platform and other seria devices. Because of the space limitations of this book, we cannot provide a detailed discussion of these methods. Refer to the associated materials for more detailed information about those issues.*

* Ying Bai, *Applications Interface Programming Using Multiple Languages*, Prentice Hall, 2003.

6 Serial Port Programming in MATLAB

6.1 INTRODUCTION

In this chapter we'll examine interface programming between serial ports and MATLAB®, a programming language and interactive environment package available from The Mathworks, Inc. MATLAB provides different ways to access serial ports and perform serial data communications, typically by calling external codes from within the MATLAB domain. MATLAB provides three general ways to access and interface serial ports:

- Calling a MEX-file developed in a third-party language, such as C/C++ or Visual C++, from within the MATLAB domain.
- Loading and accessing a dynamic link library (DLL) developed in a third-party language such as C/C++ or Visual C++.
- Using the `serial` objects defined in the Instrument Toolbox or the `serial` function.

The first two methods are closely related, and entail calling external codes or the API from MATLAB environment. The third method allows us to call the serial port directly, from within the MATLAB domain. Thus the third method involves less interface coding, and is more suitable for users who do not have much programming experience in other languages.

Section 6.2 of this chapter provides a detailed discussion of interfacing with MEX-files (MATLAB-executable files). We'll discuss configuring the system compiler for MEX-files, creating the MEX-files themselves, establishing connections between MEX-files and MATLAB's M-functions, transmitting data between MATLAB and third-party programming languages (such as C/C++). The compiler used in this section is Visual C++ 6.0 for the Windows operating system. To illustrate this interfacing method step by step, we'll use two examples:

- Interfacing with a 12-bit serial A/D converter, the MAX187, via the serial port
- Interfacing with an 8-bit serial A/D converter, the TLC548, via the serial port

In Section 6.3, we'll use the shared DLL method to interface with the serial port. The loading, accessing, and unloading processes of the DLL are illustrated with a real example: an interfacing DLL developed in Visual C++ 6.0 IDE. Several data conversions and transmissions between MATLAB and C/C++ are detailed in this section. We'll also learn to transmit data structures and arrays between MATLAB and C/C++ or Visual C++. In Section 6.4 we'll use the `serial` object to interface directly with the serial port from within the MATLAB domain. This discussion includes an illustration detailing the process of transferring data through the serial port. The `ByteAvailable` and `ByteAvailableFcn` properties of the `serial` object are implemented in this example to demonstrate the MATLAB callback function.

6.2 USING MEX-FILES TO INTERFACE WITH SERIAL PORTS

MEX stands for *MATLAB-executable.* MEX-files are dynamically linked subroutines produced from C or Fortran source code which, when compiled, can be run from within MATLAB as though they were MATLAB M-files or built-in functions. The external interface functions let us transfer data between MEX-files and MATLAB, or call MATLAB functions from C or Fortran code.

The main advantages of MEX-files are:

- Simplicity; the ability to call large existing C or FORTRAN routines directly from MATLAB without having to rewrite them as M-files.
- Speed; we can increase program efficiency by rewriting bottlenecked computations (such as For-loop) in MEX-file format.

MEX-files are not appropriate for all applications. MATLAB is a high-productivity system designed to eliminate the time-consuming, low-level programming inherent in compiled languages (such as C and Fortran). For many end users, all programming tasks can be done in MATLAB unless an application requires real-time access to the low-level hardware.

6.2.1 The MEX-File Format

Unlike MATLAB M-files (which have the platform-independent extension *.m*), MEX-files are identified by platform-specific extensions. There are different extensions for MEX-files, organized by operating system. File extensions used in different platforms are listed in Table 6.1. For update extensions used in the MEX-files, refer to the latest version of the MATLAB documentation, "External Interface/API."

TABLE 6.1
MEX-file Extensions

Platform	MEX-file Extension
Alpha	mexaxp
HP, V10.20	Mexhp7
HP, V11.x	mexhpux
IBM RS/6000	Mexrs6
Linux	mexglx
SGI, SGI64	mexsg
Solaris	mexsol
Windows	DLL

MATLAB Technology Menu: External Interfaces/API, Version 6, p. 3-2. Reprinted with permission of MathWorks Inc.

In the Windows operating system, a MEX-file is a DLL developed in a third-party language such as C/C++, Visual C++, or FORTRAN. Unlike general-purpose DLLs, in which multiple interface functions can be exported to the target program, MEX-files can transfer only one interface function; this is the *gateway function* `mexFunction`. This gateway function is the only interface between the MEX-file and MATLAB, and it works as a bridge to connect the external subroutines developed in the third-party language with the MATLAB program. MEX-files are dynamically linked subroutines that the MATLAB interpreter can automatically load and execute.

We can access and call any subroutine developed as a MEX-file just as we might call an M-Function in the MATLAB domain, by using the gateway function `mexFunction` as the program runs. We cannot directly access or call any subroutine in a MEX-file without calling the gateway function `mexFunction` first. The `mexFunction` can be considered the entry point of the MEX-file, and we must call it before we can access any other subroutine defined in the MEX-file. From the point of view of the general DLL, the MEX-file works as a single function DLL and it only exports a single interface function (the gateway function) to the MATLAB domain. All other subroutines must be called from `mexFunction`. Consequently, we need export only one DLL function, the gateway function `mexFunction`, to MATLAB when developing a MEX-file.

To successfully call subroutines developed in MEX-file from within the MATLAB domain, we must correctly perform the following steps:

- Configure the system to meet the requirements of applying the MEX-file in a specified platform and compiling environment.
- Develop and build the desired MEX-file in the third-party compiling environment.
- Set up the interface between the MEX-file and MATLAB, and connect the entry point, the gateway function `mexFunction`, with the MATLAB domain.
- Convert the data between the third-party languages and MATLAB; this is necessary because different data types and structures are used in both language systems within the MEX-file. Most of these data conversion are performed in the gateway function `mex-Function`.

We'll examine these steps one by one in the following sections.

6.2.2 System Setup and Configuration

The MATLAB package provides all the tools we need for working with the API. MATLAB includes a C compiler, `Lcc`, for the PC but does not include a Fortran compiler. If you choose to use your own C compiler, it must be an ANSI C, and in the Windows platform it must be able to create 32-bit dynamic linked libraries (DLLs).

MATLAB supports many compilers and provides preconfigured options files designed specifically to support different compilers in different platforms. The purpose of supporting this large collection of compilers is to give you the flexibility to use the tool of your choice. However, in many cases, you simply can use the provided `Lcc` compiler with your C code to produce your MEX-files.

Before we can create MEX-files on the Windows platform, we must configure the default options file, `mexopts.bat`, for our compiler. The switch, `setup`, provides an easy way to configure the default options file. To configure or change the options file at anytime, we would run

```
mex  -setup
```

from either the MATLAB or DOS command prompt.

6.2.2.1 Select a Compiler

MATLAB includes a C compiler, `Lcc`, that can be used to create C MEX-files. The `mex` script will use the `Lcc` compiler automatically if there is no C or C++ compiler installed on the system. Naturally, if you want to compile Fortran programs, you must supply your own supported Fortran compiler.

In this section and the following sections, we assume that a Visual C++ 6.0 IDE that includes the Visual C++ 6.0 compiler has been installed on your machine. We will use this compiler to develop all the MEX-files necessary for interfacing with MATLAB. To select a compiler or change from the existing default compiler (`Lcc`) to the Visual C++ 6.0 compiler, perform the following steps:

1. Type `>>mex -setup` from either the MATLAB or DOS command prompt. A prompt asks you to locate the desired compiler:

```
Please choose your compiler for building external interface
(MEX) files:
Would you like mex to locate installed compilers [y]/n? y
```

2. Enter y to allow the mex feature to locate the desired compiler. A list of the compilers available on the machine is displayed for you to choose from:

```
Select a compiler:

[1] Digital Visual Fortran version 6.0 in C:\Program Files\Microsoft Visual Studio
[2] Lcc C version 2.4 in C:\MATLAB6P5\sys\lcc
[3] Microsoft Visual C/C++ version 6.0 in C:\Program Files\Microsoft Visual Studio
[0] None
Compiler: 3
```

3. Enter 3 to select the Visual C++ 6.0 compiler. A prompt appears to ask you to confirm this selection:

```
Please verify your choices:
Compiler: Microsoft Visual C/C++ 6.0
Location: C:\Program Files\Microsoft Visual Studio
Are these correct?([y]/n): y
```

4. Enter y to confirm this section. The default option file mexopts.bat is replaced on the screen with our msvc60opts.bat, and the location of the updated file is displayed on the screen:

```
The default options file:
"C:\WINDOWS\Application Data\MathWorks\MATLAB\R13\mexopts.bat"
is being updated from C:\MATLAB6P5\BIN\WIN32\mexopts\
msvc60opts.bat ...
Installing the MATLAB Visual Studio add-in ...
Updated C:\Program Files\Microsoft Visual Studio\common\msdev98
   \template\MATLABWizard.awx
 from C:\MATLAB6P5\BIN\WIN32\MATLABWizard.awx
Updated C:\Program Files\Microsoft Visual Studio\common\msdev98
   \template\MATLABWizard.hlp
 from C:\MATLAB6P5\BIN\WIN32\MATLABWizard.hlp
Updated C:\Program Files\Microsoft Visual Studio\common\msdev98
   \addins\MATLABAddin.dll
 from C:\MATLAB6P5\BIN\WIN32\MATLABAddin.dll
Merged C:\MATLAB6P5\BIN\WIN32\usertype.dat
 with C:\Program Files\Microsoft Visual Studio\common\
msdev98\bin\usertype.dat
```

Once you've selected the compiler, MATLAB installs another useful tool, the MATLAB Visual Studio Add-In. The Add-In greatly simplifies the use of MEX-files in the MSVC environment. Once you have the Add-In set up, you can use your IDE to compile the MEX-file. In addition to compiling MEX-files in Visual C++ 6.0 IDE, the Add-In tool can also be used to call MATLAB M-functions from within Visual C++ 6.0 workspace. Any MATLAB M-function can be added to the Visual Studio environment in Active-X format. Calling a MATLAB M-function is as easy as calling an add-in function in the Visual C++ domain.

Now that we've selected our compiler, it will be used to compile all the MEX-files we develop in this section. We can use the compiler either from the command line or from the Visual C++ 6.0 IDE. Now let's have a deeper look at the components of a MEX-file.

6.2.3 The Ingredients of a MEX-file

All MEX-files must include four things:

- A Header file, `#include mex.h` (in C/C++ MEX-files only)
- The `mxArray`
- Either the gateway function `mexFunction` in C/C++ or `SUBROUTINE MEXFUNCTION` in Fortran
- API functions

The header file `mex.h` declares all the types, macros and functions necessary to interface `mex` files with the current version of MATLAB. The gateway function `mexFunction` is used as an entry point to the MEX-file. `mxArray` is a popular MATLAB data type that is widely used in the interface functions developed in MEX-files. The API functions are used to convert data, structures, and macros from the MATLAB domain to the C/C++ domain; these are applied in the MEX-file.

6.2.3.1 Header File mex.h

In MATLAB, a group of functions, which are called API functions, is defined to perform data conversion between different language environments. All protocols of these API functions are declared in the header file `mex.h`. Before our program can successfully access MEX-file from MATLAB, it must perform the correct data conversions from one language system to another.

In order to convert the data, every C/C++ MEX-file must include the header file `mex.h`. This header allows us to use the `mx*` and `mex*` routines that are defined in the API functions. Every API function in MATLAB is composed of a sequence of subroutines prefixed with `mex` or `mx`. Because of the different definitions of variables, structures, and macros in C/C++ and MATLAB, our program must perform the correct conversions; it does so by means of the API functions.

Routines in an API function that are prefixed with `mx` allow us to create, access, manipulate, and destroy `mxArrays` in the C/C++ domain. In other words, API functions prefixed with `mx` are used to convert the data from MATLAB domain to C/C++ domain. Routines prefixed with `mex` perform operations back in the MATLAB environment from C/C++ domain. In other words, the API functions prefixed with `mex` are used to convert data from C/C++ domain to MATLAB domain. For example, we would use the API function `mxGetPr()` to get the pointer to the data passed from MATLAB in the C/C++ domain, and use the API function `mexErrMsgTxt()` to display an error message in MATLAB domain and return control from C/C++ to the MATLAB domain.

Keep in mind that the header file `mex.h` must appear at the beginning of the C-languate MEX-file.

6.2.3.2 The mxArray

The MATLAB language works with only a single object type: the MATLAB array. It is unnecessary that MATLAB arrays are array type variables, because all MATLAB variables, including scalars, vectors, matrices, strings, cell arrays, structures, and objects are stored as MATLAB arrays. In C/C++, every MATLAB array is declared to be of type `mxArray`. The `mxArray` is a special structure that contains MATLAB data and it is the C representation of a MATLAB variable. The `mxArray` declaration corresponds to the internal data structure that MATLAB uses to represent arrays. The MATLAB array is the C-language definition of a MATLAB variable. The `mxArray` structure has the following components:

- Its type
- Its dimensions
- All associated data
- If numeric, an indication of whether the variable is real or complex
- If sparse, values for its indices and maximum nonzero elements
- If a structure or an object, an indication of the number of its fields and field names

If a variable includes complex numbers, the MATLAB array will include vectors containing the real and imaginary parts. Matrices, or m-by-n arrays, that are not sparse are called full. In the case of a full matrix, the `mxArray` structure includes the parameters `pr` and `pi`; `pr` contains the real part of the matrix data, and `pi` contains the imaginary data, if there is any. Both `pr` and `pi` are one-dimensional arrays of double-precision numbers. The elements of the matrix are stored columnwise in these arrays.

An `mxArray` is declared like any other variable:

```
mxArray *myarray;
```

This line creates an `mxArray` named `myarray`. The values inside `myarray` are undefined when it is declared, so it should be initialized with an `mx*` routine (such as the API function `mxCreateNumericArray`) before it is used.

`myarray` can hold any type of MATLAB variable, such as integer data, double data, strings, numeric arrays, pointer arrays, structures, and even objects.

Note that inside an `mxArray`, data is read down and then across, instead of across and then down. This is contrary to how indexing works in C, and so special care must be taken when our program accesses the array's elements. To access the data inside of an `mxArray`, we would use the API functions.

6.2.3.3 Using the Gateway Function `mexFunction` in C/C++

The gateway function to every MEX-file is called `mexFunction`. This is the entry point that MATLAB uses to access DLLs developed in the third-party language. Each MEX-file must contain this gateway function so that MATLAB can access this MEX-file. `mexFunction` must be exported explicitly in the Definition (.DEF) file to direct MATLAB to enter the MEX-file. Without this gateway function, MATLAB cannot access the MEX-file at all.

Here is the format of `mexFunction` in C++:

```
mexFunction(int nlhs, mxArray *plhs[ ], int nrhs, mxArray *prhs[ ]) { ... }
```

In Fortran, mexFunction takes this form:

```
SUBROUTINE MEXFUNCTION(NLHS, PLHS, NRHS, PRHS)
```

Definitions of the arguments for this function are listed in Table 6.2.

- **nlhs:** Indicate the number of output variables from this MEX-File back to MATLAB domain. This number is equivalent to the number of returned data to MATLAB domain. As usual, the returned data is defined in the left hand side of the function.
- **plhs[]:** Stores an array of pointers to the returned data (mxArray). Please note that this array contains an array of pointers to the output data, not returned data. Double pointer is applied to this variable.
- **nrhs:** Indicate the number of input variables to the MEX-File, and those input data is coming from MATLAB domain. As usual, the input arguments are defined in the right hand side of the function.
- **prhs[]:** Stores an array of pointers to the input data (mxArray). Please note that this array contains an array of pointers to the input data, not input data. Double pointer is applied to this variable.

TABLE 6.2
MexFunction Arguments

Argument	Definition
nlhs	Number of output variables (lefthand side) stored in `plhs[]`
*plhs[ ]	Array of pointers to the output variables
nrhs	Number of input variables (righthand side) stored in `prhs[]`
*prhs[ ]	Array of pointers to the input variables

http://www.mathworks.com/support/tech-notes/1600/1605.shtml. Reprinted with permission of MathWorks, Inc.

The variables `prhs` and `plhs` are not `mxArrays`; they are arrays of pointers to `mxArrays`. For example, if a function is given three inputs, `prhs` will be an array of three pointers to the `mxArrays` that contain the data passed in. The variable `prhs` can be declared as `const`. This means that the values that are passed into the MEX-file should not be altered. Changing these values might cause segmentation violations in MATLAB. The values in `plhs` are invalid when the MEX-file begins. The `mxArrays` they point to must be explicitly created before they are used. Compilers won't catch this problem, but it can cause incorrect results or segmentation violations.

You can place any number of subroutines or functions written in the third-party language inside the gateway function `mexFunction`. This gives us the flexibility of calling different subroutines to perform different tasks in the third-party language domain. For example, in the following sections, we will discuss how to call low-level functions written in C/C++ to access the serial port from the gateway function.

From the gateway function, our program can access the data in the `mxArray` structure and then manipulate the data in our C functions. For example, the expression `mxGetPr(prhs[0])` would return a pointer of type `double *` to the real data in the `mxArray` pointed to by `prhs[0]`. We could then use this pointer like any other pointer of type `double *` in C/C++. After calling the C/C++ functions from the gateway function, we would set a pointer of type `mxArray` to the data it returned. MATLAB would then able to recognize the output from our C/C++ functions as the output from the MEX-file.

The C MEX cycle depicted in Figure 6.1 shows how input enters a MEX-file and how output is returned to MATLAB, and demonstrates the functions performed by the gateway routine.

When the gateway function is invoked from the MATLAB domain by the M-function `[C, D] = func(A, B)`, the inputs `A` and `B` to the MEX-file are stored in the array elements `prhs[0]` and `prhs[1]`, respectively, in the `mxArray` data type. We must use the API function `mxGet()` to obtain each input data unit from `prhs[0]`, `prhs[1], ...` We can use `mxGetPr()` to get the pointer to the associated input data, and then use that pointer as a normal pointer to pick up the associated input data. To return data to MATLAB, we must use the API function `mxCreate()` to create the MATLAB array variables and assign each output data to `plhs[0]`, `plhs[1]`,.... Then we assign `plhs[0]`, `plhs[1]`,... to the associated pointer to the created MATLAB array variables.

TIP: Notice that when we call an M-function from MATLAB to access the gateway function `mexFunction` in the MEX-file, the M-function must have the same name as the MEX-file that includes the gateway function. For example, the MEX-file developed in C/C++ is named `mSerial.dll`, so the M-function we use should be `[C, D] = mSerial(A, B)`. If the names are not identical, a segmentation violation error will occur.

For example, if we invoke a MEX-file from the MATLAB workspace with the command `x = func(y, z)`, the MATLAB interpreter will call `mexFunction` with the arguments, as shown in Figure 6.2.

INPUTS

MATLAB

A call to
MEX-file func:

[C,D]=func (A, B)

tells MATLAB to
pass variables A and
B to your MEX-file.
C and D are left
unassigned.

const mxArray *8
B = prhs [1]

const mxArray *A
A = prhs [0]

func. c

void mexFunction(
int nlhs, mxArray *plhs [ ],
int nrhs, const mxArray *prhs [ ])

In the gateway routine:

- Use the mxCreate functions to create the MATLAB arrays for your output arguments. Set plhs [0}, [1], ... to the pointers to the newly created MATLAB arrays.
- Use the mxGet functions to extract your data from prhs [0], [1], ...
- Call your C subroutine passing the input and output data pointers as function parameters.

MATLAB

On return from
MEX-file func:

[C,D]=func (A, B)

plhs [0] is assigned
to C and plhs [1] is
assigned to D.

mxArray *D
D = plhs [1]

mxArray *C
C = plhs[0]

OUTPUTS

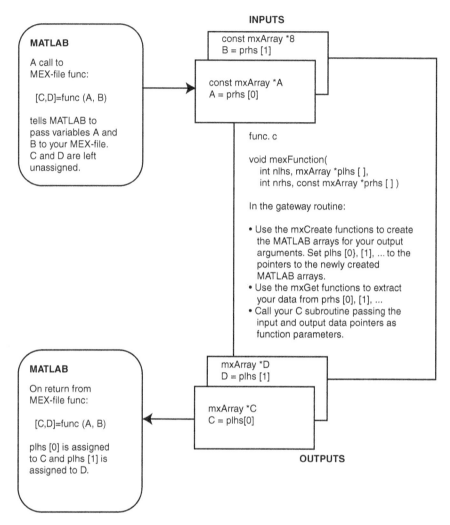

FIGURE 6.1 The C MEX cycle. MATLAB Technology Menu: *MATLAB External Interfaces/API, Version 6,* p. 4-3. Reprinted with permission of MathWorks Inc.

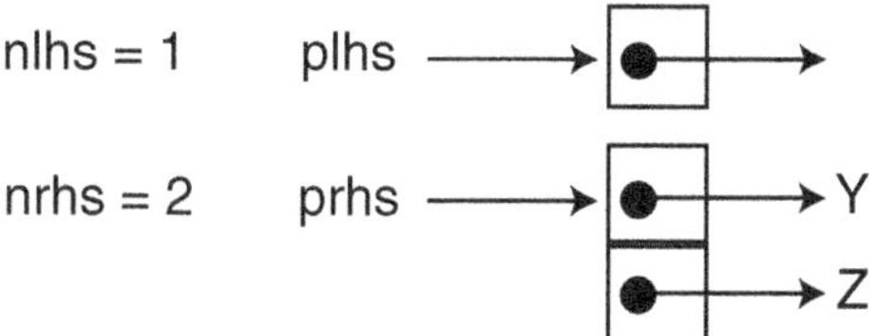

FIGURE 6.2 Calling the gateway function. MATLAB Technology Menu: *MATLAB External Interfaces/API, Version 6,* p. 4-5. Reprinted with permission of MathWorks Inc.

The `plhs` argument is a one-element C array that contains a null pointer. The `prhs` is a 2-element C array in which the first element is a pointer to an `mxArray` named `y`, and the second element is a pointer to an `mxArray` named `z`.

The plhs parameter points at nothing because the output x is not created until the subroutine is executed. It is the responsibility of the gateway routine to create an output array and to set a pointer to that array in plhs[0]. If plhs[0] is left unassigned, MATLAB will print a warning message stating that no output has been assigned.

TIP: It is possible to return an output value even if nlhs = 0. This is the equivalent of returning the result in the ans variable.

6.2.3.4 API Functions

The mx* functions are used to access data inside of mxArrays. They are also used to manage the system memory and to create and destroy mxArrays. Some useful routines are listed in Table 6.3.

TABLE 6.3
Commonly Used API Functions

Purpose	Associated Functions
Array creation	mxCreateNumericArray,mxCreateCellArray,mxCreateCharArray
Array access	mxGetPr, mxGetPi, mxGetM, mxGetData, mxGetCell
Array modification	mxSetPr, mxSetPi, mxSetData, mxSetField
Memory management	mxMalloc, mxCalloc, mxFree, mexMakeMemoryPersistent, mexAtExit, mxDestroyArray, memcpy

http://www.mathworks.com/support/tech-notes/1600/1605.shtml. Reprinted with permission of MathWorks, Inc.

Keep in mind that mxGetPr and mxGetPi return pointers to their data. To change the values in an array, we must directly change the value in the array being pointed at, or use a function such as memcpy from the C Standard Library. API functions such as mxCalloc and mxFree should be used instead of their Standard C counterparts because the mx* routines let MATLAB manage the memory and perform initialization and cleanup.

We can use the mex* API functions to access MATLAB variables directly from the C/C++ domain and transfer control back to MATLAB. On the PC there is no concept of stdin, stdout, or stderr, so it is important to use MATLAB's mex* functions, such as mexPrintf and mexError. Some popular mex* routines are listed in Table 6.4.

TABLE 6.4
Commonly Used mex* Functions

Function	Purpose
mexFunction	Provides an entry point to a C MEX-file
mexErrMsgTxt	Issues an error message and then returns to MATLAB
mexEvalString	Executes a MATLAB command in the caller's workspace
mexCallMATLAB	Calls a MATLAB function or a user-defined M-file or MEX-file
mexGetArray	Gets a copy of a variable from another workspace
mexPrintf	Runs an ANSI C printf-style output routine
mexWarnMsgTxt	Issues a warning message

http://www.mathworks.com/support/tech-notes/1600/1605.shtml. Reprinted with permission of MathWorks, Inc.

The MEX API provides several functions that allow us to determine various states of an array. These functions are used to check the input to the MEX-file and ensure that it is what is expected. All of the functions in the MEX API begin with the prefix mxIs. In some cases it may be desirable to use the mxIs function specific to a certain data type; however, it is generally much easier to use mxIsClass to perform this operation.

In order to prevent passing inputs of the incorrect type, use the mxIsClass function extensively at the beginning of your MEX-file. For example, suppose prhs[0] is a full, real-valued array. To prevent passing your function a sparse matrix, a string matrix, or a complex matrix, we would use code similar to the following:

```
if (mxIsChar(prhs[0]) || mxIsClass(prhs[0],"sparse") ||
mxIsComplex(prhs[0]))
    mexErrMsgTxt("first input must be real, full, and nonstring");
```

Putting these checks in the code will prevent the MEX-file from crashing for no apparent reason if we should accidentally pass it the wrong type of data.

We have now explored the process of developing a MEX-file using a third-party language and interfacing with MATLAB. In the following section we will build a C/C++ language MEX-file using either the default C compiler from the command line or the Visual C++ 6.0 compiler from the Visual C++ 6.0 IDE.

6.2.4 Creating a MEX-file in C/C++

Two popular methods are used for compiling MEX-files in C/C++:

- Using the default compiler to compile the MEX-file from the command line
- Using the Visual C++ 6.0 compiler from the Visual C++ 6.0 IDE

The first method is straightforward and easy. We must first create the source code for the MEX-file that will include the gateway function, and then use the mex command to compile the source code into the MEX-file. For example, if the C/C++ source file were named mSerial.c or mSerial.cpp, we would perform the compilation by executing mex mSerial.c or mex mSerial.cpp from either the MATLAB workspace or the DOS window. The completed MEX-file, mSerial.dll, would be located in the current directory, and we could access the MEX-file by using a M-function call such as [a, b] = mSerial(....).

We will now concentrate on the second method, using the Visual C++ 6.0 compiler.

To build a MEX-files in the Microsoft Visual C++ 6.0 Integrated Development Environment (IDE), following these steps:

1. Create a project of the type Win32 Dynamic-Link Library and insert your MEX source code and the mexversion.rc into it.
2. Create a .DEF file to export the MEX entry point. For example, if the MEX-file project were named mSerial, the Definition file would look like this in C:

   ```
   LIBRARY MSERIAL.DLL
   EXPORTS mexFunction
   ```

   In Fortran, the file would look like this:

   ```
   EXPORTS _MEXFUNCTION@16
   ```

3. Add the .DEF file to the project.

4. Under the MATLABRoot\extern\lib\win32\microsoft directory, locate the .LIB files for the compiler you are using. (For example, for version 6.0, you would use the files that are located in the msvc60 subdirectory.)
5. From this directory, use the Link settings option to add libmx.lib, libmex.lib, and libmat.lib to the library modules.
6. Select Tools|Options|Directories and add the directory MATLAB6p5\extern\include as the include path.
7. Select Settings from the Project menu; then select C/C++. Type MATLAB_MEX_FILE as the final entry in the Preprocessor definitions field.
8. To debug the MEX-file using the IDE, select Settings|Debug and enter matlab.exe for the option Executable for debug session.

If you are using a compiler other than the Microsoft Visual C/C++ compiler, the process for building MEX files is similar to the process just described. In step 3, however, you would locate the .LIB files for the compiler under the subdirectory MATLABRoot\extern\lib\win32. (For example, for version 5.4 of the Borland C/C++ compiler, you would find the files in MATLABRoot\extern\lib\win32\borland\bc54.)

A better way to develop a MEX-file in Visual C++ 6.0 IDE is to copy all associated MATLAB files (such as the header files, library files, and resource files) into the current MEX-file project. Then we can compile and build the target MEX-File along with all the MATLAB-related files to get one portable file. Because all related files are located in the current project folder, we can simply copy and paste that project folder into any other machines that run on the same platform. If we choose to set the link path, however, and link the header and library files to the project by means of different paths, we cannot simply copy and paste the entire project, because the related files will still be located in various folders on your machine.

In the following sections, we'll compile and build the actual C/C++ MEX-files that will interface with MATLAB. The first example interfaces between a C/C++ MEX-file and MATLAB to communicate with a serial port and thus collect data from a 12-bit serial A/D converter MAX187. The second example is a similar interfacing program that is used to collect data from an 8-bit serial A/D converter TLC548.

The advantage of using interfacing programs to communicate with the serial port to collect data from A/D converters is that we can directly analyze and process the converted data in the MATLAB domain using any mathematical functions provided by the different toolboxes, such as the signal processing, control, fuzzy logic, and identification toolboxes. If we use an interface program, we can then perform any signal processing and analysis in the MATLAB domain with no additional steps involved. In the traditional method, data is first collected by a program that has been created in a real-time programming language such as C/C++. Then the data must be copied or translated into the MATLAB domain before it can be analyzed and processed. By using this interface program, we can avoid the data translation step.

6.2.5 Using a MEX-file to Interface with the MAX187 ADC

We have used the MAX187 converter, manufactured by Maxim Integrated Products, several times in previous chapters to illustrate the design and development of interfacing programs created in different languages. In our next project, the MEX-file works as a bridge between MATLAB and C/C++ codes so that data can be collected via the serial port in the C/C++ domain and displayed by means of M-functions in the MATLAB domain.

The hardware connection for our interface circuit was originally shown in Figure 5.26 in Chapter 5; for your convenience, the circuit is presented again in Figure 6.3. The elements used with this circuit are listed in Table 6.5.

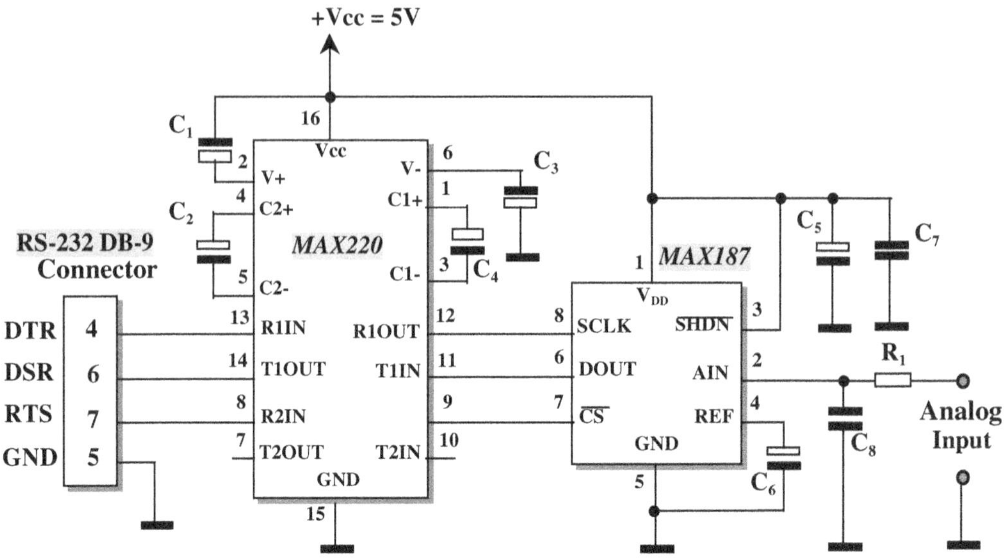

FIGURE 6.3 Interface circuit of the MAX187.

TABLE 6.5
Elements Used with the MAX187

Elements	Values	Description
R_1	10 KΩ	Current-limited resistor
C_1 through C_4	10 μF/25V	Electrolytic capacitors
C_5 through C_6	4.7 μF/10V	Electrolytic capacitors
C_7 through C_8	0.1 μF	Capacitors

Recall from Chapter 5 that the MAX187 is a 12-bit serial A/D converter. Data conversion is controlled by the `Chip Select` control signal (CS-bar), which starts the A/D conversion. A second control signal, `SCLK` (serial CLK), is a simulated clock that is provided by an external device, such as the transmission line on the serial port UART. This signal is used to shift converted data bit by bit from the output data buffer DOUT on the MAX187 after a 12-bit data conversion is finished. Both of these control signals are connected to the RTS and the DTR transmission lines. The DOUT output is connected to the DSR transmission line on the port that will receive the shifted data from the MAX187.

The MAX220 is a serial driver/converter that is used to provide enough power to the MAX187 and convert the different voltage levels between the CMOS and RS-232 levels. (For details, refer back to Figures 1.5 and 1.6 in Chapter 1). Keep in mind that the MAX220 incorporates inverting logic, so all signals output from the MAX220 are inverted. This will be important to remember as we create the code for our interface program.

The operating sequence of the data conversion is as follows. After the conversion process has begun, the PC monitors the DSR line and waits until its state becomes `HIGH`, which indicates that data conversion is complete. Then the PC sends 12 simulated clocks via the DTR line that is connected to the SCLK (serial CLK) on the MAX187 to serially move the converted data from the output shift register on the MAX187 to the DSR line. Finally, after checking the value received on the DSR line, the PC picks up the data bits one by one.

Make the circuit connection as shown in Figure 6.3. In this example, we use a DB-9 serial connector, and our serial port will be COM1. The analog input signal comes from a functional generator, with sinusoidal, triangular, and square waveform outputs.

Now let's develop our MEX-file project in Visual C++ 6.0 IDE. Launch Visual C++ 6.0 and open a new project with the following properties:

- Project name: MEX_MAX
- Project type: Win32 Dynamic-Link Library
- Location: C:\Book2_Program\Chapter 6

Create a new empty C/C++ Header File named MEX_MAX.h and a new empty C++ Source File named MEX_MAX.cpp in the new opened project. Before we can continue, we need to setup the environment of the compiler and linker in Visual C++ 6.0 to make this project compatible with MATLAB requirements.

6.2.5.1 Configuring the C/C++ MEX-file

To make this project portable, we need to add the following MATLAB-related files into the current project MEX_MAX.

Open Windows Explorer and copy the following files into the current project folder C:\Book2_Program\Chapter 6\MEX_MAX:

- libmat.lib
- libmex.lib
- libmx.lib

All of these library files are located in the default MATLAB installation folder, C:\MATLAB6p5\extern\lib\win32\Microsoft\msvc60.

Still in Windows Explorer, copy the resource file mexversion.rc, which is located in the folder C:\MATLAB6p5\extern\include, into the current project folder.

Copy the following MATLAB header files into the current project folder:

- matrix.h
- mex.h
- tmwtypes.h

All of these header files are located in the folder C:\MATLAB6p5\extern\include.

TIP: The advantage of copying all of these MATLAB related files from the MATLAB installation folders into our current project folder is that all project files are located and integrated in the current project folder, and we do not need to set any external link to locate any MATLAB related file from any other folders. Of course, we can still do that external link by setting the names of the MATLAB related libraries into the Object/library modules box in the Project|Settings|Link item, and setting the external include path in the Tools|Options|Directories item in the Visual C++ 6.0 IDE for the header files if we like.

Now close Windows Explorer and open the newly created project MEX_MAX in Visual C++ 6.0 domain. Click the Project|Add To Project|Files menu item and browse to the current project folder to add all of MATLAB related files we've copied above into the project. Those MATLAB-related files include one resource file, mexversion.rc, three library files libmat.lib, libmex.lib, libmx.lib, and three header files, matrix.h, mex.h, and tmwtypes.h. Make sure that all of these MATLAB-related files are added into the current project.

Now we can continue to develop all other files of the MEX-file project.

6.2.5.2 Designing the Header File for the MEX-file

The purpose of the header file of this project is to declare protocols and prototypes for the global variables, user-defined constants and functions used in this project. Open the empty header file `MEX_MAX.h` created in Section 6.2.5 and enter the code that is shown in Figure 6.4.

```
  /* NAME: MEX_MAX.h */
A #include <Windows.h>
  #include "mex.h"
B #ifndef _MEX_MAX_H_
  #define _MEX_MAX_H_
C #define MAX_BYTE                1
  #define MAX_BITS                12
  #define MAX_DATA                100
  #define MAX_STRING              256
  #define NOPARITY                0
  #define ONESTOPBIT              0
  #define RTS_CONTROL_DISABLE     0x00
  #define RTS_CONTROL_ENABLE      0x01
  #define DTR_CONTROL_DISABLE     0x00
  #define DTR_CONTROL_ENABLE      0x01
D #define msg(info)   MessageBox(NULL, info, "", MB_OK)
  #ifdef __cplusplus
E extern "C" {
  #endif /* __cplusplus */
F typedef struct
  {
    ULONG  ulCtrlID;
    char   cEcho;
    char   cEORChar;
    long   lTimeout;
    long   lBaudRate;
    long   lDataBits;
  } SerialCreate, *pSerialCreate;
G typedef struct
  {
    int  pcBuffer;          /* received data buffer */
    int  iMaxChars;         /* the number of the maximum characters */
    int  iMaxBits;          /* the number of the maximum bits */
    int  piNumRcvd;         /* the number of the received data */
    char cTermChar;         /* the termination character */
  } CommPortClass;
H typedef enum
  {
    OK      = 0,            /* no error */
    EC_TIMEOUT,
    EC_FOPEN,
    EC_INVAL_CONFIG,
    EC_TIMEOUT_SET,
    EC_RECV_TIMEOUT,
    EC_EXIT_CODE,
    EC_WAIT_SINGLEOBJ,
    EC_INVALIDPORT,
    EC_WRITE_FAIL,
```

FIGURE 6.4 Header file fo the MEX-file. *(continued)*

```
    EC_CREATE_THREAD,
    EC_GETMODSTATUS,
    EC_UNKNOWNERROR
  } ERR_CODE;
I FILE*  fp;
  HANDLE  hPort;
  char*  sPortName;
  bool   PortCreateflg = false;
  int      runTIMES = 0;
  /* local functions */
J int  Setup(double* pCom);
  int  ReadData(void);
  int  PortClose();
K void WINAPI ThreadFunc(void* hCommPorts);
  void Delay(int  num);
  ERR_CODE PortInitialize(char* lpszPortName,  pSerialCreate pCreate);
  ERR_CODE PortRead(CommPortClass *hCommPort);
L void mexFunction(int  nlhs, mxArray *plhs[], int  nrhs, const mxArray*prhs[]);
  #ifdef __cplusplus
  }
M #endif  /* __cplusplus */
  #endif
```

FIGURE 6.4 Header file fo the MEX-file.

A: The system header file `Windows.h` is included first because this system header file provides all object definitions applied in the Windows environment. As an example, the `MessageBox()` function is defined in this system header file.

B: To avoid multiple inclusions of the header file, we use the system macro `#ifndef`. This macro will allow the other source file to include this header file if the header file has not been included before by that source file. In C/C++ programming, it is illegal to include a header file multiple times by any source file of a project. To prevent this situation, we use the macros `#ifndef` and `#define`. We must also attach an `#endif` at the end of the header file to indicate the ending of the macro.

C: Some user-defined and system constants are defined here, and most of them are serial communication-related parameters, such as `MAX_BITS`, `NOPARITY`, `ONESTOPBIT`, `DTR`, `RTS_CONTROL_ENABLE`, and `RTS_CONTROL_DISABLE`. The `MAX_BITS` parameter defines the maximum bits of the collected data as 12 because the MAX187 is a 12-bit converter. As mentioned previously, the transmission lines used for this project are not in normal format, so it is necessary for us to set and reset each transmission line by using the function `EscapeCommFunction()`. We must configure and setup the transmission lines to either `CONTROL_ENABLE` or `CONTROL_DISABLE` state during the configuration stage in order to use that extended function to access and set/reset any transmission line.

D: We can simplify the system function `MessageBox()` by using the macro `#define`. After this redefinition, the length of the `MessageBox()` function can be greatly shortened, and thus easily placed in the program by means of a `msg()` statement with a text string as the information.

E: When we build shared libraries for C++, we must prevent the C++ compiler from decorating the function names in the final object code. To do this, we wrap the function declaration in an extern “C” clause, `extern "C" { ....}`. The codes included inside the braces are considered C codes, and the compiler converts them to C object codes, not C++ object codes. Note that if we disable C++ decoration of a function, the compiler cannot create polymorphic versions of the function.

F: Two structures are defined here to simplify port configuration. The first structure is `SerialCreate`, which contains useful port communication parameters, such as the baud rate, data bits, and timeout value, which are used to check and indicate the status of communication.

G: The second structure is the `CommPortClass`, which is used to hold parameters that will ensure the data is correctly read from the port.

H: An `enum` structure, `ERR_CODE`, is declared to define the numeric error value that is associated with each possible error that could occur when the project runs. Space can be greatly saved with this kind of definition. Each error code is sequenced from the integer `0` to the maximum integer value.

I: Global variables are declared in this section. The purpose of these global variables is to simplify the program and allow different source files to share some common variables. Although the global style is not recommended in the object-oriented programming environment, it can really simplify and speed up the process for application programs that need high-speed real-time responses. `fp` is a FILE pointer variable used to open a new data file that will store the collected data at run time. This data file can be read later and plotted as a waveform in any programming environment. `hPort` is used to reserve the file handle that represents the opened port. Any code can use `hPort` to access the opened serial port in the program. `PortCreateflg` is a Boolean variable that works as a flag to monitor and indicate whether the port setup process has been completed. This variable is set to `True` if the port configuration is successfully processed. `sPortName` is a string variable used to reserve the port name in text format, as required by the port initialization function. `runTIMES` is an integer variable used to monitor the times of calling the `ReadData()` function from within the gateway function `mexFunction`. Because a timeout error may be encountered during the call to the `ReadData()` function, we use `runTIMES` to record the time of each call and skip the first call to `ReadData()`.

J: Seven local functions are declared here, and these can be divided into two levels. The first three functions can be considered the first-level local functions because they are called directly from within the gateway function `mexFunction`. The following four functions can be considered the second-level local functions because they are called by the first-level local functions. The `Setup()` function is used to configure and initialize the serial port according to the parameters passed into the function by the `pCom` argument. The `ReadData()` function is used to collect a converted 12-bit data from the MAX187 via the serial port. The `PortClose()` function will clean up the environment of the serial communication and close the opened serial port.

K: Four local second-level functions are used to coordinate the first-level functions for passing data between the serial port and the computer. The thread function `Thread-Func()` is used to support the process of reading data from the serial port and to prevent dead cycles when the system function `WaitCommEvent()` is used. `Delay()` is a user-defined function and it is used to delay a specified period of time during the data collection. The `PortInitialize()` function is used to configure the serial port; this function has two arguments. The first one is the port name represented in text format, and the second is a pointer to the data structure `SerialCreate`, which is the address where configuration parameters are stored. The `PortRead()` function is used to directly access low-level system routines for receiving data.

L: The gateway function `mexFunction` is declared here. (Refer to Section 6.2.3.3 for detailed information for this function and a description of its arguments).

M: Attach the ending braces for the macro `#ifndef` and #ifdef_cplusplus.

Click the File|Save menu item to save the header file.

6.2.5.3 Designing the DEF File

In order to allow MATLAB M-functions to recognize the MEX-file and to identify the gateway function contained in the developed MEX-file, we must create a Definition file in the Visual C++ domain to explicitly export the gateway function. Click the File|New menu item from Visual C++ 6.0 workspace to open the New dialog box. Keep the default Files tab selected, and choose the Text File item from the list box to create a new text file named MEX_MAX.txt. Then open Windows Explorer and browse to the current project folder, right-click on the newly created MEX_MAX.txt file, and select the Rename item from the pop-up menu to rename the file to MEX_MAX.def.

Return to the Visual C++ 6.0 workspace, click the Project|Add To Project|Files menu item to browse to the current project folder and add the renamed file MEX_MAX.def into the current project.

Double-click this .DEF file to open it, and add the code that is shown in Figure 6.5.

Click the File|Save menu item to save this file.

```
LIBRARY MEX_MAX.DLL

EXPORTS mexFunction
```

FIGURE 6.5 Definition file for the MEX-file program.

6.2.5.4 Designing the Source File of the MEX-file

The source file is relatively large, so we'll divide it into several sections and discuss each of them one by one.

6.2.5.4.1 Designing the Gateway Function

First let's take a look at the gateway function mexFunction.

Open the source file MEX_MAX.cpp that we created in Section 6.2.5, and add the code that is shown in Figure 6.6 into the empty source file.

The gateway function works as an entry point to the MEX-file; any MATLAB function call should start from this gateway function. Each section of the code is explained in the following list.

N: The system header files and the user-defined header file are declared at the beginning of the source file. The header file MEX_MAX.h must be included because all functions, global variables, and constants used in our project are defined in that file.

O: The macro #define DEBUG is used to indicate whether we choose to display the debug information when the project runs. If this macro is declared here, then debug information will be displayed at run time so we can check the running status of the program by using these debug information. This is very useful during the initial development stage of the program. If this declaration is comment out, no debug information will be displayed as the program runs. After the program is developed and bug free, however, we will comment out this declaration to speed up the running of the program.

P: The local variables are declared here. The ad_data[] is an array that will store the collected data received from the MAX187. inParam, outParam, and plpr are pointer variables that support the operations of the MATLAB array mxArray. inParam is used to reserve the pointer to the input MATLAB array, and outParam works as a temporary pointer variable to store the collected data and assign it to the returned pointer variable plpr.

```
  /*****************************************************************************
   * NAME: MEX_MAX.cpp
   * DESC.: Source file for MEX-File MEX_MAX.DLL. Called by MATLAB mexmax.m
   * PGMR.:Y. Bai
   * DATE: 11/20/2003
   *****************************************************************************/
N #include <stdio.h>
  #include <stdlib.h>
  #include "MEX_MAX.h"
O #define DEBUG
  void mexFunction(int nlhs, mxArray *plhs[], int nrhs, const mxArray *prhs[])
  {
P     int ad_data[100];
      int i, m, n, ret = 0;
      double *inParam, *outParam, *plpr;
Q     m = 1; n = 100;
R     for (i = 0; i < nrhs; i++)                // Get the data passed in
          inParam = mxGetPr(prhs[i]);
S     ret = Setup(inParam);
      if (ret != OK)
          mexErrMsgTxt("ERROR in Setup() calling!");
T     outParam = (double *) mxMalloc(m*n * sizeof(double));
U     plhs[0] = mxCreateDoubleMatrix(m, n, mxREAL);
V     plpr = mxGetPr(plhs[0]);
W     #ifdef DEBUG
      mexPrintf("Port is reading...\n");
      #endif
X     ad_data[0] = ReadData();                  //wake-up reading.
Y     for (i = 0; i < MAX_DATA; i++)
      {
          ad_data[i] = ReadData();
          outParam[i] = (double)ad_data[i];
Z         *(plpr + i) = outParam[i];
      }
1     ret = PortClose();
2     #ifdef DEBUG
      mexPrintf("Port is closed...\n");
      #endif
3     return;
  }
```

FIGURE 6.6 Gateway function for the MEX_MAX project.

Q: The size of the collected data is 100, which means that we want to collect 100 converted data from the MAX187. The size of the array that will store the collected data is 1 × 100. The variables `m` and `n` represent row and column values.

R: A `for` loop is used to pick up all input elements stored in the `prhs[]` argument. The `nrhs` argument stores the maximum number of input elements, so it works as the terminator of the `for` loop. Note that only the addresses or the pointers to those input elements, not the element's actual values, are picked up and stored in the pointer variable `inParam`, by means of the API function `mxGetPr()`. The type of the pointer to those elements is `double`, which is a default data type in MATLAB.

S: The local function `Setup()` is called with the pointer variable `inParam`, which contains the address of the input elements (the MATLAB array `mxArray`) to configure and initialize the serial port. An error message will be displayed if this function call encounters any mistakes. In that case, The MATLAB function `mexErrMsgTxt()` is called to display the error information in the MATLAB workspace because on the PC, there is no concept of `stdin`, `stdout`, and `stderr`.

T: The MATLAB function `mxMalloc()` is used to create a memory space of 1× 100, with a `double` type for the temporary pointer variable `outParam`. This pointer variable is declared in the gateway function but without yet allocating any memory space.

U: As we mentioned in Section 6.2.3.3, the gateway function creates an output array and set a pointer to that array in `plhs[0]`. This means that the argument `plhs[]` is an empty pointer variable (refer to Figure 6.2); it points to nothing. In order to return any data back to the MATLAB domain, we must create the necessary memory space for that empty pointer variable and assign the starting address of the returned data to `plhs[0]`. The input argument `prhs[]` is also a pointer variable, but its memory space is allocated in MATLAB domain before it is passed into the gateway function. The MATLAB function `mxCreateDoubleMatrix()` is called to allocate the memory for `plhs[]`, and the starting address is returned to `plhs[0]`.

V: The API function `mxGetPr()` is called to get the starting address of the returned data, which is stored in `plhs[0]`; this address is assigned to the pointer variable `plpr`. Now `plpr` contains the starting address of the data to be output to MATLAB. Note that the arguments `plhs` and `prhs` are `double` pointer variables; they contain the pointers to a sequence of pointers of input/output elements. (Output pointers are empty. Refer to Figure 6.2 for more details).

W: The macro `#ifdef DEBUG` is used to display the debug information for the beginning of the data reading if that macro has been defined.

X: During the testing and debugging processes, a timeout error may be encountered for the first call to the `ReadData()` function. To prevent this error, our program must execute a wake-up reading. This means that before the formal calling, our program uses the first-time calling to instruct the function to set up the environment of the serial communication; for example, `ReadData()` will create a reading thread and begin to execute the system function `WaitCommEvent()`. Then we can formally call this function to pick up the converted data from the MAX187. In other words, this calling is only used to wake up the reading process; no data is used for this first call.

Y: Another `for` loop is used to continuously execute the `ReadData()` function, which will pick up the converted data and assign the collected data to the `ad_data[]` buffer. A 12-bit string of converted data is returned for each calling to `ReadData()`. The returned data is then assigned to the temporary array `outParam`. A cast is needed to convert the data stored in the `ad_data[]` buffer from `integer` type to `double` type, as required by the program.

Z: This step is very important. The collected data is assigned to the output argument `plhs` and returned to MATLAB. Remember that the starting address of the returned data is stored in `plpr`, so a reversed pointer operation is applied to assign the data from the temporary pointer variable `outParam` to the `plhs` whose starting address is in `plpr`. `*(plpr + i)` is equivalent to `plpr[i]`.

1: After 100 data have been collected, the function `PortClose()` is called to clean up the serial communication environment and close the opened port.

2: The macro `#ifdef DEBUG` is used to display the debug information if that macro has been declared at the beginning of this file.

3: The gateway function is ended with the `return` statement.

6.2.5.4.2 Designing the Setup Function

The `Setup()` function is used to configure and initialize the serial port according to the arguments passed into the function. The body of this function is shown in Figure 6.7.

```
  int Setup(double* pComputer)
```

```
   int Setup(double* pCom)
   {                                               //pCom[1] = baud_rate
4     ERR_CODE rc = OK;                            //pCom[2] = data_bits
      pSerialCreate pParam;                        //pCom[3] = stop_bit
5     fp = fopen("maxdata.dat", "w");              //pCom[4] = parity
6     pParam = new SerialCreate;                   //pCom[5] = timeout_value
      pParam->lBaudRate = (int)pCom[1];
      pParam->lDataBits = (int)pCom[2];
      pParam->lTimeout  = (int)pCom[5];
7     #ifdef DEBUG
      mexPrintf("data[%d] = %d\n", 0, (int)pCom[0]);
      mexPrintf("data[%d] = %d\n", 1, (int)pCom[1]);
      mexPrintf("data[%d] = %d\n", 2, (int)pCom[2]);
      mexPrintf("data[%d] = %d\n", 3, (int)pCom[3]);
      mexPrintf("data[%d] = %d\n", 4, (int)pCom[4]);
      mexPrintf("data[%d] = %d\n", 5, (int)pCom[5]);
      #endif
8     switch((int)pCom[0])
      {
          case 1:  sPortName = "COM1";
                   break;
          case 2:  sPortName = "COM2";
                   break;
          case 3:  sPortName = "COM3";
                   break;
          case 4:  sPortName = "COM4";
                   break;
          default: return EC_INVALIDPORT;
      }
9     if (PortCreateflg)
      {
          msg("Port has been Setup ");
          return rc;
      }
10    rc = PortInitialize(sPortName, pParam);
      if (rc != 0)
        msg("ERROR in PortInitialize()!");
11    #ifdef DEBUG
      else
        mexPrintf("\nPort is initialized...\n");
      #endif
12    delete pParam;
13    PortCreateflg = true;
14    return rc;
   }
```

FIGURE 6.7 The `Setup()` function for the `MEX_MAX` project.

4: The local variables are defined at the beginning of this function. The returned variable `rc` is defined as the `enum` structure `ERR_CODE`, and an `OK` is assigned to that variable to initialize it to `0`. `pParam` is a pointer variable of the structure `pSerialcreate`.

5: The system function `fopen()` is called to open a new data file named `maxdata.dat`. The returned file handler is assigned to the FILE pointer `fp`. This data file is used to store the collected data from the MAX187 A/D converter when the program runs, and this data file can be used to compare the output data returned by the argument `plhs[]`.

6: A `SerialCreate` structure variable `pParam` is generated by the `new` keyword. The `new` keyword is used to create a new structure variable and allocate the memory space for that structure variable. new returns the starting address where the structure variable pParam is stored. The variables defined inside the SerialCreate structure are initialized with the values of those elements stored in the argument array passed from the gateway function. Each element's position and definition are clearly explained in the comment statements. Only four elements' values are used in this application.

7: The macro #ifdef DEBUG is used to display the argument values passed from the gateway function. This step is useful when the program is initially tested and debugged. The MATLAB function mexPrintf() is used to display these argument values in the MATLAB workspace.

8: A switch structure is used to identify the desired port number. The condition variable for this switch structure is the first element stored in the argument array pCom[0] that corresponds to the desired port number. The string variable sPortName is assigned by the associated port name based on the port number that is the first element stored in the pCom[0] array. This translation from port number to port name is necessary because the PortInitialize() function needs a string argument in order to open and configure the serial port. In this application, the range of valid port numbers is 1 through 4. (You can modify this range as needed in your applications.)

9: If the global Boolean variable PortCreateflg is already set to True, which means that the port has been opened and configured, a message is displayed to remind the user, and the program returns to the calling function without performing any configuration.

10: If PortCreateflg is False, the local function PortInitialize() is called to open and configure the serial port. Two arguments are passed into this function: the port name sPortName, which is a string variable, and the SerialCreate structure variable pParam, which stores the configuration parameters. The function will return a 0 if it is successful; otherwise a nonzero will be returned to indicate that the function call has failed. In this case, an error message will be displayed.

11: The macro #ifdef DEBUG is used to display the debug information if that macro has been declared at the beginning of the file.

12: Because the new keyword is used to create a data structure variable pParam, the delete command must be also used to clean up the memory space allocated by the new keyword for the data structure when it is no longer to be used.

13: After the port is successfully opened and configured, the Boolean variable PortCreateflg should be set to True to indicate that the port has been opened and configured. Do not try to reopen the port if the port is already opened; if you do, you may encounter an opening error. By using PortCreateflg, we can avoid the reopening operation.

14: Finally the running status of the function is returned to the calling function.

The code for the local function PortInitialize() is shown in Figure 6.8. Each section of this code is explained in the following list.

15: Some local variables are declared at the beginning of this function. The dwError variable is a double-word integer used to hold the returned error code for the system function call. The DCB (device control block) structure is very useful for controlling the settings and configurations of the serial port. (Refer to Section 4.2.3 and Table 4.4 in Chapter 4 for a more detailed description of this structure.) All configuration of the serial devices are performed by this structure. A variable of the PortDCB structure is declared here in order to use this structure within the function. ecStatus is a variable of the enum structure ERR_CODE; it is used to hold the returned status of the user-defined function call. An initial value of OK is assigned to this variable. COMMTIMEOUTS is another useful data structure that is used to set the timeout values for the serial devices. The dBit variable is used to temporarily store the data bits value.

```
   ERR_CODE PortInitialize(char* lpszPortName, pSerialCreate pCreate)
   {
15    DWORD  dwError;
      DCB       PortDCB;
      ERR_CODE ecStatus = OK;
      COMMTIMEOUTS   CommTimeouts;
      UCHAR  dBit;
16    if (PortCreateflg)                        // check if the port has been created...
      {
         msg("Port has been initialized!");
         return  ecStatus;
      }
17    hPort = CreateFile(lpszPortName,          // Pointer to the name of the port
                     GENERIC_READ | GENERIC_WRITE,  // Access (read/write) mode
                     0,                  // Share mode
                     NULL,               // Pointer to the security attribute
                     OPEN_EXISTING,      // How to open the serial port
                     0,                  // Port attributes
                     NULL);              // Handle to port with attribute to copy
      // If it fails to open the port, return error.
18    if ( hPort == INVALID_HANDLE_VALUE )
      {
          // Could not open the port.
          dwError = GetLastError();
          msg("Unable to open the port");
          CloseHandle(hPort);
          return EC_FOPEN;
      }
19    PortCreateflg = TRUE;
      PortDCB.DCBlength = sizeof(DCB);

      // Get the default port setting information.
20    GetCommState(hPort, &PortDCB);

      // Change the DCB structure settings.
21    PortDCB.BaudRate = pCreate->lBaudRate;    // Current baud
      PortDCB.fBinary  = TRUE;                  // Binary mode; no EOF check
      PortDCB.fParity  = FALSE;                 // Disable parity checking.
      PortDCB.fOutxCtsFlow = FALSE;             // No CTS output flow control
      PortDCB.fOutxDsrFlow = FALSE;             // No DSR output flow control
22    PortDCB.fDtrControl = DTR_CONTROL_ENABLE; // DTR flow control type
      PortDCB.fDsrSensitivity = FALSE;          // DSR sensitivity
      PortDCB.fTXContinueOnXoff = FALSE;        // XOFF continues Tx
      PortDCB.fOutX = FALSE;                    // No XON/XOFF out flow control
      PortDCB.fInX  = FALSE;                    // No XON/XOFF in flow control
      PortDCB.fErrorChar = FALSE;               // Disable error replacement.
      PortDCB.fNull = FALSE;                    // Disable null stripping.
23    PortDCB.fRtsControl = RTS_CONTROL_ENABLE; // RTS flow control
      PortDCB.fAbortOnError = FALSE;            // Do not abort reads/writes on error.
      dBit = (UCHAR)pCreate->lDataBits;         // Assign data bits
24    PortDCB.ByteSize = dBit;                  // Number of bits/bytes, 4-8
      PortDCB.Parity = NOPARITY;                // 0-4=no,odd,even,mark,space
      PortDCB.StopBits = ONESTOPBIT;            // 0,1,2 = 1, 1.5, 2
```

FIGURE 6.8 The `PortInitialize()` function. *(continued)*

16: Our program must determine whether the port has been opened and configured. It determines this by inspecting the status of the Boolean variable `PortCreateflg`.

17: If the port has not been opened, we use the system function `CreateFile()` to open a new port. Seven arguments are included in this function call. The first one is the port

```
    // Configure the port according to the specifications of the DCB structure.
25  if (!SetCommState (hPort, &PortDCB))
    {
        // Could not set the timeout parameter.
        dwError = GetLastError();
        msg("Unable to configure the serial port");
        return EC_INVAL_CONFIG;
    }
    // Retrieve the time-out parameters for all read and write operations on the port.
26  GetCommTimeouts(hPort, &CommTimeouts);
    // Change the COMMTIMEOUTS structure settings.
27  CommTimeouts.ReadIntervalTimeout = MAXDWORD;
    CommTimeouts.ReadTotalTimeoutMultiplier = 0;
    CommTimeouts.ReadTotalTimeoutConstant = 0;
    CommTimeouts.WriteTotalTimeoutMultiplier = 10;
    CommTimeouts.WriteTotalTimeoutConstant = 1000;
    // Set the time-out parameters for all read and write operations on the port.
28  if (!SetCommTimeouts (hPort, &CommTimeouts))
    {
        // Could not set the port timeout parameter.
        dwError = GetLastError();
        msg("Unable to set the time-out parameters");
        return  EC_TIMEOUT_SET;
    }
29  return  ecStatus;
}
```

FIGURE 6.8 The `PortInitialize()` function.

name in text format (for example, "COM1"). The second parameter is used to indicate the open mode of the port. The `GENERIC_READ|GENERIC_WRITE` statement indicates that the port can perform reading and writing operations. The third parameter is the share mode. A `0` means that the port cannot be shared with other threads. The fourth argument is used to indicate the security attribute; it is used to determine whether the returned port handle can be inherited by child processes. If this parameter is `NULL`, then the handle cannot be inherited. The next parameter is the creation mode that is used to indicate actions that should be taken on files that exist and actions to be taken when files do not exist. The opened file is mapped to the associated serial port or device. If the file (port) does not exist, the `OPEN_EXISTING` parameter will indicate that the opening has failed. The sixth parameter is used to indicate whether the opening has additional attributes. A `0` means that there are no additional attributes for the file opening. The final parameter specifies a handle with `GENERIC_READ` access to a template file. The template file supplies attributes and extended attributes for the file being created.

18: If the system function `CreateFile()` is successful, an opened file handler should be returned. This handler will function as a unique ID for the opened port. If the function fails, an `INVALID_HANDLE_VALUE` message is returned. To get the exact error code, the `GetLastError()` system function is executed, and the error message is displayed on the screen. The `CloseHandle()` system function may be called to close the opened port if it is still opened. The user-defined error code `EC_FOPEN` is returned to the calling function to indicate this error.

19: The Boolean variable `PortCreateflg` is set to `True` if the port is opened successfully. Next we need to configure the port with the `DCB` structure. The `DCBLength` parameter needs to be filled, so the `sizeof` operator is used to get the length of the DCB structure.

20: To use the `DCB` structure for configuring the serial port, we must first obtain the default `DCB` structure by calling the system function `GetCommState()`. Two parameters are included in this function call. The first is the port handler obtained from `CreateFile()`, and the second is the `DCB` structure variable `PortDCB`, which returns the default `DCB` structure.

21: After the default `DCB` structure is obtained, we can assign new values to the elements of that structure based on our applications. The baud rate is assigned to the `BaudRate` element in the `DCB`. Other assignments are explained in the associated comments. Two elements are important to us: `fDtrControl` and `fRtsControl`. Because the serial port interface applied in this project is not configured with normal serial communication mode, the handshaking signals cannot be used as normal interfacing signals as they would with a traditional serial port. These handshaking signals should be set to `DTR_CONTROL_ENABLE` and `RTS_CONTROL_ENABLE`, respectively. Then we can use the extended system function `EscapeCommFunction()` to set or reset those transmission lines directly. These two settings are indicated by the explanation steps 22 and 23 in the Coding.

24: The temporary variable `dBit` is used to pick up and reserve the `data bits` value from the `SerialCreate` structure variable `pCreate`. This value is assigned to the `ByteSize` element in the `DCB` structure.

25: The system function `SetCommState()` is called to configure the port by using the completed `DCB` structure. If this function returns a `False`, which means that the function call has failed, an error message will be displayed and the user-defined error code `EC_INVAL_CONFIG` will be returned to the calling function.

26: Here our program gets the default timeout structure `CommTimeouts` by using the system function `GetCommTimeouts()`.

27: After the default timeout structure is obtained, we can use `SetCommTimeouts()` to set the desired timeout values for the port.

28: If the `SetCommTimeouts()` function fails, an error message is displayed and a user-defined error code, `EC_TIMEOUT_SET`, is returned to the calling function.

29: Finally the running status of the function is returned to the calling function.

We have now completed our examination of the `Setup()` function.

6.2.5.4.3 Designing the Data Reading Functions

The data reading operation is composed of three functions: `ReadData()`, `PortRead()`, and the thread function `ThreadFunc()`.

`ReadData()` can be considered the highest-level function. It is called from within the gateway function to obtain the converted data from the MAX187. `PortRead()` is a second-level function that creates a thread to actually read the data from the MAX187, via the serial port. `ThreadFunc()` is the lowest-level function used to actually collect the data from the hardware.

The reason we need to create a thread to handle data collection from the serial port is that we must prevent any dead cycles that might otherwise be caused by the execution of the system function `WaitCommEvent()`. In normal cases, an event should be created and the system function `WaitCommEvent()` should be signaled if the state of the transmission lines has changed or any software handshaking signal has occurred. In some situations, however, even if a communication event occurs, no signal will be detected by the `WaitCommEvent()` function. In these cases, the program will enter a dead cycle and wait there forever unless we use a thread to handle data collection.

The system function `WaitForSingleObject()` can be executed to monitor the running status of the thread function with the timeout's upper boundary value; a timeout error will be triggered if the `WaitForSingleObject()` has not received any feedback from the thread function during a certain period of time. This means that the thread function has entered a dead cycle. If a timeout error occurs at run time, we can specify what the program should do next, and thus avoid the possible dead cycle.

The body of the `ReadData()` function is shown in Figure 6.9.

```
   int ReadData(void)
   {
30     int ad_data;
       ERR_CODE rc = OK;
       CommPortClass* commClass;
31     commClass = new CommPortClass;
       commClass->iMaxChars = MAX_BYTE;
       commClass->iMaxBits  = MAX_BITS;
32    EscapeCommFunction(hPort, SETDTR);        //Set DTR to disable the SCLK
      EscapeCommFunction(hPort, CLRRTS);        //Reset RTS to disable the CS-bar
33    rc = PortRead(commClass);
      if (rc != 0 && runTIMES != 0)             //wake-up reading error neglected.
         msg("ERROR in PortRead()! ");
34    runTIMES++;
35    fprintf(fp, "%d\n", commClass->pcBuffer);  //Reserve data
36    ad_data = commClass->pcBuffer;
      delete commClass;
37    return ad_data;
   }
```

FIGURE 6.9 The `ReadData()` function.

30: Some local variables are declared here. The `ad_data` variable can be considered a buffer; it is used to reserve the received data from the serial port (or specifically, from the MAX187 A/D converter). The `rc` variable works as a status register to hold the returned running status of the calling function. `commClass` is a pointer variable of the data structure `CommPortClass` defined in the header file.

31: The `new` keyword is used to allocate memory space for the pointer variable `commClass` and to return the starting address of that variable. Two setup parameters, `iMaxChars` and `iMaxBits`, are assigned to the elements of the `commClass` structure variable.

32: The system extended function `EscapeCommFunction()` is executed to set the initial status of two transmission lines, the DTR and the RTS, to disable the SCLK and the CS bar control signals on the MAX187. Both `SETDTR` and the `CLRRTS` are system constants defined in Win32 SDK.

33: The second-level function `PortRead()` is called to retrieve the converted data from the MAX187 A/D converter via the serial port. `commClass` is a structure pointer variable that contains the data collection elements. An error message will be displayed if the function call fails. Note that an `AND` operation with the global `runTIMES` variable is inserted in the logical `IF` condition so that the program skips the first possible reading error. During the initialization stage, `runTIMES` is reset to `0`. If the first `PortRead()` returns an error, the associated conditions are `rc  !=0` and `runTIMES  =0`. Because we try to skip the first reading (the wake-up reading) error, no error message is displayed for these conditions. You will see in step 34 that after the first reading, the global variable `runTIMES` is incremented by `1`, and that these conditions will not be met if the following `PortRead()` encounters any error. This means that all following errors caused by the `PortRead()` will be displayed without skipping.

34: The global variable runTIMES is incremented by 1 to indicate to the program that the following errors are not the errors caused by the first calling of the function PortRead(), and those errors should be displayed if any of them occurs.

35: The received data is stored in the structure variable commClass->pcBuffer, and it is written into a data file by the system function fprintf(). The fp argument is the opened file handler obtained from the Setup() function.

36: The received data (12 bits) is also assigned to the data buffer ad_data. After this assignment, the structure variable commClass will no longer be used. The delete statement is called to delete that structure variable and to clean up the memory space allocated for it.

37: Finally, the data buffer is returned to the calling function as the received data.

The code for the second-level function PortRead() is shown in Figure 6.10.

38: Some local variables are declared inside the local function PortRead(). hThread is a handle used to hold the thread handle when a new thread is created. IDThread is a double-word integer that is used to reserve the thread ID as a new thread is opened. Ret holds the running status of some system functions, such as WaitForSingleObject(), and ExitCode is used to hold the exit code when a thread or an object is terminated. dTimeout is a double-word integer that is used to hold the timeout value. The default value for the upper boundary of the timeout is 500 milliseconds.

39: The system function CreateThread() is called to create a new thread that handles the port reading process. If this call is successful, the returned thread's handle will be assigned to the hThread. A returned value of False means that this function has failed. In this case, an error message will be displayed, and the function will return the error to the calling function. The third argument of this function is the thread function ThreadFunc. This thread function executes the thread. The thread only provides a frame; the actual thread job is performed inside the thread function. The fourth argument, hCommPort, is a pointer variable of the structure CommPortClass; it is very important to this application because it contains all data collection definitions. To pass this structure variable into the thread function, we must place it in this position and in this format. The fifth argument is a system constant that indicates the running status of the thread when it is created. CREATE_SUSPENDED means that the created thread is suspended, and will not run until the ResumeThread() function is executed.

40: A ResumeThread() function is called to begin running the thread function.

41: The system function WaitForSingleObject() is called to monitor the thread function and wait until it is completed. This function indicates when the specified object (thread function) is signaled or when the time-out interval elapses. Two arguments are passed into the function: hThread, which is the thread handle, and dTimeout, which is the value of the timeout's upper boundary. If the function returns WAIT_OBJECT_0, which is the thread handle, it means that the thread function has been executed successfully; in this case, the data is collected and the thread function is terminated automatically as it is completed. No other action is needed in this situation except closing the thread handle with the CloseHandle() system function.

42: If the function returns WAIT_TIMEOUT, it means that a timeout error has occurred and the data collection has failed (that is, no event was signaled). Two steps are needed in this situation. First we need to retrieve the exit code of the thread function by calling the system function GetExitCodeThread(). If the exit code indicates that the thread

```
/*****************************************************************************
 * NAME:     PortRead()
 * PGRMR:  Y. Bai
 *****************************************************************************/
ERR_CODE PortRead(CommPortClass *hCommPort)
{
38      HANDLE hThread;                    // handler for port read thread
        DWORD  IDThread;
        DWORD  Ret, ExitCode;
        DWORD  dTimeout = 500;             // define time out value: 500 ms.
        ERR_CODE ecStatus = OK;
39      if (!(hThread = CreateThread(NULL,                    // no security attributes
                        0,                                    // use default stack size
                        (LPTHREAD_START_ROUTINE) ThreadFunc,
                        (LPVOID)hCommPort,                    // parameter to thread function
                        CREATE_SUSPENDED,                     // creation flag - suspended
                        &IDThread) ) )                        // returns thread ID
       {
            msg("Create Read Thread failed");
            return EC_CREATE_THREAD;
       }
40     ResumeThread(hThread);                                 // start thread now
41     Ret = WaitForSingleObject(hThread, dTimeout);
       if (Ret == WAIT_OBJECT_0)
       {    // data received & process it...need to do nothing because the data
            // has been stored in the hCommPort in Thread Func. Close thread handle
            CloseHandle(hThread);
        }
42      else if (Ret == WAIT_TIMEOUT)
       {
            // time out happened, warning & kill thread
            Ret = GetExitCodeThread(hThread, &ExitCode);
            if (ExitCode == STILL_ACTIVE)
            {
                TerminateThread(hThread, ExitCode);
                CloseHandle(hThread);
                return EC_RECV_TIMEOUT;
            }
43          else
            {
                CloseHandle(hThread);
                msg("ERROR in GetExitCodeThread: != STILL_ACTIVE ");
                ecStatus = EC_EXIT_CODE;
            }
         }
         else
        {
             msg("ERROR in WaitFor SingleObject ");
             ecStatus = EC_WAIT_SINGLEOBJ;
        }
44      return  ecStatus;
}
```

FIGURE 6.10 The `PortRead` function.

function still runs (`STILL_ACTIVE`), the function `TerminateThread()` is executed to stop the thread function and to close the thread by calling the function `CloseHandle()`. If the exit code of the thread is not equal to `STILL_ACTIVE`, which means that the thread function has been terminated, we can directly close the thread by calling the function `CloseHandle()`.

43: If the function returns other values, which means that some other error has occurred during the function call, an error message is displayed and the function returns this error to the calling function.

44: The running status of the function `ecStatus` is returned to the calling function.

The code for the thread function, `ThreadFunc()`, is shown in Figure 6.11.
Each section of this code is explained in the following list.

45: All local variables are declared at the beginning of this function. The Boolean variable `fDone` works as a condition variable for the `while` loop that waits for the communication events to occur during the data collection process. `ad_data` works as a data buffer to store a single collected data. The double-word variable `dwModemStatus` works as an argument to be passed into the system function `GetCommModemStatus()`, and the returned status of the associated transmission line is stored in this argument. The variable `dwCommModemStatus` works in a similar way as the variable `dwModemStatus` did, and it returns the associated event status as the function `WaitCommEvent()` is called.

46: A casting operation (`CommPortClass*`) is performed to convert the argument `hCommPorts` that has a `void*` data type into the `CommPortClass*` structure type. This cast is necessary because the argument `hCommPorts` has a `void*` data type. Any argument included in a thread function must be in a `void*` data type without any exception. In order to use that structure, we must use a cast operator to convert the argument to the desired data type.

TIP: When passing an argument with a different data type into a `thread function`, the data type of the passed argument must be `void*`. Inside the `thread function`, in order to use the argument, the program must use a cast operator to convert the argument back to the desired data type.

47: The extended system function `EscapeCommFunction()` is called to set the RTS line to `HIGH`, which will enable the MAX187 to begin data conversion. (Refer to Figure 6.3). The RTS line is connected to the CS-bar input on the MAX187 via the inverter MAX220. A `HIGH` in RTS produces a `LOW` on the CS-bar.

48: After data conversion starts, we need to monitor the status of the DSR line because this line is connected to the output buffer (DOUT) of the MAX187. The converted data will be transmitted from the output buffer to the serial port serially via this DSR line. (Again, refer to Figure 6.3). We must use the system function `SetCommMask()` to select and mask the desired transmission line. After this setup, an event will be generated as the status of the DSR line is changed; this event can be detected by the function `WaitCommEvent()`. The functions `SetCommMask()` and `WaitCommEvent()` can be considered a pair. They work together to detect the status of a transmission line.

49: The Boolean variable `fDone` is reset to `False` so that it is ready to start the `while` loop.

50: The `while` loop here is used to wait for the event to occur and that event is associated with the desired or masked transmission line. In our case, this event is `EV_DSR`.

51: The system function `WaitCommEvent()` is executed to detect the possible event. If we use this function directly, without a thread function involved, it may cause a dead cycle, and the system could be hung up indefinitely. When this function is included inside

```
   void WINAPI ThreadFunc(void* hCommPorts)
   {
45     BOOL  fDone;
       int      ad_data = 0;
       DWORD  dwModemStatus;
       int   index, nTotRead = 0;
       DWORD  dwCommModemStatus;
       CommPortClass*  CommPorts;
       ERR_CODE ecStatus = OK;
46     CommPorts = (CommPortClass* )hCommPorts;
47     EscapeCommFunction(hPort, SETRTS);  // Set RTS to enable the CS-bar to start A/D
48     SetCommMask(hPort, EV_DSR);  // Specify a set of events to be monitored for the port.
49     fDone = FALSE;
50     while (!fDone)
      {   // Wait for an event to occur for the port.
51        WaitCommEvent(hPort, &dwCommModemStatus, 0);
52        if (dwCommModemStatus & EV_DSR)                // received the DSR event
          {
53           for (index = 0; index < CommPorts->iMaxBits; index++)
             {
54              EscapeCommFunction(hPort, CLRDTR);  //Reset DTR (HIGH in SCLK)
                Delay(10);
55              EscapeCommFunction(hPort, SETDTR);  //Set DTR (LOW in SCLK)
                Delay(10);
56              if (!GetCommModemStatus(hPort, &dwModemStatus))
                {
                   msg("ERROR in GetModemStatus()!");
                   fDone = TRUE;
                   break;
                }
57              if (MS_DSR_ON & dwModemStatus)        //DSR status is HIGH.
                   ad_data = ad_data + 0;
58              else                                  //DSR status is LOW
                   ad_data++;
59              ad_data = ad_data << 1;
             }
60           EscapeCommFunction(hPort, SETDTR);       //Set DTR (LOW in SCLK)
             EscapeCommFunction(hPort, CLRRTS);       //Reset CS to deselect A/D
61           ad_data = ad_data >> 1;
62           CommPorts->pcBuffer = ad_data;
             fDone = TRUE;
             break;
          }
      } // end of while loop
   }
63 void Delay(int  num)
   {
       int k, m, n = 100*num;
64     for (m = 0; m < n; m++)
           k++;
   }
```

FIGURE 6.11 The `Threadfunc` function.

the thread function, a timeout error will occur if no event is signaled during the waiting process.

52: The function `WaitCommEvent()` will be terminated if the desired event occurs. The returned status of the associated transmission line is stored in the argument `dwComm-`

ModemStatus. An AND operation is used to determine whether the desired event, EV_DSR, has occurred.

53: If the EV_DSR is received, a for loop is used to repeatedly collect 12-bit converted data. To retrieve each bit of data, a simulated or an external clock must be provided. This clock is generated by a sequence of instructions.

54: The function EscapeCommFunction() is called to reset the DTR line. This reset is equivalent to assigning a HIGH value to the SCLK input on the MAX187. (Refer to Figure 6.3.) A user-defined function, Delay(), is executed to make this simulated clock stable and ensure that it is received by the SCLK input.

55: Another EscapeCommFunction() is called after this delay to set the DTR line to HIGH, which is equivalent to providing a LOW signal on the SCLK input. Following this set, another delay is inserted. In this way, a completed simulated clock cycle is generated to the SCLK input on the MAX187, and one bit of converted data can be shifted from the output buffer on the MAX187 to the serial port, via the DSR line.

56: Now we need to check the level or status of the DSR line to determine whether a logical 1 or a logical 0 has been received. To do this, we must call the system function GetCommModemStatus(). This function will return the current status of the desired transmission line. An error message will be displayed if this function call encounters any mistake. The function will be terminated and returned to the calling function after an error message is displayed.

57: By using the operation MS_DSR_ON AND dwModemStatus, we can detect whether the value of the DSR line is HIGH or LOW. Note that a HIGH (ON) on the DSR line is associated with a logical 0 because of the MAX220 inverter. In this case, only a 0 is added into the data buffer ad_data.

58: If a LOW status is detected on the DSR line, which is equivalent to a logical 1 on the converted bit, the data buffer ad_data should be increased by 1 in the LSB.

59: The data buffer ad_data is shifted left by one bit to reserve space for the next bit of data. Steps 53 through 59 will be continued until all 12 bits of data have been converted and received.

60: After all 12 bits have been received, the system function EscapeCommFunction() is called to set the DTR line to HIGH, which is equivalent to resetting the SCLK input on the MAX187, and to reset the RTS line to LOW, which is equivalent to assign a HIGH value to the CS-bar on the MAX187 to deselect it. SETDTR and CLRRTS are two system constants used in the Win32 SDK.

61: During the data collection process, the data buffer is totally shifted left by 12 bits. But for a 12-bit data string, shifting left 11 times is enough because the last bit does not need to shift. So a compensation is needed to make this data processing correct. This compensation can be accomplished by shifting the final result right by one bit.

62: The final result is assigned to pcBuffer, which is an element of the data structure CommPortClass, and is then returned to the calling function. The Boolean condition variable fDone is set to True to stop the while loop. The instruction break is unnecessary, but we still use it here to ensure our program's reliability.

63: Delay() is a simple user-defined function; its purpose is to delay processing for a specified period of time. Three local integer variables are declared here.

64: A for loop is used to repeatedly increase the variable k by 1 until n = m.

Now that we have finished the code for our data collection functions, let's take a look at the PortClose() function.

6.2.5.4.4 Designing the PortClose Function

The code for this function is shown in Figure 6.12.

```
/*****************************************************************************
 * NAME:        PortClose
 * DESC:        Interface program to MAX187 Serial A/D converter
 * PGMR:        Y. Bai
 * DATE:        11/26/2003
 *****************************************************************************/
int PortClose()
{
    ERR_CODE rc = OK;
65  if (PortCreateflg)
        CloseHandle(hPort);
66  PortCreateflg = false;
67  fclose(fp);
68  runTIMES = 0;
69  return rc;
}
```

FIGURE 6.12 The `PortClose` function.

65: First we need to determine whether the port has been opened and configured. To do this, we inspect the global Boolean variable `PortCreateflg`. This flag will have been set by the function `Setup()` if the port has been successfully opened and configured. The system function `CloseHandle()` is called to close the port if the port has been opened and configured.
66: After the port is closed, the Boolean variable `PortCreateflg` is reset to `false`.
67: Other cleanup jobs include the closing of the opened file handle `fp` by the system function `fclose()`.
68: Here the global variable `runTIMES` is reset to `0`.
69: Finally the running status of this function is returned to the calling function.

We have finished all the coding for our MEX-file project.

6.2.5.5 Compiling and Building the Target MEX-file

Click the `Build|Build MEX_MAX.dll` menu item from the Visual C++ 6.0 IDE to compile and build the target file `MEX_MAX.dll`. Everything should be OK if your coding is identical with that shown in the preceding sections.

After the target file has been compiled and built, it is located in the `Debug` folder that is under the current project folder. You have three ways to go to invoke this DLL when you run your MATLAB M-functions:

- Copying this DLL file to the default system DLL folder on your machine so the system can locate the DLL file when you want to invoke it from within MATLAB domain. The default system DLL folder is `C:\WINNT\system` for Windows NT/2000 platforms, and `C:\WINDOWS\SYSTEM` for Windows 95/98/Me/XP platforms.
- Copying the target DLL file to your working directory. For example, suppose we develop the MATLAB M-functions in the default user folder (which is named `work` and is located in `C:\MATLAB6p5\work`) and want to run the M-function from that folder to interface the MEX-file. We could copy the DLL file to the `work` folder, where it could be recognized and invoked when you call the DLL from the M-function.
- Creating a user-defined DLL folder and copying the target DLL file to that folder. Note that the user-defined DLL folder must be a searchable folder on the machine, which

means that you should set the path of the DLL to the system configuration file. In Windows 2000 platform, you can set that DLL path by using the `System` icon on the Control Panel and then selecting the `Advanced` tab, clicking the `Environment Variables` button, and selecting `Path` from the `System variables` list. In Windows 95/98/Me platforms, you need to set that DLL path in the `Autoexec.bat` file.

In our application, we copied the target DLL file to our M-function `work` folder because we will develop our MATLAB M-function and run it from that folder.

In the Visual C++ 6.0 workspace, click the `File|Open` menu item and browse to our current project folder, `MEX_MAX`. Double click the `Debug` folder and select `All Files (*.*)` from the `Files of types` box to locate the target file `MEX_MAX.dll`. Select this DLL file and copy it to the MATLAB user-default folder, `C:\MATLAB6p5\work`.

Now we are ready to develop an MATLAB M-function to test this MEX-file from within the MATLAB domain.

6.2.5.6 The Design of the MATLAB M-Function

The purpose of this MATLAB M-function is to call the MEX-file developed in Visual C++ 6.0 IDE to access the serial port, which will then interface with the MAX187 serial A/D converter to collect the converted data. As previously mentioned, after the MEX-file is built, we can call it as a normal M-function from within MATLAB domain. This is very convenient if we want to collect the data in real time and analyze it in the MATLAB domain with the help of MATLAB's mathematical functions and toolboxes.

Open MATLAB 6.5 and create a new M-function; then enter the code that is shown in Figure 6.13. Name this M-function `mexmax.m` and save it in the MATLAB default user folder, `C:\MATLAB6p5\work`. Because we've already stored our MEX-file `MEX_MAX.dll` in this folder, we can directly interface with that target file.

```
% Test calling MEX-File developed in VC++ 6.0 IDE
% MEX-File name: MEX_MAX.DLL
% Y. Bai - 11/21/2003

V = 5.0;          % MAX187 full input voltage is 5.0 V.
S = 4095;         % 12-bit scalar factor is 4095.

PortNum  = 1;
BaudRate = 9600;
DataBits = 8;
StopBits = 1;
Parity   = 0;
Timeout  = 5000;

comPort = [PortNum BaudRate DataBits StopBits Parity Timeout];
[max_data] = MEX_MAX(comPort);
max_data = max_data*V/S;

t = 1:100;
plot(t, max_data, 'b-', t, max_data, 'b.');
grid;

title('MEX-File: MEX-MAX - Interface to Serial A/D Converter - MAX187');
xlabel('Sampling Points - 100 pt.');
ylabel('Real Amplitude');
```

FIGURE 6.13 The MATLAB M-function `mexmax.m`.

This M-function is straightforward. A numeric array, `comPort`, is used to store the serial communication parameters, such as the `port number`, `baud rate`, and `data bits` values. The MEX-file `MEX_MAX()` is called as a normal M-function to access the gateway function defined in that MEX-file and to interface the MAX187 via the serial port. The collected data is returned to another array, `max_data`, that is a 100 × 1 double-data array.

The converted data is multiplied by a scalar factor to get the real output voltage unit. The `Plot()` function is called to plot the received data with the desired label and title.

You can use any mathematical function defined in any toolbox to analyze the collected data in either the time domain or the frequency domain. It is very convenient!

We are now ready to test and run our project.

6.2.5.7 Testing and Running the Project

Make sure that the interface circuit is correctly connected to the serial port and to the MAX187. Turn on the function generator and set the output to `sinusoidal waveform` with an amplitude of up to five volts.

In MATLAB workspace, enter `mexmax` at the command prompt to run our new M-function. The gateway function is invoked, and the low-level functions are called to interface with the serial port to collect the converted data from the MAX187. The debug information is displayed as the program runs, which is shown in Figure 6.14.

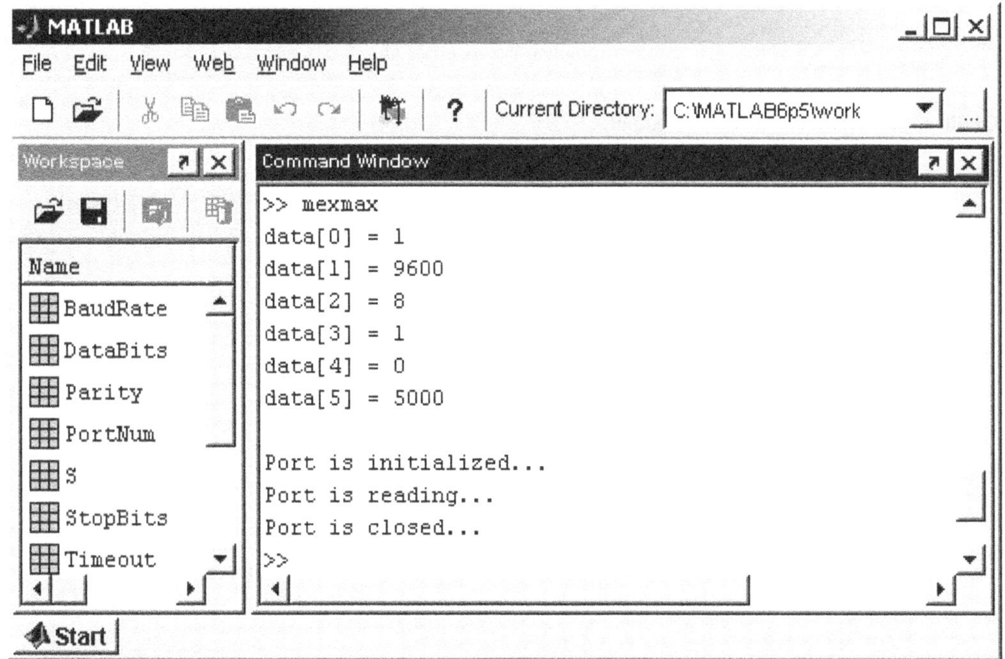

FIGURE 6.14 Running status of the MATLAB M-function.

The plot of the converted data is shown in Figure 6.15. The first waveform is a sinusoidal waveform with a frequency of around 20 Hz.

Now change the output waveform of the function generator to the triangular signal and run the M-function again. The collected data is plotted again; you can see the result in Figure 6.16. Figure 6.17 shows the plotting result when the output waveform of the function generator is a square signal.

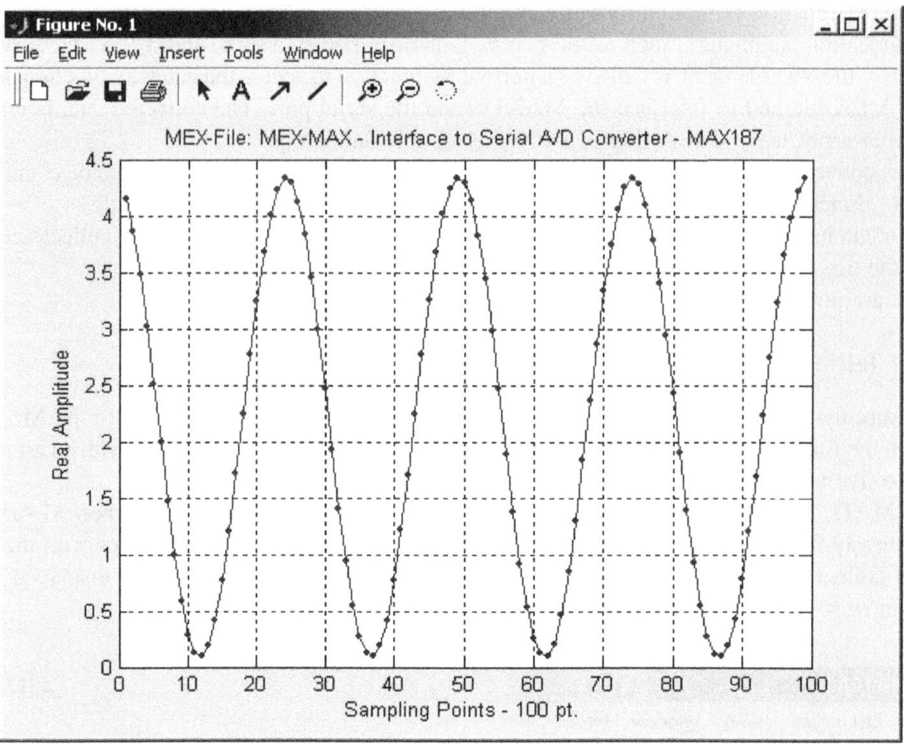

FIGURE 6.15 Sinusoidal waveform output.

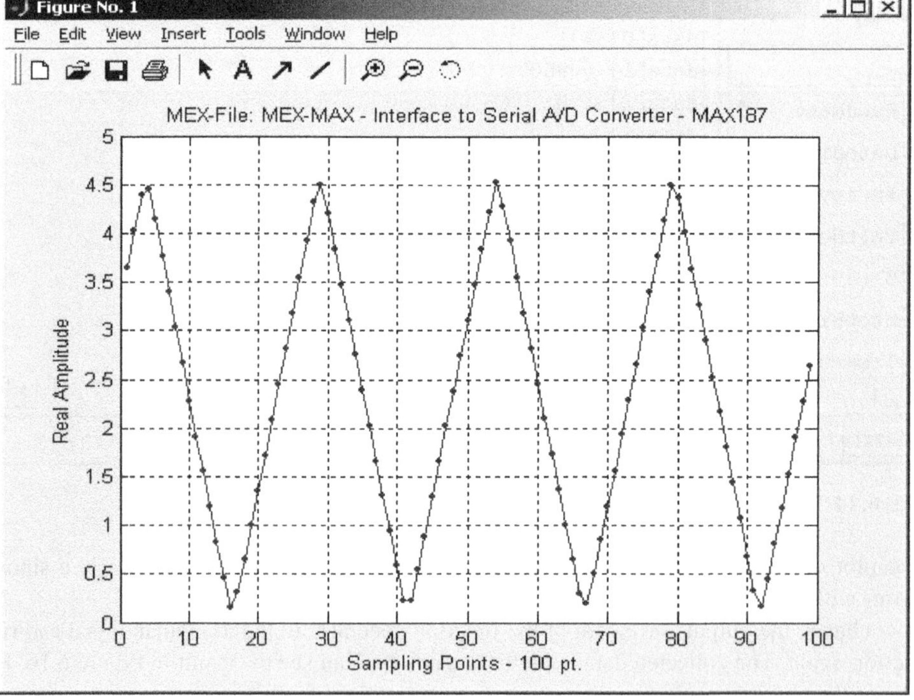

FIGURE 6.16 Triangular waveform output.

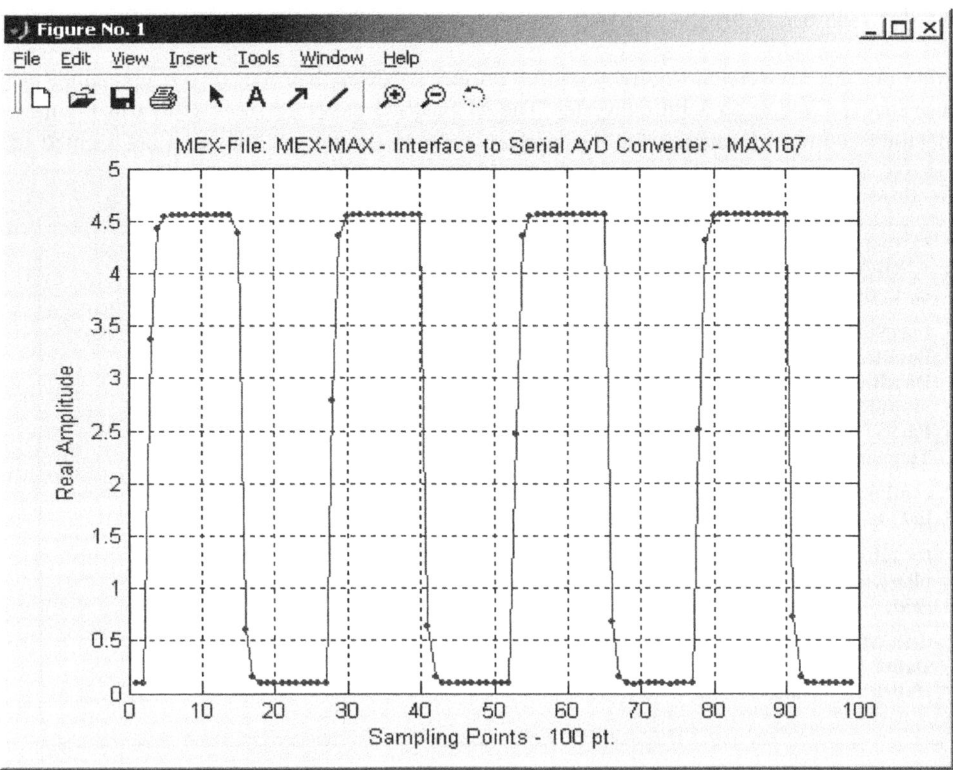

FIGURE 6.17 Square waveform output.

Notice that the output amplitude is the real voltage output amplitude, and that three signals are correctly received and plotted.

By using this project, we can access any kind of low-level hardware via the serial port to communicate with the external devices or equipment. The MEX-file handles low-level interfacing with the device driver and hardware, and returns the data to the M-function developed in MATLAB domain. In this way, we can successfully interface with the hardware via external codes from within the MATLAB workspace.

The complete MEX-file project files, including the header file, source file, definition file, target DLL file, and M-function, are stored in the folder `Chapter 6\MEX_MAX` on the attached CD. You can copy these files and store them to the default MATLAB user folder to run this project on your machine.

Now we will develop a similar project to interface with an 8-bit serial A/D converter, the TLC548.

6.2.6 Creating a MEX-file to Interface with the TLC548 ADC

This project is very similar to the last one, so here we'll provide only a quick review and some highlights.

Refer to Figure 5-48 in Chapter 5 for the detailed description of the interface circuit connection. The serial port we'll use for this project is still COM1. Development of the MEX-file for this project is nearly identical to the same process in the preceding project; The only differences are that a `PortWrite()` function is added into this project and a thread function is deleted. Communication between the serial port and the C++ functions is performed by means of the polling method (as opposed to the event-driven method), and this make the communication easier—but slower.

Note that the conversion accuracy of this project is lower than that of our preceding project because the TLC548 is an 8-bit converter. The M-function `mextlc.m` is shown in Figure 6.18. For detailed coding information for this project, refer to the project files that are located in the `Chapter 6\MEX_TLC` folder on the attached CD.

```
% Test call MEX-File developed in VC++ 6.0 IDE
% MEX-File name: MEX_TLC.DLL
% Y. Bai - 11/18/2003

PortNum  = 1;
BaudRate = 9600;
DataBits = 8;
StopBits = 1;
Parity   = 0;
Timeout  = 5000;

comPort = [PortNum BaudRate DataBits StopBits Parity Timeout];
[ad_data] = MEX_TLC(comPort);

t = 1:100;
plot(t, ad_data, 'b-', t, ad_data, 'b.');
grid;

title('MEX-File: MEX_TLC - Interface to Serial A/D Converter - TLC548');
xlabel('Sampling Points - 100 pt.');
ylabel('Raw Amplitude');
```

FIGURE 6.18 The MATLAB M-function `mextlc.m`.

To run this project, we need to copy the target MEX-file `MEX_TLC.dll` to the MATLAB default user folder, `C:\MATLAB6p5\work`, and then type the name of the M-function, `mextlc`, in the MATLAB workspace. The running status will be displayed, and the collected data will be plotted as a two-dimensional graphic in the MATLAB domain.

The code of this M-function in this project is similar to that of the M-function in the last project, so no additional explanation is needed here.

6.3 USING THE SHARED DLL TO INTERFACE WITH THE SERIAL PORTS

C/C++ programs built into external, shared libraries are easily accessed by MATLAB through a command line interface. This interface gives us the ability to load an external library into MATLAB memory space and then access any of the functions defined therein. Although data types differ between the two language environments, we can usually pass MATLAB types to the C/C++ functions without having to do the work of conversion. MATLAB can handle this issue for us.

This interface also supports libraries containing functions programmed in languages other than C/C++, as long as the functions have a C/C++ interface.

6.3.1 INSTALLING THE LOADLIBRARY INTERFACE

All operating systems provide a collection of functions precompiled into a shared library file (a dynamic link library, or `.dll`, in Windows). These libraries, provided by the operating system and other software vendors, are designed for use by one or more applications running on the system. There is significant value in being able to access the shared library functions from inside the MATLAB environment.

MATLAB 6.5 (R13) provides a way to access functions defined in Win32 Standard Dynamic Link Libraries (DLLs) from the command line in the MATLAB workspace. This feature is only available for users of Windows 98/Me/NT/2000/XP. But you need to download and install the additional software on your machine if you wish to use this feature. Follow these steps to finish this download and installation:

1. Download the installation file `GenericDll_1p1.exe` from this Web site:

   ftp://ftp.mathworks.com/pub/tech-support/solutions/s33513/GenericDll_1p1.exe
2. Save the software to the TEMP folder on your machine.
3. Double-click the downloaded `GenericDll_1p1.exe` file from the TEMP folder to start installing it on your local PC. The `WinZip Self-Extractor` dialog box opens, indicating the version of the update.
4. In the opened dialog box, the default location of the installed MATLAB will be displayed as `C:\MATLAB6p5`. You'll need to install the downloaded software to this folder. If MATLAB is installed in a different directory on your machine, specify that location instead.
5. Click the `Unzip` button to install the interface files in the appropriate directories. After the files are extracted and installed, a new dialog box will open and display a message indicating that 24 files have been successfully unzipped. The installation is complete. Click `OK` to close the installation module.
6. Exit the installation program by clicking `Close` in the `WinZip Self-Extractor` dialog box. The new interface, complete with shared libraries, is now ready for use.
7. To allow MATLAB to recognize the newly installed files, refresh your Toolbox cache by entering `rehash toolboxcache` at the MATLAB command prompt.

The new feature allows us to load a Windows DLL into the MATLAB memory space and then access any of its functions. Because the DLL may contain functions programmed in languages other than C, the DLL must provide a C interface so that we can load and use the functions from within MATLAB.

Although data types differ between MATLAB and the C language environment used to program the DLL, in most cases we can seamlessly pass MATLAB types to the functions in the library. MATLAB handles most of the data conversions necessary for transmitting data to and from the DLL.

Here are some limitations and restrictions that you need to be aware of:

- Currently, the MATLAB Interface with shared libraries is supported on Windows systems only. All Windows shared library files have the file extension `.dll`.
- Passing a `void **` argument (that is, a pointer to a `VOID` pointer) to a function in a shared library is not supported in the current release.
- Passing a complex structure argument (that is, a structure constructed from other structures) to a shared library function is not supported in this release.
- MATLAB does not currently support manipulation (for example, addition, and subtraction) of pointers returned by the functions in a shared library.

Now that we have download and installed the interface, we are ready to use any of the features provided by the software to access the Win32 DLL files.

6.3.2 Loading and Unloading the Shared Library

To allow MATLAB to access the external functions in a shared library, we must first load the library into memory. Once it is loaded, we can request information about any of the functions in the library and call them directly from MATLAB. When the library is no longer needed, we should unload it to conserve memory.

To load a shared library into MATLAB, use the `loadlibrary` function. The syntax for `loadlibrary` is:

```
loadlibrary('shrlib', 'hfile')
```

Here, `shrlib` is the DLL filename for the shared library, and `hfile` is the name of the header file that contains the function prototypes in the DLL.

As an example, we can use `loadlibrary` to load the `MAXDLL` library that is developed later in this section. The first statement below forms the directory specification for the `MAXDLL.h` header file for the C/C++ functions. The second loads the library from `MAXDLL.dll`, also specifying the header file:

```
hfile = ['C:\Book2_Program\Chapter 6\MAXDLL\MAXDLL.h'];
loadlibrary('MAXDLL', hfile);
```

There are also several optional arguments that we can use with `loadlibrary`. You can use the `help loadlibrary` statement to get more information for this issue.

To unload the library and free up the memory space that it occupied, use the `unloadlibrary` function. For example, to unload the library MAXDLL.dll, use

```
unloadlibrary MAXDLL
```

6.3.3 Obtaining Information from the Library

You can use either of two of following functions to obtain information on the functions available in the library that we have loaded:

```
libfunctions('libname')
libfunctionsview('libname')
```

The main difference between these two functions is that `libfunctions` displays the information in the MATLAB workspace (and we can assign its output to a variable), and `libfunctionsview` displays the information graphically in a new window.

To see what functions are available in the `MAXDLL` library, use `libfunctions`, as shown here, specifying the library filename as the only argument. Note that you can use the MATLAB command syntax (with no parentheses or quotes required) when specifying no output variables:

```
libfunctions MAXDLL
Functions in library MAXDLL
PortClose    ReadData    Setup
```

Three functions are available in the library `MAXDLL.dll`.

To list the functions along with their signatures, use the `libfunctions` command with the `-full` switch. Shown here is the MATLAB syntax for calling functions written in C. The data types used in the argument list and return values matching MATLAB types, not C types.

```
libfunctions MAXDLL -full
```

Functions in library MAXDLL:

```
[int32, int32Ptr] Setup(int32Ptr)
int32   ReadData
int32   PortClose
```

The `libfunctionsview` function creates a new window that displays all of the functions defined in a specific library. These methods are listed in Table 6.6.

TABLE 6.6
Functions in the GUI Window

Heading	Description
Return Type	Data types that the method returns
Name	Function name
Arguments	Valid data types for input arguments
Inherited From	Not relevant for shared library functions

MATLAB Technology Menu: *External Interfaces/API, Version 6,* p. 2-5. Reprinted with permission of MathWorks, Inc.

6.3.4 Calling Library Functions and Passing Arguments

Once a shared library has been loaded into MATLAB, we can use the `calllib` function to call any of the functions from that library. We specify the library name, function name, and any arguments that are passed to the function, using this format:

```
calllib('libname', 'funcname', arg1, ..., argN)
```

The following example calls functions from the `MAXDLL` library to test the `Setup()` function:

```
hfile = ['C:\Book2_Program\Chapter 6\MAXDLL\MAXDLL.h'];
loadlibrary('MAXDLL', hfile);
comPort = [PortNum BaudRate DataBits StopBits Parity Timeout];
ret = calllib('MAXDLL', 'Setup', comPort);
```

The argument passed to the `Setup()` function in this example is an integer array with six setup parameters.

To determine which MATLAB data types to use when passing arguments to library functions, see the output of `libfunctionsview` or `libfunctions -full`. These commands list all of the functions found in a particular library, along with specifications of the data types required for each argument. There are a few interesting things to note about the input and output arguments shown in the preceding function listing:

- Many of the arguments (such as `int32, double`) are very similar to their C/C++ counterparts. In these cases, we only need to pass in the MATLAB data types shown for these arguments.
- Some arguments in C/C++ (such as `**double` or predefined structures) are quite different from standard MATLAB data types. In these cases, we usually have the option of either passing a standard MATLAB type and letting MATLAB convert it, or converting the data using such MATLAB functions as `libstruct` and `libpointer`. (See the next section for details about data conversion between MATLAB and the external library).

- C/C++ input arguments are often passed by reference. Although MATLAB does not support passing by reference, we can create MATLAB arguments that are compatible with C/C++ references. In the preceding listing shown, these are the arguments with names ending in `Ptr` and `PtrPtr`.
- C/C++ functions often return data in input arguments passed by reference. MATLAB creates additional output arguments to return these values. Note in the listing that all input arguments ending in `Ptr` or `PtrPtr` are also listed as outputs.
- When we pass an array that has more than two dimensions, the shape of the array may be altered by MATLAB. To ensure that the array retains its shape, we store the size of the array before making the function call, and then use this size to reshape the output array to the correct dimensions, as in this example:

```
vs = size(vin)      % Store the original dimensions
vs =
     2   5   2
vout = calllib('shrlibsample', 'multDoubleArray', vin, 20);
size(vout)          % Dimensions have been altered
ans =
     2   10
vout = reshape(vout, vs); % Restore the array to 2-by-5-by-2
size(vout)
ans =
     2   5   2
```

- We use an empty array, `[]`, to pass a `NULL` parameter to a library function that supports optional input arguments. This is valid only when the argument is declared as a `Ptr` or `PtrPtr` (as shown by `libfunctions` or `libfunctionsview`).

6.3.5 Converting Data Between MATLAB and External Functions

This section describes how MATLAB handles conversion of argument data and how we can convert the data manually when that would be more efficient.

TIP: Under most conditions, data passed to and from external library functions is automatically converted by MATLAB to the data type expected by the external function. However, you may choose, in certain situations, to convert some of your argument data manually.

Procedures for which you might find this advantageous include:

- Passing the same piece of data to a series of library functions, it probably makes more sense in this scenario to convert the data once manually at the beginning rather than having MATLAB convert it automatically on every call. This will save time on unnecessary copy and conversion operations.
- Passing large structures. We can save memory by creating MATLAB structures that match the shape of the C/C++ structures used in the external function instead of using generic MATLAB structures. The `libstruct` function creates a MATLAB structure modeled from a C/C++ structure taken from the library.
- Incorporating an external function that uses more than one level of referencing (for example, `double **`). In this situation, we need to pass a reference (constructed by the `libpointer` function) rather than having MATLAB convert the data type automatically.

In the following sections, we'll discuss data conversion based on the different data types.

6.3.5.1 Primitive Data Types

All standard scalar C data types are supported by the shared library interface.

These are listed in Tables 6.7 and 6.8, along with their equivalent MATLAB types. MATLAB uses the type from the right column for arguments having the C type shown in the left column. Table 6.8 shows extended MATLAB types in the right column. These are instances of the MATLAB `lib.pointer` class rather than standard MATLAB data types.

TABLE 6.7
Mapping of Data Types Between C and MATLAB

C Type (on a 32-bit computer)	Equivalent MATLAB Type
Char, byte	int8
Unsigned char, byte	uint8
Short	int16
Unsigned short	8int16
int, long	int32
Unsigned int, unsigned long	uint32
Float	single
Double	double
Char *	string (1 × n char array)

MATLAB Technology Menu: *External Interfaces/API, Version 6*, p. 2-12. Reprinted with permission of MathWorks, Inc.

TABLE 6.8
Extended MATLAB Data Types

C Type (on a 32-bit computer)	Extended MATLAB Type
integer pointer types (int *)	(u)int(*size*)Ptr
float *	singlePtr
double *	doublePtr
mxArray *	MATLAB array
void *	voidPtr
type **	Same as *type*Ptr with an added Ptr (e.g., double ** is double PtrPtr)

MATLAB Technology Menu: *External Interfaces/API, Version 6*, p. 2-12. Reprinted with permission of MathWorks, Inc.

6.3.5.2 Converting Data to Other Primitive Data Types

For primitive types, MATLAB automatically converts any argument to the data type expected by the external function. This means that we can pass a `double` argument to a function that expects to receive a byte (an 8-bit integer), and MATLAB will perform the conversion. For example, examine the C function with types of: `short`, `int` and `double`:

```
double addMixedTypes(short x, int y, double z)
{
    return (x + y + z);
}
```

We can simply pass all of these arguments as type `double` from MATLAB. MATLAB determines what type of data is expected for each argument and performs the appropriate conversions:

```
calllib('shrlibsample', 'addMixedTypes', 127, 33000, pi)
ans =
     3.3130e+004
```

6.3.5.3 Converting Data to References

MATLAB also automatically converts an argument passed by value into an argument passed by reference when the external function prototype defines the argument as a reference. So a MATLAB `double` argument passed to a function that expects `double *` is converted to a `double` reference by MATLAB.

The function addDoubleRef is a C function that takes an argument of type `double *`:

```
double addDoubleRef(double x, double *y, double z)
{
   return (x + *y + z);
}
```

Call the function with three arguments of type `double`, and MATLAB handles the conversion:

```
calllib('shrlibsample', 'addDoubleRef', 1.78, 5.42, 13.3)
ans =
       20.5000
```

6.3.5.4 Converting to Strings

For arguments that require `char *`, we can pass a MATLAB string (a character array). This C function incorporates a `char *` input argument:

```
char* stringToUpper(char *input)
{
char *p = input;
if (p != NULL)
 while (*p!=0)
    *p++ = toupper(*p);
return input;
}
```

`libfunctions` shows that we can use a MATLAB string for this input.

```
libfunctions shrlibsample  -full
[string, string] stringToUpper(string)
```

Create a MATLAB character array, `str`, and pass it as the input argument:

```
str = 'This was a Mixed-Case string';
calllib('shrlibsample', 'stringToUpper', str)
ans =
        THIS WAS A MIXED-CASE STRING
```

TIP: Although the input argument that MATLAB passes to `stringToUpper` resembles a reference to type `char`, it is not a true reference data type. That is, it does not contain `str`, the address of the MATLAB character array. When the function runs, it returns the correct result but does not modify the value in `str`. If we now examine `str`, we see that its original value is unchanged:

```
str =

 This was a mixed-case string.
```

6.3.5.5 Converting and Passing Structures

For library functions that take structure arguments, we need to pass structures that have the same field names as those in the structure definitions in the library. To determine the names and the data types of structure fields, we can do one of the following:

- Consult the documentation that was provided with the library.
- Look for the structure definition in the header file that we used to load the library into MATLAB.

We can also determine the field names of an externally defined structure from within MATLAB using the following procedure. When we create and initialize the structure, we don't necessarily have to match the data types of numeric fields. MATLAB converts to the correct numeric type for us when we make the call using the `calllib` function. To get the structure field names, follow these steps:

1. Use `libfunctionsview` to display the signatures for all functions in the library we are using. `libfunctionsview` shows the names of the structures used by each function. For example, when we type `libfunctionsview shrlibsample`, MATLAB opens a new window displaying function signatures for the `shrlibsample` library. The line showing the `addStructFields` function reads:

   ```
   double addStructFields (c_struct)
   ```

2. If the function we are interested in takes a structure argument, we can get the structure type from the `libfunctionsview` display, and invoke the `libstruct` function on that type. `libstruct` returns an object that is modeled on the structure as defined in the library:

   ```
   s = libstruct('c_struct');
   ```

3. Get the names of the structure fields from the object returned by `libstruct`:

   ```
   get(s)
   p1: 0
   p2: 0
   p3: 0
   ```

4. Initialize the fields to the values we want to pass to the library function and make the call using `calllib`:

   ```
   s.p1 = 476; s.p2 = -299; s.p3 = 1000;
   calllib('shrlibsample', 'addStructFields', s)
   ```

   We can use an integrated method to set the structure, as in this example:

   ```
   set(s, 'p1', 100, 'p2', 180, 'p3', 220);
   ```

6.3.5.5.1 Passing a MATLAB Structure

As with other data types, when an external function takes a structure argument (such as a C structure), we can pass a MATLAB structure to the function in its place. Structure field names must match field names defined in the library, but data types for numeric fields do not have to match. MATLAB converts each numeric field of the MATLAB structure to the correct data type.

The sample shared library, `shrlibsample`, defines the following C structure and function:

```
struct c_struct
   {
      double p1;
      short  p2;
      long   p3;
   };
   double addStructFields(struct c_struct st)
   {
      double t = st.p1 + st.p2 + st.p3;
      return t;
}
```

The following code passes a MATLAB structure, `sm`, with three double fields to `addStruct-Fields`. MATLAB converts the fields to the `double`, `short`, and `long` data types defined in the C structure, `c_struct`.

```
sm.p1 = 476; sm.p2 = -299; sm.p3 = 1000;
calllib('shrlibsample', 'addStructFields', sm)
ans =
     1177
```

6.3.5.5.2 Passing a `libstruct` Object

When a structure is passed to an external function, MATLAB makes sure that the structure matches the library's definition for that structure type. It must contain all the necessary fields defined for that type and each field must be of the expected data type. For any fields that are missing in the structure being passed, MATLAB creates an empty field of that name and initializes its value to zero. For any fields that have a data type that doesn't match the structure definition, MATLAB converts the field to the expected type.

When working with small structures, it is efficient enough to have MATLAB do this work. We can pass the original MATLAB structure with `calllib` and let MATLAB handle the conversions automatically. However, when working with repeated calls that pass one or more large structures, it is sometimes better to convert the structure manually before making any calls to external functions. In this way, we save processing time by converting the structure data only once, at the beginning of the program, rather than at each function call. We can also save memory if the fields of the converted structure take up less space than the original MATLAB structure.

We can convert a MATLAB structure to a C-like structure derived from a specific type definition in the library in one step. We call the `libstruct` function, passing in the name of the structure type from the library, and the original structure from MATLAB. The syntax for `libstruct` is

```
s = libstruct('structtype', mlstruct)
```

The value *s* returned by this function is called a *libstruct* object. Although it is truly a MATLAB object, it handles much like a MATLAB structure. The fields of this new structure are derived from the external structure type specified by *structtype* in this syntax.

For example, to convert a MATLAB structure, `sm`, to a `libstruct` object, `sc`, that is derived from the `c_struct` structure type, we would use

```
sm.p1 = 476; sm.p2 = -299; sm.p3 = 1000;
sc = libstruct('c_struct', sm);
```

The original structure, sm, has fields that are all of type double. The object, sc, returned from the libstruct call has fields that match the c_struct structure type. These fields are double, short, and long.

We can also create an empty libstruct object by calling libstruct with only the structtype argument. This constructs an object with all the required fields and with each field initialized to zero:

```
s = libstruct('structtype')
```

6.3.5.5.3 Using the Structure as an Object

The value returned by libstruct is not a true MATLAB structure. It is actually an instance of a class called lib.c_struct, as seen by examining the output of whos:

```
whos sc
Name       Size          Bytes  Class
sc         1x1           lib.c_struct
Grand  total  is  1  element  using  0  bytes
```

The fields of this structure are implemented as properties of the lib.c_struct class. We can read and modify any of these fields using MATLAB's object-oriented functions set and get:

```
sc = libstruct('c_struct');
set(sc, 'p1', 100, 'p2', 150, 'p3', 200);
get(sc)
    p1: 100
    p2: 150
    p3: 200
```

We can also read and modify the fields by simply treating them like any other MATLAB structure fields:

```
sc.p1 = 23;
sc.p1
ans =
     23
```

6.3.5.6 Creating References

We can pass most arguments to an external function by value, even when the prototype for that function declares the argument to be a reference. However, at times it is useful to pass a MATLAB argument that is the equivalent of a C reference.

To construct a reference, we would use the libpointer function with this syntax:

```
p = libpointer('type', 'value')
```

To give an example, create a pointer pv to an int16 value. In the first argument to libpointer, enter the type of pointer we are creating. The type name is always the data type (int16, in this case) suffixed by the letters Ptr:

```
v = int16(485);
pv = libpointer('int16Ptr', v);
```

The value returned, pv, is actually an instance of a MATLAB class called lib.pointer. The lib.pointer class has the properties Value and DataType.

We can read and modify these properties with the MATLAB `get` and `set` functions:

```
get(pv)
Value: 485
DataType: 'int16Ptr'
```

The `lib.pointer` class also has two methods, `setdatatype` and `reshape`, that are described in the next section.

```
methods(pv)
```

Methods for class lib.pointer:

```
setdatatype reshape
```

The following example illustrates constructing and passing a pointer to type `double`, and then interpreting the output data. The function `multDoubleRef` takes one input that is a reference to a `double` and returns the same.

```
double *multDoubleRef(double *x)
{
*x *= 5;
return x;
}
```

Next we construct a reference, `xp`, to input data, `x`, and verify its contents:

```
x = 15;
xp = libpointer('doublePtr', x);
get(xp)
Value: 15
DataType: 'doublePtr'
```

Now we can call the function and check the results:

```
calllib('shrlibsample', 'multDoubleRef', xp);
get(xp, 'Value')
ans =
     75
```

TIP: Note that the reference `xp` is not a true pointer, as it would be in a language such as C. That is, even though it was constructed as a reference to `x`, it does not contain the address of `x`. So, when the function executes, it modifies the `Value` property of `xp`, but it does not modify the value in `x`. If we now examine `x`, we find that its original value is unchanged:

```
x =
     15
```

In the preceding example, the result of the function called from MATLAB could be obtained by examining the modified input reference. But this function also returns data in its output arguments that may be useful.

The MATLAB prototype for this function (returned by `libfunctions -full`), indicates that MATLAB returns two outputs. The first is an object of class `lib.pointer`; the second is the `Value` property of the `doublePtr` input argument:

```
libfunctions shrlibsample -full
[lib.pointer, doublePtr] multDoubleRef(doublePtr)
```

Run the example once more, but this time check the output values returned:

```
x = 15;
xp = libpointer('doublePtr', x);
[xobj, xval] = calllib('shrlibsample', 'multDoubleRef', xp)
xobj =
lib.pointer
xval =
      75
```

Like the input reference argument, the first output, `xobj`, is an object of class `lib.pointer`. We'll examine this output, but first we need to initialize its data type and its size as these factors are undefined when returned by the function. We use the `setdatatype` method defined by class `lib.pointer` to set the data type to `doublePtr` and the size to `1-by-1`.

Once initialized, we can examine the `xobj` output:

```
setdatatype(xobj, 'doublePtr', 1, 1)
get(xobj)
ans =
     Value: 75
DataType: 'doublePtr'
```

The second output, `xval`, is a `double` copied from the value of input `xp`.

6.3.5.7 Creating a Structure Reference

Creating a reference argument to a structure is not much different than using a reference to a primitive type. The function shown here takes a reference to a structure of type `c_struct` as its only input. It returns an output argument that is the sum of all fields in the structure. It also modifies the fields of the input argument.

```
double addStructByRef(struct c_struct *st)
{
double t = st->p1 + st->p2 + st->p3;
st->p1 = 5.5;
st->p2 = 1234;
st->p3 = 12345678;
return t;
}
```

Although this function expects to receive a structure reference input, it is easier to pass the structure itself and let MATLAB convert it to a reference. Our next example passes a MATLAB structure, `sm`, to the function `addStructByRef`. MATLAB returns the correct value in the output, `x`, but does not modify the contents of the input, `sm`, because `sm` is not a reference.

```
sm.p1 = 476; sm.p2 = -299; sm.p3 = 1000;

x = calllib('shrlibsample', 'addStructByRef', sm)
x =
    1177
```

The next part of the example passes the structure by reference. This time, the function receives a pointer to the structure and is then able to modify the structure fields.

```
sp = libpointer('c_struct', sm);
calllib('shrlibsample', 'addStructByRef', sp)
ans =
      1177
get(sp, 'Value')
ans =
p1: 5.5000
p2: 1234
p3: 12345678
```

6.3.5.8 Creating Reference Pointers

Arguments that have more than one level of referencing (for instance, `uint16 **`) are referred to here as *reference pointers*. In MATLAB, these argument types are named with the suffix `PtrPtr` (for example, `uint16PtrPtr`). See the output of `libfunctionsview` or methods `-full` for examples of this type.

When calling a function that takes a reference pointer argument, we can use a reference argument instead and MATLAB will convert it to a reference pointer. For example, the external `allocateStruct` function expects a `c_structPtrPtr` argument:

```
libfunctions shrlibsample -full
c_structPtrPtr allocateStruct(c_structPtrPtr)
```

Here is the C function:

```
void allocateStruct(struct c_struct **val)
{
*val=(struct c_struct*) malloc(sizeof(struct c_struct));
(*val)->p1 = 12.4;
(*val)->p2 = 222;
(*val)->p3 = 333333;
}
```

Although the prototype says that a `c_structPtrPtr` is required, we can use a `c_structPtr` and let MATLAB do the second level of conversion. We create a reference to an empty structure argument and pass it to `allocateStruct`:

```
sp = libpointer('c_structPtr');
calllib('shrlibsample', 'allocateStruct', sp)
get(sp)
ans =
      Value: [1x1 struct]
DataType: 'c_structPtr'
get(sp, 'Value')
ans =
p1: 12.4000
p2: 222
p3: 333333
```

When we are done, we return the allocated memory:

```
calllib('shrlibsample', 'deallocateStruct', sp)
```

You can select your data conversion style based on your applications. For the simplest data conversion, we should try to use MATLAB and allow it to automatically complete this conversion.

In the next section, we use an actual example to demonstrate the use of some of methods for loading and calling a shared DLL, developed in the Visual C++ 6.0 domain, that will interface between a serial A/D converter MAX187 via the serial port COM1.

6.3.6 Calling a Shared DLL

In this section, we use a real example to discuss how to call Win32 DLL files from within MATLAB workspace. The example is designed as an interface between the MATLAB M-function and a DLL developed in Visual C++ 6.0 domain. By using this interface, we can easily access the serial devices such as MAX187 serial A/D converter via the RS-232 serial port from within the MATLAB domain. (The hardware components and their connection are detailed in Figure 6.3 and Table 6.5. Refer to those items to finish the circuit connection between the serial port COM1 and the MAX187.)

6.3.6.1 Developing a Standard Win32 Dynamic Link Library

This DLL is similar to the MEX-file we developed in the preceding section, but several differences are listed here:

- Unlike the MEX-file, no gateway function is needed for this Win32 DLL. All interface functions should be exported to MATLAB and they can be accessed by MATLAB directly.
- No Definition file is needed in this DLL. By using the macro definition for each DLL function, we can export each of them to MATLAB.
- The tasks performed by the gateway function in the MEX-file developed in the last section were calling the different C/C++ functions to access the low-level devices and perform the setup, configuring the serial port, reading data from the MAX187, and closing the port. In our new project, these functions have been translated to a MATLAB M-function.

We must develop our Win32 DLL file before we can call it from within MATLAB workspace. Launch Visual C++ 6.0 and open a new project with the following properties:

- Project Type: `Win32 Dynamic-Link Library`
- Project Name: `MAXDLL`
- Location: `C:\Book2_Program\Chapter 6`

Open a new C/C++ header file for the newly created project; name the file `MAXDLL.h`. Then open a new C++ source file and name it `MAXDLL.cpp`.

Open Windows Explorer to copy the following files into the current project folder, `C:\Book2_Program\Chapter 6\MAXDLL`:

- matrix.h
- mex.h
- tmwtypes.h
- libmex.lib

The top three header files are located in the default MATLAB installation folder `C:\MATLAB6p5\extern\include`, and the last library file is located in the folder `C:\MATLAB6p5\extern\lib\win32\microsoft\msvc60`.

Now return to the Visual C++ 6.0 IDE and click `Project|Add To Project|Files` from the menu, and add all the copied files into the current project. We want to develop a portable project, so we need to copy all of these files into our current project folder. Then, when we compile and build the project, we won't need to set any links or paths to any external folders.

The purpose of copying the library file `libmex.lib` and the header file `mex.h` is that we still want to use the `mex*` functions to display the debug information in the MATLAB domain as our project runs. However, another two header files are required by the `mex.h` header file.

Let's take a look at the header file `MAXDLL.h`.

6.3.6.1.1 Designing the Header File

Open the newly created header file `MAXDLL.h` and enter the code that is shown in Figure 6.19.

This header file and the header file we developed in the last section are quite similar, so only the differences are explained here. (For more details about coding of the header file, refer to Figure 6.4.)

A: We use the macro `#define` to define the DLL export heading as `DllExport`. Once this definition has been made, we can directly use this symbol in front of each DLL function to export it.

B: The `DllExport` symbol is applied for each export DLL function. Three functions are needed to export to MATLAB: `Setup()`, `ReadData()`, and `PortClose()`. The `Setup()` function is used to configure and initialize the serial port. `ReadData()` is used to collect the converted data from the MAX187. `PortClose()` is used to clean up the serial communication environment and close the opened serial port.

After using this macro definition, we do not need the `Definition` file to export our DLL function; `DllExport` will export the function. Click the `File|Save` menu item to save this header file.

6.3.6.1.2 Designing the Source File

We will now create the source file for our DLL project.

6.3.6.1.2.1 Coding of the Setup Function

Open the newly created source file `MAXDLL.cpp` and enter the code that is shown in Figure 6.20.

(This code is very similar to that of the `Setup()` function we developed in the preceding section. Refer to Figure 6.8 for detailed explanations. The only difference between this example and the previous one is the function signature).

C: `Setup()` is a DLL function that should be exported to the MATLAB M-function, so `DllExport` is applied in front of the function to allow it to be exported.

D: Because the argument type is `integer`, no cast operation is needed in front of each element of the argument.

6.3.6.1.2.2 Coding the `ReadData()` Function

The code for the `ReadData()` function is shown in Figure 6.21.

This function is basically identical to the `ReadData()` function we developed in the last section. The only difference is the function signature.

E: The symbol `DllExport` is applied in front of this function to indicate that the function should be exported to the MATLAB domain.

(Refer back to Figure 6.9 for details about coding this function.)

The local function `PortRead()` and the thread function `ThreadFunc()` are shown in Figures 6.22 and 6.23, respectively.

These two functions are identical to those developed in the preceding section, so no explanation is made here. (Refer back to Figures 6.10 and 6.11 for details coding about these functions.)

```
/*****************************************************************************
 * NAME       : MAXDLL.h
 * DESC.      : Header file for MAXDLL.cpp (MAX187 A/D Converter) loadlibrary call
 * PGRMER.    : Y. Bai
 * DATE       : 11/26/2003
 *****************************************************************************/
#include <Windows.h>
#include "mex.h"
#ifndef _MAXDLL_H_
#define _MAXDLL_H_

#define MAX_BYTE                1
#define MAX_BITS                12
#define MAX_DATA                100
#define MAX_STRING              256
#define NOPARITY                0
#define ONESTOPBIT              0
#define RTS_CONTROL_DISABLE     0x00
#define RTS_CONTROL_ENABLE      0x01
#define DTR_CONTROL_DISABLE     0x00
#define DTR_CONTROL_ENABLE      0x01

#define msg(info)    MessageBox(NULL, info, "", MB_OK)

#ifdef __cplusplus
extern "C" {
#endif  /* __cplusplus */
typedef struct
{
   ULONG  ulCtrlID;
   char   cEcho;
   char   cEORChar;
   long   lTimeout;
   long   lBaudRate;
   long   lDataBits;
} SerialCreate, *pSerialCreate;

typedef struct
{
   int  pcBuffer;            /* received data buffer */
   int  iMaxChars;           /* the number of the maximum characters */
   int  iMaxBits;            /* the number of the maximum bits */
   int  piNumRcvd;           /* the number of the received data */
   char cTermChar;           /* the termination character */
} CommPortClass;
typedef enum
{
    OK       = 0,        /* no error */
    EC_TIMEOUT,
    EC_FOPEN,
    EC_INVAL_CONFIG,
    EC_TIMEOUT_SET,
    EC_RECV_TIMEOUT,
```

FIGURE 6.19 Header file for the MAXDLL project. *(continued)*

```
    EC_EXIT_CODE,
    EC_WAIT_SINGLEOBJ,
    EC_INVALIDPORT,
    EC_WRITE_FAIL,
    EC_CREATE_THREAD,
    EC_GETMODSTATUS,
    EC_UNKNOWNERROR
} ERR_CODE;

FILE*     fp;
HANDLE    hPort;
char*     sPortName;
bool      PortCreateflg = false;
int       runTIMES = 0;
/*-----------------------------------------------------------*/
A  #define DllExport   __declspec( dllexport )
/*-----------------------------------------------------------*/
/* DLL Interface functions */
B  DllExport int Setup(int* pCom);
DllExport int ReadData();
DllExport int PortClose();
/* Local functions */
ERR_CODE PortInitialize(char* lpszPortName, pSerialCreate pCreate);
ERR_CODE PortRead(CommPortClass *hCommPort);
void   WINAPI ThreadFunc(void* hCommPorts);
void   Delay(int num);

#ifdef __cplusplus
}
#endif  /* __cplusplus */
#endif
```

FIGURE 6.19 Header file for the MAXDLL project.

At this point, we have finished creating our source file code. Click the `Build|Build MAXDLL.dll` menu item from the Visual C++ 6.0 IDE to compile and build the DLL file.

The target file `MAXDLL.dll` is located in the `Debug` folder under the current project folder. Copy that DLL file to the default MATLAB user folder, `C:\MATLAB6p5\work`; later we need to call it from this folder by using an M-function.

6.3.6.2 Developing a MATLAB M-Function to Call the DLL

Now we need to develop a MATLAB M-function to access the DLL file `MAXDLL.dll` that we developed earlier. Open a new M-function named `loadmax.m`, and enter the code that is shown in Figure 6.24.

Each section of this code is explained in the following list.

- F: The scalar factors are defined at the beginning of this function. `N` represents the maximum number of sampling points for the data collection. The `max_data` is a 1×100 array used to store the received data from the MAX187.
- G: The serial port setup parameters are declared here. These parameters are the default configuration parameters for the serial port.

```
/*****************************************************************************
 * NAME        : MAXDLL.cpp
 * PGRMER.     : Y. Bai
 *****************************************************************************/
#include <stdio.h>
#include <stdlib.h>
#include "MAXDLL.h"
#define  DEBUG
C   DllExport int Setup(int* pCom)
    {                                               //pCom[1] = baud_rate
        ERR_CODE rc = OK;                           //pCom[2] = data_bits
        pSerialCreate pParam;                       //pCom[3] = stop_bit
        fp = fopen("max_dll.dat", "w");             //pCom[4] = parity
        pParam = new SerialCreate;                  //pCom[5] = timeout_value
D       pParam->lBaudRate = pCom[1];
        pParam->lDataBits = pCom[2];
        pParam->lTimeout  = pCom[5];
        #ifdef DEBUG
        mexPrintf("data[%d] = %d\n", 0, pCom[0]);
        mexPrintf("data[%d] = %d\n", 1, pCom[1]);
        mexPrintf("data[%d] = %d\n", 2, pCom[2]);
        mexPrintf("data[%d] = %d\n", 3, pCom[3]);
        mexPrintf("data[%d] = %d\n", 4, pCom[4]);
        mexPrintf("data[%d] = %d\n", 5, pCom[5]);
        #endif
        switch(pCom[0])
        {
            case 1: sPortName = "COM1";  break;
            case 2: sPortName = "COM2";  break;
            case 3: sPortName = "COM3";  break;
            case 4: sPortName = "COM4";  break;
            default: return EC_INVALIDPORT;
        }
        if (PortCreateflg)
        {
            msg("Port has been Setup ");
            return rc;
        }
        rc = PortInitialize(sPortName, pParam);
        if (rc != 0)
            msg("ERROR in PortInitialize()!");
        #ifdef DEBUG
        else
            mexPrintf("\nPort is initialized...\n");
        #endif
        delete pParam;
        PortCreateflg = true;
        return rc;
    }
```

FIGURE 6.20 The coding of the `Setup` function. *(continued)*

```
ERR_CODE PortInitialize(char* lpszPortName, pSerialCreate pCreate)
{
    DWORD  dwError;
    DCB       PortDCB;
    ERR_CODE ecStatus = OK;
    COMMTIMEOUTS   CommTimeouts;
    UCHAR  dBit;
    if (PortCreateflg)                          // check if the port has been created...
    {
        msg("Port has been initialized!");
        return  ecStatus;
    }
    hPort = CreateFile(lpszPortName,            // Pointer to the name of the port
                       GENERIC_READ | GENERIC_WRITE,  // Access (read/write) mode
                       0,                       // Share mode
                       NULL,                    // Pointer to the security attribute
                       OPEN_EXISTING,// How to open the serial port
                       0,                       // Port attributes
                       NULL);                   // Handle to port with attribute to copy
    // If it fails to open the port, return error.
    if ( hPort == INVALID_HANDLE_VALUE )
    {
        // Could not open the port.
        dwError = GetLastError();
        msg("Unable to open the port");
        CloseHandle(hPort);
        return EC_FOPEN;
    }
    PortCreateflg = TRUE;
    PortDCB.DCBlength = sizeof(DCB);
    // Get the default port setting information.
    GetCommState(hPort, &PortDCB);
    // Change the DCB structure settings.
    PortDCB.BaudRate = pCreate->lBaudRate;   // Current baud
    PortDCB.fBinary  = TRUE;                    // Binary mode; no EOF check
    PortDCB.fParity  = FALSE;                   // Disable parity checking.
    PortDCB.fOutxCtsFlow = FALSE;               // No CTS output flow control
    PortDCB.fOutxDsrFlow = FALSE;               // No DSR output flow control
    PortDCB.fDtrControl = DTR_CONTROL_ENABLE;  // DTR flow control type
    PortDCB.fDsrSensitivity = FALSE;            // DSR sensitivity
    PortDCB.fTXContinueOnXoff = FALSE;         // XOFF continues Tx
    PortDCB.fOutX = FALSE;                      // No XON/XOFF out flow control
    PortDCB.fInX  = FALSE;                      // No XON/XOFF in flow control
    PortDCB.fErrorChar = FALSE;                 // Disable error replacement.
    PortDCB.fNull = FALSE;                      // Disable null stripping.
    PortDCB.fRtsControl = RTS_CONTROL_ENABLE; // RTS flow control
    PortDCB.fAbortOnError = FALSE;              // Do not abort reads/writes on error.
    dBit = (UCHAR)pCreate->lDataBits;           // Assign data bits
    PortDCB.ByteSize = dBit;                    // Number of bits/bytes, 4-8
```

FIGURE 6.20 The coding of the `Setup` function. *(continued)*

```
    PortDCB.Parity = NOPARITY;              // 0-4=no,odd,even,mark,space
    PortDCB.StopBits = ONESTOPBIT;          // 0,1,2 = 1, 1.5, 2
// Configure the port according to the specifications of the DCB structure.
    if (!SetCommState (hPort, &PortDCB))
    {
        // Could not set the timeout parameter.
        dwError = GetLastError();
        msg("Unable to configure the serial port");
        return EC_INVAL_CONFIG;
    }
    // Retrieve the time-out parameters for all read and write operations on the port.
    GetCommTimeouts(hPort, &CommTimeouts);
    // Change the COMMTIMEOUTS structure settings.
    CommTimeouts.ReadIntervalTimeout = MAXDWORD;
    CommTimeouts.ReadTotalTimeoutMultiplier = 0;
    CommTimeouts.ReadTotalTimeoutConstant = 0;
    CommTimeouts.WriteTotalTimeoutMultiplier = 10;
    CommTimeouts.WriteTotalTimeoutConstant = 1000;
    // Set the time-out parameters for all read and write operations on the port.
    if (!SetCommTimeouts (hPort, &CommTimeouts))
    {
        // Could not set the port timeout parameter.
        dwError = GetLastError();
        msg("Unable to set the time-out parameters");
        return  EC_TIMEOUT_SET;
    }
    return  ecStatus;
}
```

FIGURE 6.20 The coding of the `Setup` function.

E

```
DllExport int ReadData()
{
    int ad_data;
    ERR_CODE rc = OK;
    CommPortClass* commClass;
    commClass = new CommPortClass;
    commClass->iMaxChars = MAX_BYTE;
    commClass->iMaxBits  = MAX_BITS;
    EscapeCommFunction(hPort, SETDTR);      //Set DTR to disable the SCLK
    EscapeCommFunction(hPort, CLRRTS);      //Reset RTS to disable the CS-bar
    rc = PortRead(commClass);
    if (rc != 0 && runTIMES != 0)           //wake-up reading error neglected.
      msg("ERROR in PortRead()! ");
    runTIMES++;
    fprintf(fp, "%d\n", commClass->pcBuffer);   //Reserve data
    ad_data = commClass->pcBuffer;
    delete  commClass;
    return  ad_data;
}
```

FIGURE 6.21 The coding of the `ReadData` function.

```
/*****************************************************************************
 * NAME:     PortRead()
 * PGRMR:  Y. Bai
 *****************************************************************************/
ERR_CODE PortRead(CommPortClass *hCommPort)
{
    HANDLE hThread;                     // handler for port read thread
    DWORD  IDThread;
    DWORD  Ret, ExitCode;
    DWORD  dTimeout = 500;              // define time out value: 500 ms.
    ERR_CODE ecStatus = OK;
    if (!(hThread = CreateThread(NULL,                  // no security attributes
                    0,                                  // use default stack size
                    (LPTHREAD_START_ROUTINE) ThreadFunc,
                    (LPVOID)hCommPort,                  // parameter to thread function
                    CREATE_SUSPENDED,                   // creation flag - suspended
                    &IDThread) ) )                      // returns thread ID
    {
        msg("Create Read Thread failed");
        return EC_CREATE_THREAD;
    }
    ResumeThread(hThread);                              // start thread now
    Ret = WaitForSingleObject(hThread, dTimeout);
    if (Ret == WAIT_OBJECT_0)
    {   // data received & process it...need to do nothing because the data
        // has been stored in the hCommPort in Thread Func. Close thread handle
        CloseHandle(hThread);
    }
    else if (Ret == WAIT_TIMEOUT)
    {
        // time out happened, warning & kill thread
        Ret = GetExitCodeThread(hThread, &ExitCode);
        if (ExitCode == STILL_ACTIVE)
        {
            TerminateThread(hThread, ExitCode);
            CloseHandle(hThread);
            return EC_RECV_TIMEOUT;
        }
        else
        {
            CloseHandle(hThread);
            msg("ERROR in GetExitCodeThread: != STILL_ACTIVE ");
            ecStatus = EC_EXIT_CODE;
        }
    }
    else
    {
        msg("ERROR in WaitFor SingleObject ");
        ecStatus = EC_WAIT_SINGLEOBJ;
    }
    return ecStatus;
}
```

FIGURE 6.22 The `PortRead()` function.

H: The setup parameters are placed into an array `comPort` that will be passed into the DLL function `Setup()` in the next.

I: The header file `hfile` is defined based on the location of the actual header file `MAXDLL.h`. This is our project's header file, and it is located in the folder, `C:\Boo2_Program\Chapter 6\MAXDLL`.

```
void WINAPI ThreadFunc(void* hCommPorts)
{
    BOOL  fDone;
    int      ad_data = 0;
    DWORD  dwModemStatus;
    int  index, nTotRead = 0;
    DWORD  dwCommModemStatus;
    CommPortClass*  CommPorts;
    ERR_CODE ecStatus = OK;

    CommPorts = (CommPortClass* )hCommPorts;

    EscapeCommFunction(hPort, SETRTS);  // Set RTS to enable the CS-bar to start A/D
    SetCommMask(hPort, EV_DSR);  // Specify a set of events to be monitored for the port.
    fDone = FALSE;
    while (!fDone)
    {   // Wait for an event to occur for the port.
       WaitCommEvent(hPort, &dwCommModemStatus, 0);
       if (dwCommModemStatus & EV_DSR)               // received the DSR event
       {
           for (index = 0; index < CommPorts->iMaxBits; index++)
           {
              EscapeCommFunction(hPort, CLRDTR);  //Reset DTR (HIGH in SCLK)
              Delay(10);
              EscapeCommFunction(hPort, SETDTR);  //Set DTR (LOW in SCLK)
              Delay(10);
              if (!GetCommModemStatus(hPort, &dwModemStatus))
              {
                 msg("ERROR in GetModemStatus()!");
                 fDone = TRUE;
                 break;
              }
              if (MS_DSR_ON & dwModemStatus)        //DSR status is HIGH.
                 ad_data = ad_data + 0;
              else                                   //DSR status is LOW
                 ad_data++;
             ad_data = ad_data << 1;
           }
           EscapeCommFunction(hPort, SETDTR);        //Set DTR (LOW in SCLK)
           EscapeCommFunction(hPort, CLRRTS);        //Reset CS to deselect A/D
           ad_data = ad_data >> 1;
           CommPorts->pcBuffer = ad_data;
           fDone = TRUE;
           break;
       }
    } // end of while loop
}
void Delay(int  num)
{
    int l, m, n = 100*num;

    for (m = 0; m < n; m++)
       l++;
}
```

FIGURE 6.23 The `ThreadFunc()` function.

J: The DLL target file `MAXDLL.dll` has been copied into the current MATLAB `work` folder, so we can directly load that library by using the `loadlibrary` function with the library's name and the header file. We also call the `libfunctions` to display all exported DLL functions in that library.

```
    % Load shared library MAXDLL.dll
    % The header file MAXDLL.h is at C:\Book2_Program\Chapter 6\MAXDLL
    % The shared library file MAXDLL.dll is at the current folder - work
    % November 27, 2003
    % Y. Bai
F   V = 5.0;        % MAX187 full input voltage is 5.0 V.
    S = 4095;       % 12-bit scalar factor is 4095.
    N = 100;
    max_data = zeros(1, 100);
G   PortNum  = 1;
    BaudRate = 9600;
    DataBits = 8;
    StopBits = 1;
    Parity   = 0;
    Timeout  = 5000;
H   comPort = [PortNum BaudRate DataBits StopBits Parity Timeout];
I   hfile = ['C:\Book2_Program\Chapter 6\MAXDLL\MAXDLL.h'];
J   loadlibrary('MAXDLL', hfile);
    libfunctions MAXDLL -full
K   ret = calllib('MAXDLL', 'Setup', comPort);
    if ret ~= 0
      ERROR('Error in Setup() calling...');
    end
L   max_data(1) = calllib('MAXDLL', 'ReadData');    % Wake-up reading
    for m = 1:N,
M     max_data(m) = calllib('MAXDLL', 'ReadData');
    end
N   ret = calllib('MAXDLL', 'PortClose');
    if ret ~= 0
      ERROR('Error in PortClose() calling...');
    end
O   max_data = max_data * V/S;
    t = 1:N;
P   plot(t, max_data, 'b-', t, max_data, 'b.');
    grid;
    title('LOAD DLL MAXDLL: - Interface to Serial A/D Converter - MAX187');
    xlabel('Sampling Points - 100 pt.');
    ylabel('Real Amplitude');
Q   unloadlibrary MAXDLL
```

FIGURE 6.24 The MATLAB M-function.

K: The `Setup()` DLL function is called by the `calllib` MATLAB function to configure the serial port. The argument `comPort` is an array containing the setup parameters that are passed into the `Setup()` function to configure the port. An error message is displayed if this function encounters any mistakes.

L: The wake-up reading is executed by calling the `ReadData()` DLL function. This function is used to prevent possible timeout errors when the program accesses the serial port and performs the thread reading. No argument is passed into this function.

M: A `for` loop is used to continuously read back all 100 converted data from the MAX187 via the `ReadData()` DLL function. The received data is stored in the data array `max_data`.

N: After all data has been received, the DLL `PortClose()` function is called by the `calllib` MATLAB function to close the opened serial port. This function call has no argument to be passed. An error message is displayed if the function encounters any mistakes.

O: The received data array is multiplied by the scalar factor to convert the data to the real voltage unit.

P: In the MATLAB domain, we use the `Plot()` function to plot the received data. The title and labels are used to identify our project.

Q: Finally, when data collection is complete and the DLL functions are no longer needed, we call the `unloadlibrary` function to unload the DLL library.

Now we are ready to test and run our project.

6.3.6.3 Testing and Running the DLL Project

Open the MATLAB workspace and enter `loadmax` on the command line to run the M-function. The M-function will call DLL functions to configure the serial port, read data from the MAX187, and close the port when data collection is complete. The DLL functions and the debug information are displayed in the MATLAB workspace, which is shown in Figure 6.25.

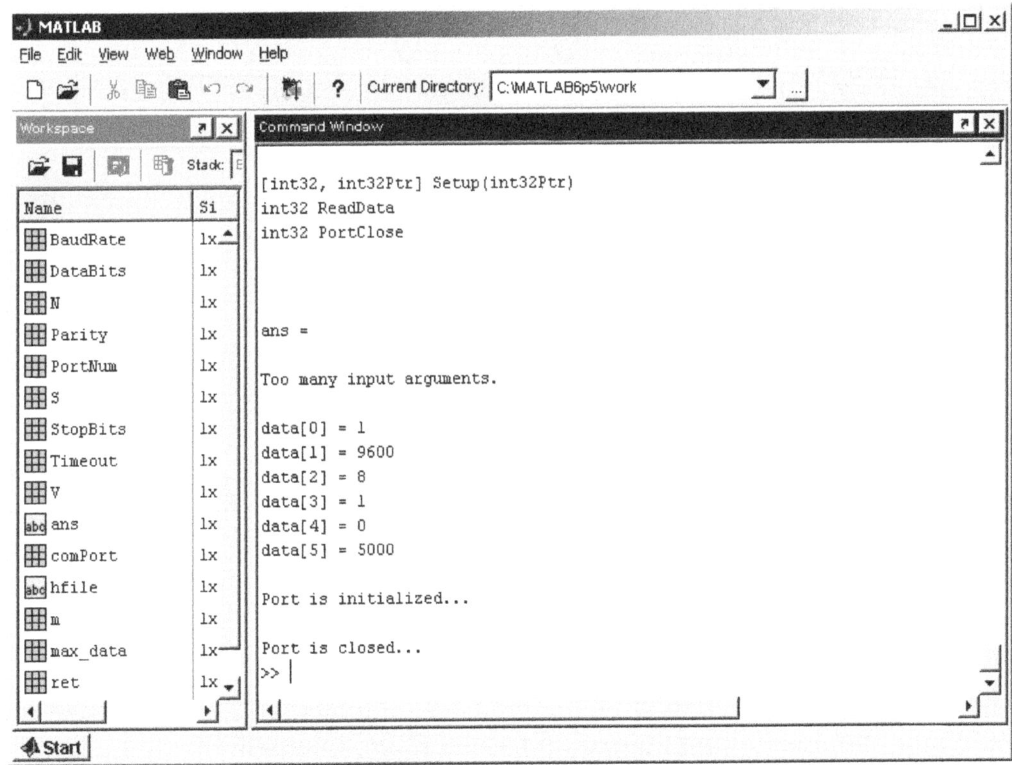

FIGURE 6.25 Running status of the M-function.

Three analog signals are used for this project: sinusoidal, triangular, and square waveforms. All of these signals come from a function generator that is connected to the analog input to the MAX187. The running results for these three waveforms are shown in Figures 6.26, 6.27, and 6.28, respectively.

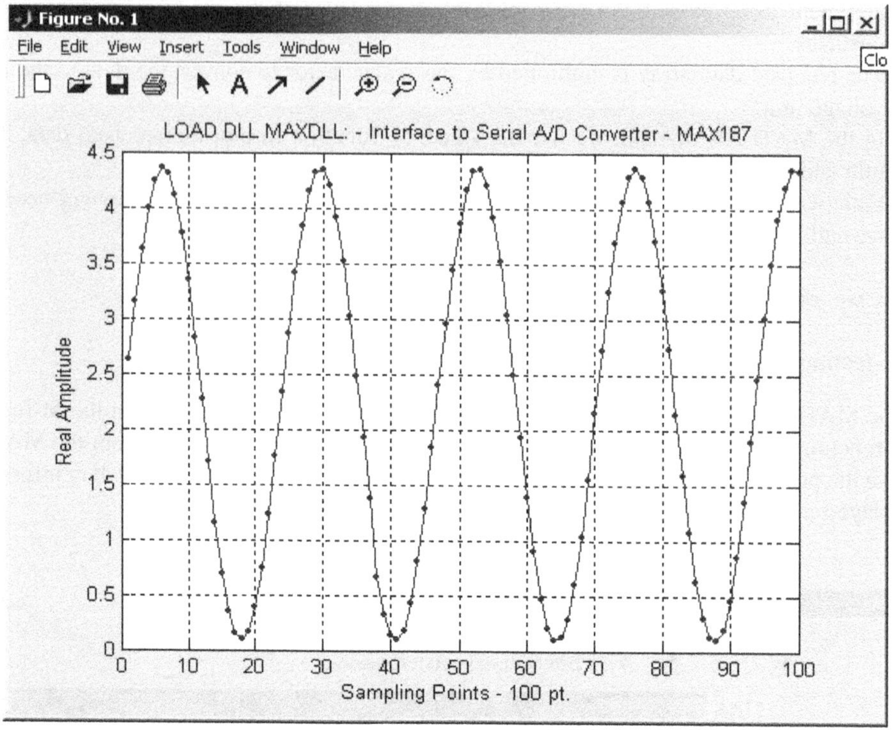

FIGURE 6.26 Sinusoidal waveform input.

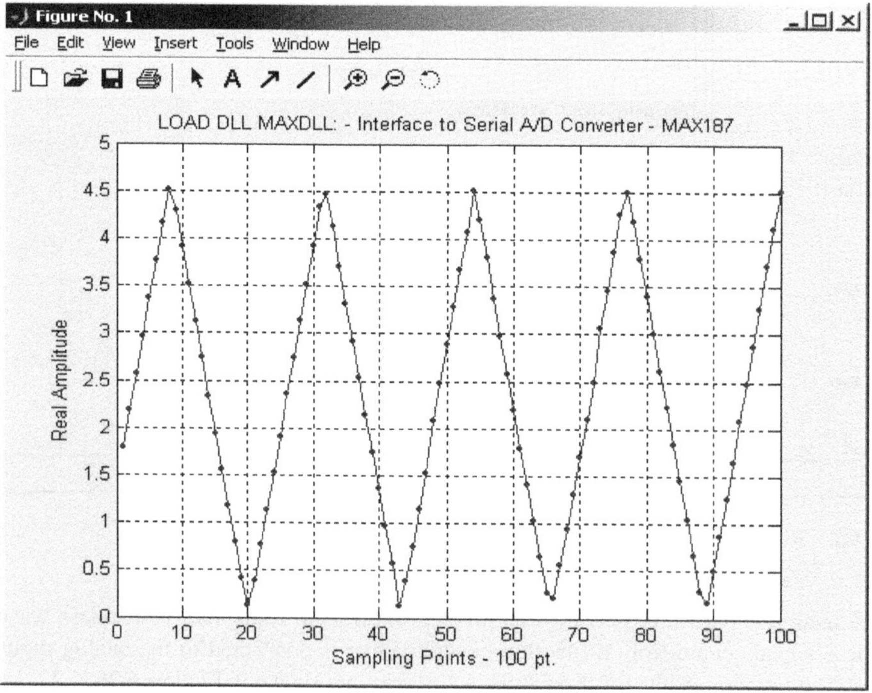

FIGURE 6.27 Triangular waveform input.

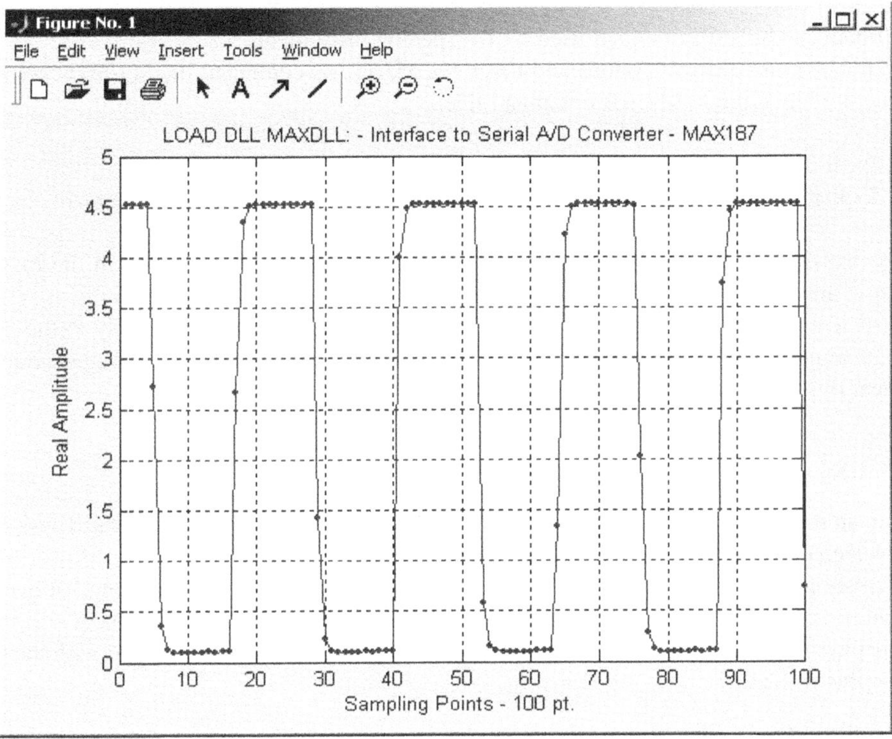

FIGURE 6.28 Square waveform input.

The complete project files, including the DLL source file, the header file, the target file, and the MATLAB M-function file, are stored in the folder `Chapter 6\MAXDLL` on the attached CD. You can copy these files and run them on your own machine. First, however, you must copy and install the target DLL file `MAXDLL.dll` and the MATLAB M-function file `loadmax.m` in the same folder on your machine, and modify the header file directory for the `hfile` function based on the actual location of the DLL header file `MAXDLL.h` in your machine.

You may wish to develop a similar DLL file for the 8-bit A/D converter TLC548 and call it from within the MATLAB domain. The process is very similar to that for our preceding example.

6.4 USING THE SERIAL OBJECT TO INTERFACE WITH THE SERIAL PORTS

In this section, we discuss to use a specific serial object provided by MATLAB to interface to the serial port.

6.4.1 The Instrument Control Toolbox

The Instrument Control Toolbox is a collection of M-file functions built in the MATLAB technical computing environment. The toolbox provides the following features:

- A framework for communicating with instruments that support the GPIB interface, such as IEEE-488, the Virtual Instrument Standard Architecture (VISA) standard, the TCP/IP, and the serial port interface (RS-232, RS-422 or RS-485).
- Functions for transferring data between MATLAB and the specified instrument:

The data can be in binary or text format.
Text data can be any command used by the specific instrument.
The transfer can be synchronous and block the MATLAB command line, or asynchronous and not block the MATLAB command line.

- Event-driven communication
- Tools that facilitate instrument control in an easy-to-use graphical environment

You can view a list of toolbox functions by typing `help instrument` in the MATLAB workspace, and you can view any function body by typing `type func_name`.

Instrument objects are used to access the instruments. They provide a gateway to the features of each instrument, and allow us to control the behavior of the instrument control application. Each instrument object is associated with a specific interface standard.

6.4.2 Creating and Configuring a Serial Port Object

To create an instrument object, we need to call the M-file object creation functions. These M-files are implemented in MATLAB's object-oriented programming style.

To create a serial port object, we need to call the `serial` function. This function needs one argument, `port number`, to identify the port to be created. Each serial port object is associated with one physical serial port. For example, to create a serial port object associated with the COM1 port, use this format:

```
s = serial('COM1');
```

The serial port object `s` now exists in the MATLAB workspace. You can display the created serial port's state and settings in the MATLAB workspace by typing `s`; the following information will appear the MATLAB workspace:

```
>>s = serial('COM1');
>>s
 Serial Port Object : Serial-COM1
 Communication Settings
  Port:               COM1

  BaudRate:           9600

  Terminator:         'LF'
 Communication State
  Status:             closed
  RecordStatus:       off
 Read/Write State
  TransferStatus:     idle
  BytesAvailable:     0
  ValuesReceived:     0
  ValuesSent:         0
```

Before the program can write or read data, the serial port must be configured with the suitable parameters. These serial port parameters should be identical to the configuration parameters of the specific instrument that is supposed to communicate with the serial port. By assigning the associated properties of the serial port object with different setup parameters, we can easily configure the serial port. Table 6.9 lists the most commonly used properties of the serial port.

TABLE 6.9
Serial Port Configuration Properties

Property Name	Description
BaudRate	Baud rate used to transmit data
DataBits	Number of data bits to be transmitted
Parity	Value used for checking parity
StopBits	Number of stop bits used in the data transmission
Terminator	Terminator character

TABLE 6.10
Serial Port Status Properties

Property Name	Indication
BytesAvailable	Number of bytes available in the input buffer.
BytesAvailableFcn	A specified number of bytes are available in the input buffer, or a terminator has been received.
BytesAvailableFcnCount	Number of bytes that must be available in the input buffer to generate a bytes-available event.
BytesAvailableFcnMode	Whether or not the bytes-available event is generated after a specified number of bytes are available in the input buffer, or after a terminator is read.
OutputEmptyFcn	The output buffer is empty.
InputBufferSize	Number of bytes that can be written to the input buffer.
OutputBufferSize	Number of bytes that can be written to the output buffer.
PinStatus	Status of the transmission lines (pins) of the port.
PinStatusFcn	M-file callback function to be executed when the pin status has changed.
ValuesReceived	Total number of values read from the instrument.
ValuesSent	Total number of values written to the instrument.
RecordDetail	Amount of information to be saved to a record file.
RecordMode	Whether data and events are saved to one record file or to multiple record files.
RecordName	Name of the record file.
RecordStatus	Whether data or events are saved to a record file.

In addition to the communication settings properties, MATLAB provides a group of state properties to reflect the current working status of the serial port. These properties are very useful during data communications. Some commonly used status properties are shown in Table 6.10.

By using the status properties of the serial port, we can design event-driven programs that use the M-file `callback` function to monitor and respond to the `BytesAvailable` event. We can thus avoid using the polling method to check the running status of the serial port.

We can access and use any property by using dot notation, just as we did for data in an object in C++ programming. For example, `s.BytesAvailable = 80` would specify that 80 data should be received in the input buffer.

6.4.3 Writing and Reading the Serial Port Object

Communicating with the serial port involves writing and reading data. The serial port object allows for writing and reading of text and binary data to and from the serial port. The functions associated with writing data are shown in Table 6.11.

TABLE 6.11
Functions Associated with Writing Data

Function	Purpose
Fprintf	Writes text data to the serial port
Fwrite	Writes binary data to the serial port
Stopasync	Stopes asynchronous read and write operations
Binblockwrite	Writes binblock data to the instrument

Instrument Control Toolbox User's Guide, Version 1, p. 2-13. Reprinted with permission of MathWorks, Inc.

TABLE 6.12
Functions Associated with Reading Data

Function	Purpose
Fgetl	Reads one line of text from the serial port and discards the terminator
Fgets	Reads one line of text from the serial port and includes the terminator
Fread	Reads binary data from the serial port
Fscanf	Reads data from the serial port and formats it as text
Readasync	Reads data asynchronously from the serial port
Scanstr	Reads data from the serial port, formats it as text, and parses the data
Stopasync	Stops asynchronous read and write operations
Binblockread	Reads binblock data from the instrument

Instrument Control Toolbox User's Guide Version 1, p. 2-19. Reprinted with permission of MathWorks, Inc.

The functions associated with reading data are listed in Table 6-12.

When writing to or reading from the serial ports, a program must follow this operational sequence:

1. The `serial` M-file function must be called to create the serial port object first.
2. The `fopen` M-file function must be called to attach the created serial port object with the physical serial port.
3. Writing or reading operations can be performed via the serial port.
4. When the data communication is complete, the following three M-file functions must be called to clean and close the opened port:

```
fclose
delete
clear
```

The program can also incorporate events and callback functions to perform writing or reading data operations with the serial port.

6.4.4 Event and Callback Functions

The Instrument Control toolbox provides the event-driven and callback functions with the serial port object to support the interface with the serial ports. The most-used event and callback functions are listed in Table 6.10. They can be divided into three categories based on their purposes.

6.4.4.1 The `BytesAvailable` Event and Its Callback Function `BytesAvailableFcn`

To use this event and its associated callback function, we need to set the following properties in the serial port object:

- We set the `BytesAvailableFcnCount` property with the desired number of bytes to be received in the `InputBuffer`. When the number of bytes that have arrived in the `InputBuffer` equals this number, the callback function assigned to the `BytesAvailableFcn` property will be signaled and called.
- We set the `BytesAvailableMode` property to `byte`.
- We assign an M-file callback function to the `BytesAvailableFcn` property. This callback function will be called as the number of bytes received in the `InputBuffer` equals the number in the `BytesAvailableFcnCount` property.

For example, a user-defined M-file function `GetByte()` that works as the callback function to respond to the `BytesAvailable` event might be called as the number of the bytes received in the `InputBuffer` on the COM1 equals 80. This would be accomplished by the following code:

```
s = serial('COM1');
s.BytesAvailableFcn = @GetByte;
s.BytesAvailableFcnCount = 80;
s.BytesAvailableFcnMode = 'byte';
fopen(s);
```

6.4.4.2 The Output Empty Event and Its Callback Function `OutputEmptyFcn`

An output empty event is generated if the output buffer becomes empty. The associated callback function that is assigned to the `OutputEmptyFcn` property can be signaled and called as this event occurs. To use this event and its callback function, we need to develop a user-defined M-file function such as `SendByte()` and assign the name of that M-file function to the `OutputEmptyFcn` property. This would be accomplished by the following code:

```
s = serial('COM1');
s.OutputEmptyFcn = @SendByte;
fopen(s);
```

This code will call the callback function `SendByte()` when the output buffer becomes empty.

6.4.4.3 The `PinStatus` Event and Its Callback Function `PinStatusFcn`

A `PinStatus` event is generated when the status of one of transmission lines has changed. The pin status includes the status of the following transmission lines:

- CD
- CTS
- DSR
- RI

To use the `PinStatus` event and its associated callback function, we need to develop a user-defined M-file function such as `RespPin()` and assign that function to the `PinStatusFcn` property. This would be accomplished by the following code:

```
s = serial('COM1');
s.PinStatusFcn = @RespPin;
fopen(s);
```

6.4.4.4 The Timer Event and Its Callback Function TimerFcn

To use this event and its associated callback function, we need to set up the following properties:

- TimerPeriod
- TimerFcn

The TimerPeriod property is used to specify the time interval between calls to TimerFcn. The time interval is measured in seconds. For example, to periodically call an M-file function TimerProcess() that works as a callback function every 10 seconds, we would use the following code:

```
s = serial('COM1');
s.TimerFcn = @TimerProcess();
s.TimerPeriod = 10
fopen(s);
```

6.4.4.5 The Break Interrupt Event and Its Callback Function BreakInterruptFcn()

The Break Interrupt event is generated when a break occurs in the serial port. The associated callback function would be called if a user-defined M-file function has been assigned to the BreakInterruptFcn property of the serial port object. To use this event and its associated callback function, we need to develop a M-file function as the callback function and assign it to the BreakInterruptFcn property. The following codes show an example to use this event and its callback function BreakProcess():

```
s = serial('COM1');
s. BreakInterruptFcn = @BreakProcess();
fopen(s);
```

6.4.5 Using the Serial Port Object to Perform Data Transmission

In this section, we'll discuss how to interface with the serial port by using a serial port object developed with the Instrument Control toolbox. We'll develop a sample program that demonstrates this interface.

6.4.5.1 Using the Graphical Tool to Create and Configure a Serial Port

In the MATLAB Instrument Control Toolbox, we can use the serial port object serial to create a new port. But here we like to use the graphical toolbox provided by the Instrument Control Toolbox to create and configure a new serial port in MATLAB domain.

To use the graphical toolbox to create and configure a new serial port, type instrcreate command in the MATLAB workspace. The graphical toolbox is displayed, as shown in Figure 6.29.

To create a new serial port, click the Serial Port radio button and click Next to go to the next dialog box, which is shown in Figure 6.30.

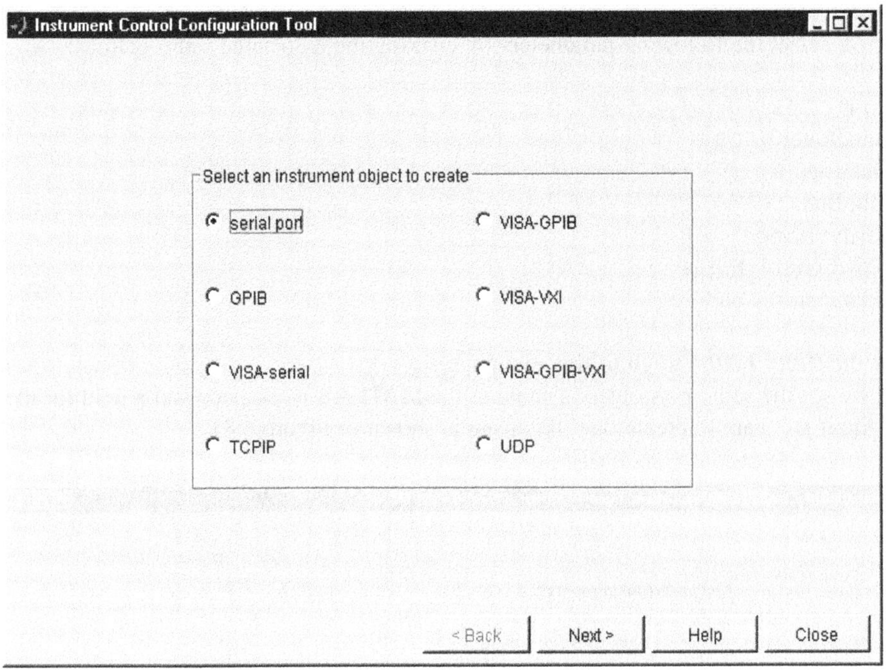

Instrument Control Configuration Tool

Select an instrument object to create

serial port
VISA-GPIB
GPIB
VISA-VXI
VISA-serial
VISA-GPIB-VXI
TCPIP
UDP

< Back Next > Help Close

FIGURE 6.29 The graphical toolbox. *Instrument Control Toolbox User's Guide Ver. 1,* p. 8–56. Reprinted with the permission of MathWorks, Inc.

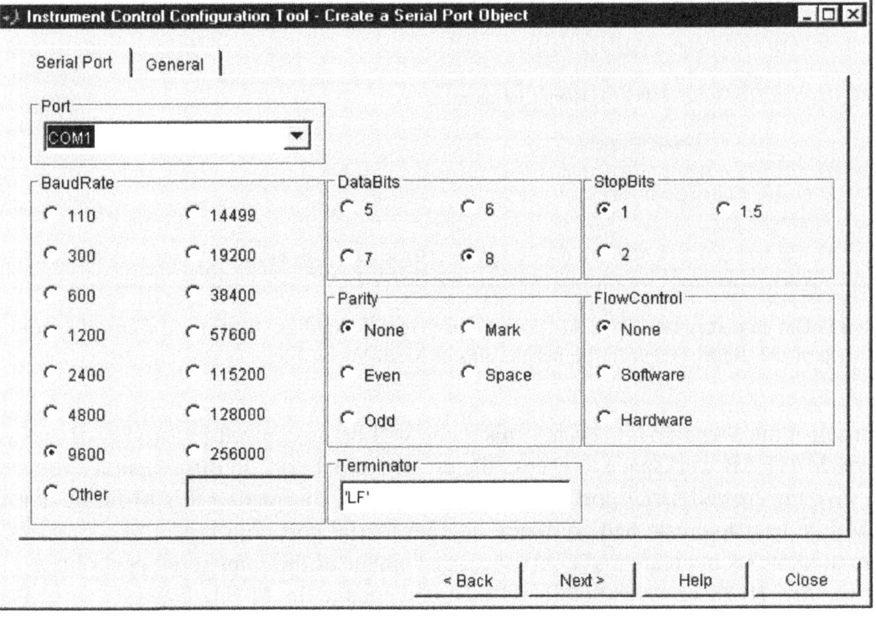

FIGURE 6.30 Graphical interface for the serial port.

You can configure the newly created serial port by setting the different parameters. For this example, we select the following parameters by clicking the associated radio buttons:

- Port: COM1
- BaudRate: 9600
- DataBits: 8
- StopBits: 1
- Parity: None
- FlowControl: None
- Terminator: 'LF'

Click the Next button to go to the next page.

Here we see the serial port object's name in the MATLAB workspace and a field for the name of an M-file if we want to create one; this page is shown in Figure 6.31.

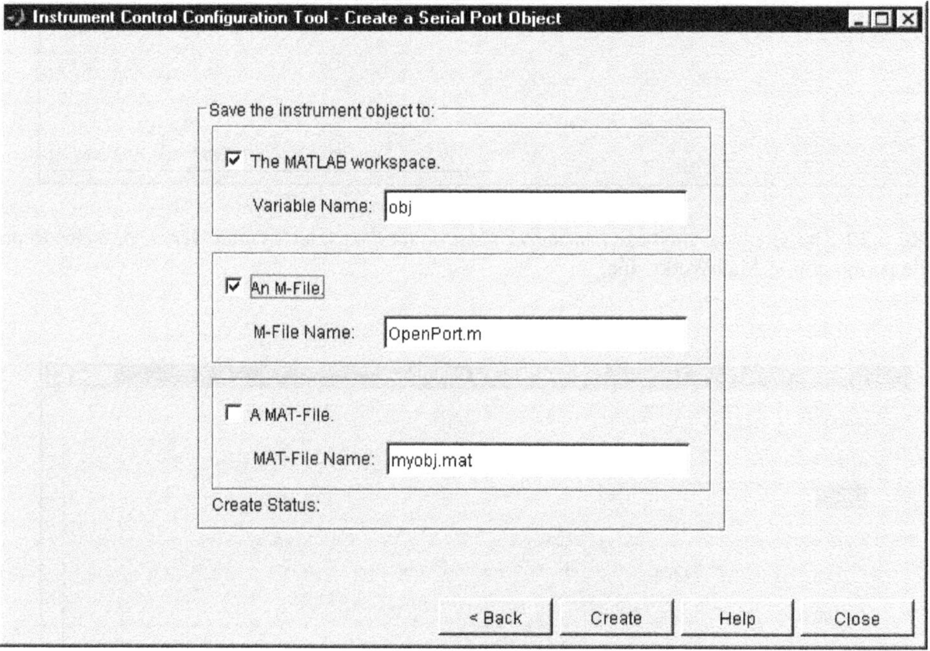

FIGURE 6.31 The Create a Serial Port Object dialog box. *Instrument Control Toolbox User's Guide Ver. 1*, p. 8–59. Reprinted with the permission of MathWorks, Inc.

If you select the Variable Name, this name will be recognized by MATLAB and you can use it in the MATLAB workspace to access the created serial port. In this example, you create an M-file to save the created serial port object. The advantage of creating this M-file is that we can call this M-File later to create and configure any new serial port object. The M-file works just as a template to allow us to create and configure any number of different serial port objects.

Click the An M-File checkbox to select it and change the M-File Name to OpenPort, as shown in Figure 6.31. Click the Create button to create the M-file.

Click the Close button to complete this creation process. In the MATLAB workspace, click the File|Open menu item to open the newly created M-file OpenPort.m. The opened M-file is shown in Figure 6.32.

```
function out = OpenPort(comPort)
% OPENPORT M-Code for creating an instrument object.
%  This is the machine generated representation of an instrument object.
%  This M-file, OPENPORT.M, was generated from the OBJ2MFILE function.
%  A MAT-file is created if the object's UserData property is not empty or if any of the
%  callback properties are set to a cell array or to a function handle. The MAT-file will have
%  the same name as the M-file but with a .MAT extension. To recreate this instrument object,
%  type the name of the M-file, OpenPort, at the MATLAB command prompt.
%  Example: obj = OpenPort;
%  Creation time: 16-Nov-2003 11:27:52
%  Create the instrument object.
obj1 = serial(comPort);
% Set the property values.
set(obj1, 'BaudRate', 9600);
set(obj1, 'BreakInterruptFcn', '');
set(obj1, 'ByteOrder', 'littleEndian');
set(obj1, 'BytesAvailableFcn', '');
set(obj1, 'BytesAvailableFcnCount', 8);
set(obj1, 'BytesAvailableFcnMode', 'byte');
set(obj1, 'DataBits', 8);
set(obj1, 'DataTerminalReady', 'on');
set(obj1, 'ErrorFcn', '');
set(obj1, 'FlowControl', 'none');
set(obj1, 'InputBufferSize', 512);
set(obj1, 'Name', comPort);
set(obj1, 'OutputBufferSize', 512);
set(obj1, 'OutputEmptyFcn', '');
set(obj1, 'Parity', 'none');
set(obj1, 'PinStatusFcn', '');
set(obj1, 'Port', comPort);
set(obj1, 'ReadAsyncMode', 'continuous');
set(obj1, 'RecordDetail', 'compact');
set(obj1, 'RecordMode', 'overwrite');
set(obj1, 'RecordName', 'record.txt');
set(obj1, 'RequestToSend', 'on');
set(obj1, 'StopBits', 1);
set(obj1, 'Tag', '');
set(obj1, 'Terminator', 'LF');
set(obj1, 'Timeout', 10);
set(obj1, 'TimerFcn', '');
set(obj1, 'TimerPeriod', 1);
set(obj1, 'UserData', []);
if nargout > 0
   out = [obj1];
end
```

FIGURE 6.32 The M-file `OpenPort.m`.

By using this M-file, we can modify any setup and configuration parameter for the created serial port based on our applications. We can assign a callback function to the desired property to call it when the associated event occurs. This provides us a very convenient way to create a new serial port object with our specified parameters. We can call this M-file repeatedly to create as many serial port objects as we like. The argument `comPort` can be replaced by any port number when the M-file is called.

Click the `File|Save` menu item to save the M-file after all modifications have been made to our file.

6.4.5.2 Developing a User-Defined Callback Function

In this application we'll develop a user-defined M-file function, `GetByte()`, to use as a callback function. This function will be called when the defined number of bytes received in the `InputBuffer` is equal to the `BytesAvailableFcnCount` property we will set in the main interface program. This M-file function will collect the data from the serial port COM1.

Open a new M-file and name it `GetByte()`. Enter the code that is shown in Figure 6.33.

```
function GetByte(obj, event)

global s;
global r_data;
global index;
pause(0.1);

for index = 1:50,
   r_data(:, index) = eval(fscanf(s));
end
```

FIGURE 6.33 The user-defined callback function.

The global variables `s` and `r_data` are used both in this callback function and in the main interface program. The `global` keyword is used to indicate that the variable can be used by all associated M-file functions in the current directory. The `pause()` function will delay the callback function for a certain period of time. A `for` loop is used to continuously pick up 50 bytes of data from the serial port COM1. The `eval()` function is used to convert the data from text format to numeric format. The received data is then stored in the global data array `r_data`, which can later be used by the main interface program.

This callback function should be stored in the same folder as the main interface program.

Now let's develop our main interface program.

6.4.5.3 Developing the Main Serial Port Interface Program

The purpose of our main interface program is to create a sequence of data in sinusoidal format and send the sequence to serial port COM1. The property `BytesAvailableFcnCount` is set to 100. This means that a `BytesAvailable` event is generated when the number of the arrived data in the `InputBuffer` on the COM1 is equal to 100 bytes. The callback function `GetByte()` we developed earlier will be called as the `BytesAvailable` event is generated. The callback function picks up 50 bytes of received data from the `InputBuffer` and stores them in the global data array `r_data`.

Finally, the program uses the `Plot` function to plot the received date to show that it is identical to the transmitted data.

Open a new M-file and name it `SerialInstr.m`. Enter the code that is shown in Figure 6.34. The detailed explanations for each coding are listed below.

A: Some local variables are declared at the beginning of the program. The variables `m` and `n` are used to define the dimensions of the data array. The variable `A` is used to define the amplitude of the sinusoidal signal that will be sent to the serial port.

B: The global variables are defined here. These global variables can be used by all M-file functions in the current directory. The `r_data` variable will be used by the callback function `GetByte()` to store the data collected from serial port COM1. The `s` variable represents the opened serial port object.

C: All data arrays are initialized to zero matrices.

```
   % Test simple COM1 with Sinusoidal signal - 11/30/2003
   % Define the dimension of the array element to be sent
   % Y. Bai
A  m = 1;
   n = 100;
   N = 100;
   A = 10;
B  global r_data;
   global s;
   global index;
   index = 0;
C  sdata = zeros(m, n);
   s_data = zeros(m, n);
   r_data = zeros(m, n);
D  s = OpenPort('COM1');
E  s.BytesAvailableFcn = @GetByte;
   s.BytesAvailableFcnCount = 100;
   s.BytesAvailableFcnMode = 'byte';
F  fopen(s);
   tt = 1:N;
G  sdata = A*sin((2*pi/N)*tt);
   for nn = 1:N,
     s.RequestToSend = 'on';
H    fprintf(s, int2str(sdata(:, nn)));
I    s_data(:, nn) = sdata(:, nn);
     s.RequestToSend = 'off';
   end
J  s.BytesAvailable
   t = 1:n;
K  plot(t, s_data, 'r-', t, r_data, 'b-');
   grid;
   title('Comparison between the sent out (red) and read in data (blue): Randn');
   xlabel('Data Point');
L  fclose(s);
   delete(s);
   clear s;
```

FIGURE 6.34 The main serial interface program.

D: The `OpenPort()` M-file function is called to create a new serial port object.

E: The callback function `GetByte()` is assigned to the `BytesAvailableFcn` property, and this callback function is called when the number of the received data in the `InputBuffer` is equal to 100 (which is the value assigned to the `BytesAvailableFcnCount` property). The '`byte`' value is assigned to the `BytesAvailableFcnMode` to indicate that the received data will be counted in bytes.

F: The `fopen()` function is called to connect the created serial port object with the physical serial port. Once `fopen()` is executed, all serial port parameters and properties we've set will become effective.

G: The built-in MATLAB function `sin()` is called to create a sequence of sinusoidal formatted data.

H: The sinusoidal data sequence is sent to serial port COM1 by executing the function `fprintf()`. The built-in function `int2str()` is used to convert the data from numeric format to text format.

I: The sent out data is also stored to the data array `s_data` that will be plotted later as the standard data compared with the received data.

J: When the number of the sent out data bytes is equal to 100, the callback function `GetByte()` is called to pick up the first 50 bytes from serial port COM1. The `BytesAvailable` property is used to display the number of available bytes in the `InputBuffer`.

K: The `Plot()` function is executed to plot the sent out data stored in the `s_data` array and the received data stored in the `r_data` array. The result can be used to compare the two sets of data to confirm that the serial port is working properly.

L: Finally, the created serial port object is deleted and the physical port is closed. The `clear` statement is used to clean up the memory space we've allocated for the serial data transmission.

Now we are ready to test and run this interface program to perform our serial data transmission between the serial port object in the MATLAB domain and the physical serial port installed on the computer. You need to install a loop-serial-connector (see Figure 3.6) on the COM1 to do this test.

6.4.5.4 Testing and Running the Main Serial Port Interface Program

In the MATLAB workspace, type `SerialInstr` to run the M-file function. The interface program will begin to run. Finally the `Plot()` function is called to plot the transmitted and received data, as shown in Figure 6.35.

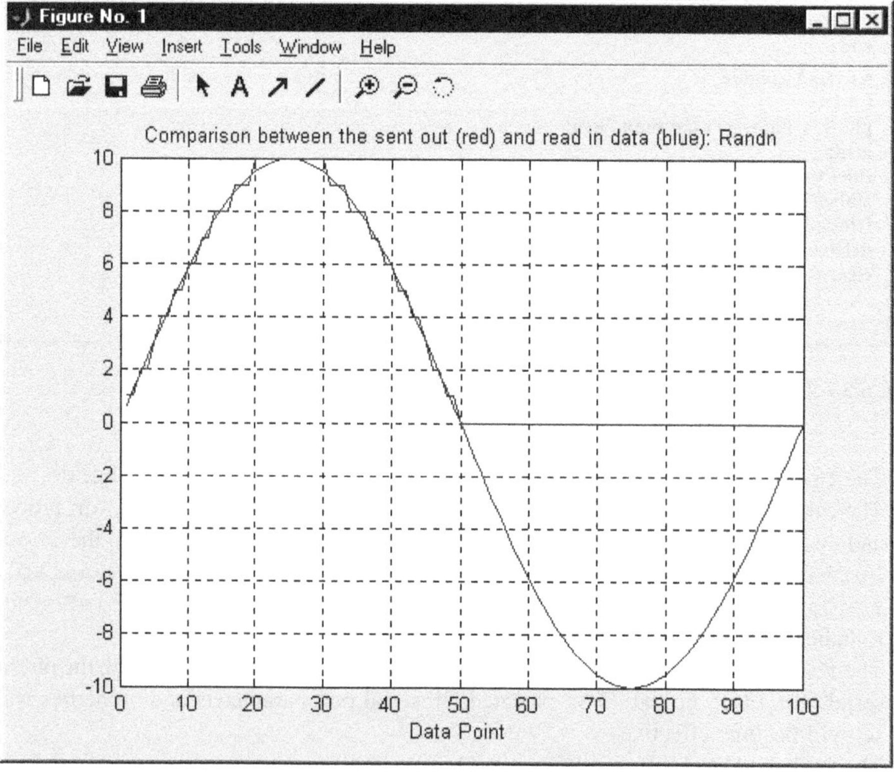

FIGURE 6.35 Results of plotting the transmitted and received data.

The complete program files for this project, including the `OpenPort()` and callback functions and the main interface program, are located in the folder `Chapter 6\InstruToolBox` on the attached CD. You can load these programs and run them on your own machine.

7 Serial Port Programming in Smalltalk

7.1 INTRODUCTION

Smalltalk was the first object-oriented programming language developed in the twentieth century. Today, object-oriented programming (OOP) is a popular term applied in software engineering and computer application fields, and many software engineers and programmers try to learn and apply this idea to solve problems around the real world. The advantages of applying OOP are obvious and understandable, especially in complicated applications and implementations for multitask controls.

Applications programming is a challenging and intellectually stimulating activity. Smalltalk is an environment that supports complex application development. Smalltalk's success is due mainly to its focus on needs of developers.

There are several manufacturers and software companies, such as IBM, Adventa Control Technologies, Inc., and CinCom Systems, Inc. that are integrating Smalltalk with graphical user interfaces to provide user-friendly development environments. These companies have developed different interfaces (IBM's VisualAge®, Adventa's ControlWORKS®, and Cincom's VisualWorks®) that communicate between Smalltalk and the application program interfaces (API). All of these products incorporate a GUI named ENVY/Developer, developed by Object Technology International (OTI) Inc.

ENVY can be considered a collaborative programming environment with version control and configuration management tools. Combining ENVY with ControlWORKS or VisualWorks simplifies the development of an OOP in Smalltalk.

This chapter is organized as follows:

- Overviews of Smalltalk and useful GUIs (such as VisualWorks and its environments).
- Introduction to VisualWorks and its development environment. Two actual examples are provided to illustrate the development of real-life programs with this tool.
- Discussion of using VisualWorks to illustrate the interface between Smalltalk and the external codes developed in third-party languages such as C/C++.

VisualWorks is discussed in detail in the following sections, and as in earlier chapters, we'll examine several sample programs. The first example uses a loopback serial port test to illustrate the interface between Smalltalk and a DLL that we'll develop in Visual C++. The second example uses a serial A/D converter to show the interface between Smalltalk and the RS-232 serial port. Both of these examples have been applied in real-life projects, and you can tailor any section of them to meet your own programming requirements.

7.2 OVERVIEW OF VISUALWORKS

VisualWorks is a complete Smalltalk development environment that includes an implementation of the Smalltalk programming language, a virtual machine for executing Smalltalk code, and a wide assortment of tools for creating applications.

VisualWorks provides an integrated environment that includes the Model-View-Controller modal, which is a very popular OOP idea. VisualWorks runs a virtual machine (an object engine) to process the data in a Smalltalk image. The virtual machine is an executable file that interprets and executes the Smalltalk byte-code stored in the image.

Developing a program in the VisualWorks environment involves these procedures:

- Making specifications and planning the program.
- Developing a graphical user interface by using the Paint Canvas.
- Creating code for each method and making that the source code for the program. (Every VisualWorks source file ends with a `.sou` extension.)
- Compiling the completed source code into the byte-code, which is called an image file, and running that file in the virtual machine. (The image file is a byte-code file that contains all the code and environmental variables for the program. Every VisualWorks image file has an `.im` extension.)
- Making any necessary modifications to the program; these will be stored in a change file (which will have a `.cha` extension).

Once a program has been developed in the VisualWorks environment, three files should exist: a source file (`.sou`), an image file (`.im`) and a change file (`.cha`). The change file is a uniquely useful file in VisualWorks environment. Unlike files created in C/C++ or Visual Basic, VisualWorks files (such as the source file, head file, library files, and resource files) cannot be stored in different folders on the machine. Instead they will be stored in different namespaces or packaged into a parcel. Keep in mind that if you don't package your program when exit VisualWorks midway through its development, then the next time you run VisualWorks, your program will not be available from the default namespaces. In this situation, you will need to use the change file to recover your half-finished program.

7.2.1 The VisualWorks Application Framework

As mentioned earlier, VisualWorks provides a Model-View-Controller modal. Similar to the `Document-View` class in Visual C++, a *Domain Model* and an *Application Model* are provided in the VisualWorks environment. The purpose of the Domain Model is to store and operate program data (application data or user data, not system data), and the Application Model is used to provide a user interface, present the data, and handle input and output from the user interface. The VisualWorks Domain Model is mapped to a `Model` class, and the Application Model in VisualWorks is mapped to a `View` class in Visual C++. The VisualWorks Controller is generally embedded in the Application Model; its duty is to coordinate the communication between the domain and Application Models. Figure 7.1 shows this structure.

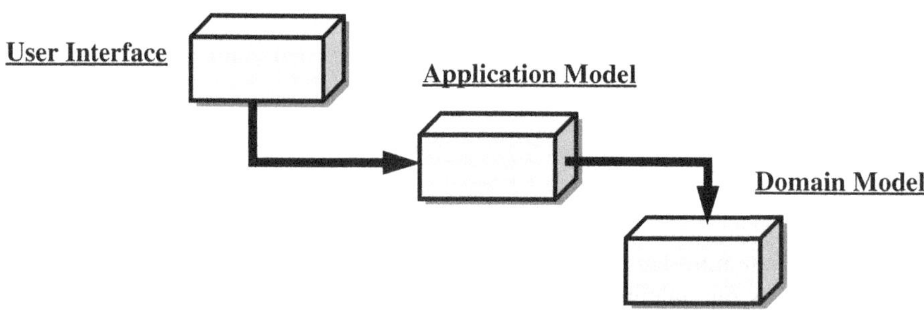

FIGURE 7.1 The Model-View-Controller structure in VisualWorks.

In VisualWorks, the mechanism that the Application Model uses is called an adaptor. An adaptor stands between the specific interfaces of the UI and the domain objects, adapting messages and values so they can work together. This adaptor is also called the value model, and one of most popular value models used in VisualWorks is the `valueHolder`, which can be used to hold the value of a variable or an object. The `valueHolder` can be considered a bridge or a temporary control unit between the domain and the UI, and it can be used to monitor and track the states and changes of variables and objects. The relationship among the user interface, the Application Model, and the `valueHolder` is shown in Figure 7.2.

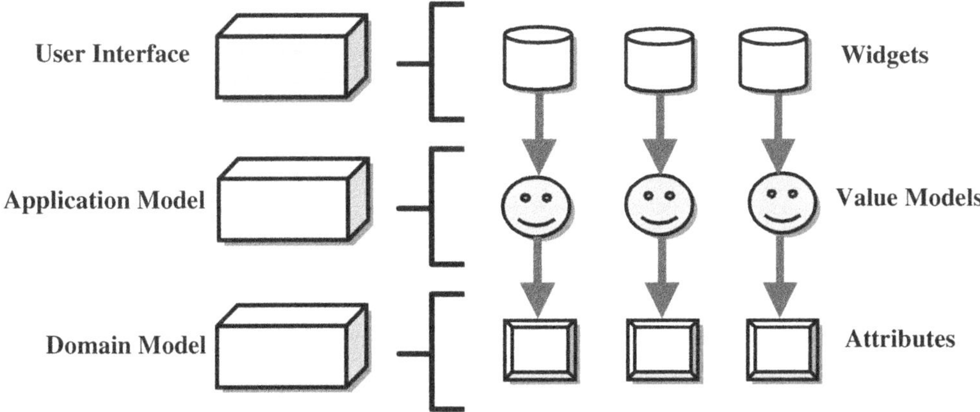

FIGURE 7.2 Relationship among the UI, the Application Model, and the `valueHolder`.

The components inserted in the user interface are called *widgets*. Widgets can be buttons, labels, text input boxes, list boxes, or combo boxes. The Application Model sets a connection between the attributes (either variables or data) in the Domain Model and the widgets in the user interface that belongs to the Application Model. This connection is established by the value model or value holder objects. These value holder objects can be considered robots that are used to monitor the states and the values of all widgets; they will inform the Application Model if an expected action has occurred. The Application Model then will pass messages into the associated attributes in the Domain Model to trigger the associated processes or responses.

In VisualWorks, all communications between objects occur via messages. There are different communication methods used in VisualWorks, such as setting up dependents and notifications between objects, and using event-based notifications. In some simple applications, the Domain Model may not be needed because the Application Model can provide all the procedures necessary for the program's implementation.

The most recent release of VisualWorks is version 7.2. The most recent version of ObjectStudio is 6.9. VisualWorks and ObjectStudio are both components of the Smalltalk package, and they can be installed together. You can download these products for free from CinCom Web site (http://smalltalk.cincom.com/downloads/index.ssp).

7.2.2 Installing and Starting VisualWorks

You can install VisualWorks and ObjectStudio from either a CD that contains the software or from the noncommercial downloads available on the CinCom Web site. Refer to the installation instructions on that Web site to complete the installation. You can copy a shortcut of the VisualWorks image to the desktop on your machine so that you can use it later easily.

Once you've installed VisualWorks, you can launch a VisualWorks session.

The virtual machine name is `visual.exe`, and the initial image file is `visual.im` (or `visualnc.im` for the noncommercial version). This file is installed in the `image` subdirectory. The image file is a read-only, write-protected file, so you won't be overwriting its contents. Instead, you will need to save your image file under a different name by using the `Save Image As...` command.

Double-click the VisualWorks image icon on the desktop or from the Window Explorer to launch VisualWorks. Three windows will appear on your screen. Two of these, the Visual Launcher and the workspace, are shown in Figures 7.3 (a) and (b). If you're using the noncommercial version of VisualWorks, a NC license agreement is displayed; read it and click `I Accept` to start the VisualWorks program.

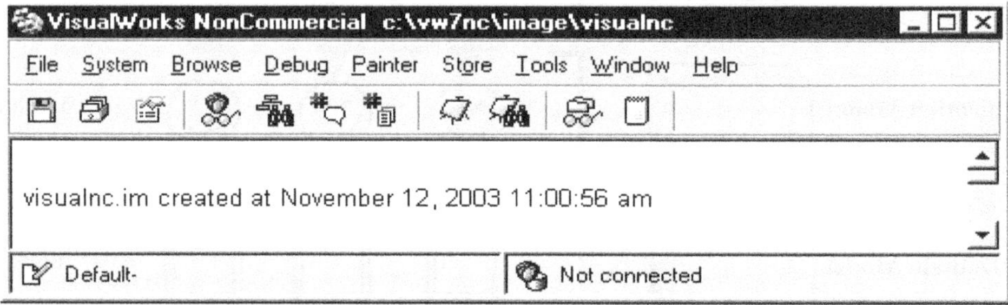

FIGURE 7.3 (a) The Visual Launcher.

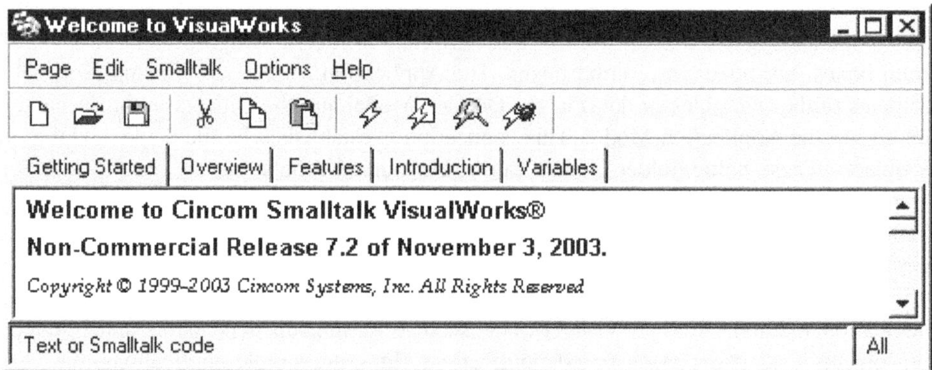

(b) The VisualWorks workspace.

The Visual Launcher is the main window; most functions and controls are located here.

The first thing we need to do is to set up the home directory of the VisualWorks image file. The correct home directory for VisualWorks should be `C:\vw7i2`. Select `File`|`Set VisualWorks Home` from the Visual Launcher; a setup window will appear, as shown in Figure 7.4.

Make sure that the default home directory, `C:\vw7i2` (or `C:\vw7i2nc` for the noncommercial version) is displayed in the text box. This directory is written into the system registry file when you install the VisualWorks software, so it must be correct. If so, click `OK`.

The second thing we need to do is to create a new working image file for our application program. The first image file you'll see is `visual.im`; this is the first image file you can see when you start VisualWorks. As mentioned earlier, this is a write-protected file. To create a new

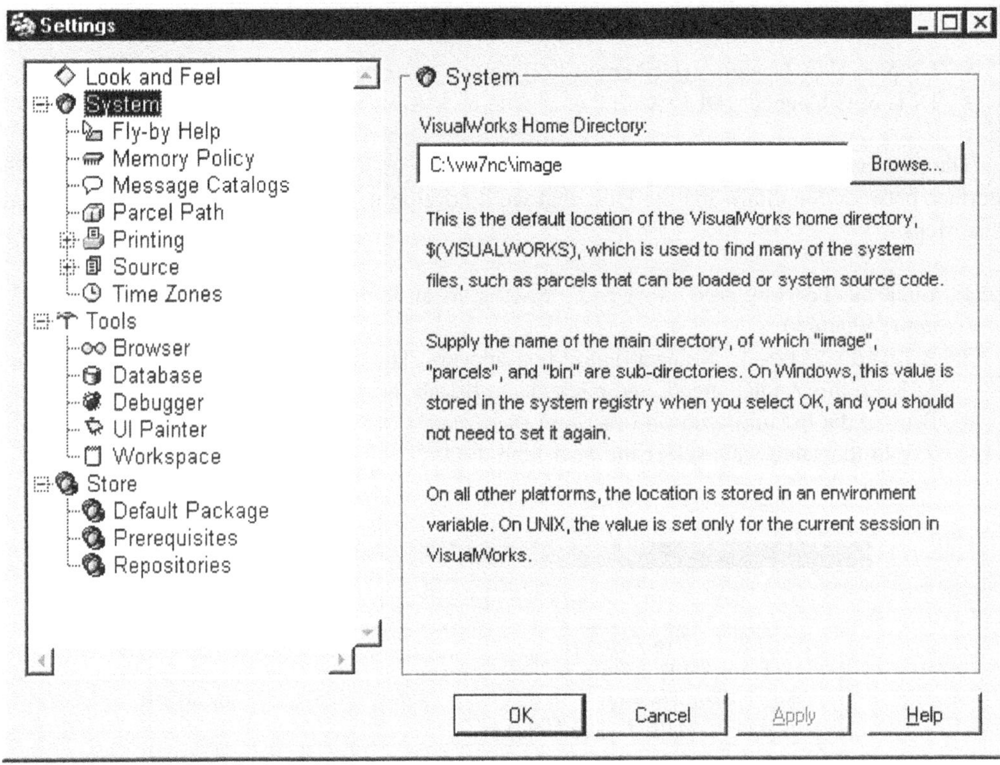

FIGURE 7.4 Setting up the home directory for the image file.

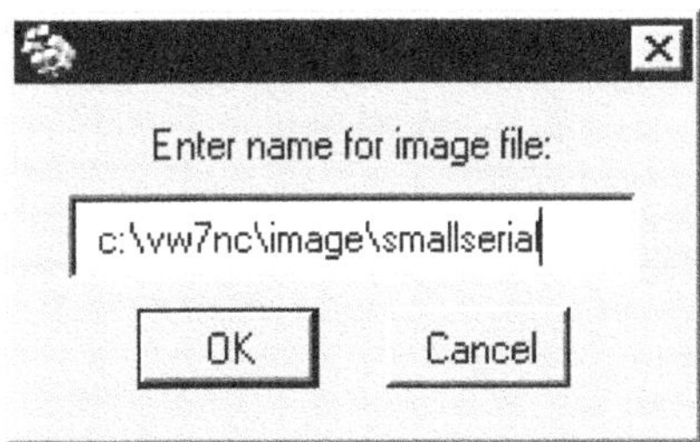

FIGURE 7.5 The Save Image File dialog box.

working image file for our program, select the `File|Save Image As...` menu item from the Visual Launcher; a new dialog box will appear, as is shown in Figure 7.5.

Enter `smallserial` as the name for the image file, and click `OK`. This will save the image file as `smallserial.im` and create a `smallserial.cha` file for our application. (You do not need to enter the `.im` or `.cha` extensions; these will be created automatically)

The third thing we need to do is to load the *parcels*. These are external Smalltalk binary and source code modules that are similar to the libraries in Visual C++. Most components in VisualWorks, such as the `DLL` and `C Connect, Database, OpenTalk, PlugIn, VisualWave, UIPainter`, and `DST`, are stored in parcels. By placing these items in separate parcels, VisualWorks can organize them more clearly. The advantage of loading parcels is that it is much faster than loading and compiling source code.

We need to load the following two parcels for this application:

- Graphic User Designer (UIPainter 7i.2)
- DLL & C Connect (DLLCC 7i.2)

The first parcel is used to design our user interface, and the second is used to develop the interface between Smalltalk and the DLL that we'll develop in C/C++. To load the parcels, follow these steps:

1. Click the `Tools|Load Parcel Named` menu item from the Visual Launcher (the upper window).
2. A `Load Parcel Named` dialog box appears. The default name in the input box is `*`. Keep this `*` unchanged, and click `OK` to list all the parcels on the parcel path.
3. Browse the list until you find the item `DLLCC 7i.2`, and select it as shown in Figure 7.6. In the same way, select the next item, `UIPainter 7i2`. Click `OK` to load these two parcels.

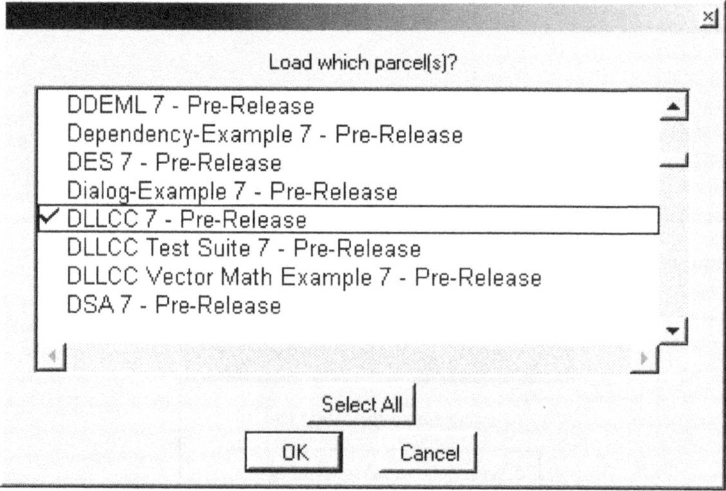

FIGURE 7.6 Loading two parcels.

Now our VisualWorks working environment is set up, and we can begin to develop our first application.

7.3 A SIMPLE SERIAL PORT INTERFACE PROGRAM

In this section, we'll create a simple VisualWorks example that incorporates both the Domain Model and the Application Model. This sample program will call DLL functions that we develop in the Visual C++ domain to perform a loopback test of the serial port.

7.3.1 Serial Port Testing Configuration

Recall that serial ports are arranged in numeric sequence (for example, from COM1 to COM8). On some computers, only a couple of ports are available to the user; typically these are COM1 and COM2. The other serial ports are used by the system hardware. Serial port testing can be divided into two categories: single-port loopback testing and dual-port loopback testing. In a single-port loopback test, the receiving data terminal (pin-2 in DB-9 connector) and the transmitting terminal (pin-3 in DB-9 connector) are connected. During the test, data is sent to the transmitting buffer, and then the same data is returned to the receiving buffer. If the port is working properly, the data that is received should be identical with the data that was sent out.

A dual-port loopback test uses a null modem cable, which means that the transmitting terminal at the first port is connected to the receiving terminal at the second port, and the transmitting terminal at the second port is connected to the receiving terminal at the first port. Data is sent from the transmitting terminal of one port, and then returned to the receiving terminal of the other port. In this way, both ports can be tested.

In our example, we'll use the single-port loopback process to test port COM1.

Shut down your computer and install a DB-9 serial connector, as shown in Figure 7.7.

Pin-number	Function
1	Not used
2	R_{XD}
3	T_{XD}
4	Not used
5	Ground

FIGURE 7.7 Hardware connection for the single-port loopback test.

7.3.2 Developing a Domain Model Class

We will first develop a Domain Model for the project and name it `SerialPort`. This model will manage and control the program data (the serial port number, baud rate, and data values) that will be sent to the serial port COM1.

To create a new Domain Model class, click the `Open a System Browser` icon on the toolbar in the Visual Launcher; then open the `Packages` dialog box, which is shown in Figure 7.8.

On the upper-left pane of this dialog box, select the `Base VisualWorks|System|System-Name Spaces` item from the `Package` list. A default prototype of the Smalltalk class will be displayed on the bottom list, as shown in Figure 7.8.

The first line indicates the class name. In this application, our Domain Model class name is `SerialPort`. Following the # symbol, enter `SerialPort` as the class name. The second line indicates the name of the super class from which this class is inherited. Enter `UI.Model` as our superclass name. The third line is used to indicate whether the class is a `named` or the `indexed` type. Most classes have the `named` type, which means that the name is an identifier for that class. Our class is a `named` type, so keep the default, #none, unchanged. The fourth line indicates whether the class is private or public. The default is public (`private: false`). Keep this default definition so that our class remains a public class. The fifth line is used to declare instance variables for the class. We will use four instance variables: `cComPort`, `cBaudRate`, `cSendDdata`, and `cReadData`. (The lowercase `c` prior to each variable stands for *current*). All these variables are instance variables and thus will only belong to an instance of this class. Enter their names one by one inside the single quotation marks, replacing the original nominal variables `instVarName1 instVarName2`. Be sure that the variable names are separated by single spaces, as shown in Figure 7.9.

The sixth line is used to declare class instance variables. We won't use any of these for this project, so just keep the sixth line empty. The seventh line indicates namespaces or other classes

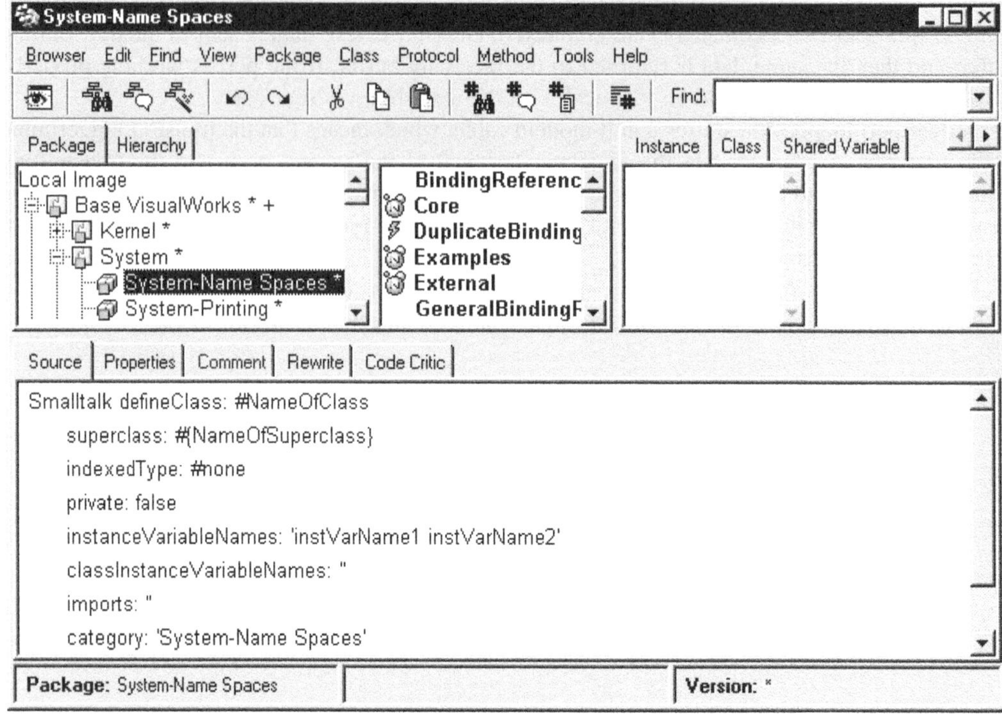

FIGURE 7.8 Creating a new Domain Model class.

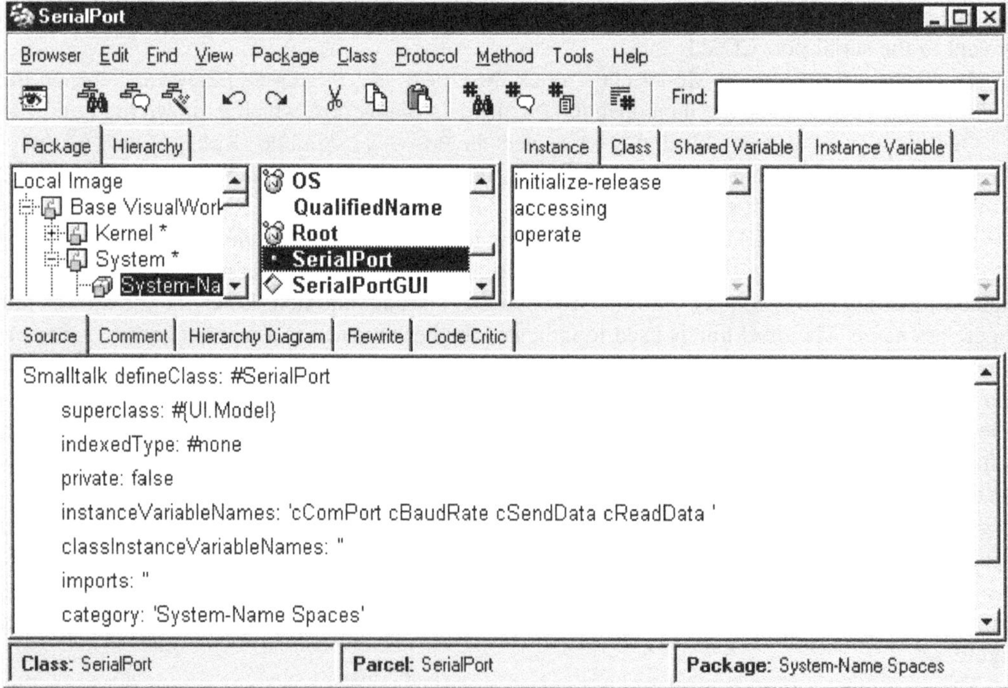

FIGURE 7.9 The Domain Model class `SerialPort`.

that will be used by the class. Currently we don't need to use any other classes, so this line should stay blank as well. The final line is used to define a category for the class; for our project, select the `System-Name Spaces` category.

After you finish modifying the class, right-click on this space and select `Accept` from the pop-up menu to save our modifications. The finished Domain Model class should match the one shown in Figure 7.9.

We must now define the instance variables and generate the associated methods for our class.

Right-click on the `Instance` pane (which is the third pane from the left, and now blank). Select `New` from the pop-up menu. In the resulting dialog box, select or enter `accessing` in the top box and click `OK`. An `accessing` protocol will appear on the `Instance` pane.

In the same way, create another two protocols: `operate` and `initialize-release`.

Click the `accessing` protocol on the third pane from the left, highlight the contents in the bottom space, and type:

```
cComPort
    ^cComPort.
```

This code will create an accessing method for the `cComPort` variable.

Right-click on the space and select `Accept` from the pop-up menu to save the code. Then, keeping the `accessing` protocol selected, highlight the code you've just entered and type the following in its place:

```
cComPort: aValue
cComPort := aValue.
self changed: #cComPort.
```

Right-click the space and again select `Accept` from the pop-up menu to save the code. You have just defined the `cComPort` variable. (The purpose of the `self changed:` entry is to send a `changed:` message to itself to automatically update the variable if it is changed).

In a similar way, we can define another three variables, `cBaudRate`, `cSendData` and `cReadData` in the `accessing` protocol and generate the associated methods, as shown in Figure 7.10.

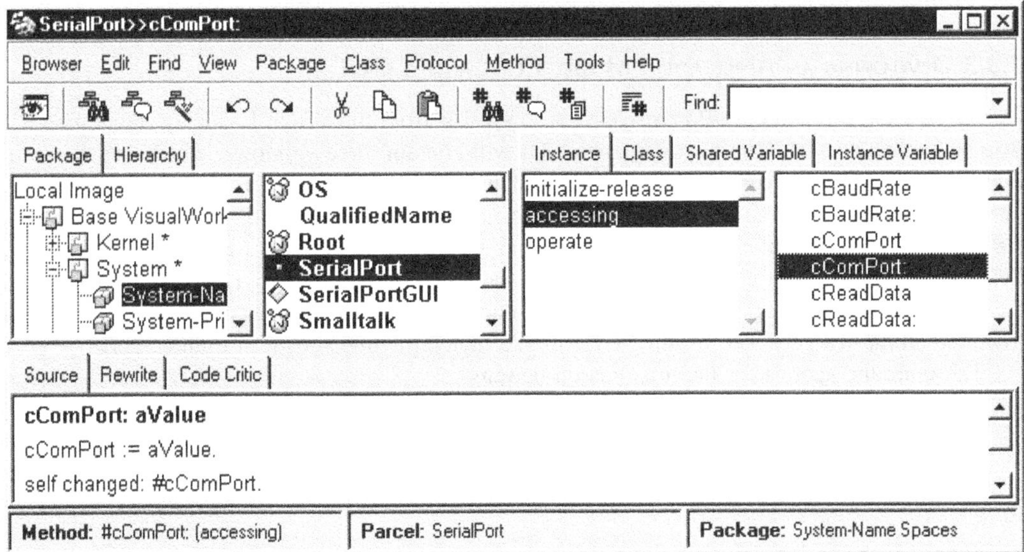

FIGURE 7.10 The instance variables.

Click the `initialize-release` item on the third pane from the left, and delete the contents of the bottom space. Enter the following code to initialize these variables:

```
initialize
   cComPort  := 1.
   cBaudRate  :=  9600.
   cSendData  :=  0.
   cReadData  :=  0.
```

Right-click on the space and select `Accept` from the pop-up menu to save the code. An `initialize` method will be added on the fourth pane from the left.

The `operate` protocol contains three control commands:

- **Setup** will call DLL functions to initialize and configure the serial port.
- **Test** will send a start command instructing the DLL functions to begin testing the serial port.
- **Exit** will send a message instructing the Object Engine to terminate the testing program.

Remaining in the System Browser, keep the `SerialPort` class selected on the second pane from the left and the `operate` protocol selected on the third pane from the left, and delete the contents of the bottom space. Enter `Setup` and right-click on the bottom space, and then select `Accept` from the pop-up menu to save this method. In the same way, create another two methods, `Test` and `Exit`.

The purpose of these methods is to directly interface with the DLL functions defined in the External Interface Class. These DLL functions will be used to access the serial port to be tested in the C/C++ domain.

We will develop the code for these methods in Section 7.3.5, based on the prototypes of the DLL functions that we will define in the External Interface Class in Section 7.3.4. All these different methods will be triggered by the associated actions (`Setup`, `Test`, and `Exit`) defined in the `SerialPortGUI` Application Model, which we'll discuss in the following section. The relationship between the Domain Model (`SerialPort`) and the Application Model (`SerialPort-GUI`) is that the Application Model is a dependent of the Domain Model.

7.3.3 Developing an Application Model Class and a GUI

Open a new GUI by clicking `Painter|New Canvas` from the Visual Launcher; label the GUI `Serial Test GUI`. The newly opened GUI will contain three windows, which are shown in Figure 7.11. Add four labels, four input fields, and three action buttons to this GUI. The four aspects that are associated with the four input fields are `comPort`, `baudRate`, `sendData`, and `read-Data`. The `Actions` of the three action buttons should be named `Setup`, `Test`, and `Exit`. Select the `Edit|Install` menu item to install and name the GUI `SerialPortGUI`, and keep the default superclass `Application Model` unchanged. Click the `Edit|Define` menu item to define all the widgets. The finished GUI should match the one shown in Figure 7.11.

These are the actions for the three action buttons:

- Setup: #Setup
- Test: #Test
- Exit: #Exit

These are the aspects of the input fields:

- Com Port: #comPort
- Baud Rate: #baudRate

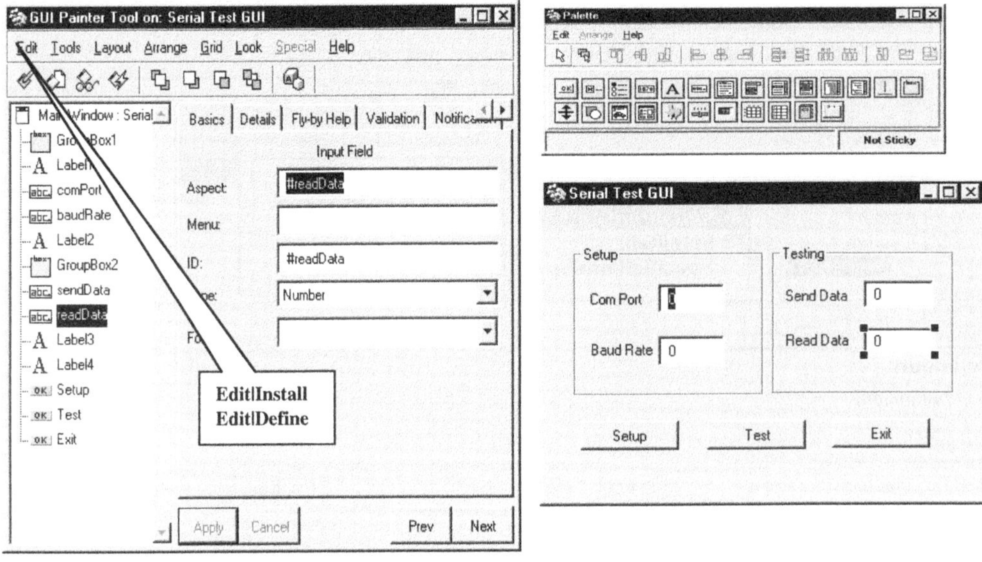

FIGURE 7.11 The completed GUI.

- Send Data: #sendData
- Read Data: #readData

The type of all the input fields should be `Number`, and the Format should also be `Number`.

To establish communication between the Application Model `SerialPortGUI` and the Domain Model `SerialPort`, we need to define the Application Model as a dependent of the Domain Model. Then the Application Model will be able to send input data entered by the user from widgets, to the Domain Model to update the data in the Domain Model. This dependent relationship will also allow the Domain Model to return any change in the data to the Application Model.

To define the `SerialPortGUI` as a dependent of `SerialPort`, create an instance variable named `serialport` in the `SerialPortGUI` class by adding it to the tail of the `instance-VariableName` of the class `SerialPortGUI`, as we did when creating our earlier instance variables. Next, create an `accessing` protocol in the `SerialPortGUI` class, and add the instance variable `serialport` to the `accessing` protocol in the `SerialPortGUI` class, as shown in Figure 7.12.

First, we create an `accessing` method for the variable `serialport` that returns an object `serialport`. Then we define a value holder for the `serialport` variable. A `changed:` message will be sent to this variable if it is updated. Finally, we need to initialize the variable to an instance of the Domain Model `SerialPort`, then initialize it as a value holder, and add the Application Model as a dependent of the `SerialPort`, as shown in Figure 7.13.

We must now create a method to remove this dependence between these two models when the class is exited. Add the system method `noticeOfWindowClose` to remove this dependence, which is shown in Figure 7.14. Now, when exiting the program, the Object Engine will call the `initialize-release` method `noticeOfWindowClose` to cancel this dependence.

7.3.4 Developing an External Interface Class

We need to develop a subclass of the External Interface Class to contain all DLL functions created in the Visual C++ domain, and use this class as an interface to communicate between Smalltalk and the DLL developed in Visual C++.

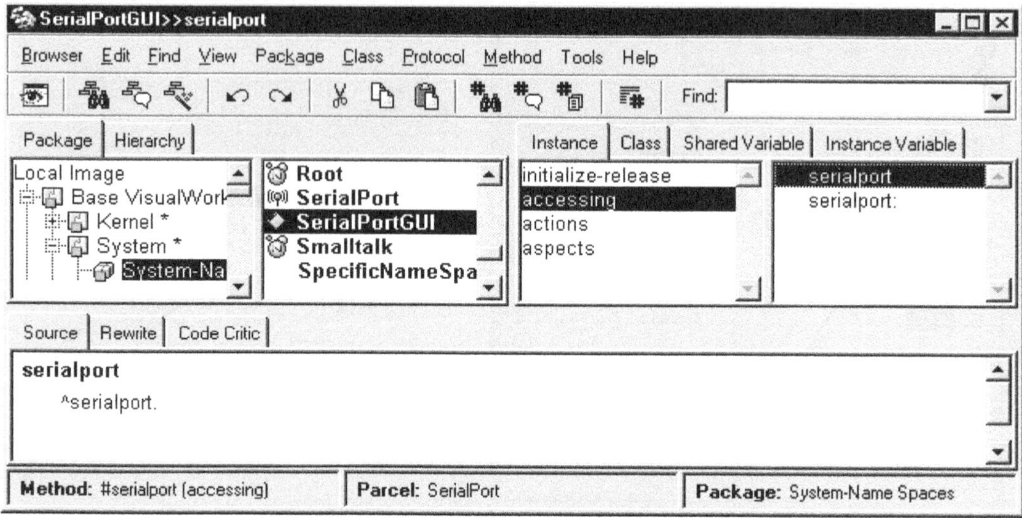

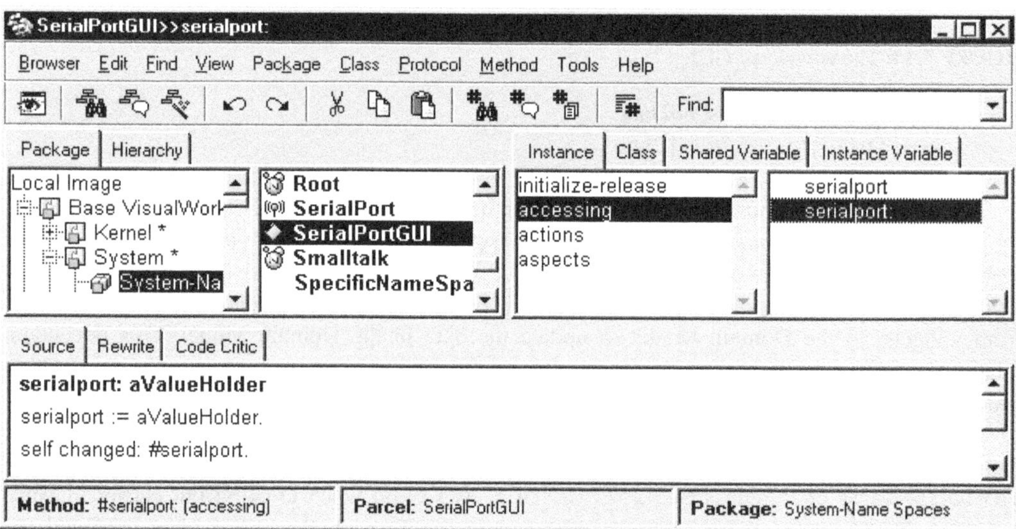

FIGURE 7.12 The instance variable `serialport`.

Open an `External Interface Finder` dialog box by clicking the `Tools|DLL and C Connect` menu item from the Visual Launcher. Click `New` to open a `Class Finder` dialog box. In this box, keep `Smalltalk namespace` selected on the lefthand pane, enter `SerialDLL` in the `Name:` field, and click `OK` to save the newly created class.

Next we need to declare prototypes of the DLL functions that are contained in the class. We want to test the serial port in real-time mode, which means that we can write some data into the port and simultaneously retrieve the data from the port, so we need to define these functions as threaded mode functions.

VisualWorks supports multitasking applications by providing a thread processing method, which can be distinguished from general functions by a pseudo-qualifier, `_threaded`, that appears prior to the function declaration in the C prototype.

In the Windows environment, the Smalltalk Object Engine is considered a separate process with one thread of control. The Object Engine uses a *process schedule* to manage all processes actively running on the Smalltalk platform. Without the thread processing method, if one process

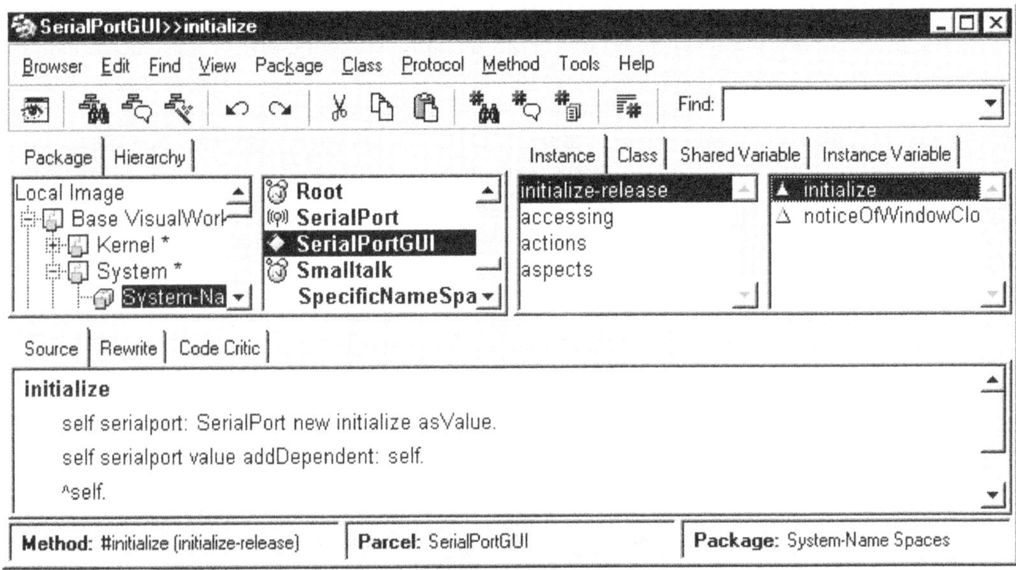

FIGURE 7.13 Setting the dependent for the `SerialPort` Domain Model.

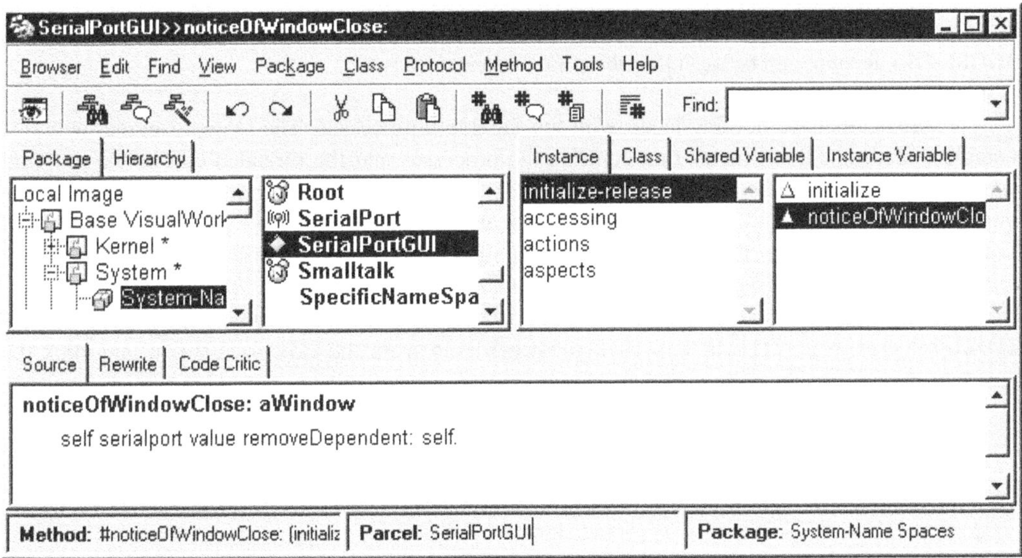

FIGURE 7.14 Removing the dependent of the Domain Model.

needed to call a DLL function to interface with a C/C++ function or a drive, a block would occur to stop the current calling process and all other processes to wait for this process to finish its function call. After that, the Object Engine would recover the schedule of the process sequence and continue to run. However, this arrangement is no good for a multitask processing system. The solution to this problem is to use thread processing, so that if a process needs to call an external function, the process will declare a thread-calling mode for the function. The Object Engine will assign a thread for this process when the process is run. When the process calls a function in threaded mode, a thread is created and used by the Object Engine to complete the function call.

The Object Engine will schedule the subsequent processes so they continue to run, and block just the calling process until the function returns. With this arrangement, none of the other Smalltalk processes need to wait for the function call to finish.

Note that these threads are not directly mapped to each Smalltalk process run by the Object Engine, but are rather used only for I/O calls via the `DLL and C Connect` interface. From the point of view of the `DLL and C Connect` programmer, the Object Engine still runs as a single thread, with the threaded interconnect calls running alongside it.

An illustration of the relationship between the Smalltalk processes and threads is shown in Figure 7.15.

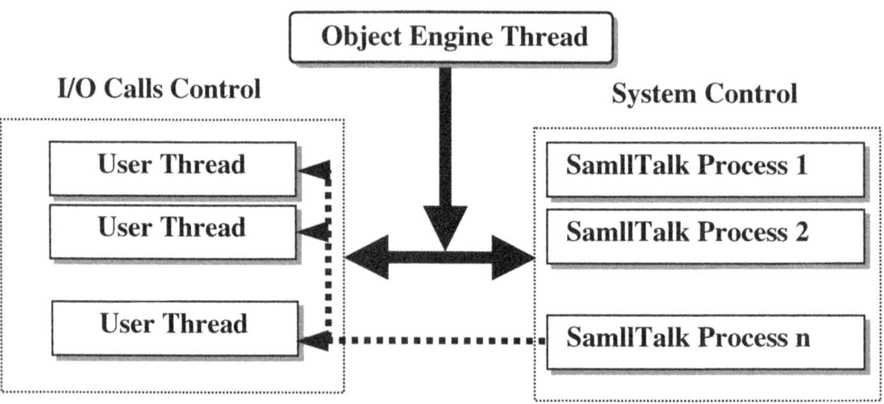

FIGURE 7.15 Relationship between the Object Engine and threads.

Threaded calls have nothing to do with the Smalltalk processes. The Object Engine, which is a single thread, is a coordinator that controls the processes and the threaded call as the program runs. If one of the processes needs a threaded call to interface with an external I/O function, the Object Engine will assign a thread to that process and allow it to wait for the function call until it returns. At the same time, the Object Engine will allow other Smalltalk process to continue to run without being blocked and waiting for the I/O function.

In the `External Interface Finder` dialog box, keep the newly created class `SerialDLL` selected in the `Class` list, click `procedures` from the `Category` list, and click the `New` button to create the following DLL functions:

- int Setup(int arg1, int arg2).
- int _threaded Write(int arg1).
- unsigned char _threaded Read(void).
- int Close(void).

The first function, `Setup`, is used to configure the serial port to be tested. The following two functions, `Write` and `Read`, are used to send out and receive the data to and from the serial port, respectively. In front of these two functions, a pseudo-qualifier, `_threaded`, is used to indicate to the Object Engine that these two functions are threaded-mode functions and need the Object Engine to assign threads to them. The last function, `Close`, is used to clean up the configuration for the tested serial port.

To create a threaded-mode function, follow these steps:

1. In the opened `New Procedure` dialog box, enter `Read` in the `Name:` input field as the function's name.

2. Select `unsigned char` as the return type from the `Return Type:` input field. Click `OK` to save the function.
3. Notice that the new `Read` function is now displayed on the rightmost pane that is named `Procedures`. Select this function, and click the `Browse` button.
4. In the resulting dialog box, select `procedures` from the middle pane and `Read` from the rightmost pane to open the function.

At this point, the displayed function should look like this:

```
Read
  <C: unsigned char Read(void)>
  ^self externalAccessFailedWith: _errCode
```

This function is not yet in threaded mode so we need to modify it.

5. Type `_threaded` just before the function name `Read`, and just after the return type `unsigned char`. The finished threaded-mode function should match the one shown in Figure 7.16.

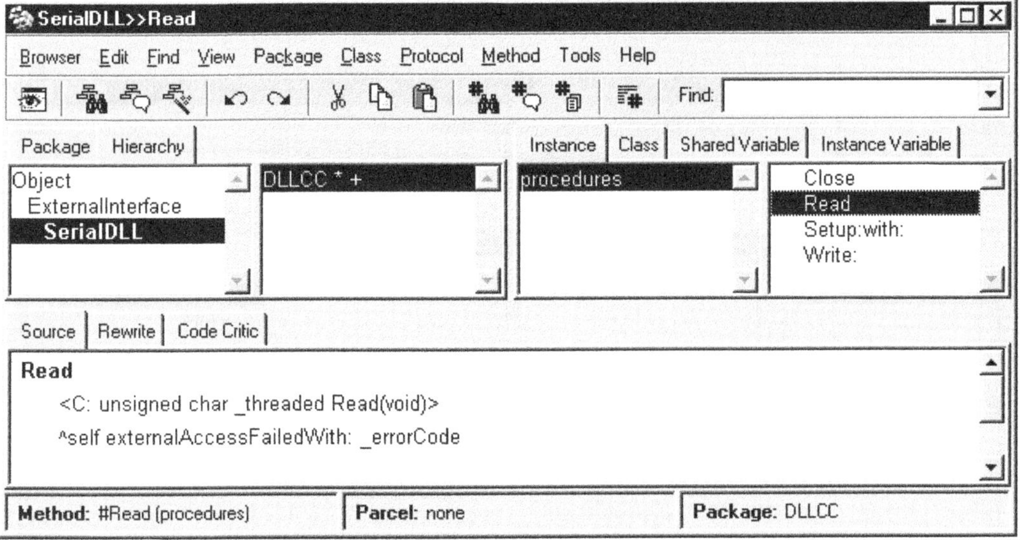

FIGURE 7.16 The threaded `Read` function.

6. You have now defined `Read` as a threaded-mode function. Close the dialog box by clicking the `Close` button on the upper-right corner of the dialog.

Follow the same procedure to create a threaded `Write` function, as shown in Figure 7.17.

The `Write` function has one argument, which is the data to be written to the serial port. The `Write` function has an `integer` return type that will work as an indicator to show the execution result of the function. A `0` will mean that the function has run successfully, and a nonzero value will mean that some error has occurred.

The `Setup` function is shown in Figure 7.18.

Two arguments are contained in the `Setup` function call; one is the COM port number and the other is the baud rate.

The completed `Close` function is shown in Figure 7.19.

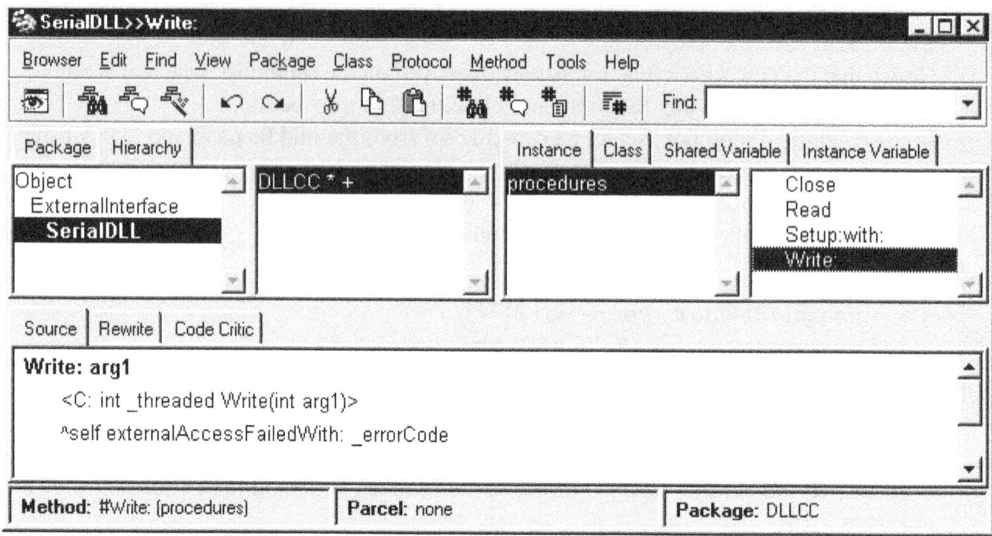

FIGURE 7.17 The threaded `Write` function.

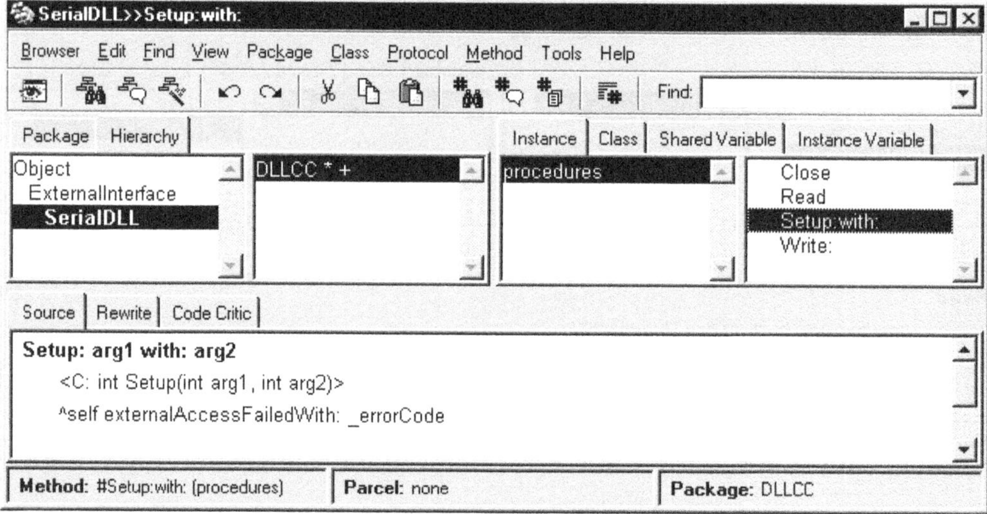

FIGURE 7.18 The `setup` function.

Notice that when you finish modifying the threaded-mode function and close the System Browser, the modified function remains unchanged, which means that the `threaded` pseudo-qualifier does not appear prior to the function name. Don't worry about this; it simply means that the External Interface Class is not yet refreshed. Click any other menu item and click the `procedures` menu item again, and you will see the updated function.

We have finished developing our External Interface Class and the declaration of the external DLL functions. (For now we needn't worry about the DLL functions; we'll create those in Section 7.3.7.)

7.3.5 Finish Coding of the SerialPort Project in VisualWorks

Figure 7.20 shows the relationship between the Domain Model, the Application Model, and the External Interface Class in our project.

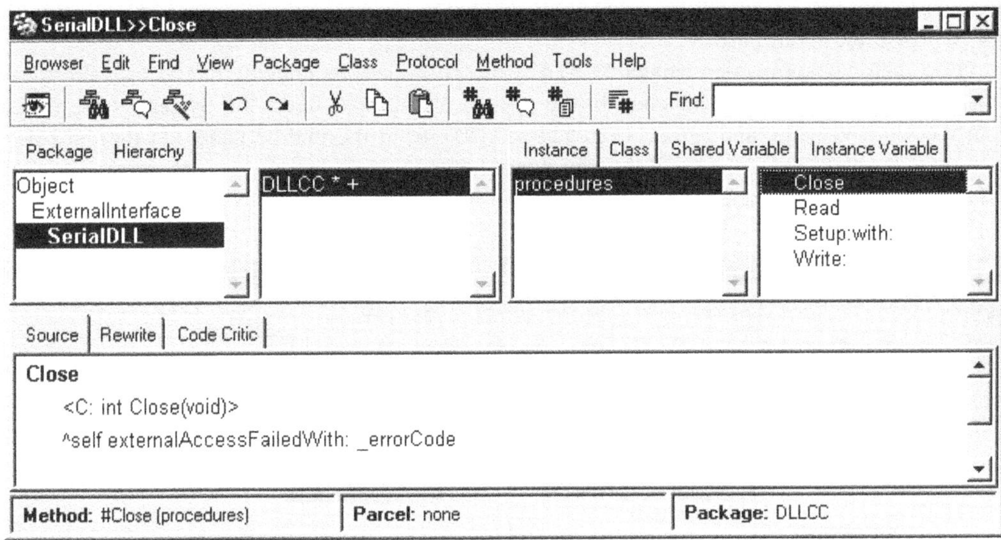

FIGURE 7.19 The `Close` function.

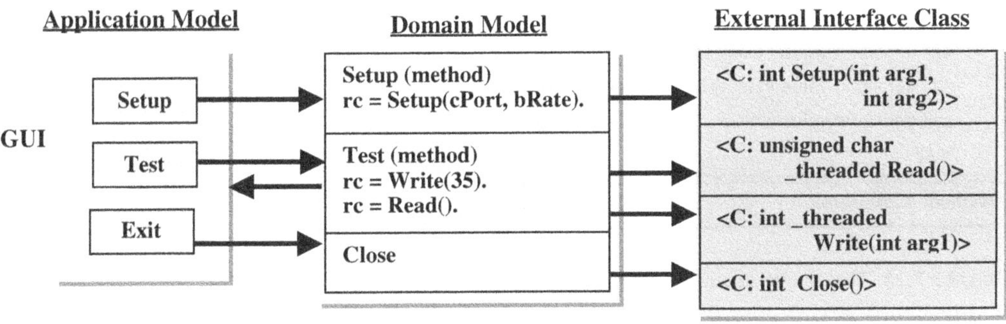

FIGURE 7.20 Relationship between the Application and Domain Models and the External Interface Class.

The Application Model is only an interface and is used to receive the input from the user. Based on the user's input, the Application Model will send the associated commands or messages to the Domain Model, and the latter will call the associated DLL functions defined in the External Interface Class to execute the commands sent by the Application Model. The Domain Model will also send the feedback coming from the DLL functions to the Application Model—specifically, to the value holder of the widgets in the GUI—to display and update the widgets.

Recall that at the end of Section 7.3.2, we defined an `operate` protocol in the Domain Model with three methods, `Setup`, `Test`, and `Exit`, under that category. In the following section, we will create the code for these methods.

7.3.5.1 Code for the Application Model

In the last section, we defined the Application Model `SerialPortGUI` as a dependent of the Domain Model `SerialPort`. At run time, when we click the `Setup` action button from the GUI, the Application Model should send the values we've entered for the `ComPort` and `BaudRate` widgets to the associated variables defined in the Domain Model's `cComPort` and `cBaudRate` instance variables. The Application Model will also send a message to the Domain Model to inform the latter to call the associated DLL functions defined in the External Interface Class to initialize and configure the serial port.

Now open the Application Model `SerialPortGUI` class by clicking the `Browse|System` menu item from the Visual Launcher. In the opened dialog box, select the System-Name spaces from the lefthand pane, and select `SerialPortGUI` from the middle pane. On the third pane from the left, click `actions`, and then on the rightmost pane select the `Setup` method to open it. In the space that appears, enter the code shown in Figure 7.21.

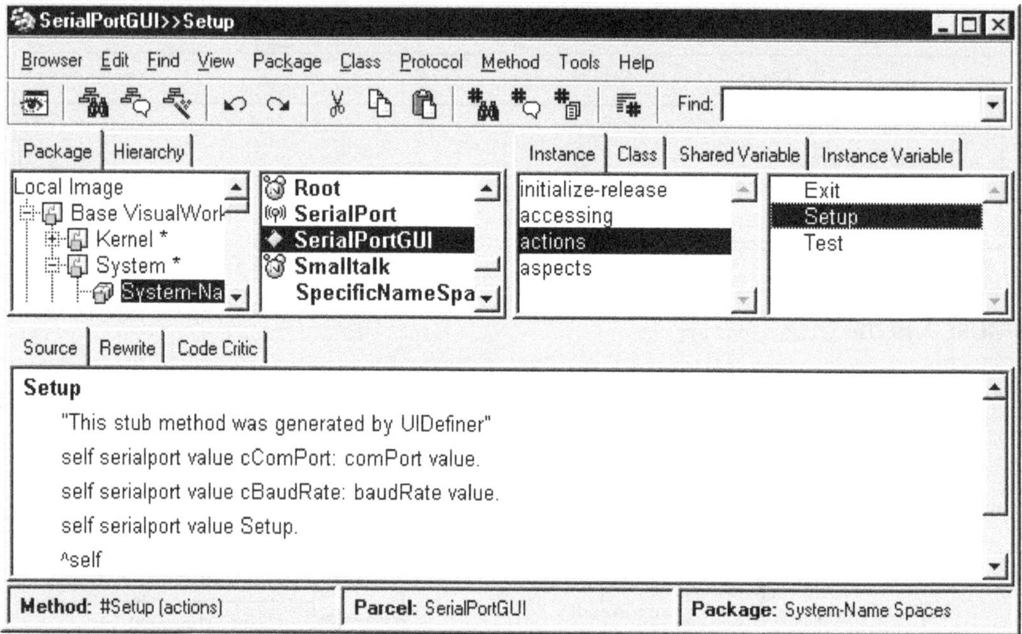

FIGURE 7.21 The `Setup` method for `SerialPortGUI`.

The first line here is a comment inserted by VisualWorks. The second line is used to assign the value of `comPort`, which is an input field widget defined in the GUI, to the variable `cComPort` defined in the Domain Model. We'll enter the value of `comPort` at run time. Here we consider the instance of Domain Model `serialport` as a value holder and use the `value:` message to assign a value to that instance variable.

The third line is similar to the second line, and is used to assign the value of the baud rate entered at run time to the associated Domain Model's instance variable, `cBaudRate`.

The fourth line is used to send a message to the Domain Model and inform the latter to execute the `Setup` method. This method will trigger the DLL function `Setup()`, defined in the External Interface Class, to perform the configuration for the serial port to be tested. Here we consider the `serialport` as a value holder and use the `value` message to assign a value to the Domain Model's `serialport` instance variable.

Right-click on the code space and select `Accept` from the pop-up menu to save the new method.

Now click `Test` on the righthand pane, and in the code space that appears, enter the code that is shown in Figure 7.22.

Again, the first line is a comment. The second line will send a message (`Test`) to the Domain Model to inform the latter to call the associated DLL functions defined in the External Interface Class to perform the testing of the serial port.

The third line is used to delay the process by 100 milliseconds to ensure that the serial port is ready for testing. You can modify this delay time based on your own applications.

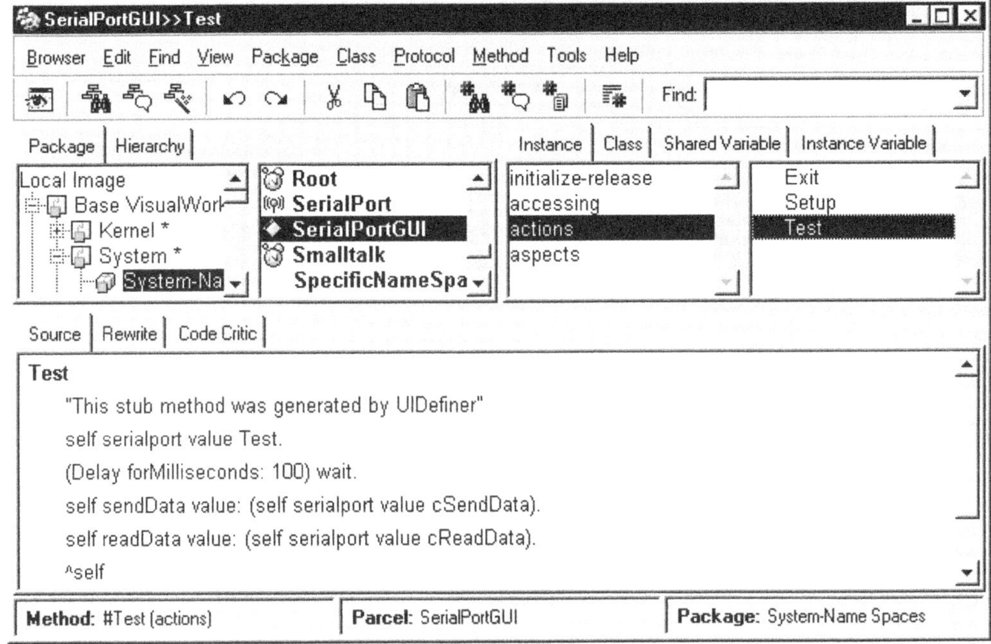

FIGURE 7.22 The `Test` method for `SerialPortGUI`.

The fourth and fifth lines are used to assign the updated data values, which will come from the serial port in real time, to the widgets in the GUI to display them on the screen. Here we use `value:` to assign these values from the associated variables in the Domain Model, which are enclosed by parentheses, to their partners in the Application Model. The parentheses indicate that the variables defined inside them have a higher precedence, and that they can be considered a single component and be assigned to the desired destination variables.

Click `Exit` on the rightmost pane to open its code space. In this space, enter the code that is shown in Figure 7.23.

This code is very simple and is similar to the code for the `Test` method. It sends an `Exit` message to the Domain Model to inform the latter to terminate the program. Then it sends a `closeRequest` message instructing the Object Engine to close the program and the GUI. The feedback will be processed by the `self changed` method.

7.3.5.2 Code for the Domain Model

Remaining in the System Browser, click the Domain Model, `SerialPort`, on the second pane from the left. On the third pane from the left, click the `operate` protocol, and on the rightmost frame, select `Setup` to open the code space for this method. The purpose of the `Setup` method is to call the associated DLL function, `Setup`, from the External Interface Class to configure the serial port to be tested. In the empty code space, enter the code that is shown in Figure 7.24.

First we create a temporary variable, `rc`, which will receive the returned value of the DLL function `Setup`. This `Setup` function will be called with two arguments, `cComPort` and `cBaudRate`. The values of both arguments are assigned by the associated variables in the Application Model. A warning message will be displayed in a dialog format if this call returns an error.

At run time, the `Setup` function will be activated by a `Setup` message sent by the Application Model when we click the `Setup` action button on the GUI.

Keep the `operate` protocol selected on the third pane from the left, and select `Test` from the rightmost pane. In the code space that appears, enter code that is shown in Figure 7.25.

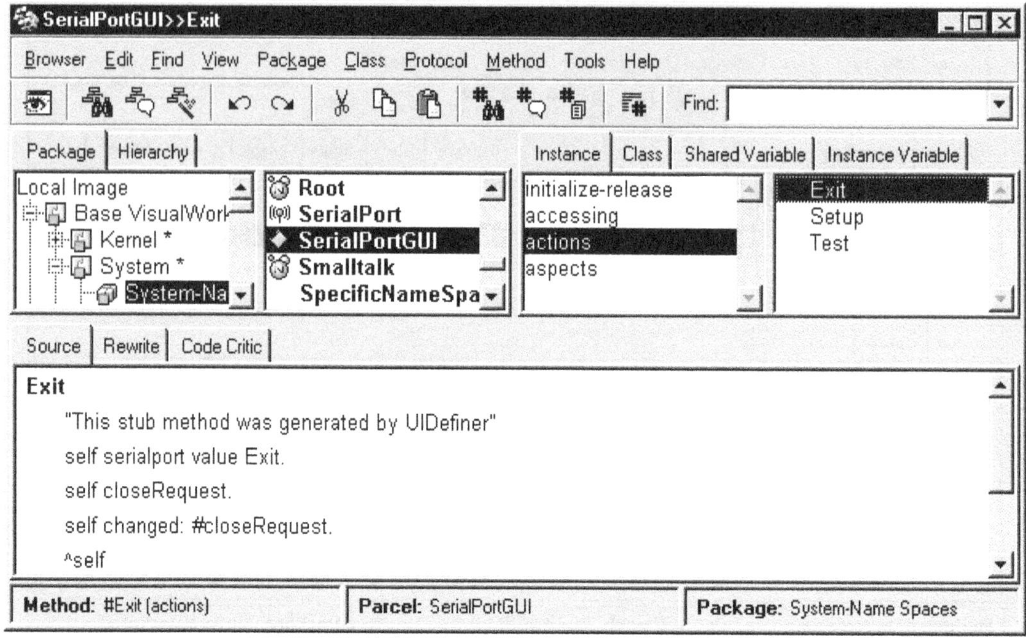

FIGURE 7.23 The `Exit` method for `SerialPortGUI`.

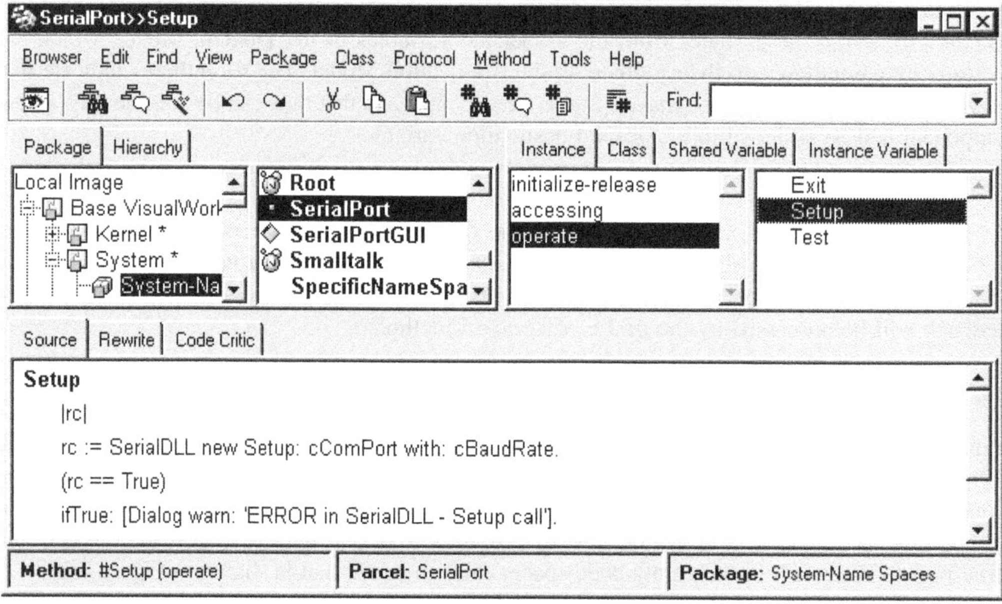

FIGURE 7.24 The `Setup` method for `SerialPort`.

First we create a temporary variable, `rc`, which will receive the returned value of the DLL function `Write`. Then we start to test the serial port by sending a sequence of integer data, `cSendData`, to the port. At run time, If this `Write` function encounters any error, a dialog box with a warning message will appear on the screen. Otherwise the test will continue; as we keep clicking the `Test` action button, the integer data is sent to the serial port one by one until the

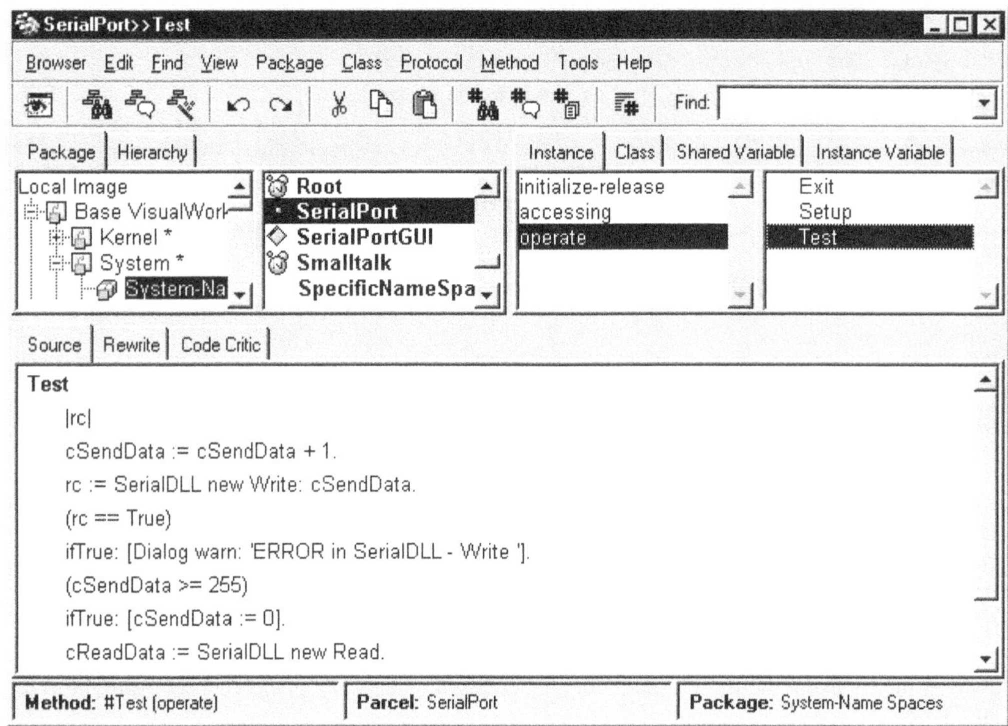

FIGURE 7.25 The `Test` method for `SerialPort`.

maximum number has been reached (255). At this point, the data value will be reset to `0` and the test will proceed.

You can insert a time delay after the execution of the `Write` function if you want to display the data more slowly on the GUI.

After successfully sending out each integer data to the serial port, we need to call another DLL function, `Read`, to receive the data from the serial port and determine whether the test has been successful. This is the purpose of the final line of code. An instance variable `cReadData` is used to store the returned data being read from the serial port. The keyword `new` is used to create an instance of the class `SerialDLL`.

Recall that in the Application Model `SerialPortGUI`, the `Test` method relies two instance variables, `cSendData` and `cReadData`, to update two input field widgets, `sendData` and `readData`, respectively. Notice that the actual update is performed in the Domain Model, exactly in the two instance variables `cSendData` and `cReadData`. Then the `Test` method in the Application Model uses the value holder for each of those variables to update the widgets in the GUI. In other words, the value holders set the connection between the variables in the Domain Model and the variables in the Application Model.

Keep the `operate` protocol selected from the third pane from the left and select `Exit` from the rightmost pane. In the code space that appears, enter code that is shown in Figure 7.26 into this space.

First we create a temporary variable, `rc`, which will receive the returned value of the DLL function `Close`. The DLL function `Close` will be called to clear the setup environment of the serial port. A dialog box with a warning message will be displayed if the call encounters any errors.

Now we complete the coding for both the Domain and Application Models of our project. Before we can continue, however, we need to save all the class files we have developed. In VisualWorks, the class files can be stored in different formats. Two popular formats are saving the

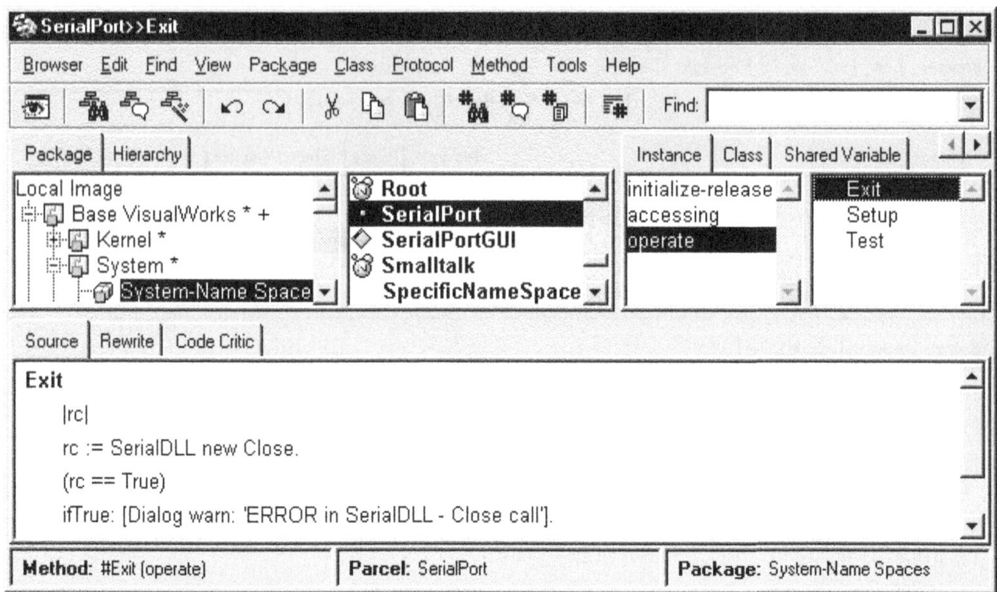

FIGURE 7.26 The `Exit` method for `SerialPort`.

class as a file by using the file-out method, and saving the class file as a parcel by using the parcel method.

7.3.6 Parceling and Filing Out the Project Files

There are different ways to parcel class files in VisualWorks. For example, we can open a System Browser by clicking the `Open a System Browser` icon from the toolbar in the Visual Launcher. The default dialog box is `Package`. You can use the `Browser|Parcel` menu item to parcel a class file. To parcel the class file `SerialPort`, perform the following steps:

1. In the opened System Browser, click the `Browser|Parcel` menu item to activate the Parcel tab.
2. Right-click on the pane (the `Parcel` list) and select `New` from the pop-up menu.
3. In the dialog box that appears, enter the name of the desired parcel file. For this application, enter `SerialPort` and Click `OK`.
4. On the second pane from the left, find the name of the newly created parcel file, `SerialPort`, and right-click on it. From the pop-up menu that appears, select `Move|All to Parcel`.
5. In the opened `Select` dialog box, click the newly added parcel `SerialPort` from the `Select parcel to move to:` list, and click `OK` to save the class file as a parcel.

You can perform the same steps to parcel the Application Model file `SerialPortGUI`. To File-out a file, you would perform the following steps:

1. In the opened System Browser, click the `Browser|Parcel` menu item to activate the Parcel tab.
2. On the leftmost pane, select the file to be filed out from the `Parcel` list.
3. Right-click on the lefthand pane and select `File Out As` from the pop-up menu.
4. Select the desired file path and enter the file name in the opened `Save As` dialog box.
5. Click the `Save` button to file out the class file.

After a class file has been parceled or filed out, you can load it either as a file or as a parcel next time you start up VisualWorks.

When you parcel your class files, you have some other selections when you right-click the newly added parcel on the second frame from the left. You can move the class file to a category, a namespace, a parcel, or a package. You can also move just the definition of the class file or selected file into a parcel or a package.

It is now time for us to complete this project by developing our dynamic link library in Visual C++.

7.3.7 Develop a Dynamic Link Library in the Visual C++ Domain

The Dynamic Link Library (DLL) that we'll create here will be used to interface with the External Interface Class in the VisualWorks domain. This DLL file is very similar to the DLL file we developed in Section 4.4 of Chapter 4. To avoid repetition, here we only show the source code for each file without detailed explanations.

Launch Visual C++ 6.0 and create a new project with the following properties:

- Project name: `SerialDLL`
- Project type: `Win32 Dynamic-Link Library`
- Project Location: `C:\Book2_Program\Chapter 7\SerialPort`

Create a new header file, `SerialDLL.h`, and a new source file, `SerialDLL.cpp`, for the newly created project.

7.3.7.1 Creating the Header File for the DLL

Open the newly created header file `SerialDLL.h` and enter the code that is shown in Figure 7.27.

The code is straightforward and easy to understand. Refer to Section 4.4 in Chapter 4 for detailed explanations of each section.

7.3.7.2 Developing the Source File for the DLL

The source file can be divided into two categories: the interface and the local functions. Developing the code will involve two steps. First we'll create code for the three interface functions, `Setup()`, `Write()`, and `Read()`. Then we'll code the local functions, such as `PortInitialize()`, `PortWrite()`, and `PortRead()`.

7.3.7.2.1 The `Setup` Function

Open the newly created source file, `SerialDLL.cpp`, and enter the code that is shown in Figure 7.28.

Two arguments are passed into this function: the com port and the baud rate. The values of two parameters will be entered at run time in the VisualWorks domain, from the `SerialPortGUI` class. The purpose of this function is to initialize and configure the serial port according to the values of these two parameters entered by the user.

7.3.7.2.2 The `Write` and `Close` Functions

The code of the `Write()` function is shown in Figure 7.29. Since the `Close()` function is very simple, so its code is also included here.

The `Write()` function is used to send a single byte of data to the transmission buffer on the serial port. The `Close()` function is used to clean up the serial setup environments during the data communication.

```
/*****************************************************************************
 * NAME          : SerialDLL.h
 * DESC.         : Header file for SerialDLL.cpp
 * PGRMER.       : Y. Bai
 *****************************************************************************/
#ifndef _SERIALDLL_H_
#define _SERIALDLL_H_
#define MAX_STRING                  256
#define NOPARITY                      0
#define ONESTOPBIT                    0
#define RTS_CONTROL_DISABLE     0x00
#define RTS_CONTROL_ENABLE      0x01
#define DTR_CONTROL_DISABLE     0x00
#define DTR_CONTROL_ENABLE      0x01
#define msg(info)       MessageBox(NULL, info, "", MB_OK)
typedef struct
{
   long      ulCtrlerID;        // serial port ID
   char      cEcho;             // echo character
   char      cEORChar;          // end of character
   long      lTimeout;          // time out value
   long      lBaudRate;         // baud rate
   long      lDataBits;         // data bits
} SerialCreate, *pSerialCreate;

typedef struct
{
   char   pcBuffer[100];        /* Buffer to store the received data */
   int    iMaxChars;            /* Max number of characters to be received */
   int    piNumRcvd;            /* Actual number of characters received */
   char   cTermChar;            /* Terminal character */
} CommPortClass;
typedef enum
{
   OK       = 0,                // no error
   EC_TIMEOUT,                  // system time out error
   EC_FOPEN,                    // file open error
   EC_INVAL_CONFIG,             // invalid configuration error
   EC_TIMEOUT_SET,              // set structure time out error
   EC_RECV_TIMEOUT,             // receiver time out error
   EC_EXIT_CODE,                // get exit code error
   EC_WAIT_SINGLEOBJ,           // WaitForSingleObject function error
   EC_INVALIDPORT,              // invalid port error
   EC_WRITE_FAIL,               // write function error
   EC_CREATE_THREAD,            // create thread error
   EC_UNKNOWNERROR              // unknown error
} ERR_CODE;

 HANDLE  hPort;
 char*     sPortName;
 bool      PortCreateflg = false;
```

FIGURE 7.27 Header file of the DLL. *(continued)*

```
/* local functions */
ERR_CODE PortInitialize(LPTSTR lpszPortName, pSerialCreate pCreate);
ERR_CODE PortWrite(char* bByte, int NumByte);
ERR_CODE PortRead(CommPortClass *hCommPort);
void WINAPI ThreadFunc(void* hCommPorts);
/*----------------------------------------------------------------*/
#define DllExport    __declspec( dllexport )
/*----------------------------------------------------------------*/
DllExport int Setup(int  cPort, int  bRate);
DllExport int Read();
DllExport int Write(int  sdata);
DllExport int Close();

#endif
```

FIGURE 7.27 Header file of the DLL.

7.3.7.2.3 The `Read` Function

The `Read()` function is somewhat complicated because a thread function is used to perform the real reading task. Without this thread support, the `Read()` function would enter an infinite cycle, and the computer would be hung up if no event were detected during the reading process. The code for the `Read()` function is shown in Figure 7.30.

A local function, `PortRead()` , is called by this `Read()` function to perform the reading operation. The `PortRead()` function creates a thread and calls the thread function to interface with the serial port and complete the data collection. A structure pointer variable, `commClass`, is passed into the function as an argument, and all data definitions are defined in that structure. The returned data is stored in a buffer that is an element defined in that structure.

7.3.7.2.4 The Local Functions

The first local function is `PortInitialize()`; its code is shown in Figure 7.31.

The second local function is the `PortWrite()` function. The code for this function is shown in Figure 7.32.

This function calls the system function `WriteFile()` to access the transmitter buffer on the serial port and send a byte to the port.

The code of the local function `PortRead()` is shown in Figure 7.33.

The `PortRead()` function has one argument, `*hCommPort`, which is a pointer structure. This pointer structure will be passed into the thread as a null pointer parameter later on when `PortRead()` creates that thread. After the thread is created, the thread function is suspended by a `CREATE_SUSPENDED` argument. The thread function will not be executed until a `ResumeTh-read()` function is called. The newly created thread returns a handler `hThread`, which will be used by all other components to access the thread.

A `WaitForSingleObject()` function is called after the thread runs. This function is used to monitor and wait for one of two events to occur. The first is a running thread completion event, `WAIT_OBJECT_0`. This event occurs when the thread function is normally completed and terminated. The second event is a timeout event, `WAIT_TIMEOUT`. This event occurs if the thread enters a dead cycle. If the first event occurs (`WAIT_OBJECT_0`), which means that the thread has successfully obtained the data written to the serial port and that the data has been stored in the buffer defined in the `hCommPort` data structure, the `PortRead()` function will close the thread handler and exit the program because the data has been obtained. If the second event occurs (WAIT_TIMEOUT), it means that the thread has entered a dead cycle and no event has triggered

```
/*****************************************************************************
 * NAME         : SerialDLL.cpp
 * DESC.        : DLL functions to interface to RS-232 serial port, called by VisualWorks.
 * PRGMER.      : Y. Bai
 *****************************************************************************/
#include <stdio.h>
#include <windows.h>
#include <stdlib.h>
#include <string.h>
#include "SerialDLL.h"

DllExport int Setup(int cPort, int bRate)
{
        ERR_CODE  rc = OK;
        pSerialCreate  pParam;

        pParam = new SerialCreate;             // create a new pointer structure
        pParam->lBaudRate = bRate;             // assign values to variables in structure
        pParam->lDataBits = 8;
        pParam->lTimeout  = 3000;

        switch(cPort)                          // check the port number
        {
        case 1:
                sPortName = "COM1";            // port is COM1
                break;
        case 2:
                sPortName = "COM2";            // port is COM2
                break;
        case 3:
                sPortName = "COM3";            // port is COM3
                break;
        case 4:
                sPortName = "COM4";            // port is COM4
                break;
        default:
                return EC_INVALIDPORT;
        }
        if (PortCreateflg)                     // port flag is true means port was set
        {
                msg("Port has been Setup ");
                return rc;
        }
        rc = PortInitialize(sPortName, pParam); // call local func. to configure port
        if (rc != 0)
           msg("ERROR in PortInitialize()!");
        delete pParam;                         // clean pointer structure
        PortCreateflg = true;                  // set port creation flag

        return rc;
}
```

FIGURE 7.28 The `setup` function.

the serial port. In this case, the `PortRead()` function also terminates the thread function and closes the thread handler, but returns a timeout error to the calling function.

In any other case, an error status is returned to the calling function to indicate that an error has been encountered during execution of the `PortRead()` function.

The final local function is the thread function `ThreadFunc()`. The code for this function is shown in Figure 7.34.

```
DllExport int Write(int  sdata)
{
        int  numByte = 1;                    // define written length as 1 byte
        char sByte[8];
        ERR_CODE rc = OK;
        sprintf(sByte, "%c", sdata);         // convert integer to character
        rc = PortWrite(sByte, numByte);      // call local func. to write the character
        if (rc != 0)
           msg("ERROR in PortWrite() !");
        return  rc;
}
DllExport int Close()
{
        ERR_CODE rc = OK;
        if (PortCreateflg)
           CloseHandle(hPort);               // clean up the port handler
        PortCreateflg = false;               // reset the port creation flag
        return rc;
}
```

FIGURE 7.29 The `Write` and `Close` functions.

```
DllExport int Read()
{
        int  idata;
        char cdata[8];
        ERR_CODE rc = OK;
        CommPortClass* commClass;
        commClass = new CommPortClass;       // create a new pointer structure
        commClass->iMaxChars = 1;            // assign value to the variable in structure
        rc = PortRead(commClass);            // call local func. to read back the data
        if (rc != 0)
           msg("ERROR in PortRead()! ");
        sprintf(cdata, "%d", commClass->pcBuffer[0]);
        idata = atoi(cdata);                 // convert the character to integer
        delete commClass;                    // clean up structure
        return  idata;
}
```

FIGURE 7.30 The `Read` function.

The thread function is the real body of the thread, which executes the task assigned to the thread. In our application, we use a thread to check and retrieve the data written to the port and to store that data into a buffer defined in the data structure. The advantage of using a thread to handle this job is to prevent a dead cycle, which would happen if no event were to trigger the port.

The thread has an argument `hCommPorts`, whose type is a null pointer. This means that the argument can be adapted and converted to hold any kind of data. This argument is passed into the thread by the `CreateThread()` function; its values are initialized by the interface function `Read()` before the `PortRead()` local function is called.

```
ERR_CODE PortInitialize(LPTSTR lpszPortName, pSerialCreate pCreate)
{
    DWORD               dwError;
    DCB                 PortDCB;
    ERR_CODE            ecStatus = OK;
    COMMTIMEOUTS        CommTimeouts;
    unsigned char       dBit;

    // check if the port has been created...
    if (PortCreateflg)
    {
        msg("Port has been initialized!");
        return ecStatus;
    }
    // Open the serial port.
    hPort = CreateFile(lpszPortName, // Pointer to the name of the port
              GENERIC_READ | GENERIC_WRITE,
                                   // Access (read/write) mode
              0,                   // Share mode
              NULL,                // Pointer to the security attribute
              OPEN_EXISTING,       // How to open the serial port
              0,                   // Port attributes
              NULL);               // Handle to port with attribute to copy
     if ( hPort == INVALID_HANDLE_VALUE )
     {
         dwError = GetLastError();                 // Could not open the port.
         msg("Unable to open the port");
         CloseHandle(hPort);  return  EC_FOPEN;
     }
     PortCreateflg = TRUE;
     PortDCB.DCBlength = sizeof(DCB);
    GetCommState(hPort, &PortDCB);
     // Change the DCB structure settings.
     PortDCB.BaudRate = pCreate->lBaudRate;   // Current baud rate
     PortDCB.fBinary  = TRUE;                 // Binary mode; no EOF check
     PortDCB.fParity  = TRUE;                 // Enable parity checking.
     PortDCB.fOutxCtsFlow = FALSE;            // No CTS output flow control
     PortDCB.fOutxDsrFlow = FALSE;            // No DSR output flow control
     PortDCB.fDtrControl = DTR_CONTROL_ENABLE; //DTR flow control type
     PortDCB.fDsrSensitivity = FALSE;         // DSR sensitivity
     PortDCB.fTXContinueOnXoff = TRUE;        // XOFF continues Tx
     PortDCB.fOutX = FALSE;                   // No XON/XOFF out flow control
     PortDCB.fInX  = FALSE;                   // No XON/XOFF in flow control
     PortDCB.fErrorChar = FALSE;              // Disable error replacement.
     PortDCB.fNull = FALSE;                   // Disable null stripping.
     PortDCB.fRtsControl = RTS_CONTROL_ENABLE;  // RTS flow control
     PortDCB.fAbortOnError = FALSE;           // Do not abort reads/writes on error.
     dBit = (unsigned char)pCreate->lDataBits;
     PortDCB.ByteSize = dBit;                 // Number of bits/bytes, 4-8
```

FIGURE 7.31 The local `PortInitialize` function. *(continued)*

```
    PortDCB.Parity = NOPARITY;              // 0-4=no,odd,even,mark,space
    PortDCB.StopBits = ONESTOPBIT;          // 0,1,2 = 1, 1.5, 2
    // Configure the port according to the specifications of the DCB structure.
    if (!SetCommState (hPort, &PortDCB))
    {
        dwError = GetLastError();         // Could not create the read thread.
        msg("Unable to configure the serial port");
        return EC_INVAL_CONFIG;
    }
    // Retrieve the time-out parameters for all read and write operations on the port.
    GetCommTimeouts(hPort, &CommTimeouts);
    // Change the COMMTIMEOUTS structure settings.
    CommTimeouts.ReadIntervalTimeout = MAXDWORD;
    CommTimeouts.ReadTotalTimeoutMultiplier = 0;
    CommTimeouts.ReadTotalTimeoutConstant = 0;
    CommTimeouts.WriteTotalTimeoutMultiplier = 10;
    CommTimeouts.WriteTotalTimeoutConstant = 1000;
    // Set the time-out parameters for all read and write operations on the port.
    if (!SetCommTimeouts (hPort, &CommTimeouts))
    {
        dwError = GetLastError();         // Could not create the read thread.
        msg("Unable to set the time-out parameters");
        return EC_TIMEOUT_SET;
    }
    return ecStatus;
}
```

FIGURE 7.31 The local `PortInitialize` function.

```
/*****************************************************************************
 * NAME        : PortWrite()
 * DESC.       : Write data to the port
 * DATE        : 12/9/03
 * PRGMER.     : Y. Bai
*****************************************************************************/
ERR_CODE PortWrite(char* bByte, int NumByte)
{
    DWORD dwError;
    DWORD dwNumBytesWritten;
    ERR_CODE ecStatus = OK;

    if (!WriteFile (hPort,               // Port handle
                bByte,                   // Pointer to the data to write
                NumByte,                 // Number of bytes to write
                &dwNumBytesWritten,      // Pointer to the number of bytes written
                NULL))                   // Must be NULL for Windows CE
    {
        // WriteFile failed. Report error.
        dwError = GetLastError ();
        msg("ERROR in PortWrite ..");
        return EC_WRITE_FAIL;
    }

    return ecStatus;
}
```

FIGURE 7.32 The local `PortWrite` function.

```
/*****************************************************************************
 * NAME        : PortRead()
 * DESC.       : Read data from the serial port
 *****************************************************************************/
ERR_CODE PortRead(CommPortClass *hCommPort)
{
    HANDLE hThread;                              // handler for port read thread
    DWORD  IDThread;
    DWORD  Ret, ExitCode;
    DWORD  dTimeout = 5000;                      // define time out value: 5 sec.
    ERR_CODE ecStatus = OK;
    if (!(hThread = CreateThread(NULL,           // no security attributes
                        0,                       // use default stack size
                        (LPTHREAD_START_ROUTINE) ThreadFunc,
                        (LPVOID)hCommPort,       // parameter to thread function
                        CREATE_SUSPENDED,        // creation flag - suspended
                        &IDThread) ) )           // returns thread ID
    {
        msg("Create Read Thread failed");
        return EC_CREATE_THREAD;
    }
    ResumeThread(hThread);                       // start thread now
    Ret = WaitForSingleObject(hThread, dTimeout);
    if (Ret == WAIT_OBJECT_0)
    {
        // Data received & process it... need to do nothing because the data is stored in the
        // hCommPort in the Thread Function. The only thing is to close thread handle
        CloseHandle(hThread);
    }
    else if (Ret == WAIT_TIMEOUT)                // Time out happened
    {                                            // Warning & kill thread
        Ret = GetExitCodeThread(hThread, &ExitCode);
        msg("Time out happened in PortRead() ");
        if (ExitCode == STILL_ACTIVE)
        {
            TerminateThread(hThread, ExitCode);
            CloseHandle(hThread);
            return EC_RECV_TIMEOUT;
        }
        else
        {
            CloseHandle(hThread);
            msg("ERROR in GetExitCodeThread: != STILL_ACTIVE ");
            ecStatus = EC_EXIT_CODE;
        }
    }
    else
    {
        msg("ERROR in WaitFor SingleObject ");
        ecStatus = EC_WAIT_SINGLEOBJ;
    }
    return ecStatus;
}
```

FIGURE 7.33 The local `PortRead` function.

After declaring some local variables and data structures at the beginning of the thread function, we need to convert the null pointer parameter, `hCommPorts`, to the destination data structure `CommPortClass`.

We need to assign a set of event masks to the serial port controller (UART) by using the `SetCommMask()` system function. We combine a sequence of event masks by using the `or`

```
/*****************************************************************************
 * NAME   : ThreadFunc()
 * DESC.  : The reason to use this thread is to overcome the hung up introduced by the
 *        : WaitCommEvent() function which waits for only the comm. event, not synchro-
 *        : nition event. The program will be dead-cycle without this thread.
 * PRMR.  : Y. Bai
 *****************************************************************************/
void WINAPI ThreadFunc(void* hCommPorts)
{
    char  Byte;
    BOOL  bResult, fDone;
    int   nTotRead = 0;
    DWORD dwCommModemStatus, dwBytesTransferred;
    CommPortClass*  CommPorts;
    ERR_CODE ecStatus = OK;
    CommPorts = (CommPortClass* )hCommPorts;
    // Specify a set of events to be monitored for the port.
    SetCommMask(hPort, EV_RXCHAR | EV_CTS | EV_DSR | EV_RLSD | EV_RING);
    fDone = FALSE;
    while (!fDone)
    {
      // Wait for an event to occur for the port.
      WaitCommEvent(hPort, &dwCommModemStatus, 0);
      // Re-specify the set of events to be monitored for the port.
      SetCommMask(hPort, EV_RXCHAR | EV_CTS | EV_DSR |EV_RLSD| EV_RING);
      if (dwCommModemStatus & EV_RXCHAR||dwCommModemStatus & EV_RLSD)
      {
         //  received the char_event & loop to wait for the data.
         do
         {
             // Read the data from the serial port.
             bResult = ReadFile(hPort, &Byte, 1, &dwBytesTransferred, 0);
             if (!bResult)
             {
                   msg("ERROR in ReadFile !");
                   fDone = TRUE;
                   break;
             }

             else
             {
                  // Display the data read.
                  if (dwBytesTransferred == 1)
                  {
                     if (Byte == 0x0D ||Byte == 0x0A)       // null char or LF
                     {
                         CommPorts->piNumRcvd = nTotRead;
                         fDone = TRUE;
                         break;
                     }
                     CommPorts->pcBuffer[nTotRead] = Byte;
                     nTotRead++;
                     if (nTotRead == CommPorts->iMaxChars)
                     {
```

FIGURE 7.34 The thread function `ThreadFunc`. *(continued)*

```
                        fDone = TRUE;
                        break;
                    }
                }
                else
                {
                    if (Byte == 0x0D ||Byte == 0x0A)        // null char or CR
                    {
                        msg("Received null character ");
                        fDone = TRUE;
                        break;
                    }
                }
            }
        }while (dwBytesTransferred == 1); //while (nTotRead < pRecv->iMaxChars);
    }   // if
  }     // while
  return;
}
```

FIGURE 7.34 The thread function `ThreadFunc`.

operator to allow multiple events to trigger the port. These events would include receiving a `char` or a `ring`, an activation of the DSR or the CTS line. If any of these events happen, the UART can immediately respond by executing the associated identifying command.

Next we use a `while` loop and a system function, `WaitCommEvent()`, to continuously monitor the events and process any of those that do occur. Note that this function only monitors serial communication events, not synchronous events. If a `received-a-char` event happens, we call `ReadFile()` to read back the character and store it in the buffer by using `CommPorts->pcBuffer[nTotRead] = Byte`.

The buffer is defined inside the data structure `CommPorts`, and the local variable `nTotRead` represents the total number of bytes to be read.

The program must determine whether the maximum number of characters to be read have arrived into the receiving buffer. When this happens, the program will set the `while` loop condition flag and exit the loop. Besides checking for the maximum number of characters, the program must also determine whether a null or CR character has been received. In some applications, the terminal string is marked by a null or CR character. The `while` loop will be terminated if either is received.

After the received character is stored in the buffer, the `while` loop will be terminated and the thread stopped. The associated event, `WAIT_OBJECT_0`, will be sent to the `WaitForSingleObject()` function in the local `PortRead()` function to inform the function that the thread has been completed successfully and that the data has been obtained and stored in the buffer. The `PortRead()` will return an `OK` status to the interface function `Read()` to indicate that the `PortRead()` function has successfully completed. The interface function will pick up the data stored in the buffer, convert it into a suitable format, and return it to the VisualWorks domain.

7.3.7.3 Developing the Definition File for the DLL

Before we can finish our dynamic link library, we need to generate a definition file for this DLL. The purpose of the definition file is to export all interface functions to VisualWorks, where they can be seen in the Smalltalk domain. The definition file for our DLL is shown in Figure 7.35.

```
LIBRARY SerialDLL.dll
EXPORTS
Setup
Read
Write
Close
```

FIGURE 7.35 The definition file.

The first line of code is used to declare the name of the dynamic link library. Following the keyword `EXPORTS`, all our four interface functions are listed. The interface functions can then be exported to VisualWorks and can be "seen" by any guy in Smalltalk domain.

TIP: This definition file is important to the interface between VisualWorks and the DLL. Without it, VisualWorks may not identify the Visual C++ interface functions defined in the DLL as the program runs. This potential bug is difficult to detect in some situations, so it is important that you define this as the DLL.

Now we have completed developing our DLL file in the Visual C++ domain. Click the `Build|Build SerialDLL.dll` menu item in the Visual C++ IDE to compile and build the target DLL file. The completed DLL file is located in the `Debug` folder of the current project. Click the `File|Open` menu item, browse to our DLL target file, `SerialDLL.dll`, and copy this file to the folder `C:\stdll`. This folder is specifically designed to store the DLL target files for this application. If you wish, however, you can create a different folder to store the files.

7.3.8 Finish Coding of the SerialDLL Project in VisualWorks

Now let's return to the VisualWorks domain to complete the code for the External Interface Class `SerialDLL` that we created in Section 7.3.4.

Most items have been built, and our program is nearly ready to be tested. One more thing we need to do is to configure the External Interface Class and set the connections between the functions defined in the External Interface Class and the interface functions defined in the DLL.

Open the `External Interface Finder` by clicking the `Tools|DLL and C Connect` menu item from the VisualWorks launcher. On the `Category` list, click `library files`, and click the `New` button to open the `Library File` dialog box, which is shown in Figure 7.36.

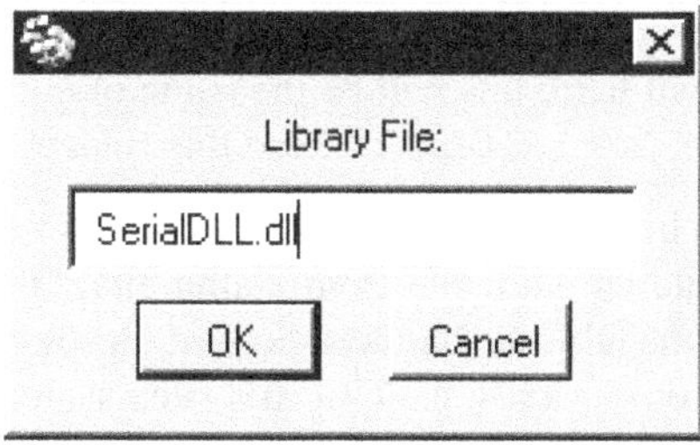

FIGURE 7.36 The `Library File` dialog box.

Enter `SerialDLL.dll` in the input field as the name for the library file, and click `OK` to save this setting.

You will see the newly added library file in the `Library files` list on the rightmost pane, which is shown in Figure 7.37.

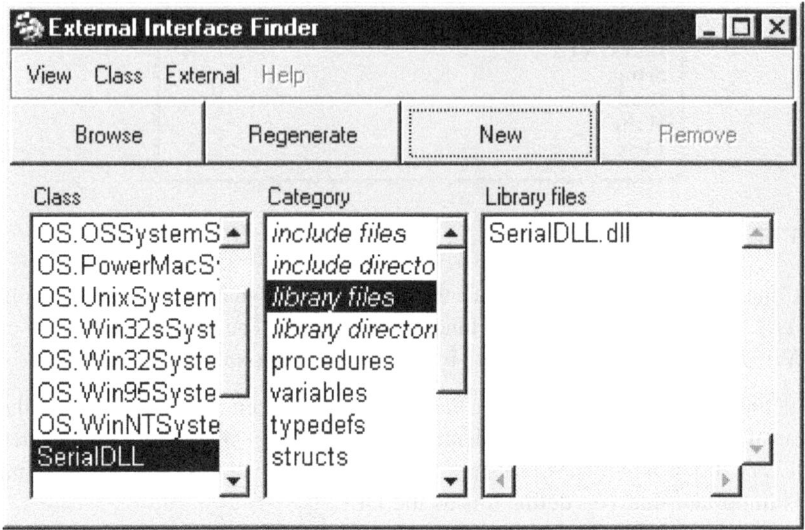

FIGURE 7.37 Configuring the library file.

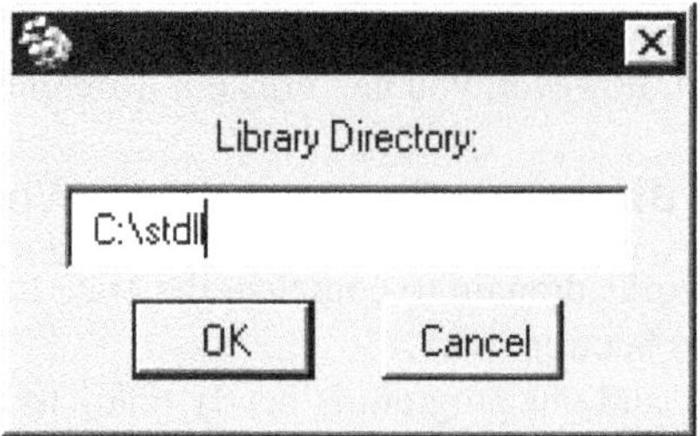

FIGURE 7.38 Configuring the library directory.

Next click the `library directories` item, which is located just below the `library files` item in the `Category` list, and click the `New` button to open the `Library Directory` dialog box, which is shown in Figure 7.38.

Enter `C:\stdll` in the input field; this will be the name of our library directory. (Recall that we've saved our DLL target file, `SerialDLL.dll`, in this folder). Click `OK` to save this setting.

TIP: After you complete these library configurations, especially for the library file, you will not be able to delete or update the DLL file from within either the Window Explorer or the Visual C++ IDE because the DLL file has been hooked together with the External Interface Class in VisualWorks. In other words, the DLL has been shared by Smalltalk. If you want to make modifications to the DLL file, you should first have to delete the file from the library file in the External Interface Class. To do this, select the DLL file and click the `Remove` button. After removing the DLL file from the External Interface Class, you can delete that DLL file from the Windows Explorer and copy a new one to the folder `C:\stdll`. Then you can create a new library file by entering the name `SerialDLL.dll` in the `library file` input field to recover the library file.

Now everything is ready for us to run and test our project in the Smalltalk domain.

You can activate the project in two ways. One way is to run it from the `Resource Finder`. In the `Resource Finder`, select our Application Model, `SerialPortGUI`, from the `Class` list, and then click the `Start` button to run the project, as shown in Figure 7.39.

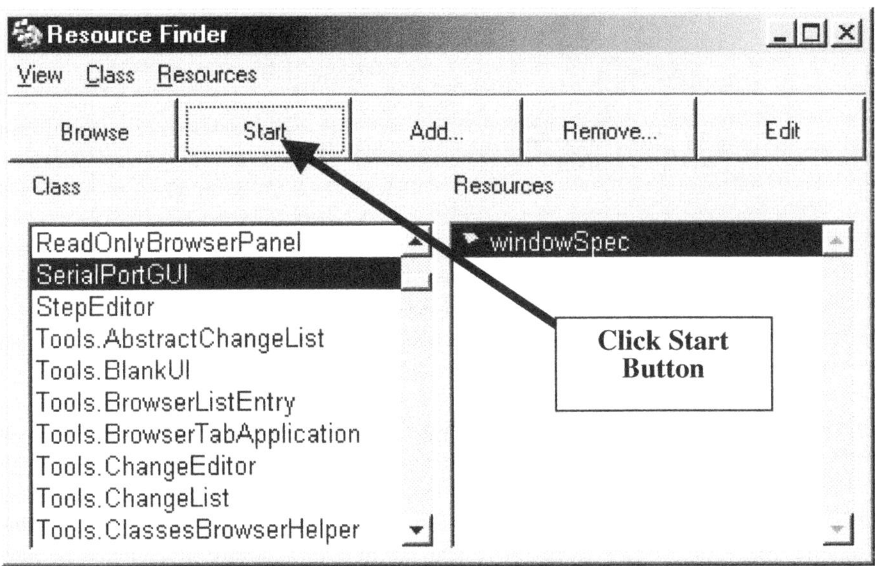

FIGURE 7.39 Running the project from the `Resource Finder`.

Another way to run the project is to type the following commands shown in Figure 7.40 in the `Workspace`, highlight it and right-click on it, and select `Do it` from the pop-up menu, as shown in Figure 7.40.

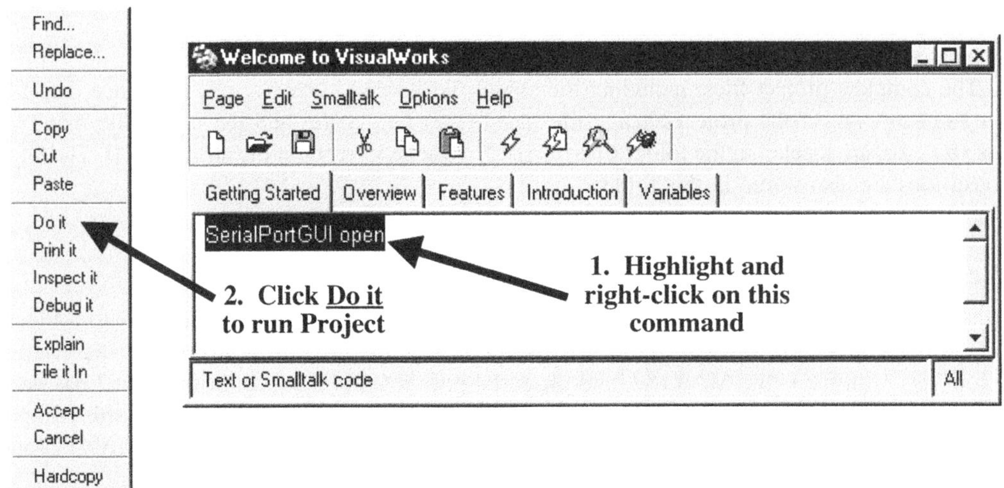

FIGURE 7.40 Running the project from the `Workspace`.

The results of running the project are shown in Figure 7.41.

As the program runs, enter `1` in the `Com Port` input field, and enter `9600` in the `Baud Rate` input field. Then click the `Setup` action button to configure the serial port. A debug message

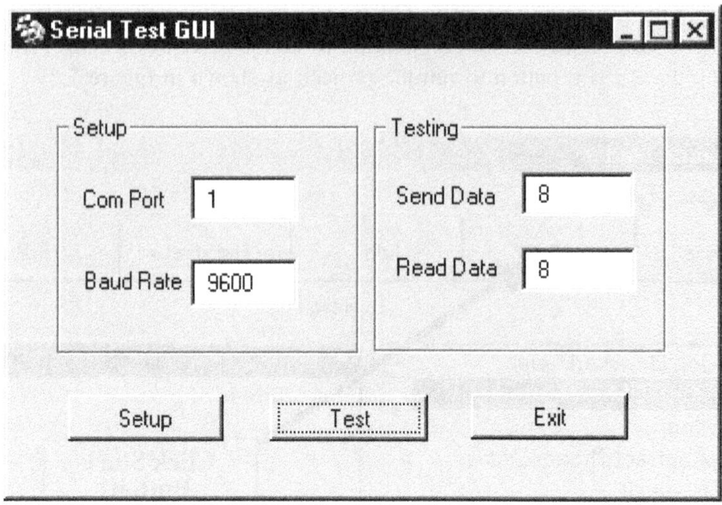

FIGURE 7.41 Results of running the Serial Port Interface project.

box will appear to display the port number and the baud rate if the DEBUG macro is enabled in the DLL source file. Click `Test` to begin to test the port by sending a sequence of integers to COM1 and read back the same data from the port. The sent out data and read back data will be displayed in the `Send Data` and `Read Data` input fields, respectively. Continue to click the `Test` button to test the next data.

Click the `Exit` action button to terminate the program.

You can add and modify the delay between the time when data is sent out and the time when it is read back. The effect will be that the data displayed in the `Read Data` input field is delayed by the period of time that you specify in the program. If the delay value is greater than 100 milliseconds, the received data will be one number less than the data sent out.

Now we have finished developing and testing our serial port project.

The complete project files, including the parcel file `SerialPort.pcl`, the office data file `SerialPort.pst`, the project change file `smallserial.cha`, and the image file `smallserial.im`, are located in the folder `Chapter 7\SerialPort` on the attached CD. The DLL project files are also stored in this folder.

7.4 AN ADVANCED SERIAL PORT INTERFACE PROGRAM

In this section, we'll develop an interface that will connect a VisualWorks program with a Visual C++ DLL to communicate with a serial A/D converter via the serial port. The serial A/D converter used in this example is the MAX187, and the serial port is COM1. Since the MAX187 has been discussed in earlier chapters of this book, we will not provide detailed description for this component. Refer to Section 2.7.3 in Chapter 2 to get more detailed information about the MAX187 and the MAX220.

Figure 7.42 shows the interface structure of this project.

As in our last project, two models are implemented here: the Domain Model and the Application Model. The storage and processing of data are performed in the Domain Model, and the input and output of the data are processed in the Application Model. The Application Model also provides a graphical user interface to the Domain Model; at run time, this GUI will allow us to perform data operations and computations. The Domain Model will pass the information between the Application Model and a DLL that we'll develop in the Visual C++ domain. The DLL can directly access the

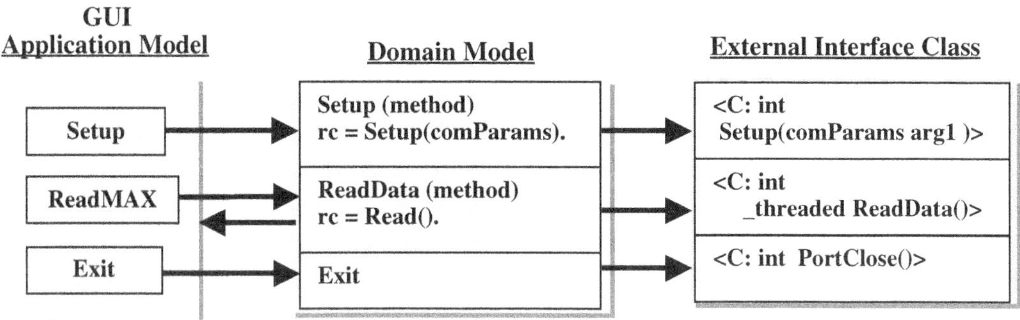

FIGURE 7.42 Structure of the Advanced Serial Port Interface program.

serial port to perform data transmission between VisualWorks and the serial port. All communications between the two models and the DLL are performed by the methods or interface functions developed in the associated domains.

7.4.1 The Interface Circuit

The interface circuit of this project is identical to that described in Section 2.7.3. A DB-9 connector is used for this project. (Refer to Section 2.7.3 to get detailed descriptions of the components and the circuit.) The interface circuit is shown in Figure 7.43.

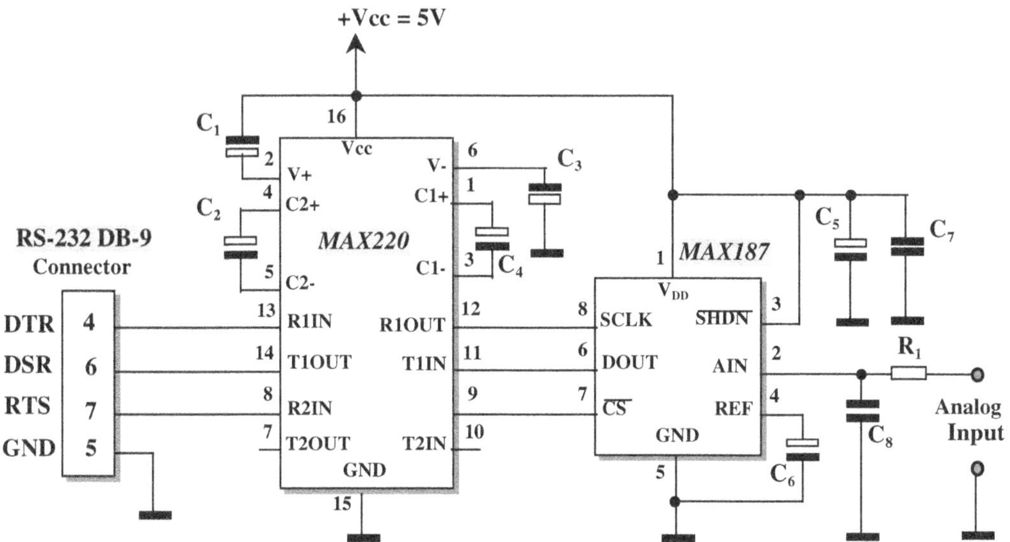

FIGURE 7.43 Interface circuit for the Advanced Serial Port Interface program.

The components used in this circuit are listed in Table 7.1.

One point to keep in mind as we develop our code is the inverted logic that exists on the serial driver/converter MAX220. Recall that the input and the output signals of the MAX220 are inverted, so in order to get a logical `0` in the terminal of the MAX187, the associated input on the MAX220 should be a logical `1`. A logical `1` in the output of the MAX187 becomes a logical `0` in the output of the MAX220.

The input signal to the MAX187 comes from a function generator or from an actual analog input system. For this project, we'll use a function generator to generate the input to the MAX187.

TABLE 7.1
The Elements Parameters

Elements	Value	Meaning
R_1	10 KΩ	Current-limited resistor
C_1 –C_4	10 μF/25V	Electrolytic capacitors
C_5 –C_6	4.7 μF/10V	Electrolytic capacitors
C_7 –C_8	0.1 μF	Capacitors

Three waveforms are tested: sinusoidal, triangular, and square signals. The maximum input voltage is 5 volts, which is the upper limitation of the MAX187.

First let's develop a Dynamic Link Library (DLL). This DLL will be called by the interface functions in the External Interface Class, which we'll develop later in the VisualWorks domain.

7.4.2 Developing the Dynamic Link Library

We must develop three interface functions for this DLL file: `Setup()`, `ReadData()`,and `Port-Close()`. (Refer to Figure 7.42). The names of these interface functions should be identical to the names of the methods developed in the External Interface Class in VisualWorks.

This DLL is very similar to the one developed in Section 4.4.3 in Chapter 4. Refer to that section to get more detailed information. There are some minor differences between that DLL and the one we will develop for this project. In the following sections, we'll discuss each piece of code separately. The code is divided into three main categories: the header file, the source file, and the definition file. In the source file, the code operates according to the different actions of the associated functions developed in the DLL. All parts that must be modified from the DLL developed in Chapter 4 are discussed in detail in the following sections.

Launch Visual C++ 6.0 and create a new `Win32 Dynamic-Link Library` project named `SmallMAXDLL`.

7.4.2.1 The Header File for the DLL

In the newly created project, add a new header file named `SmallMAXDLL.h`, and enter the code that is shown in Figure 7.44.

Each section of the code is explained in the following list.

A: Three macros are added in this header file: `MAX_BYTE`, `MAX_BITS`, and `MAX_DATA`. These macros are used to define the size of the data string to be received from the MAX187. `MAX_BITS` is defined as `12` because the MAX187 is a 12-bit A/D converter. `MAX_DATA` is used to define the total collected data units; its value is `100` in this application.

B: The data buffer `pcBuffer`, defined in the structure `CommPortClass`, is modified to an integer data type since the received data will be a 12-bit integer.

C: A file pointer is added here; it is used to open a data file to store the collected data from the MAX187.

D: An integer variable, `runTIMES`, is used to record the times of calls to the function `PortRead()`. By using this variable, we can monitor the calling times to that function and neglect the first call to that function (the wake-up call).

```
/*****************************************************************************
 * NAME        : SmallMAXDLL.h
 * DESC.       : Header file for SmallMAXDLL.cpp
 *****************************************************************************/
#include <Windows.h>
#ifndef _SMALLMAXDLL_H_
#define _SMALLMAXDLL_H_
A  #define MAX_BYTE                   1
#define MAX_BITS                   12
#define MAX_DATA                   100
#define MAX_STRING                 256
#define NOPARITY                   0
#define ONESTOPBIT                 0
#define RTS_CONTROL_DISABLE        0x00
#define RTS_CONTROL_ENABLE         0x01
#define DTR_CONTROL_DISABLE        0x00
#define DTR_CONTROL_ENABLE         0x01
#define msg(info)     MessageBox(NULL, info, "", MB_OK)
typedef struct
{
  ULONG    ulCtrlerID;        // serial port ID
  char     cEcho;             // echo character
  char     cEORChar;          // end of character
  long     lTimeout;          // time out value
  long     lBaudRate;         // baud rate
  long     lDataBits;         // data bits
} SerialCreate, *pSerialCreate;
B  typedef struct
{
  int    pcBuffer;            /* Buffer to store the received data */
  int    iMaxChars;           /* Max number of characters to be received */
  int    piNumRcvd;           /* Actual number of characters received */
  char   cTermChar;           /* Terminal character */
} CommPortClass;
typedef enum
{
  OK        = 0,              // no error
  EC_TIMEOUT,                 // system time out error
  EC_FOPEN,                   // file open error
  EC_INVAL_CONFIG,            // invalid configuration error
  EC_TIMEOUT_SET,             // set structure time out error
  EC_RECV_TIMEOUT,            // receiver time out error
  EC_EXIT_CODE,               // get exit code error
  EC_WAIT_SINGLEOBJ,          // WaitForSingleObject function error
  EC_INVALIDPORT,             // invalid port error
  EC_WRITE_FAIL,              // write function error
  EC_CREATE_THREAD,           // create thread error
  EC_UNKNOWNERROR             // unknown error
 } ERR_CODE;
```

FIGURE 7.44 Header file of the DLL project. *(continued)*

```
C  FILE*       fp;
   HANDLE      hPort;
   char*       sPortName;
   bool        PortCreateflg = false;
D  int         runTIMES = 0;
E  char        fileName[] = "C:\\stdll\\smaxdll.dat";

   #define DllExport  __declspec( dllexport )

   /* DLL Interface functions */
   DllExport int Setup(int pCom[]);
   DllExport int ReadData();
   DllExport int PortClose();
   /* Local functions */
   ERR_CODE PortInitialize(LPTSTR lpszPortName, pSerialCreate pCreate);
   ERR_CODE PortRead(CommPortClass *hCommPort);
   void WINAPI ThreadFunc(void* hCommPorts);
   void Delay(int num);

   #endif
```

FIGURE 7.44 Header file of the DLL project.

E: A string variable, `fileName`, is declared here to provide a file name and path for the data file to be opened during the data collection.

All other code in this header file is identical to the code of the header file `SerialDLL` developed in Section 4.4.3.

Click the `File|Save` menu item from the Visual C++ 6.0 IDE to save the new header file to the appropriate project folder. For our application, the project folder is `C:\Book2_Program\SerialMAX\SmallMAXDLL`.

7.4.2.2 Code for the Source Files of the DLL

As previously mentioned, the code of the source files is based on the associated actions of the different functions. We'll develop the source code in this sequence: the `Setup()` function and its associated local functions, the `ReadData()` function and its associated local functions, and the `PortClose()` function.

7.4.2.2.1 The `Setup()` Function

Open the newly created source file and enter the code that is shown in Figure 7.45.

Each section of the code is explained in the following list.

F: A `DEBUG` macro is defined at the beginning of this source file. This macro works as a flag to indicate to the program that all debug information should be displayed as the program runs.

G: The system function `fopen()` is called to open a data file that is used to store the collected data. The data stored in this file can be plotted in the MATLAB domain to confirm that the data collection has been successful later.

H: The debug information that shows the passed port parameters from the External Interface Class in VisualWorks is displayed here to check and confirm the arguments of the `Setup()` function. A temporary buffer is used to store the debug information.

```
/*****************************************************************************
 * NAME        : SmallMAXDLL.cpp
 * DESC.       : DLL functions to interface to RS-232 serial port, called by VisualWorks.
 * PRGMER.     : Y. Bai
 *****************************************************************************/
#include <stdio.h>
#include <stdlib.h>
#include <string.h>
#include "SmallMAXDLL.h"
F   #define DEBUG
DllExport int Setup(int pCom[])
{
        ERR_CODE rc = OK;
        pSerialCreate pParam;
G       fp = fopen(fileName, "w");
        pParam = new SerialCreate;              // create a new pointer structure
        pParam->lBaudRate = pCom[1];            // assign values to variables in structure
        pParam->lDataBits = pCom[2];
        pParam->lTimeout = 3000;
        #ifdef DEBUG
H       char buff[128];
        sprintf(buff, "pCom[] = %d %d %d %d %d",
                pCom[0], pCom[1], pCom[2], pCom[3], pCom[4]);
        msg(buff);
        #endif
        switch(pCom[0])                         // check the port number
        {
        case 1: sPortName = "COM1";             // port is COM1
                break;
        case 2: sPortName = "COM2";             // port is COM2
                break;
        case 3: sPortName = "COM3";             // port is COM3
                break;
        case 4: sPortName = "COM4";             // port is COM4
                break;
        default:
                return EC_INVALIDPORT;
        }

      if (PortCreateflg)                        // port flag is true means port was set
      {
           msg("Port has been Setup ");
           return rc;
      }
      rc = PortInitialize(sPortName, pParam);   // call local func. to configure port
      if (rc != 0)
         msg("ERROR in PortInitialize()!");
      delete pParam;                            // clean pointer structure
      PortCreateflg = true;                     // set port creation flag
      return rc;
}
```

FIGURE 7.45 The `Setup()` function.

The `Setup()` function needs to call a local function, `PortInitialize()`, to perform the port configurations. The code for that local function is shown in Figure 7.46.

This code is identical to the code of the same function in Section 4.4.3.

```
ERR_CODE PortInitialize(LPTSTR lpszPortName, pSerialCreate pCreate)
{
    DWORD              dwError;
    DCB                PortDCB;
    ERR_CODE           ecStatus = OK;
    COMMTIMEOUTS       CommTimeouts;
    unsigned char      dBit;

    // check if the port has been created...
    if (PortCreateflg)
    {
        msg("Port has been initialized!");
        return ecStatus;
    }
    // Open the serial port.
    hPort = CreateFile(lpszPortName, GENERIC_READ | GENERIC_WRITE, 0,
                       NULL, OPEN_EXISTING, 0, NULL);

    // If it fails to open the port, return error.
    if ( hPort == INVALID_HANDLE_VALUE )
    {
        dwError = GetLastError();              // Could not open the port.
        msg("Unable to open the port");
        CloseHandle(hPort);
        return EC_FOPEN;
    }
    PortCreateflg = TRUE;
    PortDCB.DCBlength = sizeof(DCB);
    GetCommState(hPort, &PortDCB);    // Get the default port setting information.
    PortDCB.BaudRate = pCreate->lBaudRate;    // Current baud rate
    PortDCB.fBinary = TRUE;                    // Binary mode; no EOF check
    PortDCB.fParity = TRUE;                    // Enable parity checking.
    PortDCB.fOutxCtsFlow = FALSE;              // No CTS output flow control
    PortDCB.fOutxDsrFlow = FALSE;              // No DSR output flow control
    PortDCB.fDtrControl = DTR_CONTROL_ENABLE; //DTR flow control type
    PortDCB.fDsrSensitivity = FALSE;           // DSR sensitivity
    PortDCB.fTXContinueOnXoff = TRUE;          // XOFF continues Tx
    PortDCB.fOutX = FALSE;                     // No XON/XOFF out flow control
    PortDCB.fInX = FALSE;                      // No XON/XOFF in flow control
    PortDCB.fErrorChar = FALSE;                // Disable error replacement.
    PortDCB.fNull = FALSE;                     // Disable null stripping.
    PortDCB.fRtsControl = RTS_CONTROL_ENABLE;  // RTS flow control
    PortDCB.fAbortOnError = FALSE;             // Do not abort reads/writes on error.
    dBit = (unsigned char)pCreate->lDataBits;
    PortDCB.ByteSize = dBit;                   // Number of bits/bytes, 4-8
    PortDCB.Parity = NOPARITY;                 // 0-4=no,odd,even,mark,space
    PortDCB.StopBits = ONESTOPBIT;             // 0,1,2 = 1, 1.5, 2
    if (!SetCommState (hPort, &PortDCB))
    {
```

FIGURE 7.46 The local function `PortInitialize()`. *(continued)*

```
        dwError = GetLastError();            // Could not create the read thread.
        msg("Unable to configure the serial port");
        return EC_INVAL_CONFIG;
    }
    // Retrieve the time-out parameters for all read and write operations on the port.
    GetCommTimeouts(hPort, &CommTimeouts);
    // Change the COMMTIMEOUTS structure settings.
    CommTimeouts.ReadIntervalTimeout = MAXDWORD;
    CommTimeouts.ReadTotalTimeoutMultiplier = 0;
    CommTimeouts.ReadTotalTimeoutConstant = 0;
    CommTimeouts.WriteTotalTimeoutMultiplier = 10;
    CommTimeouts.WriteTotalTimeoutConstant = 1000;
    // Set the time-out parameters for all read and write operations on the port.
    if (!SetCommTimeouts (hPort, &CommTimeouts))
    {
        dwError = GetLastError();
        msg("Unable to set the time-out parameters");
        return EC_TIMEOUT_SET;
    }
    return ecStatus;
}
```

FIGURE 7.46 The local function `PortInitialize()`.

7.4.2.2.2 The ReadData Function

The code of the `ReadData()` function is shown in Figure 7.47.

```
  DllExport int ReadData()
  {
I      int ad_data;
       ERR_CODE rc = OK;
       CommPortClass* commClass;
J      commClass = new CommPortClass;
       commClass->iMaxChars = MAX_BYTE;
       commClass->iMaxBits = MAX_BITS;
K     EscapeCommFunction(hPort, SETDTR);     //Set DTR to disable the SCLK
      EscapeCommFunction(hPort, CLRRTS);     //Reset RTS to disable the CS-bar
L     rc = PortRead(commClass);
      if (rc != 0 && runTIMES != 0)          //wake-up reading error neglected.
         msg("ERROR in PortRead()! ");
M     runTIMES++;
N     fprintf(fp, "%d\n", commClass->pcBuffer);   //Reserve data
      ad_data = commClass->pcBuffer;
O     delete commClass;
P     return ad_data;
  }
```

FIGURE 7.47 The `ReadData()` function.

Each section of the code is explained in the following list.

I: The local variables are declared here. The `ad_data` variable can be considered a buffer; it is used to store the received data from the MAX187 A/D converter. The `rc` variable works as a status register to hold the returned running status of the calling function. The `commClass` is a pointer variable of the data structure `CommPortClass` defined in the header file.

J: The `new` keyword is used to allocate the memory space for the pointer variable `commClass` and return the starting address of that variable. Two setup parameters, `iMaxChars` and `iMaxBits`, are assigned to the elements of the structure variable `commClass`.

K: The system-extended function `EscapeCommFunction()` is executed to set up the initial status of two transmission lines, the DTR and the RTS, to disable the SCLK and the CS-bar control signals on the MAX187. `SETDTR` and `CLRRTS` are two system constants defined in the Win32 Software Development Kit (SDK).

L: The local function `PortRead()` is called to retrieve the converted data from the MAX187 A/D converter via the serial port. The argument `commClass` is a structure pointer variable that contains the data collection elements. An error message is displayed if the function call has failed. Note that an `AND` operation with `runTIMES` is added into the `IF` logic condition to skip the first possible reading error. During the initialization stage, the global variable `runTIMES` is reset to `0`. If the first `PortRead()` returns an error, the associated conditions are `rc !=0 and runTIMES =0`. Because we want to skip the first reading (wake-up reading) error, no error message is displayed for these conditions. Notice that in step M, after the first reading, the global variable `runTIMES` is incremented by 1, and the above conditions are not met if the next `PortRead()` encounters an error. This means that all following errors caused by the `PortRead()` will be displayed without skipping.

M: The global variable `runTIMES` is incremented by 1 to indicate to the program that the subsequent errors caused by the function `PortRead()` should be displayed.

N: The received data is stored in the structure variable `commClass->pcBuffer`, and is written into a data file by the system function `fprintf()`. The `fp` variable stores the opened file handle obtained from the `Setup()` function.

O: The received data (12 bits) is assigned to the data buffer `ad_data`. After this assignment, the structure variable `commClass` is no longer needed. The `delete` statement is called to delete that structure variable and to clean up the memory space allocated for it.

P: Finally the data buffer is returned to the calling function.

The code for the local function `PortRead()` is shown in Figure 7.48.
Each section of the code is explained in the following list.

Q: Some local variables are declared inside the local function `PortRead()`. The `hThread` variable stores the thread handle when a new thread is created. `IDThread` is a double-word integer that is used to reserve the thread ID as a new thread is opened. `Ret` holds the running status of some system function such as `WaitForSingleObject()`, and `ExitCode` is used to hold the exit code when a thread or an object is terminated. `dTimeout` is a double-word integer that is used to hold the timeout value. The default value for the upper boundary of the timeout is 500 milliseconds.

R: The system function `CreateThread()` is called to create a new thread that is used to handle the port reading process. If this call is successful, the returned thread's handle is assigned to `hThread`. A returned value of `False` means that this function has failed; an error message is displayed, and the function returns this error to the calling function. The third argument of this function is the thread function `ThreadFunc`. This thread function is a real body to execute the actions of the thread. The thread only provides a

```
/*****************************************************************************
 * NAME:     PortRead()
 * PGRMR:   Y. Bai
 *****************************************************************************/
ERR_CODE PortRead(CommPortClass *hCommPort)
{
Q     HANDLE hThread;                     // handler for port read thread
      DWORD  IDThread;
      DWORD  Ret, ExitCode;
      DWORD  dTimeout = 500;              // define time out value: 500 ms.
      ERR_CODE ecStatus = OK;
R     if (!(hThread = CreateThread(NULL,                 // no security attributes
                  0,                                     // use default stack size
                  (LPTHREAD_START_ROUTINE) ThreadFunc,
                  (LPVOID)hCommPort,                     // parameter to thread function
                  CREATE_SUSPENDED,                      // creation flag - suspended
                  &IDThread) ) )                         // returns thread ID
     {
          msg("Create Read Thread failed");
          return EC_CREATE_THREAD;
     }
S    ResumeThread(hThread);                              // start thread now
T    Ret = WaitForSingleObject(hThread, dTimeout);
     if (Ret == WAIT_OBJECT_0)
     {    // data received & process it...need to do nothing because the data
          // has been stored in the hCommPort in Thread Func. Close thread handle
          CloseHandle(hThread);
     }
U    else if (Ret == WAIT_TIMEOUT)
     {
          // time out happened, warning & kill thread
          Ret = GetExitCodeThread(hThread, &ExitCode);
          if (ExitCode == STILL_ACTIVE)
          {
               TerminateThread(hThread, ExitCode);
               CloseHandle(hThread);
               return EC_RECV_TIMEOUT;
          }
          else
          {
               CloseHandle(hThread);
               msg("ERROR in GetExitCodeThread: != STILL_ACTIVE ");
               ecStatus = EC_EXIT_CODE;
          }
      }
V     else
      {
          msg("ERROR in WaitFor SingleObject ");
          ecStatus = EC_WAIT_SINGLEOBJ;
      }
W     return  ecStatus;
}
```

FIGURE 7.48 The local function `PortRead()`.

frame; the actual thread job is performed by `ThreadFunc`. The fourth argument, `hCommPort` is a pointer variable of the structure `CommPortClass` and is very important to this application because it contains all data collection definitions. To pass this structure variable into the thread function, you must place it in this position with this format. The fifth argument is a system constant that indicates the running status of the thread when it is created. The CREATE_SUSPENDED macro suspends the thread so that it will not run until the ResumeThread() function is executed.

S: A ResumeThread() function is called to begin running the thread function.

T: The system function WaitForSingleObject() is called to monitor the thread function and to wait until it is completed. This function returns when the thread function is signaled or when the time-out interval elapses. Two arguments are passed into this function: hThread is the thread handle, dTimeout is the upper boundary value of the timeout. If the function returns WAIT_OBJECT_0, which is the thread handle, it means that the thread function has been executed successfully; the data is collected and the thread function is terminated automatically as it is completed. No other action is needed in this situation except closing the thread handle by using CloseHandle() system function.

U: If the function returns WAIT_TIMEOUT, it means that a timeout error has occurred and the data collection has failed (that is, no event has been signaled). Two steps are needed in this situation. First we need to retrieve the exit code of the thread function by calling the system function GetExitCodeThread(). If the exit code indicates that the thread function is still running (STILL_ACTIVE), the function TerminateThread() is executed to stop the thread function and to close the thread by calling the function CloseHandle(). If the exit code of the thread is not equal to STILL_ACTIVE, it means that the thread function has been terminated. We can directly close the thread by calling the function CloseHandle().

V: If the function returns any other value, it means that some other error has occurred during the function call. An error message is displayed, and the function returns the message to the calling function.

W: The running status of this function ecStatus is returned to the calling function.

The code of the thread function, ThreadFunc(), is shown in Figure 7.49.
Each section of the code is explained in the following list.

X: All local variables are declared at the beginning of the function. The Boolean variable fDone works as a condition variable for the while loop that waits for the communication events to occur during the data collection process. The ad_data variable works as a data buffer to store a single collected data unit. The double-word variable dwModemStatus works as an argument to be passed into the system function GetCommModemStatus(), and the returned status of the associated transmission line is stored in this argument. The variable dwCommModemStatus works in a similar way as does the variable dwModemStatus, and it returns the associated event status as the function WaitCommEvent() is called.

Y: A casting operation (CommPortClass*) is performed to convert the argument hCommPorts, which has a void* data type, into the CommPortClass* structure type. This cast is very important and is necessary because the argument hCommPorts is a void* data type. (Any argument included in a thread function must be in a void* data type). In order to use our structure, a program must use a cast operator to convert that argument to our desired data type.

Z: The extended system function EscapeCommFunction() is called to set the RTS line to HIGH, which will enable the MAX187 to begin the data conversion. The RTS line is connected to the CS-bar input on the MAX187 via the inverter MAX220. (Refer to Figure 7.43). A HIGH value in RTS produces a LOW value on the CS-bar of the MAX187.

1: After the data conversion starts, we need to monitor the status of the DSR line because this line is connected to the output buffer (DOUT) of the MAX187. The converted data

```
  void WINAPI ThreadFunc(void* hCommPorts)
  {
X     BOOL   fDone;
      int    ad_data = 0;
      DWORD  dwModemStatus;
      int    index, nTotRead = 0;
      DWORD  dwCommModemStatus;
      CommPortClass*  CommPorts;
      ERR_CODE ecStatus = OK;
Y     CommPorts = (CommPortClass* )hCommPorts;
Z     EscapeCommFunction(hPort, SETRTS);   // Set RTS to enable the CS-bar to start A/D
1     SetCommMask(hPort, EV_DSR);  // Specify a set of events to be monitored for the port.
2     fDone = FALSE;
3     while (!fDone)
      {   // Wait for an event to occur for the port.
4         WaitCommEvent(hPort, &dwCommModemStatus, 0);
5         if (dwCommModemStatus & EV_DSR)                // received the DSR event
          {
6             for (index = 0; index < CommPorts->iMaxBits; index++)
              {
7                 EscapeCommFunction(hPort, CLRDTR);  //Reset DTR (HIGH in SCLK)
                  Delay(10);
8                 EscapeCommFunction(hPort, SETDTR);  //Set DTR (LOW in SCLK)
                  Delay(10);
9                 if (!GetCommModemStatus(hPort, &dwModemStatus))
                  {
                      msg("ERROR in GetModemStatus()!");
                      fDone = TRUE;
                      break;
                  }
10                if (MS_DSR_ON & dwModemStatus)          //DSR status is HIGH.
                      ad_data = ad_data + 0;
11                else                                    //DSR status is LOW
                      ad_data++;
12                ad_data = ad_data << 1;
              }
13            EscapeCommFunction(hPort, SETDTR);        //Set DTR (LOW in SCLK)
              EscapeCommFunction(hPort, CLRRTS);        //Reset CS to deselect A/D
14            ad_data = ad_data >> 1;
15            CommPorts->pcBuffer = ad_data;
              fDone = TRUE;
              break;
          }
      } // end of while loop
  }
16 void Delay(int num)
  {
      int k, m, n = 100*num;
17    for (m = 0; m < n; m++)
          k++;
  }
```

FIGURE 7.49 The thread function `ThreadFunc()`.

will be transmitted from the output buffer to the serial port via this DSR line. (Refer to Figure 7.43). To monitor that transmission line, the program must call the system function `SetCommMask()` to select and mask the desired transmission line. After this configuration, an event will be generated as the status of the DSR line is changed, and this event will be detected by the function WaitCommEvent(). The functions SetCommMask() and WaitCommEvent() work as a pair to complete the setup and detection of the status of the transmission line.

2: The Boolean variable fDone is reset to False so that it is ready to start the while loop.
3: A while loop is used to infinitely wait for the event to occur, which is associated with the desired or masked transmission line. In our case, this event is EV_DSR.
4: The system function WaitCommEvent() is executed to determine whether the event occurs. Note that if we were to use this function directly, without involving the thread function, a dead cycle would be caused by the WaitCommEvent() and the system would be hung up indefinitely. When this function is involved with the thread function, a timeout error will occur if no event is detected during the waiting process.
5: The function WaitCommEvent() will be terminated if the desired event occurs. The returned status of the associated transmission line is stored in the argument dwCommModemStatus. An AND operation is used to determine whether the EV_DSR has occurred.
6: If the EV_DSR event is received, a for loop is used to repeatedly collect 12-bit converted data. To retrieve each bit of data, either an external or a simulated clock must be provided. Our program uses a simulated clock, generated by a sequence of instructions as below.
7: The function EscapeCommFunction() is called to reset the DTR line. This resetting is equivalent to assign a HIGH signal to the SCLK input on the MAX187. (Refer to Figure 7.43). A user-defined Delay() function is executed to stabilize the simulated clock and allow it to be received by the SCLK input.
8: After the delay another EscapeCommFunction() is called to set the DTR line to HIGH, which is equivalent to assign a LOW value to the SCLK input. Following this setting, another delay is inserted. In this way, a completed simulated clock cycle is generated to the SCLK input on the MAX187 and one bit of converted data can be shifted from the output buffer on the MAX187 to the serial port via the DSR line.
9: Now we need to check the status of the DSR line to determine whether a logical 1 or a logical 0 has been received. This check is made by a call the system function GetCommModemStatus(), which will return the current status of the desired transmission line. An error message will be displayed if the function call encounters any errors. In that case, the function will be terminated and returned to the calling function after an error message is displayed on the screen.
10: By using the operation MS_DSR_ON & dwModemStatus, we can detect whether the DSR line is HIGH or LOW. Keep in mind that a HIGH (ON) value on the DSR line is associated with a logical 0 because of the inverter MAX220. In that case, only a 0 is added to the data buffer ad_data.
11: If a LOW value is detected on the DSR line, which is equivalent to a logical 1 on the converted bit, the data buffer ad_data should be increased by 1 in the least significant bit (LSB).
12: The data buffer ad_data is shifted left by one bit to reserve the space for the next bit of data. Steps 6 through 12 will be continually repeated until all 12 bits of data are converted and received.
13: Once all 12 bits of data have been received, the system function EscapeCommFunction() is called to set the DTR line to HIGH, which is the equivalent of resetting the SCLK input on the MAX187 to LOW, and to reset the RTS line to LOW, which is the equivalent of assigning a HIGH value to the CS-bar on the MAX187 to deselect the latter. SETDTR and CLRRTS are two system constants used in the Win32 SDK.
14: During the data collection process described earlier, the data buffer is totally shifted left by 12 bits. However, for a 12-bit data string, shifting left 11 times is enough because the last bit does not need to shift. So some compensation is needed to make the data

processing correct. This compensation is accomplished by shifting the final result right by one bit.

15: The final result is assigned to the `pcBuffer`, an element of the data structure `ComPortClass`, to be returned to the calling function. The Boolean condition variable `fDone` is set to `True` to stop the `while` loop. The `break` instruction is not strictly necessary, but we use it here to ensure the reliability of our application.

16: `Delay()` is a simple user-defined function; its purpose is to delay processing for a specified period of time. Three local integer variables are declared here.

17: A `for` loop is used to repeatedly increase the variable `k` by `1` until `n = m`.

7.4.2.2.3 The `PortClose` Function

The code for this function is shown in Figure 7.50. Each section of the code is explained in the following list.

18: Here the function inspects the global Boolean variable `PortCreateflg` to determine whether the port has been opened and configured. This flag should be set by the `Setup()` function if the port has been successfully opened and configured. The system function `CloseHandle()` is called to close the port if the port has been opened and configured.

19: Once the port is closed, the Boolean variable `PortCreateflg` is reset to `False`.

20: Some other cleanup jobs include closing of the opened file handle `fp` by means of the system function `fclose()`.

21: The global variable `runTIMES` is reset to 0.

22: Finally the running status of the function is returned to the calling function.

```
/*****************************************************************************
 * NAME:      PortClose
 * DESC:      Interface program to MAX187 Serial A/D converter
 * PGMR:      Y. Bai
 * DATE:      12/11/2003
 *****************************************************************************/
int PortClose()
{
     ERR_CODE rc = OK;
18   if (PortCreateflg)
          CloseHandle(hPort);
19   PortCreateflg = false;
20   fclose(fp);
21   runTIMES = 0;
22   return rc;
}
```

FIGURE 7.50 The `PortClose` function.

At this point, we have finished developing the code for our source file.

7.4.2.3 Developing the Definition File for the DLL

Before we can finish our dynamic link library, we need to generate its definition file. The purpose of the definition file is to export all interface functions to the External Interface Class in VisualWorks so that any interface function can be accessed by the associated function defined in that class.

The definition file for this DLL is shown in Figure 7.51.

```
LIBRARY SmallMAXDLL.dll
EXPORTS
Setup
ReadData
PortClose
```

FIGURE 7.51 Definition file for the DLL.

The first line here is used to declare the name of the dynamic link library. Following the keyword EXPORTS, all three interface functions are listed so that they can be exported to VisualWorks and can be accessed from within Smalltalk domain.

TIP: Keep in mind that this definition file is important to the interface between Smalltalk and the DLL. Without it, VisualWorks may not identify the Visual C++ interface functions defined in the DLL as the program runs. This potential bug is difficult to detect in some situations, so it is important that you define this file carefully.

7.4.2.4 Building and Installing the DLL Target File

We are now ready to compile and build our DLL target file. From the menu in the Visual C++ 6.0 IDE, click Build|Build SmallMAXDLL.dll to build the DLL file. The default folder for storing the DLL file should be Debug. The target DLL file should be compiled and built successfully if everything is fine.

To install the DLL file, we need to copy the target DLL file SmallMAXDLL.dll from the default project folder, C:\Book2_Program\Chapter 7\SerialMAX\Small-MAXDLL\Debug, to our user-defined DLL folder, C:\stdll. For this application, C:\stdll is the user-defined DLL folder. You can select any different folder to store your DLL file. Keep in mind that after you select your user-defined DLL folder, you need to insert the name of that folder into the VisualWorks library directories input box when you connect the DLL to the External Interface Class in VisualWorks domain.

Now we can complete all the necessary development tasks for the DLL file. We must return to the VisualWorks domain to finish our programming and to connect the DLL file with the External Interface Class in VisualWorks domain.

7.4.3 Developing a Domain Model Class

We will now develop a Domain Model for our project. The name of this Domain Model will be SerialMAX. It will be used to manage and control the program data (the serial port number, baud rate, and data values) to be sent to and received from with the serial port COM1.

From the toolbar on the Visual Launcher, click the Open a System Browser icon. The default tab of the system browser is Package. The opened Package dialog box is shown in Figure 7.52.

Click the Base VisualWorks|System|System Name Space menu item to open the package in which our Domain Model class will be located, as shown in Figure 7.52. (Review Section 7.3.2 to get a more detailed description of each line for this Domain Model class file).

On the first line, replace NameOfClass, with SerialMAX, our Domain Model's name. On the second line, replace {NameOfSuperclass}, with {UI.Model}; this will be the name of our superclass. Add seven instance variables into the fifth line. The finished Domain Model class file should match the one shown in Figure 7.53.

The instance variables are: dmComport, dmBaudRate, dmDataBits, dmStopBit, dmParity, dmDataNum, and dmReadData. The prefix dm is used to indicate to the system that each of these instance variables belongs to the Domain Model class. The first five variables are

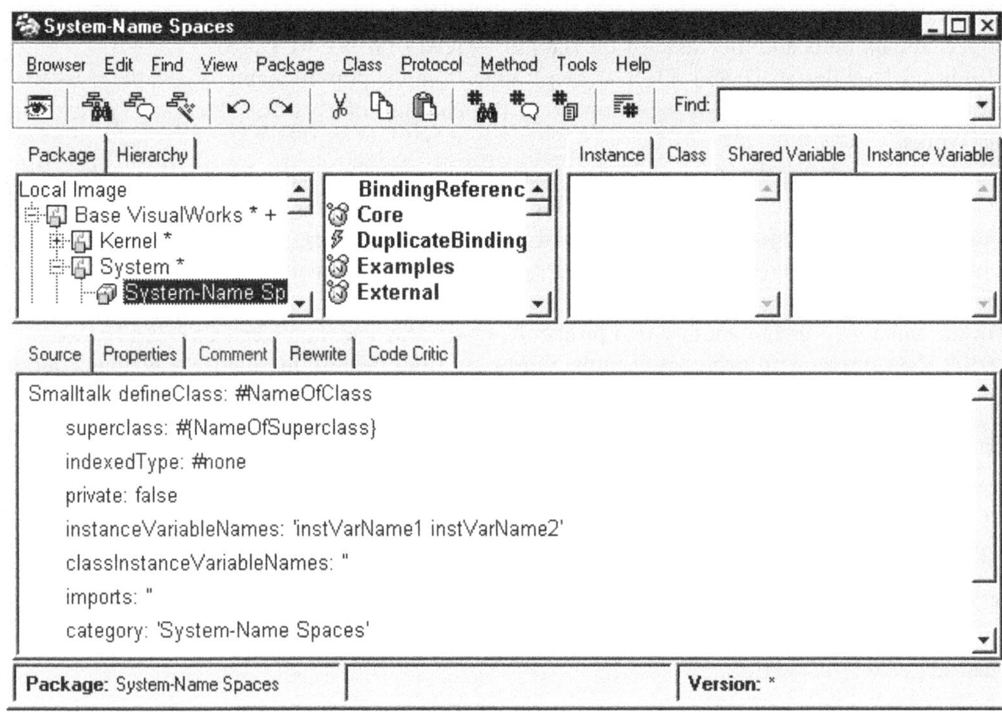

FIGURE 7.52 The `Package` dialog box.

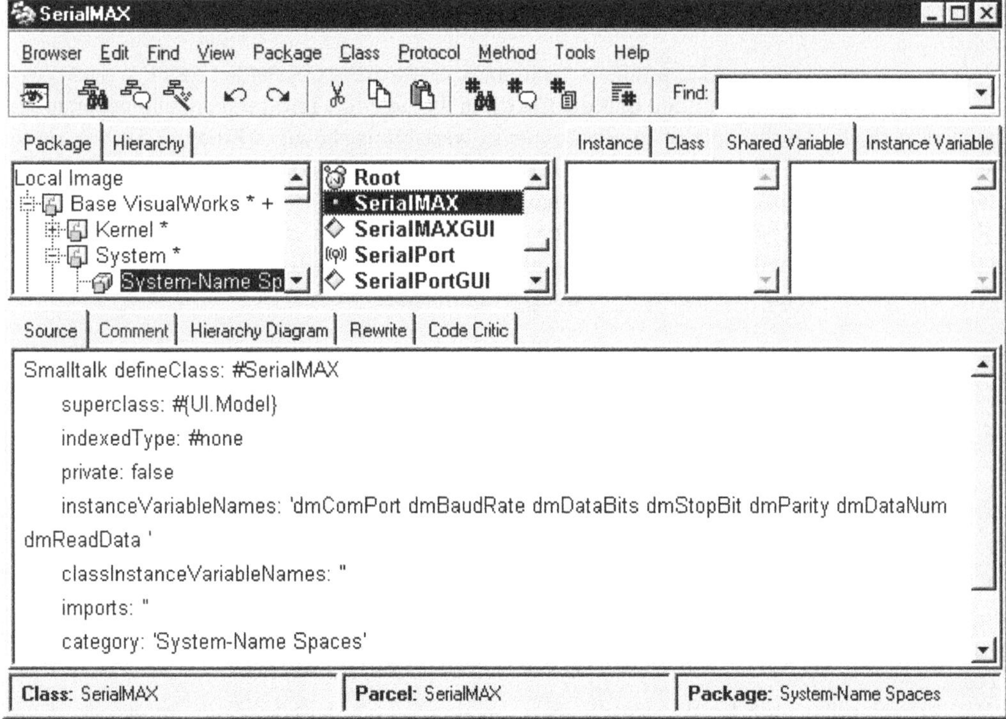

FIGURE 7.53 The Domain Model class file `SerialMAX`.

used to store the serial port configuration parameters, and the final two are used to store the number of collected data units and the value of the data to be read from the MAX187.

Right-click on this space and select `Accept` item from the pop-up menu to save the class file. A new class named SerialMAX will appear in the package of `System-Name Spaces` in VisualWorks.

We must now define the instance variables and generate the associated methods for them.

Click the `Instance` tab, right-click on the third pane from the left and select `New` from the pop-up menu (the `Operate` menu in VisualWorks). In the resulting dialog box, select or enter `accessing` in the top box and click `OK`. An `accessing` protocol will appear on the `Instance` pane.

In the same way, create another two protocols: `operate` and `initialize-release`.

Click the `accessing` protocol from the third pane from the left, highlight the contents in the bottom space, and type the following code to replace the original code:

```
dmComPort
 ^dmComPort.
```

This code will create an accessing method for the `dmComPort` variable.

Right-click on the space and select `Accept` from the pop-up menu to save the code. Then, keeping the `accessing` protocol selected, highlight the code you've just entered and type the following code in its place:

```
dmComPort: aValue
dmComPort := aValue.
self changed: #dmComPort.
```

Right-click the space and again select `Accept` from the pop-up menu to save the code. You have now defined our `dmComPort` variable. (The purpose of the `self changed:` entry is to send a `changed:` message to `dmComPort` itself to automatically update the variable if it is changed).

In a similar way, we can define another six variables, `dmBaudRate`, `dmDataBits`, `dmStop-Bit`, `dmParity`, `dmDataNum`, and `dmReadData` in the `accessing` protocol and generate the associated methods. An example of the `dmComPort` variable is shown in Figure 7.54.

Click the `initialize-release` protocol on the third pane from the left and highlight the contents in the bottom space. Enter the code that is shown in Figure 7.55 to initialize the variables.

Right-click on this space and select `Accept` from the pop-up menu to save the code. An `initialize` method will be added on the fourth pane from the left.

The `operate` protocol contains three control commands:

- **Setup** will call the DLL function `Setup()` from the External Interface Class to initialize and configure the serial port.
- **ReadData** will trigger the DLL function `ReadData()` to begin collecting the converted data from the MAX187 via the serial port.
- **Exit** will call the DLL function `PortClose()` to close the port, and will send a message instructing the Object Engine to terminate the testing program.

Click the `operate` protocol on the third pane from the left, highlight the contents of the bottom space, and enter `Setup`. Right-click on this space and select the `Accept` item from the pop-up menu to save this method. In the same way, create another two methods, `ReadData` and `Exit`.

We'll develop the code for these methods in Section 7.4.6.2, based on the prototypes of the DLL functions that we'll define in the External Interface Class in Section 7.4.5. All these methods

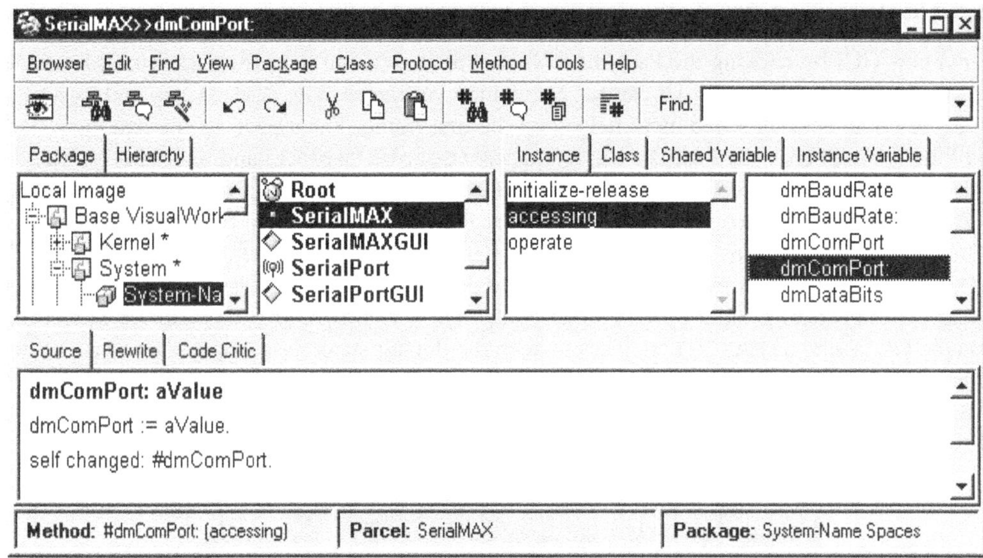

FIGURE 7.54 The instance variable `dmComPort`.

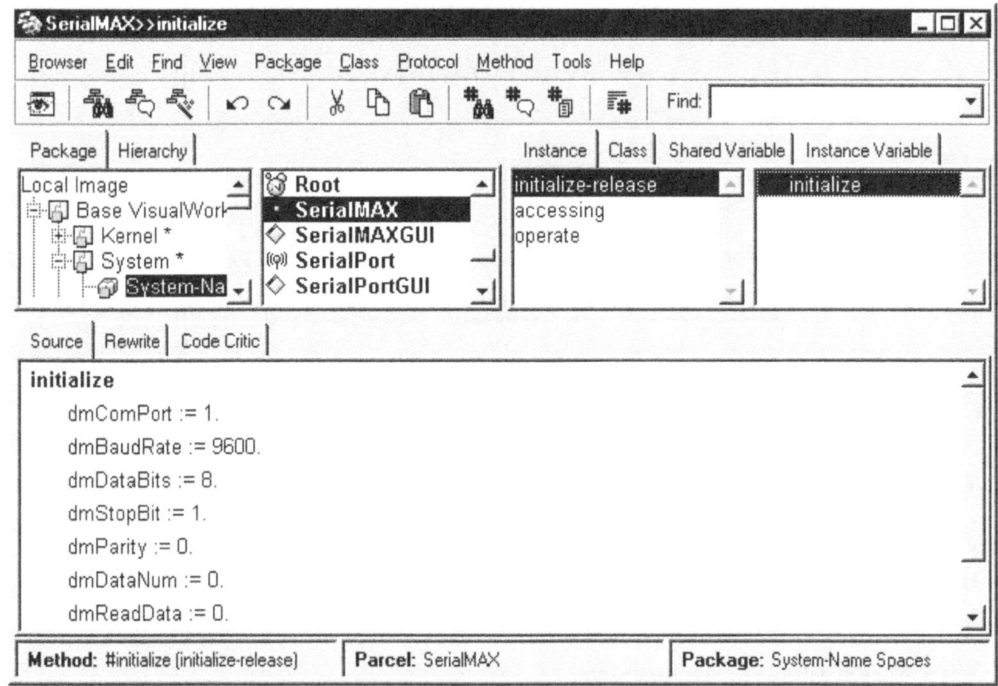

FIGURE 7.55 The `initialize` method in the `initialize-release` protocol.

will be activated by their associated actions (`Setup`, `ReadMAX`, and `Exit`) which we'll define in the following section for our Application Model, `SerialMAXGUI`. The relationship between the Domain Model, `SerialMAX`, and the Application Model, `SerialMAXGUI`, is that the Application Model is a dependent of the Domain Model.

Now let's develop an Application Model class, `SerialMAXGUI`, for our project.

7.4.4 Developing an Application Model Class and a GUI

Open a new GUI by clicking the Painter|New Canvas menu item from the Visual Launcher. Add two frames into the new GUI canvas. Name the two frames COM Settings and Reading Data. Add five labels and five input fields into the first frame. The aspects of the five input fields should be amComPort, amBaudRate, amDataBits, amStopBit, and amParity. The five labels should be COM Port, Baud Rate, Data Bits, Stop Bit, and Parity.

Add two labels and two input fields into the second frame. Name the two input fields amDataNum and amReadData, and name the two labels Data Number and Read Data.

Add three action buttons to the canvas; the Actions you should assign them are Setup, ReadMAX, and Exit. From the GUI Painter Tool, click Edit|Install to install the widgets and name the GUI SerialMAXGUI. Be sure to keep the default superclass Application Model unchanged when you install the new GUI. Then define all the widgets for the GUI by clicking the Edit|Define item from the GUI Painter Tool. The finished GUI should match the one that shown in Figure 7.56.

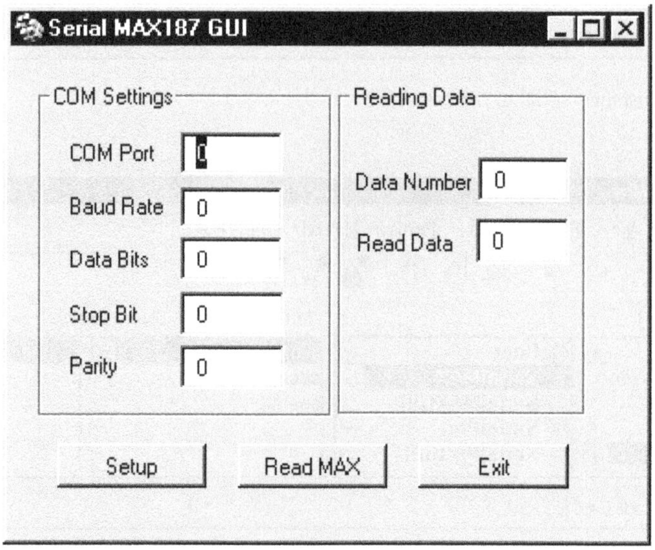

FIGURE 7.56 The completed GUI.

These are the actions for the three action buttons:

- Setup: #Setup
- ReadMAX: #ReadMAX
- Exit: #Exit

These are the aspects of the input fields:

- Com Port: #amComPort
- Baud Rate: #amBaudRate
- Data Bits: #amDataBits
- Stop Bit: #amStopBit
- Parity: #amParity
- Data Number: #amDataNum
- Read Data: #amReadData

The type for all the input fields is `Number`, and the Format is `0`.

To establish communication between the Application Model `SerialMAXGUI` and the Domain Model `SerialMAX`, we need to define the Application Model as a dependent of the Domain Model. Then the Application Model will be able to send input data entered by the user from widgets to the Domain Model to update the data in the Domain Model. This dependent relationship will also allow the Domain Model to return any change in the data to the Application Model.

To define the `SerialMAXGUI` as a dependent of `SerialMAX`, add a new instance variable named `serialmax` to the tail of the `instanceVariableName` of the class `SerialMAXGUI`. Then create an `accessing` protocol in the `SerialMAXGUI` class, and add the new instance variable `serialmax` to the `accessing` protocol, as shown in Figure 7.57 (a) and (b).

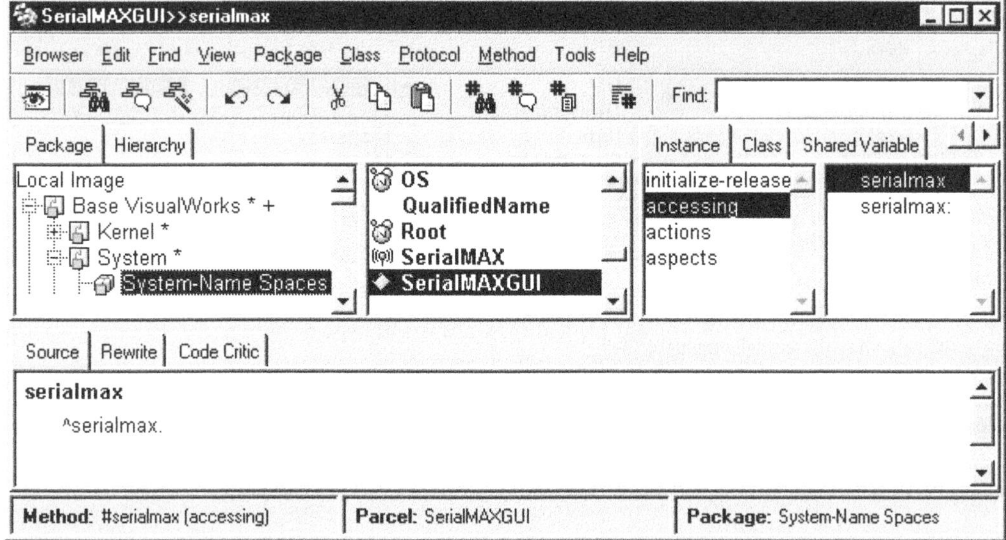

(a) The instance variable `serialmax`.

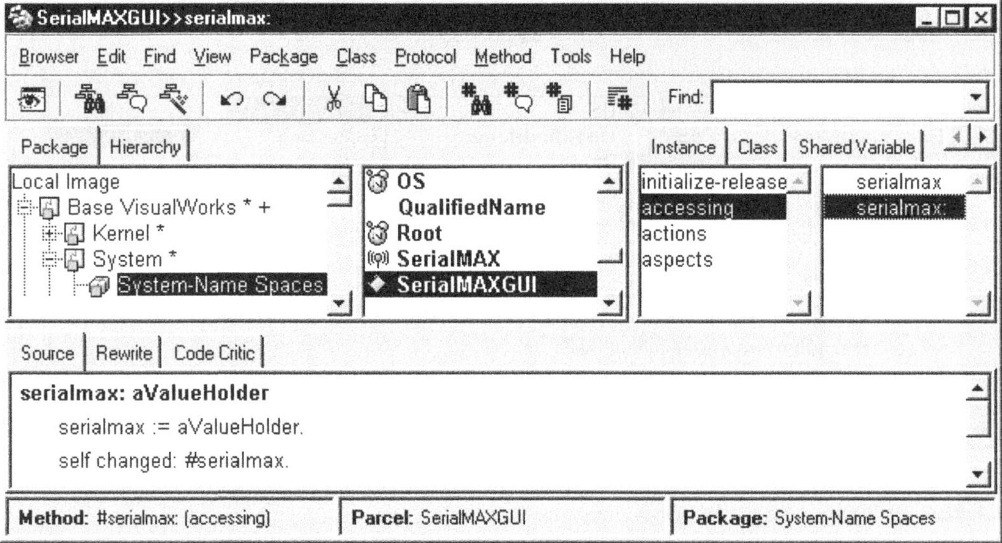

FIGURE 7.57 (b) the value holder `serialmax`.

Next we need to initialize the `serialmax` variable to an instance of the Domain Model `SerialMAX`, initialize it as a value holder as well, and add the Application Model as a dependent of `SerialMAX`. The code for the `initialize` method, which handles these processes, is shown in Figure 7.58.

We must also create a method to remove this dependence between these two models when the program exits. Add the system method `noticeOfWindowClose` to remove the dependence, which is shown in Figure 7.59.

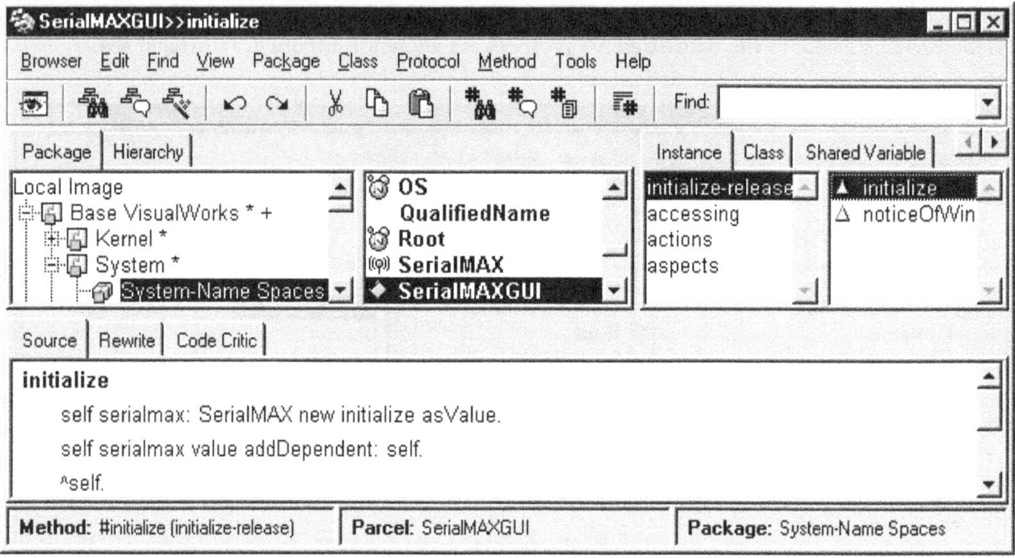

FIGURE 7.58 The `initialize` method.

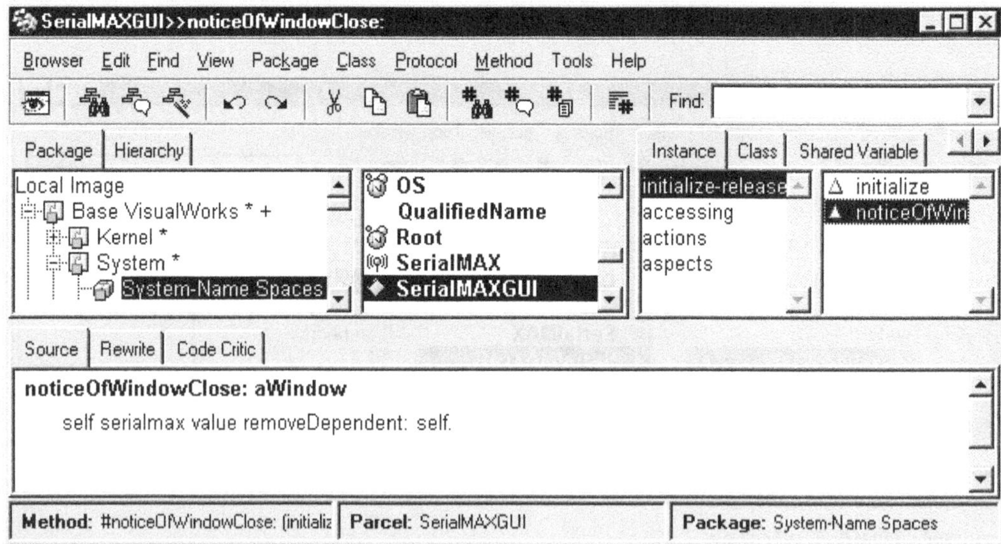

FIGURE 7.59 The `noticeOfWindowClose` method.

Now, when exiting the program, the Object Engine will call the `initialize-release` method `noticeOfWindowClose` to cancel this dependence.

7.4.5 Developing an External Interface Class

We need to develop a subclass of the External Interface Class to contain all DLL functions created in the Visual C++ domain, and use this class as an interface to communicate between Smalltalk and the DLL developed in Visual C++ 6.0.

Open an `External Interface Finder` dialog box by clicking `Tools|DLL and C Connect` from the Visual Launcher. Click `New` to open a `Class Finder` dialog box. In this box, keep `Smalltalk namespace` selected in the lefthand pane, enter `MAXDLL` in the `Name:` field, and click `OK` to save the newly created class.

Next we need to declare prototypes of the DLL functions that are contained in the class. We want to test the serial port in real-time mode, which means that we can write some data into the port and simultaneously retrieve the data from the port as other tasks are running on the machine. We need to define the `ReadData()` function in thread mode.

VisualWorks supports multitasking applications by providing a thread processing method, which can be distinguished from general functions by a pseudo-qualifier, `_threaded`, that appears prior to the function declaration in the C prototype.

In the Windows environment, the Smalltalk Object Engine is considered a separate process with one thread of control. The Object Engine uses a process schedule to manage all processes actively running on the Smalltalk platform. Without the thread processing method, if one process needed to call a DLL function to interface with a C/C++ function or a drive, a block would occur to stop the current calling process and all other processes to wait for this process to finish its function call. After that, the Object Engine would recover the schedule of the process sequence and continue to run. However, this arrangement is no good for a multitask processing system. The solution to this problem is to use thread processing, so that if a process needs to call an external function, the process will declare a thread-calling mode for the function. The Object Engine will assign a thread for this process when the process is run. When the process calls a function in threaded mode, a thread is created and used by the Object Engine to complete the function call. The Object Engine will schedule the subsequent processes so they continue to run, and block just the calling process until the function returns. With this arrangement, none of the other Smalltalk processes needs to wait for the function call to finish.

Note that these threads are not directly mapped to each Smalltalk process run by the Object Engine, but are rather used only for I/O calls via the `DLL and C Connect` interface. From the point of view of the `DLL and C Connect` programmer, the Object Engine still runs as a single thread, with the threaded interconnect calls running alongside it.

In the `External Interface Finder` dialog box, keep the newly created class `MAXDLL` selected in the `Class` list, click `procedures` from the `Category` list, and click the `New` button to create the following interface functions:

- int Setup(comParams arg1)
- int _threaded ReadData(void)
- int PortClose(void)

The first function, `Setup`, is used to configure the serial port to be tested. The argument of this function is an array or a pointer that contains the addresses of five setup parameters. The second function, `ReadData()`, is used to receive the data from the serial port. In front of this function, a pseudo-qualifier, `_threaded`, is used to indicate to the Object Engine that the function is a threaded-mode function and needs the Object Engine to assign it a thread when it is executed. The final function, `PortClose()`, is used to clean up the configuration for the tested serial port.

To create an argument with an array or pointer type, following the steps below.

1. Click the `typedefs` option on the `Category` list, and click `New` to open a `New Typedef` dialog box.
2. In the opened dialog box, enter `comParams` into the `Name:` input field.
3. Select `int` from the `Type:` list.

The finished dialog box should match the one shown in Figure 7.60.

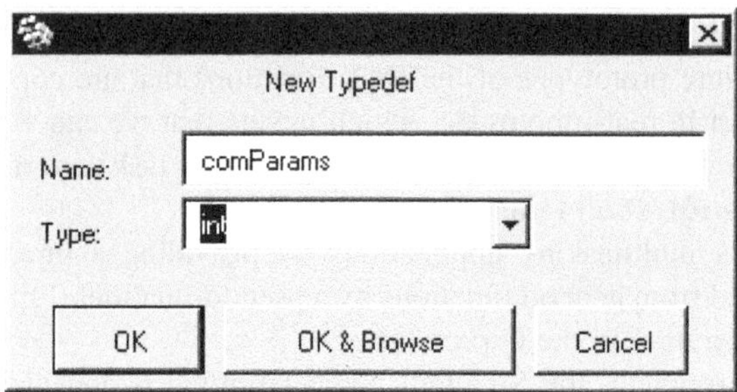

FIGURE 7.60 The finished `typedef` dialog box.

4. Click `OK` to save the new settings. You'll see that a new data type, `comParams`, is generated on the third pane from the left.

Now select `typedefs` from the `Category` list, click `comParams` on the `Typedefs` list, and click the `Browse` button to open this new data type.

Move the cursor to the end of the data type definition in the bottom space and type `[5]` at the end of the data type, as shown in Figure 7.61.

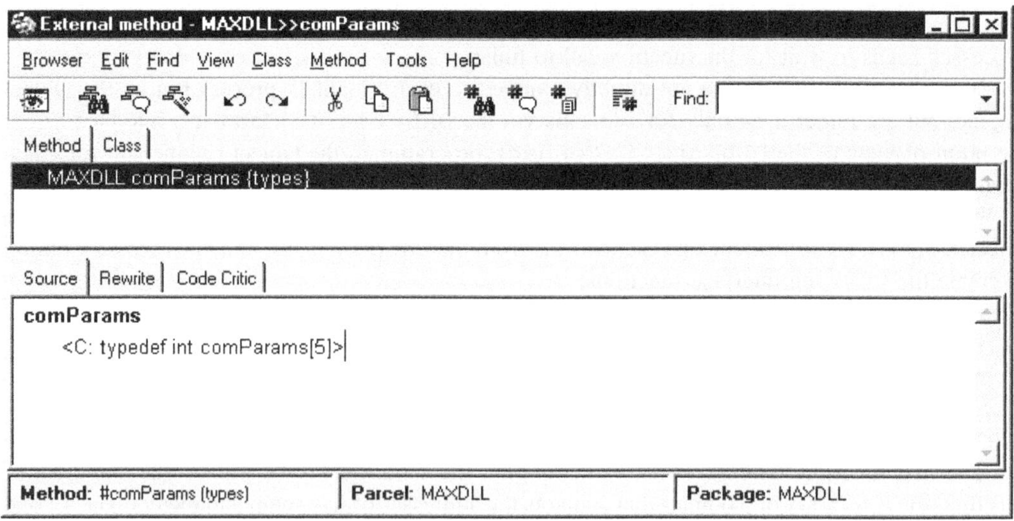

FIGURE 7.61 Adding elements to the new data type.

In this way, we define this data type as an array with 5 elements.

Close the dialog box by clicking the `Close` button in the upper-right corner of this window.

To create the `Setup()` procedure, follow these steps:

1. Select `procedures` from the `Category` list and click `New` to open a `New Procedures` dialog box.
2. In the opened dialog box, enter `Setup` in the `Name:` input field.
3. Select `int` from the `Return Type:` list.
4. Select `argument 1` from the `Argument Types:` list, and select `comParams` item from the `argument type` combox.
5. Click `OK` to save the procedure. The updated dialog box should match the one shown in Figure 7.62.

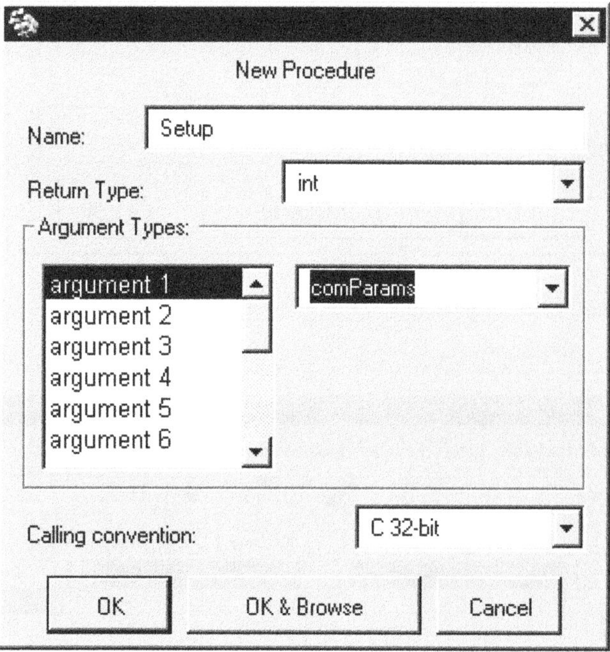

FIGURE 7.62 The `Setup()` procedure.

In a similar way, we can generate the `PortClose()` procedure.

To create the threaded-mode `ReadData()` function, follow these steps:

1. Select `procedures` from the `Category` list and click `New` to open a `New Procedures` dialog box.
2. In the opened dialog, enter `ReadData` in the `Name:` input field.
3. Select `int` from the `Return Type:` list.
4. Click `OK` to save the procedure. The updated dialog box should match the one shown in Figure 7.63.
5. Notice that our new procedure now appears on the third pane. Select this procedure and click the `Browse` button.
6. In the dialog box that appears, type `_threaded` just before the procedure name `ReadData`, as shown in Figure 7.64.

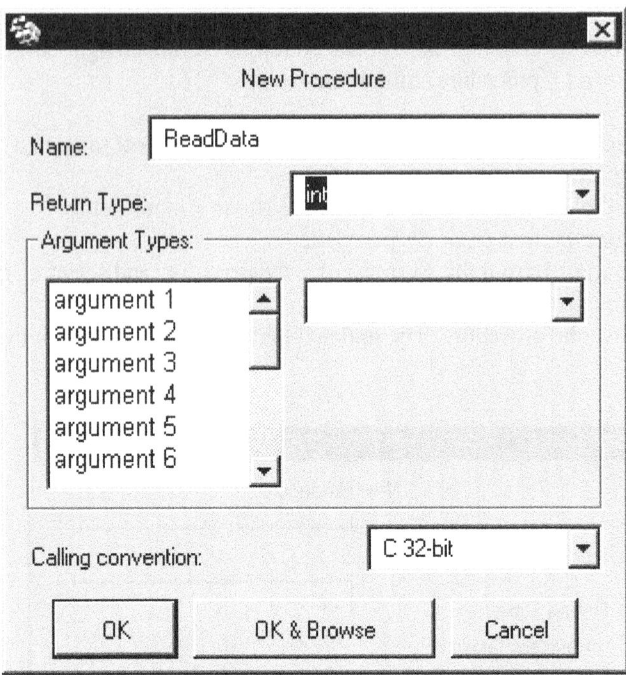

FIGURE 7.63 The `ReadData()` function.

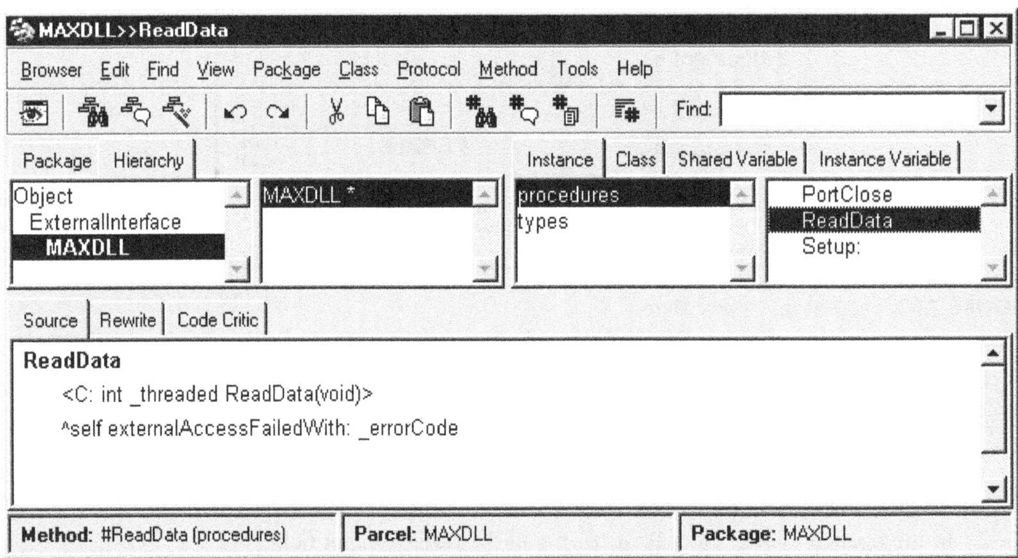

FIGURE 7.64 The threaded `ReadData()` procedure.

7. We have now defined `ReadData()` as a threaded-mode procedure. Close this dialog box by clicking the `Close` button.

TIP: Notice again that when you finish modifying the threaded-mode function and close the System Browser, the modified function remains unchanged, which means that the _threaded pseudo-qualifier does not appear prior to the function name. Don't worry about this; it simply means that the External Interface Class is not yet refreshed. Click any other menu item and click the procedures menu item again, and you will see the updated function.

Finally we need to define the path and the name of the target DLL file for the External Interface Class.

Click library directories item from the Category list and click New to open the Library Directory dialog bx. Enter C:\stdll, the name of our user-defined DLL folder into the input field, and click OK to save this setting, as shown in Figure 7.65(a).

Continue to click the library files item from the Category list, and click New to open the Library Files dialog box. Enter SmallMAXDLL.dll in the input field, and click OK to save this setting, as shown in Figure 7.65(b).

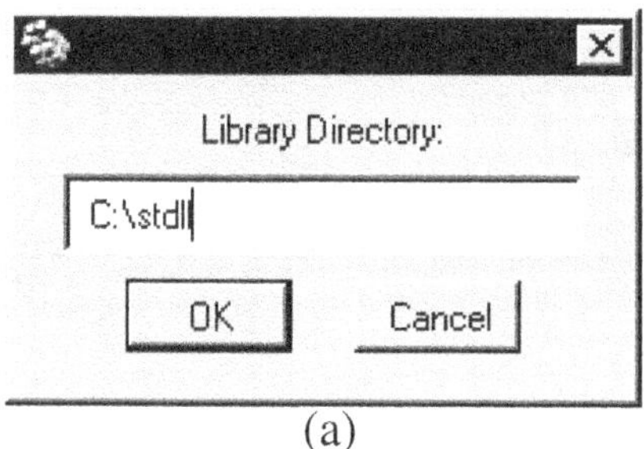

(a)

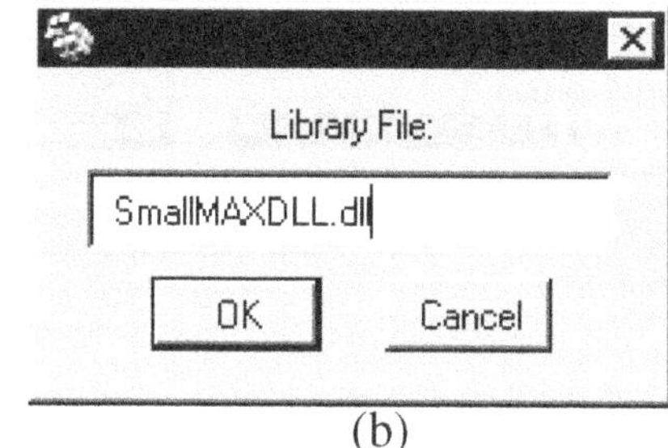

(b)

FIGURE 7.65 Configuring the library directory and name.

We have now finished developing our External Interface Class and declaring the interface procedures. (Recall that the names of these procedures names must be identical with the names of those interface functions in the DLL we developed in Section 7.4.2.)

Now let's develop the remaining code for the SerialMAX and SerialMAXGUI class files.

7.4.6 Finish Coding of the SmallMAXDLL Project in VisualWorks

We have finished creating most of the code for the Domain and the Application Model files. The following code is dependent on the code of the External Interface Class. However, we cannot develop that code until the External Interface Class is complete.

The Application Model is only an interface and is used to receive the input from the user. Based on the user's input, the Application Model will send the associated commands or messages to the Domain Model, and the latter will call the associated DLL functions defined in the External Interface Class to execute the commands sent by the Application Model. The Domain Model will also send the feedback coming from the DLL functions to the Application Model—specifically, to the value holder of the widgets in the GUI—to display and update the widgets.

Recall that at the end of the Section 7.4.3, we defined an operate protocol in the Domain Model and defined three methods, Setup, ReadData, and Exit, under that category. After we finish developing the External Interface Class, MAXDLL, we can create the code for these methods.

7.4.6.1 Code of the Application Model Class

In Section 7.4.4, we defined the Application Model SerialMAXGUI as a dependent of the Domain Model SerialMAX. At run time, when we click the Setup action button from the GUI, the Application Model should send the value of the amComPort widget to the associated variable defined in the Domain Model, dmComPort. The Application Model will also send a message to the Domain Model to inform the latter to call the associated DLL functions defined in the External Interface Class to initialize and configure the serial port.

Now open the Application Model `SerialMAXGUI`, located in the system directory `Base VisualWorks|System|System-Name Space`, and click `actions` on the third pane from the left. Select the `Setup` method from the rightmost pane to open it. Highlight the contents of the bottom space, and enter the code that is shown in Figure 7.66.

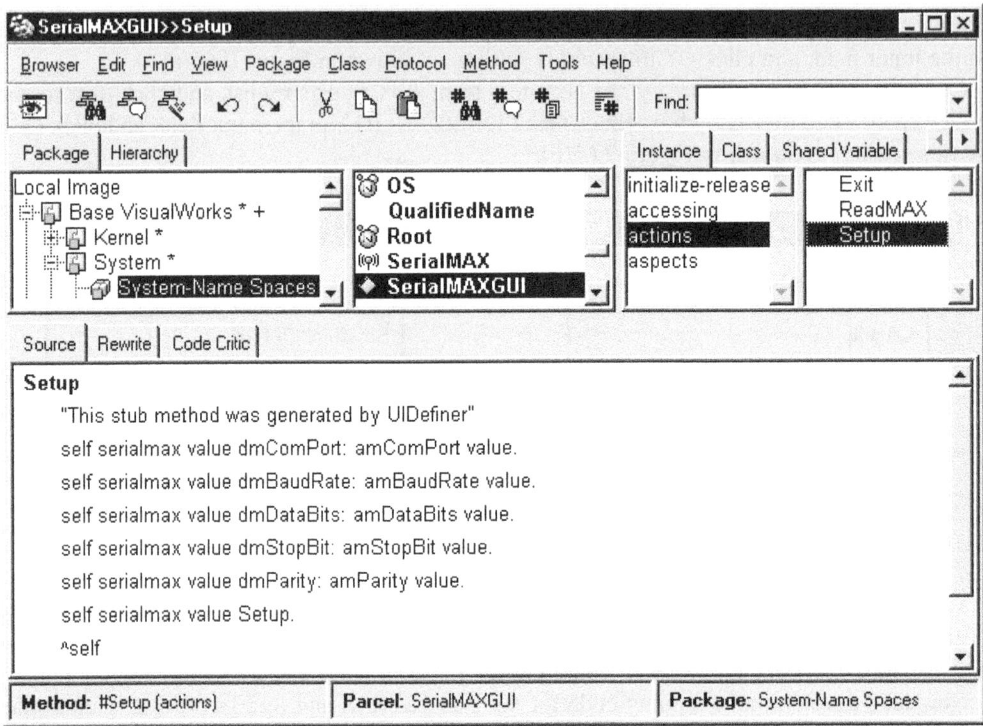

FIGURE 7.66 The `Setup` action for the application model `SerialMAXGUI`.

The second line here is used to assign the value of `amComPort`, which is an input field widget defined in the GUI, to the variable `dmComPort` defined in the Domain Model. The value of `amComPort` will be entered by the user when the program runs. Here we consider the instance of the Domain Model, `serialmax`, a value holder and use the `value` message to assign the value to its variable.

The code between the third and the sixth lines are similar to the second line; they assign the values of setup parameters, entered by the user at run time, to the associated variables defined in the Domain Model.

The seventh line is used to send a message to the Domain Model and inform the latter to begin to execute the `Setup` method, which instructs the DLL function `Setup()` defined in the External Interface Class to perform setup and configuration for the serial port. The Domain Model `serialmax` instance variable is considered a value holder, and the `value` message is used to send out this message.

Right-click on this code space and select the `Accept` item from the pop-up menu to save this method.

Click `ReadMAX` from the rightmost pane to open its code space. In this space, enter the code that is shown in Figure 7.67.

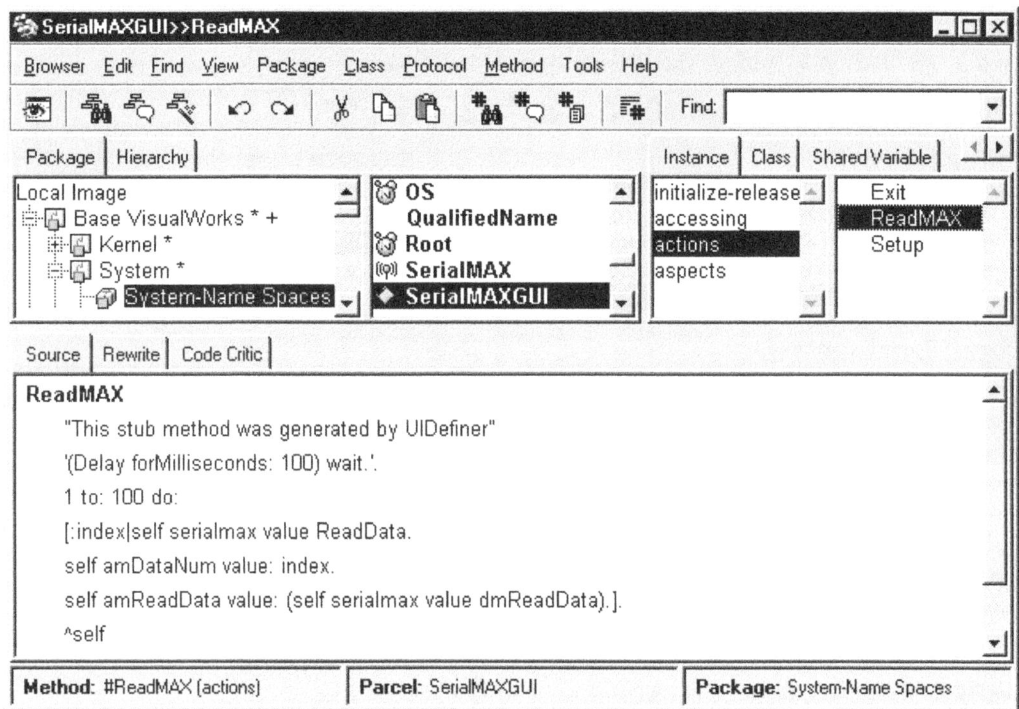

FIGURE 7.67 The `ReadMAX` action for the application model `SerialMAXGUI`.

The second line here is used to delay the process by 100 milliseconds to slow down the display of data. (This delay is not strictly necessary for real-time data collection. A single quotation mark can be used to comment out this code and thus invalidate it).

A `for` loop is used to repeatedly send the `ReadData` message to the Domain Model to collect data from the MAX187 via the serial port. The fifth and sixth lines are used to assign the updated data values, which come from the serial port in real time, to the widgets in the GUI to display them onscreen. Here we use the `value` to assign these values from the associated variable defined in the Domain Model (`dmReadData`) to their partners in the Application Model (`amReadData`). The parentheses are necessary because the variables defined inside the parentheses have a higher precedence, and they can be considered a single variable and be assigned to the desired destination variable.

Click the `Exit` action from the rightmost pane to open its code space, and enter the code that is shown in Figure 7.68.

This code is very simple. First it sends an `Exit` message to the Domain Model to inform the latter to call the associated DLL function `PortClose()` to close the serial port and terminate the program. Then it sends a `closeRequest` message instructing the Object Engine to close the program and the GUI. The feedback will be executed by `self changed` method.

Right-click on this space and select the `Accept` item from the pop-up menu to save the code.

At this point, we have finished the coding for the Application Model in this project.

7.4.6.2 Code for the Domain Model Class

The purpose of this `Setup` method is to call the associated DLL function, `Setup()`, defined in the External Interface Class to setup and configure the serial port. Open the domain model class `SerialMAX`, on the third pane from the left, click the `operate` protocol, and on the rightmost

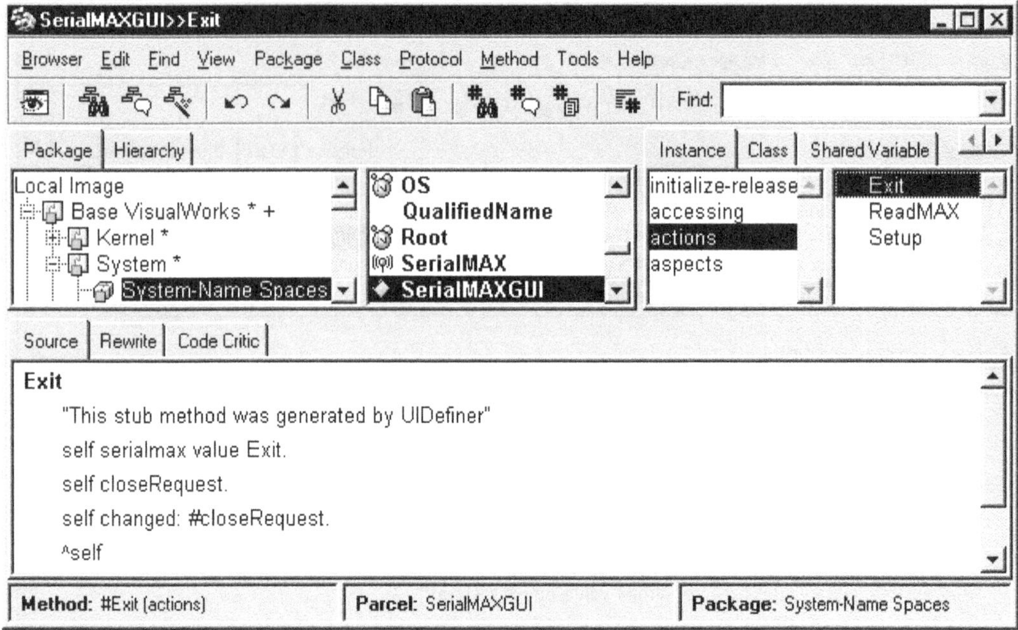

FIGURE 7.68 The Exit action for the application model `SerialMAXGUI`.

pane, select `Setup` to open the code space for this method. Highlight the contents in that space, and enter the code that is shown in Figure 7.69.

First we create two temporary variables, `rc` and `dArray`. `rc` is used to receive the value returned from the call to the DLL function `Setup()`. `dArray` is used to reserve the setup parameters to be sent to the serial port. Then an instance of the class `MAXDLL` is generated, and the system method `gcMalloc` is called to allocate five spaces for the temporary array `dArray`. The advantage of using `gcMalloc` to allocate the memory space is that at run time, we will not need to call the `delete` method to clean up the allocated space when that memory space is no longer needed; the system itself can do that cleanup job. Next, the setup parameters stored in the instance variables in the Domain Model are assigned, one by one, to this temporary array. Finally, a call to the DLL function `Setup()` is made with the temporary array `dArray`, which can be considered a pointer variable. A warning message will be displayed in a dialog format if this call returns an error.

When we click the `Setup` action button in the GUI at run time, the `Setup()` function will be activated by a `Setup` message sent by the Application Model.

Keeping the `operate` protocol selected on the third pane from the left, select the `ReadData` method from the rightmost pane to open its body. Highlight all the contents in the bottom space, and enter the code that is shown in Figure 7.70.

This code is very simple. A new instance of the class `MAXDLL` is generated, and the DLL function `ReadData()` is called when the Domain Model receives a `ReadData` message from the Application Model. This message will be activated at run time when you click the `ReadMAX` action button in the GUI.

Keeping the `operate` protocol selected on the third pane from the left, select the `Exit` method from the rightmost pane to open its body. Highlight all contents in the bottom space, and enter the code that is shown in Figure 7.71.

A temporary variable, `rc`, is generated; it is used to store the returned value or status of the DLL function call. Then the DLL function `PortClose()` is called to clean up the configuration

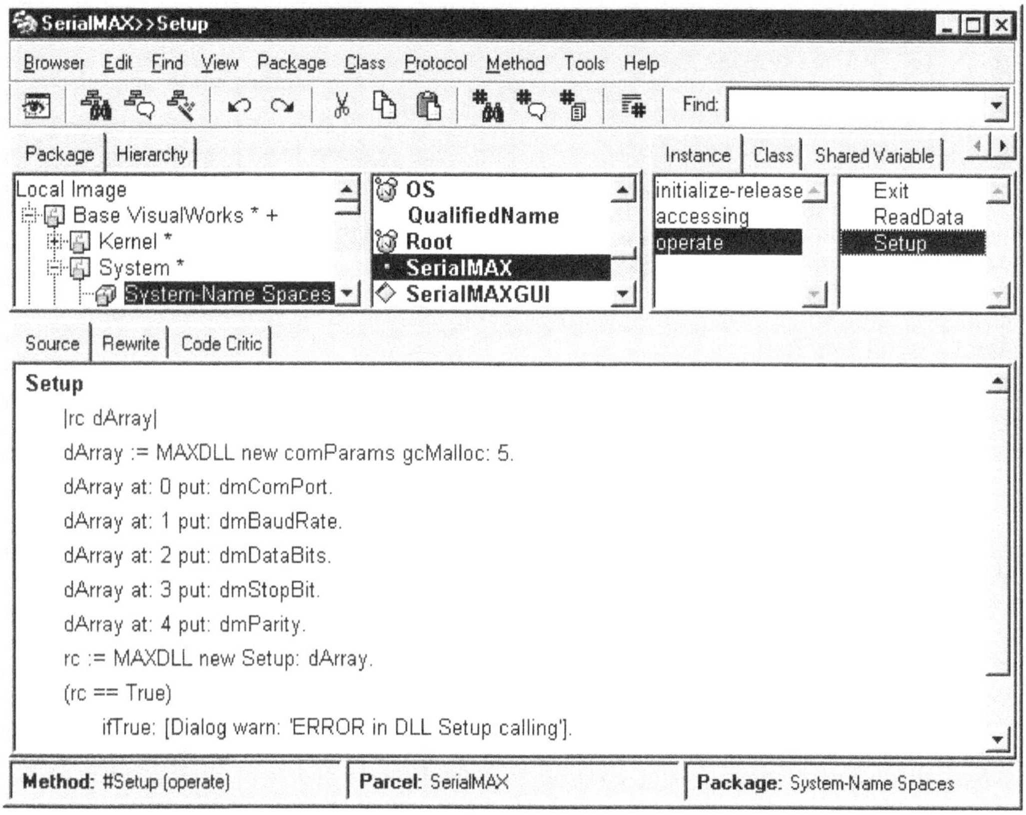

SerialMAX>>Setup
Browser Edit Find View Package Class Protocol Method Tools Help
Find:
Package Hierarchy
Instance Class Shared Variable
Local Image
Base VisualWorks * +
Kernel *
System *
System-Name Spaces
OS
QualifiedName
Root
SerialMAX
SerialMAXGUI
initialize-release
accessing
operate
Exit
ReadData
Setup
Source Rewrite Code Critic
Setup
|rc dArray|
dArray := MAXDLL new comParams gcMalloc: 5.
dArray at: 0 put: dmComPort.
dArray at: 1 put: dmBaudRate.
dArray at: 2 put: dmDataBits.
dArray at: 3 put: dmStopBit.
dArray at: 4 put: dmParity.
rc := MAXDLL new Setup: dArray.
(rc == True)
ifTrue: [Dialog warn: 'ERROR in DLL Setup calling'].
Method: #Setup (operate)
Parcel: SerialMAX
Package: System-Name Spaces

FIGURE 7.69 The `Setup` method for the domain model `SerialMAX`.

SerialMAX>>ReadData
Browser Edit Find View Package Class Protocol Method Tools Help
Find:
Package Hierarchy
Instance Class Shared Variable
Local Image
Base VisualWorks * +
Kernel *
System *
System-Name Spaces
OS
QualifiedName
Root
SerialMAX
SerialMAXGUI
initialize-release
accessing
operate
Exit
ReadData
Setup
Source Rewrite Code Critic
ReadData
dmReadData := MAXDLL new ReadData.
Method: #ReadData (operate)
Parcel: SerialMAX
Package: System-Name Spaces

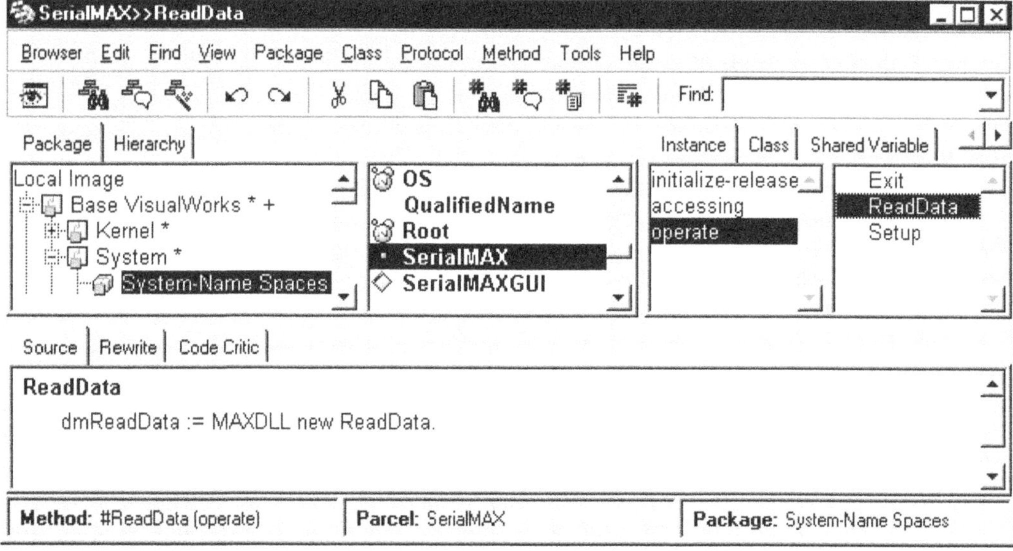

FIGURE 7.70 The `ReadData` method for the domain model `SerialMAX`.

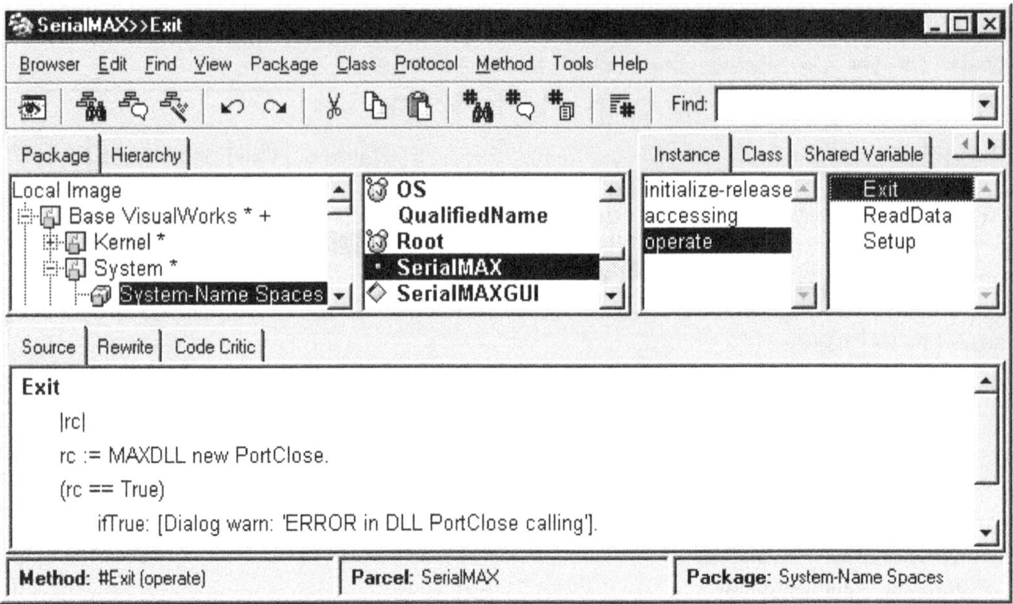

FIGURE 7.71 The `Exit` method for the domain model `SerialMAX`.

of the serial port. A dialog box with a warning message will be displayed if this calling encounters any error.

Now that we have completed the code for both the Domain and Application Models of the project, we are ready to test and run our project in the Smalltalk domain.

7.4.7 Testing and Running the Project

As we mentioned in section 7.3.8, there are two ways to activate the project. One way is to start it from the `Resource Finder`, and the other way is to start it from the `Workspace`. We will use the first method to run this project.

Click `Painter|Resource Finder` from the Visual Launcher to open the `Resource Finder`. In the opened `Resource Finder`, select the Application Model `SerialMAXGUI` from the `Class` list, and then click the `Start` button to run the project. The running project is shown in Figure 7.72.

Enter the following setup parameters into the associated input fields:

- COM Port: `1`
- Baud Rate: `9600`
- Data Bits: `8`
- Stop Bit: `1`
- Parity: `0`

Click the `Setup` action button to call the `Setup()` method in the Domain Model to send those parameters to the serial port and configure the port.

A message box is displayed with the five setup parameters. This is for debugging purposes; you can remove this step from the DLL source file if you do not want to display this message box.

Now click the `ReadMAX` button to begin collecting the converted data from the MAX187 via the serial port. The number of received data and the associated data value are continuously displayed

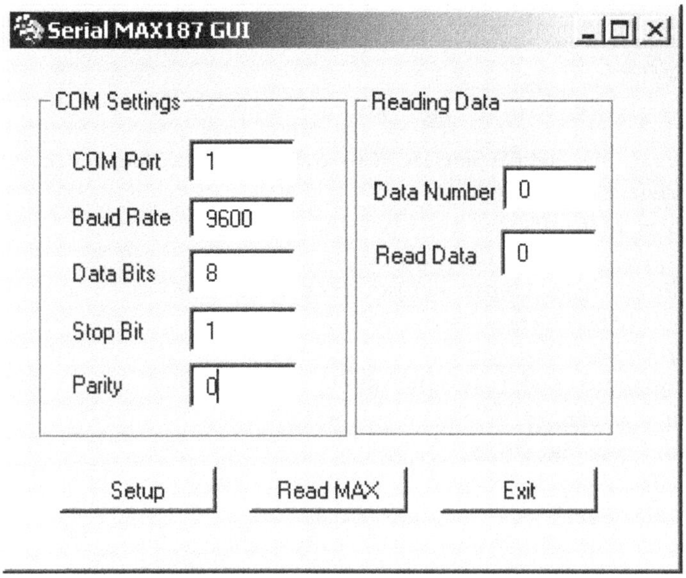

FIGURE 7.72 Running status of the project.

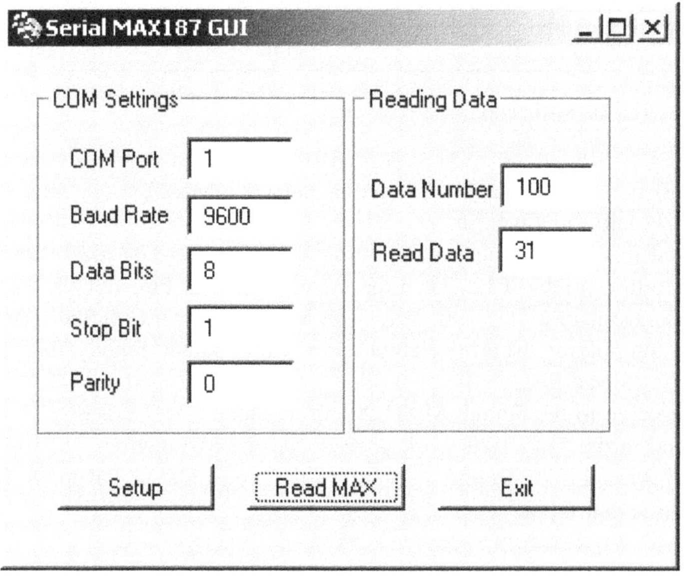

FIGURE 7.73 The data collection process.

in the `Data Number` and the `Read Data` input fields, respectively. This process is shown in Figure 7.73.

Three analog input signals are tested in this project: Sinusoidal, triangular and square waveforms. To confirm the data collection, we'll develop a MATLAB M-function to plot the received data in a two-dimensional graphic. As you know, the collected data is also stored in a data file named `smaxdll.dat` in the DLL file; for this application, this data file is located in our user-defined DLL folder, `C:\stdll`.

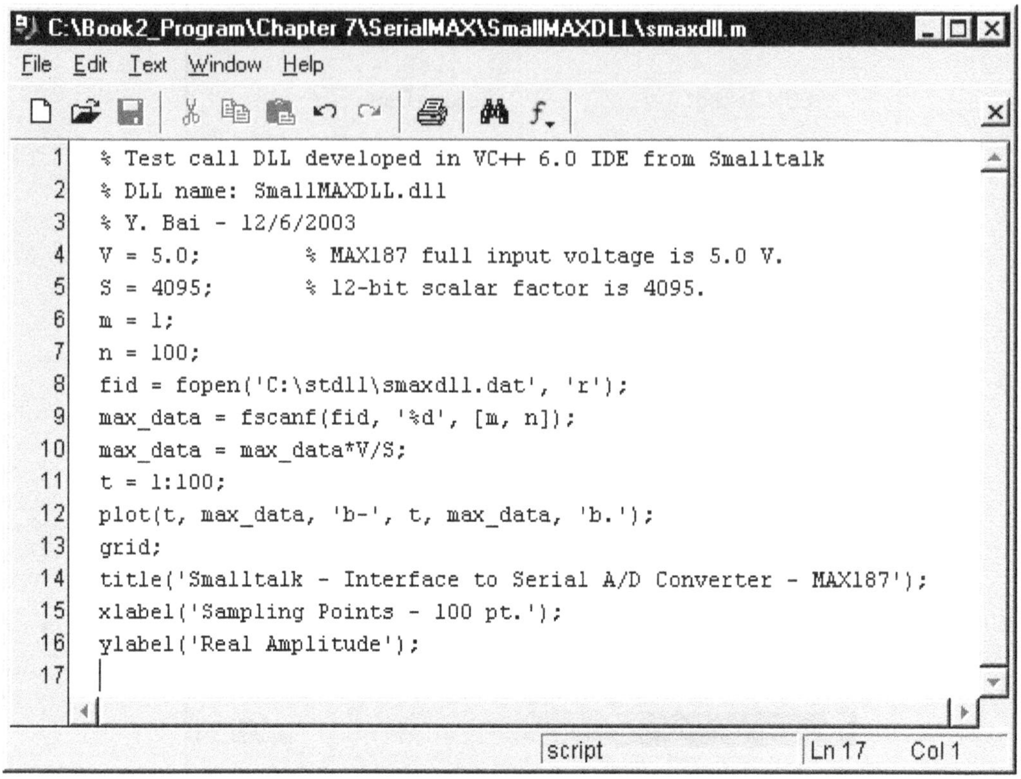

C:\Book2_Program\Chapter 7\SerialMAX\SmallMAXDLL\smaxdll.m

File Edit Text Window Help

```
% Test call DLL developed in VC++ 6.0 IDE from Smalltalk
% DLL name: SmallMAXDLL.dll
% Y. Bai - 12/6/2003
V = 5.0;          % MAX187 full input voltage is 5.0 V.
S = 4095;         % 12-bit scalar factor is 4095.
m = 1;
n = 100;
fid = fopen('C:\stdll\smaxdll.dat', 'r');
max_data = fscanf(fid, '%d', [m, n]);
max_data = max_data*V/S;
t = 1:100;
plot(t, max_data, 'b-', t, max_data, 'b.');
grid;
title('Smalltalk - Interface to Serial A/D Converter - MAX187');
xlabel('Sampling Points - 100 pt.');
ylabel('Real Amplitude');
```

script Ln 17 Col 1

FIGURE 7.74 The MATLAB M-function `smaxdll.m`.

Open MATLAB and create a new M-function named `smaxdll.m`. Enter the code that is shown in Figure 7.74 into this function.

The operation of this M-function is straightforward. First the data file is opened and the file handle is returned to the variable `fid`. Then the system function `fscanf()` is called to pick up the stored data and save it in a 1 × 100 array. The M-function converts the received data to the real voltage unit by multiplying the array element by a scaling factor. Finally, the `plot()` function is called to plot the received data.

Save this M-function to the default MATLAB user folder, `C:MATLAB6p5\work`. Enter the `smaxdll` command in the MATLAB workspace to run the M-function. The running results are shown in Figures 7.75 and 7.76. Figure 7.75 shows the sinusoidal signal input, and Figure 7.76 shows the triangular signal input.

7.4.8 Parceling and Filing Out the Project Files

To parcel the project file, follow these steps:

1. In the opened System Browser, click the `Browser|Parcel` menu item to open the project file in the parcel version.
2. Find the project file to be parceled from the `Parcel` list on the leftmost pane (for our case, the `SerialMAX` file), and right-click on the file name.
3. Select `New` from the pop-up menu.
4. In the dialog box that appears, enter the parcel name for the project file to be parceled (`SerialMAX`) and click `OK`.

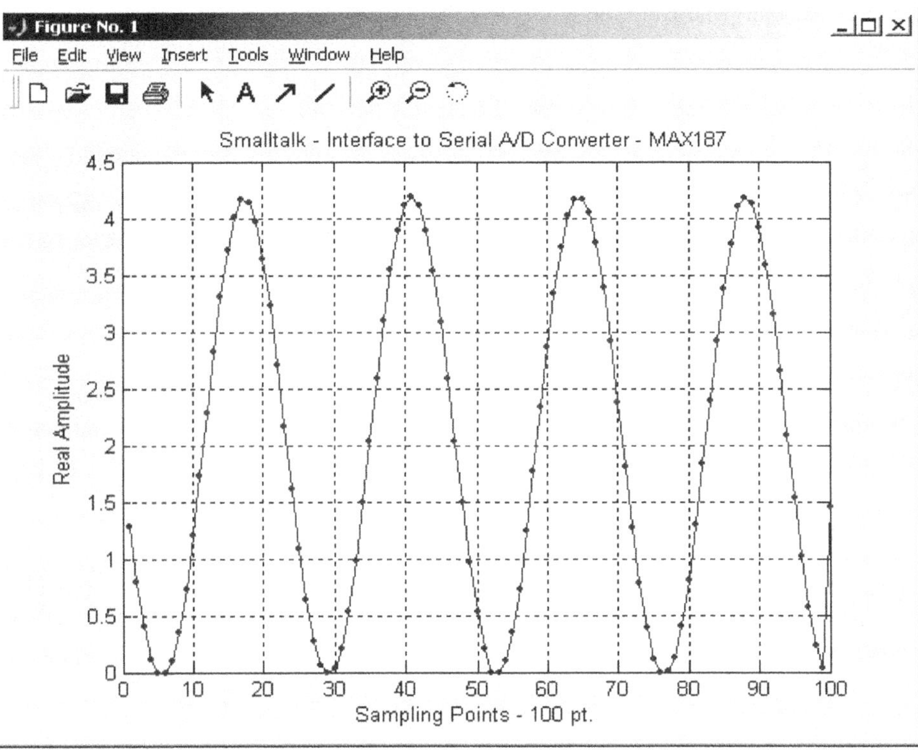

FIGURE 7.75 The received sinusoidal signal.

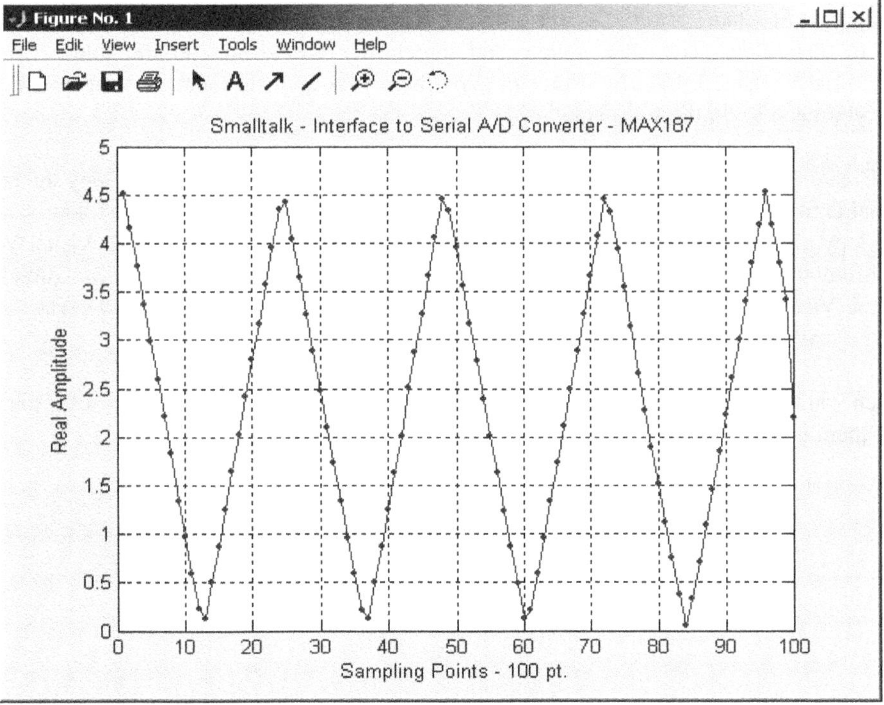

FIGURE 7.76 The received triangular signal.

5. On the second pane from the left, select the project file (SerialMAX), right-click on the file, and select Move|All To Parcel item from the pop-up menu.
6. In the opened Select dialog box, browse to find the project file (SerialMAX) from the Select parcel to move to: list. Click OK.

Now the project file can be parceled into the default image folder, C:\vw7nc\image.

To file out a project file, perform the first four steps above. Then right-click on the project file and select File Out As from the pop-up menu. In the opened Save As dialog box, select the desired file folder, enter the file name into the File name: input field, and click Save.

The next time you launch the VisualWorks, you can load the project file either in parcel or file format. You can also load a parcel file by following these steps:

1. Select the System|Parcel Manager menu item from the Visual Launcher.
2. In the dialog box that appears, select the File|Load Parcel File menu item.
3. In the Open dialog box, select the parcel file to be opened from the file list. (All parcel files have the .pcl extension). Click Open and you will see that the loaded parcel file is added to the second pane from the left.

You can also load all recent changes on the loaded parcel file by right-clicking on its file name and selecting Open in Change List from the pop-up menu. In the dialog box that appears, you can recover all recent changes to the file by right-clicking on the top line of the upper list and selecting Replay All|From the Top item from the pop-up menu. You can also recover the file in a certain position by selecting the Replay All|From Here item.

Our project is successful.

The complete project files, including the parcel and file-out files for the Domain Model and Application Model classes, the image files, and the MATLAB M-function file, are located in the folder Chapter 7\SerialMAX on the attached CD. A file folder named stdll, which contains the DLL target file SmallMAXDLL.dll and a collected data file named smaxdll.dat, is also located in this folder. The DLL source and target files are located in the folder Chapter 7\SerialMAX\SmallMAXDLL. You can copy these files and run them on your own machine, but first you need to do the following:

1. Create a new folder, stdll, under the root directory on your machine. Copy the target DLL file SmallMAXDLL.dll and the data file smaxdll.dat to that folder.
2. Copy all parcel and file-out files to the default user image folder on your VisualWorks installation directory. For example, if you've installed VisualWorks on your root directory, the VisualWorks default user image folder will most likely be C:\vw7\image (or C:\vw7nc\image for the noncommercial version).

When you have completed these two steps, you can load all the parcels and files for the project and run them in the VisualWorks environment.

8 Serial Port Programming in Java

8.1 INTRODUCTION

This chapter provides detailed information about the interfaces between Java and the serial ports, and provides some actual examples. The purpose of this chapter is to illustrate how to connect Java with the serial ports by using certain native languages.

The chapter is divided into three sections. First, an overview of the interface design using the Java Native Interface (JNI) is presented. Second, a sample serial loopback application is provided; this example illustrates the basic environment and tools used to develop an interface between Java and the serial ports with Java Native Interface (JNI), which is supplied by the Java Software Development Kit (SDK). Finally, a more complicated example is used to explain the features and tools used in the development of a serial interface between Java and a serial A/D converter.

8.2 OVERVIEW OF THE JAVA NATIVE INTERFACE

The Java Native Interface (JNI) is a key element in the interface between the Java programming language and other languages. JNI provides a convenient way for us to develop an interface between Java and the serial port. In many cases, it may seem unnecessary to develop an interface between Java and any other language if the application is limited to the Java domain. But for certain real-time applications and implementations, Java may not be a good programming language because an interpreter is always needed to execute the Java byte-code. To solve this problem, an interface between Java and a native language, such as C/C++, is necessary.

8.2.1 Why We Need an Interface Between Java and the Native Code

Java is a very popular programming language for network developments and applications because of its structure. In some real-world situations, however, you'll need to use an interface between Java programs and programs written in other languages so that your application can perform certain desired tasks and implementations. In Java, the code written in another language (such as C/C++) is called *native code*. Java provides a special tool, the Java Native Interface (JNI), to allow for interfacing between Java code and native language code.

The JNI is especially useful in the following situations:

- A program or a piece of code has been developed, debugged, and tested in another language, such as C/C++, and you don't want to spend time and energy to redevelop it, but you need to use that program or code in the Java environment.
- An application needs to access and use certain system sources or devices, such as the serial or parallel device drives. Java does not have any code that will communicate directly with the lower-level drives or the I/O manager.
- Timing is a critical issue in your applications; in other words, your applications need to run their processes in a real-time environment, and the execution speed is the first priority. Because Java code is executed by an interpreter, not a compiler, its running speed is relatively slow compared with that of compiled running mode.

Note that if you use native methods, you will lose portability because native code is not portable. For example, suppose you develop some code in Visual C++ in Windows environment, and the code will be called by Java via the JNI. You will not be able to run your application in the UNIX environment. C/C++ programming code is machine-dependent, which means that if you develop a C/C++ program using a Windows platform, it will not run in UNIX, even if your Java programming code is machine-independent.

Another point is the type-safety issue. Java is a type-safe language, but C/C++ is not and some other native languages are not. You will lose this advantage if you use the JNI.

Finally, the programs you developed by using the JNI are restricted to standard alone applications; you cannot develop applets by using JNI. This means that your programs can only be run on client machines, not on server–side machines. This is because the native library must be located on the client side since it is machine-dependent.

In spite of these drawbacks, the JNI still offers a lot of advantages to developers of real-time applications. In some situations, the JNI is an irreplaceable tool, especially for applications that either need to access the device drives or need to have real-time control of a system.

8.2.2 The JNI Development Environment

The JNI is a useful tool for developing interfaces between Java and native code. It is provided by the Java Development Kit (JDK) and is a part of the Java Visual Machine (JVM). By using the JNI, we can develop interfaces in the following two categories:

- Native libraries that contain interface functions written in native code, in which the functions can be called from the Java applications by the JNI interface. The Java application will wait for an interface function until the latter completes the operation of the calling function and then execute the next Java instruction. The interface functions are written in native code (in this chapter, Visual C++) and are located in the native library (in our case, a DLL). A block diagram of this technique is shown in Figure 8.1.

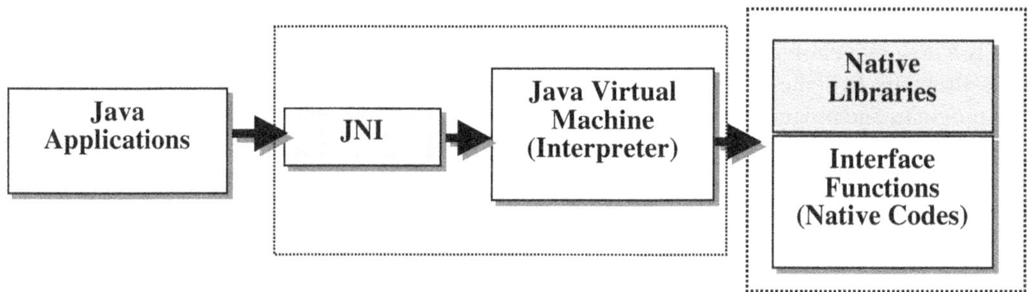

FIGURE 8.1 Using the JNI to call native code.

- Native applications that contain embedded Java Virtual Machines (JVMs). By using an invocation interface provided by the JNI, a native application can access components in Java and execute code written in the Java language via a native library. For example, when calling and executing a Java applet, a web browser might be used to download the applet from a server by means of an HTML file, and then to run a Java Virtual Machine that is embedded in the web browser to interpret and execute the applet code (bytecode) on the client machine. The web browser would be considered a native application if it were developed in C or C++ native code. A block diagram of this technique is shown in Figure 8.2.

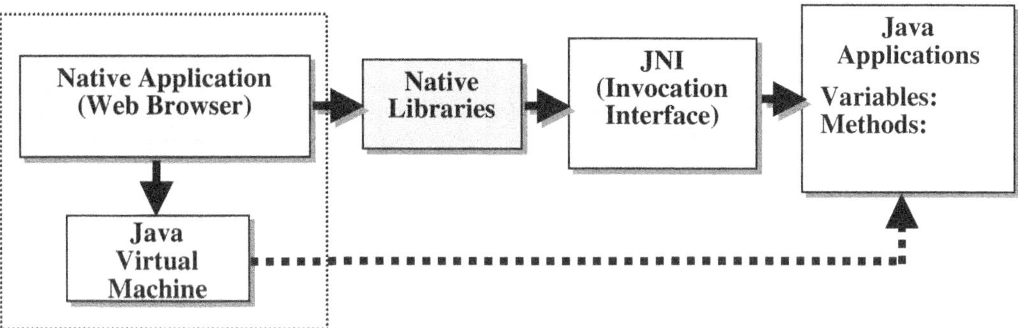

FIGURE 8.2 Embedding a Java Virtual Machine in a native application.

From the first category, a modified calling method is derived; this is called a `callback` method. A callback method is based on the native library method, which means that some interface functions are developed in native code and located in the native library. When these interface functions are called by Java instructions, the interface functions in the native library can access the variables defined in Java language and can call methods defined in the Java domain. The term `callback` refers to the fact that after the interface functions are called by Java, those functions can call back from the native domain to the Java domain.

As you examine Figures 8.1 and 8.2, notice that the JNI is a two-way interface. This means that the JNI can not only access the interface functions in the native library from the Java domain, it can also access and even modify the variables or methods defined in the Java domain from the native domain.

8.2.3 How To Develop an InterFACE

The development of an interface between Java and the native code C++ is heavily dependent on the interface between Java and the JNI, so in this section we will examine the process of developing an interface using the JNI. Here we will concentrate on the method illustrated in Figure 8.1.

This method relies on a native library to provide the interface between Java and the native language. (In our first sample program, the native language will be Visual C++). The native library works as a bridge, and the interface functions written in the native code are built and enclosed in the native library. The Java program must call the interface functions in the native library via the JNI to perform the tasks defined in those functions. The JNI defines a mapping relationship between the different variables and objects in the Java language and those in the native language.

Developing the interfacing program involves the following procedures:

- Before creating and exporting the interface functions (the DLL functions developed in C++), we need to declare the interface functions in the Java source file. This declaration is created by means of a C stub, and it resides in a class body in the Java source code.
- In order to call the newly declared interface functions from the Java domain, we must load and call the native library (the DLL) in which the interface functions are built and located. This is done by means of a special method, `System.loadLibrary()`, which is defined in a `static initializer` inside the class body following the C stub. The Java Virtual Machine can automatically run the `static initializer` first to execute any methods in the class body. In this way, the native library can be loaded and called by the Java platform.
- Compile the Java source file to obtain the bytecode by using the Java compiler `javac`.
- Use the `javah` tool to create a JNI-style C header file, which includes the definitions of all interface functions.

- Based on the JNI-style header file, finish the implementation of the interface functions in the native development environment (Visual C++). Compile and build the implementation to a native library, such as a DLL.
- In the Java domain, we can develop a test program to call and test the native library to finish this interface design.

Figure 8.3 shows a block diagram of this process.

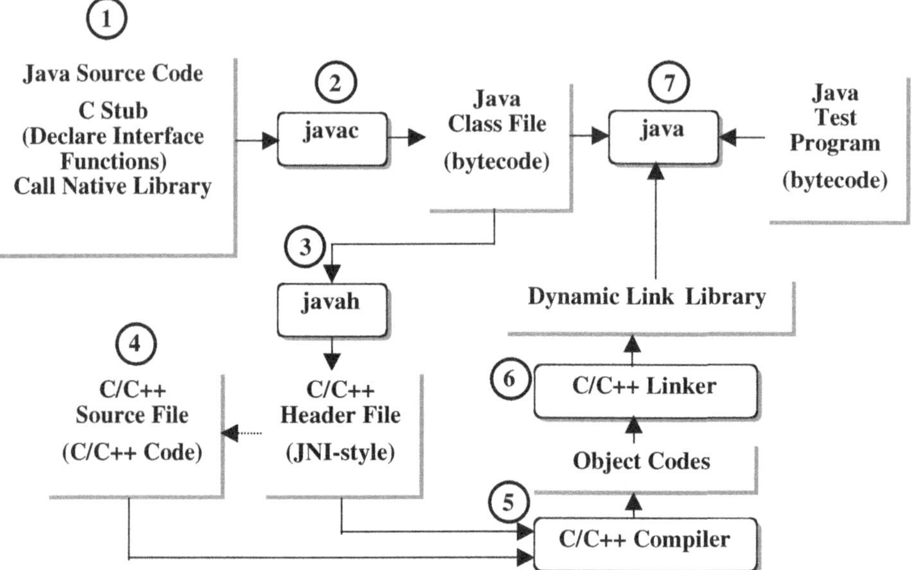

FIGURE 8.3 Using the JNI to Develop an Interface. Rob Gordon, *Essential JNI Java Native Interface* (Upper Saddle River, New Jersey: Prentice Hall, 1998), p. 20. Reprinted with permission of Pearson Education, Inc.

In the following section we will develop a simple loopback testing program to illustrate the process of developing an interface between Java and the serial port; our program will incorporate Visual C++ as the native language. The interface functions will be built in a DLL (the native library), which will be called by the Java test program to test the serial port in the Java domain.

8.3 A SIMPLE SERIAL PORT TESTING PROGRAM USING THE JNI

Before we can start developing our sample program, we must set up the Java development environment. The following three sections will explain how to set up the Java development environment in Windows 95/98/Me, Windows 2000, and Windows XP, respectively.

8.3.1 Setting Up the Java Development Environment in Windows 95/98/Me

To set up the Java development environment in Windows 95/98/Me, follow these steps:

1. Start Windows and use the Notepad editor to open the `Autoexec.bat` file, which is located on the root drive of your machine.
2. In `Autoexec.bat`, find the `SET  PATH` command line, (for example, `SET PATH=C:\...`), and move your cursor to the end of this line. If there is no semicolon (`;`) at the end of the line, add a semicolon, and then enter the full directory path to your Java compiler. For example, if your Java compiler were enclosed in the Java 2 SDK

1.3.1_01 package installed at `C:\jdk1.3`, you would enter the following line after the semicolon:

```
C:\jdk1.3\bin
```

3. Find the `SET CLASSPATH` command line (for example, `SET CLASSPATH=C:\...`), if this line exists in your `Autoexec.bat` file. Again, make sure that there is a semicolon at the end of the line, and just after the semicolon enter the following code:

```
C:\Java\SimplePort
```

If there is no `SET CLASSPATH` line, move your cursor to a new line and enter the following code:

```
SET CLASSPATH=C:\Java\SimplePort
```

4. Click `Save` from the Notepad's `File` menu and close the file.
For this application, we will use `C:\Java\SimplePort` as our user-defined project folder and store all our Java source and class files in that folder. We must define that folder as a `CLASSPATH` so that the Java SDK can identify our class files and run them properly. You may encounter an error message at run time if you have not set the `CLASSPATH` correctly.
5. Restart your computer to activate these new settings.

8.3.2 Setting Up the Java Development Environment in Windows 2000

To set up the Java development environment in Windows 2000, follow these steps:

1. Start Windows and open the Control Panel from the `Start` menu. Click the `System` icon to open the `System Properties` window. Select the `Advanced` tab and click the `Environment Variables` button.
2. At the bottom of the `Environment Variables` dialog box, go to the `System variables` table and select the `path` variable. Click the `Edit` button to open the `Edit System Variable` dialog box.
3. In the `Variable Value:` input field, move the cursor to the end of the line. Add a semicolon (`;`) if none exists, and then enter the following code:

```
C:\jdk1.3\bin
```

4. Click `OK` to save the new setting.
5. Remaining in the `System variables` table, look for the `CLASSPATH` variable. If this variable exists on your system, select it and click the `Edit` button to open the `Edit System Variable` dialog box. In the `Variable Value:` input field, move the cursor to the end, type a semicolon, and enter the following code:

```
C:\Java\SimplePort
```

If no `CLASSPATH` variable exists on your system, click the `New` button to open the `New System Variable` dialog box. Enter `CLASSPATH` in the `Variable Name:` field, and then in the `Variable Value:` field, enter the following code:

```
C:\Java\SimplePort
```

9. Click `OK` to save this setting.
For this application, we will use `C:\Java\SimplePort` as our user-defined project folder and store all our Java source and class files in that folder. We must define that

folder as a `CLASSPATH` so that the Java SDK can identify our class files and run them properly. You may encounter an error message at run time if you have not set the `CLASSPATH` correctly.

10. Restart your computer to activate the new settings.

8.3.3 Setting Up the Java Development Environment in Windows XP

To set up the Java development environment in Windows XP, follow these steps:

1. Start Windows and open the Control Panel from the `Start` menu. Click the `Performance and Maintenance` icon to open the `Performance and Maintenance` window.
2. Click the `System` icon that is located under `or Pick a Control Panel icon` item.
3. In the `System Properties` dialog box, click the `Advanced` tab and click the `Environment Variables` button.
4. At the bottom of the `Environment Variables` dialog box, go to the `System variables` table and select `path` variable. Click the `Edit` button to open the `Edit System Variable` dialog box.
5. In the `Variable Value:` input field, move the cursor to the end of the line. Add a semicolon (`;`) if none exists, and then enter the following code:

   ```
   C:\jdk1.3\bin
   ```

6. Click `OK` to save the new setting.
7. Remaining in the `System variables` table, look for the `CLASSPATH` variable. If that variable exists on your system, select it and click `Edit` button to open the `Edit System Variable` dialog box. In the `Variable Value:` input field, move the cursor to the end, type a semicolon and enter the following code:

   ```
   C:\Java\SimplePort
   ```

   If no `CLASSPATH` variable exists on your system, click the `New` button to open the `New System Variable` dialog box. Enter `CLASSPATH` in the `Variable Name:` field, and then in the `Variable Value:` field, enter the following code:

   ```
   C:\Java\SimplePort
   ```

8. Click `OK` to save this setting.
   For this application, we will use `C:\Java\SimplePort` as our user-defined project folder and store all our Java source and class files in that folder. We must define the folder as a `CLASSPATH` so that the Java SDK can identify our class files and run them properly. You may encounter an error message at run time if you have not set the `CLASSPATH` correctly.
9. Restart your computer to activate the new settings.

8.3.4 Setting Up the Hardware for the Single-Port Loopback Test

Recall that in a single-port loopback test, the receiving data terminal (pin-2 on the DB-9 connector) and the transmitting terminal (pin-3 on the DB-9 connector) are connected. During the test, data is sent to the transmitting buffer, and then the same data is returned to the receiving buffer. If the port is working properly, the data that is received should be identical with the data that was sent out. Shut down your computer and install a DB-9 serial connector with the connection, as shown in Figure 8.4.

Pin-number	Function
1	Not used
2	R_{XD}
3	T_{XD}
4	Not used
5	Ground

FIGURE 8.4 The hardware connection for the loopback test.

In this project, a run-time GUI developed in the Java domain will let us enter the setup parameters for the serial port and perform the loopback test for the associated port. The sending out and receiving in data is displayed on the corresponding text fields in the GUI in the Java domain. An interface developed with the JNI connects the Java GUI with a DLL developed in Visual C++, and allows the commands defined in the GUI to access and control the low-level serial port hardware to perform the test.

8.3.5 The Operation of the Interface Program

Our interface program will operate by calling the C++ DLL from the Java application to execute certain tasks in each interface function that is defined in the DLL. Each C++ interface function will process variables and components passed from the Java domain according to the variable types and the component types. This sequence of operations is divided into a preprocess and a postprocess, as shown in Figure 8.5.

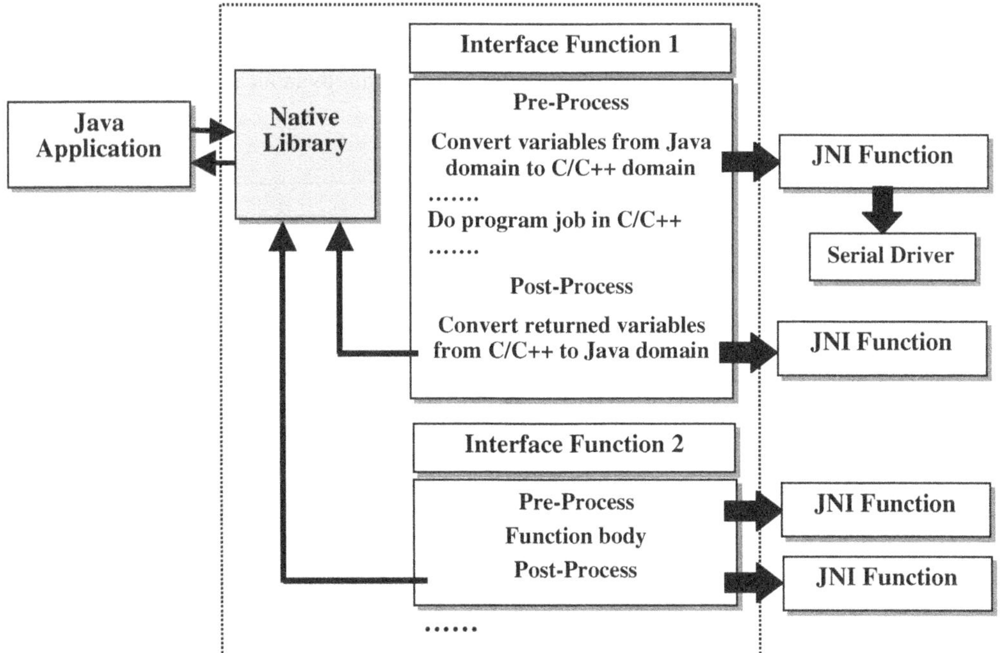

FIGURE 8.5 Block Diagram of the Interface Program.

The purpose of the preprocess is to convert variables and components, such as the primitive variables (`int`, `float`, `double`, and `Boolean`) and the object variables (`String`, `array`, and all user-defined objects), from the Java domain to the Visual C++ domain. This conversion is necessary because variables defined in the Java domain are different than those defined in the C++ domain. We cannot directly perform operations on these variables and components inside the interface function (the C++ domain); if we attempt such direct operations from the native domain, the program will halt and error messages will appear on the screen.

The purpose of the postprocess is to translate the returned variables and components from the native domain (C/C++) back to the Java domain since those variables and components will be returned and further processed by the Java program. This step is necessary because variables and components defined in C++ cannot be recognized by the Java platform.

All preprocess and postprocess tasks (that is, the conversion of the variables and components) are performed by calling the associated JNI functions, as shown in Figure 8.5. Each calling JNI function is executed according to the `JNIEnv` pointer that is located in a pointer table in the JNI.

This example will demonstrate the process of translating the variables and components between the two different language domains. The variables and components that will be passed from the Java domain to the C++ domain via the interface functions are listed here:

- A `String` component
- An `integer` data array that contains the setup parameters for the serial port
- The transmitted integer and the returned integer

Our first task is to create a Java GUI that will let us interface with the Java program at run time.

8.3.6 Developing a GUI in Java

In this project, four class files are developed according to the Model-View-Controller modal. As shown in Figure 8.6, the class `JSerialGUI` works as a graphical user interface (GUI); it provides the direct contact between the user and the project. At run time, this GUI will allow us to input information to the program and receive output from the program dynamically. The `JSerialGUI` class is considered a View object.

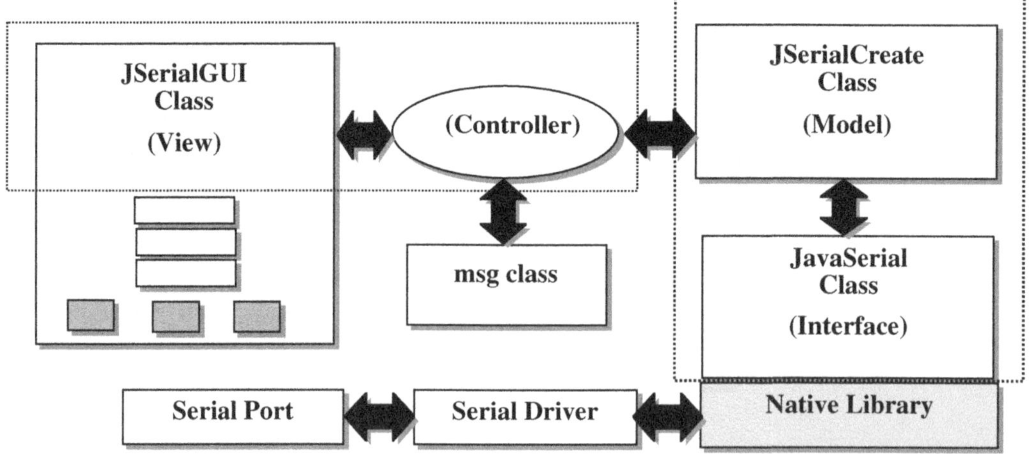

FIGURE 8.6 The Model-View-Controller modal.

The class `JSerialCreate` works as a Model object; it stores and manages the program data as the project runs. The role of this object is very similar to that of a `Document` class in Visual C++. The Controller is embedded inside the View object in this application. The `msg` class provides a template to display running and debugging information for the project. The class `JavaSerial` works as an interface between Java and the native library, allowing each to communicate with the other.

We will now develop a GUI class file named `JSerialGUI`. In Windows, open the Notepad editor and create a new Java source file named `JSerialGUI`. This GUI will include twelve components:

- TextField—COM Port number `comPort` (input).
- TextField—Baud Rate `baudRate` (input).
- TextField—Data Bits `dataBits` (input).
- TextField—Stop Bit `stopBit` (input).
- TextField—Parity `parity` (input).
- TextField—Number of data to be sent `Number` (input).
- TextField—Offset of data to be sent `Offset` (input).
- TextField—Send Data `sendData` (input).
- TextField—Read Data `readData` (output).
- Command button—`Setup`: Configure the serial port.
- Command button—`Test`: Test the serial port.
- Command button—`Exit`: Exit the program.

The top five inputs are setup parameters and are used to configure the serial port. The `Number` input is used to determine how many data should be sent to the serial port to perform the loopback test for the port. The `Offset` input works as a parameter to adjust the starting point of the data to be sent to the port. The `sendData` and `readData` are used to display the sending out and receiving in data in real time. Three command buttons, `Setup`, `Test`, and `Exit`, are used to trigger the associated event to execute the corresponding task to complete the port testing.

TIP: Recall from Chapter 7 that the Model-View-Controller modal is very popular among OOP developers. The structure of this modal is shown in Figure 8.6; the sample program in this section incorporates this modal.

The source file for the GUI class `JSerialGUI.java` is shown in Figure 8.7. Each section of the source code is explained in the following list.

A: Two class libraries, `java.awt.*` and `java.awt.event.*`, are imported at the beginning of the program. The program file needs to use the data and methods defined in these two libraries.

B: The class `JSerialGUI` is declared here. This class is a subclass of the `Frame` class, and the interface `ActionListener` is used to allow `JSerialGUI` to respond to action events.

C: We create three command buttons here by using the `Button` class with the `new` keyword. The names of the buttons are `bSetup`, `bTest`, and `bExit`.

D: An instance (`serial`) of the class `JSerialCreate` is created because we need to access that Model class to perform the associated data operations when the project runs.

E: Inside the constructor of the class `JSerialGUI`, an interface method, `addActionListener()`, is called to add this class as an event listener for the three command buttons. The keyword `this` in the parentheses represents the current class `JSerialGUI`. The size of the GUI window is set by a call to the system method `setSize()`.

```
  /*****************************************************************************
   * NAME       : JSerialGUI.java
   * DESC       : Java GUI file to test a serial port
   *****************************************************************************/
A import java.awt.*;
  import java.awt.event.*;
B public class JSerialGUI extends Frame implements ActionListener
  {
C    Button bSetup  = new Button("Setup");
     Button bTest   = new Button("Test");
     Button bExit   = new Button("Exit");
D    JSerialCreate serial = new JSerialCreate();
     public JSerialGUI()
     {
           super("Java Serial Port Testing GUI");
E          bExit.addActionListener(this);
           bSetup.addActionListener(this);
           bTest.addActionListener(this);
           setSize(450, 250);
           setLayout(new BorderLayout(2, 7));
F          Panel paneW = new Panel();
           paneW.setLayout(new GridLayout(5, 5, 8, 8));
G          paneW.add(serial.lcomPort);
           paneW.add(serial.tcomPort);
           paneW.add(serial.lbaudRate);
           paneW.add(serial.tbaudRate);
           paneW.add(serial.ldataBits);
           paneW.add(serial.tdataBits);
           paneW.add(serial.lstopBit);
           paneW.add(serial.tstopBit);
           paneW.add(serial.lparity);
           paneW.add(serial.tparity);
H          add(paneW, "West");
I          Panel paneE = new Panel();
           paneE.setLayout(new GridLayout(5, 5, 8, 8));
J          paneE.add(serial.lNum);
           paneE.add(serial.tNum);
           paneE.add(serial.lOft);
           paneE.add(serial.tOft);
           paneE.add(serial.lSend);
           paneE.add(serial.tSend);
           paneE.add(serial.lRead);
           paneE.add(serial.tRead);
K          add(paneE, "East");
L          Panel paneN = new Panel();
           paneN.setBackground(Color.gray);
M          paneN.add(new Label("Welcome to Java Serial Port Testing "));
           add(paneN, "North");
N          Panel paneS = new Panel();
           paneS.setBackground(Color.gray);
```

FIGURE 8.7 Source code for the `JSerialGUI.java`. *(continued)*

```
O          paneS.add(bSetup);
           paneS.add(bTest);
           paneS.add(bExit);
P          add(paneS, "South");
      }
      public void actionPerformed(ActionEvent  evt)
      {
Q          int m, n, ret = 0, rndNum = 0, rndOft = 0;
           int comPrms[] = {1, 9600, 8, 1, 0};
R          JavaSerial jserial = new JavaSerial();
S          rndNum = serial.getNum(serial.tNum.getText());
           rndOft = serial.getNum(serial.tOft.getText());
           Object src = evt.getSource();
T          if (src == bExit)
           {
               ret = jserial.JavaClose();
               System.exit(0);
           }
U          if (src == bSetup)
           {
               if (rndNum == 0)
                  return;
V              comPrms[0] = serial.getNum(serial.tcomPort.getText());
               comPrms[1] = serial.getNum(serial.tbaudRate.getText());
               comPrms[2] = serial.getNum(serial.tdataBits.getText());
               comPrms[3] = serial.getNum(serial.tstopBit.getText());
               comPrms[4] = serial.getNum(serial.tparity.getText());
W              ret = jserial.JavaSetup(comPrms);
           }
X          if (src == bTest)
           {
               for (m = 1; m <= rndNum; m++)
               {
Y                  n = m + rndOft;
                   ret = jserial.JavaWrite(n);
                   if (ret != 0)
                   {
                       msg warn = new msg("ERROR in Write() DLL Calling");
                       warn.show();
                       return;
                   }
Z                  serial.tSend.setText(serial.getStr(n));
1                  ret = jserial.JavaRead();
2                  serial.tRead.setText(serial.getStr(ret));
3                  if (ret != n)
                   {
                       msg warn = new msg("ERROR in the Port Testing");
                       warn.show();
                   }
               }
          }
      }
```

FIGURE 8.7 Source code for the `JSerialGUI.java`. *(continued)*

```
        public static void main(String[] args)
        {
4           JSerialGUI sGUI = new JSerialGUI();
            sGUI.show();
        }
    }
```

FIGURE 8.7 Source code for the `JSerialGUI.java`.

F: Four panels are generated in this project. Each panel is used to hold the associated components on the GUI. Here the `West` panel `paneW` is created, and a `GridLayout` manager is called to divide the panel to five by five grids.

G: Ten components, five `TextField` items and five associated labels, which are used to receive the setup parameters of the serial port (entered by us at run time), are added to this panel one by one. The sequence of adding each of these components is: add a label followed by an associated `TextField`. All these components are defined in the `Model` class `JSerialCreate`, which we will discuss next. The instance name `serial` needs to be prefixed in front of each component.

H: After all components are added to this panel, the panel is added into the `West` section of the GUI window.

I: Similarly, an `East` panel is created to hold the application parameters, such as the total number of data to be sent to the serial port (`tNum`), the offset value that is used to adjust the starting value of the data to be sent (`tOft`), the data to be transmitted (`tSend`), and the data to be received (`tRead`).

J: We add these application parameters to the `East` panel one by one. All of these parameters are defined in the Model class `JSerialCreate`, so a `serial` instance is placed in front of each parameter.

K: After all application parameters are added into the `East` panel, the panel is added to the `East` section of the GUI window.

L: A `North` panel is created here to hold the label of the project.

M: We create a new label here and add it to the `North` panel. We then add the `North` panel, with the label, to the `North` area of the GUI window.

N: A `South` panel is generated here to hold three command buttons.

O: We add the three buttons, `bSetup`, `bTest`, and `bExit`, to the `South` panel.

P: We add the `South` panel with three buttons to the `South` section of the GUI window.

Q: Several local variables are declared at the beginning of the `actionPerformed()` event procedure. `comPrms[]` is an `integer` array used to hold the setup parameters of the serial port. The default setup parameters are assigned to this array.

R: An instance of the interface class `JavaSerial`, `jserial`, is created here because we need to call the interface functions defined in that interface class in this procedure. To access those functions, we first need to create an instance of that class because all interface functions defined in the `JavaSerial` class are instance functions.

S: Next we need to pick up the total number of data items to be sent to the serial port and the offset value from the Model class `JserialCreate;` these two parameters are needed to test the port. First the system method `getText()` is used to obtain both parameters in text format. Then a user-defined method, `getNum()`, which is defined in the class `JSerialCreate`, is used to convert the parameters from text format to integer format and assign them to the associated local variables, `rndNum` and `rndOft`, respectively. The system event method `getSource()` is called to obtain the current event that triggers this event procedure `actionPerformed()`.

T: If the event is bExit, which means that the Exit button has been clicked, then the interface function JavaClose(), defined in the interface class JavaSerial, is called to close the opened serial port, and the system method System.exit(0) is called to close the GUI window and exit the project. A 0 argument means that the exit has been error free.

U: If the event is bSetup, which means that the Setup button has been clicked, we need to determine whether the total number of data items to be sent has been obtained. If the value of this parameter is 0, the program returns to the calling function without any action.

V: If the total number of data items to be sent is not 0, which means that we've already received the value of this parameter, then we need to pick up all setup parameters from the associated components defined in the Model class JSerialCreate and assign them to the local data array comPrms[].

W: Next we need to call the interface function JavaSetup(), defined in the interface class JavaSerial, to configure the serial port. Because the interface function JavaSetup() is an instance method, we need to place the instance of that class, jserial, in front of that function.

X: If the event is bTest, which means that the Test button has been clicked, a for loop is used to repeatedly send out and receive the data to and from the serial port until the loop hits the upper boundary rndNum.

Y: The actual sent out data is modified by the offset rndOft by addition of the loop counter. To send data to the serial port, an interface function, JavaWrite(), defined in the interface class JavaSerial, is called. A jserial instance is placed in front of the interface function. A warning message will be displayed if this function call has failed. An instance of the class msg, warn, is used to display this message.

Z: The system method setText() is used to display the sent out data in the tSend TextField. An instance of the class JSerialCreate, serial, is prefixed in front of the parameter tSend because this parameter is an instance variable defined in the class JSerialCreate.

1: After the data is sent out, another interface function, JavaRead(), defined in the interface class JavaSerial, is called to pick up the sent out data from the serial port.

2: The received data is displayed on the component tRead that is defined in the Model class JSerialCreate.

3: An error message is displayed if the received data is not identical with the sent out data. In the ideal case, both the sending out and the received in data should be identical if the serial port works properly.

4: The main method is the entry point of the project. An instance of the class JSerialGUI is created and displayed. In this way, the project can be started.

Save this file to our user-defined project folder, C:\Java\SimplePort. Next let's develop our Model class file, JSerialCreate.java.

8.3.7 Developing the Model Class File

The purpose of this class is to store and operate the project data according to the GUI window's events. Because there is large number of components applied in this project, we place some components in this Model class, JSerialCreate.java. Open the NotePad editor and enter the code that is shown in Figure 8.8 into this class file.

5: The system class libraries are imported at the beginning of the class file.

6: The class JSerialCreate is started from here.

```
/*****************************************************************************
 * NAME        : JSerialCreate.java
 * DESC        : Java Serial Port Object Creator - Model Class
 * DATE        : 12/15/2003
*****************************************************************************/
5   import java.awt.*;
    import java.awt.event.*;
    import java.util.*;
6   public class JSerialCreate
    {
       private int nRnd;
7      TextField tcomPort  = new TextField(10);
       TextField tbaudRate = new TextField(10);
       TextField tdataBits = new TextField(10);
       TextField tstopBit  = new TextField(10);
       TextField tparity   = new TextField(10);
       TextField tNum      = new TextField(10);
       TextField tOft      = new TextField(10);
       TextField tSend     = new TextField(10);
       TextField tRead     = new TextField(10);
8      Label lcomPort  = new Label("COM Port");
       Label lbaudRate = new Label("Baud Rate");
       Label ldataBits = new Label("Data Bits");
       Label lstopBit  = new Label("Stop Bit");
       Label lparity   = new Label("Parity");
       Label lNum      = new Label("Number");
       Label lOft      = new Label("Offset");
       Label lSend     = new Label("Send Data");
       Label lRead     = new Label("Read Data");
9      public int getNum(String nstr)
       {
10          if (nstr.length() == 0)
            {
                msg warn = new msg("No input on the Number or Amplitude Field ");
                warn.show();
                return 0;
            }
11          nRnd = Integer.parseInt(nstr);
            return  nRnd;
       }
12     public String getStr(int  dNum)
       {
            return String.valueOf(dNum);
       }
    }
```

FIGURE 8.8 The class file `JSerialCreate.java`.

7: Nine `TextField` items are declared; these components are used to hold the setup parameters of the serial port and the application parameters.

8: Nine associated labels are created here.

9: The user-defined method `getNum()` is declared. This method is used to convert the input parameter from text format to the numeric format and return the result to the calling functions.

10: Here we need to check whether the input string is an empty string by using the `length()` method that belongs to the `String` class. If the input string is empty, a `0` will be returned to the calling function, and a warning message will be displayed on the screen.

11: If the input string is non-empty, the class method `ParseInt()` that belongs to the `Integer` class will be called to convert the input string to the associated integer value. The converted result will then be returned to the calling function.

12: `getStr()` is another user-defined method in this Model class. The operation of this method is opposite to that of the last method, `getNum()`. `getStr()` is used to convert the input integer to an associated string. The class method `valueOf()`, which belongs to the class `String`, is called to complete this conversion. The converted result is returned to the calling function.

Save this file to our user-defined project folder, `C:\Java\SimplePort`.

8.3.8 Developing the Interface Class File

The class `JavaSerial` works as an interface between the Java program and the native library. All interface functions defined in this interface class should be identical with those defined in the native library.

Four interface functions are defined in this class:

- Setup()
- Write()
- Read()
- Close()

Each of these interface functions is embedded in the associated Java method, and can be accessed by calling the associated method. The code for this interface class file is shown in Figure 8.9.

13: The used system class libraries are imported at the beginning of this class file.

14: The interface class `JavaSerial` is defined and started from here.

15: A C stub, `public native int Setup();`, is used to declare the interface function `Setup()` in the native domain (Visual C++). This interface function is embedded inside this Java class, `JavaSerial`. (This is a popular format to call a native function from the Java domain.) In the same style, four interface functions are declared here. These functions are defined in the native domain and belong to that, so the keyword `native` is prefixed in front of each function. The `Setup()` function contains an integer array that holds the serial port setup parameters as the argument. The `Write()` function contains an integer argument that is the value of the data to be written to the port. The `Read()` function is used to read the data written to the serial port, and the `Close()` function is used to close the opened serial port.

16: A `static initializer` is used here to contain a call to the native library `JNISerial`, which will be developed in the C++ domain. Four native functions, `Setup()`, `Write()`, `Read()`, and `Close()`, are defined in this native library.

17: The Java method `JavaSetup()` is defined here, and the interface function `Setup()` is embedded in this method. At run time, this method will let us access the interface function `Setup()` to configure the serial port.

18: Inside the Java method `JavaSetup()`, the interface function `Setup()` is called with an integer array as the argument. The body of this interface function is defined in the native library. A warning message is displayed if this function call encounters any error. The running status of the function is returned to the calling function.

```
/*****************************************************************************
 * NAME         : JavaSerial.java
 * DESC         : Java serial interface file
 * PGMR         : Y. Bai
 * DATE         : 12/15/2003
 *****************************************************************************/
13  import java.awt.*;
    import java.awt.event.*;
    import java.util.*;
14  public class JavaSerial
    {
        int result;
15      public native int Setup(int[] comParms);
        public native int Write(int sdata);
        public native int Read();
        public native int Close();
16      static
        {
            System.loadLibrary("JNISerial");
        }
17      public int JavaSetup(int[] darray)
        {
            int ret = 0;
18          ret = Setup(darray);
            if (ret != 0)
            {
                msg warn = new msg("ERROR in Setup() DLL Calling");
                warn.show();
            }
            return ret;
        }
19      public int JavaWrite(int sdata)
        {
            int ret = 0;
20          ret = Write(sdata);
            return ret;
        }
21      public int JavaRead()
        {
            int result;
22          result = Read();
            return result;
        }
23      public int JavaClose()
        {
            int ret = 0;
24          ret = Close();
            return ret;
        }
    }
```

FIGURE 8.9 The interface class `JavaSerial.java`.

19: Similarly, the Java method `JavaWrite()` is defined here; at run time, this method will let us access the interface function `Write()`, which is embedded in the method, to send data to the serial port. The argument is the data value to be written to the port.

20: The interface function `Write()` is called to write a data item to the serial port. The running status of this interface function is returned to the calling function.

21: The Java method `JavaRead()`, which includes the interface function `Read()`, is defined here. At run time, this method will let us access the interface function `Read()` to pick up the data from the serial port.

22: The interface function `Read()` is called to access the serial port and receive the incoming data. `Read()` is a native function, defined in the native library.

23: The Java method `JavaClose()` is used to access the interface function `Close()`, which is defined in the native library, to close the opened port.

24: The interface function `Close()` is called to close the port. The running status of this function is returned to the calling function.

8.3.9 Developing the MSG Class File

The `msg` class is used to display a warning message if a method or a function encounters an error as the project runs. The code for this class file is shown in Figure 8.10. Java provides some default message boxes that appear at run time. In this application, however, we will create a user-defined message box window to display the warning message.

```
/*****************************************************************************
 * NAME        : msg.java
 * DESC        : Works as a message box for the Java program
 * DATE        : 12/15/2003
 *****************************************************************************/
25 import java.awt.*;
   import java.awt.event.*;
26 public class msg extends Frame implements ActionListener
   {
27    Button bOK = new Button("OK");
      Label input;
28    public msg(String info)
      {
29          input = new Label(info);
            setSize(300, 100);
30          Panel paneS = new Panel();
            Panel paneC = new Panel();
31          bOK.addActionListener(this);
32          paneS.add(bOK);
            paneC.add(input);
            add(paneS, "South");
            add(paneC, "Center");
      }
      public void actionPerformed(ActionEvent evt)
      {
33          Object src = evt.getSource();
            if (src == bOK)
              setVisible(false);
      }
   }
```

FIGURE 8.10 The `msg.java` class.

25: Several useful class libraries are imported at the beginning of this class file.

26: The `msg` class is defined as a subclass of the `Frame` class, and the interface `Action-Listener` is implemented to respond to action events as the project runs.

27: Two components are declared in this class: the command button `bOK` and the label `input`. The label is used to display the warning message. The button is used to activate an action event to the project.

28: The constructor of the msg class contains an argument that works as an input message to be displayed in this message box.
29: A new input label is created with the input message as an argument. The size of the message box is set by the setSize() method.
30: Two panels, paneS and paneC, are created; these are used to hold the label and the command button, respectively.
31: The system method addActionListener() is used to add the current class as an event listener for the command button bOK.
32: Both the bOK command button and the input label are added into paneS and paneC. After this addition, both components can be displayed on the two panes. Two panes are added to the South and the Center areas on the GUI window.
33: In the actionPerformed() event procedure, the system method getSource() is used to pick up the source that activates an action event, such as a click of the command button bOK. If the source is bOK, the message box is hidden from the GUI window.

Now we have completed developing all Java class files for our program. It is time for us to develop the native library, which will contain the interface functions, Setup(), Write(), Read(), and Close(), which we declared in the JavaSerial interface class. The native language is Visual C++ 6.0, and the library is the Dynamic Link Library (DLL). The name of our DLL file is JNISerial; this DLL is defined in the interface class JavaSerial. Before we can develop the DLL file, we need to create a JNI-style header file based on the Java bytecode file JavaSerial.class. This header file is C-program compatible file, and it contains all prototypes of the interface functions defined in the native library. The header file also includes the necessary protocols of the components that interface between the Java and C++ environments.

8.3.10 Developing a JNI-Style Header File

javah is a tool that is used to create a JNI-style header file. First we need to compile the interface class file JavaSerial to get the bytecode of that class file. Open a command window and type javac JavaSerial.java in the user-defined project folder C:\Java\SimplePort. The bytecode of the class JavaSerial is obtained with the name JavaSerial.class.

Remaining in the user-defined project folder C:\Java\SimplePort, type javah JavaSerial to create a JNI-style header file, JavaSerial.h. Open this header file using Visual C++ 6.0 IDE; your JNI-style header file should match the one shown in Figure 8.12.

jni_md.h is a Java system header file that provides all prototypes and protocols of the JNI variables, constants, and functions. Because the variables and constants defined in the Java domain are different than variables and constants defined in the C++ domain, the JNI provides a mapping between the variables and constants defined in Java and those in C++. All these mapping prototypes are contained in the Java system header file jni_md.h, which is shown in Figure 8.11.

JNIEXPORT is equivalent to dllexport in the C++ domain; it is used to explicitly export the interface functions. Here a full function name is needed. (The full name includes both the class name and the function name, separated with a period operator.) Note that in the JNI, the interface function is defined by using an underscore, _, to replace the period operator. A keyword, Java, is placed in front of the name of the interface function to indicate that this is a Java function. (Refer to Figure 8.12.) JNICALL is equivalent to stdcall in the C++ domain, which means that this is a standard call.

Some arguments are included with these functions. The first one, JNIEnv, is a pointer. The native code written in C++ uses the JNIEnv as a pointer to a table of JNI functions. All native code accesses the JNI functions by using this pointer. In the Java interpreter, a pointer table or a pointer array is provided, and each pointer points to a JNI function, as shown in Figure 8.13.

Four interface functions are declared in this header file. All interface functions have a returned data item with a jint data type. The Setup() function has an argument with a jintArray

```
/*
 * @(#)jni_md.h 1.11 00/02/02
 *
 * Copyright 1996-2000 Sun Microsystems, Inc. All Rights Reserved.
 *
 * This software is the proprietary information of Sun Microsystems, Inc.
 * Use is subject to license terms.
 *
 */
#ifndef _JAVASOFT_JNI_MD_H_
#define _JAVASOFT_JNI_MD_H_

#define JNIEXPORT __declspec(dllexport)
#define JNIIMPORT __declspec(dllimport)
#define JNICALL __stdcall

typedef long jint;
typedef __int64 jlong;
typedef signed char jbyte;

#endif /* !_JAVASOFT_JNI_MD_H_ */
```

FIGURE 8.11 The system header file `jni_md.h`.

data type. `jint` is a data type defined in the C++ domain; it is equivalent to an `integer` data type in the Java domain. As previously mentioned, the variables and constants defined in the Java and the C/C++ domains are different. Let's take a look at the mapping relationships between the variables and constants defined in the two domains.

8.3.11 Mapping Variables and Objects Between Java and C/C++

The variables and objects defined in the Java programming domain and those defined in the C/C++ domain are different; we cannot directly use a variable or an object that is passed from the Java domain in the C++ domain, or vice versa. We have to do some conversion or translation between the variables by using a mapping technique, provided by the JNI, to make the variables accessible in either domain.

Two categories of variables are defined in the JNI: *primitive* variables and *object* variables. The primitive variables are `int`, `float`, `double`, `char`, and `long`. The object variables are `string`, `array`, `instance`, and `class`. For mapping of primitive variables, JNI provides a table. Mapping primitive data is straightforward and this mapping relationship is shown in Table 8.1.

All these type definitions are located in the header file `jni.h` with a `typedef` statement. You can directly use this mapping to convert variables defined in either domain and use them in your program.

The mapping of the objects in JNI is not as clear as mapping of the primitive variables. This mapping happens by means of pointers that are defined in the internal data structures of the Java interpreter. To successfully convert and map the object types between the two language domains, we call the associated JNI functions. The JNI provides a set of functions to handle this conversion between the Java domain and the native domain. In this section, we will discuss two typical object types, `String` and `Array`. For other object types, refer to the following two books:

- *The Java Native Interface—Programmer's Guide and Specification* by Sheng Liang, Addison-Wesley, 1999,
- *Essential JNI—Java Native Interface* by Rob Gordon, Prentice Hall PTR, 1998.

```
/* DO NOT EDIT THIS FILE - it is machine generated */
#include "jni.h"
/* Header for class JavaSerial */

#ifndef _Included_JavaSerial
#define _Included_JavaSerial
#ifdef __cplusplus
extern "C" {
#endif
/*
 * Class:     JavaSerial
 * Method:    Setup
 * Signature: ([I)I
 */
JNIEXPORT jint JNICALL Java_JavaSerial_Setup
  (JNIEnv *, jobject, jintArray);

/*
 * Class:     JavaSerial
 * Method:    Write
 * Signature: (I)I
 */
JNIEXPORT jint JNICALL Java_JavaSerial_Write
  (JNIEnv *, jobject, jint);

/*
 * Class:     JavaSerial
 * Method:    Read
 * Signature: ()I
 */
JNIEXPORT jint JNICALL Java_JavaSerial_Read
  (JNIEnv *, jobject);

/*
 * Class:     JavaSerial
 * Method:    Close
 * Signature: ()I
 */
JNIEXPORT jint JNICALL Java_JavaSerial_Close
  (JNIEnv *, jobject);

#ifdef __cplusplus
}
#endif
#endif
```

FIGURE 8.12 The JNI-style header file.

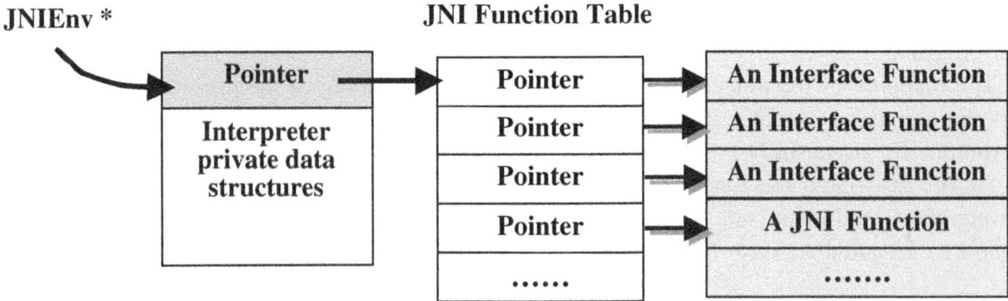

FIGURE 8.13 Calling a JNI function. Rob Gordon, *Essential JNI Java Native Interface* (Upper Saddle River, New Jersey: Prentice Hall, 1998), p. 62. Reprinted with permission of Pearson Education, Inc.

TABLE 8.1
Mapping of the Primitive Variables

Java Programming Domain	C/C++ Programming Domain	Bytes
boolean	Jboolean	1
byte	Jbyte	1
char	Jchar	2
short	Jshort	2
int	Jint	4
long	Jlong	8
float	Jfloat	4
double	Jdouble	8

8.3.11.1 Mapping String Variables

Strings in the Java programming language are sequences of 16-bit Unicode characters. C strings are null-terminated strings with 8-bit characters, so it is necessary to convert these two kinds of strings when we interface between the Java and C/C++ programming languages.

JNI provides some internal functions to support the conversion of the String variables between Java and C/C++. First let's investigate passing String variables from the Java domain to the C/C++ domain and manipulating those variables in the C/C++ domain.

Table 8.2 lists some popular JNI String operation functions and the versions of the Java SDK where they are available.

TABLE 8.2
Popular JNI String Operation Functions

JNI Function	Description	Since
`GetStringChars` `ReleaseStringChars`	Obtains or releases a pointer to the contents of a string in Unicode format. May return a copy of the string	JDK 1.1
`GetStringUTFChars` `ReleaseStringUTFChars`	Obtains or releases a pointer to the contents of a string in UTF-8 format. May return a copy of the string	JDK 1.1
`GetStringLength`	Return the number of Unicode characters in the string	JDK 1.1
`GetStringUTFLength`	Return the number of bytes needed (not including the trailing 0) to represent a string in the UTF-8 format	JDK 1.1
`NewString`	Creates a `java.lang.String` instance that contains the same sequence of characters as the given Unicode C string	JDK 1.1
`NewStringUTF`	Creates a `java.lang.String` instance that contains the same sequence of characters as the given UTF-8 encoded C string	JDK 1.1
`GetStringCritical` `ReleaseStringCritical`	Obtains a pointer to the contents of a string in Unicode format. May return a copy of the string. Native code must not block between a pair of `Get/ReleaseStringCritical` classes.	Java 2 SDK 1.2
`GetStringRegion` `SetStringRegion`	Copies the contents of a string to or from a preallocated C buffer in the Unicode format	Java 2 SDK 1.2
`GetStringUTFRegion` `SetStringUTFRegion`	Copies the contents of a string to or from a preallocated C buffer in the UTF-8 format	Java 2 SDK 1.2

As an example, suppose you want to pass a String variable, such as

```
String str = "Test a String in C/C++ Domain";
```

from a Java program to the C/C++ native method, and then manipulate that String in the C/C++ domain. You should create a native method to handle the process. A sample native method, `TestString()`, which is defined in a Java class named `Test`, is shown in Figure 8.14.

```
   JNIEXPORT jstring JNICALL Java_Test_TestString(JNIEnv *env, jobject obj, jstring str)
   {
A      const jbyte* jstr;
       char jbuff[128];
       // convert the String str in Java Domain to the String jstr in C/C++ Domain
B      jstr = (const signed char*) (env ->GetStringUTFChars(str, JNI_FALSE));
       // manipulate (printf) the String jstr in C/C++ Domain
C      printf("The Converted String: %s\n", jstr);
       // Convert the String jstr Back to Java Domain
D      sprintf( jbuff, "Returned: %s", jstr);
       // Release the Space used by Converting the String str
E      env -> ReleaseStringUTFChars(str, (const char*)jstr);
      // Return the Converted String jstr to the Java Domain
F      return env -> NewStringUTF(jbuff);
```

FIGURE 8.14 Passing a Java String variable to the native domain.

Each section of the code is explained in the following list:

A: First two C/C++ type variables, `const jbyte* jstr` and `char jbuff[128]` are created.

B: The purpose of the first variable, `const jbyte* jstr`, is to receive the converted String variable from the Java to the C/C++ domain by calling a JNI internal function, `GetStringUTFChars()`. This function returns a `const jbyte*` pointer to the Unicode Text Format (UTF) characters described in the String variable. In C++, and especially with the Visual C++ 6.0 compiler, the `const jbyte*` is defined as a `const signed char*`, so we have to cast the returned String variable to this type. This casting is necessary, and the Visual C++ 6.0 compiler would return an error message without it. Two arguments are passed to this function. The first, `str`, is the String variable (with a Java `String` type), and the second argument is a boolean variable used to define whether the variable needs a copy or not. You can put a NULL to this variable if you do not take care about it. Here we add a constant, `JNI_FALSE`, to indicate that we do not need this variable to be copied.

C: A C/C++ system function `printf()` is called to manipulate this converted String `jstr`. The function displays the contents of the String variable on the screen to show that this conversion is successful.

D: Because this native method needs to return a String back to the Java domain, we need to temporarily store this String to a C/C++ characters buffer, `jbuff`.

E: After the program obtains the converted String, we need to release the space assigned to the converted String by calling an internal function, `ReleaseStringUTFChars()`. As we executed this function call, the String variable `jstr` is no longer available. Two arguments are passed to this function. `str` is a Java String variable, and `jstr` is a C/C++ String variable. Because this function can only accept `const char*` as the data type for the second argument, we need to cast the `jstr` argument to convert it from the `const signed char*` to the `const char*` type.

F: We stored the converted String `jstr` to a temporary buffer, `jbuff`, in step D; now we want to return this String back to the Java domain. To convert the String back to the Java String type, we need to call another internal function, `NewStringUTF()`. The argument for this function is the C/C++ type String, which is stored in the buffer `jbuff`. This function returns a converted Java String.

Keep in mind that when you call any JNI internal function, you need to use an `env*` pointer to locate the function. JNI provides a table that stores all pointers that point to the associated functions.

The example in this section should give you a clear understanding of mapping the String variables in the different domains. JNI also supports some other String functions, and the Java 2 SDK 1.4 adds some new JNI String functions.

8.3.11.2 Mapping Array Variables

In Java, two kinds of arrays exist. One is the data array, with a `primitive` data type; data arrays include `int`, `float`, `double`, and `long`. Another type is the object array. Different mapping methods are used for these two types of arrays in the JNI.

For the primitive data array, the JNI uses a similar mapping method as it did for the String variable discussed earlier. Figure 8.15 shows a simple example that illustrates the conversion of a primitive data array between the Java domain and the C/C++ domain.

```
  JNIEXPORT jdoubleArray JNICALL Java_Test_Array
     (JNIEnv* env, jobject obj, jint size, jdoubleArray dArray)
  {
A    jdouble* jRandArray;

B    jdoubleArray retArray = env->NewDoubleArray(size);

     /* convert data array passed from Java domain to C/C++ data array */
C    jRandArray = env->GetDoubleArrayElements(dArray, JNI_FALSE);

     /* do some operations to the jRandArray in the C/C++ Domain */
D    ......

     /* convert data array from C/C++ domain back to Java domain */
E    env->SetDoubleArrayRegion(retArray, 0, size, jRandArray);

     /* release the space allocated to the C/C++ array jRandArray */
F    env->ReleaseDoubleArrayElements(dArray, jRandArray, 0);

     /* return the Java type array retArray to the Java domain */
G    return retArray;
```

FIGURE 8.15 Converting a primitive array.

Here a native method named `Array()` is defined in a Java class, `Test`. The argument `size` is an integer, used to indicate the length of the data array, `dArray`. The argument `dArray` has a double type, and it contains an array of double data.

Each section of the code is explained in the following list.

A: A local double array, `jRandArray`, which is a pointer variable with a C/C++ array type, is created first. This array is used to store the data value of the array converted from the Java domain.

B: A Java data array `retArray`, with a `jdoubleArray` type, is generated by a call to a JNI internal function `NewDoubleArray()` with an argument of `size`. `size` stores the size of the input array. The starting address of the new created array is assigned to `retArray`.

C: By calling the JNI function `GetDoubleArrayElements()`, we can convert the passed Java data array, `dArray`, to the C/C++ data array `jRandArray`. The conversion result is assigned to the array `jRandArray` in the C/C++ domain. A `JNI_FALSE` constant is used as the second argument to indicate that we do not need a copy of this array.

D: After the Java data array `dArray` has been converted to the C/C++ `jRandArray`, you can perform any manipulation or operation on the array in the C/C++ domain by using C/C++ functions.

E: When the operation of the data array is completed in the C/C++ domain, we can use another JNI function, `SetDoubleArrayRegion()`, to convert the C/C++ array back to the Java array and assign it to the Java array `retArray`, which is created at the beginning of this native method. Four arguments are used for this function. The first one is the destination array `retArray`, which is a Java type array. The second argument is an index that indicates the starting position of the elements in the source array `jRandArray`. In our case, we want to convert all elements in the source array, so this index is `0`. The third argument is the total number of the elements to be converted from the source array `jRandArray` to the destination array `retArray`. This argument is equal to the size of the input array. After this conversion, the resulting elements are stored in the Java data array `retArray`. The fourth argument is the source array `jRandArray`.

F: After finishing the conversion, we can delete the space allocated for the C/C++ data array `jRandArray` as we did before. We call a JNI internal function, `ReleaseDoubleArrayElements()`, to delete this space. Three arguments are used for this function. The first argument is the original Java type array `dArray` (a pointer), and the second is the C/C++ data array `jRandArray` (another pointer). The final argument is a mode parameter, and a `0` means that it will free the buffer taken by the array `jRandArray` after it updates the array elements.

G: Finally we return the converted Java array `retArray` back to the Java domain.

A mapping of all primitive data array between the Java and C/C++ domains is detailed in Table 8.3.

TABLE 8.3
Mapping of the Primitive Data Array Variables

Data Type in Java	Data Type in C/C++
boolean[ ]	jbooleanArray
byte[ ]	jbyteArray
char[ ]	jcharArray
int[ ]	jintArray
short[ ]	jshortArray
long[ ]	jlongArray
float[ ]	jfloatArray
double[ ]	jdoubleArray
object[ ]	jobjectArray

JNI provides a generic array type, `jarray`, which is an inheritance hierarchy that is shown in Figure 8.16. This inheritance hierarchy is applied to the C++ domain.

As with mapping of Strings, JNI provides a set of internal functions to map data arrays between the Java and C/C++ domains. Table 8.4 shows this set of functions.

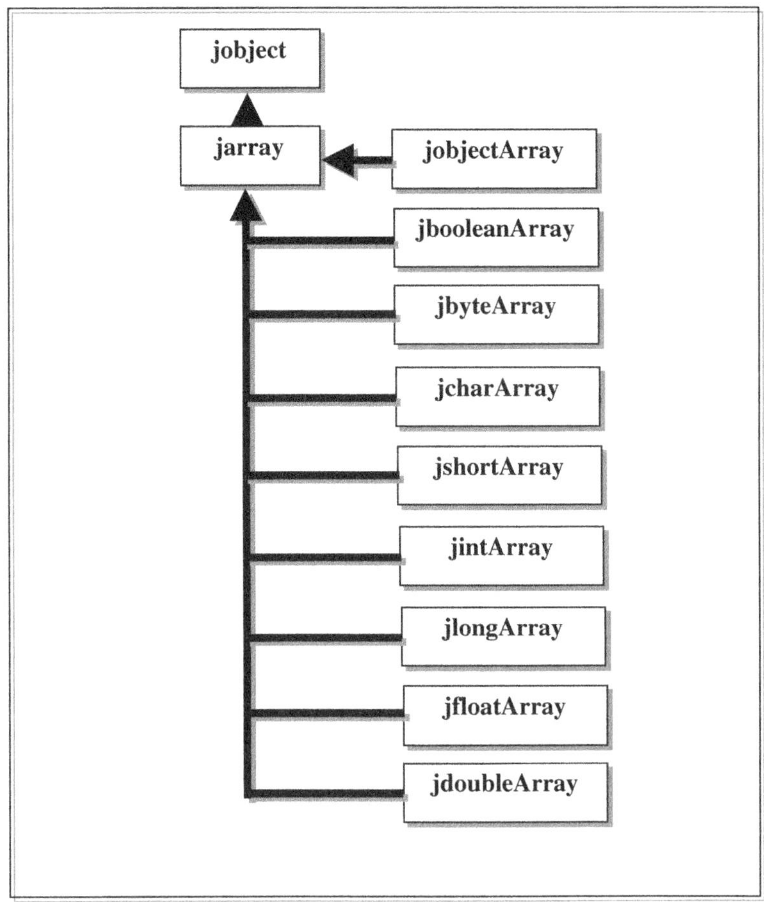

FIGURE 8.16 The inheritance hierarchy of the data array in the JNI. Cay S. Horstamann and Gary Cornell, 2002. *CORE Java 2: Volume II—Advanced Features,* Sun Microsystem, Inc. (Upper Saddle River, NJ: Prentice Hall, 2002), p. 1077. Reprinted with permission of Pearson Education, Inc.

TABLE 8.4
The JNI Mapping Functions

JNI Mapping Function[1]	Purpose
Get<*xxx*>ArrayElements	Converts a primitive data array from Java to C/C++, and returns a pointer of the converted C/C++ data array.
Release<*xxx*>ArrayElements	Cleans up the space allocated for the converted data array.
Get<*xxx*>ArrayRegion	Converts and copies a data array from Java to C/C++. The result is a C/C++ data array, not a pointer. Needs the starting position and length of the desired data array.
Set<*xxx*>ArrayRegion	Converts and copies a data array from C/C++ to Java. The result is a Java data array, not a pointer. Needs the starting position and length of the desired data array.
GetArrayLength	Returns the number of elements in a data array.
New<*xxx*>Array	Creates a new Java data array in native methods. Needs the length for the new data array.
GetPrimitiveArrayCritical ReleasePrimitiveArrayCritical	Gets or releases a pointer to the contents of a data array.

[1]The field type <*xxx*> stands for one of the primitive data types, such as int, short, long, float, char, byte, or double.

The Get<xxx>ArrayElements() converts a Java data array to a C/C++ data array, and returns a pointer that is the starting address of converted C/C++ data array.

The Get<xxx>ArrayRegion() converts a Java data array to a C/C++ data array, but this conversion is to copy all elements from the Java data array to the C/C++ data array, and the converting result is a completed C/C++ data array, not a pointer. This function needs two additional arguments compared with the Get<xxx>ArrayElements() function above, the start position (the first element's location) in the source array (Java data array) and the number of the elements to be copied.

One point you need to note is that you must use Release<xxx>ArrayElements() function to clean up the memory space allocated for the converted data array when you finish the array conversion by using Get<xxx>ArrayElements() and that array is no longer to be used.

In addition to the functions for mapping primitive data arrays, JNI provides a set of functions for mapping object arrays between the two language domains. However, this mapping is limited and only a few functions are provided:

- GetObjectArrayElement()
- SetObjectArrayElement()
- NewObjectArray()

For the GetObjectArrayElement() function, you can get only one object from the object array at the given index (position) in the object array, and for the SetObjectArrayElement(), you can set only one object according to the given index. The NewObjectArray is used to create a new object array and allocate a memory space for that array.

Now that we have a basic understanding of data and object mapping between the Java and C/C++ domains, we can begin developing the native library for our sample program.

8.3.12 Developing a Dynamic Link Library as the Native Library

After the JNI-style header file is obtained, we can begin to develop our native library. Notice the declaration of the jni.h header file. The default include format uses angle brackets: #include <jni.h>. We need to modify this format to the local include format, which uses quotation marks: #include "jni.h". The Visual C++ 6.0 compiler would not recognize that included file and compile the native library without this modification.

1. Launch Visual C++ 6.0 and create a new project with the following properties:
   - Project name: JNISerial
   - Project type: Win32 Dynamic-Link Library
   - Location: C:\Java\SimplePort

2. Open the Windows Explorer to copy the following header files to the new project folder C:\Java\SimplePort\JNISerial.
   - jni.h
   - jni_md.h

   The jni.h file is located in the Java installation folder C:\jdk1.3\include, and the jni_md.h file is located in the folder C:\jdk1.3\include\win32.
3. In the newly created project, create a header file named JNISerial.h and a source file named JNISerial.cpp.
4. Click the Project|Add To Project|Files menu item from the Visual C++ 6.0 IDE to add the following header files into the project:

- jni.h
- jni_md.h
- JavaSerial.h

The JavaSerial.h is a JNI-style header file we created in Section 8.3.9 and is located in the folder C:\Java\SimplePort.

In the following sections, we divide this project into two parts, the header file and the source file; we will code each section separately.

8.3.12.1 Developing the Header File

Open the newly created header file JNISerial.h and enter the code that is shown in Figure 8.17.

This header file is different with the JNI-style header file created by javah. All implemented variables and functions defined in the native library are declared in this header file. Besides the interface functions, there are some local functions and threads developed in the library. These local functions and threads are used to directly access the low-level driver to communicate with the serial port. The prototypes of those functions and thread are defined in this header file.

Each section of the code is explained in the following list:

A: The system header file windows.h is included first in the header file because this system header file provides all object definitions applied in the Windows environment. As an example, the MessageBox() function is defined in that system header file.

B: To prevent multiple including of the header file, the system macro #ifndef is used here. The purpose of this macro is to allow the other source files to include the header file if it has not been included before by those source files. In C/C++ programming, it is illegal for any source file in the project to include a header multiple times. When we use the #ifndef system macro, we need to attach an #endif at the end of the header file.

C: Some constants are defined here; most of them are serial communication-related parameters, such as NOPARITY, DTR, RTS_CONTROL_ENABLE, and CONTROL_DISABLE.

D: To simplify the function call, we redefine the MessageBox() function by using the macro #define. After this redefinition, the length of the function MessageBox() can be greatly shortened and then easily placed in the program by means of a msg() statement with a text string as the argument.

E: Two data structures are defined here to simplify the port configurations. The first structure SerialCreate, which contains useful port communication parameters, such as the baud rate, data bits, timeout value and other parameters used to check and mark the communication status.

F: The second structure is CommPortClass, which is used to hold parameters for receiving the data from the port correctly.

G: An enum structure ERR_CODE is declared to define the numeric error value that is associated with each error that might occur at run time. Space can be greatly saved by using this kind of definition. Each error code is sequenced from the integer 0 to the maximum integer value.

H: Global variables are declared in this section. The purpose of these global variables is to simplify the program and allow different source files to share some common variables. Although the global style is not typically recommended in the object-oriented-programming environment, it can really simplify and speed up the process of the application programs that need high speed and real-time responses. hPort is used to reserve the file handle that represents the opened port. Any function can use hPort to access the opened serial port in the program. PortCreateflg is a Boolean variable that works as a flag to monitor the port and indicate whether the port setup process has been

```
/*****************************************************************************
 * NAME          : JNISerial.h
 * DESC.         : Header file for JNISerial.cpp
 *****************************************************************************/
A  #include <windows.h>
B  #ifndef _JNISERIAL_H_
   #define _JNISERIAL_H_
C  #define MAX_STRING                    256
   #define NOPARITY                      0
   #define RTS_CONTROL_DISABLE    0x00
   #define RTS_CONTROL_ENABLE     0x01
   #define DTR_CONTROL_DISABLE    0x00
   #define DTR_CONTROL_ENABLE     0x01
D  #define msg(info)   MessageBox(NULL, info, "", MB_OK)
E  typedef struct
   {
     unsigned long   ulCtrlerID;
     char            cEcho;
     char            cEORChar;
     long            lTimeout;
     long            lBaudRate;
     long            lDataBits;
   } SerialCreate, *pSerialCreate;
F  typedef struct
   {
     char  pcBuffer[8];              /* data buffer */
     int   iMaxChars;                /* max characters */
     int   piNumRcvd;                /* number of data received */
     char  cTermChar;                /* terminator */
   } CommPortClass;
G  typedef enum
   {
     OK        = 0,                  /* no error */
     EC_TIMEOUT,
     EC_FOPEN,
     EC_INVAL_CONFIG,
     EC_TIMEOUT_SET,
     EC_RECV_TIMEOUT,
     EC_EXIT_CODE,
     EC_WAIT_SINGLEOBJ,
     EC_WRITE_FAIL,
     EC_CREATE_THREAD,
   } ERR_CODE;
H  HANDLE  hPort;
   char*   sPortName;
   bool    PortCreateflg = false;
I  ERR_CODE PortInitialize(LPTSTR lpszPortName, pSerialCreate pCreate);
   ERR_CODE PortWrite(char* bByte, int NumByte);
   ERR_CODE PortRead(CommPortClass *hCommPort);
   void WINAPI ThreadFunc(void* hCommPorts);
   #endif
```

FIGURE 8.17 The header file `JNISerial.h`.

successful. This variable is set to `True` if the port configuration is successfully processed. `sPortName` is a string variable used to reserve the port name in text format because the port initialization function needs the port name in that format.

I: Four local functions are declared here. The purpose of these functions is to coordinate the interface functions to perform data communication between the serial port and the computer. The interface functions work as the interface, and these local functions work as the executive functions to directly communicate with the low-level system routines and complete the data processing tasks. The `PortInitialize()` function is used to configure the serial port; this function has two arguments. The first is the port name, represented in text format, and the second is a pointer of the data structure `SerialCreate`, which is the starting address in which the configuration parameters are stored. The `PortRead()` and the `PortWrite()` functions are used to directly access the low-level system routines to perform the data sending and receiving processes. The thread function `ThreadFunc()` provides a method to access the serial drive and read the data from the serial port. The reason we need to use this thread is that the program would enter a dead cycle if no event were detected during the data collection process. We can prevent that dead cycle by using this thread function.

8.3.12.2 Developing the Source File

The code for the source file is divided into several sections according to the operations of each section:

- A setup section that includes the interface function `Setup()` and the local function `PortInitialize()`.
- A port writing section that contains the interface function `Write()` and the local function `PortWrite()`.
- A port reading section that includes the interface function `Read()`, the local function `PortRead()`, and the thread function `ThreadFunc()`.
- A port closing section that contains the interface function `Close()`.

Let's now develop the source file, section by section.

8.3.12.2.1 Code for the Setup Section

Open the newly created source file `JNISerial.cpp` and enter the code that is shown in Figure 8.18. Each section of the code is explained in the following list:

J: The JNI-style and user-defined header files, `JavaSerial.h` and `JNISerial.h`, are included at the beginning of this source file because both the interface functions and the local functions are defined in these two header files and the source file needs to use these functions.

K: The macro DEBUG is defined here; it is used to set a flag to display debugging information as the program runs. (This line can be commented out if you do not want the debug information to be displayed at run time.)

L: The signature of the interface function `Setup()` is declared here. This signature is modified according to the prototype of this function declared in the JNI-style header file. Compare this signature with that defined in the JNI-style header file; the modifications are that the nominal variables `env`, `obj`, and `parms` are added after each data type in the argument list.

```
    /*****************************************************************************
     * NAME          : JNISerial.cpp
     *****************************************************************************/
    #include <stdio.h>
    #include <stdlib.h>
    #include <string.h>
J   #include "JNISerial.h"
    #include "JavaSerial.h"
K   #define   DEBUG
L   JNIEXPORT jint JNICALL Java_JavaSerial_Setup
                                (JNIEnv *env, jobject obj, jintArray parms)
    {
M           jint* comParm;
            jint  rc = 0;
            pSerialCreate  pParam;
            pParam = new SerialCreate;
N           comParm = env->GetIntArrayElements(parms, JNI_FALSE);
            if (comParm == NULL)
            {
                msg("ERROR in GetIntArrayElements()\n");
                return rc = -1;
            }
O           #ifdef  DEBUG
            char buff[128];
            sprintf(buff, "comParm[] = %d  %d  %d  %d  %d", comParm[0], comParm[1],
                                  comParm[2], comParm[3], comParm[4]);  msg(buff);
            #endif
P           pParam->lBaudRate = comParm[1];
            pParam->lDataBits = comParm[2];
            pParam->lTimeout  = 3000;
Q           switch(comParm[0])
            {
              case 1:  sPortName = "COM1";  break;
              case 2:  sPortName = "COM2";  break;
              case 3:  sPortName = "COM3";  break;
              case 4:  sPortName = "COM4";  break;
              default:  return EC_INVALIDPORT;
            }
R           env->ReleaseIntArrayElements(parms,  comParm,  0);
S           if (PortCreateflg)
            {
                msg("Port has been Setup ");  return  rc;
            }
T           rc = PortInitialize(sPortName, pParam);
            if (rc != 0)
              msg("ERROR in PortInitialize()!");
U           delete pParam;
            PortCreateflg = true;
V           return rc;
    }
```

FIGURE 8.18 The interface function `Setup()`.

M: The C++ local variables are declared at the beginning of this function. `jint* comParm` is a C++ array or pointer variable that is used to hold the data values of the data array converted from the Java domain to the C++ domain. `jint rc` is a C++ variable used to hold the running status of the local functions.

N: The JNI function `GetIntArrayElements()` is used to convert the Java data array `parms` to a C++ data array. The starting address of the converted data array is assigned to the variable `comParm`. A `JNI_FALSE` constant means that we do not need this array copied. A NULL value will be returned if this function call encounters any errors. In this case, a message box with a warning message will be displayed on the screen to inform us that something is wrong with this function process.

O: The converted data array will be displayed if the DEBUG macro is active.

P: The converted data is assigned to the associated element in the data structure `Serial-Create`, and this structure will be passed into the `PortInitialize()` function to configure the serial port later.

Q: A `switch` instruction is used to find the port number and assign the `sPortName` variable with the associated port name in the text format.

R: Since we have finished converting and manipulating the data array, we no longer need the converted data array. We can delete it and clean up the memory space assigned to it by calling a JNI function `ReleaseIntArrayElements()`.

S: If the serial port has been configured, the `PortCreateflg` should be `True`. In this case, we cannot configure the port again. A message is displayed with warning information if the port has been configured.

T: The local function `PortInitialize()` is called to configure the serial port. An error message is displayed if this configuration encounters any errors.

U: The memory space allocated for the `SerialCreate` structure can be deleted before we exit this function because its mission is complete. The `PortCreateflg` is set to `True` to indicate to the system that the port has been configured.

V: The running status of the function is returned to the calling function.

The code for the local function `PortInitialize()` is shown in Figure 8.19. A detailed explanation of this function has been given in Section 5.4.3.4.5 in Chapter 5.

8.3.12.2.2 Code for the Port Writing Section

The code for the Port Writing section contains two functions: the interface function `Write()` and the local function `PortWrite()`. The code for the interface function `Write()` is shown in Figure 8.20.

This function is very simple. The local variable `rc` is a C++ variable used to hold the running status of the local function `PortWrite()`. The input data is a primitive Java data type (`jint sdata`), and it can be directly mapped to the C++ domain by using the data type `jint`. The data is first converted to the `char` type by the system function `sprintf()`, and then the local function `PortWrite()` is called to write that converted data to the serial port. An error message will be displayed if the function encounters any bug. The running status of this function is returned to the calling function. The code for the local function `PortWrite()` is shown in Figure 8.21. This code is straightforward and easy to understand.

8.3.12.2.3 Code for the Port Reading Section

This section contains three functions: the interface function `Read()`, the local function `Por-tRead()`, and the thread function `ThreadFunc()`. The code for the interface function is shown in Figure 8.22.

This code is simple. First, two nominal variables, `env` and `obj`, are added to the signature of this function. The local variable `idata` is a C++ integer; it can be directly mapped to the Java domain by the data type `jint` because it is a primitive data type. This variable is used to store the received data and return it to the Java domain after a data item is received from the serial port. The local function `PortRead()` is called to pick up the data from the serial port. An error message will be displayed if the function encounters any bug. The received data is converted from the `char`

```
ERR_CODE PortInitialize(char* lpszPortName, pSerialCreate pCreate)
{
    DWORD  dwError;
    DCB       PortDCB;
    ERR_CODE ecStatus = OK;
    COMMTIMEOUTS  CommTimeouts;  unsigned char  dBit;
    if (PortCreateflg)                          // check if the port has been created...
   {
        msg("Port has been initialized!");
        return  ecStatus;
    }
    hPort = CreateFile(lpszPortName,         // Pointer to the name of the port
                       GENERIC_READ | GENERIC_WRITE,  // Access (read/write) mode
                       0,                    // Share mode
                       NULL,                 // Pointer to the security attribute
                       OPEN_EXISTING, // How to open the serial port
                       0,                    // Port attributes
                       NULL);                // Handle to port with attribute to copy
     // If it fails to open the port, return error.
     if ( hPort == INVALID_HANDLE_VALUE )
     {
         // Could not open the port.
         dwError = GetLastError();
         msg("Unable to open the port");
         CloseHandle(hPort);
         return EC_FOPEN;
     }
     PortCreateflg = TRUE;
     PortDCB.DCBlength = sizeof(DCB);
     // Get the default port setting information.
     GetCommState(hPort, &PortDCB);
     // Change the DCB structure settings.
     PortDCB.BaudRate = pCreate->lBaudRate;   // Current baud
     PortDCB.fBinary  = TRUE;                 // Binary mode; no EOF check
     PortDCB.fParity  = FALSE;                // Disable parity checking.
     PortDCB.fOutxCtsFlow = FALSE;            // No CTS output flow control
     PortDCB.fOutxDsrFlow = FALSE;            // No DSR output flow control
     PortDCB.fDtrControl = DTR_CONTROL_DISABLE;  // DTR flow control type
     PortDCB.fDsrSensitivity = FALSE;         // DSR sensitivity
     PortDCB.fTXContinueOnXoff = FALSE;      // XOFF continues Tx
     PortDCB.fOutX = FALSE;                   // No XON/XOFF out flow control
     PortDCB.fInX  = FALSE;                   // No XON/XOFF in flow control
     PortDCB.fErrorChar = FALSE;              // Disable error replacement.
     PortDCB.fNull = FALSE;                   // Disable null stripping.
     PortDCB.fRtsControl = RTS_CONTROL_DISABLE; // RTS flow control
     PortDCB.fAbortOnError = FALSE;           // Do not abort reads/writes on error.
     dBit = (UCHAR)pCreate->lDataBits;        // Assign data bits
     PortDCB.ByteSize = dBit;                 // Number of bits/bytes, 4-8
     PortDCB.Parity = NOPARITY;               // 0-4=no,odd,even,mark,space
     PortDCB.StopBits = ONESTOPBIT;           // 0,1,2 = 1, 1.5, 2
```

FIGURE 8.19 The local function `PortInitialize()`. *(continued)*

```
    // Configure the port according to the specifications of the DCB structure.
    if (!SetCommState (hPort, &PortDCB))
    {
        // Could not set the timeout parameter.
        dwError = GetLastError();
        msg("Unable to configure the serial port");
        return EC_INVAL_CONFIG;
    }
    // Retrieve the time-out parameters for all read and write operations on the port.
    GetCommTimeouts(hPort, &CommTimeouts);

    // Change the COMMTIMEOUTS structure settings.
    CommTimeouts.ReadIntervalTimeout = MAXDWORD;
    CommTimeouts.ReadTotalTimeoutMultiplier = 0;
    CommTimeouts.ReadTotalTimeoutConstant = 0;
    CommTimeouts.WriteTotalTimeoutMultiplier = 10;
    CommTimeouts.WriteTotalTimeoutConstant = 1000;

    // Set the time-out parameters for all read and write operations on the port.
    if (!SetCommTimeouts (hPort, &CommTimeouts))
    {
        // Could not set the port timeout parameter.
        dwError = GetLastError();
        msg("Unable to set the time-out parameters");
        return  EC_TIMEOUT_SET;
    }
    EscapeCommFunction(hPort, SETDTR);    //Set DTR
    EscapeCommFunction(hPort, SETRTS);    //Set RTS
    return  ecStatus;
}
```

FIGURE 8.19 The local function `PortInitialize()`.

```
JNIEXPORT jint JNICALL Java_JavaSerial_Write
                        (JNIEnv *env, jobject obj, jint sdata)

{
    int    numByte = 1;
    char sByte[8];
    jint   rc = 0;
    sprintf(sByte, "%c", sdata);
    rc = PortWrite(sByte, numByte);
    if (rc != 0)
       msg("ERROR in PortWrite() !");
    return  rc;
}
```

FIGURE 8.20 The interface function `Write()`.

```
/*****************************************************************************
 * NAME:    PortWrite()
 * DESC.:   Write data to the port
 * DATE:    12/19/03
 * PGMR.:   Y. Bai
 *****************************************************************************/
ERR_CODE PortWrite(char* bByte, int NumByte)
{
    DWORD dwError;
    DWORD dwNumBytesWritten;
    ERR_CODE ecStatus = OK;
    if (!WriteFile (hPort,                    // Port handle
                    bByte,                    // Pointer to the data to write
                    NumByte,                  // Number of bytes to write
                    &dwNumBytesWritten,       // Pointer to the number of bytes written
                    NULL))                    // Must be NULL for Windows CE
    {
        // WriteFile failed, report error.
        dwError = GetLastError ();
        return EC_WRITE_FAIL;
    }
    return  ecStatus;
}
```

FIGURE 8.21 The local function `PortWrite()`.

```
JNIEXPORT jint JNICALL Java_JavaSerial_Read(JNIEnv *env, jobject obj)
{
        jint idata = 0;
        char cdata[8];
        ERR_CODE rc = OK;
        CommPortClass* commClass;
        commClass = new CommPortClass;
        commClass->iMaxChars = 1;
        rc = PortRead(commClass);
        if (rc != OK)
           msg("ERROR in PortRead()! ");
        sprintf(cdata, "%d", commClass->pcBuffer[0]);
        idata = atoi(cdata);
        delete commClass;
        return  idata;
}
```

FIGURE 8.22 The interface function `Read()`.

to the `integer` type by the system function `atoi()` and is returned to the calling function. The code for the local function `PortRead()` is shown in Figure 8.23.

The `PortRead()` function has one argument, `*hCommPort`, which is a pointer structure. This pointer structure will be passed into the thread as a null pointer parameter later on when the `PortRead()` creates that thread. After the thread is created, the thread function is suspended by a `CREATE_SUSPENDED` argument. The thread function will not start to execute until a `ResumeThread()` function is called. The new created thread returns a handler, `hThread`, which will be used by all other components to access this thread.

```
/*****************************************************************************
 * NAME         : PortRead()
 * DESC.        : Read data from the serial port
 *****************************************************************************/
ERR_CODE PortRead(CommPortClass *hCommPort)
{
    HANDLE  hThread;                        // handler for port read thread
    DWORD   IDThread;
    DWORD   Ret, ExitCode;
    DWORD   dTimeout = 5000;                // define time out value: 5 sec.
    ERR_CODE ecStatus = OK;
    if (!(hThread = CreateThread(NULL,               // no security attributes
                    0,                                // use default stack size
                    (LPTHREAD_START_ROUTINE) ThreadFunc,
                    (LPVOID)hCommPort,    // parameter to thread function
                    CREATE_SUSPENDED, // creation flag - suspended
                    &IDThread) ) )        // returns thread ID
     {
         msg("Create Read Thread failed");
         return  EC_CREATE_THREAD;
     }
     ResumeThread(hThread);                 // start thread now
     Ret = WaitForSingleObject(hThread, dTimeout);
     if (Ret == WAIT_OBJECT_0)
     {
         // Data received & process it... need to do nothing because the data is stored in the
         // hCommPort  in the Thread Function.  The only thing is to close thread handle
         CloseHandle(hThread);
     }
    else if (Ret == WAIT_TIMEOUT)           // Time out happened
    {                                       // Warning & kill thread
         Ret = GetExitCodeThread(hThread, &ExitCode);
         msg("Time out happened in PortRead() ");
         if (ExitCode == STILL_ACTIVE)
         {
             TerminateThread(hThread, ExitCode);
             CloseHandle(hThread);
              return  EC_RECV_TIMEOUT;
         }
         else
         {
              CloseHandle(hThread);
              msg("ERROR in GetExitCodeThread: != STILL_ACTIVE ");
              ecStatus = EC_EXIT_CODE;
         }
    }
    else
    {
         msg("ERROR in WaitFor SingleObject ");
         ecStatus = EC_WAIT_SINGLEOBJ;
    }
    return  ecStatus;
}
```

FIGURE 8.23 The local function `PortRead()`.

A `WaitForSingleObject()` function is called after the thread runs. This function is used to monitor and wait for one of two events to occur. The first is the running thread completion event that is associated with the `WAIT_OBJECT_0` event. This event occurs when the thread function is normally completed and terminated. The other is the timeout event, which is associated with the `WAIT_TIMEOUT` event. This event occurs if the program enters a dead cycle. If the first event occurs (WAIT_OBJECT_0), it means that the thread has successfully obtained the data written to the serial port and the data has been stored in the buffer defined in the hCommPort data structure; the function PortRead() will then close the thread handler and exit the program because the data has been obtained. If the second event occurs (WAIT_TIMEOUT), it means that the program has entered a dead cycle because no event has triggered the serial port. In this case, the PortRead() function will terminate the thread function and close the thread handler, but will return a timeout error to the calling function.

In any other case, an error status will be returned to the calling function to indicate that an error has been encountered during execution of the PortRead() function.

The final local function is the thread function ThreadFunc(). The code for this function is shown in Figure 8.24.

The thread function is the real body of the thread, which executes the task assigned to the thread. In our application, we use a thread to check and retrieve the data written to the port and store the data into a buffer defined in the data structure. The advantage of using a thread to handle this job is in preventing a dead cycle, which would happen if no event triggered the port.

The thread has an argument, hCommPorts, whose type is a null pointer. This means that this argument can be adopted and converted to hold any kind of data. This argument is passed into the thread by the CreateThread() function and it is exactly a pointer structure whose values are initialized by the interface function Read() before the local function PortRead() is called.

After declaring some local variables and data structures at the beginning of the thread function, we need to convert the null pointer parameter, hCommPorts, to the destination data structure, CommPortClass.

We need to assign a set of event masks to the serial port controller (UART) by using the SetCommMask() system function. We combine a sequence of event masks by using the or operator to allow multiple events to trigger the port (for example, if a char is received, if the DSR or the CTS line is activated, or if a ring is received). Should any of these events occur, the UART can immediately respond to that event by executing the associated command.

Next we use a while loop and a system function, WaitCommEvent(), to continuously monitor these events and process any that occur. (Note that this function only monitors serial communication events; not synchronous events.) If a received-a-char event occurs, we call ReadFile() to read back the character, and store it in the buffer by using CommPorts->pcBuffer[nTotRead] = Byte.

The buffer is defined inside the data structure CommPorts, and the local variable nTotRead represents the total number of bytes to be read.

Our program must determine whether the loop has reached the maximum number of characters to be read. When it does, we should set the while loop condition flag and exit the loop.

After storing the received character into the buffer, we can terminate the while loop, and end the thread. An associated event, WAIT_OBJECT_0 , will be sent to the WaitForSingleObject() function in the PortRead() local function to inform the function that the thread has been successfully completed and that the data has been obtained and stored in the buffer. The PortRead() will return an OK status to the interface function Read() to indicate that the PortRead() function has been successfully completed. The interface function will pick up the data stored in the buffer, convert it to a suitable format, and return it to the Java domain.

8.3.12.2.4 Code for the Port Closing Section

The code for this section is very simple. The purpose of this coding is to call the system function CloseHandle() defined in the native domain to close the opened serial port and terminate the native library. The code for this function is shown in Figure 8.25.

The signature of this interface function is modified by adding two nominal variables, env and obj. The local variable rc is returned to the Java domain to indicate the running status of this

```
/*****************************************************************************
* NAME    : ThreadFunc()
* DESC.   : The reason to use this thread is to overcome the hung up introduced by the
*         : WaitCommEvent() function which waits for only the comm. event, not synchro-
*         : nition event. The program will be dead-cycle without this thread.
* PRMR.   : Y. Bai
*****************************************************************************/
void WINAPI ThreadFunc(void* hCommPorts)
{
    char Byte;
    BOOL bResult, fDone;
    int  nTotRead = 0;
    DWORD dwCommModemStatus, dwBytesTransferred;
    CommPortClass* CommPorts;
    ERR_CODE ecStatus = OK;
    CommPorts = (CommPortClass* )hCommPorts;
    // Specify a set of events to be monitored for the port.
    SetCommMask(hPort, EV_RXCHAR | EV_CTS | EV_DSR | EV_RLSD | EV_RING);
    fDone = FALSE;
    while (!fDone)
    {
        // Wait for an event to occur for the port.
        WaitCommEvent(hPort, &dwCommModemStatus, 0);
        // Re-specify the set of events to be monitored for the port.
        SetCommMask(hPort, EV_RXCHAR | EV_CTS | EV_DSR |EV_RLSD| EV_RING);
        if (dwCommModemStatus & EV_RXCHAR||dwCommModemStatus & EV_RLSD)
        {
            //  received the char_event & loop to wait for the data.
            do
            {
                // Read the data from the serial port.
                bResult = ReadFile(hPort, &Byte, 1, &dwBytesTransferred, 0);
                if (!bResult)
                {
                    msg("ERROR in ReadFile !");
                    fDone = TRUE;
                    break;
                }
                else
                {
                    // Display the data read.
                    if (dwBytesTransferred == 1)
                    {
                        CommPorts->pcBuffer[nTotRead] = Byte;
                        nTotRead++;
                        if (nTotRead == CommPorts->iMaxChars)
                        {
                            fDone = TRUE;
                            break;
```

FIGURE 8.24 The thread function `ThreadFunc()`. *(continued)*

```
                        }
                    }
                    else
                    {
                        if (Byte == 0x0D ||Byte == 0x0A)        // null char or CR
                        {
                            msg("Received null character ");
                            fDone = TRUE;
                            break;
                        }
                    }
                }
            }while (dwBytesTransferred == 1); //while (nTotRead < pRecv->iMaxChars);
        }  // if
    }      // while
    return;
}
```

FIGURE 8.24 The thread function `ThreadFunc()`.

```
JNIEXPORT jint JNICALL Java_JavaSerial_Close(JNIEnv *env, jobject obj)
{
        jint rc = 0;
        if (PortCreateflg)
          CloseHandle(hPort);
        PortCreateflg = false;
        return rc;
}
```

FIGURE 8.25 The interface function `Close()`.

interface function. First we need to check whether the port has been opened and configured. (You may encounter an error if you try to close a port without opening it first.) The system function `CloseHandle()` is called to close the opened serial port if the port is opened and configured. After the port is closed, the flag `PortCreateflg` will be reset to `False`, and the running status of the interface function will be returned to the Java domain. At this point, we have completed the coding for this native library.

8.3.13 Building and Installing the Native Library

Click the `Build|Build JNISerial.dll` menu item from the Visual C++ 6.0 IDE to compile and build the native library file. The target DLL file `JNISerial.dll` is located in the `C:\Java\SimplePort\JNISerial\Debug` folder.

To allow the Java platform to recognize and interface with this target DLL file in one of the following three locations:

- The system default DLL file folder, which is `C:\WINDOWS\system` in Windows 95/98/Me/XP or `C:\WINNT\system` in Windows NT/2000.

- The searchable path on your machine. This means that you can create any user-defined folder and place the DLL file in that folder. The only requirement here is that you must set the name of that folder as a system variable to your system path.
- The folder in which the Java bytecodes are located.

In this application, we adopt the third method and install the DLL target file in our user-defined project folder `C:\Java\SimplePort`. All our Java source files and bytecode files are located in this folder. Copy the target DLL file `JNISerial.dll` to this folder.

8.3.14 Running and Testing the Project

Now let's run our project to test the serial port.

Open a command window, switch to the project folder `C:\Java\SimplePort`, and type `java JSerialGUI` on the command line to start the project. The running project is shown in Figure 8.26.

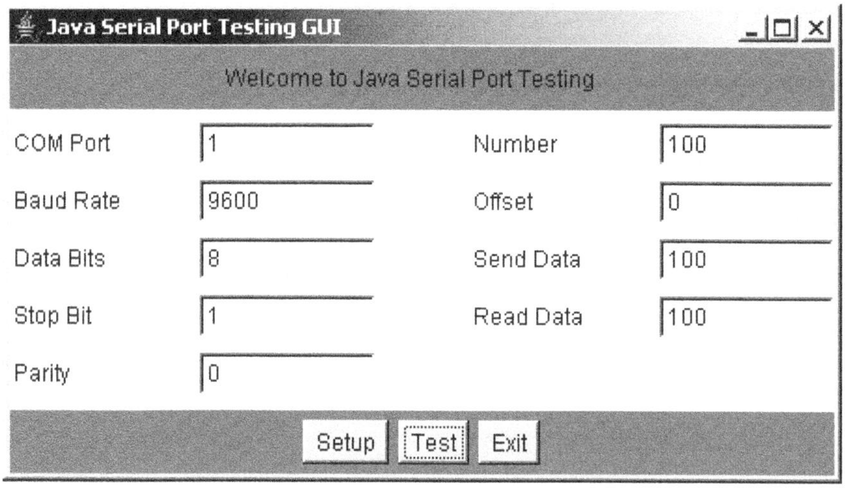

FIGURE 8.26 Running the project.

Enter the following setup parameters into the input fields on the left pane:

- COM Port: `1`
- Baud Rate: `9600`
- Data Bits: `8`
- Stop Bit: `1`
- Parity: `0`

Enter the following application parameters into input fields on the right pane:

- Number: `100`
- Offset: `0`

Click the `Setup` button to call the interface function to configure the serial port. A message box will appear displaying the setup parameters passed to the native domain, as shown in Figure 8.27.

You can comment out the debugging information and hide this message box if you do not want to display this information at run time.

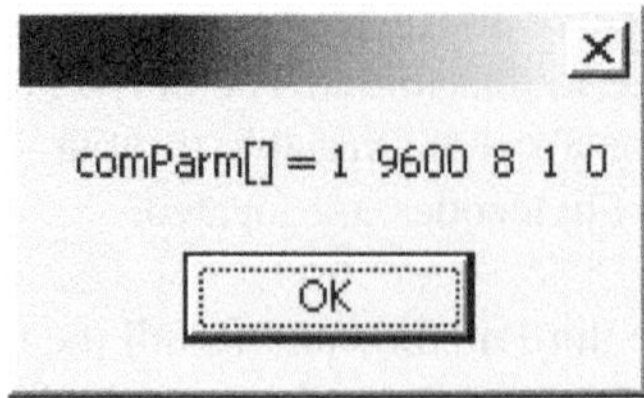

FIGURE 8.27 The debug message box.

Click OK in the message box to accept this debugging information, and click the Test button to begin testing the serial port. The testing will begin, and the sent data and received data will be displayed in the Send Data and Read Data input fields simultaneously. (See Figure 8.26.)

Now enter a new value, -50, in the Offset input field to change the starting point of the data to be sent to the serial port. Click the Test button again. This time the sent and received data start at –50 and terminate at 50. This situation is shown in Figure 8.28.

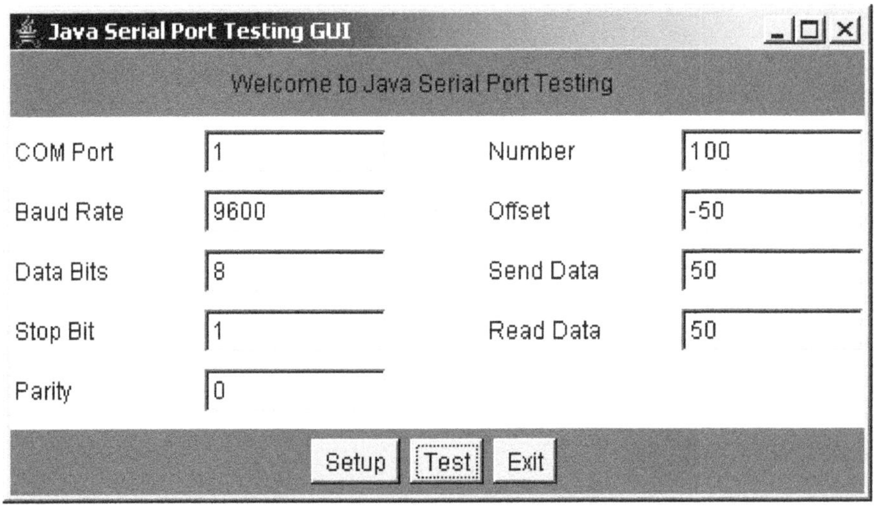

FIGURE 8.28 The modified offset value.

During the testing process, an error message will be displayed if the data sent out is not identical with the data received from the tested serial port. No error message will appear if both sets of data are identical.

All project files, including the Java source files, the bytecode files, the JNI-style header file, the native library header file, the source file and the target DLL file, are located in the folder Charter 8\SimplePort on the attached CD. You can copy all of these files and install them on your machine to test and run them. Keep the following points in mind:

- You need to configure the Java installation folder to allow your machine to recognize the Java compiler and interpreter.
- You need to install the target DLL file in one of three locations described in Section 8.3.13.

8.4 AN ADVANCED INTERFACE BETWEEN THE SERIAL A/D AND JAVA

In this section, we will develop an interface between the Java programming environment and the serial A/D converter, via the serial port, to collect data from the serial A/D converter.

The serial A/D converter is a 12-bit converter MAX187. The structure and interface circuit have been discussed in earlier chapters. The interface circuit is shown in Figure 8.29, and its components are listed in Table 8.5.

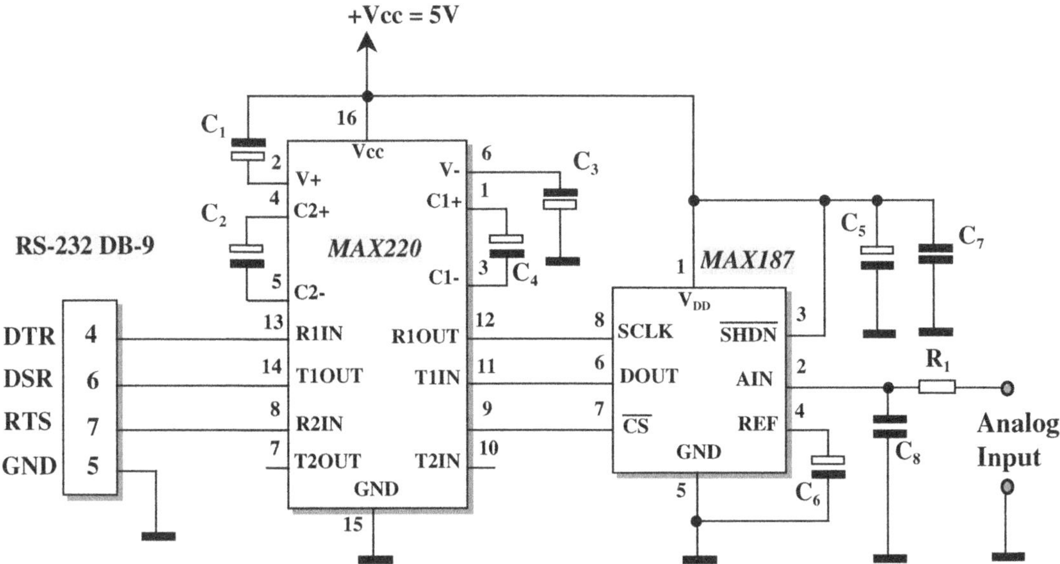

FIGURE 8.29 The interface circuit for the advanced Java project.

TABLE 8.5
The Elements Parameters

Elements	Values	Comments
R_1	10 KΩ	Current-limited Resistor
$C_1 - C_4$	10 μF/25V	Electrolytic Capacitors
$C_5 - C_6$	4.7 μF/10V	Electrolytic Capacitors
$C_7 - C_8$	0.1 μF	Capacitors

The input signal to the MAX187 comes either from a function generator or from an actual analog input system. A function generator is used in this project as the input to the MAX187. Three waveforms are tested: sinusoidal, triangular, and square signals. The maximum input voltage is 5 volts, which is the upper limitation of the MAX187.

We will use the Model-View-Controller modal to develop this project. The block diagram of this project is similar to the one shown in Figure 8.5.

Four class files are developed and implemented in this project: the View class `JMAXGUI.java`, the Model class `JMAXCreate.java`, the displaying class `msg.java`, and the interface class `JMAXSerial.java`. Because the `msg` class used in this section is identical to the one developed in the last section, we will skip the discussion of developing that class in this section.

8.4.1 Developing the View Class—Java GUI Window

This class works as a user interface to get input from the user and display output in the GUI window. Similar to the last project, this GUI is divided into four sections and contains four different types of components.

The first section contains five `TextField` items that are used to receive the serial port setup parameters, and five associated labels. The second section contains two `TextField` items. One of them is used to receive the total number of data to be collected from the MAX187 serial A/D converter, and the other is used to display the collected data in real time. The third section contains a label that displays the project title. The fourth section includes three command buttons, `Setup`, `Read_Max`, and `Exit`. At run time, we will use these buttons to trigger the associated events. The source file of the GUI class `JMAXGUI.java` is shown in Figure 8.30.

Each section of the code is described in the following list:

A: Two class libraries, `java.awt.*` and `java.awt.event.*`, are imported at the beginning of the program. The program file needs to use the data and methods defined in these libraries.

B: The class `JMAXGUI` is declared here. This class is a subclass of the `Frame` class, and the interface `ActionListener` is used to allow the class to respond to action events.

C: We create three command buttons here by using the `Button` class with the `new` keyword. The names of the buttons are `bSetup`, `bTest`, and `bExit`.

D: An instance (`serial`) of the class `JMAXCreate` is created because we need to access that Model class to perform the associated data operations when the project runs.

E: Inside the constructor of the class `JMAXGUI`, the interface method `addActionListener()` is called to add this class as an event listener for the three command buttons. The keyword `this` in the parentheses represents the current class `JMAXGUI`. The size of the GUI window is set by a call to the system method `setSize()`.

F: Four panels are generated in this project. Each panel is used to hold the associated components on the GUI. Here the `West` panel `paneW` is created, and a `GridLayout` Manager is called to divide the panel to five by five grids.

G: Ten components, five `TextField` items and five associated labels, which are used to receive the setup parameters of the serial port from the user, are added into this panel one by one. The sequence of adding these components is: first add a label and then add the associated `TextField`. All these components are defined in the Model class `JMAXCreate`, which we will discuss next. The instance name `serial` needs to be placed in front of each component.

H: After all the components are added into this panel, the panel is added into the `West` section of the GUI window.

I: Similarly an `East` panel is created and this panel is used to hold the application parameters, such as the total number of the data (`tNum`) to be collected from the MAX187 via the serial port and the value of the received data (`tRead`).

J: Here we add the application parameters to the `East` panel one by one. All of these parameters are defined in the Model class `JMAXCreate`, so a `serial` instance needs to be placed in front of each parameter.

K: After all application parameters are added into the `East` panel, the panel is added to the `East` section of the GUI window.

L: A `North` panel is created here to hold the label of our project.

M: We create a new label here and add it to the `North` panel. We then add the `North` panel, with the label, to the `North` area on the GUI window.

```
  /*****************************************************************************
   * NAME        : JMAXGUI.java
   * DESC        : Java GUI file to test a serial A/D converter MAX187
   *****************************************************************************/
A import java.awt.*;
  import java.awt.event.*;
B public class JMAXGUI extends Frame implements ActionListener
  {
C    Button bSetup  = new Button("Setup");
     Button bRead   = new Button("Read_MAX");
     Button bExit   = new Button("Exit");
D    JMAXCreate serial = new JMAXCreate();
     public JMAXGUI()
     {
          super("Java Serial Port Testing GUI");
E         bExit.addActionListener(this);
          bSetup.addActionListener(this);
          bRead.addActionListener(this);
          setSize(450, 250);
          setLayout(new BorderLayout(2, 7));
F         Panel paneW = new Panel();
          paneW.setLayout(new GridLayout(5, 5, 8, 8));
G         paneW.add(serial.lcomPort);
          paneW.add(serial.tcomPort);
          paneW.add(serial.lbaudRate);
          paneW.add(serial.tbaudRate);
          paneW.add(serial.ldataBits);
          paneW.add(serial.tdataBits);
          paneW.add(serial.lstopBit);
          paneW.add(serial.tstopBit);
          paneW.add(serial.lparity);
          paneW.add(serial.tparity);
H         add(paneW, "West");
I         Panel paneE = new Panel();
          paneE.setLayout(new GridLayout(5, 5, 8, 8));
J         paneE.add(serial.lNum);
          paneE.add(serial.tNum);
          paneE.add(serial.lRead);
          paneE.add(serial.tRead);
K         add(paneE, "East");
L         Panel paneN = new Panel();
          paneN.setBackground(Color.gray);
M         paneN.add(new Label("Welcome to Java MAX187 Testing "));
          add(paneN, "North");
N         Panel paneS = new Panel();
          paneS.setBackground(Color.gray);
O         paneS.add(bSetup);
          paneS.add(bRead);
          paneS.add(bExit);
P         add(paneS, "South");
     }
```

FIGURE 8.30 The GUI class file `JMAXGUI.java`. *(continued)*

```
     public void actionPerformed(ActionEvent evt)
     {
Q        int m, n, ret = 0, rndNum = 0;
         int comPrms[] = {1, 9600, 8, 1, 0};
R        JMAXSerial jserial = new JMAXSerial();
S        rndNum = serial.getNum(serial.tNum.getText());
         Object src = evt.getSource();
T        if (src == bExit)
         {
             ret = jserial.JavaClose();
             System.exit(0);
         }
U        if (src == bSetup)
         {
             if (rndNum == 0)
                return;
V            comPrms[0] = serial.getNum(serial.tcomPort.getText());
             comPrms[1] = serial.getNum(serial.tbaudRate.getText());
             comPrms[2] = serial.getNum(serial.tdataBits.getText());
             comPrms[3] = serial.getNum(serial.tstopBit.getText());
             comPrms[4] = serial.getNum(serial.tparity.getText());
W            ret = jserial.JavaSetup(comPrms);
         }
X        if (src == bRead)
         {
             for (m = 1; m <= rndNum + 1; m++)
             {
Y                ret = jserial.JavaRead();
Z                serial.tRead.setText(serial.getStr(ret));
             }
         }
     }
1    public static void main(String[] args)
     {
         JMAXGUI sGUI = new JMAXGUI();
         sGUI.show();
     }
    }
```

FIGURE 8.30 The GUI class file `JMAXGUI.java`.

N: A `South` panel is generated here; this panel is used to hold three command buttons.

O: Add three buttons, `bSetup`, `bRead`, and `bExit`, to the `South` panel.

P: Add the `South` panel with its three buttons to the `South` section of the GUI window.

Q: Several local variables are declared at the beginning of the `actionPerformed()` event procedure. `comPrms[]` is an `integer` array used to hold the setup parameters of the serial port. The default setup parameters are assigned to this array.

R: An instance of the interface class `JMAXSerial`, `jserial`, is created here because we need to call the interface functions defined in that interface class in this procedure. To access those functions, we need first to create an instance of the class since all interface functions defined in the `JMAXSerial` class are instance functions.

S: Next we need to pick up the total number of data items to be collected from the serial port from the Model class `JMAXCreate` because this parameter is needed for data collection. First the system method `getText()` is used to obtain this parameter in the text format, and then a user-defined method `getNum()`, which is defined in the class `JMAXCreate`, is used to convert the parameter from text format to integer format and assign it to the associated local variables, `rndNum`. The system event method `getSource()` is called to obtain the current event that is activated by an action.

T: If the event is `bExit`, which means that the `Exit` button has been clicked, then the interface function `JavaClose()`, defined in the interface class `JMAXSerial`, is called to close the opened serial port. Then the system method `System.exit(0)` is called to close the GUI window and exit the project. A `0` argument means that the exit has been error free.

U: If the event is `bSetup`, which means that the `Setup` button is clicked by the user, we need to determine whether the total number of data items to be sent has been obtained. If the value of this parameter is `0`, the program returns to the calling function.

V: If the total number of the data to be collected is not `0`, which means that we've already received the value of this parameter, then we need to pick up all setup parameters from the associated components defined in the Model class `JMAXCreate` and assign them to the local data array `comPrms[]`.

W: Next we need to call the interface function `JavaSetup()`, defined in the interface class `JMAXSerial`, to configure the serial port. Because the interface function `JavaSetup()` is an instance method, we need to place the instance of that class, `jserial`, in front of the function.

X: If the event is `bRead`, which means that the `Read_MAX` button has been clicked, a `for` loop is used to repeatedly receive the data from the MAX187 via the serial port until the loop hits the upper boundary `rndNum +1`. The upper boundary is increment by 1 is because the first data reading (called the wake-up reading) in the native library is neglected.

Y: The interface function `JavaRead()`, defined in the interface class `JMAXSerial`, is called to pick up the data from the MAX187 via the serial port.

Z: The received data is displayed on the `tRead` component, which is defined in the Model class `JMAXCreate`.

1: The `main` method is the entry point of the project. An instance of the class `JMAXGUI` is created and displayed. In this way, the project can be started.

Save this file to our user-defined project folder `C:\Java\MAX187`. Next let's develop our Model class file `JMAXCreate.java`.

8.4.2 Developing the Model Class

The purpose of this class is to store and operate the project data according to the GUI window's events. Because there is large number of components applied in this project, we place some components in this Model class, `JMAXCreate.java`. Open the NotePad editor and enter the code that is shown in Figure 8.31 into this class file.

2: The system class libraries are imported at the beginning of this class file.

3: The class `JMAXCreate` is started from here.

4: Seven `TextField` components are declared and these are used to hold the setup parameters of the serial port and the application parameters.

5: Seven associated labels are created here.

6: The user-defined method `getNum()` is declared. This method is used to convert the input parameter from text format to numeric format and return the result to the calling functions.

```
  /*****************************************************************************
   * NAME      : JMAXCreate.java
   * DESC      : Java Serial Port Object Creator - Model Class
   * DATE      : 12/19/2003
   *****************************************************************************/
2 import java.awt.*;
  import java.awt.event.*;
  import java.util.*;
3 public class JMAXCreate
  {
     private int nRnd;
4    TextField tcomPort  = new TextField(10);
     TextField tbaudRate = new TextField(10);
     TextField tdataBits = new TextField(10);
     TextField tstopBit  = new TextField(10);
     TextField tparity   = new TextField(10);
     TextField tNum      = new TextField(10);
     TextField tRead     = new TextField(10);
5    Label lcomPort  = new Label("COM Port");
     Label lbaudRate = new Label("Baud Rate");
     Label ldataBits = new Label("Data Bits");
     Label lstopBit  = new Label("Stop Bit");
     Label lparity   = new Label("Parity");
     Label lNum      = new Label("Number");
     Label lRead     = new Label("Read Data");
6    public int getNum(String nstr)
     {
7          if (nstr.length() == 0)
           {
                msg warn = new msg("No input on the Number Field ");
                warn.show();
                return 0;
           }
8          nRnd = Integer.parseInt(nstr);
           return  nRnd;
     }
9    public String getStr(int  dNum)
     {
           return String.valueOf(dNum);
     }
  }
```

FIGURE 8.31 The Model class file `JMAXCreate.java`.

7: Here we need to check whether the input string is an empty string by using the `length()` method that belongs to the `String` class. If the input string is empty, a `0` will be returned to the calling functions, and a warning message will be displayed on the screen.

8: If the input string is non-empty, the class method `ParseInt()` that belongs to the `Integer` class will be called to convert the input string to the associated integer value. The converted result will then be returned to the calling functions.

9: `getStr()` is another user-defined method in this Model class. The operation of this method is opposite to that of the last method, `getNum()`. `getStr()` is used to convert the input integer to an associated string. The class method `valueOf()`, which belongs to the class `String`, is called to complete this conversion. The converted result is returned to the calling functions.

Save this file to our user-defined project folder, `C:\Java\MAX187`.

8.4.3 Developing the Interface Class

The class `JMAXSerial` works as an interface between the Java program and the native library. All interface functions defined in this interface class should be identical with those defined in the native library.

Three interface functions are defined in this class:

- Setup()
- Read()
- Close()

Each of these interface functions is embedded in the associated Java method and can be accessed by calling the associated Java method. The code for this interface class file is shown in Figure 8.32.

10: The used system class libraries are imported at the beginning of this class file.
11: The interface class `JMAXSerial` is defined and started from here.
12: A C stub, `public native int Setup();`, is used to declare the interface function `Setup()` in the native domain (C++). This interface function is embedded inside a Java class, `JMAXSerial`. (This is a popular format or style of calling a native function from the Java domain.) In the same style, three interface functions are declared here. These functions are defined in the native domain and belong to the native domain, so the keyword `native` is prefixed in front of each function. The `Setup()` function has an integer array that contains the serial port setup parameters as the argument. The `Read()` function is used to read the data from the MAX187, and the `Close()` function is used to close the opened serial port.
13: A `static initializer` is used here to contain a calling to the native library `JNIMAX` that will be developed in the C++ domain later. Three native methods, `Setup()`, `Read()`, and `Close()`, are defined in that native library.
14: A Java method `JavaSetup()` is defined here and the interface function `Setup()` is embedded in this method. Using this method allows user to access the interface function `Setup()` to configure the serial port.
15: Inside the Java method `JavaSetup()`, the interface function `Setup()` is called with the integer array as the argument. The body of this interface function is defined in the native library. A warning message will be displayed if this function call encounters any errors, and the running status of the function will be returned to the calling function.
16: The Java method `JavaRead()`, which includes the interface function `Read()`, is defined here. At run time, this method will let us access the interface function `Read()` to pick up data from the MAX187 via the serial port.
17: The interface function `Read()` is called to access the serial port to receive the desired data from the MAX187. `Read()` is a native function defined in the native library.
18: The Java method `JavaClose()` is used to access the interface function `Close()` that is defined in the native library to close the opened serial port.
19: The interface function `Close()` is called to close the port. The running status of this function is returned to the calling function.

At this point, we have finished developing the Java source files. Next we need to develop the native library that contains the interface functions.

8.4.4 Creating a JNI-Style Header File

The prerequisite to develop the native library is to create a JNI-style header file, which will define the prototypes of all interface functions to be developed in the native library.

```
/*****************************************************************************
 * NAME        : JMAXSerial.java
 * DESC        : Java serial interface file
 * PGMR        : Y. Bai
 * DATE        : 12/19/2003
 *****************************************************************************/
10 import java.awt.*;
import java.awt.event.*;
import java.util.*;
11 public class JMAXSerial
{
   int result;
12    public native int Setup(int[] comParms);
   public native int Read();
   public native int Close();
13    static
   {
         System.loadLibrary("JNIMAX");
   }
14    public int JavaSetup(int[] darray)
   {
         int ret = 0;
15          ret = Setup(darray);
         if (ret != 0)
         {
             msg warn = new msg("ERROR in Setup() DLL Calling");
             warn.show();
         }
         return ret;
   }
16    public int JavaRead()
   {
         int result;
17          result = Read();
         return result;
   }
18    public int JavaClose()
   {
         int ret = 0;
19          ret = Close();
         return ret;
   }
}
```

FIGURE 8.32 The interface class file `JMAXSerial.java`.

1. Open a command window and switch to our project folder, `C:\Java\MAX187`, and type `javac JMAXSerial.java` to compile this interface file to the bytecode file. The bytecode file `JMAXSerial.class` is generated and stored in our project folder.
2. Type `javah JMAXSerial` on the command line to create a JNI-style header file `JMAXSerial.h`. Launch Visual C++ 6.0 IDE to open this JNI-style header file that is shown in Figure 8.33.

This header file is similar to one that is developed in Section 8.3.10 (refer to Figure 8.12). Refer to that section to get more detailed information for this coding. Note that you must modify the `include` statement from the original system statement (`#include <jni.h>`) to the local statement (`#include "jni.h"`). Otherwise you may encounter a compiling error.

```
/* DO NOT EDIT THIS FILE - it is machine generated */
#include "jni.h"
/* Header for class JMAXSerial */

#ifndef _Included_JMAXSerial
#define _Included_JMAXSerial
#ifdef __cplusplus
extern "C" {
#endif
/*
 * Class:     JMAXSerial
 * Method:    Setup
 * Signature: ([I)I
 */
JNIEXPORT jint JNICALL Java_JMAXSerial_Setup
                                    (JNIEnv *, jobject, jintArray);

/*
 * Class:     JMAXSerial
 * Method:    Read
 * Signature: ()I
 */
JNIEXPORT jint JNICALL Java_JMAXSerial_Read
                                    (JNIEnv *, jobject);

/*
 * Class:     JMAXSerial
 * Method:    Close
 * Signature: ()I
 */
JNIEXPORT jint JNICALL Java_JMAXSerial_Close
                                    (JNIEnv *, jobject);

#ifdef __cplusplus
}
#endif
#endif
```

FIGURE 8.33 The JNI-Style header file.

8.4.5 Developing the Native Library (the DLL Target File)

After the JNI-style header file is obtained, we can begin to develop our native library.

1. Launch Visual C++ 6.0 and create a new project with the following properties:
    - Project name: `JNIMAX`
    - Project type: `Win32 Dynamic-Link Library`
    - Location: `C:\Java\MAX187`
2. Open the Windows Explorer to copy the following header files to the new project folder `C:\Java\MAX187\JNIMAX`:
    - jni.h
    - jni_md.h
    - JMAXSerial.h

    The `jni.h` file is located in the Java installation folder `C:\jdk1.3\include`, and the `jni_md.h` file is located in the folder `C:\jdk1.3\include\win32`. The `JMAXSerial.h` is a JNI-style header file that we created in the last section; it is located in our project folder, `C:\Java\MAX187`.

3. In the new created project, create a new header file named `JNIMAX.h` and a new source file named `JNIMAX.cpp`.
4. Click the `Project|Add To Project|Files` menu item from Visual C++ 6.0 IDE to add the following header files we copied in Step 2 into our project:

   - jni.h
   - jni_md.h
   - JMAXSerial.h

In the following sections, we'll divide this project into two parts, the header file and the source file, and we'll code each section separately. (Note that this DLL file is very similar with one that is developed in Section 7.4.2 in Chapter 7.)

8.4.5.1 Developing the DLL Header File

Open the new created header file `JNIMAX.h` and enter the code that is shown in Figure 8.34 into this file. To avoid repetition, we won't include a detailed explanation here. Refer to Section 7.4.2.1 in Chapter 7 for more information about this code.

All data structures and local functions used in the DLL file are defined in this header file. The prototypes of the interface function are defined in the JNI-style header file we developed in the last section. Both header files are included in this project to provide the protocols of the data structures and functions used in the project.

8.4.5.2 Developing the DLL Source File

The code for the source file is divided into several sections according to the operations of each section. The Setup section contains the interface function `Setup()` and the local function `Portinitialize()`.

8.4.5.2.1 Code for the Setup Section

Open the new created source file and enter the code that is shown in Figure 8.35 into this file. Each section of the code is described in the following list:

A: Both JNI-style and user-defined header files, `JMAXSerial.h` and `JNIMAX.h`, are included at the beginning of this source file because both the interface functions and the local functions are defined in these two header files, and the source file needs to use those functions.

B: The signature of the interface function `Setup()` is declared here. This signature is modified according to the prototype of the function, which is declared in the JNI-style header file. Compare this signature with that defined in the JNI-style header file; the modifications are that the nominal variables, `env`, `obj`, and `compms`, are added after each data type in the argument list. This modification is necessary because we need to use these nominal variables in the file.

C: The C++ local variables are declared at the beginning of this function. The `jint* pCom` is a C++ array or a pointer variable that is used to hold the data values of converted data array from the Java domain to the C++ domain. `jint rc` is a C++ variable used to hold the running status of the local functions. `fopen()` is used to open a data file `jmax.dat` to store the collected data from the MAX187. This data file can be opened later in the MATLAB domain and plotted in two-dimensional graphic format.

D: The JNI function `GetIntArrayElements()` is used to convert the Java data array `compms` to a C++ data array. The starting address of the converted data array is assigned

```
/*****************************************************************************
 * NAME        : JNIMAX.h
 * DESC.       : Header file for JNIMAX.cpp (MAX187 A/D Converter)
 * PGRMER.     : Y. Bai
 * DATE        : 12/18/2003
 *****************************************************************************/
#include <windows.h>
#ifndef _JNIMAX_H_
#define _JNIMAX_H_
#define MAX_BYTE                    1
#define MAX_BITS                    12
#define MAX_DATA                    100
#define MAX_STRING                  256
#define NOPARITY                    0
#define RTS_CONTROL_DISABLE     0x00
#define RTS_CONTROL_ENABLE      0x01
#define DTR_CONTROL_DISABLE     0x00
#define DTR_CONTROL_ENABLE      0x01
#define msg(info)      MessageBox(NULL, info, "", MB_OK)
typedef struct
{
   ULONG    ulCtrlerID;        // serial port ID
   char     cEcho;             // echo character
   char     cEORChar;          // end of character
   long     lTimeout;          // time out value
   long     lBaudRate;         // baud rate
   long     lDataBits;         // data bits
} SerialCreate, *pSerialCreate;
typedef struct
{
   int    pcBuffer;            /* Buffer to store the received data */
   int    iMaxChars;           /* Max number of characters to be received */
   int    piNumRcvd;           /* Actual number of characters received */
   char   cTermChar;           /* Terminal character */
} CommPortClass;
typedef enum
{
   OK       = 0,               // no error
   EC_TIMEOUT,                 // system time out error
   EC_FOPEN,                   // file open error
   EC_INVAL_CONFIG,            // invalid configuration error
   EC_TIMEOUT_SET,             // set structure time out error
   EC_RECV_TIMEOUT,            // receiver time out error
   EC_EXIT_CODE,               // get exit code error
   EC_WAIT_SINGLEOBJ,          // WaitForSingleObject function error
   EC_INVALIDPORT,             // invalid port error
   EC_WRITE_FAIL,              // write function error
   EC_CREATE_THREAD,           // create thread error
   EC_UNKNOWNERROR             // unknown error
} ERR_CODE;
```

FIGURE 8.34 The DLL header file. *(continued)*

```
FILE*       fp;
HANDLE  hPort;
char*       sPortName;
bool         PortCreateflg = false;
int           runTIMES = 0;

/* Local functions */
ERR_CODE PortInitialize(LPTSTR lpszPortName, pSerialCreate pCreate);
ERR_CODE PortRead(CommPortClass *hCommPort);
void WINAPI ThreadFunc(void* hCommPorts);
void Delay(int num);

#endif
```

FIGURE 34 The DLL header file.

to the variable `pCom`. A `JNI_FALSE` constant means that we do not need this array copied. A `NULL` will be returned if this function call encounters any error. In this case, a message box with a warning message will be displayed on the screen to alert us that something has gone wrong during this function process.

E: The converted data is assigned to the associated element in the data structure `SerialCreate`; this structure will be passed into the `PortInitialize()` function to configure the serial port.

F: A `switch` instruction is used to find the port number and assign the `sPortName` to the associated port name in text format.

G: Because we have finished converting and manipulating the data array, we no longer need the converted data array. We can delete it and clean up the memory space assigned to it by calling the JNI function `ReleaseIntArrayElements()`.

H: If the serial port has been configured, the `PortCreateflg` should be `True`. In this case, we cannot configure the port again. A warning message will be displayed if the port has been configured.

I: Otherwise the local function `PortInitialize()` is called to configure the serial port. An error message will be displayed if this configuration encounters any error.

J: The memory space allocated for the structure `SerialCreate` can be deleted before we exit this function because its mission is complete. The `PortCreateflg` is set to `True` to indicate to the system that the port has been configured.

K: The running status of this function is returned to the calling function.

The code for the local function `PortInitialize()` is shown in Figure 8.36. A detailed explanation of this function is given in Section 5.4.3.4.5 in Chapter 5; refer to that section to get more information about this coding.

8.4.5.2.2 Code for the Data Reading Section

The code for the Data Reading section contains the coding of the interface function `Read()`, the local function `PortRead()` and the thread function `ThreadFunc()`. The code for the interface function `Read()` is shown in Figure 8.37.

L: The local variables are declared here. `ad_data` can be considered a buffer; it is used to reserve the received data from the MAX187 A/D converter. The `rc` variable works as a status register to hold the returned running status of the calling function. The `commClass` is a pointer variable of the data structure `CommPortClass`, which is defined in the header file.

```
  /*****************************************************************************
   * NAME       : JNIMAX.cpp
   * DESC.      : DLL functions to interface to RS-232 serial port, called by Java.
   * PRGMER.    : Y. Bai
   *****************************************************************************/
  #include <stdio.h>
  #include <stdlib.h>
  #include <string.h>
A #include "JNIMAX.h"
  #include "JMAXSerial.h"
B JNIEXPORT jint JNICALL Java_JMAXSerial_Setup
                              (JNIEnv *env, jobject obj, jintArray compms)
  {
C         jint rc = 0;
          pSerialCreate pParam;
          fp = fopen("jmax.dat", "w");
          jint* pCom;
D         pCom = env->GetIntArrayElements(compms, JNI_FALSE);
          if (pCom == NULL)
          {
              msg("ERROR in GetIntArrayElements()\n");
              return rc = -1;
          }
E         pParam = new SerialCreate;            // create a new structure pointer
          pParam->lBaudRate = pCom[1];          // assign values to variables in structure
          pParam->lDataBits = pCom[2];
          pParam->lTimeout = 3000;
F         switch(pCom[0])                       // check the port number
          {
           case 1: sPortName = "COM1";          // port is COM1
                   break;
           case 2: sPortName = "COM2";          // port is COM2
                   break;
           case 3: sPortName = "COM3";          // port is COM3
                   break;
           case 4: sPortName = "COM4";          // port is COM4
                   break;
           default: return EC_INVALIDPORT;
          }
G         env->ReleaseIntArrayElements(compms, pCom, 0);
H         if (PortCreateflg)                    // port flag is true means port was set
          {
              msg("Port has been Setup ");
              return rc;
          }
I         rc = PortInitialize(sPortName, pParam);  // call local func. to configure port
          if (rc != 0)
             msg("ERROR in PortInitialize()!");
J         delete pParam;                        // clean pointer structure
          PortCreateflg = true;                 // set port creation flag
K         return rc;
  }
```

FIGURE 8.35 The interface function `Setup()`.

M: The `new` keyword is used to allocate memory space for the pointer variable `commClass` and return the starting address of that variable. Two setup parameters are assigned to the elements of the structure variable `commClass`: `iMaxChars` and `iMaxBits`.

N: The system extended function `EscapeCommFunction()` is executed to setup the initial status of two transmission lines, the DTR and the RTS, to disable the SCLK and

```
ERR_CODE PortInitialize(char* lpszPortName, pSerialCreate pCreate)
{
    DWORD  dwError;
    DCB       PortDCB;
    ERR_CODE ecStatus = OK;
    COMMTIMEOUTS  CommTimeouts;  unsigned char  dBit;
    if (PortCreateflg)                          // check if the port has been created...
   {
        msg("Port has been initialized!");
        return  ecStatus;
    }
    hPort = CreateFile(lpszPortName,         // Pointer to the name of the port
                        GENERIC_READ | GENERIC_WRITE,  // Access (read/write) mode
                        0,                    // Share mode
                        NULL,                 // Pointer to the security attribute
                        OPEN_EXISTING, // How to open the serial port
                        0,                    // Port attributes
                        NULL);                // Handle to port with attribute to copy
    // If it fails to open the port, return error.
    if ( hPort == INVALID_HANDLE_VALUE )
    {
        // Could not open the port.
        dwError = GetLastError();
        msg("Unable to open the port");
        CloseHandle(hPort);
        return EC_FOPEN;
    }
    PortCreateflg = TRUE;
    PortDCB.DCBlength = sizeof(DCB);
    // Get the default port setting information.
    GetCommState(hPort, &PortDCB);
    // Change the DCB structure settings.
    PortDCB.BaudRate = pCreate->lBaudRate;   // Current baud
    PortDCB.fBinary  = TRUE;                 // Binary mode; no EOF check
    PortDCB.fParity  = FALSE;                // Disable parity checking.
    PortDCB.fOutxCtsFlow = FALSE;            // No CTS output flow control
    PortDCB.fOutxDsrFlow = FALSE;            // No DSR output flow control
    PortDCB.fDtrControl = DTR_CONTROL_DISABLE;  // DTR flow control type
    PortDCB.fDsrSensitivity = FALSE;         // DSR sensitivity
    PortDCB.fTXContinueOnXoff = FALSE;      // XOFF continues Tx
    PortDCB.fOutX = FALSE;                   // No XON/XOFF out flow control
    PortDCB.fInX  = FALSE;                   // No XON/XOFF in flow control
    PortDCB.fErrorChar = FALSE;              // Disable error replacement.
    PortDCB.fNull = FALSE;                   // Disable null stripping.
    PortDCB.fRtsControl = RTS_CONTROL_DISABLE; // RTS flow control
    PortDCB.fAbortOnError = FALSE;           // Do not abort reads/writes on error.
    dBit = (UCHAR)pCreate->lDataBits;        // Assign data bits
    PortDCB.ByteSize = dBit;                 // Number of bits/bytes, 4-8
    PortDCB.Parity = NOPARITY;               // 0-4=no,odd,even,mark,space
    PortDCB.StopBits = ONESTOPBIT;           // 0,1,2 = 1, 1.5, 2
```

FIGURE 8.36 The local function `PortInitialize()`. *(continued)*

```
    // Configure the port according to the specifications of the DCB structure.
    if (!SetCommState (hPort, &PortDCB))
    {
        // Could not set the timeout parameter.
        dwError = GetLastError();
        msg("Unable to configure the serial port");
        return EC_INVAL_CONFIG;
    }
    // Retrieve the time-out parameters for all read and write operations on the port.
    GetCommTimeouts(hPort, &CommTimeouts);

    // Change the COMMTIMEOUTS structure settings.
    CommTimeouts.ReadIntervalTimeout = MAXDWORD;
    CommTimeouts.ReadTotalTimeoutMultiplier = 0;
    CommTimeouts.ReadTotalTimeoutConstant = 0;
    CommTimeouts.WriteTotalTimeoutMultiplier = 10;
    CommTimeouts.WriteTotalTimeoutConstant = 1000;
    // Set the time-out parameters for all read and write operations on the port.
    if (!SetCommTimeouts (hPort, &CommTimeouts))
    {
        // Could not set the port timeout parameter.
        dwError = GetLastError();
        msg("Unable to set the time-out parameters");
        return  EC_TIMEOUT_SET;
    }
    EscapeCommFunction(hPort, SETDTR);    //Set DTR
    EscapeCommFunction(hPort, SETRTS);    //Set RTS
    return  ecStatus;
}
```

FIGURE 8.36 The local function `PortInitialize()`.

```
    JNIEXPORT jint JNICALL Java_JMAXSerial_Read(JNIEnv *env, jobject  obj)
    {
L       jint  ad_data;
        ERR_CODE rc = OK;
        CommPortClass* commClass;
M       commClass = new CommPortClass;
        commClass->iMaxChars = MAX_BYTE;
        commClass->iMaxBits  = MAX_BITS;
N       EscapeCommFunction(hPort, SETDTR);       //Set DTR to disable the SCLK
        EscapeCommFunction(hPort, CLRRTS);       //Reset RTS to disable the CS-bar
O       rc = PortRead(commClass);
        if (rc != 0 && runTIMES != 0)            //wake-up reading error neglected.
           msg("ERROR in PortRead()! ");
P       runTIMES++;
Q       if (runTIMES != 1)
        {
           fprintf(fp, "%d\n", commClass->pcBuffer);        //Reserve data
           ad_data = commClass->pcBuffer;
        }
R       delete  commClass;
S       return  ad_data;
    }
```

FIGURE 8.37 The interface function `Read()`.

the CS-bar control signals on the MAX187. Both SETDTR and CLRRTS are system constants defined in Win32 SDK.

O: The local function PortRead() is called to retrieve the converted data from the MAX187 A/D converter via the serial port. The argument commClass is a structure pointer variable that contains the data collection elements. An error message will be displayed if the function call has failed. An AND operation with the runTIMES value is added into this if logic condition to skip the first possible reading error. During the initialization stage, the global variable runTIMES is reset to 0. If the first PortRead() returns an error, the associated conditions are rc !=0 and runTIMES =0. Because we try to skip the first reading (Wake-up reading) error, no error message will be displayed for these conditions. You will find that in step P below, after the first reading, the global variable runTIMES is incremented by 1, and the conditions described above are not met if the following PortRead() encounters any error. This means that all subsequent errors caused by the PortRead() will be displayed without skipping.

P: The global variable runTIMES is incremented by 1 to indicate to the program that the following errors are not the errors caused by the first calling of the function PortRead(). An error message will be displayed if any such errors occur.

Q: The received data is stored in the structure variable commClass->pcBuffer, and it is written into a data file by means of the system function fprintf(). The fp variable stores the opened file handler obtained from the Setup() function. An if logic structure is used to skip the first data reading.

R: The received data (12 bits) is also assigned to the data buffer ad_data. After this assignment, the structure variable commClass is no longer used. The delete statement is called to delete that structure variable and to clean up the memory space allocated for it.

S: Finally, the data buffer is returned to the calling function as the received data.

The code for the local function PortRead() is shown in Figure 8.38.

T: Some local variables are declared inside the local function PortRead(). hThread is a HANDLE that is used to hold the thread handle when a new thread is created. IDThread is a double-word integer used to reserve the thread ID as a new thread is opened. Ret holds the running status of certain system functions, such as WaitForSingleObject(), and the ExitCode is used to hold the exit code when a thread or an object is terminated. The dTimeout is a double-word integer that is used to hold the timeout value. The default upper boundary of the timeout is 500 milliseconds.

U: The system function CreateThread() is called to create a new thread that is used to handle the port reading process. If this call is successful, the returned thread's handle is assigned to the hThread. A returned value of False means that this function has failed; in this case, an error message will be displayed and the function will return this error to the calling function. The third argument of this function is the thread function ThreadFunc. This thread function executes the actions of the thread. The thread only provides a frame; the actual thread job is performed by the thread function. The fourth argument, hCommPort, a pointer variable of the structure CommPortClass, is very important to this application because it contains all data collection definitions. To pass this structure variable into the thread function, you must place it in this position with this format. The fifth argument is a system constant that indicates the running status of the thread when it is created. CREATE_SUSPENDED means that the created thread is suspended and will not run until the ResumeThread() function is executed.

V: A ResumeThread() function is called to begin running the thread function.

```
/*****************************************************************************
 * NAME:    PortRead()
 * PGRMR:  Y. Bai
 *****************************************************************************/
ERR_CODE PortRead(CommPortClass *hCommPort)
{
T      HANDLE hThread;                    // handler for port read thread
       DWORD  IDThread;
       DWORD  Ret, ExitCode;
       DWORD  dTimeout = 500;             // define time out value: 500 ms.
       ERR_CODE ecStatus = OK;
U      if (!(hThread = CreateThread(NULL,                   // no security attributes
                       0,                                   // use default stack size
                       (LPTHREAD_START_ROUTINE) ThreadFunc,
                       (LPVOID)hCommPort,                   // parameter to thread function
                       CREATE_SUSPENDED,                    // creation flag - suspended
                       &IDThread) ) )                       // returns thread ID
      {
          msg("Create Read Thread failed");
          return EC_CREATE_THREAD;
      }
V     ResumeThread(hThread);                               // start thread now
W     Ret = WaitForSingleObject(hThread, dTimeout);
      if (Ret == WAIT_OBJECT_0)
      {   // data received & process it...need to do nothing because the data
          // has been stored in the hCommPort in Thread Func. Close thread handle
          CloseHandle(hThread);
      }
X     else if (Ret == WAIT_TIMEOUT)
      {
          // time out happened, warning & kill thread
          Ret = GetExitCodeThread(hThread, &ExitCode);
          if (ExitCode == STILL_ACTIVE)
          {
              TerminateThread(hThread, ExitCode);
              CloseHandle(hThread);
              return EC_RECV_TIMEOUT;
          }
          else
          {
              CloseHandle(hThread);
              msg("ERROR in GetExitCodeThread: != STILL_ACTIVE ");
              ecStatus = EC_EXIT_CODE;
          }
       }
Y      else
       {
           msg("ERROR in WaitFor SingleObject ");
           ecStatus = EC_WAIT_SINGLEOBJ;
       }
Z      return  ecStatus;
}
```

FIGURE 8.38 The local function `PortRead()`.

W: The system function `WaitForSingleObject()` is called to monitor and wait for the thread function until it is completed. This function returns when the specified object (thread function) is signaled or when the timeout interval elapses. Two arguments are passed into this function: `hThread` is the thread handle, and `dTimeout` is the upper boundary value of the timeout. If the function returns WAIT_OBJECT_0, which is the thread handle, it means that the thread function has been executed successfully, the data has been collected, and the thread function has been automatically terminated. No any other action is needed for this situation except closing the thread handle with the CloseHandle() system function.

X: If the function returns WAIT_TIMEOUT, it means that a timeout error has occurred and the data collection has failed (no event has been signaled). Two steps are needed for this situation. First we need to retrieve the exit code of the thread function by calling the system function GetExitCodeThread(). If the exit code indicates that the thread function is still running (STILL_ACTIVE), the function TerminateThread() is executed to stop the thread function, and then to close the thread by calling the function CloseHandle(). If the exit code of the thread is not equal to STILL_ACTIVE, which means that the thread function has been terminated, we can directly close the thread by calling the function CloseHandle().

Y: If the function returns other values, then some error has occurred during the function call. In this case, an error message will be displayed and the function will return the error to the calling function.

Z: The running status of the function ecStatus is returned to the calling function.

The code for the thread function ThreadFunc() is shown in Figure 8.39. Each section of the code is explained in the following list:

1: All local variables are declared at the beginning of this function. The Boolean variable fDone works as a condition variable for the while loop that waits for the communication events to occur during the data collection process. ad_data works as a data buffer to store a single collected data item. The double-word variable dwModemStatus works as an argument to be passed into the system function GetCommModemStatus(), and the returned status of the associated transmission line is stored in this argument. The variable dwCommModemStatus works in a similar way as did the variable dwModemStatus, and it returns the associated event status as the function WaitCommEvent() is called.

2: A casting operation (CommPortClass*) is performed to convert the argument hCommPorts that has a void* data type into the CommPortClass* structure type. This cast is very important and is necessary because the argument hCommPorts is a void* data type. Any argument included in a thread function must have a void* data type. In order to use that structure, we must uses a cast operator to convert the argument to the desired data type.

3: The extended system function EscapeCommFunction() is called to set the RTS line to HIGH to enable the MAX187 to begin data conversion. The RTS line is connected to the CS-bar input on the MAX187 via the inverter MAX220. (Refer to Figure 8.29.) A HIGH value on the RTS line produces a LOW value for the CS-bar on the MAX187.

4: After the data conversion begins, we need to monitor the status of the DSR line because this line is connected to the output buffer (DOUT) of the MAX187. The converted data will be transmitted from the output buffer to the serial port via this DSR line. (Refer to Figure 8.29.) To accomplish this transmission, we must use the system function SetCommMask() to select and mask the desired transmission line. After this configuration, an event will be generated as the status of the DSR line is changed; this event can be detected by the function WaitCommEvent(). The functions SetCommMask() and WaitCommEvent() work as a pair to complete this setup and to detect the status of a transmission line.

5: The Boolean variable fDone is reset to False to prepare for the while loop.

```
   void WINAPI ThreadFunc(void* hCommPorts)
   {
1      BOOL  fDone;
       int       ad_data = 0;
       DWORD  dwModemStatus;
       int   index, nTotRead = 0;
       DWORD  dwCommModemStatus;
       CommPortClass*  CommPorts;
       ERR_CODE ecStatus = OK;
2      CommPorts = (CommPortClass* )hCommPorts;
3      EscapeCommFunction(hPort, SETRTS);  // Set RTS to enable the CS-bar to start A/D
4      SetCommMask(hPort, EV_DSR); // Specify a set of events to be monitored for the port.
5      fDone = FALSE;
6      while (!fDone)
       {   // Wait for an event to occur for the port.
7        WaitCommEvent(hPort, &dwCommModemStatus, 0);
8        if (dwCommModemStatus & EV_DSR)             // received the DSR event
         {
9           for (index = 0; index < CommPorts->iMaxBits; index++)
            {
10             EscapeCommFunction(hPort, CLRDTR);  //Reset DTR (HIGH in SCLK)
               Delay(10);
11             EscapeCommFunction(hPort, SETDTR);  //Set DTR (LOW in SCLK)
               Delay(10);
12             if (!GetCommModemStatus(hPort, &dwModemStatus))
               {
                   msg("ERROR in GetModemStatus()!");
                   fDone = TRUE;
                   break;
               }
13             if (MS_DSR_ON & dwModemStatus)        //DSR status is HIGH.
                  ad_data = ad_data + 0;
14             else                                   //DSR status is LOW
                  ad_data++;
15            ad_data = ad_data << 1;
            }
16          EscapeCommFunction(hPort, SETDTR);       //Set DTR (LOW in SCLK)
            EscapeCommFunction(hPort, CLRRTS);       //Reset CS to deselect A/D
17          ad_data = ad_data >> 1;
18          CommPorts->pcBuffer = ad_data;
            fDone = TRUE;
            break;
         }
       } // end of while loop
   }
19 void Delay(int  num)
   {
       int k, m, n = 100*num;
20     for (m = 0; m < n; m++)
          k++;
   }
```

FIGURE 8.39 The thread function `Threadfunc()`.

6: A `while` loop is used to wait for the event that is associated with the desired or masked transmission line to occur. In our case, this event is `EV_DSR`.

7: The system function `WaitCommEvent()` is executed to detect the possible event. (If you use this function directly, without involving the thread function, a dead cycle would be caused by the `WaitCommEvent()`, and the system would be hung up indefinitely.)

A timeout error will occur when this function is included inside the thread function if no event is signaled during the waiting process.

8: The function `WaitCommEvent()` will be terminated if the desired event occurs. The returned status of the associated transmission line is stored in the argument `dwCommModemStatus`. An AND operation is used to determine whether the desired event, `EV_DSR`, is detected.

9: If the EV_DSR is received, a `for` loop is used to repeatedly collect 12-bit converted data. To retrieve each bit of data, either a simulated or an external clock must be provided. Here, a simulated clock is generated by a sequence of instructions below.

10: The function `EscapeCommFunction()` is called to reset the DTR line. This resetting is equivalent to provide a `HIGH` value to the `SCLK` input on the MAX187. (Refer to Figure 8.29.) A user-defined `Delay()` function is executed to make this simulated clock stable and send it to the `SCLK` input.

11: Another `EscapeCommFunction()` is called after this delay to set the DTR line to `HIGH`, which is equivalent to set a `LOW` value on the `SCLK` input. Following this setting, another delay is inserted. In this way, a completed simulated clock cycle is generated to the `SCLK` input on the MAX187, and one bit of converted data can be shifted from the output buffer on the MAX187 to the serial port, via the DSR line.

12: Now we need to check the status of the DSR line to determine whether a logical `1` or a logical `0` has been received. To do this, we need to call the system function `GetCommModemStatus()`. This function will return the current status of the desired transmission line. An error message will be displayed if this function call encounters any error. The function will be terminated and returned to the calling function after an error message is displayed.

13: By using the operation `MS_DSR_ON & dwModemStatus`, we can detect whether the DSR line is `HIGH` or `LOW`. Note that a `HIGH` (ON) on the DSR line means that a logical `0` has been received because of the MAX220 inverter. In this case, only a `0` is added into the data buffer `ad_data`.

14: Otherwise if a `LOW` is detected on the DSR line, which is equivalent to a logic 1 on the converted bit, the data buffer `ad_data` should be increased by 1 in the LSB.

15: The data buffer `ad_data` is shifted left by one bit to reserve space for the next bit of data. Steps 10 through 15 will be continued until all 12 bits of data have been converted and received.

16: After all 12 bits have been received, the system function `EscapeCommFunction()` is called to set the DTR line to `HIGH`, which is equivalent to reset the SCLK input on the MAX187, and reset the RTS line to `LOW`, which is equivalent to assign a `HIGH` value to the CS-bar on the MAX187 to deselect it. `SETDTR` and `CLRRTS` are two system constants used in the Win32 SDK.

17: During the data collection process, the data buffer is totally shifted left by 12 bits. But for a 12-bit data string, shifting left 11 times is enough because the last bit does not need to shift. So a compensation is needed to make this data processing correct. This compensation can be accomplished by shifting the final result right by one bit.

18: The final result is assigned to `pcBuffer`, which is an element of the data structure `CommPortClass`, and is then returned to the calling function. The Boolean condition variable `fDone` is set to `True` to stop the `while` loop. The instruction `break` is unnecessary, but we use it here to ensure our program's reliability.

19: `Delay()` is a simple user-defined function; its purpose is to delay processing for a specified period of time. Three local integer variables are declared here.

20: A `for` loop is used to repeatedly increase the variable `k by 1` until `n = m`.

Now that we have finished the coding of our data reading section, let's take a look at the port `Close()` function.

8.4.5.2.3 Code for the Port Close Section

The code for this interface function is shown in Figure 8.40.

```
/*****************************************************************************
 * NAME:          Close
 * DESC:          Interface function to MAX187 Serial A/D converter
 * PGMR:          Y. Bai
 * DATE:          12/20/2003
 *****************************************************************************/
JNIEXPORT jint JNICALL Java_JMAXSerial_Close(JNIEnv *env, jobject obj)
{
      jint  rc = 0;
21    if (PortCreateflg)
          CloseHandle(hPort);
22    PortCreateflg = false;
23    fclose(fp);
24    runTIMES = 0;
25     return  rc;
}
```

FIGURE 8.40 The interface function `close()`.

21: First we need to check whether the port has been opened and configured. To do this, we inspect the global Boolean variable `PortCreateflg`. This flag will have been set by the function `Setup()` if the port has been successfully opened and configured. The system function `CloseHandle()` is called to close the port if the port has been opened and configured.
22: After the port is closed, the Boolean variable `PortCreateflg` is reset to `false`.
23: Other cleanup jobs include the closing of the opened file handle `fp` by the system function `fclose()`.
24: Here the global variable `runTIMES` is reset to `0`.
25: Finally the running status of this function is returned to the calling function.

At this point, we have completed the coding of our source file.

8.4.6 Building and Installing the DLL Target File

Now we are ready to build our DLL target file. Click the `Build|Build JNIMAX.dll` menu item from the Visual C++ 6.0 IDE to compile and build the DLL target file. The built target file `JNIMAX.dll` is located in our project folder, `C:\Java\MAX187\JNIMAX\Debug`.

To allow the Java platform to recognize and interface with this native library file as the project runs, we need to install this target DLL file in one of the following three locations:

- The system default DLL file folder, which is `C:\WINDOWS\system` in Windows 95/98/Me/XP or `C:\WINNT\system` in Windows NT/2000.
- The searchable path on your machine. This means that you can create any user-defined folder and place the DLL target file in that folder. The only requirement here is that you must set that folder as a system variable to your system path.
- The folder in which the Java byte codes are located.

In this application, we adopt the third method and install our DLL target file in the user-defined project folder `C:\Java\MAX187`. All our Java source files and bytecode files are located at this folder. Copy the target DLL file `JNIMAX.dll` to this folder.

8.4.7 Testing and Running the MAX187 Project

Now let's run our project to perform the data collection from the MAX187 via the serial port.

1. Open a command window and switch to our project folder, `C:\Java\MAX187`, and type `java JMAXGUI` on the command line to start our project. The running project is shown in Figure 8.41.

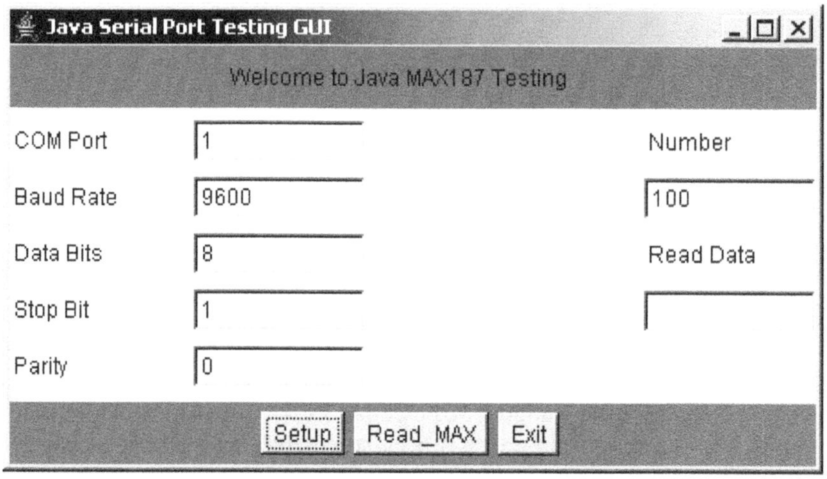

FIGURE 8.41 Running the `JMAXGUI` project.

2. Enter the following setup parameters into the input fields on the left pane:

COM Port:	1
Baud Rate:	9600
Data Bits:	8
Stop Bit:	1
Parity:	0

3. Enter the following application parameter into the input field on the right-hand pane:

   Number: 100

4. Click the `Setup` button to trigger the interface function to setup the serial port. Then click the `Read_MAX` button to begin to collect the data from the MAX187 via the serial port. The data collection process is shown in Figure 8.42.

Three analog waveforms are tested for this data collection, sinusoidal, triangular, and square signals. To confirm the data collection, you can develop a MATLAB M-function and plot the collected data in the MATLAB domain using the `plot()` M-function.

5. Launch MATLAB 6.5 and create a new M-file named `jmaxdll.m`. Enter the code that is shown in Figure 8.43 into this M-file.

As you remember, we opened a data file `jmax.dat` in the interface function `Setup()` that was developed in the native library `JNIMAX.dll`. The purpose of this data file is to store the

Java Serial Port Testing GUI
Welcome to Java MAX187 Testing
COM Port 1
Baud Rate 9600
Data Bits 8
Stop Bit 1
Parity 0
Number 100
Read Data 3726
Setup Read_MAX Exit

FIGURE 8.42 The data collection process.

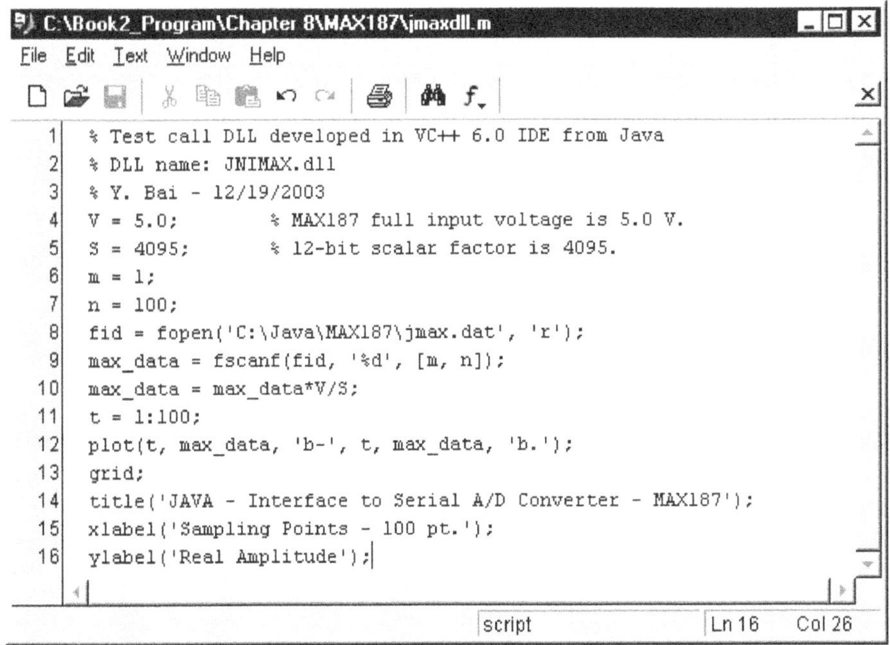


```
% Test call DLL developed in VC++ 6.0 IDE from Java
% DLL name: JNIMAX.dll
% Y. Bai - 12/19/2003
V = 5.0;          % MAX187 full input voltage is 5.0 V.
S = 4095;         % 12-bit scalar factor is 4095.
m = 1;
n = 100;
fid = fopen('C:\Java\MAX187\jmax.dat', 'r');
max_data = fscanf(fid, '%d', [m, n]);
max_data = max_data*V/S;
t = 1:100;
plot(t, max_data, 'b-', t, max_data, 'b.');
grid;
title('JAVA - Interface to Serial A/D Converter - MAX187');
xlabel('Sampling Points - 100 pt.');
ylabel('Real Amplitude');
```

FIGURE 8.43 The MATLAB M-Function `jmaxdll.m`.

collected data from the MAX187 and prepare it for future use. Now it is time for us to use this data file.

In the M-function `jmaxdll.m`, the system function `fopen()` is used to open the data file that is located at our project folder `C:\Java\MAX187` in this application. Then another system function, `fscanf()`, is used to retrieve the data from the data file and assign it to a data array, `max_data`. A scaling factor is multiplied with each element of the data array to convert the data from raw form to the real voltage of the output of the MAX187. The `plot()` function is called to plot the collected data in a two-dimensional graphic format.

Save this M-function `jmaxdll.m` in the MATLAB default work folder, which is `C:\MATLAB6p5\work` in our case.

6. Type `jmaxdll` in the MATLAB workspace to run the M-function. The resulting graphs for the three input waveforms are shown in Figures 8.44, 8.45, and 8.46, respectively.

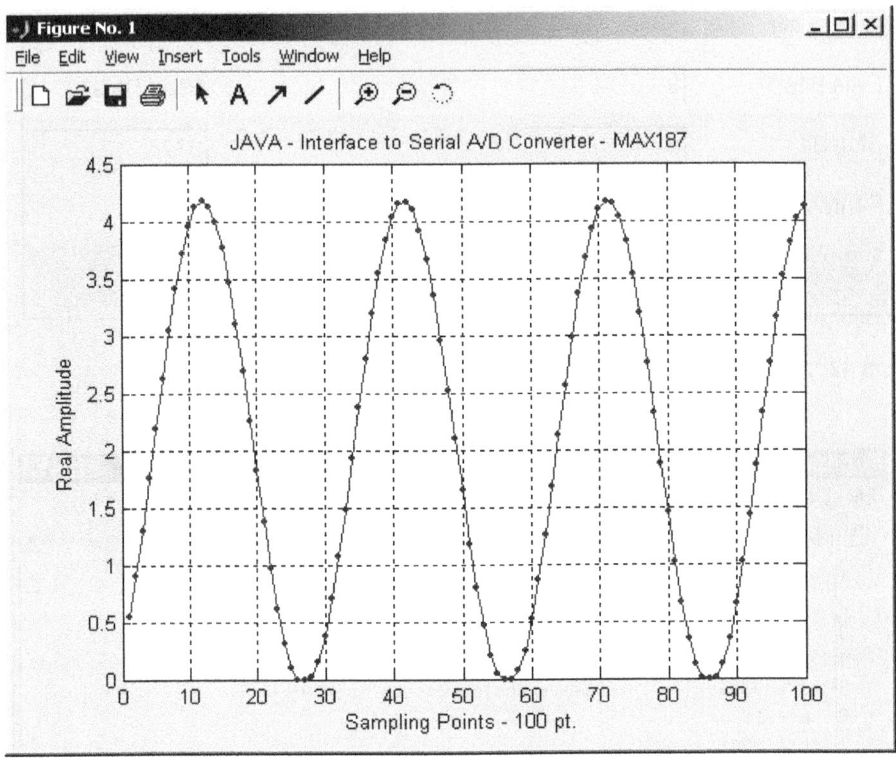

FIGURE 8.44 The tested sinusoidal waveforem.

The complete project files, including the Java source files, the bytecode files, the JNI-style header file, the DLL source file, the header file, the DLL target file, and the MATLAB M-function file, are located in the folder `Chapter 8\MAX187` on the attached CD. You can copy these files and test them on your own machine.

Generally, serial communication between Java and the serial port is realized by using the interface functions developed in the native library. In this chapter, the native library was developed as DLL in the Visual C++ 6.0 environment.

8.5 CHAPTER SUMMARY

The fundamental interface methods between Java and native languages have been discussed in this chapter. JNI is a popular method used to interface to the third-party language from within Java domain. The interface between Java and the serial port is provided by JNI. The interface steps and implementations were discussed in detail at the beginning of this chapter. Two actual examples were provided to illustrate the use of the JNI to interface with the serial ports via the native language, Visual C++ 6.0, to perform serial data communications between the Java domain and the RS-232 serial ports. You can adapt those examples to your own applications to easily perform serial data communication between Java and the serial ports.

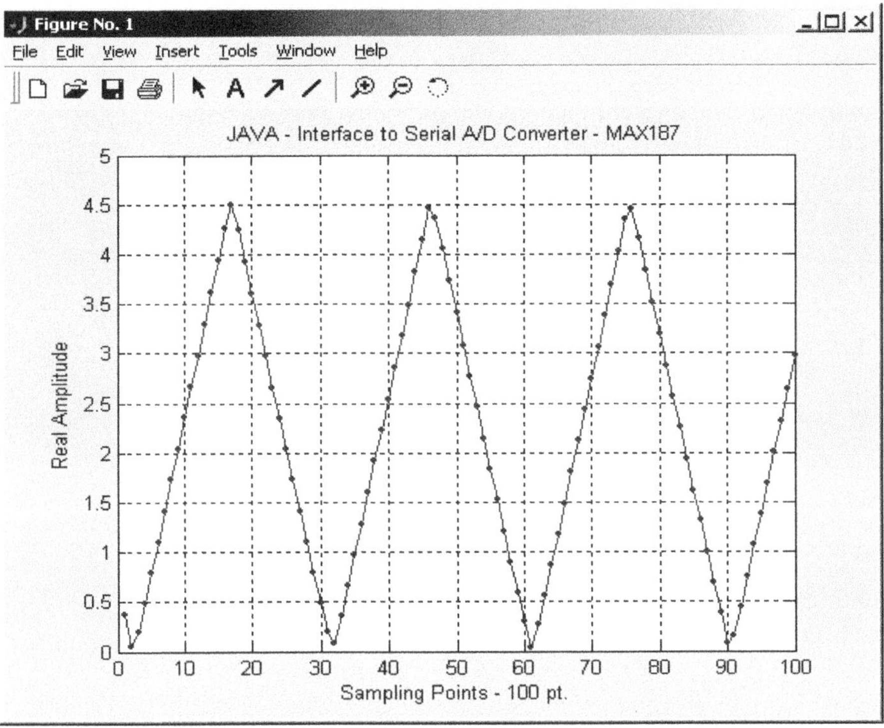

FIGURE 8.45 The tested triangular waveforem.

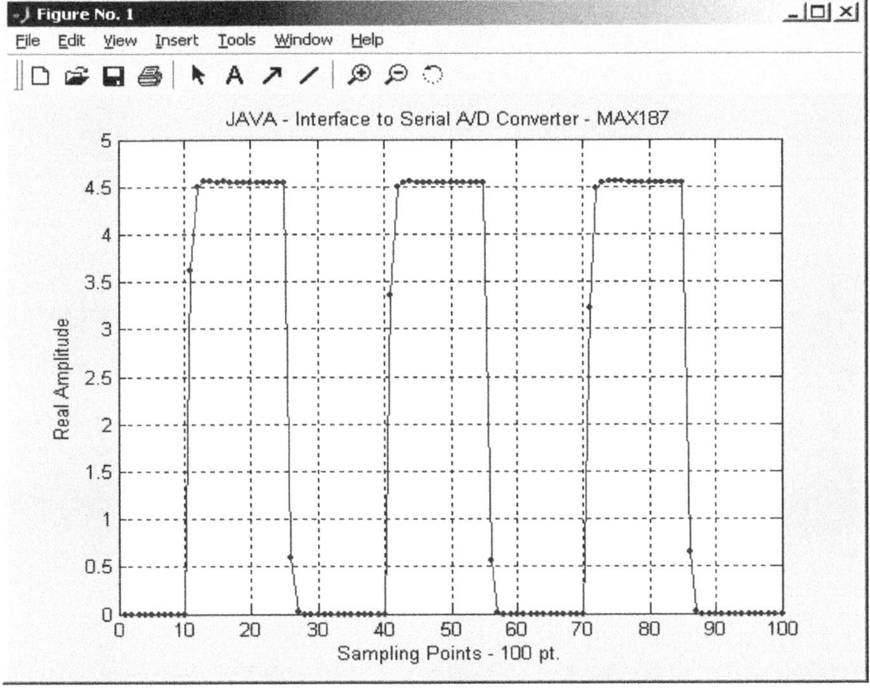

FIGURE 8.46 The tested square waveform.

A Appendix

ASCII Code Table

ASCII Value	Character	ASCII Value	Character	ASCII Value	Character	ASCII Value	Character
32	space	56	8	80	P	104	h
33	!	57	9	81	Q	105	i
34	"	58	:	82	R	106	j
35	#	59	;	83	S	107	k
36	$	60	<	84	T	108	l
37	%	61	=	85	U	109	m
38	&	62	>	86	V	110	n
39	'	63	?	87	W	111	o
40	(	64	@	88	X	112	p
41	)	65	A	89	Y	113	q
42	*	66	B	90	Z	114	r
43	+	67	C	91	[	115	s

<table>
<tr><th>ASCII Value</th><th>Character</th><th>ASCII Value</th><th>Character</th><th>ASCII Value</th><th>Character</th><th>ASCII Value</th><th>Character</th></tr>
<tr><td>44</td><td>,</td><td>68</td><td>D</td><td>92</td><td>\</td><td>116</td><td>t</td></tr>
<tr><td>45</td><td>◊</td><td>69</td><td>E</td><td>93</td><td>]</td><td>117</td><td>u</td></tr>
<tr><td>46</td><td>.</td><td>70</td><td>F</td><td>94</td><td>^</td><td>118</td><td>v</td></tr>
<tr><td>47</td><td>/</td><td>71</td><td>G</td><td>95</td><td>_</td><td>119</td><td>w</td></tr>
<tr><td>48</td><td>0</td><td>72</td><td>H</td><td>96</td><td>`</td><td>120</td><td>x</td></tr>
<tr><td>49</td><td>1</td><td>73</td><td>I</td><td>97</td><td>a</td><td>121</td><td>y</td></tr>
<tr><td>50</td><td>2</td><td>74</td><td>J</td><td>98</td><td>b</td><td>122</td><td>z</td></tr>
<tr><td>51</td><td>3</td><td>75</td><td>K</td><td>99</td><td>c</td><td>123</td><td>{</td></tr>
<tr><td>52</td><td>4</td><td>76</td><td>L</td><td>100</td><td>d</td><td>124</td><td>|</td></tr>
<tr><td>53</td><td>5</td><td>77</td><td>M</td><td>101</td><td>e</td><td>125</td><td>}</td></tr>
<tr><td>54</td><td>6</td><td>78</td><td>N</td><td>102</td><td>f</td><td>126</td><td>~</td></tr>
<tr><td>55</td><td>7</td><td>79</td><td>O</td><td>103</td><td>g</td><td>127</td><td>DEL</td></tr>
</table>

INDEX

_ AND

A

B

C

0-8493-XXXX-X/04/$0.00+$1.50

D

E

F

G

H

I

J

K

L

M

N

O

P

R

S

T

U

V

W

X-Z

Printed and bound by CPI Group (UK) Ltd, Croydon, CR0 4YY
23/10/2024
01778254-0015